CHRISTOPHER TYERMAN

God's War

A New History of the Crusades

PENGUIN BOOKS

PENGUIN BOOKS

Published by the Penguin Group
Penguin Books Ltd, 80 Strand, London WC2R 0RL, England
Penguin Group (USA) Inc., 375 Hudson Street, New York, New York 10014, USA
Penguin Group (Canada), 90 Eglinton Avenue East, Suite 700, Toronto, Ontario, Canada M4P 2Y3
(a division of Pearson Penguin Canada Inc.)
Penguin Ireland, 25 St Stephen's Green, Dublin 2, Ireland
(a division of Penguin Books Ltd)
Penguin Group (Australia), 250 Camberwell Road, Camberwell, Victoria 3124, Australia
(a division of Pearson Australia Group Pty Ltd)
Penguin Books India Pvt Ltd, 11 Community Centre, Panchsheel Park, New Delhi – 110 017, India
Penguin Group (NZ), 67 Apollo Drive, Rosedale, Auckland 0632, NewZealand
(a division of Pearson New Zealand Ltd)
Penguin Books (South Africa) (Pty) Ltd, 24 Sturdee Avenue, Rosebank, Johannesburg 2196, South Africa

Penguin Books Ltd, Registered Offices: 80 Strand, London WC2R 0RL, England

www.penguin.com

First published by Allen Lane 2006
Published in Penguin Books 2007
011

Maps 1 to 17 and 21 to 23 by Reg Piggott are reproduced by permission of
The Folio Society Ltd. Other maps are by Andrew Farmer.

Typeset by Rowland Phototypesetting Ltd, Bury St Edmunds, Suffolk
Printed in Great Britain by Clays Ltd, St Ives plc

978-0-140-26980-2

www.greenpenguin.co.uk

Contents

The Third Crusade

The Fourth Crusade

The Expansion of Crusading

The Defence of Outremer

The Later Crusades

List of Illustrations

List of Maps

Acknowledgements

This book has taken longer than even the most sluggish crusade to prepare and complete. I must record my thanks and gratitude to the Trustees of the Leverhulme Trust for the award of a Research Fellowship for the year 1998–9, which allowed me to begin to marshal evidence and ideas for this project. My agent Jonathan Lloyd has proved a tactful and potent warrior in my interests. The invitation to write this sort of book came from Simon Winder, who could not have imagined how long, in many senses, it would turn out to be. His patience and encouragement have been wonderfully sustaining. Indirectly, I have been thinking, working, teaching and writing towards this book for thirty years. Inevitably the debts to friends, colleagues, pupils and other scholars are legion and irredeemable. In particular, I should like to register my obligation for discussion, ideas, criticism and opportunities to air views to Malcolm Barber, Toby Barnard, Peter Biller, Jessalynin Bird, the late Lionel Butler, Jeremy Catto, Eric Christiansen, Gary Dickson, Barrie Dobson, Jean Dunbabin, Peter Edbury, Geoffrey Ellis, L. S. Ettre, the late Richard Fletcher, John Gillingham, Timothy Guard, Bernard Hamilton, Ruth Harris, Catherine Holmes, Norman Housley, Colin Imber, Kurt Villads Jensen, Jeremy Johns, Andrew Jotischky, Maurice Keen, Anthony Luttrell, Simon Lloyd, Jose-Juan Lopez-Portillo, Dominic Luckett, John Maddicott, Hans Mayer, James Morwood, Alan Murray, Sandy Murray, Torben Nielsen, the Oxford University Department of Continuing Education Crusades class of the summer of 2003, David Parrott, Jonathan Phillips, the late John Prestwich, Jonathan Riley-Smith, Miri Rubin, Jonathan Shepard and Mark Whittow. The intellectual vibrancy of my colleagues and pupils in Hertford College and New College provide the most stimulating of creative environments. The Principal and Fellows of Hertford gave me academic shelter for many locust years. Toby Barnard and Peter Biller have long provided personal support and intellectual stimulus with rare companionability. The responsibility for introducing me to the crusades rests with the improbable quintet of the late Ralph Bathurst, David Parry, Eric Christiansen, Maurice Keen and the late Lionel Butler, alike in little except inspiration and civility. I alone can be held accountable for the errors that stubbornly remain like mouse hairs in medieval bread. Simon Winder, editor nonpareil, and his team at Penguin UK have proved a revelation of amenable, intelligent and efficient publishing. I am grateful to those who have pointed out errata in the First Edition, in particular Paul Cobb and Eric Christiansen. For tolerating the distraction of what must at times have seemed another sibling, the book is dedicated to those most healthily but supportively sceptical of the virtues and merits of this work and its author, Elizabeth, Edward and Thomas, with love.

CJT
Oxford
15 June 2007

Preface

'The Lord is a man of war.' (Exodus 15:3)

Violence, approved by society and supported by religion, has proved a commonplace of civilized communities. What are now known as the crusades represent one manifestation of this phenomenon, distinctive to western European culture over 500 years from the late eleventh century of the Christian Era. The crusades were wars justified by faith conducted against real or imagined enemies defined by religious and political elites as perceived threats to the Christian faithful. The religious beliefs crucial to such warfare placed enormous significance on imagined awesome but reassuring supernatural forces of overwhelming power and proximity that were nevertheless expressed in hard concrete physical acts: prayer, penance, giving alms, attending church, pilgrimage, violence. Crusading reflected a social mentality grounded in war as a central force of protection, arbitration, social discipline, political expression and material gain. The crusades confirmed a communal identity comprising aggression, paranoia, nostalgia, wishful thinking and invented history. Understood by participants at once as a statement of Christian charity, religious devotion and godly savagery, the 'wars of the cross' helped fashion for adherents a shared sense of belonging to a Christian society, *societas christiana*, Christendom, and contributed to setting its human and geographic frontiers. In these ways, the crusades helped define the nature of Europe.

By forcing an otherwise improbably intimate contact with western Asia through centuries of contest over the Christian Holy Places in Palestine, the crusades encouraged European inquiry and experience beyond traditional horizons. One path to the thought-world of Christopher Columbus stretched back to Pope Urban II's first call to arms for the Christian reconquest of Jerusalem in 1095. The moral certainties fostered by crusading left physical or cultural monuments and scars from the Arctic Circle to the Nile, from the synagogues of the Rhineland to the mosques of Andalusia, from the vocabulary of value to the awkward hinterland of historic Christian pride, guilt and responsibility. Whether admired, with a contemporary of the First Crusade in the 1090s, as 'the greatest event since the Resurrection', or mocked, with Francis Bacon in the early seventeenth century, as a 'rendezvous of cracked brains that wore their feather in their head instead of their hat', or condemned, with the eighteenth-century Scottish philosopher and historian David Hume, as 'the most signal and most durable monument of human folly that has yet appeared in any age or nation', the crusades remain one of the great subjects of European history.

A familiar but baneful response to history is to configure the past as comfortingly different from the present day. Previous societies are caricatured as less sophisticated, more primitive, cruder, alien. Such attitudes reveal nothing so much as a collective desire to reassure the modern observer by demeaning the experience of the past. Within the cultural traditions of Europe and western Asia, since the sixteenth century the crusades have regularly attracted precisely such condescension from hostile religious, cultural or ideological partisans. The crusades have been dismissed as a symptom of a credulous, superstitious and backward civilization in order openly or covertly to elevate a supposedly more advanced and enlightened modern society. Yet this hardly helps understanding of past events. Another contrary vision, no less distorted, regards the past as a mirror to the present. Thus the battles of the cross are held to presage the conflicts of European imperialism, colonialism and western cultural supremacism. Yet many of the supposed links between past events and current problems are modern, not historical, constructs, invented to lend spurious legitimacy to wholly unconnected current political, social, economic and religious problems. So the crusades have been presented as symbols both of the past's inferiority and relevance. It is, by contrast, perhaps worthwhile to attempt to explore the phenomenon as far as possible on its own terms. That is the purpose of what follows.

More than half a century ago, Steven Runciman, with typical style and false modesty, imperishably pitted his pen against the 'massed typewriters of the United States'. He won. His *History of the Crusades*, published in three volumes between 1951 and 1954, became the classic twentieth-century account of the subject and remains a remarkable work of literature as much as history. It would be folly and hubris to pretend to compete, to match, as it were, my clunking computer keyboard with his pen, at once a rapier and a paintbrush; to pit one volume, however substantial, with the breadth, scope and elegance of his three. Yet scholarship and the world have moved since 1954: the former in part directly due to Runciman's inspiration; the latter in contradiction to the civilized and humane principles of faith and reason that shine from his great work. The crusades are no longer understood in quite the way they were in the 1950s either by scholars, informed by the new insights of research, or a wider public who imagine a largely spurious relevance to the twenty-first century. On these grounds, an attempt to describe again what is now perhaps the most familiar, if misunderstood, of all medieval phenomena may be justified.

The exercise is hardly straightforward. The judgemental confidence of a Macaulay – or a Runciman – is warranted neither by modern fashion nor by the discipline of the subject. All historical investigations remain contingent on surviving evidence. One of the regular temptations seducing historians and their audience is to imagine knowledge of the past. Most has been lost, by nature, accident or design. The muddle of existence is simplified both by the historians' craft, which is at root that of selection, and by the gaps in evidence. To illustrate the tenuous links that inform our knowledge, two of the most vivid, full and important contemporary narratives of the Second Crusade (1146–8) survive in a single manuscript each. Without them, our view of that remarkable event would be entirely different. Most of the evidence that once existed for the history of the crusades has been lost. Conversely, what does survive inevitably favours certain perspectives over others for which less evidence has survived. The story of the most familiar episode of all, the First Crusade and the conquest of Jerusalem (1095–9), is based on a remarkably narrow twelfth-century historiographical tradition which may, but equally may not, reveal what was of greater or lesser importance at the time. Thus any modern historical account can only be to some degree tentative. If the requirements of the narrative obscure the delicacy of the interpretive choices reached here, this in no way suggests they were easy, simple, straightforward, necessarily incontrovertible or even conclusive. They merely represent what the author, to the best of his understanding, now thinks.

The crusades were and are controversial and contentious far beyond the academic community. More than any other incident of medieval European history they have entered the sphere of public history, where the past is captured in abiding cultural myths of inheritance, self-image and identity. Many groups and nations find their memory awkward, even distressing. The massacres of Palestinian Muslims and Jews at Jerusalem in 1099 or of Greeks at Constantinople in 1204; the butchery of Rhineland Jews in 1096 or 1146, or English Jews in 1190; the defeats of Latin Christians by great Islamic leaders, Saladin and Baibars; the expulsion of western conquerors from the mainland of western Asia in 1291; the long triumphs of the Christians in Iberia, of the Germans in the eastern Baltic or the Turks in Asia Minor, the Balkans and the eastern Mediterranean; all these aspects of crusading history have left a residue of resentment, pain, anger, guilt and pride, depending on which legacy, if any, modern observers wish to claim for themselves. Therefore, for any historian the perspective taken is of importance. Yet to look at a subject from a particular vantage point is to adopt a position in order to more clearly inspect the view. It does not mean taking sides.

My perspective is western European. This accords best with my own research experience. More importantly, it matches the origins, development, continuance and nature of the phenomenon. Although having an impact far beyond western Europe, the crusade as an ideal and human activity began and remained rooted in western European culture. By adopting this stance in no way implies approval of crusading. It does not ignore the sources generated by the opponents and victims of crusading. Nor does it privilege the value or importance of the experience of western Europeans over others involved, as will be apparent in what follows. However, it is a necessary device to see the subject clearly through the fog of ignorance, obscurity, the passage of time and the complexity of surviving sources. A history of the crusades could be very different in structure if composed from the viewpoint of medieval Syrian, Egyptian or Andalusian Muslims, or European or Near Eastern Jews, or Balts, Livs or Prussians. However, the essential contours of the subject would, if observed dispassionately, look much the same, because this study is intended as a history, not a polemic, an account not a judgement, an exploration of an important episode of world history of enormous imaginative as well as intellectual fascination, not a confessional apologia or witness statement in some cosmic law suit. Readers will decide whether the view is worth the journey.

Introduction: Europe and the Mediterranean

In the eleventh century of the Christian Era, the region between the Atlantic, the Sahara Desert, the Persian Gulf, the rivers of western Russia and the Arctic Circle lived in the shadow of two great empires, Rome and the Baghdad caliphate, and accommodated two world religions, Christianity and Islam. The legacy of the classical Roman empire still determined cultural assumptions even outside the attenuated rump of the eastern Roman empire that survived as a comparatively modest but still powerful Greek-speaking empire situated between the Danube and the Taurus mountains, based on Constantinople, known to modern historians as Byzantium. In western Europe north of the Pyrenees, where Roman imperial rule had vanished five centuries before, the image of Rome, in law, art, architecture, learning and the Latin language, persisted, even in places between the Rhine and Elbe where the legions had never established their grip. The rulers of Germany claimed to be the heirs of the western Roman emperors, direct successors to the Caesars. To the east of Byzantium, the Near East, Egypt, the southern Mediterranean coastlands and most of the Iberian peninsula preserved the inheritance of the great Arab conquests of the seventh and eighth centuries, which had established an empire centred on the caliph (Commander of the Faithful, political heir of the Prophet) of Baghdad from the mid-eighth century.

Cultural divisions were reinforced and defined by religion; Christianity in Byzantium and western Europe from northern Iberia to the Elbe, Ireland to the Hungarian plain; Islam to the east and south, in western Asia, north Africa and the southern Mediterranean. Neither religious block was united. In the later tenth century, the traditional authority of the caliph of Baghdad had been usurped in Egypt by a caliph adhering to the minority Shi'ite Islamic tradition that had separated from the majority, orthodox Sunni tradition in the late seventh century over the spiritual legitimacy of the successors of the Prophet. In Spain, the Muslim community owed allegiance to an indigenous caliphate, based at Cordoba, until its disintegration and fragmentation in the early eleventh century. In Christian territories, although a sharper separation of powers existed between religious and secular authority than in Islamic states, two main distinctive forms of Christianity had developed since the later Roman empire; the Greek Orthodox tradition based on the Byzantine empire and a Latin tradition theoretically centred on the papacy in Rome but largely driven by the twin forces of local, aristocracy-led churches and a network of monasteries. In both Christianity and Islam, apparently monolithic belief systems concealed within them infinite local variety and tensions born of social, linguistic, ethnic, cultural and geographic diversity and distance. There were few non-Christians in lands ruled by Christians, although Jewish communities were spreading from the tenth century north of the Alps, especially to France and the Rhineland. By contrast, every Muslim region contained non-Muslim inhabitants, often in large numbers, mainly those Islamic law called the People of the Book, Jews and Christians, the latter from a range of local sects and confessional traditions deriving from late Roman theological interpretations different from either Latin or Greek orthodoxies.

In central areas of this Afro-Eurasian region, those of Christian and Muslim observance and rule, the religious and political structures rested on settled agrarian economies and populations. Byzantium and the Islamic states shared a flourishing commercial system that supported gold currencies and towns, while in Christian western Europe, by 1000 urbanization – or, in the perspective of the Roman empire, reurbanization – had only recently begun to accelerate along the major trade routes north of the Alps: the North Sea and north-west Mediterranean coasts, the Rhine, Rhône, Seine, Loire, Thames. In Italy towns and cities had survived more robustly since the collapse of the late Roman economy and civilization, even if on a far smaller scale than further east. The economic imbalance was reflected in the size of cities in the eleventh century. In the eastern Mediterranean, the great metropolis cities boasted populations of hundreds of thousands – Baghdad perhaps half a million; Old Cairo slightly less; Constantinople perhaps 600,000 at most. In Muslim Spain, 100,000 people may have lived in Cordoba, although some estimates make it much more. By contrast, the largest western

Christian cities – Rome, Venice, Florence, Milan, Cologne – hovered around 30–40,000. Paris and London in 1100, sustained by a largely rural hinterland, probably counted about 20,000 each, the equivalent of rather third-rate cities in the Near East or less. Elsewhere in northern Europe, cities were even smaller, while some important towns could muster only a very few thousand inhabitants. One of the striking features of the following two centuries lay in the massive growth in western urban populations, but even by 1300 cities such as Paris, pushing towards 100,000, still barely competed with the great entrepôts of the eastern Mediterranean.

Even with heightened economic and commercial activity in western Europe, the imbalance of trade remained evident, the west having to rely on an often limited silver coinage as the wealth flowed eastward and southward, gold, much of it from west Africa, never reaching or staying in large enough quantities to sustain currencies beyond the Pyrenees, Alps or Danube. International trade revolved around luxury items, notably spices and finished textiles such as silk from the east and slaves, fur, timber and some metals from the west and north. Local exchange, primarily of foodstuffs but also certain basic living materials, such as wool and woollen cloth, provided the main engine of regional commerce in the rural economies. The mosaic of local economies varied widely across the region: cereals, wheat in the more southerly areas, rye and oats further north; wine in the south, beer in the north; sugar cane in Syria; olives around the Mediterranean; fishing everywhere along the enormously long shores of Afro-Eurasia. The growth of towns in Europe between the Alps and the Atlantic indicated an acceleration in such commercialization, a process that acted as a liberating dimension for large sections of the peasant communities who were mainly tied to the land by law, hierarchy, custom, coercion and economic necessity. In market places, transactions may have been taxed and regulated but they tended to operate outside bonds of tenure. Slavery, once ubiquitous in Roman and post-Roman Afro-Eurasia, persisted in the Arab world, but was gradually dying out in Christian lands, whether through moral distaste driven by the church or economic prudence.

Rather different demographic and economic patterns survived outside the heartlands of settled communities, around the geographic margins of the region – the Atlantic seaboard, the fringes of the Sahara, the plains, forests, steppes and tundra north of the Black Sea and Carpathian mountains, north and east of the Elbe towards the Arctic Circle – as well as in the areas within the settled regions on the edge of cultivatable land – deserts, mountains, marshes and islands. Many places on the periphery of the region harboured nomadic tribes, shifting Turkish alliances in the Eurasia steppes; Bedouin in the deserts of the Near East; seasonal herdsmen such as the Lapps near and beyond the Arctic Circle. These groups depended on varying degrees of intimacy with their settled neighbours; most of the Bedouin and many of the Turkish nomads had accepted Islam; waves of Turkish invasions from the eleventh to the thirteenth centuries into the Balkans and Near East, followed by the Mongols from the Far East in the thirteenth century, highlighted this relationship. Similar mechanisms of exchange between the central lands and the geographic fringes applied to the non-nomadic peoples of northern Europe, Basques, Irish and the Scandinavians commonly known as the Vikings. In northern and north-eastern Europe, paganism flourished and resisted the cultural penetration of Christianity unenforced by commerce or conquest. Christianity (or Islam) was not necessary for the creation of stable cultural and political institutions. The eastern Baltic only began to be converted in the twelfth and thirteenth centuries. Lithuania remained staunchly pagan until the late fourteenth century and then converted on its own terms for political reasons.

The oldest institution in western Europe in the eleventh century, self-consciously tracing an uninterrupted history back a thousand years, was the papacy. Originally one of five patriarchs of the early church (Jerusalem, Constantinople, Antioch and Alexandria being the others), the bishop of Rome claimed primacy as the successor to SS Peter and Paul, the guardian of these founding saints' bones (supposedly buried beneath St Peter's basilica) and the diocesan of the seat of empire, from the Emperor Constantine (306–37) and the fourth century, a Christian empire. After the Arab invasions of the seventh century, only Rome and Constantinople remained in Christian hands; Jerusalem had fallen to the Muslims in 638. The absence of a western Roman emperor after 476 drew the pope and the eastern, Byzantine, emperor closer together, if in an uneasy relationship. The absence of effective imperial power in Italy had propelled the papacy into a position of temporal authority over the city of Rome and, in theory at least, parts of the central peninsula. Papal spiritual authority was enhanced by its sponsorship of the conversion of the Anglo-Saxons in the seventh century and of the Frisians and continental Saxons in the eighth.

In the early eighth century, the Byzantine emperors' flirtation with Iconoclasm (rejecting the religious efficacy of images, icons, etc.) and their inability to protect Rome and the pope from the Lombard rulers of northern Italy persuaded Popes Gregory III (731–41), Zacharias (741–52) and Stephen II (752–7) to enter into alliances with the Franks, the rulers of a large kingdom that stretched from modern south-west France to the Rhineland and the Low Countries. As part of this new orientation of policy, the papal court (or Curia) concocted the so-called Donation of Constantine, one of the most powerful forgeries in world history only properly exposed in the fifteenth century. This claimed that, on becoming a Christian, the Emperor Constantine surrendered his imperial authority to Pope Sylvester I (314–35), who returned it while retaining pre-eminence over the other patriarchates, theoretical temporal jurisdiction over the western empire and direct rule of Rome, its surrounding region and Italy in general. This forgery formed one basis for the later papal insistence on its claims to a state in central Italy and its wider assertion of primacy over imperial authority in western Europe.

The papal–Frankish alliance proved mutually advantageous. The papacy gained effective protection in Italy; the Franks legitimacy for their mid- to late-eighth-century conquests in Lombardy, Gascony, Bavaria and Saxony between the Rhine and Elbe. The culmination of the alliance came on Christmas Day 800 when Pope Leo III (795–816) crowned the king of the Franks, Charles the Great or Charlemagne (768–814), as the new Roman emperor in the west, inaugurating what came to be known as the Holy Roman Empire, which survived, with various interruptions and changes of fortune, nature and substance, until abolished in 1806 on the insistence of Napoleon. While the Frankish, or Carolingian (i.e. family of Charles), empire lasted, until the 880s, the papacy remained rather overshadowed. Thereafter the throne of St Peter tended to be the preserve of a dim succession of Roman nobles, some youthful, dissolute, even irreligious. Yet the reputation of their office remained high, especially in northern Europe, where papal authority still appeared as a final arbiter of ecclesiastical and spiritual issues; the newly converted King Miesco I of Poland sought papal protection in 991. In 962, the king of Germany, Otto I, who had recently conquered northern Italy, revived the western empire by being crowned in Rome by

Pope John XII (955–64), a notoriously debauched twenty-five-year-old nobleman and libertine who apparently met his death, still only about twenty-seven, after a stroke suffered during intercourse with a married woman.

By the early eleventh century the papacy alternated between grand protégés of the German emperors, such as the scholar Gerbert (Pope Sylvester II, 999–1003), and a succession of local appointees of distinctly uneven calibre usually taking the names Benedict or John. Increasingly elements within the Roman church and elsewhere in Christendom sought to reform both the papacy and the wider secular church in the west by re-emphasizing the separation and dominance of the spiritual over the secular in church appointments, management, finance and behaviour. Under the patronage of Emperor Henry III (1039–56), the reformers seized control of the papacy. A succession of German, Italian and French popes in the half-century after 1048 transformed both the papacy and western Christendom. Deliberately and innovatively international in outlook and personnel, central in the policies of the reforming papal Curia came the understanding that the church of Rome was synonymous with the universal church; that the pope held temporal as well as spiritual jurisdiction on earth as the heir to St Peter, to whom, according to the so-called Petrine texts in Matthew's Gospel, Christ entrusted the keys of heaven and the power to bind and loose on earth and in heaven (Matthew 16:19). The more general reformist agenda included the improving of the morals and education of the clergy and the eradication of simony (paying for church office) and clerical marriage (a move both moral and economic, to protect church land from being inherited by non-clerical clergy children). An attempt was made to make secular priests more like monks, wholly distinctive from their lay neighbours and relatives, and loyally obedient to Rome.

This programme met fierce local opposition as it threatened the vested interests of lay and clerical patrons of private churches and monasteries; the habits of the mass of the secular priesthood; and the power of secular rulers to control the richest landed corporations in their regions. The most acute and bitter dispute developed with the king of Germany, Henry IV, whose accession as a minor had forced the reforming popes to seek independence from the German throne in order to protect themselves from Italian enemies. At issue were imperial rights in choosing a new pope; papal rights in approving the choice of emperor; and, more directly, the authority over appointments and control of the church in imperial lands in Germany and north Italy. The dispute was encapsulated in the ceremony of investing, i.e. giving newly consecrated bishops the ring and staff, symbols of their spiritual dignity. Traditionally in Germany, and elsewhere, kings performed this ceremony. Uniquely for a layman – and inconveniently for church reformers – kings were also consecrated, 'the Lord's Anointed'. The right to invest with the ring and staff became iconic, hence the name given to the dispute and the wars it generated, the Investiture Contest, although in reality the disagreements were both more mundane – control of church wealth and patronage – and sublime – the spiritual health of those who administered the Sacraments and 'the right order in Christendom'.

This was much more than a theological spat. The power of the German kings relied heavily on control of the church, especially in Saxony. A revolt there in 1076 gave the most belligerent of the reforming popes, Gregory VII, an opportunity to put pressure on Henry IV to make concessions by publicly challenging his right to rule, claiming the pope possessed a plenitude of power that included the right to depose unsuitable monarchs, including emperors. The intransigent Henry IV was excommunicated in 1076 and again in 1080. Rival kings were put up by the papalist and anti-imperialist party in Germany. The ensuing war spilt over into Italy. In 1084 Henry IV invaded, captured Rome, installed his own anti-pope and forced Gregory VII to find refuge with the Norman conquerors of southern Italy. Over the subsequent decade, Henry's anti-pope held sway in Rome, supported by repeated imperial forays south of the Alps. The background to the First Crusade lay in this conflict, as Urban II sought to use the mobilization of the expedition as a cover to reclaim the pope's position in Italy and demonstrate his practical leadership of Christendom, independent of secular monarchs. The slogan of the papal reformers was 'libertas ecclesiae', 'church freedom/liberty/rights'. This provided the central appeal of Urban II's summons of 1095, when he called on the faithful to go to 'liberate' the churches of the east and Jerusalem. The crusade is impossible to understand outside of this context of more general church and papal reform. It was ironic that, at the very time they were asserting universalist claims, the reforming popes could never be entirely secure in Rome itself. Local nobles, deprived of control of the lucrative office of the papacy, German and pro-imperialist invaders and other Italian political rivals forced successive popes into temporary or near-permanent exile over the century following Gregory VII's exile. It was only after he had launched the First Crusade in 1095–6 that Urban II was himself able to establish his residence in the Eternal City.

The Investiture Contest, only resolved by compromise in 1122, exposed some of the weaknesses in the material and ideological positions of both papacy and empire, as well as highlighting the limitations of centralized political authority more generally. The papacy was, with the English government of the time, one of the leaders in western Europe pioneering the development of written techniques of government – communicating with local agents, subordinates and representatives abroad by standardized letters; systematic, retrievable record keeping; the creation of a bureaucratic tradition. Yet, as was later famously remarked, the pope lacked legions, having to rely on secular protectors to secure papal independence and integrity. By contrast, the German emperor was politically the most powerful ruler in western Europe, wielding vast theoretical and potential power over territories that stretched from southern Denmark to central Italy. Yet these lands, based on the eastern portion of the old Carolingian empire (known from the ninth century as East Francia), were held together by networks of dynastic alliance, personal relations, tradition, ideology, convenience and brute force, not institutional routine. This made the building of political consensus, the basis to all effective authority, a full-time and precarious exercise for German rulers in the eleventh century. Since 962, the king of Germany could hope to be crowned by the pope as Roman emperor. Despite the Investiture Contest and continued tension thereafter, most kings succeeded in persuading popes to perform this highly symbolic and important ceremony. However, some did not. King Conrad III of Germany, commander of the Second Crusade (1145–9), was one of the few medieval German kings after Otto I not to be crowned emperor, although he nonetheless exercised many of the imperial prerogatives and gave himself some of the formal titles of an emperor. The lack of imperial title reduced a German king's claims to jurisdiction in North Italy, one of the wealthiest regions of western Europe, which formed a significant and lasting element in imperial pretensions. However, Conrad's power, like that of his predecessors, depended on his position in Germany.

Politically, Germany in the eleventh and twelfth centuries comprised a number of disparate regions each dominated by its own duke and closely integrated nobilities: Bavaria, Swabia, Franconia, Saxony, Lorraine. Eastward expansion, although temporarily halted in the north by a great Slav rebellion in 983 against German rule east of the Elbe, had created marcher lordships such as in Austria, Styria and Meissen, giving local entrepreneurial margraves considerable autonomy. The power of the king depended on his own personal dynastic lands – Otto I had been duke of Saxony – coupled with a range of imperial lands, cities and rights, and alliance with the church, the only truly imperial institution (hence the threat presented by the Investiture dispute). Although tending to descend within one family – the Saxons 911–1024; Salians 1024–1125; Hohenstaufen 1138–1254 – the German kingship was elective, a right the electors, composed of the leading dukes and ecclesiastical magnates such as the archbishops of Cologne and Mainz, stubbornly maintained. While the elective element in other kingdoms, such as England, France or the Christian states of northern Iberia, withered, repeated dynastic interruptions, through either lack of direct heirs (1002, 1024, 1125, 1138, 1152) or the succession of minors (1056, 1197), entrenched an active elective principle in Germany. Nonetheless, the German kings were – and were recognized by their neighbours as being – not just sentimentally the secular heads of western Christendom by virtue of the imperial title, but practically the leading secular rulers in western Christendom.

Not the least symptom and cause of this predominance lay in the role of German rulers in the expansion of Christianity to the Slavic kingdoms of eastern Europe. It says much for the damage inflicted on German monarchic power that, whereas in the tenth and eleventh centuries the initiative in reeling the new kingdoms and principalities of Poland, Bohemia and Hungary into the orbit of western Christendom had come from the German kings, from the mid-twelfth century it was left to local east German dukes and lords, aided by the ideology of holy war and their recruiting of crusaders and immigrants, who pushed the frontiers of Latin Christendom into Prussia and the north-eastern Baltic. Although many of the earliest Christian missionaries to the western Slavs, especially in Bohemia and Moravia, and to the Magyars in Hungary in the decades around 900 were Greek Orthodox, the creation of the new western empire by Otto I, not least through his defeats of Magyar invaders, opened the region to western Latin evangelists as local rulers sought to associate themselves with the new German power. The adoption of Christianity provided a cohesive force in the establishment of settled political identities and institutions, the church providing education, literacy, civil servants, a potentially pliant and dependent new landowning ecclesiastical aristocracy of bishops and abbots, a supportive ideology of transcendent kingship and convenient national saints, such as King Wenceslas in Bohemia (d. *c.*929) and Stephen in Hungary (king 1000–1038). Poland had adopted Latin Christianity in 966 as part of the attempts of Miesco I to expand into Pomerania as a client of Otto I, a strategy giving him, he reckoned, a better chance of making good his conquests and his desire to dominate the western Slavs. A sign of Polish determination to enter the Latin world came when, in 991, Miesco placed the kingdom under formal papal protection. Hungary's position was far more liminal, sharing a long frontier with Byzantium as well as Germany. However, here too rulers consistently sought to place themselves within a German/Latin Christian orbit politically and hence culturally rather than become a client of the Greek empire. The Hungarian desire to maintain this western bias informed their consistently sympathetic and later active engagement with the crusades that passed through their lands in 1096, 1146 and 1189. In some senses the crusades confirmed the drift of Hungarian policy since the tenth century.

The only competitor for influence in the vast tracts of Slavic/Magyar lands between the Elbe, Baltic, Danube and the Black Sea remained the Greek empire of east Rome, Byzantium, with its capital of Constantinople on the Bosporus, between Europe and Asia. Both Moravia and Hungary had initially seemed likely to fall into the Greek orbit in the early tenth century before the rise of Ottonian Germany proved more attractive. Even in the eleventh century, Constantine IX (1042–55) sent the Hungarian ruler a crown, although Hungary steadfastly attempted to protect its autonomy though close ties with the German empire (St Stephen had married the sister of Emperor Henry II (1002–24)). More securely, Greek influence and the desire of the local ruler to consolidate his status by a Byzantine alliance led to the conversion of Prince Vladimir of Kiev (988/9) whose confederation of the Rus incorporated the main trading centres on the Dneiper with the original northern capital of the Rus at Novgorod. However, even the Russians gradually emancipated themselves from Greek dominance. Alliances were sought in the west; Henry I of France (1031–60) married a Russian princess, with their son,

Philip I, introducing a Greek first name that became popular in the French royal family down to the nineteenth century. In the 1040s the Russians even attacked Byzantium, and there were generally unavailing attempts to loosen the grip of the Constantinopolitan patriarchate over the Russian church. The ability to manipulate peoples around its frontiers played a crucial role in Byzantine foreign policy and survival. East of the Russians, the nomadic and Turkish tribes such as the Khazars, Pechenegs and Cumans of the southern Eurasian steppes north of the Black Sea presented a greater and more intractable threat, as did the Turkish tribes that penetrated the Near East in the mid-eleventh century.

By the early eleventh century, the Byzantine empire stretched from the Danube and Adriatic, with some outposts still retained on the mainland of Italy (at Bari, for instance), to the Taurus and Anti-Taurus mountains of eastern Anatolia and a few strongholds in northern Syria, such as Antioch. Seemingly dominant, culturally, commercially and politically, in fact the empire had only recently reasserted its position in northern Syria and the northern Balkans, where the previously independent Bulgarian state had been painfully annexed by Emperor Basil II, 'the Bulgar Slayer' (976–1025), and Serbian separatist tendencies neutralized. This hegemony did not last long. In the mid-1050s, Turkish tribes led by the Seljuk family had invaded the Near East, becoming the effective rulers in Baghdad. In 1071, the Seljuks invaded Anatolia, defeating and capturing the Byzantine emperor, Romanus IV Diogenes, at the battle of Manzikert. With their frontier defences breached, the Byzantines soon lost the interior of Anatolia, the Seljuks even establishing their Anatolian capital at Nicaea, within striking distance of Constantinople itself. Behind the Seljuk conquest of Anatolia other Turkish tribes took advantage of the political chaos to exploit the towns and settled agrarian economy of the region. The chief of these groups were the Danishmends, who established a so-called *ghazi* (i.e. holy warrior) state to the north-east of the peninsula. At much the same time, other nomadic and semi-nomadic tribes penetrated Byzantium's Balkan frontiers. Twenty years earlier, the Greeks had to accept the settlement of the Pechenegs south of the Danube in north-eastern Bulgaria, while another steppe people, the Cumans, established themselves just to the north of the Balkan frontier. Across the Adriatic, the final Byzantine holdings were snuffed out by the new power in the region, Norman adventurers led by Robert Guiscard. Bari, the last stronghold, fell in

1071. Guiscard followed up his victory by invading the Balkans. Only with the accession of the military usurper Alexius I Comnenus was the Norman threat repulsed at Durazzo (now Durres on the Adriatic coast of Albania) in 1085 and the Pechenegs finally defeated, at Mount Levounion (at the mouth of the Maritsa in southern Thrace near the modern Turco–Greek border) in 1091. Apart from the Italian possessions, only the losses to the Seljuks in Anatolia and northern Syria remained to be restored. That is where, in the eyes and strategy of Alexius I, the appeal to the west he made in 1095 and the First Crusade came in.

The shifting fortunes of Byzantium in the eleventh century were mirrored by the disorder in the Islamic Near East following the Seljuk invasions of the 1050s. After seizing control of the Baghdad caliphate in 1055, their leader receiving the apt title of 'sultan' (*sultan* is Arabic for power), the Seljuk Turks pressed westwards. After defeating the Greeks in 1071, they annexed most of Syria and Palestine by 1079. However, despite the appearance of unity, the Seljuks presided over a loose, often fractious confederation of regional powers, such as the more or less independent sultanate of Rum, i.e. Anatolia, and city states, such as Mosul, Aleppo, Antioch (taken in 1084/5), Damascus and Jerusalem. These old Arab cities, while often owing allegiance to one or other of a series of competing Seljuk lords, were often controlled by Turkish military commanders (atabegs) whose authority rested as much in their personal mercenary bands, often of slave troops (mamluks), as on higher Seljuk approval. Everywhere, ethnic and religious diversity complemented the alienation of ruled – whether town-dwellers, rural cultivators or Bedouin or steppe nomads – from ruler. In parts of Syria, immigrant Turkish Sunnis ruled indigenous Shia populations or exerted control over local Arab nobles. In Cilicia and northern Syria, significant religiously and ethnically distinct Armenian communities were squeezed between the competing powers of Byzantium, Arabs and Turks. Across this area and in the Jazira (modern northern Iraq) the political uncertainties offered opportunities for Kurdish as well as other Turkish incomers. Similar dislocation characterized the Fatimid caliphate of Egypt, which contested with the Seljuks ascendancy over southern Palestine. In Egypt, the Shia rulers dominated the majority Sunni inhabitants through powerful chief ministers, called viziers, who were often neither Egyptian nor Arab, but Turks or Armenians. The Near East presented no harmonious spectacle of civilized peace. The Turkish invasions from the 1050s destabilized the region, introducing an alien ruling elite backed by military coercion, causing as much if not more mayhem and disruption than the crusaders were able to achieve.

Elsewhere in the Muslim Mediterranean, the political pendulum was swinging towards Christian powers. After the implosion through internecine feuding of the Cordoba caliphate in 1031, Muslim Spain, al-Andalus, was ruled or fought over by competing so-called *taifa* or 'party' kings. Their weakness and disunity allowed Christian rulers north of the Ebro to take advantage of the lucrative offers of pay and alliance to extend their power southwards, a process driven by profit, not religion, but later given the accolade of the 'Reconquest' or *reconquista*, in largely propagandist reference to the Arab conquest of the eighth century. By the end of the eleventh century, distinctive political identities had been assumed by five Christian statelets: Catalonia; Aragon; Navarre; León; and Castile. These were joined in the 1140s by the creation of Portugal following conquests between the Duero and Tagus rivers along the Atlantic seaboard. Despite a Muslim counter-attack led by a puritanical north African Muslim fundamentalist sect, the Almoravids (*c.*1086–1139), these Christian principalities managed to exploit the enfeebled political system of their indigenous Muslim neighbours to forge lasting ascendancy in the northern half of the peninsula, which provided the basis for the sweeping conquests of the thirteenth century.

Across the western Mediterranean, between 1060 and 1091, the island of Sicily, a former Byzantine territory in Muslim hands since the later ninth century, was conquered by armies commanded by lords of Norman French extraction whose presence in the region exemplified the fluidity of high politics where skill in battle plus a private army could propel ambitious warriors, in western Europe as much as in the Near East, to unpredicted eminence. The collapse of an independent post-Carolingian kingdom of Italy in the tenth century had opened the north of the peninsula to German invasion and the assertion of civic independence by the commercial and manufacturing cities and entrepôts of the Po valley (Milan, Venice), Liguria (Genoa) and Tuscany (Florence, Pisa). In the south, Byzantine rule in Apulia and Calabria rubbed uneasily against squabbling local dynasts in Capua, Salerno and Benevento, providing plenty of opportunities for hired professional fighters. The most militarily and politically successful of these came from Normandy, a duchy in northern France with a surplus of arms-bearers and an insufficiency of land, patronage and preferment. Normans, attracted perhaps by a familiar pilgrimage route but certainly by the prospects of profit and improved status, began making their presence felt in south Italian politics from the 1020s. By 1030, one contingent had acquired a permanent hold on Aversa between Naples and Capua. Within thirty years, Norman warlords dominated the area. After a disastrous attempt by Pope Leo IX to put papal theories of temporal jurisdiction into practice by trying to oust them ended in a crushing papal defeat at Civitate in 1053, the Norman lords acquired titles and respectability as the reforming papacy sought protectors. In 1059 Pope Nicholas II (1059–61) recognized Richard of Aversa as prince of Capua and Robert Guiscard as prospective ruler of Byzantine Calabria and Apulia and Muslim Sicily. To reinforce the honour, when Robert Guiscard's brother, Roger, began the conquest of Sicily in 1060, the enterprise was awarded a papal banner.

The fortunes of Robert Guiscard's dynasty presaged those of many later crusaders, the family business of war now accorded religious legitimacy and gaining enormous success. Guiscard had conquered Calabria by 1060 and Apulia in 1071 with the surrender of the last Byzantine garrison in Bari. Despite Guiscard's failure to carve out a principality for his eldest son Bohemund in the western Balkans in the 1080s, to die in 1085 as ruler of southern Italy and arbiter of the destiny of the Vicar of St Peter was no mean feat for a younger son of a minor Norman aristocrat, Tancred of Hauteville. The conquest of Sicily by Guiscard's brother Roger (d. 1101) provided a new focus for profit and a centre of Norman-Italian political endeavour. Once finally subdued after a bitter three decades' fighting, Sicily proved far wealthier than the family's mainland holdings. Under Roger's son, Roger II, the two parts of the Hauteville inheritance were brought together to the anxiety of popes and western and eastern emperors. In 1130, in return for support, the anti-pope Anacletus II crowned Roger II king of Sicily, Calabria and Apulia, and acknowledged his overlordship over Capua, Naples and Benevento, titles that Roger retained by forcing the legitimate pope, Innocent II, whom he had just defeated and captured, to recognize them in 1139. The combined lands of the kingdom of Sicily created one of the wealthiest, culturally and politically most dynamic, ambitious and disruptive powers of the twelfth-century Mediterranean. By comparison, the Norman-Italian enclave founded by his cousins Bohemund and Tancred in Antioch in 1098 scarcely matched Roger's lavish regime, which, at its height, sought to emulate, rival, even usurp Byzantium itself. Such entrepreneurial opportunism supplied one vital context for the early crusades. It may have been no coincidence that Alexius I timed his invitation to the west to send military aid shortly after the end of the Sicilian conquest, when, at least in the mind of the canny Greek emperor, there would be available a rich stock of soldiery, some disappointed perhaps at the Sicilian land settlement and eager for new chances to make their fortunes and save their souls.

In many ways the rise of the Hautevilles constituted an experience typical of eleventh-century France. The disintegration of the Carolingian empire in the late ninth century not only permanently divided the constituent political entities into East Francia (essentially Germany from Lorraine to the Elbe), Italy and West Francia (between the Rhine and the southern Pyrenean marches). The chaos of civil war and invasions by Vikings from the north and Arab pirates in the south also caused effective civil power within West Francia to become devolved on to the local royal agents, the counts, who wielded vice-regal military, fiscal and judicial authority. By the end of the tenth century the kingdom of France remained a legal and ideological construct, but its kings exerted little genuine power outside their own family lands. The main political foci were the great counties ruled as autonomous principalities by comital families who rapidly acquired their own grand, if often fictional, pedigrees to match their practical status. The most important counties, some later elevating themselves into duchies, were Flanders, Champagne, Normandy, Brittany, Burgundy, Blois-Chartres, Anjou, Paris (i.e. the Ile de France), Poitou-Aquitaine, which acquired the duchy of Gascony, Toulouse and Barcelona, which was to be attracted away from the French orbit by the opportunities and successes of its Iberian neighbours. Beside these, numerous lesser counties sprang up, some owing allegiance to the greater lords, some autonomous.

To this political patchwork were added wide geographic, economic, linguistic and ethnic contrasts. Brittany was still a Celtic region; the Basques had given their name to Gascony. Elsewhere the chief linguistic divide was between those in the north who spoke *langue d'oil* (so described after the word used for 'yes', *oil*) and the speakers of *langue d'oc* in the south, the dividing line running east–west well to the north of the modern Midi. These linguistic contrasts mirrored different histories, customs and laws. The far south retained a tradition of written law and limited urbanization to match its Mediterranean climate. Elsewhere, there was no uniformity of rules of landholding, judicial systems, weights, measures or currency. A kingdom often in name alone, nonetheless in 987 the great magnates of northern France, perhaps on the promptings of pro-German interests, decided to change the royal dynasty from the remnants of the attenuated Carolingians to the family of the counts of Paris, in the figure of Hugh Capet (987–96), his descendants being known as the Capetians. The exclusion of the Carolingian claimant suited the Germans, whose kings now came from a non-Carolingian, relatively parvenu dynasty from Saxony. Once installed, the Capetians set about securing their hold on the monarchy by reducing the elective element in French kingship not least by consistent, determined and remarkably successful efforts to ensure that each Capetian king left a son to succeed him. (Louis VII had to wait until his third wife and his mid-forties before he had a son.) The unique Capetian genetic triumph, which saw son succeed father in an unbroken line from 987 to 1316, transformed the nature of the French monarchy, but only over time.

The Capetians were aided in their ambitions by three factors. Their family lands, centred on the Ile de France, were among the richest in western Europe and straddled the main trade routes: the Seine, Marne, Loire river systems, which linked eastwards to the Rhine, Meuse and Low Countries, west to the Atlantic, north to the English Channel and south to the Saône-Rhône corridor and the Mediterranean. The church lent the Capetians ideological support and material assistance. The king was patron to wealthy monasteries and controlled appointments to important bishoprics and archbishoprics outside his own lands. The final advantage possessed by the Capetians lay in the role of kingship itself. Although few of the great princes in France bothered to pay the king homage and fealty (some counts of Anjou were happy to), the office of king legitimized those of the counts. A king, however feeble, was needed, as the events of 987 recognized. When, as rarely occurred, a foreign invasion was threatened, as in 1124, the counts rallied round. The potential for the king, as legal overlord, to interfere in the affairs of any county in the realm was undeniable but only enforceable in political circumstances that did not regularly occur until the late twelfth century.

On the other hand, the political cohesion of France was undermined by another three facts of political life. For the vast majority of Frenchmen, their spheres of economic, public and private life operated entirely beyond the reach or necessity of royal influence or power, a matter of geography, communications and the absence of national institutions. This was reflected and exacerbated in the years around 1000 in an ever more local search for protection and arbitration. Even the authority of counts was challenged and ignored as provincial gangsters and racketeers commandeered lands, markets, churches, monasteries and fighting men to impose a rough order on localities often centred on the construction of castles. Although this devolution of power has been regarded by some as a sign of a collapse of social order and its replacement by anarchy, the networks linking these petty lordships with the regional counts, bishops and local monasteries suggest a structure, however undisciplined in places. The period of supposed anarchy was accompanied, perhaps not coincidentally, by the establishment of new strength by a number of active comital dynasties, such as in Normandy, Anjou, Flanders, Blois and Champagne. Yet in valleys distant from Paris, dominated by a castle and a local boss with a posse of armed thugs (later known as knights), royal power and national sentiment were for stories and romances of a glamorous Carolingian past not daily life.

The third impediment to French royal authority lay in the loose legal concept of sovereignty, which tended to be explained and conceived in personal not institutional terms. Thus a landowner, knight, lord or count could take as his overlord anyone from whom he held land, leading to a cat's cradle of overlapping lordships. In time, centripetal legal and political forces could turn this fluid system to the king's benefit, but not until the thirteenth century. This personal system of lordship also ignored the boundaries of kingdoms. The count of Flanders held lands from Artois to the river Scheldt; for those which lay in the kingdom of France, the count was a subject of the king of France; for those in the empire, the emperor was his overlord. Two masters; one count; one count, two sets of subjects with wholly different technical allegiances, the king of France or Germany; a political and legal minefield. Viewed from Capetian Paris, the most dramatic and potentially dangerous of these personal international lordships concerned that of the kings of England. In 1066, the duke of Normandy, William the Bastard, invaded England and succeeded in establishing himself as king of the English. As a consequence, from 1066, with a few brief interruptions (1087–96; 1100–1106; 1138–54), the duke or regent of Normandy was also king of England. As a result of dynastic inheritance and a military and political victory in a long English civil war, in 1154 the situation was further complicated when Henry, count of Anjou, also duke of Normandy by inheritance from his mother and duke by marriage of Aquitaine, became king of England. Henry II, the first of the Angevin (i.e. Anjou was his partrimony) kings of England, was overlord to far more of France than his supposed French sovereign Louis VII: Normandy, Maine, Anjou, Touraine, Brittany, Poitou, the duchy of Aquitaine, the Limousin, Gascony and parts of the Auvergne, with unachieved claims to parts of Languedoc. These French lands were passed on more or less intact to Henry's son Richard I, a fact that made his relations with his crusading partner Philip II of France during the Third Crusade (1190–91) awkward, to say the least. Only after Philip II's conquest from John of all the Angevin lands north of the Loire in 1202–4 could the Capetians begin to assert practical sovereignty over their whole kingdom.

Neither the Angevins nor their Norman predecessors as kings of England were in any meaningful sense English. It is wholly wrong to imagine that the lands they held in France were English lands. They were the personal dynastic inheritance of the rulers. In that sense, they typified a Europe that contained no nation states in the manner understood in modern Europe, although cultivating a sense of shared national identity was a feature of the kingdoms that emerged across Europe after the tenth century. The histories of France, Germany, Italy and Spain – and indeed of all the regions discussed including the Near East in this period – underline that the later political organization of Europe or western Asia was not inevitable; frontiers, traditions and nationalities were mutable, even accidental, certainly not innate.

This applied even to the most centralized state of western Europe, the kingdom of the English. Formed through the tenth-century conquest by the kings of Wessex of their northern neighbours, England developed a distinctive system of government in which public justice, coinage, markets, taxation and defence rested with the royal authority, as did control of the church. The king's authority was mediated through local officials, a relatively efficient and sophisticated bureaucracy and a dense pattern of aristocratic and noble patronage. In Christian Europe, only in Byzantium had the techniques and institutions of government reached a more complicated and comprehensive form. Yet England's northern and western frontiers remained uncertain, and the kingdom itself was repeatedly invaded and, in the eleventh century, twice conquered, by the Danes (1013–16) and the Normans (1066–70). The very efficiency of the English government's capacity to tap the kingdom's wealth made England an inviting target; the centralization of institutions and power facilitated successful conquest. France could not be conquered by a battle. With only a little exaggeration, England could, a sign of relative strength not, paradoxically, weakness. The European significance of the Norman Conquest can be found in the reorientation of English and hence British Isles politics towards north-west Europe rather than Scandinavia. English money transfused the economy of northern France. Continental habits of religious observance, styles of art and architecture and institutions of scholarship were now open to England and the English. In some instances the confrontation was painful, the imposition of foreign ways on a reluctant and far from culturally inferior conquest. In others, contact was as benign as the millennia of peaceful trade across the English Channel. Along with English wool to feed the cloth factories of Flanders and English scholars attending the new continental universities, notably Paris, the ease of assimilation into the continental European community was recognized by the enthusiastic participation by those who regarded themselves as English, as well as the descendants of their conquerors, in the crusades.

For all its elaborate institutions of government, the English state was created and maintained by armed force. After 1066, England was invaded in 1088, 1101, 1139, 1153, 1216–17; civil wars involving the English king or regent were fought 1087–8, 1100–1106, 1123–4, 1139–53, 1173–4, 1191, 1215–17. Yet warfare provided one building block of statehood. This was equally true of the Scandinavian kingdoms that emerged in the late tenth century from the fragmented politics of the Viking age. Denmark had received Christianity under Harold Bluetooth (950–86) and consolidated its territorial and national identity through conquest, both in the Baltic and across the North Sea. Slightly later, in the early eleventh century, Norway followed a similar pattern of royal conversion, rivalry with Scandinavian neighbours and foreign conquest. In 1066, the last Anglo-Saxon king of England had to defeat a king of Norway before he faced the duke of Normandy. From the twelfth century, crusading provided the Scandinavians with the useful mixture of legitimate war and an ideology of supremacy and colonialism to extend their interests eastwards, the Danes into Estonia and the Swedes into Finland.

At every stage and in every corner of the Afro-Eurasian region under discussion, the ubiquity of organized violence, of public and private warfare, has been inescapable. War provided the glue to cement together political institutions and assert governmental authority over areas. It supplied the pivot of civil and international disputes. It also provided occupation for nobles, aristocrats and the wider urban and rural population; by service for the upwardly ambitious, the physically suited or the otherwise unemployed; or by non-combatant engagement in the extensive social, economic and commercial networks that were required to sustain armies of whatever size. Across the whole region one of the most characteristic figures was that of the warrior plying his trade; the mamluk or Kurdish mercenaries who maintained regimes in the Near East; the Flemish and other mercenaries who supported kings and their rivals in northern Europe; the Varangian guards, northern European émigrés in the service of the Byzantine emperor. Some effectively professional fighting men did very well. The former Varangian Harold Hardrada (d. 1066) ascended to the throne of Norway; the Norman freebooter Robert Guiscard (d. 1085) became ruler of southern Italy; his great-nephew Tancred (d. 1112) rose from landless gentility to be prince of Antioch; the exiled Rodrigo Diaz, the Cid, of Castile (d. 1099), sold his sword and his soldiers to the highest bidders on all sides of the Christian–Muslim conflict before taking Valencia to rule for himself; after failed careers as a cleric and then Anglo-Norman noble, Baldwin of Boulogne (d. 1118) used his military and generalship skills to install himself as ruler of Edessa in the Jazira beyond the Euphrates before assuming the crown of Jerusalem; the Kurdish mercenary captain Yusuf Ibn Ayyub (d. 1193) became Sultan of the Near East: he is better known as Saladin.

The increasing prominence given such men can be charted in their cultural profile. By the twelfth century across western Europe, lords and even kings were for the first time depicting themselves on their personal seals as mounted warriors, knights, no longer an image of mere soldiery but of social status. The image of the armed knight, in wax, painting, sculpture, stained glass, poetry and funerary effigies, became the standard iconic representation of the ruling military aristocracy. In Byzantium, not only were the martial qualities of Alexius I emphasized by eulogists and artists, but much attention and admiration was directed at the fighting characteristics of the hired mercenaries on which the empire depended, Turks, Slavs and western Europeans. In the Near East, political propaganda caught up with political reality. A political system that relied on hiring paid private armies unsurprisingly revived the theory of holy war, *jihad*, to which any ambitious leader had to aspire. A succession of ambitious parvenu rulers, culminating but not ending with Saladin, laid claim to the accolade of *mujahid*, holy warrior.

One obvious practical reason underpinned such respect for the fighting man. The well-trained mounted fighter, even in small numbers, could dominate any battlefield and provide a decisive outcome usually in a modest period of time relative to the static slugging matches of massed, opposing, poorly armed infantry. In the Near East, these cavalrymen would be lightly armoured, using small horses, with the shorter bow as their main offensive weapon. The rapid attack, feint and ambush were their methods. In the west, archers tended to be infantry and, although useful in sieges and to control the tempo of a field battle, until the development of the great longbow were not the arbiters of victory or defeat. The western armed knight was the tank of the period; manoeuvrable; impervious to most of the fire power available to the opposing infantry. Arrows from short bows usually stuck irritatingly but harmlessly into the chain-mail coats worn over leather hauberks or tunics, so that during a long struggle knights were seen to resemble giant hedgehogs. Many famous knightly casualties to arrows came when the missile found an exposed, unprotected part of the anatomy, such as the eye or, most often, the neck when heat forced the mailed warrior to loosen his mailed neck-guard. With plate armour, arrows, even from the later longbows, tended to glance off carefully moulded front surfaces. While direct hits from spears and lances were a threat, the best chain-mail and plate armour were remarkably effective at deflecting sword-thrusts. The main use of swords, spears and maces against mounted knights was to unseat them; without the height and horse advantage, the armoured warrior became vulnerable.

Through genetics, training and diet, knights tended to be physically bigger than infantry. Mounted on increasingly well-bred, specially trained and larger horses, protected by armour and wielding heavy lances, maces and swords, a few knights could hold their own against scores of infantry. The repeated accounts of seemingly miraculous victories or escapes by hopelessly outnumbered bands of knights, while likely to be exaggerated, preserved a truth. Knightly losses in battle were modest except through the massacres that often ensued at the end of fighting. In the massed charge, lances fixed (or 'couched') or with swords and maces, western knights presented a most potent weapon. This depended for its effectiveness on the use of shielding ranks of infantry to commit the enemy so far as to prevent his withdrawal, escape or, as when faced with Near Eastern armies, feints and strong field discipline, to prevent a precipitate or piecemeal attack. The numbers involved in battles varied enormously. In the eleventh or twelfth century, an army of 10,000 was very large and difficult to handle over long periods, for obvious logistical reasons. Much larger forces were recorded, not least during the crusades, but these relied on the availability of plentiful forage or, in the invasion of England in 1066 or on crusade from the later twelfth century, the deep pockets and administrations of rulers to transport tens of thousands of troops by sea. Many battles and military forays were much smaller enterprises, consisting of a few hundred, even a few score. Some battles could feature a dozen or so knights. The nature of medieval warfare precluded the huge forces of the classical age, the mass national levies of the late eighteenth century, or the industrialized conscription of modern times.

The cost of western and eastern warriors, men and horses was high. In Europe and western Asia, money payment for fighting on campaigns was common, as were longer-term rewards, such as land, titles and the consequent social privileges and status. This even applied to the mamluks, who technically were slaves; they ended by ruling Egypt for 250 years. Warfare did not comprise pitched battles alone. In fact, most generals tended to avoid such risky and expensive encounters, preferring skirmishes and ravaging to achieve usually limited political or economic objectives. The butchery in most internal warfare, where combatants came from the same cultural and regional milieu or even knew each other well, tended to be limited, unlike conflicts that involved strangers, such as foreign invaders like the Vikings or crusaders. In the absence of effective systems of social and legal arbitration, still less international law, war was endemic and only marginally mitigated in its effects by shared warrior values, later called chivalry in the west but equally recognized in essence in the Muslim world. The main victims of war were non-combatants caught in war and forage zones and the unskilled infantry who rarely enjoyed a fair share of victory (i.e. booty) while suffering incommensurately in fighting. Skilled, trained warriors were worth their reward because they could ensure the best chance of success in most forms of warfare: battle; foraging; defended or forced marches; skirmishing. As war so often *was* politics and vice versa, with rulers across the whole Afro-Eurasian region expecting and expected to campaign every year, their value was evident.

However, in some circumstances, the mounted warrior was ineffective. Besieging cities or castles with stone walls neutralized him completely. Yet sieges played a central part in the successful prosecution of war, to annexe territory or force an opponent to come to terms. Here numbers, not equestrian panache, counted for all. Medieval warfare depended on muscle power, of men and women, horses, beasts of burden and drawers of carts. Muscle power was the medieval equivalent of modern electricity and petrol. Equally, if the besiegers either had to starve or storm a castle or a walled city into submission, the number of attackers was crucial. In addition to men, sieges required timber to build giant throwing machines and engines in and beneath which attackers could scale or undermine the city's walls. The technology of siege warfare appears to have been more highly developed in the eastern Mediterranean, especially perhaps in Byzantium where forests and cities were both in abundance. Although fleeting references exist to large wooden siege machines in western Europe before the First Crusade, only during that expedition were westerners extensively exposed to such engines, the use of which they very quickly mastered, probably with Greek help. Timber and carpentry also provided the vital accompaniment to shipping. Western European advances in shipbuilding and navigation supplied the sinews of Europe, where communications ran along coasts and up rivers. The different physical world of the Near East, where political power and much of the internal trade were landlocked and timber was in shortening supply, gave the western attackers after 1095 their one clear military advantage.

Yet even where their military training was of least use, the elite mounted warrior played a vital role. As social leaders, they provided the money, the command structures, occasionally military knowledge.

Medieval armies were collected by coercion, loyalty, the incentive of cash and idealism. The knightly classes habitually provided the first three; with the crusades they supplied the fourth as well.

The First Crusade

I
The Origins of Christian Holy War

On 12 April 1096, a young castellan, Achard of Montmerle, pledged property to the great Burgundian monastery of Cluny in return for 2,000 Lyons shillings and four mules so that he could accomplish his intention to join 'the journey to Jerusalem to fight for God against pagans and Saracens'. In a similar deal with the abbey of St Victor at Marseilles four months later the brothers Geoffrey and Guy were reported as wishing to seek Jerusalem 'both for the grace of pilgrimage and under the protection of God, to exterminate the wickedness and unrestrained rage of the pagans by which innumerable Christians have already been oppressed, made captive and killed'.[1] The experience of that campaign, which cost Achard his life near Jaffa in June 1099, convinced his companions that they were the army of God 'fighting for Christ', their casualties martyrs, their cause supported in battle by the saints of heaven themselves, George, Demetrius and Blaise, 'knights of Christ', their success assured because 'God fights for us'. They were no more than pursuing the task given them by Urban II on his preaching tour of 1095–6, who, in his own words to the Flemish in December 1095, hearing that the Turks had 'in their frenzy invaded and ravaged the churches of God in the east' and 'seized the Holy City', had at Clermont 'imposed on them the obligation to undertake such a military enterprise for the remission of all their sins'.[2]

Fifty years later, in an account of the Second Crusade, an Anglo-Norman priest called Raoul aired a general theory of justified homicide: 'He is not cruel who slays the cruel. He who puts wicked men to death is a servant of the Lord because they are wicked and there is ground for killing them.'[3] By this time, such redefinition of Christian militancy raised few eyebrows. Some years before, the austere and massively influential Bernard, abbot of Clairvaux, a sort of one-man European moral ombudsman and one of the instigators of the Second Crusade (1146–8), voiced his approval of the union of the Militia of God and the Militia of the World in the creation of the Military Order of the Knights Templar:

The knight who puts the breastplate of faith on his soul in the same way as he puts a breastplate of iron on his body is truly intrepid and safe from everything . . . so forward in safety, knights, and with undaunted souls drive off the enemies of the Cross of Christ.[4]

Bernard, in his recruiting preaching and letters for the Second Crusade in 1146–7, showed intimate knowledge of the New Testament, not least the Epistles of St Paul. The Apostle was fond of martial metaphors, but his message was wholly contrary to the abbot of Clairvaux's:

Put on the whole armour of God, that ye may be able to stand against the wiles of the devil. For we wrestle not against the flesh and blood . . . Stand therefore, having your loins girt about with truth, and having on the breastplate of righteousness, and your feet shod with the preparation of the gospel of peace . . . taking the shield of faith . . . and take the helmet of salvation, and the sword of the spirit, which is the word of God. (Ephesians 6:11–17)

Or, more succinctly, 'No man that warreth for God entangleth himself with the affairs of this world' (II Timothy 2:4) and 'For though we walk in the flesh, we do not war after the flesh: for the weapons of our warfare are not carnal, but mighty through God to the pulling down of strongholds' (II Corinthians 10:3–4).

It is a measure of the pragmatism, sophistication (some might say sophistry) and sheer intellectual ingenuity of St Paul's successors over the following millennium in expounding the doctrine of the Gospels that there was an ideology of Christian holy war at all.

WAR, THE BIBLE AND CLASSICAL THEORY

The most ringing modern verdict on the crusades has become justifiably famous. At the end of what has been described as the last great medieval chronicle, his three-volume *History of the Crusades* (1951–4), Steven

Runciman delivered his judgement: 'the Holy War itself was nothing more than a long act of intolerance in the name of God, which is the sin against the Holy Ghost'.[5] Yet intolerance of the enemies of God has a long history in the Judeo-Christian tradition. For much of the last two millennia there have been scholars and religious propagandists, often a majority, who would have taken issue with Sir Steven just as there have always been those who would have agreed with him. What may appear today to many Christians and perhaps most non-Christians as an irreconcilable paradox between holy war and the doctrines of peace and forgiveness proclaimed in the Lord's Prayer, the Sermon on the Mount and many other Gospel passages has not always been so obvious or recognized. This was certainly the case in educated circles around Urban II at the end of the eleventh century.

As it had developed by the beginning of its second millennium in western Christendom, Christianity was only indirectly a scriptural faith. The foundation texts of the Old and New Testaments were mediated even to the educated through the prism of commentaries by the so-called Church Fathers, theologians such as Origen of Alexandria, Ambrose of Milan, Augustine of Hippo and Pope Gregory I who, from the third to the sixth centuries, undertook the often tricky task of translating some inappropriate, obscure, incomplete, contradictory or idealistic apophthegms into an intelligible and satisfying system of thought and action within the context of the institutions of an active religion, a temporal church and the daily lives of believers. The Beatitudes had to be reconciled with human civilization, specifically the Graeco-Roman world, or, to put it crudely, ways found around the Sermon on the Mount. Being extravagantly well versed in the highest traditions of classical learning, the Church Fathers did this rather well. Beside these majestic exercises of the intellect, which extended even to manipulating the wording of some inconvenient biblical texts, Scripture attracted apocryphal additions and spawned a massive literature of imitative hagiography often supported by legends surrounding relics of biblical characters or events. The experience of the church over the centuries provided its own corpus of law, tradition, history, legend and saints that reflected neither the idealism nor experience of the first century AD.

The church's teaching on war early reflected this process of interpretation and exegesis. Negatively, the so-called charity texts of the New Testament that preached pacifism and forgiveness, not retaliation, were firmly defined as applying to the beliefs and behaviour of the private person. John the Baptist advised soldiers to remain in the army and draw their wages (Luke 3:14). As citizens, Christ told His followers to pay taxes to Caesar, drawing a clear distinction between political and spiritual obligations (Matthew 22:21). St Paul implied the same fundamental dichotomy of obedience in urging his disciple Timothy and his community at Ephesus to pray 'for kings and all that are in authority' (I Timothy 2:2). This distinction between the public and the private was reinforced by the Bible's very language. In St Jerome's Latin translation of the Scriptures (finished *c.*405), known as the *Vulgate*, which became the standard text of the Bible in the medieval West, the word for 'enemy' in the New Testament is invariably *inimicus*, implying a personal enemy. The Latin for a public enemy, *hostis*, does not appear in the New Testament. From this it could be argued that there was no intrinsic contradiction in a doctrine of personal, individual forgiveness condoning certain forms of necessary public violence to ensure the security in which, in St Paul's phrase, Christians 'may lead a quiet and peacable life in all godliness and honesty' (I Timothy 2:2).

While theoretically, in a perfect world, individual pacifism could be translated into political pacifism, the main thrust of Christian teaching assumed post-lapsarian sin and imperfection. The Old Testament bequeathed stories of legitimate war pleasing to God, from the Israelites, Joshua and King David to Judas Maccabeus. In contrast to modern Christians not of biblical fundamentalist persuasion, the medieval church placed considerable importance on the Old Testament for its apparent historicity, its moral stories, its prophecies and its prefiguring of the New Covenant. Bible stories operated on many levels (medieval exegetes distinguished as many as four), including literal and divine truth. In the Old Testament, the Chosen People of the Israelites fought battles for their faith commanded and protected by their God. Moses was told directly by God to enlist the Levites to slaughter the followers of the Golden Calf (Exodus 32:26–8). God ordered Saul to annihilate the Amalekites 'men, women, infant and suckling' (I Samuel 15:3). Warrior heroes adorn the scriptural landscape: Joshua, Gideon, David. In the Books of the Maccabees, recording the battles of Jews against the Hellenic Seleucids and their Jewish allies in the second century BC, butchery and mutilation are praised as the work of God through His followers, whose weapons are blessed and who meet their enemies with hymns and prayers. 'So, fighting with their hands and praying to God in their hearts, they laid low no less than thirty-five thousand and were greatly gladdened by God's manifestation' (II Maccabees 15:27–8). Many Old Testament texts, especially those concerning Jerusalem, could be construed as providing *casus belli*: 'O God, the heathen are come into thine inheritance; thy holy temple have they defiled; they have laid Jerusalem on heaps' (Psalm 79).

Even in the New Testament the Apocalypse described in The Revelation of St John is shot through with violence as part of the fulfilment of the Last Judgement:

> And I saw heaven opened, and behold a white horse; and he that sat upon him was called Faithful and True, and in righteousness he doth judge and make war . . . And he was clothed with a vesture dipped in blood: and his name is called The Word of God. And the armies which were in heaven followed him . . . And out of his mouth goeth a sharp sword that with it he should smite the nations: and he shall rule them with a rod of iron: and he treadeth the winepress of the fierceness and wrath of Almighty God. (Revelation 19:11–15)

Such imagery and language as well as the martial history of the biblical Chosen People of the Old Testament fed directly the world-view of the crusaders, providing rich quarries alike for preachers and chroniclers. Although the surviving letters from the First Crusaders contain only one reference to the Apocalypse, commentators were full of it. In a notorious passage, Raymond of Aguilers, chaplain to Raymond IV, count of Toulouse, one of the leaders of the First Crusade, who witnessed the fall of Jerusalem in 1099, described the ensuing massacre on the Temple Mount: 'it is sufficient to relate that in the Temple of Solomon and the portico crusaders rode in blood to the knees and bridles of their horses'.[6] Whatever the atrocities performed that day, Raymond was quoting Revelation 14:20: 'And the winepress was trodden without the city, and blood came out of the winepress, even unto the horse bridles.' It is hard to exaggerate the dependence of Raymond's contemporaries on the Scriptures for imagery and language. Many saw Urban II's holy war as the fulfilment of biblical prophecy or an imitation and renewal of scriptural struggles. Just as the reformed papacy of the eleventh century loudly proclaimed its adherence to the so-called New Testament Petrine texts in which Christ committed His Church to St Peter, so the holy war itself was perceived and possibly designed to revolve around Matthew

16:24: 'If any man will come after me, let him deny himself, and take up his cross, and follow me.' This was the text referred to in the deal between the south-east German abbey of Göttweig and Wolfker of Kuffern, who had decided to join the march to Jerusalem in 1096 because 'he wanted to fulfil the Gospel command, "who wishes to follow me"'.[7]

This process of translating the spiritual conflict described by St Paul into a doctrine of battle and reversing the habit of discounting the interminable wars of the Israelites as literal models for Christian behaviour was not sudden. Until the adoption of Christianity by the Roman state, public war had been rejected by theologians such as Origen of Alexandria in the third century, who insisted that the Old Testament wars should be read as allegories of the spiritual battles of the New Covenant. Thereafter, Christianity had to come to terms with more than biblical exegesis. In devising a tentative theoretical justification for war in the fourth and fifth centuries, the Church Fathers incorporated two distinct traditions of legitimate war, the Helleno-Roman and the Jewish.

The fourth-century BC Greek philosopher Aristotle coined the phrase 'just war' to describe the categories of acceptable warfare (*Politics* I: 8). War provided a natural form of acquisition for the state but should not be an end in itself. It could legitimately be deployed in self-defence, to prevent the state's enslavement; to obtain an empire to benefit the inhabitants of the conquering state; or to enslave non-Hellenes deserving of slavery. The key was the justice of the ends for which the war was fought. In his *Politics* (VII: 14) Aristotle insisted that 'war must be for the sake of peace'. There was no concept of a religious war *per se* nor of religious disapproval of war, as public religion resembled a civic cult, thus the needs of a virtuous state were almost by definition just. Even while Aristotle deplored the Spartan attitude of war for its own sake, Athenian just war in practice accommodated the tradition of victors' genocide of those they defeated. To Aristotle's just ends, Roman Law added just cause, a *causa belli* as the historian Livy put it, based on contractual relations. From the Latin for peace, *pax*, derived from the verb *pangere*, meaning to enter into a contract, it was argued that war was justified if one party was guilty of breaking an agreement or injuring the other. As a legal procedure, to jurists such as Cicero, just war required formal declaration and purposes of defence, recovering lost goods or punishment. The enemy of a just war was *ipso facto* guilty.

Cicero also argued for right conduct, such as virtue or courage, in waging a just war. The practical consequences of these theories lent the aura of justice to all Rome's wars against external enemies, especially barbarians, identified as *hostes*, public enemies, automatically legitimate targets of just war.[8]

CHRISTIAN JUST WAR

When Christianity became adopted as the official religion of the Roman empire in the early fourth century, Graeco-Roman just war confronted the Judaic tradition of wars fought for faith and not merely temporal but divinely ordained rights. The conversion of Constantine and the final recognition of Christianity as the offical religion of the Roman empire in 381 prompted the emergence of a set of limited principles of Christian just war which, by virtue of being fought by the Faithful, could be regarded as holy. The identification of the Roman empire with the church of God allowed Christians to see in the secular state their protector, the *pax Romana* being synonymous with Christian Peace. For the state, to its temporal *hostes* were added enemies of the Faith, pagan barbarians and, more immediately dangerous, religious heretics within the empire. Eusebius of Caesarea, historian of Constantine's conversion, in the early fourth century reconciled traditional Christian pacifism with the new duties of the Christian citizen by pointing to the distinction between the clergy, immune from military service, and the laity, now fully encouraged to wage the just wars for the Christian empire. Ambrose of Milan (d. 397), as befitted a former imperial official, consolidated this symbiosis of the Graeco-Roman and Christian: Rome and Christianity were indissolubly united, their fates inextricably linked. Thus the war of one was that of the other, all Rome's wars were just in the same way that those of the Old Testament Israelites had been; even heresy could be depicted as treason. Ambrose's vision of the Christian empire and the wars to protect it which constituted perhaps the earliest formulation of Christian warfare was, therefore, based on the union of church and state; hatred of foreigners in the shape of barbarians and other external foes; and a sharp intolerance towards dissent and internal debate, religious and political.

The collapse of the institutions of the Roman empire in the west in the fifth century undermined Ambrose's union of interests and could have threatened the whole theoretical basis of Christian just war without the work of a younger contemporary, Augustine of Hippo (d. 430). Augustine combined the classical and biblical doctrines of just war to arrive at some general principles outside the context of an active *imperium Romana*. Augustine's analysis depended on sin, which caused war but which could also be combated by war. In the face of the political realities of successful barbarian invasions and Donatist heretics in his North African diocese, Augustine combined the Graeco-Roman ideas of right causes and ends with a Christian concept of right intent. With Aristotle he agreed that the right end of war was peace. With Cicero he argued, 'it is the injustice of the opposing side that lays on the wise man the duty of waging war'. With Roman lawyers, he agreed that public war must be supported by authority, but cited scriptural evidence: 'the commandment forbidding killing was not broken by those who have waged war on the authority of God'.[9]

From Augustine's diffuse comments on war could be identified four essential characteristics of a just war that were to underpin most subsequent discussions of the subject. A just war requires a just cause; its aim must be defensive or for the recovery of rightful possession; legitimate authority must sanction it; those who fight must be motivated by right intent. Thus war, by nature sinful, could be a vehicle for the promotion of righteousness; war that is violent could, as some later medieval apologists maintained, act as a form of charitable love, to help victims of injustice. From Augustine's categories developed the basis of Christian just war theory, as presented, for example, by Thomas Aquinas in the thirteenth century.

However, Augustine was no warmonger. The world of the spirit was preferable to that of the flesh. Although public prayers, litanies and masses continued to be said from the fifth to the eight centuries, especially under papal instigation in Rome itself, to invoke divine aid in wars against enemies of the church, the Christian tradition of withdrawal from the world, of non-violence and condemnation of temporal aggression remained, if anything strengthened by the spread of monasticism across Christendom. Nonetheless, Augustine had moved the justification of violence from lawbooks to liturgies, from the secular to the religious. His lack of definition in merging holy and just war, extended in a number of later pseudo-Augustinian texts and commentaries, produced a convenient conceptual plasticity that characterized subsequent Christian attitudes to war. The language of the *bellum justum* often described what came closer to *bellum sacrum*. This fusion of ideas might conveniently be called religious war, waged for and by the church, sharing features of holy and just war, allowing war to become valid as an expression of Christian vocation second only to monasticism itself.

A just war was not necessarily a holy war, although all holy wars were, to their adherents, just. While holy war depended on God's will, constituted a religious act, was directed by clergy or divinely sanctioned lay rulers, and offered spiritual rewards, just war formed a legal category justified by secular necessity, conduct and aim, attracting temporal benefits. The fusion of the two became characteristic of later Christian formulations. Where Rome survived, in Byzantium, the coterminous relation of church and state rendered all public war in some sense holy, in defence of religion as well as state, approved by the church, none more so than when the Emperor Heraclius defeated the Persians and returned the True Cross to Jerusalem in 630. However, Byzantine warfare remained a secular activity, for all its divine sanction, never a penitential act of religious votaries.

THE GERMANIC WORLD

The advent of successor kingdoms in what had been the western Roman empire from the fifth century presented the Christian church with cultural as well as political problems. By the eighth century the ruling aristocracies of kingdoms in Italy, Gaul, Spain and the eastern British Isles had almost universally adopted orthodox Roman Christianity without radically altering their social assumptions and belief systems in which, in Carl Erdmann's words, war provided 'a form of moral action, a higher type of life than peace'.[10] In this new aesthetic, apparently contradictory of Christian teaching, war provided a *raison d'être* for political power and social status because, with the collapse of Roman civil institutions, war and its associated fiscal and human structures of plunder, tribute and the *comitatus* or warband of dependent warriors, provided the basis for economic and social cohesion. The army – *exercitus* – assumed the role of a central public institution in the medieval west. In the process of converting the new rulers of early medieval

Europe the church had no option but to recognize their values, even if it sought to defuse them of exclusively martial connotations by employing the new converts' language metaphorically, much in the manner of St Paul.

Nevertheless, extremely and personally violent converted heroes such as Clovis the Frank in Gaul *c.*500 or Oswald king of Northumbria *c.*635 emerge from flattering accounts of Christian apologists as warriors for the Faith even when their political, tribal or national priorities are recognized. According to fellow Northumbrian Bede, Oswald, 'a man beloved of God', prayed for divine aid in battle against the British king Cadwalla 'for He knows that we are fighting in a just cause for the preservation of our whole race'. It might be noted that Cadwalla was a Christian too. Oswald's bloody career, which ended in death, mutilation and dismemberment at the hands of pagan enemies, earned him the sanctity of a martyr's crown.[11] The concept of the Christian warrior was thus forged in the reality of political life as the church relied for patronage and protection on such violent warlords. So intimate was the symbiosis of religion and society that bishops in northern Europe, themselves usually chosen from aristocratic families, began to appear as great noblemen complete with military retinues. The process of the conversion itself was accompanied by violence; even among the Anglo-Saxons, where there was comparatively little physical hostility to the missionaries, at least one pagan priest, a South Saxon, was killed by a Christian missionary as sign of God's judgement. Perhaps even more corrosive of Christian pacifism than the political compromises reflected in accounts of conversions was the emergence of physical evangelical aggression in the burgeoning corpus of Christian hagiography: holy men were now themselves party to holy violence, a literary trend that reached maturity in the tenth and eleventh centuries.

The type of the early medieval Christian warrior was Charlemagne (d. 814) who renewed the western Roman empire as a Christian *imperium* in 800 when he was crowned emperor by the pope in Rome. Charlemagne portrayed himself, and encouraged his propagandists to regard him, as the defender of the church. In 791, Charlemagne asked the pope to pray for his success against rebels and enemies so that they would be vanquished by 'the arms of Faith'. Before campaigns against the pagan Avars of Pannonia in the 790s, special fasts, processions and masses were ordered to ensure victory and a profitable campaign (*prosperum iter*), Christ Himself being entreated to bring 'victory and vengeance', the latter a common legal justification. In 793, Frankish bishops were instructed to institute litanies and fasts for the king and the army of the Franks. Charlemagne's protracted conquest of the pagan Saxons between the Rhine and the Elbe was placed in a Christian context: the pagan Saxons were 'hostile to our religion' and felt 'no dishonour to violate and transgress the laws of God and man'.[12] The Franks were careful to attack Saxon religion and to impose Christianity by force as a civic duty on the conquered Germans. The atmosphere of holy war was deliberately fostered. Frankish kings traditionally carried into battle the relic of St Martin's *cappa* (i.e. cloak) to bring victory. According to the *Annals of the Kingdom of the Franks*, miracles displayed God's approval of Frankish imperialism and genocide, as at Syburg in 776 when flaming red shields appeared in the sky to confound the Saxons. (The *Revised Annals*, composed after the great king's death, interestingly make no mention of such divine encouragement.)[13] A contemporary Italian poem attributed the victory over the Avars achieved by Charlemagne's son Pippin to God, who 'granted us victory over the pagan peoples'. At Ingelheim near Mainz a wall painting depicted the wars of the Carolingians:

> with these and other deeds that place shines brightly;
> those who gaze on it with pleasure take strength from the sight.

In such a world, the virtues of the Frankish warrior and the good Christian coincided. In her famous advice (843) to her son William, Dhuoda of Septimania, after praying that God would 'determine that prosperity shall be his lot in all things' hoped that he would be 'open-handed and prudent, pious and brave'.[14]

Older Christian attitudes to violence did not disappear in the face of militant Carolingian Christian triumphalism. One of Charlemagne's closest advisers, the Englishman Alcuin of York, in a lament on the destruction of the Northumbrian monastery of Lindisfarne by the Vikings in 793 and the loss of the Christian Near East, North Africa and Spain to the Muslims, insisted that only by prayer and pious living would the tide be reversed. The ninth-century Irish philosopher and poet John Scot Erigena, tutor to Charlemagne's grandson Charles the Bald, proudly contrasted pagan poets' descriptions of temporal battles with his own poems on Christ's spiritual victories, although even he was not above asking that God 'thwart the scheme of our enemies and rout the pagan fleets'.[15] This was no literary flourish but highly topical. The ninth century saw the disintegration of the Carolingian *imperium Christiana* in the face of civil wars exploited by external attacks of Muslims, Vikings and Magyars, whose success seemed to threaten Christendom itself, thrusting the practice as well as theory of holy war into urgent prominence.

DEFENDERS OF THE FAITH: THE NINTH AND TENTH CENTURIES

The impact of the invasions of the ninth century was to consecrate wars fought in defence of the church, called by one contemporary 'battles of Christ'. Pope Leo IV (847–55) offered salvation and Pope John VIII (872–82) penitential indulgences, remission of sins, to those who fought and died 'for the truth of the Faith the salvation of souls and the defence of Christendom (*patria Christianorum*)' 'against pagans and infidels'.[16] Only in the secular arm lay Christianity's survival as Saracens established themselves in Sicily and southern France and Vikings penetrated the heartlands of western Francia and destroyed three ancient Anglo-Saxon kingdoms. The detached theorizing of Augustine's just war was replaced by a seeming life-and-death struggle to which the church was inescapably committed. The propaganda of Alfred of Wessex (d. 899) deliberately and consistently characterized his Danish foes as pagans; his thegns fought with swords decorated with symbols of the evangelists; prayers and alms accompanied military success. The secular and religious causes became one. The Frankish *Annals of Fulda* – a monastic source – portrayed Arnulf, king of the East Franks, urging his men on to victory over the Northmen at the river Dyle in 891: 'we attack our enemies in God's name, avenging the affront not to us but to Him who is all powerful', the justice of the cause being carefully established by reference to the pagan Vikings' atrocities against Frankish civilians and clergy.[17] The identification of religion and war extended to the clergy. A French monk, in his enthusiasm at the defence of Paris against the Vikings in 885/6, praised his own abbot of St Germain for his skill with a *ballista*, a sort of enlarged crossbow:

He was capable of piercing seven men with a single arrow;
in jest he commanded some of them to be taken to the kitchen.[18]

A few years earlier, Adelarius, a monk at Fleury in Burgundy, which claimed to possess the bones of St Benedict, the founder of his order, recorded that a Frankish commander in a skirmish against the Vikings thought he had seen monks on the battlefield; when told that none had been present he realized that he had witnessed St Benedict himself fighting for him 'with his left hand directing and shielding my cavalry and with his right hand killing many enemies with his staff'.

This remarkable recruitment of the founder of western monasticism into the armies of the beleaguered Franks strikingly evokes the fusion, or perhaps confusion, of the sacred and the profane that underpinned Christian holy war in medieval Europe. The synthesis was neither a temporary expedient nor of recent gestation. In mediating between the Christian message and Germanic values, the vocabulary of Christianity itself adopted appropriate images accessible to warrior elites. In the eighth-century Old English poem *The Dream of the Rood*, composed only a generation or so after the completion of the conversion of the Anglo-Saxons, Christ is described as 'the young warrior', 'the Lord of Victories'; His death on the cross a battle; and heaven a form of Valhalla, 'where the people of God are seated at the feast'.[19] The ninth-century Old German poetic rendering of the Gospel story the *Heliand* (i.e. Saviour), perhaps used to popularize the new religion among the recently and forcibly converted Saxons, witnesses a similar expression of what could be called vernacular Christianity. Thus, in the Sermon on the Mount, 'Blessed are the merciful; for they shall obtain mercy' (Matthew 5:7) is transformed into 'Blessed are those who have kind and generous feelings within a hero's chest: the powerful Holy Lord will be kind and generous to them.'

The language of martial lordship and the warband dominate. Christ is the liege lord of mankind (*manno drohtin*), 'a generous mead-giver', his disciples his 'gesiths', 'earls' in high-horned ships or 'royal thegns' (*cuninges thegn*). Judas is damned for changing lords and breaking his bond of loyalty. Peter 'the mighty noble swordsman' begs to fight to the death in Gethsemane; Thomas argues that Christ's followers should suffer with him 'for that is the thegns' choice . . . to die with his liege at his doom'; even Pilate, 'coming from Caesar . . . to rule our realm' resembles nothing so much as a Carolingian governor or *missus*.[20] The thrust of these images is metaphorical, but the extended equation of Christian discipleship with the social relationships and functions of temporal warriors could blur the inherent distinctions between the two, providing a mental picture in which actual physical violence for Christ needed little special pleading. In the poem on the English defeat by the Danes at the battle of Maldon (991), the doomed hero Britnoth, in the thick of the fighting, thanked 'his Creator for the day's work that the Lord had granted him'; after his death, his thegns prayed 'that they might take vengeance for their lord and work slaughter among their foes'.[21] The theme of lordship, loyalty and vengeance reached a logical if extraordinary conclusion in one version of the twelfth-century poem about the First Crusade, the *Chanson d'Antioche*, where Christ is depicted on the cross prophesying that:

> the people are not yet born
> Who will come to avenge me with their steel lances.
> So they will come to kill the faithless pagans
> . . .
> They will all be my sons, I promise them that.
> In heavenly paradise shall their heritage be.[22]

Official church teaching remained reluctant to embrace the secularization of the spiritual battle, though still eager to appropriate the values and services of temporal warriors in its defence. God was a god of victory, His best advocates godly heroes such as Charlemagne or the tenth-century conqueror of the Magyars and recreator of the western empire, Otto the Great (d. 973). Ironically, as the immediate threat from outside diminished, within Christendom the political and social role of the armed nobleman grew as larger political units imploded. Monks persisted in asserting that their 'spiritual weapons' and the 'sword of the spirit' were effective 'against the aery wiles of the devil' and thus of direct use to kings and kingdoms. As the English monk Aelfric of Cerne, the abbot of Eynsham, argued at the end of the tenth century, the religious in their monasteries were 'God's champions in the spiritual battle, who fight with prayers not swords; it is they who are the soldiers of Christ'.[23]

Yet Aelfric's own vernacular *Lives of the Saints* (mid-990s), aimed at a secular, aristocratic audience, contains laudatory homilies of St Oswald,

St Edmund of East Anglia and Judas Maccabeus. There was no pacifist metaphor here. Following Abbo of Fleury's widely popular *Passio sancti Edmundi*, Aelfric's King Edmund is a martyr for Christ at the hands of the Danes. Even though the king was shown as throwing away his weapons, his resistance is made explicit; as Abbo put it, 'I have never fled a battlefield, thinking it a fine thing to die for my country (*pro patria mori*)'; Edmund, a keen warrior, is 'a martyr for Christ'. Aelfric copied Bede in showing Oswald using force to win power and protect his people and faith; Judas Maccabeus is 'godes thegen', waging bloodthirsty war, his troops supported by angels and the prospect of remission of sins. Aelfric makes clear that unbelievers will be slain 'for their hard-heartedness against the Heavenly Saviour'. Of course, as a monk Aelfric insisted on the primacy of the spiritual conflict inherent in the New Covenant but he admits that Judas Maccabeus, through his temporal wars

> is as holy, in the Old Testament
> as God's elect ones, in the Gospel-preaching.[24]

Both Aelfric and Abbo employ the image of a secular warrior, in battle or not, aspring to martyrdom to point to their respectability.

These warrior saints were rulers who, in a sense, validated their own wars. Abbo of Fleury made great play with Edmund's status as an anointed monarch, vested with authority to defend his people. In his version of the *Passio*, Aelfric refers to Alfred of Wessex, another protector of his people against pagans. This concentration on kings ceased to match contemporary reality as both the political and ecclesiastical worlds increasingly revolved around princes, counts, even castellans and seigneurs, whose military strength supplied social control and church patronage. From the tenth century the church's express support was extended more widely to soldiers in public wars and against pagans, even their swords, arms and banners beginning to be blessed in formal liturgies. In his *Vita Geraldi Comitis Aurillac* (*Life of Gerald, count of Aurillac*), Abbot Odo of Cluny, one of the most influential ecclesiastical figures in western Christendom in the early tenth century, depicted a man of action, a saintly knight who fought in God's cause for the common good in a just war. However removed from actual life – Gerald's sword never shed blood – Odo's portrait allowed for morality in martial culture. This was particularly important as monasteries more than ever relied on the protection of just such local military bosses. Thus, in the eleventh century, Odo of St Maur-les-Fosses, called Burchard, count of Vendôme, a count 'faithful to God' because he defended churches, monks, clergy, widows and nuns: his protection of St Maur itself counted for much. This pious layman nevertheless engaged in private warfare against his neighbours and, 'confidently trusting in the Lord', killed people.[25] However, this idealized picture of the pious warrior was, in many cases, no less than the truth, as evinced in the level of lay funding and donations to monasteries. The spiritual anxieties attendant on violence as a way of life were not confined to the cloister.

Yet if the church accommodated war, it did not surrender to it, rather churchmen of the tenth and eleventh centuries sought to control and direct it in law and in practice. Across western Europe regional power was increasingly vested in the hands of landed aristocrats whose cultural world and social mentality were shaped by the practice of war. Around them emerged a class of dependants, members of their military households and tenants who in turn adopted the habits and outlook of their superiors, the future knights. While in many, but by no means all, parts of western Europe (England, areas of northern France and Germany were exceptions) political power had tended to devolve down to the localities, the years around 1000 did not witness some reversion to a Hobbesian state of nature. At a time of growing population, ownership of land was increasingly profitable, provided control of agricultural and commercial resources was tightly managed. Nucleated estates, often combined into blocs with associated public as well as private fiscal and judicial authority being exercised by the local landowners rather than by distant rulers or their representatives, may have looked chaotic from above, but supplied local cohesion, even if only that of the protection racket. This process of political, judicial and fiscal fragmentation seems especially apparent in western Francia, what is now France, but even here much power remained or was recreated by regional counts. One problem created by this mosaic of private usurpations of public rights, which applied to areas with emergent towns such as Flanders, the Rhineland or north Italy as much as to rural provinces, was the lack of sovereign or effective arbitration. Literally, counts, seigneurs and castellans took the law into their own hands in a process that sharply exacerbated the tendency towards endemic violence. Yet the perpetrators of this seemingly endless round of private violence were often themselves concerned for the destiny of their immortal souls, frenzied violence being interrupted by no less hysterical contrition. Famously, Fulk Nerra, the Black, count of Anjou, punctuated his bloody career of territorial aggrandizement in the Loire valley in the years around 1000 with three pilgrimages to Jerusalem 'driven by fear of hell'; more permanently, he founded a monastery near Loches, where monks could pray 'day and night for the redemption of his soul'.[26]

TOWARDS HOLY WAR: THE ELEVENTH CENTURY

The principles evoked by Odo of Cluny's portrait of Gerald of Aurillac and Odo of St Maur's description of Burchard of Vendôme were not merely literary models. From the later tenth century, initially across the duchy of Aquitaine but spreading to Burgundy and, after an apparent lull in the third quarter of the eleventh century, resuming in northern France and the Rhineland, bishops summoned clergy and laity to councils at which they proclaimed the Peace of God, reinforced from the 1020s with Truces of God. The Peace of God consisted of agreement by the arms-bearers, under oath, to protect those outside the pale of the military classes: monks, other clergy, the weak, the vulnerable and the poor, just those, in fact, for whom Burchard of Vendôme allegedly spent his time fighting. The Truces specified periods during which all violence should cease. Both were to be policed by the local arms-bearers, under oath and the threat of excommunication and ecclesiastical interdict. The oaths exacted at these councils were regarded as demonstrating a communal repentance as much as responsibility, all sections of free society being apparently represented in attempts to expiate sins and alleviate God's punishment in the shape not only of violence but of pestilence and famine. To this end, many councils were held in the awesome presence of the relics (i.e. almost invariably cadavers or bones) of local saints. There was an apparent contradiction in churchmen who willingly blessed the warriors' instruments of death proclaiming, as did the Council of Narbonne in 1054, that 'no Christian shall kill another Christian for whoever kills a Christian undoubtedly sheds the blood of Christ'.[27]

The Peace and Truce of God movements, sporadic, local, regional and ineffectual though they were, provided if not a model for the laity then a pattern for the clergy that directly influenced the inception of the First Crusade. The role of the knight was couched in positive language, as protector of Christian peace, specifically of the church and its interests. The clergy assumed leadership in tackling the material as well as moral ills of the temporal world and commanded the laity; oaths bound laymen into corporate action for a religious end, peace. Logically, if knights were forbidden to pursue their profession within Christendom, then just causes outside had to be found. It was no coincidence that Urban II's speech launching the First Crusade echoed in setting, style and possibly even content the exhortations of the Peace and Truce movement; his audience's vocal responses – 'Deus lo volt!' – paralleled the cries of 'Pax, pax, pax!' at earlier councils; and at Clermont Urban's council passed a decree establishing a Peace throughout Christendom which was promulgated at regional church councils over the following months. Given the revival of the Peace and Truce movement in the 1080s in the Rhineland, a centre of reforming ideas with close contacts with the papacy, the link with holy war, although not geographically universal, was evident.

The problem remained of the legitimate function of arms-bearers in a Christian society. That of benign local policeman hardly fitted the political reality or individual self-image of men who saw what violence could bring; in the case of those Frenchmen who sought their fortunes in southern Italy or England fame, fortune and riches beyond their dreams. Despite concerted attempts from the tenth century, through exhortation and the liturgy, to refine the attitudes of arms-bearers to ensure righteous motives, just cause and humility even in victory, the prevailing ideology remained that, however lawful the conflict, fighting was sinful, the occupation of arms intrinsically a sin. This traditional position was retained by the widely influential canon lawyer Burchard, bishop of Worms (d. 1025) and even in his early years by Pope Gregory VII, who was to transform papal ideas on arms-bearing. In 1066, William of Normandy had invaded England with explicit papal approval, his cause deemed just, his army fighting under a papal banner. His opponent, Harold II, was adjudged an oath-breaker, having previously promised to support William's claim to the throne, a usurper and, thanks to his patronage of a pluralist archbishop of Canterbury of contested legitimacy, a schismatic. Nonetheless, in 1070 on all who had fought with William at Hastings and had killed or wounded men penances were imposed even though the invasion was recognized as a 'public war' in the classical sense.[28] The idea that an arms-bearer could be truly penitent whilst remaining a warrior, still less use fighting itself as a penance, was a development only of the twenty years before Urban II's ideological coup of 1095 and a result of precise circumstances of papal policy and perceived threats to the Roman church from within and beyond Christendom's frontiers.

THE PAPACY AND HOLY WAR

In the later eleventh century, holy war became a particular and intimate concern of the reformed papacy, one which was to transform Christian attitudes and practices for half a millennium. The main thrust of papal reform was towards restoring to the church the pristine autonomy and spirituality of the Acts of the Apostles. This required enforcing canonical rules on the secular clergy, prohibiting abuses such as simony (buying or selling a cure of souls), clerical marriage, treating ecclesiastical office as property or political position and the intrusion of lay control over clergy and churches. A radical alteration was projected in the relationship of church and state which, since the Carolingians and perhaps since Constantine, had assumed mutual cooperation rather than separation. This carried severe political risks. At most centres of political power, the church was inextricably linked with secular rule: kings, notably in England or Germany, looked to churchmen for material and political assistance, received their prayers in scarcely disguised king cults and exercised recognized powers of patronage in church appointments. Exclusion of lay control not only undermined powerful and well-established political structures, it cut at local patronage systems whereby donor families maintained close, proprietorial interests in monasteries they had founded or subsidized or in parishes they had established on their estates. For the secular clergy, reform implied a deliberate attempt to distinguish the clerical order from the habits and behaviour of the laity. Crudely, reform aimed at making them more like monks in celibacy, in immunity from the material snares of money and personal property, and in obedience, to canon law, their ecclesiastical superiors and, ultimately, the pope. The social impact was potentially considerable, marking the end of the inheritance of clerical land and office. For the church, while there were clear economic advantages in denying the heritability, division and potential alienation of church property, there remained the argument of law and morality. The impact of papal reform was profound because of such effective combination of the temporal and spiritual.

While moral and institutional reform of the clergy had been promoted in many areas of early eleventh-century western Christendom, the annexation of the papal office by a cosmopolitan group of radicals and puritans from the mid-1040s provided reformers with the oldest, most dignified institution of church government with which to exercise authority and impose doctrinal, legal and liturgical uniformity. The challenges to the reformed papacy became those of politics and discipline as well as law and doctrine. Skilfully, if controversially, manipulating political circumstances in Italy and Germany, the reforming popes asserted not just the independence of the church, *libertas ecclesiae*, but the autonomous primacy of the see of St Peter. Trumpeting the Petrine texts in the New Testament as demonstrating how Christ gave St Peter – and therefore the pope as his heir or, more telling, vicar (i.e. representative) – rule of the church and authority in heaven and on earth (e.g. Matthew 16:18–19), the reforming popes increasingly claimed authority not just over all churches but over states and laymen as well. Ideologically and politically, this invited opposition, much of it physical. To establish and protect their 'right order' of Christendom, successive popes were forced or chose to fight with temporal weapons. The First Crusade was a direct result of this.

In recruiting allies or raising their own troops, later eleventh-century popes were fully aware of the theoretical implications as much as the political necessities. The moral standing of those who fought for the pope became a matter of acute concern. In 1053, Leo IX (1048–54) offered German troops who fought (unsuccessfully) under his personal command against the Norman bandit lords of southern Italy remission of penance and absolution of sins. In 1059, as a result of a major diplomatic revolution, these same Normans became papal vassals, with the obligation to fight for their new lord. Papal banners were granted the Norman invaders of Sicily (in 1060) and England (in 1066) and to Milanese street gangs, the Patarines, engaged in a violent and protracted struggle for the eradication of clerical abuses and control of the archbishopric of the city in the 1060s and 1070s. Holy war became part of the papal programme. The Patarine conflict was called a *bellum Dei*, a war of God, the fallen Patarine leader Erlembald (d. 1075), a martyr. The key testing ground of papal reform and power was in Germany, where any loosening of the link between church and state or challenge to imperial authority was fiercely opposed by Emperor Henry IV. From the late 1070s disagreements turned to war, the so-called wars of the Investiture Contest, although the issues were far broader than whether or not kings should invest bishops with ring and staff. To fight for papal interests, the most militant of the reforming popes, Gregory VII, even attempted to recruit knights from across Europe to form a papal army, a *militia sancti Petri*, a Militia of St Peter.

Gregory VII significantly developed the theory and practice of holy war and holy warriors. Although not given to citing Augustine of Hippo himself, his loyal henchman Bishop Anselm II of Lucca, in his *Collectio canonum* (i.e. Collection of canon law) of *c.*1083, brought together the Augustinian theories of just war in one contained, intelligible and coherent place for the first time, although its circulation was limited. Gregory, one of whose favourite scriptural quotations was 'Cursed is he who keeps back his sword from bloodshed' (Jeremiah 48:10), preferred a moral rather than legal approach. He identified two forms of occupation for arms-bearers, one secular, selfish and sinful, the other penitential, justified by legitimate rights, loyalty to a lord, protection of the vulnerable or defence of the church. Writing in the decade after Gregory's death, a vigorous papalist propagandist, Bishop Bonizo of Sutri, in his *Liber de Vita Christiana*, identified those who, 'for their salvation and the common good', fought schismatics, heretics and excommunicates and protected the poor, orphans and widows, as members of an 'ordo pugnatorum', an order of warriors to rank in the social hierarchy, precisely the group implied by the Militia of St Peter and to whom Urban II sought to direct his appeal in 1095.[29] By the end of his stormy pontificate, Gregory VII offered all who fought for his cause, in whatever fashion, absolution of their sins and the prospect of eternal salvation. Provided their motivation was grounded on selflessness and faith not gain, such soldiers could combine penance and violence. In castigating his opponents and encouraging his followers Gregory extended his rhetoric, likening service in such a just war as an imitation of Christ's sufferings against 'those who are the enemies of the cross of Christ'.[30]

Gregory was not merely a rhetorician or theorist. Even before becoming pope, as archdeacon of the Roman church, he had taken a keen interest in wars on behalf of the church, in Sicily, England and Milan. As pope, this continued. In 1076, he offered absolution of all sins to the knights of Count Roger of Sicily on a projected campaign against the Saracens as he did to those joining an attack on Byzantium in 1080 to restore, as Gregory mistakenly thought, the rightful emperor. Throughout the 1070s and 1080s, he tried to enlist *milites* in Italy, Germany and France to coerce clergy contumaciously clinging to unreformed practices of simony and fornication as much as he encouraged the civil conflict in Milan and, after 1080, armed resistance to Henry IV in Germany and Italy. Beyond the specific justifications of war and the function of the arms-bearer, this extension of papal approval and rhetoric lent these conflicts a sustained ideological quality Gregory deliberately fostered and publicized. Those involved were bombarded with rhetoric from all sides insisting on the principles for which they were fighting, conceived in terms of service to God. Many, like the *fidelis beati Sancti Petri* Raymond IV of Toulouse or the duke of Lower Lorraine, Godfrey of Bouillon, who fought for the emperor in Italy against the pope in the 1080s, were to answer the call to Jerusalem in 1096. The level of this propaganda war was such as to indicate that catching the imaginations of the knights themselves was no accident. Not all was conducted on the highest intellectual plane. One imperialist propagandist nicknamed Godfrey of Bouillon's predecessor but one as duke of Lorraine, another Godfrey, but a staunch papalist, as 'Prickfrey' or 'Shitfrey'.[31]

The ideological rhetoric of the Investiture Contest wars and the recruitment of knights to establish and protect the Peace and Truce of God depended on the susceptibility of western knights to a religiously framed ideology of war. The Anglo-Norman chronicler Orderic Vitalis left a sharp portrait of one such pious warlord. Hugh, count of Avranches in western Normandy and earl of Chester in north-west England, a nephew of William the Conqueror, had done very well out of the Norman conquest of England, a classic example of that eleventh-century aristocratic mobility and fluid opportunistic careerism that fuelled the First Crusade. In establishing his power on the fringes of the Anglo-Norman realm, Hugh, called by some 'the wolf', acquired a foul reputation; vicious, violent, addicted to gambling, a lecher and a glutton, so fat he could hardly move, he was 'a great lover of the world' (not a recommendation in the eyes of the monk who used the phrase). Brave, extravagant and generous to the point of prodigality, he attracted around him a rowdy household in which many were as debauched and sybaritic as he. Yet Hugh was also a patron of monks and an old and close friend of the saintly abbot and archbishop Anselm. He employed a chaplain, Gerold, who furthered the moral instruction of his household with stories of 'holy knights' from the Old Testament and of Christian military heroes, including the legendary William of Orange, a saintly warrior in one of the earliest cycles of *chansons de geste*. Some in Gerold's audience were so moved that they became monks; Hugh himself died (in 1101) in the habit of a Benedictine.[32] Such figures were found across western Christendom, from Denmark to Sicily. In such a raucous atmosphere of passion, carnality, militarism and piety was nurtured the mentality of the holy warriors of 1096, among them friends and relatives of Hugh, possessed of the self-righteousness of ideological conviction to add to the heady brew of hedonism, brutality, guilt, obligation, spirituality and remorse. These were precisely the skilled soldiers Gregory VII had hoped to recruit and Urban II did.

The most dramatic and quixotic of Gregory's military plans was that of 1074, when he announced his intention to lead in person an army to help the Christians of the eastern Mediterranean, who were beleaguered by the Seljuk Turks, 'to take up arms against the enemies of God and push forwards even to the sepulchre of the Lord under His supreme leadership'. The diplomatic context, involving a delicate and unstable triangle of Byzantium, the papacy and the Normans, was specific, in part a consequence of the Greek defeat by the Seljuk Turks at Manzikert (1071). However, the objects of the enterprise – apparently Jerusalem, the consolidation of relations with the eastern church, the demonstration of active papal leadership of the whole of Christendom, lay and ecclesiastical, east and west – as well as the rhetoric, pointed directly to the path his protégé Urban II later chose. The language was especially striking, with its persistent emphasis, not only on St Peter, as was usual in his calls to arms, but on Christ Himself:

> the example of our Redeemer and the duty of brotherly love demand of us that we should set our hearts upon the deliverance of our brethren. For as He offered his life for us, so ought we to offer our lives for our brothers.

Gregory hoped he could 'with Christ's help carry succour to the Christians who are being slaughtered by the pagans'; preferable even to dying for one's country, 'it is most beautiful and glorious indeed to give our mortal bodies for Christ, who is life eternal'. He called on the faithful 'to defend the Christian faith and serve (*militare*) the heavenly king' thus 'by a transitory labour you can win an eternal reward'.[33] Similar Christocentric rhetoric suffused Urban II's preaching of the First Crusade twenty years later. Before he became pope, Odo of Largery, as cardinal-bishop of Ostia from 1080, had been very close to Gregory VII, once described as his *pedisequus*, lackey or valet. Within the papal Curia in the early twelfth century, therefore among those who may have known those involved first or at most second hand, Urban II's crusade was seen explicitly as completing Gregory's abortive project of 1074.

Gregory's scheme of 1074 displayed a broad sense of history. The pope placed his desire to help and be reconciled with the eastern church in the context of papal visits to Constantinople that had ceased in the early eighth century when the Carolingian Franks were adopted as the new protectors of the church in the west. The church's legitimizing of war in the eleventh century was similarly influenced by a historical perspective. Just as Carolingian warriors gained in reputation by being seen as the champions of Christianity against pagan and infidel foes, so the perception of a turn in what had seemed an inexorable tide running against Christendom not only inspired gestures such as Gregory VII's in 1074 and Urban II's in 1095 but enhanced the status of those called upon to fight for the Faith. However important the just and holy war against enemies of the church in general, the highest justification for knighthood was the battle against the infidel, against Islam. The earliest vernacular French *chansons de geste* of the late eleventh and early twelfth century, which provide some insight into the mentality and idealism of the arms-bearing classes, while displaying little of the trappings of the crusade – war as penance, Jerusalem and the Holy Land, papal authorization – demonstrated the special status of war against the infidel, who stood both in practice and in literary type as the absolute antithesis to the Christian world, a dangerous alien aping of the familiar and the good. As the *Song of Roland*, the earliest surviving version of which seems to have been consolidated *c.*1100, put it in a notorious line: 'Paien unt tort e chrestiens unt dreit' (Pagans are wrong and Christians are right).[34] The memory of the long struggle with Islam from the seventh century was not lost 400 years later. If anything, it had grown in symbolic as well as political significance, an exaggerated exercise in collective religious and cultural nostalgia. The context of western reactions to Islam in the eleventh century was of a period of active military confrontation on all frontiers which had been preceded by one of relative stability. The First Crusade occurred at a time of shifting fortunes along the borders of Christendom, which provided the opportunity to think of aggressive campaigns even before the request for aid from the eastern emperor in 1095.

ISLAM AND HOLY WAR

The ten years after the death of Muhammed at Mecca in 632 redrew the political and religious map of the Mediterranean and Near East. The ancient rivals of Christian Byzantium and Sassanian Persia who had fought each other almost to a standstill in a war that had lasted a generation (602–28) proved easy pickings for the Arab-led armies that swept from the Arabian peninsular to conquer the Fertile Crescent: Syria and Palestine 635–41; Persia 637–42; Egypt 640–42. In classical Muslim historiography, deliberately symbolic was the entrance into Jerusalem of the caliph (i.e. successor to the Prophet as Commander of the Faithful), Umar, in February 638. The caliph was not the field commander of operations in Palestine but, with the fall of Jerusalem imminent, he arrived to supervise proceedings. Having negotiated a peaceful surrender of the Holy City whence, Islamic tradition insisted, the Prophet had made his night journey to heaven, Umar entered the city, on a donkey or camel – the sources disagree – ostentatiously dressed in coarse, dirty robes, perhaps in deliberate contrast to the lavish parades favoured by the defeated Byzantines. The religious element in the triumph was clear to both Muslim and Christian commentators. Going to the terrace on which the Jewish Temple had stood, the supposed site of Muhammed's celestial ascent but now reduced to a rubbish tip, Umar ordered the clearance of the site and the construction of a small mosque. Equally, in accordance with the surrender terms, the shrines, churches and synagogues of the Christians and the Jews were left untouched. This iconic moment resonated for centuries; it was entirely appropriate that the fullest contemporary history of crusading and the subsequent western settlements in Palestine and Syria in the twelfth century, by Archbishop William of Tyre, began with the Arab conquests and the failure of the Byzantine emperor Heraclius to resist them.[35]

The conquest of Jerusalem marked just one stage of Muslim expansion. Within a century of the Prophet's death, Muslim rule extended from central Asia and north India to Spain. In the Mediterranean basin, Constantinople had survived the great siege of 674–7, but Byzantine sea supremacy had been shattered; Cyprus had been ceded to joint rule, Muslim control on the mainland of western Asia extended to Armenia and Cilicia, and the Byzantine provinces in north Africa lost by 698. In a lightning campaign, Visigothic Spain was overwhelmed by Arab-led Berber armies in 711–13. Although defeated by the Franks at Poitiers in 732, Muslim armies continued to harass southern Gaul for some years. Although the era of conquest was followed by civil war, religious schism and a collapse of political unity, with Spain and north Africa acquiring separate rulers, the Abbasid caliphs, established since 750 in Baghdad, retained the nominal loyalty of much of the Islamic world. More significantly, an international affinity was created by Islamic culture and, to a lesser degree, religion. The question of the extent of Arabization and Islamicization of conquered lands remains obscure and vexed, but it appears that the process was slow, uneven and, by the eleventh century, still incomplete. It is not certain whether there was even a Muslim majority in Syria or Palestine when the crusaders arrived in 1097.

In part this was a consequence of Islamic law. For those Christians and Jews, People of the Book, living within Muslim lands, the so-called *Dar al-Islam* (House of Islam), religious tolerance was guaranteed by the early Islamic texts. Sura 109 of the Koran declared:

> Unbelievers, I do not serve what you worship, nor do you serve what I worship. I shall never serve what you worship nor will you ever serve what I worship. You have your own religion, and I have mine.

In return for Islamic rule and protection, the People of the Book had to recognize their subordinate status and pay a tax, the *jizya*. Despite the reaction of some modern sentimentalists, there was little of generosity but much of pragmatism in these rules. By contrast, beyond the world of Islamic order, in the *Dar al-harb* (House of War), non-Islamic political structures and individuals were open to attack. All the world must recognize or embrace Islam through conversion or subjugation. Thus on the Muslim community was enjoined *jihad*, struggle. In classical Islamic theory, i.e. traditionally from the seventh and eighth centuries but possibly later, this took two forms, the greater (*al-jihad al-akbar*), the internal spiritual struggle to achieve personal purity, and the lesser (*al-jihad al-asghar*), the military struggle against infidels. Both were obligatory on able-bodied Muslims. Unlike Christian concepts of holy war, to which the Islamic *jihad* appears to have owed nothing, *jihad* was fundamental to the Faith, described by some as a sixth pillar of Islam. In theory, fighting was incumbent on all Muslims until the whole world had been subdued, but it was a spiritual as well as military exercise from the start, and a corporate not individual obligation.

In practice, after the first century of conquest, accommodation was regularly achieved across religious and political frontiers. Islam was not in a constant state of aggression against neighbours and was no more actively militant than their enemies. Continued, almost ritualized raiding across stable frontiers in Asia Minor or Spain was lent added intensity during the collapse of Frankish power and continued Byzantine impotence in the west in the ninth century, highlighted by the conquest of Sicily by 830 and pirate bases being established in Calabria and Provence. However, much Muslim warfare was internal. By the mid-tenth century separate caliphates had been established, that of the Umayyads at Cordoba in Spain was of long standing and reached a pinnacle of success in this century, ending it with raids deep into Christian territory under the command of the effective ruler of Cordoba, al-Mansur. The Fatimid caliphate of north Africa had annexed Egypt in 969, buoyed by its Shi'ite heresy, a religious as well as political challenge to the Abbasids of Baghdad. The tenth century also saw a revival of Byzantine military power. Nicephoras Phocas (963–9) regained Cyprus and Syrian Antioch; his successor, John Tzimisces (969–76), campaigned in northern Iraq (974) and, in 975, in Syria and northern Palestine, his propaganda possibly even offering the prospect of a recapture of the holy sites of Jerusalem.

Yet such wars were hardly religious, even if some thought them just or holy. The Greeks wished to secure the eastern marches of Asia Minor; Nicephoras was perfectly willing to allow Muslim Aleppo to become a client, self-governing city. Al-Mansur posed as a holy warrior, yet he hired Christian mercenaries and his attack on the famous shrine of

St James at Compostela in Galicia in 997 was only made possible by Christian nobles who acted as guides.[36] This essentially secular pattern continued into the eleventh century, especially in Spain, where Christian adventurers rifled through the debris left by the collapse of the Cordoba caliphate from the 1030s, often in alliance with, or in the service of, Muslim princelings.

From the perspective of the western church, conflict with Islam was *ipso facto* meritorious in a religious context. Whatever the reality of ambitious Italian trading cities, Norman bandits, Spanish lords or even Greek princes, churchmen, in particular successive popes, conceptualized the conflict, fitting it into a wider picture of cosmic significance and individual grace. Whereas in the ninth century, Christendom appeared genuinely threatened, the frontier skirmishing of the eleventh century was of a very different order, yet the rhetoric was conversely gaudier. This was of considerable importance as the attitude to wars against the infidel in the earlier eleventh century coloured the whole approach of Urban II. The motives for holy war were always ever only partly practical, those directed against Muslims often being only tangentially related to any military necessity in defence of Christendom. What counted for successive popes was the place of these wars in Christian history and the opportunity they afforded for a revival of religious enthusiasm, devotion and piety, essentially concerns internal to the church and Christian society.

This is not to say that religion played no part in these wars. Pisan raids on Palermo in Sicily (1063) and al-Mahdiya in north Africa (1087) were consciously placed in the context of Christian service. The Norman invaders of Sicily after 1060, supported by papal encouragement and banner, were regarded by some as champions of the Faith. Their troops took Communion before battle; their efforts were sustained by visions of saints; and one Italian chronicler (who died in 1085, so avoiding the hindsight of the First Crusade that infected others) had the Norman leader Robert Guiscard declare his wish to free Christians from Muslim rule and to 'avenge the injury done to God'.[37]

Pilgrimage and war marched closely together. The Pisan al-Mahdiya campaign in 1087 included a pilgrimage to Rome. Frenchmen were habitués of the pilgrimage to Compostela as well as the *reconquista*. A grant of indulgences by Pope Alexander II has been variously interpreted, if genuine, as applying either to war or pilgrimage or both.[38] Gregory

VII's enigmatic reference to the Holy Sepulchre in 1074 hinted at a fusion of ideas, unsurprising in a pope so concerned with the ramifications of confession and penance as well as war. Partly no doubt as a consequence of an increase in pilgrimages, especially to Jerusalem, attested by Muslim as well as western observers and itself a result of the increase in Byzantine power in the Balkans and the eastern Mediterranean under Emperor Basil the Bulgar Slayer (d. 1025), there was a distinct frisson of outrage at the arbitrary destruction of the church of the Holy Sepulchre by the unstable Fatimid caliph of Egypt, al-Hakim, in 1009. Whether or not Pope Sergius IV (1009–12) encouraged the creation of a Christian relief fleet with a promise of indulgences, news of the outrage rang across the west. In a grim foreshadowing of the anti-Semitism of later Jerusalem holy warriors, a Burgundian chronicler, Ralph Glaber (d. 1046), recorded how Jewish communities in France were perversely blamed for inciting al-Hakim and were violently persecuted in consequence.[39] Elsewhere, chroniclers saw those fighting wars of profit in Spain or in the Venetian defence of Bari against Muslims in 1003 as inspired by faith, as indeed may have been the participants themselves. In 1015–16, Pope Benedict VIII (1012–24) openly approved a Pisan and Genoese raid on Muslim pirate bases in Sardinia. The Limousin monk Adhemar of Chabannes (d. 1034) not only recorded the Jewish libel over the destruction of the Holy Sepulchre, adding gory details of atrocities against eastern Christians, but frequently mentioned campaigns against the Moors in Spain and, in describing a supposed Muslim attack on Narbonne *c.*1018, told of the Christian defenders receiving Communion before battle. Adam, who referred to his warlike lay uncles with pride, revealed a world in which religiosity and violence were as close as his lay and clerical relatives.[40]

From 1060, the reformed papacy applied their theories of justified war with even greater vigour and legal precision to campaigns against the infidel than they did to those against their Christian enemies. In Sicily, the ethos of holy war was carefully nurtured, extending to the eccentric but politically convenient expedient of appointing the military commander, Count Roger, Robert Guiscard's equally bellicose younger brother, as papal legate, the pope's representative in running the church in the newly conquered island. Although it appears that many holy war aspects of the reconquest of Muslim Spain resulted from the First Crusade rather than the other way round, the Iberian peninsula attracted interest from popes and French knights and fitted neatly and centrally into the increasingly grandiose concepts of world destiny being peddled not just by papal apologists but by monastic reformers as well. Glaber, a Cluniac Benedictine whose order had a long and close interest both in the Christian kingdoms of northern Spain and in promoting pilgrimage, peppered his chronicle with accounts of pilgrimages to Jerusalem (which he feared had become abused as a fashionable accessory for those seeking prestige not penitence); Christian warfare against the Moors in Spain and, on one occasion, the Slavs beyond the Elbe; and the Peace and Truce of God movement. Glaber was in no doubt of the efficacy of all of them; even monks who broke their vows and *in extremis* took up arms, were seen as gaining salvation.[41] In this context, papal approval and grants of specific spiritual privileges to warriors against infidels would have occasioned little surprise. It is likely that Alexander II offered a lifting of all penances and remission of sins to campaigners in Spain in 1064. Gregory VII advertised 'eternal reward' for recruits against the infidel (and others) in 1074. In 1089, Urban II himself urged the colonization of the devastated frontier city of Tarragona on the Spanish coast south of Barcelona as a penitential act. The rebuilding of the city was described in military terms, as providing a wall of Christianity against the Muslims; those joining the enterprise could substitute it for any planned penitential pilgrimage, including that to Jerusalem, later specified as 'indulgence of your sins'.[42]

Theories and practices of morally just and spiritually meritorious warfare had developed unevenly in response to changing political circumstances, religious outlook and social behaviour. Many clung to older concepts of sin and spiritual war. Some feigned or genuinely felt shock at the unapologetic and unequivocal combination of war and penance proposed by Urban II in 1095. Yet the pre-history of the First Crusade was long and illustrious. Holy war against infidels who, by the late eleventh century, appeared if not in retreat then at least to be subject to attack on equal terms, provided one means of morally legitimate expression for a military aristocracy whose social authority and robust culture served to highlight their spiritual vulnerability. The detritus of legal justifications, scriptural, Patristic and classical, thrown into relief by actual experience in the Carolingian period and by romanticized echoes of it enshrined in vernacular *chansons de geste*, supplied material from which fresh theories of holy war could be constructed. The catalyst was as much the perspectives and interests of the reformed papacy as the external threats presented by Islam: together they set the stage for Urban II. Yet much of what was proclaimed as new by the call to arms in 1095 represented old wine in new bottles; the winepress from which it came was grimed with use and age.

2
The Summons to Jerusalem

The sermon preached by Pope Urban II outside the cathedral at Clermont in the Auvergne on Tuesday, 27 November 1095 has been seen as setting in train one of the most renowned sequence of events in the history of western Europe and Christianity. The story has resonated down the centuries; of how tens of thousands willingly uprooted themselves for the sake of liberating Jerusalem, a place of unimaginable physical remoteness yet ubiquitous immediate appeal; of how, suffering horrific losses and agonizing obstacles, they were painfully forged into an army that appeared to campaign as much in a war of the spirit as of the flesh; of how they surmounted seemingly fatal odds, of climate, terrain, local hostility and superior enemy numbers in repeated desperate battles and skirmishes; and of how, after three years on the road, the survivors stormed the Holy City, reclaiming it for Christendom, as one awed observer remarked, 460 years after its loss to Islam under the Emperor Heraclius.[1] If the response to Urban's appeal astonished all and shocked some, the outcome provided its own justification, creating a legend to feed the imaginations of western Europeans, to stir their emotions and haunt their nightmares.

The luminosity of the story of triumph over adversity in the cause of God, shining with epic, romance, adventure, excitement, glamour, heroism and the supernatural, casts shade as well as light. It suited promoters and apologists as well as the conquering heroes themselves, the proud Jerusalemites, to depict this holy war as a coherent narrative, of defined armies and a clear pattern of campaign. The story of the march to Jerusalem obscured much that failed to fit an acceptable and accepted literary and theological pattern, or challenged the embroidered reminiscences of the returned warriors of Christ. So far from a sudden clap of thunder or a leap in the dark, the devising and prosecution of what is now called the First Crusade, if unexpected, was not entirely unfamiliar, while much of the process remains unknown and unknowable.

The traditional version, largely derived from contemporary chronicles reflecting the experiences and perspectives of contingents and commentators in northern and southern France combined with a distinctive view from Lorraine, describes a series of armies leaving the west from the spring to the autumn of 1096 in explosive popular response to the inspirational and novel preaching of Urban II and his agents; their rendezvous was Constantinople, which all had reached by the end of May 1097. The earliest contingents, some associated with the charismatic preacher Peter the Hermit, often misleadingly known as the Peasants' Crusades, after engaging in destructive attacks on Jewish communities in France and the Rhineland, continued to display indiscipline as they were picked off by enraged locals during separate marches across the Balkans, those who eventually reached Constantinople being massacred in their first serious military encounter with the Turks of western Asia Minor in the autumn of 1096. The armies of the so-called Princes' Crusade, with more discipline, military skill, diplomatic contacts and money, fared better. Led by great nobles such as the dukes of Lower Lorraine and Normandy, the counts of Toulouse, Boulogne, Flanders, Blois and the brother of the king of France and count of Apulia, accompanied by important churchmen, including a papal legate, and large numbers of knights, dependent and free, as well as footsoldiers, servants, camp-followers and subsidized pilgrims, these armies coalesced at the siege of Nicaea near the Asiatic shore of the Bosporus in June 1097.

With financial and military assistance from the Byzantine emperor, this skilled but disparate army fought its way across Anatolia before crashing into northern Syria in October 1097. During an extraordinary siege of Antioch (October 1097 to June 1098), when appalling material conditions and fear of military vulnerability caused many to desert, and a near-miraculous defeat of a Syrian relief force, the western army found sustenance to their morale in visions, relics and a growing belief in their providential status. In the wake of this advance, parts of Cilician Armenia, some ports on the north Syrian coast and the city of Edessa across the river Euphrates in northern Iraq fell under western control or effective influence. After internal bickering over precedence and land following the death of the papal legate (August 1098), most of the leaders joined the final, largely unopposed march south into Palestine in May 1099, reaching Jerusalem on 7 June. After a desperate siege in arid high summer, with the threat of an Egyptian relief army ever closer, the city was bloodily stormed on 15 July, its occupation confirmed by a startling victory over the Egyptians at Ascalon a month later. Leaving a garrison established in Jerusalem under Godfrey of Bouillon, most of the troops, their vows well fulfilled, returned home, mainly by sea, their deeds exciting immediate, if unsuccessful, imitation, in particular by armies from Lombardy, Bavaria and France (1100–1102), and almost universal praise. Judged on any criteria, the achievement of the expedition to Jerusalem was stupendous.[2]

By explaining these spectacular events in terms of divine will, contemporaries found neither need nor inclination to inquire too deeply into the gestation, purpose, timing or nature of Urban's appeal. Still less were they able to produce a comprehensive view of all operations connected with the journey east. Although there was disagreement between local traditions over details (as in different provinces boasting one of their own as the first man over the walls of the Holy City), and at least one account, that of the Lorrainer Albert of Aachen (Aix), attributing the original inspiration of the whole enterprise to Peter the Hermit rather than the pope, the events themselves provided their own explanation and justification without causing anxiety over what occurred beyond the vision or hearing of the writer and his sources. Thus the direct and indirect accounts of eyewitnesses, many of which fed off each other, were partial and artificial, literary and didactic. Raymond of Aguilers, chaplain to the count of Toulouse, is frank about his concerns, lest the deeds of the victors of 1099 be distorted by rumours spread by 'misfits of war and cowardly deserters'. His openness may stand for all:

> It is a matter of record that God's army, although it bore the whip of the Lord for its transgressions, nevertheless triumphed over all paganism because of His loving kindness. But it seems too tiresome to write of each journey since some went through Sclavonia, others by Hungary, by Lombardy, or by the sea. So, we have taken care to write of the Count of Saint-Gilles, the bishop of Le Puy, and their army without bothering with the others.[3]

As a result, although the most famous episode of its age and place, there is much about the First Crusade that is confused and irrecoverable.

It is not only private motives that elude scrutiny. After the first five identifiable groups of Jew-persecuting crusaders had left the Rhineland by the beginning of June 1096, further attacks on Jewish communities occurred in June and July to the north, in Xanten, Geldern, Neuss, Wiehr and Wevelinghoren, hitherto untouched by the pogroms. Who precisely the perpetrators were, who led them and what happened to them is wholly obscure. When Peter the Hermit arrived in Constantinople in August 1096, he discovered a large army of Italians already there; again their provenance, leadership, organization and route have left no trace in the sources. When the princes' army arrived in the environs of Antioch in October 1097, they discovered that two nearby ports on the coast of north Syria, St Symeon and Lattakiah, had already been captured by western fleets that included Genoese and *angli* (literally 'English'). These may have acted in concert with crusade leaders or the Byzantine emperor, or not. For the next eighteen months, western shipping appeared regularly in Levantine waters without any clear account of their origins, such as another fleet of *angli* that reached St Symeon in March 1098, having put in at the Italian port of Lucca en route. These mariners, numerous other groups and thousands of individuals who joined the 'great stirring' (*motio valida*) have little or no history.[4] To generalize about their expectations and experiences is inherently futile and possibly distorting. The picture of the First Crusade is far from clear, well delineated or fixed despite the fierce attention it has attracted over more than 900 years. Its story can only be tentative and incomplete, the stuff of legend indeed.

When Urban II stood before the crowd at the end of the council at Clermont neither was unprepared. In March 1095, at a council at Piacenza in Lombardy, ambassadors from the Byzantine emperor, Alexius I Comnenus, appealed for military aid against his hostile neighbours, the latest in a succession of such requests. A few years earlier, Alexius had asked Urban to organize help against the Pechenegs in the Balkans. Now, according to a western account, the enemy were described as 'pagans' who threatened eastern Christians and were menacing even Constantinople itself.[5] Whatever the strategic validity of such claims, the combination of military danger and religious solidarity bore strong echoes of the schemes of the 1070s. Urban turned this opportunity to his own purposes. After years of defensiveness since Gregory VII's expulsion from Rome by the imperialists in 1084, the papal party had begun to consolidate its position in Italy, France and Germany. The Council of Piacenza, a clear demonstration of papal power as the first international ecclesiastical assembly of Urban's pontificate, witnessed Gregorianism in action, sitting in judgement on the state of the church and the morals of the clergy and debating the sins of emperors and kings, specifically the conduct of Henry IV of Germany and the adultery of Philip I, the Fat, of France. This latest Greek request could be incorporated into this new confident papal assertiveness. It was recorded that the pope exhorted 'many' to promise to help Alexius against the 'pagans' by taking an oath.[6]

To capitalize on the achievement of Piacenza, Urban planned his elaborate tour of France, the first by a pope for almost half a century. This was to culminate at the Council of Clermont, attended by at least thirteen archbishops, eighty-two bishops, countless abbots and a host of other clerics. The geographical embrace of this gathering was impressive, from the Anglo-Norman realms and Artois in the north to Upper Austria in the east to Italy in the south; the assembling of such a gathering was a matter of weeks if not months; its business neither random nor spontaneous but premeditated. However, the council provided only part of the pope's business and itinerary. Urban arrived in Provence in July 1095. During the following fourteen months before returning to Italy in September 1096, he conducted a unique papal tour, covering much of southern, central, western and south-eastern France: Provence, Languedoc, the Rhône valley, Burgundy, the Auvergne, the Limousin, Anjou, Maine, Touraine, Poitou, the Bordelais, his journey punctuated by theatrical ceremonies, assemblies and preaching in some of the most important religious and urban centres: Nîmes, Avignon, Lyons, Cluny, Mâcon, Clermont, Limoges, Angers, Le Mans, Tours, Poitiers, Bordeaux, Moissac, Toulouse, Carcassonne, Montpellier, Arles. His avoidance of the territories under the direct control of the Capetian king, in the Orléannais and the Ile de France, and those of the feuding heirs to the Anglo-Norman lands, William II of England and Duke Robert of Normandy, was political and deliberate; the French king was to be excommunicated at the Clermont Council; the Normans were too successfully old-fashioned in their control of their clergy and too ambivalent in their loyalty to the Urbanist cause for comfort. Flanders and Lorraine were too far north and close to strong imperialists. The impact of the papal visit was great, the physical presence of such an august figure attracting special excitement in regions unused to such grand progresses.

By the time he reached Clermont in November Urban had already been on the road for four months, visiting significant religious and secular centres in Provence, Languedoc and Burgundy, including his *alma mater*, the abbey of Cluny, where on 25 October he dedicated the high altar of the new church that Abbot Hugh had begun to build, the ruins of which still stand as a reminder of the awesome scale and grandeur of Cluniac monasticism. Before arriving at Clermont he had almost certainly discussed his eastern project with Raymond IV of St Gilles count of Toulouse, a veteran of wars in Spain, and Adhemar of Monteil, bishop of Le Puy, both of whom were to play central roles in the expedition, as well as the bishop of Cahors and, very probably, the archbishop of Lyons and the abbot of Cluny, in addition to the cardinals and Italian clerics in his entourage, which included Daimbert, archbishop of Pisa, later patriarch of Jerusalem after its capture in 1099. To the Clermont meeting, diocesans were asked to bring with them the most powerful magnates from their regions (*excellentiores principes*); the bishop of Arras was specifically encouraged by his archbishop to invite Baldwin of Mons, count of Hainault, who was later to join up, dying in an ambush while on an embassy to the Greek emperor in Asia Minor in 1098.[7] In Burgundy, a story persisted that at a regional council at Autun, possibly held during Urban's stay in late October 1095 on his way to Clermont, 'the first vows for the Jerusalem journey were sworn'.[8]

The consistency of Urban's correspondence with what was later thought he had said at Clermont by eyewitnesses and with contemporary perceptions revealed in charters of departing soldiers and in accounts such as that of Count Fulk le Rechin (the Sour) of Anjou, who left a description of the pope's preaching in the Loire valley in early 1096, strongly suggest that Urban travelled to France with most, if not all, the elements of his eastern project in place: a penitential journey in arms to Jerusalem to recover the Holy Sepulchre and to 'liberate Christianity' and the eastern Christians, the expedition earning warriors satisfaction of penance and remission of sin, signalled by a vow to enforce the obligation and the adoption of the sign of the cross to distinguish those who, in the words even of a grudging papal critic, had swapped the 'militia of the world' (*militia mundi*) for the 'militia of God' (*militia Dei*).[9] With him, Urban carried relics of the True Cross, one of which he used to consecrate the abbey church of Marmoutier, near Tours, in

March 1096, an event that coincided with local magnate recruits 'in the presence of the pope stitch(ing) onto their clothes the insignia of the holy cross'.[10] Taking the cross became the emblematic and defining gesture of crusading. The crosses to be worn were usually of textile, wool or occasionally silk, large enough to be noticed but small enough to be sewn on to the shoulder of a cloak or tunic.

The planning was meticulous, part of a wider programme. At the Council of Clermont, the Jerusalem decree was one of more than thirty that promulgated a general Peace and dealt with issues of penance, ecclesiastical organization and discipline, simony, clerical marriage, lay investiture and sanctuary. The call to arms sat squarely within this assertion of church discipline, moral reform of clergy and laity, and papal authority. Geoffrey, abbot of Vendôme, recalled Urban personally distinguishing between the journey enjoined on the laity and the prohibition on the participation of monks, signals of discipline confirmed in Urban's own correspondence. Papal spiritual and temporal authority was expressed by the grant of the remission of sins and the appointment of Adhemar of Le Puy as leader of the expedition 'in our place', as Urban wrote to the Flemish in December 1095; it was confirmed by the enthusiastic response.[11] The link between the Jerusalem journey and papal power politics so impressed the gossipy English writer William of Malmesbury a generation later that he insinuated that Urban dreamt up the whole idea in order to create enough upheaval and turmoil to allow him to recapture Rome.[12] Yet, if the context was a restatement of Gregorian ideals and practices, the expedition to Jerusalem was both novel and distinct, a bold, radical reformulation of Gregorian ideas and expedients concerning penance, war and moral regeneration presented in a succession of carefully designed public demonstrations of which that at Clermont was only the most lavish, and, in fact, not even the most successful.

Urban II's speech at Clermont was the first public declaration of his new concept of holy war that we know of. The event itself was carefully orchestrated, its theatricality aimed at establishing a concrete image and memory. In a partially literate society, ceremonies acted as media for information, exhortation and formalized debate, as in the regular crown-wearings by kings such as William the Conqueror, or at the Peace and Truce of God assemblies. In the repeated familiar ritual of church liturgy, the mass exposed with particular force basic issues of the relationship of God and man, sin and redemption; it provided an ideal setting for preaching the Jerusalem expedition. At Clermont, the presence of such a grand figure as the pope itself lent power to the imagery of language and action, the flavour of penance in his Christocentric message strengthened by its proclamation five days before the beginning of the penitential season of Advent. During the speech, chanting of the slogan 'Deus lo volt', probably led by a papal claque, established the participation of the congregation in the ritual as well as symbolizing the correct submissive acceptance of divine guidance.[13] At Clermont the unfamiliarity of the new ritualistic forms, notably taking the cross, and the uncertainty of the correct response presented problems. As with all revivalist meetings, Urban's sermon demanded a physical as well as vocal reaction; nothing destroys the message of ritual more certainly than unease or confusion in its performance. Later crusade preachers were in no doubt of the importance of a member of the audience to set an example, to use an analogy from modern Christian evangelists, by promptly 'coming on down' to take the cross. 'Converts' were often planted to be the first to respond in this fashion after the end of the sermon.[14] At Clermont this role was taken by Adhemar of Le Puy, who, following Urban's address, demonstrated to the rest what was expected of them by immediately taking the cross, numbers of which, some recorded, had been prepared earlier. At the end of the subsequent oath-taking, a cardinal led the congregation in the general confession, a prayer familiar to all from the mass. The ceremonial of commitment, confession, penance, oath and cross proved iconic and effective, its imagery and language lending distinctive identity to the recruits in the *exercitus Dei*. Some of those 'signed' with the cross saw themselves as pilgrims, *peregrini*, receiving the recognized symbols of pilgrimage, such as the napkin or satchel and staff. Thus novelty and familiarity could be satisfyingly and effectively blended. The crusade and the pilgrimage were originally distinct. Yet official correspondence and chroniclers suggest a rapid fusion of language, images and ideology; charters recording departing crusaders' property transactions talk of penitential journeying as often as explicit fighting, their models similar contracts struck by earlier pilgrims; it is frequently very difficult to see the difference. Members of the mass German pilgrimage to Jerusalem in 1064–5, said to number 7,000, had, according to one account, worn crosses. The attitudes and social rituals of Urban's new war and of traditional pilgrimage were often identical;

to the pope's apparent concern, many took up or followed the cross in 1095–6 with little or no soldierly skill or intent.[15] The key to Urban's success in 1095–6 lay in the incorporation of existing images and emotions into a fresh concept of secular spirituality.

In fact, as far as we can tell, at the time the Clermont speech proved something of a damp squib. Very few lay magnates attended, not even the count of Toulouse. Few bishops bothered to record the council's decree concerning the Jerusalem expedition, most retaining copies only of those canons effecting church reform. Provincial ecclesiastical councils held in the wake of Clermont, such as one at Rouen, ignored the Jerusalem business. There survives no official account of what Urban actually said at Clermont. Three eyewitnesses recorded their versions years later only after the success of the expedition had moulded attitudes and perspectives. Even then they disagreed with each other, using the speech to reflect their own visions of what they later thought worthy of recognition. The artificial literary quality of these accounts established a model for succeeding propaganda exercises, the inspirational set-piece sermon becoming a familiar stereotype of crusade literature if not practice, but they do not record Urban's own words. In November 1095, success was by no means inevitable. To a large extent, the impact of Urban's message depended on the subsequent publicity skills of the pope himself. These proved to be formidable.

A key element in a carefully devised strategy to assert the papacy's political and moral purpose, Urban's scheme reflected sentiments central to his personal understanding of Christendom, Christian history and the papacy's role in reform. Close examination of Urban's thought has revealed that his intellectual approach to the unity and integrity of Christendom, and hence his Jerusalem venture was determined by a particular schematic view of Christian history: an idealized picture of the purity of the early church; its corruption by human sins that allowed the conquest of ancient Christian centres by Islam from the seventh century; the eleventh-century Christian recovery of lands lost in Spain, Sicily and finally the eastern Mediterranean; this reconquest manifesting an opportunity for a general Christian renewal through divine grace, a process in which the pope performed as God's executor and coadjutor.[16] Hence the intrinsic duality in Urban's Jerusalem project: the material objective to aid Byzantium and the eastern Christians and recapture the Holy City enmeshed with the transcendent purpose of serving God by liberating the Holy Sepulchre as an individual and collective act of piety and redemption. Going beyond the academic debate on holy war pursued in the circle of papalist intellectuals (e.g. Anselm of Lucca, John of Mantua, Bonizo of Sutri), Urban, following the logic of his mentor Gregory VII, argued in 1095–6 that not only was the war meritorious, and thus participation not blameworthy, so too was the fighting, which, refashioned into a religious act combining penance and charity, 'for the love of God and their neighbour',[17] would earn substantial merit rather than dutiful expiation, as with William of Normandy's troops at Hastings in 1066. To emphasize the unique nature of the enterprise and the special status of participants, probably at Clermont, certainly by the end of his French tour, Urban attached regulations designed to protect crusaders' property, to prevent husbands unilaterally abandoning their wives, to prohibit indiscriminate clerical and monastic participation and to ensure advice was sought from local priests. One witness at Clermont later indicated that Urban had tried to forbid the participation of unchaperoned women, the old, the infirm and the poor, unless subsidized by the wealthy.[18] These rules merely pointed the central innovation of the plenary indulgence, remission of sins, for fighting in the holy war. This was controversial on two counts: holy war was now classed as penitential; and the pope was assuming the authority of Christ in seeming to remit sin not just penance. Whatever academic unease was aroused, neither innovation provoked much resistance, certainly not after the expedition's success.

Jerusalem formed the cornerstone of Urban's concept of penitential warfare in 1095. The Clermont decree, preserved by the bishop of Arras, and repeated almost verbatim by the pope in a letter to Bologna in September 1096, was unequivocal: 'Whoever for devotion alone, not to gain honour or money, goes to Jerusalem to liberate the Church of God can substitute this journey for all penance.'[19] Writing to supporters in Flanders a few days after his Clermont speech, Urban talked of the Muslim conquest and ravaging of the eastern church:

> Worse still, they have seized the Holy City of Christ, embellished by his passion and resurrection, and . . . have sold her and her churches into abominable slavery . . . we visited Gaul and urged most fervently the lords and subjects of that land to liberate the eastern churches . . . [and] imposed on them the obligation to undertake such a military enterprise for the remission of all their sins.[20]

Contemporary descriptions of his preaching in the Loire valley, echoed in numerous charters drawn up by monastic recipients of departing warriors' property, confirm that Urban encouraged people 'to go to Jerusalem to drive out the heathen'. As he expressed it in a letter to the monks of Vallembrosa in October 1096, his recruits 'are heading for Jerusalem with the good intent of liberating Christianity'.[21] The restoration to Christendom of the scene of the ideal church as recorded in the Acts of the Apostles represented more than a propaganda device or a sop and capitulation to ill-informed populism, as some twentieth-century historians such as Carl Erdmann have implied. Rather it signalled the ultimate *libertas ecclesiae* for which the whole church reform movement of the previous half-century had been striving.

Jerusalem in the eleventh as in other centuries defined an ideal as much as a terrestrial city. It could stand as a metaphor, 'the holy city, God's celestial Jerusalem', as an English royal charter of 1093 put it, for the world redeemed by Christ.[22] Jerusalem could represent a spiritual condition and aspiration, as in the religious life of an individual or community, or its attributes could be geographically transposed to create a virtual reality in relics and shrines. Clairvaux abbey in the mid-twelfth century was likened to Jerusalem by its abbot, St Bernard, as had been the imperial courts of Charlemagne or Byzantium. More pervasively, the liturgy recreated scenes from Jerusalem in the mass or enacted whole episodes, as in the increasingly popular Easter plays, each a glimpse of the Holy City. Yet for all its liminality, poised between heaven and earth, God and man, Jerusalem remained a place as well as an ideal, temporal as well as spiritual, corporal as well as supernatural. In the tenth and eleventh centuries its distance – *loca remotissima*, as one historian of Urban's expedition put it[23] – and association with Christ's life, Passion and Resurrection ensured Jerusalem as the most meritorious goal of pilgrimage to such an extent that the chronicler Ralph Glaber noted that such a trip was in danger of becoming a fashionable social accessory rather than an act of piety.[24] The difficulties of the journey, magnified a hundred-fold by war, secured its penitential attraction.

Scriptural history and the pseudo-history of Christian prophecy confirmed this unique numinous status. Earlier in the eleventh century the Limousin monk Adhemar of Chabannes insisted on the historical primacy of Jerusalem over Rome itself as 'the fountain of Christianity . . . the mother of all Churches'.[25] Throughout the century, notably in the 1030s and 1060s, huge bands of pilgrims trekked east, inspired by chiliastic enthusiasm condemned as misguided by one commentator, who nonetheless recorded the potency of such emotions to attract 'not only the common people but the elites (*primores*)'.[26] Jerusalem played a prominent part in the genre of eschatological literature popular in western monasteries, cathedrals and courts from at least the mid-tenth century, the setting for the final scenes of Judgement at the end of the world. There, it was widely asserted, the Last Roman Emperor would surrender his crown as a preliminary to the Last Things. Unsurprisingly, such prominence in the Divine Plan appealed to imperialists during the contest between Henry IV and the reforming popes, Benzo of Alba advising the king to fulfil these Jerusalem prophecies himself. Western obsessions with the Holy City may have been sufficiently strong to have persuaded the Byzantine emperor Alexius I to cite the liberation of Jerusalem and the Holy Sepulchre in enticing western nobles into his service in the years before 1095.[27]

Pope Urban was particularly susceptible to the pull of Jerusalem. As a monk, later prior of Cluny from the late 1060s, he was exposed to vivid images of the Holy City in the interminable liturgical round, in Psalms (e.g. Psalm 79: 'O God, the heathen are come into thine inheritance') as well as in special ceremonies surrounding Easter and Pentecost conducted in the great Burgundian abbey. As pope, Urban's interest in the Apostolic church of Jerusalem is suggested by his patronage in the years immediately before 1095 of regular canons – secular clergy who lived in a community – in whom, he insisted, the virtues of the pristine church could be renewed. As a cardinal in Rome after 1079, Urban had been surrounded by relics of Jerusalem and the Holy Land, especially the collection housed at the Lateran, then the pope's habitual Roman residence. These included Christ's umbilical chord, foreskin and some of His blood, pieces of the cross, numerous objects associated with His ministry and Passion (such as a loaf and thirteen beans from the Last Supper), relics of Holy Land saints and numerous physical specimens, such as rocks from Bethlehem, the Mount of Olives, the river Jordan, Calvary and the Holy Sepulchre itself. Such a collection fitted the growing trend in eleventh-century religious devotion away from purely local saints towards those with worldwide appeal, such as St Nicholas at Bari or the cult of the Virgin Mary. It was in trying to establish the universal importance of his Limoges patron St Martial that Adhemar of

Chabannes disparaged Rome in preference to Jerusalem, where he claimed the saint had been consecrated. Adhemar died on his own pilgrimage to the Holy City in 1034. International shrines such as St Iago of Compostela in Galicia as well as Jerusalem featured increasingly prominently in the spiritual life of western Christendom. Urban's preaching of 1095 did not create such interest or enthusiasm, however much it confirmed and extended it; rather, as elsewhere, the pope reforged a new weapon from old shards.[28]

This was obvious with the employment of the cross as military banner, personal insignia and mystical symbol; part relic, part totem, part uniform. The ceremony instituted at Clermont tapped into another well of traditional devotion conjured up by the Crucifixion and Christ's command: 'If any man will come after me, let him deny himself, and take up his cross, and follow me' (Matthew 16:24; cf. Luke 14.26: 'And whosoever doth not bear his cross, and come after me, cannot be my disciple'). Two eyewitnesses later reported Urban use this invocation, as did a veteran of the expedition itself who probably heard of Urban's appeal some months after Clermont. The theme of following Christ was a standard of eleventh-century eremitic (the ideal of the recluse) and revivalist rhetoric. On a popular as well as elite level, church reform was pursued by evangelists living and preaching a return to the Apostolic life. The idea was not confined to the Jerusalem journey; it inspired eremitical groups such as the new religious communities of Molesme and Cîteaux established in Burgundy before and during the First Crusade as well as the influential Robert of Arbrissel, founder of the Order of Fontevrault, whose preaching tours coincided with Urban's. Closer to the papacy, Peter Damian (d. 1072), hermit and cardinal, who exerted a strong influence on successive popes for a generation from the 1040s, was an enthusiast for the Jerusalem pilgrimage who propagated the cult of the cross. The two went together as symbols of practical and mystical remission of sin and redemption. From his Jerusalem pilgrimage of 1026–7, the saintly Abbot Richard of St Vanne of Verdun returned with a piece of the True Cross hanging in a bag around his neck.[29] By the 1090s many abbeys had received such relics from pilgrims, not least those, such as Moissac, that were active in support of both pilgrimage and crusade; as Urban's consecration of Marmoutier indicated, such relics were sought after.

The use of the symbol of the cross at Clermont signalled a pivotal concern for Jerusalem. Urban himself certainly presided over cross-giving at Tours (March 1096) and probably Le Mans (February), and it is likely that he or his agents distributed crosses wherever he preached. Ceremonies conducted by Urban's deputies, by local clergy or unofficially proliferated. Apparently at one such occasion at Rouen a riot ensued. Using relics of the cross as a prop to encourage participation, as Urban had done at Marmoutier, became fashionable. It could backfire. An English annalist described how, during the preaching of the Jerusalem expedition, a French abbot constructed his own cross, passing it off as having been made by God: as a punishment, he was afflicted with cancer.[30] It is an indication of the independent role assumed by Peter the Hermit, possibly retrospectively, that he carried as a preaching aid a letter from heaven rather than a relic of the cross which, within a year of Clermont, had swept all other symbols aside. Giving the cross was simple and non-discriminatory. Unlike the granting of the symbols of pilgrimage, which assumed a contractual imposition of a penance by a priest, in the first flush of the new ritual, presenting crosses was not a monopoly of those in holy orders. In June 1096, at Amalfi, as a carefully staged demonstration of piety and power, the Italian-Norman lord Bohemund of Taranto provided crosses for his men. Although never becoming the exclusive preserve of holy warriors, wearing the cross was immediately distinctive. At Amalfi, Bohemund had been particularly struck by the crosses worn by passing crusaders. Those in the army to Jerusalem themselves referred to recruits who had not yet fulfilled their vows as being 'signed with the holy cross' while in 1098 they wrote to Urban himself that he had 'ordered us to follow Christ carrying our crosses'.[31] For others these badges carried more sinister implications. One of the words employed by Hebrew chroniclers to describe the perpetrators of the Rhineland pogroms of 1096 translates as 'those bearing insignia', signs of an obsession with the Crucifixion and vengeance on those allegedly responsible who still denied Christ's divinity.[32] For Christian warrior and persecuted Jew, the cross was definitive.

Urban's message delivered at Clermont and repeated in sermons and letters over the next three years, emerged clearly: penitential warfare to rescue Jerusalem and the eastern churches from Islam; the liberation of the eastern church after centuries of bondage with the implication of the restoration of fraternal unity with, as one eyewitness at Clermont later had it, 'blood-brothers';[33] the prospect of the remission of all sins, as

Urban clearly stated in December 1095, for those warriors who had taken the cross in sign of their acceptance of their duty to follow Christ; the obligation to revenge the loss of Christ's Holy Land as a debt of honour; the realization of papal leadership of Christendom; the transformation of a sinful military aristocracy into a godly order. It is not entirely clear how far this was from what Alexius I had envisaged when he despatched yet another embassy to the pope early in 1095, but it is certain that Urban's scheme owed more to his own rather than the Greek's designs. Not the least remarkable feature of the inception of the Jerusalem expedition was that the *casus belli* was the sole invention of the aggressors, almost entirely unimagined by their target. In the west, Urban's penitential war marked a significant step on the path towards incorporating all Christendom into a *militia Dei* against unbelievers and sinners.

Urban called for a penitential holy war rather than, as many have maintained, specifically an armed pilgrimage. While no authentic account of the Clermont speech exists, the council's Jerusalem decree and Urban's surviving letters from the period emphasized the spiritually meritorious temporal goal of the expedition, the liberation of the eastern churches and that of Jerusalem. The method to be employed was unequivocally military. In a letter to his supporters in Flanders written days after the end of the Clermont assembly, Urban talked of the expedition in terms of a *procinctus*, a military undertaking.[34] To the monks of Vallembrosa a year later he referred to his hope that the knights who set out 'might be able to restrain the savagery of the Saracens by their arms and restore the Christians to their former freedom', warning the monks not to join up 'either to bear arms or go on this journey'. Urban was remembered as calling for an armed struggle in his preaching at Limoges in December 1095. Count Fulk of Anjou, who entertained Urban in March 1096, shortly afterwards noted how the pope had exhorted recruits 'to go to Jerusalem to hunt the pagan people who had occupied the city'. Many of those who received the pope's message of liberating Jersualem by force understood his meaning clearly enough, as a Gascon charter put it, 'to fight and to kill' those who had defiled the scene of the Resurrection. The countess of Flanders recalled in 1097 how the Holy Spirit had inflamed the heart of her husband, Count Robert II, to curb the perfidy of the Turks with armed force. In the surviving letters of the crusaders, the sense of the army as a militia rather than a pilgrimage is strong. When Pope Paschal II announced the capture of Jerusalem to the French clergy in December 1099, he described the expedition as a *Christiana militia*, only the following April adding the word *peregrinatio* and the language of pilgrimage.[35]

For Urban, holy war and its associated remission of confessed sin needed no additional justification; he claimed the authority of God. The Clermont decree avoided any direct reference to pilgrimage. The Clermont ceremony of taking the cross appeared deliberately novel, independent of the rite performed by departing pilgrims. *Libertas ecclesiae* by force needed no further sanction, as the Investiture Wars of Gregory VII had shown – at least to the radicals at the Papal Curia, of whom Urban was one. It has been argued that the oblique language of Urban's letters, using words such as *labor*, *via* and *iter*, implied pilgrimage. Rather, they implied an equally meritorious penitential military alternative to pilgrimage. Overt language of pilgrimage was avoided or ignored by Urban in his own correspondence, the closest evidence for what he may have been thinking. Urban's own words explicitly and unequivocally described holy war, in the style of Gregory VII; they did not refer explicitly to an armed pilgrimage even if he were conscious of the tempting parallel. However, the sacralizing of war in all its aspects, shedding blood, killing, securing booty and plunder, appeared extreme and for some, especially among the clergy, no doubt disconcerting. The point was made by the famous battle cry of the hard-pressed crusaders at the battle of Dorylaeum in July 1097 as recorded by a widely circulated anonymous author who gave the impression of being an eyewitness: 'Stand fast all together, trusting in God and the Holy Cross. Today, please God, you will all gain much booty'.[36] This was not, as many have assumed, a surrender to material greed. Instead, the chronicler was attempting to convince his audience of the spiritual legitimacy of the form of warfare in all its practical ramifications, in recognition, perhaps, of its contentious nature.

Other witnesses, such as Bishop Gaston of Cahors or Abbot Geoffrey of Vendôme, took Urban's holy war and, whether or not the pope intended it, by analogy interpreted it as a form of pilgrimage, a familiar and more clerically palatable model.[37] This was facilitated by the goal of the enterprise being the supreme pilgrimage destination, Jerusalem. The association with pilgrimage diluted the radicalism of Urban's message, even if it set up an inherent conceptual contradiction by linking extreme violence with a previously pacific activity. Earlier stories of pilgrims carrying arms for defence and fighting attackers, as on the German pilgrimage of 1064–5, simply did not embrace the idea of pilgrims whose whole purpose was to fight. The appeal of thinking of the Jerusalem expedition as a pilgrimage was obvious; the typology of journeying, penance and remission of sins was recognizable, demonstrated by the hordes of non-combatant pilgrims who tagged along with the armed forces. From the evidence of some charters, a few crusaders' letters, such as those of Count Stephen of Blois, and early chronicle accounts, it is clear that this conservative approach, probably peddled by local clergy in search of a means of comprehending this novel phenomenon, possessed force and acquired ready adherents.[38] Thereafter, pilgrimage and the holy wars of the cross became almost inseparable. This may not have been Urban's doing. His vision was more radical, more disturbing and more penetrating.

It is sometimes argued that Urban's original plan had been for a limited expedition to assist Alexius I and press on to the Holy Sepulchre rather in the fashion of Gregory VII's embryonic scheme of 1074, and that it was only the astonishing response to his call that forced him to change his rhetoric and policy. This underestimates the grandeur of his scheme. His tour of France was extensive and exhausting. At Clermont in late November and again at Tours in March, the sixty-year-old pope preached in the open air. His schedule was punishing, with the travelling followed by regular public appearances at long-winded liturgical ceremonies even without preaching. He presided over three major church councils, at Tours (March 1096) and Nîmes (July 1096) as well as Clermont. The vigour and geographic embrace of Urban's preaching argues against modest recruitment plans; his role in local consecrations of altars and the like, the ease of passage through different provinces and lordships and the orderly crowds of notables assembled reflected careful premeditation. Despite the attempts of apologists to imply otherwise, enthusiastic crowds were not gathered by chance in the early weeks of Urban's tour. On Christmas Day 1095 at Limoges he attended three separate services, progressing between them in full regalia. Within the week he had rededicated the cathedral and the chief local shrine of St Martial. Only then did he preach about Jerusalem.[39] His visit to Poitiers coincided with the feast of that city's patron saint, St Hilary (13 January). At Angers (January 1096) and at Tours and Marmoutier

(March), his preaching was linked to local ceremonies or assemblies that were far from haphazard and probably long planned (dedications of churches, translations of bodies of local dignitaries, church councils, etc.). The liturgical theatricality, emphasized by regular processions in full ceremonial finery, was not staged at random. His successor Paschal II noted Urban's attention to towns (*civitates*). While he tried to impose a southern French bishop, Adhemar of Le Puy, as leader of the expedition in his place, he still wrote to the Flemish in the north urging participation and dispatched a legate to the Anglo-Norman realms. Although the expedition lacked the cohesion Urban may have wished for, Adhemar's authority was widely accepted on the march once the armies had combined at Nicaea in June 1097. Urban's later injunctions to the Bolognese (September 1096), prohibiting clergy from joining and encouraging laymen to consult their parish priests or bishops, do not speak of alarm at numbers but canonical rectitude, very much part of the package from Clermont or even Piacenza onwards. The timing of the preaching, seen by some as oddly late in the year, suited elaborate recruitment. Urban's journey to France covered two penitential seasons, Advent and Lent, appropriate to his message of repentance, as well as the major Christocentric festivals of Christmas and Easter, when images and dramatic representations of Jerusalem accompanied church and civic celebrations. Urban's announcement that the expedition would set out on 15 August 1096 provided time for armies to be raised: in the event all the main contingents north of the Alps left by October. It also recognized the importance of waiting for the harvest, traditionally begun in northern Europe on 1 August. Thus the timetable of the church year, including the departure date, the Feast of the Assumption of the Virgin Mary, a major cult in Le Puy itself, was suited to military requirements; logistics matched liturgy.

Urban's own preaching seems to have been highly effective. From the admittedly partial and limited evidence of charters between recruits and monasteries, it has been observed that a 'high proportion' of noble recruits came from areas Urban visited or within a couple of days' ride from his itinerary. His preaching impressed eyewitnesses, and he had an advantage that Gregory VII lacked, in that he himself came from precisely the arms-bearing aristocratic milieu of the French nobility that he sought to exploit, as did his chosen legate, Bishop Adhemar of Le Puy, a nobleman reputed as an excellent horseman.[40] Like many contemporary bishops, Adhemar was evidently almost as at home on a battlefield as in a cathedral, some of his colleagues even donning armour (like Odo, bishop of Bayeux at the battle of Hastings as depicted in the Bayeux Tapestry) and wielding maces in deference to the canon law prohibition on clergy spilling blood, a ban that apparently did not include crushing and bruising.

Urban performed only as the hub of the recruiting wheel. The mechanics of spreading the word capitalized on the networks of ecclesiastical affinity and administrative efficiency developed by the reformist papacy over the previous half-century. Urban authorized local diocesans to preach the cross but probably depended more upon a concentric circle of friends, allies and supporters, such as the archbishop of Lyons. Sympathetic abbots not only preached but used their local influence to encourage lay patrons to take the cross and to exchange property for money or war materials (e.g. pack animals). As religious centres possessed of bullion and cash, monasteries were the chief bankers for the First Crusade. The holy warriors desired their prayers and their capital. The necessary financial outlay on the expedition for each landowner was likely to represent many times his annual revenue, especially as the mid-1090s were times of agricultural depression. The price of sin was incalculable. In some cases monks deliberately – and successfully – touted for trade. Elsewhere, the process was indirect, clergy instilling into the faithful over time the sense of sin which provided the spur to many to take the cross.[41]

Beside the complementary efforts of the papally directed and local ecclesiastical apparatus, news of the expedition spread though informal contacts and association. The papal legate to the Anglo-Norman provinces, the abbot of St Bénigne, Dijon, in early 1096 negotiated an agreement between William II of England and his brother Duke Robert of Normandy under which Robert pledged his duchy to William for three years in return for 10,000 silver marks, a massive sum equivalent, it has been speculated, to a quarter of royal income, only available through a heavy land tax. If nothing else, this unpopular levy publicized the crusade. More direct contacts eased publicity. In southern Italy, Bohemund of Taranto apparently only learnt of the crusade from a passing band of French (or possibly Catalan) recruits in June 1096. His ignorance of the momentous events north of the Alps is surprising and, on the face of it, unlikely. Bohemund's half-brother and nominal overlord, Roger Borsa, was married to the sister of the count of Flanders, who had taken the cross. Bohemund had close links with the pope; between 1089 and 1093 he had entertained Urban twice and had met him on at least two other occasions. His half-brother Guy was prominent in the service of Alexius I, whose attempts to recruit Italian Normans may have intensified after the completion of the Sicilian conquest in 1091–2. The anonymous writer of one of the earliest accounts of the expedition, the *Gesta Francorum*, perhaps a knight or cleric in Bohemund's army, may have accurately reflected the situation of the summer of 1096 when he wrote of the widespread rumours of Urban's message sweeping through 'all the regions and provinces of the Gauls'.[42] Even if merely relying on what he later heard from companions on the march, the author hit upon three prime recruiting officers: emulation, the courts of lay nobles and princes, and rumour.

The rapidity of the spread of news of the Jerusalem campaign is attested not only in the literary accounts but in the rate of recruitment itself. Within twelve months of Clermont perhaps as many as 70–80,000 people had already left their homes for the east. The geographical spread was wide but uneven, the bulk of known crusaders coming from a shallow crescent stretching from the Dordogne in the south-west to Flanders in the north-east, covering the Limousin, Poitou, the Loire valley, Maine, the Chartrain, Ile de France and Champagne; there were also significant groupings in Languedoc, Provence, Burgundy, parts of western Germany and in Italy. Enthusiasm for the expedition was not universal. Although support crossed the ideological and political divide between papalists and imperialists, even Henry IV's constable joining up as well as important imperial vassals such as Godfrey of Bouillon, only a minority even in areas of greatest enthusiasm took the cross. Contemporary chroniclers emphasized the magnitude of the response, which they attributed to the miraculous working of the Holy Spirit or to the potency of rumour. Although reconstruction of the details of how information spread through a semi-literate society is difficult, certain features stand out. The focal points of recruitment were lay courts and households, especially those with close links to monasteries (although this may be a distorted impression caused by the nature of charter evidence); networks of interlaced aristocratic families and, crucially, their dependants – humbler relatives, tenants, household knights and clergy, servants; and towns. Crusading was as much an urban as a rural phenomenon. In both, wealth and status provided necessities and incentives. Just as the castellan, seigneur or count were pivotal in raising the countryside, so the 'better sort' (*meliores*), as a Genoese observer of 1096 put it, gave the lead in towns and cities.[43] The expedition inspired by Urban's preaching was not assembled at random, but followed the contours of a society dominated by wealthy lords, connected by bonds of family, obedience, locality, obligation, employment and commerce. A rural/urban divide is misleading. Many influential monasteries were situated within or just outside major urban centres; lords had rights over markets and, in areas of developed urban life, such as north Italy or Flanders, town and country were mutually bound together socially and economically as well as politically. Although managing to sell or pledge most of his properties to raise money, Godfrey of Bouillon also extorted 1,000 silver pieces from the Jewish communities of Cologne and Mainz to fund his campaign. Gossip and rumours thrive when people are in close contact; ceremonies exert maximum effect if witnessed. The success of recruitment in 1095–6 relied on wealth, social order and mobility, attributes of an underlying prosperity, as well as on skilful manipulation of cultural habits of violence and spiritual fears of damnation.

According to some witnesses, at the centre of the 'great rumour', as one contemporary called it, was the charismatic preaching of a diminutive, ageing Picard evangelist known as Peter the Hermit. In Lorraine, during and immediately after the crusade, he was regarded as having inspired the whole enterprise. This cannot entirely be dismissed, not least because, whatever his status, he managed to raise armies months before anyone else, in person led one of them to Constantinople and was thereafter accepted by the princes as a member of the expedition's elite, if only in a minor capacity. Peter had experience as a preacher of apostolic poverty. It was later claimed that he was a pilgrim to the Holy City who had been entrusted with a letter from heaven to rouse Christians to liberate Jerusalem and a request from the patriarch of Jerusalem to send western help which he conveyed to Pope Urban. In fact, Patriarch Symeon may have been in Constantinople when Peter was supposed to have passed through on pilgrimage. It may or may not have been chance that one of the first contacts the Christian army made in northern Syria in 1097–8 was with the exiled patriarch, who then promptly wrote a letter to the west appealing for further military aid, perhaps an echo, repeat or inspiration of the Peter the Hermit story.

The hints of distinctive features in Peter's appeal – apocalyptic, populist, visionary, charismatic – in contrast to the uniform outline of the theologically focused message emanating from the pope reflected in most chronicles and charters – authority, penance, pilgrimage, cross, war – may be taken as a sign of Peter's insignificance or the reverse. Even hostile witnesses attest to the popular if naive element in his following. Part of the motive for the massacres of the Rhineland Jews identified in Jewish sources was a crude, vindictive and violent assertion of Christian supremacy and lust for vengeance for Christ Crucified; many of these pogroms were the work of contingents associated with Peter. That there was little or no such barbaric persecution of Jews by the armies recruited by Urban and his agents may point to a distinct difference of tone and content in Peter's preaching. However the evidence is viewed, Peter played a prominent and semi-independent role in at least some theatres of propagandizing and recruiting for the Jerusalem expedition. The Lorraine perspective contained in the chronicle of Albert of Aachen is probably as valid as others which ignore Peter.[44]

It is incontestable that the armies he inspired were on the road by Easter 1096 (13 April); even the anonymous chronicler attached to Bohemund placed Peter's as part of the 'official' campaign.[45] To organize, equip and supply perhaps up to 30,000 troops and non-combatants at the end of winter and in spring, following poor harvests, some local famines and plagues in the previous year, suggests that Peter must have begun preaching before Clermont and that his powers of organization were of an order beyond his image of a dishevelled hedge priest. It is possible that Urban appointed him to preach the Jerusalem journey weeks before Clermont: the pope had been discussing his plan with potential leaders at least as early as August 1095. It is notable that Peter's itinerary, from Berry through the Orléannais and Champagne to Lorraine and the Rhineland, avoided those areas visited by the pope. Peter, in a more demotic style, appealed to audiences not dissimilar to the pope's. He recruited a number of significant lords, one of whom, Walter, lord of Boissy Sans Avoir, whom he despatched with eight knights and a large company of infantry in early March, was already in Constantinople in July 1096, no mean logistical effort. The forces Peter raised lacked the tight social authority lent by the presence of many great lords. His preaching campaign, which he combined with leading an army, apparently operated apart from the hierarchy of religious houses that so crucially underpinned Urban's efforts: unlike the pope, Peter is absent from surviving monastic charters.[46] His message was revivalist, probably peppered with visions and atrocity stories. These were neither new nor exclusive to Peter. The Limousin chronicler and pilgrim Adhemar of Chabannes had peddled stories of persecution, assassination and murder of Christians by the Muslim rulers of the Holy Land seventy years earlier. The memory of the destruction of the Holy Sepulchre may have formed part of a propaganda campaign by the monks of St Peter's Moissac, visited by Urban himself in May 1096.[47]

On arrival in the Rhineland, Peter appears to have delegated his own preaching commission to a local priest, Gottschalk, who, demonstrating that he was no rabble-rousing bumpkin either, in turn recruited a large army in southern Germany, which reached Hungary via Bavaria only to be massacred in late July by the Hungarian army, outraged at the violent and indiscriminate foraging. Gottschalk's force may have been intended as the right flank of Peter's own army, predominantly comprised of Frenchmen and led by lords from Chartres and Champagne, which marched through the Rhineland in April before travelling down the Danube to Hungary and across the Balkans to reach Constantinople on 1 August. It is possible that Peter also delegated recruitment to another German, Volkmar, whose contingent followed a route to Peter's north, through Saxony and Bohemia before being dispersed by the Hungarians in late June. To Peter's preaching may be attributed the participation of numerous other German lords, in particular the Swabian count Emich of Flonheim and Count Hartmann of Dillingen-Kybourg, who joined forces with lords from the Ile de France as well as, apparently, some Englishmen. Even if these groups took the cross independent of Peter, his contribution was significant, possibly papally authorized and suggestive of just how much is unknown about the genesis of the First Crusade. Peter, a man of some learning and habitually boastful, may have spent his retirement at the abbey of Neumoustier in Lorraine embroidering his own legend. The tragedy of the subsequent military failure of all of his contingents and Peter's own equivocal fortitude during the sieges of Antioch ensured the relegation of his initial contribution by writers eager to emphasize the successes of their favoured leaders for didactic purposes. Yet between the two extremes, those returning to Lorraine from the Jerusalem adventure in 1099 did not dismiss him; some even remembered him as its '*primus auctor*'.[48]

Urban's initiative, like that of Gregory VII, could have been still-born. That it was not indicates a social and cultural predisposition to accept his radical concept of guiltless, meritorious violence and a skilful publicity campaign. Both are evident in the events of 1095–6. However, the question of timing remains. Why did 1095 strike Urban II as the 'acceptable year of the Lord and the day of vengeance of our God' (Isaiah 61:2)? Western aristocratic arms-bearers had been anxious for their souls for generations; Greek emperors had been asking for and receiving western military aid for decades; campaigns against Muslims in Spain, Sicily or north Africa had become an increasingly common feature of western Mediterranean warfare; church discipline of secular society had been at least notionally acknowledged though the Peace and Truce of God movement in many areas; papal thinking on holy war and penance had a long pedigree. Yet a convergence of circumstances persuaded Urban to recast Alexius's appeal; and the immediate context of 1095 allowed for its success.

There is little direct evidence that, as was later alleged, the pilgrim route to Jerusalem or the treatment of Jerusalem pilgrims had deteriorated since the conquest of much of Asia Minor and parts of northern Syria by the Seljuk Turks since the 1070s. Among Near Eastern observers, there are traces of anxiety about western (i.e. for them primarily Byzantine) threats. The Persian Naser-e Khosraw, a visitor to Palestine in 1046/7, recorded that the Fatimid rulers of Egypt had garrisoned the Nile Delta port of Tinnis 'as a precaution against attacks by Franks and Byzantines'. A century later, the Aleppan historian al-Azimi (d. 1161) referred to Frankish and Byzantine pilgrims being prevented by strong-arm tactics from reaching Jerusalem in 1093/4, adding, 'those of them who survived spread the news about that to their country. So they prepared themselves for military invasion.'[49] The neatness with which this account mirrors western propaganda invites suspicion. Visiting Jerusalem was always dangerous and ran the risk of violent confrontation, as the 1064/5 German pilgrims discovered when attacked at Ramla. There is no evidence of pilgrimages drying up in the 1090s. Roger count of Foix happily set out for Palestine in late April 1095; the Norman Odard's pilgrimage actually coincided with the crusade itself.[50]

Nonetheless, even if conditions had not in reality become more difficult, perceptions may have altered. The First Crusade did not open up the Near East to westerners. There is more and more evidence that Asia Minor as well as the Balkan areas of the Byzantine empire were crawling with French, Italians and Germans. Large numbers of south Italian Normans had entered and stayed in the service of Alexius I after the failure of the Norman campaign against him in the Balkans in 1081. When Bohemund and his force arrived in Byzantium in 1097, they were among friends and relations. Many in the post-Conquest Anglo-Saxon aristocratic diaspora had found their way into the imperial Varangian guard. The Greeks positively encouraged western knights to enter imperial employment, such was their admiration of western military tactics: this enthusiasm helped lose them the battle of Manzikert against the Seljuk Turks in 1071, when western levies under the Norman Roussel of Bailleul deserted. The pilgrimage to Jerusalem in the late 1080s of Robert the Frisian, count of Flanders, led to his sending Alexius a force of 500 knights around 1090: his son, Robert, was one of the leaders of the 1096 expedition. By the early 1090s Alexius may have been employing thousands of western troops in Asia Minor, for whom he constructed at least one base, at Kibotos, and possibly planned another, at Nicomedia, under the supervision of a Frankish monk. Western clerics as well as soldiers and pilgrims were apparently familiar figures at the Byzantine court, some of whom also made the pilgrimage to Jerusalem. After the final conquest and settlement of Sicily in 1092, a process to which Alexius paid close attention, Norman troops were more available than for a generation. While after the Council of Piacenza, Urban II looked northwards, Alexius's gaze may have been resting firmly on the south, as it had for over a decade.

Almost at every step of their journey, the armies of 1096 to 1099 encountered expatriate westerners. When Bohemund's nephew, Tancred, arrived at Adana in Cilicia in September 1097, he found a Burgundian, Welf, already in occupation with a force of Armenians. At Tarsus in the same month, Baldwin of Boulogne encountered a fleet of Flemish and Frisian pirates who claimed to have been plying their trade in those waters for eight years.[51] More sensationally, after the Christian army had invested Jerusalem on 7 June 1099, in his camp facing the Damascus Gate, Duke Robert of Normandy received an unexpected visit from a fellow countryman living locally who offered his services to his natural lord. Twenty-two years before, Hugh Bunel had committed one of the most notorious murders of the day when he decapitated Mabel of Bellême at her castle of Bures, 'where she was relaxing in bed after a bath', this in revenge for her seizing his patrimony. Pursued by Mabel's sons, William the Conqueror's agents and bounty-hunters, Hugh had fled to Apulia, then Sicily, then Byzantium before, fearful of William's 'strong hand and long arm, he left the Latin world'. He had lived among Muslims for twenty years when the crusaders arrived at the walls of Jerusalem.[52]

Although Hugh Bunel's *cause célèbre* prevented contact with the west, the presence of westerners as pilgrims, visitors, merchants, mercenaries and settlers in and beyond the Byzantine empire provided a growing medium for the transmission of news and intelligence, such as the English Jerusalem pilgrim Joseph, a Canterbury monk who met Greek-speaking friends at Constantinople, or Guillermus of Cormery, appointed by Alexius as chaplain to western troops stationed around Nicomedia in the early 1090s. The information reaching the west may have sounded an increasingly strident note in portraying the depredations of the Seljuk Turks, even if these were not in fact more onerous. There is evidence that at precisely this juncture Alexius himself played on the Jerusalem-sensitive emotions in the west by sending 'frequent messages about the oppression of the Lord's sepulchre and the desolation of all the churches'.[53] In this context the story of Peter the Hermit spreading atrocity stories does not sound too unlikely; his may have been one of many such reports. The elements in Urban's coup of 1095 begin to be apparent: the Greek appeal to the pope of March 1095, only the latest in a consistent series; increasing contacts with the east through pilgrims, mercenaries and correspondence with some of the higher nobility of the west; persistent rumours of persecution of pilgrims and attacks on eastern Christians perhaps reaching a crescendo through the accounts of travellers and Greek diplomats; the consolidation of Urban's own historical and theological vision; the coincidence of the improved political position of Urban in Italy and France. The roles of Urban, Alexius and Peter the Hermit have often been placed in opposition as explanations of the events of 1095; perhaps instead they should be seen as complementary.

The scale of the reaction to the call to Jerusalem was impressive. While large armies were not unknown in western Europe in the eleventh century – William of Normandy collected perhaps as many as 14,000 men and up to 3,000 horses for his invasion of England in 1066 – the combination of forces being raised simultaneously in so many different regions struck contemporaries as remarkable and novel. The reasons for such a response have been much debated. Generalizations can mislead as motives varied and conflicted from person to person, class to class, region to region; evidence for individual or collective decisions is extremely patchy, transmitted through the prism of clerical interpretation, whether in chronicle, charter or correspondence. However, this does not disqualify such material, as lay attitudes often found inspiration and articulation from the clergy.

A central discussion revolves around the balance between material and ideological motives. Crudely, did crusaders embark for worldly or spiritual profit? In many senses this poses a false dichotomy. The *Chanson d'Antioche* a couple of generations later declared that those who served Jesus would receive gold.[54] Subsequent accounts of Urban's speech by those who heard it unapologetically portrayed him as offering material gain:

> Take the road to the Holy Sepulchre, rescue that land from a dreadful race and rule over it yourselves, for that land that, as scripture says, floweth with milk and honey was given by God as a possession to the children of Israel. (Robert of Rheims before 1107)

> You will get the enemies' possessions, because you will despoil their treasures and either return victorious to your own homes or gain eternal fame, purpled with your own blood. (Baldric of Bourgeuil *c.*1108)[55]

The battle cry at Dorylaeum on 1 July 1097 already mentioned – 'Stand fast all together, trusting in Christ and in the victory of the Holy Cross. Today, please God, you will all gain much booty' – made good psychological and theological as well as tactical and logistic sense.[56] The emphasis was as much on 'standing fast' in faith as on the necessary material rewards of military success. The rewards of service to God need not be restricted to the spiritual; given the service was military, it could not be if success were to be achieved.

However, that is not the same thing as saying that the Jerusalem expedition attracted recruits for mercenary reasons. As a song composed at the time of the First Crusade put it: 'There we must go, selling our goods to buy the temple of God and to destroy the Saracens.'[57] The peasant-hating Guibert of Nogent recalled the economic and financial hardships they suffered in selling their homes, vineyards and fields to raise money for the journey: 'everyone bought high and sold low'.[58] A similar fate could not be avoided by knights and nobles. Whatever his hopes for future gain, a crusader began his journey suffering capital losses in converting landed property into cash and war materials. The agricultural depression of the mid-1090s only exacerbated the problem. Even for those who did anticipate a land of milk and honey, the scale of the initial investment was sobering: no money; no crusade.

As most wished to return – demonstrably so with those who left charters behind – and as most survivors did just that, putative profits of settlement and colonization were hardly an issue. Of course, the rewards of successful campaigning were accepted eagerly; opportunities for profit were taken with alacrity. Genoese crusaders were quick to establish privileged trading status with Bohemund's new regime in Antioch in July 1098. This does not mean they had taken the cross with this intent uppermost in their minds; the risks of committing a fleet to such a venture were very great. It was not as if those who took the cross did not know where they were going or were ignorant of the costs involved; their own, their neighbours' and their relatives' experiences in war and on pilgrimage prepared them. The crusaders' financial balance sheet on setting out contradicts any easy economic reductionism. Terrestrial profits were more realistically those of honour, prestige and relics. The cliché of younger sons being drawn to the Jerusalem adventure contains no truth. Almost by definition the leaders were, if not all eldest sons, possessed of significant patrimonies of their own; this applied not only to the so-called princes but to the vital second-rank nobles whose retinues formed the military backbone of the armies, such as Raymond Pilet, lord of Alès in the Limousin, who emerged as an independent leader within the army from the summer of 1098. The evidence of land-hunger is local and unconvincing; internal colonization and expanding the areas of cultivation within western Europe catered for the expanding population. What is known of individual crusaders demonstrates no special appeal for younger sons; rather the opposite. Whole families departed together; some sixty families contributing more than one member to the expedition have been identified.[59] Having broken one of the supposedly immutable rules of medieval life by mortgaging or selling patrimonies, such men were evidently moved by considerations other than the obviously material.

The cultural aspirations of the arms-bearing aristocracy were directly engaged. The growing social dominance of a self-conscious military elite was answered in the call to Jerusalem depicted in terms of honour, reputation and family pride. Robert of Rheims had Urban appeal directly to these values:

> Oh most strong soldiers and the offspring of unvanquished parents, do not show yourselves to be weaker than your forbears but remember their strength . . . upon you (i.e. the Franks) before all other nations God has bestowed outstanding glory in arms.[60]

Heroes of the Scriptures, such as the Maccabees, and of secular romance, notably Charlemagne, were held up as models for emulation. The Jerusalem expedition was perceived as an honourable duty by a class familiar with the *raison d'être* expressed in the *Chanson d'Antioche*: 'He who fears death more than dishonour has no right to lordship'.[61] In this war, the reward was social and religious justification, honour and eternal life.

It is hardly surprising that the surviving charters of departing crusaders, drafted by monks, should emphasize their overwhelming burden of sin. However, both lay and clerical observers confirmed this obsession. For Guibert of Nogent and his contemporaries, the key to the success of the Jerusalem expedition was that it offered the professionally and socially violent classes 'a new way of earning salvation' in holy war.[62] Fulcher of Chartres, a priest in the army of northern French who set out for Jerusalem in the autumn of 1096, explained:

> Let those who are accustomed wantonly to wage private war against the faithful march upon the infidels . . . Let those who have long been robbers now be soldiers of Christ; let those who once fought against brothers and relatives now rightfully fight against barbarians. Let those who have been hirelings for a few pieces of silver now attain an eternal reward.[63]

Such pious generalities were translated into active reconciliation. There are numerous examples of lords and knights taking the opportunity of the Jerusalem expedition to resolve outstanding disputes with local religious houses, some of which had been pursued with considerable savagery, such as Bertrand of Moncontour and Nivelo of Fréteval in northern France or the castellans of Mezenc in the south, whose cruelty to local villagers shocked the hard-bitten Adhemar of Le Puy, who nevertheless absolved them for their Jerusalem journey.[64] The tone of such deals may have exaggerated both guilt and penitence. While for some, the Jerusalem journey signalled a transformed life, many crusaders were and remained extremely violent. Thomas of Marle notoriously terrorized the Ile de France for years on either side of his march to Jerusalem; the pilgrim remained a psychopath. William viscount of Melun earned his nickname 'the Carpenter' because of his skills as a battlefield butcher. Stephen count of Blois, who fled the siege of Antioch and later died a hero's death at Ramla in 1102, had killed men in private wars. On his return to the Chartres region, Raimbold Croton, a hero at Antioch and Jerusalem, castrated a monk in a land dispute. Such men were not immune to religious anxieties, rather their piety was robust and practical. The lay biographer Ralph of Caen's famous portrait of Bohemund's nephew Tancred agonizing over his violent life before the Clermont indulgence reconciled warfare with God's commandments should be treated with scepticism; Tancred's dilemma was neither new nor previously unresolved.[65] Nevertheless, Urban's remission of sins for such killers was a lifeline indeed.

The success of recruiting in 1096 remains mysterious. The dilemmas of secular rule and war were hardly novel. It is difficult to reconcile eleventh-century history with a view that hundreds or even thousands of powerful arms-bearers suffered from debilitating individual or collective guilt complexes that suddenly became critical, as a literal acceptance of their charters might suggest. There was an increased focus by the church and hence by congregations and patrons on the problem of salvation for sinners. Urban II neatly summed it up: 'there are only two gates to eternal life; baptism and genuine penitence'.[66] The supernatural was perceived as real and proximate. Hell, heaven and the place between where souls waited for redemption, if not as yet fully understood as purgatory, were not abstractions. Yet it needed a combination of pressures to excite the response of 1096. Alone, ideology is insufficient explanation.

Concentration on faith by itself is inadequate to explain the genesis or progress of the war of the cross ideologically, sociologically, politically or militarily. Jerusalem was not won by faith alone; faith alone did not send men to Jerusalem. The reductionism implied by the idea of an 'age of faith' requires questioning. The picture is more complicated.

Faced with sermons repeatedly insisting on the basic merits and message of Christianity; with hagiography in which doubters featured regularly; with academics, such as Anselm of Canterbury (d. 1109), attempting to construct logically satisfactory explanations of God; and with innumerable anecdotes of lay (and some clerical) mockery of the pretentions of the church, it is hard to argue that we are dealing with an age any more credulous or unthinkingly accepting of religious truth than our own. One much-derided episode during the First Crusade concerned the story of a band of crusaders or pilgrims being led towards Jerusalem by a goose from Cambrai in northern France to Lorraine, where the creature died. The snobbish and irascible Guibert of Nogent dismissed the tale with contempt, as much social as academic, suggesting that the animal would have given more to the cause of Jerusalem 'if the day before she had set out she had made of herself a holiday meal for her mistress'. Having earlier poured scorn on the credulity of the masses who believed they saw clouds at Beauvais forming (Guibert, who was there, thought they looked like a stork or crane), the abbot explained why he had mentioned the goose at all: 'we have attached this incident to the true history (*historiae veraci*) so that men may know that they have been warned against permitting Christian seriousness to be trivialized by belief in vulgar fables'.[67] Reactions to the Jerusalem journey were hardly undiscriminating.

Contemporaries had few doubts of the genesis of the expedition. Whether described as rumour or a great stirring, the emotions whipped up in 1095–6 were neither ephemeral nor superficial. A previous 'terror' in 1064 had been observed to inspire men of all classes to leave their families and possessions for Jerusalem, including bishops and at least one scholar who entertained his companions with vernacular songs about Christ's miracles, a technique of boosting morale probably repeated in the armies of 1096.[68] The well-attested astrological episodes early in 1095 – apparently a meteor shower – could be used to agitate moods, as had Halley's Comet of 1066. Enthusiasm for the Jerusalem expedition was not the result of any famine or ergot-inspired hallucinations; if it can be described as a form of mass hysteria, it was by no means inchoate. The patterns of delivering the message and of recruitment tracked the dynamics and bonds of society; of lordship, kinship, locality, authority, towns, and of worship. Ceremony, symbolism and repetition of a simple creed provided focus for disparate ambitions involving faith, self-image and the pressure of peers. Although, as one rather bemused onlooker noticed, the huge number moved by this single objective was inspired by word of mouth, one to another,[69] the elites of church and lay rule provided the kernel of idealism as well as the prosaic but vital mechanics of action. Part revivalism, part politics, part a search for release and personal renewal, both a manipulation of popular beliefs and prejudices common to all social groups and an attempt to channel these towards a narrowly laudable yet essentially familiar and explicable end, the summons to Jerusalem succeeded because it caught the imagination of a society not necessarily ready but psychologically, culturally and materially equipped to answer the call. In the level of official enthusiasm, in the rapidity of popular acceptance, in the extremes of response, in the widespread uncertainty, indifference and regional variation shadowing extravagant and well-publicized bellicosity, 1096 was the 1914 of the middle ages.

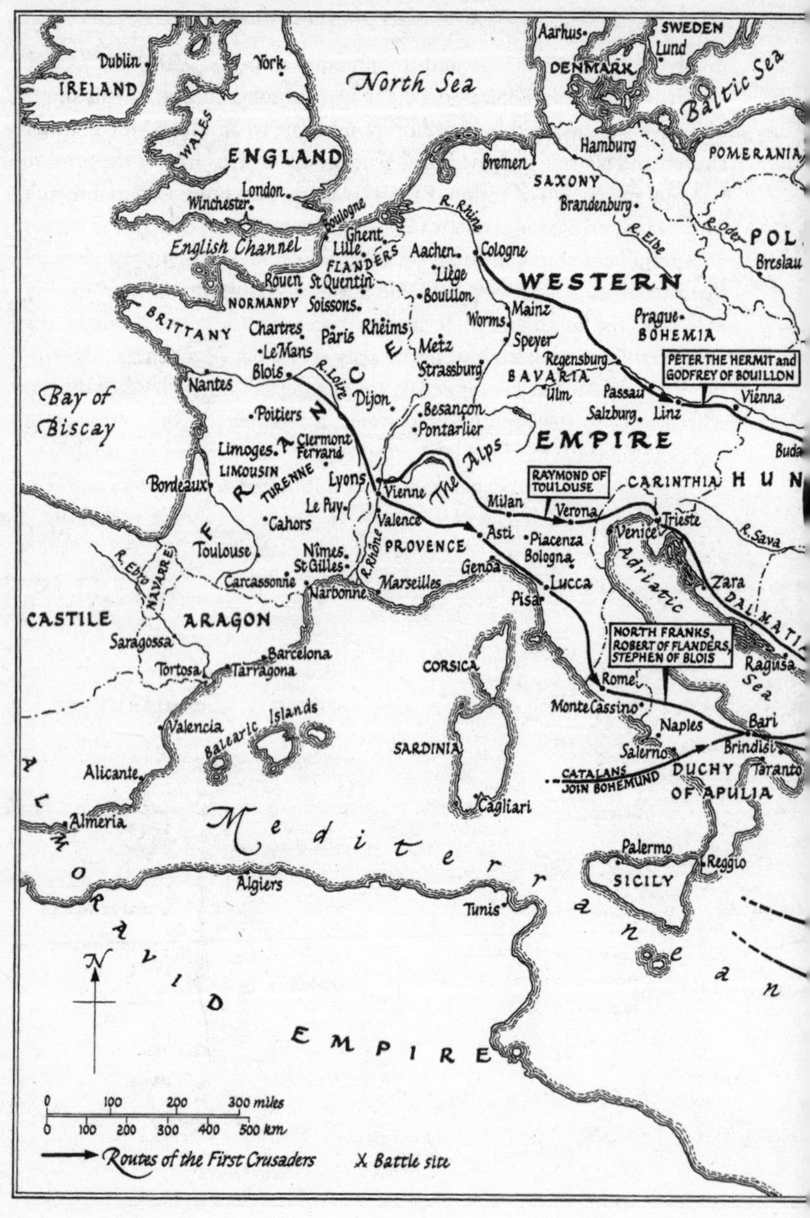

1. Europe and the Near East at the Time of the First Crusade and Preaching Tour of Pope Urban II 1095–6

Preaching Tour of Pope Urban II 1095–6
Paris
Le Mans
Vendôme
Angers
R. Loire
Nantes
Tours
Nevers
Autun
Poitiers
Cluny
Clermont
Limoges
Lyons
Le Puy
Valence
Asti
Bordeaux
FRANCE
Gap
Nîmes
St Gilles
Toulouse
Marseilles
Carcassonne
Narbonne
RUSSIAN
PRINCIPALITIES
R. Vistula
ND
R. Dniester
GARY
Belgrade
R. Morava
R. Danube
Black Sea
Nish
Sofia
Sinope
Bafra
Philippopolis
R. Maritza
Adrianople
Mersivan
Scutari
R. Vardar
Constantinople
Gangra
DANISHMENDS
Dyrrachium
Serres
Nicomedia
Ochrid
Rodosto
Nicaea
Ancyra
Palagonia
Roussa
Thessalonica
SELJUKS OF RUM
Caesarea
Avlona
Castoria
Dorylaeum
BYZANTINE
ARMENIANS
Aegean Sea
Polybotus
Philomelium
Coxon
Marash
Edessa
Antioch-in-Pisidia
Iconium
Aintab
Mamistra
Adana
Heraclea
Ravendan
Tarsus
Aleppo
EMPIRE
Antioch
Lattakiah
Ma'arrat an Numan
Jabala
PISANS 1099
Tortosa
Krak des Chevaliers
RHODES
Tripoli
Arqah
GENOESE 1097/1102
CYPRUS
Beirut
Damascus
Sidon
CRETE
Tyre
Sea
Acre
COUNT RAYMOND, GODFREY and ROBERT OF FLANDERS
Caesarea
Jaffa
Jerusalem
Bethlehem
Ascalon
FATIMID CALIPHATE
Cairo

3
The March to Constantinople

The polity of western Christendom comprised regions rather than kingdoms. Consequently, recruitment, politics, structure and command of the First Crusade were dominated by provincial lords, not kings. Writers on and of the expedition to Jerusalem took pains to identify different regional identities. Sigebert of Gembloux specified recruits from Provence, Aquitaine, Brittany, Scotland, England, Normandy, Francia (i.e. roughly, in this context, the area from the Loire to the Meuse), Lotharingia (i.e. greater Lorraine), Burgundy, Germania, Lombardy and Apulia. From his Lotharingian perspective, Albert of Aachen listed Franks, Lotharingians, Alemans, Bavarians, Flemings, 'all the people of the Teutons', Swabians, Normans, Burgundians and Bretons. From the south, Raymond of Aguilers distinguished between Franks, northern French, and Provençals, southern French, amongst whom he further separated those from Provence itself, Burgundy (probably the county east of the Saône/Rhône corridor, not the duchy), the Auvergne, Gascony and 'Gothia' (i.e. what might now be called Languedoc). Fulcher of Chartres described his companions as western Franks; Albert of Aachen mentioned East Franks. Raymond commented that the Muslims called them all Franks, clearly well informed of the Arabic catch-all for western European Christians, 'al-ifranj'. The anonymous, possibly Normano-Italian author of the *Gesta Francorum*, who often used general terms such as 'Christiani', carefully differentiated those from Italy who joined Peter the Hermit at Constantinople as 'Lombardi', from the Po region, and 'Longobardi', his neighbours from the centre and south of the peninsula. The *Gesta* retains the older name 'Gauls' for the geographic France. The fiercely xenophobic Guibert of Nogent insisted on a fabricated nationalism, arguing that Urban II had specifically summoned the 'Franks', not the Germans, to protect Christendom from the Turks, a distortion of the events that rapidly gained favour with other 'French' writers such as Robert of Rheims and Baldric of Bourgeuil: thus were invented the *Gesta Dei per Francos*, the Deeds of God through the Franks, the title of Guibert's admiring account, a national gloss that concealed the nature and structure of the expedition itself. So keen was Guibert on the Frankish monopoly on the *Gesta Dei* that he insisted that Bohemund – an Italian Norman – through his family's origins and later marriage 'might very well be considered a Frank'. Judged by their own letters, the members of the expedition called themselves 'Christiani', their clerics as 'Latini', in contrast to the local 'Graeci'.[1]

Given the fame and aura of sanctity that surrounded the First Crusade, the Francophile gloss on the racial and regional diversity of the expedition played a part in the elevation and consolidation of a new sense of national identity apparent in twelfth- and thirteenth-century France, one exploited vigorously by the Capetian kings, not least in their own crusading ventures in 1147, 1190 and 1248. This nascent consciousness of unity encouraged by historians of the First Crusade such as Guibert of Nogent or Robert of Rheims was to contrast strongly with the older traditions of particularism maintained in Germany and Italy, whose actual experience of crusading differed little but lacked any specifically national dividend. The image of the French as dominating the crusades was not entirely misplaced: the majority of those we know as participants in 1096–9 came from lands between the Rhine and the Atlantic, the English Channel and the Mediterranean. However, to equate the 'Franks' with the French ignores their wide differences of language, law, landholding, history, tradition and culture as well as the contributions of other regions, from Denmark to Apulia, and England to Austria.

Shared objectives and shared perils created the cohesion of the First Crusade. After receiving a serious fright in the first field battle with the Turks in July 1097, the expedition's military decisions were scrutinized by a common council; Adhemar of Le Puy enforced a chairman's control. At Antioch, a common fund was created to fund expensive capital projects such as a siege tower and, briefly, a commander-in-chief was appointed, Stephen of Blois, who promptly ran away. For battle, leadership was agreed beforehand. Some factions were suspicious of the Provençal monopoly on helpful visions and the discovery of the Holy Lance at Antioch, and Raymond of Toulouse remained an isolated figure, perhaps because he spoke *langue d'oc* (southern French) not, like the rest of the high command, versions of *langue d'oil* (northern French). Even at Jerusalem, the princes kept a certain distance from each other, preserving their autonomy.[2]

This reality of frequent regional and ethnic tensions reflected the basic structure of the expedition which revolved around those lords and knights with sufficient means to support an entourage. Initially such groups mirrored the local circumstances of recruitment and travel. At least seven different currencies circulated in the army, perhaps even as late as May 1099.[3] As medieval armies shared many characteristics of moving markets, such distinctions cannot have made transactions easier, exacerbated as they already were in Syria by a silver-based coinage operating within a gold currency area. Different contingents voiced different battle cries. Nevertheless, as funds ran out and leaders died, deserted or opted out of the main campaign, patronage became fluid, and not only for well-connected opportunists such as Tancred, who bartered his services between his uncle, Bohemund, Raymond of Toulouse and Godfrey of Bouillon. In the surviving rump before the walls of Jerusalem, allegiance followed sustenance and the provision of horses rather than race or region. This had not been the case at the outset.

THE FIRST WAVE, 1096

By the time Peter the Hermit entered Cologne on 12 April 1096, Easter Saturday, considerable numbers from northern and eastern France, Lorraine and the Rhineland were already mobilized. Walter lord of Boissy-sans-Avoir in the Ile de France was preparing to leave the city immediately after Easter; on 15 April he set out on the traditional pilgrim route up the Rhine and Neckar to Regensberg and down the Danube to Hungary and the Balkan routes to Constantinople. With him was an infantry force, mainly French, led by eight knights, seemingly an advance guard for Peter's larger army of levies raised on his march from Berry through the Ile de France and Champagne to the Moselle and the Rhine. Already, Peter had attracted a smattering of French nobles and volunteers from the towns he had visited. Some have seen his force as more of a pilgrimage than a military operation, yet, apart from Walter Sans Avoir, Peter established a military command under Godfrey Burel of Etampes, Reynald of Broyes from Epernay, Walter Fitz Waleran of Breteuil in the Beauvaisis and Fulcher, brother of the vidame of Chartres.[4] His concentration on the urban centres of Lorraine and the Rhineland was not fortuitous. Arriving at Trier on the Moselle in early April, Peter bullied the local Jewish community into supplying provisions by showing a letter from French Jews urging them to accede to his demands: news of threatened or actual violence against northern French Jewish communities had probably already filtered through. From Trier, Peter headed north, down the Moselle, to Cologne on the Rhine, probably as much in search of funds and supplies as of men. Cologne possessed a large Jewish community, which at about this time was being blackmailed into subsidizing Godfrey of Bouillon's expedition. A major commercial centre, although hardly on a direct route from Trier to the Danube and Constantinople, the city provided a convenient muster point for Lorraine recruits, including some German knights.

Peter's movements displayed deliberation and control. He may have threatened the Jews of Trier and elsewhere by anti-Jewish preaching, but his forces abstained from organized attacks on them, unlike the troops of the armies collected in his wake and scavenging local citizens. Even if, as hostile commentators maintained, his followers were 'the leftover dregs of the Franks' with children in tow who, 'whenever they came upon a castle or city, asked whether this was Jerusalem', Peter, a small but charismatic figure, unafraid and competent later to negotiate in person with the Byzantine emperor and the atabeg of Mosul, displayed neither ignorance nor naivety.[5] He was either well briefed or able to extemporize with skill in delegating further recruitment to the priest Gottschalk. He, in turn, raised an effective and well-funded force, 15,000 strong according to Albert of Aachen, with as many knights as infantry, sufficiently impressive and organized for King Coloman I of Hungary to negotiate a truce and the surrender of their arms, providing him with the opportunity, eagerly embraced, to massacre them at Pannonhalma in early July.

Peter may also have encouraged Count Emich of Flonheim, whose followers began killing Jews in Speyer on 3 May, although his army travelled north, down the Rhine, while Peter's, days earlier, had passed in the opposite direction. Emich's muster with significant contingents from northern France occurred at Mainz in late May, by which time Peter was far down the Danube. However, the obscurity of the gathering of Emich's south German and French force suggests local recruitment. Peter, Gottschalk or Urban may have had a focusing effect; so too did local interest, traditions and contacts. As a child, Guibert of Nogent had known one of the knights later killed at Antioch, Matthew from the Beauvaisis, who had served the Byzantine emperor.[6] His example may have exerted as much influence as Peter's evangelism, garbled accounts of Urban II's call to arms or rumours of a millennial holy war.

The orderliness of Peter's forces stands in contrast with what followed. In mid-May, his lieutenant Walter Sans Avoir, marching only days ahead of him, negotiated a safe-conduct with the new Hungarian King Coloman, including access to markets, an important privilege as the early summer, before the harvest, were the hungriest months in the middle ages. There was trouble at Semlin on the Hungarian border over purchases of arms. Once they were across the Byzantine frontier, the hazards of early summer campaigns were exposed, Walter being refused market facilities at Belgrade, causing an affray in which sixty pilgrims died. However, the Byzantine military authorities recognized Walter as an ally and, to prevent further pillaging, provided food and an escort to Constantinople, which he reached about 20 July 1096 to await Peter. It says much for Alexius's involvement in the project that he was so accommodating, not least as he must have been expecting the westerners to arrive some months later, when local provisions would have been more plentiful.

The speed in conveying Walter Sans Avoir to the imperial capital shows the Greeks knew that Peter the Hermit's larger force was only days behind, presenting a potentially dangerous competition for food. Although his regime rested on recent military success against the Pechenegs in the Balkans and some moderate successes in Asia Minor and the Aegean, Alexius I had witnessed too many political coups, one of them his own in 1081, to feel entirely secure. In 1094–5 there was a Balkan invasion across the Danube by Cumans, trouble in Serbia (directly on the crusaders' line of march), stirrings of a tax revolt and a dangerous conspiracy in the army to replace Alexius by Nicephoras Diogenes, son of the Emperor Romanus IV (1068–71), the loser at Manzikert. Pressure on food in the strategically vital Balkan provinces and, still more, in the capital itself, could erode Alexius's precarious support.[7] Alexius needed western aid but could not allow it to disrupt his delicate political arrangements. A hungry, resentful population in

Constantinople would have been very dangerous. Alexius determined to push the crusaders into Asia as quickly as possible to minimize the risk. It was less, as his daughter Anna Comnena claimed half a century later, that the emperor feared a western attack, more that he was wary of food riots or dissident Greeks recruiting the foreigners to overthrow him. From the first Alexius attempted to control his unexpectedly numerous allies through a mixture of hospitality, generosity and firm direction, careful always not to commit too many of his own stretched resources to their cause.

Peter the Hermit's army left Cologne on 20 April. It was large, perhaps as many as 20,000 including non-combatants; the line of march in the Balkans was at least a mile long. Its passage through central Europe was rapid, averaging over seventeen miles per day, with twenty-five miles on good roads.[8] Most of the pilgrims walked or rode, Peter apparently on his talismanic donkey, although some travelled down the Danube by boat. At Regensberg on 23 May, Peter's followers orchestrated a mass forced baptism of the city's Jews in the Danube. Unsurprisingly in view of the expedition's propaganda, crusaders adopted a belligerent attitude to any who stood in their way, physically or ideologically. This emerged starkly when Peter's army sacked Semlin in the second week of June after concerted assaults led by heavily armed knights and Godfrey Burel's infantry. Again, the trouble arose from disputes over supplies – apparently rumours of the ill-treatment of Walter's followers and an argument over the purchase of a pair of shoes sparked a riot that led to armed intervention – and anxiety over the prospects of help across the frontier in Byzantium. Although capable of storming a city and accompanied by carts full of treasure, under pressure Peter's army lacked discipline.

The Semlin affair put the Greeks on their guard, evacuating Belgrade, leaving it open to plunder. After a forced crossing of the river Save, the pilgrims reached Nish, the provincial capital, on 27 June, where the crisis of supplies became critical. The Byzantine governor Nicetas negotiated a market for Peter's men in return for hostages, significantly including the military commanders Godfrey Burel and Walter Fitz Waleran. When this broke down, Nicetas imposed order by force; after a failed attempt to restore peace by Peter, his forces were scattered by a concerted Greek assault. Chastened, Peter led the survivors along the road to Sofia; at the evacuated town of Bela Palanka they regrouped and gathered the local harvest. At Sofia, on 7 July, Peter was met by an escort from

Alexius that hurried them towards Constantinople, making sure they never stopped anywhere for more than three days. The battles at Nish, which cost perhaps as much as a third of his force, had been caused by Peter and his commanders losing control, particularly, Albert of Aachen recorded, of the young men.[9] Communications along the line broke down, a sign of inexperienced leadership faced with such a large and disparate force, lacking the cohesion exerted by wealthy magnates. Exhausting marches; uncertain food supplies; alien territory and people; discomfort, fear and the prospect of hunger soured idealism. Yet, once chaperoned by the Greeks and provided with secure provisions, Peter's army regained its integrity; Adrianople was reached by 22 July and Constantinople on 1 August, just five months after Peter's first rallying of pilgrims in the Ile de France over a thousand miles behind.

The shambles in the Balkans served as a prelude to disaster. Alexius advised Peter against pressing forward immediately. Evidently abreast of events in the west, some princes and probably the pope having written to him of their plans, Alexius urged waiting for the arrival of the rest of forces being assembled. Reunited with Walter Sans Avoir and reinforced by some Italian levies, Peter was provided with a well-supplied base that Alexius used for western mercenaries at Kibotos, on the Gulf of Nicomedia just across the Sea of Marmora from the capital. There, the usual difficulty of countering boredom in an army camp was exacerbated by regional rivalries and the proximity of territory controlled by the Seljuk Turks, whose capital in Asia Minor was at Nicaea, only twenty-five miles away. With Peter now reduced to a diplomatic role in negotiating the level and cost of regular supplies with the Byzantine authorities in Constantinople, leadership devolved on to the separate captains in whose interest it was to engage in lucrative pillaging of the locality, regardless of whether the victims were Greek Christians or Muslims. The objectives were food, booty and action. It was a truism of medieval warfare that an armed force was never more vulnerable than when foraging. In September, French raiders penetrated to the walls of Nicaea. Not to be outdone, a contingent of Germans and Italians, under an Italian called Rainaldo, ranged further afield, seizing a castle at Xerigordo near Nicaea. There they were trapped and massacred by Seljuks from Nicaea, allegedly only those who surrendered and embraced Islam escaping to lead lives as captives and slaves, one of them being Rainaldo himself.

Disorderly conduct and confused leadership were not the sole prerogatives of these early crusade armies; a year later the princes fared little better during some of the darker days at the siege of Antioch. The populist nature of the whole enterprise now emerged, not for the last time, as a potent force in tactical decisions. Walter Sans Avoir and most of the other leaders at Kibotos argued against any precipitate response to the Xerigordo disaster, but popular demand for revenge found a spokesman in Godfrey Burel, the majority prevailing over the cautious leadership. The popular agitation provoked the main body of the crusaders to advance from Kibotos towards Nicaea. By now the Seljuk Sultan Kilij Arslan was sufficiently alarmed to take personal direction of his forces. In a series of fast-moving engagements on 21 October, a significant proportion of the Christian knights were isolated and killed, including Walter Sans Avoir, pierced, so Albert of Aachen recorded, by seven arrows, and Reynald of Broyes.[10] With the elite of knights broken, the Christians were either massacred or fled, the Turks overrunning the camp at Kibotos three miles away within minutes. Only the arrival of a Byzantine relief force saved the remnants of the Christian army that had found refuge in a deserted castle on the shore; a large proportion of these would appear to have been knights.

Although not directly responsible for the catastrophe, Peter the Hermit's role as a leader was at an end, his presence during the rest of the campaign receiving distinctly muted acknowledgement in the eyewitness accounts. Yet his contribution, ultimately insignificant militarily, demonstrated that the journey to the east was not a fool's errand. His troops had held together as a viable force for months despite their difficulties with supplies, which were the result of timing as much as anything. He had accomplished a long march with thousands of ill-assorted followers, negotiated with local rulers and secured the patronage and favour of the Greek emperor. The tragic failure of his army in Asia pointed to the requirements for success: united leadership; significant numbers of knights; respect for the enemy; and, above all, adequate and secure supplies, of food, water, war materials and horses.

Peter the Hermit's failure looked like modest success when compared with the fate of the other large crusader bands that set out from the Rhineland area in the spring of 1096. Gottschalk's army was destroyed at the beginning of July by an exasperated King Coloman in western Hungary at about the same time as Volkmar's force was dispersed at

Nitra in the north after a career of Jewish persecution in Bohemia. The problem for the Hungarians was of order and supply. Each successive crusader army seemed less disciplined, more eager to plunder, commandeer markets and coerce locals. Beyond the scrutiny of chroniclers, a steady stream of ordinary pilgrims was flowing east, adding to the pressure on food stocks and forage. These material considerations dictated Coloman's refusal in late July to allow the passage into his kingdom of Emich of Flonheim and his south and west German followers: with a more favourable supply position three months later, the king allowed Godfrey of Bouillon a negotiated passage. However, beyond provisions, Coloman may also have regarded Emich as a dangerous liability, his reputation for violence and flouting of royal authority preceding him. In the three months since embarking on his crusade, Count Emich had, in the eyes of many, indelibly stained the holy project by the systematic persecution of Jews.

THE JEWISH POGROM OF 1096

The Jews of northern Europe shared in the economic growth of the eleventh century, especially in the revival of urban life. Attracted from the Mediterranean regions, Ashkenazic Jews became established in market towns of northern France such as Troyes or Le Mans by the late tenth century, as well as in the towns of the Rhineland. New communities continued to be established, such as in England after 1066 or in Speyer in 1084; older ones, such as those of Rouen, Cologne or Mainz, flourished under the protection of local rulers or bishops eager to promote trade. Jewish banking became a feature of the expanding markets of the area. As well as direct involvement in trading goods, with increased long-distance commerce and the persistence of varying local currencies, weights and measures, the network of Jewish financiers proved useful. Judging by Rhineland evidence, interest rates were not exorbitant, 8 per cent in one example, Jewish credit being certainly more accessible and in the long term cheaper than obtaining cash from another source of bullion, religious houses.[11] With success came dangers. In northern France there had been sporadic outbreaks of anti-Semitic persecution allied to forced conversions, in particular in the years 1007–12.[12] As holders of movable wealth, Jews were targets for casual as well as systematic larceny. As a religious minority, Jews remained tolerated if not accepted. A more consistent threat to their communities than persecution lay in conversions of successful and ambitious Jews to the majority faith, as occurred with sons of two famous Mainz rabbis. Privileged and protected status in the confined streets of eleventh-century towns presented its own problems: Bishop Rudiger's charter establishing Jews at Speyer provided for a walled enclave to protect them from 'the violence of the mob'.[13] Such communal tensions played their part in the tragedy of 1096.

On 3 May 1096, the Jewish Sabbath, Count Emich's troops attacked the Jews at Speyer, near to his estates, killing a dozen of them who refused baptism, before the bishop came to their rescue. One woman committed suicide rather than submit to the Christians. The persecutors received the help of townspeople, as Bishop John punished some of them by having their hands cut off, a penalty for theft. Those Jews who had fled to the surrounding countryside or had accepted baptism returned under the bishop's protection, the apostates allowed to revert to Judaism; a new synagogue was begun. Steven Runciman rather astonishingly dismisses this episode as 'not a very impressive attack'.[14] Perhaps the walls prescribed in 1084 proved their use. Over a fortnight later, on 18 May, Emich arrived at Worms where he managed to mobilize more effective local assistance, including peasants from the countryside as well as burghers. Given the proximity of Emich's own lands, the count was probably exploiting known local tensions. Jews found in their quarter were massacred, the Torah Scrolls desecrated; those who had fled to the protection of the bishop's palace were besieged and, on 20 May, slaughtered. Some resisted forcible conversion, one of the bishop's relatives being killed; others may have taken the route of suicide. Hundreds died.

The destruction of the Jews of Mainz attracted the most detailed attention, later held up to Jewish audiences as a model of fortitude under persecution and of holy martyrdom. Mainz was a major centre of Jewish learning and culture as well as business. Jewish leaders were prominent in commerce; the chief rabbi, Kalonymos, on good terms with the archbishop and recognized by the emperor. On Emich's appearance before their gates, which the archbishop had ordered to be shut against him, some townspeople provoked riots. The Jewish leaders bribed the archbishop to protect them and tried to buy off Emich with a gift of seven pounds of gold, to no avail. The gates were opened on 26 May; the killing and looting lasted two days. The archbishop reneged on his promise of protection and fled; the Jews sheltering in his palace, despite initial vigorous armed resistance, were slaughtered with the rest. The search for money and Jews throughout the city was thorough. The synagogue was destroyed in the mayhem; some Jews apostatized; others chose suicide. The story of the young mother Rachel's sacrifice of her four children, circulated for the edification of the faithful in the twelfth century, is grim. Her youngest, Aaron, terrified at seeing the deaths of his siblings, begged his mother to spare him, running away to hide under a box.

> When this pious woman had completed sacrificing her three children to their Creator, she raised her voice and called to her son: 'Aaron, Aaron, where are you? I will not spare you either, or have mercy on you.' She drew him out by his feet from under the box where he had hidden and slaughtered him before the Exalted and Lofty God.[15]

Surrounded by the still-twitching corpses of her children, Rachel waited to be found by the Christians; before killing her, they demanded, 'Show us the money you have in your sleeves'. Hers was not the only horrific death. Rabbi Kalonymos and fifty others escaped to seek asylum at the archbishop's country retreat across the Rhine at Rudesheim. Archbishop Ruthard, pusillanimous and discreditable to the last, tried to exploit the rabbi's predicament by offering protection only in return for conversion. Kalonymos, so furious at this self-seeking betrayal that he tried to assault the archbishop, was butchered with his companions. The amount of loot gained by Emich's men and the local Christians is unknown; perhaps about a thousand Jews died.

By the time Emich reached Cologne on 29 May, lessons had been learnt, local Jews having dispersed across the countryside or sought shelter from friendly Christians in the city, hoping to avoid trouble during the following weekend and Whit Sunday (1 June). The synagogue was burnt and the Torah Scrolls desecrated, but casualties among the Jews were light, the quest for booty more obvious: a wealthy Jewish woman, Rebecca, was murdered when found trying to smuggle gold and silver to her husband in hiding with a Christian family.[16] The Jews who had fled the city were soon being hunted down, attacks being recorded in Neuss, Wevelinghofen and elsewhere in the neighbourhood. With the best plums picked, Count Emich and his men turned south and east, along the Main towards the Danube and Hungary. Denied entry into Hungary at Wiesselberg in mid-July, Emich discovered that thuggery and bullying cut no ice against an organized armed enemy. Settling down to an elaborate siege, Emich and his French and Swabian allies showed tactical expertise and engineering skill in constructing pontoon bridges and siege-engines but, on a rumour of the approach of King Coloman, morale disintegrated. His men beginning to flee, Emich and his knights were unexpectedly worsted by a sortie from the Wiesselberg garrison, the count only escaping because of the speed of his mount. The army dissolved; the French nobles returned west to seek other routes and new leaders; Emich went home.

The Rhineland pogroms of May did not end with Emich's departure. Whether pursued by other bands of *crucesignati* or by opportunist locals, the area around Cologne continued to suffer depredations for some weeks. In June attacks spread down the Moselle to Trier and Metz, where over twenty Jews died. It was high summer, and, if not necessarily as scorching as the dry year of 1095, tempers could have frayed as hunger increased; shortages for crusaders implied shortages for the locals; prices rose in the wake of the levying of armies. A lead had been provided by Count Emich's butchers, with their sanctimonious, bloodied aprons of righteousness. In late June and July, further attacks occurred in the Cologne region and to the north, at Xanten, Mehr, Eller and Geldern. The descriptions of the assailants are vague. In places such as Mehr, neighbours played a key role in the Jews' ordeal. By late summer, the outbursts of hate had died away, perhaps as the harvest came in. Followers of Godfrey of Bouillon, recruited from adjacent regions, whose leader had done his own blackmailing of the Jews of Mainz and Cologne, caused no trouble; perhaps they thought the Jews had nothing left worth plundering.

Emich of Flonheim's campaign against the prosperous Jewish communities was deliberate, far from mindless vandalism. The rhetoric, not least that recorded in the harrowingly full Jewish accounts of the pogroms, was religious, but the motive may have been financial. It was not that the crusaders were in debt to the Jews, merely that many had sold or pledged their patrimonies and still faced further expense. For leaders such as Emich, cash meant power and authority. Locals, including some bishops, erstwhile protectors, exploited the crusaders' greed by extorting protection money from the helpless Jews as well as looting. The Mainz community offered Emich money to spare them and delayed their own fate by throwing coins at their ravaging persecutors. Albert of Aachen drily commented that the pilgrims had slaughtered the Jews 'more from avarice than for the justice of God', a sin to which he attributed their later travails in the Balkans.[17] The lust for money alone cannot explain the consistent flouting of canon law and religious teaching witnessed by the repeated forcible conversions. Nothing in official Christian doctrine justified slaying Jews. Pope Alexander II had explicitly prohibited it when drawing a careful distinction between them and Muslims in 1063. No justification of holy war could embrace victimization of those whom the Christians ruled anyway, hence the repeated attempts to blame the Jews of subversion and plotting the destruction of Christendom to excuse persecution. However, the preaching of the cross emphasized meritorious Christian violence, the legitimacy of revenge and religious vendetta and the suffering of Christ Crucified. Christian sources record how such messages were translated into a gospel of indiscriminate religious hate. Crusaders at Rouen thought it absurd to campaign against God's enemies in the east 'when in front of our eyes are the Jews, of all races the most hostile to God'. Albert of Aachen noted that recruits to Emich's army at Mainz insisted that killing the Jews was the first act of their campaign against the 'enemies of the Christian faith'. The Christian love Urban may have preached to justify his Jerusalem project was reserved for Christians; the obverse of this message of charity was intolerance and violence. According to a disapproving German witness, Ekkehard of Aura, the persecutors were zealous Christians who 'took pains to destroy utterly the execrable Jews' either by death or forced conversion.[18] Not only were Jewish communities ransacked for money and goods, their synagogues, Torah Scrolls and cemeteries were repeatedly desecrated. Jews believed the incentive for their attackers was religious. In general, Jews were enemies of the church; in particular they killed Christ. When the gates of Mainz were opened to them, Emich's followers were reported by one Hebrew source as exulting, 'All this the Crucified has done for us, so that we might avenge his blood on the Jews.'[19] All three Hebrew chronicle sources for the pogroms agree on the persistence of the theme of vengeance for the Crucifixion. Thus the mixture of demotic religious propaganda and material greed combined to create an obscene cocktail of butchery and bigotry.

Yet the anti-Jewish persecutions reflected more than mob violence and hysteria. The chronicle attributed to Solomon bar Simson, a Mainz Jew writing *c.*1140, recorded that those who set out for the Holy Land 'decorated themselves prominently with their signs, placing a profane symbol – a horizontal line over a vertical one – on the vestments of every man and woman whose heart yearned to go on the stray path to the grave of their Messiah'. The butchers of the Mainz community are described as raging 'in the name of the crucified one' and carrying banners of the cross.[20] Just as much as a shared campaign, a shared pogrom cements identity on a group. Crusaders possessed a special sense of identity; already by June 1097 one wrote of 'the army of God'.[21] In the early days of 1096, this uniqueness of purpose and community sought and found expression, warriors of the cross fighting for Christ. Theological niceties were irrelevant and, in any case, the clergy travelling with the crusaders may have encouraged the outrages while those in the towns affected were rarely able to sustain the orthodox line. The massacre of the Jews was just the first of many articulations of the corporate spirit of crusading. There also existed a local political dimension. Henry IV had explicitly and repeatedly forbidden the Jews to be harmed; they were under his protection. Emich's attacks represented a challenge to Henry's authority, an assertion of his independence, made easier by the emperor's absence in Italy. The political dividends of the upheavel of 1096 may not have been confined to the papacy.

For the Jews, the Rhineland pogroms did not mark 'the first holocaust'.[22] There had been assaults before; neither did they mark the opening of a sustained campaign against the Jews. If now more wary and uneasy, the Ashkenazic Jewish communities of the Rhineland and northern Europe survived and thrived for generations, despite further atrocities attendant on the Second and Third Crusades. Jews continued to migrate into the areas of persecution. More conductive to intolerance was the growing exclusivity and general militancy of the western church. With the battles with Islam, in Spain and the east; the conversion of the Baltic; the elaboration of canon law; and the war against heresy, the persistence of a religious minority appeared more anomalous and, to some, more offensive. 1096 was only one part of this process. Ironically, its impact on Ashkenazic memory was testimony to its lack of profound material effect on the victimized communities. It was to renewed and expanding Jewish congregations in the Rhineland itself that the image of the martyrs of 1096 spoke most eloquently, as in the liturgical prayer first mentioned by Ephraim, a twelfth-century rabbi in Bonn: 'May the Merciful Father, who dwells in heaven, in his abundant mercies remember compassionately the pious and righteous and pure, the sacred communities who sacrificed themselves for the sanctification of the Divine Name'.[23]

THE SECOND WAVE, 1096–7

The failures and excesses of the bands travelling east in the summer of 1096 attracted scorn, contempt and ridicule but hardly impinged on the project's popularity. By the date fixed by Urban II for departure, 15 August 1096, all three German expeditions had collapsed; Peter the Hermit's troops were perched precariously in their base on the rim of western Asia, soon to be annihilated; none of the princes of the west had embarked. Yet Urban II had not yet returned to Italy and recruitment was gathering momentum across western Europe. Before stopped by their local bishop, the abbot and monks of Cerne in Dorset had invested thirty shillings in a ship to take them to Jerusalem. At the same time, the pope voiced anxieties about indiscriminate enlistment, especially by clergy and young husbands with itchy feet.[24] Frustrated veterans of the first armies sought new comrades. By the end of the year, by land and sea, by boat, horse, wagon and on foot, perhaps another 50–60,000 had embarked for the east, casting the earlier efforts into a deep shade.

For each *crucesignatus* and those left behind, departure was a solemn moment. While most hoped to return, none could guarantee it. As he travelled south to rendezvous with the duke of Normandy and count of Blois in September 1096, Count Robert of Flanders was received at a monastery near Rheims by a procession of monks; there too a local magnate came to pay his respects.[25] Most adieux lacked such grand ceremony, although many would have been witnessed by parish priest and villagers and accompanied by ritualized as well as genuine grief. Fulcher of Chartres, chaplain on the march to Count Robert's companion Stephen of Blois, provided an imaginative, yet universal description:

What sighs, what weeping, what lamentation among friends when husband left wife so dear to him, his children, his possessions however great, his father, mother, brother and other relatives. But however many tears those remaining shed for departing friends and in their presence, none flinched from going ... Then husband told wife the time he expected to return, assuring her that if by God's grace he survived he would come back home to her. He commended her to the Lord, kissed her lingeringly, and promised her as she wept that he would return. She, though, fearing that she would never see him again, could not stand but swooned to the ground, mourning her loved one, whom she was losing in this life as if he were already dead. He, however, like one who has no pity – although he had – and as if he were not moved by the tears of his wife nor the grief of any of his friends – yet secretly moved in his heart – departed with firm resolution. Sadness was the lot of those who remained, elation, of those who departed.[26]

The first great western lord to set out for Jerusalem, somewhat paradoxically, was the brother of the king Urban II had excommunicated at Clermont. Hugh count of Vermandois was the younger brother of Philip I, the Fat. Distinguished only by blood, Hugh acted as a magnet for some of his brother's leading vassals, including the king's constable (Walo of Chaumont-en-Vexin) and seneschal (Gilbert of Garlande). The Ile de France was well represented in Hugh's entourage, including later William the Carpenter of Melun, Thomas of Marle and Drogo of Nesle. Capetian interest was not entirely ideological. Participation in the expedition was agreed during a council at Paris in February 1096; in July, Hugh's participation was announced to the pope by King Philip with his own submission to Urban's judgement over his adulterous marriage (to the wife of the count of Anjou, to whom Urban had presented a golden rose during his preaching tour in March). Thus Urban's Jerusalem scheme produced immediate and direct political gains for the wider papal cause by allowing Philip to be reconciled without losing too much face. The settlement suited both sides, Hugh receiving a papal banner to carry on his pilgrimage. The numerous recruits from the Paris region indicate another political benefit, this time for the Capetians, by providing a rare opportunity to exhibit practical leadership over their unruly vassals of the Ile de France, although Hugh hardly proved a dominant figure.

His journey was carefully planned; before leaving, probably in late

August, he wrote to Alexius I, informing him of his intended itinerary.[27] This took him through Italy, where he may have received the papal banner and blessing, to Bari. By this time Hugh's small contingent of knights had been swelled by the French lords from Emich of Flonheim's misadventure led by William of Melun. In southern Italy, his party was joined by one of Bohemund's nephews, William FitzMarquis, and others, including veterans of Byzantine service.[28] Crossing the Adriatic in October, after the indignity of a shipwreck, Hugh was held under comfortable house-arrest in Durazzo by the nonetheless hospitable Greek authorities before being escorted under close guard to Constantinople. Alexius seemed concerned lest Hugh linked up with the large numbers of Italians following the same route along the Via Egnatia from Durazzo to the capital; or he may have received warning that his old enemy Bohemund was only a fortnight behind the count. Hugh was welcomed at Constantinople in November, only a few weeks after the massacre at Kibotos. Alexius's treatment of Hugh betrayed nervousness; although well entertained and apparently rather embarrassingly easily flattered by the emperor's attention, the count's movements were monitored and some of his followers kept under close arrest. The emperor was beginning to appreciate the scale of his problems. Almost every day, news came of more western grandees bearing down on him while the flow of lesser pilgrims became a flood, swelled by the bumper harvest experienced in the west in the autumn of 1096. Miraculous would not necessarily have been Alexius's word for it.

Shortly before Christmas 1096, Godfrey of Bouillon, duke of Lower Lorraine, arrived at the Greek capital with a substantial army derived mainly from Lotharingia (Lorraine) and the Low Countries. He proved an awkward guest. His march through central Europe followed the pilgrims' road which had carried Peter the Hermit's armies some months earlier. In contrast to his predecessor, Godfrey's diplomacy worked all the way, a sign of meticulous preparation. Far from the selfless hero of chivalric legend he later appeared, Godfrey struck a number of hard bargains to raise funds for his expedition. Apart from extorting money from Rhineland Jews, he sold some estates; Bouillon itself he mortgaged to the bishop of Liège, with a proviso of restitution if he returned. Although unmarried, perhaps from sexual preference, Godfrey did not regard the expedition to Jerusalem as an excuse for abandoning his status in the west. The younger brother of the wealthy Count Eustace III of Boulogne, Godfrey's career had flourished as a partisan of Henry IV. Succeeding to the disputed duchy of Lower Lorraine as a teenager in 1076, Godfrey fought for Henry in Italy in 1083. In 1087, his rights as duke were confirmed by a grateful emperor: his army in 1096 attracted many imperialists from the diocese of Liège.[29] Although before his departure he had minted coins inscribed 'Godefridus Ierosolimitanus', and despite apparent political ineffectiveness, he never relinquished his duchy even after becoming ruler of the Christian enclave in Palestine in 1099. With him were two future kings of Jerusalem, his ambitious opportunist younger brother Baldwin and his cousin Baldwin lord of Le Bourcq; the counts of Toul and Hainault; other relatives such as Henry and Godfrey of Esch; and perhaps over 100 other knights. He was later joined by survivors from Peter's army, such as Fulcher, brother of the vidame of Chartres. One of his strengths on crusade, and as ruler of Jerusalem, lay in the loyalty of his sizeable military household.

Godfrey's march was prolonged but not turbulent. Leaving Lorraine in August, he negotiated a peaceful crossing of Hungary and access to markets with King Coloman who insisted, as he had with Peter the Hermit, on the security of grand hostages, in this case an extremely reluctant Baldwin of Boulogne and his Anglo-Norman heiress wife, Godehilde of Tosni. Godfrey's chief spokesman had been Godfrey of Esch, a veteran of earlier diplomacy with the Hungarians, another indication of the scale, depth and complexity of the political as well as material preparations. Reaching the Byzantine frontier in early November, Godfrey quickly struck a deal with the Greek authorities over provisions, promising not to engage in violent foraging in return for secure food supplies, the Byzantines having prepared large food dumps along the route. After a leisurely escorted progress, by the time he reached Adrianople, Godfrey, learning of the treatment of Hugh of Vermandois, become alarmed lest he was walking into a gilded trap. Given his minor role in western European politics, the duke's pride and self-importance unexpectedly came to the fore as he insisted Alexius release the Frenchmen. As later admirers and perhaps he himself liked to recall, a descendant of Charlemagne, whose mythologized exploits furnished an important corner of the mental world of aristocratic crusaders,[30] Godfrey behaved as if he were the emperor's equal, not a policy designed to endear him to Alexius. Perhaps Godfrey saw himself in some way as representing his lord, the western emperor Henry IV; certainly the chronicler of Godfrey's campaign, Albert of Aachen, placed the German king at the head of his list of rulers in 1096, above the pope.[31] Godfrey's objections to Alexius's handling of Count Hugh spilt over into violence, as Alexius cut off aid and the Lorrainers began to pillage the neighbourhood of Salabria, between Adrianople and the Sea of Marmora. Only by sending an embassy of Franks in imperial service to reassure the duke of his reception did hostilities cease, but it was a somewhat prickly Godfrey who arrived at Constantinople on 23 December 1096. Stationed on the Golden Horn, then at Pera opposite the city, for weeks Godfrey resisted Alexius's attempts, conveyed by Hugh of Vermandois and others, to arrange a meeting. Alexius again withdrew food supplies, forcing Godfrey into an abortive assault on the city (13 January 1097) and further ravaging until diplomacy prevailed. Hostages were exchanged (including Alexius's son and eventual successor, John) before Godfrey attended an audience with the emperor. The outcome was satisfactory to all concerned. Godfrey swore an oath to the emperor, of vassalage according to Albert of Aachen.[32] Alexius became his patron and helped ship his army across the Bosporus by the end of February 1097. For the Greek emperor, the presence of such a large army, even if peaceful, had presented serious logistical and political problems. Godfrey's initial refusal to reach some accommodation with Alexius or to move forward across the Bosporus to Asia presented dangers as the winter progressed and the capital and its suburbs had to absorb increasing numbers of pilgrims. Both Alexius and Godfrey were exercised by the imminent arrival of the other major commanders of the expedition; the one fearful of the implications to his capital's food supplies and security; the other eager to consult with his peers as to how best to proceed. Around 20 January 1097 Godfrey apparently received an embassy from Bohemund, then making very slow but careful progress from the Adriatic coast, suggesting a combined attack on the capital. Despite his stand-off, Godfrey rejected Bohemund's plan; later veterans of his army spoke about the Greeks without hostility or malice.[33] At a popular level, relations remained good; equally, Godfrey had not resisted manipulation by Alexius only to become a pawn in Bohemund's deep-rooted schemes concerning the Greek empire.

Bohemund of Taranto is the most controversial leader of the First Crusade. Of all the major surviving commanders, he alone failed to join the march to Jerusalem in 1099, more concerned with securing his hold over Syrian Antioch. Admired for his generalship, his pious credentials have been impugned in the light of his priorities in 1099 and his career of attempting to carve out for himself a kingdom in the Balkans at the expense of the Byzantine empire. The traditional view sees his motives as basely material, in contrast to the supposedly more elevated inspirations of some of his colleagues. This is untenable. The psychologies of the crusade's leaders cannot be reconstructed. Each can be shown to have as much avarice or as little piety as the other. The dichotomy between spiritual and mercenary possesses little meaning. Raymond of Toulouse, whose religious sincerity has been widely accepted, proved both scheming and petulant in his earnest quest for an eastern principality, which he finally achieved in the lands around Tripoli in the south Lebanon. The spiritual agonizing of Tancred of Altavilla, Bohemund's nephew, was matched by his alert political opportunism. Godfrey of Bouillon accepted power and lands when offered them in 1099. Baldwin of Boulogne, the most obviously careerist of all, devoted the last twenty years of his life to defending the Holy Places. All the leaders sought to protect their material interests rather than proceed to Jerusalem in the five months after July 1098. Bohemund was not alone in his desire to achieve status, lands and wealth; neither did this ambition automatically contradict the genuineness of his adherence to the cause of Jerusalem. With Baldwin, he undertook a tricky and dangerous journey to fulfil his pilgrimage to the Holy Sepulchre at Christmas 1099, a gesture that, for lack of evidence, cannot be assumed to have been purely for reasons of image or politics.

The picture of Bohemund the ruthless schemer derives from the *Alexiad* of Anna Comnena, Alexius's daughter.[34] Writing half a century after the First Crusade, Anna insists on the deviousness of the westerners, their consistent desire to subvert and occupy the Byzantine empire, and the heroic patience and skill of Alexius, in an attempt to exonerate the emperor from any responsibility for admitting the Franks into the empire and his subsequent failure to establish Greek overlordship over Antioch. Bohemund, who invaded the Balkans twice, in the 1080s and again in 1107–8, is one of the villains of her staunchly anti-western account that has as much to do with the tangled dynastic and imperial politics of the twelfth century as with the events of the 1090s. Seductively vivid, Anna is a confused and misleading source for the crusade let alone the motives of the western leaders. Even her famous description of Bohemund himself – tall, slim, muscular, good complexion, short light-brown hair, forbidding expression – cannot be trusted, still less Runciman's fancy that the teenage Anna was taken by his good looks, 'being, like all Greeks down the ages, susceptible to human beauty'.[35]

Nonetheless, Bohemund's position on crusade is intriguing. The dominant personality in the expedition's military leadership from April 1097 until January 1099, he founded a Norman dynasty in Antioch that outlasted the Norman kings of England and of Sicily. Yet in 1096, in contrast to all the other leaders who were at least of comital status (i.e. of a count), Bohemund was technically still a vassal of a count, his half-brother, the ineffectual Roger Borsa (1089–1111), younger son and heir of Robert Guiscard in southern Italy. The fabulous inheritance promised him by his father, Robert Guiscard, in the Balkans had come to nothing after the failure of the Norman invasion of 1081–5. Despite rebelling in 1085 and 1087 against Roger Borsa, Bohemund had failed to establish an independent territorial title for himself in the west, a political frustration that shaped his actions on crusade. Although possessed of political clout and contacts above his formal station – he knew Urban II personally – he lacked the extensive patrimony or dependent baronage that supported his fellow leaders. The army he gathered about him in southern Italy in the autumn of 1096 reflected this. The core seems to have been his close relatives, including his nephew, Tancred of Lecce and cousin, Richard of Salerno, known as Richard of the Principate, as well as his standard bearer, Robert FitzGerald. In addition there were former rebels, such as Robert of Ansa; and vassals of his half-brother, such as Robert FitzTristan, and of his uncle, Count Roger of Sicily, such as Robert of Sourdeval.[36] His whole force was small, perhaps in total between 3,500 and 4,000 men. Lacking the power of lordship or the purse, Bohemund had to rely on more overt political and military skills. Even these failed to impose cohesion on his force. One nephew, William FitzMarquis, joined Hugh of Vermandois; another, Tancred, fought under his own banner, refused to accept Bohemund's authority at Constantinople and thereafter pursued an increasingly independent line.

Bohemund's army crossed the Adriatic from Bari to the coast of Epirus in late October 1096, probably deliberately avoiding the Byzantine garrison at Durazzo. It then dawdled its way to Constantinople, taking the best part of six months, at an average of just over three miles a day, almost being caught up by the larger force under Raymond of Toulouse, who had landed at Durazzo over three months behind. Yet there was almost no fighting or local resistance. If the story of his approach to Godfrey for an anti-Greek alliance in January 1097 is credited, the initial delay in the western Balkans is explicable as Bohemund would not wish to become too closely entangled with Greek escorts or garrisons near the capital. Godfrey's rebuff may have inspired a *volte face*. As his troops neared Thrace, Bohemund left them under the command of Tancred on 1 April and hurried on to Constantinople, which he reached on 9 April. There, so far from fomenting trouble for Alexius, he proved the emperor's staunchest ally in the often tetchy negotiations with other leaders. Bohemund spent longer with Alexius than any of the other leaders, almost a full calendar month. He eagerly took an oath of fealty and tried to obtain a future role for himself as military commander or ruler of new conquests in the east as the emperor's vassal. His efforts to persuade Raymond of Toulouse to come to terms with Alexius and to force Tancred to swear an oath of fealty confirmed his alliance with the emperor. In return, Alexius employed him as his agent with the crusade leaders, Bohemund appearing to have acted as the expedition's quartermaster for the siege of Nicaea, after which he shared the vanguard of the army with Alexius's representative Tatikios. When he arrived at Constantinople, without his army, Bohemund was the least powerful of the western magnates at the imperial court; when he left Nicaea less than two months later, he was one of its undoubted leaders. Part, at least, of this must be ascribed to his private diplomacy with Alexius.

Instead of the archetype of a bumptious, threatening and deceitful barbarian as portrayed by Anna Comnena, Bohemund provided a medium of contact between east and west. He was not alone. When Godfrey of Bouillon arrived at Constantinople, he was met by a court official, Roger, son of Dagobert, a Norman who had joined the service of Alexius in the 1080s and progenitor of a family of Greek politicians. Peter of Alifa had fought with Guiscard and Bohemund against Alexius in the 1080s but, with many Italian Normans, had entered imperial service after Guiscard's death in 1085. Accompanying the crusaders after Nicaea, he received the governorship of Comana in eastern Anatolia, captured by the crusaders in the autumn of 1097, 'in fealty to God and the Holy Sepulchre, and to our leaders and the emperor'. Peter founded a Byzantine dynasty which adopted the name Petraliphas; both he and Roger, son of Dagobert, later fought for Alexius against Bohemund in the Epirus war of 1107–8.[37] Another recruit at Alexius's court was Bohemund's own half-brother, Guy; in June 1098, when Alexius decided to withdraw from his projected relief of the crusaders at Antioch, he unavailingly begged the emperor to continue to save his kindred. Another imperial servant was Bohemund's brother-in-law, William of Grandmesnil from Normandy, who travelled with Tatikios's Greek division that marched with Bohemund in the vanguard across Asia Minor. Thus, viewed in the perspective of Norman experience, not propaganda, the First Crusade appears as part of an existing process of contact, tension and reaction. When Bohemund arrived in Constantinople in April 1097 and swore fealty to Alexius, his former enemy, he was doing no more than his half-brother and brother-in-law had done before him.

Bohemund's prominence rested on establishing Byzantine credentials. Alexius need not have trusted him; but he could use him to suit his own purpose of controlling the crusade by proxy. He thought he had achieved this, as he had with so many other Italian Normans, by appealing to Bohemund's ambition and greed. Bohemund was a highly suitable agent not least because he probably spoke Greek. There is evidence that he read Greek; according to Anna Comnena he could pun in Greek; and a number of western sources indicate that he conversed in Greek with the treacherous Armenian who allowed the crusaders into Antioch in June 1098, Firuz, who expected Bohemund's troops to do the same. Bohemund's relatives at Alexius's court spoke Greek; Tancred apparently could speak Arabic (and did so at Antioch); language skills ran in the family. Indeed, Bohemund itself was a nickname, coined by his father after seeing the size of his infant son; it referred to a legendary giant. The boy had been baptized Mark, a Greek name.[38]

The timing of arrivals at Constantinople exerted a profound influence on the balance, nature and course of the rest of the expedition. That Alexius had managed to extract oaths from Count Hugh, Duke Godfrey and Bohemund, as well as the count of Flanders, who had left his travelling companions the duke of Normandy and the count of Blois behind in Italy at the turn of the year, and had shipped their troops across the Bosporus by 26 April 1097, presented Raymond of Toulouse with something of a *fait accompli* when he arrived in the last days of

April 1097. As his chaplain recorded, it was reported to Raymond that 'Bohemund, the duke of Lorraine, the count of Flanders and other princes besought him to make a pact with Alexius'.[39] His temper can hardly have been improved by what had proved a long, exhausting and increasingly violent and ill-disciplined march.

Although probably the first magnate to take the cross, and the only one certainly to have had prior warning of Urban's message at Clermont, Raymond had started late, in October 1096. His army was probably the largest and best funded; his preparations had been meticulous; his entourage filled with the eminent from the Limousin, Languedoc and Provence, including the counts of Orange and Montpellier, the viscounts of Béarn and Turenne, as well as the pope's designated leader of the enterprise, Bishop Adhemar of Le Puy and his Monteil brothers from the Auvergne. It is possible Raymond's planning lay behind the Genoese fleet despatched to the Levant in July 1097; Urban had sent a legation to the city led by Bishop William of Orange, who later accompanied Raymond east.[40] Yet Urban's grant of a papal banner to Hugh of Vermandois and legatine authority to the chaplains of the duke of Normandy and the count of Blois at Lucca in October 1096 indicated that, despite Raymond's early involvement and Urban's tour of his lands in June and July 1096, he had no claim to overall command of the enterprise beyond his seniority (he was about sixty); possibly his experience in fighting in Spain; his association with Bishop Adhemar; and his money.[41] He proved a difficult colleague; it is hard to determine whether his repeated displays of ill-temper were a cause or effect of his political isolation. However, his journey to Constantinople might have tried a saint.

Avoiding the Adriatic crossings from Italy, presumably because of the lateness of season, Raymond laboriously led his large army around the head of the Adriatic and down the Dalmatian coast across very difficult terrain. The natives proved unfriendly, provoking reciprocal atrocities. On reaching Byzantine territory at Durazzo in January, Raymond's troops discovered a resentful populace, suspicious authorities and hard-pressed escorts. It was mid-winter; food supplies were beginning to present a problem, not least because of the recent passage of Bohemund's army. There were increasing confrontations with locals and the Pecheneg police escort. Raymond of Aguilers caught the bitterness of the crusaders' reaction:

we were confident that we were in our own land, because we believed that Alexius and his followers were our Christian brothers and confederates. But truly, with the savagery of lions they rushed upon peaceful men who were oblivious of their need for self defence.[42]

In one incident, Adhemar of Le Puy was quite badly wounded; although he recovered after recuperating at Thessalonica, he appears hardly at all in the chroniclers' accounts of the negotiations at Constantinople. The problem was food. The Provençals sacked Roussa and, after Raymond had left his troops to parley with emperor in April 1097, were dispersed by imperial soldiers as punishment for ravaging. When he heard, the count was unamused and in no mood to place himself under the lordship of a ruler whose conduct had to date appeared either incompetent or mendacious.

The last army to reach the Byzantine capital contained the contingents led by Robert of Normandy and his brother-in-law Stephen of Blois. Initially, they had travelled with Count Robert II of Flanders, whose father, Robert I the Frisian, having undertaken a pilgrimage to Jerusalem, had served with Alexius in the Balkans in the late 1080s and had later sent the emperor a force of 500 knights. Robert II of Normandy's grandfather, Robert I the Devil (or Magnificent according to taste) had died on pilgrimage to Jerusalem in 1035; his father, William the Conqueror, had been asked to assist the Byzantines against the Turks in the 1060s.[43] His own crusade owed as much to his political difficulties in his duchy as to the advice of his spiritual advisers, who were credited with persuading him to join the march to Jerusalem. A poor politician, Robert was an effective military leader and warrior and a popular companion. Supported by the 10,000 marks provided by his younger brother, William II Rufus, king of England, Robert cut a finer figure on crusade than he had at home. At the head of a substantial force of Anglo-Norman nobles, including representatives of the families of Montgomery, Grandmesnil, Gournay and Percy, he picked up more followers on the journey. Eustace III of Boulogne, eldest brother to Godfrey of Bouillon and Baldwin, and a major landowner in England, probably travelled with him; in Italy Norman émigrés such as Roger of Barneville joined their ancestral lord.

Duke Robert earned glittering fame on crusade, playing prominent roles in the crucial encounters at Dorylaeum (July 1097), Antioch, Jerusalem and Ascalon (August 1099). In 1097–8, he assumed control of the vital Syrian port of Lattakiah. The second Latin bishop appointed by the Franks in the east, at Ramla in June 1099, was a Norman, Robert of Rouen; Duke Robert's own chaplain, the foul-mouthed philanderer Arnulf of Chocques, was elected Latin Patriarch of Jerusalem in August 1099. There was even talk of Robert being a candidate for the crown of Jerusalem, which he was supposed to have rejected, characteristically, 'out of fear of the work involved'.[44] This prominence was in part a function of Robert's wealth, which enabled him to maintain his independence and a sizeable retinue of knights; even as late as January 1099, he appears to have been able to maintain about 100 knights in his army, the same as Godfrey of Bouillon and twice the number supported by Robert of Flanders.[45] On his return to the west, Robert found himself the hero of instant legend, his alleged deeds enshrined in stained glass at the great royal abbey of St Denis within a decade of his death. His reputation formed an acute contrast with his totally disastrous political career, which ended in twenty-eight years' incarceration (1106–34) by his youngest brother, King Henry I of England.

His brother-in-law, Stephen count of Blois, left an even more equivocal reputation. Famously hen-pecked by his tough wife, Adela, the Conqueror's daughter, Stephen may have been a reluctant crusader, but he was one of the wealthiest. Perhaps this explained why, at a crisis at Antioch in 1098, he was chosen by the other leaders as, in his own words, 'lord, director and governor' of the enterprise, perhaps implying a chairman's role in the council of the high command.[46] He scarcely exercised any authority, deserting the siege of Antioch the day before its capture in June 1098. His presence with Robert of Normandy confirmed an intimate dynastic network that underpinned their expedition. The counts of Flanders and Boulogne were closely related; Duke Robert's mother was of the Flemish comital house; Count Stephen was the duke's brother-in-law. With them was Duke Robert's uncle, the worldly and acquisitive but now disgraced Odo bishop of Bayeux: he was to die in the winter of 1096–7, the guest of another successful Norman opportunist, Count Roger of Sicily, who provided a fine tomb for him in Palermo. The sense of family business was reinforced when the army reached Apulia, where Duke Roger Borsa's wife was Robert of Flanders's sister.

These northern French lords left for the east in late September or early

October 1096, travelling across the Alps to the Po valley. They met Urban II at Lucca in late October, before visiting Rome and Monte Cassino on their journey south to Bari. There, Robert of Flanders left them to cross the Adriatic despite the late season. Duke Robert and Count Stephen stayed in southern Italy for the winter. This delay presented some less affluent, self-funded crusaders with acute problems. Unable to forage freely in friendly territory, their costs rising, those who lacked the patronage of lords or knights faced both hunger and ruin. Many, one of the chaplains attached to Count Stephen recalled, 'sold their weapons and again took up their pilgrims' staves and returned home'.[47] However, it was still a considerable force that was shipped from Brindisi to Durazzo in early April 1097. Shipwreck and flash floods reduced the ranks, but by then supplies in the Balkans presented fewer problems. All the other armies had crossed or were in the process of crossing to Asia when the northern French reached their destination. Arriving at Constantinople on 14 May, the leaders were deeply impressed by Alexius's lavish welcome; the other ranks received guided tours of the fabulous city in select groups of five or six. None of them had seen anything like it.

CONSTANTINOPLE

The negotiations between Alexius and the military leaders of the Jerusalem expedition formed a pivot around which the nature and future perception of the campaign revolved.[48] Both sides understood the importance of what was agreed, even though they later chose to interpret events very differently. Alexius wished to use the westerners to exploit divisions among the Turks of Asia Minor and Syria to restore a measure of Byzantine control without risking a full commitment of his own military reserves. His dilemma lay in the extent to which he imposed his authority over the crusaders as paymaster and beneficiary while remaining essentially a sleeping partner in the operation. Fully aware of the obsession with Jerusalem, Alexius needed to encourage the idea that he shared the crusaders' strategic goals while being more interested in undermining Seljuk power in Anatolia and opening stronger lines of political communication with sympathetic Armenians in Cilicia and

Syria. Although he may not have been unhappy that Syrian Antioch had been taken from one of his Greek opponents in 1084–5, the fact that this great city had been lost to Islam in his own reign did not look good.[49] On the other side, while Urban II had clearly envisaged the closest cooperation with the Greek emperor, of greater urgency were immediate logistical considerations. The western armies required Byzantine advice and material aid before they headed out across hostile Muslim territory. If they had doubted it, the disasters at Xerigordo and Kibotos would have persuaded them. However, the westerners lacked unified leadership, a coherent political strategy or an agreed military plan. They knew something of what problems to expect across the frontier with the Turks; they also had no clear view as to how to deal with them. Thus, Alexius was eager to assert demonstrable but indirect leadership over the expedition, while the crusaders were equally keen to accept Byzantine assistance. What needed to be resolved were the terms of that control and the conditions of that assistance.

Traditional Byzantine foreign policy, derived from the techniques of the Roman empire, outlined the best course of action when dealing with barbarians, those outside the empire or those, like the Normans in Italy and Sicily or the Armenians and Turks in northern Syria who, in the timeless Byzantine view of the world, were squatting on former imperial lands. If such tribes threatened the empire, or the emperor wished to use them, the tactics remained much the same: smother them with hospitality; learn their customs and exploit these; divide and rule; forge links of dependence based on profit, golden chains as it were; employ them; Byzantinize them. These were Alexius's methods in the early months of 1097, to which he added a high dose of flexible opportunism. He was welcoming to all who accepted his hospitality; some, such as Godfrey of Bouillon or Tancred of Lecce, who avoided Constantinople and tried not to meet the emperor, required some small element of coercion; for the rest nothing was too much, as Alexius imposed the authority of fabulous wealth on his bucolic visitors. The oath he wished them to swear to him was, according to Anna, a 'customary Latin oath'; whatever its details, the reactions of the leaders suggest that they recognized it.[50] Alexius used Hugh of Vermandois to persuade Godfrey to come to heel and ensured Godfrey and the rest witnessed Bohemund's oath. Bohemund, Godfrey and Robert of Flanders were cited as wishing

Raymond's adherence to Alexius's contract. Bohemund was employed to extract agreement from Raymond and to force Tancred to fall into line. Once agreement and acquiescence had been obtained, Alexius lavished gifts on the westeners, whom he now regarded as his servants. The only aspect of the Greek formula that failed, and did so disastrously, was the inability of most of the westerners to become Byzantines. Although they could meet over mutual self-interest in the deals struck at Constantinople, there was a fundamental gulf not so much of understanding but of aspiration.

Alexius saw his interests as eternal: the benefit of the empire. Anything else was peripheral or secondary, not least remote Jerusalem. He probably minimized the importance of the reciprocal nature of his agreement with the crusaders, seeing them effectively as mercenaries; they regarded him as a lord with contractual obligations to preserve the interests of his vassals. When he was persuaded that the crusaders were doomed at Antioch in June 1098, Alexius preserved his strategy by withdrawing his own army from danger. For the crusaders, this withdrawal was inexplicable treachery from a lord whose help had been sworn. They, who had risked all so many times, failed to appreciate his caution. The shadow of Antioch fell deep over Graeco-Latin relations in the twelfth century, nowhere more black than in the pages of the eyewitness chroniclers who felt and experienced the betrayal in which dim light they re-evaluated all that had transpired between Alexius and the crusade leadership. It is small wonder that Anna Comnena was so frenetic in her attempts to exonerate Alexius from any suggestion of culpability over Antioch, for he had been caught out by that most politically damaging agent: events. If the westerners had been annihilated at Antioch, as common sense dictated they should have been, Alexius would have been vindicated. Unfortunately not only did they survive, they proceeded to win Jerusalem and return to tell their tale.

At the heart of the dispute lay the oaths sworn, which were solemn and serious. Despite the contrasting sensitivities locked into the descriptions of events at Constantinople, it appears that Alexius demanded and received from all the leaders except Raymond of Toulouse homage and fealty. They became the emperor's vassals, promising to restore to imperial rule all lands, towns and castles they captured which had formally belonged to the empire. This in effect meant lands lost in the relatively recent past: even Raymond of Toulouse, who became most protective of the relationship with Alexius, considered towns in Syria beyond Antioch, such as al-Bara, beyond the remit of the agreement.[51] In return, Alexius promised help for the crusaders. Some tried to argue that he had promised to join the march to Jerusalem, but this probably represents a post-Antioch gloss. Raymond of Aguilers, a very hostile source, stated that Alexius ruled out his personal involvement. More probable was a guarantee of military aid, supplies and advice, as well as promises to protect the crusaders' rear and assist reinforcements. The importance of these arrangements was underlined by Alexius's insistence at the crusaders' Asiatic base at Pelekanum just before they left for the march across Anatolia that even lesser lords took the oath. The one exception was Raymond of Toulouse, who insisted on swearing an oath more acceptable to Provençal practice, that 'he would not, either through himself or through others, take away from the emperor, life and possessions'.[52] Yet he abided by his obligations more faithfully than his colleagues, perhaps because Alexius had taken special pains to establish good relations with him after their sticky introduction.

The legal aspects of the agreements struck by Alexius and the western leaders were less important than the political implications. Only by becoming Alexius's vassals could they extract necessary help. For Bohemund, subservience offered an opportunity for self-advancement; he proposed to Alexius that he be created Domestic of the East, effectively commander of the imperial forces in Asia and, in consequence, commander-in-chief of the crusade.[53] Alexius temporized but did not reject his offer of service outright. That Bohemund came up with the idea exposes the nature of his ambition; he wanted leadership; he wanted land. Alexius was not to know the extent to which Bohemund was determined to have both without any ties of vassalage. His whole career to date had made the Norman wish to dispense with overlords. Yet for the present, Alexius suited his case.

Initially, whatever the details, the treaties of Constantinople worked. Relations between western leaders, not least Bishop Adhemar, with the Greeks were good. Nicaea reverted to imperial control after its capture in June 1097 despite Alexius's absence. A Byzantine division accompanied the army eastwards towards Antioch, under an experienced commander, Tatikios, a safe choice as a Turkish eunuch of unavoidable loyalty to the emperor rather than a Greek nobleman who could have harboured imperial longings of his own. Cities captured on the way, such as Comana, were indeed restored to Greek lordship. Optimism, if judged by a cheerful letter Stephen of Blois wrote to his wife from Nicaea on 24 June 1097, was high: 'the army of God' was looking forward to reaching Jerusalem in five weeks – 'unless Antioch holds us up'.[54] Urban's plan seemed to be working.

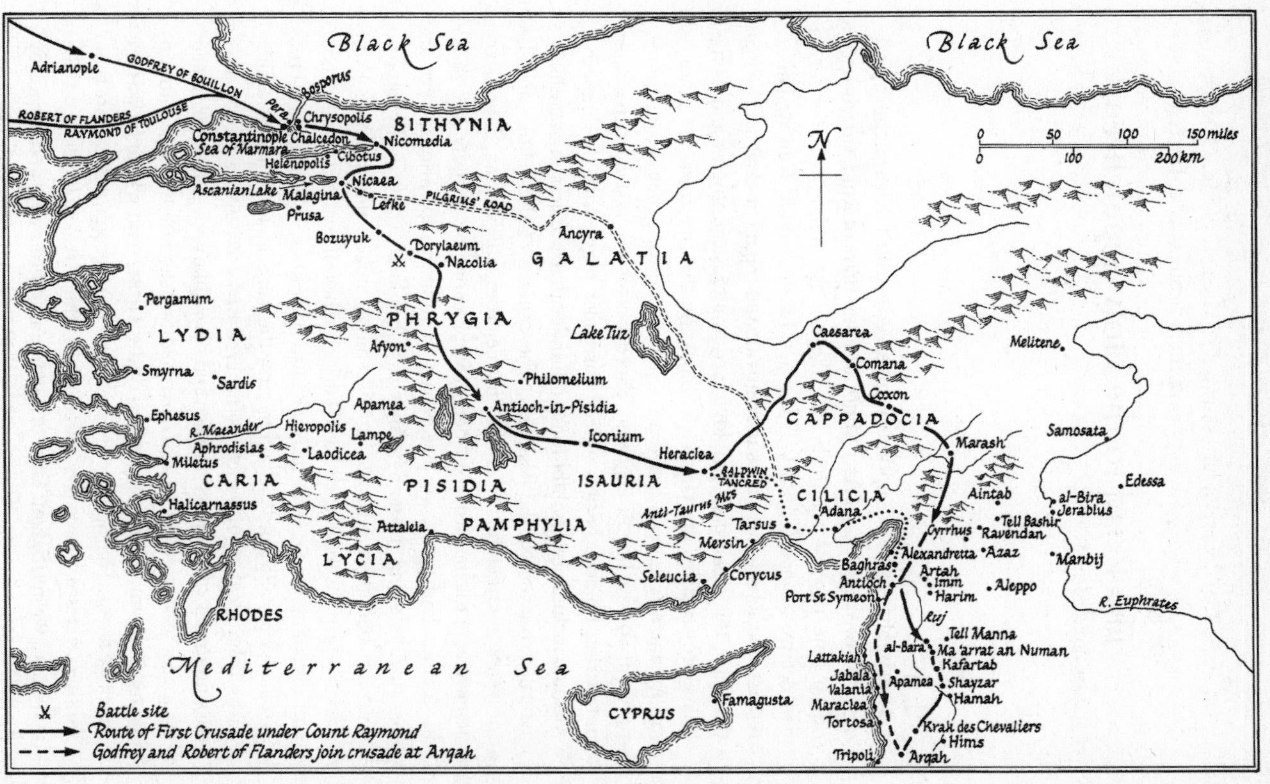

2. Asia Minor and Syria 1097–99

4
The Road to the Holy Sepulchre

Count Stephen of Blois's optimism appeared justified. Nicaea, the capital of the Turkish Seljuks of Asia Minor, the sultanate of Rum, surrendered on 19 June 1097. A month before, the still-assembling crusader force had decisively repulsed the relief attack by the sultan, Kilij Arslan, a remarkable achievement for such a novice and fragmented army. During the siege, the westerners, employing catapults, siege towers and using boats provided by the Greeks to blockade the city from the adjoining Ascanian lake, established a common fund for expenses, including payment for an Italian engineer. Faced by such a vast host, perhaps numbering 60,000, Nicaea agreed surrender terms with the Emperor Alexius, including a prohibition on plunder that was less than enthusiastically received by the besiegers. The capture of the Seljuk capital, for years a target for Byzantine mercenaries, marked an impressive achievement for the 'army of God', as Stephen of Blois proudly described it. Alexius had taken no direct part in military operations, beyond logistical help, but through his new vassals a large, strategically important city had been returned to his empire intact, undermining Kilij Arslan's grip on the largely non-Turkish cities of western Asia Minor and signalling a new force in Near Eastern politics. When the emperor assembled his allies at Pelekanum after the siege, apart from extracting oaths from recalcitrants such as Tancred of Lecce, giving advice, discussing strategy and showering rich and poor alike with gifts, he arranged for a crusader embassy to be despatched to negotiate with the Fatimid regime in Egypt, fellow adversaries of the Turks, with whom he was on amicable terms. The victors of Nicaea were thus recognized as more than another western mercenary force doing the Greeks' bidding on the margins of western Islam. Their distinctive ambitions were understood by their Byzantine patron, if not as yet by his Muslim friends and enemies.[1]

This soon changed. The Damascus chronicler Ibn al-Qalanisi (d. 1160), a young man at the time of the First Crusade, remembered the ominous rumours reaching Syria in 1097:

there began to arrive a succession of reports that the armies of the Franks had appeared from the direction of the sea of Constantinople with forces not to be reckoned for multitude. As these reports followed one upon the other, and spread from mouth to mouth far and wide, the people grew anxious and disturbed in mind.

An Armenian monk, writing in Syria during the invasion of 1097–9, described the westerners who followed 'the sign of the cross of Christ' as fulfilment of Christ's promise to come to the assistance of His people. Another, commenting from Alexandria in the summer of 1099, remarked on the 'countless multitudes' who attacked Syria with 'Divine aid inspired by Almighty God'. The significance of these intruders became apparent. In 1105, a religious lawyer teaching at the Great Mosque in Damascus, Ali Ibn Tahir al-Sulami, unwittingly mirrored Urban II's historical analysis in explaining the advance of the *ifranj*:

A number fell upon the island of Sicily at a time of difference and competition, and likewise they gained possession of town after town in Spain. When mutually confirmatory reports reached them of the state of this country – the disagreement of its lords, the dissensions of its dignitaries, together with its disorder and disturbance – they carried out their resolution of going out to it, and Jerusalem was the summit of their wishes.[2]

So marked did these dissensions appear, and so favourable to any invader, some have wondered whether Alexius and Urban deliberately timed their initiative to take advantage of them. The chroniclers who accompanied the expedition to Jerusalem well knew that the Muslim world the western host entered in June 1097 lacked unity in politics, race and religion. They distinguished between Muslim 'Turks' – the warrior elite originating in the Eurasian steppes – and 'Saracens' or 'Arabs' – the Arabic-speaking, settled population of the Levant: the anonymous veteran who wrote the *Gesta Francorum*, one of the earliest written accounts, carefully discriminated between these and also the different Christian communities – Greek, Armenian and Syrian (i.e. Greek Orthodox, Jacobite or Maronite Christians in Syria who spoke Arabic).[3] The protracted negotiations with the Fatimid rulers of Egypt between June 1097 and May 1099 revealed the potential for exploiting Near Eastern political fissures; partitioning Palestine may even have been mooted at Antioch in March 1098. Throughout their march across Asia Minor and Syria, western leaders appeared well informed of their opponents' alliances. Subsequent successes in Cilicia, at Edessa and Antioch, and the unopposed march to Jerusalem in 1099 relied on the failure of the competing Muslim powers to unite, the crusaders' appreciation of this disunity and their willingness to exploit it through diplomacy and war.

It is a persistent myth that western Christians possessed either no knowledge of or a universally blinkered hostility to Islam and Muslim rulers. In eleventh-century Spain, opportunist military adventurers, such as Rodrigo Diaz, El Cid, happily served Muslim employers when it suited them. On a military level, the soldiers of Christ of 1097 recognized the quality of their Turkish opponents. Even Pope Gregory VII, a scourge of Christian backsliders, attempted to maintain friendly relations with the Muslim ruler of Mauritania, on the startlingly tolerant grounds that 'we worship and confess the same God though in diverse forms and daily praise and adore him as the creator and ruler of this world'.[4] From the other side, so-called Muslim policy was often conducted and implemented by non-Muslims, Christians of various denominations as well as Jews. The Coptic Christian community in Egypt remained influential in administration until the fourteenth century. In many areas of western Asia under Islamic rule in the eleventh century it is doubtful whether there existed a Muslim majority.[5] Constructive contact between the Christian army and selected Muslim powers was unsurprising, especially since the Byzantines had been pursuing such strategies for generations.

From the middle of the eleventh century, the heterogeneous polity of the Near East had revolved around the dominance of orthodox Sunni Muslim Seljuk Turks in Iran, Iraq, Syria and Asia Minor controlling the decadent Abbasid caliphate of Baghdad and the faltering heretical Shi'ite caliphate of the Fatimids in Egypt.[6] In 1055, the chief of the Oghuz Turcoman tribes in north-eastern Iran, the Seljuk Tughrul Beg, seized Baghdad, appropriating for himself from the caliph the title of sultan (literally, in Arabic, 'power'). Tughrul (d. 1063), his nephew Alp Arslan (1063–72) and great-nephew Malik Shah (1072–92) created an empire including Iran, Iraq and, from the late 1070s, central and southern Syria; northern Syria, a group of client city states, was incorporated by 1086. Alp Arslan, by his decisive defeat of the Byzantine emperor, Romanus Diogenes, at Manzikert in 1071, opened Anatolia to Turcoman invasion and settlement. The sultanate created there, of Rum (i.e. the former lands of the Byzantines who always referred to themselves as Romans), was ruled by Seljuk cousins of Malik Shah, Suleiman Ibn Kutulmush (d. 1086) and his son Kilij Arslan, whose influence in northern Syria was successfully challenged by Malik Shah's brother Tutush. While the sultanate of Rum occupied southern and western Anatolia, another Turkish power, the Danishmends, established control of the north and east of the peninsula. The two powers competed for advantage, while unsuccessfully combining to resist the westerners' advance across Anatolia in the summer of 1097.

Turkish authority from the Persian Gulf to the Dead Sea rested on military strength exercised by the control of local communities by Turkish garrisons or mercenaries holding indigenous political hierarchies in check. The western invaders of 1097 acknowledged that Turkish military supremacy had 'terrorized the Arabs, Saracens, Armenians, Syrians and Greeks'.[7] Such rule varied from the militant Turkish holy warrior ethos of the Danishmends to the Great Seljuks of Baghdad, fully assimilated into the Arabo-Persian culture of the Abbasids: Malik Shah is not a Turkish name at all; it means King King in Arabic and Persian, a sort of echo of the imperial title of the ancient Persian Shahanshahs, Kings of Kings. Local power depended on standing armies of mercenaries, as the traditional Turkish nomadic life clashed with the settled rural and urban conditions of Iraq, Syria, Palestine and much of Anatolia. As effective warriors, the Turks of Asia Minor and Syria maintained their hold, real power often lying with mercenary army commanders rather than princely governors. Even the power of the Seljuk sultans in Baghdad was overshadowed by that of their vizier, Nizam al-Mulk.

One characteristic of the Seljuks was their fiercely orthodox Sunni Islam, putting them at odds with many of their subjects, not only the various Christian sects but also the Shi'ite majority among the Muslim peasantry of Syria, as well as with the heretical caliphs of Egypt, with whom they contested control of Palestine. After establishing themselves in Egypt in 969, the Shi'ite Fatimid caliphate became increasingly dependent on its mercenary troops, Berber tribesmen, Blacks (*Sudan* in Arabic) from the upper Nile, Turks and other slave warriors (mamluks). These elements fought for supremacy behind the throne of Caliph al-Mustansir (1036–94) until he appointed as his vizier the aged Armenian mamluk Badr al-Jamali, who ruled Egypt as a military dictator from 1074 to 1094. The political potential of religion was dramatically demonstrated in 1092, when a Shi'ite splinter group established at Alamut, south of the Caspian Sea, murdered the immensely powerful vizier of Baghdad, Nizam al-Mulk; the killers' sect was later known in the west as the Assassins. The Egyptian rulers were less ideologically militant or successful, their hold over the hinterland of Syria and Palestine reduced to nominal control over a few sea-ports on the Palestinian littoral. In an attempt to eject Turkish authority from Palestine Badr al-Jamali's son and successor, al-Afdal, sought friendship with Byzantium and an agreement with the Greeks' newest allies in 1097–9.

Tensions and rivalries were inherent in a polity where form disguised substance; behind the caliph a sultan, behind a sultan a vizier, behind a vizier a mamluk. Indigenous hierarchies were subject to foreign domination: Egypt and Iraq competed for Syria and Palestine; Armenian, Turcoman, Kurd or Berber adventurers subjugated local aristocracies. These fissures were deepened by a disastrous coincidence of death between 1092 and 1094, which swept away all the major political figures of the Near East. In 1092, the Vizier Nizam al-Mulk, effective ruler of the Seljuk empire, was followed to his grave a few weeks later by the Sultan Malik Shah himself. A similar pattern was repeated in Egypt in 1094, when the death of the Vizier Badr al-Jamali closely followed that of his ostensible master, the veteran Fatimid Caliph al-Mustansir. In the same year, the Sunni caliph of Baghdad, al-Muqtadi, also died. These multiple deaths provoked succession struggles and political fragmentation from Iran to Anatolia, Syria and Palestine. In Asia Minor, Kilij Arslan, held hostage by Malik Shah since the defeat and death of his father Suleiman in 1086, began to restore an independent sultanate of Rum in competition with the Seljuks and the Danishmends of eastern Anatolia. In the civil wars over Malik Shah's inheritance, his brother Tutush, ruler of Syria, was defeated and killed in 1095 by the sultan's son Barkyaruq, whose own power remained disputed by his brother Muhammed until his death in 1105. While much of the internecine fighting occurred in western Iran, political unity in Syria imploded. Tutush's bickering sons Ridwan of Aleppo and Duqaq of Damascus failed to impose their authority allowing the Turkish atabeg (i.e. guardian of prince or governor) of Mosul, Kerbogha, the opportunity to extend his authority into northern Syria, while local dynasties asserted their independence further south, such as the Ortoqids in Jerusalem or the Shi'ite Banu 'Ammar in Tripoli. At Edessa in northern Iraq, in Cilicia and northern Syria, Armenian princelings re-established themselves in the debris of Seljuk rule. The new Egyptian vizier, al-Afdal, took advantage of this instability to restore Fatimid power in southern Palestine, culminating in his capture of Jerusalem from the Ortoqids in 1098.

In this political turmoil, where power rested with military warlords with varying claims to legitimacy, the western army appeared neither as distinctive nor as threatening as it thought itself. With the main contest for power in the Near East being fought in Iran, hundreds of miles to the east, the westerners' targets – Cilicia, Antioch, Edessa, Jerusalem – were peripheral. As Tutush had discovered, rule of Syria counted for little against the forces of Iraq and Iran. Given the nature of their enterprise, the Christian expeditionary force rarely constituted a genuine threat to local dynasts. Despite the loss of Nicaea and defeats by the crusaders in 1097, the sultanate of Rum and the power of the Danishmends remained intact if dented. Only where Turkish authority had already eroded or collapsed – as in Cilicia or parts of northern Syria, including Antioch – did the crusaders threaten existing structures of authority. This new, fanatical, single-minded force apparently of Byzantine mercenaries fitted easily into a world dominated by armies of foreign hirelings – Kurdish, Turcoman or Armenian. The First Crusade was well suited to contemporary Near Eastern politics.

Such insights were far from apparent to the members of the expedition as they set out to cross Anatolia in late June 1097. Within days of leaving the area of Nicaea, the army was almost defeated, its vanguard overrun and nearly destroyed, by Kilij Arslan's field army. Four years later, similar western contingents were serially annihilated by local forces, leaving merely uneasy rumours of their fate. Such could easily have been the fate of the 1097 host. The battle, conventionally called of Dorylaeum, but actually fought over twenty-five miles to the north, attracted vivid if confused memories, recalling fear ('huddled together like sheep in a fold . . . we had no hope of surviving,' remembered one), recognition that it had been a close-run thing and certainty that victory had been God-given.[8]

By the early morning of 1 July 1097, the Christian vanguard, perhaps 20,000 strong, comprising the contingents of Bohemund, Robert of Normandy, Stephen of Blois and Robert of Flanders, with the Byzantine troops under Tatikios, had advanced about forty-five miles south-east of Nicaea, reaching a valley just under three miles north of the modern Bozuyuk. There they were confronted by Kilij Arslan and his new ally the Danishmend emir. The Turkish force was mounted and probably outnumbered the western knights in the vanguard, which had become detached from the main body of crusaders under Raymond of Toulouse and Godfrey of Bouillon, around 30,000 strong, who were still some three miles away when battle was joined. On seeing the size of the Turkish army, Bohemund, his generalship skill already recognized, ordered the infantry, priests and other non-combatants to make a defensive camp, awkwardly with its back to a marsh, while the mounted knights advanced towards the enemy. Immediately things went badly, the mobile Turkish mounted archers driving the knights back to the camp, which became assailed on all flanks. Surrounded, the vanguard fought ferociously in dogged, bloody close combat, sustained by their close formation, lack of alternatives and a burgeoning *esprit de corps*.[9] After more than five hours, the vanguard faced massacre until the arrival of the main force under Godfrey and Raymond compelled the Turks to break off their assault to engage in a series of running fights across the field before abandoning the fray when the Provençals, led, some said, by Adhemar of Le Puy, threatened to encircle them. In the pursuit, lasting some days, the westerners looted the sultan's camp, seizing gold, silver, horses, asses and camels (employed as pack-animals for the rest of the booty), cows and sheep. While proving the crusaders' mettle, the battle had exposed failures of command and the danger still posed by the Turks; disaster had come perilously close.

While the largely nomadic Turkish forces of Kilij Arslan and the Danishmends could not be destroyed in one set-piece defeat, such a reverse undermined the sultan's authority, especially over the towns of Anatolia with large Christian populations, and his recently constructed prestige amongst his Turkish supporters. Towns and cities across Anatolia repudiated the sultan, many welcoming the passing crusaders. The sheer size of the westerners' force invited respect. In crossing central

Anatolia, its main enemy was heat by day and, in the uplands, sharp cold by night, thirst, lack of supplies and fatigue. There was an almost unstoppable haemorrhaging of horses: one veteran suggested they lost most of them in a few weeks after the battle, a potentially fatal blow. While Tancred and Baldwin of Boulogne separately pressed on directly towards Konya, the main army, moving at times as little as five miles a day and never much more than ten, took a detour into more fertile territory around Pisidian Antioch to the south to allow effective foraging. Reunited at Konya in mid-August, the great army was showing signs of depletion. Goats, sheep, even dogs were pressed into service as pack animals, their backs soon lacerated with sores, while knights rode cows or walked. In high and late summer temperatures could soar to over 30 degrees. Some recalled hundreds dying, mainly of thirst; the true figure may have been thousands. New-born babies were abandoned by their mothers. The march across Anatolia scarred the memories of the survivors. The leaders were not immune, Raymond of Toulouse falling so gravely ill that he received the last rites and Godfrey of Bouillon apparently being attacked and injured by a bear.[10] The requirements of food and water were paramount, determining the routes and behaviour of the army. Without cowed Turkish opponents and the general uprising against the sultan in Christian towns, the westerners could hardly have survived. The only serious military resistance encountered was at Ereghli (Heraclea) about a hundred miles east of Konya, around 10 September.

After Heraclea, the great army divided, a decision displaying awareness of regional political conditions, local geography and topography, diplomatic opportunities, and prospects for collective and personal gain. Byzantine interests remained influential. Confronted by the formidable barrier of the Taurus mountains, the ordinary route for travellers to Syria led south-east through the steep, narrow pass known as the Cilician Gates (at its tightest about thirty yards across) down into the fertile Cilician plain, past Tarsus, Adana, Mamistra to Alexandretta and the Belen pass through the Ammanus mountain range, thence to northern Syria and Antioch, a journey from Heraclea of some 220 miles. This route was taken by two separate contingents, led by Tancred and Baldwin of Boulogne, acting on orders of the whole command or, possibly, as surrogates for Bohemund and Godfrey of Bouillon. Despite bitter, at times violent rivalry once in Cilicia, these forays in September and early October cleared opponents from the southern flank of the main army and established access to significant areas for supply and forage while denying them to the Turks of Antioch. Although Tancred and Baldwin came to blows at Tarsus, the latter being implicated in the Muslim massacre of 300 knights sent by Bohemund to reinforce his nephew,[11] and again at Mamistra, they left behind sympathetic local rulers and garrisons: Baldwin's at Tarsus, Tancred's at Mamistra and possibly Baghras in northern Syria. The evidently self-interested campaigns of these two youthful, well-connected, skilful but landless adventurers materially aided the attack on Antioch and the protection of longer-term western interests in Syria.

The main army turned northwards from Heraclea towards Caesarea in Cappadocia (Kayseri), crossing the mountains by steep but broader passes before turning south-east to Coxon (Goksum) and Marasch, through defiles almost as precipitous and narrow as those of the Cilician Gates, to approach Antioch from the north, a distance from Heraclea of just under 400 miles, a long, agonizing trek through inhospitable, barren high country, the road reaching over 5,500 feet, with the risk of snow at higher altitudes. The march from Heraclea to Antioch took about seven weeks, averaging about eight miles a day; losses in the Taurus mountains were great. The reason for this apparent diversion lay in the need to encourage Armenian Christian support and to secure the hinterland of Antioch by clearing the Taurus approaches of hostile Turks. Byzantine authority was restored in some places; at Comana, the Italian Norman Peter of Alipha or Aups, a veteran in Byzantine service, assumed command of the city 'in fealty to God and the Holy Sepulchre and to our leaders and the emperor'.[12] At others local Christians resumed control, as the Armenian Simeon at an unnamed town in Cappadocia, and Tatoul at Marasch. Tatoul was a supporter of the Greek emperor; Simeon had accompanied the army providing it with local knowledge and political contacts. The diversion to Caesarea and Marasch thus served Greek interests by liberating local Christians from Turkish dominion under the imperial aegis. Militarily, approaching from the north isolated Antioch by freeing the mountain cities, capturing the strategically important city of Artah, which controlled the city's eastern approaches, and establishing a presence in the fertile Ruj valley, east of the Orontes, on which Antioch stands. Combined with the Cilician activities of Tancred and Baldwin, the westerners stood well placed to attack Antioch.

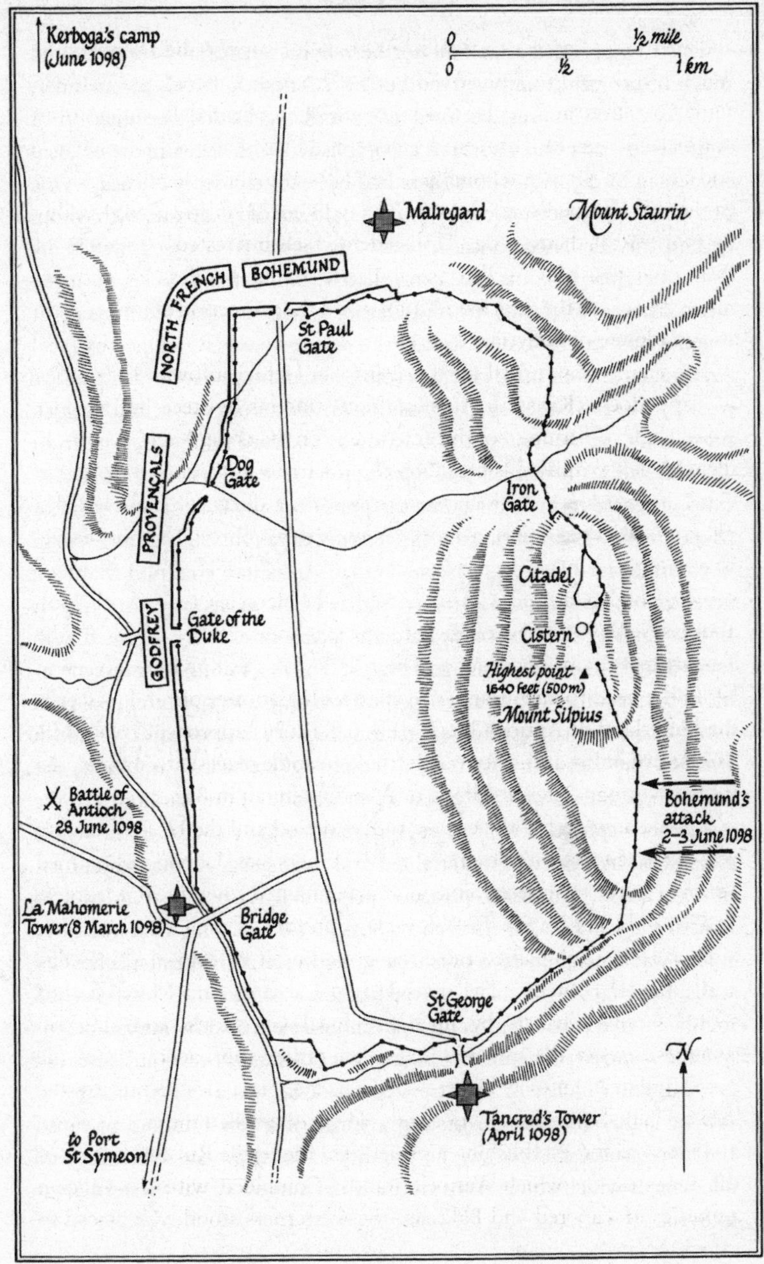

3. The Siege of Antioch, October 1097–June 1098

This two-pronged attack on northern Syria territorially reconstituted much of the principality carved out by a renegade Greek commander, Philaretus Brachamius, between 1077 and the Turkish occupation of Antioch in 1085 and had been accomplished with the support of local Armenian lords, with whom there had been contact since Nicaea.[13] One of them, Bagrat, persuaded the restless Baldwin of Boulogne, with whom he had travelled since Nicaea, to try his luck further east towards the Euphrates, also in lands once controlled by Philaretus. Leaving the army again after a brief stay in mid-October, with a small contingent of knights Baldwin moved on Tell-Bashir where he was welcomed by local Armenians as their lord. Having established military overlordship of the region up to the Euphrates, in a fashion familiar from Greek and Turkish precedents, in February 1098 Baldwin received an invitation from Thoros, the Armenian ruler of Edessa, forty-five miles east of the Euphrates, to come to his aid against the imminent advance of Kerbogha of Mosul, who was preparing a massive army to relieve Antioch and regain northern Syria from this nascent Franco-Armenian coalition. Baldwin accepted on condition Thoros recognized him as his heir. Arriving at Edessa on 20 February 1098, Baldwin tacitly or actively colluded with local dissidents in the rapid removal of Thoros, failing to intervene as his adoptive father was lynched by the town mob. On 10 March, Baldwin assumed authority over Edessa, establishing the first so-called Frankish state in the Levant. Apart from satisfying Baldwin's ambition, the addition of Edessa and the lands on either side of the Euphrates to the westerner's sphere of control proved vital for the survival of the whole expedition. A source of material aid and intelligence to the main army, in May 1098, Baldwin's presence persuaded Kerbogha of Mosul to pause in his march on Antioch to besiege Edessa. This delay of three weeks was crucial; instead of trapping the western army outside the city walls, Kerbogha's vanguard arrived just one day after the Christians had finally entered Antioch after an eight-month siege. Baldwin's campaigns in Cilicia and Syria highlighted the impact of small forces; at Edessa, so his chaplain Fulcher of Chartres recorded, he was accompanied by as few as eighty knights, suggesting a force of a few hundred at most, Baldwin's success exposing the fragility of local power structures and allegiances which contributed to the wider success of the western army in Syria.[14]

*

The siege of Antioch from October 1097 to June 1098 provided the twelfth century with its Trojan War, famed in verse, song and prose, commemorated in stone and glass, the central episode of trial and heroism in epic and romantic recounting of the First Crusade.[15] For once, legend was justified. Despite the size of the western armies, Antioch presented a formidable obstacle. Although its garrison was modest, perhaps only a few thousand, the circuit of the walls, studded with scores of towers, ran for about seven and a half miles, much of it over rough, mountainous terrain. Contained within the fortified area of about three square miles was Mt Silpius, near the summit of which perched the citadel, a thousand feet above the main city. Incapable of investing Antioch by complete blockade, the crusaders' alternative of assault offered little immediate prospect of success as they appeared at this stage to lack sufficient heavy artillery (i.e. great throwing engines such as mangonels or trebuchets) to breach the walls. A lengthy siege was in prospect, the only choice being whether to conduct it at close range or to blockade the city at a distance. Neither bore the certainty or even prospect of success as the governor of Antioch, Yaghisiyan, nominally a client of Ridwan of Aleppo, exerted much diplomatic energy to garner help. While past animosities prevented a concerted Muslim response, time lay on Yaghisiyan's side, even though many of the outlying garrisons and commanders in the area, often non-Muslim, took the opportunity to throw off the governor's unpopular rule, some Armenians regarding the westerners as liberators.

Less clear is why the siege was undertaken in the first place. The Christian army was ill-equipped for siege warfare; the success at Nicaea had been due to Byzantine diplomacy and naval power as much as anything. Given Turkish disunity, negotiation rather than attack might have cleared a path southwards. The warring jealousies of the rulers of the great Syrian cities were not greatly moved by the appearance of the crusaders; accommodation, especially in the context of the westerners' hardly secret negotiations with Fatimid Egypt, could have been achieved. When, in 1099, the Christian host marched on Jerusalem, there was little suggestion of taking Homs, Damascus or the cities on the Palestinian coast. Perhaps of greater strategic importance than Antioch itself were its ports, Alexandretta, St Symeon and Lattakiah, through which supplies of food (chiefly from Cyprus), war materials and men could reach the Christian army in Syria. Tancred had secured Alexandretta weeks before the main army reached Antioch, and a combination of Greek-sponsored and western fleets had occupied Lattakiah and St Symeon before the land army arrived.

An agreed objective between the Emperor Alexius and the westerners, evident from Stephen of Blois's comment to his wife from Nicaea, as a strategic target of the war, Antioch's role was as much political as military or logistic. Alexius, so his daughter later admitted, had hired the western armies 'to extend the bounds of the Roman (i.e. Byzantine) empire', specifically, it seems, the northern Syrian principality based on Antioch which had acted as a semi-autonomous buffer between Byzantium and the Seljuks in the late 1070s and early 1080s.[16] Its re-establishment would have greatly helped Alexius reclaim Asia Minor. The care taken by the Christian army to circle Antioch via Cilicia and the Taurus mountains and establish firm relations with Armenian rulers indicated such a policy. Although neither ignorant nor immune to the appeal of Jerusalem, Greek strategy held to more prosaic and customary ambitions, for which the emperor was prepared to lavish money, military aid, naval support and supplies on his western recruits.

Greek plans for Antioch were complemented by the ambitions and needs of the westerners. By the winter of 1097–8, the resources of many of the lesser and some of the greater leaders of the armies were reaching exhaustion. Negotiations with the Fatimids of Egypt continued: an Egyptian embassy arrived at the crusader camp in February 1098. Agreement with the Egyptians would have reduced pickings in southern Syria and Palestine, making exploitation of northern Syria urgent and necessary. In the winter of 1097–8 elements in the Christian forces eagerly established themselves as de facto rulers of significant tracts of Antioch's hinterland, even though the dangers of such loose investment of the city were well understood by a high command fearful of the army's disintegration. Alone, the requirement to find winter quarters to rest and recover from the arduous march across the mountains of eastern Asia Minor scarcely explains the siege of Antioch, especially as the decision taken in October/November 1097 to invest the city closely exacerbated the difficulty of supplying such a large army. There was more to it than logistics. Of particular significance may have been the circumstances of Bohemund, who had attached himself closely to Byzantine interests since arriving at Constantinople in April 1097. It is possible that he hoped for, or even expected, some territorial reward from Alexius in Syria. The expedition into Cilicia by his nephew, Tancred, may have been conducted on his behalf.[17] At Antioch his skills as a field commander propelled him to overall military leadership of the expedition in February 1098 against Ridwan of Aleppo. The near-disaster of the engagement with the forces of Duqaq of Damascus on 31 December 1097 in the Orontes valley, twenty-five miles south of the city, due in part to divided command, persuaded the leaders to appoint a single field commander. This suited Bohemund's political ambitions. Lacking the forces or the money to compete with Raymond of Toulouse or Godfrey of Bouillon, Bohemund may have long regarded Antioch as a prize to further his own interests, although it was only in May 1098, with the army threatened with annihilation by Kerbogha's relief force, that he showed his hand. The attempt to capture the city conformed to Greek policy. In theory, it provided a focus for a period of recuperation for the Christian host; it helped keep Egyptian friendship by threatening the Seljuk powers of northern Syria, allowing the Fatimids to recapture Jerusalem itself in July 1098. The siege of Antioch was, therefore, of general political significance as well as reflecting some misplaced confidence. Raymond of Toulouse reputedly argued in favour of the siege on the grounds that God would see them right as He had done at Nicaea and in Anatolia.[18] In fact, Antioch almost destroyed the crusade. Yet the extraordinary chain of events forged a harder unity of purpose among the mass of the army, a newly strident militant identity and confidence in divine favour expressed in the willingness of the survivors, great and humble alike, to integrate into their language and behaviour the rhetoric, symbols and theatre of visionary religious enthusiasm.

The siege of Antioch lasted from 21 October 1097 until the city fell on 3 June 1098, whereupon the Christians immediately found themselves besieged, Stalingrad-like, by the relief force under Kerbogha of Mosul until his defeat and flight on 28 June. Once committed, the Christians faced a series of potentially lethal crises stemming from their inability to surround Antioch, the precarious state of food supplies and a succession of Muslim relief expeditions. At no time during the seven and a half months of the first siege was the city entirely blockaded. Men, materials and intelligence could find ways in; the garrison was able to fire on, attack or ambush the besiegers more or less at will, inflicting both military and civilian casualties. Only in March 1098 was the Bridge

Gate that led to the road to the port of St Symeon blocked by the construction of one of three counterforts (the others were built to the north of the city in November 1097 and opposite the St George Gate to the south in April 1098). While the western troops could not force entry into the city, their numbers were too great for the Antioch garrison to dislodge. The stalemate was broken in June 1098 by treachery, not military action, and even then the garrison itself held out in the citadel a further three weeks, only surrendering the day after Kerbogha's defeat rendered its position untenable.

Such deadlock placed enormous strain on resources and morale. In late December 1097, acute food shortages prompted a major foraging expedition south up the Orontes valley towards al-Bara, only for Bohemund and Robert of Flanders to stumble across an allied relief force from Damascus and Homs led by Duqaq of Damascus and his atabeg Tughtegin.[19] Duqaq withdrew only after inflicting heavy casualties, mainly among the westerners' infantry, and preventing the collection of much-needed forage, a failure that threatened the Christians with starvation. Supplies were sought from as far away as Cyprus, Rhodes and Crete, but famine loomed; prices soared; hunger claimed men and horses. The army's debilitation reduced the number of volunteers to conduct other vital foraging sorties. The expedition appeared trapped in a vice, unable to make military progress and incapable of feeding itself. Misery and fear led to desertion; Peter the Hermit and William the Carpenter of Melun were caught trying to flee. Even Bohemund contemplated abandoning the enterprise as he saw men and horses in his modest company dying of hunger.[20] The presence in Syrian waters of friendly shipping made escape easier.

To counter collapsing morale, in January, the papal legate, Adhemar of Le Puy, instituted penitential fasting, intercessory prayers, processions and alms-giving for the laity, with the clergy celebrating masses and singing psalms. Communal participation in familiar religious ceremonies played on the psychological requirement for the beleaguered Christians to shake off fatalism, lethargy and inertia by involving the ordinary soldier and pilgrim in active contributions to the army's destiny. With a simultaneous secular crackdown on law and order within the army, the revivalist message was reinforced by the removal of all women from the camps, wives included, the association of sex with divine disapproval being widely promoted by the western clerical establishment.[21] Ritual public humiliations and punishment for adulterers were staged to underscore the evils of sexual licence, the culprits stripped naked and flogged in front of the whole army. More mundanely, an appeal for alms helped pool resources. The leaders, who reached decisions through regular councils, formed a confraternity, a sworn association which could distribute donations without complications of conflicting lordships or loyalties. The funding of the siege forts and a bridge of boats across the Orontes was organized in this way, as were payments to Tancred for him to blockade Antioch's southern gate. To meet the crisis of January 1098, Raymond of Toulouse paid 500 marks into the common fund to help knights replace their horses.[22] To further reassure their followers, the leaders swore oaths not to abandon the siege. These measures emphasized the particular corporate identity that had grown through shared experience and crisis. Correspondence to the west in October and November 1097 proclaimed that God fought for 'the army of the Lord'; in January, the bishops in the army recorded the assistance in battle of the 'knights of Christ', the Greek saints George, Theodore, Demetrius and Blaise.[23]

The bishops were appealing to the west for reinforcement. In fact, the army was receiving a constant stream of reinforcements from as far apart as Italy, England and Denmark, many travelling with the fleets that arrived in the Levant in 1097–8 providing the besiegers with vital sustenance.[24] At no time was the army of God entirely cut off from the west or its Greek paymasters. In the need to replace its devastating casualties as well as its chronic problems of supplies may lie the decision of Tatikios, early in February 1098, to leave Antioch, as he claimed, to seek food and more troops.[25] Although later condemned as a double-dyed coward by western observers intent on constructing a justification for the failure to cede Antioch to the Greek emperor, Tatikios may have harboured perfectly legitimate motives. The supply chain to Antioch had broken down; direct consultation with the imperial authorities might have improved matters. Tatikios left his staff behind at Antioch. There were rumours that he had struck a deal with Bohemund, granting him control over the Cilician cities of Mamistra, Tarsus and Adana. This would fit the actual rather than the imagined relations between the Greek general, veteran of commanding western troops in the Balkans, and the probably Greek-speaking Bohemund. They had travelled together in the vanguard to Antioch and remained in close contact. At this stage, Bohemund must have appeared one of the most philhellene of the western princes. A Greek story had Bohemund warning Tatikios to leave in order to avoid an assassination plot hatched against him by the other commanders. At the time, Tatikios's departure made little impact; contemporary letters fail to mention it. While it is possible that Bohemund may have taken some role in engineering Tatikios's withdrawal and it is certain that his absence suited the Norman's schemes, conspiracy charges against either party lack evidence untainted by later propaganda, political posturing or special pleading.

Of greater importance was the military result of the new sense of community. Thanks to Bohemund's tactics and disciplined cohesion on the battlefield, the relief army of Ridwan of Aleppo was heavily defeated near the Lake of Antioch, some miles north-east of the city, on 8 February 1098. As at Dorylaeum, the battle near al-Bara in 1097, at Antioch itself later in 1098 and Ascalon in 1099, the fate of the crusade rested on the chance and skill of fighting. The Christian troops increased in effectiveness as numbers dwindled to a hardened core of veterans accustomed to strenuous pitched battles between massed forces of cavalry and infantry. The determination for victory existed in direct correlation to the consequences of defeat. In terms of morale, this gave the Christians an advantage. The victory over Ridwan temporarily steadied Christian resolve, while the arrival of an English fleet in early March allowed the blockade of the city to be tightened by the building of a new fort opposite the Bridge Gate, protecting vital access to the port of St Symeon. However, acute problems of food, horses and morale soon returned. Even the weather was terrible, reminding Stephen of Blois of home: 'What some say about the impossibility of bearing the heat of the sun throughout Syria is untrue, for the weather here is very similar to our winter in the west.'[26] Sharp encounters with the Antioch garrison sapped men and energy without disturbing the stalemate. Some optimism for the future may have been derived from the negotiations with Egyptian ambassadors in February and March 1098 and the dispatch of Christian envoys to accompany the Egyptians back to Cairo. By April, all gates of the city faced Christian blockade. However, news of a fresh Muslim relief force exposed the army's continuing peril.

During the spring of 1098, Kerbogha, atabeg of Mosul, assembled a large coalition against the western invaders from as far apart as Damascus, Anatolia and northern Iraq. Collecting allies as he went, Kerbogha was taking the opportunity afforded by the crusaders' disruption of local power structures to create a new overlordship in Syria, ostensibly loyal to the Seljuk sultan in Baghdad. His alliance included elements hostile to the Fatimids of Egypt and Ridwan of Aleppo as well as to the westerners and their Armenian associates. The attempt to capture Edessa during the three-week siege in mid-May and the seizure of other cities and towns in the region point to a strategy in which relief of Antioch formed only a part. The atabeg's objectives may be judged from the protraction of negotiations with Yaghisiyan's son; the price of Kerbogha's assistance was high. The actual outcome of the fighting of 1098 led to the establishment of Christian power in northern Syria, yet, until his defeat before Antioch, Kerbogha's assault on Syria offered the opposite prospect of a revived Turkish authority over the region. As with the defeat of al-Afdal of Egypt at Ascalon in August 1099, the westerners' victories in 1097–9 altered the political complexion of the Near East as much by denying the alternative outcomes of Seljuk or Fatimid *révanches* as by the establishment of their own limited hegemony.

News of the approach of Kerbogha's massive army reached the besiegers at Antioch in late May when it was only a few days' march away. Although they were well informed of the diplomatic efforts to dislodge them, each relief attempt had taken the westerners by surprise. Kerbogha's appearance was the nastiest yet, catching the Christians between a huge hostile field army and the impenetrable walls of Antioch. At a crisis meeting of the high command on 29 May, Bohemund was again entrusted with the leadership: if he could capture the city, he could keep it for his own provided no aid came from the Greek emperor, this last proviso reflecting the unease at Bohemund's ambition felt by Adhemar of Le Puy and Raymond of Toulouse, who harboured his own designs on the city. This agreement did nothing to stem the panic. Desertions multiplied, the most prominent being that of Stephen of Blois. Only nine weeks earlier, he had boasted to his wife of his appointment to a prominent role in the communal leadership, in his words 'lord, guardian and governor', perhaps in charge of administrative matters or coordinating supplies.[27] Stephen fled on 2 June, yet, within hours, Antioch had fallen.

The legendary quality of so many incidents during the First Crusade is nowhere more evident than in the story of how Bohemund and an Armenian dissident in Antioch, Firuz, collaborated in allowing the crusaders to penetrate the walls of the city at a point under the traitor's command on the night of 2–3 June 1098. It appears that Bohemund had been hatching the scheme for some time, probably before the meeting of 29 May. Contact across the front line at Antioch was common, especially with local Armenians. Bohemund and his followers possessed a linguistic advantage for this: on the night of the agreed commando-style raid on his section of the walls, they were able to converse with Firuz in Greek.[28] However, the small force which established itself under cover of dark on the inside included Godfrey of Bouillon and Robert of Flanders; Tancred, Count Raymond and Bishop Adhemar had also been let into the secret and were instrumental in rousing the main army to exploit the incursion the following morning. The element of surprise devastated the civilian population waking to uproar and the sounds of massacre. The overwhelmed garrison immediately withdrew to the citadel, leaving the city below to be plundered at will by the invaders. Resistance crumpled. Yaghisiyan panicked and fled, fearful, perhaps, of reprisals for his oppressive regime; within hours he had been assassinated by local Christians, the *coup de grâce* possibly delivered by an Armenian butcher.[29]

The fall of Antioch reflected the growing self-discipline and tenacity of the western army rather than any military resourcefulness or technological supremacy. There was minimal use of siege engines or artillery, surprisingly, in view of their use at Nicaea and later sieges at Ma 'arrat al-Nu 'man (December 1098), Arqah (March–May 1099) and Jerusalem. By contrast, at Antioch the Christians appeared reactive, often, as in confronting relief expeditions, dangerously so. While, at least after the foraging battle of December 1097, excelling in set-piece battles, there was no evident superiority in western tactics or equipment. The impression left by their siege of Antioch is of a frustrated bankruptcy of ideas to resolve the struggle, more effort being expended simply in keeping the army intact. Yet the solid bravery as well as occasional gaudy heroism suggests the crusaders' continued belief in their cause. They celebrated their dead as martyrs, in Stephen of Blois's words in March 1098, whose souls were borne to the joys of paradise.[30] Conviction alone was insufficient; fear, hunger, military incompetence or realism provoked despair and desertion, witness Count Stephen himself. Without idealism, the whole enterprise would have foundered long since.

The rapid collapse of Antioch once its defences had been breached showed that the defenders had become as weakened as their attackers. When the slaughtering had ceased, the new rulers of Antioch faced a grim prospect. The Muslim garrison still held the citadel above the city; there was little food and fewer horses. Before supplies could be collected from elsewhere, just a day after the capture, the vanguard of Kergogha's army arrived on the plain to the north of the city, having swept aside the Christian forward defences. By 7 June the city was invested; over the following week, all remaining Christian outposts beyond the city were overrun and a Muslim camp established close to the citadel to coordinate attacks from that sector. Heavy fighting all day around the citadel on 10 June caused another collapse in morale; that night panic spread among the crusaders, many fleeing the city using rope ladders to earn western opprobrium as *furtivi funambuli*, shifty rope-dancers.[31] For those who remained, a sense of hopelessness was inescapable. Unable to summon help, unaware of any possibility of relief by land or sea, heavily outnumbered, ill-equipped and near to starvation, the Christians, now reduced to perhaps less than 30,000 including non-combatants, had reached their lowest ebb in fortune. Only desperate measures could avert ruin.

From this extreme crisis emerged the visionary politics that characterized the rest of the campaign until Jerusalem was won. According to the story generally accepted by immediate eyewitnesses, on the very night of the panic and desertion, a Provençal priest, Stephen of Valence, beside himself with terror at what seemed to him the imminent fall of the city, while praying in the church of the Virgin Mary experienced a vision of Christ, the cross, Mary and St Peter (traditionally the first bishop of Antioch and the city's patron saint). Christ assured Stephen that the beleaguered Christians would receive His aid in five days provided they demonstrated their faith through prayers, ceremonies and penitence for their sinfulness. After initial scepticism, insisting that Stephen swore to the truth of his statement on the Gospels, Adhemar of Le Puy exploited the vision by instituting more morale-stiffening religious ceremonies and persuading the princes to renew their oaths to stay with the expedition. More dramatically, in an almost simultaneous report, a poor Provençal pilgrim, Peter Bartholomew, claimed to have received over the previous months a number of visions of St Andrew (in the Gospels the brother of St Peter) in which the saint had urged penitence on the crusaders and, as a sign of God's favour, had indicated where the Holy Lance that had pierced the side of Christ on the cross was buried in the cathedral of St Peter. Peter's story conveniently matched Stephen's by its promise of a sign of divine aid in five days. Adhemar and many others thought Peter a fraud, yet desperation and the advocacy of Raymond of Toulouse persuaded them to verify the story. On 14 June Peter and twelve others dug around in the floor of the cathedral until, as evening fell, Peter himself discovered what he and his fellow diggers took to be the point of the Lance sticking out of the ground at the bottom of the excavations. The discovery transformed the army's mood from terrified inertia to awed encouragement, allowing the leaders to organize a military breakout with some prospect of success, further celestial sightings accompanying the preparations for battle hardly coincidentally containing saintly instructions to further penance and military discipline.[32]

The objective reality of these visions or the authenticity of the Holy Lance are immaterial. The visions fitted contemporary models of such encounters, the visual iconography of the celestial messengers borrowing from contemporary art. A scrap of metal found beneath an old, much-renovated church after a day's digging does not stretch credibility or credulity. What mattered in June 1098 was the crusaders' belief. Although at first Bishop Adhemar and, later, others, particularly among the followers and propagandists of Bohemund, regarded Peter Bartholomew as a charlatan, not least perhaps because they may have seen a 'Holy Lance' on display in Constantinople, the visions provided the leadership with a precise plan to salvage the crusade. The link with reviving morale and military purpose is clear. One eyewitness suggested that Peter Bartholomew was only believed once the connection between the Lance and the defeat of Kerbogha had been made explicit; all associated the Lance with the subsequent success in battle. The visions fitted into the wider use of religious theatre and public ceremonial of penance to reinvigorate the army. An Armenian observer, writing within eighteenth months of the events, recorded the fervent prayers of the Christians in the cathedral of St Peter, designed to stiffen resolve, without mentioning the Lance.[33]

While Stephen of Valence provided the leaders with an opportunity to impose strict discipline dressed as instructions from Christ, their heavenly commander, the poor layman Peter Bartholomew, fitted less easily into this hierarchical order. Even so, Raymond of Aguilers, guardian of the Holy Lance after its removal from the cathedral, implied Peter's association with Count Raymond's entourage and, cynics noted, his political interests. Evidently no protégé of Adhemar of Le Puy, Peter may have attached himself to the newly arrived William bishop of Orange, who helped dig up the Lance or perhaps one of Count Raymond's vassals, Peter Raymond of Hautpol, mentioned as someone to whom Peter should report St Andrew's instructions.[34] Peter claimed to have been as far as Edessa and Cyprus in search of supplies for the crusade, pointing to aristocratic employment or contacts. He knew sections of the Latin liturgy by heart, so much, indeed, that he was able to forget some and still be able to display a degree of knowledge impressive in a supposedly humble peasant; some later chroniclers thought him a clerk. Although apparently universally accepted in the summer of 1098, Peter's visions later appeared partisan, directed at elevating Raymond of Toulouse to leadership and forcing the princes to abandon their newly won possessions in northern Syria in favour of the march to Jerusalem. However, Peter Bartholomew was not necessarily a Provençal stooge. Although ultimately emerging as the champion of the popular demand for the invasion of Palestine, for months after June 1098 Raymond of Toulouse was as reluctant to cede position in Syria as Bohemund; during this period Peter's repeated heavenly messages voiced the wishes of those unable to benefit from the profits of Syrian lordship, those, by virtue of the Christian success, denied local forage, plunder and booty. Only when Raymond decided to place himself at the head of the popular party at Ma 'arrat al-Nu 'man in January 1099 did Peter's visions directly serve the count's purposes, to his cost. At the siege of Arqah (February–May 1099), factional in-fighting, allied to doubts harboured even by supporters such as Raymond of Aguilers, forced a crisis of confidence. The theatricality of the visions was challenged by an equally potent set of judicial rituals devised to determine whether Peter was inspired or a fraud. A protracted trial instigated by Arnulf of Choques, Robert of Normandy's chaplain, culminated on Good Friday 1099, 8 April, in an ordeal by fire. Although Peter satisfied his supporters by emerging alive from a corridor of flames, thirteen feet long, four foot high and only one foot wide, he succumbed to his injuries a few days later.[35]

Visions and miracles articulated the aspirations of the mass of soldiers and pilgrims who, without prospect of lasting profit from conquest, concentrated on fulfilling their vows at Jerusalem. They also mirrored the changing military and political choices facing the princes. Peter Bartholomew's equivocal fate did not mean the end of the dialogue between the terrestrial and the heavenly followers of Christ. Further visions of Stephen of Valence and another Provençal priest, Peter Desiderius, confirmed the centrality of relics, liturgy and penance in fixing the cohesion of the army of God on its march to Jerusalem, now transmitted through the politically safer medium of clergy rather than an uncomfortably radical layman. One strand of visionary politics in the final stages of the march elevated the Provençal cult of the lost leader, Adhemar of Le Puy, who had died, possibly of typhoid, at Antioch on 1 August 1098, part of an intense response to the deaths of comrades, many of whom soon reappeared to their friends in visions and dreams, witnesses to continued support from the other world. The presence in the army of Bishop Adhemar's cross and cloak provided unassailable relics of unity and leadership; the dead bishop's words inspired the troops at Jerusalem; his presence, some reported, assisted the final assault.[36] During the siege of Jerusalem, another vision of Peter Desiderius, in which Adhemar urged a penitential procession around the walls of the city, legitimized a religious framework for persuading the army to attempt the final assault. At least it did so in retrospect. While the general accretion of miracle stories, relics and religious ceremonies from the sieges of Antioch onwards is undeniable, the neatness of the visionary prophecies and saintly interventions, their correlation with political and factional conflicts, the orderly narrative of celestial advice and the precise association of relics to visions in some accounts suggest crafting at the study desk as much as experience over the camp fire. Yet the importance of the miraculous and the holy, witnessed by participants' letters, lay in the power of the perceived transcendent to transform events.

Whatever later doubts and manipulation, the discovery of the Holy Lance and the injection of religious ceremony into the political discourse of the army contributed to the startling victory achieved over Kerbogha's much greater forces by the Christian breakout of Antioch on the morning of 28 June 1098. This was Bohemund of Taranto's finest hour. The day before, Peter the Hermit and an interpreter, Herluin, probably an Arabic-speaking Italian-Norman, had visited Kerbogha's camp, a gesture of defiance as much as an attempt to negotiate or spy. Next day, under Bohemund's direction, the Christian army, employing flexible, close-ordered, well-disciplined and tightly coordinated columns, first engaged, then threw back, outflanked and finally routed the forward divisions of the Muslim army before Kerbogha's main force became involved. Much of the fighting was between infantry, at close quarters, as the Christians lacked horses. Despite greatly outnumbering the Christians, Kerbogha's coalition disintegrated once the forward positions had been destroyed. Kerbogha fled ignominiously, leaving his camp, its prisoners, women, non-combatants, footsoldiers and booty open to the victors' pleasure. The spoils were impressive: tents, camp equipment, livestock, beasts of burden, horses, camels, gold and silver, considerable supplies of food and drink. All Muslims found were killed. Unlike their co-religionists in Antioch three weeks earlier, the women were not raped; instead 'the Franks . . . drove lances into their bellies'.[37] Such unrestrained lethal warfare, characteristic of earlier medieval western conflicts against Vikings, Slavs or Magyars, had largely been replaced in the west by limited aristocratic internecine skirmishing. Its return in the aftermath of the battle of Antioch marked exultant, exhilarated release from weeks of terror.

The defeat of Kerbogha prompted the Muslim garrison in the citadel to surrender, leaving the Christians to squabble over control of the city. To seek aid, Hugh of Vermandois was dispatched to Constantinople. A few days later, on 3 July, the princes decided to postpone any further advance south until 1 November 1098, possibly to await Greek reinforcement, apparently unaware of what many later saw as a pivotal moment in the First Crusade. Around 20 June, at Philomelium in central Anatolia, the Emperor Alexius, with a substantial Greek force accompanied by thousands of western troops, encountered the deserters from Antioch led by Stephen of Blois. Persuaded by the renegades of the hopelessness of the Christian position at Antioch and fearful of exposing his army to any Muslim counter-offensive, Alexius withdrew westwards. His daughter later insisted that Alexius had intended to assist in the conquest of Syria, although, given his necessary caution and greater strategic interest in western Anatolia, this was unlikely. However, his withdrawal, when known by the army at Antioch, was interpreted as a cowardly abandonment of his allies. More than any other single event, Alexius's perceived refusal to relieve Antioch, coupled in hindsight with the earlier withdrawal of Tatikios, was exploited as the defining moment of treachery, providing those who desired one with the perfect excuse to tear up their agreements with the emperor. The consequences for relations between eastern and western Christendom were profound.[38] Yet the betrayal was more apparent than real. Constant Greek naval aid had been vital at Antioch, providing materials, reinforcements and supplies. Negotiations with the emperor over the direction of the expedition continued into the spring of 1099. Some, such as Raymond of Toulouse, persisted with the Greek alliance long after the fall of Jerusalem. Later crusaders in 1101 received and accepted Greek hospitality at Constantinople. Yet immediately, the tone of the letter to Urban II of 11 September 1098, written by the princes led by Bohemund, was bitterly hostile to Alexius and the Greeks; subsequent decisions on strategy, settlement and rule ignored the fealty to the emperor sworn in 1097.[39]

This threw open the ownership of Antioch. By swift exploitation of events before and after the city's capture, Bohemund revealed his determination to keep the city for himself. His role in its capture and preservation lent him a strong hand; as early as 14 July he issued a charter granting the Genoese privileges in Antioch in exchange for promises of military assistance.[40] His rule was contested by Raymond of Toulouse. Although sometimes portrayed as holding more elevated motives than his Italian-Norman colleague, in his desire for personal territorial gain and leadership of the expedition, Raymond displayed material ambition of some intensity, his failure to raise greater opposition to Bohemund's seizure of Antioch reflecting his own political isolation rather than the other's lack of spirituality. In sharp contrast to the personally and physically charismatic Bohemund, Raymond failed to inspire warmth or alliances. As displayed at Constantinople, exaggeratedly conscious of his status, the count was older than most of the leaders; in poor health during the siege of Antioch, his native southern French tongue, *langue d'oc* further distancing him from the rest, who spoke the *langue d'oil*. His resentments and self-interest no less than those of his colleagues threatened the enterprise with collapse.

The death of Bishop Adhemar further fractured the expedition's cohesion and direction by removing the one accepted figure of moral authority and religious stature who transcended factional and regional divisions, the appointed representative of Urban II whose leadership in council and camp had been matched in battle at Dorylaeum and Antioch. The leaders and their knights spent the summer and autumn of 1098 consolidating their possessions in Syria and Cilicia or seeking employment with Baldwin of Boulogne at Edessa. The princes' letter to Urban II in September invited him to take personal command of the expedition, indicating an aimless prevarication over the invasion of Palestine. However, while baffling to the increasingly restless poor soldiers, this delay possessed some advantages. Negotiations with the Fatimids continued, the Egyptian embassy at Antioch being accompanied back to Cairo by Christian ambassadors. The defeat of Kerbogha had helped the Fatimids recapture Jerusalem in July 1098 from his allies, the Ortoqids, radically reconfiguring the diplomatic and political map. Instead of making common cause against Turkish interlopers, the westerners' ambition now threatened the integrity of Egyptian conquests in Palestine. Negotiations continued until May 1099, with Christian envoys even celebrating Easter 1099 at the Holy Sepulchre in Jerusalem.[41] After the experience of Antioch, the last thing the western commanders would have wanted was an opposed attack on Palestine. Moreover, the lotus-eating months of 1098 extended western rule in northern Syria, laying the foundations of permanent settlement, as in the creation of a Latin episcopal see at al-Bara, some twenty miles south-east of Antioch. This suited the acquisitive habits of western lords and knights as well as the princes, each of whom vigorously pursued their own territorial aggrandizement.

Out of these material conquests and consequent political rivalries emerged the crisis that precipitated the assault on Jerusalem. On 1 November 1098, the leaders almost came to blows. Bohemund, with the tacit support of most of the other princes, claimed the whole of Antioch, while Raymond, still clinging to parts of the city, concealed his own ambitions behind an appeal to honour the agreement with Alexius. Only the newly vocal pressure from the mass of the troops forced the leaders to an uneasy peace; 'discordant' was the frank appraisal of one eyewitness.[42] Having failed to win his point in Antioch, Raymond of Toulouse tried his luck further south. With Bohemund's help, he captured Ma 'arrat in December 1098, but disputes over control of the town led to the collapse of the November treaty. Early the following month, with Bohemund back in Antioch expelling the Provençals, Raymond attempted to assume command of the rest of the expedition by offering the other princes money in return for service: only Robert of Normandy and Tancred accepted. Excluded from Antioch, Raymond's policy of expediency was increasingly driven by ordinary crusaders. At

Ma 'arrat, their plight received striking witness in the stories of apparent cannibalism practised by a daredevil but starving group called the Tafurs, whose leader was alleged to have been a Norman knight fallen on hard times.[43] For months popular demands for a resumption of the march to Jerusalem had been articulated by the visionaries. Now the troops acted for themselves. While Raymond was trying to bribe his way to leadership, his followers began dismantling the walls of Ma 'arrat to force him to leave for the south. With Antioch held against him, Raymond had little choice but to place himself at the head of this popular element, hoping, no doubt, to attract rank and file followers of his princely rivals skulking further north. In a striking gesture of piety, humility and commitment, Raymond of Toulouse led his troops out of Ma 'arrat on 13 January 1099 barefoot as a penitent, surrounded by praying clergy, while behind him the town was fired on his orders, a symbolic burning of the boats.[44] The divisions and delays of the previous six months had resolved themselves into a brave choice. Politics and the lack of options placed Count Raymond at the head of the grizzled zealots, united and justified by divine approval and the unalterable ambition to liberate the Holy Sepulchre. If only by constant refrain, this desire, coloured by visions and miracles, none more compelling than the experiences of the campaign itself, assumed a totemic driving force which gathered strength as the leaders dallied. Even so, Raymond was gambling that his rivals would bow to similar forces and rally to him.

The gamble paid off. Marching south from Ma 'arrat, Count Raymond, accompanied by Tancred and Robert of Normandy, was granted safe passage by the alarmed rulers of Shaizar and Homs. At the end of January, this modest force of perhaps only 7,000 decided to strike west, towards the coast, partly to gain access to shipping and supply lines to Cyprus. After capturing the fortress of Hisn al-Akrad, later the site of the famous Crac des Chevaliers, in mid-February, Raymond, hoping for rich pickings, began to invest Arqah, even though its ruler, the emir of Tripoli, appeared willing to come to terms. Lasting three months, the siege witnessed the final confluence of the expedition's remaining disparate contingents. By the end of February, Bohemund, Robert of Flanders and Godfrey of Bouillon had assembled at Lattakiah on the coast twenty-five miles south-west of Antioch to observe developments further south. There, Bohemund left his colleagues, returning to secure his power in

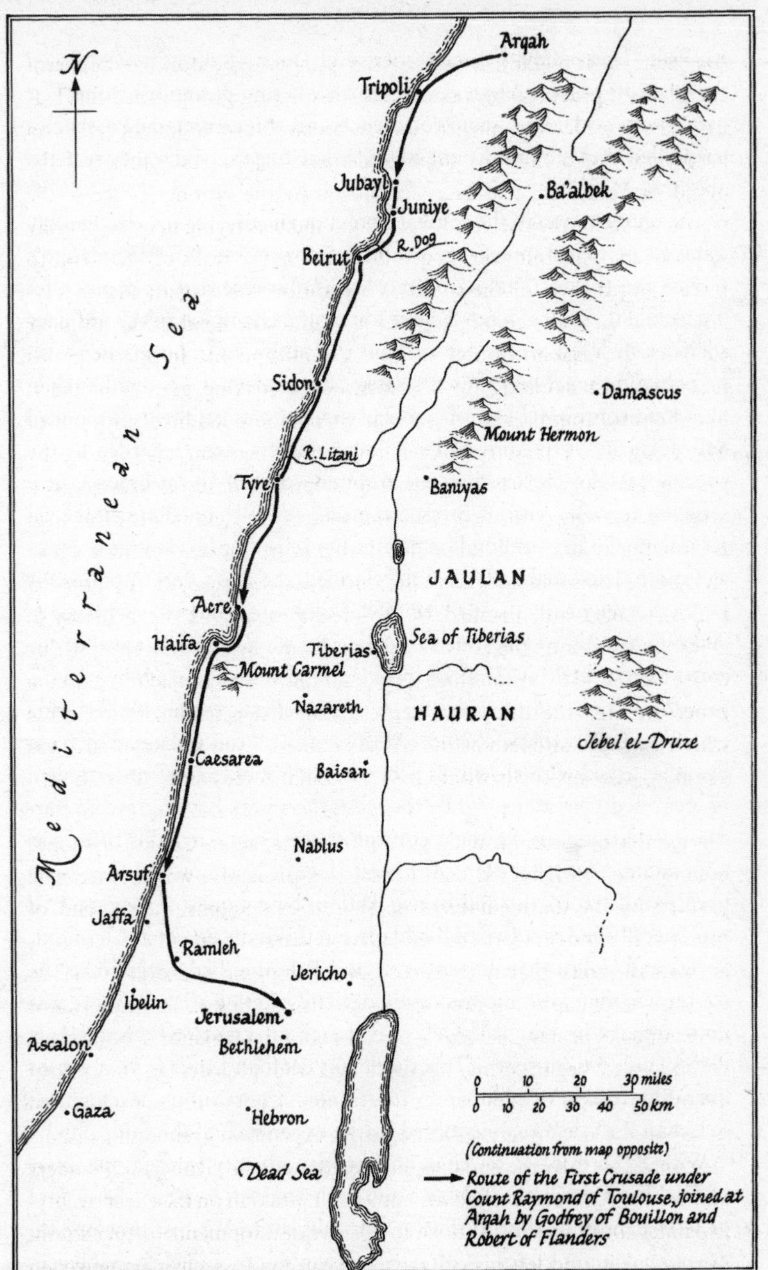

4. Palestine 1099

Antioch. Tentatively, Count Robert and Duke Godfrey moved down the coast to besiege Jubail (2–11 March), before desertions from their own troops and false rumours of a relief army threatening the Provençals persuaded them to join Count Raymond at Arqah, which they reached about 14 March.

The reunification of the combat armies reignited rivalries and feuding. Tancred of Lecce stirred up trouble by angling to desert Raymond's service for that of Duke Godfrey, who now emerged as a powerful independent political force. Count Raymond, champion of the ordinary soldier only a few weeks before, appeared stubborn in his insistence on perpetuating what was now a strategically irrelevant siege rather than marching south. His loss of popular support was reflected in the trial and death in early April of Peter Bartholomew, now regarded as the count's catspaw rather than the inspired voice of the people. A new series of reported visions pressed the case for an immediate attack on Jerusalem, Godfrey of Bouillon placing himself at the head of the popular agitation. Diplomatically, events clarified the crusaders' options. A Greek embassy early in April led to weeks of wrangling over whether to delay an assault on Palestine by waiting for the promised arrival of the emperor. On 13 May, Godfrey broke up the siege of Arqah by moving towards Tripoli, taking with him many Provençals, ending the lingering pretence of a Byzantine alliance. At this moment, the ambassadors from Egypt returned with al-Afdal's proposal for limited access to Jerusalem by unarmed Christians. While the westerners may have agreed to partition Palestine, leaving them control of the Holy City, this offer was impossible.[45] Original plans to liberate local Christians had long since been paralleled by the aim of acquisition, by conquest if necessary. It was later alleged that Urban II had offered this inducement at Clermont. Social and political reality in Syria and Palestine had revealed to the westerners that, with the fracturing of the Byzantine alliance, there was no fraternal Christian ruling class in church or state to whom the Holy Places could be entrusted. This subtle but profound shift from a war of liberation to one of occupation represented a portentous development in Urban II's schemes, one forged by the experience of the campaign.

With Byzantine aid rejected, an Egyptian alliance refused, the army of God left Tripoli on 16 May 1099 with one aim in view: the seizure of Jerusalem in as short a time as possible, a race against time and an Egyptian counter-attack. With religious symbols prominently displayed, the army reverted to type, the siege of Arqah, so far from consolidating Count Raymond's command, provoking a reversion to collective leadership. Despite its fractious nature, the army made rapid progress, covering the 225 miles from Tripoli to Jerusalem in just twenty-three days. On the often narrow coast road, shadowed by the now dilapidated English fleet that had joined the expedition at Antioch a year earlier,[46] speed dictated a diplomatic approach to the cities the army passed. Treaties were negotiated with Beirut and Acre; Tyre, Haifa and Caesarea presented no opposition, while Sidon provided only minor resistance. Signalling their inability to organize a military response, the Fatimids dismantled and abandoned Jaffa, the port nearest Jerusalem. At Arsuf, the Christian army turned inland, capturing the evacuated town of Ramla on 3 June. After resting for a few days and leaving a bishop with a garrison at nearby Lydda, on 6 June the Christians, rejecting a suggestion, possibly from Count Raymond, to attack the Fatimids directly in Egypt, climbed up into the Judean hills towards Jerusalem, camping that night at Qubeiba, ten miles from the Holy City. That evening Tancred left the army to occupy the Christian town of Bethlehem, a few miles south of Jerusalem. Although one account describes the locals as initially unsure who these invaders were, fearing more Turks, the westerners were soon welcomed, Tancred's diversion being a tribute to local intelligence and friendly contacts with co-religionists as much as to his own desire for dominion. Other elements from the army fanned out across the Judean hills, securing local villages and strongpoints. There was nothing quixotic about the march to Jerusalem. At Ramla voices had been raised warning of the dangers of besieging Jerusalem in high summer, chiefly lack of water. However, emotion and strategy compelled an immediate assault. The only hope of survival lay in capturing the city before the arrival of the Fatimid army. More than strategy drew the pilgrims on; one of them later recalled that in the final approach to the Holy City 'a few who held God's command dear marched along barefoot'; another summed up the general mood of the battered host at this climactic moment: 'rejoicing and exulting'.[47]

On Tuesday, 7 June the Christian army, numbering perhaps fewer than 14,000 fighting men, arrived at the walls of Jerusalem. The object of their quest reached, the ultimate trial began.[48] Given the threat of a Fatimid attack, the arid countryside, the impossibility of relief and the inability of such a small army to enforce a complete blockade, there was

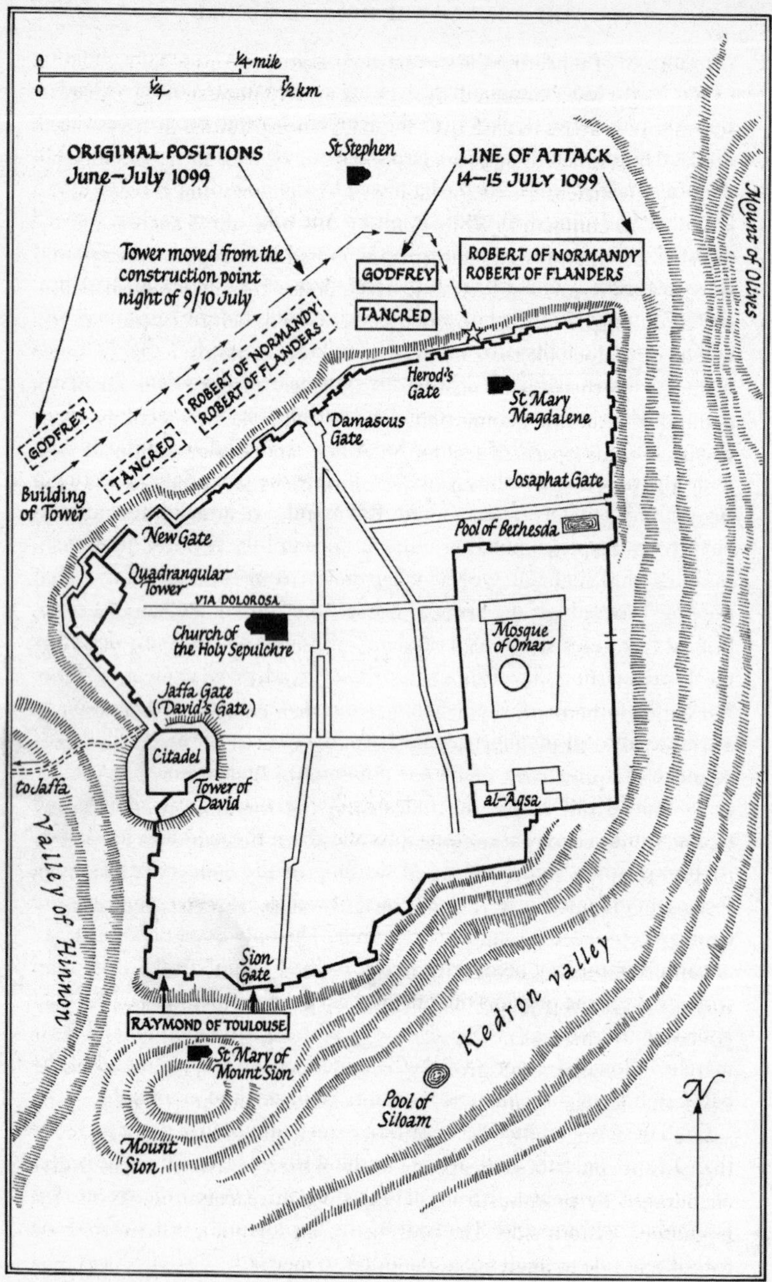

5. The Siege of Jerusalem, June–July 1099

no question of repeating the slow strangulation of Antioch. Prosecution of the siege was hampered by lack of water, necessitating elaborate schemes of water-carrying over large distances; illness, at least one of the leaders, Tancred, suffering from a bout of dysentery; the unavailability of sufficient wood for ladders, siege engines and towers; and a still divided command. While Godfrey, his new ally Tancred and the dukes of Normandy and Flanders maintained their separate camps outside the northern walls, Raymond of Toulouse initially established himself opposite the Citadel and the western walls before moving after a few days to blockade the Zion Gate in the south, almost as far removed from the northerners as possible. Thereafter, except for moments of communal ritual or planning the final assault, the two sections of the Christian army operated separately. A first, abortive attack on 13 June did not involve the Provençals at all. After the arrival of Genoese mariners who had put in at Jaffa on 17 June, with large timbers and skilled engineers, siege towers could be constructed, but each contingent made their own arrangements. Raymond, paying the construction artisans out of his own pocket, employed the Genoese William Ricau to build his tower, while the northerners, acting in concert, paid the workers out of a common fund, as at Antioch, and had Gaston of Béarn, himself a southerner from the Pyrenees, as their construction supervisor. Early in July, there were heated exchanges between the leaders over Tancred's opportunistic claim to lordship over Bethlehem and the issue of the future rule of Jerusalem. Tancred and Raymond were formally reconciled only a week before the final assault. Bitterness was probably exacerbated by the defection to Godfrey of a number of prominent Provençals before or during the siege. In such circumstances, victory was little short of miraculous.

Behind the strong obstacles of double walls, moats and natural contours, the garrison facing the westerners, commanded by the Fatimid governor Iftikhar al-Dawla, was small and surprisingly passive. Made up of professional troops from Egypt and local militias, including troops from the Jewish community, it launched no disruptive forays and scarcely challenged the building of siege machines in the later stages of the investment. Its tactics appear to have been to await help, a policy encouraged by promises from al-Afdal which reached the city via the unguarded eastern side. The prospect of an Egyptian relief force thus forced one side to aggression, the other to inertia.

To capitalize on the surge of enthusiasm at having finally arrived at Jerusalem, on 13 June, allegedly at the promptings of a hermit living on the Mount of Olives, the northern leaders launched a speculative attack between the Quadrangular Tower in the north-west corner of the city and the Damascus Gate. Relying on only one ladder, even when the outer walls were breached, no concerted attack on the inner rampart was possible, the first man up, Raimbold Croton from Chartres, losing his hand in the attempt. Losses were heavy and, although the outer walls were damaged, the defences held. This failure persuaded the leaders, at a meeting two days later, that the next assault required more careful organization and the participation of all contingents. Over the next few weeks the region was scoured for supplies; the Genoese, with their vital timbers cannibalized from their ships, were escorted to the siege and the engineers set to work. As the material preparations reached fruition, it was agreed on 6 July to hold a solemn religious procession around the walls of the city, in imitation of Joshua at Jericho. The planning and execution of this morale-boosting ritual encapsulated the expedition's spiritual history. The inspiration, some recalled, came from a vision received by Peter Desiderius; the decision to hold the procession was reached at an assembly summoned by William Hugh of Monteil, Adhemar of Le Puy's brother. After a three-day fast, on 8 July the whole army, led by the clergy bearing the growing collection of relics, processed barefoot around the walls of Jerusalem, ignoring the taunts of the locals. On completion of the circuit, the host was addressed on the Mount of Olives by Raymond of Aguilers, for the Provençals, Arnulf of Choques, the smooth-talking chaplain to the duke of Normandy, and Peter the Hermit, now under the patronage of Godfrey of Bouillon and the Lorrainers. Count Raymond and Tancred were publicly reconciled.[49] The political and religious threads of the expedition were thus drawn tightly together in a public demonstration that recognized the regional diversity of the enterprise while insisting on its single identity, shared experience and common goal. As at Antioch, it was hoped that such rededication would ignite a willingness to hazard all in a last throw of fate. News of al-Afdal's large relief army leaving Egypt had reached the Christian camp. It was now or never.

The final assault on Jerusalem begun on 13 July was a desperate affair. Attacks were launched on two fronts, by the Provençals on the narrow line of wall by the Zion Gate in the south and by the northern forces –

of Godfrey, Robert of Normandy, Robert of Flanders and Tancred – who had moved, with their siege tower and ram, to the north-east corner of the walls on 10 July. While the Provençals made little impact, the northerners' slowly wore down the defence, their tactics revolving around pushing their siege tower as close to the inner wall as possible to allow troops to gain access to the ramparts by planks and ladders. While other contingents provided ferocious salvoes of arrows and bolts, the Lorrainers under Duke Godfrey were in charge of the tower. Resistance was everywhere fierce, strongest in the south, nearest to the centre of power at the Citadel; in both sectors catapults were used by the defenders. Casualties were high; perhaps as many as a fifth or a quarter of the western armies. Contact between the two Christian assaults was maintained by signallers stationed on the Mount of Olives using reflectors. At midday on Friday, 15 July, the dispirited Provençals were encouraged to renew their attack while the northerners' siege tower was painfully edged towards the inner wall over which it towered. Albert of Aachen recorded that a golden cross was placed on the top storey of the tower, where Duke Godfrey himself stood firing his crossbow into the city.[50] When the tower was pushed right against the wall, from the storey below the brothers Ludolf and Engelbert from Tournai threw planks across the gap and entered the city, soon followed by Godfrey, Tancred and the Lorrainers. The defenders fled to the Haram al-Sharif, the Temple Mount, but were overtaken by Tancred before they could secure the precinct. The scale of the slaughter there impressed even hardened veterans of the campaign, who recalled the area 'streaming with blood' that reached to the killers' ankles. Raymond of Aguilers resorted to the language of the Book of Revelation in describing the Christian knights in front of the al-Aqsa mosque wading through blood up to their horses' knees.[51] The survivors took refuge inside the mosque, many hiding in the roof while Tancred plundered the Dome of the Rock near by before calling a halt to the killing by offering those inside the al-Aqsa mosque his protection, presumably hoping for ransom. Meanwhile, news of the entry of the Christians into the city caused the defenders in the south to withdraw to the Citadel, with Count Raymond in pursuit. Without delay Iftikhar al-Dawla struck a deal that guaranteed the garrison's safe conduct to Ascalon in return for surrendering the Citadel, although some were ransomed, at knock-down rates.[52]

The massacre in Jerusalem spared few. Jews were burnt inside their synagogue. Muslims were indiscriminately cut to pieces, decapitated or slowly tortured by fire (this on Christian evidence). Such was the scale and horror of the carnage that one Jewish witness was reduced to noticing approvingly that at least the Christians did not rape their victims before killing them as Muslims did.[53] The city was comprehensively ransacked: gold, silver, horses, food, the domestic contents of houses, were seized by the conquerors in a pillage as thorough as any in the middle ages. Profit vied with destruction; some Jewish holy books were later ransomed to the surviving community in exile. Violence overcame business on 16 July when Tancred's prisoners in the al-Aqsa mosque were butchered in cold blood, possibly by Provençals who had missed the previous day's action. The city's narrow streets were clogged with corpses and dismembered body parts, including some crusaders crushed in their zeal for the pursuit and massacre of the defenders. The heaps of the dead presented an immediate problem for the conquerors; on 17 July many of the surviving Muslim population were forced to clear the streets and carry the bodies outside the walls to be burnt in great pyres, whereat they themselves were massacred, a chilling pre-echo of later genocidal practices.

This secondary slaughter, in cold blood, perhaps even more than the initial mayhem, provoked mounting retrospective shock and outrage amongst Muslim intellectuals, religious leaders and politicians over the next century and a half. Some thousands, men, women and children, were massacred, although certainly fewer than the 70,000 trumpeted in early thirteenth-century Arabic chronicles. A few Muslim and Jewish Jerusalemites survived, managing either to escape, sometimes with their possessions and holy books, such as the belongings of the Egyptian garrison and its hangers-on, the Torah scrolls that reached Ascalon, or to be ransomed, a process that could take months, suggesting a not entirely indiscriminate policy of killing on the part of the crusaders.[54] Massacres were not a monopoly of western Christians. The recent Turkish conquests in the Near East had been accompanied by carnage and enslavement on a grand scale. When it suited, Muslim victors could behave as bestially as any Christian, as Zengi showed at Edessa in 1144 and Saladin was to prove in suppressing opposition in Egypt in the 1170s and in the killing of the knights of the military orders after the battle of Hattin in 1187. Immediate contemporary Muslim reactions appeared muted when contrasted to later polemics. Massacres as well as atrocity stories were – and are – an inescapable part of war. In the face of a Muslim counter-attack, letting the locals live may not have seemed a prudent option to the Christian victors, however obscene the alternative.

The scenes of carnage and plunder in the streets of Jerusalem attract particular notoriety through the juxtaposition of extreme violence and anguished faith. Some of the butchers thought they saw Adhemar of Le Puy urging them on. On the evening of 15 July 1099, with the din of slaughter still echoing round the city, in the midst of the almost deserted Christian quarter, recently emptied of most of its inhabitants by the Muslim governor, the conquerors went to pray at the church of the Holy Sepulchre, the object of all their labours. As one veteran put it:

> our men rushed round the whole city, seizing gold and silver, horses and mules, and houses full of all sorts of goods and they all came rejoicing and weeping from excess of gladness to worship at the Sepulchre of our Saviour Jesus, and there they fulfilled their vows.

Another, in language redolent of the Bible and the liturgy, touched on the contrasting emotions of those who, after three years of almost unimaginable effort, struggle, anxiety and fear, found themselves at journey's end:

> Jerusalem was now littered with bodies and stained with blood . . . With the fall of the city it was rewarding to see the worship of the pilgrims at the Holy Sepulchre, the clapping of hands, the rejoicing and singing of a new song to the Lord. Their souls offered to the victorious and triumphant God prayers of praise which they could not explain in words.[55]

The capture of Jerusalem, however remarkable a crowning achievement, did not end the expedition, its internal divisions or its military vulnerability. The settlement of secular and ecclesiastical authority within the city and its surrounds resurrected the simmering hostilities between the leaders. On 22 July, Raymond of Toulouse was once more outmanoeuvred. After apparently refusing an offer to accept the crown of Jerusalem, perhaps on clerical prompting, he saw instead his latest chief rival, Godfrey of Bouillon, the only other main leader willing to remain in the east, elected as secular ruler, or Advocate (the title implying ecclesiastical authority). As at Antioch, Raymond was then forced to surrender his strongpoint in the city, the Citadel. He nearly abandoned the expedition, taking himself off to sulk on a trip to the Jordan valley, only reluctantly joining the army to repel the Egyptians. On 1 August, in a further blow to Raymond's standing, the Norman Arnulf of Choques, the prosecutor of Peter Bartholomew, was elected patriarch of Jerusalem, the previous patriarch, Symeon, who had joined the army at Antioch, having died in Cyprus a few days earlier. With Arnulf's election the top posts in Jerusalem had gone to the Lorrainers and Normans. By this time a number of Count Raymond's own followers had transferred allegiance. Arnulf secured his control of the church of the Holy Sepulchre by establishing Latin canons. More significantly, he unearthed a piece of the True Cross, possibly by persuading or coercing local Christians into telling him where one had been hidden. This story of concealment and discovery, containing echoes of the Holy Lance story, may have been circulated to establish a respectable provenance for a relic whose finding was timely, convenient and iconic. The discovery of the Jerusalem relic of the True Cross brought physical symbolism to the fulfilment of the journey of the bearers of the cross. It was to play a central role in the religious ceremonial, military display and political iconography of the new Christian kingdom of Jerusalem.[56]

More vital business intruded into the feuding at Jerusalem with the arrival at Ascalon in the first days of August of a substantial Egyptian army, perhaps 20,000 strong, commanded by the Vizier al-Afdal himself. For the westerners, defeating al-Afdal was essential to secure their conquest; battle could not be shirked. By 10 August, leaving a skeleton garrison in Jerusalem with Peter the Hermit to lead prayers of intercession for their success, the Christian leaders had mustered at Ramla, with an army perhaps 10,000 strong, advancing the next day towards Ascalon on the coast twenty-five miles away. The following morning, 12 August, they caught the unprepared Egyptians encamped before the northern walls of the city. Repulsing a vigorous infantry sally, the western knights launched a concerted cavalry charge that put the Egyptian force to flight and captured the enemy camp with its rich pickings of booty. Once again, flexibility, coordination, speed, boldness and surprise allowed the westerners to overcome a force perhaps twice their size. Only continued bickering between Godfrey and Raymond prevented the surrender of the demoralized city itself, which remained in Muslim hands for another fifty-four years, a troublesome Egyptian presence in the kingdom built by Godfrey and his successors.

The battle of Ascalon marked the completion of the campaign launched from Constantinople in the spring of 1097. Jerusalem was secured; the veterans could depart. Squabbling persisted to the end. In mid-August, Godfrey forced Raymond to abandon an attempt to capture the coastal town of Arsuf. After a final reconciliation with Godfrey, Raymond and the other leaders, Robert of Normandy and Robert of Flanders, and the majority of the surviving crusaders left for the north. At Lattakiah, where they found Bohemund and the newly arrived papal legate, Daimbert of Pisa, with a large fleet attempting to dislodge the Byzantine garrison, they persuaded the attackers to withdraw. Daimbert prepared to continue south to Jerusalem to assert his authority over both church and state. Bohemund withdrew to Antioch. Raymond assumed command of the citadel of Lattakiah in agreement with the Greeks, who, in contradiction of their reputation for hostility and duplicity soon to be popularized in western Europe, helped provide the shipping to carry the crusaders back home. By the end of August, the survivors, including the duke of Normandy and count of Flanders, hundreds of other lords and knights and thousands of humbler soldiers and pilgrims, finally embarked for the west to resume their spectacularly interrupted lives.

The success of the armies called together by Urban II, whose death on 29 July 1099 robbed him of knowledge of the triumph, was neither inevitable nor incredible. The miserable failure of successive substantial western armies in Asia Minor in 1101 testified to the importance of battlefield tactics, good generalship and luck. After the near-disaster in July 1097, the main expedition performed with increasing cohesion, boldness and skill. By June 1098 these hardened troops presented a frightening proposition for the coalition armies of their opponents. Common identity was reinforced by the regular transfer of allegiances and new patterns of lordship within the contingents, as with Tancred's abandonment of Bohemund and later serial loyalty to Raymond and Godfrey; or Robert of Normandy's acceptance of Raymond's leadership in January 1099. Such permeable structures of allegiance and affinity characterized the expedition from the winter of 1097–8. The chronicler Fulcher of Chartres joined the entourage of Baldwin of Boulogne in Cilicia and at Edessa eight months before the desertion of his previous lord, Stephen of Blois. Having set out in 1096 as head of a Lorrainer army, by the time Godfrey became ruler of Jerusalem in 1099 he had attracted supporters from across northern France, a consequence of his wealth; his willingness to accept the support of knights and lords outside his original entourage; the deaths of other lords; and the casualty rate amongst his own vassals and regional allies.[57] Attrition and the search for patronage acted as powerful centripetal forces.

In their determined pursuit of victory and consequent booty, the First Crusaders bear comparison with Viking armies of the ninth to eleventh centuries. A necessary *esprit de corps* was established though always operating in potentially hostile territory, dependent on constant success for survival, in the process establishing a micro-culture of militancy, community and purpose, which found expression in extremes of violence no less than in the drive for material profit or diplomatic gain. Like those of the Carolingians, the Christian army supplied the institutional context for social, political, material and religious exchange. Militarily and politically, the First Crusade exemplified a consistent feature of medieval warfare: the effectiveness of armies, not necessarily of massive numerical superiority, operating and dominating war fronts far from home. While a familiar feature of the Islamic and Byzantine worlds, subject to regular incursions from the Eurasian steppes and dependent on foreign mercenary bands, western Europe supplied only a few analogous examples, such as the Catalan Company of the early fourteenth century, which successively terrorized Asia Minor on behalf of the ailing Greek empire and then occupied and ruled parts of Greece for themselves.[58] But it was never remotely on the scale of the First Crusade. The nature of medieval warfare allowed for such campaigns as armies, wherever they found themselves, relied on self-sufficiency in food, equipment and horses rather than being dependent, as in modern wars, on home bases.

That the First Crusade was able to achieve such results reflected the context for its operations. The expedition formed part of a pre-existing process opening the eastern Mediterranean to western adventurers, merchants, pilgrims and mercenaries. Pivotal was the role played in its inception and nurturing by the Byzantines, a debt that was soon to become embarrassing for commentators and politicians who preferred an adversarial model and the myth of an autonomous victory. Political chaos in the Near East denied their opponents unity while allowing the crusaders opportunities for diplomacy and alliances. The leaders of the western force adapted quickly not only to the diplomatic possibilities but also to the alien military tactics of their enemies.[59] Although westerners were possibly familiar with siege techniques, in the west there were few pitched battles and fewer post-conflict massacres. The central elements of war in the west were cavalry and infantry, including archers, and it was characterized by the charge and the skirmish. In the east, in addition to heavy cavalry, the impetus in battle was provided by light armed cavalry, often archers, the massed charge being replaced by the rapid and fluid tactics of the feint and the ambush, which, by early 1098, the crusaders knew how to counter. The fighting march, unknown in the west, was a staple of Levantine warfare which the westerners perfected, the march from Ramla to Ascalon on 10–12 August 1099 providing a textbook example.

Yet the political, material and military pillars of victory fail adequately to describe the structure of the First Crusade or alone explain its success. Although it is misleading to assume that all recruits and followers shared a similar intensity of religious motivation and zeal, without the element of ideology and spiritual exhilaration there would have been no march to Jerusalem, let alone a successful conquest. As the expedition shed its appearance of a Byzantine mercenary force in the winter of 1097–8, so spiritual leadership and direction came to the fore, visions, relics, liturgical ceremonies and the theatre of communal penitence binding the army together. There are contradictions here. The siege of Antioch appears in the retrospect of veterans to have been crucial to this process. Yet by then the mass of unarmed pilgrims and camp followers had been reduced to a rump, increasingly integrated into the military function of the expedition. At Antioch, too, the one acknowledged spiritual leader, Adhemar of Le Puy, died, not to be replaced, the response of the leaders appearing anything but spiritually inspired. Yet the fractured leadership after the Antioch triumph, the prospect of annihilation removed, created a vacuum of purpose that was filled by religious symbolism and exhortation expressed through increasingly vocal and organized popular elements. The language of participants from at least the early summer of 1097 points to fundamental and well-established attitudes, aspirations and beliefs that predated the crises of Antioch and Jerusalem.

When Stephen of Blois wrote in June 1097 of 'the blessed journey' of 'the army of God', he was doing more than parroting the cliché and slogans of the preachers and priests. He was expressing an understanding that the enterprise was especially holy, uniquely part of God's purpose. By March 1098, Stephen was talking of the dead as martyrs, an increasingly common theme in accounts of the later stages of the crusade: the language, images and examples of celestial help suffuse the letters sent home by clergy and laity. In two surviving letters to the archbishop of Rheims, of November 1097 and July 1098, Anselm of Ribemont, who was to be killed in February 1099 at the siege of Arqah and was reported as himself having experienced celestial visions, emphasized the unique status of the army, calling on the clergy in the west to pray for the Christian host, conscious of fighting for Christendom as a whole, spiritually bound to the western church however far removed physically.[60] The appreciation of a unique providential purpose marked out this holy war from previous conflicts with infidels in Sicily or Spain. As privations deepened and dangers grew, the awareness of the supernatural and a feeling of its proximity became more acute. This spiritual intensity did not derive solely from the conditions of the march; it was inherent from the start in the enterprise's system of belief and understanding of failure and success in terms of sin and God's favour. There was little or no perceived conflict between material and religious motives. Booty and land were justified as well as necessary reward for labouring in God's service. The crusade encompassed the pious, the adventurer, the zealot, the thug, the tourist, the driven, the bored, the penitent, the professional and the desperate within its ideology of service, warfare and faith. Grasping opportunists such as Baldwin of Boulogne observed the proprieties. The conviction of leaders and led in the transcendent worthiness of their cause had been legitimized by Urban II and the recruiters and propagandists of 1095–6, but sprang from a deeper culture of militant piety. That their casualties appeared to them as martyrs and that their efforts were crowned with victory merely confirmed them in their sense of battered righteousness.

Frankish Outremer

5
The Foundation of Christian Outremer

On 15 July 1149, fifty years to the day after the Christian capture of Jerusalem, a service was held in the southern corner of the compound of the church of the Holy Sepulchre to dedicate a complex of newly constructed chapels encasing the rock designated as Calvary, the site of the Crucifixion. To mark the event, an inscription was erected near the spot that began:

> This place is holy, sanctified by the blood of Christ.
> By our consecration we add nothing to its holiness.[1]

The formal pious humility of this sentiment concealed the revolution in the religious and political affairs of the church, city and region and in the attitudes and habits of all those elsewhere in Latin Christendom interested in their fate that had characterized the previous half-century. In the aftermath of a great, if unproductive, incursion of western help, now known as the Second Crusade, and on the eve of a major reconstruction of the church of the Holy Sepulchre itself, Patriarch Fulk of Jerusalem and his colleagues cannot have been unaware of the reconfiguration of western culture caused by the occupation of the Holy Land. Fulk himself, a pious, dogged ecclesiastical second-rater, had abandoned the awkward political compromises of an Angoulême religious house for the escapism, exoticism and opportunism of colonial Palestine. The pilgrimage to Jerusalem had become almost an obligation, certainly a mass habit, for the faithful of Europe, the image of the Holy Sepulchre a new model in art as much as for public and private devotion. Replicas proliferated across western Europe as well as symbolic representations in chapels attached to parish churches and cathedrals that played an important part in Easter rituals and liturgies.[2] The holiness mentioned in the Calvary inscription had irradiated the west through the flood of relics that streamed from Palestine in the aftermath of 1099, in the process accelerating a trend towards a greater universality of cults and a closer concentration on the historicity of the Bible and hence the humanity of Christ. The traditional rhetoric and Gregorian standard of just and holy warfare were transfigured by the memory of the first Jerusalemites, fighting for the church in Spain, the Baltic, even within Christendom itself, now being assessed and rewarded in terms of the remission of sins gained on the first journey to Jerusalem. The glory of the victors of 1099 clung to them in name and fame, their deeds cited as periods in the lives and affairs of onlookers not themselves veterans. Just as in early twenty-first-century British conversation 'the war' invariably refers to the global conflict that had ended in 1945, so the 'journey to Jerusalem' for western Europeans of the early twelfth century meant only one thing. Beyond providing a benchmark of honour and service, 'those men who obeyed the command of the pope, who left so many and so much and who, as loyal knights (*boni homines*), captured Jerusalem by arms and assault', the Anglo-Norman baron Brian Fitz-Count recalled in the early 1140s, 'established Godfrey, a good and legitimate king'.[3]

Heavenly Jerusalem may have been brought closer by the Christian liberation of the Holy Places, but the terrestrial Holy Land needed its walls defending, its fields tending and its ports to thrive. The new Christian land overseas, Outremer, provided a fresh field for ambition, endeavour and settlement. In contradiction of the hindsight of history, those gathered around the rock called Calvary did not imagine the political enterprise as any more doomed than the religious. Although nervous westerners seeking to buy property in Palestine in mid-century might prefer land 'around Jerusalem not near the border with the Turks', appreciation of the providential nature of the 1099 victory, the 'greatest event since the resurrection' as one enthusiast had proclaimed it, imposed its own confidence and anticipation of permanence.[4]

Obligation, adventure, status, profit, piety and confidence sustained the maintenance and expansion of the bridgeheads established in Syria and Palestine in 1097–9. Not all western visitors to Outremer came to fight or to pray; many arrived to settle, trade or seek preferment. In contrast to Spain, Sicily or the Baltic, as a region for western European political, social and economic colonization, Outremer was more remote. Given a mismatch of climate and cultural behaviour, notably in hygiene and diet, it faced a constant threat of demographic deficit, with high death rates, especially in infant mortality. It also had to accommodate the needs of transient pilgrims, adventurers and sightseers as well as settlers. The fate of lordships, including the very highest, could be determined by the vagaries of western politics and dynasticism. The requirements of tourism imposed particular constraints: in 1112, Arnulf of Chocques was hurriedly reappointed patriarch of Jerusalem so that there would be somebody to preside over Holy Week ceremonies for the expectant hordes of pilgrims. Pilgrims contributed to the local economy, through taxes paid at the port of entry or the flourishing trade in souvenirs: opposite the Holy Sepulchre ran the Rue des Paumiers, Palmers' Street, where the pilgrims bought the palm leaves to show they had accomplished their vows (and saving them a trip down to Jericho, where the palms grew). By mid-century, a local Frank – as all the western settlers were called by the indigenous and immigrant communities alike – Rorgo Fretel of Nazareth, had produced a convenient guide book to the now carefully managed holy geography, which had been meticulously established since 1099.[5]

Not all pilgrims ignored the military dimension of protecting this greatest of all Christian relics, many following their devotions at Jerusalem and the other Holy Sites with temporary service in the armies of the king. More lastingly, the needs of visiting pilgrims as much as local defence produced Outremer's distinctive contribution to the Latin church, the military orders. The Order of the Hospital of St John, the Hospitallers, recognized by the pope in 1113, while acquiring martial functions, never lost its duty of care for the infirm and sick, mostly visitors; the Order of the Temple of Solomon, the Templars, began *c.*1120 as a fraternity devoted to guarding the pilgrim routes from Jaffa to Jerusalem. While civilian settlement followed patterns familiar to other frontiers of Christendom, the exigencies of defence, demography and devotion lent Outremer inherently distinctive characteristics. The modest level of western settlement compared with indigenous communities contrasted with the ideological imperative that drew westerners to the Holy Land in the first place. Whatever accommodations were reached with native peoples and powers, the inspiration and justification for western rule was not social or economic or even conventionally political. Christian Outremer could never completely lose its quality of a garrison created to protect the Holy Places of its faith.

THE EXPEDITIONS OF 1100–1101

A recurrent complaint voiced by combatants throughout the campaign of 1097–9 attacked backsliding *crucesignati* for failing to fulfil their vows. The army of God's need for reinforcements always appeared urgent as massive casualties left the enterprise emaciated and vulnerable. Without reinforcements, the crusade would have failed, at Antioch as at Jerusalem. In the west preaching and recruitment had not stopped, the narrative neatness of later accounts concealing that the so-called Princes' Crusade of 1096–9 formed part of a process that slowly gathered momentum, stimulated in part by letters and news from the front. In April 1099, perhaps in response to the crusade leaders' letter to him from Antioch of September 1098 calling for the despatch of all remaining *crucesignati*, Urban II authorized a fresh preaching campaign in Lombardy, conducted by Archbishop Anselm of Milan with considerable success, for what was soon regarded by a contemporary Norman chronicler as a distinct, second expedition to Jerusalem.[6]

The modern fashion of regarding the military expeditions to the east of 1100–1101 as part of the First Crusade not only challenges twelfth-century and later historiography, it also appears to misrepresent the understanding and intentions of those concerned. While there continued to be a steady stream of westerners heading east, not least from the maritime cities of Italy, another Genoese fleet embarking in 1100, the 1101 expedition constituted a separate operation. Recruitment occurred in the clear knowledge that Jerusalem was in Christian hands. Even where many involved had taken the cross some time before, the armies only coalesced after a new call to arms by Urban II's successor, Paschal II, in December 1099, followed by a series of special councils in the spring and autumn of 1100 and a preaching tour of France by papal legates, efforts supplemented by letters from the Holy Land. The various contingents led by princes and prelates only began to march from September 1100, some not until the following spring. All the main groups crossed into Asia from the European shore of the Bosporus between April and July 1101. These campaigns constituted a self-consciously fresh initiative by the pope, his legates and local diocesans, comparable in numbers of recruits with the efforts of Urban II and his agents in 1095–6. The one difference with its predecessor was the disastrous result, fortuitously highlighting the remarkable achievement of 1099.

Recruitment in 1100–1101 appeared more regulated than in 1095–6, although this may reflect the evidence rather than the process: contemporaries were more alert to what was happening than five years before. Moreover, clear precedents had been set, to which was added the whip of unfulfilled vows. Paschal II's threat to excommunicate defaulters in December 1099 was repeated by a synod of bishops led by the archbishop of Lyons at Anse the following spring. For those *crucesignati* who had never embarked and still more for those, like Stephen of Blois, who had deserted, official strictures lent weight to social and domestic peer pressure to redeem both vows and reputations. Victory in the east in 1099 made joining up attractive for new recruits and morally imperative for defaulters. Two papal legates reinforced the message in a tour of south-western France, in the footsteps of Urban II five years earlier, visiting Valence, Limoges and Poitiers in the autumn of 1100. The embrace of the recruiting drive stretched to Burgundy and into Germany. The speed of assembly and journeys to Constantinople; the substantial quantity of money, transports and war materials assembled; and firm command structures suggested tight organization. The bishop of Nevers later complained that some of his men had been forced to go by Count William II of Nevers.[7] The enterprise was dominated by princes of church and state. Archbishop Hugh of Lyons, a veteran papal diplomat, went as the pope's chief legate along with at least eleven other archbishops and bishops. The parade of secular rulers at least equalled that of 1096, including the embarrassed veterans Stephen of Blois and Hugh of Vermandois; William IX, duke of Aquitaine; the count of Nevers; Duke Odo and Count Stephen of Burgundy; Welf IV, duke of Bavaria; and Conrad, constable to Emperor Henry IV of Germany.

Motives appeared varied as much as before. Former deserters had experienced widespread public and private abuse. Most notoriously, Stephen of Blois's strong-willed wife, Adela, daughter of William the Conqueror, waged an incessant campaign of bullying and moral blackmail, her nagging extending to their bedroom, where, before intercourse, she would urge her disgraced husband to consider his reputation and return to the Holy Land.[8] Adela's preference for being a hero's widow rather than a coward's wife cannot have been unique. Elsewhere, relatives of deserters attempted to expiate the family shame by joining up. With the deserters and vow-defaulters went those seeking penance, either with specific crimes to expunge, such as William of Nevers who had burnt the village of Molesme, or from a more general sense of the burden of sin. Eagerness to become associated with this new glorious enterprise combined with piety and devotion. As well as authorizing prayers and preaching to celebrate the new Christian enclave at Jerusalem, Archbishop Manasses of Rheims circulated copies of the letters he had received from Anselm of Ribemont in 1098 with their powerful evocation of spiritual excitement and martial achievement.[9] Fame spurred the enthusiasm of William of Aquitaine. The cause of Jerusalem transcended the political divide of the Investiture Contest, in posthumous tribute to Urban II's triumph. The disparate incentives were subsumed in ceremonies of taking the cross, now unequivocally associated with the notion of pilgrimage, which again provided the focal points of propaganda, commitment and recruitment. The earlier expedition had evidently failed to exhaust the supply of enthusiasts even in areas heavily represented in 1096, such as Aquitaine, although Burgundy, Lombardy and southern Germany loomed larger than before. Unfortunately for them, numbers and enthusiasm proved insufficient.

The Lombard army left Milan on 13 September 1100, before some other leaders such as William of Aquitaine had even taken the cross. Reaching Constantinople around the end of February or the beginning of March, the later stages of their overland journey were marked by the sort of extravagant foraging that easily slipped into pillage and casual atrocities against locals. Further trouble erupted during the Lombards' two-month stay outside Constantinople, suggesting that the leadership lacked a firm hold on their followers. In late April, the Emperor Alexius managed to ship the Lombards across the Bosporous to Nicomedia to await further western contingents. Alexius's response to this new wave of western armies was equivocal. Unlike five years before, he does not seem to have solicited fresh western aid, although his position in Asia Minor remained precarious. In his experience of the intervening years was conceived the fear and distrust of what he later described to his son as 'the commotion coming from the West' that threatened 'the high majesty of the New Rome and the prestige of the Imperial throne'.[10] According to his daughter's apologia much later, Alexius adopted an indulgent but exasperated pose in 1101, keen to avoid armed confrontation near the capital, nervous of his own security, eager to influence the westerners' strategy but prepared to subsidize their efforts by money, advice and men, and reluctantly acquiescing in their plans. As in 1097, he extracted promises that conquests in Asia Minor would be restored to Byzantine sovereignty and obtained from William of Aquitaine's party, at least, oaths of fealty. Apart from logistic help, Alexius could also offer the new crusaders a veteran commander in Raymond of Toulouse, who had been the emperor's guest since the summer of 1100, welcomed as an ally against the increasingly vexatious Norman rulers of Antioch. Raymond helped mediate agreement between Alexius and the unruly Lombards before joining the expedition itself on the arrival of his former comrade Stephen of Blois with the forces from northern France and Burgundy. Together with the small German following of the constable Conrad and a contingent of Turcopoles supplied by Alexius, the crusader army gathered at Nicomedia in early June 1101.

It was later claimed that Alexius had advised against a new assault on the Turks of Asia Minor, urging the westerners to follow the coast road through Byzantine territory to Cilicia and thence to the Holy Land. Western sources describe a fierce debate within the crusader camp, with the veterans Raymond's and Stephen of Blois's argument for a march in the footsteps of the 1097 campaign being overruled by the Lombards, who determined to attempt the rescue of Bohemond, captured by the Danishmends the year before and now held at Niksar, in the north-east of Asia Minor. There were even rumours that the Lombards planned a descent into Iraq to attack Baghdad.[11] Such grandiose schemes, fuelled by an incomprehension of geography or distance and an optimistic reliance on divine favour, however ludicrous in retrospect, were hardly more extravagant than the conquest of Jerusalem may have seemed in 1097, except that now the Turks understood their enemy better. They avoided battles and presented a more united front, the Danishmends being joined by troops from Aleppo and Harran in northern Iraq. However, the Lombard decision to free Bohemund, while offering the prospect of the release of the finest field commander of his generation, opened the prospect of reigniting the feud with Count Raymond. Yet, paradoxically, Raymond may have gone along with the plan, hoping to negotiate a favourable deal in Syria with a grateful and obligated Bohemund.

This western force, declining to await the other armies even then arriving at Constantinople, left Nicomedia around 3 June, carrying with them the Milanese relics of St Ambrose and Raymond's Holy Lance from Antioch. After capturing Ankara on 23 June, the crusaders headed north-east to Chankiri, which proved too strong to take. Thereafter, constantly harried by troops of the Seljuk sultan Kilij Arslan, the westerners fought on painfully until they encountered the main Turkish army of Danishmends and their allies near Merzifon early in August. After days of fierce fighting, Turkish pressure proved too much, panic causing the Christian army to disintegrate. Only a few of the leaders, including Raymond of Toulouse, Stephen of Blois and the archbishop of Milan and their military entourages, escaped to limp back to Constantinople; the infantry, the women and civilians and many knights were massacred.

The other armies fared no better. William of Aquitaine, who had left home in March, joined forces en route to Constantinople with Welf of Bavaria arriving at the Byzantine capital just as the Lombards were leaving Nicomedia in early June. A few days later they were joined by William of Nevers, who, for unknown reasons, decided to try to catch up with the Lombard army. By the time the Nivernais force reached Ankara, William abandoned the pursuit, turning south towards Konya and the main route to Syria. After fighting off Turks, presumably of Kilij Arslan, William reached Konya in mid-August. Finding his force insufficient to capture or intimidate the city, and too vulnerable to await the Aquitainians and Bavarians, William decided on a dash for Cilicia, pressing on to Ereghli, where his army was surrounded and destroyed. Once again the cavalry abandoned the infantry and non-combatants to their fate; once again the leaders escaped, ultimately finding their way, destitute, to Antioch.

Hard on the Nivernais' heels came the large army of William of Aquitaine and Welf of Bavaria, which included Hugh of Vermandois and, more exotically, Ida, dowager margravine of Austria. At Constantinople, rumours about the Lombards' fate persuaded some nervous Germans sensibly but expensively to embark by sea for the Holy Land; according to one them, the chronicler Ekkehard abbot of Aura, they reached Jaffa in six weeks.[12] Their comrades who chose the land route set out in mid-July along the route of the First Crusade from Nicaea, to Dorylaeum, Philomelium and Konya. Despite careful and extensive preparations, once they were out of Byzantine territory food quickly ran out, and Turkish attacks intensified. Reaching Ereghli at the beginning of September, the Christians were surprised by Kilij Arslan's army and routed. Many of the leaders, equipped with finer horses and loyal servants, escaped with their lives if not their dignity or possessions. Hugh of Vermandois died of his wounds at Tarsus; Archbishop Thiemo of Salzburg was captured and later, according to popular legend, martyred; and Ida of Austria disappeared, most likely killed but later rumoured to have ended her days in a Muslim prince's harem, the medieval west being almost as obsessed by titillating images of Muslim sexual predatoriness and licence as by their blasphemy, stories of miscegenation proving especially popular. The survivors of the Ereghli disaster, including William of Aquitaine, struggled through to Cilicia and thence to Antioch. Once in Syria, having helped Raymond of Toulouse capture the port of Tortosa, the aristocratic remnants of the three armies fulfilled their vows as pilgrims. Many returned home bankrupt in pocket and reputation. A few stayed to assist the new king of Jerusalem, Baldwin I, sharing in his mauling by the Egyptians at Ramla in May 1102, and, like the hapless Stephen of Blois, finding a martyr's crown or, like Arpin, viscount of Bourges, a Fatimid prison.

If nothing was gained by the 1101 expeditions, thousands of lives and *livres* were lost together with the westerners' local reputation for invincibility and further trust of the Greeks, who were glibly cast as scapegoats for the failure alongside the sins of the participants. Yet the campaigns possessed a wider significance. While establishing a topos of theologically explicable failure in terms of the moral deficiencies of those involved, in practical terms it imposed limits on eastern ambitions. The Lombards had envisaged capturing Baghdad; Urban II had allegedly encouraged the Milanese to think of conquering Egypt. Such dreams of a Christian conquest of the Near East died in the hills above Merzifon and the marshes around Ereghli. The enterprise of the Holy Land remained thereafter practically confined to securing Syria and Palestine; larger schemes were devised in the twelfth and later centuries, especially involving the power on the Nile, but the events of 1101 showed that Urban II's revolution of history could turn only so far.

THE ESTABLISHMENT OF LATIN RULE

The Holy Land the westerners sought to control and defend possessed geographic but not political definition. The territory that at various times came under Latin rulers in the century after 1097 stretched some 600 miles from the Gulf of Alexandretta and Cilicia in the north to the Gulf of Aqaba on the Red Sea in the south. Dominating the region is a chain of mountains running from the tall Amanus and Nosairi ranges, rising to 9,000 feet, in the north, through the parallel Lebanon and Anti-Lebanon mountains flanking the Biqa valley in the centre, to the hills of Samaria and Judea in the south, which, though lower, still rise in places to over 3,000 feet. To the west stretches a narrow, fertile coastal plain, occasionally interrupted by tongues of hill country, as along the Lebanese shore and at Haifa, irrigated by the released winter rainfall brought to the highlands by the prevailing westerly winds. To the east the mountains are bounded by a deep depression carrying the valleys of the Orontes, the Litani and the Jordan, which, except where the Anti-Lebanon rises beyond the Biqa, gives way to a plateau, fertile in places such as eastern Galilee, before the landscape merges with treeless scrub bordering the desert that stands to the east and south. In southern Palestine, where the coastal plain is wider, the hills descend gently to meet the formidable Negev desert. There were few roads from the coast to the interior, the chief routes leading from St Symeon via Antioch to Aleppo; from Tripoli to Homs; from Tyre to the Biqa; and from Acre to Galilee and on to Damascus. Although both the hills and plains were more forested than in later centuries, and many areas were agriculturally fertile and productive, particularly the coastal strip, the Orontes valley and Galilee, the climate, especially in the south, was unforgiving when compared with the areas many of the western settlers had left behind, with scorching dry summers and, as Stephen of Blois had discovered to his surprise, cool, wet winters.[13] Summer in Jerusalem, high in the Judean hills, could see midday temperatures daily reach the 90s F (mid-30s C), with an average in July and August of over 75 F (25 C), but in mid-winter see average temperatures in the mid-40s F (*c.*8 C) with frost at night. The coast, although milder in winter, experiences considerable humidity in summer, while the rift valley at Jericho and the Dead Sea, well over 1,000 feet below sea level, is stifling in summer, with temperatures well above 100 degrees F.

The physical context exerted a profound influence on power and settlement. It was a relatively small space that the westerners came to occupy, in area comparable with England or a medium-sized state in the USA, such as New York or Alabama. Even in the twelfth century, when summer military campaigns in Europe could cover hundreds of miles, Outremer was a narrow region. Warfare was intimate, witnessed by the long succession of captured Frankish commanders who languished sometimes for years in Muslim prisons. (Whether from Frankish charity, violence, incompetence or chance, few if any Muslim generals suffered similar indignities in return.) The western obsession with the region created its own imaginary space of boundless extent, a liminal world of religious contest, aliens and otherness in which usually level-headed eyewitnesses such as Fulcher of Chartres, a Jerusalem resident for over a quarter of a century, felt compelled to locate marvellous fantastical beasts against the evidence of his own eyes: basilisks, Capricorns, chimeras, dragons, etc.[14] The mundane reality determined a costive high politics at once sensitive, vulnerable and dependent on intruders from outside. Cities were crowded except where, as in Jerusalem, religion and strategy dictated social exclusion. Yet, despite the smallness of scale, and the absence of any directed policy of immigration from the west (in contrast to other areas of western conquest in Spain, the Baltic or Sicily), previous depopulation and some Muslim emigration allowed for limited but not negligible western colonization.

In terms of agricultural opportunities, while Antioch and Galilee were prosperous, the rural economy of Palestine scarcely matched that of the north and western Mediterranean, where many settlers came from. However, exploitation of the natural resources sustained an economy centred on towns, cities and trade with a prominent role for money. Power followed wealth, the fragmentation of Fatimid and Seljuk control over the region re-emphasizing the importance of the sea-ports – Acre, Tyre, Sidon, Beirut – and the linked commercial emporia of the interior, such as Aleppo and Damascus. For centuries rule had been exercised by foreign interlopers with little or no interest in creating new structures of government. Despite the political chaos of the later eleventh century, the continuity imposed by geography and economics was reflected in an underlying administrative organization left largely undisturbed by successive conquerors: the Byzantine district (*civitas*) of Caesarea of the seventh century lay behind the twelfth-century lordship of Caesarea; the Roman province of Palaestina Secunda corresponded with the Palestinian boundaries of the principality of Galilee.[15] Socially, economically and religiously, village life, outside war zones, remained largely undisturbed. Nevertheless, to enjoy the benefits of dominion, the new invaders, like their predecessors, needed to master the strongpoints, the markets and the trade routes. This required manpower, precisely what the newcomers lacked.

When most of the surviving first crusaders left Syria in the late summer of 1099, western conquests comprised the county of Edessa, the remote Franco-Armenian condominium ruled by Baldwin of Boulogne straddling the upper Euphrates; Bohemund's principality in northern Syria, based on Antioch and the lower Orontes valley but with ostensible interests in Cilicia; and a narrow stretch of land in Judea and Samaria running along the west bank of the river Jordan from the Sea of Galilee to the Dead Sea, including Tiberias, Nablus, Jerusalem, Bethlehem and Hebron, which was linked to the sea by a neck of territory surrounding the road down from the Holy City to the port of Jaffa, the nascent kingdom of Jerusalem ruled by Godfrey of Bouillon, assisted by Tancred of Lecce. In addition there remained elements of the Provençal army with Count Raymond, desperate for his own sovereign conquest; a large Pisan war fleet that had brought the new papal legate Daimbert of Pisa; and detachments of Greek troops, such as the garrison at Lattakiah, trying to make good Alexius's broken-backed policy of imposing his own overlordship in the wake of the Christian invasion of Syria. While Bohemund's military establishment appeared capable of sustained aggression, Baldwin of Edessa relied on his small, perforce tight-knit entourage of knights supported by successful diplomacy and local alliances. Together, on their pilgrimage to Jerusalem at Christmas 1099, Bohemund and Baldwin were apparently able to muster an impressive company, of hundreds perhaps even thousands, but only because it was greatly swelled by the Italians accompanying Archbishop Daimbert. In Jerusalem, Duke Godfrey had been left with as few as 300 knights and 2,000 infantry, the westerners occupying barely more than one street in the devastated city outside the manned fortifications. Manpower was insufficient to clear away all the corpses from the July massacre; the carcasses and stench of putrefaction remained evident to visitors over five months later. For some years later, visiting pilgrims noted the remains of corpses littering the roads, the devastation around Jerusalem and the constant fear of Muslim attack.[16] Although, as Tancred showed by annexing Galilee in the summer of 1099, some said with little more than a score of knights, small bands could operate effectively in the chaotic political conditions of ill-defended rural Palestine, protection of the Christian enclaves, especially Jerusalem, let alone securing their stability by extending their frontiers to stronger natural boundaries, depended on help from outside, particularly from the west. Generations successfully maintaining and expanding their holdings failed to obscure the central strategic fact. Militarily, Outremer was never entirely self-sufficient, its survival relying initially on transient western soldiers, sailors and pilgrims; then settlers from Europe; later new military orders, recruited and funded from the west, and western investment in the form of western endowments for Holy Land religious houses; and, throughout, Christian fleets, notably from north Italian maritime cities. Just as the early conquests along the Levantine coast relied on Italian sea-power and often pilgrims' muscle, so the army that faced Saladin in the final crisis of the twelfth-century kingdom of Jerusalem in July 1187 contained visiting crusaders, troops of the Templars and Hospitallers funded from Europe and local mercenaries paid with money deposited in Jerusalem by sympathetic western rulers.

Nowhere was this dependence on the west more obvious than in the conquest of the coast between 1099 and 1124, where the capture of ports relied on foreign maritime assistance as allies or mercenaries: Jaffa in 1099 (Pisa); Haifa in 1100 (Venice); Arsuf and Caesarea in 1101 (Genoa); Tortosa and Jubail in 1102 (Genoa); Lattakiah in 1103 (Genoa); Acre in 1104 (Genoa); Tripoli in 1109 (Genoa and Provence); Beirut in 1110 (Genoa and Pisa); Sidon in 1110 (Norwegian); Tyre in 1124 (Venice). Without a fleet, as at Tyre in 1111, or where a fleet was repulsed, as at Sidon in 1108, land attacks failed. The crucial importance of the maritime cities in the establishment of the Frankish principalities on the Levant coast was reflected in the privileges afforded them in the conquered cities, such as the Genoese at Antioch (1098), Jubail (1102) and Acre (1104) or the Venetians at Tyre in 1124, where they were rewarded with a third of the city and its territory. Along with the Pisans, the Genoese and Venetians gained privileged access to ports and markets, received extensive property and rights of jurisdiction over their own nationals, which allowed them to create more or less immune quarters in chosen maritime cities in which visiting merchants could stay and from which they could trade. Such was the importance of the Genoese in the creation of the kingdom of Jerusalem under its first king, Baldwin I, that later in the century they were able to make good a spurious claim that their contributions had been commemorated by an inscription erected in the church of the Holy Sepulchre.[17]

The conquest of the coast did not immediately lead to the peaceful occupation of the hinterland; the road from Jaffa to Jerusalem, the slopes of Mt Carmel and the Lebanon remained unsafe for a generation and more. Banditry, from both sides of the frontier, persisted, as did raids by neighbouring rulers. However, with the occupation of the coastal ports came security of the lifelines with the west and control of the main trade routes with the interior. Although until late in the century return on commerce probably disappointed the Italian investors, without such a hold the settlements could not have survived financially, economically or demographically. Strategically, each port gained reduced the scope of Egyptian fleets; the loss of Tyre prevented the Fatimids from threatening the trade and pilgrim routes between the Holy Land, Cyprus, Byzantium and western Europe.

It is often argued that the Italian involvement in the Holy Land venture reveals sordid materialism, even nascent capitalism at odds with devotion to the crusading ideal. This is nonsense. The typology of a conflict between 'medieval' faith and 'modern' commercialism is meaningless; faith is as much a feature of the modern world as materialism was of the medieval. At best such generalizations are literary conventions; at worst a form of condescending historical snobbery. Either way, such views belie the evidence. Writers such as the twelfth-century Genoese Caffaro suggest civic patriotism, but his *Liberation of the East* (*De Liberatione Civitatum Orientis*) and most of the other evidence available point to a mix of religious idealism and perceived self-interest familiar in many other crusaders.[18] The Italian presence in the east predated 1095; there was an Amalfitan hospital in Jerusalem in the early 1070s. The involvement of the maritime cities formed part of a process whereby the eastern Mediterranean was opened to western interests, a process that embraced the military, colonial and pious as well, the Italian merchant and the crusader playing complementary, related roles. The investment in fleets was great; the chance of disaster strong; the financial risks huge; the returns uncertain. With the resulting profits hardly matching expectations until late in the century, the Genoese privatized their holdings in Lattakiah, Jubail, Antioch and Acre to the Embriaco family, while the Venetians made over their rural possessions around Tyre to the Contarini.[19] The accusation that the privileges granted the Italians constituted them as states within a state, apparent in the thirteenth century, cannot be sustained for periods of strong secular rule in the twelfth. The commitment of these cities and their citizens to the Holy Land was neither more nor less idealistic than their fellow Latin Christians. The idea that enthusiasm for the cross failed to penetrate these bastions of early capital is inherently unlikely, based on a flawed model of human behaviour and contradicted by the evidence.

The conquest of the coast formed part of an often desperate struggle to maintain the initial conquests in Syria and Palestine from a plethora of enemies: Byzantium; the Seljuks of Iraq; the Turks of Mosul, Aleppo and Damascus; and the Fatimids of Egypt. Well might one of the settlers, Baldwin I's chaplain Fulcher of Chartres, recall in pious wonder: 'why did they not, as innumerable locusts in a little field, so completely devour and destroy us?', a vivid image from one who witnessed in his time in Jerusalem at least three serious plagues of locusts (1114, 1117, 1120).[20] Across the political and religious divide, the issue appeared the same. While contemporary Muslim poets satisfied themselves with extravagant lamentations on the violence and devastation wreaked by the Franks in successive massacres of civilian populations in the cities captured from 1098 onwards, the Damascene lawyer al-Sulami, writing *c.*1105, shrewdly noted their weakness: 'the small amount of cavalry and equipment they have at their disposal and the distance from which their reinforcements come'. He concluded that this presented 'an opportunity which must be seized at once'.[21] The Muslim rulers of Syria and Palestine needed little encouragement, less out of religious zeal promoted by the heightened rhetoric of fear and outrage, often generated by refugees from the conquered areas, than from motives of political and commercial self-interest. Although the Frankish policy of massacre and exclusion of Muslims from the cities they captured up to 1110 differed from customary behaviour, politically they were treated less exceptionally. The impression left by the twelfth-century chronicle of Ibn al-Qalanisi of Damascus, a centre for Palestinian refugees, is of the Franks as one of many fractious groups in a region of competing princelings, each jockeying for advantage. Ironically, the western interlopers immediately offered an additional diplomatic and military option for many Muslim rulers eager for allies, especially in the chronic rivalries between Mosul, Aleppo and Damascus. The creation of Christian Outremer, therefore, revolved around military security, but not just its own.

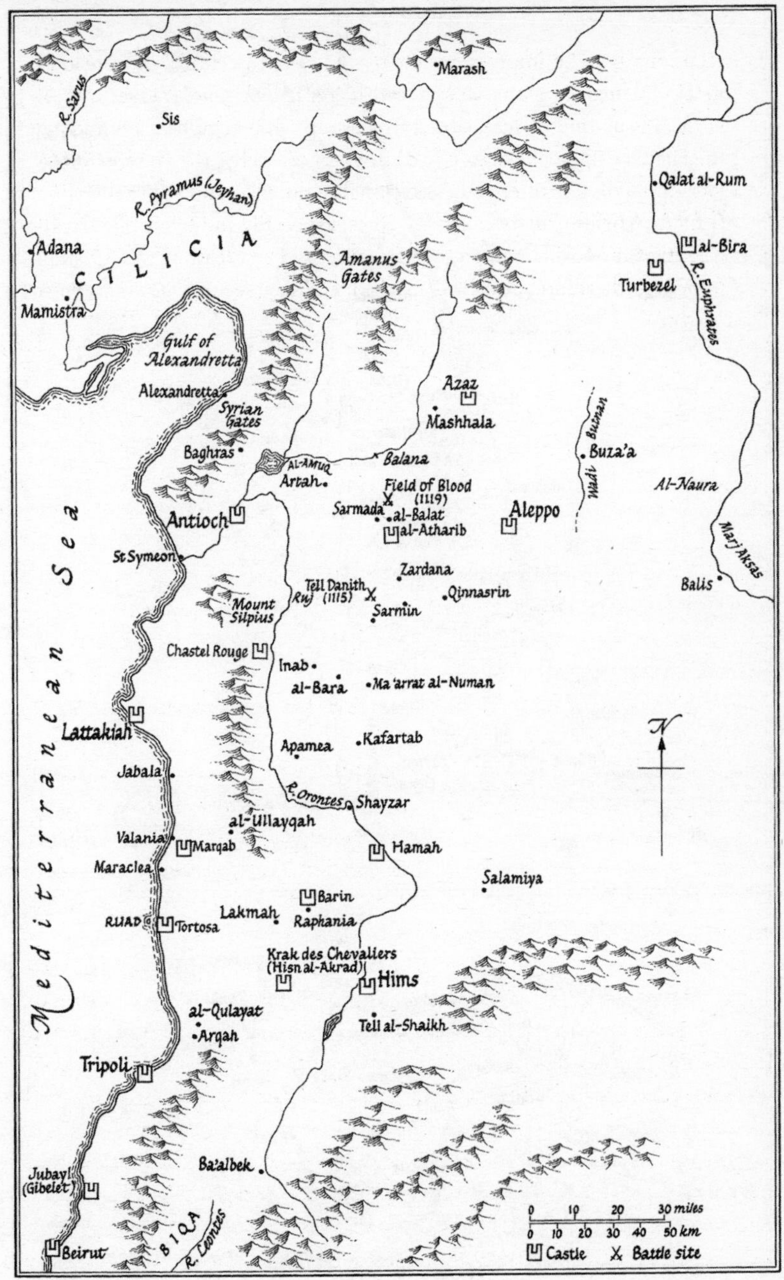

6. Syria in the Twelfth Century

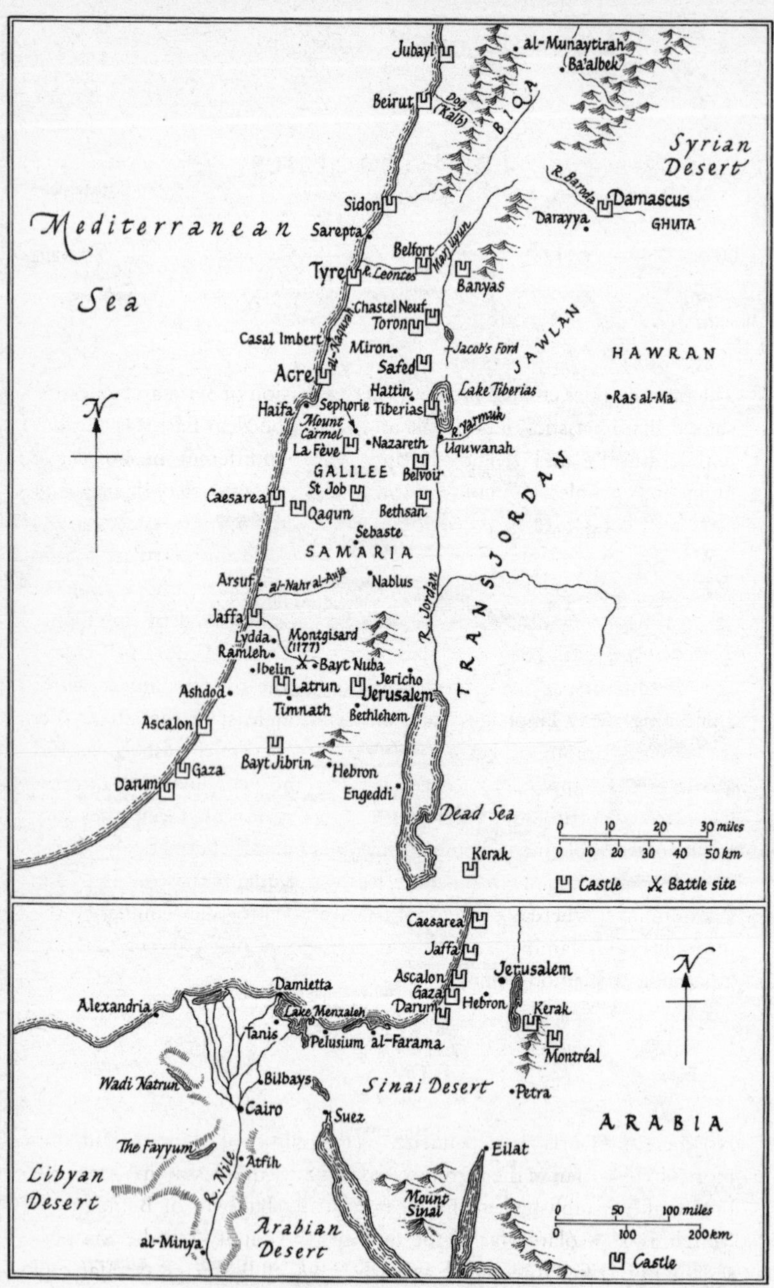

7. Palestine and Egypt in the Twelfth Century

6

The Latin States

The principalities created by the western invasion of Syria and Palestine shared characteristics of both east and west. The Near East was familiar with culturally and religiously alien elites indifferent or hostile to indigenous peoples, content to rule a heterogeneous society by means of absentee landownership, control of trade and military coercion. As exploiters, not proselytes or social engineers, Levantine rulers forged contacts across communal divisions from convenience, not conviction. The Latins, or Franks as they were more usually called by onlookers, were no different. Their new aristocracy and settlers could not ignore their neighbours; as one of them remarked in the 1120s, a *lingua franca* combining many languages soon emerged, at least in the cities.[1] Yet the political idiom of Latin rule remained severely western, as did the laws they applied to themselves and the vocabulary of government. Consequently, the vision of Outremer is bifocal. Twelfth-century Latin accounts portray a political society apparently hermetically sealed from its immediate environment, a western drama played out in exotic surroundings, whereas contemporary Arabic chronicles emphasize the normality and familiarity of Latin behaviour, one parvenu military governing elite among many.

EDESSA

Nowhere was Christian dependence on the politics of Islamic neighbours more obvious than in the fortunes of the county of Edessa, the first Latin principality established in the Near East, by Baldwin of Boulogne in March 1098. Isolated far in the interior, the county relied upon possession of fortified towns such as Turbessel (Tell Bashir), Ravendan and

Edessa, from where the fertile countryside of the Euphrates basin could be exploited and the sensibilities of the Armenian lords influenced. As a bastion defending the eastern flank of Antioch and even a potential base for assaults into northern Iraq, the county assumed great strategic importance, which was also the source of its vulnerability. For warlords from Mosul or Mardin to the east or Aleppo to the south, Edessa presented a tempting target in itself as well as a staging post on any more concerted attack on the Christian holdings towards the coast. The county's survival depended on unity among its Frankish nobility; cooperation with local Armenian lords, some of whom looked to Byzantium to guarantee their status and authority; alliances with Antioch and some, at least, of its Muslim neighbours; and, crucially, disunity among the rulers of northern Syria, the Jazira and Iraq.[2]

In 1100, when Baldwin of Boulogne succeeded his brother Godfrey as ruler of Jerusalem, Edessa devolved on to his cousin, Baldwin of Le Bourcq, who did homage to the new king for the county. After consolidating his position by marrying a local Armenian princess, Morphia of Melitene, in 1102, the new count was joined by another cousin, Joscelin of Courtenay, a veteran of the count of Nevers's crusade of 1101, to whom he gave all the county west of the Euphrates around Turbessel as a fief, thus making him almost a partner. Over the next two years, while Mosul battled with Mardin after the death of Kerbogha and further internecine feuding distracted the Seljuks of Baghdad, Joscelin as much as Count Baldwin campaigned successfully to extend Frankish rule northwards towards Armenian Marasch and south in the direction of Aleppo. In 1104, this aggression was abruptly ended when Soqman of Mardin joined with his erstwhile enemies of Mosul to crush a substantial combined Edessan/Antiochene force attempting to capture Harran, south-east of Edessa. Both Count Baldwin and Joscelin were captured. The dangers of Muslim unity were starkly underlined.

During Count Baldwin's captivity (1104–8), Edessa was ruled first by Tancred and then, after Bohemund's departure for the west in 1105, another Hauteville relative, Richard of Salerno. Tancred, busily extending the principality of Antioch in his uncle's absence, clearly hoped to annexe Edessa; it made strategic sense.[3] Consequently, on Baldwin's release, relations between Edessa and Antioch were strained beyond breaking, with Tancred trying to assert a spurious legal claim to overlordship over the county. In 1108–9, both sides to the dispute probably called on Muslim military aid, Baldwin from his former captors at Mosul, Tancred from Aleppo. Baldwin's relations with the increasingly independent Joscelin of Courtenay also deteriorated. Joscelin was arrested and exiled, Baldwin I of Jerusalem characteristically promptly recruiting him to the lordship of Galilee. However, the major invasions by Mawdud of Mosul each year between 1110 and 1113 and Tancred's death in 1112 engineered a reconciliation between Antioch and Edessa, sealed by the marriage of Count Baldwin's sister to Tancred's successor, Roger of Salerno. At the victory of Tell Danith over Bursuq of Hamadan in 1115, Count Baldwin fought side by side with the Antiochenes. Edessa's position relative to Antioch improved further after the accession of Count Baldwin to the throne of Jerusalem in 1118, due partly to the intrigues of Joscelin of Courtenay who, despite his exile in 1113, was rewarded with the county of Edessa itself. After Roger of Antioch's defeat and death at the battle known to westerners as the Field of Blood in 1119, when Baldwin II, as king, assumed the regency of Antioch, Joscelin emerged as the strongest Frankish leader in northern Syria, probably even on occasion acting as regent of Antioch himself. Although briefly held captive by Balak of Aleppo in 1123, Count Joscelin commanded a combined forced from all four Latin principalities in the same year in an attempt to free King Baldwin, who had suffered a similar fate shortly after the count. Until the king's release in 1124, Joscelin cut the leading secular figure in Outremer. Thereafter he continued to play a prominent role, joining with Baldwin II in attacking Aleppo in 1124–5 and Damascus in 1129. This did not prevent him from asserting his rights against fellow Christians by force, if necessary, or, as in 1127 during a dispute with the new prince of Antioch, Bohemund II, with the assistance of the Turks. The story of Joscelin's death in 1131 provided Outremer with one of its epic tales. Infuriated by his son's cowardice in the face of an attack from Anatolia, Joscelin, seriously ill and bedridden, insisted on leading out his troops borne on a litter. Seeing this, the invaders hurriedly withdrew. On receiving the news, Joscelin, ordering his litter to be put down on the road, died giving thanks to God.[4]

The failure of the Franks to take Aleppo in 1125 opened the way instead to the new atabeg of Mosul, Imad al-Din Zengi, to resolve the anarchy in the city by occupying it in 1128. The settled union of Mosul and Aleppo posed a serious threat to Edessa, especially after the Franks' failure in 1129 to take Damascus, which now attracted Zengi's attention.

Although primarily concerned with affairs further east and the politics of the Seljuk Baghdad sultanate, Zengi steadily increased his hold on the eastern frontiers of northern Outremer. In 1137 he captured the Frankish castle of Montferrand (Ba 'rin), the important Muslim city of Homs in 1138 and the strategically significant town of Baalbek in the Biqa valley in 1140, where he installed as garrison commander a Kurdish mercenary, Naim al-Din Ayyub, Saladin's father. The failure of an uneasy Byzantine/Antiochene/Edessan army to capture Aleppo and Shaizar in 1138 removed Greek intervention in Syria for a generation but allowed Zengi a free hand, with Damascus compelling its ruler Unur to arrange a treaty with King Fulk of Jerusalem in 1139. This increased concentration on the south left Edessa vulnerable.

Joscelin II, no great general, continued his father's active diplomacy with Muslim and Armenian neighbours, but his county appeared fair game for Turkish raiders from north, east and south. The adverse economic effect of this on the county weakened Joscelin's political hold on his Syrian and Armenian subjects and his capacity to sustain mercenaries. The political chaos in Antioch in the 1130s and the loosening of the intimate ties with Jerusalem on the death of Baldwin II in 1131 left Edessa further exposed, its viability depending more than ever on external military aid. It is perhaps significant that the Franks of Edessa, few in number and reliant on non-Frankish subjects and allies, appear not to have begun a substantial programme of stone castle building. The evidence from the Frankish stronghold of Turbessel is inconclusive, but at Edessa itself existing fortifications seem to have sufficed with local modifications. In 1122, the Armenian governor of the city, Vasil, constructed a new tower, round after an Armenian design.[5] The absence of new fortifications did not mean that the counts of Edessa were defenceless, rather that, unlike their peers elsewhere across Outremer, they lacked the wealth to undertake new building projects.

Yet the downfall of the county resulted from an opportunist raid rather than systemic collapse, although it occurred through Latin weakness and Edessan diplomacy. The kingdom of Jerusalem was embroiled in internal difficulties following the sudden death of King Fulk in 1143. Antioch, although spared a fresh Byzantine invasion by the death of John II Comnenus in 1143, remained preoccupied, relations between Joscelin II and Prince Raymond of Antioch later described as being of 'insatiable hatred'.[6] Joscelin II's alliances with Muslims opposed to Zengi gave the atabeg an excuse to attack the eastern frontier of the county in the autumn of 1144 when the count was away from Edessa on campaign towards Aleppo. Edessa itself held out for a bare four weeks before falling to Zengi on Christmas Eve 1144. Despite cursory attempts at reconquest, the county east of the Euphrates was lost. Joscelin retained the western half, based on Turbessel, where his father had begun forty years earlier. Despite the murder of Zengi in 1146, the failure of the Second Crusade (1146–8), civil war in Jerusalem and the defeat and death of Raymond of Antioch at Inab in 1149 left the rump of the county exposed. In 1150, Joscelin was captured by troops of Zengi's son Nur al-Din and imprisoned for the remaining nine years of his life in Aleppo, allegedly having to endure regular torture. His wife read the signs and sold her remaining forts to the Greek emperor Manuel I in 1150. These were overrun by Nur al-Din the following year. The Christian bulwark to the east that had posed a potential threat to the heartlands of Turkish power was lost for ever, a sign that the political chaos of the early twelfth century that had permitted, even encouraged, the political opportunism of the first two Baldwins and Joscelin I was giving place to an ominous and growing Muslim unity in Syria that challenged all Latin Outremer.

ANTIOCH

Like the county of Edessa, the principality of Antioch owed its creation to the secular impulses of the First Crusade. Any talk of Antioch as the first see of St Peter tended to be suppressed by a jealous papacy. Like Edessa, too, politics and society in Antioch followed indigenous patterns: Greek, Armenian and Muslim. Formed out of the ambitions and rivalries of the great western army of invasion in 1097–8, the principality survived by adapting and exploiting local conditions to forge a more pluralist polity than elsewhere in Outremer, embracing Greek and Sicilian institutional practices, in which marcher lords, vassals, tenants and administrators were western European, Armenian and even Muslim. Antioch's vigorous independent identity sat uneasily between regular Byzantine claims to overlordship and the repeated need for the kings of Jerusalem to rescue the principality from succession crises as prince after prince proved extraordinarily accident-prone and unlucky. Although its politics, self-image and strategic position allied its fortunes with the Holy Land, Antioch could not escape its ties with Byzantium nor its interests in Cilicia, its enforced acceptance of Byzantine suzerainty in 1137, 1145 and 1158–9 in many ways ensuring its autonomy from Jerusalem.[7]

Bohemund's establishment of his control over Antioch in 1098–9 seemed to offer the prospect of the recreation of the pre-1084 Byzantine administrative region, or *theme*, based on the city. However, he confronted stern obstacles. In Cilicia his influence faced challenge from the Byzantine emperor and the local Armenian nobility keen to win independence by playing off Greek against Latin. On the Syrian coast and to the south and east of Antioch towards the frontier with Aleppo, Raymond of Toulouse and the Byzantines competed for dominion. By the time Bohemund was captured by the Danishmends in August 1100 attempting to relieve Melitene, he had lost control of Cilicia and Lattakiah to the Greeks and failed to exert clear authority over al-Bara and Ma 'arrat. Thereafter, its charismatic founder exercised very little influence on the formation of the principality. In a Danishmend prison between 1100 and 1103, disastrously defeated at Harran in 1104, Bohemund left the east for good early in 1105 to chase his destiny against Byzantium.

The real founder of the principality of Antioch was Bohemund's nephew, Tancred of Lecce, regent 1101–3 then effectively prince 1105–12. Despite numerous reversals, by the time of his death Tancred had recovered Cilicia; extended Antiochene overlordship over Armenian princes to the north; incorporated the Ruj valley and the Jabal as-Summaq after defeating the Aleppans at Artah in 1105; effectively annexed Edessa between 1104 and 1108; occupied the ports of Lattakiah, Baniyas and, briefly, Jubail; pushed Antiochene frontiers east of the Jabal Talat and south to Apamea to threaten Aleppo and Shaizar respectively, both cities at various times paying tribute to the princes of Antioch. Despite his failed attempt to defy King Baldwin I over Edessa in 1109–10 and coming off worse in the succession dispute in Tripoli in 1109, Tancred's Antioch dominated northern Syria, sufficiently strong to withstand the invasions of Mawdud of Mosul (1110–13); he was confident that the tactic of avoiding pitched battles would not destroy the inner cohesion of his territories. A network of marcher lordships strung along the borders afforded protection to the central areas of the

Orontes valley, even when the frontiers themselves were breached. After one such incursion in 1115, Roger of Salerno won a crushing victory at Tell Danith over Bursuq of Hamadan, commander of an army sent by the sultan in Baghdad, to resecure the vulnerable south-eastern frontier. Lasting security received attention with Prince Roger's capture of the castles at Saone, Balatonos and Marqab. In 1119, Roger's luck ran out when Il-Ghazi of Mardin annihilated the Antiochene army at the Field of Blood. However, even this revealed the principality's strength. Roger had foolishly not waited for reinforcements from the south before equally rashly seeking a pitched battle. Yet Baldwin II contrived to retrieve the situation through the continued resistance of the frontier garrisons buying him time and the efficiency of the general mobilization he ordered at Antioch, and not, as some contemporaries suggested, because the victorious Il-Ghazi was an irredeemable bingeing sot.[8]

The survival of Antioch after the disaster of 1119 revealed the character of the regime built by Tancred and Roger. The administration displayed continuities with its Byzantine predecessor, as in the office of duke, *dux*, in the city of Antioch, while the princely household offices – chancellor, seneschal, chamberlain – were reminiscent of similar positions in southern and northern Norman courts in the west, perhaps unsurprisingly as many of the lords enfeoffed in the principality can be traced to Normandy or southern Italy and Sicily. Some may have gathered around Tancred during his adventurous career on the First Crusade and his territorial forays in Judea and Galilee. Others may have been supporters of Bohemund in 1098. Most importantly, the Antioch baronage appeared consistently loyal to their princes in the formative period of Frankish rule and thereafter to the principality's independent integrity. In 1135, the barons rejected overtures made to Byzantium by the wilful dowager Princess Alice. In 1161–3 they forced her flighty daughter Constance to install her son Bohemund III as prince.[9] The constant threat of invasion and dispossession; the vigorous personal support provided by the princes; and the lack of central interference in the workings of their lordships encouraged baronial loyalty. Rainald Masoir built up a strong lordship in the south of the principality, centred on Baniyas and Marqab. Despite the uncertainties and chaos after 1119, he associated himself with the regency government of Baldwin II and, after the arrival of the young Bohemund II in 1126, rose in princely favour to become constable in 1127, uniquely as a substantial landowner holding a household office. In the early 1130s, after the death of Bohemund II in battle (1130), Rainald acted as regent for a few years. The rewards were obvious. Rainald's origins are obscure, yet his son was considered grand enough to marry the daughter of the count of Tripoli and his wife, Cecilia, was the widow of Tancred and illegitimate daughter of King Philip I, the Fat, of France.[10]

Just as they relied on cooperation with the prince, Antiochene marcher lords, as elsewhere in Outremer, could not afford to adopt an inflexible siege mentality towards their Muslim neighbours. Robert FitzFulk, known as the Leper, held, among other properties, the fortress of Zardana on the frontier with Aleppo. Unsurprisingly, he established alliances with those Muslim rulers hostile to Aleppo, including Il-Ghazi of Mardin and Tughtegin, atabeg of Damascus, joining them in a military compact in 1115. Tughtegin was even remembered as being Robert's friend, although this did not prevent him personally decapitating Robert in 1119.[11] Less fraught were relations between Alan, lord of al-Atharib, another frontier fort between Antioch and Aleppo, and his Muslim physician, the chronicler Hamdan Ibn Abd al-Rahmin (*c.*1071–1147/8) whose reward for healing Alan was the grant of a village and its revenues. Hamdan assisted in regional administration, at one point presiding over the *diwan* (writing office) at Ma 'arrat al-Nu 'man. However, Hamdan's opportunism matched that of any Frank. In 1128, he transferred his allegiance to Zengi at Aleppo, returning to administer the same border region he had previously managed for the Christians after its conquest by his new master.[12] Hamdan was unusual but not unique. In 1118, Prince Roger granted three villages to a local Muslim sheikh.[13] The rhetoric of holy war, so favoured by clerical observers such as the Antiochene chancellor Walter in his account of the vicissitudes of Prince Roger, concealed inter-faith cooperation and mutual self-interest, as in the joint campaign by Prince Roger, Tughtegin of Damascus and Il-Ghazi of Mardin against the Seljuks in 1115.[14]

Internally, the non-Latin Christian communities presented not dissimilar problems and opportunities. Unlike further south in Outremer, the Muslim peasantry under Antiochene rule was probably in a minority. Greek influence was strong in language, custom, identity and religion, especially in the city of Antioch itself. However, accommodation between Latins and Greeks was complicated by the Byzantine claim to overlordship, which may have precipitated the departure of the Greek patriarch of Antioch, John IV the Oxite, in 1100. The Latin ecclesiastical hierarchy in the principality acted as a central institution of Frankish authority, led by the formidable former chaplain of Adhemar of Le Puy, Bernard of Valence (patriarch 1100–1135) and his successor Aimery of Limoges (1140–93), both of whom supplied political as well as spiritual leadership at moments of crisis, such as 1119, 1123, 1130, 1149 and 1161. Division between the secular and ecclesiastical powers weakened each, as during the turbulent patriarchate of Ralph of Domfort (1135–40) or when Prince Reynald turned on Patriarch Aimery in a dispute over exactions from the church to pay for the prince's wars. Aimery, a scholar of international repute, fluent in Greek as in Latin, translator of parts of the Bible into Castilian (the first such translation into any Romance language), was beaten up by Reynald's thugs and left chained out in the sun for a whole day, his bleeding head smeared with honey for the enjoyment of local insects. Unsurprisingly, on being released, Aimery left Antioch for the less barbarous surroundings of Jerusalem, only returning when Reynald had been captured by Nur al-Din in 1161.[15] Such internal squabbles aside, the imposition of a Latin hierarchy in northern Syria followed political conquest and matched the subordination and exploitation of the native Greek-speaking population. The political as well as economic dimension of this subjugation are clearly indicated by the contrastingly less hostile relations the Latin church enjoyed with the Jacobite and Armenian churches, both of which represented no political threat.[16]

The hostility towards the Greeks reflected Antioch's delicate international position. Although Alexius I failed to make good his claim to the city, it was over a decade before Lattakiah was finally wrested from his grasp, before which he had formally extracted recognition of his rights in Antioch from Bohemund under the treaty of Devol in 1108. Bohemund's campaign against Byzantium in 1107–8 in the Balkans, despite widespread support mainly in France, papal authority, indulgences and the declared object of assisting Jerusalem, proved a very damp squib. A long, costly, futile siege of Durazzo ended in a negotiated agreement under which Bohemund accepted tenure of a severely truncated Antioch as Alexius's vassal for life, without the prospect of hereditary reversion, the Norman being compensated with some vague promise of hereditary lands further east. The patriarch of Antioch was to be a Greek Orthodox. To rub salt into the wound, among the witnesses on behalf of the emperor were Italian Normans in Byzantine service, including relatives of Bohemund and veterans of the First Crusade.[17] In fact, the treaty was a dead letter. Bohemund's refusal to return east and Tancred's rejection of the treaty were matched by Byzantine inertia. Apart from tentative moves towards establishing a dynastic alliance in 1119, until the late 1130s Greek action concentrated in Cilicia, although in 1135 the dowager princess of Antioch, the ambitious and meddlesome Alice of Jerusalem, unavailingly proposed another Greek marriage between her daughter, the heiress, and the emperor's son as a means of preserving her own power. Only when the emperors turned their attention and armies towards northern Syria, John II in 1137–8 and 1142 and Manuel I in 1158–9, did Byzantine sovereignty aspire to practical politics, compelling Prince Raymond to perform homage in 1137 and 1145 and Prince Reynald in 1159.[18] For the princes of Antioch, the Greek claim provided an irksome context for their actions; for Outremer possibly a missed opportunity. The running tension over Antioch's disputed status, as well as the internal discrimination against Greeks and the Orthodox church within the principality, inhibited the Latin rulers further south from taking advantage of what remained the most potent twelfth-century Christian power in the eastern Mediterranean. This only changed with the diplomatic rapprochement of the 1160s signalled by the splendid theatre and political insignificance of Manuel I's entry into Antioch in 1159 and his marriage to Bohemund III's sister, Maria of Antioch, in 1161. Where Alexius I and John II sought active control over Antioch, Manuel, worried lest aggression lose him allies in the west, contented himself with acceptance of a distant, benevolent, essentially impotent overlordship. Perhaps he was making a virtue of necessity.

The Byzantines were not alone in their concern with Antioch. Repeated dynastic dislocation inevitably attracted the gaze of other western powers. After Prince Roger's death in 1119, the regency of Baldwin II of Jerusalem secured the succession for Bohemund II, then being brought up in Apulia. On arrival in 1126, Bohemund was married to Baldwin's daughter Alice in a deliberate attempt to consolidate Jerusalem's influence. After Bohemund's death in battle in 1130, apart from his infant child Constance, the nearest Hauteville relative was Roger II of Sicily, first cousin of Bohemund I and a persistent enemy to the Byzantine emperors, who feared Antioch becoming a hostile Sicilian outpost. The new king of Jerusalem, Fulk of Anjou, assumed the traditional role of regent, ensuring neither a Greek nor a Sicilian succession by choosing a Frenchman, Raymond of Poitiers, son of the former crusader William IX of Aquitaine, to marry the Antioch heiress Constance in 1136. Raymond's western affiliations lay with Henry I of England, whose daughter Matilda was married to Fulk of Jerusalem's son Geoffrey. Roger II of Sicily tried to prevent Raymond reaching the east by closing the southern Italian ports to him, the future prince having to resort to disguise and subterfuge to evade capture.[19] Raymond's vigorous rule marked the end of the Norman period in Antioch's rule and effectively the end of direct western interest in the Antioch succession.

Although administratively and tenurially autonomous, Antioch's survival repeatedly depended on interventions by the kings of Jerusalem to prevent the principality succumbing to internecine chaos or Muslim conquest. Baldwin I (in 1109–10, 1111 and 1115), Baldwin II (in 1119–26 and 1130–31), Fulk (in 1131–2 and 1133) and Baldwin III (in 1149, 1150, 1152, 1157, 1158 and 1161) ruled or installed rulers. Formal jurisdictional ties between Antioch and Jerusalem remained confused, complicated by relations of both with Byzantium. However, a presumption of Jerusalem overlordship informed the arbitrations of northern affairs by Baldwin I in 1109 and Baldwin III in 1150, as did the consistent policy of fraternal aid, which, while serving the interests of both parties, revealed a central feature of Outremer's political mentality. The pages of the Antioch chronicler Walter the Chancellor early in the twelfth century and the great Jerusalem writer William of Tyre towards the end of it were alike shot through with the sense of one shared Christian political community stretching from the Cilician mountains to the deserts of Arabia. The importance of Antioch within that community received backhanded recognition in 1130 when Bohemund II's embalmed head was sent by the Danishmend emir as a present to the caliph in Baghdad, a macabre precedent repeated when Nur al-Din delivered Prince Raymond's head and severed arm to the caliph after the battle of Inab in 1149.[20] Antioch was by no means the sick man of the Levant. Each prince conducted vigorous and often successful policies of expansion. Despite its grisly conclusion, Raymond's aggression was continued in the 1150s by his widow's second husband, the adventurer Reynald of Châtillon, who took on both Muslims and, in raiding Cyprus in 1156, Greeks. Yet each prince met an untimely end. Tancred died relatively young. Roger, Bohemund II and Raymond were killed in battles of their own choosing. Reynald's opportunism led to sixteen years in an Aleppan prison. Their fates and the survival of their principality unconquered for another century serve as a paradigm for Christian rule in Outremer, at once fragile and tenacious.

TRIPOLI

The existence of the county of Tripoli owed everything to the determination and tenacity of Raymond of Toulouse; its continued identity to the interests of the kings of Jerusalem, the wider strategic needs of Outremer and the ambitions of Raymond's squabbling Provençal heirs. Having been forced out of Antioch (1098–9), Jerusalem (1099) and Lattakiah (1102), Raymond, accompanied by veterans of the 1101 crusades, looked further south, capturing Tortosa in 1102. From 1103, he focused on Tripoli, then the major port for Damascus, as the centre of a new lordship, laying siege to the city. Raymond built a large castle on a ridge a couple of miles from the port called Mount Pilgrim, known in Arabic to this day as Qal'at Sanjil, the castle of St Gilles. Raymond of St Gilles, count of Toulouse, so often thwarted by his contemporaries, might have been content with this demotic accolade of posterity. His castle of Mount Pilgrim was to stay in Christian hands continuously from 1103 to 1289, longer than any other in mainland Outremer.[21]

When Raymond died in 1105, Tripoli still uncaptured, his followers chose as their lord his cousin, William-Jordan count of Cerdagne, despite the presence at Mount Pilgrim of the count's infant son, Alfonso-Jordan, and the existence of a bastard son, Bertrand, who had been ruling Toulouse for a decade on his father's behalf. William-Jordan's succession reflected a common problem in Outremer, where presence and possession perforce constituted the law. In Jerusalem in the early days after the conquest, absence or occupation determined ownership (the so-called *assise de l'an et jour*). Just as absentee landlords were useless to settlement and defence, so too were absent rulers, a powerful incentive to ignore strict rules of inheritance (if any existed), in Tripoli in 1105 as in Jerusalem in 1118 or Antioch in 1111 (on Bohemund's death in the west) and 1112 (the death of Tancred). Habits in the west were less cavalier. Alfonso-Jordan and his mother departed for

Toulouse, which they reached in 1108, posing an awkward problem for Bertrand, whom the church regarded as illegitimate. The same year, Bertrand left his half-brother in nominal charge of the family Provençal lands to try his fortune in the east. It is notable that no twelfth-century ruler contemplated combining eastern and western lordships to form a cross-Mediterranean empire. Although some, like Bohemund and Raymond of Toulouse, retained their old titles, others, such as Fulk V of Anjou and then king of Jerusalem, did not. This wholly pragmatic principle seems also to have applied to settler barons and seigneurs of less exalted status.

Bertrand's arrival in Outremer provoked an acrid succession contest. While William-Jordan sought the help of the dominant figure in Christian northern Syria, Tancred of Antioch, Bertrand, backed by a substantial army and a large Genoese fleet, offered homage to the equally acquisitive Baldwin I of Jerusalem, who used his royal prestige and military clout to impose a partition on the county in 1109. Shortly afterwards William-Jordan died amid rumours of murder. Meanwhile, Tripoli itself surrendered to Bertrand, Baldwin and the Genoese. The Muslim garrison was spared, but the city was plundered, its renowned library destroyed: 'the books . . . exceeded all computation' lamented Ibn al-Qalanisi from Damascus.[22]

Bertrand (d. 1112) controlled the coast from Maraclea in the north to the Dog river above Beirut in the south. At its height, the county stretched inland to Crac des Chevaliers and the Orontes valley towards Homs and northwards to Montferrand (Ba 'rin) on the road to Hamah. Although the count owed homage and fealty to the king of Jerusalem, who in times of crisis, such as the assassination of Raymond II (1152) or the captivity of Raymond III (1164), acted as guardian or regent, the county of Tripoli, unlike the not dissimilar-sized and resourced lordship of Galilee, remained outside the kingdom. The king of Jerusalem held no direct tenurial, legal or patronage rights over the count's vassals or fiefs within the county. Its ecclesiastical hierarchy maintained, against papal instructions, its allegiance to the patriarchate of Antioch, not Jerusalem, in part a result of the close political relations established between the county and principality by Bertrand's son Count Pons (1112–37). The county was divided into separate lordships based on ports such as Jubail and Tortosa and castles in the interior, with the count holding as his own domain the coastal strip around Tripoli and the eastern frontier region around Montferrand, whose loss in 1137 reduced comital resources. The vulnerability of the county led to devolution of power. In 1144, partly to counter the Assassins newly established in the Nosairi mountains and partly as defence against Homs, Raymond II granted the Hospitallers large tracts of the east of the county, including much of the Buqai'ah plain, the area towards Montferrand and the fortress of Hisn al-Akrad. In the 1150s, the Templars acquired Tortosa. Both military orders proceeded to construct major castles, the Templars at Tortosa, the Hospitallers at Hisn al-Akrad or, as it was now called, Crac des Chevaliers. The Genoese role in the county's foundation was rewarded with a quarter of Tripoli and, among other properties, the port of Jubail, which Count Bertrand gave to the Genoese admiral Guglielmo Embriaco. His descendants became vassals of the count as lords of Jubail in their own right until the last years of the thirteenth century, when, embittered by their treatment at the hands of the count of Tripoli, they briefly held Jubail as vassals of the sultan of Egypt.[23] In devolving power and responsibility, the counts of Tripoli revealed a structural weakness in their county and their resources. When Raymond III exerted influence and authority outside Tripoli, acting as regent of Jerusalem in the 1170s and 1180s, this depended not on his position as count but on his family relationship, as a great-grandson of Baldwin II and grandson of Queen Melisende, and on his marriage to the richest heiress within the kingdom, Eschiva of Galilee.

This weakness was exacerbated by rumbling succession problems, murder and captivity. During the Second Crusade (1146–8) Alfonso-Jordan of Toulouse, Raymond I's son, born at Mount Pilgrim, arrived in the east clearly possessed of a stronger formal claim than the incumbent, Raymond II, grandson of Raymond I's bastard. While Alfonso-Jordan died suddenly in Palestine in 1148, to the usual accompaniment of rumours of foul play, his own illegitimate son, Bertrand, backed by Toulousain troops, challenged Raymond's authority in 1149 by seizing the fortress of Arimah on the road to Tortosa and Homs. According to Arabic sources, Raymond dealt with this unwelcome threat by inviting Nur al-Din and Unur of Damascus, enemies only a year before during the crusaders' siege of Damascus, to dispose of his troublesome relative. Arimah was taken, razed to the ground and returned to Raymond. Bertrand was led captive to Aleppo, where he languished for the next ten years, his fate a fine tribute to the political eclecticism of Outremer politics.[24]

Another was the murder of Raymond II by Assassins in 1152. The Assassins derived from an Isma'ili sect known as the New Preaching founded in north-western Iran in the late eleventh century. Isma'ilis differed from Shi'ites in recognizing the succession of seven instead of twelve *imams*, heads of the Islamic community, descended from Caliph Ali, son-in-law of the Prophet, murdered in 661. An offshoot of the Persian Isma'ilis based at Alamut near the Caspian Sea, after a blood-chequered career in Aleppo and Damascus, from 1132 the Syrian Assassins established bases in the Nosairi mountains near Tortosa, at once a religious and political community. From 1169 to 1193 they were ruled by Sheikh Rashid al-Din Sinan, known as 'the Old Man of the Mountains'. The Assassins distinguished themselves from other Islamic sects and religio-political groups by their use of murder as a political weapon, largely to compensate for their lack of military strength. Fear, extortion and impregnable strongholds in the hills secured for the Assassins notoriety and, in the thirteenth century, some political respectability. Although occasionally available to perform others' dirty work, the Assassins possessed their own idealism, the restoration of radical Isma'ili rule over Islam. Thus their targets tended to be orthodox Sunni Muslims. Their invariable weapon was the dagger. Their nickname, common to Arabic and western sources, derived from the hashish the killers allegedly took before committing what they viewed as a pious act, seeing themselves as religious devotees prepared to face martyrdom for their faith. Raymond II was their first recorded non-Muslim victim, the reasons for his murder unknown. The consequences were severe, leading to another regency, by Raymond's widow, Hodierna, sister of Queen Melisende and aunt of Baldwin III. The immediate reaction to Raymond's murder exposed a latent racism in the Franks, who massacred the eastern indigenous population of Tripoli regardless of religion. 'In this way it was hoped that the perpetrators of the foul deed might be found.' They were not.[25]

Despite the success of Nur al-Din of Aleppo in uniting Muslim Syria in the quarter-century before his death in 1174, and Raymond III's decade in captivity (1164–74), the county maintained its precarious hold on the coast. Yet, unlike Antioch and Jerusalem, it is hard to detect much of a coherent, distinctive political culture. The very existence of the county of Tripoli, by the 1150s a loose association of semi-independent lordships, pointed to the haphazard political structure of Outremer. The creation of four separate principalities, while reflecting their respective histories and local geography, indicated a lack of strategic understanding by most of the western invaders, at least until the successes of Nur al-Din and Saladin concentrated minds. The habit of seeking immediate gratification of ambition, opportunity or claims appeared impervious even to the warnings of events and observers in the 1170s and 1180s. The pattern of building castles augmented the impression of myopia, the emphasis being on individual seigneurial administration rather than frontier defence. Perhaps only the military orders, with possessions in all principalities and fealty to none, acquired the perspective to introduce some strategic planning to their castles and campaigns. Otherwise, unity in Outremer flowed usually from the kings of Jerusalem: Baldwin I imposing a settlement in northern Syria in 1109–11; Baldwin II using the marriages of his daughters – Alice to Bohemund II of Antioch and Hodierna to Raymond II of Tripoli. Dynasticism prevailed. The childless Raymond III was succeeded as count of Tripoli by Bohemund IV of Antioch, Raymond's mother's great-great-nephew.

JERUSALEM

For a kingdom whose adherents regarded it as founded by God, the kingdom of Jerusalem exhibited disappointing fragility and disunity. It was never entirely free from the menace of invasion; civil war erupted or was threatened in 1133–4, 1152, 1182 and 1186. Its rulers, including a bigamist homosexual and another who married a bigamous wife, conspicuously failed to produce healthy male heirs. The dynastic line faltered alarmingly and damagingly. Actively disputed in 1100, 1118, 1163 and 1186, no succession went entirely uncontested, although much the same could be said of twelfth-century England. Only twice in eighty-eight years did son succeed father, in 1143 and 1174. On both occasions the heir was a minor, on the second he proved to be a leper as well. Minors inherited on three occasions. Inevitably, factional jostling and feuding marked the regime, the intimacy of political action in and around the royal court compounded by the small geographical extent of the kingdom and the lack of economic or fiscal necessity for barons to spend time of their estates. Visiting western grandees found the local political scene poisonously rebarbative and introspective.[26] Jerusalemites gained a reputation in the west, certainly from the Second Crusade, for shiftiness and decadence, in contrast to Arabic contemporaries, who noted their bellicose nature and lack of personal hygiene. Yet Jerusalem in the twelfth century remained the emotional, political and strategic heart of Outremer. Its ideology infused by militant Christianity; its rulers thoroughly acculturated to the demands of the east, four of them – Baldwin I, II, III and Amalric – marrying Armenian or Greek princesses; its fate an issue for western rulers no less than churchmen, pilgrims, settlers and crusaders, its history was already a matter of epic and legend.[27] It says much for the material foundations of the kingdom that this was so.

When Godfrey of Bouillon died in Jerusalem on 18 July 1100, only quick action by his followers prevented the newly installed patriarch, the former papal legate Daimbert of Pisa, from asserting his claims to ecclesiastical rule over the tiny enclave in Judea.[28] Desperate for military aid, the previous December Godfrey had agreed to be invested with Jerusalem by Damibert, who had just arrived in the Holy City with his ally Bohemund and Baldwin of Edessa to fulfil their vows. Armed with the power of his Pisan entourage and wealth, Daimbert had subsequently forced Godfrey to concede to him ownership of Jerusalem and Jaffa, with the duke retaining only a life interest. The departure of the Pisan fleet and the arrival of a Venetian one strengthened Godfrey's hand before he died. Afterwards, the fortuitous absence of Daimbert from Jerusalem allowed the duke's military household to launch a *coup d'état*, seizing the Citadel and sending urgent messages to Godfrey's brother, Baldwin of Edessa, to assume the inheritance. On this news, Daimbert and Tancred, fresh from conquering Galilee and Haifa and long an enemy of Baldwin, looked to invite Bohemund to come south, but he had left Antioch to campaign in the north, where he was captured by the Danishmends in August. In the event, Baldwin had to secure Antioch before in October leaving Edessa in the hands of his cousin, Baldwin of Le Bourcq, to march south. Defeating a Damascene army at the Dog river, Baldwin reached Jerusalem in November. With Tancred withdrawing to Galilee, then assuming the regency of Antioch in the new year, Daimbert was compelled to submit. Whereas Godfrey merely continued with his own title of duke and allowed others to describe him as the Advocate of the Holy Sepulchre, with Baldwin, an educated lapsed cleric himself, no equivocation over titles or authority was permitted. On Christmas Day 1100, tactfully perhaps, pointedly certainly, in the church of the Nativity in Bethlehem rather than in the church of the Holy Sepulchre, Baldwin was crowned by Daimbert as, in his later phrase, 'king of the Latins in Jerusalem'.[29]

Baldwin of Boulogne created the kingdom of Jerusalem. Always a man on the make, the youngest son of Eustace II of Boulogne, originally destined for the church, Baldwin abandoned the cloth in search of secular success, although all his life maintaining a slightly ecclesiastical air in dress and manner.[30] Married three times for worldly advancement, once bigamously, he was probably homosexual, one of his more exotic intimates being a converted Muslim who later tried to betray him during the siege of Sidon in 1110. Apparently they were inseparable, even while the king relieved himself.[31] Failing to secure a niche in the lucrative Anglo-Norman nobility through his first marriage to Godechilde of Tosni, who died at Marasch in 1097, Baldwin used the First Crusade to better his status. He matched boldness with a single-minded concentration on personal advancement, in Cilicia in 1097, where he enlisted Muslim assistance to get the better of Tancred, and at Edessa in 1098, when he showed no compunction in sacrificing his patron Thoros. His second marriage, to the Armenian Arda, served a similar function to his first, providing Baldwin with a political stake of his own. Summoned to rule Jerusalem, he proved an outstanding military leader and, unlike his somewhat supine brother Godfrey, a cunning, clear-headed politician. Constant aggression towards his neighbours, a policy of strategic conquest, and the firm imposition of royal authority over his lay and ecclesiastical vassals formed the basis of successful kingship. Not even his own chaplain, Fulcher of Chartres, claimed Baldwin was pious, nor did his later eulogists. Instead Baldwin was his people's 'shield, strength and support; their right arm; the terror of his enemies'.[32]

The early years of the reign saw the conquest of the coastal ports interrupted by some desperate defence against Egyptian invasions in 1101 and 1105, on which the survival of the kingdom depended. Damascus, the army of which Baldwin had defeated on his way south in 1100, stood aloof, not wishing to assist a Fatimid reconquest of Palestine. However, as Frankish success increasingly denied them free access to the coast, the Damascenes contested the fortification of Galilee by Baldwin's vassals and sought allies from Iraq. Between 1109 and 1115, Baldwin's attention was regularly occupied in the north, in 1109 settling the squabbles between Antioch, Edessa and Tripoli and thereafter providing military assistance against repeated attacks from Mosul. In 1113 Mawdud of Mosul, in alliance with Damascus, attacked Palestine, defeating Baldwin at es-Sinnabra in Galilee but failing to capture any towns or fortresses. Mawdud's murder by Assassins the same year produced a diplomatic rapprochement with Tughtegin of Damascus, who, as fearful of Seljuk domination as of Fatimid, reckoned the Franks served a useful purpose in balancing power in the region. With northern pressure reduced, Baldwin realized that his kingdom's security would be enhanced by extending his influence over the Bedouin and the desert trade routes between Egypt and Syria. Twice reconnotring the region south of the Dead Sea in 1100 and 1107, in 1115 and 1116 he imposed Frankish authority east of the Wadi Araba, penetrating to Petra and south to the Gulf of Aqaba. Two castles were built, at Montréal (Shawbak) in Edom and Li Vaux Moise, near Petra, although in the 1140s the centre of what became known as the lordship of Oultrejourdain was transferred north to Kerak in Moab, closer to the eastern shore of the Dead Sea and, on a clear day, within sight of the Mount of Olives. These forts allowed the Franks to tax commerce and the pilgrim traffic on the road from Syria to Mecca and Medina in the Hijaz and to impede hostile militiary activity. However, aggression from Egypt via Ascalon persisted, threatening Jerusalem (in 1113) and Jaffa (in 1115). To counter this, Baldwin led a raid in the Nile in 1118, presumably hoping to coerce the Fatimids into peace. Instead, he fell mortally ill, dying on the return journey at el-Arish on 2 April 1118.

Baldwin I's achievements were startling. He established a stable kingdom with defined and defensible borders from Beirut to Beersheba and beyond, controlled by a new, coherent political community whose power rested on exploiting existing resources of rural and commercial wealth. If he relied on force of personality and circumstance rather than law or constitutions, his idiom of authority was understood by his followers and clients. However, his career was hardly unique. From the chaos of late eleventh-century Syria, Iraq, Anatolia and Egypt, Baldwin was not alone in carving out a kingdom that survived its creator. Similar events and aptitude plotted the careers of fellow Latins Bohemund and Tancred, the Seljuk Kilij Arslan, the Mosul atabeg Zengi and his son Nur al-Din of

Aleppo, and, later, the Kurdish mercenary Saladin. For each, legitimacy derived not from long inheritance or tradition but from military force, the leadership of loyal warbands and the wealth generated by employment, plunder and tribute. They all shared the justification of religion.

In the Near East, determined use of violence, diplomacy and patronage allowed small, often tiny groups, no larger than an extended military household of a few score or hundreds of warriors, to assert authority over large, settled civilian populations largely through control of the economically and politically dominant cities. The structure of Near Eastern society rested on myriad communities, variously defined by religion, culture and ethnicity in town and country. Rural wealth was exploited by absentee landlords who also controlled the commerce that flowed though urban centres. Cities and towns dominated the rural population; military warlords dominated the cities and towns. The Franks were unusual in massacring or expelling urban populations, a habit that ceased after the capture of Sidon in 1110. Yet the importance of cities to the political economy was well understood. Baldwin I and II made strenuous efforts to attract local Christians to Jerusalem. Frankish authorities tolerated racial and religious diversity in the great ports of Acre, Tyre or Tripoli. Baldwin I's kingdom, like those of Tughtegin at Damascus or Kerbogha at Mosul, revolved around personal loyalty of a well-rewarded inner circle into whose hands power and wealth were bestowed; successful war and diplomacy; and the ready exploitation of the economy of the indigenous population. A characteristic feature of Muslim Near Eastern patronage was the grant of an *iqta*, an assignment of revenues from designated land, not its ownership. In Latin Palestine the equivalents were grants of rents and money-fiefs. While Baldwin's conquest of Palestine found parallels in Robert Guiscard's in southern Italy, Rodrigo Diaz's in Valencia or even William the Bastard's in England, it chiefly mirrored local conditions. While inevitably employing western language, customs and mentalities, Baldwin acted as a Levantine potentate. The contrast found visible expression in the mourners following his funeral bier as it wound its way up the Valley of Josaphat to Jerusalem on Palm Sunday 1118. Grieving beside Baldwin's shocked protégé, the corrupt old stager Patriarch Arnulf, and the Latin community were Syrian Christians and passing Muslims.[33]

The main legacies bequeathed by Baldwin I to his cousin Baldwin II included tight control over the disposal of lordships and fiefs; mastery of the church of a sort frowned upon in fashionable circles in the west; an understanding of the importance of maintaining the diplomatic balance between Aleppo, Damascus and Egypt; and practical overlordship and protection over the northern territories. Military generalship remained fundamental to a royal power that rested at the heart of the legal and political structure. Modified over time and reduced by dynastic failure and faction, the essence of Baldwin I's system of royal hegemony survived until 1187.

Behind the territorial conquests, the king created fiefs for his leading vassals, including the lordships of Caesarea, Arsur, Sidon, Jaffa, Hebron and Oultrejourdain. Fealty and homage were insisted on from the princes of Galilee after Tancred's show of independence under Duke Godfrey. Jerusalem was one frontier where private enterprise operated only within a clear hierarchical system centred on the crown, which retained its ability to manipulate the structure and disposition of the major fiefs in the kingdom.[34] The kings kept as their domain Judea and Samaria (with the centres of Jerusalem and Nablus) and the vastly lucrative lordships of Acre (1104) and Tyre (1124). In their domain, as the great lords in theirs, the king exercised jurisdiction through viscounts and collected or farmed taxes on trade and industry (e.g. sugar production), as well as the poll tax on Muslims. Formal relations with his tenants-in-chief, major vassals holding lands directly from the king, were conducted in the High Court (Haute Cour) attended also by leading ecclesiastics, including the heads of the military orders, and the occasional grand visiting crusader. By the reign of Amalric, the *assise sur la ligece* provided for rear-vassals (i.e. vassals of the king's vassals) to swear oaths of direct liege-homage to the king, thus, in theory, opening access to the Haute Cour to them and their litigation. Amalric also claimed the right to oaths of fealty from freemen. The desire for direct relations between the crown and free tenants finds an echo in the contemporary legal reforms of Amalric's nephew, Henry II of England. However, effective legal authority, in England or Jerusalem, depended on material wealth. Apart from income derived from his domain, the king enjoyed the profits of coining, customs and tolls in his ports, tribute from the Bedouin, highway dues, and the right of wreck. Special taxes for war and defence were agreed by the Haute Cour or wider assemblies in 1167 and 1183, perhaps a sign that ordinary revenues were being over-stretched, a phenomenon that may explain why, increasingly, secular lords passed lands to the church and the military orders. Baldwin I's successors, despite concessions agreed at the Council of Nablus in 1120s, asserted a *de facto* control over appointments to the episcopacy and the masterships of the military orders.

However, royal power was neither autocratic nor absolute. Baldwin I's pious but equally energetic successor, Baldwin II, sustained his authority at a price. Formal complaints about his regency in Antioch in 1119 were voiced by the Jerusalem nobility. At the Council of Nablus in 1120, the king and secular lords relinquished control over ecclesiastical tithes and accepted a range of penalties for breaches of the law, sexual misconduct and miscegenation. By the end of his reign, the royal habit of disposing of the inheritance of fiefs at will rather than by customary rules had begun to give way to a presumption of hereditary succession, often, given the rapid extinction rates of families in the direct male line, widely interpreted. Nonetheless the crown retained considerable authority. The cohesion of the kingdom survived Baldwin II's captivity in Aleppo (1123–4), affairs being conducted by his constable and the patriarch, including the important capture of Tyre. More generally, moves towards seigneurial hereditary succession were to be expected in the generation after the initial conquest: England after 1066 and Sicily after 1092 provided parallels. Confiscations continued for contumacious malcontents. At no time before the fall of the kingdom in 1187 were kings unable to interfere in the composition and structure of fiefs or in the disposition of unmarried heiresses. So far from consolidating territorial or jurisdictional power, many of the chief vassals – perhaps fewer that a dozen families – subdivided their fiefs or granted stretches of them to religious houses or military orders. Legally, Baldwin II managed to insist on the penalty of confiscation for prescribed offences against his rights and position both as feudal overlord and king (the *Establissment dou roi Baudoin*), although it is uncertain whether conviction and punishment lay with the king or trial in the Haute Cour. In practice, it probably made little difference as no monarch could proceed without the support of his barons. In 1133/4 Hugh count of Jaffa rebelled against King Fulk. By refusing to appear to answer in court charges and then inviting armed help from the Muslim garrison at Ascalon, Hugh's treason was not in doubt, even to his own vassals. Yet, instead of having his fiefs confiscated, he was exiled for three years with the promise of subsequent restoration of his property. Politics, in this case Fulk's unpopularity and baronial sympathy for Hugh, prevailed over law.[35]

The case of Hugh of Jaffa arose as a consequence of the personal and dynastic, not constitutional, consequences of kingship. The main weakness of the regime created by Baldwin I lay in the chance circumstances of succession, which would have undermined any Latin monarchy of the time. Baldwin I left no children. He had repudiated his second wife, possibly on the spurious grounds of her having been raped by a Muslim. His bigamous marriage to Adelisa of Sicily (1113–16), which had offered the prospect of a Sicilian succession, ended in divorce and a promise from Baldwin to his barons not to remarry. On his death in 1118, a powerful faction in his household invited Baldwin's elder brother, Eustace of Boulogne, to succeed but, by the time he reached Italy, news came that a rival group had installed Baldwin of Le Bourcq as king. Even so, Baldwin II's position was only formally recognized in 1119 by coronation at Bethlehem. Pons of Tripoli had to be forced to acknowledge his overlordship in 1122. During Baldwin II's captivity (1123–4), supporters of the house of Boulogne toyed with replacing him with Charles count of Flanders. As late as 1128, the pope had to declare Baldwin's legitimacy.[36]

Happily married, Baldwin II fathered only daughters. To secure his dynasty, he arranged for the eldest, Melisende, to marry Fulk V count of Anjou. A veteran pilgrim from 1120, Fulk arrived in Jerusalem in 1129 possessed of very grand western connections. In 1128, he had arranged the marriage of his son Geoffrey to Matilda, only surviving legitimate child and heiress of Henry I of England and his Anglo-French dominions. Henry's interest in the east was further demonstrated when a member of his household, Raymond of Poitiers, was recruited as prince of Antioch in 1133 (although he only reached Syria in 1136). As with Henry I's dispositions for his throne, Baldwin insisted on the rights of his daughter to the succession. However, Fulk expected to become king. In 1131, on his deathbed, Baldwin II complicated matters further by associating his infant grandson, later Baldwin III, as well as Melisende and Fulk in the succession, again echoing Henry I's insistence on the ultimate inheritance by his grandson, the future Henry II. As in 1118, dynastic interests created political feuds, the rights of Melisende becoming identified with those of the existing baronage resentful of the parvenu Fulk. Relations cannot have been eased by Fulk's genuine or affected amnesia for people's names or faces, even among his household and protégés, a distinctly unsettling trait, deliberate or not, in a political universe revolving round personal contact and favour.[37]

Given the lack of male heirs, the dynastic issue mattered. In 1118, a western stranger was almost imposed on Jerusalem. It occurred in Tripoli in 1109 and Antioch in 1136. In 1131, the Angevin connection in Jerusalem proved double-edged. While securing immediate stability, potentially it provided claims for Fulk's European heirs, who also happened to be the ruling dynasty of the greatest empire in western Europe. The circumstances of 1118 and 1131 in fact left a number of other western ruling families – such as Boulogne, Blois and Flanders – with dynastic interests in the east, especially as Melisende's succession had confirmed the cognatic principle of inheritance (the rights of any relative, male or female, to inherit, not just males in the male line). The protection of Baldwin's dynasty exerted a powerful influence. It was of practical as well as symbolic importance that, as was later reported, Melisende was crowned and consecrated beside Fulk in 1131, now in the church of the Holy Sepulchre not, as previously, in Bethlehem.[38] Patronage was at stake as much as who ruled. Baldwin II's accession in 1118 and his regime can be seen as depending on a close family nexus of his own kin, whose power the invitation to Fulk was designed to protect by excluding existing rivals. Fulk's subsequent confrontation with Hugh of Jaffa, prominent in Baldwin II's own Rethel/Montlhéry family mafia, reflected his desire for independence and his own men, thereby challenging the vested interests of Hugh and Melisende's other relatives.[39] Despite exiling Hugh, Fulk was forced to share authority with Melisende, as Baldwin II intended.

Although this ensured a smooth inheritance for Baldwin III on his father's death in 1143, another victim of the medieval nobleman's obsession with hunting, Melisende's autonomous power created further tensions. In contrast with the unconsecrated Matilda of England, who relinquished her claims on her son's majority, Queen Melisende continued to insist on her rights long after Baldwin III was old enough to wield power. His mother built up her own administration and support, including her cousin Manasses of Hierges, constable since 1143, and her second son Amalric. It took Baldwin's victory in a civil war in 1152 to save the integrity of the kingdom.

Factional instability, punctuated by political assassination, continued.

Baldwin III died young, without children, in 1163. His brother Amalric succeeded only after putting aside a possibly bigamous marriage. His descendants loaded the rules of inheritance to breaking. Baldwin IV was a leper; his nephew Baldwin V a sickly child of nine; his sister Sybil married an unpopular foreigner, Guy of Lusignan, whom she spatchcocked into the kingship in a manner wholly unlike Baldwin II's careful arrangements. Only *in extremis*, in 1184–5, with the leper king dying, his child-heir weak, his sister and brother-in-law in disgrace and his more distant eastern relatives eyeing up the royal prize lasciviously, did some in Jerusalem appear willing to contemplate a change of dynasty.[40] The tenacity with which the ailing royal line of Jerusalem clung to power and respect owed much to the baronage. In 1163, while forcing Amalric to annul his marriage to Agnes of Courtenay, publicly on the grounds of consanguinity but probably because she was a bigamist, the barons and prelates illogically confirmed their children as legitimate. The alternatives – the European Angevin sons of Henry II of England, the count of Flanders, great-nephew of Baldwin I and Godfrey of Bouillon, or, more credibly, the descendants of Queen Melisende's sisters, Raymond III of Tripoli or Bohemund III of Antioch – offered greater prospects of untoward intrusion into the familiar political round. After all, the Jerusalem barons could describe Amalric, a former count of Jaffa-Ascalon, as 'one of us'.

The sleaziness of Jerusalem politics was not new, with leading politicians subject to accusations of sexual impropriety and risking the murderer's knife; Hugh of Jaffa survived in 1134; the unscrupulous Miles of Plancy, accused of usurping power in the early days of the minor Baldwin IV, was not so lucky in 1174. To support this crumbling edifice, a redeeming myth of the special moral virtue of the dynasty appeared. The 1180s *Historia* of William of Tyre, Jerusalem-born, protégé of Amalric I, tutor to Baldwin IV, who may well have seen King Fulk in person, promoted an image of an almost sacred dynasty descended from the saintly Godfrey of Bouillon, Baldwin I and Baldwin II, the unimpeachable veterans of the First Crusade.[41] By a sleight of literary skill, William argued for the legitimacy of Baldwin II's succession even while admitting it breached immutable laws of inheritance. Their descent from Baldwin II was central to William's portrayal of the later kings. Melisende, who transmitted Baldwin's blood to her successors, assumed a pivotal position. Instead of the disruptive, ambitious and, some might argue, graspingly selfish, unsuccessful political menace of history, Melisende emerged from William's obituary of her as ruling wisely with her husband and son, a fount of active wisdom. As a dynastic progenitor, Fulk receded into oblivion, along with his awkwardly powerful (and healthy) western relatives. Fittingly, the carved ivory cover of the famous psalter probably written for Melisende in Jerusalem *c.*1135 shows scenes of the life of King David, the model of divinely inspired monarchy and of kings in the Holy City.[42]

All political systems require defining ideas to provide identity and purpose, whether related to reality or not. The ideology of kingship in Jerusalem centred on the person of the king, as the monarchy had been an almost parthenogenic creation. In practice the result of political opportunism and military conquest, in description the consequence of especial divine favour, the Jerusalem kingship existed without any prior tradition or contemporary authority outside the practical choices of worried men in Jerusalem in 1099 and 1100. Only subsequently did the papacy acknowledge its existence. The monarchy's survival and flourishing supplied its own legitimacy, a unique status among the new Christian monarchies of the time, all the rest of which sought the imprimatur of popes or emperors, from Hungary and Poland in the tenth and eleventh centuries to Armenia and Cyprus in the twelfth. Politically, legally and militarily, the importance of the kingship, if only to legitimize the ambitions of the baronage, remained conspicuous.

The way Baldwin IV, who died in 1185 aged only twenty-four, was portrayed by his old tutor William of Tyre reinforces this image. William's Baldwin overcame his leprosy to provide vigorous political and military leadership almost to the end of his life of a quality that would have been admirable in a ruler of maturity and health. William wrote of Baldwin's effective dealings with his nobles and household and of his battlefield leadership, even when carried in a litter. The portrait was unashamedly and deliberately heroic, perhaps to counter the damaging conclusions of those who saw in the king's leprosy, in Pope Alexander III's pointed words, 'a just judgement of God'.[43] Yet the truth was almost certainly less glamorous. Throughout the reign administration and military command were delegated. Baldwin undoubtedly appeared in council chamber and battle. Yet his disease prevented him from fighting, his experiences of horses bolting under him and being carried on a soldier's back or in a litter suggesting his presence in council and war, though astonishingly courageous, physically humiliating and painful, was iconic rather than active. Even William of Tyre admitted that some of Baldwin's most fateful decisions were due to the influence on a sick man of his mother, Agnes, and her brother, Joscelin III, titular count of Edessa and seneschal of Jerusalem.[44] The king was necessary to the cohesion of the political process. Repeatedly Baldwin's attempts to retire failed as successive schemes for regents or replacements foundered. The king was indispensable even if only as a tragic figurehead.

The reign of Baldwin IV demonstrated how the polity of Latin Jerusalem had developed since the desperate pioneer days of 1099–1102. Kings were still expected to be great warriors. Guy of Lusignan's failure to engage Saladin in 1183 cost him the regency.[45] However, by then the kingship no longer comprised the qualities of a bandit chief. Although politics not law determined relations between monarch and baron, these relations were increasingly described in legislative acts such as the *assise sur la ligece*. In common with the rest of western Christendom, royal, seigneurial and ecclesiastical administration adopted an increasingly bureaucratic mode, as in the use of written charters to record property transactions, even if the Jerusalem royal chancery remained relatively rudimentary, especially in comparison with contemporary western practices. The baronage of the kingdom assumed greater corporate identity whilst at the same time finding it harder to sustain its territorial power intact as fiefs were subdivided, partitioned, granted away or sold off. One excuse for the bitter court feuding of the 1170s and 1180s lay in the authority and patronage of the crown, not its decadence; there was something to fight for. The kingdom was not falling apart, even if a decline in resources forced the crown to appeal for a war tax in 1183. Yet this tax was granted by a national, representative assembly and conducted after a national census, indications of institutional sophistication.[46] Above all sat an ideology of rule forged from the regime's definition of itself as a garrison state protecting the Holy Places, in trust for Christendom.

7

East is East and East is West: Outremer in the Twelfth Century

There is no more haunting passage in contemporary writing on the crusades than William of Tyre's description of the young Baldwin IV, the blue-eyed (to hostile Arabic scrutiny) young prince of Jerusalem whose youthful promise turned into despair at the discovery of his leprosy. The pain of the account comes from personal involvement. William, then archdeacon of Tyre, was Baldwin's tutor; it was in his household that the first symptoms appeared. William continued to chronicle the life of his pupil, who succeeded to the throne in 1174 aged thirteen and died in 1185, a ravaged, blind, crippled wreck only twenty-four. It was as a hero of Christendom, struggling and usually triumphing for the Faith against the enormous odds of the growing power of the infidel and his own disease that Baldwin was depicted. Yet this doomed child's doctor, Abu Sulayman Da'ud, a native Syrian Christian born – like the Latin William of Tyre – in Jerusalem, had worked for the Fatimids in Egypt before being hired in the late 1160s by Baldwin's father, Amalric I, an enthusiast for Arabic medicine, as was his predecessor Baldwin III. One of Abu Sulayman's sons successfully taught Prince Baldwin to ride; another succeeded his father as Amalric's physician. After 1187, the family enlisted in the service of Saladin, the enemy against whom Baldwin IV had expended so much of his wasting energy.[1]

In common with other Levantine princelings, Baldwin grew up in a cosmopolitan court; his tutor steeped in Latin culture and learning, enhanced by a twenty-year stay in western Europe studying at Paris, Orleans and Bologna; his doctor and riding-instructor Syrians with experience of working for Muslim rulers; his stepmother, Amalric I's second wife Maria Comnena, a Byzantine Greek. However, the image the regime wished to portray through its own rhetoric, one which received elaborate and forceful corroboration from the pen of William of Tyre himself, remained that of the frontier myth, the Latin rulers in Palestine and Syria as heirs of the legendary Christian heroes of the First Crusade, the defenders of the Faith in God's own land, a myth excluding temporal realities, political compromises and social exchange. While demonstrating the nature of the Latin presence in Outremer as one of a number of communities at once cooperating, competing and coercing, William sought to explain past success and current weakness according to a two-dimensional myth of conquest and battle, not least because his audience in western Europe expected it and his eastern compatriots understood its place in such a constructed justification for their existence. Yet myth it was and remains. Much of the twelfth-century kingdom of Jerusalem for most of the time did not resemble a military frontier, nor did its social and economic and hence legal and political arrangements follow crudely racist or supremacist ideology. Despite closer frontiers with aggressive Turks, similar conditions prevailed in the northern enclaves. The Latins dominated the regions they had conquered, imposing a hierarchy of power with themselves at the apex. Yet their community was isolated neither in city nor countryside, the settlers not withdrawn from the means of their survival. The livelihood of the Latin settlers and rulers depended on using, not ignoring, their surroundings and neighbours. In the absence of overcrowding, after the military phase of conquest, exploitation of resources did not necessarily or sensibly entail systematic persecution or discrimination of other communities. Westerners came east to live for Christ just as enthusiastically as to die for Him. As the *assises* (laws) of Jerusalem noted with reference to market courts where both Latins and Syrians comprised the jurors, witnesses were permitted to swear oaths on their respective holy books, Christians on the Gospels, Jews and Samaritans on the Torah, and Muslims on the Koran, 'because be they Syrians or Greeks or Jews or Samaritans or Nestorians or Saracens, they are also men like the Franks'.[2] The great hospital in Jerusalem run by the Order of St John, accommodating many hundreds of sick at any one time, was committed to treating anybody regardless of race or religion; only lepers were excluded, on obvious medical grounds.

This was not the picture the clerical opinion formers in the west or their colleagues in the east were prepared to accept. In the years after the First

Crusade, Guibert of Nogent wishfully looked on the settlements in Jerusalem as 'Holy Christendom's new colony' (*novae coloniae*). In the late 1130s, the Anglo-Norman historian Orderic Vitalis wrote of 'the Christians who live in exile in the east for the sake of Christ', especially potent imagery as the idea of exile was closely associated by contemporaries with monastic vocation as a metaphor for absolute commitment to Christ and a godly life. Messages from the east confirmed this idealistic vision. During the grim days of 1120, the patriarch of Jerusalem struck a similar vein of emotion in describing the perils besetting Outremer from all sides: Muslims, poor harvests, grasshoppers:

> For the name of Jesus, before abandoning the holy city of Jerusalem, the cross of Our Lord and the most holy tomb of Christ, we are ready to die ... Strive to come and join the army of Christ and bring us speedy aid ...[3]

The author, Patriarch Gromond, fond of such gloomy admonitory tones, came from Picquigny in northern France, drawn to the east by such attitudes. Yet even after the pacification of most of Outremer, the rhetoric of martial solidarity and emergency persisted in official correspondence, hardly surprising, as it tended to be aimed at securing western aid. It also provided the central drama in the growing body of epic vernacular literature inspired, but significantly not written, by the Latin conquerors in the east.

The settlers' perspective scarcely matched the epic vision. Most of the castles, fortified settlements and towers were built not on exposed frontiers but in peaceful areas largely undisturbed for the central decades of the twelfth century, their function seigneurial rather than primarily military.[4] All Latin societies of the time were geared for warfare. Nobles resorted to violence as a matter of course and culture; in Outremer they behaved no differently. From the 1120s to the 1180s, much of the coastal plain northwards to Tripoli and Antioch, Judea, Samaria, western Galilee, even southern Transjordan was no less peaceful than many parts of western Europe. The imposition of precise military obligations on those who owned or held property, including farmers, did not indicate a state of perpetual ferment any more than similar arrangements did in the west. Although possibly sentimental and certainly propagandist, the impression of Outremer society left by Fulcher of Chartres, himself a settler first at Edessa then Jerusalem, while emphasizing the precarious lack of numbers, was of a growing civilian population successfully coming to terms with new surroundings. After the early days when settlers hung on the words of every visiting pilgrim in the hope of news from home, by the 1120s, Fulcher insisted not altogether plausibly, Jerusalemites had forgotten their homelands. Some had married local Syrian or Armenian Christians, even baptized Muslims, a statement corroborated by other sources. Others, once established, were joined by relatives from the west. Contact with indigenous communities was eased by the emergence of a level of *lingua franca*; sixty years after Fulcher wrote, the Spanish Muslim traveller Ibn Jubayr recorded the word 'bilghriyin', an Arabic derivation from Romance words for pilgrim (*peregrinus*, Latin; *pèlerin*, French; *pellegrini*, Italian). Usamah Ibn Munqidh of Shaizar recorded the Arabic version of the Frankish bourgeois (i.e. non-noble Franks): *burjasi*.[5] Some settlers, universally described as Franks, learnt the local languages, although interpreters, *dragomanni*, were ubiquitous, even if their role was more involved in estate management than translation. In any case, monoglot Frank lords were not alone in this polyglot society; local Arab emirs thrived without learning Turkish. Fulcher contradicted the idea, commonly held by modern historians, that Outremer society was essentially a 'crusader' society. He implied (or hoped) that immigration was a constant process not restricted to veterans of military expeditions or pilgrims who stayed on. This too is borne out by documentary evidence. Around 1150, a cobbler from Châlons-sur-Marne emigrated to Jerusalem to avoid restrictive market dues.[6] In Outremer itself secular and ecclesiastical entrepreneurs set out to attract settlers on to their estates by offering advantageous tenancy contracts; judging by their names, such offers were accepted by newcomers as well as established residents. While the aura of holiness cannot be ignored as an incentive for settlers to choose the Levant rather than areas of colonization nearer home, long-distance migration was a familiar feature of western and northern Europe. Not all settlers were religious zealots. Not all immigrants stayed. In the late 1150s, one tenant of the priory attached to the Holy Sepulchre gave up the struggle with alien and hostile agricultural conditions and abandoned his land and left. At about the same time an immigrant from Vézelay in Burgundy returned home after seven years in Outremer to find his wife had remarried; another, a married woman from the same region, who had gone east without her spouse, came back after some years to find him wed again.[7]

With settlement came accommodation. Baldwin III, described by William of Tyre as a vigorous Christian champion, waged generally successful war on his Egyptian and Turkish neighbours. This did not prevent him extending royal protection to a Muslim merchant from Tyre, Abu Ali Ibn Izz ad-Din, plying his trade with Egypt nor his funeral cortège being accompanied by mourning infidels from the hills of the interior. Such association could cause offence. William of Tyre evinced anger at the eminently sensible fashion promoted by noblemen's wives of avoiding Latin physicians in favour of 'Jews, Samaritans, Syrians and Saracens' (i.e. Muslims), although the law allowed for foreign doctors, from Europe or 'Painime' (i.e. non-Christian lands), to receive episcopal licences to practise.[8] Abroad, the unavoidable discrepancy between myth and reality earned the Jerusalemites hostile reactions. The acerbic and puritanical Anglo-Norman historian Ralph Niger was appalled at the quality of the ambassadors from the east who toured the capitals of Europe in search of aid in 1184/5; instead of austere heirs to the blessed Godfrey of Bouillon and Adhemar of Le Puy, which he might have imagined, Ralph was confronted in Paris by a parade of lavishly rich ostentation, led by Patriarch Heraclius of Jerusalem in clouds of perfume. If not the gigolo of hostile memory, a brave and skilled politician if not a paragon of celibate virtue, Heraclius, originally from the Auvergne, reinforced the contempt some in the west felt for the *poulains*, as they derisively called those who lived in Outremer. (The easterners reciprocated in kind, calling westerners 'sons of Hernaud', a tag equally obscure but certainly very rude.) William of Tyre recorded western disenchantment with the Jerusalemites dating from the Second Crusade (1146–8), the fate of which still rankled in the 1180s. He shared the view that the lustrous giants of old had been succeeded by idler and more decadent successors, even if he stopped short of Ralph Niger's fulminations against their 'dissolutior' way of life.[9] Racial and national stereotypes were familiar features of twelfth-century writing; the Latins in the Holy Land were especially vulnerable by being on view to so many visitors whose expectations had been fuelled by the popular vernacular adventure stories of the First Crusade, the pieties of wishful churchmen and the Bible.

Nonetheless, residents in Outremer were careful to provide for many of these expectations. Building on the long tradition of pilgrimage and cult sites, they meticulously fashioned a new for old sacred geography to satisfy the flood of western pilgrims, for example excavating relics of the patriarchs Abraham, Isaac and Jacob at Hebron in 1119. The pilgrim John of Würzburg in the late 1160s wrote of 'new Holy Places newly built'. At times such enthusiasm led to complications; at least two sites near Jerusalem were claimed as biblical Emmaeus; confusion surrounded certain precise locations in the church of the Holy Sepulchre; and not all pilgrims swallowed uncritically the gaudier claims of their tour guides, such as that the Tower of David by the Jaffa Gate did actually date from the time of King David.[10] In stamping a Latin religious as well as ecclesiastical mark on the Holy Land, the settlers did no more than follow a much repeated formula in remapping the sacred landscape, a process familiar from Titus and Hadrian in the first and second centuries, the Christians in fourth, the Muslims after 638, 1187 and 1291, and the Israelis after 1948. The twelfth-century Jerusalemites needed to attract and reassure pilgrims from whom as tourists they derived income and on whom the kings levied hefty taxes at the ports of entry (just as their Muslim predecessors had). They provided itineraries; physical protection (for example by the early Templars on the road from Jaffa to Jerusalem); health care (in the Hospital of St John); guesthouses; new churches at shrines designed to suit the pilgrims' needs, as with the new altars, chapels and church at the Holy Sepulchre itself; and encouragement for western shippers (mainly Italians) in their ports: at one time there could be as many as seventy pilgrim ships crowding the harbour at Acre, some capable of carrying hundreds of passengers each.[11] Central to the whole international industry were relics. A report by Gui de Blond, a monk of Grandmont, to the canons of St Junien at Condom in Gascony in the 1150s, authenticating the Holy Land relics he had distributed to religious houses across the region on his return from the east, listed their donors, including the ecclesiastical grandees of Jerusalem, the patriarch and the heads of the main religious houses associated with biblical sites, and other significant figures such as the bishop of Bethlehem, perhaps the worldly Englishman Ralph, and the abbot of the Greek monastery of St Catherine's, Sinai. In Brother Gui's treasure trove were fragments of the True Cross; earth mingled with the blood of Christ; hairs of the Virgin Mary and Mary Magdalen; pieces of Christ's cradle, the Virgin's tomb and the stone where Christ prayed at Gethsemane; and mementoes of biblical incidents and characters, Apostles, John the Baptist, Abraham, Isaac, Jacob and Stephen

Protomartyr, each a tangible reminder of the original mission that lay behind the Outremer settlements.[12]

A religious justification for conquest did not make Outremer different from Spain, Sicily or the Baltic. Its special holy status and the weight of pilgrimage did. The west adopted a proprietorial attitude to the Holy Land, even at a distance. Leaders of Outremer continually looked westwards for assistance, even if not a single twelfth-century century ruler of Jerusalem, as king or heir, visited the west, the furthest any reached being Amalric's visit to pay homage to the Greek emperor Manuel I at Constantinople in 1171. Popes circulated news, usually alarmist or depressing; monastic and clerical chroniclers from all parts of western Christendom recorded eastern events. In high politics, rulers such as the kings of England and France publicly accepted their responsibility to sustain the Christian settlement, even if between 1149 and 1187 they did little enough about it. Great magnates visited, Thierry count of Flanders four times; some went to fight, as did Philip count of Flanders in 1177; others, like Henry the Lion duke of Saxony in 1172, to pray and endow. In return, the kingdom of Jerusalem paid Peter's Pence to Rome and sent its brightest students to the west for education, such as William of Tyre, from a burgess family living in Jerusalem. Whereas, outside the faltering royal dynasty, the number of westerners claiming important secular lordships even by marriage declined in the second half of the century, the church in Outremer exhibited a tenacious dependence on immigrants. Of all the Latin bishops, archbishops and patriarchs in the kingdom of Jerusalem, only one can be identified as having been born in the east, the chronicler William, who was archbishop of Tyre 1175–86. Although this may have added to the colonial appearance of the Jerusalem church, it emphasizes the lack of available, well-educated sons of the nobility who crowded the episcopal benches of western Europe, although it might also be noted that a foreign episcopacy was not unique to Jerusalem: for sixty years after 1066, possibly more, no native Englishman was consecrated a bishop in England; in parts of the German-conquered Baltic from the twelfth century such immigrant bishops remained normal. Such a colonized church, as Heraclius discovered in 1184/5, did not necessarily endear itself to the west, not least because of the generally indifferent quality of clerical recruits in the east, men who would not have got near high office at home, at best characterized, it has been argued, by 'low-brow religiosity', at worst by material ambition and a lack of conspicuous spirituality. Unlike the rest of Latin Christendom, twelfth-century Outremer produced no successful candidates for canonization, although a sabbatical in the Holy Land could prove useful on a saint's *curriculum vitae*, such as that of the bizarre St Ranieri of Pisa, who, while living as an ascetic in Palestine *c.*1138–54, claimed to be 'God's second incarnation'.[13] It is difficult to assess whether the foreign monopoly of church leadership aided relations with the west and heightened the militancy of the Jerusalem church, or, conversely, merely produced fertile ground for opportunist timeservers and encouraged western contempt.

SETTLERS AND SETTLEMENT

The attraction of the Holy Land to ecclesiastical careerists formed only part of Outremer's history of immigration. It is impossible to calculate how many westerners settled in the Levant in the twelfth century as it is to establish what proportion of the total population they constituted. All that can be determined is that, in certain regions and cities, the Franks established a significant presence which should not be minimized just because ultimately, unlike the conquests in Sicily, Spain, eastern Europe or the Baltic, the settlement failed. Not the least consistent theme of life in Outremer was the consciousness of the need for immigration to bolster the military conquest. However, generalizations can mislead. Town and countryside (often a tricky if not false distinction); coastal plains, hills, deserts; north and south; sedentary or nomadic; Outremer presented a mosaic as varied as any that adorned the floors in the homes and manor houses of the Frankish nobility. Thus, while Jerusalem was forbidden to Muslim residents, in 1110 Tancred was encouraging Muslim settlers in the principality of Antioch and negotiating the repatriation of their wives from Aleppo.[14] Some towns and cities, such as Ramla or Jaffa in 1099, had been evacuated by Muslims; in others the Muslim population had been massacred after being stormed; while at Sidon (1110) and Tyre (1124) the indigenous communities were permitted to remain. Certain areas possessed large Christian populations before 1099, particularly in southern Samaria north of Jerusalem and in parts of Galilee; others were dominated by Muslims. Jewish communities were similarly unevenly spread across the landscape; nomadic Bedouin stalked the fringes of the desert. The economy of the plains around Tyre or Acre differed from that of the Judean hills, Transjordan or the commercial centres of Acre, Tyre and Antioch. Inevitably, the nature and distribution of settlement depended on the availability of land, the structure of landowning, the economic opportunities, military vulnerability, the attitude of indigenous communities and local entrepreneurial initiatives.

At the top of Latin society the nobles, having, like Tancred in Galilee, grabbed land or, like his successor there, Hugh of St Omer, been granted it by the king, would naturally dispose of estates to their followers. Other grants included money fiefs, rents from revenues in towns, rather than land. In return, vassals of kings and lords owed military service of knights, at least 675 by *c.*1180; others, the urban and rural freemen known as burgesses and the church, supplied footsoldiers, in theory by 1180 over 5,000. Judged by accounts of royal campaigns, the system worked at all levels: in 1170, sixty-five light-armed young men from the planted Frankish farming community of Magna Mahomeria north of Jerusalem were killed or wounded defending Gaza.[15] Unlike conquests in parts of western Europe, for example England or Sicily, grantor or grantee were not concerned to establish legal continuity with pre-conquest ownership at the level of lordships even if, in practice, they did conform to previous administrative regions, as at Caesarea. In the early days of the conquest, some land was appropriated by individual lords without formal obligations. In the kingdom of Jerusalem, the creation of lordships held directly of the crown was a process of some time, but rewarded those loyal to the king, such as Eustace Garnier, lord of Caesarea and Sidon in 1110.[16] Similarly, lesser lordships went to those in the king's or the seigneur's entourage. One of Baldwin I's knights from Edessa, Hubert of Paceo, held land from the king north of Acre; on Baldwin's death he returned to Edessa with Joscelin of Courtenay.[17] The ties were of lordship or kinship not place. Such patterns of aristocratic patronage were inevitable and commonplace. The origins of the nobility of Outremer did not derive entirely from the contingents of the First Crusade or later military campaigns. Some of the greatest in the land were enticed to the east for political advantage not military adventure: Queen Melisende's cousins Hugh II of Jaffa, actually born in Apulia, and Manasses of Hierges; the Constable Miles de Planchy; Prince Raymond of Antioch; King Fulk. Geographically, many of the earliest lords in the kingdom of Jerusalem came from northern France: Gerard of Avesnes, given a castle near Hebron by Godfrey of Bouillon; Hugh of St Omer in Galilee in 1101; Fulk of Guines at Beirut; Hugh of Le Puiset at Jaffa by 1110. However, their vassals displayed no uniform origins; Hugh of Jaffa's constable, Barisan or Balian, the founder of the fortunes of the great Outremer house of Ibelin, was probably of Italian or Sardinian extraction. Family ties, as of Joscelin of Courtenay with Baldwin II of Edessa or Richard and Roger of Salerno with Bohemund and Tancred of Antioch counted for much, possibly more than regional affinities, although the nobility of Antioch and Tripoli exhibited Italian, Norman and Provençal traces respectively.

Lower down the social scale, the evidence of clerical and secular witness lists, pilgrims' memoirs and documents relating to rural settlement projects reveals a wide catchment area of immigrant recruitment, impossible to restrict to soldierly veterans. Pilgrims outside the military campaigns arrived from as far away as Iceland and Russia. In Jerusalem, among the clergy and lay burgesses, there appear men from most regions of France, from Flanders, Normandy and Paris to Le Puy and Périgord in Languedoc, from northern Italy and Spain.[18] These hardly reflect the contingents of the First Crusade. In the 1160s, John of Würzburg listed the nationalities in Jerusalem: Franks, Lotharingians, Normans, Provençals, men from the Auvergne, Italians, Spaniards and Burgundians. Although complaining loyally at the absence of Germans, or, at least, at the lack of recognition of their original contribution, John noted the German church and hospital of St Mary in the Holy City. Among the religious communities John recorded were Germans, Scots, Celts, English, Navarrese, Ruthenians, Bohemians, Bulgars and Hungarians as well as Italians and northern French. The overcrowding in Acre caused by the press of visitors struck the Greek visitor John Phocas in 1185, who also encountered a travelling professional holy man from Spain near the river Jordan he had first met in Cilicia some years before, and a monk on Mt Carmel from Calabria.[19]

A more limited but still markedly cosmopolitan basis to immigration is traceable in the countryside by the mid-twelfth century. At the Hospitaller settlement of Bethgibelin near Ascalon, most of the incomers came from France south of the Loire, with a few from north Italy and Spain. A fuller list of settlers on land owned by the Holy Sepulchre north of Jerusalem repeats this pattern of heaviest representation from south of the Loire, Italy and Spain, although there were a significant number from the Ile de France and Burgundy.[20] Certain regions of western Europe are conspicuous by their absence: Lorraine, the German Empire and Norman Italy and Sicily, which displayed strangely little interest even in Antioch until late in the century. Part of the explanation for this uneven distribution, even given the extreme narrowness of the sample, may be the presence of easier opportunities nearer home. Yet the royal agent entrusted with attracting settlers to Casal Imbert near Acre in mid-century may have come from Valencia in Spain.[21] The motives of these families cannot be excavated: preferment, prosperity, piety; the certainty of privileged free status, a point emphasized by Fulcher of Chartres in the 1120s, all may have played a part. Most if not all must have been of individual means or attached to people of substance. Neither legally nor financially could serfs afford the trip. Yet western land charters suggest a rich pool of free, non-noble pilgrims and crusaders, villagers of property and artisans, able to raise money for the long, arduous and expensive journey.

Attracting the bulk of settlers and accommodating the largest concentrations of population, the cities of Outremer tended to be refashioned by the new rulers, who redesigned and reconfigured city centres and public spaces to suit their social, commercial and religious needs. Immigrants to cities almost certainly conformed to a similarly cosmopolitan model. Many crusaders and pilgrims originated from the growing towns of the west, so presumably did settlers. Equally, many reared in villages possessed the skills as workmen, artisans, shopkeepers and merchants appropriate to an urban as well as a rural setting. In an environment lacking plentiful wood, thereby placing a premium on skilled craftsmen, where the basic building material was stone, it is unsurprising to find numerous Frankish carpenters and masons who may have been attracted east precisely because of the more profitable market for their trades. In cities, Frankish coiners, goldsmiths, cobblers and furriers catered for a monied elite. In the countryside, in addition to these essential skilled crafts, the sources reveal Latins as blacksmiths; drovers and herdsmen of camels, goats and, distinctively, pigs; gardeners; specialists in grain or vines; butchers; and bakers. Some may have arrived in the train of invading armies, but like Constantine, a poor cobbler from Châlons, or John, a mason from Vendôme, not all, probably not most.[22]

Some settlers would not have become permanent residents and the maintenance of national distinctions apparent in pilgrims' accounts point to a transient urban population, or, like expatriate communities through the ages, groups constantly reinforced in their regional differences by visitors from home. As with all towns in the west, the cities of Outremer housed a constantly changing cosmopolitan population. Where the Italian maritime communes received privileged quarters within ports such as Acre, Tripoli and Tyre, their permanent population of residents in these trading stations remained small between the spring and autumn 'passages'. With the reduction of the power of the crown and the physical size of the Latin principalities in the thirteenth century, and the commensurately greater dependence on commerce, the Italians became powerful autonomous political forces. Despite their privileges, there is not much evidence for this in the twelfth century.

Whether rural or urban, the significance of the continued stream or trickle of non-noble settlement was reflected in the kingdom's laws. By 1110, the non-noble Frankish settler, known as the bourgeois, appeared as a recognizable social group; by the early 1130s they were allowed to hold their own courts, the *cour des bourgeois*, which operated in cities or urban and village communities in the countryside. Under Baldwin III, directed at pilgrims and the poor, in practice new arrivals, the *assise du coup apparent* exempted them from the customary legal requirement for sworn bona fides in a court of law. Newcomers would be unlikely to know anybody, yet were not immune to the usual exigencies of bad luck and the law. The presence of a substantial population of Latin non-noble freemen finds recognition in the number of sergeants whose service was claimed by the kings of Jerusalem in emergencies from towns and the extensive lands of churches and monasteries, as well as in Amalric I's *assise sur la ligece* asserting his right to demand fealty from freemen in fiefs held directly of the crown. Clearly, not all such men, as used to be thought, lived in towns and cities; the unfortunate young men from Magna Mahomeria slaughtered at Gaza testify to that.[23]

So, too, do the various attempts by Latin landlords to entice Frankish settlers to their land and other documentary and archaeological indications of immigrant rural communities. The king and his agents appear active in the plain of Acre in the 1140s to 1160s, offering competitive terms to attract settlers. The priory of the Holy Sepulchre established an extensive network of Frankish villages north of Jerusalem, often on what would now be called 'green field' sites, with distinctive advantageous tenancy agreements. The Hospitallers attracted Frankish settlers to Bethgibelin after 1136 by offering good tenancy terms with formal legal protection of rights which, in the 1160s, they further altered to ease restrictions on tenants' ability to buy and sell their holdings. The order also promoted Frankish settlement on the plain of Sharon. Such entrepreneurial initiatives were common accomplices to political settlement. Frankish customs had been established early at Ramla-Lydda, probably by the Latin bishop, and in the lordship of Caesarea, where the settlers before 1123 included a number of Lombards, possibly connected with the Italians who had helped capture the town in 1101. The pattern of settlement in the train of conquest – 'the settler's plough followed the horse of the conqueror'[24] – continued in the enclaves established in the south of the kingdom and around Ascalon such as Ibelin, Darum and Gaza, or in the fortified villages surrounding the great castles of Oultrejordain at Montréal and Kerak. These communities all contained some Franks, even if, as in the Hospitaller holdings near Ascalon or on the plain of Sharon, they lived alongside Syrian Christians. Elsewhere, Latin lords attempted to maximize their profits by encouraging settlement by locals rather than Frankish immigrants: in the 1150s Baldwin, son of Ulric, viscount of Nablus, sponsored the cultivation of new land by Muslims as well as Syrian Christians.[25]

The distribution of Latin settlement was uneven across Outremer. In the kingdom of Jerusalem, beyond the cities, farming villages, fortified or not, comprising recent immigrants from Europe as well as Latins already established in Outremer, were to be found in western Galilee, on the coastal plains from north of Acre southwards through the plain of Sharon to Ramla, Bethgibelin, Daron and the plains around Ascalon; in Transjordan at Montréal and Kerak; south of Jerusalem between Bethlehem and Hebron; around Sebaste north-west of Nablus; and in lower Galilee. The most densely settled region lay north of Jerusalem towards Sinjil (St Gilles) in southern Samaria; it was probably the first to be systematically colonized. The density of occupation in the region near Jerusalem by the 1160s prevented Duke Bela of Hungary finding suitable property to buy.[26] However, elsewhere, in eastern Galilee, central Samaria, northern Transjordan, settlement did not follow lordship, whole areas of the kingdom being populated almost exclusively by Muslims and Jews. This patchwork pattern may be explained by the Franks' tendency to settle almost exclusively in areas already dominated by local Christians.[27] In a number of places, Latin and Syrian Christians – probably in Palestine Arabic-speaking Greek Orthodox, Maronites or Jacobites – may have shared villages and sites. Baldwin II encouraged Christians from Transjordan to settle in Judea. At a number of villages, as in the great churches of the Holy Sepulchre at Jerusalem and the Nativity in Bethlehem, Latin and Syrian Christians possibly shared liturgical as well as demographic and economic space. Thus is some parts of Outremer, Frankish influence in and on the countryside was negligible, in others considerable and significant in the same way that empty Christian Jerusalem contrasted with cosmopolitan Acre, the large Muslim populations of Tyre and Tripoli or Greek and Armenian Antioch.

MELTING POT OR APARTHEID?

This raises the question posed by many twentieth-century historians of the extent, if any, to which the Latin settlers mixed with the indigenous people to create a cohesive heterogeneous society or one divided by a form of legal, religious, racial and social apartheid. Given the nature of twelfth-century society, contact between communities was inevitable. Outremer was hardly alone in Christendom in containing polyglot neighbours. Communal diversity was a characteristic of the middle ages, not least in the twelfth century: in the British Isles Celts and English, English and French, Flemish settled in Pembroke, Jews establishing quarters in commercial centres; in Sicily Greek, Muslim, Norman, Lombard; the old Jewish communities of the Rhineland; the German expansion into Slavic territory across the Elbe; the competing German and Scandinavian aggression towards the Balts and other pagans; in Spain the long interaction of Christians, Muslims and Jews. Outremer's distinction lay in the extent of the ethnic and religious fragmentation, a feature of the Near East. Nur al-Din, ruler of Aleppo and conqueror of Muslim Syria, was a Turk who surrounded himself with Kurds ruling Arabic-speaking Muslims and Christians. In Egypt the Shi'ite Fatimid caliphs employed Christian Copts and Armenians as secretaries, generals and administrators; the powerful twelfth-century Vizier Bahram (1135–7), called *Saif al-Islam*, Sword of Islam, was an Armenian Christian from Turbessel (Tell Bashir) in northern Syria; his brother was Armenian patriarch of Egypt. One of the Kurdish Saladin's physicians was a Jew.[28]

In Outremer, the Frankish invaders and immigrants discriminated between the several distinct racial and religious groups in language and law. Closest to the ruling class, and often married into it, were the Armenian Christians, mainly in the north. The Greeks, i.e. Greek-speaking Orthodox Christians, appear mainly as an urban community, periodically discriminated against politically and ecclesiastically in Antioch and elsewhere. The category of *Suriani*, Syrians, included Christians speaking Arabic and possibly Syriac, or using Syriac as a liturgical language, the Franks often not bothering to distinguish between Orthodox Melkites, Nestorians (who emphasized the humanity as opposed to divinity of Christ) and Monophysite Jacobites (who emphasized the divinity of Christ at the expense of his humanity) in Palestine and Lebanese Monothelete Maronites. However, local Christians were not confused, at least in the descriptive terms of chronicles, charters and the law courts, with Muslims. The settled Muslim population were known as *Saraceni*; the Bedouin, most but not all Muslim, could be distinguished by the description of *Arabi*, probably because of their wanderings on the desert edges of Outremer towards what the Franks rather vaguely called Arabia. Whereas local Christians, even if excluded from authority within the ecclesiastical hierarchy, lived within the pale of Frankish law, in the market courts, for instance, as neighbours, as property owners, as legitimate spouses, as priests, monks and worshippers, Muslims did not. The Council of Nablus in 1120, even if its draconian moral legislation acted mainly as a propagandist gesture, overtly discriminated against Muslims, forbidding any sexual congress with them (although the punishments for transgressors were equitable regardless of religion) and imposing dress discrimination. In reversal of the Islamic tax regime, Muslims now paid the poll tax instead of Christians. However, where it suited the Franks, for example on the frontier between northern Galilee and Damascus, cooperation in agricultural exploitation existed between Christians and Muslim; in some places, Muslim communities, their laws, customs, possibly headmen (*ra'is*), perhaps even *qadi* (judges) remained largely untouched except for purposes of taxation and profit. As a consequence Franks in Outremer displayed a form of cultural blindness towards their Muslim subjects and neighbours. The Franks recognized the very different nature of the *Turci*, the Turks, the hostile forces governed by Turks as well as the Turkish armies themselves, beyond the frontiers who constituted the main threat to the western settlers' survival. As a result of harassment, discrimination and limited economic opportunities, the indigenous Jewish communities in Outremer suffered sharp decline after 1099, although maintaining a presence in certain areas such as western Galilee. Although, like the Muslims, Jewish communities avoided active persecution after the initial murderous expulsions, and there is evidence of surviving rabbinical courts, in a predominantly Christian and Muslim landscape, the most prominent role for Jewish artisans appears to have been as dyers.[29]

To portray Outremer as a haven of inter-communal, still less interfaith, harmony would be absurd. The Muslims of Galilee in the 1180s called Baldwin IV the pig and his mother, Agnes of Courtenay, the sow.[30] There were sporadic Muslim rebellions in the principality of Antioch, where their treatment alternated between economic encouragement and extortion. While in some areas Muslims remained unmolested in others they fell under a harsh regime. Given a chance, as with the invasion of Palestine by Mawdud of Mosul in 1113 or Saladin in the 1180s, local Islamic communities aided invaders. Muslim slaves, including women in shackles, were a common sight. The massacre of all non-Franks at Tripoli in 1152 regardless of religion exposed an element of racial tension that embraced all non-Franks, particularly likely, perhaps, in crowded cities. Fulcher of Chartres expressed distaste for black Africans he encountered near the Dead Sea in 1100, 'despising them as if they were no more than sea-weed'.[31] Anecdotal evidence noted the intolerance of boorish new arrivals towards any fraternization with Islam, but William of Tyre's disapproval of fashionable Arab medicine points to a more general cultural unease, even if, unlike Norman Sicily, there were few, if any, anti-Muslim riots. As most indigenous peoples in the kingdom of Jerusalem, whatever their religion, spoke Arabic, the formal confessional solidarity could be overlaid by cultural distinction. Syrian Christians and Muslim converts could rise in Latin society, not least in the royal household, yet, beside any religious and ethnic discrimination or tolerance, social status imposed further barriers. With the exception of the Armenians of northern Syria, there were few non-Latin aristocrats within the orbit of Latin Outremer. Although patchy vestiges of a Graeco-Syrian episcopal structure remained, apart from the heads of Greek and Syrian religious houses, the higher reaches of the church were colonized by Latins. Muslim nobles had fled the early Frankish conquests. Prominent local Christians and Muslim converts tended to be professionals – civil servants, merchants, doctors – with only a few significant landowners, perhaps including the family of Muisse Arrabit, a vassal of Hugh of Ibelin around 1160.[32] While conversion as a prerequisite for marriage appears to have been common, Baldwin I's success may have prompted a number of more superior Muslim conversions. One possibly fanciful account records one such convert as governor of Jerusalem in Baldwin's absence in 1112, while a member of his entourage who received the lordship of Hebron in 1107 was known as Walter *cognomine Mahumet*. Other Muslim converts probably joined the ranks of largely Syrian Christian light cavalry in the armies of Outremer, the so-called Turcopoles. However, in general terms social and political as well as religious or ethnic barriers precluded integrated multiculturalism.

Western Christians possessed no monopoly on inter-communal friction and suspicion. One of the odder myths concerning the middle ages is of intolerant Christendom corrupting tolerant Islam. Islamic lawyers at the time of the crusades warned against fraternization, preferring clear segregation. An eleventh-century Baghdad legist, al-Shirazi, urged discriminatory dress on Christians and Jews. The Spanish Muslim traveller Ibn Jubayr intellectually disapproved of Muslims willingly living under Christian rule, behaviour for which he insisted 'there can be no excuse in the eyes of God'.[33] Conversely, just as non-Muslim communities survived under Islam, so non-Christians lived unfree but largely unmolested in Frankish Outremer. After the early massacres, displacements and expulsions of Muslims and Jews from conquered cities, coexistence rather than either integration or persecution prevailed.

No neat picture of inter-communal relations emerges from Outremer. In cities where Latin and Syrian Christians lived cheek by jowl with Muslims, accommodation was apparent. At Acre, where the two faiths shared a converted mosque as well as a suburban shrine, Muslim visitors were treated fairly and efficiently. Mosques still operated openly in Tyre and elsewhere. Muslims of substance were able to travel through the hinterland of Outremer. Although banned from living there, in 1120 Arab traders were encouraged by Baldwin II to sell cereals and vegetables in Jerusalem. In the 1180s, according to Ibn Jubayr, two of the dominant commercial entrepreneurs along the coast of Outremer were Muslim merchants from north Africa based in Damascus. In wide tracts of the countryside Muslim villagers farmed the land under Frankish ownership, paying dues in cash and kind, the lack of active resentment evinced by their political docility probably connected with the general absence of labour services required on Frankish estates. Yet some landlords exacted harsher control; Baldwin of Ibelin in the 1150s increased the poll tax fourfold and insisted on a right of corporal punishment on his Muslim tenants in villages south-west of Nablus. The general tax of 1183 almost certainly fell more harshly on the peasantry than on any other group, although there was formal equality of assessment and exaction between the religious communities. Throughout Outremer, Muslim shrines and cemeteries fell into disrepair and out of use. To visiting co-religionists old men could inaccurately recount as folk memories the epic struggles of the loss of the coastal ports early in the century, but without the presence or investment of a Muslim social or intellectual elite, popular Islamic culture stagnated.[34]

Where communities coincided, relations could be volatile. Nablus and its neighbourhood presented dramatic contrasts. Situated on the edge of the frontier zone, vulnerable to attacks and pillage, such as the raid from Damascus in 1137, it formed part of the royal domain until granted to Balian of Ibelin *c.*1177. The immediate vicinity contained Christian villages with Frankish peasants surrounded by a largely non-Christian population. In one street of the town, a Frankish wine merchant's shop stood opposite an upmarket Muslim guesthouse. A local Muslim highwaywoman exhibited a penchant for waylaying and murdering Franks, a habit possibly connected with her once having been married to one, whom she also killed. Another stylish Nablus woman, the Frank Paschia de Riveri, wife of the local draper, achieved notoriety as the alleged mistress of the Patriarch Heraclius, earning herself the nickname Madame la Patriarchesse and a wardrobe stuffed with silks and precious jewels. Although there were sufficient Franks settled there to have a Frankish court (a Cour des Bourgeois), the local Samaritan sect was permitted to continue its annual Passover ritual, which attracted devotees from all over the Near East, a tolerance of an active non-Christian religious centre unique within Christendom. The Frankish viscount, the king's representative in the town, allowed an Arab emir to witness a sanguinary trial by battle between two Franks over one party's alleged complicity in setting Muslim thieves on to his opponent's property. A bullying Frankish landlord drove a group of devout Muslims of the Hanbali sect to evacuate their villages during the 1150s and 1160s:

before that they had enjoyed full Friday prayers and sermons. In the combination of inter- and infra-communal violence, lawlessness, indifference, practical coexistence, unresolved tensions and exaggerated cultural behaviour, these stories recall the flavour of other competitive frontiers, such as the American 'Wild' West.[35]

Nablus sat on the edge of a frontier zone. Elsewhere in Outremer practical coexistence largely prevailed, even with Muslims. Religious divides could be crossed by conversion; the laws of Jerusalem insisted that former Muslim slaves, if genuine converts, became freedmen. Amongst the nobility, periods of peace, treaties or truces could lead to temporarily amicable contacts. After the treaty that ended the long and bitter siege of Tyre in 1124, the inhabitants emerged to fraternize with their conquerors and inspect the elaborate siege engines used against them. At such times of truce the loquacious raconteur Usamah Ibn-Munqidh of Shaizar, who claimed friends among the Frankish aristocracy, managed to visit his social equals throughout Outremer, even in Antioch and Jerusalem, with impunity. On one occasion Usamah managed, so he later boasted, to secure damages for the theft of part of his sheep flocks from King Fulk against Renier de Brus, lord of Baniyas. Renier's own wife, when captive in Muslim hands in the 1130s, on her own admission 'had not satisfactorily preserved the sanctity of the marriage bed', prompting her husband to divorce her on her release. Amity remained superficial. During a truce between Antioch and Izz al-Din of Shaizar in 1108, Tancred of Antioch befriended a Kurdish knight called Hasanun, who had joined in horse races with the Franks; in 1110, in renewed hostilities, Hasanun was captured and tortured, Tancred personally ordering that the young man's right eye be gouged out despite apparently having given Hasanun his personal guarantee of safety. Another Antiochene, Robert FitzFulk the Leper, struck up an alliance if not friendship with the atabeg of Damascus, Tughtegin, in 1115, although his friend later struck off his head rather than ransom him.[36]

Such stories of aristocratic exchange, largely based on the gilded self-serving memories of the rather unsuccessful Usamah of Shaizar, feature an underlying alienation between the Latins and their Muslim neighbours. Relations between Franks and the Muslim subjects were inescapable. While direct evidence of Muslim self-government is sparse, it is likely that Muslim village life continued much as before, but with heavier tax burdens, the relationship of Latin lords and their Muslim subjects remaining essentially fiscal. There was little overt attempt at conversion; those few Franks who bothered to learn Arabic probably did so to satisfy cultural and aesthetic interests or to converse with their Syrian Christian servants and tenants rather than establish contacts across the communal divide. Muslims existed outside the scope of most Frankish law, as Syrian Christians did not, or were lumped together in opposition to all Christians. Thus the *assise des bourgeois* recorded severe penalties for Muslim violence against Christians but not vice versa.[37] Any concept of an integrated society in Outremer that includes the Muslim community lacks evidence. Contact was administrative or personal, not communal or cultural, either at second or third hand, through village headmen or estate managers, bailiffs and interpreters, or through employment of individuals, such as doctors, possibly a few scribes or eccentric patronage such as that bestowed on Hamdan Ibn Abd al-Rahim by Alan of al-Atharib. The relationship never strayed from that of exploiting lord and regulated subject.

On the other hand, relations with local Christians assumed a very different guise. In some areas, notably Antioch, the institutional power of local churches could not be ignored. Despite visceral anti-Greek ecclesiastical prejudice and discrimination, as revealed in the work of Gerald of Nazareth (d. 1161), in the kingdom of Jerusalem, the ancient Greek abbey of St Sabas enjoyed the patronage of the Latin monarchs, three of whom married Orthodox princesses (Baldwin II, Baldwin III and Amalric I). Greek imperial funds helped rebuild the church of the Nativity in Bethlehem. Greek clergy were restored to the Holy Sepulchre by Baldwin I after the fiasco of the failure of the regular Easter miracle of the Holy Fire under Latin auspices in 1101, the annual ritual on Easter eve when Holy Fire is supposed to descend from heaven to light the priests' candles in the edicule of the Holy Sepulchre. The newcomers evidently had not learnt the knack. An archbishop of the Syrian and Greek communities in Gaza and Bethgibelin negotiated successfully on their behalf with the Hospitaller landlords in 1173 and was even admitted as a *confrater* of the order. Latin and eastern Christians lived together in city and country; in places they worshipped together. Arabic-speaking Syrian Christians occupied important positions as scribes and customs officers, as they did under Muslim rule. Legal rights of local religious groups could be sustained in Frankish courts even, perhaps exceptionally, against Franks. In 1137/8, the Lorraine crusader Godfrey of Asch, a companion of Godfrey of Bouillon, on the plea of the Armenian *catholicus* of Jerusalem finally gained his freedom from captivity in Egypt, where he had languished for thirty-five years. Long presumed dead by his compatriots, his Jerusalem lands had reverted to the local Jacobite (i.e. monophysite) community, the pre-1099 owners. On his release, Godfrey claimed his property back, presumably in the High Court, but, on the intervention of Queen Melisende, had to be satisfied with compensation of 300 besants (gold pieces), leaving the Jacobites in possession.[38]

Integration progressed only so far. Beneath the Frankish legal system, the Syrians held their own courts for petty crimes and civil cases, but serious criminal cases were heard in solely Frankish courts, the *cour des bourgeois*. Even in the *cour de la fronde*, possessing wide civil and limited criminal jurisdiction at Acre and probably in other city ports, where Syrians were represented as jurors, the president was the Frankish viscount. Surviving witness lists of Latin land charters include very few Syrians. Mixed Latin–Syrian marriages, entirely legal and possibly common, may be disguised behind Frankish names, however, contact, cooperation and acceptance did not mean cultural integration. The Arabic-speaking Syrian Christian communities persisted in sharp contrast to the Franks in language, law and culture even though they cohabited the same cities and rural areas. The numbers of immigrants were too small and the duration of their dominance too short for much effective cultural or social symbiosis to occur: too many to be naturalized, too few to transform.

Yet the Franks left their mark and were, in turn, marked by their environment. As elsewhere in areas of conquest and frontiers, the immigrants in Outremer expressed both the necessities of settlement and the requirements of lordship through building. The most obvious statement by the new order rose, if slowly, at the church of the Holy Sepulchre itself, but across Outremer the political, religious and economic needs of the new rulers were met by extensive construction work from grand projects such as the sophisticated concentric Hospitaller castle at Belvoir overlooking the Jordan, to town and village churches, rural fortified towers, manor houses and hall houses, residential terraces for agricultural workers in new settlements such as Magna Mahomeria, to roads, water mills, olive and wine presses and sugar-processing plants. Identifying archaeological remains as specifically Frankish rather than built during the period of Frankish occupation is, in the absence of documentary support, hazardous, yet an extensive Frankish building programme, in the countryside as well as in towns and castles, is apparent in perhaps over 200 locations. Given the hundreds of castle sites identified in post-Conquest England, such an enterprise is unsurprising, even if the building materials, mainly stone, cost more in time, money and men than the plentiful wood of the west. Frankish building in the countryside, including farmhouses and towers for seigneurial and bailiff habitation, as at the Red Tower (al Burj al-Ahmar) on the plain of Sharon, and the planned villages of Frankish farmers and labourers, such as Parva Mahomeria (Qubaiyba) north-west of Jerusalem, indicate a far from entirely absentee landowning aristocracy or exclusively urban bourgeois population.[39] The tangible remains of the Frankish settlements, alongside the records of a vibrant land market at all levels of rural society, display a level of economic viability never fully matched by political or demographic security.

The impression of Frankish society in Outremer as an alien intruder incapable of being grafted on to indigenous culture has been derived, where not from modern politicized analogies of empire, colonization, racial separate development and competing political and religious communities, from the seeming indifference of the Latins to assume a local Palestinian or Syrian identity. Part of this image relies on concentrating on the lack of contact or co-operation between the Franks and the Muslims to the exclusion of Franco-Syrian Christian association. We are told few Franks learnt local languages: 'these people speak nothing but Frankish; we do not understand what they say,' snapped Usamah, blithely ignoring his own admitted inability to speak Turkish.[40] Yet communication between linguistic groups was both essential and constant, in commerce, agriculture, estate management, taxation and justice, most obviously in the multi-ethnic *cour de la fronde*. At Qaqun (Caco) on the plain of Sharon, a mixed settlement of Franks, Syrian Christians and possibly some Muslims, the lord of Caesarea was represented fiscally and judicially by a viscount who owed him the service of one knight and probably used the fort in the village when he visited. However, administrative contact with the Syrian villagers was maintained by the dragoman, literally interpreter, one of whom, called Peter, sold to Walter I of Caesarea land worth 200 besants in 1146. Clearly of some means, Peter, like other dragomans, probably owed his lord a duty of service, conceived in western idiom as a sergeant of a rear-vassal of the lord.[41] In turn, it is possible the Arabic-speaking local Christians had their own headman to negotiate for them. While the lords of Caesarea authorized charters directly with local Syrians, the dragoman acted as the mediator. With Frankish tenants, the lord's interests rested separately with his agent, the dispensator. Thus parallel systems of administration could exist within a mixed Christian village. Physically, too, while Franks settled in areas of previous Christian settlement, it is hard to identify displacement. Rather, the Franks created new villages, resettled abandoned sites or located themselves beside existing Christian villages, even where they shared the local church. The picture emerges of linked, cooperating communities, not fully integrated or assimilated into each other, with only limited need for shared language, a model familiar in contemporary cities and on other frontiers. In such circumstances, maintenance of identity did not imply intolerant exclusivity.

Inevitably, some Franks did learn local languages as well as more generally becoming acculturated with the Near East in diet, dress, hygiene, economic activity and accommodation. A smattering of Arabic for judicial, diplomatic or administrative purposes may have been commonplace; at least one western knight, William de Preaux, managed to learn the Arabic for king, *malik*, during the Third Crusade, using it to divert the attention of Turkish troops away from Richard I during an ambush near Jaffa in 1191.[42] Learning to speak, even read, other languages came as less of a burden to twelfth-century western aristocrats than to some of their modern successors. In addition to his own local vernacular, an educated nobleman would have daily confronted Latin (if only in church or at prayers) and probably numerous other vernaculars, if only orally. Henry II of England was fluent in northern French and Latin, with a smattering of other western European languages; his son Richard I cracked jokes in Latin and recited verse in northern and southern French. To rule England or Sicily, Norman rulers or their officials needed to be trilingual; Bohemund spoke Greek. Among the Frankish nobility in Outremer, captivity provided a more peculiar school of languages; during his imprisonment in the 1160s, Raymond III of Tripoli learnt Arabic, probably not a unique pastime among long-stay prisoners. Others acquired Arabic out of curiosity, intellectual energy, political judgement or necessity. Reynald lord of Sidon (1171–1200), employed a Muslim language teacher, enjoyed religious debate and studied Arabic literature. Sufficiently fluent and adept to charm Saladin himself, Reynald used his linguistic skill to bamboozle the sultan into withdrawing from his stronghold at Beaufort in May 1189 and buy a year's grace and good surrender terms for his castle. Later Reynald acted as a diplomat in negotiations with Saladin during the Third Crusade. Another Frankish noble who, according to Saladin's associate and biographer Baha' al-Din Ibn Shaddad (1145–1234), spoke Arabic well was the effeminate Humphrey III of Toron, whose linguistic talent was in turn employed by Richard I of England in his negotiations with Saladin in 1191.[43] Both Reynald and Humphrey came from families long established in Outremer, their proficiency in Arabic, while striking Arabic chroniclers as sufficiently unusual to be worthy of note, perhaps reflecting a growing facility among the Latin rulers, surrounded as they were, even in their own households, by Arabic-speaking Christians as well as a few Muslims and Arabized Jews. Throughout the twelfth century, chance comments or descriptions of exchanges between Franks and Arabic-speaking neighbours, even at the level of spying, hint at a perhaps wide pool of linguists. The parallel may be with Anglo-Norman England, Sicily and Spain, where conquerors encountered resilient and sophisticated local languages of learning, literature, government and an indigenous social elite. Again, in the context of relations with Syrian Christians, the desire to communicate, even if not strictly imperative for political or administrative survival, appears unsurprising. Much the same could be said of other eastern elite languages. The charter recording the negotiations between the Hospitallers and Meletus the Syrian archbishop in Gaza and Bethgibelin of 1173 is bilingual in Latin and Greek. The Edessan nobleman Baldwin of Marasch, killed in a failed attempt to recapture Edessa in 1146, spoke fluent Armenian and employed an Armenian priest as his confessor.[44]

Much the same eclecticism finds demonstration in other Latin responses to the Near East. In recent centuries the Frankish settlements in Outremer have attracted attention as precursors of later European expansion and colonialism in the region. More properly, they should be seen on their own terms and in their own time. Certain elements of Latin Outremer culture and society reflected western life, notably in the church, language and law, but overlaid with a profound provincialism. The radical intellectual, artistic and legal developments in western

Europe in the twelfth century found only a thin echo in the east. Only two even relatively recent writers were represented in the library of Nazareth cathedral, the theologian Anselm of Canterbury and the canon lawyer Ivo of Chartres. There were few home-grown Outremer theologians or canon lawyers; no universities or Gothic cathedrals; the bureaucratic practices of the royal chancery appear crude in comparison with the papacy, Sicily or England; the coinage imitative and unsophisticated. Academically, Outremer existed in a backwater, distanced alike from west and east. With a few notable exceptions, such as biblical scholar and translator Aimery of Limoges, patriarch of Antioch, western immigrant clergy came from intellectual drawers below the top. Despite cathedral schools, equipped with modest, old-fashioned libraries, indigenous scholars were rare. Apart from the western-educated Jerusalemite William of Tyre, notable was Gerard of Nazareth, bishop of Lattakiah (1140–61), an anti-Greek polemicist and hagiographer. Vernacular literature similarly derived from the west; even the crusade *Chanson des Chétifs*, concerning the 1101 expeditions, which was written in the east, was produced for the immigrant Prince Raymond of Antioch (d. 1149).[45]

The plastic arts were similarly dominated by immigrant artists and models, the most notable being Byzantine influence on decorative painting, illumination and mosaics and, in architecture, southern French and Italian styles. The exquisite illuminated Melisende Psalter of the 1130s or the programme of Greek mosaics with Latin inscriptions erected at the church of the Nativity at Bethlehem *c.*1170 for an English bishop, under joint patronage of Amalric I and Manuel I Comnenus place the art of Outremer in a cosmopolitan, Mediterranean context, distinctive by the coincidence of influences rather than any specific local originality. Here, the ravine between Latin and Greek proved as serious an obstacle to effective cultural symbiosis as that between Latin and Muslim. There is some debate over the existence of a stonemasons' workshop in Jerusalem and the provenance of its artisans and skilled masons, European or indigenous. Were such skilled workers like the church hierarchy, constantly reinforced by western immigrants, or the lay aristocracy, increasingly local descendants of immigrants of previous generations? Both are plausible. One notable feature of Latin art in Outremer was provided by skill in working stone, either in sculpture, as in surviving capitals from Nazareth or the tomb of Baldwin V (d. 1186) in Jerusalem, or in the dressing of ashlar masonry of prestige buildings such as castles or churches, witnessed still in the clear, clean, sharp lines of the twelfth-century piers of Tortosa cathedral, the mighty walls of Saone castle in the principality of Antioch, or the cool certainty of the churches of St Anne in Jerusalem and at Abu Ghosh. How far the intensive labour involved in creating and erecting such stonework was conducted by slave labour, probably Muslim, is unknowable, although the contemporary account of the rebuilding of Saphet castle in northern Galilee from 1240 makes it clear that there the work was carried out by *operarii et sclavii*, workmen and slaves. Without the particular circumstances of Outremer's large resource of Muslim slaves, noted with awe and horror by Ibn Jubayr in 1184, its physical monuments would have been less impressive.[46] This, at least, did not distinguish the Franks from their Near Eastern neighbours.

Living in Outremer did not leave Franks unmarked, even if only in superficial habits of daily existence. The memoirs of Usamah of Shaizar, whose stories are frequently too good to be precisely true, mentioned an agent of his dining in Antioch with a Greek friend at the house of a Frankish veteran of the First Crusade who employed an Egyptian cook, avoided Frankish dishes and never allowed pork under his roof.[47] Such fastidious conversion to Muslim habits was uncommon; westerners in Outremer may have adopted many local comforts, but their taste for pork appeared constant. Pork butchers traded at Tyre; swineherds tended their flocks in the countryside; surviving rubbish tips evince continued consumption. A privilege of William II of Sicily in 1168 allowed the monastery of St Mary of the Latins in Jerusalem to export from Messina without paying customs 200 sides of bacon, as well as 100 barrels of tunny fish and a large shipment of lambskin cloaks, rabbit-skins, ox-hides, linen and wool: winters are chilly in the hills of Judea.[48] Perhaps the greatest dietary impact of the east on the immigrants was castor sugar; exploitation of sugar cane, especially around Acre and Tyre, became a major industry in Outremer. In dress, acclimatization went with loose-fitting clothes, cool fabrics in the summer, furs in winter, protection of skin and armour from the sun by veils and surcoats; some Franks adopted the turban.[49] Most notable in contrast to the west, Franks in Outremer imitated the high standards of hygiene practised by locals. The lack of washing and ignorance of bathhouse culture and etiquette was just one source of hilarity and contempt for Usamah, on a par with what he regarded as the Franks' lax sexual mores and poor treatment of women. Care was taken in providing water supplies for domestic use as well as irrigation, via aqueducts on the coastal plain and networks of cisterns in the arid uplands and desert. Even the Hospitaller castle at Belvoir contained a bathroom. Twelfth-century domestic architecture may rarely have reached such lavish proportions as at the Ibelin palace at Beirut, built in the first years of the thirteenth century, with its fountains, airy halls, mosaics, marble and long vistas inland and out to sea, a sort of Outremer Alhambra. However, even comparatively modest houses of the well-to-do in cities and substantial properties in the countryside boasted mosaic flooring, often with inlay of antique marble, painted plaster walls, the interiors probably furnished with carpets and textile hangings, the tables laid with pottery imports from overseas. Away from the cities, such pottery probably did not circulate, the habitations of the rural peasantry being basic in design and utensils, dependent on local produce and artefacts.

The rural economy of Outremer proved largely resistant to radical change by the western immigrants, who may nonetheless have imported their heavy ploughs to tame the thin soils of Palestine: they divided their plots of land into carrucates, as in the west, although similar land divisions and ploughs were familiar to the east. While not such a monopoly crop as in the west, cereals – wheat and barley – provided a central feature of village economy. Sesame and vegetables were planted as summer crops. The shortage of cereals apparent from imports in the early years of the century did not persist. Olives remained a staple, which would have made immigrants from southern Europe feel at home, although the orchards around the villages provided more exotic fruit. In many new villages, the central activity concentrated on winemaking.

Most evident is the degree to which the Franks in Outremer fitted into the Levantine economy, exporting dyes, luxury textiles, castor sugar and glassware and, increasingly, spices, while importing from Europe and Islamic neighbours such things as foodstuffs, metals, wood, and cotton. Outremer stimulated cross-Mediterranean commerce, in men (i.e. pilgrims) and goods. By the 1160s, one Genoese notary was recording a higher value (almost double) in trade to Syria than to Alexandria, the greatest entrepôt of the eastern Mediterranean.[50] In return, the profits of commerce increasingly sustained the economy and finances of Outremer. Thus it may have appeared to restless westerners that Outremer indeed promised a land of opportunity which its rulers and patrons of settlements struggled to realize.

Despite acculturation, the comparative brevity of the Frankish presence in the Syrian and Palestinian countryside and the truncated occupation of the coastal cities precluded further developments towards either social integration or the creation of a distinctive cohesive cultural identity. The cosmopolitan backgrounds of the settlers, their lack of numbers and the constant influx of visitors and new immigrants was reflected in the diversity of art and architecture. Outremer has been described as a fragmentary colony of western Europe, displaying only disjointed facets or incomplete bits of the mother culture.[51] Equally, it developed only a fragmentary unity with the indigenous Christian population and none at all with the Muslims. The divides of language, law, religion and status failed to coincide. Concerted attempts to convert Muslim subjects were limited. Owners resented the freeing of converted Muslim slaves. Elsewhere, conversions appeared as individual responses to circumstances, although there may have been some pull towards accepting the faith of the rulers of a confessional state, as there was in the later multi-faith Ottoman or Habsburg empires. Yet the ambiguity, if not of the Latin settlement than of the evidence for it, is well expressed in some surviving capitals from the cathedral of the Annunciation in Nazareth. While some have regarded their formalized, unrealistic depiction of Syrians as quintessential proof of the Franks' colonial blindness and policy of apartheid, two of the capitals, depicting apocryphal conversion missions of the apostles Bartholomew and Matthew, have prompted suggestions that some of the Nazarene clergy desired the Christianization of their Muslim neighbours.[52]

Twelfth-century Frankish Outremer did not disappear in the face of Saladin's conquest of 1187–9. Some of the rural population must have survived. In places, on the plain of Acre perhaps, villages may have sustained themselves, subjugated but intact, surrounded as they were by other Christian communities; certainly with the reconquest of the coast after 1191, some settlements resorted to their previous ownership and inhabitants to their former privileges. In such a geographically diverse and complicated region, numbers of Franks may have stayed, survival not necessarily dependent on the fate of the lords or even of the cities. The castle of Montréal had held out against Saladin for a year and a half before surrendering early in 1189. Twenty-eight years later, in 1217, when a German pilgrim, Thietmar, visited the town beneath the castle, still in Muslim hands and inhabited by Muslims and Syrian Christians, he stayed with a Frankish widow. On Thietmar's departure, she provided him with directions on the best route towards his destination of Mt Sinai and supplied him with provisions for his journey: twice-baked bread, cheese, raisins, figs and wine.[53] Here, at least, was one Frankish settler whose stay in the east was not temporary, superficial, transient or destitute. As Fulcher of Chartres had trumpeted optimistically a century before, the widow of Montréal was indeed an Occidental who had become an Oriental.

The Second Crusade

8

A New Path to Salvation? Western Christendom and Holy War 1100–1145

To the snobbish, mother-fixated failed abbot Guibert of Nogent, spinning his vision of 'the Deeds of God performed by the Franks' (*Gesta Dei per Francos*) before 1108, the Jerusalem campaign offered the laity a new path of salvation; the German abbot Ekkehard of Aura, a veteran of the 1101 fiasco, saw it as a new means of penitence.[1] Many western observers were quick to associate the Jerusalem enterprise's uniqueness with a general manifesto for spiritual redemption, ecclesiastical discipline and Christian expansion, such rewarded, sanctified violence exploited by a reinvigorated papacy and its supporters to reinforce the tradition of penitential war in the church's interests. However, the radical effect of the First Crusade can be exaggerated. Secular and clerical refinements of the story of the First Crusade, in poem, song, chronicle or sermon, confirmed as much as redefined long-standing cultural acceptance of the equality of physical with spiritual religious militancy. Urban II had not invented soldiers of Christ nor spiritually beneficial and meritorious warfare, a tradition that encompassed rather than surrendered to the First Crusade. While the first Jerusalemites basked in unique glory, their example did not lead to a succession of large expeditions east following the disasters of 1101. Some regions that had supplied large contingents between 1095 and 1101, including the Limousin, Champagne and Provence, provided few traceable military *crucesignati* between 1102 and 1146.[2] Those who assumed the cross and departed to fight in the east attracted admiration; the cause of Outremer received close, often anxious attention; yet, despite papal commitment and sporadic local recruitment, no mass movement emerged. The images, attitudes and actions of the First Crusade were disseminated across western society widely but fitfully, often as rhetorical evangelical tropes as much as calls to arms. Jerusalem in

Christian hands stimulated a wave of pilgrims with the occasional military adventurer or princely swell, their motives possibly as chivalric as pious. Meanwhile, popes integrated aspects of Urban's expedition into their increasingly authoritarian role as leader and protector of Christendom within as well as beyond its frontiers, encouraging use of the language and institutions of this new holy war against papal enemies in Italy or bandits in northern France as well as Muslims in Outremer or Spain.

SPREADING THE WORD

Awareness of the First Crusade pervaded elite western culture. When, around 1143 in the midst of the backsliding and compromises of the English civil war, the Anglo-Norman baron Brian FitzCount wished to expose the mendacity of the turncoat bishop of Winchester, he naturally chose a familiar reference, the golden memory of the loyalty of the *boni milites* of the First Crusade.[3] A monk from the Cambrésis on the northern Franco-Flemish frontier, writing *c.* 1133, refrained from a detailed account of the Jerusalem expedition, arguing that the events were better described in books, songs and hymns, a regrettable forbearance as he claimed to have attended the Council of Clermont four decades earlier.[4] There was no need for either baron or monk to elaborate; the story was well known. The scale and rapid production of histories of the First Crusade by eyewitnesses and others eager to interpret the startling events didactically finds no parallel in medieval historiography. Within a dozen years of Jerusalem's capture, at least four full eyewitness accounts, three major western histories and part of the great Lorraine version by Albert of Aachen were being circulated along with a bevy of other accounts, more or less derivative, imaginative or polemic. While originating in monasteries and cathedrals, these texts reflected and excited secular interests, for example in local heroes or national pride. Most of the histories sculpted stirring tales of faith, bravery, suffering, danger, tenacity and triumph. The theologians distilled the message of God's immanence and Christian duty; the no less artful eyewitnesses provided accessible tales of miracles and butchery. One of the very earliest, the *Gesta Francorum*, included elaborate scenes with stereotype exotic Orientals declaiming extravagant, bombastic nonsense much in the style of the verse *chansons de geste*. Naturalistic representation, especially of the enemy, did not feature.[5]

Signifying this artificiality, accurate knowledge of Islam and the Prophet remained almost non-existent in western Europe until the translation of the Koran in the 1140s by the abbot of Cluny, Peter the Venerable. Despite a quickening of interest after 1099, accounts of Muhammed relied on translated Byzantine polemic or mangled accounts derived from Spain or returning Holy Land pilgrims. Around 1110, Guibert of Nogent's life of the Prophet in his *Gesta Dei Per Francos* and that by Embrico of Mainz both provided Muhammed with a pet cow, presumably derived from a garbled false memory of the *Sura* of the Koran known as 'The Cow'. Most discussion of Muslims failed to rise beyond the racist ignorance and abuse of the epics and romances, a tradition in which the *Gesta Francorum*, one of the most popular and copied sources, rested comfortably.

Such texts, while sketching an increasingly fixed canon of adventure stories, fed the language of preaching, as with the invented versions of Urban II's Clermont address (i.e. all of them). A more or less distinctive, although never prescriptive or uniform, corpus of scriptural references and paraphrases became employed by popes and later propagandists and chroniclers of Jerusalem campaigns. In this narrow vocabulary of holy war a defined set of intellectual and religious attitudes and theories emerged at the precedent-obsessed papal Curia and among the propagandists and apologists of the Second Crusade (1146–8) but, until the fall of Jerusalem in 1187 once more made the story immediately relevant, not elsewhere beyond the cloister or the study. Twelfth-century circulation of even the most prominent histories of the First Crusade may have been limited, including the most 'popular', the *Historia* of Robert of Rheims. Surviving in at least thirty-nine twelfth-century manuscripts, only during the Third Crusade (1188–92) did it clearly assume the character of an exemplar. In a famous drawing of Frederick I Barbarossa of Germany, dressed as a *crucesignatus*, a copy of Robert's *Historia* is being presented by the provost of Schäftlarn. At about the same time the Cistercian monk Gunther of Pairis, near Basel, later one of the few western chroniclers of the Fourth Crusade (1202–4), rendered Robert's work into verse. Descriptions of the First Crusade and similar later expeditions may have encouraged the application of the language of the Jerusalem holy war, much of it conventional biblical rhetoric, to other conflicts, forming a specialized literary genre. This hardly constituted a demotic movement.[6]

More accessible to the partially literate communities of the twelfth century stood oral transmission of ideas, stories and news: sermons, the liturgy, living witness and the Cambrésis monk's songs, *cantica* and *carmina*, *chansons de geste*, hymns or liturgical chants. Sermons – actual, invented or remembered – sparked ideas and aspirations: the early invented accounts of Urban's Clermont speech; descriptions of addresses made in 1106 on behalf of Bohemund's eastern enterprise or in 1103 by the archbishop of Würzburg concerning a plan of Henry IV to visit Jerusalem; or a recruiting circular composed at Magdeburg in 1108 to encourage support for expansion into the lands of the Slavs beyond the Elbe. It was remembered that Bohemund began his sermon in Chartres cathedral to rouse enthusiasm for a holy war against Byzantium in 1106 by relating 'all his deeds and adventures', prominently, no doubt, his leadership to Antioch in 1098.[7] Such public performances, alive in the collective memory of historians a generation later, helped secure a crusade narrative in the minds of listeners. To reinforce his message, Bohemund may have distributed, in addition to relics, doctored copies of the *Gesta Francorum* which demonized the Greeks while praising him.

Information was conveyed by oral testimony. Chroniclers of the First Crusade relied on the reminiscences of returning veterans. Guibert of Nogent picked the memory of his acquaintance Robert of Flanders; Albert of Aachen's history depended on the testimony of returning members of Godfrey of Bouillon's contingent. The most effective medium of popular memory remained verse. Although the great verse epics, such as the *Chanson d'Antioche*, found a form stable enough to be written down only later in the century, verses for singing or recitation, perhaps with musical accompaniment, were compiled much earlier. These contain little if any historical as opposed to literary value, but they provided vivid stories. Thus, in his own lifetime, Duke Robert II of Normandy (d. 1134) was confronted with wholly fictitious tales that he had killed Kerbogha at Antioch and had been offered the crown of Jerusalem, legends that the Anglo-Norman poet Gaimar had incorporated into his vernacular *Estoire des Engleis* by the 1140s.[8] Such adventure stories fashioned the image of the First Crusade and conditioned responses to further appeals to holy war. The power of songs and verses operated on a number of levels, from taproom to court, causing disquiet even in the powerful. In 1124, Henry I of England blinded a rebel, Luke of La Barre, because of his effective slanderous songs.[9] In mid-century, Gerhoh of Reichersberg credited the medium with producing a creeping puritanism: 'The praise of God is also spreading in the mouth of laymen who fight for Christ, because there is nobody in the whole Christian realm who dares to sing dirty songs in public.'[10]

Gerhoh pointed to the close connections of the warlike laity and their families with religious houses, reflecting the interwoven social context for the varied channels of reminiscence, sermon, encyclical, chronicle and song as well as the physical context of visual reinforcement to the ideology of holy war in sculpture, painting and stained glass, of which only the ecclesiastical survives. In parish churches throughout western Europe, holy knights combated evil and qualified for salvation; in a fresco of the Apocalypse on the roof of the crypt of Auxerre cathedral Christ Himself appears as a mounted military hero. The work was commissioned by Bishop Humbaud (1095–1114), a protégé of Urban II who assisted at the Synod of Anse in 1100, which called on *crucesignati* to fulfil their vows, and who died a Jerusalem pilgrim.[11] Pilgrimage as much as holy war lay behind representations of the Holy Sepulchre itself, in manuscript illuminations, pictorial decorations, ecclesiastical carving or, as at Eichstätt in Bavaria, in the form of a full-scale physical copy.[12]

Not all media of communication told a story. Liturgical chants, hymns and songs encapsulated moods, ideas and admonition, not narrative, as in the very early twelfth-century *Jerusalem Mirabilis*: 'There we must go, selling our estates to purchase the temple of God and destroy the Saracens'.[13] More subtly, increased contemporary elaboration of the mass focused attention on Christ and the cross, their transferred vocabulary and imagery helping define the mentality on which crusading depended. To work as a focus for action, diffuse verbal and visual references depended on knowledge of the Jerusalem campaign and the motifs of holy war or pilgrimage it encouraged. The elevation of the deeds of the Jerusalemites, as they were often described, to legendary status marched in step with the programme of the post-Gregorian church and the cultural assertiveness of the *ordo pugnatorum*, the warrior class. In the overt and, after 1099, increasingly uncontested alliance between the two lay much of the significance of the events of the First Crusade for later generations.

RECEPTION AND RESPONSE

The success of the Jerusalem campaign silenced critics of the Gregorian promotion of penitential warfare, encouraging the papacy's branding of its enemies as fit targets for holy war. In 1103–4, Paschal II, in full Gregorian mode, offered unspecified remission of sins to Robert of Flanders and his knights in return for their deeds of 'just knighthood' against papal opponents in Cambrai as well as to southern German supporters against the emperor. Papal adherents in Italy were similarly encouraged: in 1135 the remission of sins granted at the Council of Pisa to those who fought against the anti-pope and the king of Sicily was explicitly equated with that decreed by Urban II at Clermont.[14] Such an association became regarded as the most potent sign of holiness, justice and honour. Elsewhere, the popularity of penitential war proved useful in essentially secular conflicts. Repeatedly after 1100 the higher clergy of northern France invoked the language of holy war and grants of remission of sins for those engaged in policing the lawlessness of the region, even where the alleged malefactor, such as Thomas of Marle, attacked in 1115, was a crusade veteran destined to epic immortality in the *Chanson d'Antioche*.[15] The distinction between brutal violence and valiant heroism lay in the eye of the beholder. For the clerics authorizing such campaigns they provided active demonstrations of the church's direction of the laity for which the First Crusade provided the most striking model.

Acceptance of the values legitimized by the Jerusalem expedition lay in reactions to the returning veterans, fêted on their homecomings laden with relics and other souvenirs from the east. One was reputed to have brought back a lion as a memento.[16] Most were content with the palm leaves that marked their status as Jerusalemites. The aura of distinction clung to many for the rest of their lives. Some retired to monasteries; others continued their pious careers by endowing religious houses or donating relics. Careers were advanced by exploiting contacts made on campaign. Most, perhaps, picked up the threads of their lives as best they could, returning, in externals at least, to the lives they had left behind. Count Robert of Flanders's crusade exploits earned admiration in chronicles and charters, his death by trampling in a skirmish in 1111 lamented as a sad fate for a 'bellicosus Jerosolimitae'.[17] Reputation could produce tangible benefits. King Henry I explained to Pope Calixtus II in 1119 that he had afforded his captive brother Duke Robert of Normandy good treatment because of his crusader status: 'I have not kept him in irons like a captured enemy but have lodged him as a noble pilgrim in a royal castle'.[18] Whether the hero of Antioch and Jerusalem appreciated such fraternal generosity over the twenty-eight years spent in his brother's prisons must be debatable.

Other veterans returned to their former lives largely unmarked. Thomas of Marle's career of rapine, if less lurid than his political opponents and their tame clerical apologists portrayed it, exposed the myth that service in the papal holy war engineered a form of spiritual conversion. As numerous commentators observed, the qualities that produced mayhem in Europe had not been suppressed, merely channelled in a good cause. Thomas of Marle's aggression had proved very useful in the desperate battles in the east. Not all crusaders attracted unrealistic sentimentality; Everard III of Le Puiset, viscount of Chartres, was accused by Abbot Suger of St Denis a generation later of having undertaken the Jerusalem journey out of pride, his evil reputation for violence in the Ile de France being in no way mitigated by the gesture. The centrality of the martial ethos in popularizing the Jerusalem expedition left some participants happy to pursue former habits. Resort to arms was forced on some: Hugh of Chaumont, lord of Amboise, faced with the loss of his inheritance, acted vigorously and violently; yet he returned east with Count Fulk of Anjou in 1128. Belligerent resolution to disputes still came naturally. Only a few years after his return, Raimbold Croton, a hero at Antioch and Jerusalem, where he lost a hand, had a monk castrated over some stolen hay. Despite a fourteen-year penance forbidding him to bear arms, effectively suspending his social status, Raimbold appealed successfully to Pope Paschal II on account of his bravery at Jerusalem, although he soon died in one of the interminable petty wars in the Ile de France.[19]

Just wars and godly knights were not invented in 1095 or first consecrated in 1099. Not all subsequent accounts of war echoed the heroics in Syria. Orderic Vitalis's description (*c.*1140) of the motives of Henry I's troops in refraining from slaughtering their defeated French opponents at Brémule (1119) rested on accepted rhetoric of Christian wars:

they spared each other . . . out of fear of God and fellowship in arms . . . As Christian soldiers they did not thirst for the blood of their brothers, but rejoiced in a just victory given by God for the good of the Holy Church, and the peace of the faithful.

In fact Henry's men thirsted for juicy ransoms. By contrast, in Orderic's description of the fighting around Fraga in 1134 between Alfonso I of Aragon and the Almoravid Muslim fundamentalists from Morocco, the Aragonese wore 'the cross of Christ' (whether Orderic meant literally or metaphorically is unclear), their battle cries 'in the name of Jesus'.[20] In the account of the battle of the Standard (1138) by the contemporary English writer Henry of Huntingdon, the English soldiers facing the invading Scots received absolution before the conflict, which was declared 'very just' by a bishop present, who promised full remission of sins to any who died in the fight in defence of their homeland ('patria'). The symbols of the church and the appeal to patriotism as well as martyrdom in this description may have been sharpened by the new holy war but in essence derived from older traditions. Similarly, although in Geoffrey of Monmouth's fanciful but widely circulated *Historia Regum Brittaniae* (*History of the Kings of Britain*) of 1136, King Arthur's troops at the battle of Bath have been 'marked with the sign of the Christian faith', i.e. the cross, they were only promised absolution from all sins if they perished in the fight. There is no explicit suggestion that fighting the pagans, however praiseworthy, was itself penitential.[21] As with Charlemagne's doomed paladins in the epic poem *The Song of Roland*, *c.*1100, paradise, where souls rested 'amid the rose-blossoms', beckoned only those slain in the good fight. Such conservatism embraced even the papacy: in December 1118 Gelasius II granted Alfonso I of Aragon plenary indulgences only to those killed fighting the Moors.[22]

While memories of the First Crusade undoubtedly influenced the sharper confidence in describing and prescribing holy war, especially against infidels and pagans, the haphazard adoption of specifically new forms of penitential warfare by writers and popes alike points to a contingent appreciation of the significance of 1095–9. Even the rhetoric lavished on the new military order of the Templars by Bernard of Clairvaux in his *De laude novae militiae* (*In Praise of the New Knighthood*) *c.*1130, for all its radical reworking of St Paul's spiritual metaphors of fighting for Christ into literal calls to arms, dwells on martyrdom and the prospect of salvation, at once traditional and immediate anxieties of the fighting classes. The images, language and ideology specifically related to penitential holy war as coined by the preachers, leaders and led of 1095–9, distinctive by association as much as by any liturgical, juridical, ceremonial or semantic coherence, formed only one part of a wider articulation of holy war and militant Christianity. In no sense did the early twelfth century knowingly witness the dawning of a pervasive 'age of the crusade'.

Instead, the dynamic force of the idealized and physical Jerusalem provided the prime focus, for travellers, in arms or not, as for theorists. Pilgrimage not holy war proved the most immediate legacy of the Christian occupation of the Holy City. King Eric I of Denmark in 1102–3 and King Sigurd of Norway in 1107–10 went east as pilgrims as well as warriors, their martial intent an extension of traditional Scandinavian service for Byzantium, which acted as host to both monarchs; fatally for the Norwegians, many dying from excess of undiluted retsina. Eric died in Cyprus before reaching the Holy Land; his wife on the Mount of Olives. In 1110, King Sigurd only allowed himself to be recruited 'to the service of Christ' by Baldwin I for the siege of Sidon once his vows had been fulfilled at Jerusalem, where he may have received the cross.[23]

Links with Jerusalem established the domestic respectability of lords, especially kings. In the winter of 1102–3, the German emperor, Henry IV, for a quarter of a century the papacy's most hated and implacable enemy, voiced his intention to travel to the Holy City, probably as a pilgrim. The public announcement at a diet at Mainz in January 1103, accompanied by solemn masses and an exhortatory sermon by the bishop of Würzburg, attracted wide interest, cynics suspecting a trick. Privately, in a letter to his aged godfather, the enormously grand Abbot Hugh of Cluny, Henry made his desire to see where Christ had lived, conversed with mortals and died conditional on a peace settlement with the papacy over the Investiture dispute. No deal, no pilgrimage.[24] In seeking to use the Jerusalem pilgrimage in helping resolve intractable secular conflicts, Henry was not alone. From England to Sicily, political outlaws, such as the would-be assassins of William I of Sicily (1160) and the actual murderers of Thomas Becket (1170), worked their passage back to respectability or found a nobler form of exile through the trip – or the promise of a trip – to Jerusalem.[25] In 1102/3, Henry IV hoped a commitment to visit Jerusalem would expedite a deal with the papacy and pacify his kingdom just as St Bernard's preaching and King Conrad III's taking of the cross did in 1146–7. It may have been the failure of such a strategy to resolve family feuding in the Danish royal house that led to the murder of Duke Canute, Eric I's son, by his cousin Magnus in 1131. Apparently, Magnus had vowed to go to Jerusalem, probably as a pilgrim, leaving his wife and children in the care of Canute, whom he then murdered as an alternative to clinching the deal.[26] In 1128, on the death of William Clito count of Flanders, many of his followers not pardoned by his hostile uncle, Henry I of England, 'took the Lord's Cross and, becoming exiles for Christ's sake, set out for His sepulchre in Jerusalem'.[27] As a technique of resolving feuds, the Jerusalem journey became embedded into the public culture of western Europe: successive treaties between Henry II and his French overlords Louis VII and Philip II featured mutual commitments to go east. However, using Jerusalem (and other) pilgrimages for political ends, to re-establish respectability and authority or as a form of temporary exile, predated the twelfth century: notable eleventh-century pilgrims included the bloodthirsty Count Fulk Nerra of Anjou, Duke Robert I the Devil of Normandy and the Anglo-Danish murderer Sweyn Godwinson, older brother of the last Anglo-Saxon king of England.

The twelfth-century explosion of peaceful pilgrimages to Jerusalem stood in marked contrast to the occasional and, after the debacle of the Second Crusade, limited enthusiasm for holy wars to the east. Yet there developed a ready association between noble pilgrims and deeds of arms, highlighted by the creation in Jerusalem of the Order of the Knights of the Temple of Solomon, the Templars, in 1119 to whom visiting grandees, such as Count Fulk of Anjou in 1120, could temporarily attach themselves. The habit began earlier. In the first decade of the twelfth century, pilgrims were repeatedly pressed into military action by inducements from the Christian rulers of Outremer. Shortly after being knighted, some time before 1111, Charles of Denmark, a nephew of Robert II of Flanders and later count of Flanders himself, underwent a pilgrimage on which he fought against the pagan 'enemies of the Christian faith'. In 1124, Conrad of Hohenstaufen, the future King Conrad III and leader of the Second Crusade, possibly after some sort of conversion experience, vowed to go to Jerusalem as a soldier for Christ, the only European monarch to campaign in the Holy Land twice.[28] Charles and Conrad were not unique. In the generation after

1100, a steady trickle of affluent French nobles visited Outremer, a few of them First Crusade veterans revisiting as pilgrims the scenes of their youthful martial glory; one or two, like Stephen of Neublans from Burgundy in 1120 or Hugh of Chaumont in 1128/9, even signed up to fight again. Interest in the east ran in families, such as those of comital Burgundy – roughly modern Franche Comté – (which included Pope Calixtus II, who proclaimed a new holy war in the east in 1119), or of the French lordships of Montlhéry and Le Puiset, a concern that embraced fighting and settlement as well as pilgrimage. Such contacts spread unevenly across western Europe, with German speakers lacking established links in Outremer 'as they . . . had no mind to stay there', to the regret of John of Würzburg in 1170.[29] Settlers' relatives provided a conduit for interest, information and material help for the Holy Land. By the 1130s, these associations could find outlet in new, permanent institutions of holy war.

MILITARY ORDERS

Hugh I count of Troyes went east three times, 1104–8, 1114 and 1125; the final visit saw him enrolling in the new religious order of the Knights Templar; he was not alone. By 1131, when the childless King Alfonso I of Aragon (d. 1134) drew up a will in which he bequeathed his possessions jointly to the canons of the Holy Sepulchre, the Order of the Hospital of St John (the Hospitallers) and the Templars, the two Levantine military orders, especially the latter, had established themselves as unique institutions within the Catholic church, combining charity with violence, religious vocation with fighting. Through attracting recruits and grants of property in the west, these orders established on a permanent footing the basic idealism of penitential warfare, a mechanism for its expression and a physical presence throughout Christendom reminding the faithful of the plight of the Holy Land.[30]

The Order of the Hospital of St John, the Hospitallers, originated in an Amalfitan hospital established in Jerusalem by 1080 to provide care for poor and sick pilgrims. Originally dedicated to St John the Almsgiver, a seventh-century patriarch, after the conquest of 1099 its enhanced role and importance in coping with the new rush of western visitors, many ill, exhausted and impoverished, led to an elevation in status and patron saint, the local historical cleric giving way to the much grander, universally recognized John the Baptist. Receiving grants of property from King Baldwin, in 1113 the order acquired papal recognition as a charitable confraternity bound together into an order through the adoption of religious vows of poverty, chastity and obedience, in outline little different from other new orders such as the Augustinian canons. While the structure of the Hospitaller order may have provided the model for the Templars, the martial function of the latter influenced the Order of St John. While never losing its essential charitable hospital function, by 1126 Hospitaller brothers were serving in the army of the kingdom of Jerusalem on campaign against Damascus, and by 1136 the order was being entrusted with garrisoning frontier fortresses.

The original function of the Templars was military yet, like the Hospital, its purpose derived from the needs of Jerusalem pilgrims. In 1119, a group of knights in Jerusalem led by Hugh de Payns from Champagne and a Picard, Godfrey of St Omer, established a confraternity to protect the pilgrim routes from the coast to Jerusalem and from there to Jericho. Licensed by the patriarch of Jerusalem and bound by the monastic vows of poverty, chastity and obedience, the knights received official ecclesiastical recognition at the Council of Nablus in January 1120. From its earliest days, although dependent on alms even for clothing, the order was lodged in and around the royal palace at the al-Aqsa mosque and elsewhere on the Temple platform, inspiring the name of the Order of Temple of Solomon (which the Franks identified with the al-Aqsa) and demonstrating the strong and consistent support of the king. The same year, their contacts were sufficiently illustrious to recruit the visiting Count Fulk of Anjou into their ranks, if only temporarily; on his return to the west Fulk endowed the order with an annual income of thirty *livres anjou*, setting an example followed by many.[31] Between 1127 and 1129, Hugh de Payns toured western Europe to attract donations and members, as well as assisting in negotiations to persuade his former *confrater* Fulk of Anjou to return east and recruiting forces for a new campaign against Damascus. Travelling widely in France and visiting England and Scotland, Hugh's success is reflected in the extensive grants made to the order in 1127–8 of land, rents, customs, war materials and, from the counts of Flanders, the proceeds from entry fines to fiefs, known as reliefs. Hugh's contacts included some of the greatest lords in France. Apart from Fulk of Anjou, Hugh of Troyes was already a member of the order, and other patrons included William Clito and Thierry of Alsace, successively counts of Flanders, and Theobald count of Blois, while his welcome in England and Scotland testified to his status.[32] His triumphal progress was crowned at the Council of Troyes in January 1129, presided over by a papal legate and attended by many from the elite ecclesiastical establishment, including the most influential of all, Bernard abbot of Clairvaux, who a few years later was to compose the famous paean of praise for the new knighthood and holy war on behalf of the new order, *De Laude novae militiae*. At Troyes, after hearing Hugh's description of the principles and practices of the new order, the council confirmed its foundation and provided a systematic Rule.

Although the Templars had received property in the west before 1128–9, Hugh's trip consolidated the order's standing as a recipient of charitable donations. By 1150, it had become an extensive and wealthy landowner from England to Italy and Portugal, and especially in northern France, Languedoc and north Spain, the extensive network of estates soon organized into regional commanderies. In some areas, the connection between crusading families and patronage of the order is obvious. In England, the Temple's chief patrons proved to be King Stephen, son of the coward of Antioch, Stephen of Blois, and his wife Queen Matilda, daughter of Eustace of Boulogne and niece of Godfrey of Bouillon and Baldwin I. King Stephen's brother Theobald and William Clito of Flanders, son of the crusader Robert of Normandy, also proved generous donors. In such concrete ways, the propaganda of St Bernard and the enthusiasm of individual recruits were lent physical expression and support, the great centres of the Temples in Paris or London, or the estates such as Temple Cowley or Knightsbridge in England acting as familiar reminders of the cause of Christianity in the east.

The clear association of the Templars with the tradition of the First Crusade found reinforcement in their enjoyment of full remission of sins for fighting and the adoption of the red cross on their white robes, showing them unmistakably as knights of Christ. However, the concept of members of a religious order, fortified by the offices of the church, riding out to shed blood could still jar, especially as other religious, such as monks, were actively discouraged from participation in holy wars. To some observers, not otherwise hostile to holy war, the vocational combination of a knight and a monk appeared monstrous. Guigo, abbot of the austere Grande Chartreuse (1109–36), expressed anxiety at the dangers inherent in this fusion of the spiritual and profane: 'It is useless attacking external enemies if we do not first conquer those within ourselves . . . first purge our souls of vices, then the lands from the barbarians'.[33] Such unease provoked lengthy apologia in support of the Templars by their adherents and supporters, most famously and polemically in St Bernard's *De Laude*. Yet, despite such honed rhetoric, the active encouragement of the great and a series of papal bulls granting recognition and extensive ecclesiastical and spiritual privileges (1139–45), doubts persisted, never entirely stilled until the order's suppression and abolition in the early fourteenth century. While in the early days of the order, the conceptual novelty disturbed some, even in the thirteenth century canonists such as Thomas Aquinas needed to spell out the meritorious connection between fighting God's war and a penitential vocation.[34]

Nonetheless the Templars and the Hospitallers, whose continued charitable function deflected criticisms, provided a model quickly copied elsewhere. Proliferation of religious confraternities was a prominent feature of the twelfth and thirteenth centuries, some designed for military purposes, such as Alfonso I of Aragon's militia at Monreal del Campo (1128–30) and the confraternity of Belchite (1122), which some have argued imitated Muslim *ribats* in combining military service and a life of prayer, or the Danish confraternity established in 1151–2 by Vetheman, a wealthy merchant from Roskilde, to police the seas against pirates, often pagan; while not specifically connected with penitential warfare, members took Communion and confessed their sins before each tour of duty.[35] Not all these brotherhoods imposed service or commitment for life: even the Templars admitted temporary members visiting Jerusalem, such as Count Fulk in 1120 or the Burgundian Humbert III the Old, lord of Beaujeu, in 1142, and provided an elite hotel service for other grandees such as Conrad III in 1148.[36]

The success of the formula pioneered in the east by the Temple and Hospital in attracting donations and organizing men, money, defence and political control of whole regions encouraged emulation in the Iberian peninsular, where local military orders were established in the struggle against the Moors: in Castile the Orders of Calatrava (1164) and Alcantara (1176); in León the Order of Santiago (1170); and in Portugal the Order of Avis (*c.*1176). In Outremer, the Order of Lazarus, founded in the 1130s mainly but not exclusively for leprous knights, possessed close ties with the Templars. Leprosy, or similar-appearing skin diseases, were indigenous to the Near East, carrying with them a social stigma and religious charge far beyond their infectious potential (which was and is small). The association with St Lazarus became widespread in Latin Christendom, leper hospitals being known as 'lazar houses'. The Templar rule became the model for the Order of Teutonic Knights (1198, based on a hospitaller confraternity formed at the siege of Acre in 1190) which in turn gave its statutes to the English Order of St Thomas of Acre (founded for canons 1190/1; militarized 1228). Such institutions closely shadowed mission and warfare on Christendom's frontiers, as with the Swordbrothers of Livonia (*c.*1202) and the Prussian Knights of Dobrin (Dobryzn, *c.*1220). The larger orders, especially the Temple and Hospital, grew into international organizations, with extensive property and political influence, comprising structures, membership and dependants far beyond the original knights, priests or hospitallers, or the sergeants and other necessary military personnel: there were even convents of nuns attached to the Hospitallers in the thirteenth century.

The military orders formed just one aspect of the great revival and extension of institutional religious life in the twelfth century. What rendered them distinctive was their function and their inspiration, the war of the cross. However, those who joined the orders as the small elite of professed knights, sometimes, especially in the early years, after long careers of secular knighthood, were not *crucesignati* in the ordinary sense; their crosses were signs of a lifetime vocation not a temporary act of penance. Entry to a military order was not an alternative to becoming a *crucesignatus*; the alternative to becoming a Templar or Hospitaller was to become a monk, an altogether more serious step into a new life not merely a temporary gesture of faith and chivalry. Even St Bernard, who repeatedly drew analogies between *crucesignati* and monks – vows, profession, liturgical entry ceremonies, special clothing, communal living – recognized that becoming a monk, or, by extension, a Templar or Hospitaller, and becoming a *crucesignatus* were neither genuine alternatives nor synonymous.

NEW WARFARE?

With the exception of the military orders, the development of new crusading institutions in the west in the early twelfth century is confused and obscure. There were few general calls to repeat the penitential warfare of 1095: Bohemund's war in 1106–8; the eastern campaign promoted by Calixtus II in 1119–20; Fulk of Anjou's expedition of 1129; the campaigns in Spain of 1114–16, 1118 and 1125–6 also attracted papal authority and indulgences. Even with these and other explicit associations of holy war and the armed pilgrimage of 1096–9, there appears little radical departure from pre-existing social and religious activities or attitudes connected with pilgrimage and church-sanctioned holy war. Little coherence existed between large-scale expeditions east (1107 or 1120–24); small, private armed and unarmed pilgrimages, many lacking any papal authority; the interests of Outremer settlers such as Fulcher of Chartres to create a process of constant reinforcement; and the emergence of the military orders. Each appeared distinct in operation even if related in terms of motive and appeal while reflecting extremely traditional responses of obligation, honour, service (to God or terrestrial lord), adventure or penitential anxiety. The First Crusade confirmed and extended existing acceptance of holy war but created no new settled legal framework, the hot rhetoric of its apologists bereft of accepted canonical formulae. In the great digest of Canon Law, Gratian of Bologna's *Decretum* (*c.*1140), the extensive discussion of legitimate just warfare (Causa 23) ignored anything that could be regarded as specifically flowing from any new institutions established during or after the holy war of 1095–9, a silence pointedly filled by an Anglo-Norman commentary on the *Decretum* later in the century that referred explicitly to *crucesignati* and the manner in which the faithful should pray for them.[37]

These new institutions scarcely amounted to a revolution in Christian habits. The legacy of the First Crusade included spiritual and temporal privileges previously associated with those enjoyed by pilgrims, which by 1145 had become recognized by the pope as comprising remission of confessed sins (not just, as in some of Urban II's pronouncements, the penalties of sin), protection by the church, legal immunity for the duration of the expedition, permission to raise mortgages and a moratorium on repayment of debts.[38] In addition the ceremony of taking the cross asserted itself as characteristic of a certain form of pilgrimage. However, implementation was erratic and at times baffling to contemporaries faced with novelty. In 1107, a committee of clerics set up to investigate a claim for protection by a recruit for Bohemund's campaign in the east failed to give a verdict because 'the institution of committing to the church's care the possessions of *milites* going to Jerusalem was new'.[39] Uncertainty was explicable. With Jerusalem in Christian hands, no incentive existed to elaborate a new form of holy war to recover it. Thus repeated calls to arms simply evoked the precedent of Urban II and Clermont rather than developing it. Pilgrimage, not war, constituted the overwhelming response to the capture of the Holy Land, the language and practice of crusading and pilgrimage increasingly fused together, pilgrims and holy warriors indiscriminately described as *peregrini* (pilgrims), a dilution of any novel aspects of Urban's holy war. This reflected reality. Not all armed pilgrims fought (e.g. Henry the Lion, duke of Saxony, in 1172) and not all who fought had taken the cross (e.g. the pilgrims employed by Baldwin I in 1102 and 1107). *Crucesignati* bore the staff and satchel of the pilgrim: pilgrims bore crosses and carried arms. Both shared the vocabulary of the *peregrinatio*, some of the same privileges and status as quasi-ecclesiastics. In twelfth-century charters it is rarely possible to distinguish the two activities. Taking the cross appeared to mark involvement in penitential warfare, yet chroniclers applied the word pilgrim. Notions of unarmed pilgrimage and armed penitential war were less discrete than the contradiction in purpose and function might imply. The cross tended to suggest violence, yet the English hermit Godric of Finchale (d. 1170) twice took the cross, the *vexillum crucis*, before visiting Palestine and yet each time, according to his contemporary biographer, he contented himself with sight-seeing, fasting and penance. In a charter of 1120 Guillaume le Veneur (i.e. huntsman) from Maine was said to have 'accepted the cross as a sign of his pilgrimage (*in signum peregrinationis*)'. A liturgical rite for taking the cross survived the events of 1095–6. Some evidence suggests that it was perceived as separate from the adoption of the signs of pilgrimage; other the opposite: for Guillaume le Veneur in 1120 and Fulk of Anjou in 1128, taking the cross was said to follow 'the custom of such pilgrimages'.[40] This may indicate regional differences similar to those found in the liturgies themselves: no standard liturgical rite for taking the cross existed for the rest of the middle ages. Such disparity, while typical of the practice if not the rhetoric of the high medieval church, hardly confirms the creation of a homogeneous movement, more a changing series of modified and conservative associations, habits and responses, stimulated by new political and ecclesiastical circumstances but rooted in tradition. Even the novel military orders grew out of existing attitudes to holy knighthood. If the new penitential warfare, especially to the east, was innovative in its eschatological resonance and its physical demands, the spiritual, social, political or economic tensions assuaged were not.

Potentially the new exercise possessed wide implications if the privileged legal and fiscal immunities claimed for *crucesignati* found guarantee with the church and support from secular power. There is little evidence before the very end of the twelfth century, from the period of the Third Crusade (1188–92) and later, for the active operation, either in church or lay courts, of these immunities. Despite a decree of the First Lateran Council (1123), the first general council of the western church in the middle ages, reinforcing the church's duty to protect crusaders' property, much depended on the local secular context and the willingness of interested parties to cooperate. When they did not, confusion ensued, as in the case of the property dispute between Hugh II of Le Puiset and Routrou of Perche in 1107, which exposed the ecclesiastical authorities as both muddled and ineffective as the case ping-ponged between secular and clerical courts, with one of the best canon lawyers of the time manifestly unable to identify clear legal cause let alone remedy.[41] Even after 1123, uncertainty persisted. As late as November 1146, Pope Eugenius III had to inform the bishop of Salisbury that the immunity only operated in regard to law suits and seizure of property after the cross had been taken. During the Second Crusade, the pope received numerous complaints that church protection simply did not work. It took another half-century for the immunities of *crucesignati* to find a place in accounts of law courts and in the records of secular government.[42] For much of the earlier twelfth century, in any given region, taking the cross was uncommon and military expeditions of the cross rare: hardly the dawn of a new age.

WARS OF THE CROSS

This ephemeral nature of the wars of the cross can partly be explained by lack of occasion. The disastrous campaigns of 1101 killed extravagant optimism. Jerusalem remained in Christian hands. The very success of the Franks of Outremer in carving out principalities militated against any sense of crisis, relatively few laymen thinking in terms of permanent holy war, fewer even than those wishing to settle in the east. Pilgrimage and later the military orders provided the main connection between the two parts of Catholic Christendom, not crusading. Yet sporadic attempts were made to summon up enthusiasm for the old cause as well as to apply its forms to conflicts elsewhere.

Bohemund of Antioch's campaign of 1107–8 demonstrated both the potential and the limitations of attempts to revive the spirit of 1096. On his release from Danishmend captivity in 1103, Bohemund was faced by the loss of much of his conquests in Cilicia to the Byzantines and, in 1104, of his eastern provinces to Ridwan of Aleppo. Western assistance provided an obvious solution; Bohemund's reputation would act as the chief recruiting officer. Arriving in Italy in 1105, after securing the approval of Paschal II, Bohemund proceeded to France early in 1106, accompanied by a papal legate, Bruno of Segni, a veteran of Urban II's preaching tour a decade before. Bohemund planned to harness concern for the Holy Land to an attack on the Byzantine empire, a sleight of hand highlighted by the presence with him on his triumphal tour of France of a spurious pretender to the Byzantine throne and other Greek exiles. During his sermon at Chartres in early April, Alexius I was identified as a target, those who joined up being promised 'wealthy towns and castles'. Writing to the pope in 1107, Bohemund argued that he sought, in the general context of aiding the Holy Land, to resolve the supposed Greek problem by ending Alexius's usurpation, the ecclesiastical schism and Byzantine hostility to crusaders. Yet Bohemund's official line during 1106–7 focused on the *via Sancti Sepulchri*. One eyewitness remembered the papal legate at a council at Poitiers in June 1106 particularly emphasizing the need to arouse enthusiasm for the journey to Jerusalem.[43] Whatever his motives, Bohemund used his fame to acquire a high-class wife, Constance, daughter of King Philip of France, and create a mood of excitement. Nobles apparently queued up to persuade him to become godfather to their children. King Henry of England, preparing his attempt to conquer Normandy from his crusader brother Duke Robert, was sufficiently alarmed as to ban him from crossing the Channel lest too many knights joined the eastern adventure. The number, geographic range and social standing of Bohemund's recruits testified to his charisma and successful propaganda. Not only did they come from lands associated with the leader's ancestry, Italy, Normandy, England, but also from large swathes of France from the Limousin and Poitou northwards across the Loire through the Chartrain and Ile de France to Flanders and imperial Burgundy. The rumour of war may also have inspired more distant interest in Jerusalem, including that of King Sigurd of Norway, although he had no practical involvement in Bohemund's plans. While piety may have played a significant part in the success of Bohemund's carefully orchestrated appeal, at least one later observer noted, perhaps with the cynicism of hindsight, that many 'set out on the road for Jerusalem like men hastening to a feast'.[44]

By October 1107, even the most purblind of his followers could see that Bohemund's intention was to revisit the battlefields of his youth in the western Balkans. Landing in Albania on 9 October, Bohemund directed his army, which marched under a papal banner, to besiege Durazzo. For all his famed military skill, Bohemund found himself completely outmanoeuvred. By the spring of 1108, his force was surrounded and cut off from reinforcements across the Adriatic. It is testimony to his determination and generalship that he resisted the logic to surrender until September. Writing a generation later of Bohemund's final interview with Alexius I before agreeing to the humiliating Treaty of Devol, Alexius's daughter, Anna, was prompted to include her famous description of this dangerous but attractive barbarian: tall, muscular, broad chest, slim waist, 'perfectly proportioned', pale skin, short, light-brown hair verging on reddish, shaven face, light blue eyes, a man of disconcerting charm, with a 'hard, savage quality' about him such that 'even his laugh sounded like a threat to others'. To rub Bohemund's nose in his failure, Alexius ensured that the Byzantine witnesses to the treaty included a number of leading Normans in his service.[45] The Treaty of Devol ended Bohemund's remarkable career. Returning to Apulia with the remnant of his army, he skulked in the west until his death in 1111, leaving a son, a famous legacy but little else. A few of those who took the cross in 1106–7 may have pursued their goal of Jerusalem after the debacle at Durazzo. Most found only disillusionment, as one commentator understated it: 'in that expedition things did not fall out as the *peregrinationes* desired'.[46]

Bohemund's failure was more than a defeat, it was an embarrassment, tarnishing not only his reputation but also the use of the *via Sancti Sepulchri*, especially sensitive precisely because of the extent of genuine devotion to Jerusalem, witnessed by pilgrimages as well as by Bohemund's own recruiting. Yet the extension by analogy of the Jerusalem expedition to other theatres of conflict with the infidel continued to flourish. In the same year as the Treaty of Devol, a Flemish propagandist associated with the archbishop of Magdeburg explicitly linked war against the pagan Wends of the south Baltic with the Jerusalem expedition, calling on his audience to 'follow the good example of the Gauls . . . sally forth and come, all lovers of Christ and the Church, and prepare yourselves just as did the men of Gaul for the liberation of Jerusalem'. By analogy, the German church became 'our Jerusalem'.[47]

Spain provided an active arena for such parallels. Although before 1095 Urban II had regarded the rebuilding of the frontier town of Tarragona south of Barcelona as a penitential exercise meriting offers of plenary indulgences, only after Clermont was the Jerusalem expedition equated with the Christian *reconquista* in Spain.[48] Thereafter, this interpretation of a common conflict between Christianity and Islam lent fragmented secular wars for territorial gain and political advantage spiritual energy and coherence, a transformation reflecting papal efforts to control the Spanish church as much as any indigenous religious revival. This ideological import conveniently and importantly coincided with the dominance of Muslim al-Andalus by the Almoravids, a fundamentalist Islamic sect from north Africa. Thus there were real battles to be fought against Muslims, which, with the eye of rhetoric, could be viewed in the context of a struggle between Faiths that embraced the Holy Land. At a council held in Santiago de Compostela in January 1126, Archbishop Diego Gelmirez, 'St James's catapult', urged his audience to imitate the conquerors of Jerusalem and 'become knights of Christ and, after defeating his wicked enemies the Muslims, open the way to the same Sepulchre of the Lord through Spain, which is shorter and much less laborious', a geographic and military fantasy with a long future.[49] Thanks to the papally inspired clerical attitude, the language and props of the Jerusalem penitential holy war began to suffuse the far from idealistic conquest of al-Andalus. The holy war tradition persisted after most of al-Andalus had fallen to the Christian kings in the thirteenth century, the link with Jerusalem never entirely fading for the rest of the middle ages. Yet in the twelfth century it was fuelled as much by evocation of an older legend; in the poem on the capture of Almeria, Alfonso VII is lauded as 'continuing the deeds of Charlemagne, with whom he is rightly compared'.[50]

The interest in warring in Spain from north of the Pyrenees reflected a tradition of itinerant fighting among the affluent arms-bearing elites of western Europe that reached back far beyond 1095. In that sense, the contest with the infidel, in the eastern or western Mediterranean, scarcely altered social mores, even if it provided fresh outlets. The new focus of holy violence exerted only a sporadic, occasional, irregular and uneven hold on the activity of the fighting classes however powerful a grip it exerted on imaginations, or, at least, those recoverable parts of their thought-world which owed most to the new orthodoxies of the western church. Victims of sordid internecine political feuding, such as Duke Canute of Denmark, murdered in 1131, could be elevated into crusader saints by association with the Holy Land adventure – which in life he lacked.[51] Yet, despite its iconic status as living proof of God's immanence and favour attracting the anxious attention of clerical and monastic chroniclers, Outremer failed to provide as popular theatre for chivalry as for pilgrims. Sustained interest tended to run in families: those with claims to Outremer inheritances, such as Bohemund II, brought up in Apulia, who arrived to claim his inheritance in Antioch in 1126, or with political influence in the east, such as the extended Montlhéry or Le Puiset affinities from northern France, who dominated Jerusalem politics and patronage under Baldwin II.[52] Even the army mustered in 1128 by Hugh de Payns and his colleagues revolved around the acceptance by Fulk of Anjou of the hand of Princess Melisende and the inheritance of Jerusalem. In the event, the 1129 sortie against Damascus failed, and many regarded the whole enterprise as a fraud, which was probably unfair as the campaign, involving most of the great leaders of Outremer as well as the western recruits, was thwarted by poor tactics and worse weather, not malice or indifference. The *Anglo-Saxon Chronicle* recorded Hugh's great recruiting success – 'so large a number of people as never had done since the first expedition in the days of Pope Urban' – and subsequent disappointment: 'He [Hugh] said that thoroughgoing war was prepared between the Christians and the heathens. Then when they arrived there it was nothing but lies – thus miserably were all the people afflicted'.[53] Different priorities and expectations of westerners and residents of Outremer persisted throughout subsequent dealings between the east and west. Much active campaigning by westerners in Outremer was opportunistic, a matter of local rulers fitting the martial skills and ambitions of chance visitors to desired objectives, such as Sigurd of Norway and the seizure of Sidon in 1110. However, a crisis in Outremer's affairs could excite widespread support however uneasily eastern setbacks stood beside the providential triumphalism that the capture of Jerusalem had originally inspired.

The disaster of the defeat of Roger of Antioch at the Field of Blood in 1119 provoked Baldwin II and his advisers early in 1120 to send ambassadors west to seek help from the papacy and Venice. A number of western lords, including Fulk of Anjou, may have answered the call. Pope Calixtus II, perhaps inspired by his abundant family ties with crusading and the east, added his weight to the appeals to the Venetian doge, Domenico Michiel, sending him a papal banner for an eastern campaign. The Doge, who acquired a well-deserved bellicose reputation, took the cross with other prominent Venetians in 1122 before embarking with a substantial fleet for the eastern Mediterranean. The Venetian expedition of 1122–4 encapsulated many of the diverse motives that propelled westerners eastwards; trade, plunder, military adventurism, colonial expansion, profit, piety and the appetite for relics. On the way out, the fleet attacked Corfu in retaliation for the reduction in their trading privileges proposed by Byzantine emperor John II. Only on hearing of the capture of Baldwin II by Balak of Aleppo in April 1123 did the Venetians proceed to the Levant, where the following month they destroyed an Egyptian fleet between Jaffa and Ascalon. While the doge claimed to be fulfilling a longstanding wish to visit the Holy Places, the Venetian credentials as soldiers of the cross operated within a frame of self-interest. Only after protracted negotiations with the regency government of Jerusalem held during Christmastide 1123 and much wrangling among the Jerusalemites as to the best target did the doge agree to an attack on Tyre, with Ascalon the last great port of the Levantine coast outside Frankish possession. In return for this aid, Venice was to receive a third of Tyre with extensive privileges in the conquered city, including free trade, the use of their own weights and measures, wide legal autonomy and immunities and an annual tribute of 300 besants. The siege lasted from February to July 1124 before the Damascene garrison surrendered. Along with the immediate booty and future privileges, the Venetians, whose commercialism never excluded piety, carried off a lump of marble on which Christ was alleged to have sat. The capture of Tyre did not end the Venetian campaign. Returning westwards, they terrorized the Aegean, sacking Rhodes and wintering in Chios, where they acquired relics of the martyred St Isidore, before pillaging Samos, Lesbos and Andros, then launching a series of raids along the Dalmatian shore of the Adriatic culminating in the plunder of Zara, after which, singing the *Te Deum Laudamus*, they returned to Venice 'full of happiness and joy'.[54] Or so it was remembered in the lagoon. Seen only from the perspective of wars of the cross, the Venetian crusade represented a serious commitment of time and investment in ships, men and money. While the Venetian fleet was at war it could not be trading as well. Yet the context for the victories off Ascalon and at Tyre was an extended, Viking-like raid on Christian Byzantine territory and property. The whole enterprise appeared designed for tangible as well as spiritual gain; it certainly reaped the former. While this did not represent as much of a contradiction at the time as it may seem now, such a layered response informed much of the interest in the cause of the cross and the Holy Land. It also serves as a foretaste and clue to the events eighty years later that led to the sack of Constantinople.

The Venetian expedition of 1122–5 illustrated how the needs of the Holy Land could be stitched into concerns of the Faithful that had little or no intrinsic association with armed pilgrimage or holy war except coincidence. Much the same could be applied to many responses to the papacy's new militant formula: social; political; chivalric; diplomatic; colonial; commercial. The striking feature of the early twelfth century appears the lack of consistent action on behalf of the cross at the same time as the image of the first Jerusalem campaign patchily suffused cultural attitudes to war and Christian society of the lay and ecclesiastical elites. As the enclaves in the east became established and their borders tentatively secured, the sense of urgency in appeals for aid slackened. The 1130s saw penitential wars on the Jerusalem model applied elsewhere, for example against the supporters of the anti-pope Anacletus.

The 1120s, despite the imprisonment of Baldwin II and the death of Bohemund II, had seemingly marked an end to major, state-threatening crises, while the failure before Damascus in 1129 ended further dramatic territorial expansion. However, both assumptions as well as the ideal of holy war itself were to be tested to their limits before the 1140s were out.

9
God's Bargain: Summoning the Second Crusade

The fall of Edessa between 24 and 26 December 1144 to the Turkish atabeg Imad al-Din Zengi, ruler of Mosul and Aleppo, rapidly assumed greater significance than its immediate strategic context demanded. The result of an opportunistic attack when its Frankish count, Joscelin II, was away, Zengi's success at Edessa helped consolidate the north-western frontier of his Aleppan-Mosul federation. Confining his habitual savagery to the surviving Frankish Christians, Zengi soon consolidated his hold on the east bank of the Euphrates. However, Zengi's main target in Syria since his annexation of Aleppo in 1128 was Damascus, while his wider political interests concerned the Jazira and Iraq more than Frankish Syria. He captured Edessa because of immediate local circumstances, such as the deaths the year before of King Fulk of Jerusalem and the Byzantine Emperor John II, which, given the hostility between Count Joscelin and Raymond of Poitiers prince of Antioch, reduced the chance of a Christian counter-attack. After his success at Edessa, revolt in Mosul early in 1145 and continued intriguing by local Armenian and Muslim princes with the Franks deflected Zengi from Damascus to further policing operations in the Euphrates valley. On one such foray, at Qal'at Ja'bar, on the night of 14 September 1146, Zengi, comatose with drink, was murdered in his bed by a favoured Frankish slave.[1] Immediately, his empire ruptured, with one son, Sayf al-Din acquiring Mosul, another, Nur al-Din, Aleppo. A Frankish attempt to take advantage of the situation by reoccupying Edessa in November 1146, led by Joscelin II and Baldwin of Marasch, failed utterly, the count fleeing ignominiously, Baldwin meeting a heroic death, the city's walls being levelled and the local Armenian Christians suffering the massacre they had avoided two years earlier.[2]

The fall of Edessa had burnished Zengi's reputation as a holy warrior.

The caliph in Baghdad conferred on him the titles: 'the Ornament of Islam, the Auxiliary of the Commander of the Faithful (i.e. the caliph), the Divinely Aided King'.[3] The accolade of *mujahid* lent religious ideology to the military power of a leader feared by his followers almost as much as by his foes, reputedly a sadistic monster, at the sight of whom one man was supposed to have dropped dead from fright, who crucified his own troops found marching out of line and trampling crops. An eager member of Zengi's entourage wrote, 'If the conquest of Edessa is the high sea, Jerusalem and all the Frankish lands (*sahil*) are its shore'.[4] Yet, while the preoccupations of Zengi's heirs precluded Islamic unity and further assault on Latin Outremer, the Franks seemingly accepted this analysis, drawing almost apocalyptic conclusions. The message brought west in 1145 was clear: Islam was on the march; all Christian Outremer was in danger; something had to be done. The result was one of the greatest international military efforts of the middle ages.

MUSLIM REVIVAL

Zengi's apologists portrayed him as champion of the *jihad*, the sixth pillar of Islam, the perpetual collective and sometimes individual obligation on all the Faithful to struggle (*jihad*) spiritually against unbelief in themselves (*al-jihad al-akbar*, the greater *jihad*) and physically against unbelievers (*al-jihad al-asghar*, the lesser *jihad*). The Christian conquest and rule over Muslim lands inevitably aroused the traditional rhetoric of holy war. As in Christendom, religion and politics operated as mutually sustaining forces within society, especially one as ethnically diverse as that of the Near East. Zengi, owing formal allegiance to an Arabo-Iraqi-Persian caliphate controlled by a Turkish sultan, was himself a Turk whose army and entourage comprised Turcomans, Kurds and slaves, chiefly from the Eurasian steppes and the northern Black Sea, and whose political ambitions embraced domination of Arab emirs and princes in Syria. Religion supported authority and defined political identity. Any Muslim ruler, like his western counterparts, surrounded himself with religious advisers and civil servants trained in religion. The Iranian Imad al-Din al-Isfahani (1125–1201), one of Nur al-Din's leading civil servants, later Saladin's field secretary and biographer, once worked as a professor at a Damascus religious school (or *madrasa*), a man learned in the Faith as well as law and administration.[5] Without a formal structure of priesthood, Islam easily pervaded secular institutions and life. As happened with holy war in western Christendom in the eleventh century, the recrudescence of *jihad* in the twelfth-century Near East relied on intellectual and spiritual movements being translated into political ambition and action, a determining alliance between the pulpit and the battlefield that found concrete expression in the *minbar* (mosque pulpit) built by Nur al-Din at Aleppo in 1168. Adorned with inscriptions praising the *jihad*, it was, as its maker had intended, installed in the al-Aqsa mosque in Jerusalem by Saladin on his conquest of the city in 1187.[6]

By 1098, when the western armies captured Antioch, the First Crusade could be seen as a continuation of traditional Byzantine border activity. No active indigenous Syrian tradition of united Islamic military response had survived centuries of coexistence. The arrival of the new Sunni Turkish zealots in the late eleventh century affected Syrian Muslims – Arab rulers or Shi'ite peasantry – more than the unbelievers. Only when the Christian army pushed south in 1098–9 did a novel threat become apparent, symbolized by the massacre of the inhabitants of Ma 'arrat al-Nu 'man in December 1098, an atrocity kept alive in the poems of exiled survivors: 'why has destiny pronounced such an unjust sentence on us?'. As Frankish conquests increased, so did the number of articulate, displaced Muslim refugees available to tweak the consciences of Muslim rulers. In Damascus some time before 1109, the poet Ibn al-Khayyat, who had worked for the emirs of Tripoli, demanded an armed response: 'The cutting edge of their sword must be blunted/And their pillar must be demolished'. After the fall of Tripoli to the Franks in 1109, its emir, Fakhr al-Mulk, settled in Bagdhad, where violent demonstrations by visiting Aleppan citizens in February 1111 successfully persuaded Sultan Muhammed to dispatch an army against the Franks. A generation later, Zengi's circle included the poets Ibn al-Qaysarani, from Caesarea (taken by the Franks in 1101), and another Tripoli refugee, Ibn Munir, both of whom urged their master to recapture Jerusalem after his capture of Edessa. Later in the century, fundamentalist émigrés from Nablus made a suburb of Damascus a centre of holy war ideology and recruits. Articulate refugees goaded the public consciences of those who posed as leaders of the faithful with tangible results: in 1136 Zengi restored property in Ma 'arrat al-Numan to its former residents or their heirs.[7]

Jihad rhetoric and action came partly in consequence of a religious revival, partly because it was good politics. The Shi'ite *qadi* (i.e. judge) of Aleppo, Ibn al-Khashshab, who organized resistance to Frankish attacks in 1118 and 1124, urged a principled stand against the infidel. During the campaign leading to the defeat of Roger of Antioch at the Field of Blood in 1119, Ibn al-Khashshab rode through the Muslim lines 'spear in hand' preaching the virtues of *jihad*, the novelty of such clerical interference causing some resentment. A generation later, such clerical cheer-leading would have seemed normal. Beleaguered Muslims in the front line naturally looked for aid from Baghdad, their appeals for military help deliberately couched in religious terms. The Aleppans' protests of 1111 targeted Friday prayers in the sultans' and caliph's mosques, preventing the sermons and vandalizing pulpits, ritual symbols of political as well as spiritual power, in an overt challenge to authority. Sultan Muhammed reacted by sending Mawdud of Mosul to Syria for a second time. In 1129, faced by another Frankish threat, such tactics were repeated by Damascene merchants led by an Iranian fundamentalist preacher 'Abd al-Wahhab al-Shirazi.[8]

The academic response anticipated the political. The *jihad*'s greater prominence in religious and political discourse operated within a Sunni revivalism originating in Iran and Iraq, initially stimulated by the fiercely orthodox Seljuk converts and the need to integrate the new Turkish rulers into Islamic culture. Heightened religious and moral commitment found tangible expression in art, architecture and literature. Twelfth-century Syria slid from its cultural backwater into the Islamic mainstream, supported by the patronage of rulers, often parvenus eager to demonstrate their spiritual credentials by endowing new orthodox Sunni schools or colleges. Such a seminary or *madrasa* acted as a focus for the mediation of the spiritual into the secular. From the 1130s, new religious schools proliferated throughout Syria; Nur al-Din himself founded half of the forty or so built in his reign (1146–74). Their often lavish endowments and rich architecture witnessed a new religious cultural energy in which *jihad* supplied one strand particularly relevant to Syrian experience. Between 1099 and 1146, the only surviving inscriptions on public buildings anywhere in the Muslim world mentioning *jihad* come from Syria, such as that on the tomb of Balak, ruler of Aleppo 1123–4 and captor of Joscelin I of Edessa and King Baldwin II: 'sword of those who fight the Holy War, leader of the armies of the Muslims, vanquisher of the infidels and the polytheists'. Another Aleppo inscription, praising Zengi in 1142, is couched in almost identical terms: 'tamer of the infidels and the polytheists, leaders of those who fight the holy war, helper of the armies, protector of the territory of the Muslims', titles that repeat those in an inscription on a *madrasa* in Damascus dated December 1138.[9]

Public expressions of idealism reflected growing Muslim awareness of the Frankish threat. Frontier warfare, justified by the ideals of *jihad*, provided useful employment for Zengi's nomadic Turcoman levies as well as security for his conquests, but a new intolerance sprang from fear. In the aftermath of the Frankish attack on Aleppo in the 1120s the city's Christian churches were converted into mosques. A blueprint for ideology and action had existed for more than a generation. In 1105, at the great mosque in Damascus, a legal scholar al-Sulami (1039–1106) had given public readings from his *Book of the Holy War* (*Kitab al-Jihad*) in which he urged moral reform (i.e. the *jihad al-akbar*) within Islam as the necessary preparation for a military reconquest (*jihad al-asghar*). Although possibly prompted by the threat to Damascus trade routes posed by the loss of Acre (1104), al-Sulami adopted a broad vision, placing the Frankish invasion in the context of eleventh-century Christian advances in Sicily and Spain and blaming Muslim failure to resist on disunity. Fearful of further Frankish conquests, al-Sulami understood that 'Jerusalem was the summit of their wishes'. Such calls for pan-Islamic solidarity were not confined to the pulpits and studies of the Fertile Crescent. At about the same time as al-Sulami was preaching religious solidarity and moral rearmament in Damascus, the Almoravid conqueror of al-Andalus, Muslim Spain, Yusuf Ibn Tashfin reputedly launched an armada of seventy ships to liberate Jerusalem, only to see it founder in Mediterranean storms.[10]

Al-Sulami's message of political unity and spiritual purity was translated into a political programme as a matter of convenience as much as Faith by rulers eager to carve out empires in the ruins of Seljuk control of Syria. Sultan Muhammed's commitment to holy war, which ceased with his last expeditionary force's defeat by the Franks of Antioch at Tell Danith in 1115, focused on restoring authority over the Muslims in the region more than driving the Franks into the sea. Thereafter, domination of Muslim Syria revolved first around control of Aleppo, then, after 1128, Damascus, a contest in which the Franks played a vigorous and by no means isolated role. For all his *jihad* rhetoric and posturing, Zengi's interests drew him eastwards, away from the Franks. However, to construct viable coalition armies, talk of *jihad* became an obligatory mask for the realpolitik of diplomacy; thus Zengi stressed the 'obligation of holy war' when raising his force to attack Edessa. As ruler of Aleppo without Mosul, Nur al-Din was forced to concentrate on Syria and so employ the language of holy war while lacking adequate economic and financial resources to conduct one. The reality of Muslim revival lay in greater political stability and direction of resources. But academics and religious leaders, with access to the courts, administration and ears of the rulers, provided a respectable ideology for the ambitions of the Zengids and their successors. While only a united Muslim northern Syria could sustain a *jihad*, religious ideas conditioned the political elites and their propaganda to accept that, regardless of temporary politicking and opportunist truces, the Franks were an eternal enemy to be expelled, by the mid-twelfth century a dimension to the language of politics no Syrian Muslim ruler could ignore. However, events, not ideas, served as the most effective recruiting officer for the *jihad*, most of all the abject failure of the Second Crusade.

THE CALL TO ARMS

News of the fall of Edessa filtered through to western Europe in the summer and autumn of 1145, arousing little particular alarm. The papal Curia was well informed of eastern affairs; there had been crises before, some leading to calls for action, as after 1119, some not. Papal involvement in Syrian politics was complicated by the need to consider Byzantine responses. By the mid-1140s, Byzantine overlordship over Antioch had been reluctantly admitted by Prince Raymond, who had renewed his homage to the new Greek emperor, Manuel I Comnenus, in 1145. An Antiochene appeal for western aid could have been regarded by Manuel as undermining his claims, especially as the head of Antioch's delegation to the west, Bishop Hugh of Jubail, had a history of opposition to the Greeks. The new pope, Eugenius III, elected in February 1145, could not afford to alienate Byzantium given his complicated and precarious position in Italy. His predecessor, Lucius II, had been killed in street fighting in Rome, which remained barred to the new pope except briefly over Christmas 1145. The rivalry between King Conrad III of Germany and King Roger II of Sicily, a longstanding enemy of Byzantium, further complicated matters. According to Otto bishop of Freising, Conrad III's half-brother, an eyewitness at the papal Curia during November and December 1145, two eastern embassies were negotiating with Eugenius at the time: Armenian bishops over possible ecclesiastical union with Rome and ambassadors from Antioch seeking help for Prince Raymond over disputes involving the ruling family. As both touched relations with Byzantium, Eugenius needed to be wary. As Otto of Freising described it, news of Edessa scarcely dominated discussions; it is likely Eugenius had heard the news already.[11] It may be that the pope's decision to issue a new call to arms, couched in terms of aid for 'the eastern church', which could be taken to include the Greeks, was partly designed to mitigate the appearance of provocative interference in a sensitive Byzantine sphere of influence, allowing Eugenius to assert his authority without jeopardizing his wider diplomatic interests.

Eugenius III's bull *Quantum praedecessores*, dated from Vetralla on 1 December 1145, contained an unequivocal statement of papal jurisdiction, including the power to grant full remission of sins 'by the authority given us by God' and 'by the authority of omnipotent God and that of the Blessed Peter the Prince of the Apostles conceded to us by God'.[12] In describing the temporal and spiritual privileges in detail, the bull provided a model for future papal exhortations. Eugenius recalled the First Crusade and the establishment of the Christian states in the east, before explaining how the fall of Edessa, with its attendant atrocities, threatened 'the Church of God and all Christianity'. Repeatedly referring to the heroic example of their ancestors, Eugenius appealed directly to 'those who are on God's side, and especially the more powerful and the nobles' to 'defend the eastern Church', a cause which would secure 'your reputation for strength'. To those who undertook 'so holy and very necessary work', Eugenius offered the remission of all confessed sins, as instituted by Urban II; the church's protection for their families and property; immunity from civil law suits begun after they had taken the cross; exemption from payment of interest on loans and debts; and the right to raise money by pledging land or possessions to churches or other Christians (by implication excluding Jewish bankers). To emphasize the redemptive, penitential quality of the enterprise, the pope, formerly of the austere order of Cistercian monks, stipulated sumptuary regulations, discouraging *haute couture*, colourful or fur-lined garments, gilded arms, hunting dogs and hawks. The loss of Edessa had been punishment for the sins of Christians; those embarking on its restoration must have regard for piety and efficiency not show. Eugenius III was restaking the papal claim to lead secular Christendom after years of schism and political weakness. In contrast to Urban II's strategy in 1095/6, Eugenius's bull and its reissue of 1 March 1146 were addressed to a monarch, Louis VII of France. By highlighting the response to Urban's summons by 'the most strong and vigorous warriors of the kingdom of the Franks and also those from Italy', Eugenius may initially have envisaged targeted, local recruitment more reminiscent of Calixtus II's plans in 1119 than 1096. He undertook no immediate general recruiting tour and, beyond approval and authorization, continued in a remarkably passive role. Leadership and organization were to lie elsewhere.

RESPONSES (I): THE KINGDOM OF FRANCE

The pope was not alone in seeing aid for the Holy Land as a chance to combine a holy cause with the assertion of political status. The decision to issue *Quantum praedecessores* may have been influenced by knowledge that Louis of France would prove receptive. Louis VII (1137–80) was a young man in a hurry to emancipate himself from the tutelage of his father's cronies and to redeem his early mistakes as king, not least his uneasy relations with leading ecclesiastics, including Bernard of Clairvaux and Pope Innocent II. Still only twenty-five, in 1145 Louis's power within his kingdom was geographically limited, politically and ideologically heavily dependent on the church. By reputation pious and modest, it has been commented that 'modern historians have generally thought that he had a good deal to be modest about'.[13] In later life he was quoted as observing contentedly that, in comparison with the riches of fellow monarchs, 'we in France have nothing but bread, wine and gaiety', an early version of a characteristic, misleading French self-image.[14] Such mellow reflection came with age, experience and repeated disappointment after a long career of energetic ineffectiveness. As a young man, the devout Louis acted with impulsive self-confidence, famously when, during a protracted feud with Theobald count of Champagne, he burnt down the church at Vitry in 1143, allegedly with hundreds of people inside. Two Second Crusade veterans who knew Louis suggested he had harboured a 'secret' desire to go to Jerusalem, whether as a knight or a pilgrim is not entirely clear.[15] As part of the general reconciliation with Champagne and Bernard of Clairvaux in 1144–5, Louis may have toyed with the idea of a penitential pilgrimage. Apart from the Vitry incident, and talk of the unfulfilled Jerusalem vow of Louis's elder brother Philip (d. 1131), Louis had incurred ecclesiastical censure over his oath to bar the archbishop of Bourges from his diocesan seat: the holding of the Christmas court in 1145 at Bourges itself may have assumed significance in this process of reconciliation.[16] The news of Edessa could have focused Louis's intentions, and it is probable that Eugenius was aware of this when he issued *Quantum praedecessores*. Before he could have received the papal bull, Louis summoned the bishops and magnates 'in greater numbers than usual' to his Christmas crown-wearing at Bourges, where he broached the subject of the eastern enterprise.

The eastern expedition provided Louis with the chance to act as king of the western Franks in a manner not seen since the Carolingians. The three assemblies gathered to discuss the matter, at Bourges (December 1145), Vézelay (March 1146) and Etampes (February 1147), personally and symbolically emphasized his sovereignty by associating princes from across France with a specifically royal policy. In charters of departing crusaders from Rheims in the north to Auch near the Pyrenees, the campaign was recognized as King Louis's expedition, 'the royal army'.[17] Louis's former adversary, Theobald of Champagne, subsequently dated charters from the king's crusade.[18] The first west Frankish king to lead a foreign conquest for three centuries, on campaign Louis established lasting relationships with magnates that in later years helped make his court more central in French politics. Immediate political dividends included a royal census, a *descriptio generalis*, preparatory to the levy of a tax for the expedition that exempted 'neither sex, nor order nor rank'; not a popular move, but if implemented offering the precedent of the king's power to tax beyond his own tenants. A more limited, but onerous levy on churches caused painful negotiations and corporate resistance.[19] Such extraordinary taxes recognized royal authority on a new level, as did his presence as crusade commander in areas outside his demesne lands. At Verdun and at Metz, where Louis mustered his large army in June 1147, his chaplain noted, 'although the king found nothing there which belonged to him by right of lordship, he nevertheless found all subject (*quasi servos*) to him voluntarily.'[20] This international adventure conferred on Louis and his dynasty the reality of national rule.

Much of this could only have been guessed at in December 1145. Beside all political calculation lay the king's personal piety, widely attested throughout his life and especially on crusade. Initially, the magnates at Bourges remained unimpressed, despite an impassioned address on the Edessa crisis by Godfrey de la Roche, the opinionated, forceful and well-connected bishop of Langres, like the pope a former Cistercian abbot. Louis's chief minister, Abbot Suger of St Denis, openly opposed the proposal, citing the dangers to which the king's absence would expose France. Journeys to Jerusalem, in arms or not, were dangerous and Louis had no son. The Bourges meeting reached no conclusion beyond possibly appealing for guidance to Bernard abbot of Clairvaux, the bishop of Langres's former superior, the most influential moral arbiter, political lobbyist and revivalist preacher of the time. The king's own brother, Henry, only that year had taken his vows at Clairvaux. Bernard transformed the prospects, conduct and nature of the whole project.[21]

Bernard of Clairvaux's decision to prosecute the crusade may not have been unexpected. The bishop of Langres was a kinsman and former colleague; the pope a pupil. Some collusion between king and abbot may have occurred before the meeting at Bourges. Some of those Bernard met during a tour of Languedoc in June and July 1145, such as the count of Toulouse, took the cross in 1146. Bernard's own links with holy war and Outremer were intimate. Although declining to establish Cistercian houses in the east, for years he encouraged the settlement of another new austere French order, the Premonstratensian monks, in the kingdom of Jerusalem, interceding with Queen Melisende on their behalf. Count Hugh of Champagne, donor of the site of Clairvaux, became a Templar, as had one of Bernard's uncles. Some years earlier Bernard had composed the *De Laude novae militiae* on the Templars' behalf and had helped secure recognition for the order. He regularly concerned himself with men journeying to Jerusalem as pilgrims or warriors, although for those with a monastic vocation he regarded the cloister as preferable, persuading one *crucesignatus* to abandon the crusade for 'something far better', 'that true Jerusalem', the Cistercian order, and threatening his fellow monks and the order's lay brethren with excommunication if they attempted to join the expedition east. Bernard was far from immune to the allure of Holy Land relics, receiving a piece of the True Cross from Patriarch William of Jerusalem (1130–45) and, in due course in 1153, being buried with a relic of St Thaddeus sent from Palestine.[22] Bernard's conspicuous spirituality, witnessed in his spare, ascetic almost frail frame, was allied with a tough, masterful clarity of intellect, eloquence and invective, making him an unnervingly effective platform orator as well as an irresistible personal advisor, at once an outstanding forensic debater, academic thinker, religious comforter, political operator and worker of miracles. As the refined intellectual aristocrat and fellow Cistercian Otto of Freising put it, 'endowed with wisdom and a knowledge of letters, renowned for signs and wonders', Bernard appeared 'as a divine oracle'; an ideal recruiting agent for the crusade.[23]

The early months of 1146 saw intense diplomacy between the French court, Bernard and the papal Curia. Once his initial, possibly formal, reluctance was overcome, Bernard insisted that he would only preach the cross with full papal authorization and legatine power. Throughout his career, legality, due authority and obedience acted as cornerstones of Bernard's temporal activities; in 1146–7 they provided him with the necessary means to discipline as well as direct recruiting operations. The inexperienced Eugenius, on the other hand, once more an exile from Rome, chose this moment to display the exaggerated fussy legalism of the chronically insecure by threatening to excommunicate the archbishop of Rheims for crowning Louis at Bourges at Christmas, a move hardly designed to encourage enthusiastic cooperation. In the end it took Bernard at his most schoolmasterly to tell the pontiff not to be so silly; the king's goodwill and the expedition to Jerusalem were far more important than ruffled vanities or procedural niceties.[24] By March, dispositions were complete. On 1 March the pope reissued *Quantum praedecessores* with minor amendments, chiefly tightening the clauses prohibiting luxury, a good Cistercian theme, and sent Louis VII a cross which he had blessed to wear. A new assembly of French magnates was called to meet at Vézelay in northern Burgundy on 31 March, Easter Day.

Bernard's preaching at Vézelay assumed almost iconic importance in perceptions of the crusade in his own time and in subsequent centuries.

The crowd gathered at the hilltop town was so large that, like Urban in 1095, Bernard preached outside the church, in the fields with their panoramic views across the Burgundian hills. Flanked on the platform by the king and other notables, Bernard used the papal bull to outline the need for action and the rewards on offer before adding his own impassioned appeal. Oddly, there survives no contemporary description, real or imagined, of what the abbot actually said as opposed to the psychological impact on his audience. Judging from his subsequent correspondence, Bernard may have argued that through the crisis in the east God had provided a unique offer of salvation. As he put it in letters to England, Lorraine and Bavaria, in return for fighting to secure the 'land made glorious by His miracles, holy by his blood . . . in which the flowers of His resurrection first blossomed' (a theme particularly suitable for Eastertide), God was putting himself 'in your debt so that, in return for your taking up arms in His cause, He can reward you with pardon for your sins and everlasting glory'. Thus the cross became a 'badge of immortality', a 'sign of salvation'. Turning from fighting each other, sinful *malitia*, to taking vengeance on the heathen, holy *militia*, 'mighty men of valour', 'men of war' were presented with a cause in which, paraphrasing St Paul, 'to conquer is glorious and to die is gain'. The exchange was a 'bargain'; for the small price of taking the cross, the return was full indulgence of confessed sins. It was no less than the 'cause of Christ'.[25]

The combination of the emotional account of the Holy Land and the direct offer of salvation, couched in very simple sets of repetitive logic, proved highly effective. The audience at Vézelay went wild, so many demanding crosses that Bernard's supply, probably made of wool, ran out, forcing him to tear up his own habit to satisfy them. Yet for all the eloquence and recorded enthusiasm, the events at Vézelay, like those at Clermont just over fifty years earlier, were hardly spontaneous. The success of any recruiting or fund-raising campaign depended (and depends) on the message being familiar, the audience already receptive. The large and distinguished congregation at Vézelay had not been assembled by accident. They knew why they were there. The event had been carefully planned and meticulously orchestrated (even if, as one source mentioned, the platform for VIPs partially collapsed), Bernard bringing with him a 'parcel of crosses which had been prepared beforehand'.[26] Presumably staged after celebration of the Easter mass, with

Louis sitting beside the preacher already wearing the cross given him by the pope, the essentially ritualistic and ceremonial nature of the occasion was evident.

Ritual embellished practical purpose. The Vézelay assembly demonstrated royal authority as well as crusade enthusiasm, the former feeding off the latter, one account even transferring the main address from Bernard to the king. Some of those not present were enjoined to follow the king of heaven as well as the king of France, a significant association.[27] The laymen taking the cross alongside King Louis bore witness to the new royal embrace. Besides his wife, Eleanor of Aquitaine, brother, Robert of Dreux, and uncle, Amadeus of Savoy, count of Maurienne, came some of the grandest independent feudatories in the kingdom, Thierry of Alsace count of Flanders, a veteran of the Holy Land; Alfonso-Jordan count of Toulouse, the son of Raymond of St Gilles, born outside Tripoli in 1104; and Henry, son of Louis's former adversary Theobald count of Champagne. The geographical reach matched the political: from central France, the counts of Nevers, Tonnerre and Bourbon; from the north, the counts of Ponthieu and Soissons and the lords of Coucy and Courtenay; from the Limousin and Poitou the lords of Rancon and Lusignan; from the Anglo-Norman realms, William of Warenne, earl of Surrey. Although not all embarked with Louis, by their presence at Vézelay they acknowledged his leadership, as one member of the assembly put it, by papal command, *apostolico praecepto*.[28]

After Vézelay, Bernard prepared for an extensive preaching tour, and diplomatic preparations began. Surprise, as at Bourges, led to meagre pickings. Local clerical and lay elites needed to be alerted to gather support and excite anticipation, Bernard's arrival completing a process of engagement with the call to Jerusalem dependent on ties of family, locality and lordship as much as religious fervour. He was at Toul in May, but only in late July did Bernard begin a journey that took him to Arras and Ghent in early August, then in a loop through Flanders and the Low Countries in September and October before turning towards the Rhineland and the empire, returning to northern France early in 1147. By all accounts, including his own, he was extraordinarily persuasive: 'towns and castles are emptied, one may scarcely find one man among seven women, so many women are there widowed while their husbands are still alive'.[29] To inspiration Bernard added organization. Places he failed to reach, such as Brittany, England, Bavaria,

Lorraine, Saxony and Bohemia, received letters or messengers, sometimes with copies of the papal privileges that the abbot insisted were the central selling points of the recruitment campaign. The network of the Cistercian order, which had helped propel Bernard to international prominence in the first place, proved central, providing many important ecclesiastical *crucesignati*. Indefatigably determined to contact as many people as possible, Bernard made the crusade his, even if professional cloistered humility prevented him from actually joining the expedition, leaving clerical leadership to other, as it happened, distinctly less able colleagues.

RESPONSES (II): THE EMPIRE

If the French were the first to be approached, numerically and politically the most significant recruits came from the German empire. For six months from late summer 1146, the imperial lands, including northern Italy, became the focus of preaching and recruiting. Eugenius III wrote to encourage Italians to take the cross.[30] After his swing through Flanders Bernard himself spent late October 1146 until mid-January 1147 criss-crossing western Germany, beginning in the central Rhineland at Worms (*c.*1 November) before turning north to Mainz and Frankfurt, where he met Conrad III, then south to Basel and Constance (12 December), before returning northwards again to attend the imperial court at Christmas in Speyer (24 December to 3 January), returning to Worms and finally taking in Cologne (9 January) and Aachen (15 January), before arriving on 18 January at Liège, which he had left three months earlier. This represented frenetic activity over hundreds of miles in mid-winter. With the exceptions of his time at Mainz and Frankurt in November and at Speyer over Christmas, Bernard rarely spent more than a night or two at any one place, in contrast to the more stately progress of Urban II through France in 1095–6. No doubt conducting Cistercian business as well, given this hurried if extensive itinerary, Bernard's crusade preaching operated as the sharp edge of a wider campaign of information and exhortation prepared by letters and emissaries, with Conrad III taking the cross at an emotional ceremony at Speyer on 27 December forming the centrepiece. As notable as the recruits Bernard secured were those who took the cross without the abbot's personal touch, such as Welf VI of Bavaria, at his own estate of Peiting on 24 December, or, further east, King Ladislaus of Bohemia, the margrave of Styria and the count of Carinthia or the large gathering at Regensburg in February 1147 run by Conrad and Bernard's representative, the Cistercian abbot of Ebrach.[31]

By his German trip, Bernard was able to retain control of a recruitment process. Twice, in late October 1146 and late January 1147, he passed near the monastery at Huy founded after 1099 by Peter the Hermit, the memory of whose remarkable but disastrous expedition remained green. On the first occasion Bernard was in pursuit of another rabble-rousing evangelist, Radulf (or Raoul or Rudolph), whose preaching threatened to confuse the plans of pope and abbot. Radulf, another Cistercian, once possibly a hermit, had undertaken a hugely popular preaching tour of the Rhineland, from Cologne to Strassburg, in the summer and autumn of 1146. Although attacked by the archbishops of Cologne and Mainz and demonized by Bernard and most subsequent commentators, some remembered Radulf fondly for his sanctity and humility, 'a splendid teacher and monk'.[32] In Hainaut, he may have received support from the Benedictine abbot of Lobbes. Even the fastidious Otto of Freising admitted Radulf's true monastic profession, his effectiveness in recruitment and his popularity, reserving his disdain for his lack of scholarship and message of violence against the Jews.[33] Initially, at least, Radulf may not have been far outside the pale of licensed preachers. Like many charismatic twelfth-century holy men, including Bernard, Radulf established himself as an arbiter of social behaviour outside the formal political and religious hierarchies: two of Bernard's main criticisms of Radulf concerned his 'unauthorized preaching and contempt for episcopal authority'. Otto of Freising noted disapprovingly how Radulf's preaching against the Jews encouraged men to rebel against their lords, who generally appeared willing to protect local Jewish communities.[34] Even Bernard's condemnation of Radulf's anti-Semitic propaganda focused narrowly on its theologically misguided incitement to murder and its reprehensible display of ambition and arrogance.

Radulf's demotic anti-Semitism was expressed in a simple argument. In summoning men to take the cross to fight the Muslims abroad, he drew the same parallel that had been drawn in 1096, as a Jewish eyewitness recalled: 'Avenge the crucified one upon his enemies who stand before you; then go to war against the Muslims,' or, as Otto of

Freising put it: 'the Jews whose homes were scattered throughout the [Rhineland] cities and towns should be slain as foes of the Christian religion'.[35] Such approaches were not the unique preserve of 'barking' demagogues (the phrase of one of Radulf's victims, Rabbi Ephraim of Bonn). Overt anti-Semitism dominated the academy of western Christendom in the twelfth and thirteenth centuries, often expressed by those unmoved by practical or communal resentment or fear. The monks, not the townspeople, of Norwich invented the Jewish blood libel of William of Norwich in 1144 to raise funds for their priory. Not all intellectuals could keep their dislike and prejudice separate from their academic detachment. Writing in 1146 or 1147 to Louis VII, Abbot Peter the Venerable of Cluny argued a point very close to Radulf's; if it is a meritorious act to fight enemies of Christianity in distant lands why are Jews allowed to live undisturbed in the heart of Christendom? If Muslims were detestable, how much more were the Jews? In profiting from Christians, even the church, through usury, they polluted Christendom. Abbot Peter was careful to follow the theologically orthodox line that Jews should not be killed but, he insisted, they should be punished as enemies of Christ. While Christians were being taxed for the crusade, why not the Jews?[36] Peter's letter mirrored the social and financial resentments, heightened by crusade preparations, on which Radulf played so effectively. Ephraim of Bonn identified the persecution of the Jews specifically with the preaching of the cross, which wrecked the normally peaceful relations between the communities of the Rhineland. Radulf, Peter the Venerable and Otto of Freising all noticed the association of Jews with other enemies of Christ. Bernard of Clairvaux, 'a decent priest' in Rabbi Ephraim's grateful memory, while rejecting simple and violent analogies, lacked sympathy or more than legal tolerance, stating:

> The Jews are not to be persecuted, killed or even put to flight . . . The Jews are for us the living words of Scripture, for they remind us always of what our Lord suffered. They are dispersed all over the world so that by expiating their crime they may be everywhere living witnesses of our redemption. Under Christian princes they endure a hard captivity . . . when the time is ripe all Israel shall be saved [i.e. converted]. But those who die before will remain in death. If Jews are utterly wiped out, what will become of our hope for their promised salvation, their eventual conversion?[37]

Radulf's robust populism represented the obverse of Bernard's refined passion, his message a product of the mass appeal to avenge the injuries done to Christ's heritage by the 'enemies of the cross' (a phrase used by Bernard and Eugenius). Although the focus of official censure, Radulf did not operate in isolation. Attacks on Jews may have begun in Mainz as early as April 1146. With the heaviest persecution in the Rhineland in the autumn of 1146, Jews in Würzburg suffered from a possibly unrelated blood libel in February/March 1147 and a rabbi at Ramerupt in Champagne was beaten up, his house looted and the Torah scroll desecrated in the spring probably of 1147 by French crusaders perhaps on their way to join the king's muster at Metz. Three other massacres were recorded by Ephraim of Bonn a quarter of a century later, although it is unclear whether they occurred in France or central Europe. In England, the new Jewish communities, planted since the Norman Conquest with royal approval, needed and received the king's protection.[38] Bernard's encyclical letter *inter alia* condemning Jewish persecution acknowledged a potentially widespread problem. Anti-Jewish motifs found extended circulation. The crusaders at Ramerupt were reported as having deliberately, almost ritualistically, inflicted five wounds on the head of Rabbi Jacob, jeering as they did so: 'Thus we shall take vengeance on you for the crucified one and wound you the way you inflicted five wounds [i.e. the stigmata] on our god.' A song composed in France in 1146 that closely echoed official crusade propaganda contained exactly the same image of the Jews, to whom God gave his body at the Passion and Crucifixion, wounding Him in five places.[39]

The scale and course of the Rhineland assaults provoked by Radulf differed from the 1096 pogroms. The secular and ecclesiastical authorities provided more consistent and competent protection for the Jewish communities, encouraged, perhaps, by the proximity of King Conrad. The Jews themselves appeared cannier in their own defence. Rabbi Ephraim of Bonn was thirteen in the autumn of 1146, living in Cologne, when he, his family and neighbours with members of other local Jewish communities, took refuge in the archbishop of Cologne's fortress of Wolkenburg.[40] The archbishop was well paid for his charity, as was his castellan. Similar precautions were followed across the Rhineland, as were Jewish payments to Christians of protection money. Radulf progressed from Strassburg to Cologne, whipping up enthusiasm for the crusade and violence against the Jews in equal measure. By the time

Bernard caught up with him at Mainz in November 1146, Radulf had established himself as a local celebrity, Bernard attracting local hostility when successfully browbeating him to return to the cloister (presumably by the threat of something much worse, probably temporal punishment by the king under whose protection the Jews lay). Unlike 1096, the impetus to attack the Jews came not from the local nobility, who seemed to have provided shelter, but from *crucesignati* and 'the poorer segment of the population who derive joy from things of no consequence'.[41] Church, town and village authorities attempted to maintain order, at a price, and even justice: one Christian murderer of Jews near Cologne was punished by having his eyes gouged out, dying soon after. The archbishop of Mainz complained directly to Bernard of Clairvaux about Radulf, perhaps suggesting the abbot's responsibility.[42] But in common with 1096, economic jealousy and financial anxiety fuelled the ferocity of the attacks at a time when converting capital into cash had become a major concern for crusaders, especially as Eugenius III's bull that excluded legitimate Jewish banking, by also prohibiting interest repayment by *crucesignati*, discouraged loans by bankers of any faith without lucrative material collateral.

If the violence appeared more random than in 1096 and the perpetrators less well connected, the horrors were real enough. Some reported large numbers of Jews seeking the king's protection as far away as Nuremberg to avoid the Christian fury.[43] Rumours circulated of massacres of hundreds of Jews; opportunist killings of men, women and children proliferated. Rabbis, synagogues, religious ceremonies and Torah scrolls became targets. Forced baptisms led to suicides as well as murder. In late summer 1146, Simon of Trier, returning from a trip to England, was caught by a mob at Cologne; on his refusal to abjure his faith, his head was severed from his body by being squeezed in a winepress. For a fee, the civic authorities returned the body and the remains of the head for Jewish burial.[44] Others drowned rather than receive baptism in the local rivers; those who submitted returned to their faith once the Christian militants had passed. After Radulf's removal, sporadic outbursts of violence continued until preaching ceased, when communal relations were restored. In contrast with England where the Jewish communities were of relatively recent origin and, on this occasion, peace reigned, areas with long-established Jewish communities had proved most susceptible to prejudice and persecution. The

Rhineland had become a centre of Jewish settlement and business but also inter-faith dialogue and dispute. One of the most famous medieval Jewish converts to Christianity, Hermann 'quondam Judaeus', i.e. the former Jew, had been born *c.*1107 Judas Levi of Cologne, where, in 1172, he rose to be a canon in the church of Sta Maria ad Gradus. Judging from his autobiography, as with many zealous converts Hermann may not have been sympathetic to his former co-religionists and relatives in their sufferings in 1146. Yet his career demonstrated contact, communication and occasional respect, Hermann arguing that conversion of the Jews would, like his own, happen through love not force or dialectic.[45] Few, anywhere in Christendom, were listening.

One of those most affected by the Rhineland disturbances was King Conrad III. Jews and their property were royal charges and undisciplined recruitment and violence threatened his own plans for the crusade, the main purpose of Bernard's mission to imperial lands. The formal story of Conrad's reluctance to commit himself when he first met Bernard at Frankfurt in November 1146, his continued reluctance at the Christmas assembly at Speyer overcome by an electrifying sermon by the abbot, conceals a carefully orchestrated process begun many months earlier which culminated in Conrad taking the cross on 27 December. It is unlikely that Radulf's tour, beginning in northern France but soon directed at the Rhineland, was accidental or, as some have suggested, determined by the need to run away from the pursuing Bernard, nor that Bernard's own evangelism had no prospect of substantial dividends. His itinerary suggests a long-planned meeting with Conrad at Frankfurt in November, his subsequent journey south to Constance received royal encouragement and his attendance at Speyer was anticipated. If startling in its success, Bernard's preaching tour was no surprise, hardly coming, as one local monk piously maintained, out of the blue, 'as if from Heaven'.[46] It is barely conceivable that Conrad's army of many tens of thousand could have been prepared to leave for the east by May 1147 if its leadership had only been settled five months before. One guest at Speyer was an ambassador from Byzantium, responding to a secret embassy earlier in the year from Conrad to Emperor Manuel, conducted by the bishop of Würzburg, on which the crusade, the subject of negotiations between Manuel and the French since the spring, almost certainly featured.[47]

Politics as well as ritual lay behind Bernard's oratory. In mid-1146, the tensions within the German nobility and between the empire and its eastern neighbours, especially Hungary, precluded Conrad's personal involvement in the eastern adventure. Bernard's visit was closely associated with attempts to engineer peace within the empire. Taking the cross could act as a focus for honourable resolution to domestic conflict under ecclesiastical supervision and guarantee. At Frankfurt in November, Bernard mediated a dispute between Count Henry of Namur and Albero of Trier, joining the crusade forming part of their reconciliation. On his visit to Constance in December, Bernard made contact with the circle of Conrad's chief domestic opponent, Welf VI, a move that led to Welf taking the cross on 24 December. In the hyperbole of the chronicler Otto of Freising, 'suddenly almost the entire West became so still that not only the waging of war but even the carrying of arms in public was considered wrong'.[48] By the time Bernard reached Speyer for Christmas 1146, it may have been clear to Conrad that his involvement was required to complete this unifying process by providing him with a share in the honour and privileges of a *crucesignatus*.

Conrad held a unique position among the monarchs of the west. By now in his fifties, an intermittently successful general and monarch caught in unpropitious times, he had previous experience of fighting in the Holy Land. His two military expeditions east, in 1124 and 1147–8, suggest, as with Thierry of Flanders's four visits (1138, 1147, 1157 and 1165), a more than formal engagement with the needs of Outremer and the appeal of holy war. No other western medieval monarch campaigned twice in the Holy Land. The German empire possessed a strong tradition of holy war, on its borders, as part of internal feuding and, since 1096, in the eastern Mediterranean. Despite a lack of prominent settlement in Outremer, no cultural or emotional barrier needed breaching, no introduction to an alien concept was required. The German crowds that flocked to hear Bernard were as primed and receptive as those further west. Conrad's elaborately staged assumption of the cross operated to a familiar pattern, a public ritual that emphasized a procedure of conversion and submission to the will of God, each participant following the choreography of a well-oiled religious ceremony. Ritual provided expression for religious and political messages as theatre. Even with interpreters in southern Germany, Bernard's message transcended language, not least when, as at Speyer, it was delivered in the context of the Eucharist. During mass on 27 December, Bernard, ending his sermon by listing the material benefits bestowed on the king, adopted the voice of God: 'O man, what is there that I should have done for you and did not?' Responding to this familiar call to reject worldly priorities, amid loud cries of excited religious fervour, Conrad fulfilled the ceremonial fiction of sudden conversion, declaring: 'I am ready to serve Him,' before receiving from Bernard both the cross and a holy banner conveniently placed on the altar. Significantly, Conrad was accompanied in taking the cross by his nephew Frederick of Swabia.[49] This was not a quixotic act. The old, dying duke of Swabia, Conrad's brother, bitterly resented the king enrolling his son as his absence might jeopardize the family holdings. That was the point. Only if as many of the great feudatories of the Empire as possible accompanied the king or, by virtue of taking the cross, were compromised if they stayed behind, could Conrad ensure both the success of the crusade and the security of his realm.

To confirm the political solidarity behind the enterprise, Conrad and Bernard's representative, Abbot Adam of Ebrach, presided over another crusade mass at Regensburg in February 1147, where Conrad's half-brother, Henry Jasomirgott, duke of Bavaria and margrave of Austria, and the bishops of Regensburg, Freising and Passau took the cross with a large press of recruits including notorious thieves and footpads, perhaps attracted by the prospect of legal immunity if not amnesty. One participant recalled the careful preparation, 'all present had been aroused by previous report', his subsequent insistence that everyone had taken the cross 'of their own accord' satisfying canonical requirements if not historical accuracy.[50] The adherence of Henry of Bavaria revealed the irenic uses of the crusade: he was now a fellow *crucesignatus* with the disgruntled and dispossessed pretender to his duchy, Welf VI. Conrad's crusade, like Louis's, embraced family, friends and foes and offered support for a sometimes beleaguered status. During his stay in the east, Conrad, although never crowned emperor, added the imperial 'semper augustus' to his titles, perhaps in response to his association with the Greek emperor or, even, a nod to the revived interest in the so-called Sibylline eschatological prophecies of the Holy Land and the Last Emperor. The image of the tall, well-built Conrad rescuing the slight, frail Bernard from an adoring mob during the Diet of Frankfurt in March 1147 by picking him up and carrying him out of the crowd provided a less cosmic but no less potent opportunity for royal association with the great forces of Christendom.[51]

PLANNING AND RECRUITMENT

A flurry of conferences and assemblies early in 1147 settled the timing and routes for the crusaders. While at Regensburg securing the Bavarians, Conrad sent ambassadors to discuss plans with Louis and Bernard at Châlons-sur-Marne in early February, prior to the French deciding on their strategy and arrangements for the king's absence at a large council at Etampes beginning on 16 February. Conrad followed suit at a diet at Frankfurt on 13 March, also attended by the tireless Bernard hot foot from Etampes. By late March, a fresh round of meetings acknowledged the presence north of the Alps of the pope. Eugenius III, making a virtue of his expulsion from Rome by its radical commune, had set out from Viterbo in January, travelling via Lucca and Vercelli to Susa, where on 8 March he discussed the crusade with Louis VII's uncle, Amadeus of Savoy, thence through imperial Burgundy to Lyons (22 March) and into France, reaching Dijon by the end of the month, where he was met by German ambassadors eager to arrange a meeting between the pope and Conrad in Strassburg. Rejecting the German overtures, Eugenius turned aside to Clairvaux (6 April), perhaps to relive his youth there, certainly to be fully briefed by his old master, before proceeding to Paris with King Louis, celebrating Easter (20 April) at St Denis. There, on 11 June, the pope presided over an elaborate ceremony marking Louis's formal departure. From St Denis Louis marched towards his muster at Metz in late June. The pope, his role as diplomatic facilitator and legitimizing observer complete, remained in France and Lotharingia for another year. Conrad meanwhile spent Easter at Bamberg, a city especially associated with the recently canonized Emperor Henry II (1002–24) and his attempts to extend Christianity (and his empire) eastwards, before moving towards the Danube via Nuremberg and Regensburg, whence he embarked eastwards in late May.[52]

The involvement of Conrad and the Germans may have influenced the French plans. After taking the cross in March 1146, Louis had explored different options for his journey east. Conrad, King Geza of Hungary, the Emperor Manuel of Byzantium and King Roger II of Sicily were each consulted over passage, supplies and support, suggesting that no immediate decision had been made between the land route via the Danube and the Balkans and a sea route via southern Italy. There was even talk of the French preparing their own fleet, perhaps to shadow any land army (as Richard I of England was to organize for his crusade in 1190), although as Louis controlled no ports himself this would have required negotiation.[53] The response to French requests, received during the summer of 1146, appeared to be universally positive, leaving the choice of route open. The likelihood of active and substantial German participation delayed any decision until the assembly at Etampes in February 1147 just after Conrad's arrangements had been communicated to the French at the Châlons conference. It is sometime argued that Louis had decided in 1146 to accept the offer of transport by sea from Roger of Sicily, only to be deflected by German involvement. Yet the Franco-Byzantine exchanges of 1146 indicated that no such decision had been reached. After a long and possibly heated debate, the assembly at Etampes decided on the land route via Byzantium.[54]

Although with hindsight condemned by some as misguided, this option presented a number of advantages. For the bulk of the French contingents, including the largest, from Flanders, and the king's, the land route was the most accessible and the cheapest, as the troops could be supplied en route by local markets and, in enemy territory, by forage. Given the difficulties in raising cash from their property, this may have appealed to most *crucesignati*. Although the prospect of travelling in the wake of the large German armies raised concerns over inadequate local provisions, it offered certain benefits; on their march the French found a number of new bridges constructed by the Germans in front of them.[55] Most French nobles had no experience of the sea, many would never have seen it, the logistics and finance involved in hiring a fleet being wholly unfamiliar. Transport of horses by sea presented further complications: those Rhinelanders, Flemings and English who did travel by sea via the Iberian peninsular in 1147 may have carried few if any horses with them, relying on local stocks when they fought on land. It is instructive that the count of Flanders chose to travel by land. Of those with access to Mediterranean sea ports, only some, like the count of Toulouse, sailed directly to the Holy Land; others, led by the counts of Auvergne and Savoy, travelled via Italy and the short ferry crossing from Brindisi to Durazzo before crossing the Balkans to Constantinople.[56] The Sicilian offer presented political difficulties. Roger II threatened German ambitions in Italy and Byzantine power in the Balkans and the central Mediterranean. Even if his offer to Louis was not simply a cover for an assault on the Greeks, Roger's participation risked alienating Conrad and arousing Manuel's justifiable suspicion for no obviously overwhelming benefit, suspicions confirmed by the Sicilian refusal to take any part in the crusade once their offer of transport had been declined. Mindful of Roger's disobedience to the papacy, the ubiquitous Bernard of Clairvaux may have tilted the balance against Roger. Despite his innovative taxation, Louis himself may have feared the cost of accepting the Sicilian proposal. By placing himself so completely into the hands of another ruler, one renowned for ruthlessly pursuing his own self-interest, Louis's independence could have been compromised. The year's delay in deciding meant the sea option would now have jeopardized coordination with the German armies. At root, perhaps, lay the fear that the sea route was too risky, too difficult for so large a landlubber army. By contrast, the land route was familiar in nature if not geography and, significantly for an adventure self-consciously undertaken in the shadow of past triumphs, had been sanctified by the heroic achievements of the First Crusade.[57] The discussion at Etampes possibly concealed a decision already taken: negotiations with Manuel I had progressed far, the emperor, and possibly the pope, assuming the land route, although this may merely represent the success of French diplomats in keeping their powder dry. In this context, Louis's much-derided decision appears thoughtful and pragmatic. Unlike his later critics, notably his crusade chaplain Odo of Deuil, Louis did not know the future.

The assembly at Etampes concluded its business by appointing regents for France, led by Abbot Suger of St Denis, appropriate for the crusade's leading critic, and fixing the muster for departure at Metz on 15 June to fit Conrad's plans and the delays since Vézelay in organizing the French contingents. Louis's formal leave-taking of his kingdom provided spectacular theatre. Held to coincide with the annual Lendit Fair at St Denis, 11 June, with the streets around the abbey church crowded with visitors, the ceremony began with Louis visiting a Parisian lazar house, a sign of humility, charity and, with its reference to the mystic royal power of healing, regality. On arrival at the recently rebuilt St Denis (parts of which still survive), before the pope, Abbot Suger, the monks and a crowd of family, courtiers and notables, and beneath newly commissioned panels of stained glass depicting the heroics of the First Crusade, Louis prostrated himself before the altar, kissed a relic of the patron saint, finally receiving from Suger the Oriflamme, the vermilion banner mounted on a gold lance that under Louis's father, Louis VI, had become the official royal ensign, and the pilgrim's scrip from the pope, visual confirmation of the three elements of his enterprise: penitential pilgrimage; holy war and national honour. Proceedings ended with the king and a few (male) companions dining with the monks in their refectory.[58] This elaborate show paraded the special relationship of the French monarchy with the papacy and between St Denis and the king, providing a ceremonial expression of leaving the kingdom in the hands of the saint and the abbot, the king becoming an associate member of the monastic community. The personal and political meaning of Louis's holy war was thus carefully spelt out for the crowds to witness and later to relate.

Conrad III also faced tricky decisions, mainly provoked by his fissiparous nobility. A general, formal peace to which all the nobility were committed by oath lay at the centre of Conrad's political strategy for the crusade. At a crowded Imperial Diet at Frankfurt on 13 March, Conrad's ten-year-old son, Henry, was accepted as heir and crowned as joint king to legitimize the regency government headed by Abbot Wibald of Stavelot, later of Corvey. The land route for the crusade was announced, the muster fixed at Regensburg in May, the presence of Bernard of Clairvaux easing agreement. Henry the Lion, the young duke of Saxony and nephew of the disgruntled *crucesignatus* Welf VI, claiming his lost Bavarian patrimony, allowed himself to be fobbed off by Conrad who 'postponed a decision until his return and persuaded him to wait peacefully'.[59] Other nobles from Saxony were less easily brushed aside. Refusing to join the eastern expedition, they saw an opportunity to elevate political expansion across their frontier with the Wends into a holy war by incorporating it into a general scheme of anti-infidel militancy, 'to take vengeance on the pagans', in Bernard's words, an argument not far removed from that used against the Jews in the Rhineland a few months earlier. Given Conrad's main aim of political harmony and his penchant for seeing the crusade as reflecting honour on his realm, the Saxons received a sympathetic hearing. Binding Saxon expansionist raiding into the larger holy war and its penumbra of sworn peace offered the added advantage of providing occupation for Henry the Lion. Using his legatine authority, Bernard accepted the Saxon proposal as legitimate, granting the participants all the trappings and privileges of the Jerusalem journey, except that the crosses they wore 'were not simply sewed to their clothing, but were brandished aloft, surmounting a wheel'. The other difference lay in the objective, again according to Bernard, of the 'wiping out or, at any rate, the conversion of these people'.[60] Neither genocide nor forced baptism was canonically legal. However, some argued that these regions had accepted Christianity from missionaries in the previous decades and so could be regarded as apostates, thus action against them was, as in the Holy Land, a matter of reclaiming lost Christian territory, theoretically defensive. To erase any doubts, during his stay at Clairvaux in April 1147, Bernard persuaded Eugenius III to issue a bull legitimizing the Wendish adventure, conversion and all, and the grant of Jerusalem privileges, conveniently placing it in the somewhat wishful context of both the Holy Land expedition and attacks on the Muslims in Spain.[61] As far as Conrad was concerned, the Baltic campaign did not materially weaken his eastern force, while it directed some otherwise possibly troublesome nobles into taking out their acquisitive instincts beyond the empire's frontiers. The importance of this was underlined by the presence in one of the raiding parties of the regent Wibald of Corvey. Despite the official ecclesiastical gloss, and the presence of a gaggle of bishops, there was little edifying in the motives or conduct of the war against the Wends and, as Wibald confessed, it failed.[62]

King Conrad's crusade mobilized or neutralized the power brokers of the German empire. With him were staunch supporters based on his family and household: his half-brothers Duke Henry of Bavaria and Bishop Otto of Freising; his nephew, Duke Frederick of Swabia; and his chancellor Arnold of Wied; and allies such as Frederick of Bogen, advocate of Regensburg. Alongside them was his arch-enemy Welf of Bavaria. No less impressive was the geographic spread, not only men from Franconia, Swabia and Bavaria, but Saxons, such as Count Bernard of Ploetzkau, and Lorrainers under the bishops of Metz and Toul (brother of the count of Flanders) and the count of Monçon, and the contingent led by the bishop of Basel, the fruits of Bernard's visit in December 1146. Joining this German coalition came the kings of Bohemia and Poland as well as the counts of Styria and Carinthia. Although the Lorrainers defected to, for them, the more congenial French at Constantinople, this gathering represented the firmest practical demonstration of the reach of German imperial power north of the Alps for almost a century.[63] The wider context of the king's leadership of Christendom in alliance with the pope was witnessed by the papal legate, Theodwin, Cardinal of St Rufina, the Curia's German expert who had helped engineer Conrad's election as king in 1138.[64] In recruitment, leadership and organization, Conrad's expedition received important support throughout the German church. Viewed in the perspective of German and imperial politics, Conrad's eastern adventure temporarily resolved domestic political tensions while making manifest his grander claims to world leadership. The febrile optimism of the summer of 1147 contrasted with the subsequent dull disillusion of defeat was well captured by one of the campaign's leaders and close royal ally, Otto of Freising:

> And so, when the rigour of the winter cold had been dispelled, as flowers and plants came forth from the earth's bosom under the gracious showers of spring and green meadows smiled upon the world, making glad the face of the earth, King Conrad led forth his troops from Nuremberg, in battle array. At Regensburg he took ship to descend the Danube and on Ascension Sunday (1 June) he pitched camp in the East Mark near a town called Ardacker . . . He drew after him so great a throng that the rivers seemed scarcely to suffice for navigation, or the extent of the plain for marching . . . But since the outcome of that expedition, because of our sins, is known to all, we have purposed this time to write not a tragedy but a joyous history, leave this to be related by others elsewhere.[65]

Except in the eyes of his own apologists, Louis VII's international prestige fell short of Conrad's. Yet, as with Conrad, the extent of recruitment and active political involvement of the leading provincial magnates encouraged his role as the driving force behind this eastern policy and, more generally, as king. The blend of pious show, military exertion and administrative direction in providing men, money, command and strategy provided Louis with a unique opportunity to establish himself and his dynasty. The muster roll of French lords who travelled east with the king testified to the potential political dividends. While the counts of Toulouse and Nîmes sailed independently from ports on the French Mediterranean coast, most of the rest of the kingdom was represented in Louis's great army: Flanders, Soissons, Bar, Ponthieu, Nevers, Tonnerre, the Bourbonnais, the Auvergne, Meaux in Champagne, Mâcon in southern Burgundy and Vienne in imperial Provence; the lords of Nogent in the Seine valley, Rancon and Lusignan in Poitou and Magnac in the Limousin. With these lords came their retinues and dependants, in considerable numbers in the case of Thierry of Flanders. The core of support rested with the king's affinity; his brother Robert count of Dreux and La Perche; his formidable wife Eleanor, duchess of Aquitaine in her own right, who presumably secured the Poitevin and Limousin contingents: Geoffrey of Rancon, later notorious for causing the near-annihilation of the army in Asia Minor, had entertained Louis and Eleanor on their honeymoon.[66] The presence of women provided a notable feature of the Second Crusade. Apart from Eleanor and her household ladies, the counts of Flanders and Toulouse travelled with their wives and the statutes agreed by the northern European fleet at Dartmouth in May 1147 assumed the same for members of that force.[67] In the French king's army, the household clerks, led by Bartholomew, the chancellor, and his personal chaplain, the monk Odo of Deuil, a coming man seconded from the abbey of St Denis, were joined by some ecclesiastical heavyweights, such as the bishops of Arras, Langres and Lisieux, the last two both claiming legatine authority, Godfrey of Langres partly on the ground of his close association with Bernard, having been his prior at Clairvaux.[68] The canon lawyer, classical scholar and acerbic wit Arnold of Lisieux contested Godfrey's pretensions, famously describing him as 'like the wine of Cyprus, which is sweet to taste but lethal unless diluted with water'. Neither behaved well, attracting gossip that they lined their pockets from alms given in return for absolution by sick and dying crusaders. Their bickering, while contributing little to the smooth running of the campaign, ignored the legate actually appointed, Guy of Florence, cardinal of St Grisogono, a man of some bureaucratic ability later displayed in Outremer after the end of the crusade, but on the march fatally hampered by his lack of fluency in French. Without Bernard, none took the role of Adhemar of Le Puy on the First Crusade.[69] Nonetheless, the dynamism that propelled so many disparate political, personal and clerical groups towards the east under the king's Oriflamme testified to a sense of secular, even national as well as religious identity. Although able to speak German and holding land in the empire as well as France, Thierry of Flanders journeyed with King Louis.[70] Among those of the king's personal bodyguard killed around him in the desperate hand-to-hand fighting in the Cadmus mountains were knights from across France but also William of Warenne, earl of Surrey, a pillar of the Anglo-Norman establishment.[71] Under the sign of the cross new bonds of loyalty could be forged.

The popularity of the enterprise helped ensure the relatively easy agreement over the grand strategy of the holy war. Heavy recruitment, across France, western and southern Germany, the Low Countries, southern England, parts of Danubean central Europe, reaching northwards to Scotland and, for the Wendish campaign, Denmark, rested on piety, idealism, loyalty to lord or family and communal enthusiasm transmitted along the arteries of social and economic exchange. Religious values found expression in secular analogies directed at various propertied elites. One set of verses composed in 1146/7 talked of a tournament between heaven and hell.[72] Bernard articulated the cultural aspirations of arms-bearers by praising their reputation for courage and of merchants in terms of an unbeatable bargain.[73] Concentric circles of contact produced substantial contingents. The economically linked networks within the Rhineland or Flanders or Normandy or East Anglia combined with an outer ring of commerce in the Narrow Seas to produce the fleet that gathered at Dartmouth in May 1147. The new community of Cistercian abbeys, Bernard's own power base, supported older secular and ecclesiastical focal points of recruitment. So did the Templars, another new order that played a significant part planning and on campaign. Templars negotiated for Louis VII in Constantinople in 1146; they acted as the king's bankers; and later held the French army together in Asia Minor during the grim weeks in January 1148. Bernard of Clairvaux's own close Templar links were shared with *crucesignati* such as the Anglo-Norman patrons of the Templars Saher of Archel, one of the commanders of the Dartmouth fleet, and Roger of Mowbray.[74] The unanimity between secular and religious authorities in promoting the expedition as spiritual profit or social responsibility contrasted with the political and ecclesiastical divisions within western Christendom in 1096. Whereas Urban II's call was clearly partisan, Bernard's transcended political barriers and boundaries, only a few religious radicals distrustful of the church's overt involvement in the world joining with the Roman commune and Roger of Sicily in openly standing aloof. Unlike 1096, potential *crucesignati* were supported by ceremonial and legal procedures, recognized in *Quantum praedecessores*, which, if not always familiar, demonstrated the progress in ecclesiastical discipline, hierarchical communication and canon law achieved in the fifty years between Clermont and Vézelay, backed by the cultural penetration of the story of the First Crusade in French and German vernacular literatures.

From the North Sea to the Mediterranean, recruits conformed to *Quantum praedecessores*, raising money on their property, in particular from religious houses, with the permission of relatives and overlords. In the increasingly competitive land market of the twelfth century, such guarantees by the king, local count or bishop were as necessary as was the compliance of interested family members, relicts and heirs who often needed firm persuasion to honour the deals of deceased crusaders. The attractive provisions regarding church protection and immunity from civil law suits required similarly careful management. In November 1146, the bishop of Salisbury had to be reminded by the pope that church jurisdiction did not extend to land disputes originating before the defendant took the cross. Even so, the popularity of the crusade with thieves, noted by Otto of Freising, may not have been coincidental.[75] The emotional or spiritual dimensions behind the legal framework emerged fitfully. In contrast to papal letters and chronicles, references in monastic land charters to taking the cross or to preaching are rare. Some charters, but not a majority, related the donations or mortgages to remission of sins; 'love and fear' apparently moved one Poitevin, Raynard *rusticus*, the countryman.[76] However, large numbers of non-combatant or otherwise militarily incompetent pilgrims did travel with the German and French armies, giving the enterprise a dogged if inconvenient revivalist tinge that drained efficiency and resources on the march and in battle. For aristocrats and arms-bearers, the imperative to translate property into cash generated expediency. Bishop Godfrey of Langres pawned gold and silver vessels from his cathedral church while promising restitution to a suspicious chapter.[77] Acquisitive religious houses skilfully played the market. In the face of royal demands for tax, the monks of Fleury protested a lack of cash, offering a miscellany of precious candlesticks and thuribles instead, yet at the same time provided money to local worthies in return for pledges of property.[78] The business could be highly lucrative, in both the short and long term. The English abbey of St Benet Holme in Norfolk made an effective profit on its deal with Philip Basset of Postwick of a minimum of 133 per cent spread over seven years, the frowned-upon usury hidden here as ubiquitously elsewhere behind the fiction of mutual gifts.[79] The cost of crusading is difficult to underestimate. Reiner von Sleiden sold outright part of his allodial (i.e. freehold) patrimony to the abbey of Klösterrad, near Aachen.[80] Dozens of land charters record landowners raising sums many times (three in Philip Basset's case) their annual revenue; they also chart those who failed to return.

The elaborate organization of the Second Crusade matched its vast human and geographic scale. The expeditions of the kings rested on the collaboration of socially, financially and politically distinct military households of the great nobles, each with their own regional and personal identity, cohesion and loyalties. However, where the armies of 1096 retained their separate regional identities to the end, Conrad and Louis, through deference and convenience, imposed an element of unity, providing, for better or worse, field leadership and chairmanship of the baronial high command. As the papally sanctioned chief organizers, they conducted the preparatory diplomacy; negotiated with local rulers during the march; set the schedule of departure and muster points; and supplied men and money. Both Conrad and Louis possessed continuing access to large funds, either cash in their own coffers or sums held on account by third parties such as the Templars. Once in Palestine in the spring of 1148, Conrad was able to reassert his authority after a disastrous journey by taking troops into his pay while Louis, using his assets in France, presumably including his church tax, as collateral, borrowed heavily from the Templars in the east; during the stumbling march across Asia Minor Louis repeatedly bailed out his impoverished nobles, knights and infantry.[81]

The geographic, political and social diversity of recruitment challenged coherent mustering, leadership, strategy, structure and timing. Yet most of the land and naval contingents for the east embarked between April and June 1147, arriving together, despite contrasting vicissitudes, a year later in the Holy Land. Planning, not chance, lay behind the musters at Dartmouth in May 1147, Regensburg the same month or Metz a month later; the adherence to the German force of Ottokar of Styria at Vienna in late May or early June; the arrival of the Anglo-Norman contingent to join Louis at Worms in late June; or the secondary French muster at Constantinople in October, where Louis waited for the counts of Maurienne and Auvergne and the marquis of Montferrat and those who had left the main army at Worms to travel via Italy, the Adriatic and the Balkans. The mechanics of such extended coordination included, from the early spring of 1146, extensive correspondence linking the major participants with each other and with those through whose territory any expedition could expect to pass: Byzantium,

Sicily, Hungary, the Christian rulers of the Iberian peninsular. Bernard of Clairvaux acted as head of a central secretariat as well as attending, in person or by agents and proxies, all the summit meetings between the main crusade leaders. On his preaching tour in 1146 Bernard contacted figures in the Flemish crusade leadership, including Count Thierry and Christian of Gistel, commander of those from Flanders and Boulogne who assembled at Dartmouth.[82] In the Rhineland, Bernard encountered civic and ecclesiastical authorities involved in raising and organizing troops, including the archbishop of Cologne, one of whose priests later wrote an eyewitness account of the siege of Lisbon. Another who sent home a description of the Lisbon campaign, the priest Duodechin, came from Lahnstein on the Rhine, which Bernard had either visited or passed by in the second week of 1147.[83]

Behind direction and strategy lay the armies' structure. The authority of the kings should not be exaggerated. Both French and perhaps to a greater degree German forces threatened to dissolve into their princely and baronial constituent parts although holding together long enough for adversity to compel unity. Political advantage, lack of alternatives, the comradeship of shared experience and hardship contributed to cohesion. Yet Louis VII failed to impose disciplinary ordinances on his nobles, his chaplain acidly commenting: 'because they did not observe them well, I have not preserved them either'. Louis's ordinances, promulgated when his army mustered at Metz, were designed 'for securing peace and other requirements on the journey, which the leaders secured by solemn oath'.[84] A precisely similar process led the leaders of the disparate contingents at Dartmouth to swear to obey mutually agreed statutes regulating the exercise of criminal and civil justice; sumptuary rules; the behaviour of women; the mechanics of corporate discussion, worship, and distribution of funds; and solving disputes between groups and leaders. Such disciplinary statutes were familiar features of medieval warfare, Richard I insisting on them in 1190 during his crusade. The commanders at Dartmouth in 1147 had in effect entered into a *coniuratio* or *societas coniurata*, a sworn association, a commune. Unlike the sworn communal statutes of Metz, those of Dartmouth retained their force when disputes emerged between the regional groups at critical points before and after the siege of Lisbon.[85] Later on his march to the east, Louis managed to establish a sworn fraternity under which his army agreed to be ruled by the Templars.[86] The readiness of the French king and the leaders at Dartmouth to create sworn communes testifies to the lack within the armies of a common legal system or political authority. Moreover, some crusaders lived outside ties of noble clientage. Across north-western Europe, urbanization had thrown up towns in which corporate identity demanded separate legal recognition. One 1147 contingent comprised of *Londonienses*, Londoners whose commune had only six years earlier decided the fate of the English crown by siding with King Stephen to prevent the coronation of his cousin, the pretender Matilda.[87] Over the previous half-century, towns and cities across the Rhineland, the Low Countries and northern France had sought rights of self-determination and justice; some of the charters granting these rights echoing the Dartmouth statutes. Sworn agreements became necessary in the absence of other political bonds, a circumstance regularly repeated on polyglot crusades. As an English writer remembered a century and a half later, the Dartmouth crusaders 'are by alliance/Sworn among themselves and are not retained'.[88] Neither the lasso of fealty nor pay held such a force together, comprising recruits from the Rhineland, the Low Countries, northern France, southern England, East Anglia and Scotland. As striking as the urban elements in the Dartmouth (and the other) expeditions appeared the willingness of secular lords to submit to such structures, even if, in the heat of battle, the agreed rules got broken, as by the Count of Aerschot and Christian of Gistel at the fall of Lisbon.[89] Experience of administering local public rights may have familiarized such lesser aristocrats to sworn associations to keep the peace; alternatively the commune may have evoked the legacy of ecclesiastical peace leagues. To view medieval Europe as hidebound by social and economic hierarchy, called by some the feudal system, ignores a perennial feature of public life which the theoretical and occasionally actual non-hierarchical nature of crusading highlighted. Sworn bonds of association were familiar and habitual. On the day they set out on crusade, at the entrance to the forest at Evry between Auxerre and Troyes in southern Champagne, Milo, lord of Evry-le-Châtel, and his knights bound themselves together with oaths to join the king's expedition.[90] Such associations can be found in similar circumstances on later crusades and are reminiscent of the fraternity formed to pay for siege engines at Antioch in 1098. Thus, beside the necessities of survival, the imperatives of enthusiasm, the community of family, friends and companions, the crusaders in the armies of 1147 were assembled and glued together by a network of mutual oaths: to the church in taking the cross; to lords and paymasters; and to each other. Time and unimaginable hardship were to put these bonds under fearful, often fatal, strain.

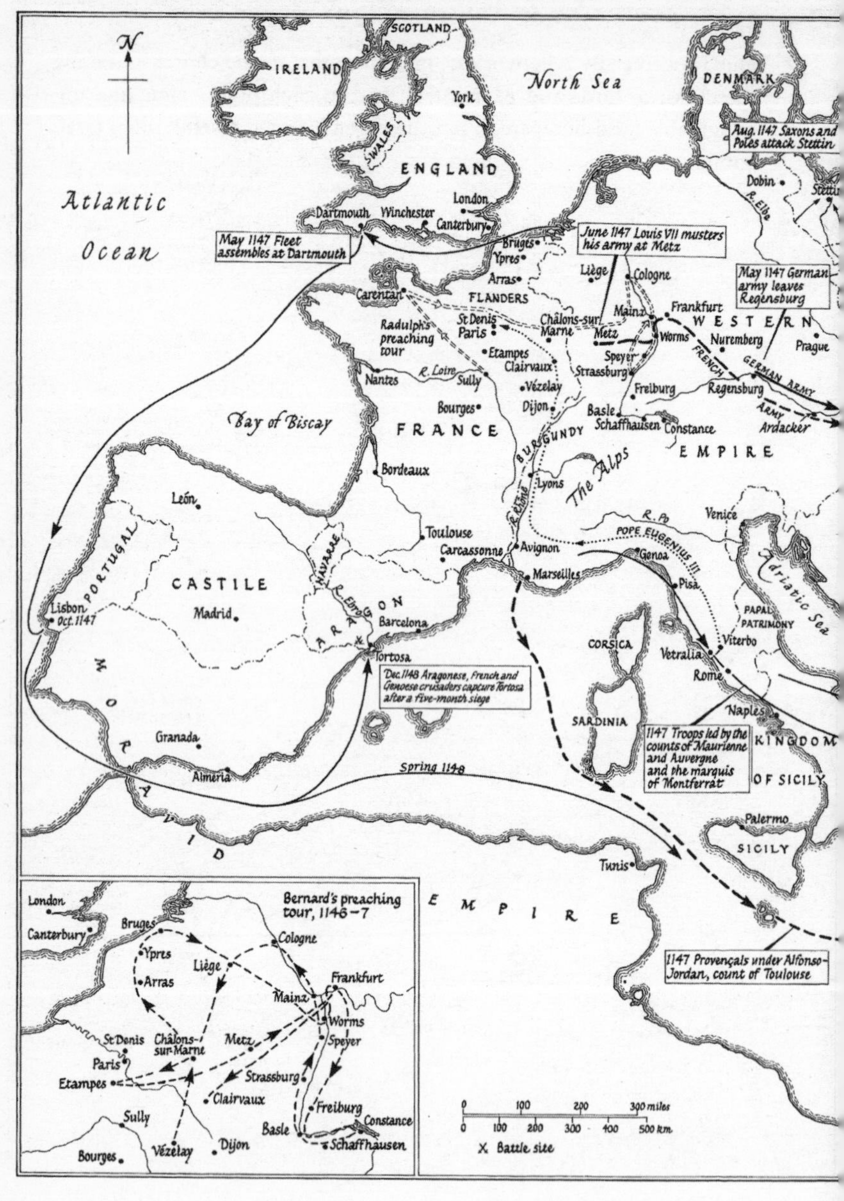

8. Europe and the Near East at the Time of the Second Crusade and Bernard's Preaching Tour 1146–7

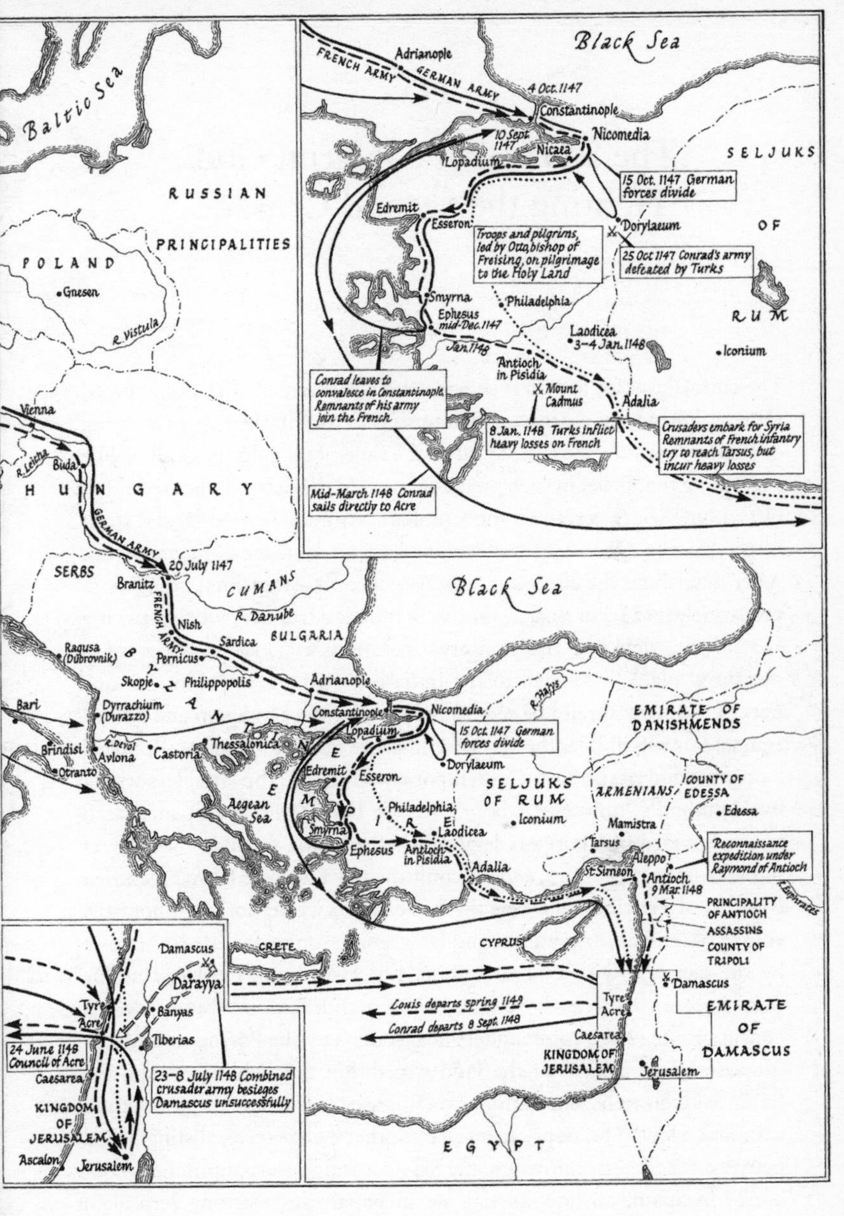

Black Sea
Adrianople
FRENCH ARMY
GERMAN ARMY
4 Oct. 1147
Constantinople
Nicomedia
10 Sept. 1147
Nicaea
Lopadium
SELJUKS
OF
RUM
15 Oct. 1147 German forces divide
Edremit
Esseron
Dorylaeum
Troops and pilgrims, led by Otto, bishop of Freising, on pilgrimage to the Holy Land
25 Oct 1147 Conrad's army defeated by Turks
Smyrna
Philadelphia
Ephesus mid-Dec. 1147
Laodicea 3–4 Jan. 1148
Jan. 1148
Iconium
Antioch in Pisidia
Mount Cadmus
Adalia
Conrad leaves to convalesce in Constantinople. Remnants of his army join the French
8 Jan. 1148 Turks inflict heavy losses on French
Crusaders embark for Syria Remnants of French infantry try to reach Tarsus, but incur heavy losses
Mid-March 1148 Conrad sails directly to Acre
Baltic Sea
RUSSIAN
PRINCIPALITIES
POLAND
Gnesen
R. Vistula
Vienna
R. Leitha
Buda
HUNGARY
GERMAN ARMY
20 July 1147
SERBS
Branitz
CUMANS
R. Danube
Black Sea
FRENCH ARMY
Nish
BULGARIA
Sardica
Ragusa (Dubrovnik)
Pernicus
BYZANTINE EMPIRE
Skopje
Philippopolis
Adrianople
Bari
Dyrrachium (Durazzo)
Constantinople
Nicomedia
R. Halys
EMIRATE OF DANISHMENDS
Lopadium
15 Oct. 1147 German forces divide
Brindisi
R. Devol
Avlona
Castoria
Thessalonica
Dorylaeum
Otranto
Edremit
Esseron
SELJUKS OF RUM
ARMENIANS
COUNTY OF EDESSA
Aegean Sea
Philadelphia
Iconium
Edessa
Smyrna
Laodicea
Mamistra
Ephesus
Antioch in Pisidia
Tarsus
Reconnaissance expedition under Raymond of Antioch
Adalia
St Simeon
Aleppo
Antioch
9 Mar. 1148
R. Euphrates
PRINCIPALITY OF ANTIOCH
ASSASSINS
COUNTY OF TRIPOLI
CRETE
CYPRUS
Damascus
Darayya
Damascus
Tyre
Acre
Banyas
Tiberias
Louis departs spring 1149
Conrad departs 8 Sept. 1148
Tyre
Acre
EMIRATE OF DAMASCUS
24 June 1148 Council of Acre
Caesarea
Caesarea
KINGDOM OF JERUSALEM
23–8 July 1148 Combined crusader army besieges Damascus unsuccessfully
Jerusalem
KINGDOM OF JERUSALEM
Ascalon
Jerusalem
EGYPT

10

'The Spirit of the Pilgrim God': Fighting the Second Crusade

The enthusiasm for holy war generated in the summer of 1147 reminded Otto of Freising of a prophecy promising victory in the east to the king of France that talked of 'the spirit of the time of the pilgrim God'. While suggesting that belief in such predictions owed much to 'Gallic credulity', Otto nonetheless described the Christian armies 'inspired by the spirit of the pilgrim God'. Others fashioned events in more concrete terms. After describing the circumstances as 'new and astonishing', the Saxon priest Helmold from Bosau, on the Baltic Slav frontier, writing twenty years later, depicted the military operations of 1147 as part of a measured plan: 'It seemed to the initiators of the expedition that one part of the army should be sent to the east, another to Spain and a third against our neighbours the Slavs.'[1] Hindsight and local interest produced a neat version of the past. Contemporary witnesses appeared less struck by Helmond's 'universal labour'. At the Diet of Frankfurt in March 1147, Bernard of Clairvaux legitimized the Saxon foray in the context of the eastern expedition, a move confirmed by Eugenius III and recorded by Otto of Freising, who was there. Yet Otto wrote nothing about the course of the Baltic operation and later confused the capture of Almeria by the Genoese with that of Lisbon, not associating the latter as the third limb of the 1147 holy war. Henry archdeacon of Huntingdon, a cousin of one of the commanders at Lisbon, saw the Portuguese adventure as the naval arm of the land expedition east while ignoring the Baltic raids entirely. The various eyewitnesses to the siege of Lisbon took a similar view. The pope, from yet another perspective, distinguished between the eastern campaign, the Slavic war and the continuing *reconquista* in Spain, all holy enterprises in papal eyes meriting Jerusalem indulgences, yet all different in motive and inception; Eugenius mentioned the Lisbon fleet not at all. Few other contemporaries drew any parallels at all, certainly not those clerics who drafted the land charters by which departing crusaders endowed religious houses in return for ready cash. Bernard's association of different theatres of holy war, possibly including Spain as well as the Baltic, appears essentially reactive rather than intentional or planned; for the pope such links merely followed policy sanctioned in use for a generation.[2] For all Bernard's bluster at Frankfurt about the Baltic army protecting the columns bound for Jerusalem, organizers and participants were bound by no calculated grand strategy embracing all Christendom's frontiers. Rather, holy warriors, inspired by much less tangible emotions, found themselves through expedience fighting at the same time at the three corners of Europe.

THE BALTIC: JULY–SEPTEMBER 1147

Of all the Christian fronts, that in the Baltic most obviously offered fulfilment of self-interest: for the secular rulers of Holstein and Saxony, reinforcements and legitimacy to their quickening efforts to spread their authority and vassals into neighbouring Slavic lands; for the squabbling kings of Denmark, a further chance to secure their southern approaches; for churchmen, an opportunity to ally force to missionary work in the hope of a permanent extension of Christendom. Viewed as a holy war, the Baltic crusade of 1147 failed; seen as larger than usual summer raids to acquire booty and to extend increasingly porous local political frontiers, the campaigns achieved limited but tangible results.

At the Diet of Frankfurt, the Saxon muster had been fixed for 29 June, the Feast of SS Peter and Paul, at Magdeburg. In April, the pope appointed Anselm bishop of Havelburg as his legate to the expedition; he also probably sent letters to the Danish Archbishop Eskil of Lund, a friend of Bernard, to encourage the participation of the warring Kings Canute V and Sweyn III whose predecessor, Eric the Lamb, may have been approached by a papal legate to join the Holy Land expedition the previous year. Further incentive came in June with the provocative pre-emptive strike on the recently re-established Christian port of Lübeck by the Wendish Prince Niklot of the Abotrites, who previously had cooperated with Adolf of Holstein in the recent German penetration of his western provinces, Wagria and Polabia. The confusion of the shifting frontier found little space for rigid political division based on religion; competition revolved around forts protecting settlements producing agricultural rents, control of trade and access to slaves. The Frankfurt holy war offered a chance to establish a military coalition to extend German authority eastwards; submission not conversion represented the central aim, despite the papal prohibition on truces and treaties with the pagans and Bernard's call for their baptism or annihilation. Canon law forbade simple war of conquest. Yet the consequences of repeated border raids, temporary annexation and repeated missions along the Saxon/Slav borderland left many pagans open to the charge, however misleading, of apostasy, such as Niklot's allies on the island of Rügen, who had briefly been ruled by the Danes in the 1130s. As apostates rather than pagans they were fair game, as were any infidels who hindered the holy war to Jerusalem, the fragile justification promoted by Bernard.[3]

Politics got the better of piety. For Henry the Lion, the enterprise allowed him to win his spurs in reasserting ducal leadership over the push eastwards, Helmold idealistically disapproving of his mercenary motives.[4] In Denmark, the holy war provided a suitably honourable good cause behind which the parties in the civil war could be persuaded to unite. In mid-July, with the archbishop of Bremen and an old Welf ally, Conrad of Zahringen, a recruit of Bernard's the previous winter, Duke Henry advanced into Abotrite country to besiege Niklot's newly fortified outpost at Dobin at the same time as a combined Danish army and fleet descended on this remote fortress from the north. Danish resolve was soon undermined, a sally from Dobin inflicting considerable damage on their army while their fleet was attacked by Niklot's Rügian allies. The consequent ravaging of the area by some besiegers alarmed Saxon crusaders hoping for territorial gain: 'Is not the land we are devastating our land? . . . Why are we . . . destroyers of our own incomes?'[5] Despite the defiant words of the spring, to extricate themselves from a militarily forlorn and politically self-defeating exercise, the crusaders soon negotiated a treaty with the Abotrites under which the garrison at Dobin accepted baptism and released Danish prisoners while Niklot agreed to return to his alliance with Adolf of Holstein and pay tribute. The terms amounted to a scanty fig leaf to allow the Danes and Saxons to withdraw, the former to resume their civil war, the latter to business as usual. The treaty fooled no one, least of all a highly critical Helmold of Bosau, who described the supposed Wendish conversion as false; Niklot's rule stayed intact with his and his people's paganism; the idols, temples and sanctuaries remained, as did the able-bodied Danish prisoners who swelled the Wendish slave market. In the context of the propaganda of Frankfurt, nothing had been achieved.

The main army of possibly some tens of thousands assembled at Magdeburg early in August under the legate Anselm of Havelburg, its religious veneer displayed by the presence of six other German bishops although the adherence of powerful Saxon marcher lords led by Albert the Bear proved more significant for its conduct. The regent Wibald of Corvey asserted the dimension of imperial leadership of this revived *Drang nach Osten*, the failure of the king's representative and the duke of Saxony to make common cause underscoring the unresolved political tensions lurking beneath the banners of the cross. Operating well away from Duke Henry's foray to Dobin, part of the legate's army battered its way over a hundred miles into Wendish territory to Demmin on the river Peene, possibly as a prelude to an assault on the strategically important island of Rügen, attacked by the Emperor Lothar a couple of decades earlier. Despite the iconic destruction of the pagan temple and idols at Malchow to the south, the siege of Demmin proved fruitless, Wendish resistance forcing a stalemate from which the Christians lamely withdrew early in September. The failure before Demmin owed much to the division of the German army. Persuaded by rapacious local margraves, the bulk of the Christian force turned further east to besiege Stettin in Pomerania, a major trading station on the Oder estuary. The difficulty in this lay in the fact, soon transmitted to the besiegers by the townsmen hanging crosses on their walls, that Stettin had already accepted 'the German God', as locals called Him, a point reinforced by a delegation from the city led by its bishop of many years, Adalbert, who pointedly suggested that if the crusaders genuinely intended to promote faith this was best achieved by preaching not fighting. He struck a nerve; as a well-informed Bohemian commentator noted, the Saxons were more interested in land than religion and so quickly agreed a truce with the bishop and the Christian prince of Pomerania, Ratibor.[6] The Wendish crusade begun with such acclaim at Frankfurt, and attracting recruits from as far afield as Moravia, Denmark and the southern Rhineland, petered out in a failed Saxon land grab.

If of little immediate tangible importance except to participants and victims, the precedent of the Wendish crusade added a new dimension to the bleak warfare across Christendom's Baltic frontier. The tacit acceptance that conversion and violence served the same end of promoting the Word of God and securing the souls of the pagans now began to be formalized. In the eyes of the Czech commentator Vincent of Prague, the bishop of Moravia had taken the cross in 1147 to convert the Pomeranians.[7] That they had already been converted by Bishop Otto of Bamberg twenty years earlier proved embarrassing but did nothing to undermine the principle which thereafter became a regular prop to campaigns of territorial aggrandizement and ecclesiastical imperialism. Conquest became the precursor to conversion and, as such, easily attracted the status of holy war and, increasingly, the legal trappings of a war of the cross. The campaigns of 1147 did not invent religious warfare in the Baltic, for Germans or for Danes; nor, thereafter, were all wars of expansion legitimized by papal grants of Jerusalem indulgences. However, the legacy of 1147 reconfigured how such wars came to be articulated and justified and, on occasion, recruited.

THE CAPTURE OF LISBON: MAY TO OCTOBER 1147

The fleet that sailed out of the Dart estuary on 23 May 1147 numbered between 150 and 200 vessels drawn from the Rhineland, Brabant-Limbourg, Flanders, Boulogne, Normandy, Lincolnshire, East Anglia, London and the major ports of southern England, including Dover, Hastings, Southampton and Bristol, with other contingents from Scotland and possibly Brittany, their destination Jerusalem.[8] The English force alone may have comprised about 4,500 men, the whole army perhaps 10,000. The muster of this polyglot armada completed a complicated process of recruitment and planning. Those from imperial lands acknowledged the leadership of Count Arnold III of Aerschot, a nephew of Godfrey of Bouillon, and so connected with the ruling house of Jerusalem as well as the aura of the First Crusade. However, the imperial crusaders had travelled separately, those from Cologne embarking on 27 April arriving at Dartmouth on 19 May to find Count Arnold from

Brabant-Limbourg already waiting. The Anglo-Norman contingents displayed marked regional diversity, reflected in their being organized into four groups: those from Norfolk and Suffolk under a local landowner, Hervey of Glanvill; the men of Kent under Simon of Dover; the Londoners; and the rest led by Saher of Archel, a lord with lands in Lincolnshire. Additionally, a distinct camaraderie existed among those from Southampton and Hastings who had been part of a similar expedition that had failed to capture Lisbon in 1142; on the 1147 campaign they and their spokesmen, the cross-Channel merchant Veil brothers, together with men from Bristol, proved awkward companions even though Saher of Archel and Hervey of Glanvill remained mutually supportive. While those from coastal Flanders and Boulogne, under Christian of Gistel, Count Arnold's men and the Germans tended to coalesce, to the extent of fighting together and later sharing texts narrating the events at Lisbon, the Fleming priest Arnulf copying the account of Winand from Cologne, the Anglo-Normans remained fissiparous. Disputatious relations between the main linguistic groups – Anglo-Norman and Germano-Flemish – persisted to the end.

Despite the precariousness of its unity, the gathering of such a heterogeneous force at the same time in the same place cannot have been coincidental. Its lack of great princes or counts as leaders and its chronic search for booty make what cohesion there was more impressive. Apart from Count Arnold and Saher of Archel, described as 'lord', other leaders came from the lesser landed aristocracy, such as Christian, castellan of Gistel, and Hervey of Glanvill, or merchant and urban elites: the Viels of Southampton and Caen; Simon of Dover; Andrew of London. Town origins appeared as prominently in eyewitness descriptions of the expedition as regional affiliations: Cologne; Boulogne; London; Hastings; Bristol; Southampton; young men from 'the region of Ipswich' (*de provintia Gipeswicensi*).[9] Such groups had been assembled by forces beyond simple social hierarchies, reflecting a complexity of relationships typical of the economically prosperous regions around the North Sea and English Channel. Without kings or great counts, the organizational impetus suggests largely hidden processes of rural and urban local self-awareness and communal action, if only in hiring and equipping ships and raising money. It may be no chance that many of the leading figures came from the prominent trading centres or some of the most densely populated areas of north-west Europe, where the ease of transmission of news and ideas was matched by a sense of community and a tradition of corporate action. Some members of the fleet were veterans of the attack on Lisbon in 1142; some may have previously been crusaders to the east. Others had felt the power of Bernard's oratory or, like Christian of Gistel, who met the abbot in August 1146, his conversation. Among the Anglo-Normans, many may have seized the opportunity to escape the conflicts and compromises of civil war; the Viels of Southampton, heavily involved in the Channel ferry and cargo business, were partisans for Matilda. Like others, they also had ready access to shipping.[10]

Some in the leadership may have anticipated fighting the Moors of Iberia. Afonso Henriques (1128–85), who was carving out an independent principality of Portugal along the Atlantic seaboard south from the rivers Mino and Duero, had maintained close links with the papacy in his as yet unsuccessful attempts to receive recognition as king. His designs on Lisbon were no secret; the crusader fleet included veterans of his failed attack on the city in 1142. In April he had captured the strategically vital stronghold of Santarem, the key to the lower Tagus valley, its investment providing an essential prerequisite for an assault on Lisbon downstream. The arrival of the crusade fleet had been anticipated by the Portuguese; an advance flotilla of five ships sailed directly from Dartmouth to Lisbon, apparently in five days, where it awaited the main fleet after its leisurely and laborious progress of more than a month. While Peter Pitoes, the bishop of Oporto, expended much eloquence and hard bargaining to attract the support of the Anglo-Normans and Rhinelanders after they arrived at the mouth of the Duero on 16 June, the Flemings under Christian of Gistel and the others from the Low Countries under the count of Arschot were still at sea. However, less than a fortnight later immediately on arrival at Lisbon the Flemings agreed to Afonso's terms to join his attack on Lisbon whereas contingents from the Anglo-Norman realms needed much persuasion. It is possible that some of those recruited from areas and by lords associated with Bernard during his Flanders tour of late summer and autumn 1146 may have agreed to cooperate with the Portuguese before setting out, although a letter from Bernard to Afonso that exists is probably not genuine.[11] The rest of the force gathered at Dartmouth came round to the idea only gradually. The idea of such action cannot have appeared entirely alien. The thrust of such action fitted the prevailing general justification for the holy war as proclaimed in 1146–7 by the pope,

Bernard and, in his awkward way, Radulf. Although Eugenius III seems not to have specifically authorized the Lisbon enterprise, in April 1147 he had extended his approval to other Iberian battles against the Moors. As recorded by a member of his audience, the bishop of Oporto echoed the rhetoric of his northern European colleagues by calling for vengeance on the infidels oppressing Christians and occupying their land: 'shall it be permitted to the adversaries of the cross to insult you with impunity? . . . the praiseworthy thing is not to have been to Jerusalem, but to have lived a good life while on the way', a criterion fulfilled by expelling the Muslims from Lisbon.[12] However, this 'just war' did not replace the vows of the Holy Sepulchre. Jerusalem remained the ultimate objective; seizing Lisbon merely a righteous act of meritorious obedience to the will of God fully in keeping, declared one of the army chaplains, with the crusaders' 'new baptism of repentance'.[13]

Thus militarily and ideologically the Lisbon campaign sat easily within established conventions, expectations and experience of fighting infidels to which the preaching and recruitment of 1146–7 had lent special urgency. A contemporary vernacular song explicitly linked the Saracens in the east with the Almoravids in Spain.[14] Even so, anxiety over the propriety of expending time, effort and lives surfaced. During violent storms in the Bay of Biscay, there was terrified talk among the seasick of their being punished for the *conversio*, the change or alteration, of their pilgrimage, perhaps referring to an already agreed plan to join the Portuguese *reconquista*. The elaborate and comprehensive arguments deployed at length by the bishop of Oporto implied resistance to the idea of diverting the expedition, while, at Lisbon itself, elements in the fleet still argued for an immediate continuation of the journey to Jerusalem, even if for reasons more of material self-interest than single-minded piety.[15] In the event, the success at Lisbon justified the endeavour in the eyes of participants, even if the achievement received remarkably scant attention from observers elsewhere in western Europe.

The lack of unitary leadership exacerbated the tensions between the different regional groups and within each contingent, the statutes agreed at Dartmouth providing a forum for dissent as well as a structure for unity. Yet sufficient discipline was retained and agreement hammered out between the various groups to ensure enough cohesion to pursue a strenuous and precarious siege. Although leaving Dartmouth together on 23 May, the fleet was soon separated, straggling into the mouth of the Duero and the city of Oporto between 16 and 26 June, the Anglo-Normans and Rhinelanders having visited Compostela on the way; the count of Aerschot arrived last. At Oporto, Afonso's plan to hire the crusaders for an assault on Lisbon was presented to the Anglo-Normans and Rhinelanders by Bishop Peter but only after the full fleet reached the Tagus on 28 June did detailed negotiations on terms for military assistance begin. While the Flemish immediately signed up, some of the Anglo-Normans, led by William and Ralph Veil from Southampton, argued that greater profits could be gained in sailing directly to the Holy Land by preying on shipping in the Mediterranean. The dissidents from Southampton, Bristol and Hastings were abetted by veterans who remembered being left in the lurch by Afonso during the 1142 attack. Although the debate revolved around payment and booty it also raised serious questions about the unity of the whole expedition. Soon after the crusaders had established a bridgehead on the beach to the west of the city, those from Flanders, Boulogne and the Rhineland, presumably having accepted Afonso's offers, moved to positions on the east of the city, where they remained a semi-detached force for the rest of the siege. The Anglo-Normans were left to thrash out their differences in a full, ill-tempered council where accusations of bad faith were hurled at the small but experienced minority – comprising eight ships, perhaps as little as 5 per cent of the fleet – who held out against serving Afonso. Apparently, only a passionate but diplomatic appeal to honour, unity and faithfulness to the Dartmouth-sworn contracts by the East Anglian commander Hervey of Glanvill persuaded the Veil faction to cooperate, and even then only after assuring them of adequate provisions and pay. The religious gloss put on events by Hervey of Glanvill's chaplain Raol, who wrote the most detailed surviving account of the expedition, cannot disguise the national and regional tensions or the anxieties over supplies, profits and possibly the justice of the whole operation.[16] That the main opposition to joining an attack on Lisbon came from hardened seamen with experience of Iberian warfare, portrayed as piratical and mercenary gold-diggers, indicated military and political risks in the enterprise that the more optimistic or more naive elements discounted.

Afonso's determination bordering on desperation to reach agreement with the crusaders was reflected in generous terms. The Portuguese ruler needed victory at Lisbon to exploit the temporary disunity among the Moorish princes of southern Iberia in the wake of the collapse of the previously dominant Almoravid power in north Africa. Securing the Tagus frontier, Afonso would reinforce his credentials as a Christian warrior worthy of papal recognition as king and further assert his independence from his nominal overlord, Alfonso VII of León-Castile. Afonso offered the 'Franks', as the treaty had it, the entire booty from the captured city and the ransoms of all the inhabitants they rounded up. Once it had been thoroughly ransacked, Afonso would then allocate property in the city and surrounding countryside to the Franks, who would also enjoy exemption from certain commercial tolls. To encourage trust, Afonso promised not to desert the siege or try to twist the treaty provisions. Additionally, guarantees for supplies and pay were presumably settled with the dissident Anglo-Normans. The whole deal was confirmed by oaths and the exchange of hostages. Thus Afonso partly hired and partly allied with the Christian fleet.[17]

The new allies invested Lisbon on all sides. Ships lay in the river to the south of the city; Afonso and the Portuguese occupied high ground to the north with the Anglo-Normans on the west and the Flemish and Germans on a hill to the east. After a fruitless formal parley with the enemy further to reinforce the legitimacy of the attack, on 1 July, following a confused melee in the steep, narrow streets of the western suburb, the besiegers managed to drive the defenders back behind the walls of the main city, in the process uncovering a vast cache of food supplies concealed in cellars. There followed a bitter attritional conflict. The small Muslim garrison, with large numbers of civilians, including refugees from Santarem, faced a grim prospect. Denied the supplies hoarded in the western suburbs, with little prospect of relief, they were reduced to reliance on the strength of the city walls, the difficulty of the hilly terrain for siege engines, crude psychological warfare in the form of abuse aimed at insulting their attackers' religion and the fidelity of their wives, and frequent costly sorties as much to undermine Christian morale as in the realistic hope of militarily forcing a withdrawal. Once attempts to persuade the governor of Evora to send help failed, the main Muslim strategy appeared to be to wait for something to turn up, most likely the disintegration of Christian harmony and the raising of the siege as in 1142. These tactics showed prospects of success when, in early August, concerted assaults from east, west and the sea by large and elaborate siege engines, including rams, trebuchets, towers, one reputedly ninety-five feet high, and precarious 'flying bridges' mounted on pairs of ships, failed utterly, with most of the machines fired, stuck in the sand or damaged by Muslim artillery. Five times men from Cologne unsuccessfully tried to undermine the walls.

With casualties mounting, the besiegers faced a major crisis. The destruction of the siege engines left the attackers 'not a little demoralized' while with the failed mining operations, the East Anglian priest Raol remembered: 'our forces again had cause for deep discouragement and, murmuring much among themselves, they made such complaints as that they might have been better employed elsewhere.'[18] Now the dividends of the hard-fought battles of May and June to maintain unity and a chain of corporate command became apparent. Stories of the hunger, privations and desperation of the Muslims circulated. To quell talk of abandoning the siege, the leaders hauled some ships on to the beaches and 'lowered the masts and put cordage under the hatches, as a sign that they were spending the winter (*hyemandi signum*)'.[19] Successful foraging expeditions around Lisbon garnered rich pickings and heavy Muslim casualties as well as securing the besiegers from any threats to their supply lines. In the new mood of optimism, even the withdrawal of most of the Portuguese forces, leaving only Afonso and his military household with the bishop of Oporto, failed to cause a panic. As September arrived, instead of seeking an excuse to leave, the besiegers sensed their advantage as more and more of the besieged crossed the lines to surrender, bearing tales of the horrors within the city. According to a Rhineland witness most were so desperate that they accepted baptism; possibly these were in fact Mozarab Christians whom the northerners could not distinguish from Muslim locals; the cultural gulf remained unbridged: some of these unfortunate refugees 'were sent back . . . to the walls with their hands cut off, and they were stoned by their fellow citizens'.[20] Perhaps this incident merely underscores the sadism inspired by prolonged close-contact warfare; perhaps it dimly echoes the blurred rhetoric of conquest and forced conversion heard by the Germans from the lips of the abbot of Clairvaux.

The final stages of the siege revolved around perfecting the mechanics of undermining or overtopping the stubborn city walls conducted in more or less security, as the defenders' ability to launch sorties had subsided in the face of starvation and a massive sustained fusillade by the Anglo-Norman trebuchets firing at a rate of more than eight stones a minute. During September, while the Germano-Flemish dug a huge galleried mine under the eastern walls, the Anglo-Normans, directed by a Pisan engineer, constructed a new eighty-three-foot tower on the western beach. The final assaults, though protracted, appeared co-ordinated. The eastern mine was fired on the night of 16 October, causing a large section of the walls to collapse, although the pile of rubble in front of the breach prevented the attackers from forcing an immediate entry into the city. On 19 October, after the ritual dimension of warfare had been observed with the blessing both of the siege tower and the troops, the tower began to be manoeuvred into place before the south-western corner of the walls. So narrow was the level area of beach that the tower became surrounded by water, cutting it off from the main force. Throughout the night of 19 October and the whole of 20 October, the garrison of 100 Anglo-Norman and 100 Portuguese knights led support troops in a desperate defence of the tower, from fire, salvoes of missiles and sorties from the walls. Seven young men from Ipswich played a crucial part in dousing the flames that threatened to destroy the engine during the night of 19–20 October. Christian casualties mounted, the Pisan engineer was wounded by a stone and the Portuguese fled, the tower garrison only being relieved on the evening of 20 October.[21] Next day saw the final assaults from both east and west. Seeing they would be overwhelmed, rather than be massacred the Muslim defenders asked for surrender terms. Negotiations became protracted, inciting restless elements in the crusader army to mutiny against the leadership, whom they suspected of selling out their rights to plunder and booty; the Anglo-Norman camp was wrecked by a group of 400 sailors led by a priest from Bristol, and the Portuguese camp threatened by a Germano-Flemish mob. Unsurprisingly, the Muslims temporarily withdrew their peace overtures until order had been restored. The treaty finally agreed on 23/4 October allowed the governor alone to retain food and property, while on 24 October 140 Anglo-Normans and 160 Germano-Flemish were peacefully to occupy the citadel and organize the despoliation of the city and its citizens. In the event the Germans and the Flemish smuggled in 200 more and the orderly occupation soon turned into looting, rape and pillage. The governor was captured; the Mozarab bishop had his throat cut.[22] Having achieved immediate gratification, the Flemish and Germans then submitted with the other crusaders to the orderly ransacking of the city and expulsion of the citizens, which lasted five days (25–29 October). To the familiar accompaniment of rotting corpses, religious processions, racketeering and refugees, Lisbon returned to Christian rule.

Given the time of year, there was no prospect of an immediate resumption of the journey to Jerusalem. Afonso was eager to entice colonists and settlers, agreeing to the appointment of Gilbert of Hastings as the new bishop of Lisbon in a signal display of cultural imperialism.[23] With the Mozarab bishop conveniently murdered, there was no question of another local; equally Afonso may have hoped to encourage settlement and to display to the papacy his orthodox international ecclesiastical connections: Bishop Gilbert introduced the Salisbury breviary and missal into his cathedral and, a few years later, returned to England to recruit more soldiers and settlers. Others remaining included the priest Raol, to whom is attributed the most detailed account of the siege; he maintained his contacts with home, some years later sending a copy of his narrative to a Suffolk clerk, Osbert of Bawdsey. Such settlement witnessed the effective end to the unity so hard won and preserved since Dartmouth. While the thirst and competition for booty had both imperilled and inspired the assault on Lisbon, the lure of profitable and privileged colonization broke up the crusader army. In early February, part of the fleet embarked for the Mediterranean to fulfil their vows separately, *per varia discrimina*, as a Rhineland crusader put it. Before passing through the Straits of Gibraltar, one group, probably Flemish and German, attacked the port of Faro, without success, an attempt to extract protection money from the Muslims proving a messy failure. Once in the Mediterranean, some contingents sailed directly to the Holy Land.[24] Others, mainly Englishmen but also Flemings and Germans, who may have lingered at Lisbon until April, tried their luck with the papally blessed Christian campaigns in eastern Iberia, culminating in the Genoese-Catalan-led siege of Tortosa on the Ebro on the southern border of Catalonia (July to December 1148), after which a few continued to Palestine while their comrades, as at Lisbon, settled. One such, Osbert 'Anglicus', the Englishman, only honoured his Jerusalem vow after two decades waxing rich in the new Christian enclave.[25]

The success of the crusaders at Lisbon confirmed the fears of the doubters. It had brought out the best and worst in them, the heroism of the young men from Suffolk, the obsessive, violent greed for a valuable horse shown by Arnold of Aerschot in the division of the spoils. The numbers and strength of the fleet became dissipated through casualties, subsequent diversion and settlement in Portugal and Catalonia. The survivors who reached Outremer in time to join the abortive siege of Damascus in July 1148, probably mainly Flemish and Germans who would have found their overlords Count Thierry and King Conrad in Jerusalem, represented only a fraction of the 10,000 who had sailed from Dartmouth in May 1147. Many of the leaders survived, including Hervey of Glanvill and Christian of Gistel, although, judging by the tone and omissions of his priest Raol's account of events, the former may not have reached the Holy Land, while the latter almost certainly did. For the development of Portugal, the capture of Lisbon, with that of Santarem a few months earlier, marked a significant as well as symbolic advance. For the *reconquista* it provided new heroes and fresh opportunities. For the cause of the Holy Land, the fall of Lisbon proved at best an irrelevance, at worst a distraction. Most of the rest of Europe ignored it.

THE ROADS TO THE HOLY LAND: MAY 1147 TO APRIL 1148

On the same October day that the Christians began the orderly ransacking of Lisbon, 2,000 miles to the east one of the largest armies assembled by a medieval king met with disaster near Dorylaeum in north-west Anatolia, close to the scene of the First Crusade's victory of 1097. The subsequent retreat westwards towards Nicaea and the coast finished what the battle had begun; losses were horrific; the rearguard wiped out; the commander-in-chief suffering a severe arrow wound to the head. The defeat of Conrad III's magnificent army, with its echoes not of 1097 but of 1101, placed the whole enterprise in jeopardy, militarily and psychologically. Although within a few weeks, Conrad could describe the traumatic events in the Anatolian hills dispassionately, others saw in them the harsh judgement of God. Veterans later wept at the memory. Louis VII's army remained in the field, but an aura of besieged failure became established, matched by the mounting practical obstacles against which the French in their turn were broken.[26]

The scale of later recriminations reflected the size of the armies led eastwards. German, French and Greek observers testified to the magnitude of Conrad III's forces on its progress to Constantinople, too numerous for Byzantine officials to count.[27] Beside the ranks of fighting men, support troops, clerical and civilian camp followers marched substantial contingents of unarmed pilgrims taking advantage of the protection afforded by the military expedition, a group large and inconvenient enough for Conrad unsuccessfully to try to separate them from the fighting units on reaching the Turkish frontier. One veteran lamented that Pope Eugenius had not insisted on the weak staying at home and, instead of banning fancy clothes, falcons and hunting dogs, 'had equipped all the strong with the sword instead of the wallet and the bow instead of the staff; for the weak and helpless are always a burden to their comrades and a source of prey to their enemies'.[28] Fresh recruits joined the German host on its way from Regensburg, down the Danube to Vienna, Hungary and on to the Byzantine border at Branitz, which was reached around 20 July. The size of Conrad's army may be reflected in its modest rate of progress, especially once it left the Danube and turned south into Bulgaria. At less than ten miles a day, with no opposition, the Germans marched considerably more slowly than the First Crusaders, who had faced resistance.[29] The weight of numbers persuaded King Geza of Hungary, Conrad's enemy of only a year earlier, to pay protection money to ensure a peaceful passage. The hulks of the large German fleet abandoned at Branitz on the Bulgarian border provided locals with plentiful firewood and building materials. Forewarned but alarmed, the Greek emperor Manuel negotiated a German oath not to cause trouble within his territories; in return he promised access to supplies and markets. It says much for Manuel's power as well as Conrad's authority that the march from the Danube to the plains of Thrace passed without serious incident, helped by the fruitful season of the year. Once in Thrace, the opportunities for forage and plunder proved irresistible, as did the local wine, the combination provoking a serious affray at Phillipopolis and the loss of drunken stragglers lagging behind the main columns, their unburied rotting carcases posing a health problem for the French coming up behind. With German discipline fraying, Manuel failed to persuade Conrad to divert his march to Asia across the Hellespont rather than the Bosporus. After further violent incidents at Adrianople and a disastrous flash flood on 8 September that hit the German camp on the plain of Choereobacchi, engulfing men, horses and large quantities of equipment, Conrad's battered and bad-tempered army reached Constantinople on 10 September to find Manuel had placed his capital on full military alert.

Manuel had good reason to be nervous.[30] He had closely followed the preparations of 1146–7 and tracked the approaching armies with almost intolerably obsequious diplomats. Yet, despite his repeated offers of cooperation and aid, the emperor faced the most dangerous coincidence of circumstances imaginable. By the time the first western troops arrived at the walls of Constantinople, relations with his erstwhile ally Conrad had deteriorated to the extent that it was believed the Germans were contemplating attacking the city. To meet the challenge from the west, Manuel had been forced to abandon his campaign against the Seljuk sultan of Rum and agree a treaty, news of which, when picked up by the crusaders, aroused suspicion, incredulity and anger. The amount of effective assistance Manuel could provide, especially on and beyond the frontier regions of western Asia Minor, would always fall short of the westerners' expectations raised by Manuel's own promises, the awesome scale of his capital, the expensive dress of imperial servants and the deliberately intimidating but gorgeous court ritual and entertainment. If relations with Conrad had turned sour, those with Louis of France promised to be no less bitter. Byzantine attempts to subjugate Cilicia and Antioch had aroused hostility from churchmen, who complained at Greeks ousting Latin clergy, and from lay nobles with close relatives in the principality: Prince Raymond of Antioch was the uncle of Louis's queen, Eleanor of Aquitaine, and many Franks throughout Outremer still regarded the king of France in some ancestral sense as an overlord. He, in turn, felt a degree of permanent responsibility for them, all of which potentially clashed with Byzantine aspirations in Syria. More ominous still for Manuel, one faction close to King Louis hankered after an alliance with Roger of Sicily, who, at the very time the crusaders were approaching Constantinople, attacked Byzantine Greece: Corfu and Cephalonia were captured; Corinth, Thebes and Euboea plundered. Manuel could have been excused for worrying lest behind these western incursions lay a plot to seize the empire by a new Franco-German-Sicilian coalition.

In the event, by a mixture of aggression, bribery and promises of help, Manuel, whose wife, Bertha of Sulzbach, was Conrad's sister-in-law, defused any immediate threat from the Germans. Despite sporadic violent clashes and a series of rather tetchy diplomatic exchanges, after almost a month camped outside the walls of Constantinople, the German army crossed the Bosporus on ships supplied by Manuel. Although rejecting a formal alliance with the Greeks, Conrad accepted guides and food before setting out to follow the route of the army of 1097, refusing to wait for the French in his eagerness to press on to Syria. On 15 October, at Nicaea, possibly to quell a threatened mutiny by those outside the nobles' retinues, his army divided, one part under his half-brother, Otto of Freising, choosing the coastal road southwards through Byzantine-held territory, the bulk of the force embarking south-east on the road towards Dorylaeum and Iconium. For ten days, the main German army advanced so slowly that food ran short, the columns becoming easy targets for Turkish skirmishers. The westerners failed entirely to adapt to Turkish tactics, despite the presence of Greek guides. On 25 October, near Dorylaeum, the German heavy cavalry fell into the classic Turkish trap, drawn away from the main body of the army by a traditional Turkish feint, leaving the infantry unprotected and open to heavy casualties while being mauled themselves. This severe setback persuaded the German high command to withdraw to Nicaea to regroup. As their food supplies were already exhausted, the retreat was slowed and the line broken by the need for forage to sustain men and horses. With increasing intensity, the Turks picked off stragglers and bombarded the main column with a constant barrage of arrows, the Germans' retreat becoming a rout once the rearguard under Bernard of Ploetzkau was cut off and overwhelmed. The enthusiastic but inept westerners waged an unequal struggle against agile Turkish mounted archers: 'these active youths . . . midway in their course, encountered winged death instead of the enemy against whom they were running swiftly and boldly with oft-drawn swords and using sheep-skins as shields'.[31] Without archers and increasingly without horses, German resistance let alone counter-attack became impossible beneath the hail of arrows: Conrad himself was hit by two, seriously wounding him in the head. A starving and broken remnant of the once magnificent army struggled back to Nicaea by the beginning of November, where many abandoned the expedition entirely, seeking Byzantine help for quick passage home. Others survived the Turkish arrows only to succumb to starvation.

The army was wrecked. Whatever the casualties, its spirit had been broken as surely as its military capability. Bankrupt, hungry, scarred physically and psychologically, the rump of the German army could do nothing except throw themselves on the mercy of the French, now encamped around Nicaea, who greeted news of the German disaster with astonishment; rumour had told them of the fall of Iconium and the opening of the road to Jerusalem. Scapegoats were identified as the Greek guides, accused of misleading the army, and the Byzantine officials for providing inadequate supplies, although Conrad placed responsibility on himself, his companions and the Turks.[32] In truth, the German crusade foundered on poor intelligence, fallible logistics, inappropriate tactics and over-optimistic strategy as much as by lack of Greek support or the skill of Turkish archers. From the rebellious, despised footsloggers and pilgrims to the mounted elite, for all their numbers and weaponry, the Germans proved in all respects except courage singularly ill-equipped for Anatolian warfare or the needs of a contested march.

Ironically, the French partially reversed the pattern of the German advance on Islam, a fractious march across Byzantium leading to a remarkably effective fighting march against fierce odds through Asia Minor before, in turn, lack of supplies and logistical support forced disintegration.[33] From the muster at Metz in June 1147, the French army, tens of thousands strong, crossed the Rhineland in late June or early July, meeting the Danube at Regensburg before following the Germans' route to Hungary, Bulgaria and on to Constantinople, reached by some units in late September and by the king in the first week in October. In the eyes of Louis's chaplain, Odo of Deuil, the provision of markets and access to supplies formed a constant anxiety and a prominent theme of his narrative. At Worms, trouble erupted because of the high prices charged by the locals, which hit both the poorer pilgrims and the army's merchants and moneychangers whose profit margins were threatened. At Regensburg Louis agreed with ambassadors from Manuel to swear not to attack any Byzantine cities or fortresses in return for guarantees of markets and reasonable exchange rates. In Hungary, King Geza provided open markets, ensuring a peaceful passage for the French despite their harbouring of Boris, a pretender to the Hungarian throne. Until the Byzantine frontier was reached at Branitz, the French march passed smoothly, helped by the new bridges constructed by the Germans. Immediately on entering Byzantine territory, problems of exchange rates and inadequate supplies provoked the French to forage for themselves 'praedis et rapinis', 'with plunder and pillage'.[34] Although the king's own retinue were kept well supplied by the Greek officials assigned to his entourage, other divisions of the army continued violent foraging, terrorizing local markets and brawling with German stragglers. As the march progressed, relations with the Greeks deteriorated. French foragers were cut down by Byzantine mercenaries; an advance guard was denied a market and attacked at Constantinople just as Louis's ambassadors were continuing their delicate negotiations with Manuel over the terms of further Greek assistance. The Anglo-Norman contingent of the bishop of Langres and William of Warenne suffered a severe mauling in Thrace. Elements in the French army increasingly regarded the Greeks as hostile, their religious observances heretical, their social conventions despicable. A siege mentality developed. One member of the king's closest circle recalled that, a day out of Constantinople, the disaffected, reinforced by news leaking out of Manuel's treaty with the Seljuks, proposed a radical new strategy: use the huge western army to occupy Thrace; enter into an immediate alliance with Roger of Sicily and, with his fleet, which was already in Greek waters, seize Constantinople.[35] Although possibly benefiting from hindsight, the story exposes mounting unease at the nature and value of Greek friendship.

As he had consistently since embarking from Metz, Louis rejected any diversion of effort, pressing on to reach Constantinople on 4 October. Any fears he may have held soon dissipated as Manuel, in stark contrast to his brusque treatment of Conrad, went out of his way to shower Louis with attention, granting him a specially favoured audience at which the king was permitted to be seated; personally conducting a guided tour of Constantinople's shrines for the famously pious monarch; and entertaining him to such a lavish public banquet that some of more boorish and hard-to-please French guests feared poison. Ignoring continued outbreaks of arson and drunken affray by French troops, Manuel provided ample markets and a good exchange rate, leaving the discipline of the unruly elements to Louis, who, typically, proved inadequate to the task. The emperor even organized a joint celebration of the Feast of Louis's patronal saint, St Denis (9 October), by Orthodox priests and Louis's own chaplains; even the hellenophobe St Denis monk, Odo of Deuil, remembered the occasion with pleasure, especially the singing of Greek eunuchs.[36] Manuel's tactics of smothering his guest with affection concealed genuine worry at French intentions, hardly assuaged by the approach of contingents from Savoy, the Auvergne and north Italy who had travelled via Brindisi in Apulia, part of Roger of Sicily's kingdom. The importance of his charm offensive immediately became clear as vocal elements in the French high command, led by the irascible Bishop Godfrey of Langres, urged an assault on the imperial capital, the capture of which would place the whole empire at the westerners' disposal. The bishop, angered at his treatment at the hands of Greek soldiers, justified his proposal by accusing the Byzantines of heresy and recalling the campaign against Antioch by Manuel's father, John II Comnenus, the replacement of the Latin patriarch by a Greek and the recent extraction of homage from Prince Raymond.[37] The emergence of Antioch as an issue exposes one strand of western policy largely suppressed in the recruitment drive of 1146–7 and by the strenuous diplomacy of the Greeks. Bishop Godfrey's complaints may well have reflected Bishop Hugh of Jubail's negotiations in the west in 1145 to which the bishop of Langres may have been a party: he certainly proclaimed the cause of Edessa at Bourges at Christmas 1145 possibly in response to Bishop Hugh's mission. King Louis appears to have consulted the pope on Antioch before departing for the east.[38] This new front of anti-Greek policy was potentially more damaging to Manuel's relations with the westerners, as it seemed more immediate to the French and less diplomatically awkward than an alliance with Sicily. However, just as in 1146, the question of Antioch subsided in the face of the claims of the Holy Sepulchre. Against Bishop Godfrey were argued the injunctions of the pope, which could not be reconciled with fighting Christians for ambition or money. Manuel, alert to the debates within the French camp, allegedly exerted pressure on the French to cross over the Bosporus by squeezing the flow of supplies, spreading false rumours that the Germans were winning great victories in Asia Minor and providing a hurriedly assembled fleet to transport the French to the Asiatic shore. The rank and file, as often on such expeditions, pushed for the simple strategy of progress towards the Holy Land; Louis agreed and on 16 or 17 October passed over to Asia, conveniently for Manuel a few days before the arrival of the armies that had come via Apulia.

Louis and his army loitered for some days in the region of Nicomedia, negotiating supplies and waiting for the counts of Savoy and Auvergne and the marquis of Montferrat. The embers of the debate over an attack on Constantinople briefly reignited as Manuel attempted to agree a treaty with Louis that would involve homage from the French, as in

1097, the return to the emperor of any captured cities and forts in exchange for supplies and a marriage alliance designed, in conjunction with the offer of a large financial subsidy, to secure the French king's support against Roger of Sicily.[39] The idea of an anti-Sicilian alliance may have been a Byzantine negotiating ploy; in view of the mood in the French camp it was certainly a bold if not cheeky proposal. After protracted and difficult talks, both sides gained their prime objectives. Manuel received the homage of the French barons and agreement over conquered land; Louis received provisions, the right to plunder where no supplies were available, Greek guides and promises of open markets on the road ahead. Manuel was not committed to provide an army; Louis escaped a binding alliance with Byzantium. Honour and politics were satisfied, even if the expedition itself scarcely benefited.

Almost immediately on leaving Nicomedia and Nicaea behind them on 26 October, ominously to some during a partial eclipse of the sun, the French learnt of the true fate of the Germans. From that moment, their march east never lost a sense of crisis, usually borne out by events. After consulting with Conrad, Louis agreed to wait for the Germans to regroup and join him at Lopadium, on the road south. Already markets had thinned and the army resorted to foraging, which soured relations with the Greek locals, who exacted reprisals on the exhausted and battle-shocked Germans struggling to catch up with the French. Too depleted to provide effective protection for the Christian column by themselves, the Germans were placed in the centre of the march, strengthened by the imperial contingents that had travelled separately through Italy, led by the bishop of Metz, who acted as Conrad's chief interpreter, the counts of Savoy and Bar and the marquis of Montferrat. Some French soldiers could not resist taunting their new comrades with cries of 'Pousse Allemand' (literally 'Push, German . . .'), which cannot have raised German morale.[40] Avoiding the long coastal road taken a month earlier by Otto of Freising, Louis headed towards Philadelphia on what he hoped were easier roads than the more direct route across Anatolia attempted by Conrad. However, reaching Esseron on 11 November, the kings decided to change course, fearful of the winter dearth of supplies in hostile, Turkish-held central Anatolia. The coastal road at least ran within Byzantine territory and offered the prospect of supply by the sea. In reaching the port of Edremit, about fifty miles away, the French army showed a worrying tendency to break up, different units losing touch with each other, a characteristic later to prove near fatal. Rain, rivers in flood, steep passes, short and expensive supplies and curmudgeonly locals conspired to sap morale further. There were reports of soldiers deserting to take service with the Greeks and of others abandoning the march to find ships to lift them off an increasingly desperate shore. It took the westerners a month to arrive at Ephesus, where they hoped to spend Christmas, a distance of about 120 miles as the crow flies.[41]

At Ephesus, the army encountered Greek messengers warning of Turkish forces massing to attack the Christians if they advanced further and advising Louis to seek shelter in Byzantine fortresses for the winter. While well meant and accurate, such intelligence hardly compensated for what later struck some crusade veterans as Manuel's highly cynical policy. He had failed to provide an adequate flow of provisions or a large enough shadowing fleet to succour or transport the western host. Even if impotent to keep Turkish incursions down the valleys of western Asia Minor from attacking the French, Manuel failed to encourage local Greek officials or citizens to show hospitality, welcome or open markets. With the German army destroyed, Manuel's policy appeared less nervous and thus less supportive, his alliance with Louis now redundant. While not wishing the crusaders ill, Manuel no longer needed to appease or promote their interests, especially if they endangered his own in Anatolia or northern Syria. While the subsequent accusations of Greek perfidy, levelled notably by Louis's chaplain Odo of Deuil, appear exaggerated and hysterical, especially as criticisms by Louis himself were muted, the king later recalling fondly his relations with Manuel, rumours of Byzantine obstruction persisted even in Greek circles.[42] At most, Manuel helped only when and how it suited him; at worst he ensured, if only passively, that the odds were stacked against the westerners disrupting his political and diplomatic arrangements. Circumstances were unpropitious; Manuel did little to ameliorate them. Unlike Alexius I in 1096, he had not called for mass expeditions from the west; he was unsure of their motives, uncertain how best to capitalize on their frankly disruptive presence and unprepared to join a united offensive against Islam. Combating the Sicilian threat in Greece loomed far larger than putative gains in the Euphrates valley. So, when Conrad fell ill at Ephesus, Manuel saw the chance to reverse his diplomacy, abandon the French to their fate, good or ill, and reconstitute the Byzantine–German alliance against Roger of Sicily. Whisking Conrad off to Constantinople by sea, Manuel personally tended to the invalid amidst generous hospitality that the German king must have contrasted with the dry, forbidding welcome he had received at Constantinople only three months before.[43] Then, he commanded one of the largest fighting forces ever sent from western Europe; now, he returned a sick old man, nursing wounds to body, spirit and reputation, only too grateful for any comfort offered.

After Conrad's departure, Louis pressed on. Turning inland from Ephesus, eastwards up the Maeander valley, the French faced a long, difficult march of more than 200 miles over difficult terrain to reach Adalia, a major port on the south coast of Asia Minor within striking distance, it must have seemed, overland to Christian Cilicia or by sea to Syria. Without a supporting fleet, the direct march across country via Laodicaea appeared sensible. It turned out to be harrowing, yet the French coped effectively with sustained Turkish attacks, more so than the German force of Otto of Freising, who, only a few days ahead of Louis's army, had suffered severe casualties beyond Laodicaea, their unburied corpses bearing witness to the French of their fate. The Turks were defeated outside Ephesus on Christmas Eve and again in a major engagement at a ford across the Maeander further upstream a week later. Given the vivid, at times lurid account of bloody close-contact battle left by the eyewitness Odo of Deuil, the French march from Ephesus to Adalia in December and January 1147/8 has been regarded as heroic, stubborn but disastrous. In fact, despite major losses suffered in the passage of the mountain range south-east of Laodicaea at Honaz Daghi (Mt Cadmus) on 8 January, due to the leader of the vanguard Geoffrey of Rancon losing touch with the rest of the column, the French forces, although depleted, remained intact after a protracted fighting march of the sort that wholly eluded the Germans. In this achievement, Louis shares credit. Although presenting no obvious skill in leadership except personal bravery and skill in arms, Louis sought ways to ensure discipline on the march, for its last stages handing responsibility to the Templars, and consistently took responsibility for ensuring as far as possible that the destitute, the poor and the 'paupers since yesterday' received enough sustenance to continue despite the general shortage of food.[44] At the fight at Honaz, Louis managed to shield his infantry and non-combatants by charging the enemy with only his immediate retinue of knights, most of whom were killed. The account of Louis's own escape reads like a scene from a pulp adventure story:

> During this engagement the king lost his small but renowned royal guard; keeping a stout heart, however, he nimbly and bravely scaled a rock by making use of some tree roots ... The enemy climbed after, in order to capture him, and the more distant rabble shot arrows at him. But ... his cuirass protected him from the arrows, and to keep from being captured he defended the crag with his bloody sword, cutting off the heads and hands of many opponents in the process. Since they did not recognize him and felt that he would be difficult to capture ... the enemy thereupon turned back to collect the spoils before night fell.[45]

In the emergency after the reverse at Honaz, Louis handed the organization of the march to the Templars under Everard of Barres, whose authority was secured by all in the army swearing oaths to form a temporary fraternity (*fraternitatem*), in which the king himself joined. Under tight order, the French fought on, repulsing at least four concerted Turkish attacks. Denied food, so they imagined, by an unholy alliance of local Greeks and Turks, the westerners survived the twelve-day march to Adalia on bread baked on their camp fires and horse meat, the last and most desperate resort of a medieval army.

The ragged army that stumbled into the plain around Adalia on 20 January 1148 had reached the end of its tether. Fatigue, the loss of horses and abandonment of equipment threatened its survival. At similar crises on the First Crusade, western and Byzantine fleets had come to the aid of the soldiers of Christ. Now the absence of such aid imperilled the entire enterprise; the great fleet of May 1147, now wintering in Lisbon, was sorely missed. Instead, reliance had to be placed on the resources of Adalia itself and any assistance procured from the Byzantine imperial authorities, who were well informed of the Frenchmen's progress and in regular contact with Emperor Manuel. Adalia sat precariously as a Greek enclave surrounded by a Turkish hinterland, neither economically nor strategically ideal as a base from which to relaunch the battered invasion force. While Louis's priorities were to re-equip his army, in particular with horses, and to organize supplies, Greek military support and, if necessary, transport, in all these respects local resources proved inadequate and expensive. After fierce debate within the army and tortuous negotiations with the city's governor and the emperor's representative, an Italian called Landulph, Louis secured the basic food needed for survival, at the cost of renewing the oath to Manuel, and the promise of ships to take his army to Antioch. Despite Louis dipping further into his deep coffers to subsidize the increasing numbers of destitute, including many impoverished knights deprived of mounts and cash, neither the available but expensive provisions nor the number of ships proved adequate. With the weather vile and the Turks continually harassing the Christian camp, morale justifiably sank. After more than a month of wrangling and indecision, in early March Louis bowed to pressure from his nobles and took ship with them and as many knights as room allowed for Syria, leaving behind the sick, the infantry, the rest of the knights and the non-combatants under the count of Flanders and the lord of Bourbon, with money to pay for a Greek escort on the long road to Tarsus in Cilicia. In the event, although the infirm and ill received treatment and care, the plan was wrecked by renewed Turkish attacks, the small number and poor quality of the available horses and Greek reluctance to embark on a hazardous land march that offered little prospect of profit and was certain to inflame their Muslim neighbours, with whom they shared local trade and markets. The appearance of more ships in the port persuaded Thierry of Flanders and Archibald of Bourbon to follow their king's example and sail directly to Syria. The abandoned infantry, trapped between an unfriendly Greek city facing famine and the Turks, took their chance in the field, only to suffer enormous casualties and the loss of thousands of men to Turkish service or slavery. Some of the survivors remained to take employment with the Greeks; others may have fought, bribed or wandered their way to Cilicia, but probably very few.

Although his chaplain later tried to exonerate Louis's actions at Adalia, others were undeceived. 'Here the king left the people on foot and with his nobles went on board ship,' remarked William of Tyre, a Jerusalem teenager at the time.[46] By doing so, Louis almost certainly saved his own skin and preserved a nucleus of a fighting force for the Holy Land. However, his escape lacked nobility, marking the final disintegration of a force he had struggled with great difficulty but considerable success to hold together in the face of terrible odds in war, disease and famine. Unlike the German armies of Conrad and Otto of Freising, the French had not been destroyed in the field, their ultimate failure to reach Syria intact the consequence of bad timing, poor strategy, flawed diplomacy, catastrophic logistics, their prospects undermined by lack of preparation and support in the face of a determined, canny and persistent opponent. Greek indifference, self-interest and occasional hostility further tipped the scales against the westerners. Numbers, faith, courage, even skill in arms could not compensate for such adverse circumstances without a measure of luck consistently absent. While not sealing the fate of the whole enterprise, the destruction of the Christian armies in Asia Minor rang through the Muslim world, one observer in Damascus recording that news of the disasters restored local confidence that the infidel invasion would fail.[47]

WAR, DISSENT AND DEFEAT IN SYRIA: MARCH 1148–APRIL 1149

King Louis landed at the port of St Symeon at the mouth of the Orontes on 19 March 1148 after a grim passage from Adalia of more than a fortnight. On landing he was enthusiastically welcomed by Prince Raymond of Antioch, who immediately began to try to involve the French in schemes to attack Aleppo and Shaizar.[48] Although now largely an army of officers without men, the French fighting potential had not been extinguished. Other contingents from the west reached the Holy Land during the following few weeks, landing mainly at Acre and Tyre, some, as with a party that came ashore at Sarfend near Sidon, only after being shipwrecked on the beaches. Otto of Freising and what remained of his German army arrived in time to spend Palm Sunday, 4 April, in Jerusalem. Later in Holy Week, King Conrad put in at Acre in Byzantine ships after spending the winter recuperating in Constantinople. From the coast he immediately journeyed up to Jerusalem, where he lodged with the Templars in their quarters in the former royal palace on the Temple Mount in and around the once and future al-Aqsa mosque; after touring the Holy Sites, Conrad marched north to Galilee before returning to Acre. The fleet from southern France led by Alfonso-Jordan count of Toulouse had reached Acre in mid-April. At about this time, too, the veterans of the siege of Lisbon finally achieved their destination.[49] Despite the distractions, defeats, desertions and high casualties, the western forces that gathered in Outremer in the spring of 1148 constituted easily the largest Christian army to arrive in Outremer since

1097–9. Not only were their leaderships largely intact, more remarkably, the bulk of the forces had arrived at the same time, roughly a year after the main armies embarked, a timetable strikingly similar to that repeated on the next great European invasion in 1190–91 and possibly deliberately planned. However reduced, the great enterprise had not yet descended into a total shambles.

For all the painful effort in reaching the Holy Land, once there, the westerners had no obvious plan of campaign. Writing home from Constantinople in late February, Conrad still looked forward to recapturing Edessa.[50] Yet after Nur al-Din had destroyed its fortifications and massacred its Christian inhabitants late in 1146, reconquest became impractical and futile. The realistic choices lay between a northern foray to reinforce the Euphrates frontier and attack Aleppo; an assault, as in 1129, against Damascus, until recently a close ally of Jerusalem but since 1146/7 uneasily allied to Nur al-Din, its lands already a target for the Jerusalemites in 1147; and, finally, an attack on Ascalon, the last port on the coast of Syria and Palestine still in Muslim hands, a base for piracy and Egyptian raids that, since the 1130s, had been circled by fortified Christian settlements designed by King Fulk to neutralize its threat. Each posed military challenges and political complications.

With Edessa no longer apparently an option, the northern strategy appeared less attractive to the westerners. Most of them had sailed to ports in the kingdom of Jerusalem to the south of the frontier with Nur al-Din of Aleppo, the main opponent in any northern campaign. For all of them, fulfilling their vows at the Holy Sepulchre appeared of paramount importance, the first objective of the recently arrived crusaders: Otto of Freising, King Conrad, the Lisbon veterans. Even Alfonso-Jordan of Toulouse, in spite of his close and potentially disruptive interests in Tripoli, after landing at Acre immediately marched south towards Jerusalem, dying suddenly at Caesarea amid rumours of poison implicating his cousin Count Raymond II of Tripoli. Of all the possible schemes, William of Tyre acutely noted, 'the hopes of the king and people of Jerusalem seemed most likely to be realised' because of the devotion to the Holy Places and the presence of Conrad.[51] Despite his landfall at Antioch, even Louis of France appeared more determined to visit Jerusalem than contemplate military action in northern Syria, rendering redundant an embassy led by Patriarch Fulk of Jerusalem to persuade him south. Some assumed piety drew him to the Holy

Sepulchre; others noted that he had fallen out badly with the prince of Antioch; later gossip ascribed this *démarche* to one of the greatest sex scandals of the age, an alleged affair between Louis's wife, Eleanor of Aquitaine, and her uncle, Raymond of Antioch. The evidence for this is suggestive but inconclusive and coloured by the hindsight of the royal couple's divorce in 1152.[52] Whether guilty of impropriety or not, Eleanor seems to have tried to persuade Louis to adopt Raymond's plan for a joint attack on Aleppo, and her husband equally clearly rejected the policy. Despite later lurid speculation and insinuation, Louis's reasons may have been based on strategic assessment not sexual jealousy. His army was ill equipped for siege warfare, lacking the footsloggers so vital, as Lisbon confirmed, in sapping, building and protecting siege engines, or providing cover for the knights. While relations between Antioch and Byzantium had soured Louis's diplomacy with Manuel, any gains effected with Prince Raymond would almost certainly be claimed by the Greeks and would raise the awkward question of the French oaths of October 1147 and January/February 1148. Louis may also have realized that, with the other contingents not interested in a northern campaign, Christian success, dependent on numbers, dictated uniting the western armies. From Louis's decision to march away from Antioch flowed the ultimately failed policy of the crusade; more widely the westerners' failure to confront directly the growing power of Nur al-Din led indirectly to the death of Prince Raymond at the battle of Inab in 1149, the capture of Joscelin II of Edessa and the subsequent evacuation of the remains of the county of Edessa in 1150.

With the northern campaign excluded, attention settled on the two southern options, especially as the suspicious death of the count of Toulouse and the continued presence of his disgruntled bastard son, Bertrand, excluded any interest Raymond of Tripoli may have harboured for western assistance on his frontiers, for example an attack on Homs, later taken by Nur al-Din in 1149. By the time Louis had completed his pilgrimage to Jerusalem in June, Conrad had already agreed with the teenaged Baldwin III, Patriarch Fulk and his recent hosts, the Templars, to take Damascus. Even before he left Constantinople, Conrad had announced his intention to raise a new army once he reached Outremer; now he did so, perhaps with Greek money, dipping into the pool of potential recruits arrived from the west, almost certainly including the Lisbon veterans, many of whom came from imperial lands in eastern

Flanders and the Rhineland.[53] On campaign, this new army was to fight efficiently together under Conrad, suggesting its construction had not been entirely random. Its presence certainly lent strength to Conrad's negotiating position.

A council of western leaders and the local baronage was convened at Acre around 24 June, perhaps after a preliminary meeting of Louis and Conrad between Acre and Tyre.[54] After what were remembered as heated arguments, the decision was reached to attack Damascus. The political context for this decision influenced the military rationale. The crusaders had stumbled on a major local constitutional clash, soon to bubble into civil war, between young Baldwin III and his mother, Queen Melisende, who, since her husband's death in 1143, had, as a crowned queen regnant, exercised power on her own behalf, increasingly jealous of her son's attempts to establish his authority. For Baldwin, a military adventure would emphasize his role as a field commander, a position denied his mother. When considering the target to attack, Baldwin and his supporters may have preferred Damascus to Ascalon, as the fall of the latter could have benefited the king's younger brother, Amalric, later count of Jaffa, a close ally of his mother, by providing an obvious fief for him to be given. More generally, despite later recriminations and modern surprise, the choice of Damascus suited the moment. The Franks had attacked it in 1126 and 1129; the treaty of the 1140s had recently collapsed; the capture of the city would not only secure fertile land and a major trading centre, the chief Syrian entrepôt in the commerce that fuelled the ports of Acre and Tyre, but would provide the Christians with the natural frontier of the desert and tilt the balance of power in Syria heavily in their favour and against Nur al-Din of Aleppo, forcing other Muslim rulers in the region to adopt at the least a more accommodating attitude. For a generation, rulers of Jerusalem had tried to control Damascus alternately by alliance or conquest. With Nur al-Din inheriting his father's ambitions to annexe the city, the attempt in 1148 conformed to traditional Jerusalem policy of asserting its interests. It also did not preclude a subsequent attack on Ascalon.

The tactics of the Christian army indicated a calculation that Damascus would either quickly surrender or succumb without much resistance. Mustering at Tiberias in mid-July, the invasion force reached Damascus in a few days, arriving on 24 July. The speed of march suggests that, although accompanied by a large baggage train and herds of livestock, the Christians had not prepared siege engines, relying on local timber from the orchards surrounding the city to fortify the camp they established to the west of the city after brushing aside the Damascene army. They also appeared to have carried limited rations with them, as food became short after only a few days of the siege. The plan appeared to be to terrify the defenders into submission or to take Damascus by rapid assault rather than to mount a prolonged investment, which, despite the numbers in the besieging forces, put by one eyewitness at 50,000, would be almost impossible given the size of the city.[55] In the event, after only two days' hard skirmishing, with no surrender imminent, the Christians moved to the less well-defended eastern suburbs on 27 July, ostensibly in search of a less well-fortified area to attack. Here, the tactics are hard to fathom. With the new position lacking cover or water, the Christians allowed themselves no time to prepare even the simplest siege engines or missile throwers, as any delay could now prove fatal. In the absence of an immediate assault, options disappeared. The defenders had reclaimed and fortified the orchards and previous camp on the west side of the city; the morale of the citizens had revived after the initial shock; and news came in of large Muslim relief armies led by Nur al-Din of Aleppo and his brother Sayf al-Din of Mosul closing on the city from the north. The retreat was sounded at dawn on 28 July, the march back to Palestine attended by constant Muslim harrying and heavy casualties.

The inevitable decision to withdraw derived from unavoidable immediate circumstance. Contemporaries and later writers, both Christian and Muslim, sought more human, accountable agencies than mischance to explain the greatest humiliation of Latin arms in the Near East, worse than any defeat in that the Christian army remained intact. Immediately there were accusations of betrayal. Conrad wrote darkly but vaguely to his regent, Wibald of Corvey, of treachery lying behind the advice to transfer the army from the west to east side of Damascus. A generation later, William of Tyre repeated the rumours that elements in the Jerusalem baronage had been bribed by the Damascenes to engineer a withdrawal. The historian Ibn al-Athir (1160–1233) reported that the governor of Damascus, Mu'in al-Din Unur, had written to Syrian Frankish leaders arguing that they were risking uniting their Muslim neighbours against them for no advantage, as the western leaders intended to keep the city for themselves, an idea echoed in William of Tyre's account of how at the beginning of the siege Thierry of Flanders extracted promises from Conrad, Louis and Baldwin, as well as some Jerusalem barons, that he would be granted Damascus when it fell. Three decades later, some veterans identified Raymond of Antioch as the culprit, driven by vengeful spite into persuading local barons to sabotage Louis of France's ambitions. There were rumours concerning the involvement of the military orders. Otto of Freising, a participant in the debate at Acre in June 1148, more generally attributed the Damascus debacle to royal pride, a moralistic view repeated across Christendom in the years ahead.[56]

Whatever the exact course of events, the charge of betrayal levelled at the local baronage became an accepted version of events, souring subsequent relations between Outremer and the west for the next thirty years, if William of Tyre, an expert witness, is to be believed. Quite why there should have been so sudden a change of heart on the part of the Jerusalemite leaders is less easy to imagine. Conrad's anger and bewilderment cannot have been unique among the westerners, who had relied on local intelligence and advice in terrain well known to many Jerusalemites. Perhaps the stories of bribery covered a semi-official payment of tribute by Unur to the Jerusalem leadership in return for their withdrawal. It is possible that in contacting the Franks, Unur offered the renewal of the lapsed treaty which actually occurred a year later in June 1149. Supporters of Melisende may have deliberately sabotaged the siege, although such callous indifference to casualties sacrificed on the altar of political feuding would have taken cynicism to new heights even for the fractious baronage of Jerusalem. Alternatively, the ambitions of the count of Flanders, married to Baldwin's much older half-sister, who accompanied him on the expedition, may have angered the Melisende faction, who apparently had hoped to secure Damascus for a partisan of theirs, Guy of Beirut; they may have feared that Baldwin wanted to use Damascus to build up his own party. The closest Muslim account, by Ibn al-Qalanisi, mentions no plot, instead emphasizing the murderously destructive nature of the Latin raid, the martyrdom of two holy men, and the heroic and vigorous defence put up by Unur. It is possible that the stiffening of resistance by religious leaders and *mujahidin* scotched any plans of appeasement within Damascus, forcing Unur to dash hopes of accommodation he may have built up with the Franks upon which the Christian strategy may have been based. However, Ibn al-Qalanisi attributed the Christian withdrawal to their fear of being trapped between the city and the advancing armies from Aleppo and Mosul. This practical analysis may be closest to the truth. Preservation of armed forces lay behind one prominent strand of strategic thinking in twelfth-century Jerusalem; faced with a choice between a brave but dangerous assault which, even if successful, ran the risk of encirclement by the relief armies, and an ordered withdrawal, retreat may have appeared the sensible path. Only it was not the path of heroes; the miracle of Antioch in 1098 was not to be repeated.

The failure before Damascus destroyed the Second Crusade. On returning to Palestine, plans were hatched to revive the scheme to attack Ascalon, a muster time and place fixed. When Conrad arrived, he waited for eight days; few joined him and he angrily abandoned the enterprise, accusing the locals of deceiving him once more, and made urgent preparations to depart to the west.[57] He embarked from Acre on 8 September bound for Byzantium and the renewal of his alliance with Manuel. Leader of the largest army to set out in 1147, Conrad had lost most and gained least. His nephew, Frederick of Swabia, returning with his reputation enhanced as Conrad's active and efficient lieutenant at every stage of the expedition, never lost his commitment to the Holy Land: forty-two years later, as Emperor Frederick Barbarossa, he set out once more to restore it to Christendom. For the rest, Conrad's brother Otto of Freising may have spoken for many when he argued, in pained explanation of God's purpose in their experiences, 'although it was not good for the enlargement of boundaries or for the advantage of bodies, yet it was good for the salvation of souls'.[58]

Louis remained in Outremer until after Easter (3 April) 1149, spending large sums of money he had to borrow to subsidize the defence of the kingdom of Jerusalem. The presence of the French king may have calmed frayed nerves, especially in the continuing feud between Melisende and Baldwin. Finally answering the appeals of Suger for him to return to his kingdom, Louis chartered some Sicilian ships for his journey west, during which one ship was impounded by the Greeks, still at war with Sicily, and even Queen Eleanor was briefly detained by the suspicious Byzantines.[59] Lacking tangible success, his achievements of leadership modest, even in the eyes of his chaplain, Louis returned to the west after an absence of two years with enhanced international status and closer personal links with many of the great princely houses of France, including Flanders and Champagne, his reputation for piety now boosted by stories of heroism and fortitude. Only the retrospective rumour derived from the gossip about the Antioch scandal tarnished the image. Although attempts in France to launch a new war of the cross in 1150, in part in response to the Antiochene defeat at Inab in June 1149, fizzled out in a tide of indifference and acknowledged impotence, Louis's affection for the cause of the Holy Land remained a feature of his public pronouncements and diplomacy; more than once he promised to return. Like many others, his visit to the Holy Land lingered in the mind as an inspiration and ideal, however disagreeable the physical reality had been. In later years, he regularly used to swear 'by the Bethlehem saints'.[60]

Elsewhere in Christendom, reactions coupled shock, sorrow and blame. While participants sought scapegoats in the Greeks or the Jerusalemites or even their own tactical naivety, observers, less charitably, condemned the whole enterprise and its leaders and participants for arrogance, lack of humility, immorality, rapacity and ultimate sterility within the traditional analysis of failure caused by sin. The promoters of the enterprise came in for heavy criticism, Eugenius III admitting that the expedition had inflicted 'the most severe injury of the Christian name that God's church has suffered in our time'. The English pope, Hadrian IV, writing to Louis VII a decade later, recalled the criticism of the papacy as the author of the crusade, although, with characteristic tactlessness, he suggested the king had undertaken the Jerusalem journey 'with little caution'.[61] Glowing with patriotic enthusiasm, Henry archdeacon of Huntingdon sought to gloss a moral point by contrasting the failure of the proud, wealthy kings with the success of humble 'ordinary rather then powerful men' on the Lisbon adventure: 'the greater part of them came from England'. Some in Germany saw behind the disasters the work of the Antichrist. A monk in Würzburg, witness to anti-Jewish atrocities in 1147, savaged both organizers and recruits: the preachers 'pseudo-prophets, sons of Belial and witnesses of Antichrist, who seduced the Christians with empty words', the crusaders mostly novelty-seeking tourists, money-grubbers, debtors, escaped convicts or refugees from harsh landlords.[62] Vincent of Prague was not alone in blaming the disaster on the presence of women; sex and holy war did not mix.[63] While Otto of Freising delicately suggested that he and the other crusaders, through pride and arrogance, had fallen short of the moral standards set by Bernard of Clairvaux, others were less charitable towards the abbot, who felt compelled to issue an extended apologia in his own and Eugenius's defence in a treatise called *De Consideratione* (completed between 1149 and 1152). Bernard remained publicly regretful but eager to make amends in a new effort, in 1150 quoting approvingly the tag: 'I go to Jerusalem to be crucified a second time.' In *De Consideratione* he admitted the sins of the crusaders and the mercilessness of Divine Judgement. Defending himself from charges of rashness, he claimed due papal authority but accepted that God's severity scandalized many. To reassure Eugenius, to whom the work was addressed, he cited the example of the Hebrews punished for their lack of faith to wander in the Wilderness, casting himself and the pope in the role of Moses, performing God's will, however painful. Thus, Bernard hoped, he and the pope could excuse themselves as agents of God's purpose, adding, in a flourish of self-righteous flagellation: 'I would rather that men murmur against us than against God. It would be well for me if He deigns to use me for his shield.'[64] Bernard's reputation survived, even if the repute of his expedition did not. King Amalric of Jerusalem used to tell of the night before a battle in Egypt in March 1167, when the long-dead abbot appeared in a dream to chide him for his sins (he was a notorious lecher), which shamed the piece of the True Cross he wore round his neck. Only when Amalric promised to repent did Bernard bless the cross; next day the relic saved the king's life.[65]

Yet King Amalric could also have talked of the falling-off of trust between east and west in consequence of the Second Crusade. In the words of William of Tyre, tutor to Amalric's son, 'fewer people, and those less fervent in spirit, undertook this pilgrimage thereafter . . . those who do come fear lest they be caught in the same toils and hence make as short a stay as possible'.[66] The searing disappointment and the rumours of treachery and misbehaviour led some to doubt the very concept of holy war and the justice of fighting and killing Muslims. Others merely mocked what appeared as wasteful, self-indulgent folly. The heady enthusiasm so powerfully and convincingly orchestrated by Bernard in 1146 and 1147 produced dust and ashes, as Otto of Freising had it, a time of weeping. For many thousands it had brought death, glorious, mundane, painful, wretched. 'So great was the disaster of the army and so inexpressible the misery that those who took part bemoan it with tears to this very day,' wrote one who knew some of the survivors.[67] All were united in acknowledgement of the personal human cost, thrown more sharply into relief by the lack of any wider material gain. Most people, complained Bernard of Clairvaux, 'judge causes from their results'.[68] Few voices were raised to contradict them; fewer still convinced.

The Third Crusade

11

'A Great Cause for Mourning':[1] The Revival of Crusading and the Third Crusade

The sour taste left by the failure of the Second Crusade undermined both the idea and practice of this method of Christian holy war, casting doubt on its motives and morality. Despite repeated and increasingly urgent appeals from Outremer, successive popes failed to inspire new general expeditions east despite employing the full armoury of religious rhetoric, spiritual inducements and diplomatic persuasion. Individual wealthy enthusiasts conducted armed pilgrimages east. Some possessed armed intent, such as the Holy Land addict Count Thierry of Flanders in 1157–8 and 1164–5 (on top of his visits in 1139 and 1148); others, such as Duke Henry the Lion of Saxony (1172), did not. Dynastic adventurers and opportunists could be lured east by the prospect of a lucrative or spectacular marriage, as in 1176, when William of Montferrat arrived to marry Sibyl, sister and heir to the leper King Baldwin IV. Yet after his death in 1177, even Sybil's attractions failed to entice a bridegroom from the west. When, in 1175, Philip of Alsace, count of Flanders, planned to follow the family tradition with a prolonged stay in the Holy Land, he felt the need to consult the redoubtable intellectual, poetess, musician, mystic and fashionable spiritual sage Abbess Hildegard of Bingen (1098–1179). Philip asked whether God, with whom his correspondent claimed to be in direct contact, would approve. For once His message lacked clarity. Hildegard's tepid endorsement only voiced approval of fighting the infidel in some imagined future, 'if the time shall come' when they threatened 'the fountain of faith'.[2] Such caution in crusading commitment touched Christendom's other frontiers. Between 1149 and 1192, there were only three papal grants of Jerusalem privileges to conflicts with infidels in Iberia, and just one in the Baltic, in 1171. The Second Crusade cast a deep shadow.

Even when events conspired to offer some prospect of success, responses were negligible. In 1176, the Greek emperor, Manuel I, hoping to bolster his position in Asia Minor and Cilicia as well as his alliances in western Europe, announced his intention of leading a joint Greek and Latin expedition to the Holy Land. Despite Pope Alexander III's vociferous urging, western support was dismal even before Manuel's advancing army was defeated by the Seljuk Turks of Iconium at the battle of Myriokephalon on 17 September 1176. When a Greek fleet of 150 ships arrived at Acre the following year, squabbling and suspicions within the Jerusalem government led to the cancellation of the proposed attack on Egypt, shenanigans that confirmed western scepticism about the plight of Outremer and the honesty of its rulers.

By 1184, the political fabric of Christian rule in Syria and Palestine had become badly frayed, worn down by increased Muslim pressure, government financial difficulties, prolonged and desperate dynastic instability in Jerusalem and tensions between its rulers and those of Tripoli and Antioch. Yet the embassy led to the west by Patriarch Heraclius of Jerusalem in 1184–5 attracted mistrust, ridicule, indifference, self-interest and caution, verging on the dismissive. The patriarch met Pope Lucius III, the German emperor, Frederick Barbarossa, and Philip II of France before begging Henry II of England to lead a new crusade; he was offered money and empty promises. Only a handful of recruits volunteered. King Henry was recorded as remarking that the patriarch sought his 'own advantage not ours'.[3] Another witness saw only the jangling jewellery, aromatic perfumes and lavish display of wealth as the patriarch's entourage passed through Paris, not the genuinely desperate plea for armed help.[4] On the eve of the greatest defeat of western arms by a non-Christian army since the tenth century, at Hattin in Galilee on 4 July 1187, crusading appeared to have run its course, a model of holy war that, in the shape taken since 1095, had served its turn and lost its fierce popular resonances. The events of that summer's day in the hills above Tiberias reignited them.

NUR AL-DIN, SALADIN AND THE MUSLIM REVIVAL

Writing in the early 1180s, the Jerusalem historian Archbishop William of Tyre, in a remarkable and justly famous passage, described how the strategic balance in the Near East had tilted decisively against the Franks. He attributed this deterioration to three developments: the sinfulness of contemporary Franks in contrast to their ancestors; the loss of the advantage that their religious zeal and military training gave the first crusaders over the then indolent and pacific locals; and the unification of Syria and Egypt:

In former times almost every city had its own ruler ... not dependent on one another ... who feared their own allies not less than the Christians [and] could not or would not readily unite to repulse the common danger or arm themselves for our destruction. But now ... all the kingdoms adjacent to us have been brought under the power of one man. Within quite recent times, Zengi ... first conquered many other kingdoms by force and then laid violent hands on Edessa ... Then his son, Nur al-Din, drove the king of Damascus from his own land, more through the treachery of the latter's subjects than by any real valour, seized that realm for himself, and added it to his paternal heritage. Still more recently, the same Nur al-Din, with the assiduous aid of Shirkuh, seized the ancient and wealthy kingdom of Egypt as his own ... Thus ... all the kingdoms round about us obey one ruler, they do the will of one man, and at this command alone, however reluctantly, they are ready, as a unit, to take up arms for our injury. Not one among them is free to indulge any inclination of his own or may with impunity disregard the commands of his overlord. This Saladin ... a man of humble antecedents and lowly station, now holds under his control all these kingdoms, for fortune has smiled too graciously upon him. From Egypt and the countries adjacent to it, he draws an inestimable supply of the purest gold ... Other provinces furnish him numberless companies of horsemen and fighters, men thirsty for gold, since it is an easy matter for those possessing a plenteous supply of this commodity to draw men to them.[5]

William's analysis found confirmation from Muslim witnesses and events.

*

The Christian failure before Damascus in 1148 did not immediately lead to the unification of Syria. Nur al-Din of Aleppo (1117–74) was perceived by some in Damascus as a greater threat to their independence than the Franks. Although providing troops for Nur al-Din's campaign, which culminated in the defeat and death of Prince Raymond of Antioch at Inab in June 1149, the Damascenes simultaneously agreed a new truce with Jerusalem which lasted almost until Nur al-Din's annexation of Damascus in 1154. A joint Damascus/Jerusalem army besieged Bosra in the Hauran region in 1151, and Damascus regularly paid tribute to its Frankish neighbour, while continuing to appease Nur al-Din by allying with him in northern Syria. Only with the Frankish capture of Ascalon in 1153 did the majority of Damascus's ruling elite decide that the Christians presented the greater threat. Even so, Nur al-Din's occupation of Damascus in April 1154 only came after an economic blockade followed by an armed assault.[6]

The peaceful terms granted the rulers of Damascus showed that Nur al-Din was more accommodating than his brutal father Zengi. The *jihad* was integrated into the substance of his policies as he regularly demanded support for annual renewals of what he announced as holy war. In 1149, he advertised the significance of his victory at Inab by bathing in the Mediterranean. Religious propagandists travelled in his armies. Palestinian émigré poets in his entourage called for the reconquest of their homeland 'until you see Jesus fleeing from Jerusalem'.[7] In practice, as his critics pointed out, Nur al-Din spent most of his career engaged in subjugating other Muslims to his rule, annexing Damascus in 1154, Mosul in 1170 and contesting control of Egypt after 1163, and was willing to agree treaties with the invading Byzantine emperor in 1159 and the Jerusalemites in 1161. However, his inheritance of Aleppo, confining him to Syria rather than his father's stamping ground of Iraq, imposed on Nur al-Din a more intense focus on his Frankish neighbours while at the same time depriving him of his father's resources to effect territorial gains at their expense, a gap covered by *jihad* rhetoric and displays of private austerity and extreme spirituality. Nur al-Din's image as the pious, just, puritanical *mujahid* was displayed on inscriptions and coins and in the patronage of religious learning, schools, scholars and mosques. He cultivated a reputation as a just ruler and judge, a knowledgeable jurist and theologian, educated, literate, orthodox, although, in the words of an Iraqi panegyrist, Ibn al-Athir, 'not a fanatic'.[8] Nur al-Din's piety apparently increased after serious illnesses, in 1157 and 1159, and a defeat by the Franks before Crac des Chevaliers in 1163, a pattern of penitential progress similar to that of another ruler who wore his faith on his sleeve a century later, Louis IX of France.

In 1161, Nur al-Din undertook the *hajj* and rebuilt the walls of Medina in the Hijaz, with Mecca the holiest cities in the Muslim world, gestures of obvious political as well as religious significance. Nominally, the Hijaz lay under the sovereignty of Egypt, although in practice ruled by local families claiming descent from the Prophet. Nur al-Din's appearance and patronage announced a new power in Islam. Convenience and devotion entwined very effectively. The inscriptions on Nur al-Din's elaborate *minbar* (or pulpit), built in Aleppo 1168–9, proclaimed his *jihad* credentials, not least in the declared intention to relocate it in the al-Aqsa mosque once the Holy City had been recaptured, a wish fulfilled by Saladin twenty years later. Such a pulpit, in which politicized polemic could be broadcast under the guise of the religious Friday sermon (the *Khutba*), represented a highly visible pledge of the unity between spiritual and political ambition, ideology and empire building. In consolidating an alliance with the newly strident and influential religious classes in law and administration, Nur al-Din hoped to reconcile political opponents to his dominance. He offered unity within Near Eastern Islam under the nominal authority of the Sunni caliph of Baghdad, whose express sanction for each conquest and annexation was deliberately sought. Not only in retrospect could Nur al-Din be seen as 'the fighter of *jihad*, the one who defends against the enemies of [Allah's] religion, the pillar of Islam and the Muslims, the dispenser of justice to those who are oppressed in the face of the oppressors'.[9] His now more famous successor, Saladin, learnt the lesson and was careful to follow it.

Yet mid-twelfth-century Outremer did not seem about to capsize. While Muslim military incursions could still threaten disaster, in the kingdom of Jerusalem at least only the immediate frontier areas were regarded as presenting much risk to settlers. Despite the recriminations following the Second Crusade and a sharp and potentially damaging conflict (1149–52) culminating in open civil war (1152) between the young King Baldwin III and his mother, Queen Melisende, the Franks managed to stabilize the position of Antioch in 1150 and resume offensive operations. Nur al-Din's attacks on Damascus were thwarted in the early

1150s. In moves to weaken Ascalon, the last remaining Palestinian port in Muslim hands, Gaza was rebuilt and given to the Templars in 1149–50. In January 1153, Baldwin III began to besiege Ascalon, which surrendered on 19 August, affording the king massive booty, a secure southern frontier and access to Egypt. By 1155, the alarmed but tottering Egyptian government began paying tribute to Jerusalem. By 1159, with Jerusalem's ally Manuel I, the dominant figure in the eastern Mediterranean, exerting his overlordship in Antioch, arranging a treaty with Nur al-Din and contemplating war with Fatimid Egypt, William of Tyre's analysis of a tightening noose would have appeared fantastic. However, the fate of Jerusalem was soon to be cast into hazard on the banks of the Nile.

The reorienting of Frankish defence strategy in the 1160s from northern Syria to Egypt marked an apparent reversal of tradition. From the reign of Baldwin I until the late 1150s, successive kings of Jerusalem had been drawn north to restore order and security in the wake of defeat, loss of leaders or internal political squabbling. The main military threats to Outremer's survival since the 1110s had come from Aleppo, Mosul and the forces of the Jazira (i.e. Upper Mesopotamia) and Iraq. Left to itself, Damascus tended towards alliance with Jerusalem, while Fatimid Egypt had long abandoned active reconquest of Palestine. Baldwin II had reinforced this northern policy by marrying two of his four daughters respectively to Bohemund II of Antioch (d. 1130) and Raymond II of Tripoli (d. 1152). However, ties between Antioch and Jerusalem became strained by the aggressive behaviour of the new prince of Antioch, the glamorous Frenchman Reynald of Châtillon, who married Constance of Antioch in 1153. After scandalizing opinion by extorting money from Patriarch Aimery of Antioch through public torture, in 1156 Reynald broke the alliance with Byzantium by raiding Cyprus.[10] Whether Reynald's capture by Nur al-Din in 1161 and detention in Aleppo until 1176 strengthened or weakened the Frankish cause is unclear; it certainly removed a source of friction. Immediately, his capture involved Baldwin III in another round of political horse-trading between supporters of Constance and her son by her first husband, Raymond of Poitiers, Bohemund III. However, the city's destiny was no longer his to decide since Manuel I's personal assertion of his lordship over Antioch in 1159.[11]

Already talking of an assault on Egypt, Baldwin eagerly embraced a

Byzantine alliance. In 1161 Manuel demonstrated his effective influence by installing Constance as ruler in Antioch after Reynald's capture, rather than her son Bohemund III. Some historians have argued that the Jerusalem kings' abandonment of northern Outremer represented a fatal error, allowing Nur al-Din's authority in the region to grow unchecked. Yet it is hard to see how Baldwin or his successor, Amalric, could have continued to act as arbiters of Antioch without conflict with Byzantium. At the height of Latin Jerusalem's power, Egypt must have seemed an almost irresistible source of ready wealth to compensate for declining revenues from the royal demesne. Nur al-Din's involvement in Egypt was reluctant and not bound to prevail. War at a distance from his Syrian bases was costly. Egyptian politicians were antipathetic to Syrian interference. Any invasion from Syria had to be launched across the desert no man's land between the Negev and northern Arabia, under the scrutiny of Frankish outposts and Bedouin spies. In such circumstances, Frankish engagement in the internal affairs of Egypt was neither capricious nor doomed; given the implosion of the Fatimid regime it was probably unavoidable.

If the reordering of alliances and policy by the Franks and their Muslim neighbours in the 1150s characterized the first phase of the process of encirclement described by William of Tyre, the second revolved around the battle for Egypt, which the Franks lost, providing Nur al-Din's erstwhile Kurdish mercenary commander Saladin with the power base from which to create a new Near Eastern empire. During the 1150s, order within the Fatimid caliphate collapsed, with power and the viziership contested by a succession of provincial governors. Taking advantage of this, Baldwin III, fresh from conquering Ascalon, extracted tribute from one of the warring factions and toyed with an invasion, plans for which he discussed with Manuel I in 1159. In 1163, Egypt descended into anarchy, three viziers succeeding each other in a matter of months, the third of whom, the former chamberlain Dirgham, refusing payment of the Frankish tribute while his ousted predecessor Shawar sought help from Nur al-Din. The new king of Jerusalem, the fleshy but energetic Amalric, intervened to exclude Nur al-Din, gain booty and consolidate his rule at home.

Amalric's first invasion, in September 1163, was only repulsed when the Egyptians breached the dykes in the Nile Delta near Bilbeis, about halfway upstream from the sea towards Cairo. The following year, Dirgham was killed and Shawar was restored by Nur al-Din's Kurdish mercenary general Asad al-Din Shirkuh, only for the restored vizier to switch sides and call for Frankish help. Nur al-Din's change of policy in 1164 from neutrality to reluctant engagement reflected a dependence on his Kurdish generals and their corps of mamluks, professional slave warriors whose loyalties rested with their commanders rather than to any nominal political overlord. Shirkuh regarded an Egyptian invasion as an opportunity to establish independent power of his own, the enterprise becoming a family business as he took with him his nephew as second-in-command, Yusuf Ibn Ayyub, better known as Salah al-Din or Saladin (1137–93). This ambition may have been detected by Shirkuh's protégé Shawar, prompting his invitation to the Franks. Certainly, during this first invasion, Shirkuh took careful stock of Egyptian resources and the potential for the establishment of an Ayyubid kingdom.

The Frankish campaign in Egypt of August to October 1164, largely taken up with a siege of Bilbeis, ended when both Amalric and Shirkuh agreed to evacuate the country. Amalric's apparent advantage in Egypt had been undermined by an attack on Antioch by Nur al-Din and his victory at Artah, about twenty miles east of the city, where Bohemund III of Antioch and Raymond III of Tripoli were both captured. However, Shirkuh, lacking reinforcements because of this war in northern Syria, could not maintain his position against a hostile local regime and its Frankish allies. Both protagonists left Egypt in 1164, their appetites for conquest far from satiated. By late 1166, Shirkuh's plans for conquering Egypt had attracted the support of the caliph in Baghdad and acquiescence of Nur al-Din. This new invasion had been anticipated by Shawar, who once more called in the aid of the Franks, the two armies arriving more or less simultaneously, in January 1167. The fighting penetrated deep into Egypt beyond the Delta and south of Cairo, where, at al-Babayn in Middle Egypt, Amalric suffered a severe defeat at the hands of Shirkuh's army in March. Despite this and the Franks' failure to dislodge Saladin from Alexandria, the subsequent stalemate led to another evacuation of Egypt by both Franks and Syrians in August, leaving Shawar in power with a Frankish representative resident with troops in Cairo and an increase in the Jerusalem tribute. The scope and intensity of the war of 1167 suggest that Amalric was determined at least to establish a protectorate over Egypt, if only to prevent it falling into the hands of Nur al-Din or Shirkuh, while the latter's intentions to annexe the country were now clear.

The crisis of the Egyptian wars came in the winter of 1168–9. Amalric attacked in October 1168, apparently intent on the conquest of Egypt, although he refused to wait for Byzantine naval assistance and lacked the support of the Templars. Amalric may have feared Shirkuh would conquer Egypt first. As it was, the Frankish advance forced the shifty but resilient Shawar into another precarious diplomatic somersault, accepting help from Shirkuh, whom he had double-crossed in 1164. After capturing and brutally sacking Bibleis, Amalric besieged Cairo. However, failing to provoke a decisive battle, the Franks were compelled to withdraw empty-handed in January 1169, leaving the field open for Shirkuh. On 18 January, Shawar, his nimble footwork at last failing, was assassinated by the Kurdish generals ostensibly on the orders of the teenaged Fatimid caliph al-Adid. Shirkuh succeeded to the viziership. However, on 22 March 1169, he succumbed to age, over three decades in the saddle, recent exertion and a longstanding heart condition exacerbated by over-indulgence, a taste for 'rich meats' and obesity (in contrast to his porcine rival, King Amalric, whose weight represented a cruel reward for moderation in food and drink).[12] Despite the reservations of more senior Turkish commanders in the army, Saladin replaced him.

Initially, Saladin's tenure appeared insecure, the fifth vizier in six years. His personal military entourage was outnumbered by the Turkish contingents from Syria, many of whom returned north with their disgruntled emirs after his accession. His remaining forces, a few thousand, were dwarfed by the Fatimid armies, especially by the 30,000 black infantry troops, the *Sudan*. His political position appeared hopelessly anomalous: an orthodox Sunni Kurd, nominally subject to a foreign overlord, sustained by a dwindling Turkish army from Syria, attempting to rule a large, unsubdued and populous country in the name of a Shi'ite caliph. Yet within a year he had destroyed the Black *Sudan* and repulsed a dangerous assault by land and sea by a combined Frankish-Greek amphibious force at Damietta. With the failure of this, Amalric's fifth invasion of Egypt in six years, and despite an attack on Alexandria by a Sicilian fleet in 1174 and the planned Byzantine naval assault of 1177, the Franks' gamble, legitimate in conception, skilfully funded by an unscrupulous monarch but bungled in execution and myopic in long-term strategic assessment, had failed, handing a major advantage to their enemies.

In 1170, Saladin went on to the offensive, capturing Gaza and Aila on the Red Sea from the Franks, harrying the remnants of the *Sudan* and extending his hold on Arabia and Yemen. Although further policing operations in Egypt and Yemen were necessary, Saladin's power was secured, not least by his careful creation of his own military corps, or *askar*, the Salahiyya, and grants of revenues (*iqta*) to his followers, especially his immediate family. His father, Naim al-Din Ayyub (d. 1173), received huge income from the Delta and its ports. In concert with Nur al-Din's policy of overt religious orthodoxy, in September 1171, on the death of the Fatimid caliph al-Adid, Saladin had the name of the Sunni Abbasid caliph of Baghdad al-Mustadi (1170–80) inserted into Friday prayers.[13] After 202 years, the Fatimid caliphate of Cairo was at an end, an achievement of religious unity for which Saladin, the reluctant executor of Nur al-Din's wishes, subsequently took credit. While the new sultan of Egypt consolidated control of the southern periphery of his empire, Nur al-Din began to prepare against this upstart. Twice, in 1171 and 1173, Saladin had withdrawn from joint expeditions against the Franks in Transjordan. Open war seemed imminent when, 'in the midst of preparations' to invade Egypt, Nur al-Din died suddenly of a heart attack in Damascus on 15 May 1174.[14] On 11 July King Amalric, after a prolonged fever, died in Jerusalem aged thirty-eight. By the end of October, Saladin had entered Damascus. The third, final stage of William of Tyre's encirclement was about to begin.

The career of al-Malik al-Nasir Salah al-Dunya wa'l-Din Abu'l Muzaffar Yusuf Ibn Ayyub Ibn Shadi al-Kurdi, known to westerners during his lifetime and ever since as Saladin, epitomized the fluidity and the opportunities of Near Eastern politics in the twelfth century.[15] Born the son of a displaced Kurdish mercenary in the service of Zengi of Mosul, he died the creator and ruler of an empire that embraced Iraq, Syria, Arabia and Egypt, the effective overlord of the Fertile Crescent, a successful dynast whose arriviste family became the political masters of the Near East for over half a century. His legend, carefully fashioned by members of his entourage after his death, received unlikely promotion by Christian authors in the west. Saladin's reputation as a noble adversary of honour, chivalry, clemency and justice, invented in the immediate aftermath of the Third Crusade (1188–92), became a staple image of crusading from the vernacular cycles of crusade epics and romances of the thirteenth century into the pulp history of the twenty-first. Such was the admiration he inspired in western commentators that they paid him the ultimate compliment of imagining he had received the belt of knighthood from a Frankish knight, identified by a writer during the Palestine war of 1191–2 as Humphrey II of Toron, constable of Jerusalem (d. 1179).[16] Such fictions of Saladin's chivalry were enshrined in verse and the visual arts across western Europe; in the early 1250s, for example, he appeared jousting with Richard I in wall paintings and tiles decorating new apartments of Richard's nephew, King Henry III of England.[17]

What struck western contemporaries most was Saladin's generosity, a quality admired equally by his contemporaries the German poet Walter von der Vogelweide (*c.*1170–1230) and the French, possibly Norman versifier of the story of the Third Crusade, Ambroise, who remarked within a few years of Saladin's death that 'in the world there was no court where he enjoyed not good report'.[18] Ironically, such admiration for the stereotype 'good pagan', as Saladin appears in Dante's *Inferno* beside Hector, Aeneas and Julius Caesar, was not universally shared by thirteenth-century Arabic writers. Saladin and his family had made too many enemies. The Iraqi Izz al-Din Ibn al-Athir's extensive history of the Muslim world, while recognizing Saladin's achievements, questioned the image and propaganda. The famous magnanimity at Jerusalem in 1187, when Saladin allowed the helpless Franks safe conduct out of the city, was tempered by Ibn al-Athir's claim that the sultan's initial instinct was to exact full revenge for the Franks' atrocities of 1099. According to Ibn al-Athir, Nur al-Din detected in Saladin a reluctance to fight the Franks 'as he should', his own emirs urging him to engage the Franks in battle at Hattin in 1187: 'because in the East people are cursing us, saying that we no longer fight the infidels but have begun to fight Muslims instead'.[19] Although his fame hardly dimmed in the west, bizarrely finding new life during and after the Enlightenment as a rational and civilized figure in juxtaposition to credulous barbaric crusaders, from the fourteenth to the late nineteenth century Saladin's repute in Islamic and Near Eastern memory paled beside that of Nur al-Din and the great Mamluk sultan of Egypt Baibars (1260–77).

The reflections of Saladin's emirs in Ibn al-Athir's account of the Hattin campaign go to the heart of Saladin's politics and reputation. Between 1174 and 1186, Saladin completed the encirclement of Outremer observed by William of Tyre, who probably died in 1186.

Through a mixture of force and diplomacy, Saladin gradually asserted his control over Syria and the Jazira, beginning with Damascus in 1174. He was not greeted with unalloyed enthusiasm. His control over most of Syria was hard won between 1174 and 1176. Aleppo was annexed only in 1183 and Mosul in 1186. Attacks on the Franks were sporadic and rare; success modest. Defeated in a skirmish in southern Palestine in 1177 (known to the Franks as the battle of Montgisard) and at Forbelet in Galilee in 1182, he captured Jacob's Ford in northern Galilee in 1179 and the waterless island of Ruad in 1180. In 1182 Beirut withstood a sea-borne attack, and a large prospective invasion following the taking of Aleppo in 1183 stalled when the Jerusalem army refused battle. In practical terms, war with the Franks appeared secondary to securing Nur al-Din's inheritance. For most of the period 1174–87 truces prevailed, the final assault on Outremer only coming when other opportunities for expansion had been exhausted. Saladin's power depended on his ability to reward followers and allies with revenues and lucrative offices. Any slackening of this rich stream of patronage threatened his authority over his mamluks, his own family members placed in command of his conquests and those non-Ayyubids, including some reconciled Zengid princes, who expected reward for subservience. Consequently, territorial expansion provided both the object and the sustenance for Saladin's policies.

Nur al-Din's legacy also included championing orthodox religion and the *jihad*. Saladin cultivated these with determination, whether, as his panegyrists insisted, out of private conviction, or from public convenience, or both, is not now possible to judge. As a parvenu Kurd, seeking to rule a largely Turkish aristocratic military elite that had once been his employer, Saladin needed the legitimacy the *jihad* could bestow. Already before Nur al-Din's death, he could boast the deposition of the heretic Fatimids and at every stage of his career he presented himself in the image of a Koranic leader. Prepared to crucify Islamic heretics, Saladin's public orthodoxy attracted the hostile attentions of the Assassins, the suicide killers of their day, until, after surviving two attempts on his life, Saladin arrived at a peaceful accommodation with their leader in the Lebanon, Rashid al-Din Sinan (1169–93), the Franks' 'Old Man of the Mountains'.[20] Public displays of religious devotion and personal piety featured prominently in Saladin's style as ruler, conveying important political messages. The ritual cleansing of the Dome of the

Rock and its surroundings performed in person with other members of his family during the physical de-Christianizing of Jerusalem in 1187 demonstrated the status of the Ayyubids as the new protectors as well as rulers of Islam.[21]

Such propagandist posing occupied a central place in the biographical eulogies by Saladin's secretary Imad al-Din al-Isfahani and his friend and official Baha' al-Din Ibn Shaddad. It also played a pivotal role in his actual political behaviour. To emphasize his loyalty to the *jihad*, he placed Nur al-Din's *minbar* from Aleppo in the al-Aqsa mosque as his predecessor had intended. Also following Nur al-Din's example, he paid especial attention to relations with the caliphs of Baghdad, whose formal recognition could lend a veneer of respectability to his conquests. In 1175 he won investiture by Caliph al-Mustadi of Egypt, Yemen, future conquests and Syria except for Aleppo, although opposition from the last great Abbasid caliph, al-Nasir (1180–1225), thwarted his designs on Mosul in 1182. Saladin peppered the court in Baghdad with flattering correspondence implying he acted as the caliph's servant, not least the newsletter he despatched to al-Nasir a few days after the victory over the Franks at Hattin in July 1187, which dripped formal obeisance to the caliph's superior authority.[22] Religious duty refined political imperative. Ibn Shaddad recorded a conversation with Saladin on the coast road between Ascalon and Acre one stormy day in 1189 during which the sultan declared his eagerness, once all the Franks had finally been expelled from Outremer, 'to set sail to their islands to pursue them there until there no longer remain on the face of the earth any who deny God'.[23] Wrapped in this rhetorical hyperbole lay the imperative of his system of patronage, loyalty and discipline; each conquest had to be followed by another.

The problem for the sultan's apologists was that before 1187 Saladin's military energies were primarily directed against fellow Muslims. For all his glamour as a conqueror of Egypt, Syria and Palestine, Saladin proved a cautious, at times nervous, field commander, better at political intrigue, diplomacy and military administration than the tactics of battle or the strategy of campaign. His successes at Damascus (1154), Aleppo (1183) and Mosul (1186) came through the application of political coercion and diplomacy, not brutal assault. Christian armies defeated him at Montgisard in 1177, Forbelet in 1182, Arsuf in 1191 and Jaffa in 1192. Indecision cost him Tyre and Antioch in 1187–8. His failure to snuff out the paltry Christian army in the early stages of the siege of Acre in 1189 remains hard to explain. Diplomacy rather than combat allowed him to withstand the Third Crusade, as it had ensured his alliance with the caliph, neutralized the Seljuks of Asia Minor and sown division in the kingdom of Jerusalem with his treaty with Raymond III of Tripoli in 1185–7. This preference for political arts cannot be ascribed to a lack of military experience or personal squeamishness; the massacres of the *Sudan* in 1169 and the butchery of the Templars and Hospitallers after Hattin give that the lie. What distinguished Saladin, as William of Tyre sensed, was a highly developed opportunism sustained by an unsentimental appreciation of how to achieve ends through blandishment rather than force, coupled with considerable skill at managing administrative systems and people. Even so, for all his qualities as a politician, Saladin's triumph over the Franks was eased by debilitating forces within Outremer for which he could claim no responsibility.

THE DECLINE OF THE KINGDOM OF JERUSALEM 1174–87

From the third quarter of the twelfth century, political society in Outremer, in western eyes prosperous, extravagant, self-absorbed, fractious and corrupt, suffered a cumulative crisis only partly the fault of its leaders. In the north, the principality of Antioch had been reduced by Nur al-Din to the coastal strip west of the Orontes. In the kingdom of Jerusalem, as has been seen, political stability was increasingly frayed by the rapid succession as monarchs of a possible bigamist (Amalric), a leper (Baldwin IV), a child (Baldwin V) and a woman (Sybil) with an unpopular arriviste husband (Guy). Protected by a series of truces with Saladin, appearances of wealth and power, noticed by Christian and Muslim travellers in the 1170s and 1180s, concealed and encouraged self-indulgent factional politicking. From 1174 to 1186 constant jockeying for control of the regency, the ill and infant kings or royal patronage diverted attention from the more intractable problems of defence and finance.

Although revenues from commerce, especially from the port of Acre, were buoyant, the incomes of the king and his greater barons seemed increasingly inadequate to meet expenditure, especially on defence. Across the kingdom there was a move towards castles and fiefs within lordships being acquired by wealthy ecclesiastical corporations, such as the Canons of the Holy Sepulchre and, especially, the military orders of the Templars and Hospitallers. These could draw on wide networks of resources from Outremer and estates in western Europe. In the lordship of Caesarea, by 1187, perhaps as much as 55 per cent of landed property was in religious hands, the bulk of it owned by the military orders. In the frontier lordship of Galilee, all the major castles except Tiberias itself seem to have been in the hands of the Templars or Hospitallers by 1168.[24] If secular lordships were withering, sustained by money fiefs rather than land, the crown retained considerable powers of patronage and wide sources of revenue, including custom and harbour dues, taxes on Muslims and pilgrims, profits from minting coin as well as from the royal demesne, including the farming-out of proceeds from local industries, such as sugar production. However, with no new lands being conquered, the demands of patronage denied the crown much scope for increasing its ordinary income. The 1167 invasion of Egypt required a special 10 per cent income tax on those who declined to join the expedition, agreed at an assembly at Nablus that apparently included representatives of 'the people' as well as the clerical and lay magnates.[25] In 1183, a comprehensive survey of landholdings in the kingdom was conducted (a *census*) to provide a basis for a new assessment of military obligation. According to the well-informed William of Tyre, chancellor of the kingdom at the time, faced with the prospect of greater pressure from Saladin, 'the king and the barons were reduced to such a desperate state of need that their revenues were entirely insufficient to provide for the necessary outlay', leading them to agree to a new national war tax on all inhabitants, regardless of language, race, religion or sex. This process of land census followed by fiscal imposition is reminiscent of the Domesday Survey of 1086 in England. The nature of the tax, 2 per cent on income above 100 besants as well as 1 per cent on land worth more than 100 besants, with a graded hearth tax below that, echoed that of 1166 and in part presaged the Saladin Tithe of 1188 and thirteenth-century English parliamentary taxation in the west, not least in the explicit element of consent described by William of Tyre: 'by the common consent of all the nobles, both secular and ecclesiastical, and by the assent of the people of the kingdom of Jerusalem . . . for the common good of the realm'.[26] This was parliamentary language.

The underlying problems were not just financial. Despite the *de facto* overlordship of the king of Jerusalem, Outremer's disjointed authority (Antioch, Tripoli and Jerusalem) militated against coherent strategic planning along the whole of the Christian frontier, although the rise of the military orders may have acted as a compensating balance to this fissiparous tendency. More damaging in the circumstances of the 1170s and 1180s was the heavy political, administrative and military reliance on the person of the ruler. The severely disabled leper King Baldwin IV was forced to preside in person over his administration and meetings of his council and to attend campaigns and battles even if he had to be strapped to his horse or carried in a litter. Whenever he tried to relinquish the increasingly intolerable burden for a partly paralysed, nearly blind invalid, whose physical disintegration caused him to shun company, he found he could not. William of Tyre's heroic Baldwin was trapped in a political system, fragile in its narrowness, vulnerable to internal faction as to external attack.[27]

In contrast with the system of consultative assemblies on display in 1167 and 1183, this lack of executive institutional sophistication matched limited military resources. An incomplete list of obligations from *c.*1180 indicated 675 knights owing to the king, which might represent about 700 in full, with service from churches, monasteries and towns, in the form of sergeants, potentially adding *c.*5,000 troops, as well as the military orders, perhaps another 700 knights and, crucially, bodies of mercenaries, such as Turcopoles or Bedouin.[28] In theory, to these more or less trained troops could be added the *levée en masse* in times of emergency. Yet, as the campaign of 1187 revealed, raising the full complement of armed forces left vital castles and cities defenceless; the castle of Le Fève in Galilee was emptied of defenders during the preliminaries to Hattin and the city of Jerusalem contained just two knights by the time Saladin began his siege in October 1187.[29] Any supplement of mercenaries required funds, which the kings and barons seemed increasingly to lack, in 1187 having to plunder the treasure deposited in Jerusalem by Henry II of England in expiation for his involvement in the murder of Thomas Becket in 1170. Yet it was lack of manpower not cash that posed the greatest threat. Small wonder that the refusal of western rulers to commit troops to Outremer in 1184–5 left Patriarch Heraclius 'much distressed'.[30]

Despite containing Muslim pressure, increasing political dysfunction corroded Jerusalem's unity of policy and purpose. The origins of the problems can be traced to the reign of Amalric. In 1163, the new king was forced at repudiate his wife, Agnes of Courtenay, sister of Joscelin III of Courtenay, heir to the lost county of Edessa. The stated grounds for the divorce were consanguinity, but some have argued that when Amalric and Agnes married in 1157, she was already married to Hugh of Ibelin, to whom she returned as wife after her separation from Amalric.[31] Whatever the truth of the royal marriage, its annulment revealed a ruling elite that calculated personal and immediate gain above destabilizing the monarchy on which their own power depended. Behind opposition to Amalric may have lurked the decline in baronial wealth and authority within their own lordships, making royal patronage even more fiercely contested, raising anxieties lest Agnes, as queen, would seek to find lordships and fiefs for her landless brother and other dispossessed Edessans. The legacy of the civil war of 1152, when Amalric sided with his mother Queen Melisende against Baldwin III, may have fuelled suspicion, as well as personal dislike. Amalric's taciturn dourness, absence of charm and lack of affability was noted even by his friend and protégé William of Tyre. Apparently, the new king was regularly heckled and insulted both in public and private, taunts he affected to ignore. More seriously, he was accused of failing to control his ministers and officials, although this may simply refer to the unpopularity of Amalric's favourite and, from 1167, seneschal (i.e. head of the civil administration), Miles of Plancy.[32] Some may have wished to annul Amalric's marriage to free him to conclude a diplomatically more advantageous match, much in the fashion of Baldwin I's marriage to Adelisa of Sicily half a century earlier (which was certainly bigamous). In 1167 Amalric did in fact marry Maria Comnena, great-niece of Manuel I.

Although the politics of Amalric's reign revolved around the Egyptian war, later battle-lines began to coalesce around Amalric's intimates and his new wife, Maria and, after 1172, her daughter Isabella, as opposed to his first wife, Agnes, and her children, Baldwin and Sybil. Even though Agnes had little or no contact with her children after her divorce from the king, the reversionary interest that surrounded them pointed to her role as future queen-mother. Agnes also established extensive contacts within Jerusalem first by her marriage (or remarriage) to Hugh of Ibelin, lord of Ramla, linking her to the fastest-rising local seigneurial family, then, after Hugh's death *c.*1169, her taking as her fourth husband (her first had died as long ago as 1149) Reynald Grenier, the ugly, intellectual lord of Sidon, noted for his command of Arabic language and literature.[33] Such affiliations were lent increased significance by an oddity of Amalric's reign, the fortuitous absence from the political scene of three leading lords who later dominated Jerusalem politics. Reynald of Châtillon, erstwhile prince of Antioch, had been in captivity in Aleppo since 1161; Joscelin III of Courtenay followed him into Aleppan captivity in 1164, as did Raymond III of Tripoli. The release of all three between 1174 and 1176, and their subsequent elevation to leading positions within the kingdom of Jerusalem, transformed the politics of the reign of Amalric's leper son.

In monarchies where an element of hereditary succession, especially primogeniture, had become established, minorities were inevitable, paradoxical destabilizing tributes to greater dynastic stability, the rights of the genetic heir overcoming the practical need for leadership. On Amalric's sudden death in July 1174, after a debate probably focusing on the already worrying signs of the thirteen-year-old heir-presumptive's illness balanced by the lack of obvious, uncontentious or available alternatives, the High Court agreed to the accession of Prince Baldwin. His elder sister Sybil was an unmarried convent girl; his young half-sister Isabella was only two. A regency would only have to last until Baldwin was fifteen, the Jerusalem age of majority. If the young king's leprosy had been diagnosed, almost certainly he would not have been chosen.[34] Yet doubts either about the prospects for his survival or his ability to have children may have already surfaced. The marriage of his sister Sybil, with its direct implication for the succession, had been discussed a few years earlier. Baldwin's accession and the rapid realization that he was a leper and would be short-lived and childless, meant that his reign was dominated by reversionary factions defined, at least in part, by the competing claims of the king's sister and half-sister, each backed by their mothers, Agnes of Courtenay and Maria Comnena.

Partly as a result of the way the highly partisan William of Tyre described events, the feuding in Jerusalem after 1174 has often been characterized as between the old, indigenous baronage, cautious, shrewd, realistic, and a court coterie of grasping Courtenays, Agnes and her brother Joscelin, titular count of Edessa and seneschal of the kingdom, allied to newcomers from the west, rash, ignorant of local conditions and dangers, provocative towards Saladin, selfish and greedy in their pursuit of power and conduct of government. The evidence fails to sustain this interpretation.[35] Under Baldwin IV the fiercest factional competition revolved around control of the machinery of government, under the king or, when he was incapacitated, through a regency, and over the succession. Separately, contrasting approaches to strategy in dealing with Saladin emerged. Some, such as Reynald of Châtillon, after his release from captivity in 1176 established as lord of Hebron and Oultrejordain, pursued an aggressive policy to distract Saladin from his conquest of Muslim Syria. Others, such as Raymond of Tripoli, advocated serial truces as a means of containing the sultan. Similarly, the importance given to diplomatic alliances with Byzantium and/or western powers provoked disagreement, not least, perhaps, after Amalric's possible acknowledgement of Manuel I as his overlord during a visit to Constantinople in 1171.

Much antagonism sprang from personal rivalries nurtured in the hothouse of Outremer's small, closed aristocracy, the complexities of which, while hard to follow, expose layers of intense suspicion and rivalry. Reynald of Châtillon's wife, Stephanie of Milly, heiress of Oultrejordain, may have blamed the murder of her previous husband, Miles of Plancy, in 1174 on Raymond of Tripoli. A broken promise of a wealthy Tripolitanian heiress in the 1170s may have lain at the root of the hostility shown in the 1180s towards Count Raymond by Gerard of Ridefort, Master of the Temple (1185–9). William of Tyre's own perspective may have been coloured by having been appointed archbishop of Tyre and chancellor of the kingdom in 1175 by Raymond of Tripoli during the regency of 1174–6 and being passed over for the patriarchate of Jerusalem in 1180, possibly at the behest of Agnes of Courtenay.[36] One notably hostile source towards the opponents of Raymond of Tripoli in the 1180s may reflect the views of the count's allies, the Ibelins.[37] They had been allied to Agnes of Courtenay at the start of Baldwin IV's reign but after the marriage of Balian of Ibelin to Dowager Queen Maria Comnena in 1177 supported the interests of Princess Isabella against her elder half-sister Sybil. In 1186, on the accession to the throne of Sybil and her husband, Guy of Lusignan, Baldwin of Ibelin quit the kingdom in disgust. There were also those whose loyalties rested not with any fixed party but with their own self-interest or with the monarch. Warriors such as Reynald of Châtillon and the constable, Humphrey II of Toron (d. 1179), remained conspicuously loyal to the king whatever their personal feelings towards whichever faction was dominant at court. Criticism of Reynald's bellicose policy towards Saladin could with as much justice be directed at Baldwin IV, whose periods of rule showed him eager to take the battle to the enemy.

The evolution of the factions demonstrated fluid self-interest. After Amalric's death most of the local baronage, including Agnes of Courtenay and Raymond of Tripoli, opposed the power of the unpopular seneschal Miles of Plancy. Yet after his assassination in October 1174, possibly organized by political rivals exploiting an old baronial feud, and Raymond's subsequent regency (1174–6), political allegiances shifted. When Raymond surrendered the regency on Baldwin coming of age, 15 July 1176, the king appointed as seneschal and chief minister his recently released uncle, Joscelin of Courtenay, and immediately reversed Raymond's policy of truce with Saladin, personally conducting two minor campaigns across the frontier in the same year. The arrival of William of Montferrat to marry Princess Sibyl in 1176 further alienated Raymond and his supporters. In 1177, on the sudden death of William of Montferrat in June, Baldwin, who was seriously ill, appointed Reynald of Châtillon as his regent, a snub less to the indigenous nobility or to Raymond personally than to the count's supine foreign policy. With Reynald Baldwin won the famous victory at Montgisard in southern Palestine on 25 November 1177, when a potentially fatal Muslim invasion was caught off-guard and routed by a much smaller Frankish army. Yet earlier in the year a far greater prize, the prospect of a new amphibious attack on Egypt by the newly arrived Philip of Flanders together with a Byzantine fleet and a Jerusalem army, came to nothing, in part because of Philip's ambitions laced with over-fastidious diplomacy, but in part because of the failure of the Outremer nobility to speak or act as one.[38]

For all his courage and determination, the longer Baldwin IV lived, the less able he was to rule. Nobody appreciated this more than the king despite his consistent political and public composure in the face of unimaginable physical and private agony. In 1177 he may have offered to abdicate in favour of his new brother-in-law, William of Montferrat. In

1178, after the birth of her son, another Baldwin, the king began associating Princess Sybil in official documents.[39] Her remarriage became a central issue of Jerusalem politics, taking precedence over the threat from Saladin. In 1180, Raymond III of Tripoli, since his marriage to Eschiva of Bures lord of Galilee and thus one of the most powerful magnates in the kingdom, with his cousin Bohemund III of Antioch attempted a military *coup d'état* to secure a marriage for Sybil more favourable to their interests than the foreigners paraded as candidates over the previous three years. They invaded the kingdom and, it seemed to Baldwin IV, threatened his deposition as well as the removal of the Courtenays from power. The insurgents' choice for Sybil's hand appears to have been Baldwin of Ibelin, a former suitor rejected in 1178, brother-in-law to the Queen Dowager Maria. The king's response was hurriedly to agree to the marriage of his sister to a Poitevin nobleman, Guy of Lusignan, recently arrived in Outremer from the west, brother of a close associate of the Courtenays, some alleged Agnes's lover, Aimery of Lusignan. As a sign of how tangled the personal and political affiliations had become in Outremer, Aimery, later (1181/2) constable and, later still, king of Jerusalem as well as ruler of Cyprus (1194–1205, king from 1197), had, on arrival in the east in 1174, married Baldwin of Ibelin's daughter. Sybil's hasty marriage to Guy spiked the plans of Raymond and Bohemund and provided Baldwin with an active male successor and available regent. As a vassal of Baldwin's Angevin first cousin Henry II of England, Guy could also claim links to a major western power. However, to supporters of Raymond of Tripoli, opponents of the Courtenays and those blessed with the perception of hindsight, the whole episode reeked of court intrigue. Within two years, Sybil's party had secured their authority and placed their adherents in key positions. Guy became the premier baron in the land as count of Jaffa and Ascalon, King Amalric's old county. With Sybil, he began to be associated in royal diplomas as the heir apparent.[40] In 1180 the patriarchate of Jerusalem went to another supposed lover of Agnes of Courtenay, Archbishop Heraclius of Caesarea, a resourceful if possibly sybaritic politician and diplomat. However, he had pipped the historians' historian William of Tyre to the job. The same year, the potentially troublesome Princess Isabella was removed from her mother and betrothed to Humphrey III of Toron, stepson of Reynald of Châtillon, the regime's chief field commander. By 1182, Aimery of Lusignan had been appointed constable, the same year that the failure of another attempted coup by Raymond of Tripoli forced him to be reconciled with the government.

Guy of Lusignan's emergence as Baldwin's probable heir did not prevent resistance to Saladin, who was now stretched between defence of his northern frontier against the Seljuks of Asia Minor, designs on Mosul and Aleppo, ambitions in Outremer and protection of the desert-land routes between Syria and Egypt. A two-year truce, 1180–82, ended with Saladin's defeat at Le Forbelet in Galilee in July 1182, failure to take Beirut and the consolidation of Frankish control of the eastern bank of the river Yarmuk. To the south, Reynald of Châtillon disrupted not only Saladin's material power but also the ideology of his political authority with a foray into the Arabian desert in 1181 and by sponsoring a prolonged raid along the Red Sea coast in 1182–3 that disrupted the annual *haj*. Saladin acknowledged the outrage by having two Frankish captives from the raiding fleet taken to Mecca itself where, at Mina outside the city, in front of crowds of pilgrims, they had their throats cut. Although of no lasting strategic impact, these raids alarmed the Muslim world, challenging Saladin's pose as the Champion and Defender of Islam. No Christian fleet had sailed the Red Sea since the seventh century; the unfortunate captives were perhaps the first Christians to have set foot in Mecca since its capture by Muhammed in 629.[41]

Reynald's southern campaigns proved the first kingdom of Jerusalem's final fling. In June 1183 Saladin finally occupied Aleppo. In August he turned his attention southwards to Jerusalem. The kingdom mobilized a large army, according to William of Tyre 1,300 cavalry and 15,000 infantry, numbers swelled by the census earlier in the year and mercenaries paid by the subsequent tax.[42] The Christian army gathered at Sephoria in Galilee. The great magnates were attending the king at Nazareth when Baldwin fell seriously ill and was thought to be dying. He summoned the High Court to his sickbed and appointed Guy of Lusignan as regent. The regency was to be permanent, Baldwin retaining only the title of king, ownership of the Holy City itself and an annual pension of 10,000 gold pieces with a promise from Guy not to alienate royal treasure or lands during the king's lifetime.

Apart from initial skirmishes, the Galilee campaign in September and October 1183 saw no military engagement. The Christian army shadowed Saladin's force as it manoeuvred in southern Galilee, but refused to confront the invaders, despite Muslim raids on Mt Tabor's monasteries and threats to Nazareth. Unable to bring the Franks to battle and lacking the numerical superiority to launch an assault on their camp, Saladin withdrew to Damascus in early October. Tactically, the Franks had prevailed with the minimum of losses. However, many in the Jerusalem high command thought that strategically they had missed an opportunity to destroy Saladin's army. Aggression had paid dividends in 1177 at Montgisard and in 1182 at Le Forbelet with far smaller forces at the Franks' disposal. Moreover, it was the duty of Christian knights to protect holy sites such as Mt Tabor from Muslim desecration. In the eyes of some observers, admittedly hostile to Guy, the management of the campaign, despite its satisfactory if not triumphant outcome, left much to be desired. Some leaders had refused to cooperate with Guy. Tactical inertia, partly the result of this inability to command confidence and unity, had been matched by inadequate provisioning of food. Many saw Guy's apparently supine performance as proof of his inability to lead. Four years later, memory of this perception proved fatal as the Franks, led once more by Guy, rejected the caution of 1183 only to be annihilated at the Horns of Hattin.

Guy's perceived shortcomings as a war leader were immediately compounded by his refusal to accede to King Baldwin's request to exchange Jerusalem for Tyre. Support for the regent ebbed. In November 1183 Saladin began a siege of Kerak in Oultrejordain while the castle was hosting the marriage between Princess Isabella and Humphrey IV of Toron. Facing this fresh crisis, Baldwin engineered a palace revolution. Guy was stripped of the regency and a new succession was arranged excluding him, signalled by the coronation of his stepson, the five-year-old Baldwin, son of Sybil and her first husband William of Monteferrat. To prevent Guy's return to power, moves were begun to annul his marriage to Sybil. Command of the relief army to Kerak was handed to Raymond of Tripoli accompanied by the now blind and partly paralysed king in a litter. After the siege had been relieved, Guy, joined by his wife Sybil, shut himself in his city of Ascalon, risking civil war by defying Baldwin's attempts to strip him of his fiefs. The process of annulment also ran into the ground. But Guy's hopes of rule seemed at an end.[43]

When the king despatched the Patriarch Heraclius to Europe in the summer of 1184 to try to induce a western ruler, perhaps one of Baldwin's Angevin cousins, to come east to assume the regency, the political landscape appeared transformed. The regent of the year before was *persona non grata*; civil war had narrowly been avoided; Guy and Sybil had effectively been excluded from the succession that now hung on the life of an increasingly infirm leper and a weak child. When the king suffered another relapse in the winter of 1184–5, Raymond of Tripoli resumed the regency he had vacated over eight years before, although under restrictive terms, with Joscelin of Courtenay acting as young Baldwin V's guardian. Acknowledging the fragility of succession arrangements, the High Court agreed that Raymond would retain the regency for ten years unless the young Baldwin died, in which case the competing claims of Princesses Sybil and Isabella would be adjudicated by the pope, the emperor of Germany and the kings of France and England. The earlier scheme of trying to attract a western regent was abandoned. Heraclius had met with no success, not having anything to offer western rulers other than temporary command of a fragile monarchy, a fractious nobility and a menacing enemy. The 1184–5 mission foundered on Jerusalem's traditional diplomatic conundrum. Outside assistance was sought but with political strings protecting the power of the local royal family and nobility, hardly an attractive proposition. Paradoxically, the new succession arrangements in 1185 merely confirmed Jerusalem's insularity.

The divisions within the ruling elite remained. Raymond held the regency, but Sybil was still married to Guy with her son, young Baldwin, in the custody of her uncle, Joscelin. Many suspected, possibly correctly, that Raymond still harboured designs on the throne while Princess Isabella's party openly supported a settlement that denied the rights of Sybil and Guy. This time Baldwin IV did not recover. By 16 May 1185 he was dead.[44] The crisis within Outremer deepened precisely at a moment of opportunity. Saladin spent the year from spring 1185 to 1186 occupied with his attempts to subdue Mosul and northern Iraq. In December 1185 he fell gravely ill. Out of action for three months, his life despaired of, Saladin's empire seemed about to fall apart. However, before leaving for Iraq, the sultan had once more agreed a truce with Raymond of Tripoli. Consequently, the Franks did nothing to intervene, despite the arrival of a few crusaders in the wake of Heraclius's embassy. The flaw in Raymond's pacific policy was exposed when, on his recovery in March 1186, Saladin finally annexed Mosul.[45] The encirclement described by William of Tyre was complete, and the Franks had done little to prevent it.

The death of the eight-year-old Baldwin V at Acre in the summer of 1186 drove Jerusalem near to civil war. While Raymond assembled a general council of the kingdom's barons and clergy at Nablus, perhaps hoping to be elected king himself, Sybil's partisans gathered at the Holy City for the young king's funeral. With Sybil were Guy, the masters of the military orders, Reynald of Châtillon, the Patriarch Heraclius and Baldwin V's paternal grandfather, William III of Montferrat, a veteran of the Second Crusade who had retired to the east in 1185. After the obsequies, despite the objections of delegates from Nablus, they proceeded to choose Sybil as queen. There was less enthusiasm about Guy becoming king. Before she was crowned, Sybil promised to divorce Guy on three conditions; their children (all daughters) were to be declared legitimate; Guy was to remain count of Ascalon and Jaffa; and Sybil was to have a free choice of new husband. However, once crowned by the patriarch, Sybil promptly selected Guy. This coup cannot have entirely pleased her supporters, but Sybil had shown that, like her father and brother, she understood her rights, knew the law and was prepared to impose her will.

In any circumstances, Sybil's election would have proved contentious given the twists in the plans for the royal succession over the previous decade. Her appointment of Guy as king and his consecration by Patriarch Heraclius displayed conjugal devotion but no political tact. Raymond of Tripoli's assembly at Nablus included the other claimant, Isabella and her husband, Humphrey of Toron, with their supporters, the Ibelins. Barred from the Holy City when Sybil's supporters barricaded the gates, they learnt of the coup through despatching a spy, a Jerusalem-born sergeant disguised as a Cistercian monk, who lurked in the precincts of the Holy Sepulchre to observe the double coronation. Once news reached Nablus, Raymond desperately proposed the assembled nobles crown Humphrey, but the young man refused to cooperate with a scheme that would have caused immediate civil war. With most of the other nobles at Nablus, Humphrey recognized that, with a king already crowned and consecrated, however hateful, they had little option but to acknowledge the *fait accompli*. He left for Jerusalem to pay homage to his new lord, thus ending any prospect of concerted resistance to Sybil's coup. Most of the rest of the Nablus gathering soon followed. Only Baldwin of Ibelin and Raymond of Tripoli remained recalcitrant. At King Guy's first meeting of the High

Court, in a show of almost constitutional propriety, Baldwin refused homage and quit the kingdom for service in the principality of Antioch. By contrast, Raymond's refusal to accept Guy provoked the king to threaten the count with military reprisal. Fearing an attack by Guy, Raymond showed his low level of statesmanship by concluding a personal deal with Saladin under which he accepted the sultan's protection and a detachment of Muslim soldiers to strengthen his garrison at Tiberias. Whatever his feelings about Guy, however disappointed he was by having power once again, and probably for ever, dashed from his grasp, Raymond's behaviour in 1186–7, as most unbiased sources agreed, was more than selfish. It was treason.[46]

THE BATTLE OF HATTIN AND THE FALL OF JERUSALEM

The general truce with Saladin was due to expire a week after Easter, 5 April 1187. It would not be renewed. Restored to health and in control of an empire that stretched from the Nile to the Tigris, Saladin could now fulfil his political *jihad* rhetoric by military action against the Franks. In Jerusalem, Guy and his Poitevin cronies hardly made themselves popular by flaunting their new power and cornering lucrative patronage. In the winter of 1186–7, Reynald of Châtillon, frustrated by the truce from contesting Saladin's attempts to consolidate his position in the Transjordanian desert, launched a successful raid on a rich Egyptian caravan travelling to Damascus. Guy's lack of political grip was exposed by his failure to force Reynald to provide compensation or restitution to the sultan. Such diplomatic exchanges between Saladin and the Franks confirm the picture left by a surprised Spanish Muslim visitor to Outremer in the autumn of 1184 who noted how trade flowed freely across the Muslim–Christian frontier despite the war. Although each side took prisoners and slaves, Muslims were not molested in Christian lands and vice versa.[47] Such accommodation may have helped persuade Raymond of Tripoli, a veteran of long captivity in Aleppo, that he would find Saladin a benign protector against his Christian king. His miscalculation no less than his ambition proved fatal.

When it became obvious that Saladin would launch an attack after the truce ended, King Guy realized he had to be reconciled with Raymond, whose control of Galilee was strategically vital. If, as it appeared, the count was prepared to allow access to Saladin's forces, not only Galilee but the west bank of the Jordan and the coastal plain around Acre were exposed. While Saladin began hostilities in late April with an assault on Kerak, a delegation was sent by Guy to negotiate with Raymond at Tiberias. Their journey coincided with a raid into Galilee in 1 May 1187 by Saladin's son al-Afdal, which was allowed free passage by Raymond in accordance with his treaty with the sultan. As the Muslim force, numbering perhaps 7,000, approached Nazareth, the locals appealed for aid to a contingent of the royal delegation led by Gerard of Ridefort, Master of the Temple, and Roger of Moulins, Master of the Hospital. Nazareth lay outside Raymond's territories and therefore outside his truce. The Masters managed to assemble a scratch force from nearby castles of about ninety Templar and Hospitaller knights, forty local knights and perhaps 300 mounted sergeants. Although hopelessly outnumbered, this small army, using its only possible tactic, attacked the Muslims at the springs of Cresson. Despite fierce fighting, the Christians were massacred, only Gerard of Ridefort and three other of the knights escaping alive. In the inevitable recriminations that followed, it was alleged that the intemperate haste of Master Gerard, against the advice of his fellow commanders, had precipitated the battle. Given the appeal from Nazareth, it is hard to see what else the Templars and Hospitallers were to do without contradicting their calling. Militarily disastrous, the heroism at Cresson soon earnt the fallen knights the accolade of legend and martyrdom, their feats admiringly retold to inspire the endeavours of troops from the west during the long siege of Acre three years later. More immediately, the victorious Muslims withdrew across the frontier carrying the heads of their slaughtered foes on the ends of their spears.[48]

While the disaster at Cresson on 1 May 1187 significantly weakened Jerusalem's resources, it produced political unity. By allowing al-Afdal's troops to cross his lands, Count Raymond could not avoid shouldering blame for the massacre. Even his own vassals and the local militia in his territories turned against him. In the days after Cresson a hasty reconciliation was patched together between Raymond and Guy, the count's truce with Saladin repudiated and the Muslim garrison at Tiberias expelled. Despite the tensions that simmered on the surface of baronial cooperation with the king, in the following weeks Guy was able to muster all the available troops from the kingdom, as well as some from Tripoli and Antioch. The Frankish host, one of the largest ever assembled, numbered up to 20,000, including around 1,200 knights. The force that Saladin led into Frankish territory around the southern end of the Sea of Galilee on 27 June 1187 was probably 30,000 strong. While the Franks, as in 1183, mustered at the springs of Sephoria, Saladin sent scouting and scavenging parties across the hills to provoke the Christians to break camp and to identify suitable battlefields. He then tried to lure the Franks into battle by leading a detachment of his main force against Tiberias on 2 July. The town fell the same day, the garrison under Raymond of Tripoli's wife, Eschiva of Galilee, withdrawing to the citadel to endure a siege. On hearing of this, the Frankish high command met in the camp at Sephoria on the evening of 2 July to decide how to respond. On their decision hung the future of nine decades of western European settlement in the Near East.[49]

Later Frankish sources favourable to Count Raymond recorded that, after Raymond had persuaded King Guy to adopt the same tactics as four years earlier and refuse battle, the Master of the Temple late at night managed to change the king's mind. Some Muslim accounts agree that Raymond urged the abandonment of Tiberias, which, he hoped, would lead to the dispersal of Saladin's army, eager to return home safely with their booty, only to be contradicted by Reynald of Châtillon, who reminded the king of Raymond's recent treachery and alliance with the enemy. Saladin's secretary, Imad al-Din, by contrast, portrayed Raymond as taking the lead in persuading Guy to march out to relieve Tiberias.[50] Whatever the immediate arguments and assessment of risks, Guy can hardly have avoided an unpleasant sense of *déjà vu*. In 1183, in similar circumstances, he had been vilified and hounded from office after failing to engage Saladin's army even though he had kept the Frankish army intact and largely unscathed. Any advice he now received from political enemies, especially Raymond, must have appeared tainted. Aggression had served the Franks well in the past; Reynald of Châtillon was living proof of that. Sephoria lay just under twenty miles from Tiberias, just possible to reach in a day of forced march across the hilly terrain. If not, the substantial springs at Hattin, just over a dozen miles distant, offered refuge for a bivouac. The Frankish army was formidably large, with experienced leaders and seasoned troops. Despite the sub-

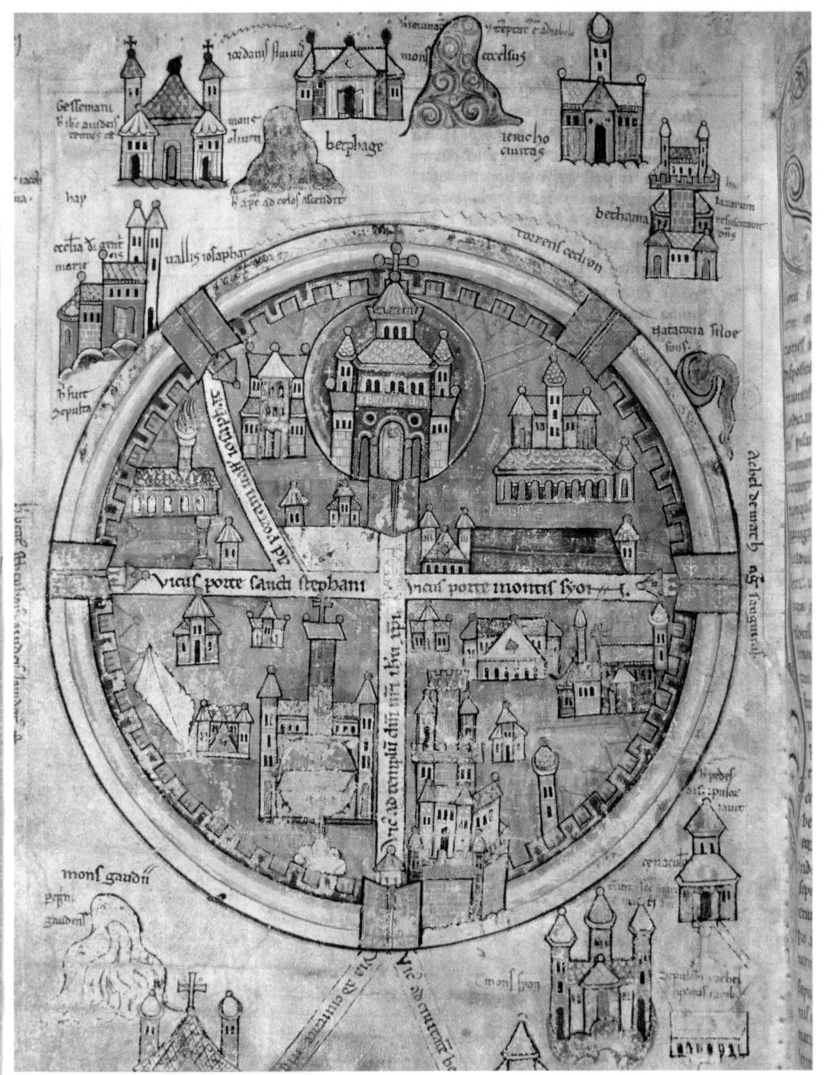

1. Jerusalem and its environs *c.*1100: the Holy City in the eyes of western Christendom.

2. Urban II consecrating the high altar at Cluny during his preaching tour of France, October 1095; see p. 63.

3. Peter the Hermit leading his crusaders.

4. Alexius I Comnenus, emperor of Byzantium 1081–1118.

5. The church of the Holy Sepulchre in Jerusalem idealized in later medieval western imagination.

6. The front cover of the Psalter of Queen Melisende of Jerusalem (1131–52); see p. 210.

7. Saladin: a contemporary Arab view.

8. The battle of Hattin, 4 July 1187: Saladin seizing the True Cross, a fictional scene visualized by the monk Matthew Paris of St Alban's (*d.* 1259).

9. Frederick I Barbarossa, emperor of Germany, dressed as a crusader *c.*1188, receiving a copy of Robert of Rheims's popular history of the First Crusade. The inscription exhorts Frederick to fight the 'Saracens'. See pp. 245, 418.

10. Embarking on crusade, showing, among others, the banners of the kings of France and England, from the statutes of the fourteenth-century chivalric Order of the Knot, dedicated to the Holy Spirit; see p. 855.

11. Women helping besiege a city, as at the siege of Acre 1190; see pp. 396–7, 415, 428.

12. The western image of war in the Holy Land: Joshua, in the guise of a Frankish knight, liberates Gibeon from the Five Kings, an episode in the Book of Joshua (10:6–13) from an illuminated Bible commissioned for the crusading court of Louis IX of France *c.*1244–54.

13. Military orchestra of the kind employed by Turkish, Kurdish and Mamluk commanders, see p. 821.

14. Pope Innocent III (1198–1216).

15. Venice *c.*1400.

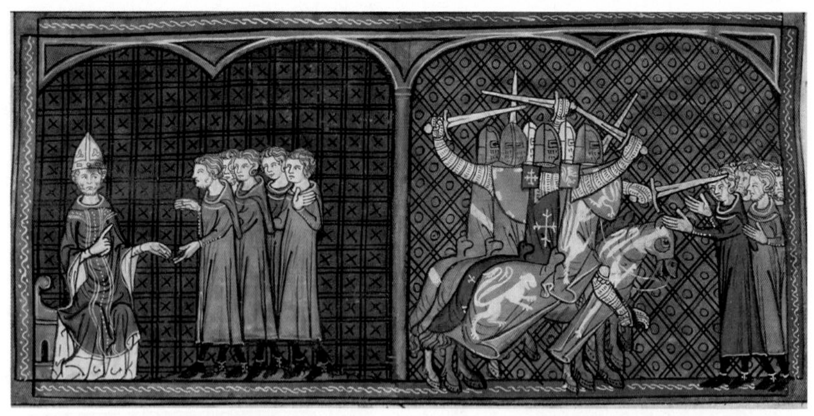

16. Innocent III and the Albigensian Crusade.

17. Neighbours at war: Moors fighting Christians in thirteenth-century Spain.

sequent verdicts of events, Guy's decision during the night of 2–3 July to break camp and march to Tiberias may not then have appeared foolish or doomed. Two years later, when he led a tiny Christian army to begin the siege of Acre, an apparently far rasher decision led to ultimate success. However, in the Galilean hills in July 1187, once committed, Guy had no prospects of reinforcement and few of ordered retreat. His choice of battle consciously provoked a confrontation that would be decisive, whatever the outcome.

The Franks left Sephoria early on 3 July, heading towards the small spring at Turan about a third of the way to Tiberias. Progress was slow and before nightfall stopped altogether. Saladin broke off his siege of Tiberias and organized his army to meet the advancing Franks. Once the springs at Turan had been passed, the Franks found themselves attacked from the right flank and rear. The sheer weight of Muslim numbers slowed the Franks until they reached Maskana on the western edge of the plateau that looked down on the Sea of Galilee. Here the leadership once more seemed at odds, whether to attempt to force their way eastwards down from the plateau to Tiberias that night, or to turn aside northwards to the large wells at the village of Hattin. In the end, they did neither, Guy ordering a halt at Maskana. The decision to camp for the night on the arid plateau with little or no water may have come from confusion and hesitancy. But Guy may have had no option. Enemy numbers harrying the army had slowed progress almost to a standstill, preventing it from reaching the springs at Hattin and threatening to turn a descent to the Sea of Galilee into a massacre or rout. The Franks do not seem to have successfully reconnoitred the enemy's strength. If they had known how heavily the odds were stacked against them, the decision at Sephoria may have been different.

By the morning of 4 July, the Franks found themselves surrounded. Their only, slim chance of success lay in pressing on towards the fresh water of the Sea of Galilee in the hope of manoeuvring the enemy into a position where a concerted cavalry charge could be mounted. The Frankish vanguard under Raymond of Tripoli made an early attempt to break the stranglehold, but the Muslims merely opened ranks, allowing the count and his followers to escape, an act that confirmed for many Raymond's treachery. Completely encircled, constantly harassed by scrub fires and hails of arrows, the Franks avoided total disintegration by establishing themselves on the Horns of Hattin, where the remains

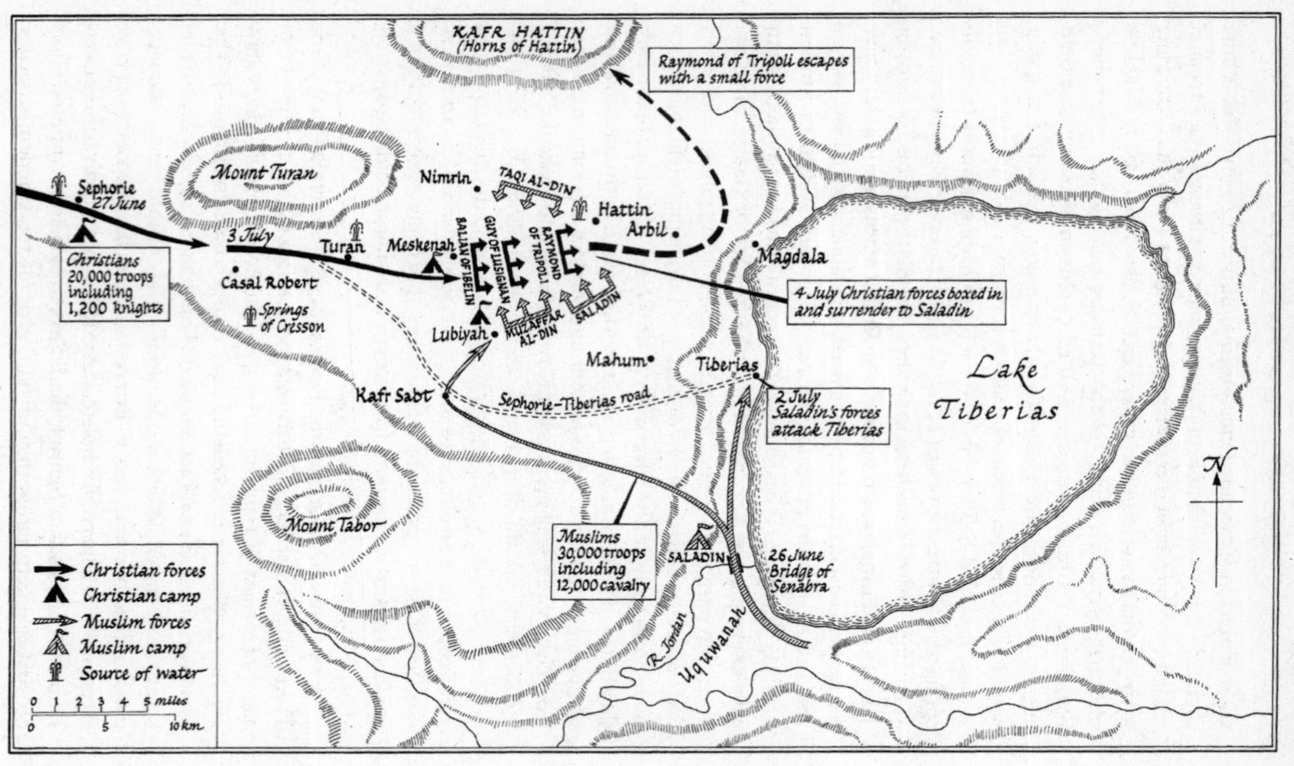

KAFR HATTIN
(Horns of Hattin)
Raymond of Tripoli escapes with a small force
Mount Turan
Sephorie
27 June
Nimrin
TAQI AL-DIN
Hattin
Arbil
3 July
Turan
Meskenah
BALIAN OF IBELIN
GUY OF LUSIGNAN
RAYMOND OF TRIPOLI
Magdala
Christians
20,000 troops
including
1,200 knights
Casal Robert
Springs of Cresson
4 July Christian forces boxed in and surrender to Saladin
SALADIN
MUZAFFAR AL-DIN
Lubiyah
Mahum
Tiberias
Lake Tiberias
Kafr Sabt
Sephorie–Tiberias road
2 July
Saladin's forces attack Tiberias
Mount Tabor
Muslims
30,000 troops
including
12,000 cavalry
SALADIN
26 June
Bridge of Senabra
R. Jordan
Uquwanah
Christian forces
Christian camp
Muslim forces
Muslim camp
Source of water
0 1 2 3 4 5 miles
0 5 10 km
N

9. The Hattin Campaign, July 1187

of an extinct volcano surrounded by the ruins of Iron Age and Bronze Age walls offered some protection. Here both cavalry and infantry made their last stand. As in the similar circumstances when the Antiochene army had been surrounded at the Field of Blood in 1119 and Inab in 1149, the outcome could hardly have been in doubt. Yet, even *in extremis*, the Christian knights refused to submit. At some point, elements of the rearguard under Reynald of Sidon and Balian of Ibelin, who had borne the brunt of attacks throughout the previous day's march, managed to break out through the Muslim lines. During the withdrawal to the Horns, a Templar attack failed to disturb the surrounding cordon though lack of support. At the end of the battle, fighting exhaustion and despair, King Guy led at least two charges from his fortified base directed against Saladin's personal bodyguard, his final throw to reverse the impending defeat. It was later reported that these attacks, even from so desperate a position, alarmed the sultan.[51] Only when the remaining Frankish knights, having dismounted to defend the Horns on foot, were overwhelmed by thirst and fatigue as much as by their enemies, did the Muslims penetrate their final defences. Lack of water may have caused the collapse of horses as well as their riders, preventing further resistance. Guy and his knights were found slumped on the ground, unable to prolong the fight. Before these final moments, Frankish morale was destroyed by the capture of the relic of the True Cross and the death of its bearer, the bishop of Acre. This relic, discovered in the days after the capture of Jerusalem in July 1099, had regularly been carried into battle by the Jerusalem Franks as a totem of God's support and promise of victory. Its loss, even more than the defeat itself, resonated throughout Christendom, raising the military disaster into a spiritual catastrophe.

Perhaps one of the most surprising aspects of the annihilation of the Frankish host was the numbers of survivors from the highest ranks of the nobility amid the carnage of thousands. Among the Frankish lords on their way to captivity Saladin had ushered to his tent after the battle were King Guy, his brother Aimery, Humphrey of Toron, Reynald of Châtillon, Gerard of Ridefort and old William of Montferrat, effectively most of the governing clique. By contrast, 200 captured rank and file Templars and Hospitallers were butchered amateurishly, almost ceremonially by Muslim Sufis, while infantry survivors were herded off to slave markets across the Levant. Alone of the grandest prisoners,

Reynald of Châtillon was executed, possibly by Saladin himself, after an elaborate charade in which the sultan expressly denied Reynald formal hospitality in the form of a drink that was offered round the other captives. The gesture was of revenge on an infidel aggressor who had dared to take war to the holy places of Arabia. The ritualistic manner of his killing as remembered by Saladin's secretary, who was present, suggested this departure from normal practice followed the needs of propaganda rather than anger. Saladin was the most calculating of politicians. He needed a head. Reynald's was the obvious victim. In western eyes, his death transformed this grizzled veteran of Outremer's wars into a martyr whose fate was promenaded to encourage recruitment for the armies that hoped to reverse the decision of Hattin.[52] Meanwhile, before leaving the battlefield, Saladin ordered a dome to be constructed to celebrate his victory; its foundations survive to this day. Less permanent testimony to the great battle presented itself to the historian Ibn al-Athir, who crossed the battlefield in 1188. Despite the ravages of weather, wild animals and carrion birds, he 'saw the land all covered with bones, which could be seen even from a distance, lying in heaps or scattered around.'[53]

The completeness of Saladin's victory was soon apparent. The army destroyed at Hattin had denuded the rest of the kingdom's defences. Saladin's progress was cautious but triumphal. Beginning with the surrender of Tiberias on 5 July and Acre on 10 July, he mopped up most of the ports within weeks, including Sidon (29 July) and Beirut (6 August). Tyre survived, and then only because of the arrival from the west of Conrad of Montferrat, son of the captured William and uncle to the dead Baldwin V, in mid-July. Most of the castles and cities of the interior fell, with the exception of the great fortresses of Montréal, Kerak, Belvoir, Saphet and Belfort. Northern Outremer awaited its turn. On 4 September 1187, Ascalon surrendered after a stiff fight, followed by the remaining strongholds in southern Palestine. After negotiations that had seen the sultan enhance his reputation for magnanimity by allowing the Queen Dowager Maria safe conduct from Jerusalem to Tyre, on 20 September Saladin invested the Holy City.[54] The garrison was commanded by Patriarch Heraclius, Balian of Ibelin, recently arrived from Tyre, and only two other knights. After a spirited show of resistance, and dramatic penances by the civilian population, the end came by negotiation. Saladin accepted payment for the release of most

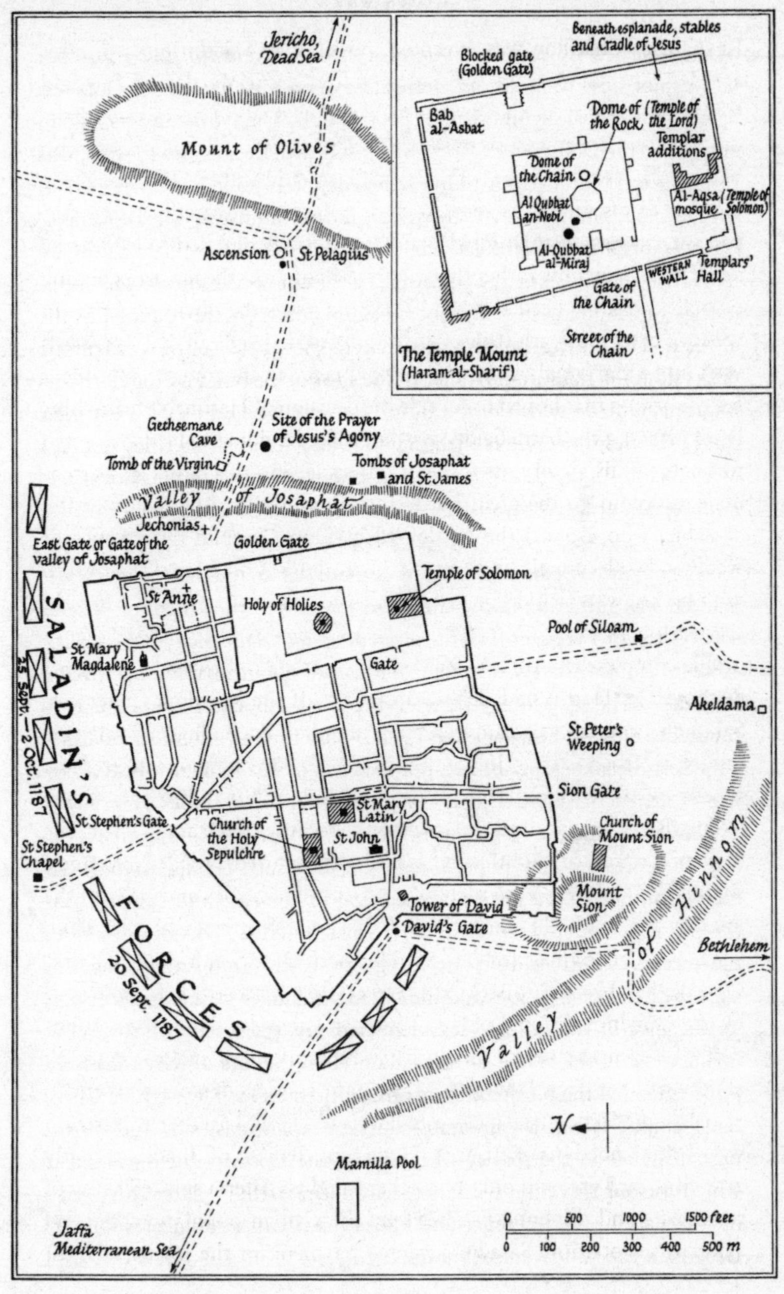

Jericho, Dead Sea
Mount of Olives
Ascension
St Pelagius
Gethsemane Cave
Site of the Prayer of Jesus's Agony
Tomb of the Virgin
Tombs of Josaphat and St James
Valley of Josaphat
Jechonias
Golden Gate
East Gate or Gate of the valley of Josaphat
Temple of Solomon
St Anne
Holy of Holies
Pool of Siloam
St Mary Magdalene
Gate
SALADIN'S
25 Sept. – 2 Oct. 1187
Akeldama
St Peter's Weeping
Sion Gate
St Mary Latin
Church of the Holy Sepulchre
St John
St Stephen's Gate
St Stephen's Chapel
Church of Mount Sion
Mount Sion
Tower of David
David's Gate
FORCES
20 Sept. 1187
Valley of Hinnom
Bethlehem
N
Mamilla Pool
Jaffa
Mediterranean Sea
0 500 1000 1500 feet
0 100 200 300 400 500 m
Beneath esplanade, stables and Cradle of Jesus
Blocked gate (Golden Gate)
Bab al-Asbat
Dome of the Rock (Temple of the Lord)
Templar additions
Dome of the Chain
Al Qubbat an-Nebi
Al-Aqsa mosque (Temple of Solomon)
Al-Qubbat al-Miraj
WESTERN WALL
Templars' Hall
Gate of the Chain
Street of the Chain
The Temple Mount (Haram al-Sharif)

10. Saladin Captures Jerusalem, September–October 1187

of the besieged Christians, a contrast with the events of July 1099 that he was not slow to point out. Jerusalem opened its gates on 2 October. Saladin milked the symbolism of his triumph. The cross the Franks had erected on the Dome of the Rock was cast down; the al-Aqsa mosque was restored and Nur al-Din's pulpit from Aleppo installed; the precincts of the Haram al Sharif purified, the sultan and his family playing a conspicuous role; prominent Frankish religious buildings, such as the house of the patriarch and the church of St Anne, were converted into Islamic seminaries or schools. On 9 October, Friday prayers were resumed in the al-Aqsa. The Holy Sepulchre was spared, some said out of a pragmatic understanding of the importance of the site not the building for Christian pilgrimage, from which in the future the sultan could profit. However, the Latin clergy were expelled. Saladin had fulfilled his titles not just as victorious king, al-Malik al-Nasir, but as Restorer of the World and Faith, Salah al-Dunya wa'l-Din. It was the pinnacle of his career.

News of Hattin reached the west by rumour, letter and messenger. While Saladin was gathering in the shattered remains of the kingdom, Joscius archbishop of Tyre set off to the west, arriving first in Sicily, where King William II immediately dispatched a fleet of about fifty ships with 200 knights.[55] The disaster produced profound shock. Pope Urban III reputedly died on hearing of it. Even before the full extent of Saladin's conquests became known, a response began to be organized. In November 1187, Richard count of Poitou, eldest surviving son of Henry II of England, became the first ruler north of the Alps to take the cross.[56] In late October, the new pope, Gregory VIII, issued a bull, *Audita Tremendi*, authorizing a general expedition to the east and summarizing the privileges offered to those who took the cross. Gregory described the horrors of the battle of Hattin, 'a great cause for mourning', lingering over the Muslim atrocities and indicated the danger facing the Holy City itself; news of the fall of Jerusalem had not yet reached Italy. While laying most of the blame for the calamity on the sins of the Franks, the pope extended the burden of responsibility to include 'the whole Christian people'. It was a Christian's duty to repent past sins and restore past mistakes in the service of God and the recovery 'of that land in which for our salvation truth arose from the earth'.[57] After forty years of complacency, indifference and lip-service, Christendom's response to Gregory's call was overwhelming.

12
The Call of the Cross

The response to the loss of Jerusalem and most of Outremer reinvented crusading. Central elements of later campaigns were introduced or confirmed: tightly organized preaching; crusade taxation, which allowed for more professional recruitment; transport by sea; and a widening strategic understanding of what was required to ensure the recovery of Jerusalem. Preachers and polemicists developed a sharper concentration on the flexible image of the cross, a banner of victory but also a badge of faith and sign of repentance. Extending the idea of communal penance contained in Gregory VIII's bull *Audita Tremendi*, crusade publicists extrapolated the act of crusading into a clear general scheme of religious revivalism. This they associated with a firmer distinctive vocabulary of personal commitment mirrored in legally more explicit privileges of the crusader, the *crucesignatus*. Taking the cross now in theory clearly separated crusading from pilgrimage, even if surviving written liturgies and chroniclers retained the link. To the crusader's special spiritual status coupled with the now customary privileges were joined precise and immediate secular benefits, such as exemption from the novel taxes levied to pay for the armies bound for the east. The experience of 1188–92 established in lay as well as ecclesiastical circles the technical name for participants in crusading even if it failed to discover an agreed term for the activity in which they were involved. Propagandists began to talk almost exclusively of '*crucesignati*', a habit that soon found its way into chronicles, histories and government records. In the accounts of the English Exchequer, *crusiatus* appeared in 1188/9 and *crucesignatus*, for the first time, in 1191/2.[1] Vernacular equivalents, such as the verbs *croisier* and *croiser*, began to appear in the poems of departing crusaders and within a generation *croisié* had become common when describing a crusader.[2] While Jerusalem dominated the language of preparation for the campaigns in the east, the failure of the Palestine war of 1191–2 to restore the Holy City to Christian rule produced a subtle but significant shift in linguistic focus that shadowed military reality. Thereafter the *iter Jerosolymitana* gave place to the broader inclusive euphemisms of *negotium Terrae Sanctae* or even simply the *negotium sanctum*, the business of the Holy Land, the holy business.

THE MESSAGE

The effort to mobilize Christendom involved every available medium of communication in a carefully organized campaign. Although published in late October and early November 1187, only days after his accession, Gregory VIII's *Audita Tremendi* had taken weeks of drafting since September when definite news of Hattin reached the papal Curia, then in Verona. Its release had awaited the arrival at the Curia, now moved to Ferrara, of Joscius archbishop of Tyre from Sicily, and been further delayed by the death of the already ailing Urban III on 20 October. The bull provided the basic ingredients of the appeal for action.[3] Proceeding from an account of Saladin's victory to a call for general Christian repentance, it emphasized the opportunity the crisis provided for the dutiful believers to follow in the path of the Maccabees and to serve the will of God. After the *casus belli* and the exhortation came the statement of the spiritual and temporal privileges, based on those declared by Eugenius III in 1145–6. With *Audita Tremendi* were sent other letters affirming papal and curial commitment and enjoining fasts and a seven-year truce on all Christian princes.

By the time they issued *Audita Tremendi*, Gregory VIII and his advisors probably guessed it was assured an eager reception. With Archbishop Joscius would have come news of William II of Sicily's plans to send a fleet to the Holy Land.[4] Already western courts were full of rumours, backed by hard evidence from correspondents from Outremer and southern Europe that preceded the formal authorization of a new crusade. Richard of Poitou's hasty and impulsive adoption of the cross at Tours in November 1187, without his father, Henry II's, permission, almost certainly anticipated the arrival of the papal bull.[5] While papal legates – Archbishop Joscius of Tyre to France and the former abbot of Clairvaux, Cardinal Henry of Albano, to Germany – accompanied the bull, by the end of the year preparations to receive the message they brought were in full swing. At an imperial diet at Strassburg in December, encouraged by the rhetoric of Bishop Henry of Strassburg, German lords had begun to take the cross, overcoming an initial wariness.[6] At the Christmas 1187 court of Canute VI of Denmark at Odense, apparently surprise and shock both at what had happened and what was being proposed inhibited spontaneous response.[7] On both the emotional and political levels, reassurance of the priority to be given any projected campaign was necessary. As elsewhere, many German lords were probably reluctant to make any move before they knew the intentions of their king-emperor, Frederick Barbarossa. Deference to rulers' decisions characterized the reception of the papal call to arms. Given the financial and political implications, it was small wonder Richard of Poitou's failure to wait for his father's lead left the old king speechless.[8]

Within weeks of the circulation and reception of the papal bull, the preaching campaign assumed coherent regional patterns. In Germany, after the Strassburg diet, it was spearheaded by Bishop Henry of Strassburg and Bishop Godfrey of Würzburg, whose eloquence helped create a mood of mass enthusiasm that culminated in a great assembly at Mainz on 27 March 1188. Billed by the papal legate Henry of Albano as a 'curia Christi', court of Christ, there Frederick received the cross. Subsidiary preaching tours were organized, such as the bishop of Strassburg's journey to Hainault, Nesle, Louvain and Lille.[9] A similarly rapid but controlled response was evoked in England and northern France. Before the end of 1187, Henry II had ordered the sequestration of the profits from the pilgrim trade at the shrine of Thomas Becket at Canterbury in order, he claimed, to assist Jerusalem and ransom Christian captives.[10] Political rivalries and resentments between Henry and Philip II of France were quickly if temporarily submerged. At Gisors in the Vexin, between Normandy and Philip's royal lands, the two rulers took the cross on 21 January 1188 in the presence of Joscius of Tyre, less than three months after the papal bull. With them were most of the counts of northern France: Flanders, Blois, La Perche, Champagne, Dreux, Clermont, Beaumont, Soissons, Bar and Nevers (King Henry himself being duke of Normandy and count of Anjou, Maine and Touraine).[11] By the time Frederick of Germany took the cross two months later, a carefully organized crusade preaching tour of Wales by Archbishop Baldwin of Canterbury was approaching its fifth week. The preaching in Henry II's lands in France and England had been organized at a conference at Le Mans in late January and Geddington, in Northamptonshire, on 11 February 1188, where sermons were delivered by the archbishop of Canterbury, who took the cross there, and his deputy, the bishop of Rochester. By the end of the month, Archbishop Baldwin was preparing his Welsh tour; the bishop of St Asaph may have already begun preaching.[12] In France, Philip II managed to gather a large assembly to Paris, also on 27 March, mid-Lent, to discuss the crusade tax and related financial provisions for crusaders. By Easter 1188, coordinated preaching and recruitment campaigns, coupled in Angevin and Capetian lands with attempts to raise the crusade tax, were well established and credited with dramatic success in attracting tens of thousands of *crucesignati*, from Germany to the Atlantic.

Central to the commitment of taking the cross was the concurrent resolution of outstanding internal and diplomatic problems. At Gisors, Henry II and Philip II agreed (only temporarily as it turned out) to shelve their territorial disputes. In Germany, the general peace was extended to Frederick's opponents, such as the archbishop of Cologne, and the troublesome duke of Saxony, Henry the Lion, who was presented with a choice of accompanying the crusade all expenses paid or exile. Henry chose the latter. Under the possibly sincere guise of promoting the crusade, Henry II attempted to assert his authority over the Welsh princes, through Archbishop Baldwin's tour, and, unsuccessfully, over Scotland, by trying to extract a contribution to the crusade tax. Despite an attached offer to settle a border dispute, the Scottish barons declined to treat Henry as their lord for crusade finance or anything else.[13] For Philip II, no less important than ensuring that his uncontrollably powerful Angevin vassal Henry II accompanied him on any eastern expedition was the similar commitment of other great feudatories, such as the duke of Burgundy or the counts of Flanders and Champagne. Philip, a calculating, cautious and resourceful opportunist who tended to wait on favourable events rather than risk grand gestures, needed to ensure that the bold undertaking of the crusade did nothing to limit his prospects of widening royal control within the French kingdom.

Although across Christendom reactions to the call to arms were conditioned by considerations of material and political advantage, as one contemporary observed, 'for the love of God, remission of sins and respect of the kings', there can be no doubt the message produced strong psychological and religious responses.[14] At its most straightforward, the effectiveness of the promotion of the crusade relied on two related elements. The shock of the loss of Jerusalem and the Holy Cross was heightened by the images of both being so familiar. Western audiences, primed by Scripture, liturgy, songs, popular stories, sculpture, stained glass, relics and the travellers' tales of returning pilgrims, could easily feel personal engagement, involvement and hence responsibility, emotions crusade publicists took care to encourage. The enormous twelfth-century popularity of Jerusalem as a pilgrimage destination encouraged identification with the place that went beyond liturgical metaphors, biblical narratives or western images, models and imitations of the Holy Sepulchre. Acquaintance with the Christian history of the Holy City and particularly the True Cross was reflected in the adoption in the west in the twelfth century of the name Heraclius, commemorating the Byzantine emperor who in AD 630 restored to Jerusalem the fragment of the cross captured by the Persians, a highly relevant historical precedent after 1187.[15] Confronted with Saladin's alleged atrocities, engagement translated horror into guilt, anger and a sense of collective duty, sentiments propaganda sought to direct. The effect was registered throughout western Christendom in hundreds if not thousands of charters drawn up for departing crusaders by monks to whom they had given or mortgaged their property for the good of their souls and, usually, for some ready cash to allow them, as the documents explicitly state, to depart for Jerusalem.

Exhortation and admonition in official letters, sermons and propagandist tracts remained consistent. The destruction of the kingdom of Jerusalem, Saladin's capture of the Holy City and, especially, the loss of the True Cross represented a disaster of biblical proportions, redeemable only by individual and collective repentance. The rhetorical themes elevated the pragmatic to the transcendent. In a tract designed to accelerate preparations, Henry of Albano declared the cross 'the ark of the vassal of the Lord, the ark of the New Testament', 'the glory of the Christian people, the remedy of sin, the care of the wounded, the restorer of health'.[16] The image of the cross dominated written and spoken appeals, Henry of Albano's formulae being mirrored, at times verbatim, by others, such as Peter of Blois, Archbishop Baldwin's secretary, one of the most insistent crusade publicists. The language of the liturgy jostled with that of the Old Testament, the Eucharist with the Psalms and the Maccabees. 'Christ's blood cries out for help,' proclaimed Peter of Blois.[17] The crusade was carefully and closely identified with spiritual renewal. Specifically this process was associated with voluntary poverty and amendment of life. One contemporary preacher of the cross, Alan of Lille, emphasized that the poverty being praised by propagandists implied spiritual humility, not economic destitution. He made this clear by citing the version of the Sermon on the Mount Beatitudes in Matthew 5:3, 'blessed are the poor in spirit', not the socially more radical Luke 6:20 ('blessed are you poor; for yours is the kingdom of Heaven').[18] The sumptuary regulations in *Audita Tremendi*, published by Henry of Albano in Germany and Henry II in England in 1188, underlined the thrust of the preaching, directed at prosperous audiences and aimed at moral regeneration, not social reform or redistribution of wealth. Adopting simple dress could be a gesture of reform only for those used to fine clothes, not an option for paupers and beggars. The repeated themes were of penance, not vainglory, humility of spirit, not in an embrace of indigence but a rejection of the mentality of wealth. As Gregory VIII put it, 'we are not saying "give up the things you have" but "send them off to the heavenly barn and entrust them to God"'.[19] Such entreaties became more urgent as political in-fighting delayed the departure of the crusade in 1189 and 1190. However, presenting this mixture of obligation and opportunity for Christian renewal through the recovery of the Holy Land was not left to metaphor. Repeated emphasis on Saladin's violence, the fate of the vanquished of Hattin, as captives or, like Reynald of Châtillon, martyrs, and the desecration of the Holy Places firmly located the forthcoming struggle in the temporal as well as spiritual sphere.

The process of disseminating the message was carefully managed. The designated papal legates recruited local ecclesiastics to proselytize their own regions. Not least this helped bridge the language barrier. Henry of Albano, legate to the Germans, reputedly knew no German.[20] Interpreters were essential members of any preaching team in alien country, whether at Mainz in 1188 or on Archbishop Baldwin's Welsh tour, when the archdeacon of Bangor performed the job.[21] Occasionally, and perhaps for the same reason, laymen were recruited to speak, as, it was later recorded, in Denmark, where Esbern, brother of the Slav-bashing archbishop of Lund, stirred his fellow nobles by evoking their Viking past, the glory of which nonetheless paled in comparison with 'the greater and more profitable conquests' of holy war.[22] Partially hidden networks of affinity underpinned the operation. Both Henry of Albano and Baldwin of Canterbury were former Cistercian abbots. Their order played a distinctive role in fostering crusade enthusiasm at this time by devising special regular prayers for *crucesignati* included in their liturgical round. Perhaps not unconnected, in the lands of the French king, Cistercians managed to win exemption from the crusade tax.

Besides official ecclesiastical support, political, social and personal contacts exerted similar pressure. After the meeting at Gisors in January 1188, the English and French kings agreed to levy a special tax of 10 per cent on movables, soon nicknamed the Saladin Tithe. The process of collecting this tax, which seems to have begun in the spring of 1188, spread the news of the enterprise perhaps more effectively than any grandiose preaching campaign. The great Paris assembly in March 1188, at which the Tithe was authorized in Philip II's lands, was attended by large numbers of clergy, nobles and an 'innumerable multitude' of knights and commoners.[23] Given that those who had taken the cross were exempted for payment, the tax may also have proved a highly effective recruiting agent. One departing crusader from the Dauphiné in the foothills of the Alps referred more generally to the 'magna mota', the great movement, of the Jerusalem expedition, suggesting a similarly wide exchange of information through the networks of trade, social dialogue and travel.[24]

The ears of the great were repeatedly bent by crusade enthusiasts. Especially vulnerable were those, such as Henry II, who could be accused of procrastination. Peter of Blois, who had first alerted the Angevin court to the shocked reaction of the papal Curia to the news of Hattin in September 1187, composed a series of exhortatory crusade pamphlets. In 1188–9, he spent much time at the king's side. In the spring of 1189, Peter witnessed a private encounter between King Henry and the abbot of Bonneval in which the abbot lamented the delays in sending any troops to the Holy Land despite the practical difficulties – essentially the problems of kingship in a wicked world – Henry self-pityingly outlined. The abbot's criticism merely echoed more public denunciations of back-sliding and internecine political squabbling, for example, by the legate Henry of Albano.[25] The effectiveness of such personal approaches on Henry cannot easily be assessed, as he died shortly afterwards, in July 1189.

News of Hattin and the loss of Jerusalem had overcome Henry's quarter-century equivocation over the Holy Land and his innate dislike of being told his military duty by the church. During the visit to the west of Heraclius of Jerusalem in 1185, Henry privately expostulated, 'these clerks can incite us boldly to arms and danger since they themselves will receive no blows in the struggle, nor will they undertake any burdens which they can avoid'.[26] Many had failed to answer the increasingly urgent appeals from Jerusalem for aid in the 1180s, so Henry was probably not alone in harbouring such doubts. Ralph Niger, a well-connected close observer of these events in northern France and a critic of Outremer before 1187, doubted the spiritual benefit of an armed crusade without a prior, commensurate spiritual transformation amongst western crusaders.[27] However, such objections became untenable in the face of both the news from Outremer and the subsequent propaganda campaign.

Successful recruitment depended on secular support. William II of Sicily had set the tone for his people by adopting a hair shirt and shutting himself away for four days, as well as commissioning a fleet to provide immediate aid for Outremer.[28] Inevitably, papal letters and legates were directed at royal courts, where their reception determined the scale of the response. In Denmark, there were some significant naval contributions, possibly concentrated in the ports of southern Jutland nearest to the Frisians with whom many of them sailed. However, without Canute VI taking the cross, noble commitment was modest, one source identifying only fifteen crusaders 'whose hearts God specially touched'.[29] The five nobles who actually embarked were all close associates of the king, and so presumably enjoyed his approval. Similarly, across the border in Norway, the leader of the small Norwegian force, Ulf of Lauvnes, was a royal favourite, but the lack of King Sverre's participation restricted aristocratic engagement. The picture appeared the same in Scotland, where William the Lion avoided entanglement in an operation led by his overbearing southern neighbour. As a consequence, only a handful of Scottish royal courtiers and officials took the cross, led by Robert of Quincy, himself of Anglo-Norman ancestry.[30]

In none of these northern European countries was preaching widespread, partly because its function was primarily to confirm existing enthusiasms rather than to stir up enthusiasm from scratch. In Germany, France and England the extensive preaching campaigns followed demonstrations of overt royal commitment, on the pattern of Louis VII and Bernard of Clairvaux in 1146. The main preaching agents were not only close to the monarch but were actively engaged in the wider organization of the enterprise. Bishop Godfrey of Würzburg, a count in his own right (of Helfenstein), followed his preaching efforts in early 1188 with a central role in diplomatic preparations and later in the conduct of the eastern expedition which he accompanied, to die at Antioch in July 1190. In England Archbishop Baldwin led the preaching, not, as it proved, for any particular oratorical skill but as the embodiment of both secular and ecclesiastical authority. Like Godfrey of Würzburg, Baldwin was committed to undertake the crusade. One of his companions recalled soon after how, on 10 April 1188, in a steep and difficult valley near Caernavon, Baldwin ordered his party to dismount and march on foot 'in intention at least rehearsing what we thought we would experience when we went on our pilgrimage to Jerusalem'.[31] Like Bishop Godfrey, Archbishop Baldwin gave his life to the crusade, dying at the siege of Acre in November 1190.

While the impact of the preaching of the Third Crusade was spectacular, it presumed prior acceptance of the message being promoted. Preaching provided ceremonial confirmation of pledges already agreed and created the conditions in which preparation, planning and recruitment could be achieved with the maximum public consent. Preaching rarely created a spontaneous response. By taking the cross the *crucesignatus* not only acquired exemptions from repayment of debts, paying the crusade tax and answering certain law suits but also gave a solemn promise to fulfil the vow, in theory enforceable through canon law. The high chances of death on crusade and the need to convert income into capital, commonly through sale or mortgage of property, required careful consideration and consultation not least with other family members. Conjugal rights also could not, in theory, be ignored nor the very real dangers to life, limb and possessions to which abandoned crusaders' wives, widows and heiresses were liable. Numerous uplifting moral anecdotes, known as *exempla*, concerned the obtaining of family agreement before the irrevocable adoption of the cross. On a social as well as political level, the crusade sermon and the ritual of giving the cross constituted an act of recognition as much as inspiration.

Tricks of theatre and stagecraft were necessary if the ritual was to work as it should, ceremonially conveying a religious and political message of identity and mutual commitment. The rhetoric's effect relied on the audience being primed by expectation, through prior advertisement, and a barrage of oratorical devices, from the lurid atrocity stories, to the metaphorical exploitation of the image of the cross, to powerful verbal refrains. The *exempla*, according to an Anglo-Norman preaching manual of a generation later, were designed to attract listeners' attention and prevent boredom as well as inspiring contrition.[32] The customary liturgical setting for the sermon was provided by the mass, with its concentration on the sufferings of Christ, the cross and repentance. Conveniently, in 1187–8 preaching coincided with the seasons of Christocentric festivals of Christmas and Easter, and the penitential period of Lent. Before the Second Crusade, Louis VII had announced his desire to go to the Holy Land at Christmas 1145, Bernard of Clairvaux preached at Vézelay at Easter 1146 and Conrad III took the cross at Christmas 1146, occasions not forced by events as in 1187–8.

If the timing and ceremonial setting were carefully chosen, so were the props. Congregations were accustomed to understand wordless messages, such as those conveyed by relics. When Philip II of France finally left on crusade in June 1190, he received the scrip and staff of a pilgrim at the royal abbey church of St Denis in front of an array of relics that encouraged all present to pray not just to the saints on show but also to the Virgin May and to Christ Himself 'for the deliverance of the Holy Land'.[33] The transcendent was a potent presence. Fragments of the True Cross had proved popular since the First Crusade. Crucifixes, increasingly prominent in the rituals of the mass in the twelfth century, probably served as well, reflecting the centrality of the cross in Third Crusade propaganda. In Wales during Lent 1188, the preachers shared a cross that each handed to the next member of the team when it was their turn to speak.[34] More striking visual aids may have been employed, although testimony comes only from two Muslim observers. According to the well-informed Iraqi historian Ibn al-Athir (1160–1233), a picture was circulated in the west showing Christ being struck in the face by an Arab. Saladin's friend and chief judge in his army, Baha' al-Din Ibn Shaddad, recorded that Conrad of Montferrat, whose timely appearance had saved Tyre in July 1187, commissioned a large painting of Jerusalem showing a Muslim cavalryman trampling over the Holy Sepulchre on which his horse was urinating. 'This picture he publicised overseas in the markets and assemblies, as the priests, bareheaded and dressed in sackcloth, paraded it, crying doom and destruction.'[35] Both Muslim writers strongly disapproved of such representational religious art, which may be why they mentioned these pictures. But Ibn Shaddad accurately commented that 'images affect [Christians'] hearts, for they are essential to their religion'. If used, such large illustrated screens would have provided telling support for the preachers' message to audiences already well versed in how to read sacred wall paintings and stained glass, although they may have been startled and impressed by the pictures' immediacy and direct relevance.

A full array of persuasive artifice was displayed on Archbishop Baldwin's Lenten tour of Wales from 2 March to 23 April 1188 as described by one of its leading members, the royal clerk Gerald of Wales, prolific chronicler, ethnographer, polemicist and frustrated careerist, whose *Journey through Wales*, drafted within months of the event, served the dual function of historical account and immediate crusade propaganda.[36] As with many crusade preaching campaigns, Baldwin's mission combined ecclesiastical and secular politics with its religious purpose. By celebrating mass in each of the Welsh cathedrals, Baldwin was asserting the authority of Canterbury over an independent-minded and occasionally recalcitrant provincial church. Involving the Welsh princes in the crusade restricted their capacity to cause trouble in the event of the king of England's absence as well as publicly binding them into the English royal polity. When Owain Cyfeiliog 'alone of all the Welsh princes' failed to present himself to take the cross he was excommunicated. The meticulous organization reflected these multiple purposes. Magnates and bishops were visited in turn, and, given the frequency with which local leaders met the archbishop's party on entering their territory, almost certainly by pre-arrangement. Gryffydd ap Cynan of Gwynedd even apologized for being late. The preaching of the cross formed a central part of the wider plan. Once they were *crucesignati*, the Welsh princes were obliged to support Henry II's crusade, a role of potential subservience that the Scottish nobility studiously and successfully avoided.

In his characteristically self-regarding style, Gerald frankly admitted the careful stage-management and theatrical manipulation of the preaching and cross-taking ceremonies. He recalled the role he played at New Radnor on 4 March after the archbishop's opening sermon of the tour:

I myself who have written these words, was the first to stand up. I threw myself at the holy man's feet and devoutly took the sign of the cross. It was the urgent admonition given some time before by the King which inspired me to give this example to the others, and the persuasion and oft-repeated promises of the archbishop and the Chief Justiciar [Ranulf Glanvill, himself a *crucesignatus*], who never tired of repeating the King's words . . . In doing so I gave strong encouragement to the others and an added incentive to what they had just been told.

Gerald later confessed that the king had added the *douceur* of promising to pay his crusade expenses.[37] The essential manoeuvre was to set an example, to show the rest of the congregation what to do, as Adhemar of Le Puy had done at Clermont in 1095. Directing crowd psychology was important. Gerald's taking the cross was thus premeditated, not at all dependent on the quality of Baldwin's sermon, an experience that was unlikely to have been unusual in 1188 even if the part played by the greatest in the land was.

Although local interpreters were employed, what was actually preached may have mattered less than how and by whom it was spoken. The language of third-party descriptions of crusade sermons in 1187–8 across Europe stressed the formality of proceedings, rather like the Latin liturgy itself. Gerald's personal testimony confirms this. His greatest popular success at Haverfordwest on 23 March provoked over 200 to adopt the cross, yet he preached in Latin and French, which many of his audience could not understand. The force of delivery apparently counted for more than the detailed content of the speech. After Archbishop Baldwin's address had flopped, Gerald, on being handed the portable cross as a prop, roused his audience to surge forward to take the cross in three carefully contrived rhetorical climaxes. A resentful wife of one of those who took the cross by being caught up in this crowd enthusiasm later allegedly complained of Gerald's bewitching 'soft words' and 'simple looks' without which her husband and the rest 'would have got clear off, as far as the preaching of the others was concerned'.[38]

However incomprehensible the actual words, the ceremonial religious context underlined the message. On one level, as indicated in Gregory VIII's *Audita Tremendi*, preaching the cross was a general call to repent. For Baldwin's team, as for Henry of Albano and Godfrey of Würzburg in Germany, this penitential purpose matched the season of

Lent. The archbishop's sermon at Chester on Easter Day, 17 April, marked the climax of the Welsh part of his tour. Other festival days with special appropriateness were also set aside by preachers of the Third Crusade to reinforce the ubiquitous symbolism and cult of Jerusalem and the cross: 14 September, Holy Cross Day, or 'Laetare Jerusalem' Sunday, chosen by Henry of Albano for Frederick Barbarossa's 'court of Christ' and by Philip II for his Paris assembly in March 1188.[39] Crusade sermons were often placed immediately after the celebration of mass, whose elements of confession and penance feature prominently in Gerald's account. The concentration on the figure, passion and redemptive nature of Christ Crucified within the mass provided the closest association with the aims of crusade sermons and the rituals for adopting the cross. More precisely, a sermon delivered immediately after the mass invited audiences to choose to follow or reject Christ in the very presence of His body and blood, the consecrated and, as was increasingly believed, transubstantiated elements of the Eucharist. (The doctrine of transubstantiation, insisting on the real presence of Christ's body and blood in the Eucharist, while previously widely accepted by academics and others, only became the official teaching of the Roman Catholic church at the Fourth Lateran Council in 1215.) Where no mass preceded the preaching, as on Anglesey on 11 April, the General Confession was recited, as it had been at Clermont in 1095. For some recruits, such as a group of criminals – 'robbers, highwaymen and murderers' – at Usk, adopting the cross was likened to a form of conversion.[40] An aura of sanctity, at least in remembrance, attended the expedition, Gerald recording a number of miracles of healing associated with spots where the cross had been preached as well as littering his narrative with miraculous and uplifting anecdotes.[41]

Although Gerald omitted any details of the content of his or the archbishop's sermons, as opposed to their delivery, something of their nature may be drawn from contemporary tracts, such as those by Peter of Blois and the papal legate Henry of Albano. Their form is suggested by Gerald's description of his address at Haverfordwest, which employed repeated climaxes to stir his audience into successive waves of enthusiasm. A generation later, an English preaching manual, known as the *Ordinatio de predicatione Sancti Crucis in Angliae* (*The Ordinance for Preaching the Holy Cross in England*, c.1216), indicated how this effect was achieved. Exempla were used liberally to attract the audience's attention, sometimes through alarming moral stories, such as the nasty one used by Gerald of the mother who overlay and smothered her beloved little son as God's punishment for trying to prevent her husband joining the crusade. Complex theology was conveyed through simple images, metaphors and references to familiar cults, such as that of the Virgin Mary, or even parallels with everyday life. In the *Ordinatio* the cross is portrayed as confirming salvation 'as if by charter', just like any ordinary land deal, except that the estate was 'the inheritance of Christ'. Much of the material for sermons, as for propaganda pamphlets, comprised a series of meditations on the allegorical significance of Christ, the cross, the Crucifixion, the paradox of life though death, the snares of fleshly delight and the spiritual rewards of the *crucesignatus*. Unlike many later sermon collections, the English *Ordinatio* includes a model address, 'the Call to Men to Take the Cross', clearly designed for a lay audience: the punchlines of some of its *exempla*, drawn from edifying exploits of earlier crusaders, are in the French vernacular. The sermon is structured around a single, simple message, repeated in a variety of different ways and punctuated by variants on the traditional crusade refrain 'Arise, therefore, take up my (sic) cross and follow me' (Matthew 16:24) modified to fit the preceding *exemplum*. Thus, the dreadful pun of the Englishman Hugh of Beauchamp's supposed last words on the field of Hattin, 'Although my name is Beauchamp, I was never in *beau champ* (i.e. paradise) until today', is followed by the preacher's exhortation 'Arise so that you may come to the *beau champ*.'[42] Gerald of Wales's Haverfordwest sermon probably employed very similar techniques. Each anecdote and refrain feeds a central message, the repetition of phrases, especially if accompanied by audience responses, inducing an almost trance-like enthusiasm in large congregations.

Another *crucesignatus* of 1188–9, the English royal official and chronicler Roger of Howden, who, unlike Gerald, actually went to the Holy Land, recorded exactly such a populist poetical sermon-lament devised by a cleric, Berthier of Orléans, who may possibly be identified with a clerk working at the French court in Philip II's chancery. The verses confirm the ubiquity of the message being drummed into audiences across Christendom. Familiar themes are rehearsed: vengeance for the insult to Christ; an attack on soft-living; the loss of the True Cross, 'the ark of the New Testament'; the obligation on believers to recover it; the association with the Eucharistic sacrifice; the debt laid up by the

Redeemer's Crucifixion; the call to 'take up your cross'. At each separate stage in the poem-sermon comes the refrain: 'The wood of the cross, the banner of the chief, the army follows, which has never given way, but has gone before in the strength of the Holy Spirit.'[43] The psychological impact of such relentless propaganda cannot be measured, but was widely felt. The same moral tone of shame, self-sacrifice and chivalry directed on the gaining of paradise, not earthly reward, suffuses a song composed in 1188 or 1189 by Conon of Béthune, an important Picard lord who fought on both the Third and Fourth Crusades.[44] Otho of Trazegnies in Hainault, in making a pious donation to his local monastery prior to embarking for the east, declared his journey was 'to avenge the insult to God'.[45] However delivered, the message was received.

RECRUITMENT AND FINANCE

Recruitment and finance formed part of a single process of converting enthusiasm into action. The assemblies at Geddington in February and Paris in March 1188 discussed arrangements for taking the cross and the administration of the Saladin Tithe together. The source of funding influenced the construction of the armies. In Germany, Frederick tried to insist that each crusader should pay his own way, placing the emphasis for organizing recruitment and recruits firmly in the hands of local magnates and urban communities beyond the king's own extensive military entourage, for which he paid out of his own resources, possibly supplemented by a tax on Jews and a form of hearth tax levied on royal lands.[46] However, the bulk of his huge force, which some estimated at 20,000 knights and 80,000 infantry, was not raised or funded directly by the crown, perhaps a factor in its disintegration when Frederick himself died before the Holy Land was reached. Similarly, the failure of Philip II of France to collect the Saladin Tithe and his limited authority outside his own royal lands restricted his personal contingent to the 2,000 knights and squires for whom he negotiated a transport contract with Genoa in 1190. The rest of the large French contribution came from provincial nobles and other lords. By contrast, Richard I's access to large sums from the Saladin Tithe and his own fundraising ploys in 1189–90 allowed him to command a royal army numbering perhaps 6,000, while subsidizing a fleet of over 100 ships that may have carried almost 9,000 soldiers and sailors, some of whom, at least, were in the king's direct pay, 'retained', as one of Richard's officials later put it.[47] Just as an English expatriate in France, Ralph Niger, noted the difference in the nature and level of fundraising between the German and western monarchs, so a German observer paid tribute to the lavish scale of the English king's preparations and finances.[48] The ability before and during any crusade campaign to convert what in theory constituted a volunteer army into a paid or retained force added enormously to its cohesion and the authority of the paymaster. Philip II increased his hold over the disparate French contingents at Messina at Christmas 1190 when he provided large subsidies to the duke of Burgundy (1,000 marks) and the count of Nevers (600 marks). On arrival in the Holy Land in 1191 Richard I and Philip II competed in offering wages to unattached troops, Richard's deeper pockets winning the day. This secured Richard's dominance of the ensuing Palestine campaign, for which he financially bailed out the count of Champagne and slipped 5,000 marks to the commander of the remaining French troops, Duke Hugh of Burgundy.[49]

The Saladin Tithe exerted another direct impact on patterns of recruitment. As the tax was designed to aid *crucesignati*, they were exempt. Hearing this, claimed Roger of Howden, himself a *crucesignatus*, 'all the rich men of his (Henry II's) lands, both clergy and laity, rushed in crowds to take the cross'.[50] In addition to the now customary crusader privileges, they could expect not just the tax exemption but also the proceeds from their non-crusading vassals and tenants. These could be lucrative and consequently could become subject to legal dispute. An East Anglian *crucesignatus*, Robert of Cokefield, unsuccessfully tried to appropriate the tithe from two manors he held as a life tenant from the abbey of Bury St Edmunds. The abbot may have been especially alert to the legal niceties as he had been refused permission to take the cross in February 1188 by Henry II despite appearing before the king brandishing a cloth cross, needle and thread.[51] For the non-crusader, the Saladin Tithe was bitterly resented, partly because of its unprecedented rate of 10 per cent on movables (i.e. surplus income after essentials had been paid for). Partly, too, because it fell equally on church as on lay lands, challenging vociferous ecclesiastical sensitivities over immunities and separation from the secular state. Given the lack of immediate moves to set off for the east, some taxpayers suspected the eagerness of the habitually rapacious Angevin government to collect the tax; it was no coincidence that the Saladin Tithe provided a model for subsequent lucrative extraordinary taxes. Collectors' misappropriation and individual peculation left a sour taste.[52]

In most regions of Europe, no such direct incentive existed. Even in France, Philip II, despite gaining agreement to the Saladin Tithe from the large assembly of clerics, nobles and knights at Paris in March 1188, was forced to cancel the grant the following year and even apologize for having introduced it in the first place.[53] Some tax collection did occur. The count of Nevers, the king's cousin, imposed a levy of 12d a house in his lands, but this may not have been part of the Saladin Tithe. It was a fixed-sum, not fixed-rate, tax, was imposed only after negotiation with the local clergy and nobility and made no mention of exemption for *crucesignati*.[54] Here, as in most places, the material pressures to take the cross operated in line with lordship, kinship and community. Although the surviving evidence overwhelmingly derives from the propertied classes, those lower down the economic and social scale were unlikely to be able to fund themselves. One English crusader assumed that those who set out shared their tears with 'their household servants (*familiaribus*), relatives and friends'.[55] The provisions of Gregory VIII's bull, the Saladin Tithe and the French debt and mortgage ordinance of March 1188 assumed that crusaders, typically 'clerks, knights and sergeants (*servientes*)', had property to dispose of, otherwise the details about raising money would be redundant. Under the Saladin Tithe, crusaders were to receive the tithe receipts from 'their lands and their men'.[56] Frederick Barbarossa's insistence on his followers being of a certain material sufficiency suggests the same. Not only did the poor not take the cross, lacking the economic or legal freedom to do so, many who did were prevented from departing by subsequent poverty. An inquiry into the non-fulfilment of crusade vows conducted in Lincolnshire in England a decade after the Third Crusade found that for twenty out of twenty-nine named *crucesignati* the cause of default was poverty.[57] So, whether or not tax avoidance was available, the reality of crusade recruitment rested on the ability to pay or be paid for, from monarchs down to prosperous peasant farmers and urban and rural artisans.

This failed to do much to inhibit the scale of recruitment. From the Baltic to the Mediterranean observers noted the extraordinary response. 'Enthusiasm for the new pilgrimage was such that already [1188] it was not a question of who had received the cross but of who had not yet done so.'[58] Recruiting fanned out from the great assemblies at Gisors, Mainz and Paris early in 1188, mainly propelled by the lords and their retinues, with the active encouragement of secular clergy and monasteries which, as on earlier crusades, supplied important financial resources in the way of cash in return for gifts and mortgages of property. While preaching provided the focus, in towns, cities and the courts of nobles, rumour and word of mouth created a public mood, the Dauphinois crusader's 'great movement' ('magna mota').[59] Peer group pressure and the fear of shame inevitably acted as effective recruiting officers. Poets cast those who failed to answer the call as 'recreants and cowards'. Chroniclers, perhaps in similarly imaginative vein, noted that waverers received 'wool and distaff' as a hint that any who remained 'were only fit for women's work'.[60] Wives and mothers added their voices to the chorus, perhaps the most persuasive of all. As a sign of commitment, some recruits wore hair shirts (often, like Abbot Samson of Bury, making sure that everybody around them knew), abstained from meat and followed the simple dress code laid down by the sumptuary laws instituted by Gregory VIII's bull and repeated in sermons and local legislation during the following three years. While reflecting an element of theatrical showing-off, such sartorial demonstrations helped create and sustain the atmosphere of engagement.

That said, it must be recognized that the impression of, in Arnold of Lübeck's words, 'rich and poor as one' demonstrating a universal adherence to the crusade may mislead.[61] Many who took the cross in 1188 out of sudden emotion or careful calculation abandoned their vows 'having saluted Jerusalem from afar', as one English monk acidly observed.[62] Many others did not take the cross at all, including William Marshal, who famously made a whole career out of the pursuit of courtliness and chivalry. He preferred to remain at home with his new, rich wife and a job in Richard I's regency government. In mitigation, he had only recently returned from two years in Outremer (1184–6). However, his failure to sign up in 1188–9, when he was close to Henry II, points to the exercise of common sense in response to the crusade. Especially in the entourage of monarchs, such a defining commitment was not undertaken indiscriminately. Life and politics in western Europe were not suspended. In Germany and Italy, Barbarossa's son and viceroy, Henry VI, vigorously pursued his claim, through his wife, to the kingdom of Naples and Sicily, while his opponents, led by adherents of the exiled duke of Saxony, Henry the Lion, encouraged revolt. In France and England, despite crusade preparations beginning in the first months of 1188, deteriorating relations between Philip II and Henry II increasingly took precedence in 1188–9. This culminated in a damaging war over the succession to Angevin lands between Henry and his son Richard of Poitou, vigorously supported by Philip II. All three were *crucesignati*. Once Richard departed on crusade in 1190, his brother John schemed to control the government, which was being run by bureaucrats, many of whom had taken the cross in 1188 only to be released by the pope in 1189 on account of their important civil office.[63] The king's crusade failed to prevent a sharp tussle for power that led to the overthrow of Richard's Chancellor, William Longchamp, in 1191. Although the personal involvement of ruling monarchs drew with them much of their ruling elites and many of their officials, many remained. Central and local administration continued. The bulk of the lay and clerical populations stayed put. The crusade was profoundly interesting for some; a matter of indifference to others. Not all contemporary chroniclers appeared obsessed with it. In England, monastic writers such as Gervase, sacrist of Christ Church Canterbury, or Jocelyn of Brakelond at Bury St Edmund's, only recorded concern with the crusade when it impinged on their religious houses. Gervase was, in retrospect at least, positively hostile, blaming Archbishop Baldwin, a particular *bête noire*, for the onerous Saladin Tithe and portraying his Welsh tour as a jaunt devised to avoid facing messy litigation with the Canterbury monks. Gervase gave events in the east in 1190–92 short shrift and, with hindsight, described the whole venture as 'unfortunate'.[64] Commitment to the crusade was frequently proportionate rather than consuming.

Recruitment for the Third Crusade was distinguished by the leadership of monarchs and their ability to secure their nobilities behind the enterprise to a degree surpassing even the Second Crusade. Secular governmental power in each kingdom – royal, comital and urban – reinforced or subsumed the ecclesiastical mechanisms for recruitment, most notably in the Angevin lands, especially in England. There, from an early stage, the relatively centralized royal administration took over all aspects of crusade planning and operation. The commitment of monarchs, while facilitating recruitment and material provision, extended the notion and traditions of good lordship to the enterprise, a visible expression of the moral dimension of rule that lay at the heart of consensual authority.

Lacking coercive force, twelfth-century kings relied on their subjects' acceptance of the mutual benefits of their rule. Leadership of such an unequivocally praiseworthy and virtuous cause as the crusade enormously enhanced the scope for kings to display the transcendent aspects of their position and, thereby, demand the respect and support of their subjects. Practical limits remained. Frederick Barbarossa could use the crusade to demonstrate his pre-eminence in German politics and impose a national peace on political factions, represented by the negotiated exile of the dissident Henry the Lion. However, in return he was expected to subsidize his own crusade himself. Similarly, Philip II of France could command the almost universal support of the church and the regional counts of France in 1188 for the crusade as such, but he could not impose the Saladin Tithe. Suspicion of novel fiscal exactions proved stronger than political trust. An essential ingredient in establishing moral leadership was the public, personal obligation created by taking the cross. That was why the ceremonies at Gisors and Mainz were so important. They bound the royal *crucesignati* to the crusade in a contract with church and people that only action could fulfil or papal absolution untie. Henry II of England well understood the implications of such a commitment, which was one reason he had avoided it for twenty-five years.

The tangible result of royal participation was early demonstrated in Sicily. To William II's rapid action in sending a fleet to the Holy Land in 1188 some attributed the survival of the remaining Christian outposts. Yet despite his display of formal grief and mourning on hearing of the catastrophe of Hattin, William did not take the cross. Although he may have discussed a joint enterprise with his brother-in-law Henry II, William seemed not to have organized his nobility for the crusade. By his death, in November 1189, no firm undertakings had been reached by the king or his nobles. In the ensuing power struggle, his eventual successor, his dwarfish illegitimate cousin Tancred of Lecce, recalled the Sicilian fleet from the Levant. The only residual Sicilian involvement in the crusade lay in William's lavish, if perhaps fanciful, bequest to Henry II of grain, wine, money, gold plate and a hundred galleys equipped for two years. This may have represented what William imagined he would contribute to the crusade. In the event his legacy provided a source of conflict and an opportunity for extortion for Richard I when he arrived in Sicily in the autumn of 1190.[65] The contrast between the Sicilian experience and that of Henry II's Angevin lands was sharp. Even if dissipated in the succession war of 1188–9, by the time of his own death in July 1189, Henry's preparations had raised men and money. Perhaps more importantly, they had committed large sections of the nobility on both sides of the English Channel to the crusade through the collective action of taking the cross. His successor Richard was one of them. Continued Angevin royal and noble interest assured sustained dedication to the crusade. Without the king's lead, the movement would have lost cohesion and drive, as happened in Sicily.

The depth of Angevin engagement was impressive.[66] The inner circle of recruits was drawn from the political and administrative elite; representatives of the higher clergy, led by Archbishop Baldwin and Justiciar Glanvill's nephew, Hubert Walter bishop of Salisbury; powerful nobles such as the earls of Leicester and Ferrers, Nigel of Mowbray and Richard of Clare; former sheriffs, such as Roger Glanvill; ministers, such as Roger's brother, the Justiciar Ranulf, whose sacking in 1189 allowed him to fulfil his vow; royal friends, agents, household officials and government bureaucrats, a number of whom, including Gerald of Wales and the future Justiciar Geoffrey FitzPeter, had their vows absolved unfulfilled. Compared with France or Germany the list of great magnates is short, a reflection of the political structure of the Angevin regime but also a matter of chance; a number of English earldoms had lapsed; others were held by minors. The core of the Angevin recruitment centred on the king's court. Beyond the immediate circle of royal patronage or acquaintance, the characteristic *crucesignati* were local aristocrats, knights and gentry, many with close links to the higher nobility. Fifty-nine *crucesignati* named in the government financial records as exempt from a levy to pay for defence against the Welsh were men of substance from across the whole kingdom, from Sussex to Yorkshire, Wiltshire to Suffolk. For convenience, such knights tended to travel in groups based on tenurial, political, geographic or family association. The collective enthusiasm of taking the cross could persist in action. According to one Yorkshire observer, the massacres of Jews during Lent 1190 at King's Lynn, Stamford and York were led by bands of young crusaders acting together. No less than the followers of the great, local networks survived from recruitment to campaign. At the siege of Acre in 1191, the royal judge and chronicler Roger, the parson of Howden near the Humber in the East Riding of Yorkshire, found a group of fellow countrymen from the region of his parish: John of Hessle, Richard and

Berengar of Legsby, the parson of Croxby, Robert the Huntsman of Pontefract.

Urban as well as rural associations lent structure to recruitment in England as in the rest of western Europe. Ships from London formed a distinct part of the large north European fleet that assembled at Dartmouth in May 1189, taking Silves in Portugal from the Moors that September. The next year at least one ship carrying eighty Londoners followed. These were led by figures from the city's merchant oligarchy, such as Geoffrey the Goldsmith and William FitzOsbert, nicknamed Longbeard, as well as members of the chapter and clergy of St Paul's cathedral. A further source of unity lay in the adoption by these citizens of Thomas Becket, a fellow Londoner, as their patron saint, an illustration of how crusading fed off wider streams of contemporary spirituality. The leading role of beneficed secular clergy among the Londoners was mirrored elsewhere. According to some sources, even monks caught crusade fever, in contradiction of their vows: 'a great number went from the cloister to camp, threw off their cowls, donned mail shirts, and became knights of Christ in a new sense, replacing alms with arms'.[67]

While clerics, beyond their important morale-building religious duties, could expect to act as scribes, accountants, secretaries even quartermasters, the bulk of recruitment was aimed at those, like the 3,000 Welsh recruits described by Gerald of Wales, 'highly skilled in the use of the spear and the arrow, most experienced in military matters and only too keen to attack the enemies of our faith at the first opportunity'.[68] The appeal was not restricted to warriors; many *crucesignati* were artisans: blacksmiths, skinners, tanners, cobblers, tailors, millers, butchers, vintners, potters and bakers, who could, in theory at least, usefully ply their trades on crusade. They were probably joined by genuine non-combatants, pilgrims, but their numbers may not have been overwhelming, especially given the emphasis on professional troops in an attempt to avoid the mistakes of the Second Crusade, where non-combatants had allegedly compromised military efficiency. A final group of recruits were women. The ordinances for the crusade restricted female recruitment to old washerwomen, who doubled as delousers for the troops, 'as good as apes for picking fleas'.[69] However, these provisions were ignored. Women fought at Acre, to the admiration of western sources and the fascinated horror of Arabic ones. In a list of forty-seven Cornish recruits there were at least four *crucesignatae*.[70]

Although England is possibly the best-documented region of Europe for the preparations for the Third Crusade, the pattern revealed there is matched elsewhere, for example in Normandy. If royal authority and money were less pervasive in Capetian France or Hohenstaufen Germany, the role played by the monarchs was just as important. In France, Philip II taking the cross at Gisors in January 1188 provided the cue for almost all the higher nobility of his kingdom to follow suit, their decisions eased as both Philip's Angevin rivals, Henry II and Richard of Poitou, later Richard I, had also signed up. In addition to the counts of Flanders, Blois, Perche, Champagne, Dreux, Clermont, Beaumont, Soissons, Bar and Nevers, who took the cross with the king, other *crucesignati* included the duke of Burgundy and the count of Sancerre. The only significant magnate not to take the cross was Count Raymond V of Toulouse. (Despite his close family ties with the county of Tripoli, Raymond, whose father had died suddenly and some said suspiciously in Palestine during the Second Crusade, was old – dying in 1194 after ruling for forty-six years – and beset by rivalries with Richard of Poitou and the problem of heresy in his dominions.) Lords such as the counts of Flanders, Burgundy and Champagne were effectively autonomous princes. At Gisors this was recognized when it was agreed that followers of Philip II should wear red crosses; those of Henry II, white; and those of the count of Flanders, green.[71] Recruitment followed regional power. All across France from Hainault to Poitou, Normandy to the Dauphiné lords and knights took the cross and began making provisions for departure. Although narrative sources emphasize the role of Richard I and his Anglo-French followers, charter evidence indicates that the contribution from the rest of France may have outstripped it. Whole regions lost their lords. Across the frontier in Limburg, the absence of Duke Henry III and his two sons removed any check to civil unrest and local violence.[72]

The same story was told in the German lands stretching from Flanders to Austria, the Baltic to the Alps. The lead was given by Frederick Barbarossa: 'by his own example he inspired all the young men to fight for Christ'.[73] The urgency and thoroughness of his preparations stimulated recruitment, which, as in 1146–7, constituted the active dimension of the establishment of a general peace under which disputes were settled or postponed, as crusade privileges not only advantaged the *crucesignati* but obliged non-crusaders to respect their rights and property. By May 1189, when the great German army mustered at Regensburg on the Danube, Frederick and his second son, Frederick duke of Swabia, had been joined by seven bishops, an abbot, the duke of Dalmatia, the count of Holland and over twenty counts and margraves from all corners of the *Reich*, from the Low Countries, to Swabia, from Bavaria to Saxony. At much the same time, other German *crucesignati* left by sea, including the counts of Guelders and Altenburg and the landgrave of Thuringia, who was accompanied by a large military household. In the land army, with the magnates marched 'the dreaded and orderly array of *ministeriales* and chosen knights'.[74] *Ministeriales* were a particularly German social group, technically unfree but materially and culturally indistinguishable from free knights. The first to take the cross in Alsace from the local bishop of Strassburg had been 'a certain powerful and active knight called Siegfried, one of count Albert of Dagsburg's *ministeriales*'.[75] Such bonds lent further unity to the army. As in England, urban crusaders played a prominent role. Citizens from Metz accompanied the land army. Eleven ships from Bremen and four from Cologne joined the expeditionary fleets in 1189, which attracted support from Denmark and Frisia as well as the Rhineland, the Low Countries and England. The Cologne flotilla apparently carried as many as 1,500 men and supplies for three years.[76]

These patterns of recruitment across Europe are striking for two reasons; their scale and their cause. The emotions of those who took the cross mixed devotion, anger, adventure, peer-group pressure, escapism, and the insistence of social superiors and employers. The success in mobilizing such huge armies from such a large area testifies to the coherence of the appeal as much as to the efficiency of organization. That organization depended heavily on the leaders, especially the kings. Subsequent disappointments and failures should not colour perceptions of the impulses that raised these massive armies in the first place. One overwhelming emotion for any *crucesignatus*, notable for the prominence it held in crusade sermons, was fear; fear of pain, hardship, alien surroundings, physical torment and likely death. Leopold V duke of Austria sailed from Venice in the autumn of 1190. After wintering in Zara in the Adriatic, he arrived at Acre the following spring. His personal following was modest. A contemporary German chronicler of the Third Crusade named ten chief companions. Of these, nine died, the tenth only surviving after illness.[77] The preachers and propagandists knew what they were talking about. To become a *crucesignatus* was to invite the torments of the cross.

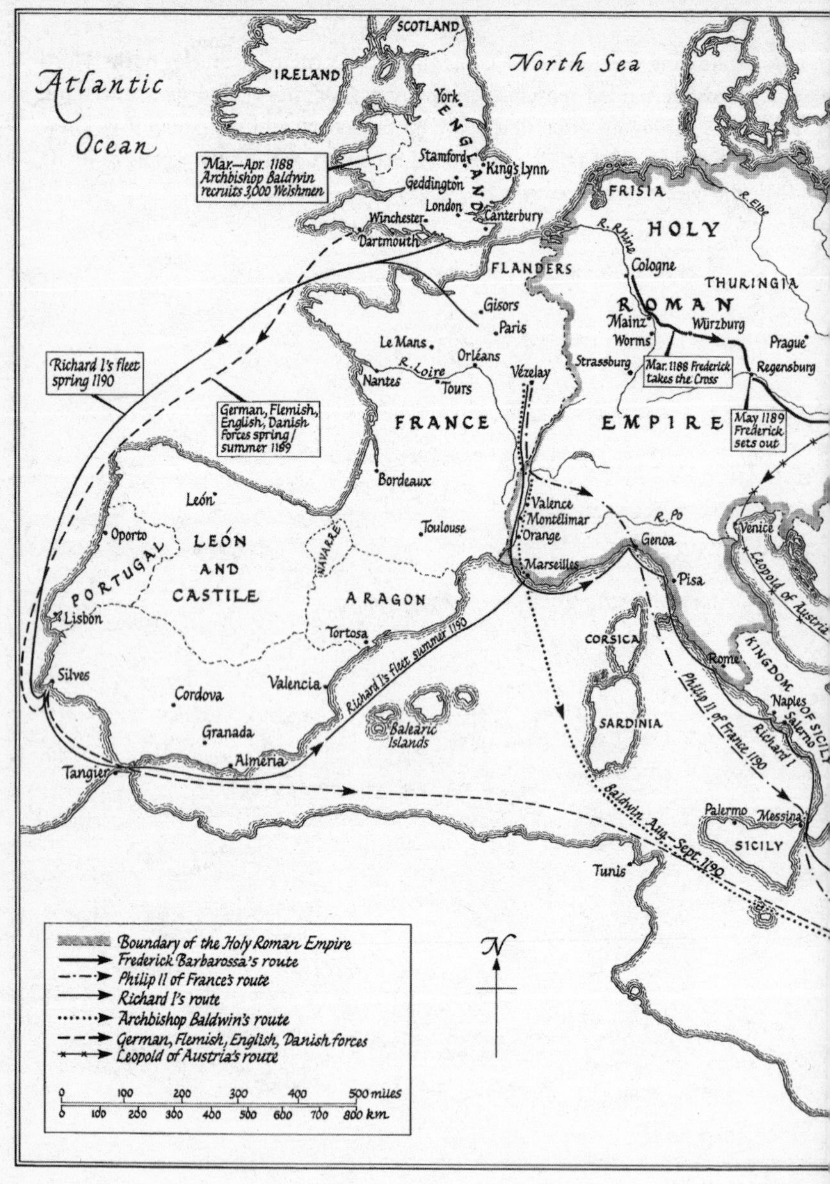
Atlantic Ocean
North Sea
SCOTLAND
IRELAND
York
ENGLAND
Mar.—Apr. 1188 Archbishop Baldwin recruits 3,000 Welshmen
Stamford
King's Lynn
Geddington
London
Canterbury
Winchester
Dartmouth
FRISIA
R. Elbe
R. Rhine
HOLY
ROMAN
EMPIRE
Cologne
THURINGIA
FLANDERS
Gisors
Paris
Mainz
Worms
Würzburg
Prague
Le Mans
Orléans
Strassburg
Mar. 1188 Frederick takes the Cross
Regensburg
Richard I's fleet spring 1190
R. Loire
Nantes
Tours
Vézelay
German, Flemish, English, Danish forces spring/summer 1189
FRANCE
May 1189 Frederick sets out
Bordeaux
León
Valence
Montélimar
Orange
R. Po
Venice
Toulouse
Oporto
PORTUGAL
LEÓN AND CASTILE
NAVARRE
Genoa
Marseilles
Pisa
Leopold of Austria
ARAGON
Lisbon
Tortosa
CORSICA
KINGDOM OF SICILY
Rome
Silves
Valencia
Richard I's fleet summer 1190
Philip II of France 1190
Naples
Salerno
Cordova
Balearic Islands
SARDINIA
Richard I
Granada
Almeria
Tangier
Baldwin Aug.–Sept. 1190
Palermo
Messina
SICILY
Tunis
Boundary of the Holy Roman Empire
Frederick Barbarossa's route
Philip II of France's route
Richard I's route
Archbishop Baldwin's route
German, Flemish, English, Danish forces
Leopold of Austria's route
N
0 100 200 300 400 500 miles
0 100 200 300 400 500 600 700 800 km

11. Europe and the Near East at the Time of the Third Crusade

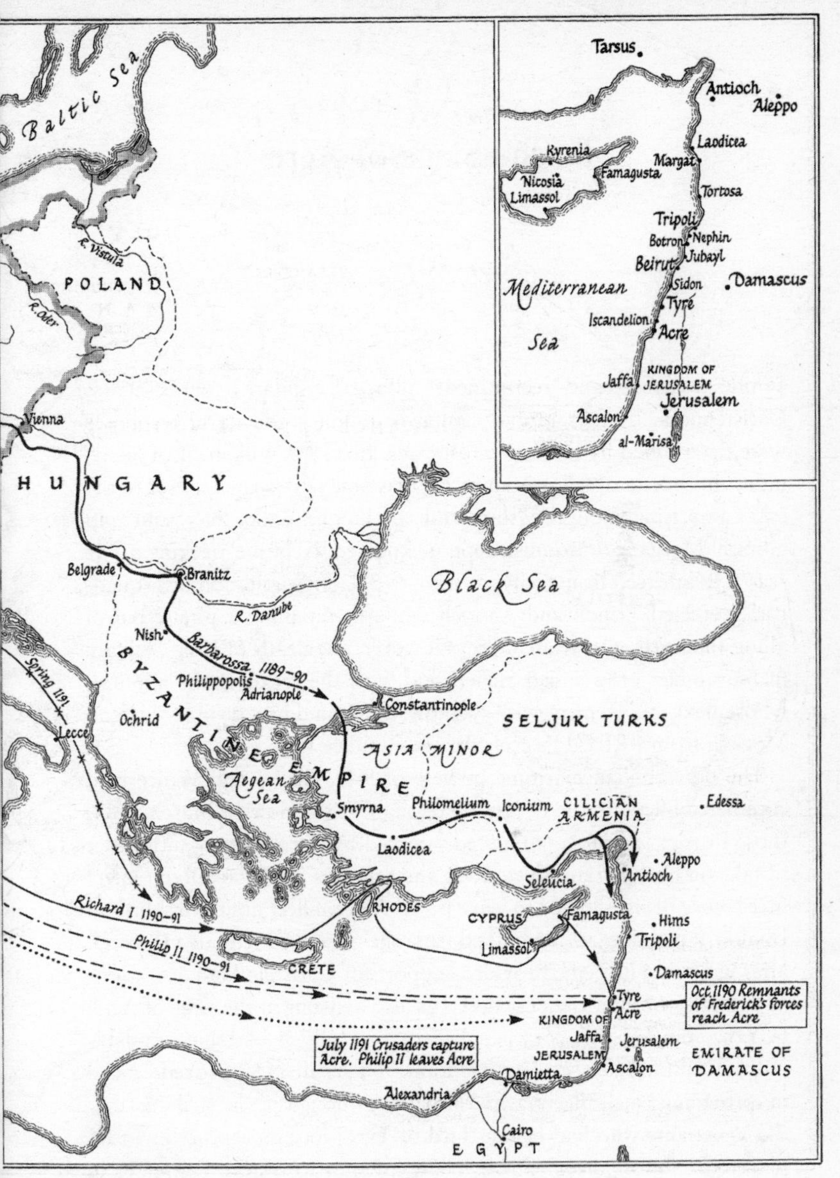

Baltic Sea
R. Vistula
POLAND
R. Oder
Vienna
HUNGARY
Belgrade
Branitz
R. Danube
Nish
Barbarossa 1189–90
BYZANTINE EMPIRE
Philippopolis
Adrianople
Spring 1191
Ochrid
Lecce
Constantinople
Black Sea
SELJUK TURKS
ASIA MINOR
Aegean Sea
Smyrna
Philomelium
Iconium
CILICIAN ARMENIA
Edessa
Laodicea
Seleucia
Antioch
Aleppo
Richard I 1190–91
RHODES
CYPRUS
Famagusta
Hims
Philip II 1190–91
Limassol
Tripoli
CRETE
Damascus
Tyre
Acre
Oct. 1190 Remnants of Frederick's forces reach Acre
KINGDOM OF JERUSALEM
Jaffa
Jerusalem
July 1191 Crusaders capture Acre. Philip II leaves Acre
Ascalon
EMIRATE OF DAMASCUS
Damietta
Alexandria
Cairo
EGYPT
Tarsus
Antioch
Aleppo
Laodicea
Kyrenia
Margat
Nicosia
Famagusta
Limassol
Tortosa
Tripoli
Botron
Nephin
Jubayl
Beirut
Mediterranean Sea
Sidon
Damascus
Tyre
Iscandelion
Acre
KINGDOM OF JERUSALEM
Jaffa
Jerusalem
Ascalon
al-Marisa

13
To the Siege of Acre

While preaching and recruitment followed similar patterns across Christendom, the nature and timing of military and naval responses were determined by local circumstances. In 1188, William II of Sicily, unlike his northern fellow monarchs, was able to despatch a fleet to the east comprising about fifty ships and 200 knights under the resourceful admiral Margarit of Brindisi, soon nicknamed 'Neptune' or 'king of the seas'.[1] Reinforced from Sicily in 1189, to Saladin's irritation this squadron protected Tripoli and Antioch while maintaining a piratic patrol along the northern Syrian shore. However, the death of King William in November 1189 ended Sicilian aid with the recall of the admiral, whose next involvement with the holy war found him trying to defend Messina from Richard I's crusaders in October 1190.

The other Italian maritime powers of Pisa, Genoa and Venice held commercial fleets in the Levant on permanent rotation. In March 1188, those in Alexandria were reputedly forced by the Egyptian authorities to take on board Frankish captives and refugees from the fall of Outremer before being allowed to leave port.[2] A Pisan fleet under Archbishop Ubaldo, a papal legate, embarked from the west at the end of 1188 and, after wintering in Sicily, provided support for Christian land operations in 1189. By 1190, a Genoese fleet was also assisting at the siege of Acre; in 1191 another was contracted to carry Philip II of France and his military entourage east. The retention of Tyre in 1187 proved crucial in providing such fleets with a base, although it is striking that the Venetians, who had held a third of Tyre since its capture in 1124, played an almost invisible role in the attempt to restore Outremer in 1188–92, perhaps because they initially feared their rights in Tyre had been overborne by the city's saviour and protector in 1187–8, Conrad of Montferrat.

By contrast, recruits from the rest of western Christendom had to plan their transport from scratch, even where equipment and supplies were readily available, as with shipping around the North Sea. As a consequence, the Third Crusade constituted a series of distinct but associated expeditions that reached the Holy Land in irregular and uneven waves. Apart from the Sicilians and Pisans, some westerners, such as Geoffrey of Lusignan, King Guy's brother, landed in Palestine and Syria in 1188 or early 1189. Substantial fleets from northern Europe only began to arrive in Palestine in the summer of 1189, followed over the next two years by a more or less constant stream of reinforcements, all, except for the vestigial German force in 1190, by sea. The largest armies were those organized by the monarchs of the west, Frederick Barbarossa, who set out by land in 1189, and Richard I and Philip II, who left together in 1190 using the sea route. The target was Acre. In July 1187, the city had capitulated to Saladin in two days; from August 1189 it took the Christians two years of hard pounding to regain it.[3]

THE SIEGE OF ACRE: CHRISTIAN REVIVAL 1188–90

By the winter of 1187–8, Frankish Outremer lay shattered at Saladin's feet, the few remaining fortresses of the interior without hope of relief and the surviving ports vulnerable to assault, siege and naval blockade. Most were mopped up in the new campaign of 1188. Of the major Frankish cities, only Tripoli, Tyre and Antioch survived in Christian hands. Two of the last castles to hold out, Belvoir and Montréal, surrendered in January and May 1189, leaving Tortosa, Margat and Crac des Chevaliers in the county of Tripoli and, temporarily, Beaufort in northern Galilee outside Saladin's grasp. Although Saladin commissioned works on the *jihad*, such as that by his future biographer Baha' al-Din Ibn Shaddad in May 1188, and constantly reminded his coalition of followers of the transcendent significance of his conquests, his approach was pragmatic.[4] At Antioch in September 1188 he agreed a truce with Bohemund III. On a military and political level he treated the remaining Frankish resisters as he would any other opponent. Confident in his overwhelming supremacy, Saladin was prepared to negotiate their surrender. If diplomacy failed, crushing force was at hand.

However, this strength was not absolute. Crucially, after failing to capture Tyre in July 1187 because of the unexpected arrival there of Conrad of Montferrat from Byzantium, Saladin was unable to press home the siege he began in November 1187. Accompanied only by a single ship's company of knights, a few score at most, Conrad brought leadership, determination, energy and optimism to the defence of Tyre. Saladin's move northwards at the start of 1188 left a vital Palestinian port in Christian hands, a haven for Frankish refugees and a base for the naval squadrons that were beginning to arrive from the west. Elsewhere, conquest and occupation were patchy. Each castle, town or city that chose to resist, even in the face of apparently certain defeat, presented a separate problem. The capture of one castle did not secure a region. While whole Frankish populations seemed to have been removed from cities such as Jerusalem and Acre, the fate of the rural Frankish population may have been less clear-cut. Some, like the Frankish woman encountered by the German pilgrim Thietmar at Montréal in 1217, may have stayed on as servile tenants or slaves.[5] Where Frankish farmers had mixed with the local Syrian Christian peasantry, it is not inconceivable that some continued to work the land unmolested. Frankish administrative units may have survived the conquest intact. Certain settlements quickly resumed their previous legal identity after the Christian reconquest, as at Casal Imbert near Acre, restored in 1191. Whether or not pockets of Frankish settlers survived under the Muslim interregnum of 1187–91, the nature of the conquest did not require annihilation or complete deportation. Palestine was a long-settled land of many different communities, some ancient, some recent. The new Kurdish imperialists hardly altered that. Saladin's conquest, despite the startling triumphs of 1187, belied the apocalyptic simplicity encouraged by his own and his enemies' propagandists.

This was vividly illustrated by the fate of Beaufort.[6] For four months from April 1189 Saladin, camped outside the castle, was persuaded not to attack by a series of negotiating ploys from its quick-witted, Arabic-speaking lord, Reynald of Sidon. Despite careful surveillance, Reynald managed to use the time to reinforce the castle's defences. His repeated promises of surrender made to Saladin in Arabic were contradicted by his orders in French to his troops inside the castle to resist. The Franks' move towards Acre in August 1189 caused Saladin to lift the siege, retaining Reynald as a captive. In April 1190, a new round of negotiations ended in the simultaneous surrender of the castle and release of Reynald. This pattern of threat and negotiation, coupled with Saladin's habitual caution in committing his troops to action, marked the campaigns in 1187–9, during which he was happy to bargain surrenders of castles for safe-conducts and the release of prisoners. One unsympathetic observer, the Iraqi historian Ibn al-Athir, blamed this tactic for allowing the Franks to regroup.[7] This reliance on negotiation not just brute force carried forward into Saladin's handling of the Frankish reconquest from August 1189. Implicitly, the policy recognized that, however strategically victorious, only his or his generals' local physical presence with their troops denied Franks space to manoeuvre. At least from the summer of 1188, small Frankish armed bands were able to travel between the northern enclaves of Antioch and Tripoli and Tyre despite Saladin's continued operations further inland. Provided some of their outposts remained, Christian recovery was possible.

In Saladin's essentially political rather than ideological or fanatical approach to his conquests lay both his success and his failure. The iconic, theatrical killing of Reynald of Châtillon after Hattin proved an exception to his usual dealings with important Frankish enemies and captives. While Christian resistance continued, Saladin pursued the traditional pre-1187 policy of accommodating Frankish nobles as prisoners and using their release for tangible, costless rewards. Thus Montréal was exchanged in May 1189 for Humphrey of Toron and Beaufort in 1190 for Reynald of Sidon. During his second attack on Tyre, in the last weeks of 1187, Saladin tried unsuccessfully to use old William of Montferrat as a bargaining chip to persuade his son Conrad to surrender the city. Less obvious were his reasons for releasing most of the surviving defeated Jerusalem leadership in the early summer of 1188, including King Guy, his brother, the Constable Aimery, and the Master of the Templars, Gerard of Ridefort. If he had hoped to undermine Conrad of Montferrat at Tyre or sow dissension in the thin Frankish ranks, he was not immediately rewarded. Gerard of Ridefort promptly led the successful defence of the Templars' citadel at Tortosa in July 1188. Guy immediately repudiated the oath he had sworn to gain his freedom, by which he had promised to abandon the struggle in Outremer. Initially, he did not attempt to challenge Conrad of Montferrat's control of Tyre, preferring to reassemble his family and supporters at Antioch and Tripoli. One direct and possibly intended consequence of the stubbornness of the castle garrisons of the interior was that Saladin was distracted and his forces stretched. The Iraqi intellectual, diplomat and lawyer Baha' al-Din Ibn Shaddad, who met Saladin and entered his service in the spring of 1188, has left a telling account of the sultan's necessary restlessness simply to hold his newly created empire together let alone extinguish the embers of Frankish opposition.[8]

While he was attempting to reduce Beaufort in August 1189, Saladin received the startling news that King Guy was marching south, apparently intent of besieging Acre. The richest port on the Palestinian coast, after its surrender a few days after Hattin Saladin turned Acre into one of his main garrison towns and arms depots. The sultan's eagerness to secure Beaufort delayed his response, allowing Guy to negotiate the awkward coastal march to begin what proved to be the start of the Christian counter-attack. It is often said that King Guy's attack on Acre demonstrated, in Runciman's phrase, 'desperate foolhardiness'.[9] Outnumbered, isolated and exposed, Guy's force, perhaps only a few thousand strong in all, was pitted against a well-protected walled city defended by a substantial garrison probably larger than the initial besieging army. At Guy's rear lay a hostile Christian rival, Conrad of Montferrat, controlling the only serviceable friendly port, and a significant, battle-hardened Ayyubid army under Saladin himself only a couple of days' march away. Yet Guy's attack on Acre may not have been so rash, surprising or unexpected. Both Arabic and western sources record the building-up of Frankish forces in and around Tyre and in the county of Tripoli in 1189. Skirmishing and raiding from Tyre increased in intensity. The gathering pace of reinforcements from the west, as well as the release of the Jerusalem leaders, demanded some form of action, if only to provide occupation for the growing crowds of arms-bearers congregating in Tyre and Tripoli. Saladin's forces had been reduced to save money and ease the political tensions involved in maintaining a large coalition army in the field for long periods without plentiful new supplies of booty. Successful conquest left the sultan's victorious army unable to plunder newly won territories now controlled by their own leaders. With their strength increasing, a Frankish advance was inevitable. Early in July 1189, an attempted foray towards Sidon was repulsed after some sharp exchanges.

By this time, the military options of the Frankish leadership had become mired in political conflict. In the early spring of 1189, Guy led his small army south from Tripoli to Tyre to reclaim the last remnant of the kingdom he had lost two years before. Conrad of Montferrat refused to countenance Guy's restoration and forbade his entry to Tyre. Conrad's grounds, depending on the account followed, rested on a sort of right of conquest argument. He wrote to Archbishop Baldwin of Canterbury of his achievements: 'for the salvation of the Christian people ... I have preserved and am preserving Tyre', a fact 'grievous and insupportable' to Guy. Arabic sources have Conrad claiming regency in Tyre on behalf of the monarchs of the west, who would eventually settle all claims to kingship, an echo of the succession schemes floated in Jerusalem in 1184–5.[10] Conrad could have learnt of these from the refugees who fled to Tyre after Hattin, including Raymond III of Tripoli, a central figure in the succession crisis of 1183–6 and the leading opponent of Guy. Although he died soon after, Raymond was still alive in Tyre in August 1187, weeks after Conrad's arrival.

A king denied his kingdom, Guy decided to dig in outside Tyre, presumably in the hope of winning political adherents from the western crusaders, who were beginning to arrive in large numbers. However, after four months, he had made no progress against either Conrad or Saladin. His options were narrowing. Saladin's army was besieging Beaufort, uncomfortably close to any assault on Sidon, as the raid of July 1189 demonstrated. To survive, let alone regain authority, Guy needed to take action. His lack of alternatives provided him with an opportunity when western reinforcements came on the spring passage from the west, notably the Pisans. Arriving in April under the papal legate Archbishop Ubaldo, they soon fell out with Conrad over competing rights in Tyre. With other western recruits and Outremer Franks alienated by Conrad, they joined Guy outside Tyre. Conrad may have underestimated the effect of the post-Hattin propaganda in the west. Instead of a rank failure, Guy was portrayed as one of the heroic defenders of the cross, a companion of the martyred Reynald of Châtillon. He was also the anointed king of Jerusalem and still married, happily it appeared, to the accepted heiress Sybil. The Templars, whose reputation remained high in the west, continued to give him their

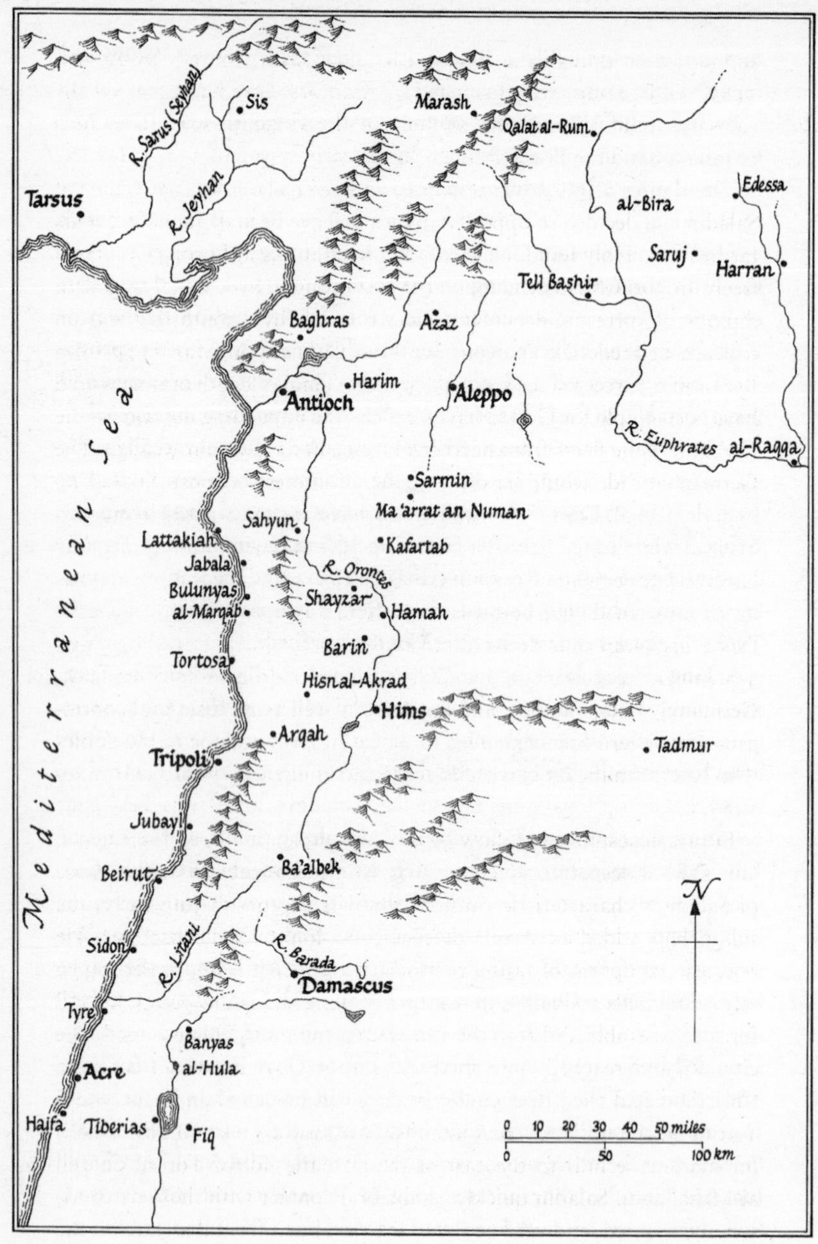

12. Syria at the Time of the Third Crusade

support, even though the Hospitallers sided with Conrad. By August 1189, with Saladin still distracted at Beaufort, Guy had amassed the core of a useful fighting force of a few hundred knights, some thousands of infantry and the Pisan fleet.

The timing of his advance south, an extremely risky manoeuvre if Saladin had decided to oppose it, may also have been dictated by events far from the Holy Land. News of the preparations in Europe circulated freely in the Christian camps at Tyre, brought by crusaders and in diplomatic correspondence. It was to take only five months for Saladin to learn of Frederick I's departure from Germany in May 1189 from Byzantine sources via his son at Aleppo.[11] A similar length of time would have been ample for Guy to have heard of the impending descent on the Levant of large fleets from northern Europe in the autumn passage. The German crusade would hardly serve Guy's interests against those of an imperial vassal, Conrad of Montferrat, unless he had already reimposed his leadership in the field. The prospect of massive reinforcements may have helped persuade Guy that the dash for Acre was not as reckless as it at first seemed. The coincidence of timing is compelling. Guy established his camp outside Acre on 28 August 1189. Before the end of September, he had been joined by large squadrons from Denmark, Germany, Frisia, Flanders and England, as well as a substantial contingent of northern Frenchmen led by James of Avesnes, one of the nobles who had taken the cross with Henry II and Philip II at Gisors in January 1188.[12]

Even so, despite his following and the prospect of reinforcements, Guy's was a desperate adventure that avoided destruction only because of Saladin's characteristic caution. Since its capture in July 1187, the sultan had added to Acre's defences and improved its harbour. He rejected the option of trying to stop Guy reaching Acre, preferring to rely on its walls and garrison resisting for long enough to permit his full force to assemble and trap the Christian army on the plain outside the city. Saladin reached Acre three days after Guy, by which time the Christians had tried to encircle the city, had launched an unsuccessful assault on the walls and had established a fortified base camp on a tell (or man-made hill) to the east of the city, the hill of Toron, or Tell al-Musallabin. Saladin quickly established contact with the Acre garrison and secured landward access to the city, but a frontal assault on the Christian camp on 15 September failed to dislodge or overrun it.

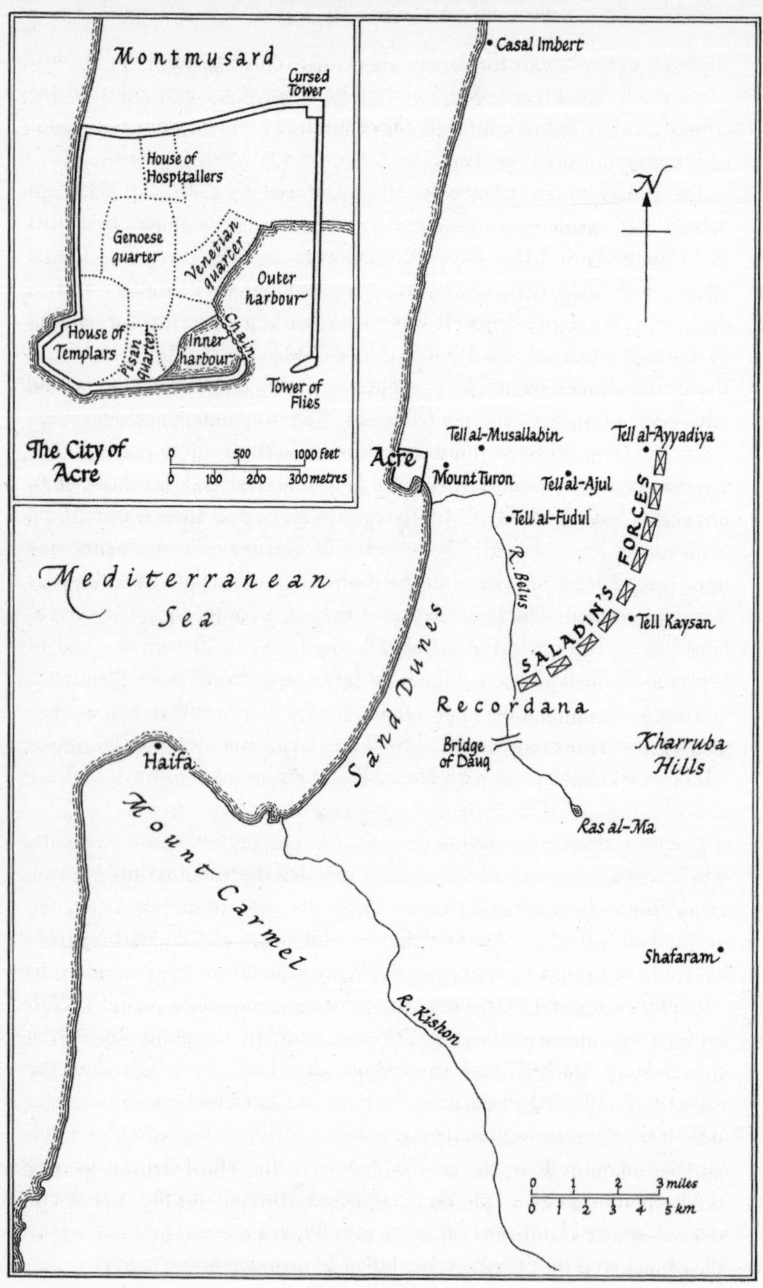
Casal Imbert
Montmusard
Cursed Tower
House of Hospitallers
Genoese quarter
Venetian quarter
Outer harbour
Chain
House of Templars
Pisan quarter
Inner harbour
Tower of Flies
The City of Acre
0 500 1000 feet
0 100 200 300 metres
N
Tell al-Musallabin
Tell al-Ayyadiya
Acre
Mount Turon
Tell al-Ajul
Tell al-Fudul
R. Belus
SALADIN'S FORCES
Tell Kaysan
Mediterranean Sea
Sand Dunes
Recordana
Bridge of Dauq
Kharruba Hills
Haifa
Mount Carmel
Ras al-Ma
Shafaram
R. Kishon
0 1 2 3 miles
0 1 2 3 4 5 km

13. The Siege of Acre 1189

The key battle was fought on 4 October. Guy's army had grown to more than 30,000 according to one Arabic estimate and now included, alongside the thousands of westerners, a reluctant Conrad of Montferrat and his supporters from Tyre, their presence showing that, politically at least, Guy's gamble had paid off. Seeing the danger of allowing the Muslim field army to grow while the Acre garrison remained untouched, the Christians decided to try to destroy the sultan's force or, at least, drive it off. A full-scale assault was launched on Saladin's camp. After a fierce pitched battle with heavy casualties on both sides, including Gerard of Ridefort, the Christians were bloodily repulsed, but their camp stayed intact. Saladin's confidant, Ibn Shaddad, claimed to have firm evidence that over 4,000 Christians had been killed on the left wing alone.[13] The heaps of rotting corpses set off infection and disease in both camps. Despite the defeat, one Christian objective was achieved when, in mid-October, Saladin withdrew from front-line investment of the Christian positions to await more troops and a fleet from Egypt. The following weeks and months saw both sides receiving reinforcements, but with neither able to press home a decisive military advantage or dislodge the other, a grim stalemate ensued. The two armies dug in; the Christians, only partially encircling the city by land, were themselves partially surrounded by Saladin's field army. A form of trench warfare began, the Franks constructing a great protective ditch and rampart around their camp. Frequent raids and close-combat skirmishes sparked across the no man's lands between the camps and between the Christians and the city, with no advantage gained by anyone. With the arrival of Egyptian fleets from late October, the Christian hold of the sea was contested and placed in jeopardy.

The survival of the Christian force at Acre depended almost entirely on the appearance of fleets from the west. Only the large numbers of crusaders sustained a siege that developed into a struggle against disease and low morale as much as with the sapping attritional fighting. While fleets played significant if underreported roles in both the First and Second Crusades, the new enterprise, the great German host excepted, was overwhelmingly dependent on naval transport. For the shipwrights and sea captains from Norway to Dalmatia, the Third Crusade proved both a bonanza and a risk, their services in demand as never before but their payment and profits often a matter of dispute and at the mercy of the elements or the chances of war. The preponderance of sea transport, the variety of vessels available, the certainty of planning and routes, the awareness of naval logistics, the distances covered and the accurate predictions of timing reflected the exponential growth in maritime activity and exchange around the coasts of Europe in the twelfth century. Of this, the traffic of crusading and pilgrimage formed only a part, at once symptom and stimulus. The local pride in these fleets was reflected by glowing accounts preserved by citizens of their home ports, such as London, Bremen or Cologne, as well as by the witnesses and chroniclers of the fighting in the Holy Land. Both demonstrated the large scale of engagement in crusading: these fleets carried thousands of men.

Western and Arabic sources leave no doubt as to the scale of the reinforcements. Christian sources recorded the arrival in early September 1189 of a fleet of Frisians and Danes in fifty cogs, large round cargo sailing ships capable of carrying companies of upwards of a hundred each, apparently commanded by some Danish nobles. The North Sea and Atlantic seaboard had been alive with crusade shipping since early in the year. Sixty ships, including four very large vessels, possibly 'busses' capable of carrying 150 crew and passengers provided by the city, had left Cologne in February 1189 with, it was optimistically suggested, 10,000 men. The Cologne squadron left Lisbon in late May or early June. Before sailing into the Mediterranean this fleet captured the small port of Albuferia in the Algarve, after which some of the Cologne crusaders cashed in their booty and returned home. By mid-September the remaining ships had reached Palestine.[14]

Their landfall was immediately followed by the arrival of a Flemish and northern French squadron, who may have sailed via Italy, under James of Avesnes. A nobleman with an enviable reputation for wisdom, integrity and chivalry, later elevated by his death at the battle of Arsuf in 1191 into an international hero, James apparently assumed leadership of the westerners in the Christian camp, perhaps by virtue of his close connection with the French royal court and his involvement in the discussions on the crusade between the kings of France and England and the count of Flanders early in 1188. By the end of September, these crusaders had been joined by the cousins of the French king, Peter count of Dreux, and his brother, Philip bishop of Beauvais, 'a man more devoted to battles than books'; the French counts of Brienne and Bar and many lesser French magnates; contingents from the Anglo-Norman-Angevin realms with William Ferrers earl of Derby; and a smattering of

Flemish, Italian and Sicilian notables. Before reaching the siege in the last week of September, Louis III, landgrave of Thuringia, at the head of an imperial contingent drawn from Germany and Italy, had put in at Tyre, where he persuaded Conrad of Montferrat to swallow his opposition to Guy and join the Christian army at Acre. This German force earned the contempt of one compatriot, who complained that by taking the sea route rather than following Frederick Barbarossa overland, they had chosen 'a short voyage that reduced the fear from enemy pagans'.[15] Once established at Acre, Louis seems to have joined James of Avesnes as the dominant voices in the crusaders' high command.

These fleets secured the Christian bridgehead at Acre at a high cost. Casualty rates assumed gruesome proportions. One contemporary tried to convey the losses by claiming that after two years at the siege, out of 12,000 who had arrived in the autumn of 1189, barely 100 survived. Small wonder that morale-boosting tales of heroic martyrdom were concocted for circulation in the camp to reassure those in daily fear and danger of death.[16] The desperate and to modern audiences highly evocative nature of the warfare was vividly captured in an account almost certainly compiled by one who had been there, a crusader at Acre in 1191–12 if not before:

> The Turks were a constant threat. While our people sweated away digging trenches, the Turks harassed them in relays incessantly from dawn to dusk. So while half were working the rest had to defend them against the Turkish assault . . . while the air was black with a pouring rain of darts and arrows beyond number or estimate . . . Many other future martyrs and confessors of the Faith came to shore and were joined to the number of the faithful. They really were martyrs: no small number of them died soon afterwards from the foul air, polluted with the stink of corpses, worn out by anxious nights spent on guard, and shattered by other hardships and needs. There was no rest, not even time to breathe. Our workers in the trench were pressed ceaselessly by the Turks who kept rushing down on them in unexpected assaults. The Turks reduced them to exasperation before the trench was eventually finished.[17]

The fleets of the autumn of 1189 were followed by possibly even more substantial forces over the following months. The largest of these, which may have reached Acre before the winter of 1189–90 but more likely only the next spring, comprised scores of ships from north Germany, the Rhineland, Flanders and England. One flotilla, including ships from

London as well as ports around the North Sea, mustered at Dartmouth in May 1189, where, following the precedent of 1147, they entered into a formal communal alliance before embarking for Lisbon on 18 May. Just over a week later, eleven ships that had embarked from Bremen on 23 April, possibly under their archbishop, after sailing down the English coast from Lowestoft, reached Dartmouth. The two fleets made a rendezvous at Lisbon on 4 July, the twenty-four ships of the Dartmouth commune having arrived on 29 June. Having missed the main German and Flemish force, of fifty-five ships, including the Cologne ships, by a month, this fleet of thirty-five or so ships was hired by the king of Portugal to help capture the port of Silves in the Algarve. Despite their naval supremacy and troops numbering perhaps 3,500, the siege lasted from 17 July until 6 September before the Muslim garrison surrendered. This delayed the fleet, which only left for Palestine on 20 September, passing the Straits of Gibraltar on 29 September before finding its way to Marseilles over the next month. Although associated in some accounts with the other northern European arrivals at Acre of the autumn of 1189, it is more likely that this fleet did not venture further in the winter months, reaching its destination the following spring.[18]

The campaign season of 1190 at Acre began with high expectations only to end in depression, disease and threatened disintegration. Both sides knew of the impending arrival of the great German host led by Frederick I. Saladin kept an especially wary eye on the emperor's progress east. In October 1189, on hearing of Frederick's departure the previous May, Saladin had despatched his new minister Ibn Shaddad to summon his allies from northern Syria and Iraq 'for the *Jihad*'.[19] These new contingents reached Acre in May and June 1190, giving Saladin a marked if temporary advantage. The Christians, meanwhile, had consolidated their defensive position around the Tell of Toron. During the winter, food ran short, with control of the sea-lanes challenged by the Egyptian fleet. On land, despite continued skirmishing, stalemate prevailed, to the retrospective annoyance of some Muslim partisans. The Iraqi Ibn al-Athir, never one of the sultan's unalloyed panegyrists, criticized Saladin's failure to destroy the Christian defences while they were still being constructed. The well-informed Syrian Abu Shama alleged that the nobles on each side punctuated the desultory round of fighting by fraternizing with each other, exchanging views, even joining together in singing and dancing. There was allegedly even a mock-combat staged between two boys from each side.[20] This did not seem to curb the violence on the battlefield, but may have exacerbated the sense, apparent among the Christian rank and file, that their leaders were reluctant to risk their lives in combat. According to Saladin's secretary, Imad al-Din, less exalted contacts were made at a carnal level, with Mamluks and other troops availing themselves of the opportunities afforded by the large red light district of the Christian camp. So intrigued or shocked was the scholarly and verbose Imad al-Din at the presence of these apparently highly skilled prostitutes that he was moved to pen an extended pornographic descant condemning their charms and erotic athleticism, achieving over twenty-five different metaphors for penetrative sex.[21]

With reinforcements for both sides beginning to arrive, any element of phoney war began to dissipate amid preparations for offensive action. By March 1190, Conrad of Montferrat had recognized the dangers of his intransigence and agreed to be reconciled with King Guy in return for possession of Tyre and, when reconquered, Beirut and Sidon. Just before Easter (25 March) Conrad reinforced his faithful credentials by returning by sea from a refitting trip to Tyre with food, men and equipment, managing to break a Muslim naval blockade. The survivors of one captured Egyptian galley were dragged ashore to be humiliated, tortured and finally killed by a group of termagant Christian women.[22] After Beaufort finally surrendered to Saladin on 2 April, the sultan began to concentrate his forces on what he hoped to be a decisive engagement at Acre. On 28 April, perhaps warned of the impending arrival of more of Saladin's allies, the Christians launched a concerted assault on the walls of Acre with three great siege engines. While these wooden towers were slowly manoeuvred against the walls of the city, Saladin tried to disrupt operations by attacking the Christian camp. A week of fierce fighting ended on 5 May, when the siege towers were destroyed by Greek fire. With Acre's walls secured and its garrison relieved by a supply flotilla, Saladin began a series of forays to test the strength of the Christian positions. If his intention had been to provoke the enemy to break out and try the luck of action on the open plain, the plan worked. On 25 July, what may have begun as a fast-moving attempt to turn the Muslim right flank soon became a general engagement between the two armies. Christian sources hinted at a failure of discipline, with the commanders and the patriarch of Jerusalem unable to dissuade a mass of disorganized, leaderless knights from seeking battle. If so, it proved a disastrous collapse of control and unity. The Christians were severely mauled, narrowly avoiding total rout. Western and Arabic sources agreed that over 4,000, and perhaps more than 5,000, Christians were killed.[23] If, as alleged, unruly knights and impatient sergeants chafing under the privations of a beleaguered camp and their own leadership's inaction had precipitated the battle, their folly, and their generals' wisdom, was confirmed just three days after the battle. On 28 July a very large crusader fleet arrived offshore carrying many of the greatest lords of northern and eastern France under the command of the count of Champagne.

Henry II, count of Champagne since 1181, was one of the wealthiest and best-connected nobles in western Europe, nephew to both Philip II of France and Richard I of England. He led what was effectively the advance guard of the French crusade being prepared by Philip II. Henry had taken the cross with King Philip, the count of Flanders and Henry II of England in January 1188. A later commentator in Outremer remembered that he brought with him to Acre some of the French king's *matériel* and siege engines, possibly in prefabricated sections.[24] He was accompanied by his uncles, Count Theobald of Blois, seneschal of France, and Count Stephen of Sancerre, with Count Robert of Clermont, constable of France, and a dozen other lords from northern France. In recognition of his status and the men and equipment he brought, Count Henry assumed effective command of the Christian army from Louis of Thuringia and James of Avesnes, a sign that western crusaders far outnumbered the Outremer Franks of King Guy and Conrad of Montferrat. Henry's arrival raised Christian morale and allowed renewed bombardment of the walls of Acre using the newly arrived French trebuchets.

However, the significance of Henry's landfall was almost completely overshadowed by news from the north. Saladin had been kept informed of the march of the German army across Asia Minor in the spring of 1190. To meet this threat, the sultan despatched troops from Acre to Aleppo and northern Syria. This meant that, when faced with the crusader reinforcements under Henry of Champagne, Saladin felt compelled to withdraw most of his remaining army to a distant blockade of the Christian lines. But by that time he knew that his northern forces were facing a rather different threat to the one he had imagined for most of the previous year. Some time in late June or early July, Saladin learnt that, on 10 June, while crossing the river Saleph in Christian Cilicia, the German emperor Frederick Barbarossa had died suddenly.[25] Although the scale of the subsequent disintegration of the German army only became apparent to the watchers at Acre in late July, the death of Frederick proved disastrous for the prospects of the whole enterprise.

THE GERMAN CRUSADE 1189–90

When Frederick I took the cross from the papal legate Henry of Albano at Mainz on 27 March 1188, he confirmed his position as the leading monarch of western Europe. As one contemporary close to the German crusade remarked, Frederick had undertaken 'the management of Christendom's affairs'.[26] Not only did the ceremony recognize his efforts to translate imperial claims into political authority within Germany, it also represented the consolidation of a new European order based on alliance between empire and papacy after decades of hostility and conflict that had dogged Frederick's domestic and international policies for most of his reign. Frederick had been negotiating with successive popes in the 1180s to reach a settled accommodation over ecclesiastical jurisdiction in Germany and political influence in Italy. With the exception of the prickly Milanese Urban III, the generally aged and cautious popes were willing, if not eager, to secure a lasting reconciliation with the emperor in order to shore up the papacy's increasingly desperate financial situation and maintain some element of integrity in its political and territorial position in Italy, where Frederick's son, Henry, had occupied the papal states in 1186. Henry's marriage to Constance, aunt and possible heiress to the childless King William II of Sicily, further encouraged papal cooperation. The imperial–papal treaty of Strassburg in April 1189 sealed this successful diplomacy as well as providing a necessary context for Frederick's departure east.

However, Frederick's commitment to the Holy Land transcended political convenience. He had played a leading role in the Second Crusade as Conrad III's chief lieutenant. In the autumn of 1184, responding to the mission from Jerusalem of Patriarch Heraclius, he had promised Pope Lucius III that he would begin immediate preparations for an eastern expedition. Now in his late sixties, having overcome internal opponents, survived defeat by the Lombard cities in the 1170s and established his son, Henry, as his heir in Germany, Frederick could afford to give substance to his chancery's claims to world authority and simultaneously fulfil personal and imperial ambition. Only the accident of events denied Frederick a central role in the Third Crusade. Although Frederick's expedition followed the traditions of the past, these proved more robust than hindsight has allowed. In some ways, Frederick was refighting the Second Crusade or even the First; and until 10 June 1190 it looked as though he was doing it rather well.

The influence of history permeated Frederick's preparations and the management of the enterprise. He was even the recipient of a glossy new edition of Robert of Rheims's popular and influential account of the First Crusade.[27] Frederick's plans embraced the idealism but avoided the errors of the past. His army was to be adequately funded by participants, well disciplined and very large. Some estimated 20,000 knights and 80,000 infantry mustered under Frederick's command; others put the fighting force at nearer 85,000. Arnold of Lübeck a generation later claimed that a census taken during the crossing of the Balkans had revealed 50,000 knights and 100,000 infantry. Even if these figures exaggerate, on two occasions the host was recorded as having taken three days to pass a single point.[28] The path of this mighty force was paved by careful diplomacy, with the rulers of central Europe, the Byzantine emperor, the Seljuk sultan of Rum and even Saladin. Although the naval option was apparently considered, the land route was more convenient for the bulk of his followers, in terms of access and the ease of supply for such a substantial force, which was, in any case, too large to be transported by sea in its entirety or at the same time. While feasible for the extended military entourages of Louis of Thuringia in 1189, Leopold of Austria in 1190–91, or even Philip II of France in 1190, Italian maritime city fleets did not have the capacity to accommodate Frederick's host. Nor, probably, did Frederick have the ready cash or the diplomatic clout to secure the necessary contracts. The land route was familiar from the First and Second Crusades, as well as diplomatic and commercial exchanges with Hungary. Henry the Lion, duke of Saxony, had followed the Danube and the Balkan route to Constantinople on his elaborate pilgrimage in 1172, before resorting to the sea for the voyage to Acre.[29] By taking the overland route, Frederick could hope to maintain political control both of his army and of his destiny.

As has been described, the 'Christ's court' at Mainz in March 1188 provided a focus and a confirmation of plans and commitments already established. These were extended in the next few months. At Mainz, the muster had been fixed for 23 April 1189. A series of assemblies, courts and diets reaffirmed recruitment and established certain rules, such as the stipulation for crusaders to be able to fund themselves for a year. Just as in 1147, political conflicts were resolved under the aegis of the higher cause and imperial authority was lent added moral force. Henry the Lion, whose youthful ambitions had been temporarily deflected by Conrad III's crusade, now was presented with a choice of acknowledging his rival's lordship by joining Frederick on crusade at the emperor's expense or of accepting imperial judgement by going into exile for three years. Henry chose the less humbling of these two unwelcome options by choosing exile at the court of his father-in-law, Henry II of England (although he was soon back). Ambassadors and letters were despatched along the German's proposed route, to Bela III of Hungary, Stephen, the ruler of Serbia, and Emperor Isaac II Angelus of Byzantium. A Franconian knight, Godfrey of Wiesenbach, visited Sultan Kilij Arslan II of Rum (1155–92), grandson of the Seljuk sultan defeated by the First Crusade, with whom Frederick had been allied for some time. According to western sources, but not those Arabic writers closest to the Ayyubid sultan, the count of Birstein, Henry of Dietz, was sent to Saladin.[30] News of Frederick's preparations and the huge response to the call to arms seem to have intimidated those living in his projected path. At a diet in Nuremberg in December 1188, representatives from Hungary and the Balkans promised cooperation, as did a delegation sent by Kilij Arslan II. This constructive diplomacy with the Seljuks, and, if not apocryphal, the mission to Saladin, conformed to a consistent pattern evident in German planning and especially during the campaign itself. Throughout, Frederick kept his eyes fixed firmly on the goal of the Holy Land and Jerusalem. He saw himself as a knight of Christ bound to avenge the events of 1187, not an indiscriminate hammer of Islam or anybody else. The Byzantine ambassadors were less convinced, asking that another German embassy be sent to Constantinople to reassure Isaac II that neither he nor any western monarch harboured hostile intentions towards the Greek empire; more shades of 1147. Only when Frederick agreed to continue negotiations by sending the requested new delegation did the Byzantine representatives commit their government to helping the crusaders with guides, markets, security and transport for the crossing to Asia Minor. The German envoys would help coordinate this assistance. Even so, Greek fear was hardly assuaged. So large an army, whatever its motives, would have the material effect of an invasion.

Despite Frederick's energetic preparations, the need for haste was loudly proclaimed, not least by Henry of Albano, who lamented the backsliding of some crusaders and the in-fighting of others, which he likened to dogs returning to their own vomit.[31] In fact, compared with the kings of England and France, Frederick moved with vigour and drive, at the head of a genuinely popular movement that redirected the lives and funds of nobles, their *ministeriales* and knights, lesser lords, higher and lower clergy, urban and rural elites and freemen from all parts of Germany. As a sympathetic contemporary noted, Frederick, 'who had been the last king to make his vow of pilgrimage, hurried to be the first to discharge it'.[32] The experience of 1147–8 prompted Frederick to maintain a very tight grip on his huge coalition. Twice on the march to Constantinople, he refined disciplinary ordinances for his disparate troops and non-combatants, establishing a system of justice and punishment sworn by the whole army and, later, dividing the host into self-regulating judicial units within this agreed communal system. In sharp contrast to Louis VII's ordinances for his crusade army in 1147, Frederick's were enforced. Loutish behaviour led to loss of hands; theft to execution. Such harsh discipline was coupled with a constant emphasis on the pious nature of the operation. At Vienna, Frederick purged the army of undesirable elements, including the prostitutes. The general effect on morale and military effectiveness stood in marked contrast to the shambles into which Conrad III's army had descended in Asia Minor in the autumn of 1147. Frederick remembered. His army's reputation for order and piety became notorious. Ibn Shaddad recorded a possibly genuine letter to Saladin by the Catholicos of the Armenian church in northern Syria, Gregory IV, written in 1190, which testifies at least to the nature and success of German propaganda if not their piety:

They are of varied races and strange ways. Their cause is a great one and they are serious in their enterprise and of prodigious discipline, so much so that, if one of them commits a crime, the only penalty is to have his throat cut like a sheep. I was informed about one of their nobles, that he did wrong to a page of his and beat him beyond the limit. The priests gathered to give judgement and the case by general decision demanded that his throat be cut. Many petitioned the emperor on his behalf, but he paid no attention and had his throat cut. They have forbidden themselves pleasures even to the extent that, if they hear that anyone has allowed himself any pleasure, they treat him as an outcast and chastise him. All this because of grief for Jerusalem.[33]

The image of a 'Christian militia' fostered by Frederick's later panegyrists may not simply have been a construct of preachers, observers and historians but, as on the First Crusade, an integral part of the army's own mechanisms of self-regulation and morale. Chroniclers' comparisons with the Theban legion and the Maccabees may have seemed appropriate to the troops themselves as they struggled across Asia Minor in the spring of 1190. In letters home in the autumn of 1189, Frederick himself described his followers as 'the army of the Holy Cross' or 'of the life-giving Cross', in clear association with the central image of the recruiting campaign.[34] This sense of identity and destiny underpinned the whole enterprise. The tone for the expedition had been set by the careful orchestration of Frederick's adoption of the cross in March 1188 and his receiving the scrip and staff of a pilgrim at Hagenau in April 1189. However, throughout the German march, the maintenance of morale and a sense of purpose ran in tandem with Frederick's careful planning and judicious use of force.

The German contingents for the land route mustered, as arranged, at Regensburg on 23 April 1189. On 11 May, the army or, more realistically, armies, moved off down the Danube, the high command in boats, the rest on shore. Progress was rapid and peaceful, past Vienna to Bratislava (Pressburg), where disciplinary regulations were promulgated. By 4 June the Germans reached Esztergom (Gran) on the Hungarian frontier. They were greeted with lavish hospitality by King Bela III and his wife Margaret. Poised between Byzantium and the west, Hungary's involvement in crusading reflected an eagerness to be associated with Latin Christendom, not least as a means of ensuring independence. Queen Margaret, daughter of Louis VII of France, Frederick's companion in arms on the Second Crusade, embodied this policy. More immediately, the Hungarians supplied the crusaders with provisions, equipment and access to plentiful if expensive markets. After what appeared, in retrospect at least, a comfortable passage through Hungary, the crusaders reached the Byzantine border at Branitz (Brnjica) on 2 July.

Relations with the Byzantine empire were complicated by Isaac II's uneasy hold on his Balkan provinces, his need to secure his eastern frontier by a treaty with the Seljuk Turks, past tensions with the Germans in Italy, a tradition of hostility with Sicily, now allied with Frederick, and with the west more generally over Italian trading rights and Antioch.[35] There persisted a fear, especially among the Constantinopolitan elites, that all western armies held as an ulterior motive the conquest of the Greek empire. On the westerners' side, the religious schism sharpened the feeling that the Greeks were poor Christians in their apparent indifference to the Holy Land. Isaac Angelus had acquired the throne in 1185 after a coup marked by mob sadism unusual even in Byzantium, the previous emperor Andronicus I Comnenus, himself a murdering usurper, being torn to pieces in the streets of the capital. Isaac balanced his political weakness with petulant diplomatic bluster. Having promised assistance to the Germans, in the summer of 1189 Isaac suddenly threw the German ambassadors he had asked for into prison. He continued to pursue amicable relations with Saladin, whom he kept informed of the German progress.[36] Saladin's envoys were in Constantinople when the German ambassadors arrived and allegedly received the horses of the unfortunate westerners when they were incarcerated. It is hard to divine the immediate advantage for the Greeks in the Ayyubid alliance, a feature of Byzantine foreign policy after 1182. Isaac may have hoped to counteract any agreement Frederick had reached with the Sicilians or the Seljuks or use it as a lever to engineer recognition of suzerainty over Antioch and other former Greek territories that the crusaders conquered. Yet such hopes were fatally undermined by Isaac's lack of adequate military strength to exert pressure on the crusaders. More immediately damaging was his failure to prevent the German army from being attacked more or less the entire length of their journey from the Danube to the plains of Thrace. The net result of Isaac's policy, if such a farrago of myopic expedience and folly can be so described, was to provoke Frederick into contemplating precisely what the Greek feared most, an attack on Constantinople.

From Branitz, the Germans threaded their way to Nish, which was reached on 27 July. Given the awkward terrain and the length of the crusader marching line, the army was divided into four divisions.[37] Despite the persistent harassment from locals acting, many believed, on

Isaac's orders, Frederick was reluctant to throw in his lot with Serbian rebels who met him at Nish. The journey though Bulgaria to Sofia increasingly resembled a fighting march, familiar to eastern tactics and from the First and Second Crusades. At Sofia, on 13 August, the Germans found that the promised markets and currency exchange had been removed on imperial orders and that the route to the Maritsa valley and Thrace had been fortified against them. After battering their way through the mountains, on 24 August the crusaders reached Philippopolis, which had been abandoned by its inhabitants and its defences destroyed on Isaac's orders by the governor of Thrace, the civil servant and historian Nicetas Choniates. Years later, in the shadow of the loss of Constantinople to the Fourth Crusade in 1204, Nicetas painted an intimate but unflattering portrait of Byzantine confusion, duplicity and impotence at this time.[38]

By the time Frederick entered the deserted Philippopolis on 26 August, he had learnt of the arrest of his ambassadors in Constantinople and of Isaac's demands for German guarantees of good behaviour and a share of future crusade conquests. Despite a growing problem of supplies, Frederick was in no mood to compromise, especially as he held a clear military advantage. Isaac's diplomatic tactlessness, such as failing to afford Frederick his proper title in correspondence, soured relations further. While angry diplomatic exchanges continued, the release of the German ambassadors without what Frederick regarded as adequate reparations did little to resolve the central issue of Byzantine assistance in transporting the crusaders across into Asia Minor. Having occupied Philippopolis and the surrounding region, securing food and markets, by early November Frederick had decided on a strategy to force Greek cooperation.

Perhaps mindful of the disastrous crusader advance into Asia Minor in the winter of 1147–8, Frederick, choosing Adrianople as his headquarters, proceeded to occupy Thrace. At the same time, he made contact with provincial rebels in the Balkans and appeared to contemplate an assault on Constantinople. Both the occupation of Thrace and an attack on the Greek capital had been policies proposed to Louis VII in 1147. In mid-November, Frederick wrote to his son and regent, Henry VI, requesting he raise a war fleet from Italian ports to meet the German army in mid-March for an attack on Constantinople. At the same time, signalling that his ultimate goal had not changed, he asked Henry to arrange with his officials and the Venetian banker Bernard the German the transfer of imperial funds to Tyre, 'since you know that we shall need large amounts because of the unexpected delays facing us'. The money was to come from outstanding sums owing the crown, especially, Frederick mentioned, Ancona, Metz, Bremen and the count of Hanau. Whether this revenue represented unpaid hearth tax, regalian obligations or some other dues is unclear, but Frederick's demands indicate a substantial financial apparatus and fiscal base for his expedition. How seriously he intended, as he put it, 'bringing the entire imperial territory under control' is less certain.[39] Five months gave little time in which to hire and equip a war fleet and have it arrive on station. Cities such as Genoa, one of those mentioned by Frederick, were able to supply transport on demand; early in 1190 the Genoese struck a deal to carry Philip II of France's military entourage the following August. However, German policy in Italy as well as the commercial rivalries between the cities made such alliances difficult. Venice had only recently entered into a new treaty with Byzantium and would refuse to cooperate with Genoa and Pisa. Although unknown to Frederick, at the same moment he wrote to Henry proposing the fleet, one potential maritime ally, William II of Sicily, died, his throne being seized by his anti-Hohenstaufen bastard cousin Tancred of Lecce. Thereafter, Henry VI's interest in Italy was focused on securing the Sicilian inheritance of his wife Constance, William II's aunt and heir, rather than supplying ships for his father. Even in Frederick's instructions of November, the simultaneous arrangements for additional funds to be sent direct to the Holy Land rather than Greece indicates that the proposed conquest of Byzantium was either loud diplomatic sabre-rattling or a sop to the war party within the German high command. By the time envoys from Pisa caught up with Frederick at Gallipoli in March 1190, plans to attack Constantinople had been abandoned.[40]

Whatever his intentions, Fredrick maintained the pressure on the Greeks by openly negotiating with Serb and Vlach delegations towards an anti-Byzantine alliance. Relations with the Greeks deteriorated as the Germans tightened their hold on Thrace, even where they suspected the local wine, which was not to their taste, of being poisoned as opposed to being merely nauseating. The Byzantine armed forces made no impression on the German garrisons and foragers, undermining whatever credibility Isaac's regime retained. Seriously alarmed, Isaac reopened negotiations only to break them off on Christmas Eve 1189 just as agreement appeared imminent. Diplomatic inconsistency and military feebleness caused Greek policy to implode. Nicetas Choniates disdainfully recorded Isaac's flailing vacillation. Without the military capacity to unsettle the Germans, in the end Isaac was forced to capitulate. On 14 February, a treaty was solemnized in the church of Hagia Sophia in Constantinople which repeated the essence of the agreement of Nuremberg of December 1188. As well as various clauses resolving immediate issues of contention that had arisen since August 1189, the treaty guaranteed the crusaders free passage through imperial territory, ships to carry them across the Hellespont at Gallipoli and access to markets at reasonable exchange rates. In return, Frederick promised to avoid Constantinople and refrain from indiscriminate foraging while in Byzantine lands. The whole tortuous episode had delayed the Germans for over six months. Although this may have fortuitously forestalled a winter campaign in Asia Minor, it allowed Saladin, well informed by Isaac, to marshal his defences in northern Syria. For Byzantium rebels and opponents as well as the watching western powers, Isaac's erratic behaviour exposed his inability to control events. In Nicetas's hostile view, a profligate sybarite of negligible political acumen, for all his thrashing about and bravado, Isaac had merely accelerated the disintegration of his own empire.[41]

The Germans crossed the Hellespont between 22 and 28 March, either side of Easter (25 March), before setting out towards Philadelphia, Hierapolis and the Seljuk border. Once again avoiding the errors of 1147, Frederick's orderly divisions remained in ostensibly friendly Byzantine territory for as long as possible. However, again echoing the crusaders' experience forty-two years earlier, the locals proved hostile and resentful, reluctant to open their markets and granaries to the westerners just as the hungry months of spring were upon them. At Philadelphia, after four weeks' march from the Hellespont, the mixture of brawling and banditry spilt into connected violence, a major armed confrontation being only narrowly avoided. Leaving Greek territory in the last days of April, the German host followed the main road via Philomelium (Akshehir) to Iconium (Konya), the Seljuk capital. The march proved a mirror image of the journey across the Byzantine empire, only more strenuous and more deadly.

For more than a year, most recently before the Germans left

Adrianople, amicable diplomatic exchanges with the Seljuk rulers of the sultanate of Rum, Kilij Arslan II and his son Qutb al-Din, had produced promises of friendship, unopposed passage and open markets for the crusaders. As in Byzantium, internal tensions, particularly between Kilij Arslan and his son, contradicted any formal agreements. Qutb al-Din was Saladin's son-in-law. Having effectively usurped his father's position, he encouraged local Turkish opposition and prepared to confront the advancing Germans. Moreover, Asia Minor swarmed with nomad Turcoman raiders who had been operating in the region since 1185 independent of any Seljuk political authority but eager to profit from the well-equipped if poorly provisioned Christian army as it lumbered through the Anatolian hills. In a sharp encounter near Philomelium on 7 May, Duke Frederick of Swabia's division repulsed a dangerous ambush, inflicting heavy casualties. Duke Frederick lost some front teeth, knocked out by a stone.[42] By now the persistent attacks of the Turks, some prominent casualties, such as the minnesinger (i.e. poet and minstrel) Frederick von Hausen, and the shortage of food and water were beginning to tell. As conditions worsened and losses mounted, some deserted; others merely gave up, collapsing at the side of the march to await death or captivity. Horses and mules killed in the fighting reduced the military effectiveness of the army but were eagerly consumed by ravenous troops.

Despite their weakened state and unrelenting Turkish attacks, the Germans cut their way through to Iconium, protected by military discipline, weight of numbers and lack of alternatives. The encounters with the enemy grew in size and intensity as the Christians closed on the Seljuk capital, which Frederick insisted on capturing rather than leave as an enemy base at his rear. On 18 May, outside Iconium, the Germans encountered Qutb al-Din's main army in a pitched battle. By dividing his forces into two, with Duke Frederick leading an assault on the city itself while the old emperor faced the Turkish field army, Frederick seems to have wrong-footed his opponents. The city fell easily, suggesting it had been denuded of defenders. After desperate fighting involving the emperor himself, the Turks outside the city were defeated, apparently against the numerical odds, leaving Iconium at the mercy of German pillaging and looting.

The victory at Iconium saved the crusade militarily and restocked it with food, supplies and money. His strategy in ruins, Qutb al-Din was replaced by his father, who resumed his pacific policy by coming to terms with the Germans. After a brief rest, the re-equipped German army left the region of Iconium on 23 May, with important Turkish hostages to guarantee the safety of their march. On 30 May the vanguard reached Karaman on the border with Christian Cilicia. Frederick Barbarossa had achieved what the crusaders of 1101 and Second Crusade could not. In two months since crossing to Asia, he had brought his vast army, depleted but intact, in the face of sustained Turkish hostility, difficult terrain, heavy casualties and shortages of supplies, to welcoming Christian territory. On its own terms, this compared with the most remarkable achievements of the whole Third Crusade. A generation later a writer in Outremer reckoned that Saladin had been so frightened of Frederick's approach that he dismantled the walls of Syrian ports lest they were captured and used against him by the Germans.[43] But Frederick's effort proved to no purpose. Pressing forward to Antioch, now only a very few weeks ahead, as the German army negotiated the crossing of the river Saleph, Frederick somehow slipped, fell or was thrown from his horse into the river. He may have fallen in because of a heart attack or, having fallen, the shock of the cold water brought one on. Alternatively, and less credibly, he drowned after going for a cooling swim. The sources disagree, some insisting that Frederick survived his ducking only to die some days later. What is certain is that the emperor died on Sunday 10 June 1190 as a consequence of fording the river Saleph and that his death, through heart failure, drowning or other injury, was connected in some way with immersion in the river.[44]

Practically and symbolically, the shock of Frederick's death was profound. It cast doubt on his cause. Even in retrospect it was impossible to recast him as a new Moses deprived of the Promised Land, as there was to be no ultimate victory for his people. At the time, his sudden death in such circumstances snapped the army's morale and unity. Freed from the imminent threat of attack from hostile locals, the great army that had held together for over a year in the face of all vicissitudes began to disintegrate. Elements peeled off to return home from the ports of Cilicia or, later, Syria. Others left the main force to sail from Tarsus for Tyre. The rest continued to Antioch, by land and, with Frederick of Swabia and the funeral cortège of his father, by sea. Duke Frederick reached Antioch on 21 June 1190, where he was joined by his depleted land army. There, disease ravaged the survivors, including a number of significant figures in the high command and royal administration. Frederick Barbarossa's body was boiled and filleted. The flesh was buried in the cathedral of St Peter in Antioch. The separated bones, now elevated to the status of relics, were destined for the Holy Sepulchre, although they ended in the church of St Mary in Tyre. This scarcely compensated for the lack of his personality and leadership.

His son, while possessing both bravery and military skill, lacked his father's authority, drive and determination. With diminished resources, Duke Frederick toyed with the idea of establishing himself as a power in northern Syria, being offered by Bohemund III, or, in other accounts, insisting upon control of Antioch.[45] This made some strategic sense, as military pressure in the north played on the relative weakness of Saladin's hold over parts of the region and had the effect of forcing the sultan to divert even more troops from Acre. The Christians' recovery from the defeat outside Acre of 25 July and the ease with which Henry of Champagne subsequently established himself may have been fruits of Duke Frederick's Antioch policy. However, Duke Frederick, perhaps because of his diminishing armed force, decided against a northern campaign. Leaving Antioch on 29 August, he led his troops south, picking their way down the coast to Tripoli and Tyre, sustaining further losses to Turkish attacks on the way. Having made contact with Conrad of Montferrat at Tyre, Frederick, with a meagre and bruised rump of the great German host, finally reached the Christian camp at Acre on 7 October 1190.

The scene he found would have inspired little confidence. The siege was locked in a violent stalemate that cost lives and achieved little. Even wives of crusaders joined in the menial tasks of siege warfare, such as filling the city ditch so that siege engines could approach the walls. One of these, mortally wounded by a Turkish arrow, begged her husband to bury her in the trench she was helping to fill.[46] The remnants of the German crusade inspired some concerted action against both the city and the surrounding Muslim forces, but they failed to make a difference. Morale was hardly raised by the departure of Louis of Thuringia shortly after Duke Frederick's arrival. National rivalries simmered dangerously, exacerbated by fresh reinforcements. At about the same time as Duke Frederick, the advance guard of the English royal army landed at Acre, led by Archbishop Baldwin of Canterbury, the recently dismissed justiciar, Ranulf Glanvill, and his nephew, soon the rising star of Angevin government, Hubert Walter bishop of Salisbury. They had left Richard I at Marseilles in August 1190, taking two months to reach Palestine. The English helped with manning the front lines and leading forays against the enemy, but their presence also reinforced a growing political division within the Christian camp in which they were pitted against the Germans.

Some time in October 1190, the disease that appears to have become endemic in the fetid conditions of the Christian camp, carrying off many of the recent arrivals, claimed Queen Sybil of Jerusalem and her two daughters. This threw the Jerusalem succession once more into doubt, as Guy was only king by virtue of being Sybil's husband. Guy's enemies among the Outremer baronage, led by Balian of Ibelin and his wife Maria Comnena, mother of the new heiress to the kingdom, Isabella, promoted the proven military success, Conrad of Montferrat, to replace the man who lost Jerusalem.[47] To achieve this they needed Isabella to divorce her existing husband, the Arabic-speaking and allegedly effeminate Humphrey III of Toron, and marry Conrad. The childlessness of Isabella and Humphrey made the scheme easier to contemplate. The uncomfortable fact that Conrad already had a wife living in Constantinople, and possibly another in Italy, seemed to have been brushed aside. The Germans, the papal legate, the archbishop of Pisa and the French vassals of Philip II lined up behind Conrad and his marriage to Isabella. Ranged against them were the Patriarch Heraclius, now too ill to act, and the Angevins under Archbishop Baldwin, who supported Guy. Baldwin proved an awkward opponent, and even the docile Humphrey of Toron seems to have briefed Ralph of Tiberias, a noted advocate, to plead his case. However, Baldwin died suddenly on 19 November, and five days later, after Humphrey had been exposed to enormous political and personal pressure and scarcely veiled physical threats, Isabella's first marriage was annulled and she was summarily married to Conrad by Philip II's cousin, the bishop of Beauvais, with the approval of the papal legate. To some, the crown of Jerusalem now lay with a couple united only by politics and bigamy. To others, it seemed the most sensible outcome, especially as they produced a child the following year. For the army at Acre, it risked schism, as Guy still insisted he was king. Only the withdrawal of the couple to Tyre and the intensification of the epidemic in the camp calmed emotions.

The coup of Conrad's marriage represented a final achievement for

Frederick of Swabia. Within weeks he had been struck down by illness, dying on 20 January 1191. He was buried in the cemetery of the field hospital established at Acre earlier in 1190 by citizens from Bremen and Lübeck.[48] It had been dedicated to St Mary's, Jerusalem, a reference to the German hospital in the Holy City before 1187. By 1196, this community caring for the sick had been organized as a religious hospitaller order on which, in 1198, was imposed the duty to fight the infidel. The Teutonic Order of St Mary's Hospital in Jerusalem, the military order of the Teutonic Knights, thus constituted the most important and lasting legacy of the German involvement in the Third Crusade. Ironically, it owed nothing to the initiative and efforts of Frederick Barbarossa. The collapse of the German expedition constitutes one of the great 'what ifs' of crusading, indeed of medieval history. If Frederick had brought his army, still tens of thousands strong despite the heavy losses, to Acre in the summer of 1190, the city might have fallen a year earlier than it did. Saladin confessed to serious alarm at the danger. His authority would have been severely weakened long before the arrival of the kings of France and England. In turn their forces would not have been deflected by the need to take Acre. The political rivalries would not have diminished. Frederick was old and imperious. Neither Richard I nor Philip II would have been over-eager to bow the knee to him. However, a joint campaign by such large forces from an already secured base at Acre in 1191 might have placed Jerusalem within Christian reach. As it was, the last great western European land attack on the eastern Mediterranean ended in frustration and almost complete failure.

All that was left for the demoralized crusaders at Acre, as Hubert Walter wrote anxiously from there in the early weeks of 1191 to the mandarin English bureaucrat, Richard FitzNeal bishop of London, was to 'maintain their efforts and withstand the discomforts of the siege until the coming of our kings'. He hoped they would arrive at Easter (14 April). Perhaps he expected them to. Without them, Hubert prophesied, 'the hope of worldly consolation will die away'.[49] All eyes, Christian and Muslim, were strained westwards, awaiting the appearance of the kings of France and England.

THE ANGLO-FRENCH EXPEDITION 1190–91

The delay in the arrival of the kings of France and England at the siege of Acre constituted one of the scandals of the age, evidence of Satan at work.[50] Frederick Barbarossa was dead before his fellow monarchs had even set out. Chroniclers, chanteurs and clerics united in condemnation of the unseemly politics that enveloped royal preparations in France and England after Henry II and Philip II had taken the cross together at Gisors in January 1188. By the end of March, both monarchs had issued instructions for the Saladin Tithe and details of how crusaders' privileges would operate. However, unrest, rebellion and war in Richard of Poitou's lands in Aquitaine distracted attention from the crusade and drew Philip II and Henry II into another round of military thrust and parry. As 1188 wore on, Philip successfully managed to entice Richard into an alliance against his father by suggesting that the old king was planning to disinherit him in favour of his youngest son, John. As John had conspicuously not taken the cross, and so was available to rule the Angevin lands in the absence of Henry and Richard, the idea seemed plausible. Despite repeated attempts at negotiation, tension over the Angevin succession, heightened by Henry's ill-health in the winter and spring of 1188–9, turned to open warfare between the old king on one side and Philip and Richard on the other. Yet pressure for the crusade continued. At a peace conference on 4 July 1189, the three protagonists, among other things, agreed to muster for the crusade at Vézelay in late February, mid-Lent, 1190. Three days later, Henry II died.[51]

Given the upheavals and arrangements consequent on a new reign in Angevin lands in France as well as in England, the remarkable feature of the crusade preparations was not delay but their acceleration on both sides of the Channel. Although twice, in November 1189 and in March 1190, the date for departure was postponed, first to 1 April, then to 24 June, both kings set about preparing their realms administratively and politically for their absence and arranging for their transport east. Remarkably, even the deaths in childbirth on 15 March 1190 of Philip's queen and the twins she was carrying scarcely deflected the king's resolve. The French succession now rested on a three-year-old child,

Prince Louis. Not only Philip, but also possible claimants such as Count Robert II of Dreux, a first cousin, left for the east. Their participation in the crusade echoed that of heir-less Louis VII and his brother Robert I of Dreux in 1147 by imperilling Capetian dynastic security, the rock on which the royal house's fortunes had rested for two centuries. As for Richard he was unmarried and childless, with a younger brother and nephew who inevitably would (and after 1199 did) compete for his inheritance. In such circumstances, embarkation a year after Henry II's death was not unduly dilatory. Much criticism of Henry, Philip and Richard appears polemical or wishful. There would have been no participation by the French and English kings of any kind without the resolution of outstanding disagreements over the succession to Angevin lands in France and the honouring of past treaties. More widely, critics underestimated the extent of non-royal crusade activity, especially in France.

By the time Philip II and Richard I finally left Vézelay together on 4 July 1190, thousands of Frenchmen, some vassals of Philip II, some of Henry II, had already reached Acre in the fleets of James of Avesnes and Henry of Champagne, including many of the leading barons of Philip II's early years, such as the count of Dreux in 1189 and the counts of Blois, Clermont and Sancerre a year later. Englishmen and Anglo-Normans such as William Ferrers earl of Derby, who joined French contingents in northern France in 1189,[52] or Ralph Hauterive archdeacon of Colchester, who had travelled with other Londoners by sea in 1189, were already entering the rich folklore of heroes in the crusader camp long before their king had ever reached the Mediterranean. Even in England and Normandy, with their centralized mechanisms of royal administration and control, independent action, based on lordship, town, region or kin, accounted for many departures beyond the ambit of the crown's preparations. Among the arrivals at Acre in 1189–90 were representatives of the London clerical and commercial elites, including members of the chapter of St Paul's and civic swells such as Geoffrey the Goldsmith and William 'Longbeard' FitzOsbert, who had to raise a mortgage on some of his city property to pay for his journey. In 1190, a significant contingent from Normandy came, probably with Henry of Champagne, linked by kinship as well as regional and lordship ties: Richard of Vernon and his son; Gilbert of Tillières and his military entourage, 'manu valida bellatorum', literally, 'with a strong hand of warriors'.[53] Some of these companies may have been modest, Ivo of Vipont on one occasion commanding a mere ten men on a trip from Acre to Tyre.[54] Archbishop Baldwin was accompanied by an extensive household, domestic servants and, possibly, dozens of fighting men. Other contingents were very substantial, such as the knights of Richard of Clare or the extended Glanvill affinity, which included, as well as the ex-justiciar, his uncle, nephew and steward and their respective military and civilian followers. Less formal associations among the English may be found in the list of Lincolnshire and Yorkshire crusaders who died at Acre in 1190 recorded by their fellow countryman Roger of Howden, who, on arriving with Richard I in June 1191, seems to have made contact with the survivors of this group.[55]

However, although these Anglo-Norman crusading journeys in 1189–90 paralleled those from the nobility of the rest of France, French and Anglo-Norman, specifically English, experiences of the Third Crusade differed significantly. Despite similar royal attempts in Angevin and Capetian lands to raise the Saladin Tithe and to regulate crusaders' privileges, especially in relation to debt and financial transactions, Philip II was unable to impose his authority, lacking both the political and bureaucratic tradition to organize or compel on a national scale.[56] The level of royal subsidy to any individual or group of crusaders is hard to estimate. In England and probably Normandy, crusaders had access to the proceeds of the Saladin Tithe, collected under the aegis of the government, while their French colleagues had not. More important, once the decision to travel by sea had been reached, a significant proportion of the followers of the Angevin king could travel in ships prepared by royal administrators with royal cash. At every stage of the crusade, from commandeering ships in English ports to Palestine, Richard hired men as well as materials. Most strikingly, while Philip II may have sent some siege engines and troops ahead of him, the force he paid the Genoese in 1190 to be shipped to the Holy Land numbered 650 knights and 1,300 squires. By contrast, Richard equipped his own fleet of more than 100 vessels and hired another small fleet of ten cargo ships and twenty galleys at Marseilles. The army he was transporting, when mustered in Sicily in the winter of 1190–91, including sailors may have numbered as many as 17,000. Not only was Richard 'the first crusader king to equip and take his fleet to Outremer', the armada he led remained one of the largest.[57]

*

Active crusade preparations had in fact begun under the much-maligned Henry II. The Saladin Tithe was vigorously collected even if, as many assumed, much of it actually went on the wars of 1188–9. Initially, Henry, and therefore Philip, who had agreed to travel with him, toyed with the idea of the land route. Archbishop Baldwin may have been expecting it when he forced his reluctant team to walk rather than ride up steep Welsh valleys in training for the journey to come.[58] An embassy was sent in 1188 to Frederick Barbarossa, Bela III of Hungary and Isaac II requesting and receiving promises of safe passage and open markets for the Capetian and Angevin armies. At this stage, Richard of Poitou may already have decided to go his own way, by sea. Perhaps news of the German choice of the land route put Henry off; the precedent of 1147 was not auspicious. It seems that at some point, perhaps to preempt his attention-seeking son, Henry switched his plan and began negotiating with William II of Sicily, his son-in-law. The substance of these negotiations may have been reflected in King William's will, in which he left Henry treasure, grain, wine and a hundred armed war galleys.[59] As William died five months after Henry, these provisions must date from at least the spring of 1189, if not earlier. If so, they indicate the scale of the royal expedition envisaged by Henry; such a fleet was capable of carrying up to 8,000 men.

Government financial accounts for September 1188 to September 1189 suggest activity below that of grand strategy, even if some of it dated from after Henry's death in July. A separate depository for the Saladin Tithe was established at Salisbury, with a tiny staff of ten tellers. Chroniclers complained of the enormous amounts raised. The highly critical monk Gervase of Canterbury put it at £70,000, while the well-informed Roger of Howden thought that Henry left a treasure, from all sources, worth more than 100,000 marks (£66,666). Even if such witnesses exaggerated Henry's rapacity, the Salisbury depository did not let the money lie idle. Two hundred marks were sent to Bristol, perhaps for hiring ships, 2,500 marks to Gloucester, perhaps for horseshoes from the of Forest of Dean, 5,000 marks to Southampton, over the following year a major centre of crusade preparations.[60] Whatever the contortions of high politics, many Englishmen, Normans and Poitevins conducted their own arrangements with official blessing. For Henry II, domestic and dynastic political calculation had always taken priority over quixotic or pious gestures. This remained the case until the day he died. However, after 1187 help for the Holy Land was no longer an option: it had become a requirement of state.

On his accession Richard I brought to the crusade his experience as a general, his ability to push forward a scheme through administration as well as politics, and a strong personal commitment. Like his father, he recognized there was probably no limit to the treasure needed to finance the planned expedition, especially as it had been decided, possibly before he became king, to equip a massive royal fleet as well as a substantial royal army. However much there remained in Henry II's coffers, Richard sought more in spectacular fashion. As Roger of Howden observed with only mild exaggeration, 'he put up for sale all he had, offices, lordships, earldoms, sheriffdoms, castles, towns, lands, everything'. Famously, Richard quipped he would have sold London itself if he could have found a buyer.[61] Sheriffs were sacked and fined; their successors appointed at a price; town charters, forest rights, earldoms, high government offices and bishoprics exchanged for cash. The scale of preparations matched this auction. Royal agents scoured the ports of England, Normandy, Brittany and Poitou for vessels, the crown offering to pay two-thirds of the cost of hire and the wages, for a year, of the sailors (2d a day) and steersmen (4d a day). In the financial year from Michaelmas 1189, Henry of Cornhill, the official most involved in arrangements for the fleet, spent more the £5,000. If, as well-informed observers calculated, the fleet collected numbered over 100 ships, the combined bill for wages and hire could have exceeded £14,000, more than half the king's annual revenue from England. On top of that, each ship carried military equipment, horses, infantrymen, food and barrels of silver pennies for expenses. Royal accounts reveal the scale of the crown's purchasing: as well as 50,000 horseshoes from the Forest of Dean and 10,000 from Hampshire, 14,000 cured pigs' carcases from Lincolnshire, Essex and Hampshire, arrows, crossbow bolts, and huge quantities of cheeses and beans. The urgency of such demand drove up prices.

The fleet could have carried, on one well-informed estimate, 8,750 soldiers and sailors, with equipment and horses for a further 4,000 or more knights.[62] Richard's own army, which he led to the Mediterranean in the summer of 1190, may have numbered as many as 6,000, including his own military household of perhaps between 2,500 and 3,000 and the contingents under Archbishop Baldwin and Ranulf Glanvill. The combined fleet that left Messina in 1191 may have contained as many as 219 vessels with perhaps 17,000 troops and seamen.[63] Although the king had not paid for all his followers, the preparations had enabled such a large force to travel together. The terms of wages indicated a clear central strategic grasp. Richard had budgeted to pay his crews for a year from, at the latest, June 1190. Thus his measured progress to Sicily, his wintering there 1190–11, fitted a prearranged timetable. Although deflected by the storm of April 1191 and his subsequent lightning conquest of Cyprus (6 May–1 June 1191), he reached Acre on 8 June 1191, more or less on schedule.

The progress of the fleet itself provides further evidence of Richard's control over crusade planning. There were at least three separate elements in Richard's armada, one that left England from Dartmouth in April 1190; another under Richard of Camville, a knight who was an important English curial official, and Robert of Sablé, a powerful Angevin baron, which left the mouth of the Loire in mid- to late June; and a final squadron of thirty-three ships under the Poitevin William of Fors of Oléron in early to mid-July.[64] Although drawing on ships and companies from all over the Angevin lands, the bulk of the fleet, as of Richard's army as a whole, probably came from England. It was placed under strict disciplinary regulations promulgated by Richard I at Chinon in June, when he also appointed justiciars to oversee them. Apparently he also distributed some vessels to *crucesignati* from his household while he retained the rest for his own use.[65] Although clearly a collaborative venture, the Angevin crusade fleet would not have been assembled in such as well-organized manner without royal subsidy and direction. The first muster point was Lisbon, at the mouth of the Tagus, where members of the first two contingents, comprising sixty-three vessels, found ready distraction from waiting. Fuelled as much by alcohol as religion, they attacked the Muslim and Jewish quarters of Lisbon, extending their rape and plunder to the Christian population before being brought under control, with some difficulty, by King Sancho I of Portugal and their own officers. The whole fleet was united at the mouth of the Tagus in late July. The next agreed rendezvous was with Richard's army at Marseilles at the beginning of August. This clearly proved impractical, but when the fleet put in at Marseilles on 22 August it had only missed an impatient King Richard by three weeks. Undaunted, after a refit, the fleet sailed on to the final planned rendezvous at Messina, which it reached at much the same time as the king in late September. The ability to organize in advance such an operation involving a huge fleet and a significant land army working in concert over hundreds of miles and without ready communication says as much about the twelfth-century development of the experience of sea travel around the Atlantic and Mediterranean coasts as it does of the ability of Richard I's government to translate extravagant ambition into efficient action.

The contrast with Philip II's preparations, while exaggerated by the comparative lack of surviving documentation, appears stark. Failure to collect the Saladin Tithe threw Philip and his nobles on to their own, separate and independent demesnal resources, although before the end of September 1189 the king seems to have received a windfall of 25,000 marks from Richard I in fulfilment of an outstanding debt.[66] This may explain the apparently rather modest contract negotiated with the Genoese to transport his force to the east. In February 1190, Duke Hugh of Burgundy was appointed to arrange details with Genoa. For 5,850 marks (whether of Paris weight or the much heavier sterling is unclear), the Genoese would provide a fleet for 650 knights and 1,300 squires, their horses, food for men and beasts for eight months and wine for four.[67] This may have represented only Philip's immediate military entourage. Even though the duke of Burgundy acted as Philip's agent, it is possible that he made separate arrangements for the transport of his followers, as did Count Philip of Flanders. While the presence with King Philip of these wealthy provincial magnates suggests that the French army was not negligible, very considerable French armies had already left for the east over the previous two years without needing to wait for the king. However large the total French force in 1190, it seems to have put a strain on Genoese resources, as Philip at Genoa in August was already trying to borrow galleys from Richard. That Philip desired to control his vassals is witnessed by his payments at Christmas 1190 in Sicily of 1,000 marks to the duke of Burgundy and 600 marks to the count of Nevers.[68] Nevertheless, most sources say Philip was outspent, outnumbered and outmanoeuvred by Richard.

Such was the size and complexity of Richard's cross-Channel inheritance in July 1189 that he was only crowned king of England at Westminster on 3 September. Richard's crusade preparations exposed the existence of a wider political community beyond the nobility, knights and urban elites. The combination of fundraising, recruitment and revivalist crusade preaching created wide public involvement with occasionally violent consequences. All coronations acted as rituals of political demonstration and dialogue. In Richard's case, denying access to the coronation feast to Jews who had come to pay their loyal respects provoked a riot when Jews were discovered in the crowds pressing to witness the banquet. The violence spread to Jewish districts in the city of London, where houses were destroyed and Jews murdered. Rioting soon turned to indiscriminate looting of property regardless of the owner's religion. The perpetrators included retainers of the nobles gathered for the coronation as well as Londoners. At one point, Ranulf Glanvill and other leading officials unsuccessfully attempted to quell the rioters. This personal involvement of government ministers on one side and a combination of nobles' households and a cross-section of locals on the other emphasized the link between public policy and popular political action. Some believed they were following royal instructions; others talked providentially of Christian destruction of the 'enemies of the Cross of Christ', the very theme of crusade preaching and recruitment campaigns.[69]

Such manifestations of popular response to precise public policies, even if based on partial misunderstanding, were a feature of crusading. So, too, during the recruitment for the Third Crusade in England in 1190 were attacks on the Jews, especially vulnerable with the king's campaign for funds, his approaching departure and the immediate financial requirements of the crusaders who converged on English towns, ports and main roads in the early months of the year. In Lent 1190, bands of English crusaders, some motivated by a misguided notion of serving God and the cross, began looting Jewish property in commercial centres such as King's Lynn and Stamford. The violence reached a ghastly climax at York in mid-March. Well-connected local crusaders led a concerted attack on the Jewish community that culminated in a mass suicide and massacre at the royal castle, now Clifford's Tower, after which, revealingly, the bloodstained crusaders went to York Minster to destroy the Jews' bonds of credit stored there.[70]

The link between royal action and Jewish persecution was direct. In Germany, on news of the imminent crusade, many in the Jewish communities in the Rhineland evacuated to fortified strongholds until the crusading fervour had subsided. Others, in Mainz, stayed even during the 'curia Christi' of 27 March 1188, when Frederick Barbarossa took the cross, protected by imperial officials and later imperial edicts supported by the church hierarchy.[71] In England, the official and ecclesiastical response was less certain. The message received by the crowds at Richard's coronation seemed equivocal to say the least. Yet where royal authorities followed official policy, which was to protect Jewish property and lives, as both legally belonged to the king, atrocities were prevented. At Lincoln in March 1190 the threatened Jewish community was able to take secure refuge in the royal castle, in stark contrast to what happened a few days later in York, when the Jews also fled to the royal castle, only to be betrayed to the mob. Richard's absence from England during Lent 1190 may have weakened official resolve to protect the Jews from cash-strapped crusaders, resentful at what they perceived to be wealthy Jews who may also have been their creditors and inflamed by a possibly sincere belief that they were pursuing their crusading vocation by attacking all enemies of the cross. Whatever else, the Jewish assaults of 1189–90 showed how the crusade could penetrate popular consciousness and group behaviour in ways outside the narrow confines of social control or church precept.

By the time of the Jewish massacres, Richard had long gone from his kingdom, crossing from Dover to Calais on 12 December 1189. The previous month, through the French ambassador, Count Routrou of Perche, he had agreed on a tight schedule with Philip of France to resolve outstanding differences and depart for the east in the spring of 1190.[72] He was away for four years, far longer than he had hoped, planned or imagined. However, Richard, although an absent king, was not a neglectful one. Over the two years on crusade he maintained contact with affairs in France and England. He took with him large numbers of officials and bureaucrats; one, the vice-chancellor Roger Maceal, was drowned off Limassol in April 1191 still wearing the royal seal round his neck (later recovered when Roger's body was washed ashore).[73] The crusade saw the royal administration at war as if the king were campaigning in France and not the far reaches of the Mediterranean. A stream of messengers kept Richard in touch with his dominions. In return he sent home newsletters announcing significant events, such as the fall of Acre and the victory over Saladin at Arsuf. Very exceptionally the journey from England to the Holy Land may have taken as little as two to three months.[74] If not in control, Richard, like his fellow crusade leaders, was well aware of events at home.

In the spring of 1190, the priority was to bring together the naval, military and diplomatic dimensions of the enterprise. Cooperation between Richard and Philip provided the cornerstone of the operation. Once close allies in prising Henry II's grip off power, Richard and Philip became increasingly wary of each other's motives. Richard, the older man (thirty-three; Philip was twenty-five), was the more mercurial and experienced in war. Philip, already into his second decade as king, was only in the early stages of developing what grew into matchless skills of feline diplomacy and political intrigue. A series of meetings between them ensured that arrangements were deftly orchestrated. Each monarch put their dominions in what they hoped would be order. Richard toured Aquitaine in May and June, arriving at Chinon in Anjou on 18 June, then moving on to Tours. There, on 24 June, the date agreed for the beginning of the crusade, he received the scrip and staff of a pilgrim just as, at exactly the same time, Philip did at St Denis, outside Paris, accompanied by the duke of Burgundy and the count of Flanders, a veteran of his own crusade in 1176–7. As arranged, the two kings met at Vézelay on 2 July, a place at once convenient for the march south, in neutral territory, and sanctified by the precedent of Bernard of Clairvaux preaching the Second Crusade. At Vézelay, the kings agreed to rendezvous at Messina in Sicily and, more controversially, to share any acquisitions they made, whether separately or only jointly is, and perhaps was, crucially unclear. For all the gaudy show of unity on display, the Vézelay agreement provided an accurate barometer of mistrust between the two leaders.[75]

Richard and Philip led their armies out of Vézelay on 4 July, three years to the day after Hattin. They began by travelling together, with only their household troops, their armies and the other contingents which were joining them all the time following behind. At Lyons, the armies divided, Philip heading east then south to Genoa while Richard followed the Rhône due south to Marseilles, where he arrived on 31 July. The journey was uneventful after the collapse of a bridge across the Rhône at Lyons beneath the weight of crusaders; Richard had it replaced by a pontoon, the sort of practical and decisive leadership for which he became famous. The arrival of such large forces taxed the capacity of the Mediterranean ports of southern France and Italy to provide shipping, especially outside the central contracts agreed with the kings. Some crusaders had to find passage from as far away as Venice or Brindisi.

Nevertheless, the agreed muster point for most if not all of those who travelled south in the early summer of 1190 was Messina. Even those delayed, such as Count Philip of Flanders, who only made his way to Sicily in the early months of 1191, regarded it as such.[76]

With characteristic impatience, Richard, after waiting a week for his fleet, decided not to delay further in Marseilles. He hired a substantial flotilla, one part of which, under Archbishop Baldwin and Ranulf Glanvill, sailed directly to Acre, which they reached on 21 September. This division of forces may have been prompted by the desire to send immediate help in response to news of Frederick Barbarossa's death. Alternatively, it may have been designed to conserve Richard's political interests in the Acre besieging force now dominated by French nobles such as the count of Champagne. For the remainder of his troops at Marseilles, Richard provided ten busses and twenty galleys, probably capable of carrying between 2,500 and 3,000 passengers and crew.[77] Again, Richard's improvisation, backed by clear strategy and cash, confirmed his reputation for firm action. On the leisurely summer cruise down the Italian coast to Sicily that followed, the king behaved equally in character, by turns tricky, aggressive, inquisitive, reckless and showy. He enjoyed robust diplomatic exchanges with Philip II at Genoa; snubbed Pope Clement III by avoiding Rome while bullying his legate; engaged in strenuous sightseeing at Naples and Salerno; and provoked a needless but dangerous fracas with some local Calabrian peasants before performing a grand public entry to Messina on 23 September.

This jaunt allowed the full crusade force to assemble. Philip had slipped into Sicily a week earlier and Richard timed his arrival to coincide with his grand fleet, which had chased him from Marseilles. Although Philip made a rather petulant show of immediately trying to leave for the Holy Land, the season was effectively too late for a crossing before the following spring. The kingdom of Sicily, which included most of southern Italy as well as the island itself, although economically prosperous with a strong maritime tradition, proved an uneasy billet. The death of William II in November 1189 had led to a succession dispute between his cousin Tancred, who had seized the crown, and William's aunt, Constance, and her husband, Frederick Barbarossa's eldest son Henry VI, now king of Germany. When the crusaders arrived, Sicily, a polyglot society of Greeks, Normans, northern Italians and Muslims, was a volatile place, nervously expecting Henry VI's invasion and threatened by a Muslim revolt on the island itself. The crusaders were faced by Tancred's uneasiness at their military strength, the overt hostility of the mainly Greek inhabitants of Messina and the occupational problem of high food prices. Their stay was marked by intricate diplomacy punctuated by violence as Richard, in particular, sought to impose himself through high-handed aggression.

Riots between locals and his men prompted Richard and his Angevin army to sack Messina on 4 October, ignoring the presence of Philip of France, who was lodged in the city, let alone the fact that the citizens, despite crusaders' dark comments about miscegenation with Muslims, were Christian subjects of a friendly power. The pressure on Tancred was maintained by building a wooden castle outside the walls nicknamed 'Mategriffon', roughly 'kill the locals'.[78] Tancred bowed to the pressure on 6 October by agreeing to pay 40,000 gold ounces in lieu of William II's legacy to Henry II and the dower of William's widow, Richard's sister Joan, who had been under house arrest since her husband's death. To keep Philip sweet, on 8 October Richard, in the spirit of the Vézelay compact, gave a third of his winnings to the French king, who used some of it to bail out his followers. Thereafter, at a popular level, there were no more disturbances, as the kings worked hard to control prices and imposed new discipline on the crusaders' behaviour by regulating gambling and repayment of their debts.

During the winter of 1190–91 Richard found time to refit and expand his fleet, to extend rather patronizing largesse to Philip by giving him some ships in February, and to redraw part of the diplomatic map of western Europe. In the October treaty with Tancred, he had promised a marriage alliance between his nephew, Arthur of Brittany, and Tancred's daughter, as well as help against any invasion of Sicily. Attempts by Philip to cast doubt on Richard's sincerity came to nothing. For himself, Richard completed arrangements for his own marriage to Berengaria, daughter of the king of Navarre. She arrived in Messina, escorted by the indefatigable septuagenarian *femme fatale* of the Second Crusade, Eleanor of Aquitaine, at the end of March 1191. By this time Philip, fresh from his failure to turn Tancred against the English king, had reluctantly absolved Richard from his longstanding obligation to marry his sister Alice in return for another 10,000 marks. Armed with this subsidy and the English ships, Philip sailed from Messina on 20 March 1191, arriving at Acre on 20 April. According to a Muslim observer,

Ibn Shaddad, Philip came with just six large cargo ships carrying his supplies, horses and retinue. A hostile western source depicted him as sneaking to shore in only one ship, without fanfare. Elsewhere his companions are described as including the count of Flanders, who probably travelled with the count of St Pol, the duke of Burgundy and a group of curial nobles and officials led by Count Routrou. One Muslim witness implied that Philip of Flanders travelled separately.[79] The group around Philip II mirrored the structure of Richard's own force, some great nobles but the core provided by the king's own household and court, but on a smaller scale and probably lacking infantry. Muslim sources recorded the defenders' relief at the modest size of the French royal fleet. Once established in the Christian camp, Philip took the lead in pressing forward new attacks on Acre as Saladin brought up reinforcements to combat the new threat of the western monarchs. Whatever Philip's intentions, the final push for the city waited on the appearance of King Richard.

Having received his future bride Berengaria at Messina, Richard put the finishing touches to his great fleet, which was to carry food, treasure, siege engines and even the dismantled wooden castle of Mategriffon, as well as horses, arms and men. On one plausible set of calculations, the fleet of 219 ships could have carried 17,000 passengers and crew.[80] This armada left Sicily on 10 April heading for Crete. Three days later a westerly gale started to blow, scattering the formation. At least twenty-five ships had become detached from the main squadron, including that carrying Richard's sister Joan and fiancée Berengaria. Waiting at Rhodes between 22 April and 1 May, Richard learnt that some of the missing ships had been blown by the storm as far as the southern coast of Cyprus, where three of them had been shipwrecked and their survivors ill treated by the locals. The remainder, including the princesses' ship, stood offshore. The independent Greek ruler of the island since 1184, Isaac Comnenus, fearing an invasion, fortified Limassol, sought a treaty with Saladin and tried to entice the princesses into his clutches, perhaps to serve as hostages against an attack by Richard, risky policies in the face of internal opposition and the crusaders' overwhelming military superiority. Limassol had most likely been fixed as a rendezvous for the fleet from Sicily and Richard may have already contemplated subduing the island to assist the crusaders on the mainland of Palestine with a ready, secure source of supplies. The affray at Limassol and Isaac's belligerent behaviour provided Richard with an excuse and a reason to intervene in Cyprus. Richard himself explained three months later that, because of Isaac's behaviour towards the shipwrecked crusaders, 'we were spurred to revenge'.[81]

What may have begun as a rescue soon became a conquest. Richard arrived off the south coast on 5 May. Having forced a landing at Limassol, pressing inland he made Isaac withdraw after a brief skirmish. On 12 May, in the chapel of St George at Limassol, Richard, Europe's most eligible (and, some hinted, most confirmed) bachelor and Berengaria of Navarre were married. By this time, Isaac had sued for peace terms. Richard also received an embassy from Acre led by Guy of Lusignan, who asked for the king's support against attempts to replace him as king of Jerusalem by Conrad of Montferrat, who enjoyed the backing of the French. A few days later, French ambassadors joined in urging Richard's presence at Acre. Meanwhile, the truce with Isaac had broken down and Richard embarked on a systematic investment of the whole island. His fleet sailed round the island capturing strategic ports. From Famagusta, Richard led his troops westwards. After defeating Isaac's army once more, at Tremetousha, he captured Nicosia unopposed and then Kyrenia on the northern coast after a siege by land and sea. A few days later, Isaac surrendered. Richard had promised not to clap him in irons, so Isaac was bound by chains forged of silver, a characteristic Ricardian touch.

The conquest of Cyprus enhanced Richard's reputation, filled his coffers with treasure, partly derived from a tax levied on every Cypriot, and provided a source of provisions for his army and for those at Acre. Initially, in his eagerness to exploit Cyprus's resources for the crusade, Richard retained direct overlordship over the island, appointing Angevin castellans and two administrators, the fleet commanders Richard of Camville and Robert of Thornham. As their rule proved unpopular and provoked resistance, and as his own costs in Palestine rose, within a few weeks Richard decided to sell the island to the Templars for 100,000 Saracen bezants, of which he actually received 40,000. When, in April 1192, the Templars, who also found ruling Cypriots an unacceptably draining experience, surrendered the island back to Richard, he found a new buyer in the recently displaced king of Jerusalem, Guy of Lusignan, who stumped up another 60,000 gold bezants for the privilege.[82] Guy, and after his death in 1194 his brother Amaury, established a ruling

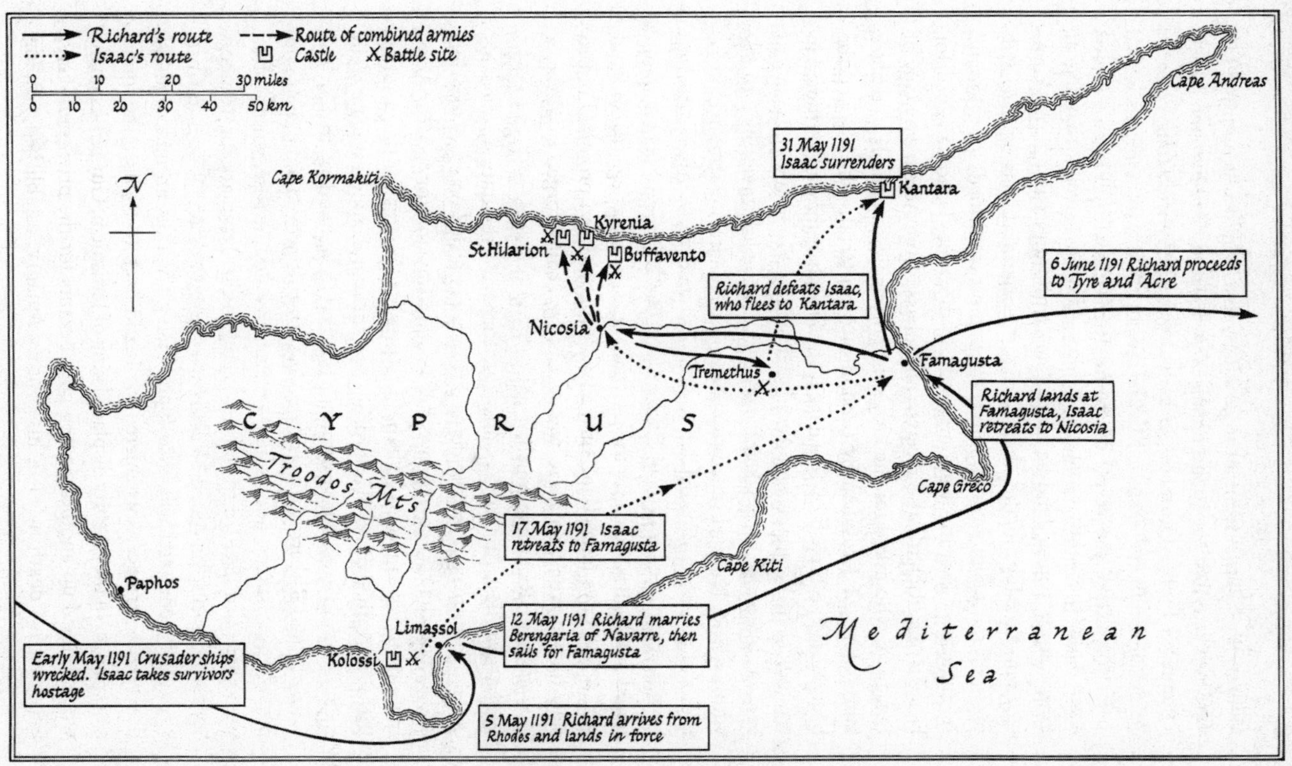

Richard's route
Isaac's route
Route of combined armies
Castle
X Battle site
0 10 20 30 miles
0 10 20 30 40 50 km
N
Cape Andreas
31 May 1191 Isaac surrenders
Kantara
Cape Kormakiti
Kyrenia
St Hilarion
Buffavento
6 June 1191 Richard proceeds to Tyre and Acre
Richard defeats Isaac, who flees to Kantara
Nicosia
Famagusta
Tremethus
Richard lands at Famagusta, Isaac retreats to Nicosia
CYPRUS
Troodos Mts
Cape Greco
17 May 1191 Isaac retreats to Famagusta
Cape Kiti
Paphos
Limassol
12 May 1191 Richard marries Berengaria of Navarre, then sails for Famagusta
Mediterranean Sea
Early May 1191 Crusader ships wrecked. Isaac takes survivors hostage
Kolossi
5 May 1191 Richard arrives from Rhodes and lands in force

14. Richard I Captures Cyprus, May 1191

dynasty in Cyprus, from 1196 as kings, that would last until the late fifteenth century. The island remained in western Christian hands until conquered by the Ottoman Turks in 1571, the most lasting crusader achievement in the eastern Mediterranean. While its annexation had been fortuitous, the result of storm, Richard's temperament, Isaac's aggression, unpopularity and incompetence, and a growing realization of how useful to the Christian cause Cyprus could be, the island subsequently provided food, military and naval bases and ultimately a refuge for crusaders and Frankish émigrés from the Holy Land. It also developed its own Frankish political structures and ruling elites, which proved more successful and lasting than those of mainland Outremer.

Isaac's surrender on 1 June freed Richard to complete his journey to the Holy Land after the most decisive Christian military operation in the Levant since the First Crusade. That the victims were fellow Christians dampened the ardour of Richard's panegyrists not at all. The Cypriots were demonized as treacherous and malign, the conquest another display of Richard's courage and determination. On 5 June he sailed from Famagusta. Taking the shortest crossing to Syria, he landed at the Hospitaller castle of Margat, where he deposited the unfortunate Isaac. The next day he reached Tyre, where the garrison, on orders from Conrad of Montferrat, refused him entry, forcing him to camp overnight outside the walls. Cruising south the next day with the fleet's rearguard of twenty-four galleys, Richard fell in with and sank a large Muslim sailing ship from Beirut carrying supplies and reinforcements for the Acre garrison. The loss of this vessel landed a heavy material and psychological blow on Saladin's forces while further elevating Richard's already formidable renown.[83] Richard finally arrived at the Christian camp outside Acre, to lavish displays of enthusiasm, on 8 June, three and a half years after he had impulsively taken the cross at Tours. The crisis of the crusade had finally been reached.

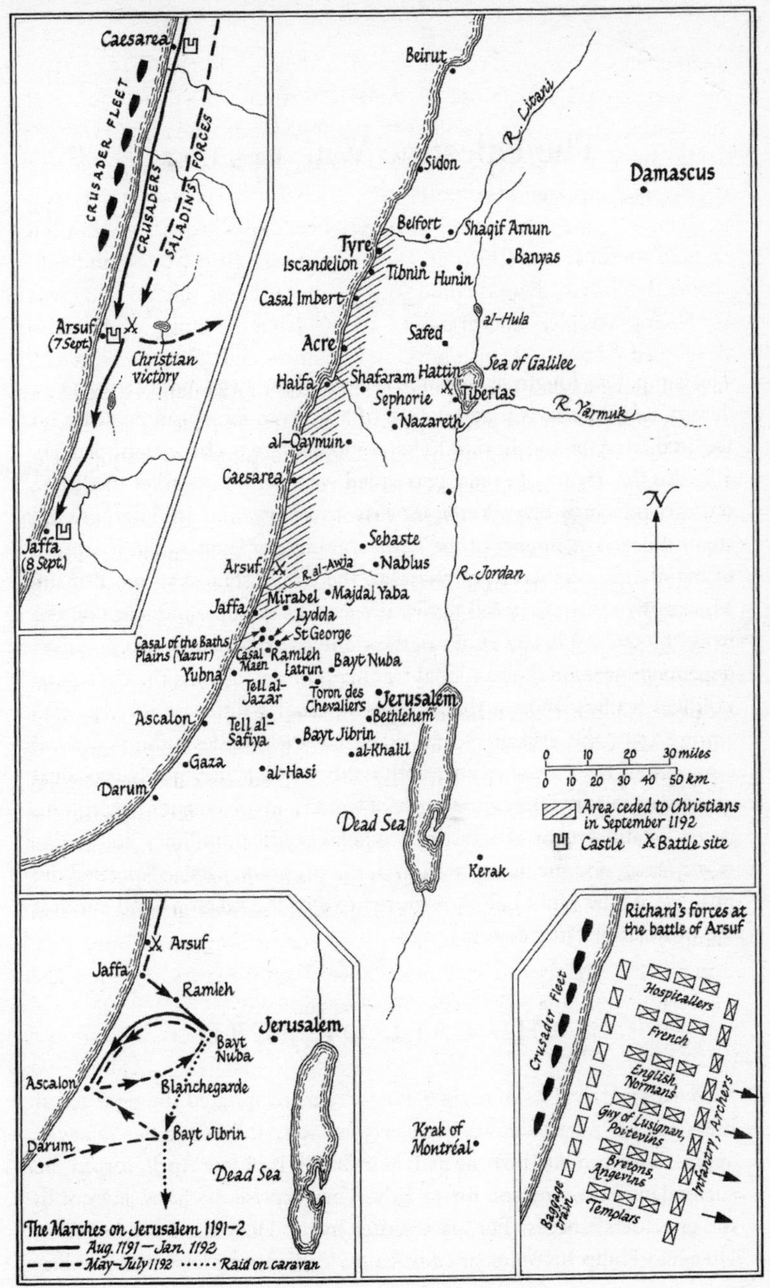
Caesarea
CRUSADER FLEET
CRUSADERS
SALADIN'S FORCES
Arsuf
(7 Sept)
Christian victory
Jaffa
(8 Sept)
Beirut
R. Litani
Sidon
Damascus
Belfort
Shaqif Arnun
Tyre
Iscandelion
Tibnin
Hunin
Banyas
Casal Imbert
al-Hula
Safed
Acre
Sea of Galilee
Haifa
Shafaram
Hattin
Tiberias
Sephorie
Nazareth
R. Yarmuk
al-Qaymun
Caesarea
N
Sebaste
Arsuf
R. al-Awja
Nablus
R. Jordan
Mirabel
Majdal Yaba
Jaffa
Lydda
St George
Casal of the Baths
Plains (Yazur)
Casal Maen
Ramleh
Bayt Nuba
Yubna
Latrun
Tell al-Jazar
Toron des Chevaliers
Jerusalem
Bethlehem
Ascalon
Tell al-Safiya
Bayt Jibrin
al-Khalil
Gaza
al-Hasi
Darum
0 10 20 30 miles
0 10 20 30 40 50 km
Dead Sea
Area ceded to Christians in September 1192
Castle
Battle site
Kerak
Arsuf
Jaffa
Ramleh
Jerusalem
Bayt Nuba
Ascalon
Blanchegarde
Bayt Jibrin
Darum
Dead Sea
The Marches on Jerusalem 1191–2
Aug. 1191 – Jan. 1192
May–July 1192
Raid on caravan
Krak of Montréal
Richard's forces at the battle of Arsuf
Crusader Fleet
Hospitallers
French
English, Normans
Guy of Lusignan, Poitevins
Bretons, Angevins
Templars
Baggage train
Infantry, Archers

15. Palestine with the Campaigns of 1191–2

14
The Palestine War 1191–2

The campaigns fought in Palestine between June 1191 and August 1192 determined the survival and nature of a western European presence on the mainland of the Levant. The combat of two charismatic leaders allied to the drama of events persuaded writers on both sides to elevate the struggle into epic. Yet it is easy to exaggerate its international significance. The impact of the Latin conquest of Cyprus and recapture of mainland ports were peripheral to the circumstances of most of the Muslim world. In material terms, it exerted negligible influence on the lives of western Europeans. Even the viability of the Christian conquests depended more on international trading patterns outside the control of political leaders and on the factious internal politics of the Ayyubid empire once the crusaders had departed. Nonetheless, the equivocal outcome of the Palestine war, with neither side achieving their central objectives, ensured the continuance of western involvement in the region, the re-establishment of a distinctive local political, military and diplomatic force, and the incorporation of the *negotium Terrae Sanctae*, 'the business of the Holy Land', as normative in the religious and cultural life of western Christendom.

THE FALL OF ACRE

Richard I's arrival at Acre on 8 June 1192 precipitated the final act of the siege of Acre. Six weeks' heavy assault, following the renewed aggression stimulated by the arrival of Philip II in late April, forced the surrender of the garrison on 12 July. The surprise, perhaps, lay not in the crusaders' success but, as a writer in the Holy Land a generation later had Philip II comment caustically, 'considering how many noblemen have been at this siege, it is extraordinary how slow they have been to take it.'[1] Saladin's failure to dislodge the Christians in 1189–90, prevent their reinforcement by sea or secure uninterrupted naval supply lines to the city rendered the ultimate outcome almost certain. With the arrival of the western monarchs, he lacked any fresh tactics beyond stepping up raids on the Christian trenches and a systematic scorched earth policy in the surrounding countryside. Even so, the defenders mounted fierce and skilled resistance until overwhelmed by force of numbers and firepower. Such was the tenacity of the besieged that the attackers almost literally had to demolish the defences of Acre stone by stone. Although a damaging blow to Saladin's carefully constructed warrior image, the manner of Acre's fall suggested that Jerusalem would be no pushover for the Christian invaders.[2]

The last weeks of the siege were dominated by the contest of the Christian siege engines, catapults, sappers and scaling ladders against the defenders' incendiary missiles, stone-throwing machines and counter-sappers. Each Christian commander possessed his own great stone-throwers. The duke of Burgundy, the Templars, the Hospitallers and the Pisans each had one. Philip II had many, his best, called 'Malvoisine' or 'Bad Neighbour', constantly needing repair as it was a prime target of enemy bombardment. The count of Flanders ran two, which, after his death on 1 June, were taken over by Richard I, who built two more as well as a couple of mangonels and a siege tower. Philip also constructed a protected shooting platform and an elaborate scaling device, although both were destroyed by fire. The common fund, established in the Christian camp at least since the autumn of 1190, paid for its own stone-thrower, 'God's Petrary'.[3] This display of advanced military technology was supported by manpower. Casualties seemed to be no deterrent to the attackers, a profligacy with human life which negated the garrison's defensive advantage of the protection of the well-built walls. Saladin's repeated assaults of the now vast crusader camp never threatened to disrupt the relentless battering against the city. Numbers clearly mattered. There may have been only a few thousand fighters within Acre, while Saladin's army, despite regular reinforcement, cannot have matched the gathered strength of the Christians, whose army may have numbered by this time well over 25,000 men. Both Philip and Richard were freely able to recruit mercenary knights when they arrived. Realistically, only famine, disease or political implosion could have prevented the Christian victory. As it happened, two of these did threaten the crusader juggernaut.

Within days of Richard's arrival, both kings were struck down with what contemporaries called 'Arnaldia' or 'Leonardie', perhaps a form of scurvy or trench mouth, which caused the victims' hair and nails to fall out.[4] Richard almost died. Although both recovered, Richard more slowly than Philip, the effects of the illness remained. Philip, despite surviving another thirty-two years, never entirely lost the traces of this debilitating condition, while Richard's health remained bad for the rest of his time in Palestine, more than once influencing his conduct of diplomacy and, perhaps, the war itself. Immediately, the sickness of the two kings shook morale. To counter any sense of drift or crisis, once the worst of his illness had passed, Richard had himself carried in a litter to within range of the city walls. There, under the protection of a specially constructed circular hut, he amused himself and inspired his troops by taking pot shots at the enemy with his crossbow.[5]

Potentially no less debilitating was the rivalry between the two kings. Philip's sense of grievance at his treatment in Sicily, slighted when Richard seized Messina and insulted by Richard's repudiation of his sister in favour of Berengaria, was exacerbated at almost every turn. Richard received the allegiance of the Pisans; their competitors, the Genoese, supported Philip. The French king's demands for half of Cyprus under the terms of the Vézelay agreement were brushed aside. While Philip hired knights at three gold coins a month, Richard offered four. When the count of Flanders died, it was Richard not Philip who acquired his siege engines. Each king attempted to negotiate separately with Saladin over surrender terms for Acre. This partly grew out of their respective support for the opposing claimants to the Jerusalem throne. Philip had formed a close alliance with Conrad of Montferrat, while Richard promoted the interests of Guy of Lusignan, once his vassal in Poitou. Guy, with a small army, had already campaigned with Richard in Cyprus. It says much for Philip's political weakness and Richard's practical dominance that, in spite of the French king having the favour of a majority of the important local Outremer barons and with most of the crusade leaders being his vassals, Conrad's succession remained blocked. Such rivalry at times endangered the military operations, as one side or the other failed to coordinate attacks, which consequently failed. The cumulative effect of this rancour fatally undermined Philip's commitment to the enterprise. A flavour of the bitterness of the kings' relations was captured in a nasty little story that circulated in Outremer some years later. This had Richard telling a sick Philip that his only son, Louis, had died. He hoped Philip would die of shock and grief. In fact, Louis was not dead at all. But, the story went on, Philip was so shaken that he immediately arranged to return to the west.[6]

Above all, Philip may have resented the personal dominance Richard asserted as soon as he reached Acre. With the most treasure and probably the largest number of troops in his pay, Richard was a veteran of proven ability and success. The seizure of Messina and conquest of Cyprus had merely confirmed his reputation, which he delighted in playing up to. He had embarked on crusade with what he claimed to be Excalibur, King Arthur's sword. A useful prop, he traded it for transport ships and galleys with Tancred of Sicily. The gorgeous apparel, prancing steed, glittering saddle and gold- and silver-decorated sword with which he greeted Isaac Comnenus outside Limassol on 1 May was carefully designed to show 'he was an exceptional knight'.[7] Such visual pyrotechnics proclaimed a direct propagandist message readily understood by observers. When Richard landed at Acre on 8 June, the strenuous celebrations included recitations of stories of ancient heroes 'as an incitement to modern people to imitate them'. Richard deliberately presented himself as just such an epic warrior, perhaps even in his lifetime earning the nickname 'cœur de lion'.[8] In all that he did, even if not always successful, Richard was formidable, in politics, in administration, in battle, in public relations and in diplomacy.

Throughout the Third Crusade, Richard's political objective was unequivocal: the restoration of Outremer, and especially the kingdom of Jerusalem, at least to its pre-Hattin extent. However, within days of landing, Richard opened channels of negotiation with Saladin, primarily though the sultan's brother al-Adil. These he never entirely closed during his seventeen-month stay in the Holy Land. His conduct at Acre and after showed willingness to fight and to kill, but also to talk and to reach accommodation. As in the west, Richard used force as a means to an end. If Saladin could be threatened or intimidated into granting Richard's demands, then battles and sieges were not necessary for their own sake. However, if Saladin refused terms, then Richard was prepared to force them from him. This elaborate and often delicate diplomatic dance, performed to the accompaniment of hard military campaigning, characterized the Palestine war of 1191–2, setting a precedent for subsequent crusades in the east. The struggle for advantage between Richard and Saladin was dominated by the mounting military and political problems each faced, yet it was far from the crude slogging match between enemies blind to each other's interests or character that some portrayals of crusading, including those by contemporaries, imply. Richard was not alone in seeking a negotiated settlement; according to one eyewitness, Philip was involved in the early approaches to Saladin.[9] However, according to Ibn Shaddad, who was also there, the policy proved controversial, at least before Acre fell, meeting with opposition from other Christian leaders. This was hardly surprising as, at the time, the events of the Third Crusade were depicted spiritually as a test of religious faith and temporally as a global contest, infidel Asia and Africa ranged against Christian Europe, the siege of Acre a new Trojan War. According to Ibn Shaddad, Richard brushed aside any criticism in typical style: 'The reins of power are entrusted to me. I rule and nobody rules me.'[10]

The negotiations, which began on 17 June, probed each side's aims and vulnerability. Gifts were exchanged and initial bargaining positions staked out. Roger of Howden shrewdly identified Saladin's irreducible insistence on retaining Jerusalem and Transjordan, the one the propaganda totem of his empire, the other the vital land bridge that held its Syrian and Egyptian halves together. However, Richard saw no need to compromise when the military situation increasingly favoured him, with the Christian siege machines maintaining an incessant bombardment of Acre's walls. Saladin's attacks and scorched earth policy failed to impede progress. Christian optimism was sustained by the traditional accompaniment of divine visions and stories of individual heroism. More prosaically, with neatly judged psychology, Richard offered to pay for every stone removed from the city walls, starting at two gold coins each but rising to four, a popular move with soldiers 'as greedy for glory as for gain'.[11] By extending his hiring of mercenaries, Richard was adding cohesion and direction to the siege. With no let-up in the attacks, it soon became apparent to the garrison commanders that they were facing an unpleasant but unavoidable choice: surrender or death. Saladin was reluctant, but his commanders in Acre capitulated on 12 July. The terms agreed, apparently negotiated mainly though the mediation of Conrad of Montferrat, spared the lives of the defenders, their wives and children, in return for a ransom of 200,000 dinars, the release of over 1,500 Christian prisoners, and the return of the relic of the True Cross taken at Hattin. Conrad received a hefty negotiating fee of 10,000 dinars. The entire contents of Acre, Saladin's main armaments depot in the Holy Land, with provisions, artillery and perhaps as many as seventy galleys, were handed over to the Christians. The loss of much of his navy was as damaging militarily to Saladin as the fall of the city was to his prestige, Ibn Shaddad remembering that he 'was more affected than a bereft mother or a distracted lovesick girl'.[12] Now Saladin could only withdraw, prevaricate over the details of the surrender agreement and wait on events, perhaps hoping, not unreasonably, that in victory Christian rivalries would re-emerge to undermine their hard-won success.

If so, he almost had his wish. As the two kings set about dividing Acre between them, those in the army attached to neither protested. Despite their contribution to the siege, they were to receive nothing. Duke Leopold of Austria seems to have felt especially aggrieved that his claims to a share of the booty had been brusquely rejected. Some said that, on Richard's orders, Leopold's banner had been thrown down after the entry into Acre to signal the denial of his claim to the spoils. Leopold and others left the Holy Land in disgust.[13] Although Richard received most of the blame for this policy, both kings clearly agreed to it. It fulfilled the assumptions that lay beneath the Vézelay accord and, more widely, recognized the special position of authority the barons of Jerusalem had for years been prepared to afford western monarchs in the Holy Land. As it was, both kings displayed a sense of this responsibility by sending help to Antioch. However, this unity proved deceptive. As Richard laconically wrote a few weeks later to his unpopular chancellor and viceroy in England, William Longchamp bishop of Ely, 'within fifteen days the king of France left us to return to his own land'.[14]

Even Philip II's most ardent apologists found his sudden abandonment of the crusade hard to justify. It was easy to explain. The death of Philip of Flanders at Acre on 1 June activated a series of rearrangements to the lordships of the territories between the royal lands around Paris and the county of Flanders, which were vital to Capetian security. Philip stood to gain the strategically and economically important region of Artois and be able to manipulate the contested Flemish succession to his material advantage. But he needed to be present to ensure the process went smoothly. His own health, fears for that of his infant son, the need for him to find a new wife as well as the persistent humiliations, real or imagined, he had to endure from Richard added to Philip's conviction that he must return home immediately. His departure, especially as he left most of his troops behind, may not have displeased Richard unduly as it consolidated his control over the enterprise.

The speed with which Philip acted after the fall of Acre suggests he had already made up his mind but, with characteristic circumspection, had successfully concealed his intention, not least from his own allies, particularly Conrad of Montferrat, whose prospects were closely bound up with the French king's presence and support. Having already declined to commit himself to remaining in the Holy Land for three years or until Jerusalem was captured, on 22 July Philip announced his decision to leave. This went down very badly with most of his followers. But when a hardly serious request to be given half of Cyprus in return for a commitment to stay was refused by Richard, the die was cast. On 28 July, after a two-day hearing on the merits of the claims of Guy and Conrad to the throne of Jerusalem, the two kings announced a compromise that reflected Richard's ascendancy. Guy was to remain king for life, but the succession would devolve after his death on Conrad and Isabella and their heirs. The revenues of the kingdom were to be divided equally between Guy and Conrad, while the latter was granted a lordship in the north based on Tyre. To balance this, Guy's brother Geoffrey was to receive the county of Jaffa and Ascalon if and when it was recaptured. There were echoes of the deal done in 1153 that transferred the English royal succession to Richard's father, Henry II, but allowed the anointed King Stephen to retain the crown until his death. Guy, too, was an anointed monarch, but only by virtue of his now deceased wife. Unlike the 1153 agreement, the arbitration of July 1191 failed to stick.

On 29 July Philip swore publicly that he would do no harm to Richard's lands in the west. The next day he appointed the duke of Burgundy as leader of the remaining French troops and gave his half share of Acre to Conrad. The following day the Muslim prisoners were divided between Philip and Richard and on 31 July the French king, with his prisoners and a small entourage, left Acre for Tyre. There he transferred his prisoners to Conrad, thus giving him a share in the promised ransom from Saladin. On 3 August, Philip sailed from Tyre for home. His behaviour attracted almost universal opprobrium, even from normally sympathetic observers. His own followers made their views transparent by refusing to accompany him. Accusations of greed, fear and dereliction of duty compounded the shame heaped on him. Only his later successs in elevating royal authority in France to heights unseen since the Carolingian heyday of the ninth century redeemed his international reputation. Nevertheless, Philip's actions left a sour taste for generations. At the time, although plainly anxious about the damage a resentful and humiliated Philip could do to Angevin lands in his continued absence, Richard could allow himself some understated sarcasm at the French king's expense. Describing Philip's departure, Richard remarked a few days afterwards: 'We, however, place the love of God and His honour above our own and above the acquisition of many regions.'[15]

FROM ACRE TO JAFFA

Philip's absence both simplified and complicated the situation facing the crusaders. Richard quickly moved to assert his influence over the remaining French army by lending their commander Hugh of Burgundy 5,000 marks, presumably until the French share of the Acre prisoners' ransom was paid. But Conrad of Montferrat actually held these prisoners at Tyre, and only reluctantly handed them over to Duke Hugh on 12 August. Conrad's independence had been bolstered by Philip's grant of half of Acre as well as the confirmation of his autonomy in Tyre. Whenever members of the local Jerusalem baronage became disenchanted with Richard, Conrad offered a focus for dissent. More immediate was Saladin's reluctance to honour the surrender terms. Although the relic of the True Cross had been inspected by Richard's envoys in the Muslim camp on 2 August,[16] negotiations stalled, only partly because not all of the prisoners had been returned from Tyre. Saladin evidently hoped that delay would increase the divisions within the Christian army, lower morale and delay Richard's march south. Withholding the lucrative ransom and the True Cross appeared useful bargaining counters. The Christian desire for the return of the Cross and their leaders' eagerness for the ransom money seemed to play into the sultan's hands. With Acre lost, stalemate now served Saladin's purpose.

On 20 August, ten days after the deadline for the exchange of the first instalment of prisoners and ransom money, Richard called Saladin's bluff. However much he wanted the relic and the money, Richard knew that further delay would only undermine the preparedness of his army for the tough campaign in prospect. He later described what happened:

On Saladin's behalf it had been agreed that the Holy Cross and 1,500 living persons would be handed over to us, and he fixed a day for us when all this was to be done. But the time limit expired, and, as the pact which he had agreed was entirely made void, we quite properly had the Saracens we had in custody – about 2,600 of them – put to death. A few of the more notable were spared, and we hope to recover the Holy Cross and certain Christian captives in exchange for them.[17]

Ibn Shaddad was in Saladin's camp a few miles away when the massacre occurred. Understandably, his account is more vivid.

When the king of England saw that the sultan hesitated to hand over the money, the prisoners and the Cross, he dealt treacherously towards the Muslim prisoners ... He and all the Frankish forces, horse and foot, marched out at the time of the afternoon prayers on Tuesday 27 rajab (20 August). They ... moved on into the middle of the plain. The enemy then brought out the Muslim prisoners for whom God had decreed martyrdom, about 3,000 bound in ropes. Then as one man they charged them and with stabbings and blows with the sword they slew them in cold blood.

The stunned Muslim advance guard watched helplessly while they sought orders from the sultan. By the time they tried to intervene, the killing was over. Next day they inspected the corpses and, Ibn Shaddad added, 'were able to recognize some of them'.[18]

Richard I's butchery of his Muslim captives was an atrocity not uncommon in war. It was not an act of random sadism, less so, for example, than Saladin's own execution of the Templars and Hospitallers after Hattin. It ranks, perhaps, with Henry V's slaughter of his French prisoners at Agincourt in 1415, except that then the battle was still in progress. Even Ibn Shaddad recognized that Richard's action contained logic: revenge for Muslim killing of surrendering Christians during the siege of Acre 'or that the king of England had decided to march to Ascalon ... and did not think it wise to leave that number in the rear'.[19] Richard and his apologists, and many observers not noted for their sympathy towards him, insisted on the justice of the killings, even their legality. One favourable source declared that, without the agreement with Saladin, the lives of the defeated garrison were forfeit *jure belli*, 'under the rights of war'.[20] The contrast between the control displayed when Acre fell and the cold-blooded savagery of the mass execution weeks later showed Saladin clearly the sort of adversary he faced. The sultan probably recognized the massacre for what it was, a deliberate act of policy for which his own actions were in part responsible. Over the following weeks he treated captured Christian soldiers with summary execution, occasionally allowing their corpses to be mutilated out of revenge. More seriously for the strategy of the war, he recognized that Richard had raised the stakes for all subsequent besieged Muslim garrisons. To avoid such consequences, Saladin moved quickly in September to dismantle the fortifications of Ascalon, one of Richard's prime objectives, the key port in southern Palestine and the bastion on the route to Egypt. Yet Saladin understood the game both were playing and, judging from the respectful tone used of Richard by his close colleague Ibn Shaddad, appreciated the king's skill at it. Whatever his public emotions, only a fortnight later he authorized his brother to resume face-to-face talks with Richard.[21]

By that time, Saladin's own options had diminished severely in the face of the Christian advance. Five days after the massacre, on 25 August, Richard had fully assembled his forces and began the march south, along the coast road past Mt Carmel, Haifa, Caesarea and Arsuf to Jaffa. The eighty miles from Acre to Jaffa proved hazardous and exhausting. In the debilitating summer heat, with little shade, the Christians marched for the most part under arms to resist the repeated attacks of Saladin's troops. The sultan shadowed the host, constantly harrying the line, especially the rearguard. This was entrusted to the Hospitallers. The Templars were in the vanguard. Between them were four separate divisions: the Angevins and Bretons; Guy of Lusignan, his Jerusalem followers and the Poitevins; the Anglo-Normans under the king; and the French, under Hugh of Burgundy and Henry of Champagne. The infantry and archers were divided into two columns, one of which marched on the landward side to provide outer defence for the knights against attack from mounted Turkish archers, while the other accompanied the baggage train on the seaward side. The large Christian fleet shadowed the army offshore, affording rest, food and protection. Before the crusaders lay a scorched landscape, its forts levelled, its crops burnt. Frequent and intense skirmishes cost both sides dear. Richard himself, constantly rallying the lines, was wounded. Progress was slow, barely five miles a day. However, as long as the battered Christian army remained intact it posed an increasingly menacing threat to the ports of Jaffa and Ascalon and thus Saladin's whole position in southern Palestine even without a direct assault on Jerusalem. Saladin's loss of sea-power was proving as significant as the land defeat at Acre. Recognizing the urgency of stopping the crusaders' advance, on 4 September, with the Christians nearing the plain of Arsuf, Saladin agreed to Richard's request to reopen negotiations. For Saladin it offered a chance to buy time to allow more reinforcements to arrive; for Richard it formed part of his consistent strategy of allying diplomatic with military pressure. On 5 September, Richard, with the jilted Humphrey of Toron as his interpreter, held a private interview with al-Adil which ended in acrimony, with Richard sticking to his demands for a return of the pre-1187 kingdom of Jerusalem.[22] Nothing was achieved except to convince Saladin that his only option was to risk a pitched battle. With the failure of diplomacy as well as Fabian tactics, Saladin was compelled to try to convert what should have been the undoubted advantages of a home base, easy access to supplies and manpower, a sympathetic population and local knowledge into an immediate decisive victory.

On 7 September, just south of the Forest of Arsuf and north of the town itself, the increased pressure of the Turkish attacks forced Richard to halt the march and turn his column to face the enemy, as Saladin intended. The tactics of each side were clear. Turkish light cavalry would harass the Christian line to provoke a disorganized counter-charge which, by breaking the crusaders' formation, would open them to piecemeal slaughter by fast-moving mounted archers. Failing that, a series of feints to draw a more concerted charge would have a similar, if riskier effect, exposing the Christians to Turkish counter-attack, provided the Turks avoided becoming trapped by the full force of a concerted enemy cavalry assault. The Christians' aim was to withstand the Turkish archers, using the screen of infantry to shield the waiting cavalry, until the Muslims were committed to close combat on tiring horses, at which point a mass cavalry charge would be launched to annihilate the enemy and sweep them from the field. The two chief problems for Richard were to survive the hail of arrows and missiles for long enough, without taking too many casualties, to make this effective; and to maintain sufficient control over his separate divisions to ensure that, when it came, the cavalry charged as one to guarantee maximum impact.

Once battle was joined about nine o'clock in the morning, the Christian lines were pounded incessantly for hour after hour but they held. Just as Richard was preparing a decisive encircling attack on all fronts at once, the bruised and battered Hospitallers, on the left (i.e. northern) flank, goaded beyond endurance and worried at the loss of horses, charged, taking with them the French division on their right. Richard immediately grasped the tactical imperative and ordered a general attack that threw the Turks back. As Saladin regrouped, Richard, having kept the Anglo-Norman brigade in reserve as a rallying point around the royal banner, the dragon standard, the ensign of English monarchs at least since Harold Godwinson, managed to restore order to his lines, preventing them breaking up in pursuit of the enemy.[23] He was thus able to repulse the Turkish counter-attack and, in the final mêlée, launch a series of renewed charges of his own that eventually forced the Turks from the field. After a brief rest, the Christian army resumed its march, reaching Jaffa on 10 September.

This was no revenge for Hattin. Saladin's army had escaped destruction. Some accounts, including Richard's own brief despatch,[24] discounted any climactic quality to the battle, portraying it merely as a sharper, more intense contest among many that had marked the Christian march south. One report suggested that the Christians had only lost just over 100 horses. The most prominent crusader killed, or at least the most mourned, was James of Avesnes, who had first arrived at the siege of Acre in September 1189. He later became the star of a secular chivalric cult, a familiar hero of uplifting anecdotes used by crusade preachers, poets and chroniclers in the thirteenth century.[25] On the Muslim side, Ibn Shaddad identified only three important casualties. Yet, whatever the emphasis, Saladin had precipitated a direct attack, engaging larger numbers than previously, and he had been decisively repulsed, if not defeated. His object of halting the crusaders' march to Jaffa, the port of Jerusalem, had failed. Ibn Shaddad recorded how inconsolable Saladin appeared on the evening of his defeat. Although his army remained intact and continued to shadow the Christian advance, it was now seemingly powerless to prevent its progress. After Arsuf, although the Christian army was still isolated in hostile territory, far from its base, its size, confidence, naval support and cohesion meant that militarily Saladin was reduced to reactive tactics; he was unable to dictate the course of events. This led him into uncharted territory with his restless allies, facing the prospect of keeping a field army at a plausible fighting strength for an indeterminate period. Saladin's success had been based on offering the military *askars*, or standing armies, of the rulers of the Near East a share in profits: land, revenues, booty. Now he had little immediately to offer but doubt, debt, struggle and prayer.

JERUSALEM?

With the second crisis of the Palestine war surmounted, the Christian army established itself at Jaffa and the surrounding area in the weeks after the battle of Arsuf. The crusaders were now within striking distance of their goal. However, Richard's grasp of strategy was subtler than many of those he commanded. An intelligent reading even of the history of the First Crusade would have revealed the need to secure as well as capture the Holy City. As with the leaders of the 1090s expedition, Richard, as well as Guy, the local barons and the military orders, understood that Egypt could determine the fate of Palestine. Equally, experience of campaigning in the west demonstrated that the chances of a successful siege increased if the attackers were in control of the surrounding region. For all these reasons, Ascalon occupied a central place in Richard's calculations. Before he left Acre, he had intended to take the port, probably in order to make it his base for any operations against Jerusalem and Egypt.[26] At the very least, occupation of Ascalon would hinder Saladin's ability to reinforce his field army in southern Palestine. Alive to the danger, Saladin forestalled him by demolishing its fortifications shortly after the battle of Arsuf. Richard's failure to persuade his allies at Jaffa in mid-September 1191 to prevent this has been seen by Richard's apologists, then and now, as a crucial tactical error.[27]

This did not remove the strategic choices. While turning Saladin's tactics against him by a series of foraging and harrying raids that led the Turkish army to withdraw from the coastal plain around Jaffa, Richard was still faced with alternative policies based on Jerusalem or Ascalon/Egypt. To placate his followers and wrong-foot Saladin, he tried to ride the two horses simultaneously. In October, while still holding out the prospect in a newsletter of taking Jerusalem by mid-January 1192,

Richard floated a plan to the Genoese for a joint invasion of Egypt the following summer, which would require more men and ships to accomplish.[28] How seriously he meant this scheme is unknowable. It may simply have been a ploy to keep the Genoese sweet while he remained in alliance with their rivals the Pisans. However, suggestions of an invasion of Egypt usefully added to the diplomatic pressure on Saladin. Negotiations with al-Adil intensified. Both sides seemed willing to explore a wide, even bizarre, range of possibilities. In mid-October Richard apparently offered his sister, the widowed Joan, to be one of al-Adil's wives as part of a deal based on a Muslim–Christian condominium in Palestine ruled by al-Adil and Joan under Saladin's suzerainty. The Christians would receive the coast, as Joan's dowry, and free access to Jerusalem, while the Muslims retained nominal sovereignty over the whole and direct rule over the hinterland. Although later claimed by Richard to have been a joke, perhaps because on hearing of the plan his sister flew into a Vesuvial rage so characteristic of her short-tempered family, the suggested terms, the question of marriage and suzerainty apart, outlined a partition very similar to what was finally agreed a year later in the Treaty of Jaffa (2 September 1192). To complicate matters further, at the same time, the disaffected Conrad of Montferrat, who had held aloof from a campaign dominated by his rival Guy's overlord, began to seek a separate treaty with Saladin, using the sultan's old adversary, the fluent Arabic speaker Reynald of Sidon, as intermediary. Conrad apparently proposed swapping Acre for Sidon and Beirut, already promised him under the arbitration of July 1191, in order to establish a new Lebanese state for himself. Saladin could afford to keep both camps talking until the serious issues of the war in Palestine were resolved.[29]

In one respect, whatever his misgivings and clever schemes, the immediate course of Richard's policy was determined for him. To the mass of his followers, the attraction of Ascalon, even Egypt, paled before the allure of Jerusalem, less than fifty miles away from their base at Jaffa. Within Richard's cosmopolitan army there could only be one strategy that would gain majority support: a march on Jerusalem. This was especially true for crusaders from the west who had joined up specifically to answer the call to recover the Holy City. Many of them had been in Palestine for more than a year, some since 1189. The privations of the siege of Acre were for a purpose defined rhetorically and emotionally in traditional, First Crusade terms. With hindsight many sources argued that Jerusalem, even if captured, would have been impossible to hold against Saladin's undefeated field army. It was argued that the Christians lacked adequate manpower to secure both Jerusalem and Jaffa and the supply lines to Acre, especially as the bulk of crusaders would depart for their homes in the west. For the local veterans, the lessons of the twelfth-century Outremer spoke loudly. Yet, the only reason any of them, Richard included, found themselves in southern Palestine at the turn of the year was the quest to recapture the Holy City. All Richard's schemes were ultimately directed to that end. The providential nature of the enterprise had been proclaimed and reinforced at every turn by stories of heroism, reports of visions and, from the perspective of September 1191, success. As Saladin could not afford to bargain away Jerusalem, his most iconic triumph, Richard's attempt to exert pressure by means other than a frontal assault on the Holy City lacked credibility. If there were too few to take or hold Jerusalem, the same was patently true, if not more so, for any attempt to invade Egypt. In fact, this lack of manpower, added to the factional difficulties within the Christian army, the rival negotiations with Conrad of Montferrat and the overwhelming fact that Richard, unlike Frederick Barbarossa, was not intending to devote the rest of his life to Outremer, indicated that the only chance of success, even in the terms Richard envisaged, lay in a military coup that brought Saladin to his knees. The stalemate after Arsuf required a new triumph. So even the logic of Richard's own policy dictated an attack on Jerusalem. Given the fissiparous nature of the coalition he led, it had to be conducted as soon as possible, even though it was mid-winter and the weather was foul.

Despite being overruled by the council of leaders when he proposed an expedition to Ascalon in September, Richard understood his position. Whatever his instincts as a secular general, this was no ordinary war, at least in its objective if not conduct. If the army was to stay together and his leadership recognized, both prerequisites for the effectiveness of his continuing diplomacy with Saladin, he had to march towards Jerusalem. The manner in which he did so suggested a serious intent; what precisely that was appeared less obvious. After a brief trip by sea to Acre, on 31 October Richard set out from Jaffa on the Jerusalem road. It had taken the First Crusaders a week to march from the coast to Jerusalem. After two months, Richard's vanguard had only reached Bayt Nuba, on the edge of the coastal plain, still twelve miles from Jerusalem. Along the way, as well as fighting off repeated Turkish attacks, the Christians had rebuilt the castles of the plain ruined on Saladin's orders. A six-week stop at Ramla allowed for provisions to be stockpiled. Richard spent Christmas at Latrun, still only a day's ride from Jaffa. To Saladin, the advance seemed worryingly inexorable in its measured pace, although the dreadful weather contributed to its glacial progress. By the beginning of January 1192, Richard had achieved mastery over the coastal plain between Jaffa and the Judean hills. This may have been the limit of his ambition. But such occupation was also crucial if a realistic attack on Jerusalem were to be attempted. Throughout these manoeuvres, Richard kept up his talks with al-Adil, although sticking to his demands for a complete return to the pre-1187 frontiers. Urgency was added when Reynald of Sidon was seen inspecting the skirmishing between the Turks and crusaders while out riding with al-Adil.[30] By November the discussions between al-Adil and Richard and their agents, and their friendly tone, were public knowledge, with open exchanges of gifts, mutual entertainment and feasting. This apparently contradictory behaviour for a warrior of Christ shocked many of Richard's followers. To avoid the taint of appeasement and show that 'he lacked not loyalty to God and Christianity', when the negotiations faltered and fighting resumed, Richard compensated by eagerly slicing the heads off Turks and displaying them as trophies around the camp. Such bizarre turns of behaviour did not pass unnoticed even by Richard's keenest fans.[31]

Having finally arrived at the feet of the Judean hills, the Holy City in normal conditions just a day's march away, in the mud and rain of a bad Palestinian winter the crusaders reached the third crisis of the war. The decision over Jerusalem could be deferred no longer. For a week (6–13 January 1192) the fate of the crusade was fiercely debated by the high command. Their dilemma revolved around whether they should gamble all in advancing on the chance of rekindling the glory – and the good fortune – of 1099 or risk the disillusionment and disintegration of the army by adopting a more prudent line. The attitude of the local baronage and the military orders proved crucial. The grizzled veterans of the east argued that an immediate attack on Jerusalem was unwise; the weather was atrocious and worsening. The problem of retaining a captured Jerusalem remained unresolved. The locals advised marching to refortify Ascalon as a base to prevent Saladin reinforcing his army from Egypt and thus exerting a stranglehold on his operations in southern Palestine. This argument fitted exactly Richard's earlier plan, as the king presumably knew it would. A contemporary Iraqi observer recorded that Richard presented the tactical reasons against a siege himself.[32] Rash in battle, cautious in politics but expert in military science, on 13 January, Richard gave the order to withdraw.

Instantly the army's morale collapsed. 'Never since the Lord God made the world was such deep grief displayed'.[33] The leadership was cursed. Inevitable rumours circulated, telling of the parlous state of the Turks and how easily the Holy City would have fallen, if only ... However, contemporary writers, Christian and Muslim, and not just his panegyrists, were, perhaps surprisingly, ready to explain and excuse Richard's decision. Ibn Shaddad ignored the whole issue. However, pursuing the accountancy of tactics rather than the foolhardiness of piety fuelled divisions between Christian factions and interest groups. While Henry of Champagne remained with Richard, Hugh of Burgundy withdrew, although staying in southern Palestine. Others left for Acre or to join Conrad of Montferrat at Tyre: if diplomacy rather than force were to determine the crusade's outcome and allocate the winnings, Richard was not the only player with a prospect of success. The retreat from Bayt Nuba also confirmed the flaw in Richard's own strategy by demonstrating to Saladin the Christians' military weakness and inadequate manpower. The collapse of his authority in Syria, still less the overthrow of his empire, no longer threatened. All the diplomatic talk from Richard was of condominium. As the crusaders slogged their way back through the rains to Ramla, Saladin gave his army home leave.[34]

Defenders of Richard's decision, then and now, praise his sagacity. Yet, alongside his acute understanding of the problems that confronted any attack on Jerusalem, Richard may also have lost his nerve or, rather, the confidence in his own ability to impose himself on events. Alternatively, if he had never intended to attack Jerusalem, and the manoeuvring around the coastal plain was merely to rattle Saladin while showing his own troops how impossibly difficult the project had become, then his cynicism was matched by his miscalculation. His limitations were exposed. Such a physically, politically and psychologically damaging exercise to achieve an abortive diplomatic advantage speaks poorly of his judgement. Assuming them not be wholly capricious, the best that can be said of Richard's policies and decisions in the winter of 1191–2 is that they allowed him to retain as many options as possible for as long as possible. The verdict of Bayt Nuba closed many of these down and immediately began to restrict further expectations of future success. What would have happened had Richard pressed on up the road to Jerusalem is unknowable. Another Hattin or a repeat of 1099; both were possible. The failure to trust in righteousness probably forced not a few to wonder what, if anything, the westerners were now doing in Palestine. Whatever view is taken of the merits of the decision of 13 January 1192, whether it can be ascribed to shrewdness or loss of conviction at the ultimate test, its consequences reconfigured the contours of Holy War in the east, not just for the following nine months but for the next century and more.

Richard countered the gloom and disillusionment by action. The *volte face* at Bayt Nuba was portrayed as a tactical withdrawal, not a retreat.[35] Never were Richard's personal qualities as a daring, or, as Saladin himself thought, foolishly rash knight more useful.[36] The stories of Richard's exploits increased in inverse proportion to the overall military success of the expedition. By the end of January, Richard had arrived at Ascalon and had set his army to work rebuilding its fortifications on a grand scale, 'making it the strongest fortress on the coast of Palestine'.[37] This strenuous outdoor relief engaged his depleted army for the next four months. But their labours did little to dilute the popular desire to spend their energies reclaiming the Holy Sepulchre. Arguably, all that was achieved was to confirm Richard's place at the now rather crowded negotiating table by virtue of his command of a still formidable army, control of Jaffa and now Ascalon. Even that was endangered by ferocious fighting between the various factions in Acre, which required Richard's presence between late February and the end of March 1192.

The absence of Turkish menace or Christian advance allowed free play of the competition for the lucrative port of Acre. Conrad of Montferrat, supported by the Genoese, the French under Hugh of Burgundy and elements of the Jerusalem baronage, contested the authority of Guy of Lusignan, backed by the Pisans and the *de facto* ruler of Christian Palestine, Richard himself. As Richard had pointedly reminded al-Adil, he too possessed a dynastic interest as King Amalric of Jerusalem's great-nephew in the male line.[38] But he was already envisaging his own departure for his responsibilities in the west. At his camp at Ascalon in early April Richard had learnt of the deposition of his viceroy in England,

William Longchamp, and the attempted coup by his brother John. Planning for the future became urgent. Not just the lordship of Acre but the succession of the crown of Jerusalem needed to be settled, especially as Conrad's disaffection continued to vitiate Richard's attempts to reach a negotiated settlement with Saladin. Richard's bullying alone had little effect as Conrad's support was powerful, obstinate and threatened to break up the crusade. Opinion was hardening that Guy could never provide the stability required to maintain the kingdom after the crusaders' departure. On the advice of his own army council, Richard, willingly or not, was forced to agree. In mid-April he abandoned Guy and accepted Conrad's claims to be king, a decision influenced perhaps by his learning that Conrad's negotiations with Saladin were nearing a successful conclusion. Guy was amply compensated by the lordship of Cyprus transferred to him by Richard from the Templars.

No sooner agreed, the succession deal collapsed. In Tyre on the evening of 28 April, walking home after dining with the bishop of Beauvais, Conrad of Montferrat was stabbed to death by two Assassins. Circumstantial evidence implicated Richard as having bribed the Assassin leader, Rashid al-Din Sinan. Equally plausible cases could be made against Saladin or Sinan himself, uneasy at Conrad's Lebanese pretentions.[39] Conrad's death caused another brief intense spasm of conflict, with Hugh of Burgundy attempting to wrest Tyre from Conrad's pregnant widow. However, a new candidate presented himself, literally, when Henry of Champagne arrived at Tyre from Acre. With the blessing of Richard, on 5 May, Henry, now a Holy Land veteran of two years, was married to the twenty-one-year-old Princess Isabella as her third husband (in the end she managed four). The marriage suited almost all parties. Henry, as a grandson of Louis VII and Eleanor of Aquitaine, was nephew to both Richard I and Philip II, his elevation satisfying the honour of each. The opinion of Humphrey of Toron, Isabella's first husband and currently leader of Richard's negotiators with al-Adil, was not recorded.

Freed from the succession problem and, for the first time since Acre fell, with united support, Richard pursued his game of two-handed chess in southern Palestine: military action shadowing detailed negotiations. One of Richard's latest offers included a proposal for a new partition that included a divided city of Jerusalem, the Muslims retaining control of the Haram al-Sharif (Temple Mount) and the Tower of David.[40]

This found no favour. Agreement over the partition of Jerusalem and Palestine was a Sisyphean task. To try to force Saladin into an acceptable deal, Richard laid siege to Darum, one of the few strongholds Saladin had left intact, which fell on 22 May. Next day his army was joined by Henry of Champagne, to whom Richard presented the town, and Hugh of Burgundy with the remaining French troops. This new unity produced an awkward alliance. In late May, the French lords joined with Richard's own from England, Normandy, Maine, Anjou and Poitou to decide that they would launch an attack on Jerusalem whatever Richard thought, with or without him. By leaking their decision to the army, they totally outmanoeuvred Richard. While the camp rang with celebration, the king sulked, his hostility to the plan – or his anger at being bested – undisguised. It may have been a symptom of his recurrent poor health, but he seems to have sunk into a temporary but deep depression, worried by the prospects for the Jerusalem escapade and ever-worsening news from the west. Apparently it took a confessional pep talk from a priest appealing to Richard's reputation, knightly prowess and providential destiny to persuade the king to resume positive leadership by promising not to leave the Holy Land until Easter 1193.[41]

Although the essential strategic arguments against besieging Jerusalem had not changed since January, the fortification of Ascalon, the capture of Darum and the annexation of the whole of the coastal plain north of the Negev desert gave the Christians greater freedom of movement. Saladin's position was weakened by the problems of maintaining his coalition for yet another campaign season, the sixth in a row (1187–92), as well as the removal of Conrad of Montferrat. The one clear improvement lay in the excellent facilities for gathering intelligence his drawn-out diplomacy had provided. However, the new advance towards Jerusalem was a contradictory and confusing, perhaps confused, affair. The second march to Bayt Nuba presented a complete contrast to the first. Richard remained dubious, if not overtly hostile. The weather was hot. Water was scarce, the more so after Saladin ordered the destruction or poisoning of the Judean water cisterns. The march from Ascalon, begun on 6 June, took five days to reach Bayt Nuba, instead of two months, a sign either that the Christians intended a rapid assault or that they now discounted Saladin's capacity to cut their supply route to the coast. Yet the Christians then stayed camped at Bayt Nuba from 10 June until 4 July, simultaneously indicating a seriousness of intent and casting doubt on their unity of purpose. The delay allowed Saladin, who had initially been caught badly off guard, to regroup. The advance to Bayt Nuba also seems to have surprised elements of the Christian coalition; from Acre Henry of Champagne only managed to catch up with the host in late June.

The chief activity in the crusader camp at Bayt Nuba was debate about whether to press on, spiced with regular forays across the surrounding countryside in search of forage, game and Turks. On one such sortie, it was said, Richard caught sight of Jerusalem in the distance, possibly from Montjoie, the hill on the Jaffa road where pilgrims received their first view of the Holy City.[42] On another, tipped off by local spies, Richard led an attack on a large Muslim caravan as it was crossing the northern Negev; Saladin regarded its loss as a serious blow. Christian morale was boosted by the discovery of yet another relic of the True Cross. Saladin and his generals began to panic. His tactics had failed to dislodge or much inconvenience the camp at Bayt Nuba or to cut the crusaders' supply line to Jaffa. With the seizure of booty and camels from the desert caravan, it looked in the last days of June that an attack on Jerusalem was finally imminent. As eyewitnesses testified, memories of the First Crusade were alive in the crusader camp;[43] it would not have been forgotten that in 1099 the Holy City had fallen on 15 July. In Jerusalem, Saladin's high command was as divided as Richard's, some urging a stand in the city, others the deployment of the army to confront the crusaders in the field. Saladin began to take emergency measures for the security of the city. Despite intelligence reports of the divisions in the Christians, on 3 July it was decided Saladin should leave the city for his own safety. At Friday prayers that day in the al-Aqsa mosque, he wept openly.[44]

Whether he had good reason to be alarmed is less obvious. Uncertainty was rife in the crusader ranks. The French under the duke of Burgundy were consistent in calling for an attack on Jerusalem, their views being relayed to Saladin by his agents: 'The only reason we have come from our countries is Jerusalem. We shall not return without it.'[45] The spies also reported Richard's response: the need to forage for clean water would break the besiegers' formation and invite annihilation. However, the crude logic of the French position attracted the support of the mass of the ordinary crusaders. Relations between the Angevin high command and the rest frayed. The camp divided into national enclaves, groups from one hurling insults at the other. Hugh of Burgundy even sponsored an obscene song about Richard, which was widely sung, provoking Richard, an experienced song-writer, to retaliate with one of his own.[46] The situation became unsustainable. The fourth crisis of the crusade had arrived.

To resolve the issue, Richard skilfully used his authority as the undoubted commander-in-chief to convene a supposedly objective committee to decide on whether to attack Jerusalem or pursue Richard's preferred southern Palestine policy of threatening Egypt. The composition of the committee guaranteed the result of its deliberations: five Templars, five Hospitallers, five Jerusalem barons and five Frenchmen. All except the French were well known to favour caution and, thus, the Egyptian policy. By excluding any of his own vassals Richard could be seen to be acting impartially, but on the side he exerted heavy pressure and moral blackmail. The committee opted for withdrawal. Even so, doubt prevailed until the last moment before, on 4 July, Richard ordered a general retreat to the coast. Disappointment inadequately describes the bitterness recorded even by writers sympathetic to Richard. Saladin watched the disconsolate and acrimonious march down to the plain. It turned out to be a decisive moment. The next hostile western European army to come as close to Jerusalem as Richard's crusaders was led by General Edmund Allenby in December 1917.

Any semblance of Christian unity now collapsed. Blame was freely flung about, the retreat costing Richard's reputation dear. The remaining French left in disgust, refusing to follow an Egyptian scheme. In any case, this much-promoted plan was increasingly revealed as at best impractical and at worst wishful thinking. Richard lacked the men, money or ships and was eager to return to the west to save his dominions from the rapacity of John and Philip II. A policy of raids on the Nile Delta or hopes of exploiting possible divisions within the Ayyubid empire after Saladin's death belonged to a hypothetical future not the circumstances of the summer of 1192. Immediately, the strategic and diplomatic options became clearer. Saladin was safe in Jerusalem: Richard in Ascalon and Jaffa. Richard, directly or through Henry of Champagne as lord of the Jerusalemite Franks, was openly pushing for a quick settlement. He now admitted total victory was beyond his reach. He also judged that Saladin too was in trouble: 'you and we together are ruined'.[47] Claims to Jerusalem were abandoned. New, ingenious ideas for partition were proposed, even a post-crusade military alliance. However, Saladin demanded the demolition of Ascalon as the price for any agreement. The balance of power in southern Palestine had to be shifted if either side were to agree to what both desired, the end of the war.

In late July, Richard returned to Acre ostensibly to plan an attack on Beirut in an attempt to lure Saladin away from the new Christian bases in southern Palestine. In Richard's absence, Saladin launched a surprise attack on Jaffa. If he could take the port, the whole Christian position in the region would be seriously undermined if not destroyed, their conquests split, their shipping vulnerable and the precariousness of Richard's position exposed. The Turks would reap huge and immediate diplomatic as well as military advantage. The stalemate would be broken. This fifth, final crisis of the Palestine war would determine its outcome.

The Turks began their assault on 28 July. By 31 July, their mangonels and sappers had destroyed whole sections of the walls. The modest garrison agreed to surrender the town, withdrawing to the citadel while Jaffa was sacked. That night, as the garrison prepared to evacuate the citadel under the supervision of Saladin's agent, Ibn Shaddad himself, Richard appeared offshore with a small fleet. He had learnt of Jaffa's plight just three days earlier. A relief column hurriedly despatched from Acre under Henry of Champagne had been stopped at Ceasarea. However, despite contrary winds, the king's flotilla arrived while most of the citadel still remained in Christian hands. On 1 August, after some confusion over whether the Turks had already occupied the citadel, Richard, heavily outnumbered, launched his famous attack, being one of the first to wade ashore from his boats at the head of his small army. Shock, surprise and the power of his crack force gave Richard a highly improbable, if dramatic, victory. Ibn Shaddad, who watched Richard lead his men through the breakers, was impressed: 'He was red-haired, his tunic was red and his banner was red, as was his device.'[48] More significantly, after clearing out the astonished and alarmed Turks from both the citadel and town, Richard consolidated his hold by repulsing a concerted Muslim surprise counter-attack begun on the night of 4/5 August that literally caught Richard and his companions with their breeches down.[49] This victory against heavy odds – apparently Richard had only seventeen knights and a few hundred infantry – infuriated Saladin, who must have recognized its importance. The fighting at Jaffa secured more than Richard's legendary status as a warrior and general. It restored the strategic stalemate. Richard could not take Jerusalem; Saladin could not drive him from southern Palestine. While Saladin's assault on Jaffa had been brilliantly opportunist, its failure dealt deep psychological as well as military blows. Negotiation became the only option for both sides who increasingly resembled tiring heavyweight boxers slugging it out while dropping from injury and fatigue.

Richard's exertions at Jaffa proved almost more fatal than the weapons of the Turks. His health had been wretched ever since Acre. He now fell dangerously ill. To this was added the growing alarm that his possessions in France were in danger of being lost to the conspiracy between John and Philip II. Urgency to reach agreement transcended all other considerations. With his physical and political energy sapped, Richard capitulated to Saladin's insistence on the demolition of the walls of Ascalon he had spent so much time and effort constructing only a few months earlier. That obstacle removed, agreement soon followed; the Treaty of Jaffa was formally sworn on 2 September. In return for a three-year truce, which included Antioch and Tripoli, Palestine was to be partitioned. The Christians were to retain their conquests of Acre, Jaffa and the intervening coast; the walls of Ascalon were to be demolished; the coastal plain around Ramla and Lydda was to become a condominium. Freedom of access was guaranteed to members of each faith across the other's territories.[50] Specifically, Christian pilgrims were permitted to visit the Holy Sepulchre unmolested. With a mixture of excitement and understandable unease at the presence of so many Turkish soldiers, many crusaders fulfilled their vows and visited the Holy Places before returning to Europe. Hubert Walter bishop of Salisbury, who led one of the three parties of crusaders to go up to Jerusalem, was even entertained by Saladin, a reminder of the courtly manner in which the diplomatic aspects of what otherwise had been a desperate and bloody conflict had been conducted. Bishop Hubert was shown the relic of the True Cross, which had been a significant omission from the final treaty, and discussed Richard's qualities with the sultan. More practically, Hubert extracted from Saladin a promise to allow a skeleton staff of Latin clergy to officiate at the Holy Sepulchre, at the church of the Nativity in Bethlehem and the church of the Annunciation in Nazareth. Either from genuine conviction or as a face-saving device, or both, Richard declined the opportunity to fulfil his vows at the Holy Sepulchre, deliberately leaving open the prospect of a return. Thus, he never met Saladin except in the legends and romances that began to be concocted within a few years. The crusade was at an end.

Richard sailed from Acre on 9 October not, as he may have hoped, to a hero's welcome, nor, as he may have feared, to a political crisis. Instead he found himself in a German prison for over thirteen months. After shipwreck near Venice, he was apprehended at Vienna on 21 December by his enemy Leopold of Austria when trying to find a way back incognito to Normandy and England. A few weeks later he was handed over to Henry VI of Germany, in whose custody he remained until February 1194. It was a remarkable fate for the most famous Christian warrior of his time and provided, as had so many of the events since news of Hattin first reached the west in the autumn of 1187, much food for moralists' judgementalism. Ironies and bitter chance had coursed the Third Crusade, this final act not least. Earlier in 1192, Richard had vowed to remain in the east until the spring passage of 1193.[51] If he had, he would have been on hand when, on 4 March 1193, Saladin died in Damascus.

Contemporary responses to the Third Crusade were as equivocal as its outcome. None questioned the heroism; many seemed to have doubted both the cost and the achievement. A vociferous apologist for the expedition and of Richard as its leader, Ambroise, possibly a Third Crusade veteran himself, acknowledged the criticism:

> Yet many people ill-informed
> Said in their foolishness that naught
> Of good in Syria was wrought,
> Since they won not Jerusalem.[52]

He also admitted the crushing casualties, from disease as much as battle. On the day the Treaty of Jaffa was sworn, Balian of Ibelin told Ibn Shaddad that he reckoned that perhaps as many as 20 per cent of crusaders had died in battle, but many more through illness or drowning. He thought that less than 50 per cent of the total Christian force survived, an impression, if not numbers, confirmed by western sources. William of Newburgh, writing shortly afterwards in northern England, pitched the losses at over 75 per cent: 'not a quarter returned home'.[53] One stock justification of the discrepancy between sacrifice and tangible success was to emphasize, as did William and Ambroise, the celestial 'other Jerusalem' these victims had won.[54] Not all were convinced. Before the expeditions had even departed some sceptics, with a certain logic, had argued that God 'could avenge himself without all these soldiers having to cross the sea'.[55] After 1192, God's purpose seemed more clouded than ever. Even if the theology remained unchallenged and human sin lay behind terrestrial failure, the loss of so many invited the charge of waste. Introducing a long list of notable casualties of the crusade, Gilbert of Mons squared this circle of blame by wondering at the extremes of sin that could have resulted in so many fine princes and knights from all parts of Christendom achieving so little: 'they recovered only the city of Acre'.[56]

In fact, on the material side of the crusade's balance sheet, the capture of Acre proved a major triumph, providing the otherwise ateliotic restored kingdom of Jerusalem with a commercial centre of international importance. The effective conquest of significant parts of the coastal plain allowed for the establishment of a territorial state that, with further additions in the decade after 1192, lasted intact until the 1260s, a modest but not the most insignificant player in the increasingly desperate contest for control of the Fertile Crescent from the Persian Gulf to the Nile Valley. The Third Crusade cast a long shadow over the future. The incorporation of Cyprus into Christian Outremer provided a new base and source of wealth and aristocratic opportunity. The Treaty of Jaffa of 1192 acted as a model for future diplomacy. For most of the next seventy years truces determined the relations between the Christian rulers of mainland Outremer and their Muslim neighbours, only unreflective or partisan westerners regarding the practice as irreligious. Every significant crusade that reached the Levant between 1192 and 1254 either sought or was forced to accept treaties with the infidel. The experience of the Third Crusade enshrined the understanding of the significance of sea-power to Christian prospects in the eastern Mediterranean. No new expeditions went by land for another 200 years. Richard's Egypt strategy quickly became orthodoxy. Partly this resulted from the most glaring failure of the Third Crusade, Jerusalem. The arguments of Richard and his apologists that the key to the Holy City lay in Cairo seemed to have been persuasive. The continued Muslim occupation of Jerusalem supplied another lasting legacy. Unlike in the years 1099–1187, the Holy Land stood as a permanent, unavoidable criticism of Christian sin or disobedience, keeping the *negotium Terrae Sanctae* at the centre of religious politics and devotional populism for more than another century. Perhaps in that sense, those who argued for the spiritual success of the Third Crusade were right. The limited temporal achievement in Palestine paled beside the effect on the spiritual landscape of western Christendom.

The Fourth Crusade

15

'Ehud's Sharpened Sword'[1]

Two decades after Richard I left the Holy Land in 1192, James of Vitry, prominent preacher, intellectual, monastic patron and ecclesiastical insider, future bishop of Acre and cardinal, was drumming up support for a new expedition to the east. His message was simple and uncomfortable. As long as Jerusalem remained under infidel occupation, all faithful Christians had an unavoidable moral duty to help regain Christ's patrimony, in the same way that vassals were legally obliged to help their secular lords, except that God's service transcended law and offered eternal rewards. The task was clear. But, he asked, where now was the zeal of the Old Testament heroes Mattathias, the Maccabees, Phinehas, Shamgar or Samson? 'Where is Ehud's sharpened sword?'[2]

By this time, during the preaching of the Fifth Crusade after 1213, such rhetoric was standard. It reflected in detail the theology of James's master, Pope Innocent III, which gave a new precision to a universal concept that equated service to God with crusading. For Innocent, the trials of the Old Testament Israelite heroes were of contemporary relevance not just oratorical resonance. 'Wounds that do not respond to the healing of poultices must be lanced with a blade.' Fighting for God was the 'servant's service' to his Lord, a test of faith 'as gold in a furnace' which determined salvation or damnation, not just for warriors but for all Christians. For Innocent the crusader was 'following the Lord', his 'service to Jesus Christ' regarded in quasi-liturgical as well as feudal terms. It was imperative that all Christians were able to join this 'war of the Lord'. In his great crusade encyclical *Quia Maior* of 1213, Innocent tellingly refashioned the central crusading text from Matthew 16:24: 'If any man will come after me, let him deny himself, and take up his cross, and follow me': 'To put it more plainly: "If anyone wishes to follow me *to the crown*, let him also follow me *into battle, which is now proposed as a test for all men*."'[3] The elevation of the Holy Land war into the epitome of Christian devotion rested on the unique plenary indulgences offered to participants, access to which Innocent wished to extend to non-combatants. In turn, this depended on the emotional and psychological pull of the Holy Land, a place where God 'accomplished the universal sacrament of our redemption',[4] a sanctified space that provided inspiration on all four levels of contemporary scriptural exegesis: literal, the site of the historical events of the Old and especially New Testaments; allegorical, as a representation of the Church Militant; moral (or tropological), a metaphor of the inner life and struggle of the soul; and mystical, an image of paradise.

These categories existed beyond clever theological dialectic, or even the formalized pleadings of preachers, evangelists and recruiting agents. The German lyric poet Walter von der Vogelweide numbered among his patrons Dukes Leopold V (d. 1194) and Leopold VI of Austria (d. 1230), whose combined crusading experience covered the Third, Fourth and Fifth Crusades, as well as campaigns in Spain and Languedoc. Walter's *Palestine Song* illustrated this fourfold potency of the Holy Land, attractive to the sinner as the place of God's incarnation where earth and heaven touched and, as such, the rightful possession of Christianity:

Now my life has found a purpose,
for my sinful eyes behold
that pure land and very country,
of which glorious things are told.
This has been my prayer of old:
I have seen the place which God
in a human form once trod.

Many a rich and splendid country
have I seen, but of them all
you deserve the highest honour,
where such wonders could befall.
That a maid to birth could bring
one who was the angel's king –
was not this a wondrous thing?

Christians, Jews and also heathen
Claim this land as rightly theirs.
May God make our cause to triumph
by the threefold name he bears.
All the world has come to fight,
but to us belongs the right;
God defend us by his might![5]

Such commitment required direction, focus, organization and explanation if the obligations of service were to be translated into effective military, material or devotional action. Preachers such as Gerald of Wales and James of Vitry described this process as a form of conversion. Innocent III referred to Holy Land crusaders as having 'converted to penance'. The Cistercian chronicler Gunther of Pairis (d. *c.*1210) described his abbot, Martin, 'converting many to the militia of Christ' at Basel in 1201. Another Cistercian, Cesarius of Heisterbach, in his *Dialogus Miraculorum* (*c.*1223), placed his discussion of crusading under the heading 'Concerning Conversion' (*De conversione*). Caesarius and James both likened becoming a *crucesignatus* to entering a monastic order, crusaders in general, not just those who had taken vows in the military orders, constituting a distinct *religio*.[6] In the two decades after the Third Crusade, this construction of crusading and the realization of Innocent III's theology of God's war were given ceremonial and administrative substance by the development of specific ecclesiastical institutions. Coupled with the political consequences of the Third Crusade and a newly confident papacy after Innocent's accession in 1198, these turned ideology into regular church practice.

INNOCENT III AND THE BUSINESS OF THE CROSS

Lothar of Segni was elected pope on 8 January 1198, taking the name Innocent III. The nephew of Clement III, he had been associated with the Roman Curia since the late 1180s, a cardinal since 1190. Trained in theology at Paris and, probably, law at Bologna, aged only thirty-seven, Innocent revivified the papacy. His immediate predecessors had tended to be cautious, experienced old men – Celestine III had lived into his nineties – seeking to protect rather than promote or extend papal interests. The three pillars of Innocent's pontificate were the assertion of papal authority – he popularized the title 'Vicar of Christ'; the development of spiritual and ecclesiastical reform though evangelization and canon law; and prosecution of the crusade, which incorporated both.

Innocent regularly described crusading as the *negotium crucis*, the business of the cross, or, more pointedly, the *negotium crucifixi*, the business of the crucified, specifically Christ but also, by analogy, all Christians.[7] In a theological work written before his election as pope, *c.*1195, *De miseria humane conditionis (Concerning the misery of the human condition)*, the young Cardinal Lothar, explained, 'the just man "denies himself" crucifying his body on the cross of its own vices and lusts so that the world is crucified to him and he to the world'.[8] The metaphor of the cross – or, as Innocent saw it, its spiritual reality – ideally suited the crusade projects. In some circles they became synonyms. Caesarius of Heisterbach was one of a long line of theorists and propagandists who used *crux transmarina* and *crux cismarina* to describe crusades to Outremer and in Europe. The absence of a formal canonical word defining the activity, as opposed to its participants (*crucesignati*), did not prevent the emergence after the Third Crusade of a vernacular crusade vocabulary based on the cross: the verbs *croisier*, *croier/croisé* in northern French (*langue d'oil*); the nouns *crozeia*, *crozea* and *crozada* in southern French (*langue d'oc*).[9] Taking the cross was, after all, the earliest ceremony that distinguished this form of religious activity, invented by Urban II. Now, a century later, the Latin term *crucesignatus* became firmly entrenched, a consequence of the insistence on the image of the cross in crusade propaganda and exhortation after 1187. This chimed theologically with the emphasis on the wider personal commitment of the faithful Christian servant of the Lord, who bore a cross in imitation as well in honour of Him. A contemporary (*c.*1200) English liturgy for the ceremonial adoption of the cross listed its virtues in this vein: 'an especial means of assistance, a support of faith, the consummation of his (the crusader's) works, the redemption of his soul and a protection and safeguard against the fierce darts of all his enemies'.[10] As military ensign, mystic symbol, badge of penance, talisman or charm, no icon was more potent. Although ubiquitous in liturgy and as a public Christian symbol, worn equally by the non-crusading religious orders, members of confraternities or reformed heretics, the cross, with its particular association with the Jerusalem, lent the crusade an almost infinite plasticity of application, association, meaning and metaphor while retaining its precise central point of reference.

Innocent III established an institutional framework within which his crusading theology found concrete expression, even if much of his construction rested on earlier foundations. There was little absolutely original in his policies. He was a codifier as much as an innovator. Nonetheless, Innocent's contribution could be regarded as a sort of creation. The bull *Quia Maior* of 1213 and the decree *Ad Liberandam* of the Fourth Lateran Council in 1215, contained a set of coherent legal, liturgical and fiscal provisions that brought together a range of previous expedients to form the basis and model for future crusades. Earlier propaganda themes were rehearsed: service to God; the offer of salvation; charity to oppressed Christians; the Holy Land as Christ's patrimony; a test of religious devotion.[11] The apparatus of inducement was given a new clarity, putting an end to a century of papal obfuscation, hesitation and reluctance to define whether the crusade indulgence remitted the sin or the penalty of the sin. Through the power vested by Christ in the pope, full remission of all orally confessed sins (annual oral confession was to become mandatory for Roman Catholics at the 1215 Lateran Council) were granted to those who took the cross and campaigned in person; to those who sent and paid for proxies to fight in their stead; and to those proxies. Those who provided *matériel*, donations and alms for the crusade were to receive an indulgence proportionate to their contribution, picking up an idea canvassed as early as 1157 by the English Pope Hadrian IV and repeated by Innocent himself in 1198.[12] Consonant with his desire for military effectiveness and his theology of the Lord's war, Innocent, extending and clarifying a precedent set by Clement III, invited 'anyone who wishes' to take the Cross 'in such a way that this vow may be commuted, redeemed or deferred by apostolic mandate when urgent need or evident expediency demand it'. The means of redemption was payment. Vow redemption helped alter radically the funding of crusading, the manner in which the cross was preached, the methods of recruitment and planning, and even the reputation of the exercise itself as the system became vulnerable to charges of 'crosses for cash'.

Characteristic of Innocent III and his fellow Paris-trained ecclesiastics was the practical and social application of theology. Financing the crusades formed a part of this. In 1199, Innocent unsuccessfully attempted to levy a compulsory fortieth on clerical surpluses to pay for mercenaries for the crusade.[13] *Quia Maior* suggested a voluntary aid, with equal lack of response, so the decree *Ad Liberandam* imposed a three-year tax of a twentieth on the church to be collected by centrally appointed papal officials. Equally practical were the restatements in 1213 and 1215 of the temporal crusader privileges of immunity from taxes and usury to Jews, moratorium on debts and general church protection for the crusaders and their property. While bishops were to enforce some of the provisions, the secular arm was called upon to police those against Jewish credit collection. Secular individuals and communities were encouraged collectively to supply warriors, as in 1198. Following a similar injunction of 1199, special chests were to be deposited in parish churches to receive indulgence-earning almsgiving for the Holy Land, visible reminders of a permanent obligation.

These material considerations were balanced by the organization of penance and preaching more systematically than before to ensure the *negotium crucis* became a permanent feature of lay devotional life, 'to fight in such a conflict', Innocent proposed, 'not so much with physical arms as spiritual ones'.[14] Special prayers and liturgical devices had been instituted by Gregory VIII and Clement III. Within the liturgy of the Cistercian Order in the 1190s prayers for *crucesignati* and 'pro terra Ierosolymitana' were introduced. Bidding prayers and *clamor* now included the needs for the Holy Land.[15] *Quia Maior* provided for monthly penitential processions throughout Christendom, accompanied by preaching, fasting and almsgiving. A new intercessory ritual was added to the daily service of the mass between the Kiss of Peace and the reception of the Communion. In addition to a specially composed intercessory prayer calling for the restoration of the Holy Land, this included the familiar crusading Psalm 79, 'O God, the heathen are come into thine inheritance; thy holy temple have they defiled; they have laid Jerusalem on heaps.' The rite underlined the association of the crusade as a physical public duty and personal spiritual obligation with the mass. Confession, penance and the mystical presence of Christ Crucified (transubstantiation was another dogma accepted by the 1215 Lateran Council) provided an appropriate ceremonial as well as spiritual context for, as the intercessory prayer of 1213 put it, the liberation of 'the land which thine only-begotten son consecrated with his own blood'. A few years later, masses for the Holy Land were marked by the ringing of a bell during the recitation of the Lord's Prayer.[16] Such formal rituals acted within the wider process of crusade evangelism, to which Innocent gave clear direction by constructing an elaborate network of crusade preachers in every province and diocese of western Christendom under the direction of papal-appointed legates. In these ways, the cause of the Holy Land became a habitual feature of the parochial liturgical round in ways it had not been before 1187. The business of the cross was the business of Christianity.

This had extensive practical consequences. Until the Third Crusade, application of crusaders' privileges had lagged behind the rhetoric of holy war in establishing recognized, coherent conventions. Given the infrequent nature of large-scale wars of the cross, this was unsurprising. This changed with the enormous convulsion of 1187–92, when tens of thousands of *crucesignati* were recruited in all parts of western Christendom. The implications did not end with the Treaty of Jaffa. The failure to recapture Jerusalem embedded the recovery of the Holy Land into western European politics, with hardly a year passing without an attempt to mobilize a new expedition somewhere in Christendom. The human detritus of the Third Crusade included not just those who departed on that campaign, with their relicts and dependants at home, but also the substantial numbers of *crucesignati*, who for reasons of accident, poverty or convenience had failed to fulfil their vows in the first place. Church authorities repeatedly attempted to insist on the performance of crusade vows, a problem that had dogged every expedition; the First Crusaders at Antioch in January 1098 had complained about the backsliders at home, threatening them with excommunication. After the Third Crusade, the problem appeared endemic. Celestine III in 1196 and Innocent III in 1200 and 1201 addressed the issue by instructing local ecclesiastical authorities to force compliance on pain of excommunication, to persuade lapsed *crucesignati* to send proxies, or, in Innocent's instructions, to allow the poor and infirm to redeem their vows.[17] Lists of defaulting crusaders drawn up by the Third Crusade veteran Hubert Walter, from 1193 archbishop of Canterbury, reveal the social range of the business of the cross as well as some of its attendant problems. In a list of forty-seven names from Cornwall, local artisans featured prominently – miller, blacksmith, tanner, tailor, cobbler, etc. – as well as four or five women *crucesignatae*. Crusaders may have lacked social elevation, but they needed legal freedom and economic substance. This social profile was repeated in a similar list from Lincolnshire, where the main cause of non-fulfilment was poverty. Such evidence confirmed the need for central funding Innocent III had identified in 1199 when he proposed the clerical crusade tax.[18] These lists of English crusaders, paralleled in the records of secular government, reveal two important features of crusading at the end of the twelfth century; its wide social embrace and, in common with governments across Europe, its increasing bureaucratization.

The efficacy of crusading always depended on the alliance of ecclesiastical authority with secular power. Alongside the institutionalization of crusading in the devotional life of the west, governments became involved in securing the temporal status and privileges of crusaders in addition to their traditional role in organizing and conducting the military expeditions. Crusaders' temporal privileges were consolidated through the circumstances of the Third Crusade, which required secular authorities to recognize and protect the various immunities enjoyed by *crucesignati* if they were to be effective. Famously, church protection of one crusader's property, Richard I's, despite loud papal concern, proved futile in the face of the ambitions of Philip II and Richard's brother John in 1192–4. Temporal privileges regarding property, civil and criminal litigation, debt and interest repayment, fiscal exemption and the disposal of assets, relied on the cooperation and active support of lay power. Indeed, much of the surviving evidence for the operation of such privileges comes from the records of secular justice and administration. The basic principle behind crusader privileges that withdrew the *crucesignatus* from a purely lay condition involved its acceptance by lay courts and lords. It was their responsibility to establish case by case claims by individual crusaders to protection and immunities and, frequently, to restrict or define these in accordance with local custom and effective justice or administration. For instance, it was of considerable practical importance that a secular legal inquest at Rouen in 1205 acknowledged that a *croisé* enjoyed similar legal status to a cleric.[19]

The Third Crusade set the pattern. Gregory VIII's bull *Audita Tremendi* provided an inadequate guide to tax and debt immunities. Angevin and Capetian royal ordinances on the Saladin Tithe and debt clarified how the exemptions would work. Interest payments supplied a particularly sharp problem. The crusader's exemption from interest on loans protected his goods and his state of Grace from usury while simultaneously destroying his creditworthiness and hence limiting his ability to fulfil his vow and thus his access to the means of Grace. As a result, some thirteenth-century crusaders voluntarily waived this exemption. The assembly of prelates and barons at Paris in March 1188 established detailed rules in an attempt to stabilize the banking system, avoid a flood of litigation and prevent debtors taking the cross simply to escape their obligations. Although subsequent papal decrees on crusaders' immunities became more precise, the gap between ecclesiastical theory and secular practice persisted. A French royal ordinance on crusade financial and legal exemptions and privileges of March 1215 declared the intention of safeguarding the 'law and customs of Holy Church and similarly . . . the law and customs of the kingdom of France'.[20] Secular approval was vital for the system to work, as many of the crusader's privileges directly affected lay judicial procedures. Thus in 1204 the English justiciar Geoffrey FitzPeter intervened in a case of *mort d'ancestor* (determining the right to inheritance) because the defendant was *crucesignatus*.[21] Across western Europe secular courts had to recognize crusaders' immunity from certain civil and non-capital criminal law suits, the postponement of their cases and the standing of their attorneys. Legal and chronological limits had to be determined and modified; in England the so-called crusaders' term, during which the privileges were effective, was set at three years in 1188 but was regarded by some lawyers fifty years later as five years or indefinite.[22] Tax collectors needed instructions to exempt crusaders' property and methods to establish who they were. On local justices and policing agents, such as sheriffs in England, fell the responsibility to implement the church's protection of crusaders' possessions and families.

The potential domestic repercussions of a decision to take the cross could be considerable. For some, crusading offered lasting advantages. The development of proxy crusaders, while expensive for the noncombatant *crucesignatus*, benefited the representative often with more than the cost of passage, equipment, travel expenses and wages. To secure proxies' services, added incentives or bribes were provided, usually land, which then remained in their family's ownership. As all crusaders were *ipso facto* legally free, if a landowner chose a possibly easily persuadable unfree tenant to perform his vow, this would imply, at the very least, manumission (i.e. being set free) for the proxy. Hugh Travers, an English servile tenant manumitted as a Jerusalem proxy in the early thirteenth century, was released servile dues and allowed to hold his previously servile tenure as a free tenancy, a move that enabled his descendants to thrive in an increasingly competitive agrarian land market.[23] More widespread benefits accrued to those who provided cash or materials in return for gifts, leases, mortgages or sale of property.

While Innocent III's programme of extending social access to the crusade indulgences further integrated the activity into society, there were casualties far removed from the battlefields of the cross. Improvident or unlucky crusaders could inflict lasting damage to their patrimonies through debt or alienation. It was no accident that so many preachers' anecdotes concerned wives trying to prevent their spouses from taking the cross. Although many women took the cross, accompanied expeditions and bequeathed funds for the Holy Land in their wills, crusaders' wives stood to lose income, status, livelihood, even life itself. Ironically, Innocent III, who elsewhere strongly promoted the ideals of Christian marriage, crucially diminished the rights of women married to crusaders. Traditionally, in canon law, conjugal rights operated with complete equality between the partners, neither having the right unilaterally to deny the other. In theory, before Innocent III, putative crusaders required the permission of their wives to go. Innocent relaxed this provision, effectively giving permission for wives to be abandoned without their consent. Crusade widows, metaphorical and actual, especially if they held or guarded property, were potentially very vulnerable. The protection of the courts often failed to prevent land being stolen, still less offer compensation for any financial hardship consequent on the crusader's absence. Although a crusader needed his wife's consent to any land deals that involved dower land set aside to provide for her widowhood, for obvious domestic reasons such permission was regularly forthcoming, exposing that property to the depredations suffered by the rest. Illicit deprivation or expulsion from family land were not the worst outcome. William Trussel left his English lands on crusade in 1190. Six weeks later his wife was murdered by his bastard half-brother and her body flung into a nearby marl pit.[24] Property rather than passion was the likely motive. Contrary to modern fantasies, it was not a chastity belt that a crusader's wife required (in any case an invention of the seventeenth century) but a good lawyer or a strong guardian.

The proliferation of evidence from the decades after 1187 showing the penetration of crusading into the interstices of social and cultural life reflected the increasing acceptance of written record keeping in politics, administration and the law. Yet it also charted genuine developments in how the business of the cross was presented, operated and perceived, in organization, preaching, liturgical prominence and social penetration. This process did not cease with the pontificate of Innocent III. New theories reconciling the holy war of the crusades with the just war categories of the canon lawyers became increasingly fashionable after 1216. Preaching grew more systematic and standardized, with a proliferation in handbooks and manuals on how to do it and what to say coupled with the emergence as a standing army of evangelism of the new orders of friars, the Dominicans and Franciscans, founded in the second decade of the thirteenth century. As members of orders that held no possessions, begged for their sustenance (hence the name Mendicants) and, while living in communal houses, conducted an active ministry in the outside world, the friars were, in theory at least, ideally suited as preachers. Crusade finance was transformed by the increase in the income from vow redemptions, donations, alms and legacies as well as by regular clerical taxes for the cause. By the mid-1270s, all western Christendom was divided into collection regions. Stronger and more settled central governments were able to mobilize more coherent state responses, even to the extent of levying lay subsidies for the crusade, as in France in 1248 and England in 1270. Recruitment, as a consequence, was based on more professional, contractual and mercenary lines, the link between taking the cross and military service no longer inevitable or essential. To be a *crucesignatus* could denote spiritual status, not physical activity. Indulgences were applied even more extensively, to include sermon audiences or congregations, crusaders' non-*crucesignati* family members and even, on occasion, deceased relatives. Within a century, indulgences were sold directly to the faithful. Although abuses were inevitable, this institutionalization was not so much a racket as an expression of managed commitment.

Few of these developments were untouched by the legacy of Innocent III, who saw the crusade with moral and religious reform – sabbatarian (i.e. Sunday observance), anti-usury, anti-materialist – as central to his mission. They were the reasons he announced for summoning the Fourth Lateran Council in 1215.[25] All the great crusade preachers of his reign combined the call of the cross of holy war with that of personal penitence and a return to Apostolic poverty, the way of Christ in public arms and private devotion. The ordinances contained in *Quia Maior* and *Ad Liberandam* demonstrated a world view allied to administrative details that exerted an extraordinary hold over succeeding papal legislation, even if their lack of precise definition of the canonical status of holy war or the exact relationship between taking the cross and the actual vow may have continued to trouble academics. By equating the crusade with his general moral agenda rather than confining it to a narrow, military or foreign policy, Innocent left the papacy and church free rein to use the mechanics and language of preaching, recruitment, cross, vow, indulgence, temporal privileges, alms, taxation and redemptions. No longer simply a matter of marching or sailing to Palestine, the crusade found itself a more pervasive role in Christian society paradoxically at the same time as its exclusiveness, some might argue distinctiveness, was diluted.

THE GERMAN CRUSADE 1195–8

The enforced revival of active crusading in the east after 1187 encouraged the application of wars of the cross elsewhere, as it had in the early years of the twelfth century and again during the Second Crusade. Propaganda, recruitment and rounding up vow shirkers for the Holy Land scarcely ceased, keeping the crusade and the associated sense of Christendom in crisis prominently in view. Other frontiers seemed to demand attention. The success of the north African Berber Islamic reformist political sect the Almohads since the 1150s, and especially under Ya'qub (1184–99), in annexing much of Muslim southern Spain and driving back earlier Christian advances, reached a climax in their defeat of Alfonso VIII of Castile at Alarcos in 1195. In 1193, Celestine III had authorized a crusade to bolster Iberian resistance. Similarly in the Baltic, in 1195 Celestine associated the crusade and its privileges with attempts to conquer and colonize Livonia (roughly modern Latvia) by Saxon entrepreneurs, adventurers and blood-stained penitents directed by Archbishop Hartwig II of Bremen (1185–1207) and his protégé Berthold, *soi-disant* bishop of the Livs.[26] The precedents for such extensions of the crusade reached back a century in local practice and found legitimacy in the decrees of the First Lateran Council

(1123) and Bernard of Clairvaux at the Diet of Frankfurt (1147). The Third Lateran Council of 1179 had sidled towards a further extension involving Christians, not just infidels. Decree XXVII offered plenary indulgences to those who were killed helping local bishops fight Cathar heretics in southern France or mercenary companies who were terrorizing and devastating whole regions 'more paganorum', like pagans. Those who joined up for these campaigns and did not die were to receive only limited indulgences, although they and their goods were to be placed under the same church protection as those who visited the Holy Sepulchre.[27] Innocent III developed these precedents into an unambiguous programme of religious warfare on all fronts.

However, the Holy Land retained its primacy of concern and effort. Innocent ascended the papal throne in January 1198 just as a major crusade to the east was at the point of disintegration, its failure providing the new pope with the *casus belli* for a new endeavour. The German crusade of 1195–8, for all its modest achievements, provided a model of nation-based expeditions followed regularly over the next century, as the political impediments to assembling international campaigns led by more than one monarch mounted. In 1194, after the death of King Tancred of Sicily, the German emperor Henry VI conquered the kingdom in the right of his wife Constance, being crowned king at Palermo on Christmas Day 1194. As king of Sicily as well as Germany, Henry's rhetoric sketched universal pretensions. His policies now developed a number of facets in which the crusade featured: good relations with the papacy in order to secure papal acceptance of his schemes for a united hereditary monarchy in Germany and Italy; the assertion of German imperial leadership of Christendom in the manner of his father Frederick Barbarossa; and traditional Sicilian interests in Byzantium and the central and eastern Mediterranean. In pursuit of all of these, during Easter week 1195, Henry privately took the cross from the bishop of Sutri. This allowed him, in the fashion of Louis VII at Vézelay in 1147, to present himself at a diet held to proclaim a new crusade at Bari on Easter Day (2 April) already a *crucesignatus*.[28]

At Bari, as a sign of his commitment and an incentive to recruitment, Henry announced that he would pay for 1,500 knights and 1,500 sergeants for a year; the knights were to receive thirty gold ounces (Troy weight) and provisions for themselves and two servants; the sergeants ten gold ounces. To pay the 5,000 gold pounds (Troy) needed for this,

Henry demanded a tribute from the new Byzantine emperor, Alexius III, who had deposed and blinded his brother, Isaac II, on 8 April 1195. This formed part of Henry's deliberate bullying of the Byzantine emperor, attempting to extract promises of material assistance for the crusade as well as restitution for Sicilian losses during the wars of the 1180s and, more pertinently, damages for those of Frederick Barbarossa in 1189–90. Henry's new power gave substance to his diplomatic belligerence. Alexius submitted to the bullying and, after failing to get political support for a general property tax, fell back on appropriating ecclesiastical alms and bullion, apparently amounting to over 7,000 pounds of silver and a much smaller quantity of gold. This highly unpopular levy was known derisively as the 'Alamanikon' (i.e. German tax).[29] Arrangements for its delivery were in hand when news of Henry's death from one of his recurrent fevers (28 September 1197) halted payment. However, these negotiations with Byzantium charted a clear western attitude to Byzantium and the eastern crusade. As well as the tax, the Greeks were asked to provide their own help for the Holy Land in conjunction with a western expedition, their past reluctance noted and present hesitation or opposition cited as grounds for a possible future invasion. The assumptions and attitudes of the leaders of next great eastern crusade, in 1202–4, boasted a long pedigree.

Right up to his death, Henry had closely supervised recruitment, helped by papal legates and local bishops authorized by Celestine III in July and August 1195 to preach the cross throughout Germany as well as in France and England.[30] At a series of diets at Gelnhausen (October 1195), Worms (December 1195) and Würzburg (March 1196), crusaders enrolled, preparations were put in train and plans agreed. Departure from Germany was set for Christmas 1196 for muster at southern Italian and Sicilian ports, in particular Messina, in time for the next spring or, at the latest, autumn passages to the Levant. To avoid unnecessary conflicts of jurisdiction in the east of the sort that dogged the Third Crusade, as well as demonstrating high imperial prestige, at Gelnhausen Henry agreed with envoys from Cyprus to accept the homage of Aimery of Lusignan, who had succeeded his brother Guy as ruler of the island in 1194, in return for a crown. Beyond natural aspiration, Aimery may have wanted such an alliance to protect him from Byzantine attempts to reconquer his island. Shortly after, a similar deal was struck with Leo II of Cilician Armenia. If in the event unrealized, this extension of German imperial authority almost to create a new eastern empire possessed wide implications, not least for the cohesion of the Christian states of the Levant and for Byzantium, now increasingly surrounded by Henry's satellites. Henry's rhetoric of universal empire was acquiring reality. Within Germany, Henry signalled his control of the enterprise by sitting for hours in Worms cathedral while *crucesignati* took their vows. Whatever the canonical niceties, the initiative and direction of this war of the cross belonged not to the pope but to a secular ruler with extremely elevated ambitions in which leadership of the crusade formed only a part.

In geographic extent and aristocratic involvement if not in actual numbers, recruitment matched that in 1188–9. The core contribution came from the imperial household and the emperor's allies. Such was the dominant appearance of Henry VI that a thirteenth-century Outremer observer imagined he promised to pay the expenses of all the German crusaders.[31] When the emperor's notoriously feeble health and his still uncertain grip on his new southern kingdom persuaded him not to lead the expedition in person, he appointed as commanders the imperial chancellor, Conrad of Querfurt, bishop of Hildesheim, and the imperial marshal, Henry of Kalden, who had led the embassy to Constantinople in 1195. Clerical leadership was provided by Archbishop Conrad of Mainz and Archbishop Hartwig of Bremen, a holy war enthusiast who in 1195 persuaded Celestine III to initiate one against the Livs on the river Dvina. Both their dioceses had previously been centres of crusade support. The leading lay crusaders tended to come from western and southern Germany including Duke Henry of Brabant, Henry the Lion's son Count Henry of the Rhine Palatinate, Duke Frederick of Austria, the dukes of Dalmatia and Carinthia and the landgrave of Thuringia. Many of them were heirs to family crusading traditions and a significant proportion had only succeeded to their titles in the previous five years or so. They may have felt they had something to prove beyond the customary appeal of the cross or the attraction of doing what their ruler wanted. Other former centres of crusade enthusiasm in the Rhineland or the northern river valleys contributed extensively. Lübeck apparently sent 400 citizens.[32] The scale of the operation was reflected in the time and varied routes taken for the muster in Italy and Sicily. Some contingents that had probably travelled from southern Germany by land left for the east as early as March 1197. The duke of Brabant reached the

Holy Land in the late summer, probably August. However, a northern fleet of forty-four vessels carrying possibly many thousands of recruits under Henry of the Palatinate and the bishop of Bremen, only reached Messina in August after its long voyage around the Iberian peninsular. This combined with the emperor's paid troops to form the main body of the expedition that sailed from Messina for Acre early in September 1197. A distant observer, Arnold of Lübeck, claimed it carried 60,000 crusaders. It may have been a quarter or a fifth that size, but still constituted a substantial force. While a contingent under the bishop of Hildesheim stopped off in Cyprus to crown Aimery, the bulk of the fleet reached Acre on 22 September.

For once, a western crusade appeared in the Holy Land when it was needed. The truce of 1192 had expired and, twelve days before the main German force arrived, Henry of Champagne had died in a bizarre accident when he fell out of an open window while reviewing troops at his palace in Acre. Already the Ayyubid chief, Saladin's brother al-Adil, was on the move. The death of Saladin in March 1193 prompted a decade of internecine feuding within his family. This was won by al-Adil, who, from his original base in northern Syria and Iraq, managed to supplant his nephews in Damascus (1196), Egypt (1200) and Aleppo (1202). In 1197, al-Adil was quick to respond to a raid into Galilee by the early German arrivals under Henry of Brabant, driving them back to the suburbs of Acre before swinging south to besiege Jaffa. It was the relief force for Jaffa that Henry of Champagne was inspecting when he met his death. Days later the port fell, imperilling the fragile *status quo* established in 1192. However, once the full German expeditionary force had assembled after 22 September, it was agreed to strike northwards to the ruins of Sidon and the Muslim base at Beirut rather than attempt to recover Jaffa immediately. This made immediate strategic sense, taking advantage of the recovery earlier in the year of Jubail further up the coast; cooperation from Bohemund III of Antioch, whose son, the future Bohemund IV, was now also count of Tripoli; and help from the Pisans and Amalric of Cyprus, anxious about the pirates operating out of Beirut. Led by Henry of Brabant, in the absence of a Frankish ruler now in temporary overall control, the Christian forces, after taking possession of the rubble of Sidon, occupied Beirut in late October. The land bridge from Tripoli to Tyre and Acre was restored.

Security for these coastal ports was less certain. Al-Adil's response to the earlier German raid into Galilee had demonstrated even Acre's vulnerability to a hostile hinterland. Before any attempt on Jerusalem, the Germans, on the advice of the local baronage, decided to consolidate the Christian position in western Galilee by attacking the castle at Toron. After initial success, the siege, which began on 28 November 1197, got bogged down. The proximity to Acre and Tyre of the German army both at Toron and before, on the Beirut campaign, may have carried a political dimension. The death of Henry of Champagne had once again opened the question of the succession to the throne of Jerusalem. His widow, Isabella, now had three young daughters, two by Henry; the eldest, Maria, daughter of Conrad of Montferrat, was still only five. Isabella, a veteran of three marriages but still only in her twenties, remained the legitimate queen. Some proposed a marriage to a local nobleman, the seneschal, Ralph of Tiberias, but the Germans, supported by the military orders and the chancellor, Joscias archbishop of Tyre, advocated the recently widowed Aimery of Cyprus. The attraction of a union of Cyprus and Jerusalem was compelling in economic, military and political terms, especially given the tensions between the two since 1192. Personally, Aimery possessed experience, close family connections with the Jerusalem nobility (his late wife's Ibelin first cousins were Queen Isabella's half-brothers) and had recently become a client of the German emperor. A united Cypriot–Jerusalem kingdom under German overlordship offered prospects of entrenching Hohenstaufen imperialism across the Mediterranean, thereby providing a permanent conduit of aid for the Holy Land without necessarily compromising the jealously promoted rights of the indigenous nobility, Italian cities or military orders. The presence of a large German army reinforced this optimism. Joscias of Tyre, who successfully negotiated Aimery's acceptance of Isabella's hand and the Jerusalem throne in October 1197, may also have reflected on these cross-Mediterranean advantages.[33] He had been Jerusalem's leading ambassador to the west in the desperate days after Hattin.

In January 1198, Aimery married Isabella and was crowned king of Jerusalem. The same month, the archbishop of Mainz crowned Leo II in Cilician Armenia. Yet the Hohenstaufen grand design was already defunct. The sickly Henry VI had died at Messina on 28 September 1197, leaving only an infant son, Frederick, not yet three years old, and a restless, fissile and violent inheritance from the Baltic to the Tyrrhenian

Sea. Another casualty of Henry's death was his crusade. On hearing the news, and faced by the prospect of a Muslim counter-attack, the Germans raised the siege of Toron on 2 February, effectively ending the German crusade. The Franks of Outremer with their new monarch preferred accommodation with al-Adil to any further provocation or grand gestures. Beirut gave them a useful bargaining chip, as well as an important compensation for the loss of Jaffa. Aimery secured a renewal of the truce in July 1198 until 1204. The conquests of 1197 were to stand on each side, al-Adil with Jaffa; the Franks with Beirut, which was given to Aimery's new brother-in-law, John of Ibelin, later known as the 'Old Lord of Beirut'. Impotent in the Holy Land, the leaders of the German army were anxious to return home to cope with the new political uncertainties. Apart from the capture of Beirut, which remained in Christian hands until 1291, the installation of Aimery as king of Cyprus and then king of Jerusalem, and of Leo II as king of Armenia, the German crusade flattered to deceive. Even the opportunity created by Ayyubid division proved counter-productive, as al-Adil increased his reputation as the strong man of the region who faced down the western infidels. Henry VI may have hoped his patronage of the fledgling military order of Teutonic Knights, for whom he obtained papal privileges in 1196, would provide a permanent magnet for German support for the Holy Land, but the failure of the crusade prevented any major expansion of its position for a generation.

The immediate future of Outremer, at least until the expiry of the 1198 truce, seemed to rest with diplomacy, internal consolidation and only tactical military excursions against hostile neighbours rather than general confrontation. In the west, the chances for a new mass crusade to the Holy Land faced serious impediments as the political balance promised by Henry VI's imperialism collapsed. Germany slid into civil war over a disputed succession. Italy resumed its fractured insecurity. The Spanish kings were fully occupied with the insurgent Almohads, while the kings of France and England continued a twenty-years' war (1194–1214) over the Angevin inheritance. The election of Innocent III in January 1198 did not obviously alter these political realities. However, the new pope preferred to set, not follow, the patterns of Christendom's public and private lives.

INNOCENT III AND THE NEW CRUSADE

In letters sent across Christendom dated 15 August 1198, Innocent III called for a new crusade to the Holy Land. Specifically, he cited the withdrawal of the Germans after the capture of Beirut and the fears of a Muslim counter-attack. As if to signal a more energetic papal regime, Innocent combined heightened rhetoric, an awareness of past failings and a desire to control organization. The communal endeavour was emphasized by appealing to nobles and cities to provide enough armed men. The troops were to serve for two years on the eastern campaign. Preaching was instituted.[34] One papal legate, Peter Capuano, was to try to impose a five-year truce in the war between Richard I and Philip II, which had been continuing ever since Richard's release from Henry VI's prison in 1194. Another, Soffredo, cardinal priest of St Praxedis, was to travel to Venice to investigate transport. The plenary nature of the indulgences, offered through the mercy of God, was more explicit. Its clarity found its mark in the memory of at least one who answered the call, Geoffrey of Villehardouin, marshal of Champagne, who described it simply as 'remission of any sins they have committed, provided they have confessed them'.[35] The only element of obviously wishful thought in Innocent's appeal lay in the proposed deadline for muster and departure, set for March 1199. However, from its inception to its ragged and bitter conclusion in 1205, most things that could go wrong for Innocent's crusade did. The Fourth Crusade, as it is now known, became the most controversial of them all, provoking Steven Runciman's famous Philippic: 'there was never a greater crime against humanity than the Fourth Crusade'.[36]

The reason for the notoriety of the Fourth Crusade lay and lies in its outcome, the conquest of large tracts of the Christian Byzantine empire after its capital Constantinople had been sacked by the crusaders in April 1204. Yet Innocent's intention had been to reverse the hung verdict of the Third Crusade and the disappointment of the German expedition in Palestine, not revive Henry VI's threats to the Greeks of 1195–6. Byzantium inevitably figured in Innocent's calculations, as it had to in those of all planners of major eastern crusades since 1095. However a hostile assault on Constantinople formed no part of the original papal scheme. Innocent's motives, as revealed in his bull of August 1198, in so far that they embraced considerations beyond the need to recover all of the Holy Land, concerned his promotion of papal authority, in the operation of the crusade itself and in his interference in secular politics to achieve it. There was no mention of Byzantium in the 1198 or subsequent bulls for the enterprise. The controversy surrounding the Fourth Crusade revolves centrally around the issue of intent. If the violent capture and barbaric pillage of Constantinople and the subsequent dispossession of the Greeks were crimes, were they the result of deliberate malice, conspiracy or a series of accidental decisions that led to unforeseen although consciously embraced consequences? Was the destruction of Byzantium murder, manslaughter or even self-defence?

Immediately, crusade recruitment proved another damp squib. It is sometimes argued that Innocent III wished to exclude reigning monarchs from commanding his crusade. The bickering during the Third Crusade presented a clear warning of potential difficulties, while Henry VI's crusade appeared to contest papal authority itself. Yet Innocent's eagerness to resolve the political conflict between Philip II and Richard I, prominent in the bull of August 1198, indicated an understanding that the financial and political resources of rulers offered the best chance for a successful crusade. It was less the success of papal planning than the failure of papal diplomacy and continuing international instability that threw the burden of military leadership on counts, not kings. Peter Capuano's mission to France served to irritate rather than pacify. By turns tactless, ingratiating and sanctimonious, Cardinal Peter, a notably effective preacher, seems to have combined the Gladstonian manner of addressing individuals as if they were public meetings and the Disraelian habit of laying on emotion with a trowel. In December 1198, when Peter suggested to Richard I that the king might agree to a truce with Philip II, Richard was so infuriated at being lectured at that he threatened the legate with castration.[37] Richard's unexpected death in April 1199, from a crossbow bolt wound suffered while besieging a rebel castle at Chalus in the Limousin, and the subsequent succession crisis in the Angevin lands that lasted until Philip II's treaty with King John at Le Goulet in May 1200, further precluded royal involvement. The only benefit the crusade derived from this long crisis lay with those lords who found themselves on the wrong side of events and were thus open to recruitment for a conveniently good cause 2,500 miles away.

The preaching campaign promised to be more efficient. A chain of authority reached from the pope to legates, local ecclesiastical hierarchies and specially appointed preachers with the powers to conscript deputies, including monks and canons. The problem lay not in the message but the promotion and reception. In November 1198, Innocent pulled off a public relations coup by enlisting the charismatic French evangelist Fulk of Neuilly, who already enjoyed a large popular following for his brand of austere moral rearmament.[38] A parish priest of imposing bearing, a notorious gourmand, Fulk had honed his rhetorical skills during a stay at the sophisticated theological schools in Paris, where the pope as young man may have encountered him. Despite this elite training, Fulk affected the common touch in his career as an itinerant holy man. He made his reputation in the late 1190s preaching a return to apostolic virtue, the practice of simplicity and poverty and a rejection of outward signs of corruption such as usury, luxury and sexual licence. He attracted stories of miracles based on those found in the Gospels and Acts of the Apostles: healing the sick; curing the blind, dumb and lame; exorcism; reforming prostitutes; and escaping from chains and prison. Although covertly something of an establishment figure himself, Fulk – and his admirers – cultivated the figure of the prophet apart, John the Baptist or even Peter the Hermit. This carefully fashioned image of plain-talking fearless pursuit of the truth and redemption, so useful for a professional evangelist, was greatly enhanced by his well-publicized encounter with Richard I. He accused the king to his face of pride, avarice and sensuality, drawing Richard's neat riposte: 'I give my pride to the Templars; my avarice to the Cistercians; and my sensuality to the Benedictines.'[39] Fulk lacked shyness; in mock humility and floods of tears he told an audience of Cistercians in 1201 that he had personally signed up 200,000 crusaders, a preposterous claim, but one that reflected a possibly necessary self-belief. In the words of his contemporary eulogist and fellow preacher, James of Vitry, Fulk was a star ('stellam in medio nebule').[40]

As such, Innocent was evidently keen to harness his fame, popularity and promotional ability to the crusade. Fulk embodied Innocent's attempt to integrate the war of the cross into the wider reform movement, loosely described as Apostolic Poverty. Fulk's appointment as a preacher of the cross in November 1198 allowed him free rein, not least in choosing his own evangelizing lieutenants. His crusade preaching took him to Flanders, Normandy and Brittany as well as his home region of the Ile de France.[41] A measure of his impact is the indelible impression his preaching left in the memories of contemporaries. Two *crucesignati* who wrote accounts of their experiences, the grand Geoffrey of Villehardouin, and a Picard knight of modest means, Robert of Clari, both opened their histories of the Fourth Crusade with Fulk's preaching. To emphasize the importance of Abbot Martin of Pairis near Basel in preaching the cross, his panegyrist Gunther took pains to associate him with Fulk's mission. Yet the tangible results of Fulk's preaching were elusive, at least in regard to enrolling lords and property owners on whom the success of any expedition depended. No important recruits came forward for another year, by which time Fulk's appeal may have faded.

Despite Innocent III's theology of redemption and the Lord's War, aspects of the alliance of Apostolic Poverty with crusading jarred. Robert of Clari noted that, as well as preaching the cross, Fulk had collected 'much wealth to be carried to the Holy Land overseas', presumably in the form of alms and donations, as encouraged by the papacy. James of Vitry's account is less innocuous and more revealing.

> [Fulk] began amassing a great sum of money from the alms of the faithful which he had undertaken to pay out to poor men who took the cross, both soldiers and others. But through avarice or other base motive, he did not make these payments, and from that time, by God's hidden judgement, the power and influence of his preaching swiftly declined. His wealth grew, but the fear and respect he had commanded fell away.[42]

According to James, following these charges of embezzlement, his reputation shot to pieces, Fulk slunk away into retirement and death. In fact he continued to play an important, if only iconic, role, at least in observers' memories.

He was not the last evangelist to find preaching and the crusade a corrosive mix. In the sermons of many of the Paris-trained moralists who promoted Innocent III's crusades, the concentration lay as much, occasionally more, with the redemptive and reforming dimensions of the message than with the military or material. One of those Fulk recruited to preach the cross, Eustace abbot of St Gemer de Flay, after preaching tours of England in 1200 and 1201 was remembered for his vitriolic attacks on illicit trading and breaches of the Sabbath rather than for his urging of holy war.[43] Fulk's difficulty lay in a series of potential conflicts and contradictions between his usual stance against usury and the requirements of the crusade. Insistence on the rejection of usury (i.e. credit) and the abandonment of wealth in favour of the rigorous *vita apostolica* presented aspirant crusade contributors and participants with material and moral quandaries. Fulk found himself preaching poverty and the evils of money, which he was simultaneously salting away. Whether he was actually corrupt hardly mattered: as always, there were fellow clerics eager to cast the first stone. Fulk had built his name on perceptions; he lost it the same way. Yet, despite the whiff of scandal, his efforts were remembered as seminal. It may have been no coincidence that some of the areas he toured in northern France, including Flanders, produced large contingents of crusaders. Both the Champenois Villehardouin and Picard Robert of Clari stressed Fulk's probity; perhaps they had heard the stories of embezzlement. Despite the rumours, Fulk remained attached to the crusade venture until his death in May 1202, attending on the crusade leaders at Soissons in May 1201 and addressing the General Chapter of the Cistercians, an order heavily involved in the preaching campaign, in September the same year.

Despite the claims made by and for Fulk, most recognized the guiding hand of Pope Innocent behind the charismatic French preacher. Whatever success the preachers enjoyed, in 1198–9 the crusade hardly progressed publicly, not least because of Innocent's difficulties. Fulk's own travails indicated one of Innocent's problems: money. In December 1199, with his proposed deadline long past and no prospect of royal involvement, the pope proclaimed a tax on clerical profits of a fortieth (2.5 per cent) in order to pay 'for the upkeep of fighting men'.[44] To try to forestall resistance to this novel demonstration of papal authority, he promised the levy would create no precedent, an indication that Innocent's conception of papal power still lacked general consensus. Hiring paid troops on crusade was not a new idea. Conrad III had done it in the Holy Land in 1148, as had both Philip II and Richard I on their arrival in 1191. Richard had paid for his fleet and its sailors. Henry VI had provided wages for a mounted regiment at least 3,000 strong in 1195. If, as James of Vitry reported, Fulk of Neuilly was raising funds to pay soldiers, then Innocent had recognized the need for such a pool of men and money from the start. Finance and mercenaries were to lie at the centre of how the Fourth Crusade operated and developed.

In 1198–9, Innocent's eastern schemes were taking time to coalesce. Elsewhere, grants of crusade privileges, as against the Livs renewed in 1198, cost little, the burden of action being taken by locals. The wars in France and Germany were partly responsible for the delay in the Holy Land enterprise. More pressing were political difficulties in Italy, where a German adventurer and former imperial steward, Markward of Anweiler (d. 1202), was attempting to carve out a territory for himself from the lands of his former master Henry VI in southern Italy and Sicily. Innocent as guardian of the rights of Henry's infant son Frederick II, sought to organize resistance. In January 1199, he toyed with the idea of granting Holy Land plenary indulgences to those resisting Markward on the mainland. By November, perhaps as a last resort when it appeared that Markward and his Muslim allies had Sicily at their mercy, Innocent offered Holy Land indulgences to those prepared to fight the invaders, in part because he professed to regard Markward's ambitions as a hindrance to the Palestine project. War in Italy and Sicily clearly influenced arrangements for any crusade to the east, if only by denying crusaders safe passage to ports and access to transport. The effect of Innocent's grant is hard to judge. It does not appear that the other central crusading features of preaching and giving the cross were employed, even though the conflict has been called the first 'political crusade'.[45]

Besides distracting the pope from the eastern question, the wars in Italy and Livonia confirmed Innocent's inclusive interpretation and use of the holy war of the cross. His theology was in place. Preaching had begun to raise the consciousness of the faithful. The bull of August 1198, coming so soon on the heels of Innocent's accession and the end of the German crusade, had confirmed a near-permanent position for Holy Land crusading in the ecclesiastical and religious polity of the western church. However, to convert ambition into action required the initiative not of the pope, legates and clergy alone or even the masses enthused by crusade evangelists. To get anywhere, Innocent's new crusade, as he had admitted in his bull, relied on the commitment and leadership of the secular rich and powerful.

16

The Fourth Crusade: Preparations

The central irony of the Fourth Crusade sprang from its achievements. The capture of Constantinople in April 1204 and the subsequent annexation by western lords of large tracts of the Greek empire constituted for many participants and witnesses a memorable and admirable triumph of western chivalry. Against great odds, as one of their leaders Geoffrey of Villehardouin was later at pains to emphasize, the crusaders had overcome 'the greatest, most powerful, and most strongly fortified city in the world'.[1] Yet every step of the way – from the treaty with Venice that insisted on a general muster there in 1202; to the attack on the Dalmatian port of Zara; to the diversion to Byzantium in 1203 – was accompanied by divisions, doubts, arguments and defections. The triumph itself seemingly required constant justification, at the time and subsequently. The Greek conquests failed to ignite much western interest or support, at least once the great holy booty of relics had been secured. This 'new France', as Innocent's successor Honorius III called it, failed to capture the imagination to compete with the Holy Land. While Byzantium never fully recovered from the trauma of defeat and partition, the effect of the Fourth Crusade on most of western Europe remained peripheral. The exception was Venice, a city that had gambled and gained hugely on this unexpected inauguration of its international empire. Yet the image of a Christian army of crusaders laying waste the ancient Christian capital of Constantinople appeared, at the very least, striking, if not actively disturbing. The pope was appalled.[2] A victory of pragmatism, perhaps even desperation, over idealism, conscience, even, some argued, law, the Fourth Crusade left its main purpose unrealized, the recovery of Jerusalem. Whatever the religious dimension of attacking the schismatic Greeks, the essential excuse for the events of 1203–4 depended on a variety of just war explanations allied to the rationale of expediency. By the time the enterprise to fight for the Holy Land was effectively called off in the summer of 1205, there had been no holy war. The crusade had been cancelled before it had begun.

RECRUITMENT AND FINANCE

Early recruitment for Innocent III's crusade owed much to a ghost. Looking back half a century later, a knowledgeable Cistercian, Alberic of Trois-Fontaines, characterized the enterprise as 'an overseas expedition of nobles signed with the Cross who had formerly abandoned King Philip when King Richard attacked, as well as other barons'.[3] Half a decade of intense conflict had forced most of the higher nobility of France to choose between allegiance to the Capetians or alliance with the Angevins. In the late 1190s, Richard's partisans included the counts of Flanders, Blois and St Pol, all prominent future leaders of the crusade. The death of Richard in April 1199 transformed prospects. While he lived, few nobles in any region of France would have been happy or sensible to leave for the east with the contest between the kings of France and England active and unresolved. No amount of fine words from Fulk of Neuilly could shift political necessities. The value of church protection for absent crusaders had been starkly exposed by the fate of Richard's own French lands in 1193–4. However, on Richard's death, new accommodations were reached, not least because of the rebarbative personality of Richard's successor John, one of the most unsuccessful medieval monarchs who lost an empire and united his own baronage in dislike, resentment, fear and, ultimately, rebellion. The awkwardness facing Richard's former allies could honourably be resolved by a decision to take the cross, a move that would serve the interests and win the approval of the king of France. Many of the great lords of northern France were young men. In 1199, the counts of Flanders, Blois and Champagne were all in their twenties, childless or with infants as heirs. For King Philip, their absence on crusade would remove proven or potential troublemakers and offer chances for lucrative royal intervention in their territories through regency or wardship arrangements.

In the winter of 1199–1200 a closely related group of great nobles from northern France accepted the cross, the counts of Champagne and Blois during a tournament at Ecry-sur-Aisne on Advent Sunday,

28 November, and the count of Flanders in Bruges on Ash Wednesday, 23 February.[4] Theobald of Champagne and Louis of Blois were cousins. Baldwin of Flanders was married to Theobald's sister, Marie, who took the cross with him, although heavily pregnant. The dates were not coincidental, each falling on the first days of the two great penitential seasons of the Christian year, Advent and Lent, familiar times to take the penitential vow of the cross. These were far from spontaneous acts, each count having assembled large numbers of important vassals to take the cross. The timing may also indicate wider preparations involving the pope, although there is no direct evidence for this. A month after the ceremony at Ecry, Innocent issued his bull announcing his own financial provision for the expedition.[5] The pope may have been waiting for news of the public commitment by the French nobles. Certainly the preamble to the bull of 31 December implied that action had already begun to which the pope wished to be seen to contribute. He also assigned two papal legates to travel to the Holy Land. At the same time, the preaching campaign was revived or extended, for example to Germany and the British Isles.[6]

The preaching campaign for the Fourth Crusade was organized through three agencies: papal legates; local bishops; and the Cistercians. Even Fulk of Neuilly fitted this scheme. Innocent declared that his appointment to preach the cross had been made with the 'advice and assent' of the legate to France, Peter Capuano.[7] A well-informed Cistercian source insisted that Fulk had previously adopted the cross at the order's general chapter at Cîteaux on 4 September 1198 and subsequently had failed to persuade many Cistercians to help in the preaching campaign. It was later alleged in Outremer that some of Fulk's 'innumerable wealth' was deposited with the Cistercians, who sent it to the Holy Land to pay for repairs to the walls of Tyre, Beirut and Acre.[8] Whatever the truth or pious fictions associating Fulk with the Cistercians, other members of the order played significant roles both in preaching and accompanying the crusade. Abbot Martin of Pairis roused considerable enthusiasm at Basel, probably in May 1201, after a modest response to the earlier preaching of the local bishop. He subsequently joined the Basel crusaders on their journey to the muster at Venice in the summer of 1202. The abbots of Loos and Les Vaux de Cernay were leading figures on the expedition itself, although finding themselves on opposite sides of the argument over the diversion to

Byzantium. Cistercians, including the abbot of Luciedo, were among the entourage of Boniface marquis of Montferrat when he arrived in France to accept the leadership of the crusade in the late summer of 1201; they may have been instrumental in persuading him to accept the task. In September 1201, the Cistercian General Chapter at Cîteaux played host to Boniface and other crusade leaders at an assembly that included Fulk of Neuilly and, possibly, Martin of Pairis.[9] The evangelical tradition of St Bernard and the Second Crusade, which had sustained Cistercian enthusiasm for the crusade after 1187, provided the expedition's organizers with a useful web of proselytizing, information and influence. The order was exempted from the clerical tax of 1199. Its role perhaps added spice to Richard I's gift to them of his greed.

However, as before, preaching operated as part of a process of public commitment. When Martin of Pairis preached at Basel, his audience were bursting with expectation, filled by rumours of preaching elsewhere, 'prepared in their hearts to enlist in Christ's camp . . . hungrily anticipating an exhortation of this sort'.[10] Whatever frisson of excitement or moment of epiphany struck congregations, the decision to take the cross depended on a long chain of conscious individual and collective calculations and decisions. This deliberate and complex activity took time to gain the acceptance, permission and support of family, lords, tenants or vassals, and to begin the necessary material as well as spiritual preparations. The sermons stood as ritualized representations of this, taking the cross confirming as much as inspiring enlistment. But months and years were required to convert the commitment into action, because, unlike the First Crusaders in 1095–6, their successors increasingly knew what to expect and took pains to anticipate the difficulties.

Between 1199 and 1202, crusade recruitment extended from the Irish Sea to the Adriatic, from Saxony to Lombardy and Provence. Yet the core regions stretched from Flanders southwards through Champagne and the Ile de France to the Loire. It gave the appearance of a very French affair. The carefully crafted ceremony at Ecry lent important momentum. One of those who took the cross there with Count Theobald, Geoffrey of Villehardouin, marshal of Champagne, noted that 'people throughout the country were greatly impressed when men of such high standing took the cross'.[11] Whatever private conviction or enthusiasm prompted responses to the call of the cross, networks of family, lordship, region, community and tradition exerted a powerful influence. As with a number of the German crusade leaders four years earlier, the youth of some of the French counts may have encouraged adventure. Preaching alone was insufficient. Many noble *crucesignati* boasted distinguished crusading pedigrees. Theobald of Champagne's father, Count Henry I, had twice visited the Holy Land, the first time with the Second Crusade; his elder brother, Count Henry II, from whom he had had inherited the county, had been one of the commanders of the Third Crusade and ruler of Jerusalem 1192–7. Louis of Blois, as a teenager, had campaigned with his father in Palestine on the Third Crusade. Baldwin of Flanders was heir to one of the most distinguished of all crusade traditions, stretching back to Count Robert II on the First Crusade and including three other twelfth-century counts. Other veterans included Geoffrey of Villehardouin, who had spent four years in a Muslim prison after being captured outside the camp at Acre in 1190, and Simon de Montfort, who had only just returned from the Holy Land.[12]

In retelling the story of the Fourth Crusade, eyewitnesses grouped noble recruits in regional or lordship associations. The Picard knight Robert of Clari described bodies of crusaders from Picardy, Flanders, Burgundy, Champagne, the Ile de France, the Beauvaisis and the Chartrain, dividing them between the very rich and those he called 'poor', men of his own modest but knightly standing who demonstrated and shared in the 'prouesse' of the chivalric elite, if not always their pick of the booty.[13] Villehardouin similarly listed recruits according to family and regional affinities, although he arranged them more hierarchically under the precedence of their local counts. When Baldwin of Flanders took the cross, his wife and brother, Henry, and a significant entourage of local nobles accompanied him. His example was soon followed by neighbouring lords in Artois and Picardy, such as Hugh IV count of St Pol and his nephew Count Peter of Amiens, one of whose vassals was Robert of Clari. In Flanders, as in Champagne and Blois-Chartres, the public commitment of the great regional overlord drew in wider aristocratic circles. In Burgundy, by contrast, with Duke Eudes III declining to participate, numbers of prominent lords recruited were fewer, and included Odo of Champlitte and his brother William, who were closely related to the Champagne comital family. However, recruitment was not confined to the networks of locality, kin and clientage in northern France. Although there was minimal enrolment in England, by 1202, crusaders from southern Burgundy and Forez were making their way east via Marseilles. Southern Germany and the Rhineland had been evangelized from early 1200 to some effect. The force from Basel that set out in 1202 included Abbot Martin of Pairis, who had led some of the local preaching. This alternative focus of support around local bishops or a monastic order, such as the Cistercians, was shown by the bishops of Autun in Burgundy, Soissons and Troyes in Champagne, the abbot of Loos in Flanders and, more eccentrically, the bishop of Halberstadt in Saxony, an unorthodox crusader.

In 1202, Conrad of Krosigk, the new bishop of Halberstadt, was excommunicated by the papal legate, Cardinal Guy of Palestrina, for his fierce partisanship on behalf of Philip of Swabia, whose claims to the German throne were then being strongly opposed by Innocent III. Undaunted, Bishop Conrad took the cross on 7 April 1202, 'judging it wiser to fall into the hands of God than into the hands of men'.[14] After accompanying the main crusade force from Venice to Zara and Constantinople, he fulfilled his vows in the Holy Land late in 1204. Only then did he receive absolution for his excommunication, reluctantly confirmed by the pope in June 1205. For the whole of his crusade, Bishop Conrad was an excommunicate. His equivocal status did not seem to interfere with his contacts with ecclesiastical authorities nor inhibit his acquisition in the Greek capital of choice relics, silks, precious stones and other lustrous fabrics and tapestries. Conrad's status and enthusiasm cut across legal niceties. He seems to have arranged for his memoirs to be recorded during his retirement in 1209. In them, acceptance by the mass of sceptical crusaders of the decision to divert the crusade to Constantinople in 1203 was ascribed to the crusaders being 'swayed partly by prayers, partly by price'.[15] Prayers and price: rather a neat description of the whole crusade.

The piety of crusaders in the cause of the Holy Land should not be discounted. Documentary as well as chronicle evidence for the now traditional pious bequests and arrangement of affairs survives in some abundance. The testimony of events proves personal and collective commitment even to death. As *crucesignati* poets put it, the choice between the lady love and the cross is an unfair contest, 'whether to go to God or to remain here'.[16] Theobald's enthusiasm seems to have played a significant part in setting the crusade in motion, even if his early death allowed him to be given the role of the lost leader unsullied by the compromises of subsequent events. However, the importance at least of the comital commanders, Theobald especially, was due as much to their wealth as to their status or conviction. When Hugh count of St Pol complained that, by July 1203, when the crusade army arrived outside Constantinople, he was heavily in debt, this reflected the expense of the campaign rather than his original financial position.[17] Baldwin of Flanders and Theobald of Champagne were probably the richest nobles in France, their combined resources rivalling those of the king. Louis of Blois, also by the right of his wife count of Clermont, controlled another extensive and rich block of territory. The ability of these lords to subsidize their followers provided the necessary mixture of incentive and control.

Crusading had developed into a joint enterprise operation. Great lords paid the expenses of their immediate entourage as well as any mercenaries. Beyond that, almost as an attribute of lordship, many leaders saw it necessary to subsidize their aristocratic vassals as well. Fleets, such as Richard I's, could also be partly funded by a commander. The experience of twelfth-century crusading had suggested that central funding contributed to efficiency and order in planning and execution. Against this, the canonical assumption of payment by the individual *crucesignatus* remained strong, although, with Innocent III's financial expedients, beginning to weaken. The Fourth Crusade occurred during a period of change from mainly self-financed expeditions to those predominantly underwritten by the leaders and the church that became a feature of the mid-thirteenth century and later. In this, crusading armies reflected patterns of military organization emerging across Europe. In 1199–1202, at the very least, to attract support, the crusade leadership, as the pope recognized, needed to be prepared openly to offer financial support to their followers. However, as they were to be forcibly reminded, the paymaster retained authority only for as long as he remained solvent. No cash, no control and, ultimately, no crusade. The experience of the Fourth Crusade stripped aside sentimental views of the material basis of crusading, its course almost wholly determined by finance and the constant quest for resources. From the outset, the crusade leaders understood this. Theobald of Champagne had calculated he needed 25,000 livres to pay his own retinue and proposed another 25,000 livres to retain other troops. Innocent III assumed the conscription of warriors for pay. On campaign at Constantinople, Hugh of St Pol reckoned knights as well as mounted sergeants and infantry required wages, if only to cover expenses.[18] Baldwin of Flanders provided Gilles de Trasignies, later a hero of a vernacular verse romance and one of his sworn vassals (*home lige*), 500 livres to go with him on crusade. The count also hired experienced troops. Along with clothing, food and other provisions, Baldwin sent some of these in his own ships with a fleet that sailed from Flanders in the summer of 1202 under the command of the governor of Bruges and others. This was evidently a comital project. When they arrived at Marseilles at the end of the year they sought Baldwin's orders as to where to go next.[19] Without such investment by the leaders there would have been no crusade.

Funds were sought across Europe. Count Baldwin was one of the richest men in Europe, his county the centre of a woollen cloth industry and trade that stretched from the British Isles to the Mediterranean. Even so, in 1202 he tried to raise money directly from his subjects, with the permission of their immediate overlords.[20] Bishop Conrad of Halberstadt received 550 silver marks from the dean of Magdeburg.[21] Apart from the apparently unsuccessful clerical tax of 1199, a voluntary lay tax of a fortieth was proposed in England and France in 1201. This may have aroused Philip II's hostility, as did other ecclesiastical crusade ordinances.[22] In England some money may have been raised and paid out, possibly including 1,000 marks King John of England gave his nephew Louis of Blois.[23] Odo of Champlitte and Guy of Thourotte, poet and castellan of Coucy, may have received money collected by Fulk of Neuilly.[24] Lesser crusaders resorted to traditional methods of fundraising. Hilduin of Villemoyenne in Champagne, in a series of land sales, received at least 280 livres, 200 of which was paid over by the monks of St Peter of Montier-le-Celle in pennies.[25] A 'fidelis' of Baldwin of Flanders, Romond, mortgaged property for a six-year loan of 140 livres in Hainault money.[26] The problem with all these measures, as on previous campaigns, lay in the inability of *crucesignati* to budget accurately for future expenses. Hugh of St Pol was not the only one forced into debt by the expenses of the campaign. Finance may have determined the initial structure of the crusading armies but, again in common with earlier crusades, the need to find large sums of money during the expedition itself exerted a no less overwhelming influence on strategy, objectives and outcome.

PREPARATIONS AND THE TREATY OF VENICE 1201

Preaching, recruitment and planning were not sequential processes but ran in parallel. Until late 1199, there is little evidence of the last. However, Innocent's appeal of August 1198 was not produced in a vacuum. In terms of international strategy, thanks to the German crusade, knowledge of events in the Holy Land was recent and vivid. The following year, the pope elicited a report on the situation in the Holy Land from Patriarch Aymar of Jerusalem.[27] One of the striking features of the Fourth Crusade was the acute awareness of the high command of the politics of the Near East and the constant stream of communication between western planners and the Franks of Outremer. Given the Palestine truce of 1198, an expeditionary force to the Holy Land would not have been welcome. This seemed to be of some importance to the crusade high command. In their 1201 treaty with the Venetians to mount an attack on Egypt, they explicitly agreed the fleet would sail direct to Egypt, implying an avoidance of a landfall in mainland Outremer, which would compromise King Aimery's diplomacy.[28] This insistence on deferring to the 1198 truce may partly explain the leadership's consistent and strident hostility to any who wished to leave the army to sail straight to Palestine. However, even if Egypt had been suggested to or by the pope in 1198–9, no evidence of it emerged, and circumstantially it seems unlikely. The propaganda talked exclusively of Jerusalem and the Holy Land. Even in 1201 the choice of Egypt as a destination was deliberately kept secret. In a sign of the fluidity rather than clarity of strategic planning, the Flemish fleet that sailed into the Mediterranean in the summer of 1202 had no exact idea where they were going to rendezvous with Count Baldwin, still less their ultimate destination. Despite distant orders to the contrary, left to themselves, in the spring of 1203 they proceeded to Acre.[29] Countless others who embarked in 1201–2 did the same.

From the start, Innocent cast his diplomatic net wide. He sought to engage the Byzantine emperor Alexius III in his plans more constructively than Henry VI had treated Alexius and his predecessor. Between 1198 and 1202, the pope and the Greek emperor exchanged at least eight embassies and twelve substantial letters.[30] At first, Innocent conducted an intensive diplomatic effort to persuade Alexius to accept church union and give material assistance to the crusade, beginning by proposing Greek participation in the expedition in return for crusade indulgences. This offer presupposed Byzantine acceptance of papal authority that Innocent assumed as a *sine qua non*. Repeated references to the example of Manuel I stood as coded criticism of Greek failure to help the crusade. After some cautious encouragement from Alexius, in the winter of 1199–1200 the negotiations soured. Alexius called for the restoration of Cyprus and restated imperial independence from Rome. This prompted a harder line from the pope, who had also been securing alliances with neighbours of Byzantium: King Emeric of Hungary took the cross, and Kalojan of Bulgaria received coronation from a papal legate. However, Alexius III's ultimate rejection of Innocent's approaches failed to persuade the pope that Byzantium merited destruction or conquest. As late as the spring of 1203, with the crusade fleet already under sail for Byzantium, Innocent expressly forbade any attack on Constantinople.[31]

If diplomacy and gathering intelligence had begun in 1198, no grand scheme could be devised until a crusade army and leadership were in place. At meetings at Soissons and Compiègne in the summer of 1201, the French crusade leaders discussed timing and objectives. The Compiègn meeting of the crusader counts and barons – a *parlement* according to Villehardouin, who was there[32] – provided a foretaste of how the crusade was to be run, by committee and deliberative assembly. Although Theobald of Champagne had provided the initiative for the enterprise and was, in some senses, accepted as its prime mover, in the absence of a royal overlord, command was collegial. The crusaders at Compiègne held a lively debate, chiefly it seems on transport, but possibly also on the destination of the expedition. It was decided to send to Italy six ambassadors, drawn from the affinities of the three dominant figures, the counts of Flanders, Champagne and Blois, to choose and negotiate with a carrier for transport east. Given that Egypt appeared in the agreement reached by this delegation, it is possible that the Compiègne *parlement* proposed it. At least four of the ambassadors, who were given plenipotentiary powers to seal a treaty binding their principals, were veterans of the Third Crusade: Villehardouin himself and Milo of Brébant (Champagne); Conon of Béthune (Flanders); and

John of Friaise (Blois). Egypt had been regarded as the key to the fate of the Holy Land since before the Third Crusade, but Richard I's campaign had emphasized its importance, a theme of various accounts of the Palestine war of 1191–2 that were already beginning to circulate. It had now become something of an orthodoxy, a convenient one in view of the 1198 Palestine truce.

Despite Innocent's diplomacy in central Europe, the decision to travel east by sea was inevitable, even if the Nile Delta had not been the objective. It had been proved to be quicker, safer and more conducive to professional control, although requiring more initial capital outlay. Crusading fleets had been sailing from northern European waters to Syria for over a century. They had materially sustained the efforts of the Second Crusade as well as the siege of Acre in 1189–91. Baldwin of Flanders was preparing to send a squadron of his own, as had Richard I in 1190. However, as in 1190, embarkation of the whole expeditionary force from North Sea and Channel ports was precluded by the numbers of crusaders, their political affiliations and geographic locations, the length of the voyage around the Iberian peninsular and a general land-lubbers' fear of the sea and seasickness. The shortest passage with the most experienced carriers was necessary. This meant Italy.

The options facing the ambassadors were limited. Genoa and Pisa had played central roles in the Third Crusade, but were still locked in fierce, hostile competition. Robert of Clari recorded the rumour that the Genoese refused help outright, perhaps in reaction to their possibly less than satisfactory experiences with Philip II. The Pisans apparently balked at the sheer size of the contract. This may have persuaded the ambassadors to try the greater shipbuilding capacity of Venice first. Innocent III had already despatched Cardinal Soffredo of St Praxedis to Venice in 1198 'to help the Holy Land' ('pro Terrae Sanctae subsidio'), although there is no evidence of Franco-papal collusion.[33] Venice could claim a crusading tradition only little less consistent than her Ligurian and Tuscan rivals. For a century, pilgrims and crusaders had used Venice as a port of embarkation for the Holy Land and Venetians as carriers for their return journeys. For the Venetians, piety and profit were not mutually exclusive but, ideally, complementary. In a demonstration of enthusiasm for the cause of the Holy Land, a significant Venetian fleet had travelled to Palestine in the wake of the First Crusade in 1099–1101, assisting in the capture of Haifa but also acquiring the relic of

St Nicholas of Myra. Their crusade of 1122–5 was designed to put pressure on the Byzantines to renew trading privileges.[34] It included raids on Adriatic ports and plundering Greek islands for booty and relics. However, the Venetian fleet also fought an Egyptian fleet off southern Palestine and supplied vital assistance in the capture of Tyre in 1124. That this help came at the price of extensive commercial and legal rights in the conquered port did not contradict the material and human cost. Campaigning in the Levant represented a hugely risky venture, individually and civically. The potential rewards were great, but so too were the dangers of ruin. Ships engaged in war were unavailable for trade. The twelfth-century balance sheet of Venetian involvement with the crusades was not exclusively financial.

Nonetheless, any bargain struck between Venice and the crusaders needed to be realistic for both sides. On it depended the fate of the whole enterprise, a significance evidently not lost on the crusade planners at Compiègne or their representatives, still less the doge of Venice, Enrico Dandolo (1192–1205) and his advisors. The French ambassadors arrived in Venice in early February 1201. Weeks of careful negotiation ended in agreement in April. After a highly theatrical ceremony in St Marks's designed to symbolize the corporate sanction and commitment of the Venetian *popolo*, a treaty was sworn, signed and sealed. Under it, the Venetians engaged to provide specialist transport vessels (*uissiers*) for 4,500 horses with 9,000 squires, as well as ships (*nefs*) for 4,500 knights and 20,000 foot sergeants, with provisions for men – water, wine, wheat, flour, fruit, vegetables, etc. – and horses for a year. In return, the crusaders would pay four marks per horse and two per man, a total of 85,000 marks. The Venetians themselves would contribute their own fleet of fifty galleys on condition that each party shared equally all conquests, by land or sea, for the duration of the contract. The crusaders were to muster at Venice by 29 June 1202. Payments were to be made in four instalments: 15,000 marks on 1 August 1201; 10,000 on 1 November; 10,000 on 2 February 1202; the balance of 50,000 at the end of April 1202. To allow building of the fleet to begin immediately, the crusader ambassadors borrowed 5,000 marks, which they deposited with the doge. A secret understanding that the destination of the armada would be Egypt, specifically Cairo, 'because from there the Turks could be more easily crushed than from any other part of their territory', was omitted from the text of the treaty for public relations reasons.[35] However, the nature of the fleet, including the specialist *uissier* landing craft and the large squadron of Venetian galleys, clearly indicated an intended attack on hostile beaches and fighting at sea or in rivers, the Nile Delta, not the friendly port of Acre or the hills of Judea.

The Treaty of Venice became possibly the most famous and notorious transport contract in European history. As the ultimate cause of determining the course of the Fourth Crusade to the walls of Constantinople, it has attracted enormous controversy, starting with some of the crusaders themselves, who lived with its consequences.[36] The terms of the treaty acted as a vice from which the crusaders were unable to escape for the simple reason that the fundamental calculation on which the agreement was based proved spectacularly wrong. The fixed price in the treaty assumed an army of 33,500. This cut two ways. The crusaders had to collect the numbers because part, at least, of the price would have to be met by the individual *crucesignati*, even if the bulk of the money was expected to be met by the crusade leadership. The Venetians had to insist on the agreed price both because the fleet had to be prepared before the crusaders arrived and because of the effect of its construction on the Venetian economy. As Robert of Clari reported the doge arguing in 1202,

> as soon as your messengers had made the bargain with me I commanded through all my land that no trader should conduct any business but that all should help prepare this navy. So they have waited ever since and have not made money for a year and a half.[37]

On top of that, unspecified in the treaty, but unavoidable, the Venetians needed to provide the crews for the fleet. On one recent calculation, these could have numbered over 30,000. Deprived of a large proportion of commercial income for a year, investing in a highly risky venture that promised no immediate dividend, the Venetians, especially the doge, whose pet project it so evidently was, were gambling as much as the crusaders.

Thus the treaty became a potentially ruinous trap for both parties. The central issue revolved around the numbers. Per head, the sums negotiated for carrying the horses and men were not exorbitant. They were in line with Philip II's contract with Genoa in 1190. But was it realistic to expect so many crusaders to enlist and, equally uncertain, follow the provisions of a contract drawn up only by one group of leaders? For all their wealth and political clout, the French counts had no authority to bind any but themselves and their vassals. Were the crusade ambassadors, therefore, ignorant, naive or just hopelessly optimistic? Not necessarily. In 1198, the pope had invited counts, barons and cities to raise troops according to their resources. His proposed clerical tax had been intended to pay for an army of mercenaries whose numbers could, presumably, have been calculated with some degree of accuracy. It may have been just such a force that Theobald of Champagne envisaged supporting with his treasure of 25,000 livres. The 20,000 'serjanz à pié' of the Venice treaty possibly referred to this division of soldiers paid out of central funds. If so, the figure had probably been reached by the crusade leaders at Compiègne. If Robert of Clari is correct, Villehardouin and his colleagues already knew the massive scale of their proposed army before they reached Venice; it was what persuaded Pisa not to join the bidding. Veterans of the Third Crusade had seen tens of thousands of troops shipped to Palestine between 1189 and 1191. Richard I's fleet when it sailed from Messina in 1191 probably comprised over 200 ships. A recent estimate of the number of war galleys, horse transports and passenger ships needed to fulfil the 1201 treaty puts the total figure at over 240 vessels, a figure not far from Nicetas Choniates's estimate at the time. According to two independent crusader witnesses, the fleet that actually embarked from Venice in October 1202 numbered around 200 ships, still capable of carrying upwards of 20,000 men and crew.[38] The Treaty of Venice may have exaggerated the putative size of the crusade host that would arrive at Venice, but the figures agreed were not beyond reason.

Neither did inflated figures serve the interests of the Venetians, who stood to bear a massive loss if the contract was broken. The idea that the Venetians deliberately overpriced their services or increased the size of the contract in order to subvert the enterprise for their own advantage lacks circumstantial evidence unless it is assumed that they had a deep-seated plan to use the crusade to establish an empire of their own. Both the treaty and recent Venetian history makes this appear unlikely. There is nothing in the 1201 agreement to cast doubt on the sincerity of the plan to attack Egypt. There was no pressing need for war with Byzantium. Although Venetians had suffered badly from Greek hostility in 1171 and 1182, losing commercial privileges and their base in Constantinople, by 1187 their trading quarter had been restored and in 1189 reparations for the expulsion of 1171 agreed. Dandolo himself successfully negotiated a final settlement and confirmation of Venetian rights in the Byzantine empire in 1198. This secured Venice special status in the empire and free access to its markets, although Alexius III's increasing favour towards the Genoese, who were especially dominant in the Black Sea, may have caused disquiet.[39] More generally, Venice was not, in 1201, an imperial power in a political as opposed to commercial sense. Nothing in Doge Dandolo's career suggested he was contemplating a radical departure from the vigorous pursuit of traditional Venetian interests. Nicetas Choniates thought Dandolo was motivated by revenge for long-standing personal as well as civic injuries done him by the Greeks.[40] Yet despite the almost certainly groundless rumours that he had been blinded in Constantinople during the troubles of 1171, Dandolo seemed to be content with a pacific policy towards the Byzantines and the new *status quo* of the 1198 treaty. With well over half of Venice's eastern trade coming through Byzantium, peace offered a more secure future than war.

Egypt and the great entrepôt of Alexandria presented a very different option, a greater risk for a much greater potential profit. The centre of the hugely lucrative spice trade, handling the spices that had been shipped from south-east Asia to the Red Sea ports and thence to the Nile before forward transit to Europe, as well as a source of wheat, sugar and alum (used in dyeing and leather making) and a market for timber and metals, Alexandria had accommodated western traders since the eleventh century. However, compared with Genoa and Pisa, Venice maintained only a modest presence there, trade with Egypt constituting perhaps 10 per cent of the city's eastern business. Dandolo had seen the opportunities at first hand during a visit to Egypt in 1174. In 1198, perhaps in response to Cardinal Soffredo's mission, the pope granted a licence to Venice to continue trading with Egypt in non-military materials (i.e. not metal and timber) despite the general, and largely ignored, ban decreed by the Third Lateran Council.[41] A successful crusade presented Venice with the chance to expand its share of the richest market in the Levant. The stipulation in the 1201 treaty for equal shares in any conquests recognized Venice's enormous risk as well as its huge material and human contribution, with the war galleys and numbers of crew amounting to only little less than the estimated crusader army. It also echoed the so-called *Pactum Warmundi* of 1124, under which the

Venetians had agreed to assist the Franks under Patriarch Gormund of Jerusalem capture Tyre in return for a third of the city.[42] In a new Frankish Alexandria, Venice would control most of the trade. Thus the crusade presented Venice with a unique commerical opportunity, a chance to assert civic patriotism and the undying glory of winning back Jerusalem, which the city's Genoese and Pisan rivals had failed to achieve ten years before. It is profitless to disentangle these motives; each complemented the other in reinforcing what was an unprecedented act of corporate faith in both the crusade ideal and its practical achievement. The grand public ceremony in St Mark's to accept the treaty – attended, Villehardouin insisted over-excitedly, by 10,000 people – formed an appropriately lavish act of civic dedication.

THE MUSTER

After leaving Venice, four of the French ambassadors unsuccessfully tried to interest Genoa and Pisa in a share of the crusade's business, presumably hoping the Venice treaty would act as an incentive. Villehardouin and one of Count Baldwin's envoys pressed on towards France.[43] Crossing the Mont Cenis pass, they encountered a group of Champagne crusaders travelling south, bound for Apulia, where their leader, Walter of Brienne, held claims. His small company found service with the pope fighting Markward of Anweiler. None of them reached Venice. This chance meeting underlined one of the most obvious faults in the Venice treaty. Those who could afford the journey east for themselves or who had no contacts with the three great French counts were under no obligation to abide by the treaty. Villehardouin's account of the crusade is peppered by asides lamenting or criticizing the contingents that avoided Venice and made their way east independently. These included not just those outside the Champagne–Flanders–Blois orbit, such as the bishop of Autun, the count of Forez and crusaders from the Ile de France, but also many who had received financial help from Theobald of Champagne, including Renaud of Dampierre, the count's own substitute. The same was true of some Flemish lords, such as Gilles de Trasignies, who enjoyed Count Baldwin's largesse. The Flemish fleet also fell outside the Venice treaty; probably it was never intended to rendezvous at Venice. The binding nature of the oaths sworn at Venice that Villehardouin insisted upon appeared less obvious to others. The surprise is less that so few mustered at Venice but that so many with no direct association with the crusade leaders took advantage of the transport on offer, including the Basel crusaders with Martin of Pairis, lords from the middle Rhine under the count of Katzenellenbogen and the companions of the bishop of Halberstadt in Saxony.[44]

The cohesive nature of the enterprise was further threatened by the death on 24 May 1201 of Theobald of Champagne shortly after Villehardouin's return from Venice. A seemingly charismatic enthusiast, despite his inexperience, his fellow crusading counts may have recognized him as their leader, possibly because of his youthful political neutrality in the contest between his uncles Philip II and Richard I. He left the 50,000 livres for the crusade, half for his own followers and half to help cover the crusade's general expenses, which presumably included the Venetian transport fee. If his money had gained Theobald authority over the expedition, his legacy acted as a bait to tempt another to take his place. The manoeuvres during the early summer of 1201 to find a replacement for Theobald with the now explicit brief to command the expedition ('la seigneurie de l'ost')[45] remain obscure despite or perhaps because one of main players was Villehardouin himself. According to his testimony, he was part of a delegation of Champenois notables who offered Theobald's money and the leadership first to Duke Eudes of Burgundy and then to another of Theobald's cousins, the count of Bar-le-Duc. Both refused. Finally, at another gathering of the crusade leaders in June or July at Soissons, whose bishop, Nivelo, had already become established as the most influential bishop attached to the enterprise, Villehardouin proposed an unexpected candidate, Boniface marquis of Montferrat in northern Italy. The assembled lords agreed he should be approached.

The choice of Boniface was both something of a coup and something of a mystery. The Montferrat family was immensely grand, related to the Capetians and the Hohenstaufen and with a pluperfect crusading pedigree. Boniface's father had fought on the Second Crusade and at Hattin; his eldest brother, William, had been the first husband of Sybil of Jerusalem in 1176 and father of Baldwin V. Another brother, Renier, had tried his luck in Byzantium politics, marrying Manuel I's muscular daughter Maria in 1179 and losing his life in the coup against his brother-in-law Alexius II by Andronicus I in 1182. A third brother,

Conrad, married Theodora Angelus, sister of the Byzantine emperor, Isaac II, before avoiding the fate of his brother by sailing to Tyre in the summer of 1187 just in time to save the port from Saladin and begin his quest for the crown of Jerusalem. Boniface himself had been Isaac's first choice for the hand of Theodora but, showing more scruples about bigamy than Conrad was later to display, declined as he was already married. This rather mixed record catalogues an important context for the events of the Fourth Crusade. Western aristocrats had been seeking their fortunes in Byzantium since the eleventh century, often with Greek encouragement. From mercenary chiefs to adopted members of the imperial family, the status of westerners rose, as more of Byzantine military and naval service were subcontracted to non-Greeks in the twelfth century. So, too, did local xenophobia and hostility. The family history also highlighted the differences between Boniface's background and those of most of the French nobles who now sought his leadership.

Yet if Boniface possessed unusually apposite credentials for a crusade commander – immense wealth, exemplary connections, chivalric repute – his selection was unexpected. A whiff of conspiracy hangs over the whole episode. Villehardouin may have played a more significant role than he was prepared to recall. The first peculiarity lay in who was not chosen as the new leader. By virtue of wealth, commitment, size of following, traditional crusading ties and familiarity with the plans already in place, the most obvious replacement for Theobald was Count Baldwin of Flanders. His leadership may have caused problems for the Champenois, witnessed by their search elsewhere, or for Louis of Blois, Theobald's cousin. More clearly, Baldwin's elevation, giving him added authority, status and access to funds, would scarcely have been welcomed by Philip II, against whom he had allied only a few years earlier. The approaches to the duke of Burgundy and the count of Bar-le-Duc may have represented a case of 'anyone but Baldwin'.

The second oddity rested with Boniface himself. Even Villehardouin admitted that his nomination was controversial, with many opposing the marquis.[46] Until 1201 the crusade had been run by a close-knit group of young, related French counts. Boniface was a middle-aged Italian who may not even have spoken *langue d'oil*, the vernacular of his would-be companions. He had not taken the cross and was probably personally unknown to most of those who endorsed his candidacy. The only one who may have encountered the marquis was Villehardouin, who possibly met him in Italy on his return from Venice. Another who knew Boniface was Philip II. According to a life of Innocent III, the *Gesta Innocenti*, written only a few years later, it had been King Philip who had proposed Boniface in the first place. Certainly when Boniface came to France, before accepting the leadership, he visited Philip first. His formal acceptance of the cross and the 'seigneurie de l'ost' at Soissons was presided over by Bishop Nivelo, who enjoyed royal favour.[47] The evidence of Capetian political intrigue is circumstantial but neither incredible nor unlikely. It would not only have been out of character but politically foolish for Philip not to try to influence events of profound tenurial and diplomatic significance.

The sense of Boniface's detachment from the other leaders persisted. After his appointment, he conducted his own independent diplomacy surrounding the crusade involving his cousin, Philip of Swabia, and the succession to the Greek throne. He was late arriving at Venice in 1202, leaving most of the arrangements for paying the Venetians to Baldwin of Flanders. He did not sail to Zara with the fleet in October 1202, arriving there only after the city's fall in November. He delayed leaving Zara for Corfu in April 1203 to wait for his protégé, young Alexius Angelus, whose bid for the Byzantine throne Boniface had championed. This is not to suggest that Boniface subverted the crusade for his own ends or never intended to campaign in the Levant. However, his perspectives and interests were not those of his French colleagues. As the crusaders were securing Constantinople after its fall on 12 April 1204, Greek citizens apparently came up to westerners crying, 'Aiios phasileos marchio,' or 'Blessed king marquis': 'they did so because they thought the marquis, whom the Greeks had known well . . . was undoubtedly about to be king of the captured city'.[48] Boniface's actual relationship with the French counts was made clear a few weeks later, when, despite being the nominal leader of the crusade, he failed to gain election as the new Latin emperor of Constantinople. That went to Baldwin of Flanders. Philip II would have been pleased. Count Baldwin would not be returning home.

In August 1201 Boniface was installed as leader of the crusade, seemingly with more powers than had been accorded Theobald. The other leaders probably swore oaths of fealty to Boniface to establish some hierarchical order in what at the best of times remained a quarrelsome and fissiparous command structure. Importantly, Boniface added his own sworn ratification to the Treaty of Venice.[49] He then left the other commanders to settle his affairs and visit Germany. There, at Philip of Swabia's Christmas court at Hagenau, he met the exiled Byzantine pretender and Philip's brother-in-law Alexius Angelus, whose appeals for help added a new dimension to the crusade's strategic possibilities. Boniface's tour may have encouraged further German recruitment, not least among supporters of Philip of Swabia, such as Bishop Conrad of Halberstadt.

These German contingents were among the last to reach Venice in the late summer of 1202.[50] Before them, from Easter 1202 onwards, thousands of *crucesignati* and hired troops, who may or may not have taken the cross, had converged on the Venetian lagoon. Their travel experiences evidently differed. Abbot Martin of Pairis with his Basel company received enthusiastic hospitality at Verona, where they stayed for some weeks in May or June, even though the city was already crammed with crusaders heading eastwards. Another visitor at Verona at the time was Alexius Angelus, trying to drum up support for his cause. Others encountered a different sort of Lombard welcome, with crusaders denied markets and hurried on, not being allowed to stay anywhere for more than one night, an indication that local resources and charity were equally finite.[51] Lombardy was particularly affected, with the German and most of the French contingents passing through, even if some of them decided to sail from the ports of southern Italy rather than Venice. This soon became a serious problem. Baldwin of Flanders, one of the first important lords to reach Venice, was sufficiently worried about the commitment even of Louis of Blois to send Villehardouin and Hugh of St Pol to meet him at Pavia to stiffen his resolve. Even this failed to persuade many travelling with or at the same time as Count Louis not to seek transport elsewhere. Reaching Piacenza, some well-connected Frenchmen from the Ile de France, Champagne and Flanders turned south to Apulia, probably to Brindisi.[52] Even those who did proceed to Venice arrived well after the supposed deadline of late June.

This haemorrhaging of troops exposed two central flaws in the planning. The lack of generally accepted authority, not uncommon on crusade, was compounded by the leadership's decision to keep their strategy a secret, at least from many recruits outside the orbit of the inner circle. If the expedition had been bound for Acre, the Fourth Crusade could have followed the Third and anticipated the Fifth in seeing waves of autonomous armies reaching the Holy Land over a number of sailing seasons or passages. However, many crusaders not only felt no obligation to honour the Venice treaty but, perhaps like the Flemish fleet that embarked in the summer of 1202, had little idea that the target was Egypt, still less what the timing and tactics were to be. They followed precedent and expectation in heading for Palestine. Despite Villehardouin's blaming them for the subsequent problems encountered by the main crusade army, it is hard to see they were in any way at fault. Responsibility for the prospect of the terms of the Treaty of Venice coming unstuck, and with it the whole elaborate and possibly over-prescriptive crusade plan, lay squarely with those who had agreed to it in the first place. They now had to cope with the consequences.

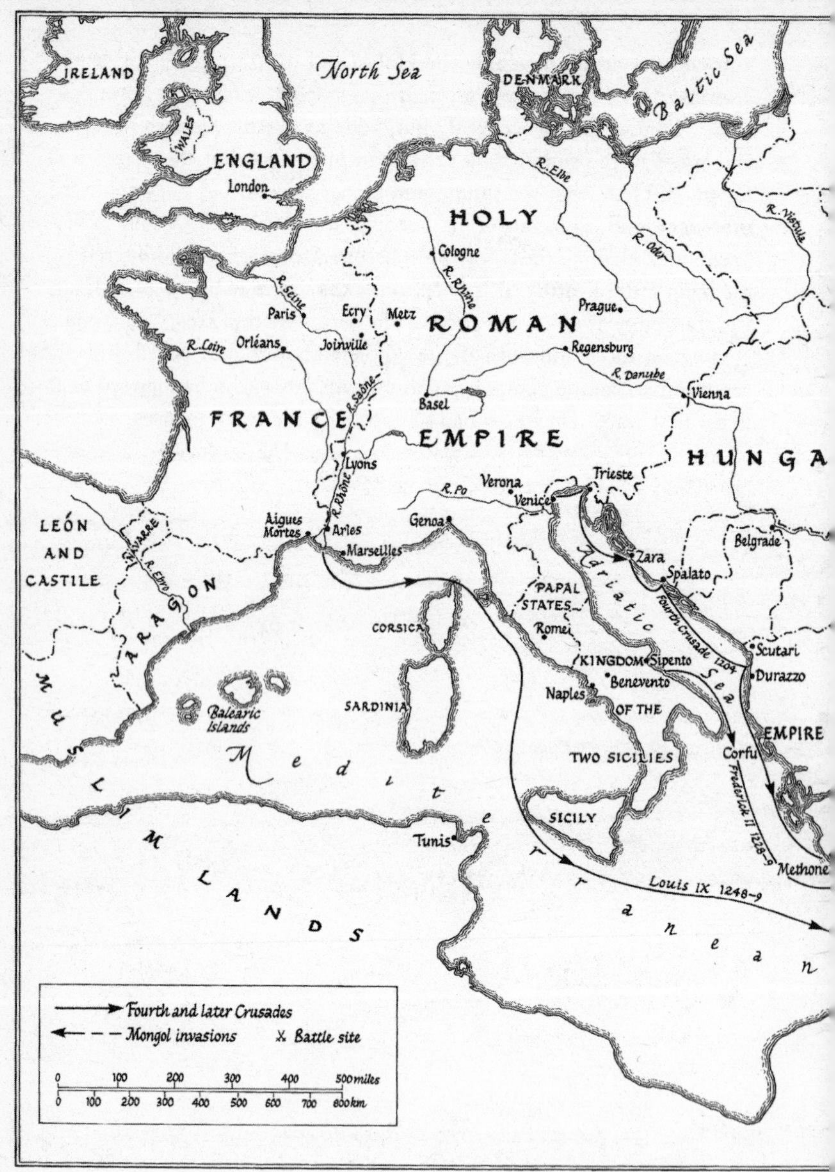

16. Europe and the Near East in the Thirteenth Century

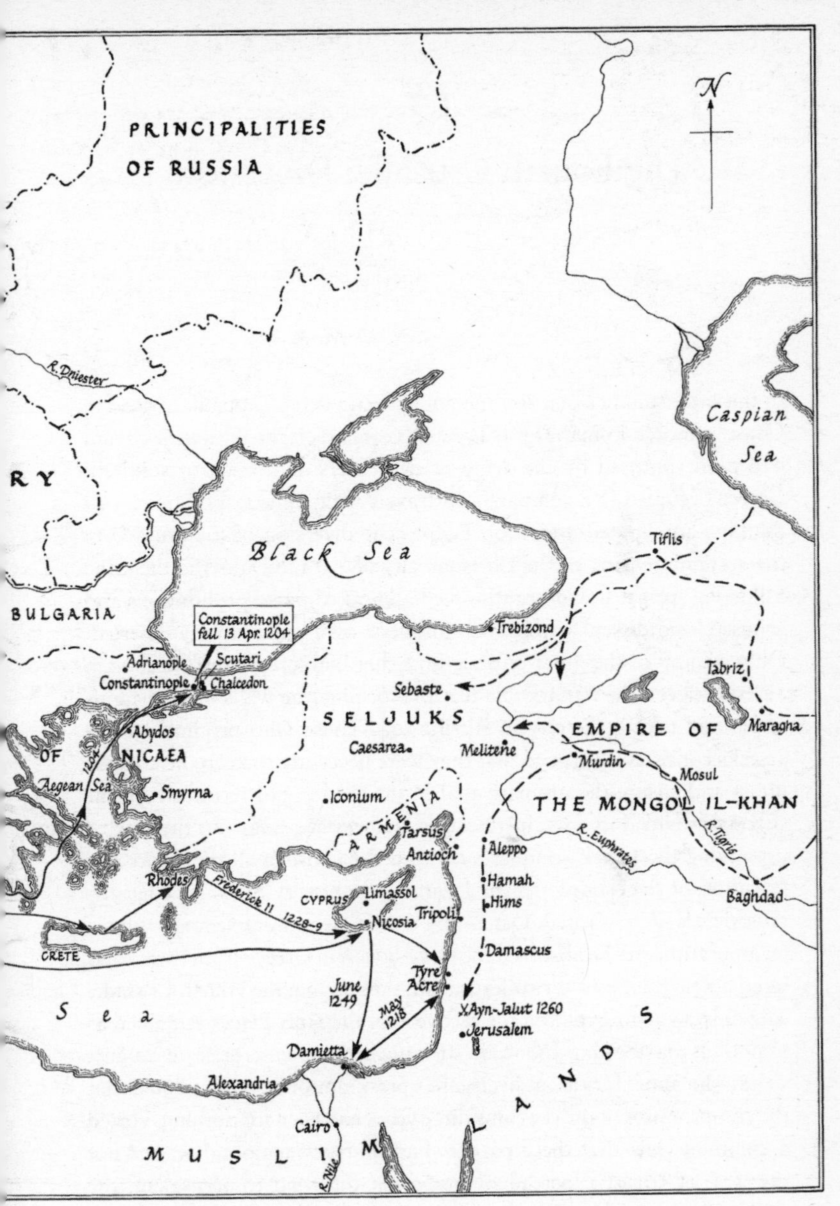

N
PRINCIPALITIES
OF RUSSIA
R. Dniester
RY
Caspian
Sea
Black Sea
Tiflis
BULGARIA
Constantinople
fell 13 Apr. 1204
Trebizond
Adrianople
Scutari
Constantinople
Chalcedon
Tabriz
Sebaste
1204
Abydos
SELJUKS
EMPIRE OF
Maragha
OF
NICAEA
Caesarea
Melitene
Murdin
Mosul
Aegean
Sea
Smyrna
Iconium
ARMENIA
THE MONGOL IL-KHAN
Tarsus
Antioch
Aleppo
R. Euphrates
R. Tigris
Rhodes
Frederick II 1228–9
Hamah
CYPRUS
Limassol
Hims
Baghdad
Nicosia
Tripoli
CRETE
Damascus
Tyre
Acre
June
1249
May
1218
Ayn-Jalut 1260
Sea
Jerusalem
S
Damietta
D
Alexandria
N
A
Cairo
L
MUSLIM
R. Nile

17
The Fourth Crusade: Diversion

In the early summer of 1205 the papal legate Peter Capuano arrived in Constantinople from the Holy Land. A year earlier, the Byzantine capital had been captured by the army of westerners and much of southern Greece occupied in a campaign portrayed at the time as preliminary to the long-anticipated attack on Egypt. The diversion of the crusade in the autumn of 1202 to the Christian city of Zara in Dalmatia then, the following spring, to Constantinople had flouted papal prohibitions and aroused loud dissent within the crusaders' own ranks. Many deserted. Only a rump of the great crusade host that had left western Europe in 1202 achieved the remarkable feat of storming the walls of Constantinople and taking the city in April 1204. Those who promoted these attacks consistently argued that they were necessary to keep the crusade intact and ensure the ultimate goal of the recovery of Jerusalem. Their success provided its own justification. However, a year on, the task of preserving the Greek conquests continued to absorb all the effort and attention of the crusaders. The legate had a history of doing what the crusade's leaders wanted. Ostensibly on his own initiative and with his legatine authority he absolved the *crucesignati* in Greece from their vows to complete their journey to Jerusalem, thus ending the Fourth Crusade. The objective of Egypt and the recovery of the Holy Places remained as remote as on the day Innocent III launched the enterprise in August 1198. The pope, furious at his legate's presumption and humiliated that the compromises of the previous three years had been for nothing, voiced a common view that the crusaders had 'pursued temporal wages' not the way of Christ.[1] Instead of preparing the road to Jerusalem, the campaigns of 1202–4 had, in retrospect, not been diversions at all, but the sum of the crusade's ambition. How this had happened, whether through malign conspiracy, organized hypocrisy or accidental concatenations of events, became and remains a subject of fierce debate, not least because the outcome was, on any standard, remarkable.

VENICE

As the crusaders gathered at Venice in the summer of 1202 they were quartered on the island of the Lido on the eastern edge of the lagoon.[2] The growing anxiety over fulfilling the terms of the 1201 treaty soon turned to alarm. Despite the large numbers gathering in Venice during the summer of 1202, it became clear that they would fall far short of the estimated complement. Villehardouin implied only a third of the 33,500 arrived; Robert of Clari thought only a quarter of the knights and half of the infantry.[3] An army of perhaps 12,000 represented a huge logistic and human undertaking, especially when the Venetian crews and galley companies are added. But, as the rows of empty ships, galleys and horse transports in the lagoon mutely demonstrated, it fell far short of what was required to fulfil the contract, exposing a measure of confusion as to who would pay what proportion of the costs. Was each man to find his own costs or to contribute to the central fund that would be subsidized by the leaders? If each were to pay his own costs, why should he be obliged to follow the formula agreed in 1201 of two marks per person and four per horse? The calculations were complicated by the networks of support provided by lords for their followers and by the probable attendance of larger numbers of hired troops. The papal legate, Peter Capuano, who arrived on 22 July, compounded the funding crisis when he absolved the destitute, sick, women and non-combatants from their vows, enhancing military efficiency while reducing the numbers available to pay. One Rhineland witness, perhaps talking of those he consorted with, remembered that 'a minority remained in Venice'.[4]

The delay caused by the lack of money was matched by the slowness of the muster. Although Baldwin of Flanders had been in Venice since early summer, Boniface of Montferrat only arrived in mid-August. The conditions in the crowded crusader camp on the Lido varied from the comfortable to the desperate, depending on status, wealth and association with the entourages of the great. The Venetian control of access to the island, to the city and to markets could be used to put pressure on the crusaders to honour their contract. The political cohesion of the expedition proved stubbornly elusive. The high command's attempts to negotiate with the Venetians were always subject to the approval not just of the other baronial chiefs but the wider body of *crucesignati*, a three-tiered structure reminiscent of both the First Crusade and the Third in Palestine. As the doge began to press for payment, the responses of these different groups became crucial to the survival of the expedition.

The first expedient was to insist that every crusader paid his own passage. According to Robert of Clari, unlike the treaty of 1201, where payment had been calculated per capita, the leaders fixed rates according to function and perhaps ability to pay: a knight paid four marks, mounted sergeants two and infantry one, with horses, as before, costing another four marks each. As even this proved too much for many, 'each man paid what he could'.[5] The burden of collecting what amounted to a tax on movables fell on the barons, who were nonetheless faced with the problem that the sums raised were less than half the agreed price. A proposed further discretionary levy on those still with cash was refused by many, who not unreasonably objected that they had already paid for their passages; if the Venetians would not take them then they would go elsewhere or abandon the enterprise altogether. Embarrassed but determined not to allow the disintegration of the expedition, the high command was forced to hand over great quantities of their own gold plate and silverware. Baldwin of Flanders and perhaps others supplemented their contributions with borrowed money, adding to the debt. Many crusaders were left unmoved by such commitment. Some regarded the Venetians as simply rapacious.[6] Only a minority seemed to have shared Villehardouin's sense of impugned honour at the prospect of breaking the oath he had sworn to the 1201 contract. More than any previous large-scale crusade to the east, the Fourth Crusade had become the victim of confused and contradictory expectations.

After all efforts, the crusaders remained 34,000 marks – 40 per cent – short.[7] Many crusaders on the Lido had barely enough left to survive as winter approached. However, what appeared a disaster for the crusaders also placed the Venetians, especially Dandolo, in a very awkward position. The doge had invested much political as well as financial, industrial and commercial capital in the project, his own and the city's. By presenting the plan as a corporate enterprise, he had pinned Venice's civic pride to the expedition. The option of keeping the money and allowing the crusaders to go home, while possibly legally sustainable, would incur a great loss in prestige as well as finance. If Dandolo wanted a return on the venture, it was in his interest to devise a way to keep the contract alive and acceptable to the crusaders and to his citizens. In any scheme to rearrange the crusaders' debt, Dandolo knew how eager the high command – if no one else – was to save face and advance the objectives of the crusade. The ingredients of any solution were the existence of a huge bespoke armada; the crusaders' guilt, debt and physical vulnerability; the presence of one of the largest and potentially most effective fighting forces seen in the Adriatic since classical times; the sustained commitment of Venice to the ultimate goal of the crusade; and immediate Venetian political interests. Dandolo's scheme to break the deadlock relied on all of these.

Some time in September 1202, the doge proposed a temporary moratorium on the crusaders' debt, which would now be held on account to be paid off by the proceeds of future conquests. In return, the crusaders were to embark in the already prepared fleet to assist the Venetians capture the Dalmatian port of Zara, with their share of any booty, it was hoped, satisfying the debt. This move was portrayed as the first step towards Egypt which, given the time of year, was out of reach until the spring. To sweeten the pill, and allay doubts as to Venetian sincerity, in a carefully theatrical performance, the aged Dandolo himself took the cross and promised to accompany the expedition.[8] Despite the agreement of the crusade high command, who presumably saw little alternative, the plan to attack Zara was highly controversial. Zara was a semi-independent Christian maritime city that had spent much of the twelfth century under the control of Venice. However, from the 1180s, despite numerous Venetian attacks, Zara enjoyed the protection of the king of Hungary, and in 1202 King Emeric was a crusader. Any campaign against Zara would attract the condemnation of the pope on the grounds that Zara was Christian and its overlord, as a crusader, entitled to the protection of the church. The leaders of the crusade who struck the deal were well aware of its sensitivity. Although they were told the good news of the freezing of the debt, according to Robert of Clari, who was there, 'the host as a whole did not know anything of this plan, save only the highest men'.[9] The leadership clung to the line that the end justified the means, a dominant theme of Villehardouin's account: anything rather than 'the army broken up and our enterprise a failure'. When challenged by the bishop of Halberstadt, Peter Capuano, the papal legate, acknowledged the problem, insisting that the pope 'would prefer to overlook whatever was unbefitting of them rather than have this pilgrimage campaign disintegrate'. The legate was entirely wrong. As soon as he heard of it Innocent III sent letters prohibiting the attack and threatening all those involved with excommunication.[10]

ZARA

Whatever the murmurings and dissent, temporarily, the leadership's obfuscation worked. Early in October, the great fleet set sail. Strangely, it left without its supposed leader, Boniface of Montferrat. Nervous, perhaps, at such a controversial operation, he may have been more concerned to explore the wider diplomatic possibilities for the crusade army opened up by the presence in Italy for most of 1202 of the Byzantine claimant, Alexius Angelus. Boniface was hardly missed. The size and quality of the fleet impressed not just those it carried. The citizens of the coastal cities of the northern Adriatic in its path quickly submitted to Venice. Zara would have followed suit if the unity of its opponents had not suddenly collapsed. Confronted with the prospect of dispossessing co-religionists, the consciences of many rebelled, ironically provoking not just a serious crisis for the crusade but the very thing they most opposed, a violent attack on the Christian city. The day after the fleet arrived on 11 November 1202, the Zaran authorities sought a negotiated surrender that would give the Venetians the city and its possessions in return for sparing the lives of its inhabitants. With the approval of most of the crusader leadership, Dandolo was prepared to accept the terms. But the Zarans withdrew their offer after contact with a group of crusader dissidents led by Simon of Montfort and Robert of Boves. They told the Zarans that the crusaders would never help the Venetians fight for Zara, so the city had nothing to gain by surrender, as there would be no attack. Unfortunately for them, the Zarans believed this, thus passing up a chance of a peaceful settlement.[11] Whatever else, the crusader force knew how to invest a city. Scores of siege engines, presumably carried with the fleet in pre-fabricated sections as on the Third Crusade, were erected. When direct assault achieved nothing, mining was begun. The odds were clear. On 24 November Zara surrendered. The lives of the surviving citizens were in theory spared, although some killing occurred. The city and its contents were divided between the crusaders and the Venetians, who settled for the winter as uneasy neighbours in the conquered port.

The failure of the initial peace negotiations exposed the divisions of opinion within the crusader army and its peculiar political dynamics. Having scuppered the discussions with the Zarans, the faction hostile to the diversion provoked uproar when Abbot Guy of Les Vaux-de-Cernay, an associate of Simon of Montfort, produced a letter from Innocent III expressly forbidding an attack on Zara on pain of excommunication and cancellation of the crusade indulgences. The Venetians, incandescent with rage and unmoved in purpose, insisted that the crusaders honour their agreement to help capture Zara, Dandolo declaring: 'I will not in any degree give over being avenged on them [the Zarans], no, not even for the pope'.[12] Abbot Guy only narrowly avoided being beaten up. Once again the crusade leaders found themselves in a moral trap, to keep faith with their allies or to obey the pope (and canon law). Either way incurred dishonour. There seems to have been a view among those most committed to the Venetian alliance that the conundrum could be solved satisfactorily and honour saved by fulfilling their obligations, even the distasteful ones, in sequence. Once all intervening agreements with the Venetians had been concluded, then the original oath to recover Jerusalem would fall into place. This perception of the crusade as a series of contracts was shared by participants on opposite sides of the arguments over the diversions. Those wishing to preserve the Venetian alliance – and transport – could claim that the best interests of the crusade were served by keeping the expedition and abiding by accords freely negotiated, a sort of moral pragmatism. Their opponents countered with a far simpler slogan. Simon of Montfort was recorded as saying, 'I have not come here to destroy Christians'.[13] Yet, as in Venice, the pragmatists prevailed. Simon withdrew from the crusader camp, taking no part in the siege. The following spring, he left the army altogether with a large group of sympathizers. After some help from the king of Hungary, 'our enemy' Villehardouin called him, they reached Italy and sailed to the Holy Land.[14]

The crisis at Zara revealed just how secular the direction of the crusade had become. A striking feature of the whole campaign was the lack of ecclesiastical lead, partly the result of the absence of a papal legate. Peter

Capuano, after his mealy-mouthed approval of the Zara plan, had not accompanied the fleet from Venice but had gone to Rome, whence he departed for the Holy Land to await events and, he presumably hoped, the arrival of the crusade. Without the authority of even a pusillanimous legate, the churchmen with the crusade army alternately squabbled among themselves on partisan lines mirroring those within the soldiery or followed the wishes of the commanders. At Zara, the majority – how large is impossible to guess – of the barons persisted in supporting the Venetians. Their actions were later justified to the pope as driven by necessity rather than choice. Yet to maintain the approval of the rank and file, they deliberately suppressed the papal letter. It would be facile to argue that the less exalted crusaders possessed greater religious commitment than their more sophisticated leaders. However, away from the baronial council, the issues appeared clearer, the ambition to recover Jerusalem more direct, attitudes reflected in a number of surviving accounts from sources not privy to the pressures on the high command. The profile of popular opinion in the army of the Fourth Crusade matches those found during the First and Third. The 'commons', their own term, were far from simple or ignorant.[15] They appeared well informed, articulate and capable of exerting organized, precise, effective political influence, reminiscent of the early weeks of 1099 or the Palestine war of 1191–2. Leaders could not ignore the led; hence the repeated concealment during the Fourth Crusade. A number of eyewitnesses away from the baronial council were highly critical of the Venetians, if not their own leadership, and recorded extensive discontent with some of the decisions reached. After Zara fell there was serious rioting between crusaders and Venetians; little love appeared lost. A sense of exploitation was, perhaps, inevitable. In the winter of 1202–3, defection became endemic, some giving up altogether, but most apparently intent on travelling directly to the Holy Land. This raises the two related questions of how the leadership was able to push through their decisions and why they chose to do so.

One largely passive factor working for the leaders lay in the accustomed acceptance of decisions by troops tied into command structures by loyalty or cash. Robert of Clari's attitude of neutral acceptance of the turns of events may have been widespread. His complaints revolved around the treatment of the less important or poor in the distribution of booty, not how or where it was won. Yet, deference was a negotiable commodity rather than a fixed asset. Without money or the means to provide largesse, lords lost authority. It is no coincidence that the crusade followed the course determined by the wealthiest lords, in particular Boniface of Montferrat and Baldwin of Flanders. Neither can it be surprising that the consent or instigation of the Venetian shippers exerted a decisive influence, especially once the crusade left Venice. As Simon of Montfort discovered in the winter of 1202–3, finding alternative travel arrangements was not easy. Groups of 'menues genz', non-aristocrats, sought to hire merchant ships or even horse transports. One ship carrying 500 defectors foundered with all hands. Escape overland risked attack by local bandits.[16] Without a strong contrary motive, staying with the Venetian fleet made sense.

The leadership may also have possessed another trump card. The process of reaching decisions in the crusader army followed an almost constitutional pattern. Whatever the high command of perhaps a dozen or so magnates decided required the approval of the wider council of barons. Counsel and consent lay at the heart of all western European political structures of the period. The crusade army, a political society in microcosm, formed no exception. Some major decisions were put to an even wider body of all self-funding *crucesignati*. However, beyond them, perhaps literally when they met together, were the ranks of the paid troops. Baldwin of Flanders led more archers and crossbowmen than any other commander; many were probably professionals retained for pay. The division of paid soldiers envisaged in the Treaty of Venice, if, as is probable, a proportion had been recruited, were presumably under the control of Boniface of Montferrat. At the first assault on Constantinople in July 1203, the marquis's division was described as 'mult granz', very large, and was in the rear while Count Baldwin's professional force was in the van.[17] Paid troops lent their commanders considerable, if mute, practical influence over the direction of the crusade as their support – and menace – did not demand consultation. The presence of mercenaries proved vital in another sense. From November 1202, defections from the army were frequent and significant. As the numbers left dwindled, a narrowly avoided split at Corfu in May 1203 threatened the whole expedition. By that time it is possible that more *crucesignati* had either abandoned the crusade or had gone to the Holy Land than were with the leaders in the Adriatic. Without the mercenaries the rump of the army could not have continued, still less triumphed.

The reasons why the leadership were so eager to endorse the diversions to Zara and then Constantinople were pragmatic, ambitious and opportunistic: to secure the expedition's funding and material resources on the one hand and, on the other, to attempt to realign the politics of the eastern Mediterranean in favour of Rome, Outremer and the crusade. They were fully aware of the moral difficulties, even without the words of Simon of Montfort and the abbot of Vaux ringing in their ears. The apparent contradiction of crusaders fighting Christians – 'detestable and unlawful' according to Gunther of Pairis[18] – was balanced by claims of justice, recorded by a number of witnesses: justice for past Venetian wrongs at the hands of Zarans; justice for the wronged Alexius Angelus. The Greek claimant provided what Dandolo was recorded as seeking for an attack on Byzantium, a 'raisnable acoison', a reasonable cause or good excuse.[19] Writing to the crusader army in January or February 1203, Innocent III, while forbidding the crusaders from 'invading [or] violating the lands of Christians in any manner', entered a caveat: 'unless, perchance they wickedly impede your journey or another just or necessary cause', in which cause an exception could be made but only with papal guidance.[20] At the time, Innocent may have had the Venetians rather than the Greeks in mind, especially as he had already rejected Alexius Angelus's attempt to win papal approval for his restoration. The crusaders at Zara could not be so detached or theoretical. Legal and moral niceties could cost lives and decide the fate of the crusade, in the winter of 1202–3 far from simply academic considerations. However, moral posturing was not the preserve of only one side of the argument. Despite the outrage expressed against it, crusader attacks on Christians had not been seen as too shocking in the past – except by the victims. Towns on the Danube–Balkan road east had been attacked or threatened on each of the first three major expeditions. The cities of Thrace and Cyprus, and Messina in Sicily, had all fallen to the soldiers of the Third Crusade. As even the pope admitted, there were circumstances where such fratricidal violence by *crucesignati* was legally permissible, notably obstruction, a conveniently vague concept and reality. The principle proclaimed by Simon of Montfort was not as immutable as he pretended, as his own later career as leader of crusaders in Languedoc amply demonstrated.

In early December, Boniface of Montferrat finally reached Zara, followed, by the end of the month, by a delegation from Philip of Swabia and his brother-in-law Alexius Angelus. In return for placing Alexius on the Byzantine throne, they offered the crusaders union of the Greek Orthodox church with Rome; a gift of 200,000 silver marks; provisions for every man in the army; 10,000 Greeks to accompany the crusaders to Egypt; and the promise of a permanent Byzantine garrison of 500 knights in Outremer.[21] The timing and content were well judged to appeal to their audience, suggesting at the least careful preparation if not active collusion with elements of the crusade leadership, especially Boniface of Montferrat. What was being offered amounted to the realization of western expectations regarding Byzantium and the crusade and a revolution in relations between the Greek church and Rome. The well-informed Venetians probably recognized the inflated implausibility of some of the details, while acknowledging the potential benefits of changing the Greek regime, not least to their commercial position. The convenience of the plan's presentation just as the crusaders were contemplating the next season's campaign was hardly fortuitous. But the prospect on offer was little short of momentous.

BYZANTIUM AND THE CRUSADE

No such thing as a 'western attitude' to Byzantium existed in the twelfth and early thirteenth century. It remains a myth of crusading historiography. Instead, a variety of responses was determined by region, status, the nature of the contact or its timing. On the levels of silks, saints, soldiers, trade and icons, exchange between western Europeans and the Greeks was habitual, customary and usually mutually beneficial. While differences in religious observance increasingly grated on a western ecclesiastical establishment eager to impose discipline and achieve uniformity, there were few awkward diplomatic or political absolutes, except, perhaps, for Byzantine foreign policy's single-minded Palmerstonian pursuit of material interests rather than set alliances or ideological posturing, a stance that so irritated successive popes and crusade leaders. Over the politics of Italy, the Danube basin, the Balkans, the eastern Mediterranean, the Black Sea, Outremer and the Near East, western European powers and Byzantium competed, cooperated and coexisted. Whatever else, the scheme put to the crusader army at Zara spoke of contact, not alienation. It also recognized the implosion of Byzantine power since the death of Manuel I in 1180.[22]

Byzantium under Manuel I presented an image of universal power and a reality only little short of it. Although under Manuel's predecessors Alexius I and John II the recovery from the defeats of the eleventh century – in Italy, Asia Minor, Syria and the Balkans – was territorially modest, by reasserting control over the ports of western Asia Minor and restoring the integrity of the Danube frontier, internal stability and the conditions for economic prosperity were secured. By 1180, the Byzantine empire included the Balkans south of the Danube, the islands of the Ionian and Aegean seas, Crete, Cyprus, western Asia Minor, Cilicia and the coastal ports of the southern Black Sea. A gold currency underpinned a comprehensive tax system and a centralized bureaucracy almost unknown further west. Diplomatically, the Greek emperor retained interests and correspondence from the Atlantic to the Persian Gulf, the Baltic to the Sahara Desert. Byzantine fleets operated from the Black Sea and the Adriatic to the Nile Delta. Satellite states sporadically festooned the frontiers, including Frankish Antioch and Seljuk Konya. Constantinople remained easily the grandest, largest and richest Christian city in the world, its population still about 375,000–400,000, six or seven times the size of Paris, despite its slums, inequalities of income, public affluence and private squalor, a magnet for trading communities from all over the Mediterranean and beyond. The imperial guard recruited from as far as Scandinavia and the British Isles; visitors came from Nubia. The quarters occupied by the commerical representatives of Venice, Pisa and Genoa were matched by a large Jewish settlement and a Muslim presence recognized by a number of mosques in the city.

The serenity of Manuel's empire masked certain underlying problems. The Comnenan rulers since 1081 relied more than previous emperors on their own family rather than on state officials, on the army rather than the civilians. Power became increasingly focused on the person and immediate entourage of the emperor rather than the civil servants and system of government over which he presided. Public centralization was eroded by a sort of privatized centralization, a deliberate policy of subcontracting military, commerical and fiscal functions of the state to foreign mercenaries – Turks, Franks, Armenians, Slavs – Italian traders, provincial landlords and defence contractors. The enormous consumption of Constantinople unbalanced the economy as well as politics. Academic uncertainty remains about the extent of economic growth in some provinces, but many parts of the empire clearly seemed highly attractive to acquisitive outsiders. The empire faced active or potential threats from the kings of Sicily; German emperors; Slavs beyond the Danube; Bulgarian and Serb freedom fighters in the Balkans; Armenians in Cilicia; and Turks in Asia Minor and Syria. As with many later cosmopolitan and imperial capitals, xenophobia stalked sections of the Greek population of Constantinople, inducing paranoia that spilled over into violent anti-western riots in 1171 and 1182. This undertow of Greek nationalism, evident in the strand of self-conscious Hellenism in the culture of twelfth-century Byzantium, counterbalanced Manuel's eclectic pro-western policies, which included holding Frankish-style tournaments and taking a German and then an Antiochene Frankish wife.

Two central weaknesses persisted despite the political success of the Comnenans; the vulnerability of the long and intricate frontiers; and the dependence on the individual emperor. For the centralized system to operate effectively, the territorial base for taxation needed to be as wide, peaceful, prosperous and secure as possible. For the system to function at all required a united court supporting or led by an unchallenged emperor. The last quarter of the twelfth century saw both conditions disappear and with them the power of the empire. Manuel himself was defeated at Myriokephalon in 1176, ending his hopes to extend the reconquest of Turkish Asia Minor. Thessalonica, second city of Greece, was briefly occupied by the Sicilians in 1185. Large parts of the north-east Balkans threw off Greek overlordship in the 1180s to form the Second Bulgarian Empire (the first having been destroyed by Basil II the Bulgar Slayer in the early eleventh century). Other parts of the Slavic Balkans, such as Serbia, slid out of imperial control. The governor of Cyprus declared independence in 1184 and the island was conquered by Richard I in 1191. Local military commanders in Asia Minor, in central Greece and the southern Peleponnese followed suit. Remoteness from central control aided the secession of outposts such as Trebizond or Adalia. Villehardouin commented on the scene that confronted the crusaders: 'each Greek man of note . . . for his own advantage, made himself master of such lands as he could lay his hands on'.[23] The Fourth Crusade accelerated this fragmentation but was not its cause, and after 1204 the new Latin rulers of Constantinople tried hard to reverse the process. Paradoxically, the fissiparous pressures that undermined the Byzantine empire allowing the Latins to seize power also ensured Greek political survival, as the westerners failed to rebuild a centralized empire based on Constantinople.

The regional disintegration after 1180 mirrored the collapse of the Comnenan dynastic system itself. Manuel had been succeeded by a minor, Alexius II. There followed a rapid slide into untrammelled political factionalism and chaos, exacerbated by invasion and provincial rebellion. Between 1180 and 1204, fifty-eight coups, rebellions and conspiracies against the existing emperor have been counted, at least five successful, in 1182–3, 1185, 1195, 1203 and 1204. The westerner's involvement in those of 1203–4 followed their compatriots' roles in 1182 and 1187. Few political systems could survive such instability intact, certainly not one whose spirit lay in autocracy. This political collapse fed off itself. The territorial losses reduced the tax base, weakening the military and patronage props that sustained imperial control, thus prompting further disintegration. Two of the most striking features of the crusaders' campaign in Byzantium in 1203–4 were the foreign complexion of the Greek defence forces and the absence of an effective Greek navy. Where Manuel's fleet had seen action from the Adriatic to the Nile, in 1203 the Greeks could not raise even a flotilla to challenge the crusaders' passage of the Hellespont. Whether or not Alexius III was a sybaritic incompetent, as described with perhaps professional disdain by Nicetas Choniates, head of Alexius's civil service, there seemed inadequate funds to maintain a paid army to protect Constantinople as well as a fleet to prevent an attack in the first place. Only when Alexius III learnt of the crusaders in Greek waters in the spring of 1203 did he bother to discover that his fleet comprised barely twenty 'rotting and worm-eaten small skiffs'.[24] They sat as a metaphor not for the culture and society of Byzantium but for its imperial system. To the decline of this system the Fourth Crusade added a lethal concentration of violence and purpose.

Whether this can be represented as the fulfilment of a century of conflict, in particular concerning the crusade – what could be called the 'Byzantium confronts the west' interpretation – is doubtful.[25] Each major crusade of the twelfth century created its own particular problems, only some of which, like the difficulties over markets, especially around the capital, or the status of Antioch, were perennial. A historiographical literary topos emerged among western clerical chroniclers that portrayed the Greeks as devious, deceitful and, most importantly, religiously as well as politically suspect. This was matched by a Byzantine convention, shared by Anna Comnena, John Kinnamos and Nicetas Choniates, that depicted westerners as intemperate, untrustworthy and greedy, always eager for a chance to conquer the empire. Alexius I's testament in 1118 had voiced anxieties over large armies from the west.[26] Both Manuel I and Isaac II had enormous difficulty in managing the transit of tens of thousands of crusaders in 1147 and 1190.

On the other side, the desire to win lands in Greece and the Balkans had been a staple of Norman Italian and Sicilian foreign policy ever since they had expelled the Greeks from their last Italian mainland base at Bari in 1071. The campaigns of Robert Guiscard in the 1080s began a series of assaults, some of which were or could be interpreted as forming part of crusades. Bohemund's attack on Durazzo in 1107–8 masqueraded as a crusade to the Holy Sepulchre. Roger II of Sicily's campaigns in 1147, which seized Corfu and raided Corinth, Athens, Thebes and the southern Peleponnese, coincided with the Second Crusade. In the 1190s, Henry VI inherited this tradition, as well as the imperial rivalry between Frederick Barbarossa and Manuel I in Italy and elsewhere. Henry's threats and bullying in 1195–6 were associated with his crusade but formed a continuation of an essentially secular power struggle. Alexius III's acceptance of Henry's terms and his difficulties in raising the agreed reparations served as a sharp comment both on the Greek emperor's weakness and the decline of his empire's taxation system.

Yet these conflicts ran concurrently with the usually more prosaic relations between Byzantium and its commerical clients of Venice, Genoa and Pisa. Many western immigrants, the so-called 'phrangopouloi', did very well in twelfth-century Byzantium. Intellectuals such as the Pisan Hugh Eteriano in the 1160s were attracted to Byzantium, as was the more obscure Englishman John of Basingstoke, who claimed to have learnt the rudiments of Greek from the glamorous intellectual daughter of the archbishop of Athens, Michael (1182–1204), elder brother of the chronicler Nicetas Choniates.[27] In such a cosmopolitan society as Constantinople, Greek relations with foreigners were not necessarily confrontational. In 1204 Nicetas Choniates, a harsh critic of the westernizing appeasement, owed his and his family's life to his acquaintance with a Venetian wine merchant.[28] Contact and mutual dependence just as much as mutual suspicion characterized the relationship of Byzantium and the west. The events of 1203–4 were a direct product of that. Even the running sore of church union and the differences in theology and observance did not create insuperable barriers or entrenched enmity. In Sicily, Calabria, Cyprus and Outremer, Greek and Roman clergy coexisted. Innocent III still hoped for church union and endeavoured to maintain good relations with Alexius III. Without equivocation, he opposed any armed attack on Byzantium. When he learnt of the sack of Constantinople, Innocent angrily observed that the Greek church 'now, and with reason, detests the Latins more than dogs'.[29] In Byzantium there flourished a fiercely anti-western, anti-Roman church party. For Byzantines, with the implosion of the state, the Greek church became increasingly a focus for identity, the disciplinarian uniformity of Rome seeming increasingly threatening and unacceptable. Yet the issue of the motives behind the diversion lies not with what the Greeks thought of westerners but what westerners thought of the Greeks. The previous century of contact had created certain stereotypes and embedded certain assumptions that informed the crusaders' responses to events in 1202–4 but did not inspire their actions.

THE 'GOOD EXCUSE'

The plan to help Alexius Angelus depose his uncle Alexius III presented to the crusaders at Zara in December 1202 came neither out of the blue nor from conspiratorial shadow. By the end of 1202, Alexius's ambitions were such an open secret as not to have been a secret at all as he hawked his claims around Europe. Alexius had escaped to the west with the help of the Pisans in 1201, making his way to the court of his sister Irene's husband, Philip of Swabia. At Philip's Christmas court at Hagenau, Alexius met Boniface of Montferrat, but there is no evidence that any deal was struck; circumstantial evidence suggests the reverse. Early in 1202, perhaps in February, Alexius tried his luck at the papal Curia and was met by Innocent's absolute refusal to countenance support for his claim. Not least, Innocent was hardly likely to favour a plan or a puppet sponsored by Philip of Swabia. However, these negotiations were conducted quite openly, Alexius's presentation at the Curia attracting a large crowd of cardinals and other notables. On leaving Rome, Alexius returned to consult Philip of Swabia. The muster of the crusade gave

Alexius renewed hope. During his stay at Verona in the summer, according to Villehardouin, he made contact with Boniface of Montferrat again and with the crusade leadership.[30]

Both the pope and Alexius III were aware of these discussions in November 1202, by which time the crusade 'principes' had despatched Peter Capuano to discuss a possible attack on Constantinople. While the pope reiterated his opposition to any such scheme, he made clear to Alexius III his desire for church union and the emperor's own vulnerability.[31] The chronology hinted at in Innocent III's letter shows that the essentials of the December proposals were in place before the crusade fleet sailed for Zara in October, even if those outside the circle of leadership were unaware of them. Given papal opposition to the Zara campaign and to Philip of Swabia, and the sensitivity of the mass of crusaders to any perceived deviation of purpose, discretion was important. Peter Capuano came to Rome to obtain papal approval for further negotiations. There, he found ambassadors from Alexius III, very worried about precisely the same thing. It was another measure of how detached Innocent had become from the realities of the crusade that he could imagine his strictures would exert any influence. Throughout 1202 to 1204, Innocent was handicapped by poor or delayed information mediated though those who pandered to his wishful thinking. Even after his prohibition on the attack on Zara had been blatantly disregarded, Innocent clung to the hope that the object of the crusade would be achieved in the end.[32] Once Peter Capuano and the crusade parted company at Venice, one for Rome, the other for Zara, Innocent's dilemma was fixed. The only control over the expedition left him was its cancellation.

The prospects for young Alexius improved as the crusaders' debts rose. Crucially, Boniface of Montferrat was persuaded to back the scheme, perhaps during his absence from the crusade fleet between October and December 1202, confirming that the diversion to Constantinople to some degree represented a revival of Hohenstaufen eastern policy evident in Henry VI's crusade plan. The Venetians were greatly in favour of the move, officially as it would secure the funding and provisioning of the expedition to Outremer. From their privileged position within Byzantium, the Venetians knew how feeble the Greek naval defences were and how the provinces were splitting away from the centre. Backing a successful coup would enhance Venice's privileged position in the empire, stealing a march on the Genoese and Pisans, whose links with young Alexius could usefully be severed in the process. The young Alexius's promised bounty offered full compensation for the Venetian capital expended in building and provisioning the crusade fleet. Armed with a highly dangerous army and equipped with a magnificent fighting fleet, the Venetians saw Alexius's offer as a unique opportunity. Although there is no reason to suppose the Venetians had planned it, they would have been eccentric not to embrace it.

The crusader high command agreed, effectively settling the crusade's future course. Alexius was summoned from Philip of Swabia's court. However, the arguments reflected profound divisions within the army that could not easily be dismissed by the leadership's *force majeur*. Hugh of St Pol argued that, without the proposed Greek subsidy, the Jerusalem journey was impossible, with no money for wages for knights and men-at-arms or siege engines.[33] The Venice treaty now only had six months to run. While some thought this argued for an immediate dash for the Nile or Holy Land, others, of the leadership's persuasion, insisted Alexius's proposal provided funding for an additional year at least. Money talked. In retrospect, Gunther of Pairis identified five reasons for the adoption of Alexius's scheme: political – the influence of Philip of Swabia; legal – the legitimacy of young Alexius's claim; pragmatic – the assistance available for the crusade; religious – the end of the schism; and opportunist – the Venetians' eagerness for Alexius's money and the chance to assert 'sovereignty over the entire sea'. As Gunther noted, Venetian opinion mattered; they were providing the transport wherever the crusade went.[34]

The arguments appeared both simpler and more difficult in the camp at Zara. On news of the proposals and the willingness of the leadership to agree, defections accelerated. Reactions varied. Two separate objections emerged, one of principle, that fighting Christians was wrong; the other more practical, that the crusade should not delay in attacking Egypt. The leadership's arguments were crafted to refute the former, insisting the diversion was just, and to reassure the latter, by presenting the Greek strategy as supportive and preparatory to the war further east. Not all were convinced. Some simply left, including, damagingly, the cousin of Louis of Blois, Reynald of Montmirail, who went to the Holy Land. Robert of Clari noted the opposition, but seemed more swayed by the stories of Greek atrocities against Alexius and Boniface of Montferrat's family, and by the religious sanction given by the pliant clergy on the grounds that Alexius, the rightful heir, had been disinherited. Thus the diversion 'would not be a sin but a righteous deed' (*grans aumosnes*, literally 'a great charitable act').[35] The suggestion that the diversion would constitute a just war, designed to counter the opposition of principle, cut little ice with some rank and file, who apparently swore oaths not to go to Greece.[36] Even the leaders who accepted the terms faced the awkward problem of trying to persuade the pope to lift the excommunication placed on them for attacking Zara, even if they could not gain his blessing for the Constantinople venture. The messy scramble for the army's support and the pope's approval hardly indicates a carefully laid plot. Nonetheless, the acceptance by the high command of Alexius's scheme reduced to two the options facing the crusaders at Zara: to stay with the fleet and sail to Byzantium; or to find their own way home or to the east.

The pope bowed to pressure and assurances from the crusade high command of their penitence for the attack on Zara, which they argued was forced on them by necessity.[37] However, anxious lest their rights to Zara be undermined, the Venetians remained unrepentant and excommunicated, although Innocent forgave Boniface of Montferrat for suppressing publication of this bull of excommunication in the interests of army unity. The continued excommunication of their carriers reduced the crusaders and the pope to intricate sophistical contortions to allow soldiers of Christ to accept transport from those under the church's anathema. More generally, the pope had placed himself in an increasingly false position. His refusal in February to condone any further attack 'on the lands of Christians', was diluted by his acceptance that a 'just and necessary cause' might allow an exception.[38] To some observers, Alexius's offer to submit the Greek church to Roman authority simply followed Innocent's own stated policy, making his disquiet less easy to understand or even believe. His repeated prohibition of 21 April came as the fleet was leaving Zara for Byzantium. In June, he publicly rejected the justification for the diversion put up by the army's bishops:

> not one of you should rashly flatter himself that he is allowed to occupy or prey upon the land of the Greeks because it might be too little obedient to the Apostolic see and because the emperor of Constantinople usurped the empire . . . it is not your business to judge their crimes.[39]

Too little: too late. As the letter was being drafted, the crusade fleet was already edging its way into the Sea of Marmara.

By the time the crusade sailed from Zara in April 1203, their ranks had been further depleted by the departure of Simon of Montfort and the abbot of Vaux. At least this removed a vociferous source of dissent. However, even after leaving Zara, the issue of the crusade's destination was not finally settled. The fleet left Zara in stages, agreeing to muster at Corfu. The young Alexius only arrived at Zara on 23 April 1203, where he was greeted by Boniface of Montferrat and Doge Dandolo. After a propaganda stop at Durazzo to allow Alexius to receive the public, although hardly unforced, approval of a Greek city, the marquis, doge and pretender caught up with the main army camped on Corfu. There the crusade almost fell apart. Faced by the Greek pretender, a large section of the army, as much as half, Villehardouin remembered, balked at the final commitment to restore him. Most of the ideological dissidents may have already left at Zara, but on Corfu many still worried about the propriety of the diversion as well as the practical commitment to the Holy Land. Only strenuous argument, earnest promises, histrionic pleading and emotional blackmail by the small coterie of the high command preserved what was left of the expedition intact. Among the most committed to the Constantinople venture were at least three of the deputation who had negotiated the 1201 treaty of Venice, as well as the count of Flanders and the Hohenstaufen faction, including Marquis Boniface and the bishop of Halberstadt. Once again, money, the control of the paid troops and the support of the Venetians probably swung the day. Even so, Alexius had publicly to swear to abide by the terms of an agreement, which now specified that, after Michaelmas 1203, when the Venetian treaty expired, the leaders were obliged to provide any member of the army with ships to take them to Palestine. While there is no evidence that the leaders dissembled in their acquiescence to this – in August 1203 Hugh of St Pol was still envisaging an attack on Egypt in the spring of 1204 – such a bargain, after all the contractual problems the expedition had already experienced, reveals a surprising degree of trust and optimism.[40]

This optimism was immediately challenged as both the local citizens of the port of Corfu and the Greek ecclesiastical hierarchy made their hostility to Alexius and his western alliance very plain.[41] As the fleet pulled away from Corfu on 24 May 1203, its prospects looked far from certain. Since Venice the previous summer, the expedition had lost much of its fighting force, some as casualties, more to disease, but most to desertion, an army now, it was observed not entirely speciously, 'as insignificant as it was underrated'.[42] The pope, from whom the crusaders derived their summons and their privileges, had forbidden them to take the path they were pursuing. Half of 'the Christian army',[43] the Venetians, were actually excommunicate. Their candidate for the throne, Alexius, was an untested young man of breeding but no experience or proven popularity. Past western involvement in Byzantine dynastic feuding had been less than happy. Over a century of assault from Norman Sicily had failed to secure any permanent territorial gains at Byzantine expense. Constantinople had never been captured by a foreign enemy since its foundation 900 years earlier. Success seemed to rest on believing Alexius's own questionable estimation of his likely Greek support. This hardly smacked of some deep-seated, long-planned plot to subvert the crusade. As it was, and had been since Venice, expectations were to be repeatedly undone by events.

The Fourth Crusade found itself before the walls of Constantinople after a series of contingent decisions each of which created new unforeseen problems. Neither some fanciful conspiracy nor a general mind-set allegedly susceptible to anti-Greek propaganda adequately explains the course of events. Instead, conflicting ties of solidarity, honour, obligation and advantage exerted the strongest pressures, not least because the expedition was run on remarkably consensual lines. Although a small, possibly unrepresentative group determined the eventual destination of the crusade, their decisions were always subject to debate, scrutiny and dissent among the wider body of *crucesignati*. Proponents of the diversions were openly unapologetic. Villehardouin saw them as a matter of honour; Hugh of St Pol, in the context of the union of the churches, called the attack on Constantinople in 1203 'the business of Jesus Christ', a clear association with holy war.[44] The diversion to Byzantium was no accident, but rather the result of conscious choices painfully, openly and controversially reached. The motives behind them were immediate, contradictory, self-deluding and muddled rather than treacherous or malign.

CONSTANTINOPLE

The Fourth Crusade went to Constantinople to install Alexius Angelus as emperor before continuing their voyage east. In the eleven months after they reached the Bosporus, the crusaders were involved in two sieges, a number of major battles and three changes to the regime, the last producing a new Veneto-Latin order in Byzantium that changed the Greek empire for good. The protracted failure of Alexius Angelus's scheme drew the crusaders so firmly into Byzantine domestic politics that they were unable to extricate themselves without risking their own destruction. In the end their very success in surmounting successive crises destroyed their capacity to pursue their original intention. What had been meant to secure the crusade ended it.

After a leisurely cruise around the coast of Greece, during which the fleet fanned out in raids and to collect supplies, the crusaders arrived at Chalcedon, on the Asiatic shore opposite Constantinople, on 24 June 1203. Two days later they transferred their camp to Scutari, further north on the east bank of the Bosporus. Two central facts became clear within a few days. Alexius III refused to surrender and his subjects entirely failed to share the crusaders' enthusiasm for his nephew. When Alexius was paraded on a galley in front of the sea walls of Constantinople, none of the watching inhabitants seemed to know who he was, still less voice any support.[45] His entourage of Venetians and western crusaders cannot have enhanced his attraction for the locals. Realization of this sullen indifference, especially so publicly demonstrated, must have been a nasty moment for the crusade leaders. They were too far committed – and too bereft of funds – to withdraw. Their only option was war.

On 5–6 July, a forced landing secured a bridgehead on the European shore at Galata while the Venetian galleys breached the chain across the Golden Horn, Constantinople's natural deep-water harbour on its northern flank. The fleet transferred to the shelter of the Golden Horn, with the troops establishing a camp outside the Blachernae Gate at the north-west angle of the city walls and close to the imperial palace. On 17 July a concerted amphibious attack was launched, the Venetians managing to establish control of a long section of the walls to the east

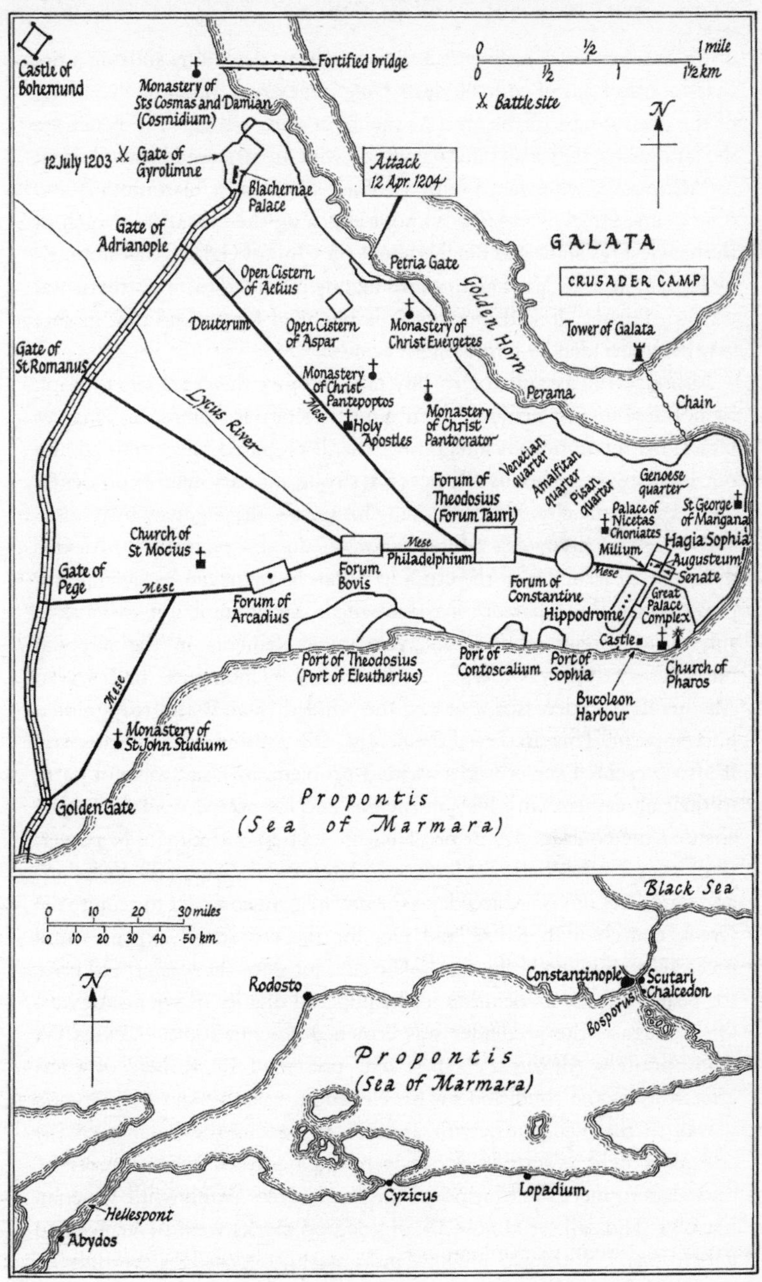

17. Constantinople at the Time of the Fourth Crusade

of the Blachernae Palace, which they sought to defend by starting a fire that soon ran out of control, destroying large areas, perhaps 120 acres, of the central part of the city. As the main army struggled to penetrate the land walls, they also had to contend with an attempted encirclement by Alexius III, who, faced with a robust advance by his outnumbered opponents, lamely retreated without engaging the crusaders. Much of the heaviest resistance, at Blachernae as on 5 July at Galata, was mounted by Italians and the Varangian guard mainly recruited from northern and western Europe. It said much for the plight of Byzantium that its fate was being decided by two western armies.

Although the assaults of 17 July failed to give the crusaders the city, its political impact achieved their aims. His city in flames, his enemies intact, his reputation disintegrating, the ill-prepared, discomposed and out-manoeuvred Alexius III, never a strong military figure, prudently chose to flee the city. By abandoning his post – 'driven away by no one' was Nicetas Choniates's contemptuous if unfair comment[46] – Alexius did more to wrong-foot the crusaders than he managed by his military ploys. Once his departure was known, in an attempt not to have to submit to foreign conquerors, remaining elements in the imperial bureaucracy, many of whom, like Nicetas Choniates, had served Alexius III's predecessor, released the blinded Isaac II and reappointed him emperor. This preserved the fiction of Byzantine imperial integrity. It also presented the crusaders with a problem, as Isaac was not party to their agreement with his son Alexius and his presence on the throne ensured the continuance of pro-Hellenic factions proximate to power. Only after a rather tense conference with representatives of the Venetians and crusaders did Isaac accede to the Zara/Corfu compact to reunite the Greek church with Rome and pay for the crusaders' expenses and projected campaign in the east.[47] The guarantee for the westerners' price for peace was the association in the imperial dignity of young Alexius. On 1 August, the pretender was crowned co-emperor as Alexius IV. Appropriately Alexius IV's first act, presented by Robert of Clari effectively as the condition for his elevation, was to hand over 50,000 marks to the Venetians, with another 34,000 as the balance of the crusaders' debt. A further 16,000 went to pay off the debts incurred by crusaders to meet the transport charges in 1202, mainly with Venetian bankers. Thus all, or almost all, of 100,000 marks went to Venice and her citizens.[48] Nothing could have more starkly exposed the centrality of the 1201 treaty and the continued Venetian role in the whole enterprise.

Unlike his father, whose support was feeble enough, Alexius IV had no political base within the Greek establishment. Recognizing his survival depended on the crusaders' continued presence, Alexius IV, a frequent visitor to his patrons in the western army's camp and knowing how they operated, privately offered to hire them to stay as his protectors in Constantinople until March 1204, when it was thought the expedition to Egypt could begin. In return he would subsidize the crusaders for a full year from the expiry of the Venice treaty, Michaelmas 1203 to Michaelmas 1204, thus underwriting a summer campaign season in the east.[49] The leaders' reaction revealed with startling clarity how the crusade was organized. After being told of Alexius's scheme, the wider council of barons insisted they could not give their approval without the general consent of the army, 'le comun de l'ost'. A *parlement* was summoned, attended by the barons, company commanders ('li chevetaigne') and 'most of the knights' ('des chevaliers la graindre parties').[50] Those who at Corfu had only consented to stay with the expedition on condition they would be assisted to travel to Outremer in the autumn passage objected to yet another delay: 'Give us the ships as you swore to do'.[51] After the now familiar wrangling over what would best serve the interests of the Holy Land, to reassure the impatient and doubtful yet another deal was struck with the Venetians. After Alexius IV had 'paid them enough to make it worth their while', they promised to keep their fleet on station and at the crusaders' disposal until Michaelmas 1204. To signal their serious intent, the leadership announced they had sent envoys to Egypt to challenge al-Adil.[52] With transport apparently secured and underwritten by Alexius IV, the crusaders agreed to the emperor's proposition. The immediate benefit to Alexius was realized when he hired Boniface of Montferrat, Hugh of St Pol and Henry of Flanders, among others, to escort him on a tour of Thrace to begin to establish his authority in provincial Byzantium and prevent a counter-coup by Alexius III. Allegedly huge amounts of gold were showered on the crusade leaders who accompanied Alexius IV, and even then some felt underpaid.[53]

The new agreement with the western invaders hardly endeared them to the locals. Relations were further damaged when a raid by pious louts from the crusader camp at Galata on a mosque situated outside the walls on the opposite shore of the Golden Horn provoked a general affray when Greek residents came to assist their Muslim neighbours.[54] To protect themselves, the westerners set fire to the mosque and surrounding properties, deliberately intending to create as much destruction as possible. With a northerly wind fanning the flames, the fire burned for three days, cutting a devastating swathe through the centre of the city from the Golden Horn to the Sea of Marmora, consuming 440 densely built-up and populated acres. Unsurprisingly, Constantinopolitans turned against members of the western communities living within the walls, thousands of whom fled across the Golden Horn for the protection of the crusader camp, a mixed blessing for the invaders, at once providing more manpower and skilled labour while further testing the supply of provisions.

The deteriorating relations between the westerners and the Greeks was compounded by growing disenchantment with the new regime from both sides. The Greeks complained no action had been taken to restrict the fire or assist the destitute survivors. Despite the ravaged city, the new government continued to ransack churches for bullion to pay the their western protectors. On their side, the westerners feared that they would be sold short, with Alexius and Isaac unable to honour their commitments. Tensions grew between the co-emperors as Isaac failed to conceal his resentment at the growing prominence of his son, slandering Alexius with unguarded talk of his weak character and the louche company who joined him in sessions of homoerotic sado-masochism.[55] After Alexius's return to the capital in November, the political situation deteriorated. Payments to the crusaders dried up as the Greek resentment at the co-emperors' exactions turned to violence in a series of riots directed rather randomly at both the government and their western allies. One drunken mob destroyed Phidias's great statue of Athena Promachos that had once stood in the open air on the Acropolis of Athens. Within the palace Isaac and Alexius drifted further apart, the father retreating into astrology, the son to drinking bouts and undignified horse-play with his western allies in their camp at Galata.[56] Neither appeared much concerned to retain the public dignity demanded by Byzantine imperial protocol. Rumour and astrologically inspired scare stories heightened a sense of impending crisis. By December, the westerners' camp increasingly resembled a beleaguered fortress in hostile territory. Their ally Alexius faced an intractable conundrum. To maintain power, he needed to retain the support of his western protectors in the short term while not alienating the Greek populace for his long-term prospects of survival. Yet to pay his western allies to keep their favour incited the hostility of the Greeks, while appeasing his subjects by ending payments risked provoking a western attack. For the westerners, now seemingly stranded at Galata, the issue increasingly became one of survival, while for the Greeks, reeling from defeat, fire and rapacious taxation, the continuation of the current regime seemed to risk further ruin and loss of political independence and integrity. Once more, the lack of money and the consequences of misplaced optimism had cornered the crusade.

Throughout December, strained, often heated diplomatic exchanges were accompanied by increasingly open violence. An anti-western faction began to challenge Alexius's appeasement, led by Alexius III's son-in-law Alexius Ducas, nicknamed Murzuphlus because of his large eyebrows that met in the middle of his forehead. The emperors were rapidly losing contact with events. On 1 January 1204, the Venetian fleet, the crusaders' lifeline, narrowly avoided destruction by Greek fireships. A week later, the army had to beat off a land attack led by Murzuphlus, who was increasingly conducting a belligerent policy of his own. Alexius IV quickly lost control. On 27 January, a rival emperor, Nicholas Kannavos, was set up by the Greek ecclesiastical establishment. Alexius tried to call in the crusaders to protect him by offering them access to the Blachernae Palace. This precipitated a coup led by Murzuphlus with the backing of the military, clergy and civil service. Alexius IV was arrested and imprisoned on the night of 27–8 January; Isaac was incarcerated, soon to die. A few days later, after assuming the imperial regalia himself as Alexius V, Murzuphlus removed Nicholas Kannavos, thereby in a few days efficiently disposing of all three rivals. In February, war began against the westerners. After his initial forays proved unsuccessful, Murzuphlus's attempts to negotiate were met by the crusaders' politically unrealistic insistence on his abiding by their agreement with his deposed predecessor Alexius IV. The final collapse of relations between the westerners and the Byzantine authorities came with the murder of Alexius IV, probably on 8 February, if western propaganda is to be believed by Murzuphlus in person.[57]

The removal of Alexius IV swept away the intrigues, contradictions and confusions of the previous year. Any hope that the crusaders' treaties with Alexius would be honoured died with him. With their ships requiring overhaul and refitting, their supplies under serious threat as Murzuphlus closed the capital's markets to them, and the anti-western militancy of the new Byzantine government, the crusaders held limited options. Murzuphlus no longer wished to bargain, beginning to reinforce the city walls and prepare for battle. Unlike Louis VII in 1147 or Frederick Barbarossa in 1189–90, the crusaders at Galata in 1204 controlled no fertile Greek provinces for easy forage. Extended raids to find provisions risked exposing the camp to Greek attack while provoking hostile intervention from Joannitza, king of Bulgaria, who saw great opportunities in the chaos at Constantinople to embellish his power. Bulgaria had only recently re-established its independence from Byzantium; it now sought any pickings from the imperial carcase. Crusader inaction would ensure famine and likely destruction. To survive, let alone have any chance of fulfilling their vows to journey to Jerusalem, the crusaders' path led through the city. Only there lay the necessary supplies and funds. Only by defeating Murzuphlus and seizing the city could they guarantee they would get them. 'Perceiving that they were neither able to enter the sea without danger of immediate death nor delay longer on land because of their impending exhaustion of food and supplies, our men reached a decision.'[58] Step by step, the crusade had marched, stumbled and been driven to contemplate conquering Byzantium for themselves. While complicit in their own fate, neither the crusaders nor the Venetians had intended this frightening, dangerous and bloody denouement.

With conquest the only choice, Doge Dandolo, Boniface, Baldwin, Louis of Blois and Hugh of St Pol sensibly prepared for an orderly occupation of the city, government and empire. The so-called March Pact decreed that all booty – gold, silver, expensive textiles – was to be collected centrally and divided according to a formula that ensured that the Venetians would receive full and final reimbursement for the various obligations to them outstanding, to the value of 200,000 marks. Once this had been satisfied, the crusaders and the Venetians were to split the profits equally, as under the 1201 treaty. During the pillaging, women and clergy were to be respected, and rape and despoiling churches were banned, on pain of death. The future ruler of Constantinople and Byzantium was to be chosen by a committee of twelve – six crusaders, six Venetians – and was to receive a quarter of the capital as well as the two imperial palaces. He was forbidden to do business with any enemies of the Venetians, a canny if naked piece of self-interest on Dandolo's part, yet no more blatant than the whole treaty was for all parties involved. If the lot as emperor fell on a crusader, the new Latin patriarch would be a Venetian, a secular intervention in the process of clerical election that insouciantly contradicted 150 years of fundamental papal policy. The rest of the empire would be granted out by another committee, of twelve Venetians and twelve crusaders, as fiefs to be held of the emperor. To secure the new political settlement, it was agreed that the army would stay together in Byzantium for another year, to March 1205, deferring the invasion of Eygpt for the fourth time since 1202. Anyone breaking the terms of the pact was threatened with excommunication.[59]

Yet even on the brink of war, which all could see by looking across the Golden Horn at Murzuphlus's energetic preparations had become unavoidable, doubts remained. The Fourth Crusade has been damned as unholy, a betrayal of the original inspiration of the war of the cross. Yet the constant self-appraisal within its ranks and repeated insistence by the leadership and their clerical stooges that they were engaged on a just cause belies any such verdict. The consciences of many crusaders remained as tender as the day they took the cross. According to Villehardouin, even in the desperate plight of the army in February and March, the leadership staged a public presentation of the case for war to reassure their followers of the legitimacy and justice of what they were doing. The clergy declared 'that this war is just and lawful' on the grounds that the Greeks were schismatics, their emperor a regicide and a usurper, crimes in which his subjects were accomplices. This inspirational invective followed the line pursued at Corfu. It acknowledged the increasing penetration of academic ideas of just war in the conceptualizing of holy war. However, faced with imminent military action, the clerics at Galata added spiritual incentives to emphasize the holiness of the cause and boost morale: 'if you fight to conquer this land with the right intention of bringing it under the authority of Rome, all those of you who die after making confession shall benefit from the indulgence granted by the pope'. If this was the actual formula employed, it copied Canon XXVII of the Third Lateran Council in offering full remission of sins, but only to those who died fighting.[60] Whether or not the army's bishops, with the legate still cooling his heels in Acre, actually possessed the claimed delegated papal authority to make such grants, they fell short of designating Constantinople a target of the crusade. The battle would be just and earn spiritual rewards for the genuinely penitent casualties, in common with much religiously approved warfare since the ninth century, but it cannot be regarded as an extension of the crusade. That would require the attack on Byzantium to have been equated exactly with the Jerusalem war and for participation in it to fulfil the crusader's vow. These, the bishops were apparently not offering. Villehardouin's version may have been flavoured by special pleading and a retrospective desire to justify what happened, but Robert of Clari recorded an identical set of arguments preached to the troops on 11 April, the day before the final assault. He also remembered that on this occasion the bishops promised absolution to all, not just the fallen, because the Greeks 'were worse than the Jews', 'enemies of God'.[61] While these accounts were designed to present the events of April 1204 as unequivocally righteous to later audiences, they suggest that the crusaders needed convincing reassurance. It was not assumed that attacking Constantinople, while undoubtedly necessary, was self-evidently just. Faith and obedience in the middle ages were neither blind nor simple, relying on reason not credulity.

On 9 April, the crusader attacks began along the northern shore of the city between the Blachernae Palace and the monastery of Christ Euergetes. Highly sophisticated techniques of amphibious warfare were involved, with the Venetian ships acting both as troop carriers and aggressive siege engines. After the initial assault failed, fighting reached a climax on 12 April when, amid scenes of desperate hand-to-hand fighting, the walls were breached and the invaders established a secure bridgehead on a substantial front within the walls, slaughtering indiscriminately. As part of their tactics, the westerners determinedly killed and plundered their way into the city, making no distinction between soldiers and civilians. Once again, fearing counter-attack, they started a fire, which quickly spread from the north to the south of the city, consuming much of what had been left or rebuilt after the two earlier conflagrations. Even though the Varangian guard was prepared to fight on, Murzuphlus saw the game was up and fled during the night. By 13 April, the crusaders found no serious resistance was left. The city had been won, a startling tribute to the naval skill of the Venetians, the engineering ingenuity that converted their ships into fighting castles and the military training, perhaps even the military culture, of the western troops.

The sack of Constantinople proceeded in two stages.[62] The first, the indiscriminate violence and pillage of the assault, was reined in the day after the crusaders' entry. With substantial Greek forces still in the city, a descent into disorganized mayhem could have put the victory at risk. The second stage, perhaps more chilling than the first, saw the systematic plundering of the capital, the customary penalty suffered by cities taken by storm. For three days the crusader captains allowed their troops to vent their anger, relief and greed in an orgy of looting the thoroughness and lack of finesse of which appalled most of those who heard of it. The main savagery was reserved for the pursuit of treasure and property, including houses, palaces and churches, rather than people. Two of the most hysterical Greek eyewitnesses, Nicetas Choniates and Nicholas Mesarites, while lamenting in lurid terms the drunken rapine and sexual violence, both record individual instances where Greeks were treated with respect and afforded protection by the invaders. Much of the Greek shock was stimulated by the wholesale desecration of holy places, an aspect of the sack that western observers, proud of their purloined relics, rather admired. The worst excesses against citizens appeared concentrated only on the first day while the victims, according to one account, amounted to a couple of thousand, about half of one per cent of the city's pre-1204 population.[63] Sufficient control was exerted on the looters to ensure the collection of much of the looted treasure in the three churches chosen as central depositories. When the looting was called off on 15 April, the official treasury had deposits worth 300,000 marks, along with 10,000 horses. This constituted perhaps less than half the total value of the goods plundered, the rest being kept by the looters, possibly as much as 500,000 marks, enough to fund a European state for a decade. The figures also exclude the boat-loads of relics stolen by 'holy robbers' like Bishop Nivelo of Soissons and Abbot Martin of Pairis.[64] During the sack and for the difficult days immediately afterwards, anecdotal evidence suggests a measure of discipline and order in the plundering, including some respect for the lives at least of the Greek upper classes.[65] The sack of Constantinople was an atrocity, but in the terms of the day not a war crime. The fire of August 1203 may have caused as much physical damage, not to mention those of July 1203 and April 1204 or the riots of the winter of 1203–4. Alexius IV's own rapacity in stripping churches and icons for gold and silver to pay the crusaders' tribute exactly matched the behaviour of the western conquerors. The loss of classical and Byzantine art, architecture and libraries is incalculable, although possibly not on a par with the cultural devastation wrought by the destruction of Baghdad by the Mongols in 1258. The intensity of human butchery pales beside the bloodlust in Jerusalem on 15 July 1099. If the victors had proceeded to the Holy Land the following spring, the fall of Constantinople may have never acquired its reputation for unique barbarism.

ROMANIA AND BYZANTIUM

The immediate distribution of Byzantium's spoils caused some disappointment that so much had been diverted into private streams. Among the rank and file it provoked fury as they accused the leaders themselves of being the worst hoarders, denying the ordinary crusaders ('the commons of the host'), the poor knights and the sergeants 'who had helped to win the treasure' their due.[66] The ratio of payment to knights, twenty marks, clerics and mounted sergeants, ten marks, and infantry, five marks concealed the injustice, as Robert of Clari saw it, of the common soldiers being fobbed off with plain silver while the choice gold, jewels and precious fabrics found their way into the coffers of the great. Some hoarders were convicted and hanged.[67] Nonetheless, the sense of achievement rang through the memories of the conquerors. The greatest city in the Christian world had fallen to an army of 20,000.[68] God's will seemed clear.

It soon became less pellucid. By mid-May, Baldwin of Flanders had been elected the new Latin emperor. The Venetian Thomas Morosini became patriarch. Baldwin grandly proclaimed on his election his intention to proceed to the Holy Land once his new realm, so providentially granted him by God's manifest will, had been pacified and secured.[69] Although Murzuphlus was soon apprehended and executed, pacification of the area around the capital, let alone exerting control over the rest of the empire, proved much harder. Many of the crusade leaders were eager to receive and secure new lands, notably Boniface of Montferrat, who had been given Thessalonica as consolation for not gaining the imperial diadem. Relations between Baldwin and Boniface, perhaps understandably, deteriorated to the point of outright hostility. Others struck out on their own, such as Geoffrey of Villehardouin's nephew and namesake in the Peloponnese. From the start, the Latin emperor in Constantinople lacked adequate manpower. In the provinces, where the same was true, the new Latin lords sought accommodation with local vested interests, religious and secular, of a sort denied the Latin emperor. The pope's initial enthusiasm for the union of the churches turned to disillusion and anger when he learnt of the carnage and destruction of the sack and the cancellation of the crusade in 1205. He was soon opening diplomatic channels to the Byzantine successor regime in Asia Minor.[70] For Innocent, the Fourth Crusade had proved a disappointment and a lesson. He proved an adept pupil.

The fissiparous nature of Byzantium did not suddenly end. While the Latins achieved some success in policing mainland Greece, Alexius III's son-in-law, Theodore Lascaris, established a self-proclaimed legitimist Greek empire in Asia Minor around Smyrna and Nicaea, its ecclesiastical capital. Epirus in western Greece and Trebizond on the distant south-eastern shore of the Black Sea emerged as other centres of Greek resistance and particularism. More immediate danger was presented by Joannitza of Bulgaria, whose overtures to the crusaders in 1203–4 for an alliance against the Greeks had been rebuffed.[71] It was not in his interests to have any powerful ruler on the Bosporus, Latin or Greek.

Emperor Baldwin inherited the weaknesses as well as the palaces of his predecessors. Tentative moves to embrace the Greek tradition achieved little, wrecked by the issue of church union and the bitter memory of 1204. Continuity was limited. At Acre, on the news of Baldwin's election, Bohemund IV of Antioch hurried to do homage to the new empress, Countess Maria of Flanders, who had arrived there expecting to meet her husband.[72] She died before embarking for Greece. The new regime lacked money, as its tax revenues remained proportionate to its limited territorial grip. Much of Constantinople remained in ruins, its public buildings dilapidated. The Venetians, especially after Dandolo's death in Constantinople in 1205, concentrated on securing their hold on their portion of the empire, the strategic islands of Euboea, Crete and the Aegean and trading posts such as Methone and Coron. They were, in any case, of limited use in helping Baldwin defend and extend his holdings on land.

More worrying for the future of the new Latin realm, the fall of

Constantinople created no great rush of excitement and enthusiasm, still less colonization to compare with the impact of the capture of Jerusalem in 1099. As the Fourth Crusade showed, the pull of the Holy Land cast other destinations into the shade even if, as in the case of those thousands who reached Palestine in 1202–4, little could be achieved there. Except for Venice, a few French families, especially from Champagne, the papacy and later the Angevin rulers of Sicily, no consistent help or material commitment came from the west. Indifference or a sense of a burden characterized reactions. Successive popes pleaded for aid for 'Romania', as the western conquests were known, and began proclaiming crusades for its aid, but, by the 1230s, the response of western knights was to swear oaths to prevent their crusade vows being deflected to Greece. No significant expedition, crusade or garrison ever came to aid or maintain Romania.

The Latin empire was a failure, politically, financially, culturally and dynastically. Exactly a year after the triumph of Constantinople, on 14 April 1205 Emperor Baldwin was captured and Louis of Blois killed in battle at Adrianople, where a Greek rebellion had been joined by Joannitza of Bulgaria. It was in the precarious aftermath of this defeat that Peter Capuano ended any fanciful lingering hopes for a campaign to the Holy Land by absolving from their Jerusalem vows those fighting for the Latins in Greece. The succession of disasters after 1205, including the death in battle of Boniface of Montferrat in 1207, severely limited the extent of Latin rule. Boniface's so-called kingdom of Thessalonica was annexed by the Greeks of Epirus in 1224. The apparent unravelling of the achievement of 1204 provided a context and possibly a spur to the works of veterans such as Villehardouin (writing before 1212/13) and Robert of Clari (*c.*1216) in praise of deeds of the Fourth Crusade. While western rule in Athens, the southern Peloponnese and the Venetian maritime colonies persisted, and in places flourished, into the fourteenth century and beyond – Crete only fell to the Ottoman Turks in 1669 – the imperial centre soon degenerated into a bankrupt husk, having to pawn relics such as the Crown of Thorns (in 1237) and, from the 1220s, sell the lead from the roofs of churches and palaces to survive.[73] Emperor Baldwin II cut a pathetic, forlorn figure when he toured the west in the 1240s trying to drum up support for his failing cause. The succession of regents, minors and guardians who held the imperial title (Henry of Flanders; Peter of Courtenay; Robert of Courtenay; Baldwin II; John of

Brienne), after surviving the crisis of 1205–6, when the existence of the empire seemed in doubt, played an increasingly minor local role in the politics of the region, increasingly insignificant in comparison with the Greeks of Nicaea and, briefly, Epirus, and the Bulgarian empire. In 1261, Constantinople was recaptured almost without a murmur by a Nicaean reconnaissance force taking advantage of the absence of the Latin garrison on a raid up the Bosporus. The suddenness of its fall even caught the new emperor Michael VIII Palealogus of Nicaea totally by surprise. Yet the end could not have long been delayed. In contrast to parts of the Peleponnese, the Latin emperors' attempts to reach accommodation with the Greeks failed. No attempts were seriously pursued to create a new imperial cultural identity. Latin Constantinople appeared a shabby outpost, increasingly irrelevant as well as impotent, neglected by the nobility and people of the west, to whom its original conquest had been represented as being such a vindicating triumph.

The prime export of the Latin empire, from the night of 12–13 April 1204 onwards, lay in relics. Such was the flood of them on to the western market that Innocent III issued instructions on how rationally to authenticate them. In Constantinople, tourists and sacred bargain hunters sought certificates guaranteeing that the piece of bone, wood, cloth or stone was genuine. Gunther of Pairis's account of Abbot Martin's grand larceny amid the fires and chaos of Constantinople sought to validate the great haul that constituted the most tangible profit of the enterprise for his abbey. Martin and his chaplain had stuffed their folded habits with over fifty treasures from the monastery of Christ Pantocrator, ranging from relics of the True Cross and Holy Blood, to stone chips from the main Holy Sites to miscellaneous physical detritus and body parts of saints, including 'a not inconsiderable piece of St John'.[74] Similar motives of validation lay behind the descriptions of the deeds of the bishops of Soissons and Halberstadt, both of which listed the sacred booty acquired by their episcopal heroes, in Conrad of Halberstadt's case including distinctly secular trophies: jewels, silks and tapestries. Bishop Nivelo of Soissons stayed at Constantinople in 1204–5, sending home a number of choice high-prestige objects associated with the Virgin Mary and John the Baptist and, when he returned, bringing with him pieces of the True Cross. Even Robert of Clari's memoirs may be seen as adding lustre to his gifts of relics of the Passion at the monastery of St Pierre, Corbie.[75] These relics provided the Fourth Crusade's most positive and lasting legacy in western Europe. The recipients of the holy treasure across northern France hoped to benefit through increased visitors to their new shrines. In places, entrepreneurial clerics transformed the fortunes of previously impoverished and obscure religious houses and churches. The struggling Cluniac house at Bromholm in Norfolk made its fortune after acquiring a piece of the True Cross purloined from the imperial chapel by an English priest in 1205.[76] The key to success lay in miracles. Across western Christendom, this new influx of divine favour manifested in these fresh agents of the miraculous provided its own justification for the enormities of 1204. More tangibly, miracles attracted pilgrims. Church income rose. The new buildings erected to house the relics and cater for the tourists employed local labour and skilled craftsmen. The increase in church profits generated higher incomes, which were used to improve estates, roads and bridges.

Whatever transcendent gains accrued, the relics of Byzantium contributed to patches of economic prosperity across Europe. Some relics could even play a political role. The Crown of Thorns pawned to the Venetians in 1237 and later sold to Louis IX of France prompted the construction of the luminous Sainte Chapelle in Paris and played a significant part in the manufacture of a Capetian religion of monarchy. The acquisition by wealthy nations of the cultural icons of conquered or exploited weaker lands is a staple of world history, as shown by glancing at Ancient Rome, nineteenth-century England or the United States of America in the past century. Byzantium was another prime example, a storehouse of classical and Christian artefacts, many of which had been translated, stolen or otherwise removed from provinces of the empire. After 1204, this process took another step, if in an unrefined, vicious and unwelcome manner. The transfer of treasure and relics stood as symbol of defeat, the four horses from the Hippodrome erected in front of St Mark's in Venice, although only placed there after 1260, a careful, considered celebration of victory and a new imperialism.

The consequences of the Fourth Crusade were not measured in spiritual or material profit and loss alone. In his history of the Crusades, Runciman's pro-Hellenist complaint has two barbs; the duplicitous destruction of a civilization and the gratuitous weakening of a bastion of Christendom against invasion from the east. The Byzantine empire never recovered from the events of 1203–4. Much of the damage was self-inflicted by the political chaos and myopic self-interest so vividly displayed in the tawdry or desperate parade of emperors. Much of the physical destruction in Constantinople came from the secondary effects of the conquest, the fires of 1203–4 and Alexius IV's frenzied scrabbling for bullion. There is no convincing evidence that the crusaders plotted the violent overthrow of the Byzantine system until they were presented with no viable alternative in 1204. That is not to say that Greeks were not demonized, their religious observances despised and feared by western elites as much as the rest. Doctrinal differences and the traditional Greek lukewarm response to the call of the cross could be and were exploited. Baldwin declared in his coronation circular that Constantinople had been stormed 'for the honour of the Holy Roman Church and for the relief of the Holy Land', a not completely mendacious justification.[77]

However destructive the sack of 1204, ultimately more damaging to the cohesion of Byzantium was the effect on church union and the inability of the Latins to re-establish a thriving capital. The failure of Latin–Greek accommodation and the inability of the Latins to suppress opposition changed the nature of the Greek polity as much as it failed to create a new Latin one. After 1204, independent, autonomous Greek statelets emerged, as at Nicaea/Smyrna, Epirus and Trebizond, with no constitutional relations with each other and owing no allegiance to a central Greek political authority. By 1261, this separatist tradition, unknown before 1204, had become enshrined as a feature of Byzantium, which persisted until the Ottoman conquests. Before 1204, Greek regional opposition had been reflected in central, imperial politics. Now the regions appeared entire to themselves. The Fourth Crusade had unstringed the lyre of universal order and degree. Between 1204 and 1261 Constantinople was no longer a centre of bureaucracy or consumption, had ceased to be a functioning capital except in name only. The restoration of 1261 could not recover its imperial dominance. The absence of metropolitan authority that had underpinned Byzantine power and unity before 1204 allowed the Orthodox church to fill the void. The role of emperor after 1261 was permanently weakened as the Christian religion rather than the Christian state acted as the chief source of cultural cohesion and political identity. This shift in authority was emphasized when successive Byzantine emperors over the next two centuries sought church union with Rome as the price for western military help. Thus the Fourth Crusade destroyed but redefined

Byzantium, enshrining a political fragmentation that included the remaining western enclaves and was to be so brilliantly exploited by the Ottomans from the mid-fourteenth century.

This does not necessarily establish the Fourth Crusade's blame for the later woes of eastern Europe, the second of Runciman's complaints. He saw Byzantium so undermined by 1204 that it could 'no longer guard Christendom against the Turk'. This ultimately handed 'the innocent Christians of the Balkans' to 'persecution and slavery'.[78] This is a view clouded by a crude religious and cultural analysis. Many Christians in the Balkans, innocent or not, had fought for generations against the Greeks – Serbs, Bulgars, Albanians – just as they later fought against the Turks. Byzantium had hardly been universally beneficent in its rule. Equally, the failure of Byzantium to retain its own territorial integrity from 1180 or defend itself in 1203–4 did not suggest it could necessarily have presented much of a bastion against later Turkish attack. However unpleasant, the Fourth Crusade did not precipitate the triumph of the Turk. The occupation of parts of the Greek empire by Latins and Venetians at least ensured some continuing western investment in resistance to the Ottomans that outlasted the Byzantine empire itself. More widely, the assumption that Ottoman rule was *per se* bad, 'worse' than Greek imperial rule or that of fractious and often vicious Christian groups in the Balkans, depends upon racial and religious stereotypes and prejudices. Not all fourteenth-century Greeks preferred Byzantium to Latin or Turkish rule. The translation of later historical, religious or cultural prejudices to explain past phenomena is here unprofitable. However, it reflects the most enduring legacy of the Fourth Crusade, one that as recently as 2001 elicited an apology from Pope John Paul II. The Fourth Crusade, the subsequent failure of the victorious Latins to build firm bridges between the Latin and Greek communities and the exploitation of the catastrophe by the Orthodox church to buttress its sense of unique righteousness confirmed and deepened the still unresolved and perhaps irrevocable estrangement of Greek and Roman Christendom. At least Innocent III was right about that.

The Expansion of Crusading

18

The Albigensian Crusades 1209–29

On 24 June 1213, in a field outside the walls of Castelnaudary, between Toulouse and Carcassonne, Amaury of Montfort was knighted by Bishop Manasses of Orléans. Amaury's father, Simon of Montfort, commanded the forces summoned by the pope in 1208–9 to extirpate heresy in Languedoc and dispossess its adherents, promoters and protectors. He now insisted the reluctant bishop 'appoint his son a knight of Christ and personally hand him the belt of knighthood'. In a very public show, Amaury was presented by both his parents:

> they approached the altar and offered him to the Lord, requesting the Bishop to appoint him a knight in the service of Christ. The bishops of Orléans and Auxerre, bowing before the altar, put the belt of knighthood round the youth and with great devotion led the *Veni Creator Spiritus*.

'A novel and unprecedented form of induction into knighthood', some said.[1]

The Castelnaudary ceremony distilled many of the elements that distinguished the twenty years' war sponsored by the church and fought between the Dordogne, Mediterranean and Pyrenees. It represented, in a ceremony previously uncommon so far south in France, the rededication of the Montfort clan to Pope Innocent III's vision of holy violence by creating almost a fresh category of knight, dedicated to Christ's war yet without the religious vows of the military orders. It signalled an alien cultural imposition, witnessed by two northern French bishops and an army almost exclusively containing warriors, like the Montforts themselves, from north of the Midi, conquerors who brought their own churchmen, laws, hierarchy and military self-sufficiency. Simon claimed, by right of conquest and ecclesiastical sanction, to be ruler of large swathes of Languedoc. At Castelnaudary, Simon demonstrated that his

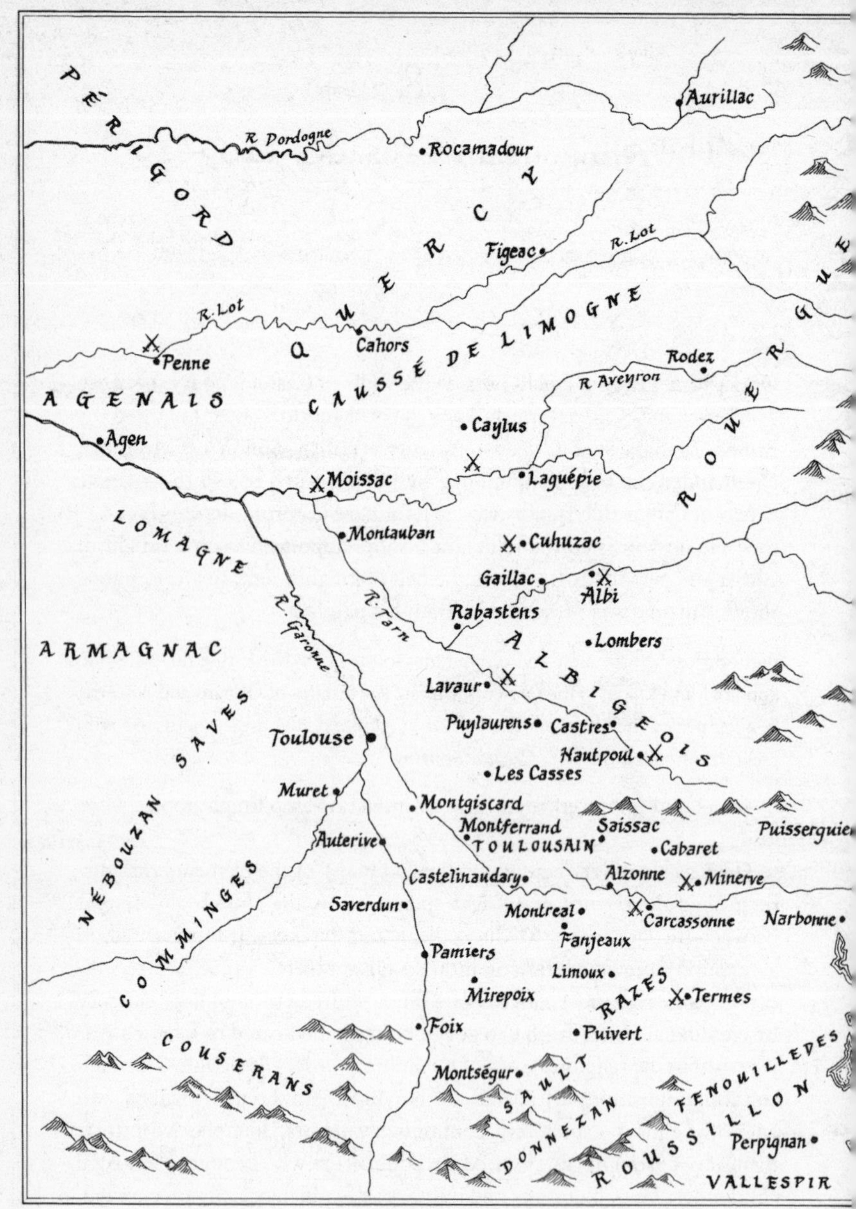

18. Languedoc, France and the Albigensian Crusade

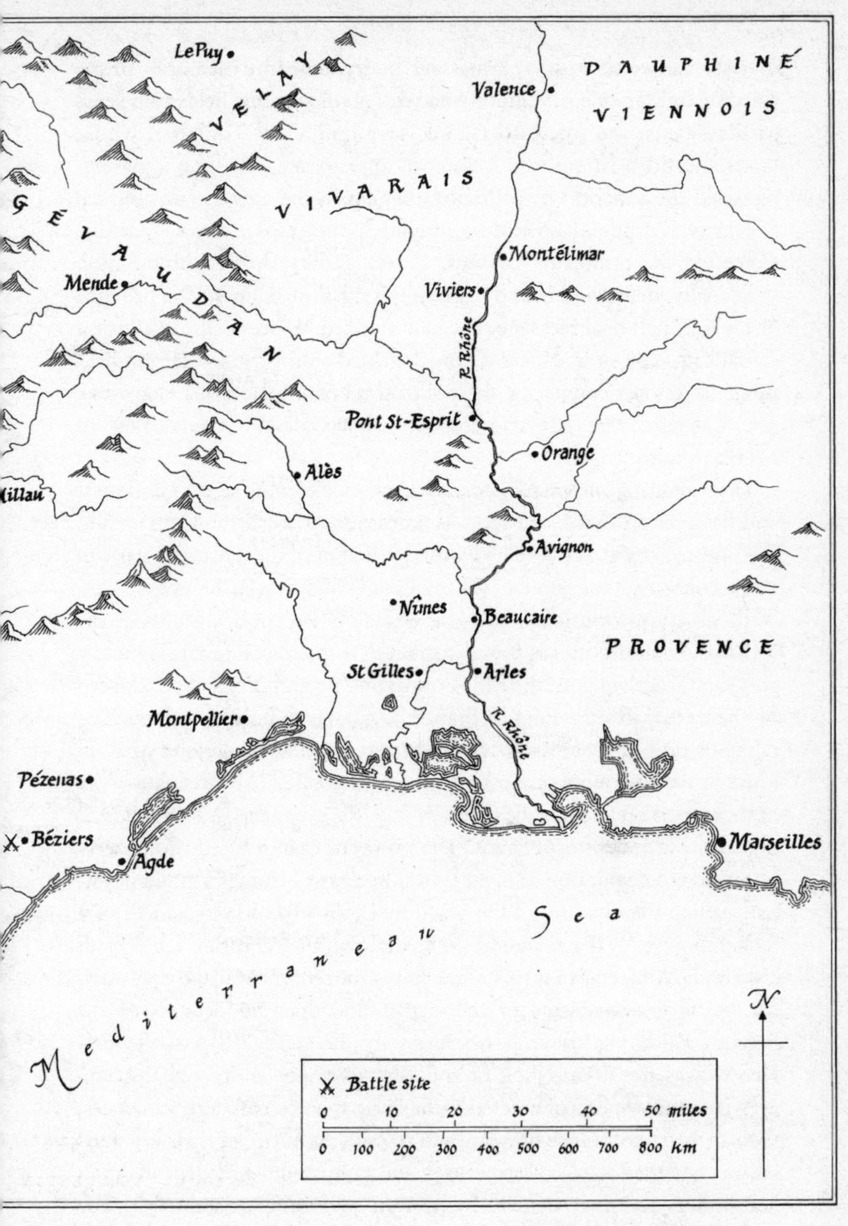

Le Puy
VELAY
Valence
DAUPHINÉ
VIENNOIS
VIVARAIS
GÉVAUDAN
Mende
Montélimar
Viviers
R. Rhône
Pont St-Esprit
Orange
Alès
Millau
Avignon
Nîmes
Beaucaire
PROVENCE
St Gilles
Arles
R. Rhône
Montpellier
Pézenas
Béziers
Agde
Marseilles
Mediterranean Sea
N
Battle site
0 10 20 30 40 50 miles
0 100 200 300 400 500 600 700 800 km

dynasty had come to stay, a message underpinned by memories of the startling military victory Simon had won on those same fields two years earlier against the forces of Count Raymond VI of Toulouse, whose lands and titles Simon was seeking to appropriate. The knighting emphasized the sanction of orthodox religion in the exercise of political authority, a crude identification of church and secular power that disconcerted the bishop of Orléans. Castelnaudary showed how Simon specifically identified his and his family's mission as holy. The primacy of the anti-heretical message that had inspired Innocent III to call for a crusade in 1208–9 was increasingly drowned out by the secular implications of Simon's conquests: the political reorganization of Languedoc. The Castelnaudary rite consecrated a new religious cause, that of Montfort authority.

The knighting of Amaury formed part of the campaign of conquest and destruction that had begun as a crusade to crush the Cathars and their protectors in 1209.[2] The fighting lasted until the Treaty of Paris in 1229 confirmed the annexation of Languedoc by the French crown. With Simon of Montfort's holy war ending in violent death outside the walls of Toulouse in 1218 and Amaury's subsequent failure to make good his father's claims, the Montfort rights and ambitions were adopted by their overlord, the king of France, in 1224, on political as much as religious grounds, heresy surviving better than did the counts of Toulouse or the viscounts of Béziers and Carcassonne. The sweeping away of the *ancien régime* in south-west France stirred anger and nostalgia at the time but much more since. The crusades that assisted the process attracted condemnation as cynical frauds, a hostile English monk pointedly calling the invasion of the south by Louis VIII of France in 1226 a 'bellum injuste'.[3] The theme has echoed down the centuries. Later criticism of the Albigensian wars has tended to the sentimental and unhistorical, as have assessments of the virtues and open-mindedness of the heretics. Faith, bigotry and atrocities were the prerogatives of all sides. Heresy was not a yardstick of southern liberality and sophistication, even if certain aspects of heretics' behaviour appeal to modern audiences, such as their acceptance of women in roles of authority or their vegetarianism. Languedoc social structures and culture did not depend upon heresy nor were they defined by it, even where they sustained it. The Albigensian crusades failed in their objective of eradicating heresy while succeeding in reordering political society and the local Catholic church.

This failure paved the way for the introduction of the Inquisition, which, through reason and judicial process not the arbitrariness of the sword, achieved what eluded the crusaders, the destruction of heresy.

Church-approved violence against heretics could claim a tradition reaching back to Augustine of Hippo in the early fifth century and found renewed justification from twelfth- and early thirteenth-century canon lawyers. The novelty of the Albigensian crusades lay in the church's recruitment of an international force rather than rely on local secular Christian rulers to combat heresy, and the application to the campaigns of the privileges of Holy Land penitential warfare. It also exposed a ready acceptance by churchmen of allowing lay powers to kill heretics more or less at will, an eagerness reined in by the calmer procedures of the Inquisition after the wars ended. The exploitation of these wars by Simon of Montfort and the Capetians did not pass unnoticed by Innocent III and his successors. Yet, to dismiss the Albigensian crusades simply as ideologically corrupt or cynically manipulative is to adopt the position of the pacifist heretic Peter Garcias of Toulouse, who was reported in 1247 as fulminating against the crusades because 'God desired no justice which would condemn anyone to death'. 'All preachers of the Cross are murderers; and the cross which preachers give is nothing than a bit of cloth on the shoulder'.[4] Many Catholics disagreed. It is also clear that adherents of heresy were equally willing to take the physical fight to their attackers.

The Albigensian crusades violently altered the political destinies of Languedoc, its social structures as well as religious and cultural orientation. They have been accused of the wilful destruction of a uniquely vibrant and tolerant culture. However, given the wealth of the region, its weak political and ecclesiastical authorities, its ties with neighbouring rulers of church and state, and its strategic importance at the hub of a circle uniting north Italy, the Ebro valley, the Atlantic and the Mediterranean, it is in every way unlikely that the fate of early thirteenth-century Languedoc would have been ignored by its distant and not so distant overlords, the kings of France, England and Aragon and the emperor. Their involvement was anticipated rather than created by the pope's concern with the enfeebled state of the Languedoc church and the threat, as he saw it, to its survival and to that of the whole Catholic church from a particularly robust and attractive heresy.

THE CATHARS

Near the heart of the Christian religion sits the problem of suffering, traditionally interpreted as a consequence of sin, of the fall of man as described in the Book of Genesis and, therefore, of the existence of evil. Both the Creation stories and experience of the material world suggested to Christians that evil existed in terrestrial matter, the city of Man, in contrast to paradise, the city of God. Much of the reform initiated within the western Catholic church from the eleventh century had been directed precisely at mitigating some of the implications of this by developing explanations, mechanisms, sacraments and devotional practices through which the consequences of inevitable sin could be alleviated, its penalties satisfied or purged and heaven attained. The penitential strand in crusade ideology and its plenary indulgence formed part of this process, as did the Fourth Lateran Council's acceptance of individual oral confession and transubstantiation in 1215 and the thirteenth-century elaboration of a coherent doctrine of purgatory and a Treasury of Merits endowed by God to save souls.

While going some way to assuage the anxieties of the faithful, this concentration on the redemptive sufferings of Christ exposed a central conundrum of belief. Christ the Son could save from sin the world created by God the Father. If the material world was sinful, it was still by definition the creation of an eternal, omnipotent and presumably loving God. Some devout and godly people found (and find) the orthodox Christian explanations for this problem of evil opaque, evasive and unconvincing. This was not a new phenomenon in the twelfth century, but the added concentration by orthodox Christians on the corruption of the world and the implications of sin and evil may have lent added encouragement to those who sought alternative and more satisfying doctrines. The *vita apostolica* trumpeted by reformers, not least Innocent III's own teams of licensed preachers, explicitly condemned many of the church's temporal accretions. More fundamentally, the sharp distinction between the spiritual and temporal spheres that lay at the heart of the Gregorian reformist critique highlighted the eternal paradox of God and Matter, the presence of evil in a world created by a beneficent Deity. Incentive to question belief and practice followed perennial orthodox interest in the nature and immanence of God, expressed by theologians such as Anselm of Canterbury, preachers such as Bernard of Clairvaux and generations of academics at the university of Paris. This was matched by official concern with the state of the church and its ministers, constantly lashed by the criticisms of Gregorian papal reformers. By challenging traditional assumptions and structures and by posing fundamental questions about the nature of the church and the place of religion in society, Catholic reformers, while engineering a transformation in their church, indicated paths that led away from disciplined uniformity. Heresy, defined as systems of belief unacceptable to prevailing ecclesiastical authority, flourished as the church's leadership proclaimed first principles; as Gregory VII commented, 'Christ did not say I am Tradition but I am the Truth.' Radicalism rarely flows along neat channels. Heresy became reform's inescapable companion in the search for solutions to these central issues of faith and observance. The western medieval church's age of reformation *c.*1050–1300 was therefore also its great age of heresy.[5]

Some heresies sprang from academic debate and hardly left the lecture room; others from evanescent personality cults; others from wider social dissent and alienation. Many shared an element of biblical fundamentalism; all a rejection of church authority in favour of direct personal or communal appreciation of scripture and faith outside official norms, mediation and control. Often flourishing in areas of weak or disputed secular and ecclesiastical authority, few regions of western Christendom escaped entirely as church leaders strove to maintain control lest reform turned to licence and destroyed the institution it was intended to improve. Even traditional, conservative and closely governed England attracted its small crop of heretics in the 1160s.[6] Boundaries between orthodoxy and heresy could be narrow and shifting; passage between the two was frequent, despite the apocalyptic rhetoric of mutual hate and demonization. Most heretical groups succumbed rapidly after the removal of a charismatic leader or through the customary factious divisiveness of the righteous. However, some established lasting identity in distinct theologies, liturgies, literature and organization. The most successful such group to challenge the institution as well as the theology of the Catholic church in this period were the Cathars, whose success in promoting their solution to the problem of evil in the area nominally under the rule of the counts of Toulouse provoked the Albigensian crusades.

The word Cathar derives from the Greek *katharos* meaning clean or pure. The central insight of the Cathars explained the existence of evil as the result of creation being determined by two principles of Good and Evil. The Cathars were thus dualists, but, in common with the seventh-century eastern Christian dualist sect of Paulicians, Christians, unlike non-Christian dualists such as the Manichees and Gnostics of the late classical world. For Cathars, the material world was logically the creation of an evil creator, not the Good God, whose realm was of the spirit. Two identifications of this evil creator were proposed by different Cathar traditions. The so-called mitigated dualists saw the evil creator as a fallen angel, Satan, who had seduced numbers of the eternal angelic souls in heaven and imprisoned them in material bodies. Alternatively, according to the more extreme or absolute dualists who dominated western Catharism from the later twelfth century, the material world had been created by an co-eternal power of evil, in some texts Lucifer's or Satan's father, into whose material human bodies of fallen angels the Good God had breathed divine life. In both versions, the goal of man was escape from the material body though the ceremony of *consolamentum* (from the Latin for comforting). Ultimately, when all the angelic souls of humans had been released to rejoin their guardian spirits in heaven, the two worlds of Spirit and Matter would be restored to their entirely separate spheres. Given the burden of sin in the world, the journey of some souls to the *consolamentum* could involve periods locked in other material objects and animals.

Cathar theology accepted parts of the New Testament and a few passages of the Old while radically reinterpreting them. The Catholic doctrine of the Trinity was rejected as, inevitably, was the Incarnation, although a reordered trinitarian hierarchy seems to have been accepted. By definition, God could not become material, and therefore the Crucifixion and Resurrection could not have occurred, except perhaps in some metaphorical or symbolic show in the spiritual world. The rejection of Catholic sacramental teaching was, consequentially, absolute. One appeal of Catharism may have lain precisely in this challenge to the increasingly prescriptive penitential and sacramental systems imposed by the church and the consequent perception of its growing intrusion and financial profiteering in social and private life. Cathars followed the Donatist heretics of the early church in arguing that the spiritual power of priests and the efficacy of their ministry depended on their own moral state, which made their own priestly hierarchy vulnerable to the slightest charges of hypocrisy, backsliding or corruption. Once again, this addressed current orthodox concerns. Gregory VII himself had flirted with similar ideas. Given the paucity of surviving Cathar texts, unmediated by hostile interpreters or the judicial formulae of the Inquisition, aspects of their theology and mysticism remain obscure, but its themes ran parallel to the concerns of orthodox theologians with sin, the means of salvation and the sacraments. In many respects the asceticism of the Cathars, the flight from the secular, the awareness of the snares of materialism and the sense of the reality of evil mirrored Catholic spirituality. The segregated Cathar communities of men and women found echoes in monasticism. Like Catholicism, Catharism was 'a written church', literate, founded on liturgical as well as theological and mystical texts.[7] Unlike another tenacious contemporary heresy, the scriptural fundamentalist Waldensians, Catharism was not a discarded offshoot of the Catholic church but an independent Christian denomination whose theological antecedents and continuing intellectual affinities lay with similar churches in the Byzantine Balkans rather than in the west. Nonetheless, the flourishing of Catharism, even if in an apparently remote orbit, occupied part of the universe of western religious, intellectual and cultural revival and expansion known to historians as the Twelfth-century Renaissance.

The structure of the Cathar church reflected the rigorous austerity of its theology. Most adherents were unprepared or unable to comply with the denial of materialism and human comforts prescribed for the full initiates. The church was organized into dioceses, each led by a bishop and two assistants, called elder and younger 'sons', who constituted the order of episcopal succession, supported by deacons. *Perfecti* or *perfectae*, men and women who had taken the *consolamentum*, acted as the church's priests, also known as *Boni Homines*, Good Men, sometimes itinerant, sometimes living communally in segregated houses, sometimes distinguished by the dark cloaks they wore as a sign of their status of purity. Major decisions affecting the church were discussed at diocesan or provincial councils. Before the beginning of the crusades in 1209, when such encounters began to court arrest, imprisonment or death, formal disputations were often conducted with Catholic preachers, another sign that the Cathar church was far from a nest of bucolic sectaries ministered to by an obscurantist order of hedge priests. There were numerous halls of residence for *perfecti*, and extensive networks of formal and informal study groups of believers, involving men and women of all social classes. There were even special Cathar cemeteries. Of central importance to the spread of informed belief, and to the impression of a genuinely popular as well as sophisticated religion, were the vernacular Cathar translations from Latin of religious texts, especially of the Vulgate version of the Bible and the Cathar liturgies.

The attraction of Catharism to women is well attested, if equivocal. Although child bearing was considered evil, the Good God made no discrimination between the souls of men and women. Nature was diabolic, so women were no more so than men. Cathar women could, like their Catholic equivalents, preside over religious communities, except that they were able to attain the ranks of the perfects/priests that were denied Catholic nuns and abbesses. However, the undisguised Cathar hatred of female bodies spoke of entrenched misogyny. *Perfectae* were not permitted to act as deacons, 'sons' or bishops, nor were they customarily engaged in hearing confessions or giving the *consolamentum* without a *perfectus* present. Nor, it seems, were Cathar women, even *perfectae*, much engaged in transmitting or even reading texts, an activity which seemed, accidentally or not, a masculine preserve. The Cathar hostility to procreation, specifically pregnancy, may well have dissuaded lay women from believing: pregnant women were denied the right to receive the *consolamentum*, in theory even if *in extremis* during labour. Modern feminists see Catharism as actually off-putting for most non-aristocratic women because of the desexualized existence of *perfectae*, the ubiquitous condemnation of all carnality, the inequalities in hierarchical opportunities and the belief that salvation abolished sexual difference.[8]

Lay Cathars, the large majority, were known as *credentes*, believers, who supported the *perfecti* financially and materially, and expected to receive the *consolamentum* when nearing death, a procedure reminiscent of Catholic extreme unction and the popular practice of deathbed admission into a religious order. On one occasion, a donor to the abbey of St Sernin in Toulouse was received into the order on his deathbed only for it to be discovered after his burial that he had also received the *consolamentum*, a neat double indemnity that revealed the Cathar habit of outward or occasional conformity, a trait that greatly worried the

Catholic hierarchy. In this case the corpse was quickly dug up and burnt.[9] While dual allegiance may have been prudent or simply sociable, it indicated how Cathars could coexist with a Catholic society, as did evidence of genuine conversions of the devout on both sides of the religious divide. Heresy and orthodoxy shared interests, anxieties and learning. In the 1170s, two *perfecti* were converted to Catholicism and promptly preferred to canonries in Toulouse. Two other thirteenth-century *perfecti* became prominent Dominican inquisitors into former associates, Rainier Sacconi in Lombardy, who composed an important description of his previous faith, and the brutal Robert le Bougre, i.e. the Bugger or Bulgar, a reference to where it was thought Catharism originated. Traffic also passed in the opposite direction. Theodoric, a leading Cathar theologian who disputed with Catholic preachers in 1207, had once been a canon of Nevers.[10]

THE CATHARS IN LANGUEDOC

Dualist Christianity in western Europe almost certainly derived from Byzantium, specifically the dualist Bogomil church (named after its founder) established from the early tenth century in Bulgaria, Macedonia and Thrace. Although the evidence is patchy, uncertain and much contested, while some Bogomil evangelists probably visited the west in the early years of the eleventh century, their greatest impact only began a century later, borne on the newly vitalized trade routes linking eastern and western Europe. One source of this proselytizing may have been the dualist church set up by western settlers in Constantinople in the years following the First Crusade. This distinct 'Latin' dualist community probably provided western converts with Latin translations of the Greek Bogomil texts including the *consolamentum* ritual and the New Testament, collated with the Vulgate.[11] The first unequivocal signs of recognizably Bogomil/Cathar beliefs in the west date from the mid-twelfth century. Their geographical spread, including the Rhineland, Champagne, Lombardy and western Languedoc; institutional organization as early as the 1140s in Cologne, Champagne, and later Languedoc; as well as subsequent rapid expansion to Lombardy and Italy indicate the presence of well-grounded networks of evangelism. The initial Cathar conversion of Lombardy may have come from northern France and the

Rhineland rather than directly from Bulgaria, Thrace or Constantinople, but the early leadership in the west seem to have remained in close touch with the mother churches to the east. By the 1170s at the latest, Cathar bishops had been established in 'France' (i.e. northern France), Albi and, probably, Lombardy. In common with elements of the Bogomil church, which was also in the process of evolving its doctrines, these western Cathars espoused mitigated, not absolute, dualism. With the conversion of the western Cathars to absolute dualism, the heretical church, especially in Languedoc, came more clearly into historical focus – and into the line of concerted orthodox Catholic fire.

At some date either in 1167 or, more likely, between 1174 and 1177, a council of western Cathar *perfecti* and *perfectae* was held at the village of St Félix de Caraman south-east of Toulouse. An earlier Languedoc Cathar assembly had been held in 1165 at Lombers south of Albi, where heretics held a futile theological disputation with local Catholic partisans. The St Félix gathering attracted an international attendance, including the Cathar bishops of 'France', Lombardy and Albi as well as members of the churches of Carcassonne, Agen and Toulouse. A representative of the Cathar church of Constantinople, *papa* Nicetas, persuaded the assembly to adopt absolute dualism, established three new dioceses, of Carcassonne, Agen and Toulouse, and consecrated their new bishops as well as reconsecrating the bishops of France, Lombardy and Albi and giving all a renewed *consolamentum*. Nicetas had previously converted the Lombard church to absolute dualism on his way to Languedoc. The theme of his address to the St Félix assembly emphasized the importance of unity, a necessary reminder in the face not just of the incipient fragmentation and factionalism of religious groups but also of the split in dualist ranks between Nicetas's own absolute dualist church of Thrace and Constantinople and the continuing moderate dualism of the Bulgarian Bogomils. Almost immediately, the Italian dualist church was divided by a mission from the Bogomil Petrach.[12] However, the Languedoc churches remained united and thrived.

By the beginning of the thirteenth century there may have been between 1,000 and 1,500 *perfecti* in the region centred on the area between Toulouse and Carcassonne but stretching north to the Lot valley and the Cahorsin and south to the Pyrenean foothills.[13] The number of *credentes* is impossible to gauge accurately, partly because of the nature of the surviving records but partly because their faith only revealed itself unequivocally through receipt of the *consolamentum*, by its nature often a hurried private ritual conducted at the bedsides of the sick and dying. More generally, *credentes* merged into a wider spectrum of response to Cathar belief, from the commitment of the *perfectus*, lay belief, general sympathy and familial or social contact through hedging religious bets and indifference to distaste, suspicion, opposition and persecution. The fact that each Cathar diocese of Languedoc geographically covered a number of Catholic ones, while reflecting cheaper running costs, may indicate a relatively limited scale of adherence. Languedoc did not become a Cathar province. Donations and recruits to Catholic religious orders continued, the heretics operating as just one of a number of manifestations of piety and religious enthusiasm. The suggestion that Catharism somehow especially embodied a distinctive Languedoc culture is fanciful. For instance, none of the great magnates and few if any of the local troubadours, however critical of the church authorities, were heretics. At least two prominent troubadours, Bertrand of Born and Fulk of Marseilles, became monks, Fulk ending as the anti-Cathar bishop of Toulouse. However, the Cathar church retained hierarchy, structure, organization and funding even beyond the period of the crusades. The raw numerical strength may have been less significant than the quality and social status of many believers and the implications of the mere existence of these organized radical anti-clerical beliefs. The nature of Cathar threat perceived by the Catholic authorities was famously indicated by a knight, Pons Adhemar of Roudeille, in 1206 or 1207. In reply to Bishop Fulk of Toulouse asking why he did not expel heretics from his lands despite admitting the superiority of Catholic theology, he confessed 'we cannot; we were brought up with them, there are many of our relatives amongst them, and we can see that their way of life is a virtuous one.'[14]

The prevalence of heresy in Languedoc should not, therefore, be exaggerated. Neither should the geographical, political or cultural identity of the region be assumed. Although it is now fashionable to talk wistfully of the lost glories of Occitania, the land where people spoke the *langue d'oc* included such diverse regions as the Limousin in the north, the foothills of the Pyrenees in the south and the Alps in the east, the wastes of the Camargue in the Rhône Delta, the volcanic outcrops of Le Puy, the Massif Central, the Provençal hills and the commercial

Mediterranean towns of Narbonne and Montpellier. Even within the part of region more commonly now understood as Languedoc, roughly from the lower Garonne and Dordogne valleys eastwards and southwards to the Pyrenees, Mediterranean and Rhône valley, largely associated, often very tenuously, with the county of Toulouse, geography contradicted politics. Toulouse, although less than 100 miles from the Mediterranean, sat on the Garonne, whose waters flowed into the Atlantic, for much of its course though lands ruled by the Angevin kings of England, who, until the early thirteenth century, as dukes of Aquitaine controlled most of the region from the Loire to the Pyrenees as well as Normandy and Anjou. The twelfth-century counts of Toulouse had to resist Angevin attempts at domination and continued to hold the Agenais as an Angevin fief. Much of the region to the south and east of Toulouse, which drained into the Mediterranean, looked more to Catalonia and Aragon than northern France or even northern Languedoc; the king of Aragon was overlord of the viscounts of Béziers and Carcassonne, as well as parts of the Gévaudan and the Pyrenean counties such as Foix and Comminges. East of the Rhône in Provence, suzerainty lay with the distant German emperor.

The term 'Albigensian' (literally 'of' or 'from Albi', a cathedral city on the river Tarn forty miles or so north-east of Toulouse) to describe the Cathars of Languedoc is something of a misnomer. Despite the earliest Cathar diocese being based there, the heaviest concentration of Cathars existed further south. The name 'Albigensian' gained wide currency only after the crusades had begun with the northern invaders, possibly because their first target in 1209 was Raymond Roger Trencavel, lord, among other places, of Albi. Innocent III used the term only once. Its use by the French conquerors illustrated their ignorance of the land they annexed.[15] Until the Albigensian crusades, little integration of southern and western Languedoc into the kingdom of France was apparent. Just as the victories of Philip II of France against King John in the early years of the thirteenth century reoriented the political direction of north-west France, so the victories of Simon of Montfort and later Louis VIII under the banner of the cross determined that the French crown would have direct access to the Mediterranean and the surrounding region would look to Paris and the Seine not Barcelona or the Ebro. Within this region, the Cathars prospered in only a relatively small area, their presence increasingly peripheral to the wider political conflict that their armed suppression provoked. The Albigensian crusades settled the fate of nations more readily than it did the destiny of souls or faith.

The health of the Cathar church in Languedoc rested on weak or competing political authority; a feeble and impoverished church hierarchy; and a failure of cooperation between church and secular lords. To this could be added a lack of centres of Catholic learning. It was no coincidence that the university of Toulouse was only founded as part of the settlement that ended the crusades in 1229 in preparation for the judicial eradication of heresy. In northern France and western Germany, secular authorities were persuaded by active and well-funded bishops that heresy posed a threat to social as well as religious order. By contrast, in Languedoc local lords were alienated from the church, especially with the influx of reform-minded Gregorian churchmen, over control of church tithes and first fruits, the bulk of which tended to remain in the hands of laymen, with a smaller proportion left for parish clergy and nothing for the bishops. Bishop Fulk of Toulouse complained that on entering office in 1205 he found his revenues amounted to ninety-six sous; he could not afford to protect his train of mules in public and was confronted by creditors in his own chapter house.[16] Lay appropriation of ecclesiastical funds not only weakened the church, it denied any material incentive for the local lords to succour it.

Attempts by the church or magnates to impose social or religious discipline sat ill with an aristocratic culture that militated against hierarchical control in favour of clannish independence. The structure of rural aristocratic society was characterized by what contemporaries described as *paratge*.[17] Literally, this meant the free right to one's inheritance. Perhaps almost 50 per cent of lands in the Toulousain were held as allods, owing no dues to a lord. Freedom was a feature of rural as well as urban society, where towns, even parts of towns, insisted on separate autonomy and rights. Vassalage was weak, especially compared with parts of northern France or England; military obligations rare. Equality, not subservience, typified how relations between lords and tenants were conceived. Knighthood denoted status and a mutually respectful position at a lord's court rather than a niche in a pyramidal social hierarchy. If *paratge* implied independence from external pressure on the disposal of lands it also protected the rights of all possible heirs within the family, which led to a sharing of fiefs. Primogeniture had not come to dominate Languedoc inheritance customs as it had further north. One consequence of partible inheritance was the proliferation of co-lords; at the extremes dozens at one time.[18] Another was the preservation of the inheritance rights of women, which were being sharply eroded further north. While the economics of partible inheritance and *paratge* encouraged infra-family cohesion, they discouraged wider social cohesion.

However, contemporaries in Languedoc seemed to invest the *paratge* system with almost transcendent cultural significance as a symbol of nobility, of the free customs of a whole society and of a system of aristocratic life, from courtly entertainments to independence, knightly generosity, personal honour and public morality. His enemies depicted Simon of Montfort as deliberately trying to destroy this world of *paratge*.[19] Yet, while some have seen in *paratge* the principle of personal freedom, it might just as well be held responsible for noble selfishness, which produced a failure of public law and order. Violence between the clan groups of Languedoc may have been petty but it could be vicious; the sight of so many small castles perched on their neighbouring crags still provides evidence of this insecurity. Landholders felt little obligation or loyalty to their nominal overlords. As a direct consequence, to maintain and impose authority, great magnates had to resort to hiring mercenaries, an unpleasant feature of Languedoc life that drew condemnation from the Third Lateran Council in 1179.[20] The absence of peace in Languedoc formed one of the twin themes of crusade propaganda, which frequently described the conflict as the *negotium fidei et pacis*, the business of the faith and of peace. The inability of the count to impose order exposed the feebleness of the episcopacy and encouraged the flourishing of heresy.

The patronage of Catharism by local noble families proved crucial to the heretics' success and represented one of the Languedoc heresy's most distinctive features. Elsewhere, from Bulgaria to Italy and France, Germany and Flanders, popular heresy appeared particularly attractive to urban artisans and the rural poor. Yet despite Cathar communities in Toulouse and the much smaller towns such as Béziers and Carcassonne, urbanization in the areas of Languedoc most affected was limited. There was little or no heresy in Narbonne, the second great city of the region. Rural Catharism revolved around the small castles, fortified villages and households of the local nobility, whose adherence to the radical faith was eased by the sophisticated literary cosmology imported by Nicetas from Constantinople, which was not predicated on hierarchical social or economic tensions or guilt. Lords had much to gain from opposing Catholic assertion of financial ecclesiastical rights and from the Cathars' absolute, rather than the Catholics' conditional, separation of church and state. In return, support from social leaders afforded Catharism material protection and financial support; physical centres for study and proselytizing; and networks for the transmission of the faith both laterally, through extended aristocratic family contacts, and vertically, to the servants, tenants and peasants of the lords. One of the common accusations levelled against Cathar *perfecti* was that they preyed on the vulnerable – the sick, dying or anxious – with promises of unconditional salvation through the *consolamentum* in return for gifts and legacies of money and property. True or not, the financial viability of the Cathar church, which distinguished it from other heretical sects, including the smaller Waldensian community in the region, probably depended less on deathbed larceny than well-heeled patrons.

The patronage of the nobility politicized the Languedoc Cathars, encouraging a political response: war. Although there is no evidence that the greatest magnates, such as the counts of Toulouse or the Trencavel counts of Albi, Béziers and Carcassonne, were heretics themselves, Cathar *perfecti* were to be found in some of the grander local aristocratic families. As early as 1178, Raymond V of Toulouse was lamenting 'the plague of infidelity' that had claimed 'the most noble of my lords' and many of their followers.[21] When inheriting his title as a child, Viscount Raymond Roger Trencavel (1194–1209) had been placed under the protection of a patron of heretics, Bernard of Saissac. Count Raymond Roger of Foix (1188–1223) earned an evil reputation among Catholic observers for his depredations against local monasteries and churches, on one occasion slaughtering monks who had been disrespectful of his *perfecta* aunt, Fais of Durfort.[22] The count's wife and sister were also *perfectae*, although his anti-clerical behaviour probably had more to do with money and jurisdiction than faith. The mother and two of the sisters of the wealthy and powerful Aimery, the lord of Lavaur and Montréal west of Carcassonne, were Cathars who established a flourishing house for *perfectae* at Lavaur. The family castles became centres of extensive networks of Cathar *perfecti*, *credentes* and sympathizers, provoking the ferocity following Simon of Montfort's capture of Lavaur, the 'synagogue of Satan', in May 1211. Aimery was hanged; eighty of his knights were put to the sword and between 300 and 400 Cathars burnt. Aimery's sister, the *perfecta* Girauda, lady of Lavaur, was flung screaming into a well and rocks thrown on top of her.[23] However, the atrocities at Lavaur contained a political purpose and message. Aimery's power had already been severely undermined by the crusader invasion; his knights were regarded by Montfort as traitors, regardless of their devotional practices; the butchery served to discourage further resistance to the northern conquerors. The intimate association of secular lords with heretical networks put each in additional jeopardy from an adversary as intent on subjugating lordships as in eradicating error.

Heresy in Languedoc had been recognized as a problem for over sixty years before the start of the Albigensian crusades. The iconoclastic anti-sacramentalist Peter of Bruys enjoyed some notoriety before his execution at St Gilles in 1131. In 1145, Bernard of Clairvaux conducted a concerted and apparently successful preaching campaign in pursuit of Henry the Monk, an itinerant anti-clerical Donatist who had established a base in Toulouse after a long career evangelizing in western France. By 1178, the rise of Catharism sufficiently alarmed Raymond V of Toulouse for him to appeal Louis VII of France and Henry of Marcy, abbot of Cîteaux for help. Although this may have had as much to do with Raymond's problems with the Trencavels, in whose lands the heretics prospered most, as with his dislike of heresy, it shows there was no inevitable anti-crusading alliance of Languedoc nobility with heresy. After all, Raymond's father had gone on the Second Crusade and his grandfather Raymond IV had been one of the heroes of the First.[24] In response to Raymond V's appeal, a combined force of soldiers and preachers arrived to conduct inquiries at Toulouse, exposing and punishing a few local heretics. Abbot Henry excommunicated two prominent Cathars, including Bernard Raymond, Cathar bishop of Toulouse. In 1179, Canon XXVII of the Third Lateran anathematized heretics and, significantly, those protecting or conversing with them and called for military action, which would earn participants two years' remission of sins and church protection equivalent to that for Jerusalem crusaders.[25] In pursuance of this canon, in 1181, Henry of Marcy, now a cardinal, led an army into Languedoc and besieged Lavaur. Local discretion prevailed. Lavaur submitted. The two Cathar leaders Henry had encountered in 1178 publicly converted and were rewarded with canonries in Toulouse.[26] The expedition went home. In contrast with 1209, there was no thought given to replacing the local ecclesiastical or secular authorities in the pursuit of heresy, merely providing assistance and a slightly menacing incentive to act.

While the activity of 1178–81 led nowhere, church policy towards heresy was clarified in Lucius II's decree *Ad abolendam* (1184), which provided for convicted heretics to be handed over to the secular authorities for punishment, unspecified.[27] Yet in Languedoc, Catharism became, by the early years of the thirteenth century, so rooted 'that it could not easily be dug out',[28] a process assisted by limp ecclesiastical control and absentee bishops. Until the accession of Innocent III in 1198, the main Catholic vigour in the area seemed to have been reserved for the patronage of Cistercian monasteries. The new pope adopted a typically active if cerebral approach. As early as April 1198,[29] Innocent despatched his confessor to investigate and followed this with a series of legatine missions, in 1198, 1200–1201 and 1203–4. The pope's alarm seems to have grown as he became aware of the ineffectiveness of his legates' preaching and disputations, the full extent of the crisis in Languedoc and the strength of Catharism not just in southern France and Italy but throughout the Balkans as well. He began a radical overhaul of the Languedoc episcopacy and urged his legates to a more aggressive stance. In 1204, when adding Abbot Arnaud Aimery of Cîteaux to his fellow Cistercians Master Ralph of Frontfroide and Peter of Castelnau, Innocent offered Holy Land indulgences to those who 'laboured faithfully against the heretics'.[30] In tune with his crusading policies elsewhere, Innocent was moving towards a military solution. This was encouraged by the stalling of his latest legatine mission, apparently through the indifference or obstruction, as the legates saw it, of the secular rulers such as Raymond VI of Toulouse (1194–1222). A fresh approach in 1206–7 adopted by new recruits to the preaching campaign, the Spanish Bishop Diego of Osma and his canon Dominic Guzman, achieved little.[31] They travelled as if in mirror image of *perfecti*, in simple clothes, walking barefoot along the footpaths and byways to a series of disputations with Cathar leaders. Although this later bore fruit in the creation of Dominic's Order of Preachers, the Dominicans, immediately it produced no tangible reversal of the heretic tide. Still less did it deal with the problem of the Cathars' powerful protectors.

Local solutions, as envisaged in 1179 or even by Innocent III himself as late as 1204, had not worked. Unlike Peter II of Aragon, who took measures against heretics in his realm, the count of Toulouse appeared unwilling or unable to act in the church's interests. This problem was compounded by the poor relations that developed between Raymond and the legates, one of whom, the brusque Peter of Castelnau, made himself extremely unpopular with local opinion.[32] To force the issue, the legates excommunicated Count Raymond in 1207 and 1208, draconian action that merely served to expose their impotence. If Raymond refused or was unable to take measures against the heretics, some external force would be required to compel or replace him. In 1205 and 1207 the pope attempted to interest Philip II of France in intervening. On the second occasion, in a letter of 17 November 1207, Holy Land indulgences were offered. Implicit was the pope's recognition that the enemies of such a campaign stood to be disinherited and their lands confiscated. Not even this incentive could attract Philip, who argued that he was busy enough defending himself from his enemies John of England and Otto IV of Germany, awkwardly one of Innocent's protégés. The pope's own strategy was still hedged with qualifications: 'we want you to bear in mind', he told the French king, 'the needs of the Holy Land, so that no aid is prevented from reaching her'. However, Innocent's attitude towards the Cathars and their supporters was ominously clear: 'wounds that do not respond to the healing of poultices must be lanced with a blade'.[33] Almost immediately, the pope was presented with a perfect *casus belli*. On the morning of 14 January, the legate Peter of Castelnau was assassinated on the west bank of the Rhône north of Arles, ten miles from the abbey of St Gilles, by a servant of the man with whom the legate had held a fierce row the previous day, Count Raymond VI of Toulouse.[34]

THE CRUSADE

The murder of Peter of Castelnau failed to elevate the victim to sanctity, even the pope admitting to the absence of customary martyr's miracles.[35] Otherwise it matched the more famous death of Archbishop Thomas Becket in 1170 in propaganda value and easily outstripped the Canterbury martyrdom in direct political consequences. News of the assassination was taken to Rome by Peter's fellow legate, Abbot Arnaud Aimery, who convinced Innocent of Count Raymond's complicity. The count was excommunicated, and, on 10 March 1208, Innocent III delivered a fulminating call to arms. The culprit was unequivocally identified as the 'changeable, crafty, slippery and inconsistent' Raymond. Full Holy Land indulgences were promised the 'knights of Christ'. Innocent's language avoided compromise. 'According to the judgement of truth we must not be afraid of those who kill the body', so 'the strong recruits of Christian knighthood' must attempt 'in whatever ways God has revealed to you to wipe out the treachery of heresy and its followers by attacking the heretics with a strong hand and an outstretched arm, that much more confidently than you would attack the Saracens because they are worse than them'. Even if he repented, Raymond's penalty should be the confiscation of his and his followers' lands. 'Catholic inhabitants must be put in their place.'[36] Combining religious conquest with political annexation complicated this new papal holy war. By legitimizing land grabbing, Innocent invited exploitation by acquisitive adventurers he proved characteristically powerless to restrain.

The new crusade was regarded as an extension of the previous legatine missions, recognized by the appointment of Arnaud Aimery as chief propagandist and recruiting agent. The theoretical justification rested on subtly different bases than the Holy Land crusades even if the rhetoric evoked similar images and the privileges tapped identical spiritual aspirations. Greater emphasis was placed on the crusade being a just as well as holy war, a slant made easier by the material crimes of heresy and murder. In his bulls of 10 March 1208, Innocent set out the juridical argument for violence against the heretics as a form of defence both spiritual and material: 'the perverters of our souls have become also the destroyers of our flesh'. Raymond VI was an excommunicate and a murderer. In a manner impossible when tackling Islam, the Cathars were portrayed as 'rebels' against Christ and His church, their heresy 'treachery', in that legalistic sense 'worse than Saracens'. These are categories of just war, increasingly familiar to contemporary canon lawyers and, as Innocent hinted, more amenable to explanation than the transcendent demands of holy war. Revenge was common to both – vengeance for the death of legate Peter but more fundamentally vengeance for the insult to Christ. The full panoply of vow, cross, plenary indulgence and temporal privileges were deployed, a logical extension of twelfth-century precedents, such as Canon XXVII of the Third Lateran Council, as well as patristic theory derived from Augustine of Hippo.

The crusade was being applied to a just war to restore the order of Christendom.

As such the Albigensian crusade displayed familiar features to emphasize Innocent III's conception of the universal embrace of holy war. The plenary indulgence and cross, absent in 1179, were prominent. Crusade temporal privileges were insisted upon and the crusade leaders attempted to impose sumptuary rules on their followers.[37] A Burgundian benefactor to the Cluniac monks in 1209 was recorded as joining the Albigensian campaign for the traditional reason of 'the remission of my and my parents' sins'. In a charter in favour of the abbey of Cluny, Odo III duke of Burgundy, the grandest of the 1209 recruits, is described as 'crucesignatus contra hereticos Albigenses'.[38] Sympathetic contemporary chroniclers refer to the crusaders generically as *peregrini*, pilgrims, although the object of any penitential pilgrimage is hard, if not impossible, to identify. During the fighting at the sieges of Lavaur in 1211 and Moissac in 1212, the crusader army clergy sang the hymn *Veni Creator Spiritus*, which became the crusaders' anthem.[39] The crusades' opponents were 'enemies of Christ' to the recruited as well as the recruiters and war propagandists. To his enemies, Raymond was 'the cruellest persecutor of Christ'. Innocent and preachers, such as James of Vitry and the Englishman Robert of Curzon (Courçon), succeeded in creating an atmosphere of spiritual crisis and crusading duty. Within a few years a crusade preaching manual in England was including uplifting stories of heroic deaths in Languedoc to set beside the deeds of Holy Land martyrs.[40] According to James of Vitry, his pet holy woman, Mary of Oignies, was a great enthusiast for the cause, experiencing visions showing Christ's care for the fate of Languedoc and, usefully for recruiters like James, angels lifting the souls of dead crusaders 'to heavenly bliss without any purgatory'.[41] This congruence with Holy Land wars of the cross was reinforced by the presence in the ranks of the Languedoc *crucesignati* of veterans from other crusades, including four prominent Fourth Crusade dissidents at Zara in 1202–3 – Abbot Guy of Les Vaux-de-Cernay, Enguerrand de Boves and Simon and Guy of Montfort – and the inveterate *crucesignatus* Leopold VI of Austria, who was recruited in 1210, as were the brothers Philip bishop of Beauvais (who went again in 1215) and Count Peter of Dreux, who had seen service in Palestine on the Third Crusade. Other recruits later joined the Spanish crusade against the Almohads in 1212, led by the Languedoc legate

Arnaud Aimery. Such international experience of crusading lent flesh to Innocent's ideology of almost eternal armed struggle against the spiritual and material forces of evil.

The regularity and persistence of this preaching sustained an atmosphere of immediate spiritual crisis. One unexpected and not entirely welcome response later became known as the Children's Crusade (discussed in the next chapter). Stirred by the claims of the dangers besetting Christendom, a series of revivalist penitential processions in northern France converged on St Denis in the summer of 1212, calling for general moral reform, a clear echo of the papal programme of reform. The heretic scare and the annual round of preaching and cross-giving contributed to the sense of alarm. A Norman chronicler suggested that many of those who marched were later recruited to the Albigensian crusade.[42] The war against heresy formed an important religious as well as political context for the Fourth Lateran Council announced by Innocent in 1213 to be held in Rome in 1215, the council's third decree expressly dealing with the Albigensian crusades, which were equated with aiding the Holy Land.[43]

However, not all the language or practice of the Albigensian crusades replicated Holy Land models. The euphemism of 'the business of faith and peace' represented a more temporal legalistic slogan than 'the business of God' or other tags attached to the eastern campaigns. Fighting within Christendom, for most within their own kingdom, with authorized territorial profit held particular repercussions. To cement local support in Toulouse, Bishop Fulk instituted the White Confraternity, a militia aimed at combating heresy and usury (a very Innocentian combination). Members received the cross and remission of sins so they would 'not be deprived of the indulgences which were being granted to outsiders'. Although reflecting civic identity as much as piety, and challenged by a rival Toulouse association called the Black Confraternity, Bishop Fulk's association possessed sufficient cohesion and commitment to supply troops at the siege of Lavaur in May 1211.[44]

The Albigensian crusades were the first great political as well as anti-heresy crusades, aimed as much against Christians as against heretics. Participants understood that the Languedoc war, however equal in merit, was not the same as the Jerusalem war. There was almost no military involvement by the military orders, despite their strong presence in the area. Wars in Languedoc were easier to fight than in Palestine, more accessible, less physically demanding, less time-consuming. The 1208 offer of indulgences invited a rather casual approach, if not blatant abuse. Recruits showed little commitment or staying power, judging a brief appearance in the field adequate to gain spiritual reward, and perhaps hoping for a share of the clerical taxes being raised for the project. The latter was not forthcoming, many crusaders probably reckoning that the war in fact offered them no profit, only loss, and, until the 1220s, served the material interests solely of the Montforts. By the autumn of 1210, the legates had become seriously alarmed that indulgences were distorting the military viability of the operation. Peter of Les Vaux-de-Cernay, nephew of Abbot Guy, wrote a detailed and well-informed contemporary account of the crusades, often as an eyewitness. He recorded the measures taken to mitigate the problem:

> the papal legates, aware that most of the crusaders were somewhat lukewarm in their enthusiasm for the campaign and perpetually anxious to go home, had laid it down that the indulgence promised to the crusaders by the pope would not be granted to anyone who failed to complete at least one full period of forty days in the service of Jesus Christ.[45]

This contractual finesse to the indulgence became a unique central aspect of the Languedoc crusades. It did not always work. In the autumn of 1210 the bishop of Beauvais and count of Dreux's army abandoned the siege of Termes to return north before their forty days were up.[46] Paradoxically, the legates' attempt to stabilize Montfort's reinforcements merely had the effect of institutionalizing an inconveniently brief period of frontline duty, especially awkward in a war characterized by lengthy sieges rather than lightning *chevauchées*. The problem was exacerbated by Montfort's chronic lack of funds preventing him hiring crusaders to remain. By 1226, the forty-day term was being claimed by the count of Champagne, eager to leave the siege of Avignon, as a right, 'de consuetudine Gallicana', according to Gallic/French custom.[47] A later thirteenth-century preaching anecdote detailed how one knight struck a bargain that he would only extend his forty days' service for another forty if Archdeacon William of Paris, who usefully doubled as crusade preacher and Montfort's chief siege engineer and tactician, would grant the second plenary indulgence the crusader felt he was earning to his deceased father. A dream confirmed the ruse worked.[48]

Such spiritual bargaining, while of interest to schoolmen, had little place on the campaigns against the infidel. Nor did it feature in Innocent's original scheme. Just as he could not have foreseen the diversion of his 1198 crusade, so the pope could not have prophesied in March 1208 how this new crusade would develop. It is likely Innocent anticipated a sharp policing operation that would remove the protectors of heresy and install a rigidly orthodox Catholic secular regime that, with the cooperation of a newly invigorated episcopacy, would proceed to extirpate the heresy and exterminate the heretics. The failure of the crusade to complete a quick conquest led to a laborious struggle almost for each valley and strongpoint. The crusade's political dimensions competed with religious certainties. Before the battle of Muret in 1213, after four years of the crusade, when Simon of Montfort's troops faced an army led by the Spanish crusading hero Peter II of Aragon, a recent ally of some of those now ranged against him, the bishop of Comminges was recorded as having to reassure the Montfortians that he would stand surety for the promise of martyrdom to those who, having confessed their sins, fell in battle.[49] Only a few months earlier Innocent III had temporarily ended the general offer of crusade indulgences to those who helped Montfort conquer the county of Toulouse.[50] As a war against Christians, enemies could become allies and vice versa, without clear lines of conflict much beyond the ambitions of Simon of Montfort. The war was more or less continuous for over a decade, but its status as a crusade was not. After the initial euphoria of victory in 1209, while rhetoric gained recruits from the north, it failed to hold them for long or lift the operation in the south far above a regional power struggle. When his new-won political rights were at stake, Montfort fell out even with his former leader Arnold Aimery, over jurisdiction in Narbonne, to whose archbishopric the abbot had been elevated in 1212.[51] In Languedoc, Innocent III's perception of holy war as a constant necessity imposed compromise with the integrity of the ideal itself.

The focus of Arnaud Aimery's recruitment in 1208 was northern France. From his own province of Burgundy among the first to be signed up were Duke Odo and Hervé count of Nevers. By contrast, Philip II was concerned at the pope's attempt to confiscate the fiefs of his vassals and, in the process, reduce the pool of soldiers available for the king's wars. Philip had not successfully resisted Innocent's interference in his conflict with King John of England over the Angevin lands in northern France in 1202–4 only to allow the pope to parcel out lands in the south. Neither, until the Angevin struggle was resolved, would Philip dissipate his energies in Languedoc. However, he abandoned attempts to limit the recruitment of his major vassals. Philip's response in 1208–9 fixed the subsequent Capetian position, one determined more or less openly by considerations of politics and self-interest. Even though his pious son, Louis, proved here, as in England in 1216–17, a willing military adventurer, his interventions in Languedoc, in 1215, 1219 and, as king, in 1226, were conditioned by royal security in the north and clear opportunities for dynastic advancement in the south.

Confident in the support of Odo of Burgundy and Hervé of Nevers and their promise of 500 knights, Arnold Aimery began the formal preaching campaign at Cîteaux on 14 September 1208, Holy Cross Day, six years to the day since another Cistercian general assembly had listened to Fulk of Neuilly preach the Fourth Crusade in the presence of Boniface of Montferrat. As then, the Cistercians dominated the evangelism for the Albigensian crusades, as they had for the Second and Third as well. In contrast with previous general Holy Land crusades, the area of preaching was restricted, chiefly to northern France. The count of Auvergne and the archbishop of Bordeaux also gathered an army in western France which launched a brief foray into the Agenais and Quercy in May 1209, terrorizing the Lot valley before tamely withdrawing. How far this incursion was motivated by frontier rivalry rather than enthusiasm to destroy heresy must remain obscure, although a number of heretics were tried and burnt. A similar raid into the Rouergue by the bishop of Le Puy seemed more concerned with profits from tribute than imposing religious orthodoxy.[52]

The main army raised in 1208–9 depended heavily on secular networks of lay and ecclesiastical lordship and financial inducement. The clerical tenth authorized by the pope was concentrated on the provinces where the crusaders came from, notably the archdiocese of Sens, while a voluntary lay subsidy was proposed for those living on the lands of the crusader nobles.[53] Raising troops was left to the lay leaders. The future leader, Simon of Montfort, was recruited by Odo of Burgundy, with 'substantial gifts' with more to follow when Simon agreed.[54] The lay commanders' underwriting of the enterprise invited division, especially as it transpired during the 1209 campaign that the immensely grand duke of Burgundy and parvenu opportunist count of Nevers detested each other to such an extent that it was daily expected that either might resort to murder.[55] Disunity on crusade was perhaps normative. However, the Albigensian campaigns proved especially vulnerable to squabbles among its short-stay generals.

The search for an acceptable lay leader foundered on Philip II's repeated refusal to countenance his own or his son's involvement, especially once he learnt of an anti-French alliance early in 1209 between John of England and his nephew Otto IV of Germany, both of whom held overlordship claims to different parts of Languedoc. However, Philip, still mired in marital problems that had aroused the censure of the pope, needed to maintain some association with the crusade to safeguard his interests. At an assembly at Villeneuve-sur-Yonne on 1 May 1209, in the presence of Arnaud Aimery, Odo of Burgundy and the counts of Nevers and St Pol, Philip reiterated his inability to campaign in person, although he promised a royal contingent. By emphasizing that the French crusaders undertook the campaign with their king's approval, Philip implicitly reserved the right to intervene. Any rearrangement of Languedoc's tenurial structure would require royal approval, offering the French king further opportunities to assert his suzerainty throughout his kingdom.

The absence of an uncontested lay leader left the nominal command to Arnaud Aimery, who appeared wholly unabashed by the task. The main expedition mustered at Lyons on 24 June 1209 and set out down the Rhône at the beginning of July. By this time the whole strategic context of the expedition had been thrown into confusion from which it never properly emerged. The expected target, Raymond of Toulouse, suddenly became an ally, no doubt to the relief of those of his vassals and close relatives who were marching with the crusaders. After trying desperately to shore up his diplomatic position and failing to persuade his nephew, young Raymond Roger Trencavel viscount of Albi, Béziers and Carcassonne to make common cause against the invaders, Raymond VI opened negotiations with the pope. Innocent was disinclined to cancel the crusade even if Raymond submitted and equally unwilling to compromise the work of his legate Arnaud Aimery. Nevertheless, he despatched two new legates to impose conditions for Raymond's submission and readmittance into the church. At St Gilles on 18 June, Raymond accepted a long list of grievances against him, agreed to surrender certain lands, and was scourged by the legate Milo before being paraded half-naked before the coffin of the murdered Peter of Castelnau. On 22 June, Raymond took the cross, aligning himself with the invaders while securing the church's protection from them. From St Gilles, Raymond hurried north to meet the advancing crusaders at Valence.[56]

Cheated of their expected victim, the crusaders turned their attention to the Trencavel lands, incontestably riddled with heretics, even though the young and engaging viscount himself was recognized as orthodox. This made little difference. The crusade needed an enemy; Raymond of Toulouse short-sightedly promoted an opportunity to destroy a troublesome vassal while escaping attack himself. Viscount Raymond Roger's attempt to deflect his fate by submitting to Arnold Aimery was brushed aside; the legate's Christian lexicon seemed to lack charitable forgiveness. Advancing from Montpellier, the crusaders entered Trencavel territory on 21 July. Raymond Roger fell back before them, leaving Béziers at their mercy. On 22 July, the crusaders began to dig in outside the walls of Béziers. The bishop of Béziers attempted to persuade the citizens to hand over or abandon the heretics in the city, of whose names he claimed to have a list. His overtures were rejected. The inhabitants believed their defences and food supplies would withstand assault. Reinforcements were expected. There were probably at most only 700 heretics in a population of 8–9,000. Béziers saw the besiegers in political and military, not Christian, terms; their city and their independence were being attacked. This, they reckoned, accurately as it turned out, the sacrifice of a few eccentric neighbours was unlikely to alter. However, the offer made by the bishop formed a crucial element in Catholic apologetics for what followed. The Christians of Béziers had placed themselves beyond the pale of humanity by consciously rejecting the bishop's terms and choosing to harbour and sustain heretics. In the words of the legates' subsequent report to the pope, their blood was on their own heads.[57]

Even so, Catholic reports on the sack of Béziers were keen to emphasize that the attack was not led by the nobles and knights but by the *servientes*, sergeants, and the unarmed mass of camp-followers, a reversal of social norms suggesting literary uneasiness with events. Whoever began the attack, it seems most of the army joined in to make it quick, ruthless and devastating. The legates laconically recorded 'our men spared no one, irrespective of rank, sex or age'.[58] The citizens appear to have panicked and put up little resistance. In a later, possibly apocryphal, anecdote, when asked by priests how they could distinguish whom to kill, Abbot Arnaud Aimery, worried lest heretics escaped by pretending to be Catholics, ordered, 'Kill them. The Lord knows who are his own.'[59] Even the crowds who sheltered in the main churches were not spared. The legates estimated that 20,000 died in the carnage and called it a miracle.[60] The true figure was almost certainly far less. The massacre may have been premeditated. Rumours suggested that discussions at the papal Curia in 1208 had authorized the destruction of any who resisted the crusade. The Navarrese cleric William of Tudela (d. *c.*1213), who composed a Provençal verse account of the early stages of the Albigensian crusades, noted that the crusade leaders decided to make examples of the inhabitants of any town taken by storm *pour encourager les autres*. 'They would then find no one daring to resist them, so great would be the terror produced . . . that is why the inhabitants of Béziers were massacred; they were all killed, it was the worst they could do to them.'[61]

In that respect, the massacre at Béziers initially worked. Narbonne immediately sent in its unconditional submission and the army met no resistance as it advanced towards Carcassonne, as the countryside, towns, villages and castles were evacuated by terrified locals. In the longer term, however, the sack of Béziers hardened Languedoc opposition to the invasion across religious divisions. Thereafter adherence or opposition to the crusaders was determined largely by secular considerations. The chief religious element in the campaigns of the following two decades found expression in periodic military atrocities and regular mass execution, usually by burning, of captured heretics. However, despite the gaudy rhetoric of holy war and Simon of Montfort's carefully constructed reputation as a warrior of Christ, between his appointment as crusade leader in 1209 and death in 1218, Cathars were hardly his main target. Most of the places where Cathars are known to have lived he left untouched, and at only a small minority of the castles and towns Montfort captured was the presence of heretics recorded.[62] As Béziers demonstrated, strategy rested on realpolitik, not religion.

Béziers set the tone for what developed into one of the nastiest of medieval wars, partly because of the high stakes of dispossession and conquest, partly because of the collapse of social order and erosion of the rule of civil law in a region that became a perpetual war zone. The religious gloss wore thin. In May 1213, Innocent III admitted that 'their protectors and defenders . . . are more dangerous than the heretics themselves'.[63] Little trust existed between opponents as surrender terms were breached. Guerilla warfare and local exploitation of the absence of settled political authority spread violence far beyond the paths of the main campaigns. The presence of mercenaries, a staple of Languedoc warfare for decades, ensured that many engagements ended with the slaughter of defeated troops, despised as paid soldiers. Stubborn garrisons received little mercy. Massacres became regular events, from most of the inhabitants of the modest *castrum* of Les Touelles near Albi (January 1212) to the 5,000 civilians despatched at Marmande on the Garonne in the Agenais in June 1219 by the army of Prince Louis of France after the town had surrendered.[64] Captured heretics went to the flames. The first was burnt without trial on Simon of Montfort's orders at Castres in August 1209.[65] Thereafter, the holocaust flickered intensely rather than raged across the province. At Minerve in July 1210, Abbot Arnold Aimery tried to scupper a negotiated surrender, so keen was he to make sure the heretics burnt; at least 140 of them did. Over 300 *perfecti* were burnt at Lavaur in May 1211 and at least sixty at Les Casses a few days later, places, the great historian of the Inquisition H. C. Lea memorably remarked, whose names 'suggest all that man can inflict and man can suffer for the glory of God'.[66] The relative dearth of such horrors as the war dragged on might indicate a lack of persecuting zeal on the part of the invaders or the chroniclers' growing indifference.

Atrocities were not the sole preserve of the crusaders. At the end of 1209, Giraud of Pépieux had captured the castle of Puisserguier from the crusaders. At the approach of Montfort he abandoned the place, burying alive the captured sergeants under debris in the moat. He also had two of Montfort's knights blinded and mutilated. At about the same time, William of Rocquefort, whose brother was the bishop of Carcassonne, murdered the abbot of Eaunes and a lay brother apparently 'for no reason except they were Cistercians'. During the siege of Moissac in September 1212, the defenders regularly mutilated crusaders' corpses. Bernard of Cazenac and his wife Elise – a 'second Jezebel' – conducted a reign of terror in the Dordogne valley in the years to 1214, including leaving 150 mutilated men and women in the Benedictine abbey of Sarlat with hands cut off, feet amputated or eyes put out. Elise specialized in removing women's thumbs to prevent them working and ordering the nipples of the poorest peasant women to be ripped off. Behind such lurid sadism lay a sustained attempt by this local noble couple to preserve their independence. One critic of the invaders portrayed Bernard as an epitome of chivalry.[67] The 'business of faith and peace' managed, if only temporarily, to brutalize a society that had not been exactly peaceful and harmonious before. Under the cover of war, when allegiances could shift with ease and rapidity, and with the region full of dispossessed nobles (known as *faidits*), lawlessness could prove the best source of profit. Two Montfort loyalists in the Toulousain, Foucard and Jean from Berzy in the Ile de France, tortured, starved, degraded and extorted money from prisoners of war on a regular basis as an adjunct to their normal pursuit of sustained banditry. As a later pro-crusade commentator from the area they ravaged acidly remarked: 'they did not perform the tasks for which they had come originally; the end did not match the beginning'.[68] Others might argue it did precisely that.

THE CONQUEST OF LANGUEDOC

The initial phase of the crusade that had begun at Béziers ended when Carcassonne surrendered on 14 August 1209 after a fortnight's siege. The international significance of these events was recognized by the brief appearance in the crusader camp of Peter II of Aragon, the nominal overlord of the Trencavel lands. The crusaders' decision to spare Carcassonne the destruction of Béziers was prompted not by humanity but by a realization that whoever was to inherit the lordship of the area needed to rule more than ruins and smouldering charnel houses. The inhabitants of Carcassonne were expelled and Viscount Raymond Roger deposed and incarcerated, to die in prison of dysentery three months later. Some felt outrage at his fate; the Dauphinois troubadour Guillem Augier lamented what he saw as his murder.[69] The viscount's removal proved highly convenient for the crusaders as they redrew the political map of the region.

The first step came within days of the occupation of Carcassonne with the election of Simon of Montfort to rule the Trencavel lands. By no means the first choice, Odo of Burgundy and Hervé of Nevers having declined, Simon became the secular leader of the crusade. A self-righteous, sanctimonious prig, Simon possessed qualities, lineage and reputation far beyond his modest lordship of Montfort l'Amaury in the Ile de France. A bull-like man of great physical presence, like many successful leaders he boasted a mane of lustrous hair. His single-minded piety and unusually strict personal morality were matched by remarkable military skills: tenacious on campaign, resourceful in logistics, audacious in battle, inspiring to his followers, ruthless to his enemies. Without him, the war could have foundered through rivalry, lack of men and money, awkward terrain and stubborn opposition, all of which Simon managed to scramble though and ultimately surmount often by sheer determination. His principled stance at Zara in 1202–3 and subsequent crusading in the Holy Land established his credentials for self-confidence, conviction and commitment. Before 1209, he had held a vicarious claim to the English earldom of Leicester through his mother. By 1210, his exploits in the south had gained such prestige for him to be discussed as a possible replacement as king of England. His appointment as ruler of the Trencavel lands, by 1210 accepted formally by Raymond Roger's widow and son, subtly changed the nature of the crusade.[70] While the enterprise continued to be promoted by the church in northern France, Germany and the Low Countries as a holy war, in Languedoc the conflict became increasingly an assertion of one lordship over another, of powerful centripetal authority over a traditionally fissiparous and independent nobility, and of dispossession and land seizure. The *casus belli* of heresy lent a sharp edge to rhetoric and occasionally action, but Simon of Montfort, however sincere an 'athlete of Christ', fought to establish a realm on earth.

The Albigensian crusades fell into four distinct phases; the annexation of the Trencavel lands (1209–11); the conquest of the county of Toulouse and the Pyrenean counties (1211–15); the revival of southern resistance (1216–25); and the Capetian conquest (1226–9). Not all the fighting could be classed as crusading, and the full panoply of the war of the cross was temporarily suspended in 1213.[71] Nevertheless, the tinge of holy war coloured the entire conception and operation of the war, even though its aims revolved around a series of essentially secular objectives. As a major political enterprise, the wars sucked in those with rights in the area. The king of Aragon, no friend to heretics but fearful of a new Montfortian power in the region, intervened diplomatically for years before he tried to assert his interests against the crusaders by force in 1213. He was defeated and killed at Muret by people with whom he had been closely negotiating only a few months earlier. In 1214, King John of England toured northern Languedoc as part of his campaign to regain his ancestral lands lost to Philip II of France in 1204. As overlord of the Agenais, he received the homage of locals at La Réole in April and visited Périgord the following August. John had no wish to see a strong pro-Capetian Montfort principality dominating his southern frontier. Direct confrontation was usually avoided, but in the summer of 1214 Montfort's assault on Marmande on the Garonne was resisted by a garrison of John's troops commanded by Geoffrey of Neville, one of the king's chamberlains.[72] It is likely that had John been more successful in defending his French lands in 1202–4 or in trying to retrieve them in 1214 he would have intervened more aggressively in Languedoc. In such ways, the Languedoc war touched on the politics of most of western Europe. Philip II's victory over Otto IV of Germany and his English allies at Bouvines in July 1214 secured Montfort's hold in the south almost as certainly as the victory at Muret a year earlier.

At every stage, the fighting revolved around sieges, the physical seizure of territory, valley by valley, castle by castle. There were very few pitched battles; Castelnaudary (1211), Muret (1213), Baziège (1218). A key figure in Montfort's entourage between 1210 and 1214 was Archdeacon William of Paris, his siegecraft expert, quartermaster, engineer and designer of siege engines. Montfort was constantly short of funds. Church taxes failed to cover expenses. Revenues from the conquered land fell short of requirements. Montfort ran the crusade on a shoestring; at the siege of Termes in 1210 it was said he was 'beset by extreme poverty' and short of food.[73] Booty thus remained an important element in the crusades' viability, especially as ravaging was precluded in lands under Montfort's control. In 1216, to pay for his siege of Toulouse, Montfort levied a tribute on his Languedoc lands hoping to raise 30,000 marks, earning a rare rebuke from a local chronicler that he was 'blinded by money'.[74] The crusade was habitually short of manpower. Each winter's preaching effort produced only a trickle of grand recruits who usually stayed for the barest minimum period of under six weeks regardless of the military situation. When the French contingent abandoned Montfort during the siege of Termes in 1210, the crusaders were only bailed out by the subsequent arrival of a company of Lorrainer infantry.[75] Recruitment attracted individuals from across north-western Europe and as far east as Austria, but little continuity was effected, squabbling was endemic, commitment was consistently feeble. Montfort was often reduced to relying on a very small cadre of household knights; apparently only thirty knights remained in the autumn of 1209.[76] Only a clear tactical sense, driving optimism, careful harbouring of resources and the divisions among his opponents saw Montfort through. The effort was complicated by the fast cross-currents of local allegiances and shifting perceptions of advantage. The war was never as simple as a northern invasion of the south yet increasingly at the higher levels of society it appeared to be, as the numbers of dispossessed and outlawed *faidits* grew. Securing the acquiescence or loyal submission of the local baronage proved elusive, hardening the cultural, linguistic and hence political barriers. Repeated betrayals persuaded Montfort of the intrinsic untrustworthiness of the people of Languedoc, one of whom commented that he 'began to eschew association with knights who spoke our tongue'.[77]

The parting of the ways had come early in 1211, when, in the face of deliberately excessive demands by the legates, Raymond VI had refused to be reconciled with the crusaders, who promptly turned the war of the cross against the county of Toulouse, signalling a contest for the future of the whole of the region. At the same time Peter of Aragon, having failed to broker a compromise between Raymond, Montfort and the legates, reluctantly accepted Montfort's homage for the Trencavel lands. This final split with Count Raymond had been long prepared. The count had withdrawn from the crusader army at Carcassonne in August 1209 and had been re-excommunicated the following month. The central issue, according to the legates, concerned the count's refusal to persecute the Cathars, while Raymond saw his authority being compromised by the punitive demands of vindictive churchmen. The pope was far more prepared to allow Raymond's reconciliation than his legates, who displayed almost visceral hatred of the count. Repeatedly, papal compromises foundered on the rock of legatine intransigence. Montfort, sensing his own advantage, backed the legates.

After the last Trencavel lands had been subdued in May 1211, Montfort turned his attention to Raymond's county of Toulouse and the Pyrenean lands of his allies, the counts of Foix and Comminges. Although unable to capture Toulouse, because of an insufficient number of troops, Montfort defeated a Toulouse–Foix army at Castelnaudary in September 1211 and the following year made sweeping gains from the Agenais to the Pyrenees. To show his confidence in the permanency of the northern French settlement, in December 1212, at an assembly of his lay and ecclesiastical followers at Pamiers, he issued statutes regulating the government of his conquests.[78] These secured the rights of the church and insisted on the strict obedience to public and tenurial comital rights, including military service from his vassals. Clear distinctions were drawn between 'French' and locals: heiresses could marry the former freely but the latter only with Montfort's permission. Treatment of heretics and former heretics was specified, as were regulations concerning inheritance and the economy. The underlying colonial purpose emerged in a codicil to the statutes Montfort added regarding the customs to be observed by those to whom he had given property, the incoming barons, knights, burgesses and peasants, who were guaranteed the 'usages and customs observed in France around Paris'. Although still technically only viscount of the former Trencavel lands, Montfort's Pamiers statutes were clearly intended to apply to all his conquests.

Early in 1213, a combination of neat diplomacy by Peter II of Aragon with Innocent III's desire to promulgate a new, general Holy Land crusade briefly threatened Montfort's authority. Failing to overcome the settled refusal of the legates to accept reconciliation and an end to the war at a council at Lavaur in January, Peter succeeded in persuading the pope that Montfort and the legates had exceeded their brief. In a series of letters dated 15–17 January, Innocent cancelled the granting of crusade indulgences, effectively ending the crusade, and ordered Montfort to return the lands of Foix, Comminges and Béarn to their rightful rulers (all vassals of the king of Aragon) and insisted that Raymond's lands and rights be restored. His previous doubts over the crusaders' motives now crystallized into harsh words directed at Arnaud Aimery and Montfort: 'you have extended greedy hands into lands which have no ill reputation for heresy . . . you have usurped the possessions of others indiscriminately, unjustly and without proper care'.[79] This diplomatic coup encouraged Peter to break with Montfort and the legates, taking Toulouse, Foix and Comminges under his protection. However, in May, Innocent, now fully apprised of what had happened at Lavaur, after intense lobbying by Montfort and the legates revoked his letters of January. This did not revive the crusade on quite the same basis as before, as in April, Innocent's great bull *Quia Maior* launching the new Holy Land crusade restricted indulgences for the Albigensian crusade only to those living in 'Provence', i.e. Languedoc.[80] The general uncertainty was compounded when Louis of France took the cross in February 1213, presumably unaware of the papal cancellation.

The diplomatic manoeuvres of the first half of 1213 ended with at least partial vindication for Montfort, witnessed at Amaury's knighting in June. They left Peter of Aragon, if he wished to influence events and prevent Montfort's annexation of south-west France, no option but war. His defeat and death at Muret on 12 September appeared to some providential.[81] A much smaller force under Montfort had seized their chance and through bold, well-disciplined action had routed a larger, complacent enemy. God had spoken. Peter lay dead on the field, his infant son a hostage and his ally Raymond VI in flight, to Spain and then England. Yet the consequences were more equivocal. While Montfort, with new recruits from the north, tightened his grip towards the Dordogne valley in 1214, Innocent III tried once more to broker a settlement based on justice, not force. A new legate, Peter of Benevento, secured the release of the child King James of Aragon and the absolution of Raymond VI. However, the count's lands were administered by Montfort, who ignored attempts at compromise. In January 1215, a large church assembly at Montpellier, presided over by Legate Peter, recommended that Montfort be chosen as 'chief and sole ruler' of all the count of Toulouse's lands. However, Montfort remained unpopular: at Montpellier he narrowly avoided assassination by disaffected citizens.[82]

The Montpellier decision required papal ratification. The dispossessed, led by Raymond VI and Raymond Roger of Foix, who had been deprived in 1214, took their case to Rome, where their fate would be decided at the general church council. Montfort's position was recognized by Louis of France, who, free since Bouvines from the threat of John and Otto IV, visited Languedoc from April to June 1215 in fulfilment of his 1213 vow. His large and distinguished army conducted a triumphal tour, rather than a crusade, seeing no military action but demonstrating, for the first time, active Capetian overlordship of the region. With such powerful support, it came as a surprise that the Montfort cause had such a stiff challenge at the Lateran Council in November, a reflection of the unease felt by the curial lawyers at Montfort's and successive legates' pugilistic exercise of church authority. The count of Foix, a vituperative but effective debater, at least in one sympathetic poet's imagination, challenged the legitimacy of the transfer of power as well as impugning the motives and methods of Montfort, the papal legates and the crusaders.[83] He clearly had some effect as the pope ordered the return to Raymond Roger of lands occupied by the invaders. However, with the county of Toulouse, the logic of Innocent's previous acquiescence produced a judgement in favour of Montfort, except the pope reserved the comital lands east of the Rhône in Provence to be held by Montfort in trust for Raymond's young son, the future Raymond VII.[84]

As in 1209, 1211 and 1213, no sooner won than victory slipped from Montfort's grasp. Although he received Philip II's investiture of the Languedoc counties at Melun in April 1216 and managed by the end of that year to have secured control over the troublesome Toulouse, rebellion, led by the younger Raymond, had already begun to sap his control. Montfort's failure to relieve Raymond's siege of Beaucaire in August 1216 encouraged further insurrection across the south. As well as the presence of a large pool of disinherited noblemen who knew the people and the country, later pro-crusade commentators pointed to the unpopularity of Montfort's subordinates fuelling discontent. 'They held the land for their own satisfaction, not for the purposes for which it had been acquired, or in Christ's interests, but for their own ends, slaves to lusts and pleasures'.[85] The Montfortians steadily lost ground as the dire cycle of violence and hard campaigning renewed itself. Despite increasing depression recorded by a writer close to his entourage, Montfort slogged on, notching significant successes without managing to prevent Raymond VI and his son re-establish a political presence across the county. The French monarchy gave no help to its new vassal, being distracted by its adventure in 1216–17 to place Prince Louis on the English throne. In September 1217, Raymond VI re-entered Toulouse, restricting the Montfortians to the citadel of the Narbonnais castle on its southern wall. Montfort began yet another siege of the city. Despite reinforcements arriving in January 1218, little progress was made. After nine months, the city, fearful of massacre, showed no signs of capitulation. The deadlock was resolved on 25 June. While inspecting forward siege engines, Montfort was struck on the head by a stone thrown from one of the city's mangonels, operated, some said, by women, crushing his skull. He died instantly, one of the most revered and reviled men ever to have fought for the cross.[86]

The removal of Montfort shifted the balance of power. Encouraged, young Raymond took the offensive, defeating the crusaders at Baziège late in the year. Pope Honorious III read the auguries and renewed the crusade indulgences in August 1218. A counter-offensive in 1219 led by Louis of France, who had again taken the cross in November 1218 and remained allied to the surviving Montfortians, captured Marmande on the Garonne in June with Montfort's son and heir Amaury, before laying siege to Toulouse. However, on 1 August, Louis abandoned the struggle, returning to France, as one writer laconically and perhaps without irony remarked, 'after continuing his crusade for the required period of service'.[87] It is hard to see in this foray much more than Capetian flag waving to remind whichever side emerged triumphant of where the ultimate suzerainty lay.

Louis's withdrawal from Toulouse exposed the full weakness of the Montfortians, dependent on French royal indifference and a pope engaged in prosecuting the crusade in Egypt (1218–21). The main support came from the largely new southern episcopacy, who owed their places and revived finances to the crusade. Amaury of Montfort, lacking his father's ability, could do little to prevent the unravelling of Simon's achievement. The clerical tenth proposed in 1221 to assist him provoked fierce resistance.[88] By 1222, the year he died, Raymond VI had recovered most of his lands, mainly though the efforts of his son, who succeeded as Raymond VII (1222–49). Foix retained its independence. Even the Trencavel lands reverted to the control of Raymond (1209–47), son of the dispossessed Viscount Raymond Roger. A truce was agreed between Amaury of Montfort and Raymond VII in 1223. The following year Raymond entered the Monfortian stronghold of Carcassonne while Amaury resigned his claims to Louis of France, now Louis VIII. The Albigensian crusade seemed over and lost.

This did not suit Louis VIII, who saw Languedoc not only personally as unfinished business but as part of the wider problem of Capetian control of south-west France, the more urgent since the annexation of Poitou from the king of England in 1224 and the French failure to hold on to Gascony in 1225. Louis managed to get a papal legate to reject Raymond VII's attempts to get his titles recognized as legitimate at a council in Bourges in December 1225. Both sides prepared for war. Honorius III once more cranked up the machinery of the crusade at the king's behest; a new clerical tenth was authorized, to the dismay of the

French clergy.[89] Unlike his father, Louis had no qualms in embracing the status of *crucesignatus*. As his son Louis IX was to do to even greater effect, Louis sought to identify his kingship and dynasty with a holy mission, to the advantage as he saw it of both church and state. A pall of legitimacy was lent the new crusade by the undeniable recrudescence of heresy in Languedoc in the wake of the Montfortians' defeat. King Louis took the cross in January 1226 and marched south in June. Despite a long and costly siege of Avignon (10 June–9 September), which ended in a negotiated surrender, Louis's passage through Languedoc was largely unopposed. Although Raymond persisted in refusing homage, most lords submitted. Louis died on his way back north on 8 November, probably of dysentery, but this time a fortuitous death did not reverse the trend of events.

In a series of brutal campaigns in 1227 and 1228 led by Humbert of Beaujeu, backed by a nascent network of local Capetian administrators and agents, the annexation of Languedoc was completed. Politically, Raymond VII had nowhere to turn. In January 1229 he agreed terms at Meaux, ratified at Paris on 12 April, when the count underwent public penance in return for reconciliation with the church and his new overlord. The Treaty of Paris ended the Albigensian crusades.[90] Raymond retained some lands but crucially his inheritance was to pass on his death to his daughter Jeanne, who was to marry a Capetian prince. Languedoc's independence was ended. Despite rebellions by Raymond Trencavel in 1240 and Raymond VII himself in 1242, the decision of Meaux/Paris was not reversed. On Raymond's death in 1249, his lands passed to his son-in-law Alphonse of Poitiers, brother of Louis IX. When he and Raymond's daughter Jeanne died in 1271, Toulouse was united with the French crown. The Treaty of Paris had summed up the paradox of the Albigensian crusades. Ultimately of radical political effectiveness, in their prime declared objective they failed. At Paris in 1229, Raymond VII promised to prosecute heretics, precisely what his father had been accused of failing to do twenty years before.

AFTERMATH

With the Treaty of Paris the religious and political future of Languedoc was freed from the association with crusading. The revival of Catharism in the 1220s that coincided with the decline of Montfortian power was checked and reversed through the concerted efforts of the new mechanisms of the Inquisition.[91] Established from 1229, and spearheaded by the Dominicans, the Inquisition in Languedoc operated as a series of essentially *ad hoc* diocesan judicial inquiries. Although standard procedures of investigation, evidence, examination and sentencing were developed, the Inquisition did not become the sinister bureaucratic institution of repression of legend. Its lurid later reputation was largely a creation of the Spanish Inquisition of the late fifteenth and early sixteenth century and disapproving Protestant polemicists. The object of each Inquisition was, as its name suggested, to discover who were heretics and to eradicate disbelief by persuasion and reconciliation. Although the accused were prevented from knowing the identities of witnesses, they were permitted to mount a defence. Torture was rare and unsophisticated. Reason, not terror, was the inquisitors' weapon. A university was founded at Toulouse in 1229 to underpin the ideological basis of the Catholic mission. The combination of new pastoral methods; effective, professional preaching; the dissemination of the systematic moral theology of the schools; and the simplicity and directness of the friars who largely conducted the Inquisition combated Catharism at every level, intellectual, parochial and personal. The punishments reflected the purpose of evangelism. The vast majority of those found guilty of heresy received non-custodial penances. Contumacious or obstinate offenders could expect prison. Only a tiny minority of convicted heretics were handed to the secular authorities to be burnt at the stake. One calculation from hundreds of penalties imposed in mid-thirteenth century Languedoc estimated that death sentences made up 1 per cent, imprisonment 10–11 per cent; the rest lesser penances, including the compulsory wearing of a cross to denote a former heretic. Out of 930 sentences presided over by Bernard Gui, the Dominican inquisitor in Carcassonne from 1308 to 1323, author of a famous inquisitor's manual, made notorious by Umberto Eco's *Name of the Rose*, only forty-five carried the death penalty, less than 5 per cent.[92] Given the prevalence of capital punishment in other areas of justice, this may not appear especially brutal.

As between 1209 and 1229, the greatest violence was provoked by an alliance of religion and politics. The infamous burning of over 200 *perfecti* at the fall of Montségur to royal troops in March 1244, including Bertrand Marty, the Cathar bishop of Toulouse (1225–44), came in retaliation for the assassination of two chief inquisitors at Avignonet, twenty-five miles south-east of Toulouse, in May 1242. However, the context for the nine-month siege of Montségur was the rebellion of Raymond VII in 1242–3 in alliance with Henry III of England and dissident Poitevins. The protection afforded the Cathars by the lords of Montségur epitomized resistance to the new Capetian and Catholic order. The holocaust of March 1244 spoke not of the Inquisition but the methods inherited from Simon of Montfort.[93] The difference lay in the increasing inability of Catharism to sustain such losses to its institutional leadership. Here, in undermining the patronal organization and public networks of heresy, the crusade had contributed directly to the weakening, if not to the eradication, of the Cathars. After the bonfires and dispossessions of 1209–11, Catharism was denied open civil expression, forcing it on to the defensive. With the coalition of church and Capetian state, Cathars were under constant attack, as were their lay sympathizers and protectors. However popular Catharism had been, the decapitation of an effective diocesan structure ensured a slow decline, especially marked after 1250. The Cathars possessed less and less political, social or even ideological protection against the inquisitors and their ecclesiastical and secular allies. Furtive, beleaguered and increasingly seeming parochial, obscurantist and unfashionable, the failure of the brief revival in the Pyrenean foothills in the early fourteenth century to capture the support of the social elites sealed its fate. A flurry of inquisitorial action snuffed it out.[94] By the 1330s, Languedoc was free of organized Cathar heresy.

The political legacy of the Albigensian crusades was less equivocal than the religious, suitably for a series of military campaigns in which the secular repeatedly dominated the spiritual. This is not to decry the sincerity of those who saw themselves as soldiers of Christ, nor of those laymen and clerks who genuinely feared the cancerous growth of heresy. However, it remains inescapable that the Albigensian crusades failed to destroy heresy while succeeding in annexing Languedoc to the Capetian dynasty. This may not have been the intention of the crusaders of 1209, yet Innocent III had persistently tried to involve Philip II, recognizing the force of using a strong state to recreate a strong church. It is equally apparent that this new order established the necessary conditions in which heresy could be destroyed. To the committed, this may mitigate the religious failure of the Albigensian crusades.

The crusades did not destroy a region. The economy of Languedoc proved very resilient.[95] Once the fighting was ended, prosperity returned. What was lost was religious and political pluralism, always hard to sustain, not just in thirteenth-century Europe. The career of Oliver, heir to the Corbières lordship of Termes, famously charted the process.[96] Termes had been a Cathar centre lost to the crusaders in 1210. By the early 1220s, Oliver had regained it after submitting to Capetian authority in 1219. However, throughout the 1220s, Oliver supported Languedoc resistance, first Raymond Trencavel, then, after 1226, Raymond VII of Toulouse, while retaining close links with Cathar *perfecti*. Despite losing Termes and being forced to renew fealty to the French king in 1228, Oliver continued to oppose the new regime and the Inquisition from his vertiginous stronghold of Queribus, north of Perpignan, which became a refuge for Cathars and other political dissidents. After joining the revolts of 1240 and 1242, Oliver was excommunicated. Reconciliation with the Capetian authorities ironically only came with his agreement in 1247 to join Louis IX's crusade to Egypt. Many Languedoc rebels, including Raymond VII, found the Holy Land crusade imposed as a penance. Oliver seems to have taken to it. He stayed east until 1255 and returned to Outremer in 1264, 1267–70 and, in 1273–4, as commander of the French garrison at Acre, where he died in 1274. The *quid pro quo* for his service was the return of lands in Languedoc and his and his family's absolute loyalty and orthodoxy: no more independence in politics or religion. Oliver's late devotion to holy war suggests a fluid but serious piety grounded in the reality of temporal opportunities. Not a pacifist, he serially supported two highly contrasting strands of thirteenth-century belief, Catharism and crusade, each determined by conflicting political allegiance but indicating that the contending ideologies reflected a shared cultural desire for active religious purity.

Oliver was not alone among Cathar sympathizers or even *credentes* in taking the cross as a positive sign of reconciliation with the church.

However, such a path was denied the hapless Raymond VI, one of the most excommunicated men of the middle ages. His fate was to find himself in an impossible position. Unable to mount effective diplomatic or military resistance to his enemies, neither could he achieve what they asked of him even if he had been disposed to do so. The contrast with his father Raymond V's attempt to suppress the Cathars in 1179 probably lay not with Raymond VI's personal religious tastes; he was an active patron of the Hospitallers. Rather, by his accession in 1194, the Cathars had become too entrenched socially as well as religiously. Short of a disruptive and devastating conquest of his own lands, for which he had neither the appetite nor the resources, it is hard to see what Raymond could have done to appease Innocent III's implacable legates and their military enforcer Montfort, who, in any case, was after Raymond's lands. The personal bitterness directed at Raymond is difficult to understand; his iconic significance less so. He was the epitome of the *fautor*, the heretic's accomplice. As such, there appeared no forgiveness, even beyond the grave. In 1222, Raymond had died technically excommunicate, prevented by his final stroke from making oral confession to the abbot of St Sernin.[97] His body, covered in a pall provided by the Hospitallers, was refused burial. Despite repeated appeals by his son and numerous ecclesiastical inquiries, his coffin remained unburied in the precincts of the Hospitaller house in Toulouse, where it was still to be seen over a century later, the shrouded body half-eaten by rats. By 1515, the worm-ridden coffin had collapsed in pieces and the bones had gone, except for the skull. This was kept by the Hospitallers, who, as late as the 1690s, used to show it off to the morbid and the curious.[98] There was something appropriate in this exhibition of antiquarian bad taste. The gruesome relic represented both the eternal vengeance of a church so badly rattled that it could not forgive or forget and the only too obvious corruption of the flesh. A Cathar might have drawn a succinct moral.

19

The Fifth Crusade 1213–21

Writing in an optimistic mood in 1208 to the crusade enthusiast Duke Leopold VI of Austria, Innocent III characterized holy war as an imitation of Christ, an act of unconditional devotion. In recognition of this he sent Leopold a cloth cross and letters conveying the plenary indulgence.[1] This innocuous exchange encapsulated the distinctive elements of Innocent III's crusade policy: theological precept, moral conviction, papal authority, pastoral care, administrative control and bureaucratic precision. The developments set in train by the Third Crusade reached new levels of thoroughness as Innocent sought to accomplish what he had failed to achieve in 1202–4, the destruction of Ayyubid Egypt, the recovery of Jerusalem and the spiritual renewal of Christendom. To this end, the so-called Fifth Crusade, planned in 1213, launched in 1215 and fought in a series of running expeditions between 1217 and 1229, marked the climax in papal cooperation with secular power. Innocent is often depicted as the most successful promoter of papal monarchism, wishing to control, even exclude, lay domination in his crusading policy after the debacle of 1202–4. It is frequently asserted that the Fifth Crusade represented the church's greatest and last serious attempt to run a holy war though its own leadership. Yet although the last acts of the Fifth Crusade were conducted in a hail of mutual recrimination and mistrust between popes and the emperor, Frederick II, leading to the bizarre, but not entirely unprecedented, scene in 1228 of a Holy Land crusade under an excommunicated leader, as with the Albigensian wars, Innocent III and his successor Honorius III based their policy on trying to obtain the cooperation and support of lay monarchs. The Fifth Crusade was intended to marry the universal ambitions of the papacy with the imperialism of the Hohenstaufen rulers of Germany and southern Italy. Innocent's involvement of the young Frederick II opened the prospect of a new order in Christendom. A mutually advantageous acceptance of the respective authority of pope and emperor would be signalled by the fulfilment of the eastern aspirations of Conrad III, Frederick I and Henry VI no less than those of Urban II, Eugenius III or Gregory VIII. The failure of the enterprise, and the reciprocal demonization that dominated papal-Hohenstaufen relations for the subsequent fifty years, obscured this central feature of Innocent's conception. If historical turning points exist, the Fifth Crusade was one; the direction of international high politics could have been set on a very different course.[2]

The organization and conduct of the Fifth Crusade witnessed growing bureaucracy. In concert with developments in secular government and law, increasingly the crusade was becoming a written phenomenon.[3] Preachers received licences and based their sermons on circulated papal bulls. Recruitment and finance was sustained by central and local record keeping, lists of *crucesignati*, accounts of moneys raised and expended, and written authorization for individuals' legal and fiscal privileges. While the creation of new technologies of record may not coincide with changes in what is being recorded, the weight of writing indicated the growing institutionalization of crusading as a social and religious activity.

THE CHILDREN'S CRUSADE OF 1212

Crusade preaching, taxation and liturgical propaganda reached an extended audience beyond the ranks of those who were able to join up: the poor, the old, the landless, the rootless and the young, all in their ways disenfranchised from direct involvement in the increasingly highly structured armies of the cross. The broader social and religious demands of crusading stimulated engagement in what would later be described as civil society, as observers, commentators, critics and participants, by sections of the community not necessarily included in the ruling hierarchies. The Albigensian crusades were attended by so-called *ribaldi*, low-born camp followers, as well as local peasants.[4] The organization of some contingents, such as the fleets from northern European waters, revolved around sworn communes, wide consultation across social groups and a measure of general debate, even occasionally, as at fraught moments during the Fourth Crusade, public consent.[5] The collective commitment to the crusade evinced in communal ceremonies of dedication, in cities from London to Cologne to Venice, was matched by the development of regular parochial rituals of devotion and support. Taking the cross, like sermons, assumed the witness of congregations. Innocent III's offer of the indulgence to those not themselves soldiers of the cross and the spread of crusade taxation further lent the *negotium sanctum* a genuinely popular, public dimension. Political and social anxieties could be articulated through support for the transcendent cause of the Holy Land by groups habitually excluded, ignored, marginalized or simply disorganized by virtue of low material status. An extraordinary demonstration of this penetration of the crusade into wider political consciousness and communal action came with the phenomenon known as the Children's Crusade.[6]

In the winter and spring of 1211–12, Innocent III's habitual concerns at the sinfulness of the faithful, the heretics in Languedoc, the Moors in Spain and the precarious plight of Outremer were focused by papal decree and battalions of preachers on just two: the Albigensian crusades and the advances of the Almohads of north Africa in the Iberian peninsula. An intensive recruiting campaign for the Languedoc war in the Rhineland and northern France was led by James of Vitry and Archdeacon William of Paris, Simon of Montfort's siege expert.[7] At the same time, Almohad victories in the autumn of 1211 prompted Innocent III to appeal for aid for the Christians in Spain, instituting a series of special penitential processions to be held in mid May. The impression of heightened crisis, reinforced by repeated calls for Apostolic simplicity and active penance, through taking the cross or collective liturgical contrition, stimulated unlicensed popular response. In at least two regions this coalesced into demonstrations of public support for the defence of Christendom from those not normally associated with leadership of formal crusading.

In the spring and summer of 1212, crowds of penitents assembled in the Low Countries, the Rhineland and northern France, areas heavily evangelized for the crusade. They called for an amendment of life and, in places, the liberation of the Holy Land. Some contingents apparently crossed the Alps into Italy in search of transport to the Levant. Details of intentions varied locally, but all these marches were seen to have been inspired in part by the rumours of the threats to Christendom, the dissemination of a redemptive theology emphasizing the crusade as a collective penitential act and the failure of the leaders of society to perform their obligations on either count. The most striking feature of these marches lay in that they were conducted by '*pueri*', literally children. In fact, these '*pueri*' may have been less juvenile than the name implied. To a Cologne chronicler, who may be reporting eyewitness memories, the *pueri* 'ranged in age from six years to full maturity'.[8] Norman and Alpine monks recorded that the marchers were adolescents and old people.[9] Accounts indicated that participants came from outside the usual hierarchies of social power – youths, girls, the unmarried, sometimes excluding even widows – or economic status: shepherds, ploughmen, carters, agricultural workers and rural artisans without a settled stake in land or community, rootless and mobile. Signs of anti-clericalism and the absence of clerical leadership accentuated this sense of social exclusion. Yet despite the absence of ecclesiastical authority, there was little church condemnation. The popular movements of 1212 demonstrated the success of Innocent's evangelism. The marches sprang from communal anxiety, not specific social or economic hardship. Dissatisfaction with the inability of the leaders of the social hierarchy to secure victory in Spain, Languedoc or Palestine may have coincided with a more diffuse trend whereby rural populations were attracted to towns, especially at a time of increasing demographic pressure in the countryside. Yet the immediate impulse appeared to be religious.

The recorded chronology of events is confusing. There were two distinct areas of enthusiasm, one in northern France, south-west of Paris, the other in the Low Countries and the Rhineland. From chronicle accounts it is possible to argue that the Ile de France marchers combined with those from the Rhineland, or, less likely, that the Rhinelanders joined the French uprising or that the two movements remained separate, coinciding only in timing. According to the Cologne chronicler, around Easter (25 March) and Whitsun (13 May) 1212 large processions of youths from the traditional crusade recruiting grounds of the Rhineland, the Netherlands, north-eastern France and western Germany, defying family and friends, began to move in the general direction of Italy. Although some groups assembled in Lorraine, a number being stopped at Metz, the main body gathered at Cologne, where a leader emerged called Nicholas, a youth from the surrounding countryside. As reported, their declared purpose was the relief of the Holy Land. A contingent of crusaders from Cologne under the provost of the cathedral had joined Simon of Montfort in Languedoc in April that year, but this commitment had been too restricted in scope to satisfy the spiritual expectations aroused by the attendant evangelizing.[10] Instead, the failure of the experienced, rich and proud (an apparent reference to the Fourth Crusade) was to be redeemed by the innocent, pure and humble. Some of the German marchers adopted the pilgrim's scrip and staff as well as the cross. Their leader, Nicholas, was remembered as carrying a tau cross, a symbol elsewhere associated with Francis of Assisi and his dynamic brand of poverty and humility.

The German processions were reported to have assembled at Speyer on 25 July 1212 before heading south through Alsace to the Alpine passes, probably the St Gotthard or the Simplon, before arriving at Piacenza on 20 August. This sequence of events fits badly with the Cologne chronicle's dating of the beginning of the movement to March, April and May. Other accounts trace marchers at Liège and Trier earlier in July, which might find confirmation in the Cologne writer's mention of trouble at Metz. Some modern historians have tried to combine the Lorraine, Netherlands and Rhineland crusaders as mustering together at Speyer, while others have explained the Lorraine marchers as coming from further west, from the uprising in northern France.[11] There, the link between the official programme of special penitential processions appeared even more specific. Here the leader who emerged from the crowd, Stephen from Cloyes, near Vendôme, was a shepherd, a highly symbolic occupation in the context of Christian populist fundamentalism. The area of enthusiasm, the Dunois, Chartrain and Ile de France, like the Rhineland, had recently witnessed recruitment for the Albigensian war. In June 1212, Stephen led groups of penitents – boys, girls, youths, old men – to St Denis near Paris, coinciding with the annual Lendit Fair, the high point of the abbey's pilgrim and commercial calendar. Stephen's followers carried crosses and banners, the trappings of liturgy, while chanting 'Lord God, exalt Christianity! Lord God, restore to us the True Cross!' echoing papal preaching.[12] Some of Stephen's companions may have been recruited for the Albigensian war, but there is no exactly contemporary evidence linking his march with the recovery of the Holy Land or the simultaneous German enterprise. If the Cologne chronicle's dating is accepted, then it is possible that rumours of the marches in the Rhineland provoked emulation in northern France. If the Lorraine and Speyer July dates reflect the chronology of the eastern expedition, then the inspiration, and even reinforcements, may have travelled in the opposite direction.

The fate of those penitents and crusaders who reached the Mediterranean is similarly clouded, not least by later lurid romantic fantasies. The German bands, once in Italy, dispersed. Some may have reached Genoa, or even Brindisi and Marseilles. Others – a handful of the many thousands who set out – returned home. Stories circulated that some embarked for the east while others had been sold into slavery or worse. There is no convincing evidence of the French marchers making a separate journey to the Mediterranean ports. All soon vanish from the record, leaving only startled memories or eccentric morality tales. Unlike similar subsequent popular uprisings associated with crusading, these outbursts left no trace in the surviving papal registers. However, whatever its fate, the so-called Children's Crusade reveals a popular and ordered reaction by sections of the usually silent public, in this case it seems predominantly rural, to the propagandizing of the church authorities. This was no outpouring of inchoate mass hysteria. The zeal may have been untempered by official direction. Ecclesiastical unease was evident. Yet few demonstrations of the effectiveness of the thirteenth-century church's redemptive message could have been more potent. The events of 1212 reveal the success of Innocent's policy of using crusade preaching and ceremonial to promote reformist as well as militant messages. The depiction of those involved as shepherds or *pueri* captured the preachers' insistence on a return to apostolic simplicity, free from the snares and obligations of materialism. Like the friars who were soon to become the shock troops of church evangelism, the marchers in 1212 were mendicants. Initially at least, some clerical observers were distinctly sympathetic to the marchers' aspirations. The extent and potential of spiritual excitement throughout the wider Christian public exposed in 1212 may have encouraged Innocent to launch a new general crusade to the Holy Land the following year. One Alpine monastery preserved an apt, if possibly *ben trovato*, tradition that Nicholas of Cologne himself joined this new expedition and found himself a few years later facing the infidel at Damietta on the Nile.[13]

SUMMONING THE NEW CRUSADE 1213–15

The papal encyclical *Quia Maior* of April 1213, the conciliar decree *Ad Liberandam* of November 1215 and the attendant papal instructions to preachers, legates and tax collectors set in motion a vast new enterprise to recover Jerusalem while establishing rhetorical, legal, fiscal, liturgical and administrative norms of official crusading for the next century and a half. The circumstances seemed propitious; the planning meticulous. In July 1212, the Almohads had been destroyed at the battle of Las Navas de Tolosa. Simon of Montfort, after successfully completing his annexation of the Trencavel lands in Languedoc in 1211, had secured control of most of the Toulousain. With the political objectives of the anti-heresy war seemingly achieved or even exceeded, Innocent III suspended that crusade in January 1213.[14] By contrast, in Outremer, the truce between the Franks and Sultan al-Adil of Egypt, renewed in 1211 and due to expire in 1217, barely concealed the Christians' weakness, penned up in a few northern Syrian enclaves. John of Brienne, king of Jerusalem, regent for his infant daughter Queen Isabella, doubted that the truce would hold and urged a new crusade. While al-Adil showed no willingness to provoke a western challenge, the recent fortification of Mt Tabor in western Galilee by his son, al Mu 'azzam of Damascus, posed a potential threat to Acre and the Franks' precarious presence on its surrounding plain. Given western sensitivities, it took little to arouse a Holy Land scare. Mt Tabor, 'where Christ revealed to his disciples a vision of his future glory', supplied the pope with a *casus belli*.[15]

The secular politics of western Christendom provided an equal, if riskier, opportunity. The German succession remained in dispute between the fading former papal protégé Otto IV and the then pope's new favourite, Frederick of Hohenstaufen, son of Henry VI. Their struggle reverberated across Germany and Italy, subsuming and focusing myriad local rivalries and political contests. The consequences of Simon of Montfort's conquests in Languedoc had created a whole class of dispossessed nobles as well as a legion of angry, suspicious or fearful neighbours, beginning with Peter of Aragon. England had been under a papal interdict since 1208 over King John's refusal to accept Innocent's nominee Stephen Langton as archbishop of Canterbury. Now, faced by an assassination plot in 1212, hints of a papal deposition and French preparations for invasion, John was eager to reach a settlement that would allow him to take the offensive to recover his lost French lands. Modern historians have commonly assumed that the distractions of these warring monarchs allowed Innocent III to fashion the crusade to his own design. Yet, so far from regarding these divisions as a hindrance, Innocent exploited them as an opportunity. He began *Quia Maior* by insisting that the transcendent cause of the Holy Land demanded the active support of all Christian faithful on pain of damnation. This required a decisive turning away from material concerns to follow Christ. To assist such a commitment, the goods and property of *crucesignati* would receive the protection of the church, thus reinforcing the moral imperative to resolve temporal conflicts with practical security. Innocent placed the resolution of civil conflict at the heart of the preaching of the new crusade. Crusading had traditionally been associated with management of disputes, witnessed by the persistent links with the Peace and Truce of God throughout the twelfth century. It provided a context within which disputing parties could resolve their differences without loss of face or advantage, as, notoriously, between the Angevins and Philip II. Innocent, with characteristic intellectual clarity, administrative verve, and the experience of fifteen years as pope, now used this passive tool as a weapon to impose ecclesiastical arbitration on material as well as spiritual problems. This was no accident, rather a recognized property of crusading in the academic circle around the pope. One of the leading preachers of the Fifth Crusade, the Englishman Robert of Courçon, legate to France from 1213, explained in an academic treatise how 'recently' a number of barons had used the crusade to remove themselves from an awkward choice of rebellion or disinheritance, probably a reference to the counts of Flanders, Blois and Perche after the collapse of their alliance with Richard I against their lord Philip II in 1199.[16]

Quia Maior established a comprehensive practical as well as religious framework for a new crusade. After presenting the universal moral obligation, the continuing scandal of Christians in Muslim captivity and the immediate crisis threatening the Holy Land, the pope announced an unequivocal plenary indulgence for all who took the cross and served or sent proxies at their own expense and to the proxies themselves: 'full forgiveness of their sins of which they make truthful oral confession with contrite hearts truly repented of'. Familiar temporal privileges were rehearsed: ecclesiastical protection of crusaders' property; moratorium on debts to Christians and their cancellation if owed to Jews. Citing his authority to 'speak as Vicar of Christ for Christ', Innocent instructed the clergy, civil communities and non-crusading lay magnates to supply troops for three years out of their resources and demanded naval help from maritime cities. The pope promised that he would also contribute. Income from clerical benefices could be pledged for three years. Trade with Muslims was banned, as was consorting with pirates. The efficacy of the practical rested on the penitential. Special monthly processions were to be accompanied by the preaching of the cross. Prayers for the Holy Land were to be supported by fasting and almsgiving with special chests placed in churches to receive pious donations. A new intercession was to be inserted in the mass. More controversial, but no less pragmatic, was Innocent's invitation 'that anyone who wishes, except those bound by religious profession, may take the cross in such a way that his vow may be commuted [i.e. replaced by another penance], redeemed [i.e. dispensed in return for a cash payment equivalent to the cost of crusading] or deferred by apostolic mandate when urgent or evident expediency demands it'. Poverty, incapacity, illness, age, gender or legitimate prior calls no longer prevented the enjoyment of crusade indulgence, a measure at once reducing the delays in checking suitability of putative *crucesignati* and increasing their numbers and social range. To focus attention and resources on the Holy Land expedition, Innocent cancelled the crusade indulgences for those fighting the Moors in Spain or the heretics in Languedoc who came from outside those regions. Knowing from the experience of the previous quarter of a century how long recruitment could take, Innocent preferred to wait until recruits had taken the cross before setting a deadline for the crusade muster.

Quia Maior operated within a wider policy. Simultaneously, Innocent summoned a general council of the church to meet in 1215 to discuss church reform and the crusade, and instituted elaborate systems to preach the cross. Papal control was central. The pope himself took the lead in Italy. Legates were appointed for France and Scandinavia. In Hungary, each bishop was authorized to preach the cross. Elsewhere, panels with legatine powers were established in every province to delegate the work of recruiting to deputies. Preachers were instructed to use the details of *Quia Maior* as the basis of their message. To avoid the controversy that swamped Fulk of Neuilly before the Fourth Crusade, they were to refuse money for themselves and, reminiscent of the bishop of Osma and Dominic Guzman in Languedoc, to travel modestly and set a good example by sober behaviour. On the ground, preachers kept written records of those they recruited and were ordered by the pope to deposit any crusade donations with local religious houses before rendering annual returns to the papal Curia so Innocent could assess the progress of the vast operation.[17] The pope maintained close scrutiny over his agents across Europe. To the dean of Speyer's request for clarification, Innocent reiterated the need to deflect Languedoc crusaders to the Holy Land, to allow recruits to take the cross despite their wives' opposition, and to follow the encyclical's radical extension of vow redemption and commutation, which was clearly arousing some concern. At his request, Bishop Conrad of Regensberg was allowed a grander entourage than Innocent had proposed. He was also permitted to absolve certain categories of criminals provided they took the cross. The abbot of Rommersdorf in Austria compiled a collection of *Quia Maior* and other papal letters as a reference tool while other preachers, such as James of Vitry, descanted on Innocent's themes.[18]

While the preaching campaign began, Innocent prepared the diplomatic ground, once more aided by events. John of England's submission to the pope in 1213, the defeat of his allies by Philip II of France at Bouvines in 1214 and the subsequent English civil war prompted the king to take the cross on Ash Wednesday (4 March) 1215, using his new status in *Magna Carta* three months later to postpone settling disputed judgements from his predecessors' reigns.[19] John's intentions probably owed more to politics than penance, adopting the cross may have been an attempt to facilitate a settlement with his enemies, many of whom were or were about to become *crucesignati*. The commitment to the crusade among the English propertied classes reached levels similar to the Third Crusade. The context of civil war also influenced Frederick II of Germany and Sicily's decision to take the cross in the same year, a move encouraged by papal agents now actively supporting his cause.[20] Further east, Leopold VI of Austria and King Andrew of Hungary were already *crucesignati*. Such was his determination to involve the whole of Christendom, Innocent even called on the Venetians to honour their still unfulfilled and unabsolved crusade vow of 1202.[21]

The array of monarchs, princes and cities added to a sense of united purpose when the 1,300 ecclesiastical delegates from all parts of Latin Christendom from the Atlantic to Syria met at the Lateran Palace in Rome in November 1215. These included most of those appointed to preach the cross, the Latin Patriarchs of Constantinople and Jerusalem, and representatives from the Maronite church in Lebanon (in communion with Rome since 1181) and of the Melkite (i.e. Syrian and Egyptian Greek Orthodox) archbishop of Alexandria, with whom the pope had maintained a regular correspondence over the conditions of Frankish prisoners in Egypt.[22] The business of the council was Christian renewal, reform and the crusade, regarded by Innocent as different aspects of the same religious enterprise. The decisions concerning the crusade suggest some hard bargaining, with the pope not necessarily getting his way. Innocent's defence of Raymond VI of Toulouse failed to convince the council, who condemned the count in favour of Simon of Montfort, whose activities had long since given the pope pause. More general papal anxieties over the legal proprieties of the war against heretics were seemingly brushed aside in the council's third decree, which established their canonical legitimacy as attracting the equivalent indulgences and privileges 'as is granted to those who go to the aid of the Holy Land'.[23] This may mark a victory for the bellicose French hierarchy, which had consistently been more robust in prosecuting the Languedoc campaigns than the more legally fastidious pope. The reverse may have been true regarding the plans for the Holy Land crusade, with the implementation of the provisions in *Quia Maior* regarding vow redemptions, debt and tax exemption causing disquiet in French official circles as being too radical.

The council's final decree (no. 71), *Ad Liberandam*, largely endorsed *Quia Maior* but with additions, modifications and omissions.[24] It established the 'sanctum propositum', the 'negotium Jesu Christi' in canon law. After two years of active preaching and recruitment, the tone was urgent. The muster was fixed for June 1217, significantly in the ports of the Sicilian *regno*, the lands of the new papal protégé and imperial candidate Frederick II. For those intending to take a land route, a legate would be appointed. Clerics were encouraged to participate and allowed to fund themselves from their benefices. The pope contributed 30,000 pounds and a ship for the contingent from the city of Rome. Tax exemption was clarified, although behind the scenes concessions may have been made to Philip II, who already in March 1215 had published an ordinance restricting crusaders' legal immunities in accordance with French customs.[25] The direct encouragement to indiscriminate adoption of the cross and vow redemption, another bone of contention, was dropped, although not explicitly contradicted, a convenient obfuscation.[26] Proportionate indulgences for 'aid' remained. Tournaments were banned for three years and a general Peace, backed by the threat of excommunication, was instituted for four years.

By far the most important innovation involved the imposition of a tax of a twentieth on ecclesiastical incomes for three years. Perhaps as a *quid pro quo*, the pope and cardinals agreed to pay a tenth. Innocent's earlier attempt to tax the church on papal authority in 1199 had failed. Now, to ensure compliance, the explicit approval of the general council, 'sacro concilio approbante', was invoked, in the conciliar decree and in every letter sent out concerning the tax's collection.[27] Both Roman law and political custom across Europe, as, famously, in Clauses 12 and 14 of *Magna Carta* five months earlier, indicated the importance of representative consent for extraordinary fiscal burdens.[28] To effect his financial and legal arrangements, Innocent was simply bowing to contemporary constitutionalism to bind all parties more absolutely than any unilateral recourse to papal absolutism. Clerical crusade taxation combined with the extension of full and proportionate indulgences redeemable by material and cash contributions, the detailed provision for alms and donations, and the beginnings of an international ecclesiastical network of collection and audit, to transform the way crusades operated. All subsequent major crusading enterprises sought similar financial provision, especially ecclesiastical taxes, often to the consternation of local churchmen. The translation of the ideology of inclusive obligation to the cause of the Lord's War into cash deposits, while arousing the cynicism of some, allowed for more central control of operations by crusade commanders with access to these funds. This made crusading attractive to magnates and kings while encouraging greater professionalism in recruitment, funding and military organization. Immediately after the Lateran Council, the fiscal scheme lent a new coherence to fundraising and papal control. In law, finance and management, Innocent left an indelible imprint on the business of the cross.

RAISING CRUSADERS

By the time *Ad Liberandam* received the council's approval on 14 December 1215, preaching and recruitment had been going for over two years. It was to continue intensively for another six years then, more sporadically, for at least a further six. The undertaking was massive, in every province and diocese from Scotland to France to Sweden to Hungary to the Mediterranean and even Acre itself, whose new bishop James of Vitry was despatched east in 1216 to drum up local support. It is the first such campaign that has left detailed evidence of every stage of its operation: the reception and dissemination of papal letters; chronicle and personal accounts of the preaching and its effect; the contents of sermons; the mechanics of spreading propaganda between preachers; accounts of money raised and spent. All indicates the grandeur of Innocent's design. However, its success depended on innumerable local encounters and individual responses.

The success of crusade preaching depended on skilful manipulation of listeners' aural, intellectual, emotional and visual perceptions. Evidence from the preaching tours after 1213 shows few opportunities were missed to provide the most receptive circumstances for the papal message. Oliver, *scholasticus* (i.e. teacher) at the cathedral school at Cologne, later bishop of Paderborn, recorded his experiences preaching the cross to Netherlanders in 1214.[29] At the village of Bedum in northern Frisia he preached after mass to a crowd that overflowed the church into the fields outside, a familiar literary and possibly actual scene. His text, Galatians 6:14 ('God forbid that I should glory, save in the cross of our Lord Jesus Christ') exploited the rhetoric of the cross and Christ Crucified in *Quia Maior*, the language of its special crusade prayer and the liturgy of the Eucharist to emphasize penance, obligation, vocation. On cue, so Oliver reported, a vision of three crosses appeared on the sky, two empty, the one in the centre bearing the image of the crucified Christ. Witnesses, apparently about a hundred drawn from all social and age groups, literally saw the point. One recognized the crosses as predicting the recapture of the Holy Land. Another, who had been following Oliver's preaching tour for some time, was finally persuaded by this visible evidence to take the cross. Other similar apparitions in Frisia confirmed the message of Bedum. Such celestial manifestations were increasingly common in accounts of crusade preaching and usually credited, as here, with inspiring heavy recruitment. In the Cologne region, the success of John of Xanten was directly attributed to such phenomena.[30] The link between cloud-gazing and the spoken message, in sermon and liturgy, was clear. At Bedum, Oliver recorded, the vision lasted for as long as it took to sing mass. However the effect was contrived during actual sermons, news of such wonders spread by letter to fellow preachers and, from them, to later chronicle descriptions.

Other techniques included prophecy. One circulated after the accession of Honorius III as pope in 1216 told of how in 1187 the future pope had been apprised by a mysterious old man, later presumed to be St Peter, that Jerusalem would be regained during his pontificate.[31] This clutching at straws seemed to provide a necessary adjunct to the official programme of evangelical preaching that the abbot of Rommersdorf kept in his letter book. The use of the supernatural reflected the context of the preaching. In Frisia and the Rhineland in 1214 the emphasis lay on collective, public visions, with reports careful to record details of time and place. A decade later, a mission to Marseilles under the provost of Arles, which claimed to have enlisted 30,000 citizens for the cross, was accompanied by a series of private miracles and personal visions. Women in ecstatic trances saw 'many secrets of the cross'.[32] Although numerous anecdotes favoured by crusade preachers or poets cast women more often as obstacles to male recruitment, either as wives or lovers, female commitment could be presented as further evidence of universal appeal. At Genoa in the autumn of 1216 James of Vitry managed to attract large numbers of noblewomen to take the cross as a prelude to enlisting their husbands.[33] At Genoa and Marseilles, the preachers were careful to publicize their experiences and to establish that their crusade work formed part of a more general campaign to assert orthodoxy.

The wider political dimensions of the recruitment campaign emphasized the resolution of conflict. Just as in Marseilles, where reception of the crusade acted as a ritual of reconciliation between the church and a city under the ban of excommunication, so Oliver of Paderborn's tour of western Germany and Netherlands seemed to be aimed at areas supportive of Otto IV, even though the crusade was sponsored by Hohenstaufen partisans such as the Fourth Crusade veteran Bishop Conrad of Halberstadt, as well as by Frederick II himself. James of Vitry's preaching in Genoa was aimed at securing peace between the city and its enemies. Between 1214 and 1219, disputing factions within Bologna were drawn together to sponsor and join a crusade contingent. Similar procedures characterized the activities of crusade preachers across Tuscany and northern Italy, led, from 1217, by Cardinal Ugolino of Ostia, the future Pope Gregory IX. He helped engineer pacification of disputes at Lucca, Pisa, Padua, Pistoia, Genoa, Bologna and Venice. By 1221, armed with money from the clerical twentieth, Ugolino was easing his diplomatic path with grants of funds to mercenaries for the eastern enterprise as well as *crucesignati*, a distinction that reflected the changes wrought in crusade recruitment by the relaxation of conditions for taking the cross and the arrangements for central church funding.[34] More prominently, Robert of Courçon, crusade legate in France from 1213, attempted, without success, to resolve the Anglo-French conflict for the sake of the Holy Land. While managing to recruit a few magnates, Robert failed prevent the campaigns in northern France of 1214, which ended in the defeat of King John, or the French invasion of England in 1216–17. John's adoption of the cross in March 1215 and Prince Louis of France's crusading jaunt to Languedoc that spring owed nothing to Robert's efforts.

These different aspects of the function and conduct of crusade preaching and recruitment were reinforced by the sermons' contents. Playing on the mutually supporting emotions generated by the plight of the Holy Land, personal penitence, corporate guilt and communal anger, preachers' *exempla* – uplifting anecdotes – were crafted to match theology and recruitment by encapsulating common assumptions, anxieties and expectations. According to the collection of preaching materials assembled during the raising of the Fifth Crusade in England, known as the *Ordinatio de predicatione Sancti Crucis*, *exempla* were designed to attract attention, prevent boredom, inspire contrition and encourage the rejection of earthly vanities.[35] Their form may have been deliberately demotic, punchy vignettes in the French vernacular in contrast to the Latin meditations on the figure of Christ Crucified that comprised the bulk of the *Ordinatio*. While much of the text explains the significance of the cross and the requirement on the faithful to imitate and follow Christ, a section, 'The call (or Vocation) of men to the cross', uses repeated refrains and the *exempla* to transmit the message to the audience's memory and arouse immediate engagement through the frisson of almost trance-like emotion, a sort of flexible liturgy. Many *exempla* involved crusade heroes and heroics, stressing the heavenly reward for those who died. Other anxieties concerning the process of becoming a *crucesignatus* were addressed: family pressure, difficulty with obstructive spouses, the pain of leaving children, the value of the indulgence. The two strands, heroic and domestic, signified the double battle waged by the *crucesignatus*, against the enemy within – doubt, luxury, sin, the devil – and the enemy without, the Saracen. While some anecdotes did the rounds of crusade preachers, assuming common currency, others attempted to explain the theology of crusading with more local resonance. The divine guarantee to *crucesignati* was confirmed 'as if by charter', a familiar legal image to the property owners of western Europe.[36] One rather charming *exemplum*, recorded after the Fifth Crusade, was aimed at the sort of Netherlandish audience to whom Oliver of Paderborn preached. Just as people in Flanders pole-vaulted over small canals, so the crusade indulgence allowed *crucesignati* to pole-vault across purgatory.[37] Elsewhere, gender resistance to crusading was addressed in stories of the consequences – uniformly dire – of women obstructing their spouses from taking the cross, just as later in the century more sympathetic accounts of the involvement of the Virgin Mary and miracles of the Holy Blood were thought to encourage female support. Accounts of local heroes and their martyr's deaths spoke directly to the practical fears of potential *crucesignati* as well as to their wider patterns of devotion and belief.

Tapping into popular religious enthusiasm and anxieties at the same time as offering social respectability, the patronage of the church and money appeared to be highly successful. Oliver of Paderborn asserts that his labours among the coastal settlements and islands of the Netherlands netted at least 15,000 fighters, who, with the Rhineland recruits, required a fleet of 300 ships to carry them east. Such a prominent and potentially disruptive church enterprise inevitably did not pass without controversy. In France, the activities of Robert of Courçon ran foul of royal interests and magnates' rights. Official apologists criticized the whole approach to vow redemption and commutation inaugurated by *Quia Maior*, a hostility that may have contributed to the toning down of such provisions in the crusade conciliar decree in 1215.[38] Another consequence was possibly less predictable. The wide authority delegated to regional agents allowed for highly devolved recruitment. Despite Innocent III's conciliar proclamation in November 1215 that the expedition should be prepared to depart on 1 June 1217 from the ports of southern Italy and Sicily, no mechanisms were devised to coordinate the gathering of so many autonomous local, regional or national groups. Innocent knew from his experiences of 1198–1202 and memories of 1187–90 how long a major eastern expedition could take to assemble, so his deliberately long preparation period of four years was prudent. However, the pope's and the council's failure to address the issue of unified leadership and planning of the sort seen in 1146–7, 1188–90, 1201–3 and even 1095–6, bequeathed a distinctive character to the Fifth Crusade, at once universal and endemically fissiparous. The scope of papal centralization grated with the complexity of its own devolved operation, producing damaging and potentially fatal political weakness. In the very size and ambition of the project lay the seeds of its failure.

By contrast, too, with previous mass expeditions, the Fifth Crusade was not dominated by recruits from the kingdom of France. Many important French magnates took the cross, including the dukes of Burgundy and Brabant and the counts of Bar, la Marche and Nevers, the last a veteran of the Languedoc wars. Recruitment from eastern France and Champagne, traditional areas of crusade enthusiasm, appeared brisk, even though it was complicated in Champagne by becoming entangled in a protracted succession dispute. Anecdotal evidence indicated large-scale adoption of the cross from all sections of society in town and country. However, the Albigensian adventure and Prince Louis's invasion of England in 1216–17 offered alternative occupation, even to *crucesignati* waiting to go east. At the same time, a combination of Robert of Courçon's wider puritanical agenda and the legal and fiscal implications of the papal arrangements aroused conflicting emotions, including resistance. Philip II and some leading nobles objected to what they regarded as papal interference in French customs and the prohibitions on usury loudly endorsed by Legate Robert. Odo of Burgundy objected to the church's blanket protection given to crusaders and their property, their immunity for repayment of debts and the ban on Jewish credit. There were stories of tensions between lords and the mass of *crucesignati* and complaints that French crusaders were still being forced to pay taxes, despite earlier promises to them to the contrary. A formal agreement between Philip II and the French episcopacy in March 1215 sought to limit the impact of the fiscal, credit and legal implications of

Quia Maior, for example by removing immunity from those charged with capital crimes and certain civil suits concerning obligations to lords.[39] Crusaders' protection risked disrupting tenurial as well as financial obligations. Negotiated limitations on privileges became a common feature of thirteenth-century crusading, a seemingly important prerequisite for the harmonious cooperation of church and state over the intrusion of canon law into the habitual conduct of secular life and the rights of governments increasingly conscious of their legal jurisdiction.[40] Yet, whatever the reaction to his controversial mission in France, Robert of Courcon, one of western Europe's leading intellectuals, was to die in the fetid camp before Damietta in the last days of 1218.[41] The crusade depended for its success on thousands of similar commitments.

In England, recruitment was interrupted by the civil war of 1215–17 to which, with ecclesiastical encouragement, some protagonists as well as observers applied the instruments and rhetoric of holy war.[42] Following King John's reconciliation with the papacy in 1213, his rule was supported by the presence of a succession of papal legates. Preaching the cross was in the hands of a team of academics, Walter, archdeacon of London, Philip of Oxford, a veteran of organizing the Fourth Crusade, John of Kent and, after 1214, William of London and Dean Leo of Wells. The crusade became an important political gesture with the king's adoption of the cross in March 1215, a precedent followed, on John's death, by his nine-year-old son and successor, Henry III, immediately after his coronation in October 1216. Both sides in the civil war were led by *crucesignati*, some of whom were offered commutation of their vows if they fought for the royalist cause while others may even have been induced to take the cross to fight for the king, an early and rather confused example of a crusade with an essentially secular political purpose. Despite attempts to the contrary, in England the crusade not only failed to achieve a political reconciliation, it may have temporarily exacerbated divisions as one side tried to appropriate a cause common to both. Only once the civil war had ended, when magnates from both sides left for the east, did the reconciling aspects of the Holy Land crusade emerge. Between 1218 and 1221, departing crusaders included rebels, such as the earls of Hereford and Winchester and the rebel leader Robert FitzWalter, and royalists such as the earl of Chester, who may, as John's executor, have been fulfilling his late master's crusade vow, and the loyalist captain Savaric of Mauléon. Savaric's contacts with crusading illustrate the futility of judging crusaders' motives and perceptions, still less the integrity of the institution itself. He fought against Simon of Montfort's crusaders at Castelnaudary in 1211 and seems to have temporarily commuted his crusader vow in favour of defending the Angevin cause in England in 1216, before joining the Fifth Crusade in Egypt and, finally, accompanying Louis VIII's crusade to Languedoc in 1226. A professional fighting man, Poitevin lord and royal servant, Savaric seemed attracted to paymasters and respectability. His actions reveal much about the cosmopolitan reach of the western European aristocracy but little of any inner spiritual life.[43]

The English contingent was not negligible but without royal leadership it lacked cohesion in structure or timing of departure. Groups, based around lordship or regional affinities, reached Egypt on each biannual passage from western ports. The earl of Chester, briefly a strong voice in the crusade's high command, left soon after the capture of Damietta in November 1219 after two years' stay, while the earl of Winchester had arrived only shortly before. Some, such as Philip of Aubigny, only appeared in eastern waters after Damietta had been returned to the sultan in 1221, while the bishop of Winchester, Peter des Roches, the controversial former justiciar, only took the cross eleven days after the city had, unknown to him, fallen. Repeatedly during the Egyptian campaign, the English presence was noted.[44] The earl of Arundel played a prominent role in acrimonious debates on strategy. It was later recorded that, after the capture of Damietta in 1219, to honour the English presence two converted mosques were dedicated to the national saints Edmund the Martyr and Thomas Becket. The new church of St Edmund was decorated with wall paintings of the martyr's passion commissioned by an English knight, Richard of Argentan, who during the expedition made himself something of an expert on eastern customs and legends. Whatever their military impact, the English crusaders re-ignited a habit of involvement in eastern crusading that lasted for generations. Philip of Aubigny, royalist and tutor to the young Henry III, arrived off Damietta in September 1221 to find the Christian evacuation in full swing. His father, Ralph, had died in the Third Crusade. In 1228 Philip again took the cross and, with his nephew Oliver and a significant company of knights, embarked for Palestine in 1235. He died in Jerusalem (which had been restored by treaty in 1229) the following year and was buried outside the church of the Holy Sepulchre in view and under the feet of all who visited. Philip's tomb slab, bearing his arms, name and inscription 'May his soul rest in peace', still survives. In the words of his contemporary, the St Alban's monk Matthew Paris, it was a grave 'he had long yearned for in life'.[45]

This process of piecemeal departures, fragmented leadership and almost permanent recruitment stretched across Germany and Italy. From the time he took the cross in 1215 with papal encouragement, Frederick II, king of Sicily as well as Germany, became the putative commander of the crusade. His departure for the east was repeatedly predicted and constantly expected. From his southern Italian ports, Innocent III announced in 1215, the main fleets were supposed to depart. Frederick's failure to fulfil the vow, which he repeated at his imperial coronation in 1220, deprived his subjects of a focus for engagement. However, given the nature of his kingdoms as well as the role the crusade played in resolving a whole series of local and national disputes, Frederick's delay, while central to the expedition's weak leadership, was not crucial to the response, except in the kingdom of Sicily. There, the main contribution came as a direct result of Frederick's command. When it became obvious he would be unable to travel east in the immediate future, the king despatched Matthew Gentile count of Lesina to Egypt in the summer of 1220 with seventy knights and six galleys and another fleet a year later under Count Henry of Malta. However, these expeditions were sent as tokens of good faith, neither being substitutes for the major Sicilian force that would have accompanied Frederick himself. In his German lands, Frederick's procrastination inhibited the active involvement of *crucesignati* among his political partisans. Only in the spring of 1221, after his coronation as emperor at Rome in November 1220, did he send Duke Louis of Bavaria, a *crucesignatus* since 1215, to represent him on the Egyptian campaign, which was then about to enter its disastrous final phase. Other Italian contingents timed their departures east according to local conditions; Lucca, Genoa and Rome in the summer and autumn of 1218, Bologna a year later, followed by Milan and Venice in spring 1220.[46]

This lack of cohesion was reflected in the time spent in the east. The main campaigns, in the Holy Land 1217–18 and in Egypt 1218–21, lasted four years in total, yet the average length of time lay and clerical aristocrats stayed in the east was about a year, the precedent of Philip II, not Richard I, still less the veterans of the first two great eastern enterprises.[47] Even the expedition of the only western crowned head to embark, King Andrew of Hungary, although oversubscribed when it assembled at Split in August of 1217, fizzled out after its leader left the Holy Land in January 1218, a few weeks after arriving. While such insouciant disregard for the wider interests of the enterprise may have been unusual and Andrew possibly an unwilling crusader, this lack of staying power was typical. Due directly to the fragmented nature of assembly and command, the transient fluidity of tours of service between 1217 and 1221 ensured that the best funded, most widely preached and professionally recruited crusade to date failed to convert numerical popularity into lasting achievement.

This was far from apparent in the summer of 1217, the deadline for departure. Despite the pope's unexpected death on 16 July 1216 at Perugia, where his corpse, stripped by thieves of its rich vestments, was seen by James of Vitry, the momentum of preparations scarcely slackened.[48] A new pope, Honorious III, the aged papal financial expert Cencius Savelli, was quickly elected, commended by his experience, understanding of the fiscal relationships between the Curia and ecclesiastical provinces and his past association with Frederick II, whose tutor he had been. Arrangements for the crusade became his prime concern. Within a year, two great armies gathered at opposite ends of Christendom, in the Adriatic and the North Sea. In August 1217, the armies of King Andrew of Hungary and Duke Leopold VI of Austria assembled at Split in Dalmatia. A longstanding *crucesignatus*, Duke Leopold's contingent included partisans of both sides in the recent German civil war. By contrast, King Andrew appears to have been more reluctant, forced by papal pressure to honour the crusade vow of his father, Bela III (d. 1196), his crusade less of a process of pacification than an exercise in expiation. Andrew had rebelled against his brother King Emeric (d. 1204), another *crucesignatus*, and was accompanied largely by his own supporters from Slavonia and Dalmatia. Their combined forces were substantial. While Leopold sailed for Acre almost immediately, taking only sixteen days to complete the passage, Andrew found difficulty securing adequate transport for his followers. His shipping contract with Venice, secured by the formal ceding of Zara to the city, provided for at least ten large ships, with an unspecified number of smaller vessels, suggesting an expected military complement of perhaps as many as 1,000 knights and 5,000 infantry. In the event, in ironic and diametric distinction with 1202, the number of troops exceeded the Venetians' immediate capacity to carry them. Surplus local shipping may have been requisitioned by the Germans, who were not covered by Andrew's agreement, or by a number of other groups who arrived at Split, including some from France. Entering Split on 23 August, Andrew was not able to reach Acre until late September. If, as is just possible, he had been expecting to find or have news of the impending arrival of the great northern fleet, he would have been disappointed. In a failure of coordination that came to typify the whole enterprise, the Germano-Hungarian crusaders found themselves an isolated vanguard of the larger forces massing rather slowly in the west.[49]

In late May and early June 1217, flotillas from Frisia, the Netherlands and the Rhineland left their home ports to rendezvous, like their predecessors in 1147 and 1189, at Dartmouth. Led by William count of Holland and George count of Weid, and carrying their recruiting officer Oliver of Paderborn, the combined fleet may have comprised between 250 and 300 ships, including numerous cogs capable of shipping upwards of 500 people each, implying a force of many, perhaps tens of thousands.[50] Their leaders appeared to regard their expedition as part of the greater design to be led, in due course, by Frederick II, but there was no indication of any direct imperial direction. During a brief stop at Dartmouth they again followed precedent by forming what amounted to a commune under which 'new laws' to secure peace within the army were agreed. Although at the same time they appointed 'communiter' the count of Weid as 'lord of the army', subsequent decisions and disagreements operated within a communal rather than command structure. New arrivals in the fleet were incorporated into this sworn commune, from those who met the main armada off Brittany later in June 1217 to those from Civitavecchia in Italy in March 1218 who joined the Frisian contingent, which had spent the previous winter there. While the commune may have provided the means of maintaining peace and discipline within the fleet, it failed to impose political unity. Reaching Lisbon in late July after a stormy and costly passage of the Bay of Biscay, the fleet split. The main part, under the counts of Weid and Holland, accepted the proposal of local bishops and commanders of the military orders to attack the troublesome Muslim garrison at al-Qasr (Alcazar do Sal). The Frisians under the abbot of Werde refused to join them, insisting that their duty was to press forward to the Holy Land and that, in any case, Innocent III had refused support for such a campaign at the Lateran Council. Leaving Lisbon on 28 July 1217, the eighty or so Frisian ships entered the Mediterranean and, hugging the northern shore, finally wintered at Civitavecchia, where they enjoyed papal protection. Meanwhile the counts, with possibly up to 160 ships, helped in the costly investment of al-Qasr, which fell on 21 October. As in 1147 and 1189, the effort of this act of vigorous fraternal charity seemed adequate service for some, who managed to obtain absolution from their crusader vows. The rest remained in Lisbon until March 1218 before sailing to Acre. In late April and May, the various surviving elements of the great fleet that had gathered at Dartmouth almost a year earlier arrived in the Holy Land. A year from the North Sea to Palestine repeated patterns established on the Second and Third Crusades. As with those earlier campaigns, this northern fleet found that, by accident or design, they had timed their arrival to coincide with the most significant action of the crusade.

WAR IN THE EAST

A decision to attack Egypt had been taken at the Fourth Lateran Council in 1215.[51] Unlike in 1201–2, there was no need for secrecy, the new strategic orthodoxy being apparently well established and accepted. Preliminary operations in northern Palestine in late autumn and early winter of 1217 by the newly arrived Germans and Hungarians provided employment for restless western troops, badly needed food supplies for Acre and a measure of increased security for the Frankish enclave without provoking any serious counter-attack by al Mu 'azzam of Damascus. From their camp south of Acre, the crusaders, careful to avoid a pitched battle with local Ayyubid forces, conducted a leisurely promenade across the river Jordan and a circuit of the Sea of Galilee, followed in December by two fruitless assaults on the Muslim fortress on Mt Tabor, Pope Innocent's *casus belli* of 1213. A subsequent foray by a splinter group of 500 Hungarians into the Lebanese mountains ended in disaster. However, the success of the earlier foraging excursion was followed in the New Year by the crusaders' refortification of two vital links on the road south, the Templar castle of Athlit or Château Pèlerin south of Haifa (now the site of an Israeli naval base) and Caesarea. Although this did not foreshadow an immediate march on Jerusalem, re-establishing these strongholds put pressure on Muslim strategists as well as protecting Acre. These manoeuvres may also have played a part in an alliance with Kay Kavus, the Seljuk sultan of Rum, who invaded northern Syria and attacked Aleppo in 1218. Given the westerners' Egyptian plan, such Syrian diversions were extremely useful in stretching the resources and resolve of Sultan al-Adil's family and allies who controlled Muslim Syria and Palestine in uneasy cooperation or competition.

The sense of a carefully prepared strategy was reinforced in the early months of 1218. Even Andrew of Hungary's precipitate departure from Acre with many of his Hungarian followers in January 1218 may have played an incidental role. Unusually, he travelled west overland, giving money to northern Syrian castles, arranging marriages for his sons with Armenian and Greek princesses as well as probably passing through Seljuk territory.[52] There may well have been a subsidiary diplomatic purpose in this unusual itinerary to assist shoring up the crusaders' distant northern flank. To allow Acre or Antioch to be attacked while the main armies fought in the Nile Delta would have made no sense. That the Egyptian attack was planned by this time cannot be doubted, as immediately the northern fleets arrived in late spring an assault was launched. When the fleets' commanders assembled with the duke of Austria and the local lay, clerical and military order leadership, their support for the Egyptian campaign was, according to James of Vitry, who was there, unanimous. The only issue in the mind of the king of Jerusalem, John of Brienne, was whether the crusaders should sail for Alexandria or Damietta. Regarded by common consent in Outremer as 'the key to Egypt', the choice fell on Damietta.[53] By the end of May, the crusaders had established a bridgehead on the left bank of the Nile opposite Damietta and began to probe the city's formidable defences. For the next three and a half years, this narrow waterlogged region of flats, marsh, canals and rivers remained the focal point for the thousands who joined the crusade from the west, the longest static campaign in the history of the eastern crusades.

Damietta, set among the silt, lagoons, sandbars, dunes and mud flats at the mouth of the main eastern estuary of the Nile, was, in Near Eastern terms, a relatively minor port, with a population of perhaps 60,000, smaller than Alexandria, much smaller than Cairo. However, because of its strategic importance, guarding one of the main routes of access to Cairo, it was well fortified with walls and protected by canals and river channels. The warfare around Damietta fell into four phases. After the initial landings in late May 1218 and the establishment of a camp opposite Damietta, strenuous assaults led to the taking of the so-called Tower of Chains, which stood in the Nile, midstream between the crusaders' camp and the city, on 24 August 1218. A series of increasingly desperate efforts to secure a hold on the right bank of the river, as well as some fruitless sallies against the city walls led, in February 1219, to the complete investment of the city when the new Sultan, al-Kamil, withdrew from his camp at al-Adilyah. During the summer of 1219, despite some heavy mauling, the crusaders held their positions. At this moment Francis of Assisi arrived in the crusader camp.[54] After accurately predicting the crusaders' failure to dislodge the Muslims from their camp at Fariskur, he was reluctantly given permission to cross through the lines on a hopeless mission to convert the sultan. Francis barely escaped with his life. The failure of Ayyubid relief, increasingly dire conditions within the city and consequently negligent defence led to the fall of the city in November 1219. The nearby port of Tinnis fell soon after. The third phase witnessed a long, curious twenty-one-month period of edgy diplomacy and phoney war, during which the leadership squabbled as to the best strategy to adopt; whether to accept Muslim peace terms, as preferred by King John of Jerusalem, or to press forward to capture Cairo, a policy supported by the increasingly assertive Cardinal Pelagius. These disagreements were conducted against a backcloth of regular crusader departures for which new arrivals failed to compensate. A growing impatience at inaction was exacerbated by the failure of Frederick II to honour his commitment to join the Egypt campaign. The final act saw a failed march on Cairo in August 1221 and the Christian evacuation of Damietta the following month. While a few crusaders remained to help defend Outremer and a trickle of new recruits continued to travel east, the surrender of Damietta marked the end of the central action of the crusade. The lesser expeditions of 1227 and of Frederick II in 1228 acted as codas for the Damietta enterprise as well as setting a pattern of continual small-scale western military assistance for Outremer that characterized the rest of the thirteenth century, with the exception of the French crusade of 1248–50.

The Damietta campaign of 1218–21 revolved around problems of leadership, reinforcement, technology and diplomacy. The delay in capturing Damietta raised questions over the central thrust of the Egyptian strategy. Were the crusaders there to conquer Egypt or to force a panicked Ayyubid sultan to restore the kingdom of Jerusalem? All the central features of the operation touched on this issue. Who determined the crusade's objectives? Did the western host possess the technical ability successfully to prosecute a campaign in the Delta and an attack on Cairo? Were there enough troops to achieve and sustain such a conquest? How far could negotiation with Ayyubids or other Near Eastern powers guarantee the security of a restored Jerusalem? In the event none of the answers to these questions proved satisfactory for the crusaders. It said much for the enthusiasm and levels of commitment aroused during the recruitment process that the effort was maintained for so long despite very modest material gains.

The problem of leadership arose as soon as the vanguard of the crusader fleet reached Egyptian waters on 27 May 1218. In the absence of most of the more important leaders, delayed by contrary winds, the crusaders elected Count Simon of Saarbrücken to lead the landing and the establishment of a camp on the west bank of the Nile opposite Damietta.[55] Born of immediate military necessity, this was only a temporary measure, probably reflecting the Rhenish composition of the ships in the vanguard. Once the full army had assembled, 'with the agreement of all' (*par accort de toz*),[56] John of Brienne king of Jerusalem was chosen as leader of the host. Although his partisans later claimed that he had also been promised rule of any conquests made, his position was considerably less dominant than that of Richard I or even Conrad III on earlier campaigns. John's leadership was of military convenience rather than recognition of political authority. Western lords were unlikely to accept his orders unconditionally, not least because they led their own contingents, many tied to their lords by close regional, tenurial or familial association. The papacy, in the form of the legate Pelagius cardinal bishop of Albano, who arrived in September 1218, demanded influence, supported by the significant amounts of treasure derived from the 1215 clerical tax, redemptions and donations. Control of these funds placed great practical power in the legate's hands. Oliver of Paderborn recorded at least two occasions when he used the central fund: in May 1219 to help the Pisans, Genoese and Venetians conduct an assault on the walls of Damietta and in 1220, when he hired French and German troops to join his retinue.[57] A papal account of 1220 recorded payments made to Pelagius from the papal Camera (i.e. treasury) and the 1215 tax of well over 35,000 silver marks and more than 25,000 gold ounces.[58] This pivotal role in funding as much as his supposed arrogance and imperious self-confidence propelled Pelagius into playing a key part in tactical decisions in an army whose lay recruits continually found themselves running short of cash.

King John's own position was less than secure. John of Brienne, a nobleman from Champagne, had carved a career for himself out of his military usefulness in high places. However, despite a number of golden opportunities, through lack of political acumen or luck, he repeatedly failed to translate his skills into a throne of his own. In 1210 he had arrived in Palestine and married Queen Maria, the daughter of Conrad of Montferrat and Isabella I. She had died in 1212, leaving John technically regent for their infant daughter Isabella II. John was remarried, to an Armenian princess, daughter of King Leo II (d. 1219), through whom and on behalf of their son he laid claim to the Armenian throne. These foundered on his wife's and son's deaths at Acre in 1220 only shortly after he had withdrawn from the crusade army in Egypt to pursue their Armenian inheritance.[59] Losing even his Jerusalem position when Isabella II married Frederick II in 1225, John campaigned in Italy for the pope and finally served as regent for Baldwin II and co-emperor in the Latin Empire of Constantinople. The political vulnerability of King John was emphasized by the crusade's collective leadership with its constantly changing membership. This was partly a product of the expedition's composition, partly of its constitution. The insistence that decisions were reached collectively could involve, as they had during the Fourth Crusade, the wider military community of the host. The crucial debate in the spring of 1220 on whether or not to advance from Damietta to attack Cairo was decided, against the advice of Cardinal Pelagius, the archbishop of Milan and other luminaries, by the opinion of the knights, not the divided leadership.[60] The crusaders stayed put. At Sharamsah in July 1221, the mass of crusaders overruled John of Brienne's counsel to withdraw.[61] As on every previous large crusade, decisions of the high command had to pass the close and critical scrutiny of their troops' public opinion in ways unusual in normal contemporary western warfare. The lack of political cohesion, the rhetoric of voluntary service and the reality of sworn communal rules of discipline created a robust and, for the leadership, at times awkward and unpredictable climate of participation.

Overshadowing everything was the promise of the appearance of Frederick II, held out from the arrival of the Germans in 1217–18 and Pelagius in the autumn of 1218 to the appearance of Matthew of Lesina in 1220–21, repeated regularly by the pope and earnestly desired by crusaders. Frederick, although not yet the figure of self-promoted glamour and outrageous ambition he was to become, seemed, in his inheritance of Sicily, Germany and the imperial dignity, to represent a new secular order in Christendom, for the moment allied with the papacy. His arrival was regarded as totemic of optimism and success. As Peter of Montague, Master of the Temple, put it, the emperor was 'long expected'.[62] As late as 1221, one compelling argument against accepting apparently generous peace terms was that Frederick had forbidden any deal prior to his own arrival.[63] No secular figure could replace him, not even his representatives in 1220–21. Frederick's absence unsettled tactical considerations and strategic planning. Cardinal Pelagius, representing the other universal power, had the unenviable task of trying to maintain the crusade until the emperor was ready to join it.

This was made considerably more difficult by the rhythm of departures and arrivals. The regularity of the two annual passages, the number of ships and crusaders carried provided remarkable testimony to the development of Mediterranean shipping and trade routes during the twelfth century. It did little to support an effective military campaign. A key element in previous long crusading expeditions had been the emergence of an *esprit de corps* based on shared expedience rather than shared origins – 1097–9, 1191–2, 1203–4. During the operations around Damietta from May 1218 to September 1221, death or departure deprived the Christian army of consistent command. Not a single great western lord remained in the Nile Delta for the complete duration of the war. Oliver of Paderborn was one of a very few leading clergy who did. In contrast with the Third Crusade, the Outremer barons, clergy and the masters of the military orders, spent significant passages of time away from the front line. Pelagius's continuous presence from the autumn of 1218 of itself added to his influence. Each newly arrived contingent was balanced by the departure of others.[64] Few seemed reconciled to staying until the Egyptian campaign was completed or Jerusalem recovered. As with the Albigensian wars, *crucesignati* appeared to believe that seeing only limited active service in the cause of the cross was sufficient to merit the indulgence. Although *Quia Maior* and *Ad Liberandam* indicated that Innocent III envisaged a campaign lasting three years or more, in neither was any conditional time limit set for the enjoyment of the plenary indulgence. The temporary quality of the crusaders' commitment exerted a powerful influence. Even the legate's threats of excommunication failed to prevent some, such as the count of Katzenellenbogen in 1220, from deserting.[65] In October 1218, the news of crusaders leaving encouraged the Muslims to attack the Christian camp. Later, the pressure to retain as many troops as possible on station prompted Pelagius in 1220–21 to argue for a more aggressive policy. Without fighting and the prospect of booty or success, hanging about in Damietta indefinitely was hardly an attractive or sustainable option. Equally damaging, the incessant merry-go-round of arrivals and departures consolidated the regional, national and social divisions that dominated the public and private debates on the course the campaign should take, a disunity fed by the lack of an accepted single leader.

Technology assumed a central place in the Egyptian campaign. Eyewitnesses noted when new crusaders brought with them siege equipment, as they had during the siege of Acre during the Third Crusade. Apart from the contest of throwing machines on both sides, much of the fighting was determined by the respective merits of the attackers' and defenders' engineering and shipping as the struggle was played out across the Nile around Damietta and later, in the summer of 1221, upstream towards Cairo. Water protected and threatened by turns in a landscape where military aggression was fraught with hazard as it almost invariably required crossing rivers or canals. The first great obstacle, the seventy-foot-high Chain Tower, situated in the Nile between Damietta and the crusader camp, was separated from the Christian-held left bank by a narrow channel. From the tower to the city walls ran a chain, restored by Saladin, that was raised to prevent unwelcome river traffic proceeding up the Nile. It was only captured in August 1218 thanks to an elaborate floating fortress designed by Oliver of Paderborn himself.[66] Although paid for and built by the Germans and Frisians, the design – a fortified platform equipped with scaling ladders suspended above two large ships lashed together – resembled the devices constructed by the Venetians before the walls of Constantinople in 1204. A number of Venetian maritime experts may have been on hand, left behind to find new clients when Andrew of Hungary decided to return home overland.

Oliver's engine was needed because the garrison of 300 in the Chain Tower could not be starved out as a bridge of boats supplied the tower from Damietta. Another pontoon bridge further upstream protected the Ayyubid camp at al-Adilyah, south of the city, as well as allowing Muslims to attack crusader positions across the river. This bridge became the focus of operations for both sides, producing one of more remarkable engineering feats of the campaign. To outflank the bridge, the crusaders dredged and enlarged the al-Azraq canal, which ran for some miles, linking the Mediterranean coast to the Nile south of the Christian camp and upstream of Muslim defences, which now included hulks scuttled in the main channel of the river.[67] The enlargement of the canal took a month. Any immediate advantage was dissipated by a devastating storm and flood of seawater in late November that almost engulfed the two hostile camps, followed by an epidemic, possibly of scurvy. Christian fatalities may have been as high as 20 per cent.[68] However, after a grim and unsettled winter, the engineering efforts of the previous autumn contributed to the occupation of the Ayyubid camp on the right bank of the Nile in February 1219 which had been deserted as a consequence of an attempted coup against the new sultan al-Kamil.[69]

Thereafter, the lack of adequate technological capacity first blunted the crusaders' attempts to take the city during the summer of 1219 and later, on the march south in July and August 1221, placed the western host at a fatal disadvantage. The lack of manpower, exacerbated by the departure in the spring of 1219 of Leopold of Austria and many others the following autumn, proved significant. This left the crusaders outnumbered and unable to press forward attacks. Muscle power, human or animal, provided the energy upon which the army depended, a role taken in much later centuries by gunpowder, petrol and electricity. Among the skills well represented on all crusading expeditions, those of the carpenter stand out. John of Brienne employed one of his, Aubert the Carpenter, to reconnoitre the deserted Ayyubid camp in February 1219.[70] On land or water, wood technology occupied a central place in medieval warfare. The Nile Delta presented peculiar problems, not least its lack of suitable local timber, a point recognized by Innocent III's attempt to ban western exports of wood or ships to Egypt in 1213 and 1215. From the winter of 1218–19, although able to maintain a blockade of Damietta once the city was encircled in February, the crusaders made no progress and were only barely able to resist counter-attacks by Sultan al-Kamil, now stationed further to the south. In the event, the blockade worked, starving the city so that resistance slackened, an unguarded section of wall leading to its fall in November 1219. The main bulk of the Muslim forces were deliberately never engaged. When, finally, almost two years later, they were, the crusaders' technological limitations were exposed. They lacked sufficient flat-bottomed barges to carry the bulk of the army and so had to maintain a precarious link between the land army and many of its leaders, including the legate, on board ship. This form of amphibious warfare was beyond the experience of many, the departure of Frisians and Netherlanders over the previous two years being keenly felt. The absence of adequate craft in sufficient numbers allowed the Egyptians to outmanoeuvre the crusaders. By using shallow side canals, the Muslims cut them off from their base at Damietta and imperilled any chance of retreat once the Christians pressed southwards into the heart of the Delta beyond Sharamsah in late July 1221.[71]

Yet these problems of leadership, manpower and technology did not prevent the crusade from threatening the survival of the Ayyubid empire, if only, but especially, in the minds of Egypt's defenders. From their discomfort came a policy of military containment and appeasing diplomacy, which unlike the Richard–Saladin negotiations over Palestine in 1191–12, nonetheless failed seriously to engage the Christians. On this failure, traditionally blamed on the myopic stubbornness of Cardinal Pelagius, the crusade has been seen by many to have foundered. In fact, the objectives of each side were incompatible. The fragile unity of the Ayyubid empire was severely shaken by the death of Sultan al-Adil in August 1218, just after the fall of the Chain Tower.[72] Thereafter, no claimant to the succession among his sons or nephews could realistically have surrendered control of Palestine, still less the Holy City of Jerusalem, any such offers being so territorially circumscribed as to be unconvincing. The Ayyubid military weakness exposed by the simultaneous attack on Egypt by the crusaders and on Aleppo by the Seljuks in 1218 imposed a temporary unity of self-interest on the rival dynasts. Hard-pressed al-Kamil, al-Adil's son and successor in Egypt, received vital help from his brother al Mu 'azzam of Damascus. Al Mu 'azzam campaigned in Egypt in 1219 and 1221 and launched a series of assaults on Frankish positions in Syria, recapturing Caesarea late in 1219 and in

1220 threatening Acre and Château Pèlerin. Yet it was entirely unclear whether al-Kamil exerted sufficient control over Palestine for any promise to restore Jerusalem to the Christians to be implemented. The Franks may have known this. The hollowness of any negotiated return of Jerusalem was emphasized when al Mu 'azzam dismantled its walls in 1219 and ordered further demolition in the city in 1220.[73]

The perceived threat from the crusaders was real enough. Taking the fight to Egypt dealt a profound blow to morale and hence was a key element in support for the Ayyubids, whose power had been grounded on their ability to unite and protect Islam against the infidel invaders. Al-Adil had been careful to avoid risking direct confrontation or a pitched battle. Al-Kamil had no option, especially as his own position was challenged at least once by a failed palace coup implicating another brother, al-Faiz, early in 1219. This had caused al-Kamil to abandon his frontline camp at al-Adilyah in February 1219 and regroup further south. Just as the crusaders' long failure to capitalize on the fall of the Chain Tower sapped their morale in 1218–19, so their opponents' inability to expel them from Egyptian soil placed great strain on Egyptian logistic, military, defensive and financial resources. The mere presence of the crusaders in the Nile Delta, supported by fleets from a number of Italian trading cities, threatened Egypt's immensely lucrative commerce far more certainly than the wishful papal bans on trading. Al-Kamil, rebuilding his army early in 1219, had to resort to increased taxes on the Coptic and other Christian communities. The sultan's anxiety over the military threat in 1219 led him to devote attention to the fortifications of Cairo itself. Two years later, news of the crusaders' long-awaited push towards Cairo caused panic.[74] Some members of the political elite tried to ingratiate themselves with Christian captives in Cairo as insurance against a crusader victory. The sultan announced a general call-up probably as much to stiffen morale as to provide effective additional military strength. Both the old and new cities of Cairo were evacuated. Ayyubid rule had arisen from Frankish attempts to occupy Egypt, with Frankish troops stationed in Cairo and Alexandria in 1167 and Cairo besieged in 1168. They feared that their rule might end the same way. The total number of combatant crusaders, peaking at perhaps 30,000 fighting men in 1218 and gradually if irregularly decreasing thereafter, with a casualty rate among the leaders of around a third, may never have been adequate to achieve or maintain such a conquest.

Yet the threat to political stability and the prospect of a return to the factional chaos of the last days of the Fatimids was a distinct possibility. According to Oliver of Paderborn, whose figures are impressively precise and possibly based on official estimates at the time, the army that set out for Cairo in July 1221 included a modest 1,200 knights and 4,000 archers, with a fleet of 600 boats of various sizes, as well as unspecified, perhaps a few thousand, auxiliary cavalry, such as Turcopoles and infantry.[75] This would have been unlikely to have been able to lay serious siege to Cairo, even if the army had used the timber from its ships to construct siege machines. However, the danger for al-Kamil lay in the loyalty of his emirs and of his and their *askars* or professional military households. Sustained warfare on home soil denied participants much chance of booty or profit, placing a strain on the military system that supported Ayyubid political authority. As it was, the crusaders received some local support, including, according to Oliver of Paderborn, 'a great multitude of Bedouin', resentful of the fiscal exaction of the parvenu Ayyubids.[76] Fears of such internal dissent, exacerbated by the attempted coup of February 1219, prompted al-Kamil at least twice to offer what he thought the crusaders might accept for withdrawing their forces from his territory, the return of Jerusalem.

The first offer came after al-Kamil had successfully repulsed the crusader attack on his camp at Fariskur in late August 1219, when it became clear that a quick military solution was unlikely. The worsening conditions in both camps and in Damietta, the inability of either side to establish a clear military advantage and the strains within both leaderships indicated that a negotiated settlement might find sympathetic hearing. Francis of Assisi's intervention at this precise moment hinted that a peaceful agreement was being considered by the Christians as well as the Muslims. Francis may have inclined to pacifism, but his mission to Sultan al-Kamil was rather different. He went to convert, not to secure a lasting armistice. He sought no accommodation with Islam, rather its eradication through reasoned evangelism. However, the naive grandeur of his vision failed to conceal that immediately in the crusader camp and more generally among the intellectual elites there existed a Christian alternative to military crusading. The idea of removing Islam's grip on the Holy Places and as a threat to Christendom by conversion, not conquest, attracted more adherents as the size, racial and religious diversity of the world became more apparent to western Europeans during the thirteenth century at the same time as warfare failed to achieve the desired objectives of crusading.[77] Whatever else, in the circumstances of the depressed, divided and wretched Christian camp on the Nile in the late summer of 1219, Francis's mission to al-Kamil expressed, however eccentrically, the desire of many to arrange an honourable end to their difficulties.

As reported by western writers, the sultan proposed, in return for the crusaders' evacuating Egypt, to restore the Holy Cross lost at Hattin as well as Jerusalem with all castles west of the Jordan to Christian rule, with a financial subsidy to help rebuild the walls of the Holy City demolished earlier in the year.[78] Unsurprisingly, John of Brienne urged acceptance, as it would, at a stroke, incontestably provide him with a greatly expanded kingdom. Despite the assumptions of sympathizers, John's claims to any Egyptian conquests were opposed both by the legate, acting on papal instructions handing him the power to dispose of any territorial gains, and by the representatives of the emperor. Swapping an uncertain acquisition for the traditional goal of the expedition made complete sense to the king, as it did to most of the northern crusaders and the Teutonic Knights. However, the legate, the rest of the clergy and the Italians disagreed. For the Italians this was not necessarily, as has usually been supposed, a simple question of a material desire for control of a commercial centre in Egypt for their own profit. Rather, many of them, like the Venetians in 1203–4, sought compensation for the interruption to business with Egypt. The restoration of the kingdom of Jerusalem hardly offered them this. In the light of the anger from the rank and file at the lack of booty when Damietta was captured two months later, it is likely that many of those advocating acceptance of al-Kamil's terms might similarly have felt disgruntled in the event of the deal being achieved. Crucially, King John's essentially self-interested position was contradicted by the Hospitallers and Templars, the military orders which, unlike the Teutonic Knights, had institutional and corporate memories of the problems of the twelfth century. They argued that the absence of Kerak, Montréal, and with them control over the Transjordan region, made Jerusalem untenable. During 1191–2, they had supported Richard I in believing that even if captured Jerusalem could not be held because of the departure of most of the western crusaders. Now they again stood on strategic realities. Al-Kamil's terms, even in the unlikely event of being acceptable to the

Ayyubids of Syria, offered no lasting peace or security to a revived kingdom of Jerusalem, any more than had the treaty of Jaffa in 1192. By insisting on the retention of Transjordan, al-Kamil signalled his intention to retain his hold on the vital sinews of Ayyubid power uniting Egypt and Syria, and that his proposals came from self-interest not generosity. His seriousness was further impugned by the memory that Saladin, when he had promised to return the True Cross, had failed to find it. Any evacuation of Egypt after the struggles of 1218–19 would almost certainly have led the crusade to break up, exposing Outremer to immediate vulnerability. After a debate further damaging the unity of the enterprise, the sultan's offer was rejected.

Two years later, as the crusaders were preparing to advance on Cairo in August 1221, al-Kamil repeated his peace offer: Damietta for Jerusalem. Seriously alarmed at the potential erosion of his political position any prolonged fighting in the Egyptian hinterland would cause, let alone the prospect of defeat, al-Kamil may have reckoned that this proposal would sow dissension in the crusader ranks and encourage delay. This would allow more time for his Syrian allies to assemble as well as bringing the timing of the Christian advance awkwardly close to the annual Nile flood. It is possible that the deal had been presented to the crusaders more than once; Oliver of Paderborn described the terms as 'so often proffered by the enemy'.[79] A striking but unsurprising feature of the Egypt war 1218–21 was how much informal contact existed between the two sides as they manoeuvred for advantage in the narrow region around Damietta; spies, renegades, prisoners of war, ambassadors all featured prominently. Each side had a shrewd idea of the circumstances, motives and fears of the other. Once again, as in 1219, al-Kamil's diplomacy split the army, although this time even some of Pelagius's admirers seemed, with hindsight, less than enthusiastic at his steadfast refusal to countenance compromise. In Oliver of Paderborn's case this may reflect the different stages of composition, his earlier support for Pelagius being written before the failure of the crusade had occurred.[80] While it is likely that the arguments of 1219 were still canvassed, by August 1221 both the pope and the emperor had expressly forbidden their representatives in Egypt to agree to a treaty. In those circumstances, negotiations could not succeed. The crusade's fate would be determined on the battlefield.

In retrospect, this final rejection of al-Kamil's peace terms appears

18. The Fifth Crusade: a clash between Frankish and Egyptian forces outside Damietta, June 1218, from Matthew Paris's *Chronica Majora*, *c*.1255.

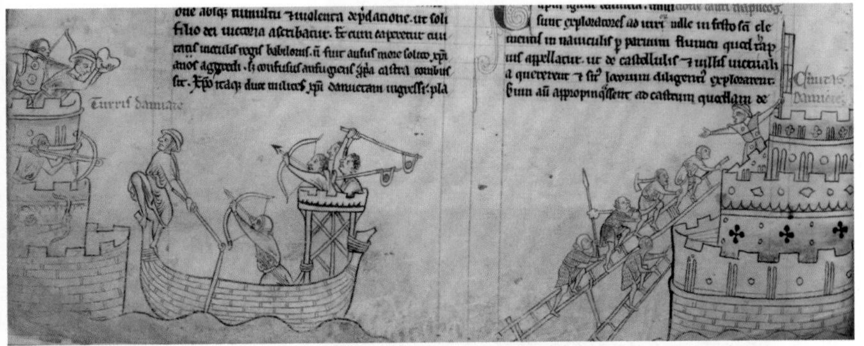

19. The Fifth Crusade: the capture of the Tower of Chains by Oliver of Paderborn's floating fortress, August 1218 (*left*), and the fall of Damietta, November 1219 (*right*), from Matthew Paris's *Chronica Majora*, *c*.1255.

20. Frederick II, emperor, king of Germany 1212–50, ruler, crusader, polymath and falconry expert.

21. Louis IX of France captures Damietta, June 1249, from a manuscript produced at Acre *c.*1280. Not a cross in sight; instead the crusaders bear the royal emblem of France, the fleur de lis; see p. 909.

22. Outremer's nemesis: Mamluk warriors training.

23. Outremer's nemesis: a Turkish cavalry squadron.

24. The battle of La Forbie, October 1244: a Khwarazmian and Egyptian army annihilate a Frankish-Damascene force; see p. 771.

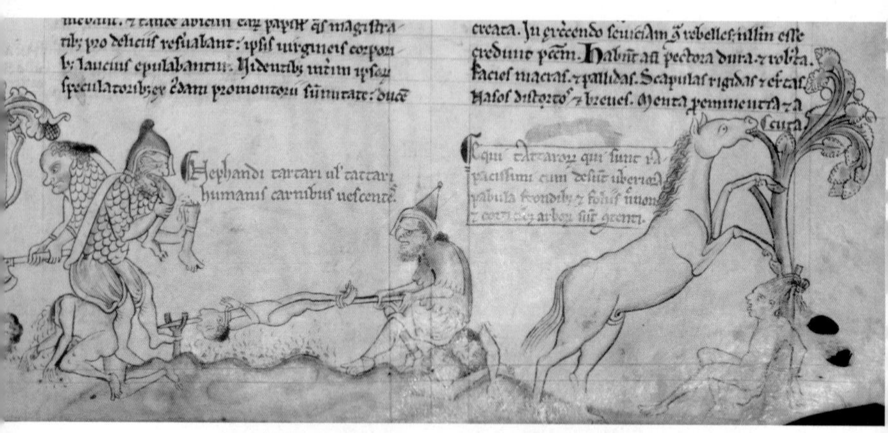

25. Matthew Paris imagines the Mongols as cannibalistic savages, *Chronica Majora*, *c.*1255.

26. (*opposite*) The fall of Tripoli to the Mamluks, April 1289; see p. 817.

27. Charles V of France entertains Charles IV of Germany during a banquet in Paris in 1378 with a lavish show of the siege of Jerusalem of 1099, possibly stage-managed by Philip of Mézières, perhaps the figure in black shown in the left foreground; see p. 887.

28. Andrea Bonaiuti's fresco 'The Church Militant' in the Spanish Chapel, St Maria Novella, Florence, portraying the leading lights in crusading at the time (*back row, right to left, beginning with the black-bearded noble carrying a sword*): Amadeus VI count of Savoy, King Peter I of Cyprus, the Emperor Charles IV, Pope Urban V, the papal legate in Italy, Gil Albornoz; (*back row, fourth from far left*) Juan Fernandez Heredia, master of the Hospitallers; and, standing in front of Peter of Cyprus, Thomas Beauchamp earl of Warwick, wearing the insignia of the Order of the Garter below his left knee. See p. 832.

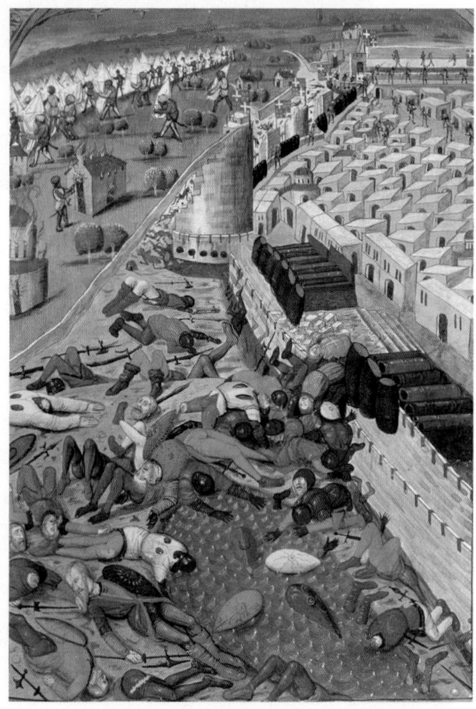

29. The failed Ottoman Turkish siege of Rhodes, 1480.

30. Mehmed II the Conqueror (1451–81) by Gentile Bellini, 1480/81.

31. The battle of Lepanto, 1571; see pp. 903–4.

stupendously perverse or foolish. The prohibition of the pope and emperor hardly seems adequate explanation for the imbalance of chances between a risky campaign in alien territory soon to be inundated with flood water and the peaceful return of the Holy City and most of Palestine. Richard I may have jumped at such terms. Yet Richard's pragmatism had failed to deliver lasting success. It seems that, just as John of Brienne may have been too openly moved by self-interest, Pelagius had begun to believe his own propaganda, which had been fed in unexpected ways. Resident for these years on the rim of Asia, the crusaders grew familiar with the complexity and, to a westerner, exoticism of regional politics. They acquired news of events further east and north, from Georgia to the great Eurasian steppes. Distorted rumours of the extraordinary conquests of Genghis Khan (d. 1227) filtered through. By 1220, the Mongols seemed to threaten Iraq and the Baghdad caliphate. Even though al-Ashraf of Greater Armenia, another of al-Kamil's brothers, judged the crusaders a greater menace than the Mongols, the stories of a non-Muslim conqueror to the east of the Islamic world aroused considerable excitement in the crusader camp. Genghis Khan, or rather a garbled version of him, became King David of the Indians commonly called, as James of Vitry wrote to the pope, Prester John.[81] This figure of legend, the Christian priest king who combated Islam from the east as the crusaders did from the west, had haunted western imagination since the mid-twelfth century, when stories of Nestorian Christians in the Far East and great victories over Muslims in the Eurasian steppes first reached western Europeans. To wishful observers shut up in Damietta, keen to clutch at signs of grace for their enterprise, the great events in the east presaged another reordering of temporal affairs in a manner similar to the First Crusade. In this vein James of Vitry described the privations of the camp at Damietta in words taken verbatim from William of Tyre's account of the First Crusade.[82] History, they hoped, was about to repeat itself. For this they had additional and unusual confirmation in a series of prophecies that very conveniently came to light in the months before and after Damietta fell in November 1219. The prophetic tradition formed a powerful element in preaching and the promotion of the crusade. Now, it appeared, there was more to it than fancy biblical exegesis and intellectual prestidigitation.

Even before the capture of Damietta, an apparently prophetic work in Arabic had been brought to the crusaders' attention predicting the capture of the city. Rumours circulated of a pan-Christian rising against the power of Islam. Such heady influences formed the emotional context within which the peace diplomacy of 1219–21 was conducted. The atmosphere of cosmic expectation was further heightened after the capture of the city by the supposed discovery of further prophetic works that were widely circulated though the crusader ranks in translation, their content directly informing official propaganda and preaching.[83] One of these, the *Prophecy of Hannan, son of Isaac*, while purporting to be by a ninth-century Persian Nestorian doctor, was probably composed by local Egyptian Nestorians in 1219–20. Another associated the prophecy of ultimate success with an unimpeachable Christian source, *The Revelations of the Blessed Apostle Peter by his Disciple Clement*. These rather esoteric works were provided with suitably hoary provenance, complete with references to ancient languages, local custody and old bindings. While evidently feeding directly into the stream of optimism that sustained the clerical propagandists in the crusader camp, these prophecies seemed to gain credence when combined with the contemporary news of the events in the east, of 'King David' and of Prester John, even if there was some confusion over the location of the latter's kingdom, in eastern Asia or east Africa. Pelagius and his high-powered intellectual advisors, such as James of Vitry, seemed to have been convinced of the essential accuracy of these prophecies of triumph. They had them translated, sent to the west and broadcast to the troops, especially in the prelude to the advance south in July 1221. These auguries combined with the instructions from the leaders in the west to incline the clerical leadership against throwing away what all sides agreed was an advantage by agreeing to the sultan's terms. Imperialist support in 1220–21 stiffened this resolve.

Pelagius did not hope the crusaders would win; he thought he knew they would. While it is impossible to reach into the minds of the protagonists, the acceptance of what struck intelligent witnesses as objective prophetic documents, while anathema to most sane modern observers, fitted well into the mind set that placed crusading within a frame of universal history. To reject the possibility of prophetic truth would have been to deny the crusade mentality itself. To ignore the prophetic message in favour of the naked short-term self-interest of John of Jerusalem would have seemed treason to God's purpose. The forged Damietta prophecies of 1219–21 exerted such an impact because they operated with, not against, the grain of expectation and understanding of the progress of human history towards Judgement Day. Only in retrospect did the refusal to accept al-Kamil appear foolish. The central failure of the Fifth Crusade was not diplomatic but military.

THE FAILURE OF THE EGYPT CAMPAIGN

The outcome of the Egyptian campaign surprised and appalled in almost equal measure. The canny Iraqi pundit Ibn al-Athir called it 'unexpected'.[84] Western observers were less charitable, attaching blame variously to Pelagius, the pope, the dilatory Frederick II, the clergy, the crusade leaders, sin, pride, materialism and avarice. Many remained confused, by the decisions taken on the ground and the judgement of God on his followers. 'What mass of evil caused it?'[85] Reaction on all sides was sharpened by the appreciation of how near to success the crusaders had come. A major Egyptian port had been secured in the face of fierce opposition, an undefeated land army and hostile terrain, in its way an achievement to rank with the taking of Acre in 1191. The Ayyubid empire had been severely shaken, especially in the aftermath of the death of al-Adil in 1218. The perceived seriousness of the threat to Egypt had briefly united the rival Ayyubid factions across the Near East. For two years Sultan al-Kamil had been prepared to offer superficially generous terms simply to get the crusaders out of his territory. The prospect of the crusaders' assault on Cairo in 1221 had caused widespread alarm. Yet that final foray into the heart of the Nile Delta in the summer of 1221 exposed the westerners' consistent weaknesses of leadership, control and manpower. The army in 1221, as for the previous three years, was too hesitant, too divided and too small. Traditionally these problems have been seen in terms of a personal conflict between Pelagius and John of Brienne. The reality was more complex.

The lack of a settled army of itself need not have undermined the crusade. Regional or national divisions were never submerged during the Third or even the First Crusade. However, in Egypt in 1218–21 these divisions were not balanced by a decisive command structure, which went some way to explaining the lethargy that gripped the expedition between November 1219 and July 1221. When Damietta fell, the high command failed to distribute the booty and plunder in ways regarded as equitable by the mass of their troops, reminiscent of events following the fall of Constantinople fifteen years earlier.[86] The conflict was triangular. Pelagius, as controller of the central fund, bore responsibility for dispersing the plunder and incurred the anger of the common crusader for perceived meanness. He was also opposed by John of Brienne, who insisted on his right to rule the city and, supported by his barons, resorted to arms to press his case. While Pelagius received the support of the imperialists, eager to preserve any future rights of Frederick II, John could play on Pelagius's unpopularity to secure a favourable compromise. He was granted the city until the arrival of Frederick and the division of spoils was increased. This represented a hollow victory, as the city's property and mosques were assigned to separate western national groups whose distinct identities were preserved by the constant arrival of fellow countrymen. Neither Pelagius nor John was in control of events, these national groups pursuing their own policies with an inconsistency that meant that neither could rely on their support. As the legate discovered with some of the French and Germans, not even cash guaranteed loyalty.[87] Elaborate military operations were often conducted as separate private enterprises by one contingent or another. For once, corporate leadership did not work.

This serial dislocation of command and control not only frustrated Pelagius's policies but encouraged King John to leave the army around Easter 1220 for more than a year.[88] His departure drew criticism from the legate's adherents and weakened the king's standing among the veterans at Damietta, who remembered the promises of unwavering support before the campaign had begun in 1218. John's withdrawal prompted many others to leave, further emasculating its offensive capacity. John was attempting to secure a claim to the Armenian throne though his wife, Stephanie, eldest daughter of Leo II of Armenia, and their infant son. Leo II died in the summer of 1219, leading to a damaging succession dispute between his great nephew, Raymond Roupen, a recently failed prince of Antioch, and Leo's daughters Stephanie and his preferred heir Isabella. While John may have despatched troops to support his cause in Armenia, his claim was negated by the deaths of his wife and son in Acre shortly after he arrived from Egypt. John's failure to return to Damietta for another year after the collapse of his Armenian hopes further eroded his position. By the time he reappeared, seemingly reluctantly, in July 1221, while the familiar divisions between the aggressive and defensive parties remained, the army had been joined by influential newcomers, especially imperialists led by Louis of Bavaria and the count of Lesina, who owed no allegiance or respect to John's rights or authority. In his absence, *faute de mieux*, Pelagius had assumed a more dominant role. Thus, when John sensibly advised caution in the face of the risks of a Delta campaign, he lacked the political credit to impose his will, a weakness not entirely of his enemies' making. However, John's absence may have served the crusade's interests in ways not recognized by his opponents at Damietta. By remaining in his kingdom in 1220–21, John was on hand to blunt al Mu 'azzam's and al-Ashraf's continued probing of the Franks' Syrian and Palestinian defences, including attacks on Château Pèlerin and Acre.

One of the most remarkable features of the Egypt campaign was its tenacity, first in the face of the desperate warfare of 1218–19 and then during the long period of defence and inactivity 1219–21. By the summer of 1221 the Christian host remained intact. But action now appeared an absolute necessity if the army were to remain in Egypt.[89] Certainly the clerical elite around Pelagius believed the whole enterprise was becoming mired in corruption, indolence and sin by the enforced inaction. Only activity would raise morale, morals and the integrity of the army. Nonetheless, with hindsight, the decisions reached by the crusade high command in July and August 1221 seem to defy reason. The first was to launch an attack on Cairo in early July perilously close to the annual flood season with a force, perhaps a minority of the troops available, far smaller than the combined Egyptian and Syrian Ayyubid armies facing them and comprising too few to take the Egyptian capital by siege or even protracted assault. The plan to march on Cairo was unlikely to have been made suddenly. In Louis of Bavaria, who reached Damietta in May, the legate found an ally for his strategy and a commander for his troops. The arrival of King John and a large force on 7 July precisely coincided with the Damietta troops reaching battle readiness. However, the final muster at Fariskur, on 17 July, came with only a month left before the Nile flooded. The leadership also knew of the Syrian reinforcements coming to aid al-Kamil. Yet such had been the effort in preparing the expeditionary force that further delay or even acceptance of the sultan's renewed peace terms would not only have split the leadership but risked the complete disintegration of the Christian army. This, in turn, would have encouraged the sultan and his allies to renege on any offer made while the crusader army was strong and threatening. Once embarked upon, the advance could scarcely be cancelled. Although he expressed his doubts, at no stage did King John withdraw his troops. Indeed, he had timed his return to Egypt precisely to coincide with the advance.

The second fateful decision was to continue the march southwards from Sharamsah, a town twenty miles south of Damietta on the Cairo road, at the end of July. To that point, progress had been relatively unopposed. The prevailing insistence of the mass of the crusaders to press on came as a direct consequence of the effort to mobilize the force in the first place. It also provided testimony to the fragile hold over public opinion within the army. Once again, although vociferously unhappy with the outcome, King John loyally remained with the army as it picked its way towards Mansourah. He had declined to break up the army when he had a final chance at Sharamsah to remove his own contingent. The details and motives behind the leaders' debate are irrecoverable. However, it was not be the first or last occasion when contested military judgement was proved wrong. It should be remembered that up to its departure from Sharamshah, the army had only made contact with the enemy's Turkish light cavalry. The Christian failure to see the trap being prepared for them suggests a collapse in intelligence rather than cussed obstinacy or myopic amateurism.

The third decision was less finely balanced. The crusaders had marched, open-eyed, into a position opposite Mansourah between the Nile and the al-Bahr-as-Saghir, a canal that linked the river to Lake Manzalah to the north-east. From one aspect, they were protected from attack by these waterways. From another they were cornered. During their march south, the crusaders ignored a side channel that flowed into the Nile north of Baramun. Now the Muslims used it to blockade the river downstream from the Christian camp opposite Mansourah. At the same time the Syrian levies moved to positions on land north-east of the crusaders, obstructing access to their base at Damietta. The Christians were trapped. Once this became apparent, a debate began on whether to withdraw or to dig in, hoping for relief from Damietta or from the promised arrival of Frederick II. With provisions for only twenty days, trying to hold such an advanced, exposed position made little sense. On 26 August, the crusaders began a ragged but not entirely disorderly retreat. Beset by constant enemy attack and the rising waters of the Nile, the Christian army struggled northwards. Many common crusaders decided to drink the wine supplies they could not take with them, reducing their military effectiveness still further. As a final throw, the sultan opened the sluices, flooding the Christians' camp near Baramun, catching them, in the words of the Master of the Temple, 'like a fish in a net'.[90] Pelagius bowed to the inevitable and asked John of Brienne to sue for peace.

Despite appearances, the crusaders still held some bargaining chips. The large garrison at Damietta remained unconquered. The substantial field army, although badly mauled and carrying heavy casualties, remained intact, largely thanks to the organization imposed by the Templars. Reinforcements from Europe were expected to arrive any day. Al-Kamil's priority remained the same as before: the removal of foreign troops from Egyptian soil. He had no desire to press for a definitive military solution, not least because the continued presence of his Syrian brothers and their armies in his kingdom presented a potential threat to his authority. A siege of Damietta could take months. After some ineffectual sabre rattling by both sides, terms were agreed on 29 August that struck Oliver of Paderborn as 'excellent'.[91] This stretched a point. In return for the surrender of Damietta, the Christians were to be allowed to evacuate Egypt freely, without ransom. All prisoners were to be exchanged and a truce of eight years established that was not to be binding on Frederick II if he chose to campaign in the east. As a fig leaf to conceal Christian disappointment, the return of the True Cross was promised, by now a formal, not realistic, part of such treaties. After some trouble when the news of the treaty reached Damietta, the evacuation was conducted in orderly fashion, even though a new imperial force under the count of Malta had just arrived in port. The crusaders dispersed, some travelling to Acre, others sailing directly for the west.

However brave a face apologists presented, the failure of the Egyptian campaign stood in barren contrast to the hopes raised in 1219 and, more widely, to the prodigious efforts made across Christendom after 1213. While the fundraising and recruiting continued, the political appetite for a renewed general crusade ceased. Increasingly, the relationship between the pope and the new emperor, upon which the success of whole enterprise had come to be predicated, became marred by recrimination and mutual suspicion, leading to Gregory IX's excommunication of Frederick in 1227 following his failure to embark on crusade that year.[92] Other contingents journeyed east, including a substantial army with the English bishops Peter des Roches of Winchester and William Brewer of Exeter in 1227. This was intended as part of Frederick II's crusade, and some of its members stayed to join the emperor when he finally arrived in the Holy Land in 1228.[93] However, the sight of an excommunicated crusade leader, shunned by large sections of the Frankish political and clerical hierarchy, eagerly securing a deal with al-Kamil that had eluded the crusaders on the Nile was hardly the result envisaged by Innocent III and his army of preachers and recruiting agents a decade and a half earlier.

Perhaps the surprise of the Fifth Crusade lies less in its failure than in how nearly it succeeded, at least in destabilizing the Ayyubid empire at a critical moment of insecurity on the death of al-Adil in 1218. This is the more remarkable as it appears unlikely that the expedition ever contained enough troops to attempt a serious conquest, still less occupation of Egypt. Its disturbing impact on the region testified to the fragility of Ayyubid power structures. However, lasting achievements in the east were few. The fortification of Château Pèlerin stood the test of time. It was never captured by the Muslims, only being evacuated in August 1291 after the fall of Acre had rendered further resistance impractical. The experience of regular traffic of seaborne armies across the Mediterranean set a trend for the rest of the thirteenth century which sustained the mainland outposts of Outremer as its Muslim neighbours became increasingly united and bellicose. The financial, propagandist and penitential systems that were perfected during the crusade's preparations formed the basis for the conduct of future expeditions. Ironically, even the strategy of an assault on a Nile port was deemed to retain the promise of success. It was rehearsed, with even more disastrous results, in 1249–50 by Louis IX of France and remained a staple of crusade planning for another century. Although many blamed the defeat in Egypt in 1221 on excessive church control, the integration of ecclesiastical wealth into the 'holy business' transformed the nature of the exercise for succeeding generations, as did the availability of cash vow redemptions and donations. The crusade failed to secure a lasting papal–

imperial alliance, but did not necessarily point to mortal combat between the two. More generally, the reaction to the Fifth Crusade was not, as it could have been, the abandonment of the ideal or practices of crusading.[94] Instead, contemporaries took the lesson that their efforts needed to be more sharply focused in terms of logistic preparations, military organization and religious commitment. The Fifth Crusade met military defeat for itself while securing institutional success for its cause.

20

Frontier Crusades 1: Conquest in Spain

To the Damascus scholar al-Sulami in 1105, the recent arrival of the western armies in Syria formed part of a wider Christian attack on Islamic lands. Everywhere encouraged by Muslim disunity, the Franks had conquered Sicily and made extensive conquests in Spain, where they had 'gained possession of town after town', before descending on the Near East.[1] Al-Sulami's vision mirrored Urban II's encouragement for certain Catalan counts to restore the town and church of Tarragona rather than depart for Jerusalem: 'it is no virtue to rescue Christians from the Saracens in one place, only to expose them to the tyranny and oppression of the Saracens in another'.[2] To both, the First Crusade formed part of a larger political struggle between the two religions in which control of territory and lordship stood as a vindication and imperative of faith. While the Muslim concept of *umma*, the universal community of the faithful, derived from the religion's earliest days, its rough Christian equivalent, the idea of Christendom, *Christianitas*, inhabited by a homogeneous Christian people or race (*gens*), was markedly consolidated by the papal reforms of the eleventh century. This emphasized doctrinal and devotional uniformity. Where opponents were of different faiths, the material could be associated with the transcendent. Configuring frontier conflicts in terms of religious identity allowed the language and institutions of holy war to be applied to frontier wars against Muslim and pagan neighbours.

This was no new phenomenon in the late eleventh and twelfth centuries. Christian rhetoric had surrounded the wars of Charlemagne against the then pagan Saxons in the eighth century and those against Vikings, Magyars and Saracens in the ninth and tenth centuries. In the eleventh century, certain frontier conflicts became suffused with doctrines of penitential warfare developed by the reformed papacy for

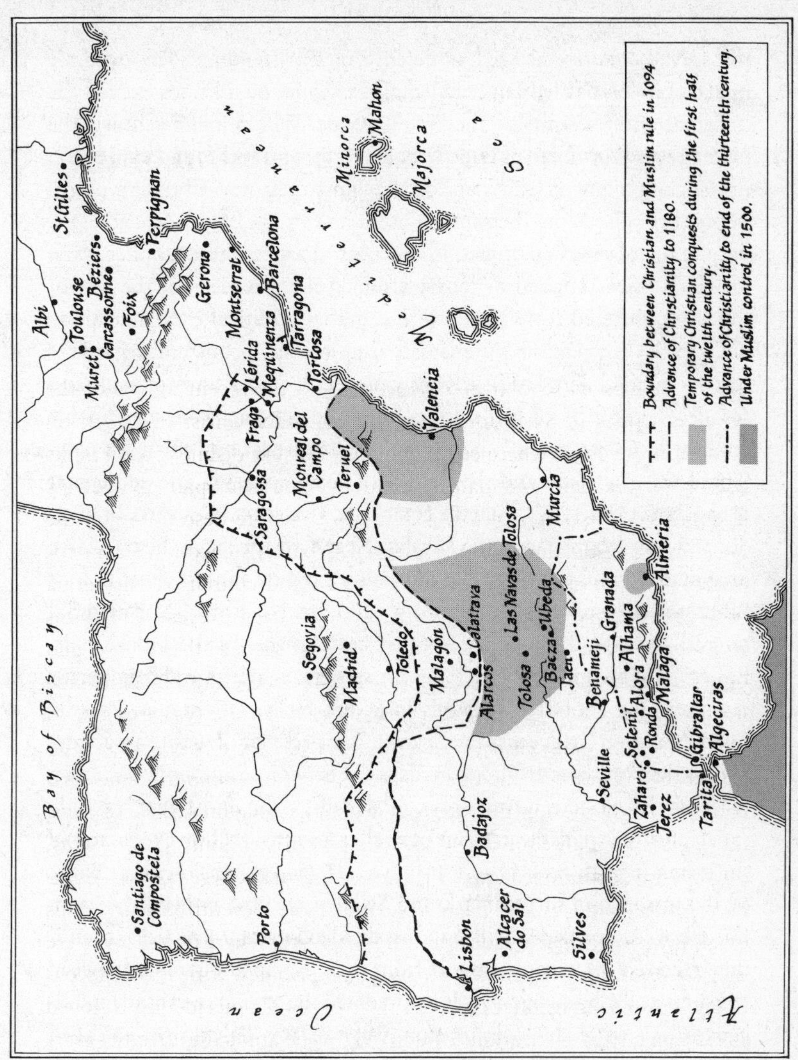

19. The Spanish *Reconquista*

the spread (*dilatio*) as well as defence of Christendom. The dynamic image of an embattled faith challenging enemies on all sides excited the imagination of recruits on the First Crusade. Within half a century, the ideology and formulae of Pope Urban's Jerusalem war found expression in the campaigns of Christian lords against their non-Christian neighbours throughout the Iberian peninsula and in the Baltic. Nonetheless, despite the obvious analogies, in one central aspect these frontier wars, to which popes applied or locals assumed the privileges of the war of the cross, differed from the eastern crusades. Political exchange along and across Christendom's immediate frontiers was a constant, regardless of new-fangled ways of justifying violence. Competition for land and resources, conflicts of lordship, culture and religion were inescapable features of Christendom's borderlands, long predating Urban II's penitential war. In Spain and the Baltic political expansion and settlement drove the crusades, not, as in the Near East, vice versa. Western Christendom had no frontier with the Muslim Near East except in the collective imaginative empathy of a religious culture fed by endless repetition of Bible stories in preaching, the liturgy and art. No strategic or material interest compelled the presence of western knights in the Judean hills. Easier if not always richer pickings for settlers, colonists and conquerors lay along the contested marches in Spain, Sicily, Pomerania, Prussia, Livonia or even Greece and the Aegean. The presence of western warriors and settlers on these frontiers made some economic and political sense, whereas the western adventures to Palestine, Syria and Egypt are only satisfactorily explicable in terms of a religious mission, however material the means used to achieve and sustain it. German expansion in the Baltic or the integration of Denmark and Sweden into the polity of western Europe were not dependent on crusade ideology and practices, even if they received important support from them. In Spain, conflict between Muslims and Christian rulers long predated the arrival of crusade indulgences. As with the colonization wars in the Baltic, the so-called Reconquest (*reconquista*) of Spain by Christian powers in the twelfth and thirteenth centuries, even where embracing the spiritual, legal and fiscal benefits of the *negotium crucis*, retained distinct characteristics unmediated by the idea of the crusade.[3]

THE SPANISH RECONQUEST

The political history of early medieval Spain bore closer similarities with the experience of north Africa, the Levant and the Mediterranean islands than with western Europe north of the Pyrenees. Indeed, it has been argued that the application of crusading formulae to the wars in the peninsula provided a barometer of northern influences and the integration of Spanish society and culture within the norms of Latin Christendom. By the early eighth century, the former Roman province of Hispania was dominated by a Christian Visigothic kingdom based at Toledo, which had emerged two centuries earlier. This Visigothic kingdom was then destroyed by a power that owed nothing either to the Roman or Germanic inheritance. In 711 largely Berber armies led by Arab generals invaded the peninsula, defeating and killing the last Visigothic king, Rodrigo, at the battle of the Guadelete (711). Rapidly, the political structure of Spain was transformed. The Visigothic state imploded, to be replaced by a Muslim emirate (756–1031) with its capital at Cordoba, transformed in 929 into an autonomous caliphate, under the descendants of the earlier seventh- and eighth-century Ummayyad caliphs of the whole Islamic empire. The new rulers asserted their political authority over almost all of the Iberian peninsula, with the exception of the far north beyond the Duero valley, in the Cantabrian mountains and the Basque country. There some enduring Christian lordships coalesced during the century and a half following the Arab invasion. More slowly, the Arab conquest led to the creation of an Islamicized and Arabized culture in the lands they occupied. Berber settlers assumed the orthodoxy of their Muslim Arab commanders and gradually, over many generations, significant numbers of the indigenous Romano-Hispanic population that had not emigrated adopted the customs, language, laws and religion of the conquerors. Although by 900 only about 25 per cent, in 1000, perhaps about 75 per cent of the population of Muslim Spain, al-Andalus, 'the land of the West', may have been Muslims.[4]

This produced neither cultural apartheid nor an Eden of multicultural harmony. As elsewhere under Islamic rulers, Jews and Christians were afforded subordinate status as people of the Book, liable to the habitual poll tax. They lived side by side with Muslim neighbours and adopted the customs and language of their masters, Arabic-speaking Christians being known as Mozarabs. Early medieval Spain under the Ummayyads of Cordoba was a land of diversity as well as *convivencia* (literally 'living together'), but not always harmony. Central authority was often patchy, cultural identity frequently confused by conversion, intermarriage and ambition. Claiming Arab ancestry, even if ersatz, was almost a *sine qua non* for political success under the Cordoba caliphate. The peninsula was crossed by a series of political, social and cultural frontiers to match its intractably divisive physical geography. Such frontiers produced synthesis and contact alongside competition and hostility. The independence of the northern Christian enclaves centred initially around Oviedo in the Asturias largely depended on the early Muslim withdrawal from the region rather than any resilience of their own. Only by the early tenth century had this principality expanded southwards into the wide frontier zone south of the Cantabrian mountains to incorporate a new capital, León, as well as the county of Castile around Burgos and the headwaters of the Ebro. By this time another murkily identifiable lordship had coalesced around Pamplona in the western Pyrenees, later known as Navarre. South-east of Navarre, the valley of the river Aragon, a tributary of the Ebro, also became a focus of power that grew into a separate kingdom in the eleventh century. At the eastern end of the Pyrenees, Catalonia, a political and cultural link with the Christian shores of the Mediterranean and conduit for people and ideas from southern France, had been established by Louis the Pious, Charlemagne's son, in the early years of the ninth century. Charlemagne's own attempts to create a Frankish march further south around Zaragoza on the Ebro failed dismally in 778, a campaign made famous by the defeat of its rearguard at Roncevalles.

With the exception of Catalonia, whose counts remained in the orbit of trans-Pyrenean Frankish politics, these tiny Christian principalities remained insular, locked in a close dependency on rivalries between each other and raiding across the long and wide frontier with the caliphate of Cordoba, bandits and rustlers, not warriors of God. The transformation in the *Song of Roland* of the disastrous massacre of a Frankish regiment by Pyrenean Basques in 778 into an epic contest pitting Christian chivalry against the massed exotic malignity of Spanish and north African Islam owed everything to religious rhetoric, social values, cultural experiences and imaginative constructions north of the Pyrenees. The development of the *Song of Roland*, its earliest written version only surviving from the early twelfth century, after the First Crusade, in no way reflected Iberian realities. However, the idea of the immediate Iberian military frontier with Islam played its part in the formation of Urban II's world-view. In the second half of the eleventh century, Spanish frontier wars attracted recruits from southern France and, possibly, even papal indulgences a generation before the Council of Clermont, signs, at the least, of greater interest from outside the region. When and how far these wars of survival, profit and conquest were regarded by those engaged in them as possessing any transcendent religious purpose or spiritual value remains both unclear and controversial.

Most national identities rest in part on a series of shared pseudo-historical myths. Christian Spain, that of Ferdinand and Isabella, Philip II or General Franco, defined itself in the context of the Reconquest from the Moors (literally people from the old Roman province of Mauretania, i.e. Berbers from what are now coastal Morocco and Algeria), a process begun with the eighth-century Asturian resistance to the Muslim conquerors and finding its culmination in the capture of Granada in 1492. This construct gave shape to an otherwise messy political history; it explained and justified the elements of religious, even racial exclusivity in early modern and modern Spanish culture; it provided a link between late medieval Christian rule and its remote Visigothic predecessor; and it lent to Spanish history the aura of providential destiny. Holy war operated at the centre of the Reconquest myth. The leading patron saint of Spain, St James, became an archetype of holy warrior. In war as in peace, church marched in militant step with state. It was no coincidence that Spanish *bula de la cruzada*, papally sanctioned grants of spiritual privileges in return for cash payments to secular or ecclesiastical authorities, a direct legacy of medieval crusade instruments, resisted many attempts at their abolition from the sixteenth century onwards. Only with the Second Vatican Council (1962–5) were these crusading remnants finally laid to rest.[5]

However closely associated, the Reconquest and crusading were not synonyms. The conquest of Muslim Spain by Christian princes was a long political process; regarding it as a *re*-conquest, a state of mind. A crusade was an event, Spanish crusades punctuating the larger narrative of conquest and settlement. Crusaders conquered but if subsequently they settled in these newly acquired lands, they did so not as crusaders *per se*. Frontier settlements may have been established by warriors of the cross but they were not 'crusading communities', with the possible exception of those areas and castles controlled by the military orders. Some historians have designated certain regions in terms of the ideology of conquest, as in the thirteenth-century 'Crusader Kingdom of Valencia'.[6] This may appear something of a misnomer. The ideology of penitential warfare lent an edge to pre-existing reconquest mentalities, but it is notable that the development of communal and religious intolerance and the rise of a new biological racism that marked the persecution of Jews, Muslims and Muslim converts (*moriscos*) in the late fifteenth and sixteenth centuries post-dated the period when crusades were a regular feature of Iberian politics.

Early versions of the Reconquest myth emerged among propagandists associated with the royal court of the Asturias in the late ninth century. Their object lay in asserting a legitimate continuity for Asturian kingship from the Visigothic past, the purging of the former sins that had lost Spain to Christendom and the providential mission to restore Christian rule and liberty to the peninsula. Ninth-century concerns fashioned accounts of the creation of the Asturian kingdom by a King Pelayo, ostensibly of Visigothic royal blood, after a victory over the Moors in 722. In this triumph against the odds, so the myth insisted, the inevitable recovery of Christian Spain was born. Although such claims were fictive, this fashioning of perceptions established important and lasting traditions. Wars of defence and conquest against the Moors were projected as possessing a fundamental religious purpose, the salvation (*salus*) of Spain.[7] Aggression, portrayed as recapturing territory lost by Visigothic predecessors, was intrinsically just. The struggle with Muslim neighbours became elevated into a sort of Manichaean contest of religions and cultures which bore very little actual relation to the nature of frontier competition and exchange, still less to the continuous internecine conflicts between the Christian lordlings of the north. As elsewhere in western Europe, the church, its bishops and its saints became intensely involved in promoting political identity. The permanent presence of the infidel aided the development of religious warfare, in ways parallel to contemporary war rhetoric in Alfredian Wessex or late Carolingian Francia. Religious symbolism and church liturgy had long been incorporated into the rituals of war. There was an elaborate liturgy blessing a departing warrior king in the Visigothic *Liber ordinum*, and it is possible that the tradition of bearing into battle a cross, or a relic of the True Cross, survived in the Christian kingdoms.[8]

However, warfare framed by religious language is hardly the same as a self-conscious religiously backed Reconquest or even religious war. Religious approval of war was a commonplace to inspire loyalty, establish united purpose, salve consciences and assuage doubts on both sides of the Iberian frontier. The great Cordoban vizier al-Mansur (i.e. 'the Victorious', 976–1002) attacked churches and monasteries during his devastating raids into Christian territory (985–1102), in which he plundered from Barcelona and Pamplona to León, the Duero valley and Coimbra. In 997, he carried off the bells of the basilica of St James at Compostela to adorn the mosque at Cordoba. Al-Mansur made a public virtue of his piety, allegedly carrying his own autograph fair copy of the Koran on campaigns, which he publicized as *jihad*. This did not prevent him from employing Christians as mercenaries and guides or being remembered by his own people as 'our provider of slaves'.[9] All Iberian rulers conducted aggressive warfare for profit. Although by 1000 much of this was conducted across the frontier region around the Duero valley stretching north-east towards the Upper Ebro and the foothills of the Pyrenees, there existed many petty frontiers in early eleventh-century Iberia, those caused by religion only the most obvious. The political authority and material resources of the Cordoban caliphate rather than its religious complexion made it a threat and a target for its Christian neighbours. Competition for resources and power pitted Christian against Christian and induced political alliances across religious divides. This was not how it looked to later observers and some foreign contemporaries, such as the Burgundian monk Ralph Glaber (*c.*980–1046), who wrote of resistance to al-Mansur in terms of faith and heavenly reward.[10] However, recourse to the encouragement of religion in an idealized vision of a conflict of faiths ignored the realities of eleventh-century Spain.

Politics and cash, not religion, provided the impetus for the Reconquest. The collapse of the Cordoban caliphate through internecine feuding in the generation leading to its extinction in 1031 and its replacement by a patchwork of so-called *taifa* or 'party' kingdoms provided Christian rulers with a chance to intervene in affairs of the south, a reversal of the politics of al-Mansur's time. Muslim Spain was transformed into competing principalities, many no stronger, some weaker than their

Christian counterparts: Badajoz, Seville, Granada, Malaga, Toledo, Murcia, Valencia, Denia, Zaragoza, Lerida and the Balearic Islands. Strong Christian rulers, such as Ferdinand I of León-Castile, his son, Alfonso VI, and Ramon Berenguer I count of Barcelona (1035–76), exploited these divisions by establishing a network of proprietorial protection rackets. Formal treaties were drawn up under which the Christian ruler would agree to defend his *taifa* client in return for vast quantities of the key commodity that fuelled these relationships, gold. Although the material weakness of *taifa* emirs allowed for territorial expansion, such as Ferdinand I's annexation of Coimbra in 1064, intense competition revolved around *taifa* gold through annual tributes, or protection money, known as *parias*. Historically, the prosperous urban economy of al-Andalus had been rich in gold that came from the west African Gold Coast across the Sahara to the Mediterranean. Now the Christian kings managed to harness this wealth for themselves. By the 1060s, Ferdinand I, for example, enjoyed *parias* from Zaragoza, Toledo and Badajoz. Control over Zaragoza had been contested between León-Castile, Navarre and Barcelona. On Ferdinand's death, it passed briefly to Sancho IV of Navarre. Al-Andalus became the milch-cow for Christian assertiveness. The wider circulation of large quantities of gold, in the rest of western Europe a very scarce commodity, funded the consolidation of royal power, the formation of stable states and the expansion of Christian frontiers. As well as enriching those in military, religious, civilian or commercial royal service, the influx of gold to the Christian realms attracted interest from beyond the Pyrenees, both military adventurers and diplomatic allies. In that indirect fashion, the *parias* system contributed to opening Spain to ideas of holy war increasingly fashionable north of the Pyrenees.[11]

Religion was no determinant in these arrangements. In his deal with the emir of Zaragoza for the year 1069, Sancho IV of Navarre explicitly agreed not to assist any 'people from France or elsewhere' crossing his kingdom to attack Zaragoza or ally with any Christians or Muslims against the emir, with whom the king would be bound 'in one brotherhood'. For these promises, the emir agreed to pay 1,000 gold pieces a month.[12] These deals rightly assumed an inherent instability that allowed entrepreneurial freebooters to sell their swords and armed following to the highest bidder or even to establish themselves as independent rulers. This occurred across the peninsula, making it, for the first time in centuries, a single, if chaotic political system. One Muslim political entrepreneur from the south, Ibn Ammar (1031–84), had won and lost control of Murcia. After years in exile at the court of Zaragoza, he was murdered by his former boss, the emir of Seville, using an axe given by Alfonso VI of León-Castile. The most famous example of a freelance taking advantage of this fluidity of preferment and power was the Castilian nobleman Rodrigo Diaz, El Cid (*c.*1045–99). A valued general and diplomat under Ferdinand I, after falling out with Alfonso VI, Rodrigo served the emir of Zaragoza (1081–6), becoming rich from his victories over Catalans and Aragonese. After a brief reconciliation with Alfsonso, from 1089 Rodrigo maintained a private army through successful and lucrative campaigning against Christian as well as Muslim rulers in eastern Spain before establishing his own independent *taifa* lordship at Valencia (1094–9), which survived until 1102.[13] Such were the opportunities of political instability.

These opportunities stimulated the ideology of Reconquest, not vice versa. Instead of relying solely on indirect exploitation, racketeers like Alfonso VI, partly to secure their income, looked to run their client states themselves. The strand of Reconquest justification came in useful, particularly, it seems, for Alfsonso VI. When gathering *parias*, his agents talked of the strategy of ultimate recovery of lands that 'originally belonged to the Christians'. When establishing the new archbishopric at Toledo in 1086, a year after its capture, Alfonso VI talked of restoring the city, after 376 years, 'under the leadership of Christ ... to the devotees of His faith'. Muslim rule was described as usurpation by blasphemers; the conquest of Toledo as a recreation of 'a holy place'. Sancho I of Aragon echoed this theme, talking of his conquests as 'the recovery and extension of the Church of Christ'. Both Gregory VII and Urban II, who like many popes of the eleventh and twelfth centuries displayed particular concern for Iberian Christianity, picked up the theme of the liberation of former Christian lands. Toledo, Urban purred, was 'restored' by Alfonso VI 'to the law of the Christians'.[14] The Reconquest was not a war of conversion but conquest and, in places, expulsion. Yet, despite the realities of inter-faith political collaboration, the language and symbols of religion came in useful. When Peter I of Aragon attacked Zaragoza in 1101 he was described as bearing a cross (*crucifer*).[15] By then he had a grander model to copy: the expedition to Jerusalem.

THE SPANISH CRUSADES

While the convenient idea of the just political and religious war of Reconquest may be traced to indigenous peninsula origins, the stimulus to the application of holy war was probably a foreign import. In tune with papal policy elsewhere, Alexander II may have offered 'knights destined to set out for Spain' remission of penance and confessed sin in 1063, although the authenticity of his bull has been questioned.[16] Whether or not Alexander was suggesting that war against the Moors was itself penitential, a Catalan-Aragonese campaign that briefly occupied Barbastro, north-east of Zaragoza, in 1064–5 attracted troops from Burgundy, Normandy, Aquitaine and possibly Norman Sicily who, in their short occupation of the town, committed the sort of atrocity for which western knights became notorious in the Muslim world. The Barbastro expedition, while hardly meriting the title of a 'crusade before the crusades',[17] showed increased trans-Pyrenean interest in Spanish affairs. In its wake came harsher attitudes towards Muslims based on ignorance, unfamiliarity and the martial spirituality of the reformed papacy. Spain became something of a testing ground for the Roman church's claims to leadership of Christendom on two fronts: the imposition of a Roman rather than Mozarab liturgy on the Spanish church and the struggle against Islam. In 1073, Gregory VII characteristically asserted that Spain 'from ancient times belonged to St Peter'. Despite long occupation by the Moors 'it belongs even now . . . to no mortal but solely to the Apostolic see'. Small wonder four years later Alfonso VI began to style himself 'emperor of all Spain' to retain freedom of action.[18] Ecclesiastical interest was supported by the penetration of Cluniac monasticism into northern Spain during the eleventh century. In another sign of quickening religious and cultural transmission across the Pyrenees, in 1064 Ramon Berenguer I of Barcelona promulgated the Peace and Truce of God.

By the 1080s, foreign military participation in the profitable Iberian wars had become familiar, as had the habit of Spanish princes and princesses seeking spouses north of the Pyrenees. In 1068, Sancho I Ramirez of Navarre married the sister of Count Ebles of Roucy, perhaps as part of a deal to attract the count's military support against the *taifa* kings, a scheme still being promoted by the papacy five years later. Alfonso VI managed five wives over an extended and complicated marital career: a daughter of the duke of Aquitaine (William VIII, a veteran of the Barbastro campaign, 1064–5), a sister of the duke of Burgundy as well as two further Frenchwomen and an Italian. His daughters' husbands (he had no legitimate surviving sons) included two close members of the ducal house of Burgundy and Roger II of Sicily. Of his illegitimate daughters, one married Raymond IV of Toulouse, veteran of Spanish wars and a leader of the First Crusade, another the nephew of the duke of Burgundy. Dynastically, León-Castile had entered the family of western European rulers, even if domestically Alfonso retained local tastes; one of his mistresses, Zaida, was the daughter-in-law of the emir of Seville.[19]

Two events transformed the redefinition of the Reconquest apparent in some later eleventh-century texts into a tradition of holy war; the invasion of Spain by the Moroccan fundamentalist Almoravids and the development of the papal policy of penitential war that led to the First Crusade. From their original base on the fringes of the Sahara, by the early 1080s the Almoravids, a sect of austere Islamic fundamentalists, had conquered Morocco. Representing a very different cultural perspective than the Arabic Mediterranean sophistication of the rulers of al-Andalus, the Almoravids combined the fanaticism of converts with the militancy of outsiders. They were the *al-Murabitun*, 'people of the *ribat*', armed monasteries on the frontiers of Islam, who imposed strict observance on their followers, subjects and neighbours by force of piety and arms. Religion lay at the heart of their aggressive politics. By the mid-1080s they were ready to extend their authority across the Straits of Gibraltar into al-Andalus whether the local Muslim rulers welcomed them or, as was almost universally the case, not. The Almoravids regarded what they saw as the corrupt decadence of the *taifa* kings with as much contempt as they despised the Christian infidels. In return, the emirs of al-Andalus no less than their Christian neighbours and partners saw the Moroccan invaders as threatening their power and the whole mutually beneficial political system. However, with the pressure growing from the north, in the aftermath of Alfonso VI's capture of Toledo in 1085, the *taifa* emirs, led by Seville, had little option but to invite Almoravid aid. The invasion, led by Yusuf Ibn Tashfin, led to the defeat of Alfonso at Sagrajas in 1086. Over the next quarter of a century, by force, coercion and diplomacy, the Almoravids absorbed remaining *taifa* emirates into their empire, the last, Zaragoza, falling in 1110.

The adoption of a newly aggressive idea of Christian holy war came in direct response to this new threat to territory and the cosy system of *parias*. However, despite official ecclesiastical pronouncements, this was not perceived as a simple blanket religious conflict. Twelfth-century Christian Spanish writers repeatedly drew the distinction between the Muslims of al-Andalus, sometimes called 'Hagarenes', with whom business could be done, and the alien invaders, referred to as 'Moabites', with whom it could not.[20]

Into this new political situation arrived foreign soldiers with the ideology and institutions of penitential warfare. In 1089, perhaps in response to news of the Almoravid invasion of that year, Urban II offered the same remission of sins to those who helped rebuild the city and church of Tarragona as that granted to those on penitential pilgrimage to Jerusalem, an offer repeated in 1091. Contributing to the defence of Tarragona, over the border on the coast fifty miles south of Barcelona, constituted a penance, as the city was intended as a 'wall and bastion (literally 'ante-mural') against the Saracens for the Christian people'.[21] Such mingling of defensive religious just war and remission of sins defined by analogy with the extreme penance of the Jerusalem pilgrimage showed how papal ideas were moving. The launch of the First Crusade did not deflect Urban from support of the Tarragona enterprise. He tried to insist that local counts should not fulfil their Jerusalem vow in the east but fight the Muslims nearer home. This hope was not entirely successful. There is little evidence that the cause of Tarragona proved popular but rather more for Spanish involvement in the Jerusalem campaign itself. However, the success of the First Crusade had its impact on Spain as elsewhere. Peter I of Aragon had taken the cross to go to Jerusalem in 1100. A year later, still trying to annexe Zaragoza, he displayed banners of the cross at the siege of the city and built a castle to intimidate the citizens nicknamed 'Juslibol', i.e. 'God Wills It', the slogan of Clermont.[22]

The incorporation of the formal apparatus of crusading – bull, indulgence, temporal privileges, cross – sprang from the wider, older association of Christian conquest and religious war. The past, as revealed by twelfth-century accounts of earlier campaigns against the Moors, was reconfigured to include holy war. From *c.*1115, the patronal saint, James the Apostle, began to be referred to as a 'knight of Christ', apparently shocking a visiting Greek, a story that suggested the novelty of the saint's new role.[23] Other saints, such as George in Aragon and Catalonia, and even, bizarrely, the seventh-century scholar Isidore of Seville, popular in León, were recruited to the providential mission of reconquest, as was the cult of the Virgin Mary. These local or adopted celestial allies outflanked papal arguments promoting St Peter as the peninsula's proprietary saint. There were other limits to the acceptance of the crusade. Twelfth-century writers close to the action continued to chronicle the non-violent interaction between Christian and al-Andalus Muslims. Even the early thirteenth-century epic on Rodrigo Diaz, the *Poema de Mio Cid* (*The Poem of the Cid*) admits to the hero's friendship with Muslims and catalogues the deficiencies of Rodrigo's Christian associates as much as those of the Moors. As with the *Historia Roderici* of a century before, this is hardly 'crusading' literature.[24] Despite the trickle of papal bulls from the early decades of the twelfth century, holy war was grafted on to the Spanish conflicts only gradually and, from an Iberian perspective, incompletely. Not all subsequent wars against Muslims were crusades. Crusading did not, as often in the eastern Mediterranean, set the military and political agenda but followed it, shaping mentalities, not strategy. The association of holiness to defence and conquest paid practical dividends, in the use of military orders in front-line settlements as well on campaign, or in the access to ecclesiastical and lay taxation. However, Iberian Muslims rarely attracted from Iberian Christians the consistent demonization concocted by western rhetoric far from the crusade frontier. Spanish *convivencia*, while never the Edenic state of multicultural harmony some have imagined, precluded the worst excesses of religious hatred in the contest for supremacy that rumbled and spat for a century and half after the First Crusade. The tainted legacy of entrenched intolerance and the racist persecution and expulsion of non-Catholic Spaniards belonged more to the period after the effective completion of the Reconquest, Granada excepted, in the mid-thirteenth century than to the previous period of active crusading.[25] Nonetheless, crusade stereotypes did influence the creation of Spanish Catholic exceptionalism in the late fifteenth and sixteenth centuries, providing a justification for internal discrimination with an abiding external incentive, the recovery of Jerusalem. The self-image of warriors of Christ, specially favoured and specially commissioned, that permeated Spanish official culture by 1500 was thus an indirect product of the historical Reconquest crusade experience.[26]

HOLY WAR

By analogy, the First Crusade lent definition to the application of holy war to the Spanish Reconquest. While remissions of sins were attached to various Spanish campaigns by Paschal II, the full panoply including cross-giving was applied to the ephemerally successful Pisan-Catalan-southern French assault on the Balearic Islands in 1113–14, and possibly to the unrealized attack on Tortosa planned in 1115. The successful siege of Zaragoza by Alfonso I of Aragon in 1118 drew a papal indulgence for those who died or, in the tradition of Urban II's Tarragona appeal of 1089, contributed to the establishment of the city's new church and clergy. The consistent papal line was that the Spanish war against Islam was as useful and therefore as meritorious as the wars for the Holy Land, even in the absence of equivalent symbols and privileges. The First Lateran Council of 1123, summoned by Calixtus II, a former papal legate to Spain, confirmed the equation by lumping together those who had taken the cross for Jerusalem and Spain (Canon XI).[27] At the same time, Calixtus granted to *crucesignati* in Spain 'the same remission of sins that we conceded to the defenders of the eastern church' for an expedition planned in Catalonia under the legates of the archbishop of Tarragona.[28] On the other side of the peninsula, in 1125, Archbishop Diego Gelmirez of Santiago took up the linguistic and theological association in a grandiose scheme apparently aimed at reaching Jerusalem via north Africa: 'let us become soldiers of Christ . . . taking up arms . . . for the remission of sins'.[29] However, as with the papal plan for a general crusade in Spain in 1123, the archbishop's ambition proved stillborn. In general, crusading apparatus was most effective when it fitted existing plans rather than of itself stimulating action in the manner of many eastern Mediterranean campaigns. It is notable how regularly papal crusade grants came in response to requests from local Iberian rulers. Perhaps of greater significance than the operation of the formal paraphernalia of the Jerusalem holy war in Spain was its influence on aspirations. Increasingly, wars in Spain were regarded by their promoters in terms of the wider conflict defined by the Jerusalem war. This redefinition was neither universal nor constant. Yet its penetration was evident in Leonese and Castilian chronicles and, most startlingly, in the 1131 testamentary arrangements of Alfonso I of Aragon-Navarre (d. 1134), who left his kingdom jointly to the Templars, Hospitallers and the Canons of the Holy Sepulchre. Ten years before his death Alfonso had attempted to found a *militia Christi*, modelled on the Templars, entrusted with the task of fighting all Muslims and, in the fashion of Archbishop Gelmirez, cutting a new path to Jerusalem.[30]

The experience of the late 1140s emphasized how Iberian holy war was influenced by local demands coinciding with grander crusading designs, in this case the Second Crusade. In 1146, the Genoese had attacked the port of Almeria on the southern coast of Granada, an expedition described by contemporaries in wholly secular terms. The following year, in alliance with Alfonso VII of Castile, a renewed Genoese attack had been elevated into a holy war, complete with remission of sins. Alfonso attracted allies to join the venture with promises of 'redemption of souls' before he obtained from Eugenius III retrospective confirmation of the status of the new attack on Almeria in the bull *Divina dispensatione* (April 1147).[31] Almeria fell to the Christians in October 1147. In conception and execution, the Almeria campaign had no direct connection with the larger eastern expedition beyond the availability of crusade privileges. In 1148, a further papal grant of crusader indulgences 'which Pope Urban established for all those going for the liberation of the eastern church' was applied to the Catalan-Genoese attack on Tortosa at the mouth of the Ebro, which fell after a five-month siege in December 1148.[32] Among others, the Tortosa campaign recruited veterans from Almeria and the successful siege of Lisbon (July–October 1147). However, it is notable that, unlike the Aragonese and Catalan ventures of 1147–8, the Lisbon enterprise seems not to have elicited an explicit, separate papal crusade bull, the Portuguese invitation to the Holy Land crusaders, however long contemplated, appearing by comparison rather more opportunist.

The failure of the Second Crusade in the east dampened papal and probably popular enthusiasm for crusading holy war. However, local conditions, in Spain as in the Baltic, encouraged continued identification of secular conflict with religious war. This was lent added force by a new threat to Christian gains from the Almohads, *al-Muwahhidun*, the 'Upholders of the Divine Unity'. These fundamentalist unitarians, originating like the Almoravids in southern Morocco, sought to purge the increasingly corrupt Almoravid regime and restore to the Maghrib and al-Andalus the spiritual purity and intensity of early Islam. The

Almoravids had emphasized legalistic rules and operated a very loose theocratic regime even before they declined from their initial austerity. The Almohads, under their founder Muhammed Ibn Tumart (declared the *mahdi* by his followers in 1121, d. 1130) and his successor 'Abd al-Mu 'min (1130–63) destroyed Almoravid power in the Mahgrib and, from 1146, began to infiltrate across the Straits into Spain. (They founded a town at Gibraltar in 1159.) While initially a threat chiefly to the emirs, who had regained a measure of autonomy as the authority of the Almoravids had decayed from the 1120s, soon the Christian rulers felt the force of this new power. By 1173, mainland al-Andalus had been annexed by the Almohads under Yusuf I (1163–84). In the next quarter of a century, the Almohads reversed many of the Christian advances of the previous generations. In 1195 they defeated Alfonso VIII of Castile at Alarcos on the river Guadiana and proceeded to raid into the Tagus valley. Yet, even here, the complexity of Spanish politics overlay any religious conflict. At least one disaffected Castilian noble fought for the Almohads at Alarcos and in 1196 led a Muslim regiment in the army of Alfonso IX of León which invaded Castile.[33] The Almohad advance served only to add another potential ally for the warring Christian kings. In an attempt to impose Christian unity, in 1197 the nonagenarian pope, Celestine III, was even induced to authorize the full eastern crusading privileges for those who fought against the renegade Alfonso IX.[34] Only in gilded memory was the Spanish crusade a simple religious war.

Celestine III's use of the crusade against the Christian Alfonso IX, although eliciting little obvious response, demonstrated how far the mechanics of the Jerusalem war had come to dominate church-sanctioned violence. In 1166, a church council at Segovia had proposed Jerusalem indulgences for those who defended Castile from invasion. By the early thirteenth century, crusade privileges became a regular, accepted element in church warfare. However, Celestine had a more personal concern with Iberian politics. As Cardinal Hyacinth he had twice been on legatine missions to the peninsula, in 1154–5 and 1172–3. On each occasion he had promoted the Reconquest as a crusade, an association he revived during his pontificate, when he sent his nephew, Gregory of Sant' Angelo, as legate to Spain.[35] While Celestine's commitment exposed the contrast between the rhetoric of holy war and the reality of secular politics, his long career witnessed the consolidation of a crusading tradition which, although reflecting both the general absence of crusading between 1149 and 1187 and its revival and extension thereafter, presented distinctive features.

Most obvious was the use of international and local military orders to garrison the frontier regions from southern Aragon to Portugal.[36] As recipients of alms, estates, villages and castles, the military orders played a central role in the politics as well as campaigning of the Reconquest, a position reflected in successive rulers' determination to control them. Each kingdom created its own orders, as well as patronizing the Templars and Hospitallers, who stood as the models for the rest. In the 1140s, these two international orders had begun to be employed in a military capacity as opposed to merely receiving grants of land. Within thirty years, every kingdom except Navarre had established their own orders, while retaining the services of the Temple and Hospital, especially in Aragon and Catalonia. Among the lasting foundations were Calatrava (1158) in Castile; Santiago (1170) and St Julian of Pereiro, later known as Alcantara (by 1176), in León; Evora, later Avis (by 1176), in Portugal. During the same periods a number of more ephemeral orders were established, each, like the more permanent orders, based on frontier castles which, in many cases, gave them their names as well as headquarters. One order, of La Merced (*c.*1230), was founded in Barcelona to ransom captives of the Moors, a task it shared with the French Order of the Trinity.[37] Although the details are often obscure, the initiative to found these orders appears to have come from pious noblemen (or in the case of the Mercedarians a wealthy merchant), with the encouragement and patronage of kings and ecclesiastical hierarchies. The larger orders soon began to resemble the Holy Land military orders in attracting international investment; by 1200 the Order of Santiago held estates from the British Isles to Carinthia. The chronology of foundation, the second half of the twelfth century, suggests that the institutionalization of holy war was not an immediate consequence either of the Reconquest successes of the previous century or of the First Crusade. The presence of these orders influenced the way the Reconquest was pursued, as well as playing a prominent role in national politics and internecine warfare between Christian rulers. However, only when the major conquest in al-Andalus were nearing completion did the Orders of Alcantara (1238) and Calatrava (1240) receive permanent privileges from the pope granting indulgences to any who fought with them against the Moors, creating for them the sort of 'eternal crusade' seen later in the thirteenth century, applied to the activities of the Teutonic Knights in the Baltic. Consistently, Spanish crusading, while providing a framework for lay enthusiasm and, in the military orders, institutions for maintaining conquests, remained secondary or complementary to secular considerations and an older association of Christian conquest with religious war.

Another characteristic of Spanish crusading lay in the two distinct audiences courted by papal grants. Within the peninsula, crusading privileges merely underpinned the pre-existing sense of mission and righteousness involved in fighting armies of infidels and winning land ostensibly for Christianity. It is difficult to gauge the autonomous effect of such appeals on recruits. The wars would have been fought in any case, their cause identified as religious and just. Raising armies followed secular patterns of military obligations and clientage. Troops were summoned as to any other war, their terms of service, chronological and financial, being the same as for secular or non-crusading warfare. Pay or shares in booty held the armies together. The church may have felt more obliged to contribute to crusading ventures as it stood to gain new bishoprics and lands. Crusade privileges, especially those contained in general appeals of the kind instituted by Calixtus II in 1123, were also designed to attract foreign assistance, the crusade as an international recruiting device constituting one of its chief roles in the Spanish Reconquest. Certain areas, such as southern France, were also specifically targeted. There were exceptions, as in 1189–90 and 1217, when crusaders en route to the eastern Mediterranean assisted locals rulers in new conquests along the southern coastline of the peninsula on the pattern familiar from 1147–8. Even so, the significance of cross-Pyrenean aid was largely limited to the period up to the greatest Reconquest victory at Las Navas de Tolosa in 1212. Thereafter, although foreigners continued to campaign in the peninsula and to settle in new conquests such as Seville (conquered in 1248), the crusades were increasingly overt adjuncts to national territorial expansion and internal state building. The failure of successive rulers in Catalonia and Languedoc to create a unified kingdom stretching from the Ebro to the Rhône compounded this patriation of the Spanish crusade.

The Las Navas de Tolosa campaign was instrumental in this process. The battle of 16 July 1212 was won by a coalition of Spanish kings, Alfonso VIII of Castile, Peter II of Aragon, and Sancho VII of Navarre.

Although a few northern allies under Archbishop Arnaud Amaury of Narbonne remained in the Christian army for the battle, the bulk of the French recruits had deserted the campaign a fortnight earlier, disappointed at the lack of action or booty and oppressed by the summer heat, while the duke of Austria had not yet arrived. The victory over al-Nasir (1199–1214) and his large Almohad force could thus be proclaimed as a specifically Spanish achievement and fitted into a providential narrative of Spanish revenge for the 'Spanish' defeat of 711. Although surrounded by the panoply of crusading, the campaign relied on the secular resources of Castile. Alfonso VIII bankrolled the whole enterprise, paying for the bulk of the coalition troops, including stipends for Peter II and his Aragonese army, and providing the unreliable French with horses. To allow him to do this, Alfonso had extracted a massive forced aid of 50 per cent of annual revenues from the Castilian church. The muster had been fixed at Castilian Toledo for Pentecost 1212. The consequences of the Las Navas campaign were profound, if equivocal. The Reconquest's association with crusading institutions failed to disguise the dependence for success on the national strength of, in particular, Castile, re-emphasized following the death during the Albigensian crusade at Muret in 1213 of Peter II, a crusader killed by crusaders. The victory of Las Navas opened Andalucia to Castilian aggression. It fatally undermined Almohad prestige and power both in Spain and Morocco, where a demoralized al-Nasir died in 1214. The financial precedent exerted possibly the most direct material influence as successive Iberian monarchs exploited the church to fund their wars, in particular appropriating a third of ecclesiastical tithe income (*tercias*) as well as attempting to syphon off clerical taxation designed to help the Holy Land. Combined with a range of extraordinary lay levies and forced loans, the needs of the Reconquest materially strengthened the fiscal and hence political power of the state in thirteenth-century Iberia, a lasting legacy of the expedients that won the triumph at Las Navas.[38]

Within forty years, all that remained of Muslim al-Andalus politically was the emirate of Granada, reduced to a Castilian tributary. As the disintegrating Almohad empire fell with accelerating rapidity into Christian hands, crusading in Spain adopted a settled local flavour. There were no more Muslim counter-attacks to excite the fear of all western Christendom. When the kingdom of Navarre devolved on to Theobald IV count of Champagne (1201–53) in 1234, its new French ruler preferred to take the cross for the Holy Land, not Andalucia. The great warrior kings of the thirteenth century, Ferdinand III of Castile (and of León from 1230) and James I, 'the Conqueror' of Aragon, rolled back the Muslim frontier self-consciously in the name of God. Each flirted with carrying the fight beyond the peninsula, to Africa or Palestine. Yet neither found the commitment that led their contemporary Louis IX of France to the Nile (1249–50), even though, as Christendom's elder statesman, James I sent an Aragonese regiment east in 1269 and played a central if hardly positive role in plans for a new eastern crusade in 1274. Some conquests were accompanied by gestures of religious restoration and purification, with a stated goal of extending the Christian faith. When Ferdinand III captured Cordoba in 1236, he returned to the cathedral of St James in Compostela the bells al-Mansur had seized in 997, which had been housed in the Cordoban great mosque ever since. Elsewhere, the siege of Valencia (1238) attracted English and French recruits and Seville (captured 1248), was partly settled by foreign Christians to replace the expelled Muslims. Yet much of the Reconquest involved negotiation and accommodation of the religious, legal and civil liberties of the conquered, as with James I's annexation of Mallorca (1229) and Valencia (1231–8) and Ferdinand III's occupation of Murcia in 1243. In the kingdom of Valencia, the majority Muslim population remained, despite James having taken the cross in 1232 to symbolize his religious credentials. The few attempts at conversion amounted to little, although some Muslims apostatized, such as Abu Zayd, the king of Valencia deposed in 1229 and ally of James I. He adopted the Christian name Vincent. In 1245, his son, al-Hasan, by then governor of the Moroccan Atlantic port of Sale, abortively offered to convert and turn his city over to the Order of Santiago as a start to the conversion of the Maghrib.[39] In many ways, after the conquests, Muslims and Christians changed roles, the *mudejars* now becoming the protected second-class citizens. The sound of calls of the muezzin to prayer persisted in some areas for centuries, to the growing annoyance of their Christian neighbours. Although new sacred and secular landscapes and spaces were created, from encouraging Christian immigration and changing Arabic place names to converting mosques into churches, initially, at least, holy war did not impose a holy settlement on the ancient Muslim communities of conquered al-Andalus. Accommodation survived. In regions such as Valencia, non-Christian communities negotiated their own futures, their subordinate status only very slowly succumbing to concerted discrimination. However, the status and rights of the *mudejars* did deteriorate, until the recrudescence of militant neo-crusading led to the imposition of intolerant and increasingly racist Christian uniformity under the Catholic monarchs Ferdinand II of Aragon and Isabella of Castile and their heirs Charles V and Philip II. Yet, the expulsions and persecutions of *mudejars* and *moriscos* testified to the hold not of the crusading ideals familiar to the twelfth and thirteenth centuries, but to a newly configured aggressive militancy that engaged the crusade tradition as well as the Reconquest myth to drive its chariot's wheels.

With the fall of Seville in 1248, the main thrust of the Reconquest had been completed. Thereafter, and arguably for years before, the crusade in Spain was almost entirely subsumed in the mainstream of Spanish life, distinguishable largely in name only as a separate exercise of religious devotion, military enterprise or financial expedient. The occasional recrudescence of war, such as the campaign against the Marinid invaders from Morocco, which ended with their defeat by Alfonso XI of Castile at the river Salado in 1340, still elicited crusade bulls. The religious mentality crusading fostered and bequeathed to the conquerors was more truly reflected in the fiscal and penitential instruments it had created, such as the *bula de la cruzada*. These became obstinately cherished elements of Spanish public life, especially in Castile, after the early thirteenth century the only Christian kingdom with a land border with the Moors of Granada. The ideology of crusade and Reconquest, reflected in the continued material prominence of the military orders, induced a providential tinge to the rhetoric of state power and national identity.

Although the decline in active frontier militarism after *c.*1300 may be traced in the fading of the cult of Santiago before that of the Virgin Mary, the holy war tradition remained available in its crusading wrapping. Despite intimate social and economic exchange across confessional divides in Andalucia, Murcia and Valencia, for the knightly and noble classes and their royal and ecclesiastical sponsors engaged in wars against infidels – Muslim or heathen – in Granada, the Mediterranean, north Africa or the Atlantic, identification with the crusade remained a living cultural force as well as a stereotype. While his captains were observing west Africans outside the straitjacket of crusading aesthetics, the Portuguese prince Henry the Navigator (1394–1460) embraced crusading aspirations and campaigned in north Africa.[40] As late as 1578, a Portuguese king, Sebastian, died commanding an international force, armed with indulgences and papal legates, fighting the Moors of Morocco at the battle of Alcazar. The penetration of Latin Christendom into the islands of the eastern Atlantic in the fourteenth and fifteenth centuries attracted papal grants for the extension of Christianity.[41] The Iberian tradition ensured a sympathetic hearing for the Genoese crusade enthusiast Christopher Columbus. The crusade provided one strand in the conceptual justification for the conquest of the Americas and, more tenuously, in the mentality of the slave trade, which some saw as a vehicle for expanding Christianity. This was made possible by the idea popular by *c.*1500 that Spain itself constituted a Holy Land, its Christian inhabitants new Israelites, tempered and proved in the fire of the Reconquest, champions of God's cause against infidels outside Christendom or heretics within.[42]

In the later fifteenth century, a revival of the crusading mission, with papal bulls for the war against Granada in 1485, depended as heavily on this recasting of, in particular, Castile, as itself a new Holy Land with a providential task as it did on genuine Aragonese and Castilian crusading traditions. The fall of Granada in 1492 and persistent attempts in the sixteenth century to conquer the coast of Morocco and Tunisia breathed new life into the myth of the Reconquest and the manifest destiny of Catholic Spain. Domestically, this was turned to justify the expulsions of Moors, Jews and *moriscos* and underpinned the development of an openly exclusive and racist sectarian society. Externally, the appropriation of crusading into the projection of national identity informed the creation of the Spanish empire, sometimes with bizarre consequences. In faraway central America, local allies of the conquistadors at Tlaxcala, a city state east of Mexico, marked the treaty of Aigues Mortes between Charles V and the French king Francis I in 1538 with a lavish pageant showing the anticipated conquest of Jerusalem by the king of Spain. On Corpus Christi Day 1539, in the presence of the consecrated host, a lavish display included two Christian 'armies' laying siege to the Holy City, one comprising Europeans, the other commanded by the Viceroy Antonio de Mendoza, with the Tlaxcalans and other 'New Spaniards' in their own war costumes, complete with 'feathers, devices and shields'. Seemingly, a good time was had by all. A few weeks earlier, the Mexicans to the east had laid on a similar show depicting the Turkish siege of Rhodes.[43] Through these traditional images of past and future crusading, New Spain was being assimilated into the culture and faith of the old. The association was not accidental. Peace between the great Christian powers of early sixteenth-century Europe habitually came with hopes of a new holy war against the Turks. For some Spanish propagandists, the duty to defend and extend Christendom had devolved uniquely on to Spain, 'Mother of the heroes of war, confidant of Catholic soldiers, crucible in which the love of God is purified, land where it is seen that Heaven buries those who to Heaven will be borne as defenders of the purest faith'.[44] The words are those of Miguel de Cervantes. The crusade and Reconquest fed a new national messianism that became inextricably bound into Spanish imperial ideology and, more diffusely, into cultural identity. Further in time than Mexico was in space from the medieval battlefields of the cross, but oddly closer in sentiment, the power and longevity of the Spanish crusade myth, and its practical social and political implications, still found mighty confirmation in the twentieth century through its insidious but effective appropriation by General Franco and his fascist apologists.

21

Frontier Crusades 2: the Baltic and the North

'They shall either be converted or wiped out.'[1] So Bernard of Clairvaux announced the extension of Jerusalem indulgences to the summer campaign of 1147 against the pagan Slavs, or Wends, between the rivers Elbe and Oder. This decision, reached at the Diet of Frankfurt in March 1147, set the tone for perhaps the most radical and effective association of holy war and territorial expansion. Crusading in the Baltic touched the destinies of every region east of the Elbe in a great arc stretching along the coast eastwards and northwards to Livonia, Estonia, Finland and the Gulfs of Finland and Bothnia. Bernard's analogy with wars fought for the Holy Land of Palestine provided ethnic cleansing, commercial exploitation and political aggrandizement with a religious gloss, a potent, lasting and, for some, sincerely believed justification for the cruel process of land-grabbing, Christianization and Germanization that brought the pagan communities of the eastern and northern Baltic littoral into the pale of Christianity and western European culture.

BEGINNINGS

Yet Bernard had not invented the religious excuse for conquest in the Baltic. He had been anticipated by the Magdeburg appeal of 1108, encouraging support for an attack on the Wends, probably composed by a Flemish clerk in the archbishop's household. The campaign being urged was to liberate 'our Jerusalem', an ambiguous reference to the vulnerable Christian lands along the Elbe frontier and the lost ecclesiastical provinces beyond, briefly established by the tenth-century Ottonian kings of Germany before being abandoned after the Slav rising of 983. This challenging analogy prefigured the way crusading influenced

20. The Baltic

German eastward expansion by exploiting the new impetus and definition given to holy war by the eastern Jerusalem campaigns in emphasizing the need to defend all Christian frontiers and by implying that, in the Baltic, as in Palestine, the battle was for the recovery of Christian lands. In a mood of realism no less prophetic of the future Baltic crusades, the Magdeburg clerk augmented these emotional triggers and legal niceties with the harsher attractions of blatant materialism and spiritual reward:

> These gentiles are most wicked, but their land is the best, rich in meat, honey, corn and birds; and if it were well cultivated none could be compared to it for wealth of its produce . . . And so, most renowned Saxons, French, Lorrainers and Flemings and conquerors of the world, this is an occasion for you to save your souls and, if you wish it, acquire the best land in which to live. May He who with the strength of his arm led the men of Gaul on their march from the far West in triumph against his enemies in the farthest East give you the will and power to conquer those most inhuman gentiles who are nearby and to prosper well in all things.[2]

The material greed of Christian Saxon lords in their dealings with the pagan Slavs stood as an uncontested if lamented commonplace amongst even the most sympathetic regional Christian apologists.

As much as in the Christian territories of the region, religion helped define cultural, social and political identity across the frontiers in the pagan lands that stretched along the Baltic shore to the Gulf of Finland and beyond. Although subdivided into numerous principalities, tribes or groups of extended families, the most prominent general division among the pagan peoples remained linguistic. Between Kiel and the Vistula lived the western Slavs, known to the Germans and Scandinavians as Wends, related but distinct from the Slavic Poles, Russians and Czechs and the Sorbs to the south and east. Among the Wends, tribal and political groups were sustained by an organized and resilient polytheist religion run by an ordered and powerful priesthood presiding over a network of regional cults and a system of rich local temples stocked with images and idols. Wendish paganism was closely bound up with the tensions between rural territorial princes and the market and trading towns, mainly on the coast, whose religious affiliations reflected often competitive aspirations for autonomy and power. To the Germans and

Danes, Wendish princes and towns displayed recognizable political structures and habits. This was less the case further east. From the Vistula to the Dvina and up to the shores of the Gulf of Riga, the Balts were divided into four separate peoples: Prussians, Lithuanians, the Latvians and Curonians. Within these ancient tribal groups, political and religious authority operated on a smaller, less centralized scale than among the Wends. The power of local chiefs depended on their ability to organize the warrior aristocracy of their areas; to dominate the agricultural population from behind substantial earthworks rather than creating settled rural estates; and to exploit an array of fertility cults revolving around numinous places, plants, animals and the dead as well as gods. The tenacity and continued vibrancy of the paganism of the Balts testified to its importance to social and political cohesion. From the Gulf of Riga and Estonia into the Gulf of Finland and beyond were settled a range of Finno-Urgian-speaking communities, some of which existed on the very fringes of settled cultivation. Social structure rested on extended families, who combined when economically or militarily necessary into larger, although still very localized, political associations. The harshness of the environment imposed an intimacy with nature reflected in the religious cults, which helped explain the natural world and offered a chance to mitigate its severity.

Although nothing seems to have come from Magdeburg's isolated exhortation, the Wendish crusade of 1147 emerged from an indigenous German context that displayed growing interest in fusing political, ecclesiastical and religious aggression. Despite John of Würzburg's gloom at the lack of German prominence in Palestine in the 1170s, interest in holy war penetrated German lands as much as those further west.[3] The Emperor Henry IV had toyed with at least a pilgrimage and possibly a military expedition to Palestine in 1103–4. Twenty years later Conrad of Hohenstaufen, the future Conrad III, campaigned in the Holy Land.[4] The ideology of holy war, even if imported by westerners such as the Flemish clerk at Magdeburg, soon infected German literature as much as politics, with such familiar epic figures as Roland appearing in the unmistakable guise of a crusading *miles Christi*.[5] On the German–Slav borderlands, the early twelfth century saw an escalation in conflict over religious and ecclesiastical orientation. Religious observance defined communal identity and political authority on both sides of the shifting frontiers. Conquerors, such as the Christian Boleslav III of

Poland (1102–38) in Pomerania, regional lords, such as the Pomeranian princes who accepted baptism in the 1120s, or local rulers, such as Henry, the Christian lord of the pagan Wendish Abotrites (d. 1127), used or embraced Christianity and Christian mission to assert their power, in particular over urban elites wedded to a thriving and well-organized paganism. Much of the progress of Christianity between the Elbe and Oder valley revolved around the subjugation of independent towns, with their civic cultic shrines and priesthood, to a more amenable church structure run by prelates and priests sponsored and employed by the landed princes. The evangelism of Bishop Otto of Bamberg in Pomerania in 1124 and 1127 involved the violent destruction of pagan temples and the submission of cities such as Stettin.[6]

The new God was unambiguously a German God, His success accompanied by German settlers. Rejection of political subjugation was expressed in religious opposition. Henry of the Abotrites, his rule buttressed by German and Danish mercenaries, having himself converted, allowed Saxon missionaries to lay waste Wendish cultic shrines in his territories. With the Christian priests came the prospect of church taxes, land-grabbing and a loss of political and economic as well as ecclesiastical autonomy. However strong the private or corporate devotional ties to the old beliefs, the political consequences of the choice of paganism or conversion were unmistakable. Religion was politics. After the death of Christianizing Henry, Wendish independence reasserted itself under the vigorously pagan prince Niklot. The end of the independence of the Rugians was marked by the destruction of the temple and public pagan worship at Arkona in 1168 by Valdemar I of Denmark, a more lasting repeat of the enforced baptism of the Arkona garrison by the Danes between 1134 and 1136. Apostasy, as of the Rugians after 1136 and the Wends after 1127, expressed communal identity. Conversion was more important than a matter of faith. Long before the 1147 crusade, political confrontation had been articulated in religious terms.

Bernard of Clairvaux's stark and canonically suspect choice, baptism or death, implicitly acknowledged this religious component to competing perceptions of ethnicity, cultural identity, political autonomy and racial awareness. He referred to the conversion or extermination of the pagan races. While this may have appeased legal experts by avoiding direct approval of forced individual conversion, equating the threat of collective destruction of the pagan nation with the alternative of personal baptism exposed a clear contradiction to canon law. More obviously, Bernard's direct exhortation to arm the faithful 'with the Holy Cross against the enemies of the Cross of Christ' invited a far simpler interpretation and response.[7] The Wendish crusade of 1147 was a missionary war not cloaking but glorifying and legitimizing a campaign of undisguised material aggrandizement. The distant memory of the conquests beyond the Elbe by Saxon and Salian German kings in the tenth and eleventh centuries combined with the confused recent history of conversion ebbing backwards and forwards according to the political and ecclesiastical interest of local rulers to allow a retrospective justification in the concept of a reconquest of lost Christian lands.[8] In practical military or political terms, such excuses made little difference to the reality while intellectually and rhetorically, if not entirely spurious, they formed a convenient exercise in double-speak. Nonetheless, the easy acceptance of the trappings of crusading in the Baltic revealed how far a positive ideology of legitimate religious violence had penetrated the western Christian world and how far cultural and territorial acquisitiveness marched with spiritual imperialism.

The longer-term implications scarcely intruded directly into the circumstances of the 1147 crusade. A generation later, the frontier missionary priest Helmold of Bosau, following Bernard's lead, sought to equate the desultory fighting of the summer of 1147 with the struggle for the Holy Land, characterizing the expeditions in terms of vengeance against Slavs occupying previously Christian lands and retribution for attacks and atrocities on Christians. Yet he also described the complicated cross-frontier relations between one of the crusade's leaders, Count Adolf of Holstein, and Niklot of the Abotrites, one of its targets. They had entered into an alliance shortly before the 1147 campaigns.[9] The context of the decision to extend the Holy Land privileges to the Saxon princes included the need of King Conrad III to leave a peaceful realm behind him when he departed for Palestine. Unwilling to accede to Henry the Lion's demands at the Diet of Frankfurt of March 1147 for restitution of his ancestral claims in Bavaria, Conrad nonetheless sought to bind the potentially dissident magnate within the general Peace of the crusade. Henry's uncle joined Conrad's army, but Henry's Saxon allies refused to join the eastern campaigns. By extending the crusade vow and obligations to the annual summer raids across the Wendish frontier, Conrad and Bernard performed a neat trick of offering ecclesiastical approval to traditional autonomous regional conflict in a manner that implicitly tied the participants to royal policy, if only temporarily. Significantly, among those mustered at Magdeburg in August 1147 was Wibald abbot of Stavelot, a leading member of the regency government, his presence signalling the element of royal sanction, if not control. The unusual, local and distinctive nature of the German Wendish crusade was recognized symbolically. According to Otto of Freising, a Holy Land *crucesignatus*, the Saxon crusaders' crosses 'differed from ours in this respect, that they were not simply sewed to their clothing, but were brandished aloft, surmounting a wheel', to all appearances as much a totem of religious aggression and triumphalism as a badge of penance.[10]

For all the religious propaganda, and the large turnout of German bishops (at least eight), many of whom, wielding temporal as well as ecclesiastical authority in their cities, were able to raise substantial armies of their own, the nature of the 1147 campaigns to Dobin and Demmin was more accurately captured by the complaint of Saxon crusaders when the siege of Dobin turned to a war of attrition:

> Is not the land we are devastating our land, and the people we are fighting our people? Why are we, then, found to be our own enemies and the destroyers of our own incomes? Does not this loss fall back on our lords?[11]

The temporal dynamic was more embarrasingly exposed when one of the crusader armies found itself besieging the Christian city of Stettin until the local Pomeranian bishop pointed out their mistake. The 1147 crusade was regional warfare under a new flag of convenience. As a crusade, it achieved nothing; as Abbot Wibald reflected, 'it didn't work'.[12]

However, the potential in holy war was suggested by the involvement of the two warring claimants to the Danish throne, Canute V and Sweyn III. They temporarily ceased their contest to join together with a German force under the archbishop of Bremen and Henry the Lion in the attack on Dobin. Domestically, the crusade acted in Denmark as elsewhere in western Christendom, legitimizing the annexation of territory, providing a respectable context for the resolution of political conflict and encouraging the development of the institutions of the state by associating royalty with a recognizable divinely inspired mission. Like the Saxons, the Danes had appeared reluctant to join Conrad III's eastern expedition, but the prospect of what must have seemed easy pickings at the Wends' expense combined with the offer of crusade indulgences to prompt the royal rivals to joint action. The year before, Sweyn had translated the bones of his uncle, Duke Canute, murdered by Canute V's father in 1131, to a monastic tomb preparatory to canonization (which came in 1169). Duke Canute had fought against the Wends in campaigns later characterized as holy wars. His son, Valdemar I (1157–82), while continuing to fight the Wends, secured his father's status as a saint, incorporated the image of a holy warrior in his coinage and became a patron of the Hospitallers. Although involvement in the 1147 expedition proved a flop, subsequent Danish rulers eagerly associated their kingship and their conquests across the Baltic with religious warfare, some of which attracted the formal apparatus of crusading, introducing a competitive element in the Christian grab for the Baltic over the next two centuries.[13] Yet, to define the Denmark of Valdemar I and his successors as a 'crusading state' places too precise an emphasis on what was a more general concept of armed expansionism that, by virtue of its Christian tinge, was held up in favourable comparison with the glorious Viking past. As Esbern, brother of the Slav-bashing Archbishop Absalon of Lund, declared at the start of the Third Crusade, the crusade offered 'greater and more profitable conquests' than those achieved by the heroes of former times.[14] The profit was spiritual; it was also material.

DEVELOPMENT

Crusading in the Baltic contributed to the twelfth-century German expansion into territory between the Elbe and Oder and western Pomerania; thirteenth-century German penetration into the southern Baltic lands between the Vistula and Nieman, Prussia, Courland and, in the fourteenth century, Pomerelia west of the Vistula; the transmarine colonization of Livonia in the thirteenth century by a combination of churchmen and merchants from German trading centres such as Lübeck and Bremen; the aggressive expansionism of the Danish crown, especially in northern Estonia; and the advance of the Swedes into Finland. As secondary involvement, these theatres of war expanded to include Greek Orthodox Russian Novgorod and, from the later thirteenth century, Lithuania, a front of religious as well political contest that sustained the idea and practice of holy war in increasingly quaint and attenuated, if still bloody, forms into the fifteenth century. Yet to ascribe responsibility to the crusade for the harsh barbarism of aspects of German, Danish or Swedish imperialism would mislead. One might as well accuse the medieval western church. Equally, it should be remembered that Baltic pagans were just as enthusiastic about massacring opponents and eradicating the symbols of an alien faith when opportunity arose. The secular reality of these wars was brutal for the conquered and only little less harsh for the conquerors or the Germans and Flemish who settled in their wake.

After 1147, formal crusade bulls were not again issued for Baltic warfare until 1171 and only became a regular feature of Christian conquest there from the 1190s. Appearances could deceive. Local observers such as Helmold of Bosau or the Danish historians Sven Aggeson and Saxo Grammaticus invoked the language of holy religious war. In 1169, Pope Alexander III described Valdemar I's conquest and forced conversion of the islanders of Rügen the previous year as 'inspired with the heavenly flame, strengthened by the arms of Christ, armed with the shield of faith and protected by divine faith'.[15] The crusade bull of 1171 looked forward to an extension of holy war from Wendish Pomerania to distant Estonia. Yet, that bull excepted, the institutions of crusading – vow, cross, indulgence – were absent.[16] Saxo depicts the motives for Danish attacks on their pagan neighbours as revenge and imperialism. Helmold famously decried Henry the Lion's secular greed: 'in the several expeditions the young man has so far undertaken into Slavia, no mention has been made of Christianity, but only of money'.[17] One of the veterans of 1147, Albert the Bear (d. 1170), did not need crusade bulls to carve out a principality of Brandenburg beyond the Elbe, even though his acquisitiveness was predictably portrayed by apologists as attracting the approval of God, 'who had given him his victory over his enemies'.[18] For pagans too, motives concerned the material as much as the eternal. In 1156, Pribislav of Lübeck was prepared to accept baptism, erect churches, even pay tithes, provided 'the rights of Saxons in respect of property and taxes be extended to us'.[19] Until the turn of the century, the extension of German and Danish power along the southern and eastern shores of the Baltic, while susceptible to holy war interpretation, remained largely unmoved by holy war priorities.

Crusading in the Baltic directly served political, economic and ecclesiastical ambitions: the extension of German or Danish rule; the establishment of new towns, trading posts and privileged immigrant rural communities; the creation of bishoprics and the proliferation of, in particular, Cistercian monasteries. The crusading dimension assumed the highly distinctive element of being allied with conversion, Bernard of Clairvaux's choice, baptism or death. Converts were welcomed; resisters were degraded or exterminated. Innocent III freely used the language of compulsion, in 1209 encouraging Valdemar II of Denmark to pursue 'the war of the Lord ... to drag the barbarians into the net of orthodoxy'.[20] This unsound doctrine acknowledged the assistance religion lent to political aggression. It also recognized the religious component in practical as well as theoretical distinctions of ethnicity, cultural identity and racial awareness. In contrast with Spain or the Near East, in the Baltic crusades conversion came as a corollary and recognition of conquest. Although destructive and brutal during initial contact, paradoxically the insistence on conversion as the price of constructive coexistence allowed for greater long-term cultural accommodation. As pagans could become Christians, so, as Pribislav of Lübeck was hinting, Slavs, Letts, Balts and Livs could become Germans.

This process rested on self-interest as much as self-image. The Wendish Abotrite ruler Niklot had been killed by Christian forces in 1160. Despite converting the same year, his eldest son Pribislav had been disinherited. He spent much of the 1160s in revolt against the new ruler of the area, Henry the Lion, until at the end of the decade he was finally installed as ruler of Mecklenberg, essentially as heir to his father's principality. For much of this period, according to Christian sources, Pribislav had emphasized that he was fighting for Slavic independence against the new German yoke. Once reconciled politically with the new regime, he embraced its Christianizing policies, helping Valdemar I destroy the idols and temples on Rügen in 1168, allying with the leading missionary to the Abotrites, Bern of Amelungsborn, and becoming an active patron of the Cistercians. In 1172, Pribislav accompanied his overlord Henry the Lion on his elaborate pilgrimage to Jerusalem. His own son was baptized with a politically correct non-Slavic name, Henry. In subsequent generations of his family German and Latin names predominated over Slavic ones. His heirs, the dukes of Mecklenberg, become patrons of the Hospitallers. In 1147 Pribislav's father had been the target for a crusade. In 1218 one of his descendants joined a crusade to Livonia.[21] On the southern shores of the Baltic, at least, the scramble for status, wealth and power, and the desire to exploit the opportunities for conquest and redemption further east, dictated such transformations. Even the heirs of the strongly pagan princes of Rügen, forcibly converted in 1168, joined in the assaults on the pagans of the east Baltic in the thirteenth century.

However unpalatable to the religiously fastidious, when allied with material advantage, enforced conversion worked. By 1400, the Baltic had become a Latin Christian lake, even at the cost of sustained conflict with the Greek Orthodox Christians of Russia as well as the various pagan communities and peoples. Beneath the surface, elements of pagan culture swam freely. But in towns, cathedrals, churches and forts; in new liturgical calendars, even where infected by older beliefs and ceremonial custom; in new saints' cults; in the payment of tithes; in the presence of western-trained scholars and church leaders; in new laws for the western immigrants; in literature, both Latin and vernacular; in ideologies of rule; and in the actual presence and activities of rulers, lay, clerical and that peculiar mixture of the two, the military order, Latin Christendom imposed itself indelibly on the physical, mental and human landscape. Conversion not backed by coercion, painful and laborious as it was, may have experienced a harder struggle, especially in regions removed from the immediate frontier with Latin Christendom in eastern Germany and Poland. The survival of paganism in Lithuania derived from effective political and military resistance and the development of a strong, pagan state. Only in 1386 did the Lithuanians accept Christianity, on their own terms, as a consequence of their king Jogaila's acquisition of the Polish throne. Everywhere, popular religious conversion followed, if at all, far behind the imposition of Christian political and ecclesiastical authority. Formal observance or occasional conformity may have been necessary for social and economic survival. But, equally, Christian conquerors of the Baltic coasts needed to retain open commercial links with pagan or Orthodox Christian interiors. Alone, it is hard to see missionaries having the same success as the killers, the adventurers, the entrepreneurs and the empire-builders. The application of crusading incentives to German, Danish and to a lesser extent Swedish political and economic competition did not create the link between force and faith. The process of cultural and territorial imperialism was established well before 1147 and already articulated by enthusiasts in religious as well as racial terms.

The real impetus towards fixing the technical apparatus of crusading – vow, cross, indulgence and so on – to Christian conquest in the Baltic came when attention shifted in the late twelfth century from the Wends and western Slavs of the southern Baltic to the heathen tribes further east, first Livonia (modern Latvia), then Estonia, Prussia and Finland. These theatres dominated the crusading operations for the century after the 1190s. Celestine III authorized a crusade to Livonia in 1193, a call repeated by Innocent III in 1198. Formal crusade bulls and crusading recruitment were then sporadically attached from the early thirteenth century to the increasingly belligerent Danish attempts to colonize Estonia and its neighbouring islands, the conquest of Prussia and to Danish and Swedish attacks on Finland. The new focus followed the revival of crusading formulae and consciousness after 1187, evident both in ideology and practice. It came with the commitment to the broadest prosecution of the Lord's War by successive popes from Celestine III, an enthusiastic crusade promoter in Spain and Palestine as well as the Baltic, and Innocent III. It also reflected the commercial and ecclesiastical ambition of German mercantile cities, Bremen, Lübeck even Cologne. Political and civil unrest and social conflict within Germany from the 1190s created a pool of people willing to take risks to establish new lives as colonists and conquerors. Arnold of Lübeck described the recruits for the disastrous Livonian crusade of 1198 as including bishops, clergy, knights, the rich, the poor and businessmen or merchants (*negotiatores*).[22] Across the Baltic in Denmark and Sweden, the prospect of ecclesiastically condoned wars of expansion appealed to monarchs eager to assert their authority through martial expansion beyond traditional frontiers. The pagan communities of the east and north Baltic appeared vulnerable in their relative lack of technological sophistication, political disunity and openness to commercial exploitation. Their attraction lay rather more in their furs, fish, amber, wax and slaves than the need to reform their benighted beliefs. The Baltic crusades rode a new, decisive balance of power in the region to which it gave a reassuring ideology and a cruel edge. The pagan Estonian defenders of Fellin in 1211 saw the point. After a short, brutal siege, marked by uncompromising butchery by the Christian besiegers, the garrison surrendered in return for baptism: 'We acknowledge your God to be greater than our gods. By overcoming us, He has inclined out hearts to worship Him.'[23]

The identification of Baltic warfare as religious adopted different guises. In Livonia or Estonia, around 1200, expansionist conquest could be justified narrowly as defence of missionary churches. Previous Christian evangelism and conversion lent legitimacy to wars against the Wends or in parts of Pomerania. The theme of apostasy and restoration of lost Christian territory became pervasive, from Prussia to Finland, when each transient summer raid by Christian fleets produced temporary submission by local pagans, and the Baltic coasts were littered with the remains of abandoned or destroyed mission stations and a few surviving ones. Henry of Livonia, committed mission priest and triumphalist Christian apologist for the Livonian colony and its wars, significantly described the Livs as 'perfidious', breakers of faith.[24] The campaigns of the kings of Denmark along the southern Baltic shore or in northern Estonia were conducted by monarchs who wrapped themselves in the aura of Christian warriors, 'active knights of Christ'.[25] By rooting out paganism, the conquerors were performing holy tasks, their conquests, by incorporation into Christendom, *ipso facto* holy. More generally, the areas attacked were assigned a new holy status, mimicking the Holy Land of Palestine or the lands of St Peter or St James in the Iberian peninsula. This allowed for a very particular form of military and political management. From *c.*1202, the missionary bishop of Riga, in Livonia, recruited a religious order of knights, the Militia of Christ or Swordbrothers, to defend and extend his diocese on the river Dvina. Their symbol was a sword surmounted by a cross. In 1207 they were granted a third of the Christian settlement. In 1210 an agreement between the Swordbrothers and the bishop established a permanent condominium in Livonia and neighbouring Lettia (Latvia south of the Dvina). A few years later, the missionary bishop on the Polish–Prussian border assembled a similar body, the Militia of Christ of Livonia against the Prussians, also known as the Knights of Dobrin (or Dobryzn) after their original headquarters on the Vistula. Recognized by the pope in 1228, their emblem comprised a sword topped by a star. Although deriving their rules from those of the Templars and sharing characteristics in defence and settlement with the military orders on the Muslim–Christian borderlands in Spain, these orders displayed unique characteristics. Officially they held land and authority from the local bishop. Their resources came almost exclusively – and meagrely – from what they seized for themselves. Unlike the international orders, they had no lush estates in the prosperous west to cushion them from the impoverished realities of the barren frontiers and wastes of the Baltic interior. They were also confronted by the legal and practical problems of dealing with pagans and forced converts. Yet the model of a permanent garrison of Christian warriors who sustained the frontiers and colonies between crusades, helped plan and direct the expeditions that did arrive and, most distinctive, ruled over the conquests they secured, was one that, in the form of the Teutonic Knights from the 1220s onwards, came to dominate Christian aggression in much of the eastern Baltic for the rest of the middle ages.[26]

The sanctification of the Baltic wars recast the region as holy space. In 1212 Innocent III declared Livonia to have been subjugated for St Peter, a claim his successors attempted to make good over the next quarter of a century. Prussia became a papal fief in 1234. Thirty years earlier, at Riga in Livonia in the first decade of its settlement by German missionaries, knights and merchants, a cathedral was dedicated to the Virgin Mary, the settlers' protectress, and a church to St Peter, guarantor of ecclesiastical privileges. Recruits to defend the colony were urged to 'accept the Cross of the Blessed Virgin'. At the Fourth Lateran Council of 1215, Albert of Buxtehude, bishop of Riga, declared Livonia to be the land of the Virgin Mary, just as Jerusalem was the land of her Son. This designation of the Virgin as patroness of the Riga colony, the land of Livonia her dowry, allowed apologists to describe crusaders as pilgrims or the 'militia of pilgrims', in line with *crucesignati* elsewhere, even in Languedoc.[27] When the Teutonic Knights assumed direction of war and government in Prussia and then Livonia in the 1230s, absorbing the other military orders in the process, identification with the cult of the Virgin Mary was reinforced, as she was the order's own patroness. In Livonia the knights bore her image as a war banner. By the end of century, in the view of the religious knight in the rhyming history of Livonia, the *Livlandische Reimchronik*, Mary had become a war goddess. In the absence of a genuine historic justification, the author, possibly a Teutonic knight, insinuated a transcendent context. Beginning by recounting the Creation, Pentecost and the missions of the Early Church, he admitted that no apostle reached Livonia, in contrast to the myth of St James converting Spain. Instead, a higher mission was being conducted in the wilderness of the eastern Baltic. The holy task begun by the Apostles of proselytizing the world was now being prosecuted through service and death in the armies of the Mother of God in defence of Her land.[28]

Such literary and rhetorical devices reassured participants and attracted recruits partly by refusing to disguise the true nature of the wars in their bitterness, difficulty, frustrations and violence. Some aspects could not so easily be translated into such robust edification. Christian efforts were marked as much by rivalry and competition as by the unity of faith. In Livonia and Estonia, the Danes contested the ambitions of the Swordbrothers and later the Teutonic Knights. In 1234, the Swordbrothers of Riga displayed their contempt for the pope's authority by killing 100 men employed by the papal legate and then heaping their bodies into a pile, sticking 'one of the slain who had been too faithful to the Church on top of the other dead to represent the Lord Pope'.[29] As reported to Gregory IX, by this atrocity these knights of Christ wished to show themselves to 'converts, Russians, pagans and heretics to be greater than the Roman Church'. Later in the century, the brutality of the Teutonic Knights faced criticism. The Oxford scholar Roger Bacon argued in the 1260s that the Knights' desire to rule and enslave the pagan Prussians presented a barrier, not an incentive, to conversion. In his advice to the Second Council of Lyons in 1274, the Dominican preaching expert Humbert of Romans challenged the premise that the pagans posed a genuine threat to Christian lands, a perception hardly shared by frontiersmen in Livonia or Lithuania.[30]

The almost Manichaean view of a conflict between world forces of good and evil hardly matched the very different practical realities of conquest and colonization. Contact, compromise and change filtered across the innumerable political and religious boundaries from the Elbe to Lake Lagoda. In Prussia, especially the western parts, German and Flemish settlement appeared substantial. In Livonia and Estonia, accessible only by a tricky and expensive sea voyage when the water was free of ice, western colonization was negligible, limited almost exclusively to fortified trading posts on the main rivers. Prussia witnessed a slow process of acculturation similar to the earlier experience between the Elbe and Oder. Slavs became Germans, an uncomfortable notion for later racial nationalists on both sides of the linguistic divide. The judicial pluralism and segregation familiar from other crusading fronts did not prevent the Prussians adopting elements of German inheritance laws and, more awkwardly for the invaders, German military technology. Over generations, the brutality of forced conversion, occupation, dispossession, alien settlement and discrimination transformed Prussia into a distinctively German province. By contrast, only a small military, clerical and commercial elite was established in Estonia and Livonia, largely confined to the coast and river valleys, especially the Dvina. Power depended on solid fortresses; technological superiority in artillery, siege machines, armour and weapons; uneasy alliances with native rulers who sought the invaders' protection from other regional enemies; and Christian control of the ports and access to maritime trade routes for local produce from the pagan interior. These different colonial experiences cast long shadows. In March 1939, Adolf Hitler insisted that Lithuania cede Memel, established by German invaders in 1252, to the Third Reich, an act that provoked Britain's guarantee to protect Poland. No part of historic Prussia was to be outside Greater Germany. Yet, five months later, Hitler was content to consign Latvia and Estonia as well as Lithuania to the lot of the Russians as if they were, in a sense crucial to the Nazi perversion of the past, less 'German'.

CRUSADES AND CRUSADERS

Livonia 1188–1300

The origins of Christian dominion in Livonia were prophetic, combining genuine missionary enthusiasm, church politics, cultural imperialism and profit, the building blocks of conquest. Drawn by growing trading links between western German and Baltic ports such as Bremen and, especially, Lübeck, an isolated mission to the Dvina valley by a German canon, Meinhard, was taken over by his ecclesiastical superior, Archbishop Hartwig II of Bremen (1185–1207), who elevated the missionary into a bishop and began to solicit papal support for a Christian invasion. Meinhard's failure to secure any lasting converts, despite showing the locals how to construct stone fortresses, encouraged a more vigorous policy after his death in 1196. Hartwig, eager to secure a new ecclesiastical empire for Bremen, which a century earlier had dominated the north, despatched a new bishop, Berthold. A futile initial foray in 1196–7 was succeeded by an armed expedition in 1198 recruited with the help of papal privileges. Despite the German army's military success, Berthold managed to get himself killed. The expedition achieved nothing beyond coercing a few temporary converts and showing off the effectiveness of German scorched earth tactics.

Archbishop Hartwig was not so easily deflected. He was not content just to preside over a series of piractical raids or even the creation of trading stations on the Dvina. His concept was of a new ecclesiastical missionary state, under episcopal not secular control. For this he needed a suitable cleric, political backing and papal support. Each were conveniently to hand, in the shape of his nephew, Albert of Buxtehude; Canute VI of Denmark and his brother Valdemar; Philip of Swabia, Hohenstaufen candidate for the contested German throne; and Pope Innocent III, for whom Hartwig's scheme represented a practical demonstration of the sort of theocratic authority that chimed precisely with his own grander ambitions. Albert became the new bishop of Livonia (1198–1229) while in October 1199 Innocent III issued an unequivocal call for a crusade to defend the Christians of Livonia, a fiction made possible by reference to Meinhard's evangelizing and the Livs' subsequent apostasy. The news of the crusade bull reached Philip of Swabia's Christmas court along with Bishop Albert, who engaged in a strenuous tour of preaching and diplomacy. The cross was preached in Saxony and Westphalia, but the most important backing was garnered by Albert's visits to the mercantile community at Visby in Gotland, where 500 apparently took the cross, and his meeting with King Canute, his brother, and the veteran holy warrior Archbishop Absalon of Lund. Although Danish support was vital to allow recruits to sail unimpeded from Lübeck to Livonia, it was later regarded by them as an acceptance of overlordship, a clash of interests only too characteristic of colonization in the eastern Baltic.[31]

Bishop Albert's crusade to Livonia in 1200 provided the basis of the new Christian state, setting the military and ideological pattern for its conquest and occupation. The central dynamic combined ecclesiastical with commercial imperialism. More than most other crusade locations, Livonia was unequivocally a colony, of north Germany and Latin Christianity. For a quarter of a century, Bishop Albert followed a routine of more or less annual recruiting tours of Germany and the west Baltic. In 1204 he received a papal bull effectively authorizing him to sign up crusaders whenever he wished.[32] Although the Holy Land crusade was regarded as paramount – Albert's new colony contributed its own share, for example, to the church tax for the Fifth Crusade – the habitual support of crusade privileges lent a special quality to the bishop's sales pitch and responses to it. As Eric Christiansen has observed, 'the Lübeck–Livonia run became a steady source of profit and absolution for skippers, knights, burghers and princes'.[33] Within a decade, Bishop Albert had subdued the pagan tribes of the coast and lower Dvina, built a new capital at Riga with a port to accommodate the great trading cargo ships from the west, begun his new cathedral and created his permanent garrison of Christian knights, the Swordbrothers. In the process, like any conquering lord, he provided a bonanza for members of his own family. Albert's brothers, a brother-in-law and cousins were rewarded with important, potentially lucrative positions in church and state, founding dynasties that formed part of the nucleus of the German settlers' establishment.

The Livonian state rested on volatile foundations. Bishop Albert faced challenges to his sovereignty from the papacy and the king of Denmark. Internally, clerical rule depended on the support of the German merchants, whose interests were primarily economic, not spiritual, and the nominally subservient but actually autonomous Swordbrothers, who controlled a third of all territory and claimed the right to the same share of all future conquests. Critics saw little difference between the businessmen and the knights, accusing the Swordbrothers of being crooks, wealthy renegade merchants from Saxony. The mercantile elite refused to allow Bishop Albert to surrender Riga to the Danes as part of a settlement of jurisdictional rivalries in 1222. The Swordbrothers were increasingly a law to themselves, especially after Albert's death in 1229. Both knight and trader were self-evidently entrepreneurial in their attitude to Livonia, as was the ecclesiastical hierarchy. The spreading of Christianity became indistinguishable from the creation of privileged trading depots, commercial cartels and fresh estates for the military order alongside the foundation, endowment or annexation of bishoprics (such as Dorpat, founded in 1133) and monasteries, like Dunamunde. The regular Livonian crusades of the first third of the thirteenth century were central to sustaining the practical aspects of this congruence of material and spiritual expansionism by providing physical reinforcements for defence and attack. These wars of the Cross maintained the ideological credentials of the operation, even in the face of exploitation, scandal and corruption, which by the mid-1230s threatened the colony's very survival.[34]

The first wave of conquest to 1209 brought the lower Dvina valley under Rigan control, as well as the subjugation by a combination of alliance and force of the Semigallians south and west of the river and the Letts to the north and east. One advantage the Germans held was their perceived ability to protect local rulers from their traditional enemies, the Lithuanians to the south and the Estonians to the north. The ruler of Polotsk, upstream from the Livonian enclave, came to terms with the new settlers in order to ease commerce. From 1209 to 1218, the Livonians pressed northwards into Estonia, but were then checked by the intervention of Valdemar II of Denmark, who claimed sovereignty there. After an initial alliance of convenience between the Livonian Germans and the Danes in 1219, acrimonious rivalries threatened to undermine not only the new conquest in Estonia but Bishop Albert's lordship in Livonia itself. Estonia was partitioned in 1222, leaving the Danes in control of the north coast around their new fortress of Reval (now Tallinin, built in 1219), and with a measure of recognized overlordship over the rest. The problem for Bishop Albert lay in King Valdemar's stranglehold over Baltic shipping and over Lübeck in particular. Without Lübeck as a base for recruits and cargoes, German Livonia, whoever exercised power, could hardly exist. Thus Albert bequeathed an essentially unstable political system, contested between distant or absentee foreigners, the Danes and the papacy; local settlers and merchants; the Swordbrothers; the indigenous population of converts, allies and pagans; and nervous or aggressive neighbours, such as the Curonians, the Lithuanians and the Russians of Novgorod. This hardly made for a model Christian state, whatever the rhetoric of pilgrimage and the cross.

In the generation after Bishop Albert, despite further conquests, the main challenges to the viability of German Livonia remained invasion, rebellion and internal disintegration. The islanders of Osel and the Curonians had capitulated by 1231, and a network of defensive barrier forts begun to consolidate a sort of frontier with the Samogitians and Lithuanians in the south and the Russians in the east. The modest returns on land led to fierce competition between the Swordbrothers and other ecclesiastical and lay landowners. Rapacious exploitation of local peasantry and commercial tolls provoked rebellion in 1222 and, in concert with military defeat of the Swordbrothers by the Lithuanians, in 1236. Between 1225 and 1227, the Swordbrothers, keen to maximize their income, seized the Danish areas of northern Estonia, including Reval, which they held until 1237, in direct contravention of the 1222 partition. By this time the Swordbrothers' unruly independence had attracted the disapproval of the papacy as well. Despite, or perhaps because of, their success, the knights, who never numbered more than about 120, had developed a taste and earned a justified reputation for loutish thuggery and barbaric cruelty. Wenno, the first Master, had been murdered with an axe by a fellow brother. His successor, Folkwin, a nobleman from Hesse, pursued a policy of vigorous military enterprise and self-interested gangsterism. The Swordbrothers were content to ally with Livonia's enemies to gain territorial advantage. After Bishop Albert's death, they ignored the 1204 and 1207 agreements by encroaching on episcopal property. Cistercian monasteries were plundered, converts were massacred and baptisms prevented. For the Swordbrother, the best Liv or Lett was a slave, not a co-religionist. The atrocity of the massacre of the papal legate's men in 1234 further alienated the papacy, which had been critically investigating the order for years. By the mid-1230s, the Swordbrothers were isolated. The pope had condemned them; the king of Denmark had been made an enemy. In 1236, Folkwin and fifty brothers, at the head of an army of crusader recruits, were killed by the Lithuanians at the battle of Saule in Samogitia. The following year, the order was wound up, the remaining members absorbed by the Teutonic Knights who now assumed their responsibilities in Livonia.

The arrival of the Teutonic Knights restored the territorial integrity and political coherence of the Livonian colony that had almost been swept away in 1236, helped by their extensive international resources, the backing of the pope and the acquiescence of the Danish king, to whom northern Estonia was restored in 1238. Through a winning combination of military strength, alliances with neighbours and a measure of tolerance towards client rulers, the Teutonic Knights made themselves undisputed masters of Livonia. Bishop Albert's ecclesiastical experiment was abandoned as the bishops (after 1253 archbishops) of Riga ceded two-thirds of conquests to the order. But the settlement remained precarious. A further general revolt in 1259–60, aided by Russians and Lithuanians, threatened to sweep away the whole edifice of German power in the region. The uprising was based on those client states that the Teutonic Knights had carefully nurtured around its key holdings, while Livonia and Prussia, despite the hardness of their rule, remained loyal. For the rest of the century, the Teutonic Knights fought to reclaim territory and secure Livonia's frontiers. This they achieved, at a high cost in devastation and death. Semigallia was laid waste and depopulated as its inhabitants fled to Lithuania. Samogitia remained outside Livonian grip. The victory of the Knights was won at the cost of a new, even longer confrontation with Lithuania that lasted into the fifteenth century. Yet the Livonian branch of the Teutonic Knights, with its own provincial Master, survived until 1562, when Gotthard Kettler abandoned his religious vows and turned himself into the duke of Courland and Semigallia, thirty-seven years after the secularization of the order in Prussia. By then, the German order appeared as something of a relic, faced with Muscovite pressure on Livonia's borders and Lutheran converts within.[35]

The Conquests by Denmark and Sweden

The spectacular colonizing achievement of the Germans in Livonia and Prussia should not obscure the wider aspects of the invasion of the northern and eastern Baltic by outsiders. Just as relations between Latin Christians, indigenous pagans, converts and Greek Orthodox Christians were as much of accommodation and compromise as of visceral or racial enmity, so the conquerors were not all German or ecclesiastical. At the same time as Scandinavian kings were eager to enter the orbit of Latin Christendom, so they were keen to expand their interests and power eastwards. The two processes went together to consolidate new national ideologies and the cohesion of power elites. The motives for attacks on Estonia and Finland may have been commercial, the need to combat or regulate piracy and increase profits; the means – naval raids and the settlement of religious centres and trading stations – prudential rather than ideological. Yet, even without the assistance of their own military orders, the kings of Denmark and Sweden managed to attract the approval of the church for their wars of Baltic conquest.

Danish fleets had operated in the eastern Baltic on a number of occasions in the later twelfth century, from Finland to Prussia. The Swedes were also said to have launched occasional raids on the coasts of the Gulf of Finland and the Gulf of Riga. These transitory forays allowed later propagandists to assert supposed historic political, religious and ecclesiastical claims. More directly, by 1200, any Latin Christian war against non-Christians could expect to find religious backing. Locally, church-building and the construction of cathedrals, dioceses and monasteries anchored political and commercial imperialism. In alliance with the crown, the church ruled its tenants, collected raw materials and taxes (tithes) and dispensed justice on their estates. To such administrative structures was added social policing through conversion of the natives, at once a symbol and guarantee of local acceptance of the new order. The church gave the conquest, the conquerors and their allies a clear, shared communal identity. Internationally, conquests depicted as extending or defending Christianity could gain for the monarch who conducted such campaigns the recognition and sanction of the papacy, a valuable asset in elevating regional kingship above domestic challenge. Whether or not it actually produced material dividends, the attempts by Scandinavian kings to align their status with the great monarchs of western Christendom suggested that they believed such policies offered tangible rewards.[36]

In 1171, Alexander III offered to those who campaigned against the pagans of the eastern Baltic, probably the Estonians, a year's plenary indulgence as given to pilgrims to the Holy Sepulchre. Those who died on the expedition would receive full remission of confessed sins. Although not technically exactly equivalent to a crusade – no vow, no cross and smaller spiritual privileges – such incentives recognized the direction of papal thinking.[37] Despite Valdemar I's interest in the area, nothing came of this initiative. It seems that the first full-blown Danish crusade in the eastern Baltic, complete with *crucesignati*, accompanied Valdemar II's attack on Osel in 1206.[38] This produced no lasting occupation, but whetted the king's appetite for the creation of Danish colonies and protectorates across the region. In 1218, Honorius III backed Valdemar's east Baltic ambitions by proclaiming a crusade against the heathens of Estonia. Danish crusading forces invaded in 1219 and 1220 as part of a coalition that included the Livonian Swordbrothers, attacking Estonia from the south, and King John of Sweden capturing Leal on Estonia's west coast. In 1219 Valdemar established a garrison at Reval that controlled the chief natural harbour in northern Estonia. There the Danes built a new city and colonized it with Germans, from Saxony, Holstein and Westphalia, the king content to act as absentee ruler skimming off the profits of trade and the income from extensive estates that the crown assigned to itself. In the long run, this allowed increasing autonomy for the burghers and landowners of Reval and Estonia. Danish interests were decreasingly engaged. In 1346, Valdemar IV sold northern Estonia to the Teutonic Knights, who loosely integrated it into Livonia.

The earliest threat to the Dano-German plantation in northern Estonia had come from former allies. Although the Swedes soon evacuated Leal, the Swordbrothers, as already discussed, continued to advance from the south, occupying Reval itself in 1227. Conflicts of jurisdiction led to an appeal to Rome. Only after the settlement with the new Livonia authorities, the Teutonic Knights, in 1238 was Danish overlordship accepted, at least by fellow Latin Christians. Thereafter, the main interest of the Danish kings concerned the prospects for further eastwards expansion into the Vod region controlled by the Russians of Novgorod. The limits to Danish expansion were set in a series of wars along Estonia's eastern frontier. Valdemar II became involved in the anti-Russian crusade of 1240–42 beside the Teutonic Knights from Livonia and the Swedes moving east from their bases in Finland. However, the Swedes were defeated on the river Neva in 1240 and, after early success against Pskov, the Teutonic Knights were defeated at and on Lake Chud-Peipus on 5 April 1242 by Alexander Nevsky of Novgorod, an incident glamorously imagined in Eisenstein's famous nationalistic film. Papal policy after the 1220s consistently branded the Russians as schismatics, who had to be opposed by force, as well as harbouring fanciful schemes for the conversion of the pagans at the eastern end of the Gulf of Finland. Papal hopes for concerted anti-Russian crusades encouraged Eric IV of Denmark (1241–50) to take the cross in 1244, but without consequence. Pope Alexander IV revived the crusade in 1256, appealing to the faithful in Prussia and Livonia to assist the conversion of the pagans further east. In fact, the modest expedition that followed simply helped a local landowner consolidate his hold on the lower Narva; baptisms were not attempted. Future campaigns in the region, against Novgorod or the pagans of Finland, were entrusted to the kings of Sweden, who had already established a presence on the northern shore of the Gulf of Finland. The political and economic returns from such remote and intractable lands appeared increasingly peripheral to the Danes, while relations between Livonia and the Russians were largely determined by commercial traffic, not religious controversy.[39]

*

Swedish interest in Finland reached back to the twelfth century.[40] Missionizing the Suomi of south-west Finland began after 1209, accompanied by some colonization from Sweden. Attempts to convert the wilder Tavastrians further east ran into religious and political difficulty. The locals were less amenable. By trying to penetrate Tavastria, the Swedes came into competition with the neighbouring Karelians, who were controlled by the Russians of Novgorod. A crusade to bring the Tavastrians to heel was proclaimed in 1237. Further campaigns were conducted by Birger Jarl, Eric XI's brother-in-law, in 1249. In 1257 the pope called on the Swedes to attack the Karelians, a war that was aimed at the Russians as well as the pagans. Another expedition in 1292 pushed Swedish influence further into Karelia. Ostensibly organized by King Birger (1290–1319) to promote Latin Christianity in the region, its objective was control of the lucrative north-east Baltic trade, not the cure of souls. Fame and profit, not faith, drove the Swedish armies into the wastes of the Finnish interior.

Frontier war continued between the Swedes and the Russians into the fourteenth century. A Swedish base was established at Viborg in Karelia. Some attempt was made to elevate these conflicts into the sort of permanent religious war familiar in Livonia and Prussia. In the later thirteenth century an appropriate royal saint, the twelfth-century Eric IX, was promoted as the model holy warrior against the Finns, on shaky if not wholly spurious grounds. Dimly remembered martyrs in Finland were brought into the light of ecclesiastical propaganda. The cause of conversion receded in fact, but not as an ideal that could justify the violent aspects of aristocratic power and culture. In the 1340s, Bridget of Sweden urged on her cousin King Magnus II (1319–63) the spiritual merits of a holy war to be fought by a select army of the pious, a penitential and redemptive act of faith and charity.[41] More practically, church taxes continued to be raised in expectation of crusading wars, money that could be assigned to the king if he gave the appearance of sympathizing with the cause. Even the religiously refined and later canonized Bridget argued that the king could more justly raise funds for a crusade than for more secular warfare, thus recognizing that the idea of a holy war could still be made to underpin royal authority and neutralize opposition to kings raising men and money.

After a generation of accommodation along the Karelian frontier after the 1320s, in 1348 and 1350, Magnus II launched two new crusades along the Neva either side of the appearance of the Black Death. Backed by yet another crusade enthusiast on the throne of St Peter, Clement VI, Magnus sought to bolster his position at home by attacking the Novgorod Russians when their potential allies in Lithuania and Muscovy were distracted. Orekhov on the Neva was captured and briefly occupied before its recapture by the Novgorodians early in 1349. In 1350, after a futile promenade around the eastern end of the Gulf of Finland, Magnus arrived at Reval, where he tried to achieve by commercial blockade against Novgorod what he had failed to take by arms. Further papal approval in March 1351 allowed Magnus to try to continue throwing his weight around, supported by the prospect of a new church crusade tithe. Despite healthy profits from the tax, Magnus failed to drum up support, either at home or elsewhere in the Latin Baltic. His crusading enterprise fizzled out. Soon Magnus faced rebellion in Sweden and an unwelcome change of policy at the papal Curia; in 1355 they asked for their money back. This marked the end of serious crusading by the Swedes in the Baltic. Attempts to revive the crusade against the Russians were made in the 1370s by King Albert (1364–89); Urban VI offered indulgences in 1378. Raiding across the Karelian frontier sporadically spluttered into life into the fifteenth century. The final Swedish crusade bull, issued by another, if improbable, crusade devotee, the venal and libidinous Alexander VI in 1496, failed even to reach its destination, intercepted by a hostile king of Denmark. The triumph of internecine Christian politics over sentimental, hypocritical or pious manipulation of the institutions of holy war provided a fitting coda to what had become one of the longest and least glamorous of all the conflicts to which the crusade had been attached. Yet it should be remembered that Finland remained part of the Swedish kingdom until 1809.

Prussia

Crusading in Prussia was of a very different stamp to the dingy campaigns of the far north and left a more obvious mark. If anywhere could be described as a 'crusader state' it was the principality created by the Teutonic Knights in thirteenth-century Prussia. Even more than Livonia, medieval Prussian institutions and identity were forged out of a continuous holy war and rule by a military order whose authority, while repeatedly challenged by natives and pagan neighbours, was recognized by pope and emperor alike and sustained by permanent access to crusade privileges, preaching and formulae. Whereas in Livonia or Estonia, the order had to compete with the urban patriciate, ecclesiastical hierarchy or Danish kings, in Prussia by the 1240s the order was supreme domestically and already enjoyed the privilege of declaring crusades on their own, not papal initiative. If not the sadistic ghouls of certain black legends, the order's rule was effective and transforming. Although suffering repeated military disasters, the order's international resources and a ready supply of recruits prevented its disintegration. Despite unease at some of the Teutonic Knights' methods and behaviour, the model of a military order ruling a colonizing state was borrowed by planners of new ways to win back the Holy Land in the fourteenth century. The order provided the aristocracy, commanding the castles, controlling commerce and holding vast tracts of land. From conquered marcher lordship, Prussia became a new heartland of Germany and Germanness. Whilst one of crusading's more awkward and, for some, uncomfortable legacies, this was also one of its most influential and enduring.[42]

The crusades in Prussia predated the involvement of the Teutonic Knights by more than a decade. The efforts of Christian, a Cistercian missionary in the region since 1206 and appointed bishop of the Prussians in 1215, received the backing of papal crusading bulls from 1217. For the next few years, in alliance with Germans and Polish lords from the upper Vistula, the bishop tried to extend Christianity to the pagan tribes of the lower Vistula without success. The fierce reprisals after such raids persuaded Conrad duke of Mazovia in 1225 to invite the Teutonic Knights to support the enterprise, freeing him to pursue his ambitions within Poland. The Knights had made a name for themselves since 1211, employed by King Andrew of Hungary defending eastern Transylvania from the Cumans. Founded as a German hospitaller order in Acre during the Third Crusade, the order had enjoyed the patronage of Henry VI, who secured them papal recognition, and later his son Frederick II, who confirmed their privileges in 1215 and vastly increased their endowment. Adopting the rule of the Templars more or less wholesale, although the order's main theatre of operation, ideologically if not always materially, remained the Holy Land, by the 1220s it had become a landowner across all western Christendom. Just as importantly, in their Master, Hermann of Salza (1209–39), the order possessed a skilled political leader, close to Frederick II. In 1226, in an imperial bull issued at Rimini, Frederick authorized the order to invade Prussia under its own authority; Hermann was to hold its conquests in Kulmerland and Prussia as a *Reichsfürst*, an independent imperial prince. Conrad of Mazovia was also seemingly persuaded to recognize the order's autonomous authority in Prussia. Hermann exploited the competition between the pope and Frederick by obtaining in 1234 Gregory IX's papal designation of the order's lands in Prussia as a papal fief, under the protection of St Peter, but held by the Teutonic Knights.[43] This canny charting of the choppy waters of international politics gave the order a very free hand, especially when Bishop Christian, the only nominal check to their activities, was captured by the Prussians in 1233 and held until 1239. This was a vital period in the consolidation of the order's leadership of the conquest and organization of the regular crusades proclaimed to help them. They made few obvious efforts to secure the bishop's release. Recognition of the order's role in orchestrating outside military reinforcements was recognized in Innocent IV's grant in 1245, allowing the Teutonic Knights to recruit crusades at will without express papal authority each time.[44] This devolution of crusade authorization was logical in dealing with military orders permanently in the front line, and had parallels in Livonia and Spain. In Prussia it consolidated the order's supreme position as the principal political authority in the new state that was emerging in the wake of conquests they had secured as much by being managers of crusades as through their own unaided efforts.

Hermann of Salza had not been unconditionally impressed by Conrad of Mazovia's first invitation in 1225. He postponed committing the order until his return from accompanying Frederick II's crusade to the Holy Land in 1228–9. Then a small reconnaissance force under Hermann Balk established a garrison on the Polish–Kulmerland frontier in 1229 preparatory to an assault down the Vistula. As in Livonia, the key battleground lay along the rivers, the riparian forts and trading posts providing the bases for control of the surrounding countryside and for further advance. However, in contrast with the war along the Dvina, the invasion of Prussia came from upstream, strangling Prussian commerce with the interior. Equally unlike Livonia, the order and its crusading allies operated close to home bases, in Poland and Pomerania, within easy reach of the rest of northern Germany. This was reflected in the much greater numerical popularity of the Prussian crusade of the 1230s than any fought in Livonia, Estonia or Finland. It also meant that, unlike the sometimes beleaguered German outposts at Riga and Reval, there was little prospect of the Germans in Prussia being driven into the sea. This did not prevent a series of revolts and counter-attacks challenging and occasionally reversing the process of conquest.

In 1230, the advance down the Vistula began. Over the next decade careful progress was made down river towards the Baltic and the Frisches Haff. Supported by regular and significant crusading armies from across eastern Europe, fortresses were built from Thorn (1231) to Marienwerder (1233) and Elbing (1237) on the shores of the Frisches Haff. Forts in the eastern hinterland of the Vistula were erected at Reden (1234) and Christburg (1237), a significantly chosen name. By using local forced labour, and attracting German colonists and Dominican missionaries, these centres became symbols of domination as well as military bases. In 1233 Silesian immigrants to Kulmerland were granted civic rights in Thorn and Chelmno according to the laws of Magdeburg. Rural estates along the Vistula began to be parcelled out to German lords. On its capture, Elbing was immediately colonized by citizens from Lübeck. From Elbing the invaders advanced north-east towards Samland, thereby cutting the Prussians off from the coast, encouraging some to come to terms with the new foreign power. In 1239, a castle was built at Balga on the Frisches Haff. Having assumed responsibility for Livonia along with the Swordbrother rump in 1237, the Teutonic Knights were well placed to complete the encirclement of the recalcitrant Prussians and link their two provinces to create a swathe of Latin Christian territory from Pomerania to Estonia.

The rapid success of the conquest produced a violent and effective backlash by the Prussian tribes of the interior. They allied with the severely discomposed Duke Swantopelk of Danzig, whose nose had been put well out of joint by the Knights and crusaders, who appeared happy to usurp his political and commercial ambitions in the Vistula valley and along the coast towards Samland. The order's defeat by the Novgorodians at Lake Chud made them vulnerable. The Prussian revolt began in 1242 and lasted for more than a decade. Initially, the order lost most of the conquests of the 1230s. Only in Pomerania and a few outposts such as Elbing and Balga did the order hold on. The technological advantages in open battle, based on heavy cavalry and massed crossbow fire, and dominance of the waterways proved less decisive for the order than they may have hoped. The Prussians were able to use ambushes and the equivalent of guerrilla tactics to deny the order control of territory away from the fortresses, to launch successful ambushes and to achieve some significant victories. However, sieges tended to be beyond them.

Thus exposed, the fragility of the early conquests produced two complementary results. The order prepared for a long, stern war of repression, witnessed by Innocent IV's 1245 grant allowing a more or less perpetual crusade. At the same time, a subtler policy of engagement with the native Prussians led to the peace of Christburg in 1249, under which Prussian converts were afforded civil liberties provided they adhered to Christian laws and customs administered by church courts, in practice under the thumb of the Teutonic Order. Faced with more severe native challenges after 1260, the policy of creating a specially privileged elite of Christianized Prussians became a lasting feature of the order's Prussian polity, integrating the few, tolerating the traditional social structure of a complaisant local aristocracy, while discriminating against the many: pagans, the unfree and the recalcitrant, some of whom, if they had the means, emigrated to more sympathetic regimes beyond the Lithuanian border.

The decade after the treaty of Christburg saw the order outmanoeuvre its competitors. The conquest of Prussia was never simply a question of the Teutonic Knights and their German crusader allies against the rest. Crusading was not permitted to interfere with diplomacy, politics and the chance of lasting success, although it contributed to all three. Accommodation for control of the lower Vistula was reached with Duke Swantopelk in 1253 after he had been threatened by a crusade but, more importantly for the order, to pre-empt Polish designs on the area. The conquest of Samland (1254–6) with the help of the crusade of King Ottokar II of Bohemia prevented its annexation by Hakon IV of Norway, who had been offered the region by the pope. The conquest also allowed the order to trump the Lübeckers, who had begun to organize colonization of Samland in 1246. Russian pressure on the powerful east Prussian Yatwingian tribes induced the king of Lithuania, Mindaugas, to seek a rapprochement with the order and accept baptism. This, in turn, allowed for the peaceful building of two strongholds north of Samland and the Kurisches Haff, along the river Niemen, at Memel (1252) and Georgenburg (1259 – another significant name).

The crisis of the Teutonic Knights' rule in Prussia, in many ways the crisis of the whole Baltic crusade, came with the great revolt of 1260. A general rising of the Prussian tribes or nations almost reversed the tide completely. Aided by Swantopelk's son Mestwin of Danzig and involving all the strongest Prussian nations, this time the rebellion was well organized and well equipped. The Prussians had learnt from their conquerors. They now possessed crossbows, knew how to construct siege engines and perfected tactics for open battle, no longer having to rely on furtive campaigning in the backwoods. Between 1260 and 1264, two Prussian Masters of the Teutonic Knights were killed, a crusading army annihilated at Pokarvis, south of Königsberg, colonists massacred and many of the order's forts lost, including Marienwerder, which had been held since 1233. The savage nature of the war reflected the stakes. On both sides, atrocities in the name of faith punctuated campaigns of devastation and brutality. Whole regions were reduced to waste, whole peoples given a choice of death, slavery or emigration. Only with regular reinforcement of substantial crusade armies and the sustained support of the pope and church in preaching, raising men and funds were the Teutonic Knights able to claw back their position. By 1277, most of the Prussian tribes had submitted or had been destroyed. The Yatwingians surrendered in 1283, with many choosing to emigrate to Lithuania rather than bow to foreign rulers and a foreign god. The end to Prussian resistance brought with it the conquest of the Curonians and Letts. In 1290, the Semigallians were subdued. Failed revolts in 1286 and 1295 merely tightened the vice of the order's rule. In Prussia and elsewhere, the cost of defeat was exile or enslavement, except for a few aristocratic loyalists and quislings. The price of victory was the creation of a confessional militarist state. Although most thirteenth-century states in western Christendom were to some degree confessional and militaristic, Prussia and its dependencies were unique in being so closely defined institutionally and socially by religion and war, the so-called *Ordensstaat*.[45]

The German crusades of the 1260s had saved the Teutonic Knights' hold on Prussia. The status and resources of the crusaders who joined the Teutonic Knights gave them a clear advantage in comparison with the comparatively threadbare recruitment for the Livonian wars of the cross. The first decade of conquest had attracted important Polish nobles: Conrad of Masovia, his son and Duke Vladislav Odonicz; the German princes Duke Henry of Silesia and Cracow, Margrave Henry of Meissen and Duke Henry of Brunswick. With them came burghers from Silesia, Breslau and Magdeburg as well as Lübeck, and lesser lords in search of new lands, for example from Saxony and Hanover. In the following decades, Prussian crusaders included some of the most important figures in German politics, such as Rudolf of Habsburg (1254), Otto III of Brandenburg (1254 and 1266) and King Ottokar II of Bohemia (1254–5, when he lent his title to the new castle of Königsberg – i.e. King's Mountain – in Samland, and 1267), Albert I of Brunswick and Albert of Thuringia (1264–5) and Dietrich of Landsberg (1272).[46] This political weight of support was the more remarkable as it coincided with prolonged and damaging civil war in Germany from the late 1230s. Such foreign adventures may well have served German nobles well in avoiding awkward choices at home. Among recruits were some leading anti-Hohenstaufen figures, but equally the Teutonic Knights were careful not to sever relations with Frederick II and his family. The long struggle between the Hohenstaufen kings and the papacy allowed the order a measure of independence that otherwise would have been impossible. However, to an extent they made their own luck, diplomatic skill proving crucial in handling difficulties with popes occasionally uneasy at the order's policies and powers. This task was rendered easier by the order's good relations with William of Savoy, cardinal of St Sabina (d. 1251), a regular and highly sympathetic legate in the Baltic (1225–6, 1228–30 and 1234–42). William generally promoted the order's interests, in sharp contrast to his bullishly independent successor Albert Sürbeer, archbishop of Prussia 1246–53 and of Riga 1253–73.

One key to the order's survival lay in its ability to retain control of its own destiny in the face of pressures from German kings, foreign crusaders, immigrant settlers, the papacy, native rebels and neighbouring powers. With their patron still in Prussian captivity, Bishop Christian's Militia of Dobryzn was absorbed in 1235, possibly with the connivance of Conrad of Masovia, who wanted their property, certainly to the displeasure of some of its Knights. The Livonian Swordbrothers were taken over two years later. The disintegration of Hohenstaufen power after 1250 assisted the order's legal autonomy and control over lay settlers. In common with contemporary rulers in France and England, the order, as a secular sovereign authority, brooked no unnecessary interference from the pope or local bishops. Even the aggressive papal legate Albert Sürbeer ended his career forced not to make any appeals to Rome against the Knights, having spent a brief period as the order's captive after a failed coup in Livonia in 1267–8. The difficulty for advocates of papal or ecclesiastical power rested on the remoteness of the Baltic; the divisions and hostility generated by the wars against the Hohenstaufen; the privileges already granted to the Teutonic Knights; and the order's undeniable military record. In 1243, the number of Prussian bishoprics, potential jurisdictional rivals, was limited and the order permitted to divide possessions two-thirds to one-third.[47] The 1245 grant by Innocent IV, no natural ally, of Jerusalem indulgences to all recruits for the order's wars who 'without public preaching' took the cross devolved on to the order the power to summon fully fledged crusades.[48] This did not stop subsequent papal crusade appeals or the authorization of widespread preaching by the friars. However, Innocent's grant established the mechanics of a permanent crusade run by and for the Teutonic Knights without constant recourse to specific papal approval. This was reinforced in 1260 by Alexander IV's permission for the order's priests to preach the cross on their own initiative on terms similar to those granted the Dominicans, Franciscans and local bishops.[49] In the circumstances of the revolts of 1242–9 and 1260–83, and in the eternal crusade with Lithuania in the fourteenth century, this special status allowed the order to run its affairs as an autonomous business.

The Later Middle Ages

By 1300, the Teutonic Knights were secure in Prussia, Livonia and southern Estonia, over the following generation consolidating their rule through subjugation and selected favour of 'Old Prussians' and the sponsorship of trade and rural and urban immigration by German 'New Prussians'. Eager to dominate as much of the southern and eastern Baltic as possible, the order annexed Danzig and eastern Pomerania in 1308–10. In 1337, the emperor Louis IV authorized the order to conquer the whole of eastern Europe, by which he meant primarily the growing power of pagan Lithuania and its regular allies in Poland, even though frequent attempts were made by successive popes to recruit the nobility in the latter, a Christian power, as crusaders themselves, against Mongols and, confusingly, Lithuania. In 1346, the order purchased northern Estonia from Valdemar IV of Denmark. The reasons for this expensive and sustained programme of expansion lay in the nature of Baltic politics and of the order itself. Expelled with the rest of the Latin Christians from the Holy Land after the fall of Acre to the Mamluks of Egypt in 1291, the Teutonic Knights relocated their headquarters to Venice. It says much for the respective status of the enterprises that, while it had entrenched itself as sole ruler of a large state in northern Europe, at the cost of unimaginable treasure and more blood, the High Masters, as they called themselves, remained in the Mediterranean. It took a crisis on three fronts to persuade the leadership to move north.[50]

In Livonia, challenges to the order's rule by the archbishop and citizens of Riga led to a messy civil war in 1297–9 similar to the feuding that had marked the last decades of Christian rule in Acre. The Knights appeared willing to prosecute their rights even by physical violence against the clergy. The protagonists appealed to the pope. At least since the Second Lyons Council of 1274, the role of the Teutonic Knights had come in for critical scrutiny. While the order's credentials and role as a bastion against the pagan Lithuanians was praised by Bishop Bruno of Olmütz in a memorandum written for Gregory X in 1272, others doubted the order's methods and motives.[51] Baltic crusade appeals petered out towards the end of the thirteenth century, only reviving in the fourteenth. The Livonian conflict added weight to charges against the order that rumbled on at the papal Curia for years. In 1310, Clement V ordered an inquiry into claims that the order was waging war 'against Christ'.[52] Such legal action coincided with concerted efforts by the powerful and still pagan Lithuanians under Grand Prince Vytenis to conquer Livonia and Prussia. Even more alarming was the arrest and trials of the Templars begun by Philip IV of France in 1307 and confirmed by Clement V a year later. For over a generation there had been serious talk about merging all military orders so as to more effectively defend or recover the Holy Land. With the Templars under the cosh, the Hospitallers established themselves in Rhodes (1306–10), moving their central convent there in 1309. The Teutonic Knights followed suit. In 1309, they moved their headquarters to Marienburg in the safety of their own realm, symbolizing their commitment to the continuing struggle against the infidel. Even then, their Christian enemies almost succeeded in their undoing, the Livonian brothers being excommunicated in 1312 for a year.

In the fourteenth century the crusade against Lithuania served a variety of rather different purposes. It provided the Teutonic Knights, who never numbered more than about 1,000 to 1,200 unevenly split between Prussia and Livonia, with necessary reinforcements on the ground and political capital abroad. Crusades legitimized, at times to the scandal of observers, the order's long struggle with Lithuania, which, in turn, assisted the maintenance of their grip on their own territories. The regular frozen winter and soggy summer raids, or *reisen*, provided a reassuring focus for Christendom's longstanding self-image of religious mission. Until 1386, Lithuania remained a vigorous and aggressive pagan kingdom, although hostilities were not concerned with conversion so much as power and profit. More precisely, these campaigns offered adventurous nobles opportunities to show off. Glamorous in repute but difficult, dangerous and sordid in practice, the raids across the wildernesses that marked the Prussian/Livonian/Lithuanian border, were often run by the order as chivalrous package tours, complete with special feasts, displays of heraldry, souvenirs and even prizes. Perfected by Grand Master Winrich of Kniprode (1352–82), these festivals of knighthood became almost *de rigueur* for the chivalric classes of western Europe, a rather different clientele to the more habitual Baltic crusaders from Germany and central Europe.[53] The dozen prize winners who dined at the Table of Honour after the 1375 *reisa* each received a badge bearing the motto 'Honour conquers all', a far cry from the Jerusalem decree of Clermont ('Whoever for devotion alone, not for honour or money goes to Jerusalem . . .'). While remaining popular throughout the fourteenth century, especially during truces in the Hundred Years War in the 1360s and 1390s, the strategic significance of these crusading enterprises waned. Their ideological foundation collapsed after the conversion of Lithuania. Promoters and apologists increasingly fell back on what has been described as the language of illusion to justify what had become simply a matter of secular politics.

The longevity of crusading in the Baltic was impressive. From 1304 until 1423, repeated contingents of German recruits arrived. John of Luxembourg, king of Bohemia, campaigned three times, as did William IV count of Holland and the Frenchman Marshal Boucicaut. William I of Gelderland went on no fewer than seven *reisen* between 1383 and 1400. Armies could be substantial for summer campaigns (the winter *reisen* usually accommodating only a few hundred). Duke Albert III of Austria arrived in 1377 with 2,000 knights of his own. It has been calculated that at least 450 French and English nobles made the journey over this whole period, a habit recognized by Geoffrey Chaucer when giving his Knight a suitably grand chivalric pedigree:

> Ful ofte time he hadde the bord bigonne
> Aboven alle nacions in Pruce;
> In Lettow hadde he reysed and in Ruce,
> No Cristen man so ofte of his degree.[54]

Evidence from England exposes networks of family involvement, wide social embrace and the relationship between the Baltic front and other wars for the faith.[55] Between 1362 and 1368, during peace with France, knights and their retinues left England for the Baltic on an almost annual basis, reaching a crescendo of activity in the winter of 1367–8, when licences were granted to at least ninety-seven men to travel to Prussia. These ranged from the large and well-funded retinues of the sons of the earl of Warwick, himself a Baltic veteran from two years before, to an esquire, William Dalleson, who was apparently accompanied by a single yeoman, two hacks and thirty marks.[56] The exercise could be expensive and dangerous. However packaged, the fighting was real enough. The Marienkirche at Königsberg became a mausoleum as well as monument to the international dimension of the Lithuanian wars; there John Loudeham, killed on a *reisa* to Vilnius, was buried with military honours in 1391. A number of those who joined the Teutonic Knights also saw service against the infidel in the Mediterranean. Thomas Beauchamp earl of Warwick's vow of 1365 was regarded by the pope as interchangeable between Prussia and Palestine.[57] Humphrey Bohun earl of Hereford was on the Vistula in 1363; he had also been with the king of Cyprus at the capture of Satalia in southern Turkey in 1361, as had one of his companions in Prussia, Richard Waldegrave from Bures in Suffolk, a future Speaker of the English House of Commons (1381).

Such recruits saw themselves as answering a higher calling. Sympathetic observers described these recruits as pilgrims. Many of them visited the various shrines dotted around Prussia that offered indulgences to visitors. Even though it is difficult to be sure whether or not those who fought with the Teutonic Knights had actually taken the cross in a formal ceremony, traditional language was still applied, one contemporary depicting Henry Bolingbroke, the future Henry IV of England, as going to Prussia in 1390 'against the enemies of Christ's cross' to 'avenge the Crucified'.[58] Whatever the precise legal niceties, foreign participation in these Baltic campaigns can only be understood in the context of the crusade and its continuing tradition. This did not mean that the displays of piety and chivalry necessarily transformed behaviour. Henry Bolingbroke in 1390–91 spent £69 on gambling debts and only £12 on alms.[59] Secular considerations abided. The order was sensitive lest their commercial rights were compromised by foreign infiltration arriving in the wake of foreign armies. Concerted efforts were made to try to break into the Baltic trade in the teeth of opposition from the Hanseatic League and the Teutonic Knights. Fish wars broke out in the North Sea. In 1373, Edward III of England's government encouraged a York bowyer to establish a bow-making factory in Prussia. The following year, a Norwich vintner was allowed to try to dump vinegar on the Prussian market, fourteen tuns of Spanish plonk that because of 'its weakness and age . . . may not be advantageously sold in England'.[60] English merchants settled in Danzig and Königsberg. Lord Bourgchier owned a house in Danzig. This did not make for harmonious relations despite all the free military assistance the Teutonic Knights received. By the early years of the fifteenth century, the English exchequer was paying substantial damages to the Prussian authorities to compensate for trading irregularities. The warriors were not immune. Bolingbroke became involved in a dispute over herring traders in 1391. The same year his uncle, the duke of Gloucester, was authorized to negotiate with the Teutonic Knights, probably over the failed trade agreement of 1388, as well as joining the *reisa*. In the event, bad weather put paid to both.[61]

The conflation of the material and the idealistic that patterned the whole tapestry of crusading and holy war could lead to its unravelling. The decades of war in the Baltic had created no lasting advantage to either side. Lithuania had not driven the Germans into the sea; the Teutonic Knights, despite some notable triumphs, failed to restrain the rise of Lithuania or prevent its union with Poland and consequent conversion in 1386. Once their main adversary had abandoned paganism, the *raison d'être* of the crusades and, some argued, of the Teutonic Knights' rule in Prussia and Livonia itself was called into question. Despite the rhetoric of holy war against a now non-pagan 'infidel', the political battle lacked any obvious religious element, as the order jockeyed for position and control by trying to set Lithuania and Poland against each other. With each, the order achieved some successes in the

1390s, coinciding with a revival of foreign military aid, on occasion with larger armies even than those of the 1360s and 1370s. Dobryzn was briefly annexed in the 1390s and Samogitia occupied between 1398 and 1406. Yet the strategy of divide and rule collapsed when Grand Master Ulrich von Jungingen, almost all the upper hierarchy and 400 brothers were killed at the battle of Tannenberg (or Grünwald) on 15 July 1410 by a much larger Lithuanian-Polish army.[62]

The defeat at Tannenberg did not end the Teutonic Knights' rule in Prussia. Marienberg held out against the Lithuanians and the final territorial losses were minimal. It did not end the Baltic crusade. There had been a significant number of crusaders from across Germany and possibly even a few Frenchmen at the battle, and further reinforcements arrived over the next three years from Germany and Burgundy. But there is no hard evidence that non-Germans campaigned after 1413, perhaps because of the renewal of the Hundred Years War in 1415 following a quarter of a century's interlude. Already before Tannenberg, there had been a decline in non-German crusades. After, traditional wells of support such as England seemed to have dried completely. From 1423, even the Germans stayed away. It was difficult to persuade onlookers to regard Tannenberg as a Hattin-like defeat for Christendom, not least because it was not. The Council of Constance (1414–18), which healed the great papal schism (1378–1417), witnessed a violent debate between the order's apologists, eager to gain conciliar approval for a condemnation and crusade against Poland, and the Polish advocate Paul Vladimiri, who with conviction but unsound canon law attempted to cast the Teutonic Knights as unchristian in their wars and alliances and illegitimate as rulers of Prussia.[63] Although Vladimiri's case, including a radical assault on non-Holy Land crusades, gained few adherents, the council effectively conducted a trial of the order's methods and mission. In 1418, the order escaped censure, but it failed to gain support for a crusade against its enemies. Instead, the rulers of Poland and Lithuania were appointed papal vicars-general in their promised war against the schismatic Russians. Any suggestion that, as some of the order's more extreme partisans tried to insist, the Poles were unchristian was thereby decisively repudiated. The proceedings at Constance left a stain on the order's reputation of hypocrisy, tyranny and making war on Christians which proved indelible.

The last foreign crusade to help the Teutonic Knights ended in 1423.

The rest of the fifteenth century saw the order's rule in Prussia pared on two sides, by their own landowners and burghers and by Poland. After a thirteen years' war (1454–66), these two opponents combined to wreck the integrity of the order's rule in Prussia. At the Treaty of Thorn in 1466, west Prussia was relinquished, including the order's seat at Marienberg and most of the earliest conquests dating back to the mid-thirteenth century. The new capital of the eastern rump was fixed at Königsberg; the Grand Masters became Polish clients. Occasionally, Teutonic Knights engaged in holy war. In 1429 a detachment fought the Ottoman Turks on the invitation of their ally and protector Sigismund, Holy Roman Emperor and king of Hungary. In Livonia a semblance of the order's original function remained, in the interminable struggle with the Russians. However, the order seemed no longer able to recruit crusaders for itself and popes, quite willing to issue crusade bulls in wars against Turks and heretics, declined to reintroduce formal crusading into the politics of what was now eastern Latin Christendom. Even when repeatedly begged for a crusade bull to help the Livonia order against the Russians between 1495 and 1502, Alexander VI refused. The Baltic crusade was over, an experiment in holy war that had run its course. In 1525, the Prussian order secularized itself, to be followed by the Livonian convent in 1562.

In a sense, the decline of the Teutonic Knights and the Baltic crusade came as a consequence of their success. Together, they made the Baltic part of Christendom and thus became redundant. The Baltic crusades played their part in one of the most decisive processes of infra-European colonization since the barbarian invasions of Late Antiquity. While this expansion rode commercial and technological advantages, it adopted, at least into the fourteenth century, a self-consciously religious definition of identity. The crusades did not drive the expansion of German, Danish or Swedish power. Wider cultural, economic, demographic and social forces did that. By articulating these expansionist and aggressive impulses in religious terms, crusading offered a particular vocabulary, at once practical and inspirational, that could service self-referential ideologies and self-righteous policies of domination. Holy war gave Prussia, Livonia, Estonia, even Finland a pedigree as well as a legitimacy to compensate for a lack of history, always a difficulty in conquered lands and new polities. Holy symbols – physical, human, institutional – achieved political, social and legal significance, the Catholic churches and churchmen presiding over the transmission of a distinctive western European culture even where the underlying processes of trade, settlement and land ownership remained resolutely secular. It says something for medieval rationality that at no time was this alliance of the material and religious taken for granted. When its contradictions became too egregious, crusading in the Baltic was abandoned, not necessarily because it was bad business, but because it had degenerated into at best a sham and at worst a lie.

The Defence of Outremer

22

Survival and Decline: the Frankish Holy Land in the Thirteenth Century

The century after the Treaty of Jaffa in 1192 and Saladin's death the following year established a wholly new political configuration in the Near East. The twelfth century had been dominated by warring emirs, atabegs, seigneurs and mercenary captains from competing city states in shifting coalitions and alliances that cut across region, race and religion. A hundred years later, the area had become dominated by an empire based on the Nile, incorporating Palestine and Syria, which faced a Mongol successor state of the il-khanate of Persia, which included Iraq, a division of the Fertile Crescent that survived into the sixteenth century.[1] To this process, the Christian enclaves on the rim of western Asia were far from passive bystanders.[2] The century of renewed Christian occupation of Acre saw the golden age of crusading in terms of the number of significant military expeditions east, as well as the integration of crusading institutions into the lives of the Christian faithful. The so-called second kingdom of Jerusalem lasted longer than the first. Control of the ports of the Syrian and Palestinian littoral allowed the Christian authorities, an often messy and volatile alliance of local nobles, foreign adventurers and competitive Italian businessmen, to exploit international trade routes that found access to the Mediterranean in their territories. Only with the shifting of these trade routes in the wake of the Mongol invasion of the late 1250s, and the consequent economic decline of Syria, did mainland Outremer's commercial function as well profits decline. This coincided with the emergence of the aggressive Mamluk sultanate of Egypt, which found the Christians of the Levant coast useful whipping boys to establish internal authority and international éclat. Yet this outcome was hardly inevitable.

THIRTEENTH-CENTURY OUTREMER

The structure of Christian Outremer in the thirteenth century differed significantly from that of the twelfth. Jerusalem or, more properly, Acre, constituted the sentimental and commercial heart of mainland Outremer. However, Cyprus became an independent principality (1192) and then a kingdom (1197), while retaining a semi-detached relationship, through family and tenurial ties and the recognition of a common judicial inheritance, the laws, customs and precedents from Jerusalem being accepted in Frankish Cypriot courts. Ruled by a cadet branch of Isabella I's heirs until the crowns were united in 1269, Cyprus remained heavily engaged with the mainland while asserting its own integrity as a kingdom. The fate of the island did not depend on that of the mainland, or, as it proved, vice versa. Latin rule in Cyprus outlasted Christian Acre by nearly three centuries.[3] To the north, although Antioch relinquished formal claims of overlordship of Cilician Armenia in 1194, close dynastic and political relations threw the two Christian principalities into a long struggle that only ended in 1219 when the count of Tripoli succeeded in securing his rule in Antioch as Bohemund IV against the Armenian claimant. As has been seen, the opportunity presented by the death of Leo II in 1219 of Armenia being ruled by his son-in-law, John of Brienne, king of Jerusalem, faded when John's wife, Leo's daughter Stephanie, and their child died in 1220.[4] The Hohenstaufen imperial project briefly offered a prospect of a united Outremer. Cyprus and Armenia had received crowns under the auspices of Henry VI in 1197–8. His son, Frederick II, who married the heiress of Jerusalem in 1225, tried to assert his overlordship in Cyprus in 1228–9. His and later his agents' failure ensured Outremer's fissiparous status quo.

One of the most striking features of post-1192 Outremer was the manner in which in legal terms the caesura in ownership in most parts of the restored lands was ignored or sidestepped. Where possible, old lordships or the rights of landowning corporations, such as the church or military orders, were revived. Nobles retained titles even of lands long lost. Many land deeds and charters seemed to have survived the catastrophe of 1187, at least in the archives of ecclesiastical landlords. Lawbooks of the thirteenth century lovingly, if possibly imaginatively, cherished twelfth-century precedents and traditions, not least in fostering the kingdom's creation myth of Godfrey of Bouillon and his pious knightly companions.[5] While modern observers tend to divide the history of the kingdom sharply in 1187, thirteenth-century residents, *pullani*, preferred to emphasize continuity. In some ways, the rulers at Acre created a virtual kingdom, moving the institutional capital and the headquarters of the great ecclesiastical corporations, such as the military orders and the canons of the Holy Sepulchre, to the new capital while retaining the fiction of a kingdom based around the Holy City. Even when Jerusalem was in Christian hands between 1229 and 1244, the capital remained at Acre.[6]

The real difference with the pre-1187 kingdom lay in the lack of secure, settled rural territory. The countryside was to an even greater extent than previously a place from which to extract rents and resources rather than to settle immigrants, although there is some evidence of attempts to encourage new settlement after 1191/2. Whether or not any Frankish peasants survived the Ayyubid conquest of 1187–91/2 in situ, some estates, at least near Acre, were recreated as if nothing had happened.[7] Further from the Frankish ports and cities such continuities were not possible. Yet the lack of land may not have been a source of disastrous weakness. New settlers in the thirteenth century tended to congregate in the cities, along with internal refugees. An increase in population at Acre was witnessed by the urbanization of the substantial northern suburb of Montmusard, enclosed by walls between 1198 and 1212.[8] Acre gave its rulers a source of incalculable benefit. The well-informed, if in this case possibly optimistic, English observer Matthew Paris learnt from Richard of Cornwall after his crusade in 1240–41 that Acre brought in annually £50,000 (sterling), a huge sum comparable with entire royal incomes in western Europe.[9] By law, the crown retained a monopoly on profits of international trade. Acre occupied a pivotal position on the lucrative east–west trade routes. In addition with the exchange of foodstuffs with other Levantine markets, eastern spices, metalware, porcelain, glass, sugar, perfume, wine, jewels and slaves were traded with western textiles, base metals, wood and pilgrims. Niche markets included the Christian taste for salt pork and the Near Eastern demand for Tuscan saffron. Acre's wealth allowed its thirteenth-century rulers to maintain a military establishment numerically similar to that of the territorially much larger pre-1187 kingdom at least into the 1240s.[10] It also threw the city of Acre itself into prominence as a forum in which wider political issues were rehearsed and disputed. In 1231, a group of barons, knights and burgesses established a sworn Commune at Acre that lasted for more than a decade, its members claiming, wishfully and partisanly, to represent the community of the whole realm.[11]

Acre's wealth reflected in its political clout was also on display in its architecture and the new building to accommodate the needs of a capital. This opulence, mirrored in descriptions of the lavish marbled halls of John of Ibelin's palace at Beirut, adorned by mosaics and elaborate fountains, built between 1197 and 1212, underpinned the survival of the Christian enclaves.[12] As part of a wider commercial system involving the Muslim hinterland and trade routes that reached from far Asia to the Atlantic, this economic prosperity reflected and guaranteed generally pacific relations with the Franks' neighbours until the irruption of the Mongols in the Near East from the 1250s diverted caravans northwards and southwards, away from the Syrian ports. Thereafter, the economic and financial decline mirrored an increasingly bleak outlook for Christian Outremer. This was not lost on alert contemporaries. In the early fourteenth century, the Venetian writer, merchant, diplomat and crusade propagandist Marino Sanudo Torsello (*c.*1270–*c.*1343), who visited Acre in the 1280s, insisted that a successful Christian counter-attack to recover the kingdom of Jerusalem had to be preceded by an economic war against Egypt.[13] Trade gave power.

The dependence of the kingdom of Acre-Jerusalem from 1192 on the contrasting supports of defence and commerce propelled into prominence the military orders and the Italian communes, each bent on pursuing their sectional and corporate interests. Increasingly, the few inland and coastal fortresses that remained or came into Christian hands were assigned to the military orders. They had the international resources from their estates in the west to build and maintain them and a constant if modest supply of men to command the garrisons. Even small fortified sites gravitated to the orders.[14] The orders' headquarters were among the most impressive and best-fortified buildings in Acre, as their central role in the defence in May 1291 showed. Of the representatives from the Italian communes, initially Venice was dominant in Tyre and Genoa and Pisa in Acre, until from the 1260s Venice asserted its power in Acre too.[15] The Italians provided both the merchant marine, carrying pilgrims as well as goods, and the navy for the kingdom of Jerusalem. Their trading stations attracted significant home investment. Their local commercial and legal privileges, most of which dated back to the twelfth century, posed awkward problems of politics, customs tax, finance and justice for the local authorities. Yet without their presence and support, Acre, Tyre and the rest would have become untenable. In the absence of strong central government, these powerful military and commercial corporations became the arbiters of state affairs.

Whatever the lurid propaganda circulated in the west, thirteenth-century mainland Outremer did not experience the perpetual threat of annihilation. An account of the rebuilding of the fortress of Saphet in northern Galilee in 1240 leaves a flavour of the delicate mix of competition, aggression, accommodation and frailty on both sides of the Christian–Muslim frontier. A Christian fortress before its capture by Saladin in 1188, Saphet was returned under the treaty agreed between the visiting crusader Theobald IV of Champagne and the Sultan of Damascus. During the truce, Benedict d'Alignan bishop of Marseilles (1229–67) visited the shrine of St Mary at Saidnaya, an unusual Greek Orthodox pilgrim site north of Damascus venerated by Muslims as well as Latin Christians. The Templars displayed particular interest in the cult. While in Damascus, where he received very civil treatment, the bishop was asked by locals whether the Christians were intending to rebuild Saphet, which, they insisted, would threaten their city's security. On his return journey to Acre, Bishop Benedict conducted a careful survey of Saphet and its surroundings, unimpeded even though he was in part scouting lands still under Muslim control. He learnt that with a rebuilt Saphet would come control of the whole district. At Acre he bullied a reluctant Master of the Temple to organize the reconstruction of the castle, even though the promise by Count Theobald's now departed crusaders to pay for it came to nothing. In December 1240, the teams of builders, which included Muslim slaves, began the work, the bishop laying the foundation stone after a suitably exhortatory sermon. More immediately useful, perhaps, he also left a 'silver gilt jar of money to support subsequent work'.[16] The cost of rebuilding Saphet was enormous, 1,100,000 bezants over two and a half years. The garrison's daily complement included mercenaries and as many (fifty) Turcopoles, probably local Christians, and Templar Knights. The reliance on slave labour, local levies and mercenaries indicates how the shrunken Frankish elite had become adept at manipulating the widest social resources from its subject communities. When Bishop Benedict revisited the site twenty years later, still in Christian hands the castle presented an impressive picture of strength and power; through it the Templars wielded control of the rich surrounding area and its resources, apparently up to 260 villages. Six years later it fell to the Egyptians.

This story reveals contact, exploitation and understanding by each side of the other's interests and opportunities, as well as of the narrow terrain in contention. Residents of Outremer remained dependent and closely linked to their neighbours and opponents. Occasionally, fraternization turned sour. The assassin who attacked Edward of England during his stay at Acre in 1271–2 was a recent local convert from Islam retained by Edward as a spy.[17] While Edward, not being a *pullanus*, needed an interpreter, many locals were more linguistically adept. The knowledge of Arabic by some Outremer nobles proved useful during the crusade on the Nile in 1250.[18] The author of the fullest eyewitness account of the last days of Christian Acre, known misleadingly as 'The Templar of Tyre' (in fact probably a Cypriot by birth and certainly not a Templar) read and spoke Arabic, being closely involved in the network of espionage run by the Master of the Temple, William of Beaujeu (1273–91) linking the Frankish ports of Syria to the Mamluk court in Egypt.[19]

THE THREAT TO OUTREMER

By then, of course, prospects for the Franks were grim. Yet this had not always been the case. Neighbouring Muslim rulers were repeatedly willing to enter into agreements to avoid conflict, some of them including the return of territory lost in 1187. Truces with Jerusalem-Acre covered seventy of the ninety-nine years between Richard I's Treaty of Jaffa in 1192 and the final loss of Acre in 1291. The later Ayyubids seemed to accept the Christian enclaves, their extinction desirable but not a determining political necessity. Only with the advent of the new rulers of Egypt, the Mamluks, in 1250 did a harder Muslim ideology emphasizing the commitment to *jihad* return to the rhetoric and politics of Outremer's enemies.[20] In thirteenth-century Syria, the aggressive, more militant Mamluks overrode the undemanding *convivencia* of the later Ayyubids in a manner reminiscent of, but more successful than, the

Moroccan fundamentalist Almoravids and Almohads in Spain challenging Christian power by displacing the accommodating indigenous Muslim rulers of al-Andalus.

Western awareness of events in the Holy Land existed on many levels. Innocent III had requested information from the patriarch of Jerusalem before the Fourth Crusade.[21] In the century that followed, newsletters and diplomatic correspondence were circulated to courts and through the networks of the preaching mendicants and monastic orders. Such material found its way into the works of chroniclers such as Roger of Wendover and Matthew Paris in the English abbey of St Alban's. Matthew Paris also tapped returning crusaders and passing travellers for his information.[22] Personal appeals for aid, for example from the bishop of Beirut in 1245, provided a focus for renewed commitment.[23] Gregory X, in planning a new crusade in the 1270s, asked for memoranda on the whole range of crusade issues including the state of the Holy Land and the ways it could be defended.[24] Beyond this elite circulation, repeated preaching disseminated news of the successive crises to a wider audience primed by the new crusading liturgies and the embrace of crusade taxation. The engagement of alert and critical public opinion was confirmed by the French popular movement known as the Shepherds' Crusade of 1251.[25]

The image of Outremer presented in the west was largely one of challenge, crisis and threat. The reality in the Holy Land was somewhat different. Exploiting Ayyubid divisions, through a mixture of local action, alert diplomacy, superior sea-power and western military assistance, by the early 1240s the Franks had re-established control of sorts over the coastal plain from Tortosa to Ascalon; Jerusalem and Bethlehem had been restored by treaty in 1229. After further agreements in 1240 and 1241, while Samaria, Hebron and Transjordan remained in Muslim hands, the coastal plain and Galilee were reabsorbed and a number of key inland fortresses reoccupied, such as Saphet and Beaufort, or refortified, such as Crac des Chevaliers.[26] In the north Antioch remained apparently secure within a rump of a principality based on the lower Orontes valley, since 1219 united dynastically, if separate geographically, with Tripoli.

One key to the Frankish revival had been a deliberate policy of tactical rebuilding of castles and the refortification of important coastal sites. This became a particular role for visiting crusades: in 1217–18 at

Athlit and Caesarea; Caesarea, Sidon and Jaffa in 1227–9; Ascalon in 1240–41; Caesarea in 1250–54; Acre in 1271–2. Even the rebuilding of Saphet in 1240 was stimulated by western visitors and an unfulfilled promise of crusader money. Control of territory meant ownership of strongholds and lordship, not physical occupation and settlement of the countryside. In this respect, even more than in the twelfth century, the Franks were falling into line with successive Muslim overlords in Syria at least from the Seljuks onwards. This strategy only unravelled in the face of Sultan Baibars's systematic destruction of Frankish strongholds in the 1260s. Before this, parts of the coastal plain, western and northern Galilee and many castles in the interior remained in Christian hands.[27]

The collapse of the Ayyubid sultanate in Egypt in 1250, the eradication of the Ayyubids of Syria by the Mongols in 1260 and their subsequent defeat by the Mamluks and withdrawal from the region presented the Franks with a more tenacious and aggressive threat. The Mongol challenge to Mamluk control of Syria persisted for the next four decades, punctuated by border warfare and occasional invasions.[28] The eradication of any potential allies of the Mongols became a Mamluk priority as it had not been for the Ayyubids. The Franks were thrown on to constant defence, the truces with the Mamluks increasingly desperate and disadvantageous. After the crusade of Louis IX of France (1248–54), western assistance comprised small crusades and the despatch of professional armed contingents. The French were especially wedded to this form of support. Louis IX had left the commander of his bodyguard, Geoffrey of Sergines, as commander of a garrison of 100 knights in 1254. In 1259, Geoffrey rose to become *bailli*, effectively regent. On his death in 1269, the French regiment was led by Oliver of Termes, the former Cathar sympathizer and veteran of Louis's first crusade.[29] It was later estimated that between 1254 and 1270 the French crown had spent an average of 4,000 *livres tournois* a year on men and subsidies for the Holy Land.[30] Others contributed, notably Pope Gregory X, who had learnt of his election as pope when visiting Acre in the winter of 1271–2. One of his first acts was to send a contingent of 500 troops.[31] Edward of England left a paid garrison at Acre in 1272; in 1278 he made over the defence of a tower he had built at Acre to an otherwise ephemeral Order of St Edward.[32] The funds of the three great international military orders still flowed east, where, at Acre, each still maintained its headquarters. Such cross-Mediterranean assistance, puny as it was, provided a sketch for what could have been effective military and material support. However, no substantial military assistance was forthcoming. The anguished west largely consigned Outremer to its own fate.

THE POLITICS OF OUTREMER

The internal politics of the kingdom of Jerusalem in the thirteenth century presents the observer with an almost impenetrably dense pointillist picture of confusion, competition and conflict. The military vulnerability of mainland Outremer was compounded by perennial political and dynastic bickering. While hardly responsible for the collapse of Outremer, the enervating effect of the labyrinthine rivalries scarcely encouraged consistent planning or political direction. Occasionally, as in the late 1220s and 1230s, it prevented full advantage being taken of favourable opportunities to consolidate gains. Not all the dissension was home grown. To customary jealousies within a nobility jostling for preferment in a very small pool of patronage were added the attempted annexation of Jerusalem by Frederick II and the Hohenstaufen as well as the clashing interests of the Italian communities and the three great military orders. The absence of a significant rural dimension to Frankish settlement in the thirteenth century and the insistence in the regular truces of free passage and intercommunal tolerance limited inter-faith tensions in Jerusalem-Acre. However, in Antioch during the succession struggle 1201–19 Frankish supporters of Bohemund IV were pitted against the Frankish and Armenian adherents of his nephew Raymond Roupen, son of Bohemund IV's elder brother, with the large Greek community in the middle, by turns flattered and bullied for their favour.[33]

No medieval monarchy could have flourished under the genetic handicaps and physical accidents of the house of Jerusalem. Queen Isabella I, daughter and sole surviving heir of King Amalric, married four times between 1183 and 1197, her last three husbands meeting extravagantly unlikely deaths. Conrad of Montferrat was assassinated walking home after dinner (1192). Henry of Champagne walked backwards out of a high window (1197). Aimery was said to have died of a surfeit of fish, white mullet (1205).[34] Perhaps perplexed at the workings of providence, Isabella herself followed soon after, still only thirty-three, before other husbands could be put at risk. Her heir, Maria, was a teenager. Maria's daughter, Isabella II, succeeded in 1212 as a tiny infant. She, in turn, after marrying Frederick II of Germany in 1225, died in 1228 aged sixteen, only a few days after giving birth to her successor, Conrad II of Jerusalem (IV of Germany). Although Conrad reached manhood (dying in 1254), he never visited his eastern kingdom. Nor did his son Conradin, who nominally succeeded aged two as Conrad III of Jerusalem, and was executed in 1268, aged only sixteen, by Charles of Anjou, his rival for the Sicilian throne.[35] It says much for the reverence for the form of law, the respect for the blood of the old house of Jerusalem, or merely the convenient habit of an absentee lord that this extraordinary sequence was accepted, continuing a run of unsurpassed dynastic calamities reaching back to the 1170s. Yet the kingdom endured, supplied by its fleets, protected by the walls of its cities and castles and for more than six decades tolerated by neighbours who saw no easy way either to capture Acre or avoid it as an entrepôt for commerce.

Following the death of Saladin, holding little more than Acre, Jaffa (lost 1197–1204) and a strip of the coastal plain, Henry of Champagne established a pattern that characterized the new kingdom: peaceful diplomacy with Muslim neighbours where possible; dependence for defence on the military orders; alliance with the Italian maritime communes; and a wary acknowledgement that, without a large royal landed fisc, his powers of independent action and patronage and hence authority over his barons were circumscribed. Henry's main asset was Acre. After Henry's death in 1197, the succession was passed to Aimery of Lusignan, brother of Guy and since 1194 ruler and, on receiving a crown from Henry VI of Germany in 1197, king of Cyprus.[36] To gain the Jerusalem crown he married Henry's widow, Isabella I. However, he failed to unite the crowns of Cyprus and Jerusalem.[37] Although keen for an alliance, the prospect of a dual monarchy may have proved too much for the Jerusalem barons who had offered Aimery the crown. Only in 1269 was Isabella I's and Henry of Champagne's great-grandson, Hugh III of Cyprus, accepted as legitimate king of Jerusalem.

Throughout Aimery's reign the balance between Frankish – or rather Italian – naval power and Muslim land advantage encouraged compromise. The renewed six-year truce of 1204 restored Jaffa and Ramla to the kingdom, as well as confirming Frankish control of Sidon and improving pilgrim access to Nazareth in Galilee, a business convenience for both sides. The deaths in quick succession in 1205 of Aimery and Isabella I proved the wisdom of the diplomatic approach. The heiress, Maria of Montferrat, was under-age and unmarried. The regent of Jerusalem, Maria's uncle, Isabella's half-brother, John of Ibelin (1177–1236), so-called 'Old Lord of Beirut', son of Balian of Ibelin and Maria Comnena, could plan what to do when the 1204 treaty expired in 1210. His regency signalled the arrival of a baronial dynasty that came to dominate the politics of Cyprus and Jerusalem for the next century.[38] The solution to the succession was unexpected. In a revival of twelfth-century tradition, a husband for Maria had been sought in the west, the choice falling on an energetic, dogged but strangely unsuccessful adventurer from a noble house in Champagne, John of Brienne. Armed with French royal approval, a large subsidy and a small army, he married Maria in 1210, becoming king of Jerusalem, a title he retained after his wife's death in 1212 as regent for their daughter Isabella II.[39] A new six-year treaty was agreed with al-Adil in 1211. On the expiry of the truce, the Fifth Crusade of 1217–21 led to the construction of fortifications at Athlit and Caesarea; the further fragmentation of the Ayyubid empire after the death of al-Adil in 1218; the collapse of John of Brienne's Armenian ambitions; and another truce.[40] More ominous, for John of Brienne personally and the kingdom as a whole, the crusade revealed the interest and influence of Frederick II.

The beginning of the Hohenstaufen period in 1225 saw Isabella II married to Frederick II, who became king in her right, immediately depriving John of Brienne of his position. John was left without a kingdom (he later went to Greece in search of another one) and the kingdom without a king, as Isabella and her husband stayed in the west 1225–8. By the time Frederick finally arrived to claim his realm in 1228–9, Isabella was dead and he no longer king. As discussed in the next chapter, his rights as king were challenged at every step by elements of both church and state. Thereafter Frederick attempted to assert by proxy power as regent for his infant son Conrad IV/II. This provoked an extended and bitter civil war, known as the War of the Lombards (1228–43), largely conducted between Frederick's representative, Richard Filangieri, and local barons led by John of Ibelin, the former regent, and, after his death in 1236, by his son Barisan, and then, from 1239, Philip of Montfort, lord of Toron and Tyre, a nephew of John and relative of the Albigensian crusader Simon of Montfort. The war involved Cyprus, where Frederick claimed overlordship, as well as the mainland.[41] Filangieri, even when recognized as Frederick's legal representative, was denied authority under the cloak of traditional Jerusalem law. Filangieri was based at Tyre and supported by the Teutonic Knights, Hospitallers, Bohemund V, the new prince of Tripoli-Antioch, the Pisans, and a few Cypriot and Jerusalemite enemies of the Ibelins. His only symbolic trump was his control of Frankish Jerusalem. Most of the rest of the mainland and Cypriot nobility, Acre, the Templars and the Genoese were behind the Ibelins, whose family lands included Beirut, Caesarea and Arsur. In 1231, a commune was established based on the church of St Andrew at Acre to give some corporate cohesion to opposition to Filangieri beyond the legalisms of the High Court; John of Ibelin was its mayor in 1232.[42]

In May 1232, the imperialists defeated the Ibelins at Casal Imbert but, taking the fight to Cyprus, Filangieri was badly beaten at Agridi the following month; within a year, his supporters had been driven out of Cyprus altogether. The conflict spluttered on acrimoniously until 1242.[43] The year before, Simon of Montfort, younger son of the Albigensian crusader, earl of Leicester, and later famous as the leader of the baronial rebellion against Henry III of England in 1258–65, had been offered the post of *bailli* of Acre by the barons and commune. Married to the sister-in-law of Frederick II, brother-in-law to the king of England and, through his cousin, Philip of Montfort, related to the Ibelins, Simon looked an ideal candidate to reconcile the warring parties. But nothing came of it.[44] The Lombard War ended the following year, when Conrad IV/II's majority was declared. Frederick's claim to the regency was rejected by the High Court in favour of Alice of Cyprus, wife of Hugh I and daughter of Isabella I and Henry of Champagne. She promptly announced the rejection of any authority wielded by Conrad IV/II or his agents. Tyre was seized by the Ibelins and Filangieri arrested. For the next twenty-five years, Jerusalem was an established regency, rather than monarchy.

The main winner from this disorder was the local baronage, especially the Ibelins, who remained the dominant dynastic affinity in both Jerusalem-Acre and Cyprus. Whatever rights of the crown persisted amidst the incessant round of legal and constitutional wrangling were further undermined by the loss to the royal demesne of Tyre. After its capture by the Ibelins in 1242 it quietly slipped into the firm grip of Philip of

Montfort, a leader of the Ibelin faction until his assassination in 1270. At the same time, Philip's cousin John of Ibelin received the exposed county of Jaffa, again with dubious legality. The regencies of Alice of Cyprus (1242–6) and Henry I of Cyprus (1246–53) were almost as ineffectual as the absent Conrad IV/II. From 1253 to 1258 the regency devolved on to rival members of the dominant Ibelin clan while, for selfish rather than prudent reasons, on the death of Conrad IV/II in 1254, the barons accepted as king his two-year-old son Conradin (Conrad III of Jerusalem). However, during his stay in the Holy Land in 1250–54, Louis IX of France exercised effective authority through a sort of parallel administration based on his royal household, military establishment and money. The appointment of Geoffrey of Sergines, commander of the regiment Louis left behind, as marshal, seneschal and, after 1259, lieutenant of the kingdom, finally regent (1261–3, 1264–7), exposed the serial inadequacy and failure of the indigenous politicians.[45]

THE END OF THE KINGDOM OF JERUSALEM

By no means did the Jerusalem baronage hold a monopoly on power or selfishness. From 1256, Genoa and Venice conducted a vicious war, known as the War of St Sabas, that sucked in the Holy Land nobility. The balance of power between the Italian communities had shifted since 1200. In the twelfth century the most committed Italian city had been Pisa, but from the early thirteenth century the Venetians' interest had grown steadily both in and beyond their headquarters at Tyre.[46] By the 1250s, the Genoese, long commercial rivals of Venice, were challenging for dominance throughout the eastern Mediterranean from the Black Sea to Egypt. Violence over disputed property in Acre within a year developed into full-scale war involving and dividing the whole political elite. Venice received the support of the Pisans, the Templars, the Teutonic Knights, most of the Ibelins and the Provençals, while the Genoese could depend on the Hospitallers, the increasingly important Catalan merchant community and two leading Ibelins, John of Arsuf and Philip of Montfort, who took the opportunity to try to expel the Venetians from Tyre. The Genoese Embriaco family, who ruled Jubail, rebelled against their overlord Bohemund VI of Tripoli-Antioch, who was trying to force his vassals to support the Venetians, causing a civil war that guttered until 1282. The War of St Sabas lasted intensely until 1258, then sporadically until almost the end of the kingdom, the Italian rivalry played out on the seas and in the ports of the Levant, spreading in the 1260s to the restored Byzantine empire. A peace of sorts between Venice and Genoa was brokered by Louis IX in 1270, but the Venetians returned to Tyre only in 1277 and a treaty between Genoa and Pisa waited until 1288. The waste of resources, the weakening of Acre as a market and commercial centre, the damage to the cities fought over and the consequent impossibility of planning a united western crusade armada further undermined the chances of the kingdom's survival.

To add legal absurdity to political tragedy, in 1258 the Jerusalem baronage was persuaded to recognize a child, Hugh II of Cyprus, as regent for the absent child king Conradin/Conrad III. The remaining authority was exercised by Hugh's mother, Queen Plaisance (d. 1261). The arrangement reflected less constitutional propriety than an elaborate tussle for power involving the Cypriot and Antiochene interest (Plaisance was the daughter of Bohemund V of Antioch as well as the widow of Henry I of Cyprus) and two competing Ibelins, John of Arsuf and his cousin John of Jaffa, whose mistress Plaisance shortly became.[47] During the 1260s, the complexities of legal and actual authority spun even further from clarity while Sultan Baibars began his systematic destruction of the kingdom. As a sign of the kingdom's disintegration, individual lords made their own truces with their hostile neighbours: John of Jaffa with the sultan of Damascus in 1255 and 1256, and with Baibars of Egypt in 1261; Philip of Montfort for Tyre in 1266 and 1267; and Isabella of Ibelin, heiress of Beirut, with Baibars in 1269. This had happened before – famously as early as Raymond III of Tripoli's treaty with Saladin in 1186–7 – but it began a trend that only ended with the kingdom itself in 1291.[48]

The experience of Isabella lady of Beirut showed how far the kingdom had sunk into disarray and become in practical terms a Mamluk dependency. Inheriting Beirut in 1264 from her father, who had also engineered an agreement with Baibars, Isabella had been betrothed to Hugh II of Cyprus when he died in 1267. After securing her own truce with Baibars, in 1271–2, Isabella, after an affair with Julian of Sidon, married Hamo L'Estrange, a wealthy lord from the Welsh Marches. When he died a few years later, to prevent Isabella, clearly a lady of independence, having to accept a new husband chosen for her by King Hugh I, Hamo committed his widow to the protection of Baibars. Extraordinarily, supported of all people by the Templars, Baibars's protection was upheld in the Jerusalem High Court against King Hugh's claim of lordship. To ensure compliance with her freedom, Isabella installed a Mamluk guard in Beirut. On Baibars's death in 1277, Isabella sought and found the protection of two further husbands before her own death in 1282.[49]

Yet while this bizarre and sordid pantomime of self-interest and desperation whirled towards oblivion, one of its major players, John of Jaffa (*c.*1216–66), was putting the finishing touches to his great codification of the laws of the kingdom of Jerusalem, *Le Livre des Assises* (completed between 1264 and 1266).[50] This gave no hint of the chaos and weakness around him. Son of John, 'the Old Lord Beirut' (d. 1236), John, since 1246 count of Jaffa, cut a grand figure in Frankish Outremer. Joinville was deeply impressed by his large war galley at Damietta, propelled by 300 oarsmen and decorated all over with his heraldic device. In the French crusader's account of Louis IX's stay in the Holy Land, John was portrayed as a man of practical but notable piety, of energy and generosity to his followers, whose advice was sought and heeded.[51] His *Livre des Assises*, part original, part a compilation from older materials, purports to describe a legal system of harmony, clarity and efficiency. The taste for legal theory and practice appeared strong in certain quarters of Outremer. John's great work followed the precedents of the *Livre au Roi* (*c.*1200), the early thirteenth-century *Assises d'Antioche* and the more nearly contemporary Acre *Livre des Assises de la cour des Bourgeois*, the work of Geoffrey Le Tor, and Philip of Novara's *Livre de forme de plaint* (1250–*c.*1260). The interest in compiling lawbooks was one shared across Latin Christendom in the thirteenth century. Law was not yet everywhere the preserve of professional lawyers (as it had precociously become in England); intellectual nobles who spent their time pleading their rights or sitting as judges unsurprisingly developed an interest in legal codification, if only as an outlet for academic enthusiasm otherwise denied. Most aristocratic laymen had no access to the higher education of the new universities, especially in Outremer, where there were none. Just as tales of chivalry acted as a form of escapism for those conducting unpleasant real warfare, so John's evocation of a perfect legal system that had descended and developed intact and unimpaired from the legendary foundation of the kingdom stood in similar distorted relation with the actual world in which he wrote and defended his fief on the fraying edge of Christendom. Although most if not all medieval (and modern) law codes express ideals as much as current or even past reality, John's lawbook was not a work of romance, even if in tone one of some fiction. It dealt with hard law and difficult cases, with principles and precedents. As with that other great legal text of the period, once known as Bracton's *Laws of England*, the construction of a lawbook creates law. John's was still in active use in Cyprus as late as the 1530s.[52]

The career of John of Jaffa reveals another side to Outremer. His father had built the cool, shaded halls of his grand palace in Beirut. An associate, Philip of Novara, was a chronicler as well as legist. Acre housed an exceptional set of ateliers from which luxury illuminated manuscripts were produced, which bear witness to a distinctive artistic style, synthetical but not derivative of local, Greek and western forms.[53] The great buildings of Acre or the massive fortifications of castles and city walls compare with the most impressive in Christendom.[54] The particularly intense local eremitic spiritual tradition gave rise to a new religious order, the Carmelites, which soon established itself in the west in a rare example of reverse colonization.[55] Frankish Syria was not a society creeping in material and aesthetic penury to a predestined annihilation. Yet, as the political turmoil continued, and the territorial base withered, the finances upon which the culture of Outremer rested began to evaporate. John of Jaffa had been able to reward his knights lavishly from preying on caravans crossing between Egypt and Syria, carrying, for instance, luxury textiles.[56] Yet Jaffa fell to Baibars in 1268, just two years after John's death. With the loss of such bases, profits and income dried. Yet even before this, John himself had been in debt. Increasingly, lay lords were forced to sell out to the military orders for reason of finance not protection. No amount of shuffling of the rapidly diminishing property could mitigate the damage of chronic political dysfunction.

A semblance of constitutional if not political order was restored with the acceptance of Hugh of Antioch-Jerusalem, since 1267 Hugh III of Cyprus, as regent for Conradin/Conrad III in 1268 and his ascent to the throne of Jerusalem as Hugh I the following year after Conradin's execution in Italy, the first monarch resident in the east since 1225. From his base in Cyprus, Hugh could do little to direct affairs on the mainland. Brief help came with the crusade of Edward of England, the truce of 1272 and the death of Baibars in 1277. Yet, as the case of Isabella of Beirut's marriage showed, Hugh's authority was circumscribed, contingent on barons whose jealous guarding of what they perceived as their rights outweighed any sense of impending disaster. Some may have believed their own national myths of the providential status of Outremer. Others, more prosaically, could not imagine the annihilation of their *patria*. It is misleading to view the last years of Frankish Syria solely through the lens of hindsight or from the perspective of western Europe. The Ibelin family may stand for many. They were probably descended from an Italian immigrant, perhaps from Sardinia or Pisa, who became castellan of Jaffa in the second decade of the twelfth century. Perhaps because of their relatively humble place in the Jerusalem aristocracy, in the twelfth century the Ibelins married within the kingdom, rather than seeking spouses from the west. The family waxed rich and grand in the years around and after 1200, not least by their association and marriage with members of the royal family such as Maria Comnena, although they rarely, even in the thirteenth century, married directly into the royal house of Cyprus or Jerusalem. Men such as John of Jaffa were not colonists, even if they saw themselves as manning an outer bastion of Christendom. They were indigenous Jerusalemites and Cypriots, part of Latin Christendom but as autonomous in law, custom, tradition, history and expectation as any other. From the early twelfth to the late fourteenth centuries, when the male line in Cyprus died out, for the Ibelins Outremer was home, the only one they knew.[57] Lacking the hawk-like vision of western observers or modern historians, their political in-fighting may not have seemed myopic, merely business as usual.

This tendency of the Jerusalem baronage to compete and disagree was tested once more before the end. The political mess had thickened still further in 1277, when Maria of Antioch, a granddaughter of Isabella I who had contested the succession in 1268, sold her rights in Jerusalem to Charles of Anjou, brother of Louis IX of France, papal champion in the Italian war against the Hohenstaufen, executioner of Conradin/Conrad III and acquisitive new king of Naples and Sicily. While the Mamluks battered their gates, the Franks contented themselves with recognizing two kings. Acre, Sidon and the Templars opted for Charles of Anjou and his *bailli*, Roger of San Severino (1277–82); Tyre and

Beirut for Hugh I.[58] The schism only ended with Charles's death in 1285. The following year Acre submitted to the new king of Cyprus (since 1285) and Jerusalem, Henry I, Hugh I's son. The discord at the centre was matched elsewhere as the rump of mainland Outremer confronted internal divisions as dangerous as external attack. In Tripoli, Bohemund VII only concluded a civil war with the Templars and Guy II Embriaco of Jubail (1277–82) by having Guy's followers blinded and Guy himself, with his brothers and cousins buried in the moat of the castle at Nephin and left to starve to death. Little wonder the surviving Embriacos sought the suzerainty of the Mamluk sultan.[59]

Ironically, the apparent unity achieved by Henry I, witnessed by his lavish and misleadingly optimistic coronation at Tyre in 1286, coincided with a new Mamluk offensive that negated all shows of solidarity. The series of piecemeal truces agreed by harassed local rulers, such as a condominium deal arranged for Tyre in 1285, availed little. Since the 1260s, such partitions of land or revenues had failed to assuage the Mamluk appetite for conquest. By now the kingdom was beyond repair. Sultan Kalavun of Egypt's treaty with Acre in 1283 excluded Tyre and Beirut as if they no longer belonged to the same kingdom.[60] One by one the last Frankish strongholds succumbed, including Tripoli in 1289. As will be described in Chapter 24, the final crisis came in May 1291 with the fall of Acre itself to Sultan al-Ashraf Khalil (1290–93) after a grisly six-week siege.[61] Further resistance evaporated. No great western fleets hovered just over the horizon. There was no relief. By mid-August 1291 Tyre, Sidon, Beirut, Tortosa and Athlit had capitulated or been evacuated. Peter Embriaco of Jubail negotiated submission to the sultan and held his city as a dependency for a few more years. The Templars clung on to the waterless island of Ruad until 1303. A few individual Franks, released captives, freed or abandoned slaves, lingered in Outremer for more than a generation, stranded, impoverished and debased relics of a lost dominion.

Almost half a century later, two old men encountered by a German pilgrim by the Dead Sea turned out to be French Templars captured at Acre in 1291. They had worked for the sultan, married and had children, living in the southern Judean hills, entirely isolated and ignorant of events in the west. They now became minor celebrities. They and their families were shipped back to Europe and received with honour at the papal court at Avignon before retiring on pensions to end their days in peace. What they, their wives, children or new neighbours made of this turn of fortune is unknown. Yet their fate stood as a suitably confusing epitaph for Frankish Outremer: glamour, courage, strain, wishful thinking, strenuous endeavour, the international stage and unmistakable domesticity.[62]

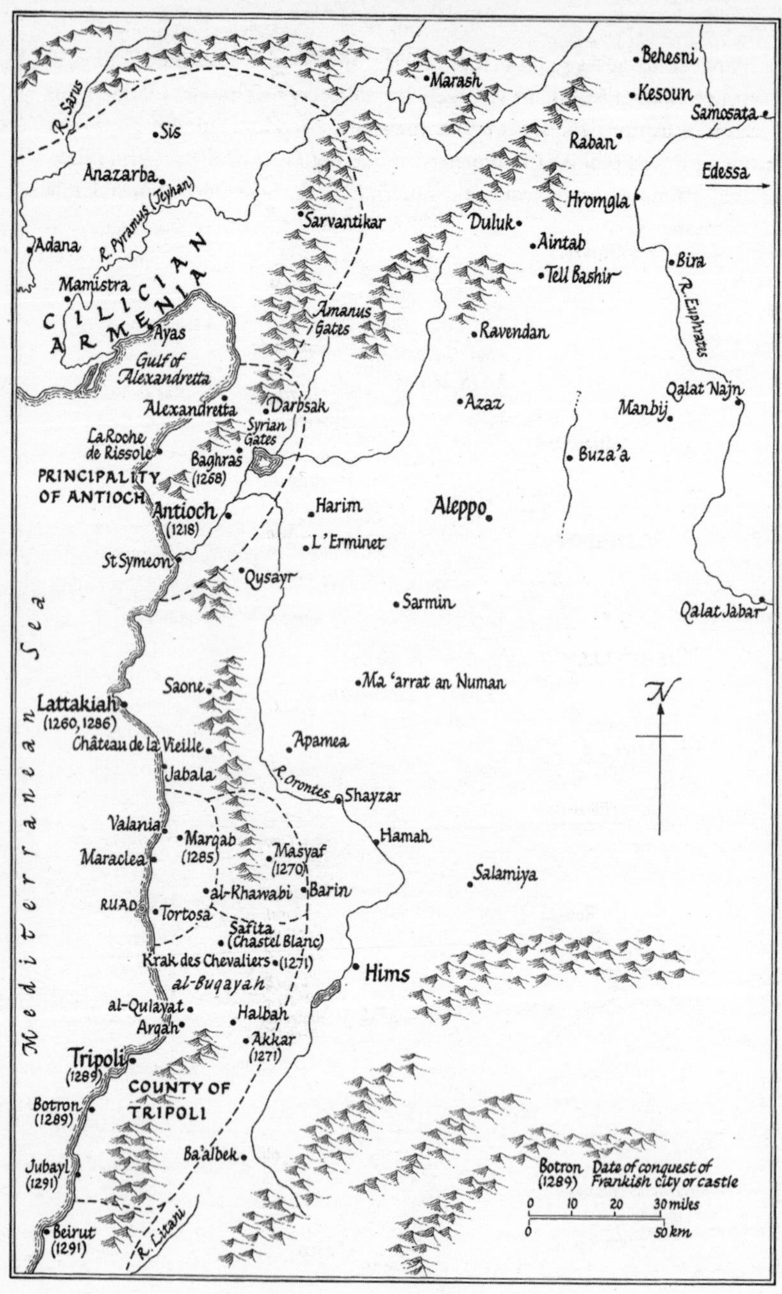

21. Syria in the Thirteenth Century

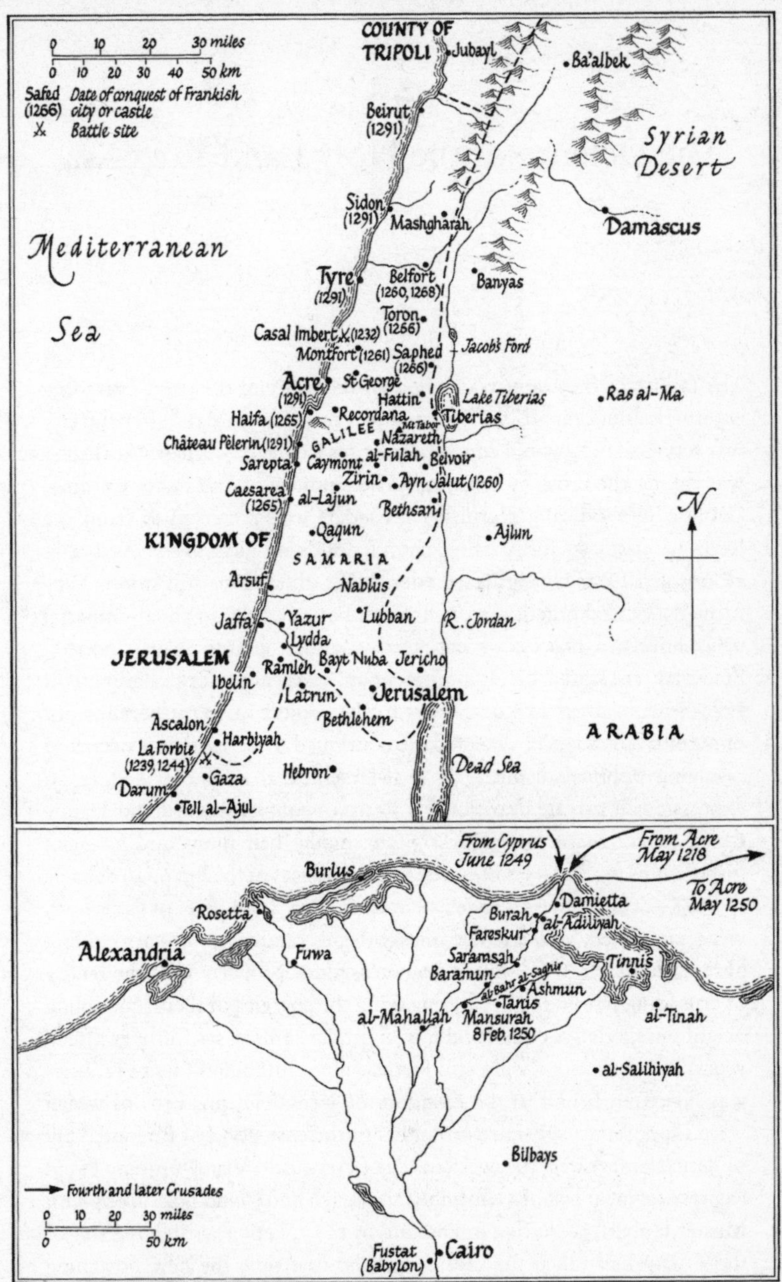

22. Palestine and Egypt in the Thirteenth Century

23
The Defence of the Holy Land 1221–44

The failure of the Damietta campaign did not end the great crusading enterprise Innocent III had initiated in 1213. Eleven days after the city was returned to Ayyubid control, Peter des Roches bishop of Winchester was taking the cross in England.[1] The summer of 1221 saw Cardinal Ugolino methodically recruiting crusaders and mercenaries from the lords of northern Italy, using church funds as incentives.[2] As far as Honorius III was concerned, Frederick II's obligations still stood. They formed a central practical as well as symbolic element in papal–imperial negotiations, a process of preparation and a guarantee of sincerity. Frederick reiterated his commitment in 1223 and 1225. Philip II of France bequeathed 150,000 *livres* to the project in 1223, perhaps out of a guilty conscience. The crusade continued to be used as a means of resolving political disputes, as in Marseilles in 1224, as well as an expression of private devotion.[3] A Parisian couple, Renard and Jeanne Crest, *crucesignatus* and *crucesignata*, made their pious and financial dispositions in 1224–5 before departure.[4] Stories of the Egyptian debacle of 1218–21 by witnesses such as James of Vitry and Oliver of Paderborn were circulated widely. The messy legal ramifications surrounding absent, deceased or presumed dead crusaders' property kept the reality of crusading painfully alive by engaging the energies of their squabbling neighbours, relatives and local law courts in some cases for over fifteen years.[5] Contributions were still forthcoming. In England in 1222 a tax was levied on behalf of the kingdom of Jerusalem, proceeds of which were supposed to subsidize crusaders to the east. John of Brienne, king of Jerusalem visited the west in 1223, trying to drum up aid. Papal legates and local bishops continued to preach and round up *crucesignati*; Master Hubert, recruiting in England in 1227, kept a written register of those who had taken the cross.[6] For the first time the new preaching order of the Dominican friars was employed in England under the patronage of Peter des Roches.[7] Within a few years they and the Franciscans came to dominate the *verbum crucis*, the word of the cross.

More generally, the decades after 1221 saw the 'business of the Holy Land' embedded into the religious culture of western Christendom. Away from specific campaign appeals, the special prayers, liturgy, bell-ringing, processions and invitations to donate alms that had been established since 1187 assumed habitual places in the devotional round of the faithful laity. The democratization of penance after the Fourth Lateran Council through oral confession, the improvement in the educational standards of the clergy and the extra-parochial presence of friars and, for the prosperous, private confessors was matched and reflected by a growing prominence of lay spirituality expressed in religious confraternities, which sprang up across Europe, most obviously in towns, and in the personal lives of lay *dévots*. Stress on the spiritual life and moral behaviour of individuals recognized the validity and value of personal and collective lay religious observance. The crusade epitomized just this sort of secular commitment, a number of contemporary observers likening *crucesignati* to converts or even a religious order, a *religio*.[8]

Crusading perceptions and practices altered in the thirteenth century. Taking the cross signalled inner spiritual commitment not limited to specific military endeavour alone. The crusade became braided with personal religious identity in a system of practical spirituality channelled through regular devotional exercises; confession, penance, alms-giving, prayer and conduct. Louis VII of France had been a pious monarch and crusader, but the role crusading played in his spiritual life, as far as external appearances are any guide, pales beside its importance to his great-grandson Louis IX. For the younger Louis, the crusade occupied a central place in his life, a means to achieve personal and spiritual emancipation, self-expression and fulfilment. Similar prominence of the crusade in a broader spiritual life of puritanical seriousness was demonstrated by another leading thirteenth-century *dévot*, Simon of Montfort the Younger. Son of the leader of the Albigensian crusades, himself a *crucesignatus* and campaigner in the east in 1240–41, it was entirely in character that in the great crisis of his life, the civil wars in England of 1263–5, Simon called on the images of crusading to sustain his cause.[9] Even for a lukewarm crusader such as Simon's opponent, Henry III, the cross became an accepted way of displaying religious credentials, almost regardless of whether he embarked. Henry took the cross on at least three occasions (1216, 1250 and 1271). Neither the first or last occasion represented a serious decision to campaign. The first signalled the newly crowned boy-king's renewal of the papal protection vital to the survival of his dynasty. Fifty-five years later, the old ailing king's gesture spoke of rededication of a soul mindful of salvation and troubled by the unfulfilled commitment of two decades before. For Henry's uncle, Richard I, crusading had been a much more specific ambition, no less intense perhaps, but less central to his regular spiritual life or religious observances. A century on, the crusade had become, as F. M. Powicke remarked, inseparable from the air men breathed.[10]

In the years after the evacuation of Damietta, the flow of *crucesignati* to the Levant never entirely ran dry, even if the 40,000 names allegedly on Master Hubert's roll of 1227 cannot be credited. No less telling of this diffuse commitment, the stock figures of the armchair crusader, nicknamed 'ashie' because he stayed by his hearth, and the *décroisié*, the man who had redeemed or abandoned his vow, entered literary vocabulary and convention.[11] This pattern of constant, often low-key activity of raising men, awareness and funds set the pattern of western engagement for the rest of the century and beyond. Periodically, the involvement of one of the great lords of western Christendom lent focus to such efforts, leading to the organization of large crusading expeditions, in 1227–9, 1239–41, 1248–50 and 1269–71. Some enterprises, as in 1248 and 1269, were ostensibly sparked by a crisis, the loss of Jerusalem or Antioch. Others owed more to the political moods or demands in western Europe rather than any threat to Outremer. Contact with the east was maintained at a number of different levels, trade, pilgrimage, even diplomacy. Both Frederick II and Henry III of England maintained diplomatic relations with Ayyubid rulers, the English king using as his ambassador a Genoese entrepreneur one of whose lines was to supply the English court with crossbows.[12]

THE CRUSADE OF FREDERICK II, 1227–9

The crusade that coalesced around Frederick II in the late 1220s has tended to be dismissed as a sideshow, a self-indulgent and politically inept expression of the hubris of a ruler scarcely bothered by the motives that drove most crusaders, an expedition contradictory in genesis and barren in result. This view distorts. Polymath, intellectual, linguist, scholar, falconry expert and politician of imagination, arrogance, ambition and energy, Frederick II was no less sincere in his crusading ambition than Richard I. The cause took a central place in Frederick's policies for almost a decade and a half, its implementation risking disaster at home and defeat abroad. Only in the hindsight of the decline of the kingdom of Jerusalem after the 1240s and the simultaneous parting of the ways between papacy and empire in the west did the events of 1227–9 come to appear futile, eccentric or irrelevant. At the time, for all his political jockeying, Frederick's actions exposed an ambition inexplicable without a conventional religious purpose.[13]

Although attracting large numbers of recruits, the organization, leadership and military core of Frederick's expedition depended on the tight control imposed by central finance in the form of royal or ecclesiastical subsidies to individual leaders as well as lay and clerical taxation. As such, it probably constituted the most professional expedition to the Holy Land to date in the sense that many, perhaps most of the troops involved were paid as well as transported by their employers. Although conceived as an exercise in papal–imperial cooperation, Frederick's failure to depart as promised in 1227 caused the new pope, Gregory IX, to excommunicate him, even though the reason for delay, illness, was genuine. Frederick's determination to proceed regardless in 1228 in turn placed the pope in a false position as his ban failed to deter thousands of crusaders and had minimal impact in Outremer. The scene of the Christian emperor wearing his crown in the church of the Holy Sepulchre in March 1229 while hotly pursued by clerics eager to place the Holy City itself under an interdict was hardly edifying. Neither were papal efforts to prevent a church crusade tax being raised in Frederick's lands, which papal armies were invading.

However, Jerusalem was restored by treaty, without bloodshed. What Richard I had failed to win by force and the Fifth Crusade had rejected as unworthy or unworkable, Frederick achieved through dogged negotiation, in the teeth of the pope's enmity. The three holiest sites, Jerusalem, Bethlehem and Nazareth, were restored to Christian hands; the kingdom of Jerusalem given a new viability with increased territory and strengthened fortifications in cities and castles. If Frederick's campaign marked the culmination of Innocent III's crusade, it also marked the greatest challenge to Innocent's vision of papal monarchy. At least in the emperor's eyes, it seemed to vindicate the independent imperialism of a Hohenstaufen empire that Frederick had bullyingly tried to impose on the states of Outremer. Frederick's campaign possessed a Janus-like quality, harking back to crusading precedent while offering fresh diplomatic, political and logistic solutions. One of the expedition's more bizarre consequences certainly caught echoes of Innocent's crusade while casting auguries for the future. At the moment of Frederick's triumphal appearance in Jerusalem, his southern Italian lands were being attacked by papal forces under the joint command of John of Brienne and Cardinal Pelagius.[14] In the event, the reunion of these two sparring partners of the Fifth Crusade in an attempt to dismember the power of a current crusader was no more successful than their previous association.

Like many thirteenth-century rulers, Frederick II was a serial *crucesignatus*. He first took the cross at his coronation as king of Germany at Aachen in July 1215. There, probably deliberately, he aped his father Henry VI's ceremony at Worms in December 1195 by personally presiding over the mass distribution of crosses to his new subjects.[15] The problems encountered in establishing his rule prevented Frederick honouring this vow, yet the obligation remained indelible. At his imperial coronation in Rome in November 1220, he again received the cross, this time from Cardinal Ugolino, a personal confrontation that bore bitter fruit when the cardinal, as Pope Gregory IX, excommunicated Frederick seven years later. Frederick publicly vowed to help the Holy Land twice more, at conferences at Ferentino in March 1223 and San Germano in July 1225, ten years to the day (25 July) since he had first taken the cross. This proliferation of commitment reflected the reverse of empty bombast. Just as taking the cross in 1215 had associated the young King Frederick with papal approval, and that of 1220 with joint leadership of Christendom, so the vows of 1223 and 1225 marked stages of the development of a detailed crusade plan in response to acerbic criticism of his inaction during the Damietta campaign.

Frederick's problem lay in his eagerness or insouciance in setting himself precise deadlines for action. In 1220, he promised to go east in August 1221. Instead he merely despatched a fleet and an army under the duke of Bavaria, which reached Damietta just in time for the final debacle. In 1223 Frederick guaranteed departure in 1225; domestic politics intruded. In 1225 the date for his crusade was pushed back to 1227, but this time with the agreed additional sanction of excommunication if he failed to honour his pledge. Given that at Ferentino and San Germano Frederick had committed himself to providing large numbers of paid troops, a fleet and large reserves of cash for the expedition, the precision of the dates may have been designed to convince potential followers, tax payers and bankers of his sincerity. They also helped counter charges of dishonour levelled since 1221. Most important, the promises of 1223 and 1225 appeased the well-inclined but suspicious Pope Honorius III. Frederick needed papal support to consolidate his authority in Germany, Italy and Sicily. Yet these negotiations constituted no imperial surrender. By recognizing Frederick's command of the crusade, even on the tough, restrictive terms reached at San Germano, the pope was affording him the position in Christendom the emperor had chosen for himself, that of the foremost secular authority under God.

At the same time as he began to raise money, troops and allies for the expedition, Frederick developed his wider eastern strategy. In 1223 it was agreed with John of Brienne that the emperor would marry his daughter, Isabella II, giving Frederick direct claim to jurisdiction in mainland Outremer. The marriage took place in 1225. Frederick promptly relieved his new father-in-law, John of Brienne, of his role as regent, thereby, rather characteristically, making an enemy for life. Despite King John's bruised feelings, the Jerusalem barons, many of whom attended the wedding in Brindisi in November 1225, accepted the new arrangements even where they harboured reservations on the actual extent and exercise of royal power in Jerusalem. At least on campaign, as king of Jerusalem in the right of his wife, Frederick would hope to avoid the disputes over authority and sovereignty that marred the Fifth Crusade. More widely, the king of Jerusalem being present at the head of a western crusading force rather than acting as a more or less reluctant or enthusiastic local host promised to resolve a tension inherent in all expeditions launched to the Holy Land since 1099. Frederick's plan offered a new departure for eastern crusading, a unitary model that a century later became very fashionable in circles trying to revive the idea of the recovery of the Holy Land, even though by then Frederick's pioneering scheme was denied any credit. The crown would allow Frederick to fight the war, acquire conquests and negotiate peace with full, unchallenged legitimacy. Perhaps as early as 1226, Frederick had begun direct and detailed negotiations with Sultan al-Kamil of Egypt (1218–38) over the return of Jerusalem, although he needed the prospect of his appearance in the Levant to persuade the sultan to consider accepting him as an ally.[16] The royal title also complemented the claim to authority over Cyprus as an imperial fief, Frederick's father Henry VI having granted Aimery of Lusignan a crown in 1197. The tentacles of Hohenstaufen power were expansive. Henry VI had also granted a crown to Cilician Armenia. Frederick's new bride was the granddaughter of Conrad of Montferrat, an imperial vassal and a member of a house loyal to the Hohenstaufen in the years of civil war in the western empire after 1197. As heir of the Hauteville kings of Sicily (Roger II was his maternal grandfather), Frederick possessed a wider strategic and commercial interest in Mediterranean politics. The 1225 marriage seemed to bring a step closer the realization of the ambition of a cross-Mediterranean empire of the sort envisaged by Henry VI. It also fed the grander universalist imperial policy and rhetoric inherited from Frederick Barbarossa; his propaganda and acts showed Frederick II was well aware of both. However, the Treaty of San Germano could also be seen as encompassing the cooperation of church and state in the recovery by a Christian monarch, the king of Jerusalem, of his lost territories. Despite his later reputation as a sort of elemental political force, *stupor mundi*, and despite some of his own posturing, Frederick's grand designs were founded on often prosaic traditional, immediate and sustainable rights and claims.

Rhetoric did not win wars. Money, men and ships could. At the heart of negotiations with the papacy in 1223 and 1225 lay finance, logistics and recruitment. Frederick's commitments to subsidize the expedition served to reassure the pope, encourage his own subjects and attract followers beyond his territories. They also guaranteed a measure of imperial control over the whole project, another lesson learnt from the events of 1217–21. After the agreement at Ferentino in 1223, Frederick had agreed to prepare a fleet to carry 10,000 infantry and 1,000 knights east. The treaty of San Germano specified his own military entourage would number 1,000 knights to be maintained for two years, with transport to be provided for a further 2,000 knights, each with three horses, as well as their *familia*, squires and valets. The muster was fixed for 15 August 1227.[17] To underwrite the expenses of this force once in Outremer, Frederick agreed to deposit 100,000 gold ounces for withdrawal at Acre. Over the following two years Frederick extended his commitment by offering free transport and supplies to all *crucesignati*, however grand. It was clear that his campaign was not going to match the scale of those recruited in 1188, 1202 or 1217, a point reflected in the absence of a general clerical tax, as well as the concurrent distractions of the Languedoc war, campaigns against the Moors in Spain by Ferdinand III of Castile and James I of Aragon and in 1227 a crusade authorizing the king of Hungary to attack dissident Bosnians. Frederick fell back largely on the resources within his Italian and Sicilian kingdom, although he received John of Brienne's share (50,000 marks) of Philip II of France's crusade legacy in a moment of rare rapprochement with his father-in-law. Local sources suggest monasteries bore the brunt of a heavy clerical tax, calculated, levied or soon converted into gold, the currency of the eastern Mediterranean. Throughout the 1220s, Frederick appeared eager to increase his gold reserves, insisting that visiting merchants to the kingdom use gold for all financial transactions. While this policy may have been designed to build up stocks preparatory to his bold scheme of producing a gold currency in 1231–2, it may also have been instituted with the crusade in mind. As well as being the currency of the east, the relative value of gold made it far less bulky to transport than the same value of silver. Other crusaders, such as the bishop of Winchester, seemed to share Frederick's appreciation of gold in financing the journey east.[18]

The effect of the treaty of San Germano was almost immediate. Earlier attempts after 1223 to raise forces in Germany and elsewhere by John of Brienne and the Master of the Teutonic Knights, Frederick's close friend and adviser Hermann von Salza, had met with a very cool response. Now the reaction was very different, especially in Germany, Italy and England. Frederick's commitments were broadcast across western Europe. In England, for instance, a papal nuncio, Otho, circulated copies of the San Germano agreement to each diocese.[19] Papal orders to preach the cross were similarly distributed. The promise of imperial aid secured the support of important German magnates, such as the dukes of Thuringia and Limburg, the count of Urach, numbers of imperial *ministeriales* and contingents from traditional crusade centres such as the Netherlands, and the cities of Worms, Cologne and Lübeck. Frederick could also rely on his network of officials and supporters in southern Italy and Sicily, such as Thomas of Aquino count of Acerra. Independent *crucesignati* were encouraged to associate themselves with the muster fixed at Brinsidi for August 1227.[20]

One of the more distinct contributions, from England, demonstrated the narrowness of recruitment for the 1227 crusade in comparison with more generally popular expeditions.[21] The leading figure was the recently disgraced former Justiciar bishop of Winchester, Peter des Roches, through his support for King John and the ideals and practices of authoritarian kingship, one of the most controversial politicians in England of the first third of the thirteenth century. He had taken the cross in 1221 amid rumours that he had been nominated as archbishop of Damietta. News of Frederick's plans in 1225 seems to have stimulated des Roches's preparations. From 1226, he was in direct contact with the emperor, coordinating plans, and probably booking his passage in the imperial fleet. The timing was convenient for the bishop personally, as he had recently been excluded from power. However, the young King Henry III and his advisers were looking to reconquer Angevin ancestral lands in France rather than help the Holy Land or the disgraced former minister. Apart from releasing his debts at the Exchequer, forcing payment of loans owed to him and defending some property rights, perhaps in recognition of his crusader status, the government made no financial contribution to des Roches's expedition, although the pope allowed him to raise money from his diocese. As the see of Winchester was one of the wealthiest in western Europe and des Roches was privately a very rich man, the absence of official subsidy may have made little difference. On crusade, he appeared amply supplied with funds. However, not a single English magnate accompanied him to Syria. The only fellow crusader of substance was William Brewer bishop of Exeter. Taking the cross in 1226–7, Brewer stood proxy for his uncle and namesake, a veteran civil servant who had taken the cross as long ago as 1188 but had been allowed to postpone fulfilling his vow by the pope. To pay for his nephew's crusade, the older Brewer deposited 4,000 marks with the Templars at Acre.[22]

As the bishops had not previously been linked socially or politically, the coincidence of their crusades did not indicate any great enthusiasm among the ruling classes in England. In 1227, des Roches was accompanied by a suitable clerical and military entourage and acquired a small army, probably mercenaries from England or the Continent. A smattering of other traceable English crusaders accompanied them. A year later Philip of Aubigny, a survivor of the Damietta campaign, took the cross. Yet the figure of 40,000 *crucesignati* given by the St Albans monk Roger of Wendover appears a gross exaggeration.[23] However, in the reduced army that embarked from Brindisi in August 1227, the English contingent assumed some prominence, which was confirmed during the crusade's stay in Outremer. Des Roches became a confidant of the German leadership, and the English force played a major role in the refortification of coastal towns, especially Sidon and Jaffa. The bishops witnessed the Treaty of Jaffa in 1229, which restored Jerusalem, and des Roches supervised the reconstruction of St Stephen's Gate and the Tower of David. While widely praised in English sources, the bishops' cooperation with the excommunicated emperor earned them papal censure. This hardly seemed to affect them. At Acre, des Roches transformed an existing English hospital dedicated to St Thomas Becket, which possibly dated from the Third Crusade, into a military order. Within a few years the order had adopted the rule of the Teutonic Knights; it continued as a military corporation for a century and as a religious order for a further two.[24] On their return to their dioceses, Brewer in 1229 and des Roches in 1231, they were greeted as heroes. Yet their, and the crusade's, achievements, while diplomatically startling and politically controversial, were, compared with earlier campaigns, modest.

Until the summer of 1227, Frederick's preparations had gone smoothly. Recruiting hardly seemed designed to produce a mass response. The context for Frederick's campaign was limited and precise, focused on the assertion of his royal and imperial rights in Outremer; fulfilling political obligations to the papacy as part of consolidating his power in Italy and Germany; and exploiting the diplomatic opportunity presented by al-Kamil of Egypt. Aware of the emperor's plan to come east, in 1226 the sultan had sent Emir Fakhr al-Din to Frederick offering an alliance against his brother al-Mu 'azzam emir of Damascus. Al-Mu 'azzam was challenging for supremacy in the Ayyubid empire and had recently allied with Jelal al-Din, the ruler of the Khwarazmians, a Turkish federation from the steppes between the river Oxus and the Caspian Sea. Khwarazmian raiders could tip the balance of power in Syria decisively against al-Kamil.[25] As a lure, the Egyptian sultan proposed the return of Jerusalem and other towns to the Christians, in effect reviving his offers to the crusaders in 1219–21. Frederick evidently got on well with Fakhr al-Din, apparently even knighting him; in 1249 the emir still bore the emperor's arms on his banner.[26] An imperial embassy travelled to Egypt in 1227 and went on to Damascus, where they were rebuffed by al-Mu 'azzam. For the treaty with al-Kamil to be realized, Frederick needed to appear in Outremer with an army. However, as the abortive talks in Damascus suggested, Frederick probably wondered how far al-Kamil was in a position to deliver on his promises. The death of al-Mu 'azzam in November 1227 reconfigured the political map. With al-Kamil and another brother, al-Ashraf, concentrating on trying to annexe Damascus, their need for Frederick ceased. According to Ibn Wasil, a well-informed Ayyubid official of the next generation, Frederick had become 'an embarrassment'.[27] Yet the sultan could not afford to fight him either, as this would deflect from his aim of subduing Damascus. Yet, by honouring his promise to Frederick, al-Kamil risked hardening opposition to his rule from the Damascenes, who regarded Palestine as part of their sphere of influence. When news of the 1229 treaty reached Damascus, it provided al-Kamil's enemies with a fine propaganda weapon as the city went into public mourning, with preachers and poets fanning a sense of Islamic outrage.[28] Thus Fredrick's Egyptian diplomacy required a far more delicate use of military strength than had initially seemed in prospect.

This was not apparent in the summer of 1227, when the roads from Germany to Apulia were clogged with crusaders.[29] The muster at Brindisi attracted many thousands, although the core comprised a force of over 1,000 knights in the emperor's pay. The crowding and summer heat took their toll as plague broke out in the crusader camps. As victims mounted, some abandoned the journey. The main German fleet sailed in mid-August, probably including the English bishops. Frederick and the landgrave of Thuringia embarked with Sicilian levies on 8 September. Within days, probably from the effects of plague, the landgrave was dead and Frederick incapacitated, forcing him to put in at Otranto to recuperate. As a token of his continuing commitment, he despatched Hermann von Salza and the patriarch of Jerusalem to Syria with twenty galleys to join the main force, whose command he entrusted to Henry, the new duke of Limburg. What in other circumstances would have seemed an unfortunate but unavoidable setback became the pivot around which the crusade was transformed from an enterprise of Christian solidarity into one of confrontation and division. Despite being told the reasons for this further delay, on 29 September Pope Gregory IX excommunicated Frederick for having broken the terms of the Treaty of San Germano.[30]

The unreasonable vehemence of Gregory's condemnation and his refusal to accept Frederick's subsequent restrained defence suggested that the pope had been waiting for a chance to strike against the emperor. Unlike his predecessor, Honorius III, whom he had succeeded only in March 1227, Gregory was not by nature a conciliator. A nephew of Innocent III, an early patron of the friars, a canon lawyer and papal diplomat of wide and long experience, Gregory had come to mistrust Frederick personally and politically. Fearing an extension of Hohenstaufen power across all Italy and suspicious of Frederick's imperious attitude to ecclesiastical independence within his kingdom, Gregory presumably hoped excommunication would force Frederick into a new submission or overt disobedience. Frederick thought Gregory's stance a form of papal monarchic extremism that ran counter to and undermined the traditional just order of Christendom. Within a year, the remarkable spectacle arose of an excommunicated crusader sailing to restore Jerusalem, while the pope was organizing armies, one of which was led by the former king of Jerusalem, to secure the crusader's political overthrow in the west.

Frederick now needed the crusade more than ever to wrong-foot the pope and reassert his credentials for honesty and Christian leadership. He announced his departure for May 1228, began to raise more troops in Germany and Italy, and imposed a tax of eight gold ounces per fief in the kingdom of Sicily. In April 1228, the imperial marshal Richard Filangieri sailed for Acre with 500 knights to add to the 800 knights already there under the duke of Limburg's command. Frederick himself followed in June with perhaps seventy ships.[31] If this figure is accurate, such a fleet could have carried a few thousand men. At Acre, Frederick's army could only be accommodated in a camp outside the city, at Recordana, behind the coastal sand dunes to the south of the city. One unreliable but knowledgeable source put the number of infantry as high as 10,000.[32] If not a mass expedition, Frederick had assembled a significant and cohesive fighting force sufficiently strong to persuade al-Kamil to negotiate and to preside over a substantial refortification programme. The duke of Limburg had begun a rebuilding programme a year earlier. When news of Frederick's delay caused many immediately to return home, to keep an army intact, Duke Henry marched down the coast to refurbish the defences of Caesaerea and Jaffa. Some of his troops dreamt of an assault on Jerusalem itself. On hearing of the death of al-Mu 'azzam in November 1227, a separate group of crusaders left in Acre annexed the Muslim-held half of Sidon. During the winter of 1227–8 German crusaders and Teutonic Knights cooperated in constructing a castle on one of the order's estates at Montfort about twenty miles north-east of Acre in the Galileean hills. This soon became the Teutonic Knights' headquarters.

The activities of Henry of Limburg and the English bishops in 1227–8 were consciously preliminary to Frederick's arrival. After an increasingly venomous war of words and despite the risk of leaving his European lands under the threat of papal confiscation, Frederick sailed from Brindisi on 28 June 1228, arriving at Limassol on 21 July. During five stormy weeks in Cyprus, Frederick sought to assert imperial overlordship, attempting to call John of Ibelin to account for his management of the kingdom on behalf of the young King Henry I (1218–53) and install a Cypriot regency more amenable to imperial interests. Only Frederick's higher purpose prevented an open breach. Both John of Ibelin and King Henry were in the emperor's entourage when he sailed for Acre on 2 September 1228, arriving five days later. There, for the first time in Outremer, Frederick encountered the inconvenience of excommunication. The pope's refusal to lift the ban forced the patriarch of Jerusalem into opposition and elicited a rather nervous response to Frederick's leadership from the Templars and Hospitallers. Frederick had to chart a careful course around Frankish sensibilities, appointing separate nominal commanders of the army's divisions to avoid pious crusaders having to be seen to obey an excommunicate. The English bishops showed no such qualms and, in practice, the papal ban scarcely restricted Frederick. Even the litigious Jerusalem barons did not try to reject his authority because of the excommunication; they had quite enough to attack him under their existing law code.

Frederick's challenge was threefold: to insist on his rights as king of Jerusalem; to keep his army together; and to secure the projected treaty with al-Kamil. In the first his position had seriously been weakened by the death of his teenage wife Isabella II, in May 1228 after childbirth. Technically, Frederick could thereafter only wield power in the kingdom of Jerusalem as regent for his and Isabella's infant son Conrad IV/II, compromising his insistence on exercising regalian rights. More awkwardly, with the removal of al-Mu 'azzam, al-Kamil had no need to honour his earlier promises over Jerusalem as he and al-Ashraf began military action against Damascus to remove their young nephew, al-Nasir Dawud. Al-Kamil had agreed with al-Ashraf to partition al-Nasir's territories, keeping Transjordan and Palestine for himself. Any concessions to the Franks might appear superfluous if not risky. However, for Frederick a satisfactory diplomatic outcome was essential, and, with rumours of papal armies attacking his lands in Italy, a speedy one at that. In the footsteps, at times literally, of Richard I three and a half decades earlier, permanent dialogue backed by a show of force was the only option available. However, unlike Richard's, Frederick's army was palpably incapable of conquering inland Palestine, still less conducting an effective siege or defence of Jerusalem. The most pressure that Frederick could exert over the Egyptian sultan was as a nuisance in the path of the new Ayyubid settlement.

As soon as he landed Frederick reopened negotiations with al-Kamil. After an initial friendly but empty exchange of gifts, talks proceeded between Frederick and Fakhr al-Din. During these exchanges, Frederick showed himself in his element, skilfully exploiting his cosmopolitan culture to charm the Ayyubid negotiators and persuade them of his sincerity and good intentions. The widespread but largely false accusations by his opponents in the west of his sympathy for Islam and general irreligious scepticism finds a rather more approving parallel in Arabic observers, who liked to depict him as a man of reason and faith, tolerant if not sympathetic to Islam. Frederick enjoyed showing off, from elaborate royal ceremonial to swapping esoteric academic arguments. Accompanied in Palestine by his Arabic logic tutor, with whom he was apparently reading Aristotle, Frederick sent al-Kamil a list of detailed questions on philosophy, geometry and mathematics.[33] This kind of intellectual showing off reflected Frederick's Sicilian education, as did his refusal to engage in crude anti-Islamic posturing once Jerusalem had been restored. He was critical of decisions by the local Jerusalem *qadi* to suspend the call of the muezzin. While preventing Christian priests insulting Muslim sensibilities by carrying copies of the Bible into holy places in the Haram al-Sharif to which the treaty specified joint access, he allowed his Muslim bodyguards from Sicily to say their midday prayers there. While such behaviour left Arabic commentators favourably impressed, it allowed Latin critics to attack what they perceived as decadence or, worse, a lack of sincere faith. The Patriarch Gerold, uncomfortably placed on the spot but loyal to the papal ban, accused Frederick of enjoying the sultan's gifts of not just mathematical solutions but 'singing girls and jugglers, persons who were not only of ill repute but unworthy even to be mentioned by Christians' (although naturally that did not stop the patriarch doing precisely that). There were stories that Frederick reciprocated by providing his Muslim guests with Christian dancing girls.[34] Alleged miscegenation was almost guaranteed to summon the interest if not blood of watching monastic commentators in the west.

However cosy their social relations, Frederick and al-Kamil's negotiators had no easy task. Al-Kamil felt he needed a settlement with Frederick to free his hands in Syria but was nervous at the price in prestige of a peaceful settlement or surrender, as his opponents would say. He could not be seen as giving too much too freely. On the other hand Frederick, although desperate for a treaty to restore his reputation in Christendom and allow him to return to defend his Italian territories, could not appear as a suppliant. Both had to be cautious but persistent. One member of Frederick's forces, the poet Freidank, likened the process to watching two misers trying to divide evenly three gold pieces.[35] In November 1228, with negotiations deadlocked, al-Kamil moved to southern Palestine. Frederick followed in a show of force, almost a copy of Richard I's march of September 1191, leading a coalition of local barons, the military orders and the western crusaders down the coast road to Caesarea and Jaffa, ostensibly preparatory to an assault on Jerusalem itself. So as not to appear to be serving under an excommunicated commander, the Templars and Hospitallers followed the main body a day behind. However, on reaching Arsuf they realized the folly of such division and the armies united before reaching

Jaffa unopposed. There, supplied by the sea, Frederick completed the refortifications and built up supplies. At the same time, news from the west of papally sponsored invasions of his Italian territories sharpened the emperor's dilemma. Although he sent for more galleys from Sicily, a winter return passage was hardly feasible for the whole of the emperor's force.

The stalemate was broken by al-Kamil's agreement to most of Frederick's terms. While insisting to his subjects that any territorial concessions could easily be reversed once the crusade army had departed and exaggerating the threat posed by Frederick's continued stay, al-Kamil's acceptance of a treaty recognized the priorities of Ayyubid policy.[36] Damascus and Transjordan were more important than Judea; peaceful relations with the Frankish masters of the coastal entrepôts more crucial to the rulers of the hinterland than stubborn points of principle. A sign of successful diplomacy, each side was able to gloss the details of the treaty to suit their domestic needs, and critics on both sides could condemn the whole deal as unprincipled. Reminiscent of the 1192 agreement between Saladin and Richard I, the Treaty of Jaffa of 18 February 1229 gave both parties what they immediately wanted.[37] The Ayyubids' priorities concerned political strategy; the Christians' what could be called religious strategy. Jerusalem, Bethlehem and Nazareth, the sites of the Crucifixion, Nativity and Annunication, were restored to Christian rule, with territorial corridors linking them to the Frankish-held coastal plain. The whole of Sidon was relinquished to the Franks, as was Toron in western Galilee, although with a stipulation that it should not be fortified, a restriction that, despite al-Kamil's claim to the contrary, did not apply to Jerusalem or elsewhere. Prisoners of war, always a very sensitive issue, from the Fifth Crusade and since, were to be returned. A truce was established that was to last for ten years. Excluded or ignored by the terms were the castles of the Templars and Hospitallers and the lands of Bohemund IV of Antioch-Tripoli, perhaps in revenge for his refusal to swear fealty to Frederick in the summer of 1228. Within Jerusalem, the Temple Mount, al-Haram al-Sharif, was to remain under the jurisdiction of Islamic religious authorities, the Dome of the Rock and the al-Aqsa mosque to remain Muslim places of worship. Christians were allowed free access to these sites, just as Muslim pilgrims were to be protected in their devotions, with their own resident *qadi*. Otherwise, the Muslim population was evacuated, being replaced by Franks, who immediately began to refortify the city, even though the political capital effectively remained at Acre.

The Treaty of Jaffa appalled sections of the Muslim world, especially al-Kamil's enemies in Damascus. Even writers sympathetic to al-Kamil acknowledged the distaste provoked by the surrender of Jerusalem, reversing, as one pointedly commented, 'one of Saladin's most notable achievements'.[38] On the Christian side, the Templars and Hospitallers had few reasons to rejoice, especially as Frederick had so very obviously favoured the Teutonic Knights during his stay. Few were more vitriolic in their condemnation than Patriarch Gerold of Jerusalem, who lambasted Frederick for his temerity, disobedience, deceit, misbehaviour and pride.[39] The restoration of Jerusalem posed an awkward problem for local churchmen and their allies in the baronage and military orders. Recovery of territory offered a return of property that, if opposed, could be in danger of being given to another. Alice of Armenia had to appeal to the High Court to prevent Toron remaining in the hands of the Teutonic Knights, to whom Frederick had given it.[40] Most pilgrims relished the prospect of fulfilling their vows at the Holy Sepulchre despite not having shed any infidel blood. Denying access to the Holy Places or insisting on violence rather than diplomacy placed churchmen in a tricky situation, especially as some clerics, notably the bishops of Winchester and Exeter, supported Frederick, earning themselves papal censure. Quite quickly, self-interest won over the Templars and Hospitallers to the benefits of reoccupying Jerusalem and the other restored areas. Christian opposition to the 1229 treaty had far more to do with its architect, Frederick, than its content which in essence repeated much of what Richard I had suggested in 1191–2.

Frederick could afford no such doubts. On 17 March, before an interdict could reach him from Patriarch Gerold in Acre, Frederick entered Jersualem. After visiting the Muslim shrines in the company of the local Islamic authorities, the following day he led his followers into the church of the Holy Sepulchre. There, in one of the most memorable pieces of political and religious theatre of thirteenth-century Christendom, Frederick took his crown from the high altar in the great twelfth-century Romanesque nave of the church and placed it on his own head. This was not a Napoleonic self-coronation as king of Jerusalem so much as an imperial crown-wearing, a demonstration of his unique authority, a reminder of his pre-eminent role in the order of the Christian society and, boldest of all, an assertion of his inheritance of the special favour once bestowed by God Himself on King David. One of the most skilled propagandists and self-promoters of his age, Frederick made this very clear in his letter to Henry III of England describing the scene:

> we, as being a Catholic emperor ... wore the crown, which Almighty God provided for us from the throne of His majesty, when of his especial grace, he exalted us on high among the princes of the world; so that whilst we have supported the honour of this high dignity, which belongs to us by right of sovereignty, it is more and more evident to all that the hand of the Lord hath done all this: and since His mercies are over all His works, let the worshippers of the orthodox faith henceforth know and relate it far and wide throughout the world, that He, who is blessed for ever, has visited and redeemed His people, and has raised up the horn of salvation for us in the house of His servant David.[41]

During the crown-wearing ceremony, Hermann von Salza read out a statement, once in German and then in French, justifying Frederick's actions surrounding the crusade and attacking his critics. The Jerusalem ritual was to serve purposes far beyond the Holy Land. The scene in the Holy Sepulchre was woven prominently into Frederick's self-image. When later in 1229 his armies took the field against those of the pope in his successful attempts to regain his kingdom in Italy, sympathetic writers described them as 'the army of crusaders (*crucesignatorum*)'.[42] As he reputedly said to Fakhr al-Din, his reason for taking Jerusalem was primarily because 'I simply want to safeguard my reputation with the Christians.'[43] Immediately this seemed unlikely. Only the next day the archbishop of Caesarea arrived to impose the patriarch's interdict on the Holy City. However, the bird had flown, Frederick decamping for Jaffa that day, eager to return to the west to make sure he did not become an emperor with no empire. Yet even while he had been in Jerusalem, some clergy had accompanied him and others, such as the Dominican Walter, who had preached the cross in England in 1227, celebrated mass for crusaders just outside the city walls. Once the emperor had gone, the bishop of Winchester and the military orders began rebuilding the city's fortifications and, so one jaundiced English observer noted, clerics from grand prelates downwards crowded back into the Holy City, 'their churches and old possessions restored to them'.[44] However controversial, the restoration of Jerusalem to Christian occupation lasted, with one brief interlude, for fifteen years. There is evidence that it benefited economically from a revived pilgrim trade; at least one new holy site was constructed, the Coeniculum on Mt Zion, the reputed site of the Last Supper. A well-funded, staffed and equipped scriptorium seems to have been established in the Holy City and large sums of money expended on its walls. Its loss briefly in 1240 and permanently in 1244 proved the wisdom of those who, since 1191, had argued for the impracticality of trying to defend Jerusalem without a larger militarized hinterland and control of the castles of Transjordan. As it was, after 1229, there was a Muslim military base stationed a few miles away at al-Bira, site of the former Frankish settlement of Magna Mahomeria. Discounted by subsequent events, nonetheless Jerusalem's recovery in 1229 was a significant actual as well as symbolic achievement in the context of the emotions, blood and treasure so profligately expended on it since 1187.

Frederick's haste to depart contributed to a further souring of relations with the clergy and local baronage. As in Cyprus in 1228, Frederick wished to impose a subservient regime in the kingdom, clipping the wings of the Ibelins. On his return to Acre he also found ranged against him the Templars, the patriarch and many of the Italian merchants in the city nervous at Damascus's extremely hostile reaction to the surrender of Jerusalem. Patriarch Gerold was planning a coup with the Templars to wrest Jerusalem from the hands of imperial agents. Frederick's attempt to instal Thomas of Acrerra as his – or rather his infant son Conrad's – *bailli* met fierce resistance. After trying to browbeat the Templars and the patriarch by force, Frederick admitted defeat. He maintained the imperial presence by leaving a garrison in Acre and securing Montfort for the Teutonic Knights as well as endowing them with as much property as his opponents could not legally challenge. But he had to bow to local pressure and appoint two loyal but Syrian barons as his regents. The future of Hohenstaufen control in Jerusalem or Cyprus was to be resolved by war over the next decade and a half; Frederick's allies lost.[45]

The politics of Outremer meant that Frederick's diplomatic success, still more his grand gesture in Jerusalem, was greeted with widespread derision, on both sides of the Ayyubid frontier. A Damascene contemporary drew a neat literary contrast between Frederick's political and intellectual pretensions and his unprepossessing appearance. Quoting one of the janitors of the Dome of the Rock, Ibn al-Jawzi noted that

Frederick was red-faced, balding and myopic: 'Had he been a slave he would not have been worth two hundred *dirham*.'[46] The Franks of Acre were even less charitable. As Frederick hurried to embark from the city on 1 May 1229, local butchers pelted him with offal.[47] Yet the doubters and critics were wrong. Al-Kamil's victory over Damascus soon after allayed fears in Acre of a threat to their trade with the Syrian capital. Frederick's own defeat of papal forces in 1229–30 and the subsequent reconciliation with Gregory IX at the Treaties of San Germano and Ceprano in 1230, secured official ecclesiastical acceptance of the Outremer settlement of 1229. Frederick's crusade had potentially laid the basis for constructive relations with the Ayyubids in the development of a wider condominium in Palestine. When instability returned to the region on the death of al-Kamil in 1238, the territorial and castle base established in 1229 could have formed a platform for further Frankish advances. Frederick retained an almost proprietary interest in the affairs of Outremer and the need to assist the defence of the Holy Land. Yet the rejection by the Outremer nobles of Hohenstaufen control, the fissures in their own polity and the collapse of imperial–papal relations in the west prevented more than a very modest western response when the 1229 truce expired. However, Frederick never forgot his crusade. When his porphyry tomb in Palermo was opened in 1782, the emperor's body was found to be wearing, on the left shoulder, his crusader's cross.[48]

THE CRUSADES OF 1239–41

While the ten-year truce of 1229 focused minds in the west on preparations for a new expedition, political circumstances in the west were hardly conducive to fresh mass recruitment. In England and France, the ending of their kings' minorities stimulated internal faction and rebellion. In 1230, Henry III of England attempted to recover his ancestral lands in Poitou by force. Relations between Frederick and Gregory IX, chiefly over imperial policy in Italy, slid towards a final parting of the ways in 1239. The monarchs of Iberia were vigorously pursuing their own expansion and consolidation of conquests from the Moors and each other. In eastern Europe, rumours and refugees alerted rulers to a new danger from Mongol advances westwards beyond the

Eurasian steppes that culminated in the great campaign (1236–42) by Batu, grandson of Genghis Khan, which brought him first to the marches of Latin Europe then, in 1241–2, to Poland, Hungary and, briefly, the Adriatic coast of Dalmatia. The Latin empire of Constantinople stumbled towards financial and political bankruptcy, despite vigorous leadership from the new co-emperor, the ever available and willing, if now rather shop-soiled, John of Brienne. In the Baltic, the energies of local rulers were engaged in the subjugation of Prussia, the collapse of the Swordbrothers in Livonia (1236) and growing rivalry with Novgorod.

Yet out of this apparently unpropitious setting, a new series of expeditions was fashioned. One collector of heroic tales and good stories, no friend to the emperor, noted that once Pope Gregory 'realised that Frederick was not going to put forward any plan for freeing the Holy Land from the unbelievers' he initiated preaching the cross in England and France.[49] This was unfair. Frederick continued to take a close interest in plans for a new crusade and, even in 1239, when again excommunicated, retained at least diplomatic hopes of finding a role for himself or his son, Conrad, the absentee king of Jerusalem. However, Gregory saw in the crusade a unique instrument of ecclesiastical and specifically papal authority with wide application. He authorized crusading campaigns against allegedly heretical peasants in the Netherlands and the Lower Weser in the 1220s and early 1230s, and against Bosnians in 1227 and 1234. His commitment to prop up Latin Constantinople produced crusading plans in 1231 and 1236–8. In the Baltic he authorized the Teutonic Knights' conquest of Prussia and supported them with repeated crusading appeals including, in 1240, war with Novgorod. From 1234, he employed the Dominicans and Franciscans on a regular basis to preach the *verbum crucis*. Finally in 1239–40 he began the series of crusades against Frederick that marked the start of a thirty-year contest to destroy the Hohenstaufen.[50]

Yet, in all this holy war, the plight of the Holy Land retained its special resonance.

> Any man who will not set off at once
> for the land where God lived and died,
> any man who will not take the Holy Land's cross
> will have but little chance of going to heaven.[51]

Although hardly impartial, these verses of Count Theobald IV of Champagne (1201–53, king of Navarre from 1234) marking his own determination to sail for Syria, such sentiments permeated the literature, liturgy and diplomatic rhetoric of the west. By 1234, prospects appeared at least realistic. In Outremer the War of the Lombards had temporarily died down after the defeat of the imperialists in Cyprus in 1232–3. The pope was involved in efforts to gain acceptance of the imperial administration on the mainland. In the west, after Louis IX of France achieved his majority in 1234, the severe political unrest of the previous years gave way to acceptance of the royal regime. In England a sharp political crisis of 1232–4 appeared over and protracted civil war averted. In both countries, just as during the preaching of the Fifth Crusade, the institution of a new expedition to the Holy Land offered a useful political ritual through which disputes and rivalries could be settled and political consensus restored.

Gregory IX launched his new enterprise in letters to the English (4 September 1234) and French (6 November 1234).[52] The plan he devised was a sophisticated if logical development from the experience of 1213–21 and 1227–9. In addition to the crusaders themselves, Gregory proposed the creation of a ten-year garrison (or 'militia') funded by lay tax contributions earning non-plenary remission of sins.[53] To subsidize the crusaders, the clergy were taxed and the pope instituted a campaign to attract vow redemptions and offered indulgences for material contributions. While the preaching was committed largely to the friars, the moneys raised were held in diocesan depositories from which sums were released by direct papal command or the instructions from a papal legate. The funds were given to the regional commanders of the crusade for their own expenses, those of their followers and for mercenaries. Some recruits, such as Count Amaury of Montfort, had their debts settled, while for others, including the count of Champagne, such subsidies made involvement possible.[54] The leading English recruit, Henry III's brother, Richard earl of Cornwall, stood in a different category. From Cornwall he received huge revenues from the growing tin industry, making him one of the richest men in Europe. Nonetheless, he was eager to supplement his resources to pay for the equipping, maintenance and transport of a small army to the Holy Land. Earl Richard received 3,000 marks levied from the increasingly hard-pressed English Jewish community in 1237. The next year, the pope assigned to him legacies bequeathed for the Holy Land and cash vow redemptions, to be handed over once the earl reached Outremer. In fact, the elaborate funding system encountered severe administrative difficulties. Collection of Earl Richard's grant of redemptions proved glacial, lasting into the 1250s, but lucrative. As late as 1247, when efforts to settle the account were revived by Pope Innocent IV, one archdeaconry was alleged to have raised 600 pounds. Yet by this time, as critics observed, it was evident that little of the money had been used on the actual crusade. Just as some expressed distaste at preachers' emphasis on fund raising, so others saw the incongruity of supplying the fabulously wealthy earl with a form of regular pension derived from the payments of the pious, the halt, the lame and the poor.[55] In France, bureaucratic confusion led to the same funds from the diocese of Poitiers being assigned simultaneously to two different crusaders, Geoffrey of Argentan and the duke of Brittany, while proceeds from three dioceses in the province of Lyons were directed to the duke of Burgundy, having previously been allocated to Count John of Mâcon.[56]

In addition to these papally organized levies, crusaders resorted to traditional means to raise capital, chiefly from their own property and their lords' generosity. Richard of Cornwall cut down and sold off his woods after taking the cross in 1236.[57] His brother-in-law and fellow *crucesignatus*, Simon of Montfort, Amaury's younger brother and earl of Leicester, received 1,000 pounds from the sale of his wood at Leicester.[58] Others were supported by the king, especially the entourage of Richard of Cornwall. The earl's 'chief of staff', the prior of the English Hospitallers, Thierry of Nussa, was lent 1,000 pounds. Royal officials who had taken the cross received advances on their salaries or outright gifts. Other *crucesignati* were able to obtain mortgages from the crown, Across the English Channel, Louis IX was encouraged by the pope to provide funds for the expedition in 1237.[59] The stimulus given to the land market by departing crusaders' need to raise cash on their landed assets is unquantifiable but everywhere apparent.

Although some contemporaries noted, perhaps formally rather than arithmetically, the participation of large numbers of the 'mediocrium' or 'menu peuple', the commons or 'ordinary' people[60] – and there is evidence of involvement by some non-noble or knightly freeholders – the core of the crusade comprised the subsidized entourages of earls, counts and dukes, around whom gathered political and dynastic affinities. Superficially, the French crusaders fell into certain broad groups – royal baronial officials, such as Amaury of Montfort, the constable and the butler Robert of Courtenay – and circles of nobles associated by blood or allegiance with a few great lords who had taken the cross: Duke Hugh IV of Burgundy, Theobald of Champagne and Count Peter of Brittany. The muster, from all parts of the kingdom except the south, represented the most extensive commitment of French nobles since the Fourth Crusade, including the counts of Bar, Mâcon, Joigny, Sancerre, Soissons, Grandpré and Nevers. Yet this conceals the most striking feature of the recruitment. Each of these lords, as well as many of their crusading followers such as the counts of Bar, Châlons and Nevers, had been central to the largely anti-royalist disturbances of the late 1220s and early 1230s. Taking the cross formed part of a process of reconciliation with Louis IX and his mother, the powerful regent Blanche of Castile. It is perhaps significant that in the end the most loyalist baron who took the cross, Humbert of Beaujeu, actually went to defend Constantinople and did not accompany his former adversaries to the Holy Land. Taking the cross afforded former rebels protection and served as a guarantee of future conduct as well as presenting a respectable opportunity for political losers to absent themselves from the kingdom. The government could feel secure and the ex-rebels escape further harassment. A key role of the crusade in secular politics was to assist the process of achieving political consensus, the absence of which rendered any medieval polity ungovernable.

In England, the pattern was similar. The symbolic taking of the cross by the most important political recruits in 1236 represented an attempt to reconcile dissidents with the royal court after the near civil war of 1233–4, in which the king and his foreign advisors, led by the former crusader Peter des Roches, were challenged by a baronial coalition under Richard and Gilbert Marshal. Between 1236 and 1239, the cross was taken by a range of former allies and opponents. By taking the cross together, the alliance between Richard of Cornwall and his brother-in-law Gilbert Marshal was consolidated. The crusade encompassed complex currents of personal and factional hostility, including the outlaw Richard Siward, a longstanding enemy of Earl Richard, and the man who engineered his arrest in 1236, Simon of Montfort. At Northampton in 1239, the *crucesignati* swore an oath not to be deflected from the Holy Land as the goal of the expedition. They included former dissidents such as Siward and Gilbert Marshal as well as royal captains instrumental in combating the Marshals, such as Henry of Turbeville.[61] Those who embarked in 1240 ranged from close allies, servants and relatives of the king to previously fierce opponents such as Robert Tweng or Philip Basset.

Yet although the vows of prominent political figures in England and France, the main areas for recruitment, may have been sworn in the context of the political in-fighting of the 1230s, the structure of the crusading armies that embarked scarcely reflected the urge to unity that their original commitment apparently symbolized. The great English and French lords had mostly taken the cross by the end of 1236. Yet, despite the enterprise being conceived by Gregory IX and even Frederick II as a single operation, there appeared only partial co-ordination of effort. The main French wave left in 1239. The English contribution was divided into three distinct armies, under Richard of Cornwall, who set off in June 1240 and sailed via Marseilles; Simon of Montfort who left independently and travelled via Brindisi; and William of Forz, who left in 1241. Each attracted a distinctive constituency of followers. With Richard went his own extended *familia*, courtiers and close relatives and allies such as his cousin William Longspee and half-brother Eudo. Simon of Montfort led a mixed Anglo-French retinue, while William of Forz seems to have been followed by his fellow expatriate Poitevins. Each group retained independence of structure, policy and action once in the east.[62] As one of the more bizarre, yet suggestive features of the 1239–41 crusading effort, Richard of Cornwall timed his arrival at Acre just weeks after Theobald had left the city for home.

Yet the French armies were no more unified. After delaying their departure until 1239 out of deference to Frederick II's opposition to a precipitate breaking of the ten-year 1229 truce, a delay possibly secured by the emperor's promise to provide Theobald of Champagne with funds once he reached the Holy Land, the French crusaders displayed little cohesion.[63] Although most sailed from Marseilles, others used the ports of Apulia. Both before embarkation and in the Holy Land, an apparent primacy was afforded Theobald of Champagne, perhaps in deference to his grand crusading pedigree rather than his diminished wealth or conspicuous lack of political talent. Although Theobald had abandoned the 1226 Albigensian crusade at the siege of Avignon, his father (d. 1201) had been the lost leader of the Fourth Crusade; his uncle, Henry, had ruled Jerusalem 1192–7, and his predecessors and county had been central to crusade enthusiasm since the 1090s. However, on campaign in Palestine, he appeared unable to impose unity within the crusade force despite being recognized as commander of the crusade at an assembly of crusaders and Franks on arrival at Acre. At different times, Peter of Brittany, Hugh of Burgundy and Henry of Bar pursued their own separate tactics. The duke of Burgundy operated throughout as a semi-detached ally, remaining in the east a year after Theobald and most of the French had departed in 1240. When a private raid of Peter of Brittany's managed to seize a considerable haul of booty, livestock and meat were distributed to other commanders and 'the poor', but only as gifts, arousing jealousy and resentment. The duke of Burgundy and the counts of Bar and Montfort decided, disastrously, to forage and plunder for themselves because 'they were just as powerful as the count of Brittany' and they would be shamed if they failed to follow his example.[64] Attempts by Count Theobald to stop them, even his appeal to the fealty they had sworn him at Acre as leader of the army, failed. Such divisions reflected funding as much as the politics and personalities of the French operation. There was no central fund in the hands of a unified leadership. Each noble had funded himself and his followers and had received individual grants from the ecclesiastical depositories. None of the great lords depended financially on another. No pay; no discipline. One commentator remarked that by the end of his stay in Outremer, in the late summer of 1240, Theobald of Champagne lamented how members of his army disliked him so much that 'they did not obey his orders, as they had promised to do at the beginning when he landed in Syria'.[65]

This lack of unity was not entirely the crusaders' own making. Just as recruiting for the Holy Land was reaching completion towards the end of 1236, Gregory IX complicated arrangements by suggesting a parallel expedition to help defend the ailing Latin empire of Constantinople against a new menacing coalition of Greeks and Bulgars. Despite assumptions by later historians, the Latin empire never attracted much support from the west beyond the relatives of those French nobles who had established themselves in Greece. As reaction to the pope's new demands in the 1230s confirmed, in no sense did the Latin presence in Greece, or Romania as they called it, deflect western aid for the Holy Land. Rather the reverse; money raised in England for the Latin empire had to be assigned to the Palestine crusade because no English lord would change course for the Bosporus instead of Acre.[66] Gregory's appeal in 1236–8, made in conjunction with the mission to the west of the co-emperor Baldwin II, failed to redirect many *crucesignati* from the Holy Land. The pope's strenuous efforts on his behalf failed to disguise Baldwin II's own poor showing as an impecunious and unimpressive political mendicant with nothing to offer but relics, such as the Crown of Thorns eagerly acquired by Louis IX of France, and the sale of some vestigial western patrimonial lands. More damaging to the Palestine project were the pope's attempts to persuade or insist that crusaders commute their vows from Jerusalem to Constantinople. His main target in France was Peter of Brittany and his associates, including the counts of Bar and Soissons. Although negotiations drifted on for a couple of years, resistance to the Greek crusade hardened. The counts of Brittany and Bar both explicitly refused to commute their vows to the Greek scheme.[67] Of the French barons, only Humbert of Beaujeu and Thomas of Marly went with Baldwin II to Constantinople in 1239; Peter of Brittany and his colleagues went to Palestine. In England, Richard of Cornwall also resisted papal blandishments to commute his vow and divert his crusade money to subsidize Baldwin II's campaign.

If the papal dalliance with Greece sowed confusion and resentment, his renewed excommunication and subsequent crusade against Frederick II in 1239 provoked open disobedience. For one thing, the breach with Frederick potentially closed various routes to the east, especially the ports in Apulia. At least one army, that of Simon of Montfort, ignored this by using Brindisi. Frederick's son, Conrad, was titular king of Jerusalem, and the emperor retained agents in Outremer with access to funds and troops useful to any crusade. They held the Holy City itself. Many in France and England did not share Gregory's paranoia over the Hohenstaufen. Beyond the practical lay the principle. When faced by papal demands for a clerical tax to fund the Hohenstaufen war, the rectors of Berkshire in England repudiated the whole idea of the war, pointing out that Frederick had not been condemned as a heretic.[68] More pointedly, if the biased anti-papal Matthew Paris of St Alban's can be trusted, on 12 November 1239, Richard of Cornwall and other English *crucesignati* swore an oath confirming their intention to relieve the Holy Land 'lest their honest vow be hindered by the objections of the Roman Church and diverted to shedding Christian blood in Greece or Italy'.[69]

While attempt to divert the crusaders and their funds largely failed, they exacerbated the confused and divided nature of the Holy Land enterprise. The absence of a clear command structure, a united army or even a shared strategy contrasted with the financial discipline imposed within some of the contingents themselves. Yet the crusades of 1239–41 showed that the transition from the traditional expeditions of often rather loosely allied military households to those relying on central funding and organization could be more apparent than real. Although each noble contingent had access to a share of the central funds, their viability depended, as had all earlier crusade armies, on pre-existing bonds of clientage, association and dependency. Traditional means of self-finance persisted. One crusader poet, Philip of Nanteuil-le-Hardouin, later complained bitterly from an Egyptian prison that ordinary knights and freemen, once the money they had raised by mortgaging their lands had run out, received 'no kindness or help or comfort from the great lords'.[70] Other evidence reveals how cohesion within noble contingents was based on written contract, specific promises of agreed cash payments rather than less concrete ties of loyalty and expectation of patronage. This may be an accident of evidence. Earlier crusades had contained paid troops and retained knights, even nobles, since the First Crusade. By the mid-thirteenth century, such techniques had developed written records and, perhaps, a greater precision in the process.

The entourage of Richard of Cornwall revealed this combination of the obviously traditional and the possibly new, serving as a balance to the chroniclers' accounts of support for the crusade in terms of grand political gestures and popular emotion. Richard himself stood as financial guarantor for his followers, many of whom, such as his steward John FitzJohn, belonged to his *familia*, his paid household, which included knights as well as officials. Three days after landing in October 1240, Richard proclaimed throughout Acre that he would take any crusader into his pay.[71] Amongst his followers, similar but more formal contracts were drawn up. Philip Basset, one of Richard's followers, agreed with another, the king's forester, John of Neville, that they would travel together, with Philip paying for his own passage with two knights and four horses. Once at Acre, Neville would take Basset and his two knights into his paid *familia*.[72] Such relationships provided the bones to support all the campaigns of 1239–41 as suggested by the cohesion within the different retinues on the French crusade of 1239–40 and the contrasting inability of Theobald of Champagne to weld them into a single unit. Money can bind and sever. After another generation of use, by the 1270s, such contracts were commonplace throughout crusading hosts, as indeed they later became across the armed forces of western Europe.

The subtleties of internal organization and material preparations could not prevent the perfunctory nature and mixed military fortunes of the campaigns. Diplomatic achievements depended on continuing divisions between the Ayyubid rulers of Damascus, Transjordan and Egypt. The death of al-Kamil of Egypt in 1238 had left the succession to be disputed between al-Kamil's sons, al-Salih Ayyub and al-Adil II, and their uncle, al-Kamil's brother, al-Salih Isma 'il. Holding the ring as an important powerbroker stood the ruler of the crucial region around Kerak, al-Nasir, the former ruler of Damascus deposed in 1229, who could negate any settlement made by the others as to the future of southern Palestine. In 1240, al-Salih Ayyub, with the help of al-Nasir of Kerak, ousted al-Adil II from Egypt, having previously surrendered control of Damascus to his uncle al-Salih Isma 'il. The tensions between these rulers provided the Franks with an opportunity at the same time as making any territorial concessions difficult to guarantee. Within the kingdom of Jerusalem, different factions argued for different alliances. Consistency was impossible in the face of such volatile regime changes in the Ayyubid empire. A large, concerted crusader-Frankish army might have exerted considerable influence in the region. But no such force was assembled and, even if it had been, no obvious strategic plan was available.

The crusade that arrived at Acre under Theobald of Champagne in early September 1239 comprised in some near-contemporary estimates well over 1,000 knights. Most of the fleet had left from Marseilles, others using the southern Italian ports. Well stocked with great lords, the army lacked horses, a potential penalty of sea travel. Some knights were apparently reduced to riding donkeys.[73] The total number of non-knights could have reached a few thousand. The diplomatic and military options were complicated. Neither Damascus nor Egypt, the main military threats to the Franks, were in control of Jerusalem and southern Palestine during the crusaders' stay. At the expiry of the truce in 1239, the Holy City was threatened instead by al-Nasir of Kerak, who eventually occupied it at the end of the year. Yet the council at Acre that accepted Theobald's leadership agreed a potentially disastrous policy of threatening both Egypt and Damascus. First Ascalon would be refortified to secure the south and perhaps dissuade the Muslims from attacking Jerusalem. Then the Christians would launch a campaign against Damascus. This account of the plan may owe more to subsequent events than to what was decided at Acre.[74] However, a policy to unsettle both Damascus and Egypt may have appealed during the unresolved Ayyubid succession conflict. The logic, if any, to this scheme also reflected the divisions and interests within the local baronage. A recent prominent newcomer to Outremer, Walter of Brienne, a vassal of Theobald of Champagne in the west and married to the sister of Henry I of Cyprus, held the county of Jaffa in the right of his mother-in-law, Alice of Champagne. Ascalon traditionally formed part of that county, and Walter held a powerful voice in the local baronage. The concern of many, not least from the merchant community in Acre, lest relations with Damascus be harmed, may also have encouraged a foray southwards, as would the desire of the crusaders to visit the Holy City. Egypt in the winter of 1239–40 may have seemed a softer target than Damascus, while direct assistance for the garrison at Jerusalem would mean aiding the imperialist garrison there. Throughout the proceedings, although Theobald had hoped for a subsidy from Frederick II when he reached Acre, the hostility of the local barons led by the Ibelins ensured that the emperor's agent in the east, Richard Filangieri at Tyre, would remain excluded from operations.

As in 1228–9, the military manoeuvres of Theobald's crusade appeared chiefly designed to produce a diplomatic solution. This was achieved, but more by internal Ayyubid politics than Christian action. The march to Ascalon began on 2 November, reaching Jaffa ten days later. En route, the count of Brittany conducted a successful raid on a large convoy of herded livestock bound for Damascus, his success supplying the army with necessary food but feeding internal resentment at his independent action.[75] Once at Jaffa, news of an Egyptian army approaching from the south provoked a large division of nobles and knights under the duke of Burgundy, Walter of Brienne and the counts of Bar and Montfort, together with other local barons and members of the military orders, to offer battle. Ignoring warnings and pleas for unity from Count Theobald they advanced during the night to pitch camp beyond Ascalon, near Gaza. Omitting to post sentries, by morning this splinter expeditionary force found itself surrounded. Some of the leaders managed to break out and escape. The rest, led by the counts of Bar and Montfort, remained to be overwhelmed by the Egyptians. Henry of Bar was killed; Amaury of Montfort and many others captured. The defeat at Gaza, although modest in numbers lost, seriously undermined any potential diplomatic strategy by weakening the crusader army in repute if not materially. It provided the Egyptians with scores of well-connected aristocratic hostages. Hamstrung militarily and diplomatically, Theobald abandoned plans to rebuild Ascalon and withdrew from Jaffa back to Acre, seemingly waiting for something to turn up.

The activity during the rest of the count's stay was fashioned by events within the Ayyubid empire. In the autumn of 1239, al-Salih Ayyub had been expelled from Damascus by his uncle, al-Salih Ismai 'il and imprisoned by his cousin al-Nasir of Kerak. At the turn of the year, al-Nasir occupied Jerusalem. In the early months of 1240, the kaleidoscope received a further series of twists. In the north the change of government in Damascus prompted the emir of Hamah, a supporter of al-Salih Ayyub, to offer an alliance with the Franks against the lord of neighbouring Homs, an ally of the new Damascus regime. This prospect drew Count Theobald north to Tripoli, only for his presence to cause the lord of Homs to ease the pressure on Hamah, whose emir promptly withdrew from the promised alliance with the crusaders. While Theobald was being manipulated by political factions in northern Syria, in Egypt al-Adil II was deposed by a new partnership between al-Nasir and his erstwhile prisoner al-Salih Ayyub, who now assumed the sultanate. By May 1240, with no contribution by the crusaders or Franks, the political landscape had altered significantly from the one that Count Theobald had found nine months earlier. Jerusalem was under the control of al-Nasir of Kerak; his new ally al-Salih Ayyub was installed in Egypt, but retained the Gaza hostages won under his ousted predecessor al-Adil II; and the authority of al-Salih Isma 'il had been consolidated over Damascus and its northern Syrian dependencies. The diplomatic options facing Theobald were thus dictated for him. If he wished to regain the hostages, a treaty with Egypt was necessary. But to secure territorial concessions further north and appease the mercantile interests in Acre, a Damascus alliance was desirable. To acquire lands west of the

Jordan and recover Jerusalem, a deal with al-Nasir of Kerak had to be struck.[76]

The new ascendancy of al-Salih Ayyub in Egypt inclined a nervous Damascus and the shifty but nimble al-Nasir to reach agreement with Theobald, who launched a brief military foray into Galilee to press his case for a treaty. The details of this and subsequent negotiations remain obscure, victims of highly partisan reporting at the time and later. It appears that Theobald, despite the lack of military success, negotiated a superficially advantageous treaty with al-Salih Isma 'il of Damascus. Beaufort, the area behind Sidon, much of Galilee, including Tiberias and Saphet, Jerusalem, Bethlehem and, possibly, most of the rest of southern Palestine were assigned to the Franks. Much of this agreement could only be implemented by a parallel treaty that was reached with al-Nasir of Kerak, who was actually occupying Jerusalem and the surrounding region. On completing the treaty with Damascus, Theobald again marched south and possibly visited Jerusalem, manoeuvres which may have persuaded al-Salih Ayyub of Egypt to release some of the Gaza prisoners in August 1240. Without any prospect of further gains, nervous of possible competition for leadership from the impending arrival of Richard of Cornwall and with relations with Damascus fraying, in September 1240 Theobald left Acre for the west, in a hurry, some said.[77] He left behind a precarious but viable model of territorial recovery, an imperialist garrison in a restored Jerusalem, the resentment of local barons and the duke of Burgundy, supported by a Champenois garrison, still bivouacked at Ascalon.

A few weeks later, Richard of Cornwall, with a well-equipped fleet, reached Acre. Richard's crusade marked his coming of age on the international stage as befitted his wealth from Cornish tin and dynastic contacts of birth and marriage. It also provided an opportunity for his distinguished powers of self-publicity. The generally favourable reception of his exploits in the east, trumpeted by sympathetic chroniclers, rested on his own estimation circulated by newsletter on his return to Europe in July 1241, in which he lauded his treaty with Egypt, implicitly denigrating the achievements of Count Theobald.[78] In fact, Richard's brief stay in Outremer from October 1240 to May 1241 remained largely barren of significant results.

Richard possessed some distinct advantages; deep pockets, a close-knit entourage and, remarkably, the approval of both the pope and the emperor. Supported by papal subsidies, Richard had nonetheless kept Frederick informed of his progress and may even have received some sort of imperial accreditation. Although potentially a source of friction with anti-imperialists in Outremer, this imperial connection offered some hope of a compromise in the debilitating political infighting. In the summer of 1241 it was suggested by the baronial faction that Richard's brother-in-law, Simon of Montfort, be appointed imperial lieutenant.[79] More immediately, Richard faced the same choice as Theobald, whether to shore up the Damascus treaty, as supported by the Templars, or ally with Egypt, the Hospitallers' choice. Again, in the footsteps of Theobald, Richard's force of about 800 knights, later possibly joined by the contingent of Simon of Montfort (William of Forz's expedition probably arriving too late to play a part in Richard's campaign) marched south to Jaffa in November 1240. There he opened negotiations with Egyptian ambassadors before proceeding to join the duke of Burgundy at Ascalon. While the diplomacy continued, Richard supervised the reconstruction of a new fortress in the citadel at Ascalon, building on foundations laid half a century earlier by his uncle Richard I.[80] On completion, the new fortress was handed over to Walter Pennenpié, the imperial agent in Jerusalem.[81] This represented a balancing act, on the one hand signalling Richard's acceptance of imperial authority, on the other pursuing what most local barons wanted, a deal with Egypt. Like his uncle, Earl Richard presumably hoped that the re-establishment of a powerful stronghold on the southern Palestinian coast would encourage Egypt to agree terms. If so, the tactic worked. On 8 February a treaty was settled with al-Salih Ayyub. This ostensibly confirmed the territorial settlement of the previous year between Count Theobald, Damascus and Kerak, giving the Franks control of Palestine west of the Jordan, including Galilee but excluding Samaria and Hebron. In fact, Sultan al-Salih Ayyub had no control over the lands he granted to the Christians. His agreement to the treaty asserted a nominal lordship as part of a longer contest to regain his former lands in northern Syria to which the Franks were merely spectators. More important for Richard's western reputation than notional territorial gains, the treaty secured the release of the remaining prisoners from the battle of Gaza. Richard used the truce to order the interment of the remains of thirty-three nobles and 500 other troops that lay still unburied on that battlefield.[82] A pensioner of the pope, a friend of the emperor, this act of charity made him a hero to the French. It did nothing at all to reshape the destiny of Outremer, as the treaty with Egypt was entirely dependent on the good will of al-Nasir of Kerak and the acquiescence of the emir of Damascus.

His gestures and building complete, after the customary tour of the Holy Places, Richard departed, sailing from Acre on 3 May 1241. One unimpressed observer remarked: 'Thus all these men did almost nothing in the Holy Land that was of any use.'[83] Despite restoring the kingdom to its greatest extent since Hattin and consolidating a fortified frontier, the crusades of 1239–41 appeared wholly insignificant compared with the great events that were soon to engulf the region, the displacement of the Khwarazmians and the advent of the Mongols. The crusades failed to resolve, hardly address even, the debilitating internal tensions of Outremer. During a period of intense Ayyubid instability, the crusaders appeared by turns bystanders and puppets, manipulated according to the changing ambitions of competing Muslim princes. Yet in organization and awareness of the modest, incremental possibilities of all campaigns except the most massive of western invasion, the crusades of Theobald and Richard confirmed a pattern in western aid. Gregory IX's scheme for a permanent garrison sponsored by western money became a reality a decade later, forming a vital element in the final defence of the Holy Land. More ambiguously, the experience of the 1239–41 crusades revealed a new professionalism in how the business of the cross could be organized at the same time as showing how its success could so easily be compromised by this very professionalism. The increased distinction between crusade enthusiasm that could be expressed by donations not service and crusade campaigning that depended on complex systems of military recruitment and funding reduced the uniqueness of such enterprises, if not in ambition then in organization. As crusading became ever more firmly a matter for state governments, this at once offered greater prospects of achievement and greater vulnerability to those governments' distractions, one of the central paradoxes of Holy Land crusading in the later thirteenth century and beyond. Only where a ruler made the Holy Land his main policy could this tension hope to be resolved. In all the thirteenth century, this applied to one monarch alone.

24
Louis IX and the Fall of Mainland Outremer 1244–91

In the eyes of western Christendom, Louis IX's crusade of 1248–50 was one of the great events of the thirteenth century. This unsuccessful attempt by a major western European power to conquer Egypt hastened the collapse of Ayyubid rule, triggering the elevation of a military elite of professional Turkish slave warriors, the mamluks, to political power in their place. The defeat of the most professionally organized and carefully funded of all the eastern crusades reduced Christian strategy in the Near East to piecemeal treaties amid increasingly desperate attempts to shore up the rump of the Frankish kingdom in Palestine. Fresh political configurations in the region were recognized by attempts to establish contacts with the advancing Mongols that opened further the west's window on previously fabulous lands beyond the Caspian Sea. The knowing self-importance of Louis and his crusaders contrasted cruelly with their insignificance in the scheme of Asian affairs. Louis's attack on Egypt promised a wholesale reversal of generations of Christian failure. Its fate exposed the remains of mainland Outremer to new forces over which the Franks held no influence. Ironically, precisely from the total defeat of such high ambitions flowed the luminous reputation that Louis and his crusade earned in a sorrowful but admiring west.

PREPARATIONS

In 1244, the uneasy and confused Palestinian settlement left by the 1239–41 crusades was rudely swept away. Previously, prospects for the Franks had appeared brighter than at any time since the 1170s.[1] In 1243, a new treaty with Damascus promised to entrench Frankish security in Syria. Yet a year later, the Franks were unexpectedly faced by the irruption into Palestine of the Khwarazmians, allies of Sultan al-Salih Ayyub of Egypt. Turkish freebooters originally from the steppes of central Asia, they had been driven west by the Mongol advance in the 1220s. Surviving as a mercenary band in northern Iraq, they had formed an alliance with al-Salih Ayyub when he was ruling the Jazira in the 1230s. In his efforts to control Syria, the sultan called on their assistance with offers of pay and land. In 1244, a large Khwarazmian force launched a destructive raid from Iraq through Syria to Palestine before joining al-Salih Ayyub's Egyptian army coming up from the Nile. On the way they attacked Jerusalem on 23 August, easily overcoming the feeble defences, killing any Franks they found and desecrating the Christian Holy Places. Christian rule in the Holy City was ended, not to be revived until the ending of Ottoman rule in December 1917 by a British army. The Franks in Acre summoned their full military forces and elicited the help of their allies the rulers of Damascus and Homs. Together they marched south to confront the combined Egyptian-Khwarazmian force near Gaza. On 17 October, the Egyptians and Khwarazmians annihilated the substantial Franco-Syrian Ayyubid army at La Forbie (Harbiya) near Gaza. Although a military disaster for the Franks from which Outremer never entirely recovered, the battle of La Forbie was as much a contest, as one observer put, of 'Saracen against Saracen',[2] exposing just how peripheral the Franks could appear in the wider regional conflicts. The last thing at stake was religion. The Khwarazmians proved unruly allies and violent employees. After helping al-Salih Ayyub conquer Syria, Damascus falling in 1245, they were dispensable. For some years, the sultan had been building up his personal *askar* or regiment of trained mamluks, known as the Bahriyya (from their base on the Nile, Bahr al-Nil) or Salihiyya. They provided more efficient military support for the regime. In 1246, the Khwarazmians were destroyed by the Ayyubid emirs of Homs and Aleppo without any Frankish involvement. Meanwhile, most of the Frankish gains of 1240–41 in southern Palestine were lost, Ascalon falling in 1247.[3]

The disaster in the east threw the survival of the Frankish kingdom into doubt. Pleas for help were despatched to the west. Yet the concerted memory in western Europe attributed the inspiration for a new general relief expedition to a domestic event. In December 1244, Louis IX of France took the cross after surviving a near-fatal illness. It is unclear whether he received the cross for its mystical healing properties, a belief widely held by contemporaries, or as a token of gratitude after hovering between life and death. He may have known of the loss of Jerusalem in August. Pope Innocent IV, in exile at Lyons, had certainly heard of it by the end of December.[4] However, the driving motive behind the French king's commitment lay in Louis's own personality, piety and ambition. Despite apparently strong initial opposition from his domineering mother, Blanche of Castile, and possibly other members of his entourage, Louis stuck to his decision, repeating his vow when in sounder body if not mind and persuading his brothers and court to follow suit.[5]

The public support of the royal family revealed how carefully Louis laid his plans. By the mid-1240s, the conquests of 1203–26 within France by Philip II and Louis VIII had not only extended the royal demesne massively but had left much of provincial France in the hands of cadet members of the dynasty, Louis's brothers Robert in Artois, Charles in Anjou and Alphonse in Poitou and heir to Toulouse. The kingdom became a family firm. The adherence of his brothers to the crusade scheme was a political prerequisite for the policy to work, not just a sign of cosy family harmony. Louis had taken the cross, possibly from the bishop of Paris, the scholarly academic William of Auvergne, without any apparent prior papal authorization. Beside his ecclesiastical role, Bishop William was an unusually dispassionate expert on branches of Arabic philosophy and had become something of an expert on eastern affairs. If the well-informed gossip Matthew Paris can be credited, this may have lent weight to the doubts Paris claimed William expressed about the wisdom of Louis's decision.[6] Yet in the teeth of maternal, episcopal and probably political opposition, Louis pressed ahead in such a determined fashion that it is hard not to subscribe to the idea that his crusade marked a personal and political as well as spiritual rite of passage, an occasion and process of individual emancipation.

The legend of Louis may distort the picture. The near-death experience, the almost miraculous return to health and the assumption of the 'life-giving' cross, as the phrase went, may appear too dramatically neat to be credited. Within weeks, Innocent IV was sending out summonses to a new church council, to be held at Lyons, at which the plight of the Holy Land was to be discussed, although the council's agenda was dominated by the struggle with Frederick II, the eastern crisis being cited alongside possible campaigns to defend Latin Constantinople and resist the Mongols.[7] Louis's decision to hazard life, treasure and reputation on an eastern adventure may not have been as spontaneous as admiring or wondering observers suggested. Buoyed by a strong domestic political position won by victories in 1242–4 over disaffected magnates, including the count of Toulouse, as well as over the king of England (in 1242), such a grand gesture might have seemed timely even without the stimulus of grave illness. The crusade provided an excuse and opportunity to tighten and reform royal administration, extend the king's judicial and fiscal grasp and increase revenues. As a decade earlier, it could serve as a mechanism to consolidate or impose reconciliation of dissident regional and baronial factions. Command of a new eastern expedition placed a convenient distance between Louis and the embattled emperor without his having to take sides against the Hohenstaufen as the pope's poodle. The whole scheme enhanced Louis's moral authority, his particular brand of political puritanism signalled by the use of friars as agents in the reform of government and the collection of clerical taxes. With control of the holy business, Louis could fashion more directly and strongly than in any other way a new cult of holy monarchy with the elevation of France itself as a cradle of holy warriors, conscious of its special, divinely inspired mission, itself a holy land. The single-mindedness with which Louis pursued all these ends might indicate that the decision made in his sick room at Pontoise in December 1244 came at the end of a lengthy process of deliberation. As with most crusaders, while in no way diminishing its sincerity, it is too crudely simple to explain Louis IX's devotion to the cause in terms of piety alone.

Within two months of Louis taking the cross, the pope had issued a crusade bull and preaching had been authorized, led in France by the legate Odo of Châteauroux, cardinal bishop of Tusculum (1244–73), who additionally legitimized regional preachers and collectors of funds.[8] As before, preaching combined the practical with the persuasive to create an atmosphere or mood to encourage the faithful to take the cross, purchase vow redemptions or provide the more disengaged assistance of donations and prayers. All of these featured in Cardinal Odo's sermons. While never far from the church's rhetorical lexicon, the plight of the Holy Land needed to be placed in a suitably moving emotional and cultural frame to attract the sort of active involvement the king sought. So beside the reminders of the spiritual rewards, the religious duty and the Christian obligation of the cross, in one sermon Odo reminded his audience of those 'nobles of former times who left the kingdom of

France, captured Antioch and the land of Jerusalem'.[9] The enticement of nostalgia may have been easier to effect in lay aristocratic circles because of the popularity and circulation of vernacular adventure poems known today as Crusade Cycles, which had transmuted the events of the First and Third Crusades into epics of chivalry. Nostalgia only works if the images being refurbished retain contemporary resonance. However, stimulating a warm glow of religious, cultural and, in the case of Odo's preaching, French national pride was insufficient. Odo and other preachers had also to spell out how the faithful could contribute, in person, with money or through prayer.

The preaching campaign of 1245–8 did not run entirely smoothly, hampered less by public indifference or hostility than by official contradictions and institutional bickering. Outside France, preaching was organized in the British Isles, Scandinavia, Germany and the Low Countries. Henry III of England, licking his wounds after his defeat by Louis IX in 1242 in Poitou, was suspicious of getting involved in what from the outset appeared to be a French project, prompting him to bar entry to the bishop of Beirut, who had hoped to visit England to drum up support.[10] In Languedoc, the French government deliberately associated the Holy Land crusade with the suppression of the rebellion of 1242–4 and the eradication of heresy. Rebels, such as Raymond VII of Toulouse or Oliver of Termes, were induced to take the cross as a symbol and shackle of loyalty to the Capetians, while reformed heretics received sentences that insisted on taking the cross for Palestine, although many chose exile instead.[11] Elsewhere, the claims of other papal holy wars were simultaneously being pressed on the faithful. After the Council of Lyons (June–July 1245) deposed Frederick II, a crusade against him began to be preached in large parts of Germany. This led directly to conflicts of interest and effort. In July 1246, Cardinal Odo was instructed by Innocent IV to tell Holy Land preachers in Germany to preach the war against Frederick II. Innocent recognized the sensitivity of this order by commanding Odo to keep the instructions secret.[12] This hardly assisted administrative clarity. In Frisia, as in other places, the two preaching campaigns tripped each other up. One preacher began by preaching against Frederick II before being transferred to the Holy Land war. Holy Land recruits in the dioceses of Cambrai, Louvain, Metz, Toul and Verdun were forbidden to swap their vows to fight Frederick, even though the anti-Hohenstaufen crusade was being preached there. Unsurprisingly, this competition for recruits carried over to the raising of vow redemptions, offering unscrupulous operators the chance of illicit profits as control and audit broke down.[13] In places, the crusade to defend the Latin Empire of Constantinople was promoted. In Provence, while the Holy Land crusade was being preached with mixed success in neighbouring Languedoc, the Dominicans of Provence were bombarded with papal bulls concerning the crusade against the Greeks.[14] Whereas the Holy Land crusade could be preached successfully throughout Christendom, recruitment for other crusading enterprises, in Frankish Greece (or Romania), Germany, Italy or the Baltic, suited geographically more limited, targeted constituencies.

Recruitment away from the French court was regionally vigorous, but in places slow to develop. Louis's youngest brother Alphonse of Poitiers' army was only ready in the spring of 1249. Even in northern France, men were still joining up into 1250.[15] Holy Land recruitment was concentrated in the kingdom of France, Burgundy, Lorraine and the Low Countries between the Meuse and the Rhine. Small contingents were raised or promised elsewhere, such as England and Norway. However, the evangelizing demonstrated this was a French expedition, as did the way King Louis used it to consolidate and extend his domestic authority. Apart from the king and his brothers, there were loyalists such as the crusade veteran Duke Hugh IV of Burgundy and Count William of Flanders, whose close adherence to the king was secured by Louis's favouring him in the disputed Flemish succession. Old reprobates such as Peter Maulcerc, the now retired count of Brittany, another veteran of the 1239–40 crusade, were enlisted alongside a range of former or recent rebels including Raymond of Toulouse and Hugh of Lusignan. Recruits came from across the kingdom, from Flanders and Brittany to Poitou, the Bourbonnais and Languedoc. From Brittany it appears that practically all the major landowners participated, a pattern that may have been repeated elsewhere. Although Theobald of Champagne rather pointedly declined to join, the Champenois provided a substantial contingent of perhaps as many as 175 knights in a total of about 1,000 men.[16] A significant number of clergy, including bishops, took the cross. There is evidence of members of rural and urban elites, artisans, even some prosperous peasants signing up. Not being necessarily associated with a lord, they seemed to have been mobilized rather more slowly. Others identified local ways to implement commitment. By the spring of 1247, crusaders at Châteaudun, with the approval of the legate, Odo of Châteauroux, had formed a confraternity (*confratria*) to ease the purchase of war materials, hiring of ships and funding for those who went to 'fight for the Lord', as well as a focus for further donations by non-*crucesignati*. The establishment of such a confraternity served as a reminder of the material costs of the enterprise and the increasingly diverse responses to both the vow and its implementation. To ensure acceptance for this exercise in business sense reminiscent of earlier crusading communal action, members obtained papal approval.[17] The motives of other recruits caused some alarm. The crusader's temporal privileges granting certain legal immunities had always run the risk of attracting those wishing to avoid answering law suits and the downright criminal. In 1246, at Rouen, it was pronounced that *crucesignati* were not permitted to avoid law suits involving fiefs and pledges. The same year, Louis IX complained to Innocent IV that many crusaders, instead of abstaining from excess as befitted their privileged status, were enthusiastically indulging in theft, murder and rape. The pope ordered bishops not to protect such miscreants, crusade privileges notwithstanding.[18]

While the social aspects of crusade recruitment were largely out of the king's hands, the political dimension of the recruiting process was manifest, not just in signing up rebels. In October 1245, Louis gathered a national assembly of barons to receive their agreement and support for the crusade. In the spring of 1248, Louis summoned another baronial gathering in Paris to swear fealty to his children in the event of his not returning from the crusade. One of those summoned was John lord of Joinville-sur-Marne and seneschal of Champagne, whose extraordinary account of Louis's crusade remains the most detailed and vivid personal description of any crusade.[19] Although as a vassal of the count of Champagne John refused to give his oath, the king's intention in summoning him was plain enough, to extend the network of direct loyalty to the monarch into previously autonomous regions of the kingdom.

This political dimension embraced administrative reform.[20] All thirteenth-century western European regimes faced the problem of reconciling what they regarded as effective rule with what their subjects perceived as good government. Rights and liberties cut two ways, especially as writing laws down and recording legal decisions and precedents were increasingly fashionable. In France, as in England at the time, the government was potentially in a double bind. Inefficient or archaic administrative practice denied the king revenues and subjects effective justice. At the same time, suspicion of royal officials was encouraged by the abiding difficulty of arbitration in administrative disagreements. Who could provide impartial justice if the complaints were levelled at the agents of the supreme judicial authority, the crown? Reform of royal administration in the provinces could threaten vested interests and arouse popular suspicion. However, with preparations for the crusade, the practical need to maximize royal revenues combined with the opportunity presented by an almost universally admired public policy to drive change.

Reform operated through two mechanisms. From 1245 the salaried local royal fiscal and administrative agents (*baillis* in the king's lands in the north, *sénéschaux* in the south) began to replaced, often by what one modern scholar has called troubleshooters.[21] This reduced the agents' independence, improved their sensitivity to royal interests and demands, emphasized their accountability and increased revenues reaching the king's coffers. From some areas of the royal demesne, income rose dramatically, the crusade acting as a convenient and not wholly mendacious justification. Besides the tightening of local administration, in the early months of 1247 Louis appointed investigators (*enquêteurs réformateurs*) to inquire into complaints against royal officials. Traditionally, departing crusaders sought to settle outstanding grievances of their subjects. By relying heavily on friars to conduct these inquiries, Louis underlined the link between governmental reform and religious mission. They also lent the exercise a possibly spurious but politically necessary gloss of impartiality. These investigations, covering the royal demesne and the lands held by his brothers (known as apanages), contributed to the changes in methods and personel of the *baillis* and *sénéschaux* in 1247–9.

With the advantages of such reforms creating a consensus of support for the monarchy came fiscal pickings. It was later calculated that between the Ascension audit of 1247 and that of 1257, Louis's expenses on the crusade ('pro passagio ultramarino' in the accounts) came to 1,537,570 *livres tournois* 13 *sous* 5 *deniers tournois*, perhaps six times the king's annual revenues.[22] The king's bill for troops alone may have run at 1,000 *l.t.* a day. Although Louis was largely able to cover this from sources other than his ordinary revenues, the hidden costs of administration and government for and during the crusade needed to be covered and the regency administration adequately funded. The increase in royal revenues and income from the administrative reforms supplied an important part of Louis's general fundraising. Certain specific measures were clearly related to the expedition. In 1248–9, Jewish moneylenders were expelled from the kingdom, their property confiscated, a hardening of the king's habitual and notorious anti-Jewish policies and prejudices. More income for vacant church benefices was sought. Most striking of all, 'gifts' from towns, sometimes explicitly 'pro auxilio viae transmarinae' ('to help the overseas journey') were collected on a massive scale. At least eighty-two towns from across northern and central France raised over 70,000 *l.t.* in 1248, a figure that excluded contributions from Normandy likely to have almost matched this sum. It appears that the total figure of the urban 'gifts', including widely levied supplementary grants from towns that had already paid up, may have reached almost 275,000 *l.t.*[23] Louis's taxation of towns was not unprecedented; royal towns may have helped pay for Louis VII's crusade. However, the extent and thoroughness mark it out as a symbol of the new authority wielded by the French king in his realm. Although not entirely transparent, the accounting system appeared able to identify crusade income so that Louis could either arrange with his agents how to spend it or could convey the surplus to the Templars, the usual royal bankers, for transmission to the east, where it could stay on deposit or be used to purchase supplies to await the arrival of the king's army.

The bulk of Louis's funding, and the largest single resource for other crusaders, was money derived from or through the church. This came in two forms; private sources – vow redemptions, legacies and alms – collected by the clergy; and clerical taxation. The Council of Lyons in 1245 had encouraged crusade legacies, as had Odo of Châteauroux. Vow redemptions now operated as a central accompaniment to the preaching campaign. By 1247, redemptions were systematically being offered and collected by diocesan agents, usually friars.[24] In Normandy in 1248, two groups of papal agents quarrelled over the right to collect the crusade redemptions.[25] In the same year, Innocent IV expressed concerns lest the conditions for redemption were too lax and the rates accepted too low.[26] The potential for peculation and fraud was evident. Early in the preaching campaign, a Franciscan in Frisia took advantage of feeble supervision to pass himself off as an authorized collector of redemptions and legacies which in fact went straight into his own pocket.[27] Aware the system could degenerate into a vast racket, in 1247 Innocent IV imposed a form of audit. The process of scrutinizing redemptions appeared meticulous. A knight's redemption, for instance, may have been around 200 *l.t.*, a year's wages.[28] However, secular policy actually may have encouraged corners to be cut by preachers, collectors and the *descroisiés* alike. Louis, in seeking appropriate fighting men and support units, apparently left many behind when he embarked in August 1248. These presumably had little option but to redeem their vows for cash on the best, i.e. cheapest, terms available in order to enjoy the anticipated spiritual privileges.

While it is impossible to calculate how much was raised for Louis's expedition by redemptions, legacies and alms, of clerical taxation there is little doubt. The Council of Lyons authorized a general clerical tax of a twentieth. The French clergy offered a tenth over five years. The distraction of the anti-Hohenstaufen crusade and the clear identification of the Holy Land venture with the French reduced international contributions, the English and German churches staying largely aloof. However, along the eastern frontiers of France, in Burgundy and Lorraine, the tax was levied, a sign of the growing assimilation of the regions beyond the Rhône and Meuse into French politics and culture. The combined proceeds from the clerical tenth, over five years, may have come to as much as 950,000 *l.t.*[29] As in 1239–41, individual crusade commanders received subventions, notably the king's brothers. They, and other property owners, also raised funds from their own lands. However, the bulk of crusade funds and clerical taxes probably found their way into the royal coffers. With the increased income for the king's own demesne, this centralized system of financing the expedition gave Louis unprecedented control over his main followers.

The experience of John of Joinville was typical. Refusing to swear fealty to Louis in 1248, he embarked with his cousin in a ship they hired together at Marseilles with a company of twenty knights. John recorded that despite mortgaging most of his lands, by the time he reached Cyprus in the autumn of 1248, after paying for his passage, he had in hand only 240 *l.t.*, or, at best, about enough for only a couple of knights' annual expenses. His retinue became mutinous, forcing John to enter the king's service, in return for which he received an immediate grant of 800 *l.t.*[30] This pattern of debt rescued by royal aid was widespread, involving even substantial lords such as the counts of Flanders and Forez. Alphonse of Poitiers enjoyed substantial clerical grants and income from his vast estates (Auvergne alone contributing 7,500 *l.t.*). Yet he was forced to seek his brother's financial help.[31] The success of Louis' financing of the operation found extraordinary testimony in his ability, even in the extremes of defeat, to find over 200,000 *l.t.* to pay his army's ransom in 1250 and then still be able to finance his subsequent stay in the Holy Land, even though expenditure there reached over one million *l.t.* over 1250–53. Only in 1252–3 does it appear the money ran out, which may reflect the difficulties experienced in France after the death of the regent Blanche of Castile.[32] Even with his improvement of royal finances and administration, it is hard to imagine that Louis's solvency could have been achieved without the church's money, a precedent that possessed wide and controversial future implications for clerical funding of the state.

Translating funds into crusading required similarly strenuous royal organization. The core of the expedition lay in the king's fleet, based around the ships he hired, sixteen from Genoa and twenty from Marseilles. The contracts drawn up in 1246 specified delivery at Aigues Mortes, an unpromising little port with a small, shallow harbour in an obscure corner of the Rhône Delta.[33] Although prone to silting and with an awkward channel to the Mediterranean, Aigues Mortes possessed one advantage. It had recently become part of the royal demesne. This allowed Louis to avoid negotiating with the patriciates of other, more obvious and better-equipped ports, some of which resented the growing royal power in the region. Other convenient ports were controlled by foreign powers, for example Montpellier by the king of Aragon. The ports of Apulia and Sicily were effectively closed by Frederick II's excommunication. Nonetheless, the choice of Aigues Mortes showed Louis's determination to preside directly over his crusade. It was not his best decision. Political expedience prevailed over practical efficiency. A new port, with sufficient access by land as well as sea, had to be built from scratch. It speaks for the energy and resolve of Louis's government that the king was able to gather his army and navy there just three and an half years after deciding to go east.

Other problems concerned the nature and equipment of the fleet. Alongside the hired vessels, both Genoa and Marseilles agreed to supply additional shipping initially at their own expense which would later, once in the Levant, be available for the king's hire. Some at least of the ships were horse-carriers, *tarridae*. But the fleet lacked landing craft, which had to be constructed once Louis had reached Cyprus in the winter of 1248–9. Although the contracts of 1246 contained details of each ship's equipment, royal agents in 1248, as well as gathering food and wine, spent at least 5,926 *l.t.* on basic naval supplies, including canvas, rope, yard arms and rudders.[34] There may also be a possibility that the shippers had driven an excessively hard bargain, knowing that, as at Venice in 1201–2, this was a very strong seller's market. When returning from the Holy Land in 1254, Louis was told by his Genoese master mariners that his flagship, which had just run aground off Cyprus, was worth 4,000 *l.t.* when fully loaded with cargo. In 1246, Louis had paid up to 7,000 *l.t.* for the largest ship.[35] However, in general Louis's alliance with Genoa proved mutually highly beneficial. Crusade business was spread widely through the city. In return Genoese not only crewed ships and supplied significant military assistance in Egypt, but also provided important banking facilities for the king throughout his stay in the east.

The force that sailed with Louis from Aigues Mortes in late August 1248 may have been of comparable size with Richard I's army when he left Sicily in April 1191, well over 10,000 strong. With Louis and separately went troops not directly in his pay or service. Not all followed the king to Aigues Mortes. The count of Toulouse, who died before he could depart, arranged a contract with shippers at Marseilles, as did John of Joinville and his cousin. Some vessels seem to have come a long way. The count of St Pol, another who died before setting out, apparently if improbably hired a ship from Inverness, while one of the transports for Raymond of Toulouse's force had to come to Marseilles from the Atlantic coast via the Straits of Gibralter, a delay that kept the count in port for the winter 1248–9.[36] Even the best-funded commanders, such as Alphonse of Poitiers, ran out of their own money and found raising an army more time-consuming than originally intended. Alphonse only sailed east in 1249. If the logistics of his followers ran less smoothly than his own, Louis also recognized the limits of what could be prepared in France. By the time he reached Cyprus, the designated muster point, his agents had spent two years stockpiling vast quantities of food. Joinville described the stacked barrels of wine as resembling great wooden barns while the heaps of wheat and barley looked like hills: 'the rain had made it sprout on the outside so all you could see was green grass'.[37] Salt pork, another staple of western military diet consumed in great quantities, was either purchased in Cyprus or shipped with the army from France. By hiring, paying, buying or manufacturing, Louis appeared determined to leave as little as possible to fate or chance.

*

Crusading was never a matter of logistics alone. The personal and domestic were no less central than the public and material. Joinville, his memory gilded by sixty years' nostalgia, left a vivid picture of the rituals of a propertied crusader's departure.[38] Joinville's crusading pedigree was impeccable. His grandfather had died on the Third Crusade. Two uncles had joined the Fourth Crusade, one of them travelling to Palestine, where he was killed. His father, Simon, had fought in the Albigensian wars and in Egypt during the Fifth Crusade. To prepare for his departure in 1248, Joinville raised money through mortgaging most of his lands, possibly to bankers in Metz, and entered into a joint venture with his cousin to hire a ship at Marseilles to carry their combined retinue of twenty knights, which possibly implied a total force of over 100. Complying with the tradition of the crusade providing a context for justice, at Easter 1248, Joinville held an assembly of his fief-holders where, amidst an enthusiastic round of feasting, he settled all outstanding law suits and grievances held against him. The need to put affairs in order found repeated confirmation in the records of disputes that clogged the courts after every crusade, especially, Joinville admitted to his tenants, as it was quite likely the crusader would not return. Such general settlements went some way to ensure the continued integrity of the crusader's lands. In Joinville's case, his tenants and relatives at the same time probably recognized his recently born son as his heir. Western Europe was littered with examples of battered or murdered crusaders' wives and deprived heirs. The jollifications and judgements at Joinville thus shared a common purpose.

After sending his luggage on ahead, Joinville received the scrip and staff of a pilgrim from the Cistercian abbot of Cheminon. So armed, and dressed as a penitent, barefoot, in only a shirt, Joinville toured local shrines to emphasize the religious character of his enterprise and to equip his soul as well as he had his soldiers. He recalled how, as he conducted these pilgrimages, 'I never once let my eyes turn back towards Joinville, for fear my heart might be filled with longing at the thought of my lovely castle and the two children I had left behind',[39] one of them only a few weeks old. Reunited with his luggage at Auxonne on the Saône, Joinville travelled south by river, with his war-horses being led along the riverbank. Once at Marseilles, with men, horses and baggage stored on board, the ship weighed anchor and set sail with the whole ship's company, led by priests, singing *Veni Creator Spiritus* as the vessel began its journey.

Joinville, like many reluctant medieval mariners, was frightened of drowning and fearfully seasick on the three-week voyage to Cyprus.

Joinville's experience, even if tidied by six decades of retelling, displayed the characteristic crusading mixture of pragmatism and ritual. Few understood the importance of this more than Louis IX himself. His carefully orchestrated departure displayed striking parallels with Joinville's. He had invited his subjects to demand redress of grievances through his *enquêteurs*. As preparations neared completion, Louis stage-managed his progress towards Aigues Mortes to resemble a religious procession as much as a royal progress. The climax of the ceremonies marking his departure from his capital saw him participate in April 1248 at the dedication of the new Sainte Chapelle in the royal palace on the Ile de la Cité in Paris. This had been built as a giant reliquary to house the relic of the Crown of Thorns which Louis had redeemed in 1239 from the Venetians, to whom it had been pawned by Baldwin II of Constantinople. With the Crown of Thorns were other major relics of the Passion acquired, at great expense, from the Latins in Constantinople, including a piece of the True Cross. Louis was signalling that France was now the heir of Israel, the protector of the holiest relics in Christendom, almost a second Jerusalem, a new Holy Land. The 'Most Christian' king of France (an honorific title dating from the twelfth century) was assuming the leadership of Christendom vacated by the excommunicated emperor. Before leaving Paris for the south in June, Louis received the insignia of a pilgrim and, following ancestral precedent, the oriflamme at St Denis. Louis was conducting his crusade as a penitent but also as a king of France; the two were inseparable in propaganda and policy. From St Denis, Louis, dressed as a penitent, walked to Notre Dame to hear mass before continuing to the abbey of St Antoine, still just like Joinville on his local pilgrimages, barefoot. On his slow journey south, Louis was careful to be seen in the garb of a pilgrim in a series of civic festivals and public appearances. After meeting Innocent IV at Lyons, he travelled towards the Mediterranean, dispensing justice as he went, the first French king to visit the region since his father in 1226. On 25 August, Louis sailed from Aigues Mortes, reaching Limassol in Cyprus on 17 September.[40]

THE ATTACK ON EGYPT 1249–50

Later Louis allegedly claimed he would have been happy to sail directly to Egypt.[41] With hindsight this may have appeared an attractive option. In 1248 Sultan al-Salih Ayyub was out of the country, fully engaged in Syria trying to conquer Homs during another round of Ayyubid feuding. By June 1249, when the crusaders finally landed, he and his army were back home. There was little doubt that Egypt was the destination; otherwise there would have been no need to stockpile supplies in Cyprus. Long before Louis's attack began, the sultan had strengthened Damietta, as if he knew where to expect the Christian assault, which, given the prevalence of espionage, he probably did. The delay in Cyprus from September 1248 to May 1249 devoured supplies, sapped morale and gave the Egyptians time to prepare their defences. However, Louis was not to know that Damietta, once again the chosen target, would fall such easy prey as it did. Wintering in Cyprus allowed Louis to wait for the stragglers, such as Alphonse of Poitiers who had yet to leave France, or the duke of Burgundy, who spent the winter in Sparta, the guest of William of Villehardouin, the Frankish ruler of that part of the Peloponnese. Contingents who had found harbour at Acre, Tripoli or Antioch were also given time to rejoin the main armada. Holding court at Nicosia, Louis managed to attract gifts and reinforcements from Christians of the eastern Mediterranean, including William of Villehardouin with a fleet of twenty-four ships, and large sections of the local Jerusalem-Cypriot baronage, led by John of Jaffa. Louis appears to have played on his status as king of the local Franks' ancestral lands; the king of Cyprus declared he would take Louis 'as his friend and lord'. Although prolonged by a characteristically messy and violent dispute between the Genoese and Pisans, Louis's stay in Cyprus allowed him to consolidate his control over his followers by bailing out many of them as their private funds ran out, plan his Egyptian strategy and construct the necessary landing craft and subsidiary vessels required for warfare in the Nile Delta.[42]

While in Cyprus, Louis received direct intimations of how his providential understanding of his mission failed to grasp the realities of Eurasian politics. For many in eastern Europe and the Near East, the most significant and alarming recent development lay not in the ownership of a Judean hill town, however numinous, but in the advance of the Mongols on a front from Russia to Iraq.[43] In the wake of the Mongol invasion of central Europe in 1241–2, the prospect of a crusade to the Holy Land that denuded Christendom of warriors astonished and alarmed Bela IV of Hungary, who lived in annual fear of a new attack. In the autumn of 1244, Bohemund V of Antioch-Tripoli had made a well-publicized appeal to Frederick II for help against a Mongol army menacing Syria. Innocent IV was well aware of the Mongol threat. In 1245, before the Council of Lyons had discussed the problem, the pope had sent at least three separate missions to the east with the dual purpose of contacting the various Mongol armies but at the same time building up a broad coalition of eastern Christian, even Muslim allies against them. While the response of many Orthodox and other eastern Christian rulers and communities appeared positive, or desperate, the Dominican Andrew of Longjumeau made no headway with the Ayyubids, while the Franciscan John of Plano Carpini, who penetrated all the way to Mongolia to see a new khan, Guyuk, enthroned in 1246, returned with news of the khan's outright rejection of anything other than Christian submission to the world-conquering Mongols.[44] John's accounts of the Mongol court and customs, while making him a minor celebrity, also conveyed the extent of Mongol power and future ambitions of seemingly limitless western conquest. Evidently, one of Friar John's tasks had been to spy. The idea that Innocent IV and his envoys sought an alliance with the Mongols against the Muslims appears unlikely. The actions of his envoys suggested a policy of resistance and containment; their reports indicated that neither was liable to succeed.

Mongol disdain did not exclude Mongol diplomacy. In December 1248 at Nicosia, Louis received ambassadors from the Mongol general in Persia, Elijigidei.[45] Ostensibly, the Mongol embassy sought Louis's help in alleviating the plight of eastern Christians living under Frankish rule in Outremer. Under Mongol rule they enjoyed, it was alleged, freedom from the poll tax and forced labour. There were suggestions that Elijigidei was himself a Christian and that Khan Guyuk was sympathetic, a view that had been peddled only a few months earlier in a letter from Samarkand by an Armenian prince, Sempad, which Louis had seen on arrival at Cyprus. Some witnesses even remembered talk of Mongol help in recovering Jerusalem and the rest of Holy Land. After grilling Elijigidei's ambassadors, Nestorian Christians from the Mosul region, Louis was sufficiently impressed to send an embassy in reply, led by the old Mongol hand, Andrew of Longjumeau, who had recently arrived in Cyprus. In retrospect, Louis's involvement appears naive. He himself was said later to have regretted it.[46] While some Mongols were converts to Christianity and the Olympian Mongol cultural superiority complex accommodated tolerance of other religions and the employment of their adherents, their policy was uncompromising. To them, Muslims and Christians came alike, potential subjects, not allies. Elijigidei's initiative probably had more to do with countering the papal approaches to the Ayyubids and neutralizing Louis's impact on Syrian politics where Mongol influence was already securing clients. A crusader attack on Egypt would nicely distract the Ayyubids, allowing further Mongol advances in the region. That Louis had been willing to go along with Elijigidei's advances suggests a lack of strategic grasp, or one badly discoloured by excessively pious wishful thinking.

It was not as if Louis or his advisors were ignorant of the Mongol threat or their past history. Papal correspondence and appeals from rulers of eastern and central Europe had been full of both for much of the previous decade. Possibly only the death in 1249 of Khan Guyuk prevented immediate exploitation of the chaos that engulfed the Ayyubid empire during Louis's invasion of Egypt. Andrew of Longjumeau's mission achieved nothing except confirmation that the Mongols refused to regard others as equals and that they were not about to become a new Christian power. This diplomatic interlude says as much for Mongol skill in exploiting the mentality of their opponents as it does for the myopia of a future saint. It also added to the awareness of the world beyond the customary horizons of western thought witnessed by the popularity of news, or, rather, stories of the exotic new power that had intruded into western consciousness.[47] While crusading interest in the Near East may have accelerated contacts between western Europe and Asia before the Mongols appeared on Christendom's frontiers in the 1240s, in this context, as in many others, it is hard to see Louis's adventure as much more than a sideshow.

In the middle of May 1249, the allied Christian fleet began to set out for Cyprus. It carried perhaps upwards of 15,000 troops, impressive for battle, rather modest for a conquest.[48] Louis's French army had been joined by recruits and allies from Frankish Outremer and Greece. More were yet to reach eastern waters, including Alphonse of Poitiers's large force, perhaps of some thousands, and a select English regiment of perhaps as many as 200 knights, including a number retained for pay by its leader, Henry III's cousin William Longspee.[49] These only joined the main army in Egypt in the late autumn. According to the royal chamberlain, John Sarasin, one of Louis's finance ministers who accompanied the crusade, apart from 2,500 knights and the heavy cavalry, backed by mounted sergeants and infantry, a striking feature of the forces Louis led towards Egypt lay in the 5,000 crossbowmen.[50] They played a crucial role throughout the campaign in the Nile Delta, laying down devastating barrages of bolts in support of attacks or to cover retreats. The acquisition of crossbow bolts had been of especial concern during the crusade preparations, contracts to supply them being given to the Genoese admirals employed to command the royal fleet. The necessary landing craft had been assembled, some built or hired in Cyprus, others, such as John of Jaffa's galley, which could be driven up the beach, belonging to the Outremer barons.[51]

As with most military enterprises, despite meticulous preparation, things went wrong. A storm dispersed the fleet, many ships seeking refuge in the Syrian ports, only later joining the crusade after the landings in Egypt. Those remaining arrived off Damietta on 4 June 1249 only to discover their plan had been anticipated. Sultan al-Salih Ayyub had left a strong garrison in Damietta under the veteran commander Fakhr al-Din, Frederick II's old sparring partner who, according to Joinville's memory, still displayed the emperor's arms on his war banner in honour of their friendship.[52] However, a bold massed attack on the shore opposite Damietta on the morning of 5 June managed to secure a bridgehead on the beach, even though some of the troops, including Louis himself, had to wade ashore with water up to their armpits. The superior firepower of the crossbowmen probably clinched success for this ambitious amphibious operation. By nightfall, while the crusaders were establishing a camp, the Muslim defenders panicked. Many of those routed on the beach fled southwards. There the sultan waited with his main army upstream from Damietta, mindful of the need not to repeat the events of 1218–19 by becoming engaged in a sterile and costly conflict around the port itself. This left the garrison in the city badly exposed. Rather than risk death by assault or starvation, the defenders evacuated the city without a fight, leaving the stockpiles of food and war materials intact behind them. To the astonishment, incredulity and delight of the invaders, Damietta had fallen in hours instead of the seventeen months it had taken in 1218–19. It was symbolic, as Sarasin recorded, that the victors found fifty-three Christian captives in the city who claimed they had had been incarcerated there since the Fifth Crusade.[53] As welcome, the fleeing garrison had left the well-stocked city intact. News of the abandonment of Damietta brought widespread opprobrium on Fakhr al-Din and panic to Cairo.[54]

Unfortunately for Louis, the fall of Damietta after only a day's fighting marked the high point of his whole campaign. It has been argued that if he had seized the moment, a great triumph was there to be won. Cairo was in a turmoil of fear. In his new forward camp, established as his father's had been in 1219–21 at Mansourah, the sultan was dying, probably from tuberculosis; his heir was out of the country; and jealous rival factions within the Egyptian high command and the sultan's own military entourage were greedily or anxiously circling the throne. Yet the problems that delayed the embarkation from Cyprus had left the crusaders little time to organize a march south before the Nile flooded. The precedents of the Fifth Crusade were vivid on both sides. To the surprise and horror of Louis when they met after the king's capture, at least one veteran of John of Brienne's army, from Provins in France, had stayed behind, converted to Islam and married an Egyptian, rising to a position of some importance at court.[55] Staying safe in Damietta must have appealed to many in the army, including the clergy who busied themselves with reclaiming mosques as churches, and Italian merchants securing quays and quarters. Louis may also have reckoned that, before attempting any hostile action, he needed to wait for the arrival of his brother Alphonse's army, other contingents from the west, such as the English, and those scattered by the storm off Cyprus. Alphonse only reached Damietta on 24 October.

However, if the annual Nile flood precluded immediate action, plans could be laid. A seemingly sensible scheme to attack Alexandria rather than risk the Delta streams in marching on Cairo was discussed, provoking, according to Joinville, the impetuous Robert of Artois to exclaim, 'If you wish to kill the serpent, you must first crush its head.'[56] Robert urged an advance on Cairo, as did the king. Hindsight blamed Count Robert for the decision to attack Cairo taken, Joinville alleged, against the near-unanimous opposition of the rest of the French barons. It seems that Louis's support was sufficient to win the day for Robert's minority view. This may say much for Louis's personal authority, or for his deep pockets, which were now supporting many, perhaps most of the crusade leaders. The ultimate defeat of the Cairo strategy as well as the death of Robert of Artois has clouded later perspectives. Robert became the scapegoat for the defeat of the crusade, his strategic advice at Damietta compounded by his reckless and suicidal behaviour at Mansourah in February 1250. Yet staying cooped up in Damietta or acquiring another Nile port only made sense if the plan had been to use any conquests as bargaining chips for the return of Jerusalem and the Holy Land. However, if, as is possible, Louis planned to conquer Egypt, even to convert the local Muslims, there were excellent tactical and strategic reasons for pressing home the Christian advantage in an attack on Cairo, especially in the light of deepening Ayyubid disarray.

Al-Salih Ayyub, alarmed at how the invasion was developing and now in the final stages of his fatal illness, remained at Mansourah. Protected by the Nile and its side channels, the site afforded level dry ground for his camp outside a defensible town. It barred the direct route to Cairo but was close enough to Damietta to maintain some pressure on the Christians. The sultan's immediate problems were the internal tensions in his high command produced by his failing health and exacerbated by the French invasion. Although he had executed members of the spineless Damietta garrison, *pour encourager les autres*, he felt unable to dismiss Fakhr al-Din. Any sudden interregnum would need the support of such veteran loyalists to hold the line against both the crusaders and internal challenges to the Ayyubid succession. Yet the sultan's impending demise disturbed his increasingly powerful and assertive mamluks, the Bahriyya, who feared a loss in status or worse under his heir, al-Mu 'azzam Turan Shah. Rivalries were further complicated by the ambitions of al-Salih Ayyub's Turkish wife, Shajar al-Durr, who as eagerly embraced the prospect of being a power broker as, according to legend and some fact, she did the bodies of some of the powerful.[57] Politically, therefore, the crusaders' delay at Damietta from June to November did not obviously improve the unity of their opponents, who, militarily, were as hampered as the invaders by the annual flood.

On 20 November 1249, with his army now at its strongest, Louis IX led his troops out of Damietta, leaving behind his wife, five months pregnant, and a well-equipped garrison, supported by Genoese and Pisans. The months since June had been employed in strengthening Damietta's defences, some thought excessively.[58] But Louis's meticulous planning, which extended to his allocation of palaces and churches in the city, was a feature of his whole enterprise. It also confirmed his general intention to conquer, not bargain. His chief problem lay in whether, even with his careful organization and massive reserves of treasure, he possessed adequate forces and the right equipment to force a path through the Delta and mount a successful assault on Cairo. He may have been relying on the implosion of Egyptian resistance following the death of the sultan, the seriousness of whose illness was likely to have been reported to the Christians. Not only was he disappointed in this, he underestimated the stake the sultan's mamluks held in the survival of some version of the existing Egyptian regime.

More immediately damaging, the crusaders' march south proved painfully slow, covering an average of less than two miles a day. While the bulk of the army marched along the river banks, it was shadowed by a large fleet mainly, it seems, of heavy transport vessels, as well as some lighter, shallow draft galleys, more appropriate for Nile warfare. Progress was hindered by a strong southerly wind, slowing the preponderant sailing ships, which lacked manoeuvrability. Yet in spite of the measured pace, Louis appears not to have placed a series of supply dumps or protective garrisons along his route, the same mistake as 1221. Unlike his predecessors, Louis had not even secured Tinnis or other local strongholds. Perhaps he recognized he lacked sufficient manpower and preferred to confront the enemy in a decisive engagement with the maximum force at his disposal. It took the army thirty-two days to arrive at the same point between the Nile and the Bahr al-Saghir opposite Mansourah as the Fifth Crusade had reached in only seven in July 1221. One difference lay in the large amount of food supplies and war materials, especially timber, that Louis carried with him. These allowed him to establish a camp opposite Mansourah without fear of starvation and to build protective vehicles for his engineers and large throwing machines.[59] The Fifth Crusade had travelled lighter, with fatal results.

As the crusader army and navy gingerly picked their way southwards through the canals and streams of the Delta, in late November al-Salih Ayyub finally died in the camp at Mansourah. His death was hushed up while his widow, Shajar al-Durr, engineered the effective transfer of power to the military commander-in-chief, Fakhr al-Din, while al-Salih Ayyub's son and heir, al-Mu 'azzam Turan Shah, was summoned from Hisn Kayfa, his base in the upper Tigris valley in northern Iraq. It took him three months to reach Mansourah, during which time authority inevitably devolved increasingly on the sultana, on Fakhr al-Din and on the late sultan's Bahriyya Mamluks. The urgency in managing a smooth transition of power was evident in the gathering crisis on the Nile. While the Muslim camp flanking the river shore outside Mansourah was strengthened and a battery of throwing machines prepared, Egyptian skirmishers harried the Christians, a sharp encounter with the Templar-led vanguard on 7 December failing to halt the advance. A fortnight later, Louis's army and flotilla of support ships reached the bank opposite the Egyptian camp, separated only by the Bahr al-Saghir branch of the Nile. There they dug in, against attacks from the land, and constructed eighteen wooden ballista, throwing machines, which they used to pepper their enemies on the far shore, who returned fire in kind.

DEFEAT, FEBRUARY–MARCH 1250

For the next six weeks, under an unrelenting mutual barrage across the Nile and Bahr al-Saghir, the Christians attempted to construct some sort of causeway across the Bahr al-Saghir, presumably to allow for passage of their war engines as well as cavalry.[60] The efforts failed. So too did Egyptian attacks by land on the Christian camp and by water, using fireships to try to disrupt or destroy the Christian fleet. Stalemate beckoned until Egyptian defectors informed the crusaders of a deep ford downstream across the Bahr al-Saghir. This offered Louis a risky but excellent chance to outflank and surprise the enemy. He had little choice. The longer he remained stuck opposite Mansourah, the nearer the new sultan, the shorter his supplies and the fewer his tactical options. His perimeter defences could not hold indefinitely, nor could his fleet hope to remain unscathed. Louis presumably had planned on a war of movement, punctuated by battles in open terrain, not frittering away weeks and provisions in futile, if skilful, engineering works. Unless he could engage and destroy the enemy, his campaign was doomed. Unlike Richard I in Palestine in 1191–2, Pelagius and John of Brienne in Egypt in 1221 or even the crusaders of 1228–9 and 1239–41, Louis had no alternative strategy. He held no jurisdiction over the actual or hoped-for kingdom of Jerusalem, and so could hardly negotiate for it, although powerful Frankish lords, such as John of Jaffa, were in his army. His dispositions at Damietta had made it clear he regarded Damietta definitively as his, not part of Jerusalem, and so hardly negotiable for territory there. Louis was an intensely pious man. He seems to have believed that God would reward that conspicuous piety, even where temporal preparation proved insufficient to guarantee victory. Otherwise, his strategy in Egypt made little sense, a quixotic gesture of optimism rather than a sober exercise of Christian generalship.

The attack across the ford, so deep that only the cavalry could cross with their horses having to swim, began at dawn on 8 February. The infantry and engineers were left in the camp under the duke of Burgundy and the Outremer barons to wait for a chance to cross once the opposite bank had been secured by the knights' bold outflanking move. The choice of only the French regiments indicated an understanding of the need for discipline. The tricky manoeuvre worked and almost paid off. The advance guard under Robert of Artois, stiffened by Templars and Hospitallers and afforced by the English squadron under William Longspee, successfully crossed the river. But instead of staying at the bridgehead to wait for the king and the rest of the cavalry, the count's force immediately charged the enemy camp outside Mansourah, catching the defenders completely off guard. The Muslim commander and effective ruler of Egypt, Fakhr al-Din, was killed in the attack; unarmed, he had been interrupted during his morning ablutions.[61] The terrified Egyptians fled towards the refuge of the town. Flushed with sudden victory, Robert and his division flouted clear previous orders. Instead of pausing while the whole army could gather, they pressed on in pursuit of the fleeing enemy into Mansourah itself. A fortified town where the bulk of the Egyptian forces were billeted, Mansourah's narrow streets rendered the Christian cavalry ineffective. Count Robert's triumphant foray turned into a massacre, as his knights became separated, hemmed in and trapped. The morale of the Muslims held, buoyed by the leadership of the Bahriyya Mamluks stationed in the town. The crusader advance-guard was soon wiped out. Louis and the main cavalry force, now safely across the Bahr al-Saghir, were left with their backs to the Nile to face the brunt of a newly confident Egyptian counter-attack.

The battle lasted all day, with desperate fighting along the whole front. The king's tactics were to force a path towards a position directly opposite the Christian camp from where he could expect reinforcements, especially of infantry and crossbowmen. In places, the line broke into splintered skirmishes. Elsewhere, the cavalry were sorely harried by enemy arrows. Joinville claimed to have been hit by five, his horse by fifteen.[62] Protected by armour and padded quilts, they must have resembled monstrous pin cushions. The weight of constantly reinforced enemy troops prevented the deployment of the usual Frankish cavalry charge, much of the fighting reduced to hand-to-hand combat, 'maces against swords' in Joinville's phrase, adding, rather sententiously, 'it was a truly noble passage of arms, for no one there drew either bow or crossbow', weapons regarded by knights like Joinville as plebeian.[63] However gilded by memory, composition and the subsequent need to explain, justify and glorify his saintly hero, Joinville's account of the battle of Mansourah provides one of the most vivid pictures of the experience of medieval fighting, the chaos, cameraderie, improvisation, horror and sheer bravery of the battlefield. In the heat and stress of combat, even the chivalric patina cracked. In a rather Wellingtonian moment, Count Peter of Brittany, veteran crusader and political intriguer, wounded and fearful of the press of his own men as they scrambled to the safety of the main formation around the king, spitting blood from his mouth, swore at them, 'Good Lord, did you ever see such scum!'[64] As the day ended, the Christians held the field. Reinforcements had arrived from their camp opposite, giving them covering fire and access to supplies. The Egyptians withdrew into Mansourah. But their army had not been destroyed. The road to Cairo remained blocked.

The bitter-sweet victory outside Mansourah was the prelude to catastrophe. Apart from showing Louis's personal courage, in his gilded helmet and sword of German steel,[65] the battle exposed the weakness of his strategy. He had driven his army into a cul-de-sac that could easily become a trap. The consequences of the failure to annihilate the Egyptian army were so dire that blame needed to be directed away from the future saint. Robert of Artois's rashness supplied the ideal excuse for chroniclers attempting to deflect responsibility from the king. Louis himself declined to condemn Robert and characteristically blamed himself for defeat. While commended for his bravery, and praised in memorial sermons devised and delivered at Louis's court in the Holy Land over the next few years, Robert's reputation fared far worse than some of his colleagues whom he led to slaughter.[66] Robert may have been placed among the martyrs, but no heroic secular cult of crusading sainthood attached itself to him as it did to the 'manifest martyr', William Longspee, in England.[67]

Within a few years, an elaborate Anglo-French vernacular romance was circulating alongside legends of how he died. The uneasiness about Robert of Artois was to a degree mitigated, at least in official circles, by regarding his sacrifice as another demonstration of how the French had become the new tribe of Judah, leading the faith and providing examples of Christian behaviour, agents of divine providence.

No amount of subsequent interpretation of events could alter the problem confronting Louis's army. As the days passed, the tactical balance tipped increasingly against the crusaders. By the end of February, the new sultan, Turan Shah, had arrived at Mansourah. Although unable to dislodge the Christians from their entrenched position on the site of Fakhr al-Din's camp on the right bank of the Nile, the Egyptians' strength grew. Reinforcements and war materials, especially shipping, joined the Muslim army while the crusaders had to rely on what they already had with them. Louis lacked adequate physical resources to batter his way past the enemy ranged against him, even though reports of his victory incited renewed panic in Cairo.[68] His only realistic hope lay in the internecine rivalries that were emerging between the military households of the former and new sultan breaking out into open civil war. Yet Louis's very presence acted to postpone any Muslim bloodletting until after his defeat. As the weeks of stalemate dragged by, the Christians were hit by food shortages and disease, including scurvy and dysentery. The traumatic details were etched on Joinville's memory. When surgeon-barbers cut away putrefying flesh around the gums of the sick, 'it was pitiful to hear the screams: it was just like the cry of a woman in labour'.[69]

No less serious, the Egyptians had managed to drag overland on carts a number of boats, some sources say fifty galleys, and launch them on the Nile downstream of the crusader camp.[70] This established an effective blockade between the crusaders at Mansourah and their supply base at Damietta. Twice large convoys from Damietta carrying bread, wine, salt meat and other provisions were intercepted and failed to get through. Towards the end of March, worsening conditions, and concerted Muslim attacks throughout Holy Week (20–27 March) forced Louis to abandon his position before Mansourah and return to the old camp across the Bahr al-Saghir. By then, morale had sunk as low as food reserves. It was reported that some openly voiced doubts about the whole enterprise as 'they could see God did not approve of it'.[71] Desultory negotiations over a possible exchange of Damietta for Jerusalem led nowhere as the sultan, seeing his growing advantage, offered unacceptable conditions to a deal. In any case, Louis had little tangible with which to bargain. Finally, on the evening of 5 April, Louis ordered the retreat. The logic of remaining for so long in such an exposed position remains obscure unless Louis recognized his strategy had failed yet still hoped for the implosion of Egyptian unity – or a miracle.

Hampered by enemy forces, illness, hunger, fatigue, difficult terrain and collapsing morale, the shattered army on land, shadowed by a rag-bag navy increasingly vulnerable to enemy shipping on the Nile, effectively disintegrated. Charles of Anjou later claimed, perhaps with some exaggeration, that the army had already lost 80 per cent of its knights.[72] A handful of ships managed to break through to Damietta by river. Louis himself, his dysentery so acute that his trousers had to be cut off, refused escape despite the seriousness of his condition, which brought him close to death. He had entered a fatalistic mood of acceptance of God's will that clung to him for the rest of his life. Others were less impressed by such pietist passivity. One of Joinville's cellarers (whose presence suggests the style in which aristocratic crusaders customarily campaigned) disagreed with the decision to surrender, preferring that they 'should all let ourselves be slain, for thus we shall go to paradise'. His advice was ignored.[73] On crusade as elsewhere, religious enthusiasm did not dispel pragmatic self-preservation. As the Christian forces struggled northwards, unsurprisingly at a considerably faster rate than they had marched south four and a half months earlier, the Egyptians took no chances. Fearful lest some of the Christians reach the safety of Damietta, the sultan saturated the landscape with troops, who skirmished, looted and killed more or less at will. Within two days the crusade army ceased to exist. Even if he had not been so physically helpless, Louis would have been unable to assert even the sort of discipline John of Brienne maintained in 1221. The enemy forces proved irresistible, led by the Bahriyya Mamluks, described by one Egyptian observer, in a telling backhanded compliment, as 'Islam's Templars'.[74] The cohesion of the Christian army disappeared as it struggled north. By the time the king surrendered on 6 April, he had barely reached Sharamsah, less than half way back to Damietta, while the advance guard managed to make it to Fariskur, perhaps only a couple of days' march from safety, before they were overwhelmed by the Egyptian forces. Left to his own devices on his galley and witnessing repeated atrocities suffered by the crusaders on shore, Joinville consulted his knights and the rest of his entourage on the only decision left to them, whether to surrender to the sultan's fleet or his killers on shore. In a collective decision typical of how crusade armies operated, Joinville's company opted for the galley commanders, as those on land, they thought, would sell them as slaves, as indeed many crusaders were. Everywhere similar surrenders by individual companies were occurring. King Louis's surrender on 6 April was negotiated directly with the sultan by the Outremer baron Philip of Montfort. The king and his entourage were taken in chains to Mansourah, where they were joined over the next days by other prominent captives mopped up by the exultant Egyptians. Their victory was total.[75]

Across the Muslim Near East, the response to this astonishing reversal was immediate and celebratory. Turan Shah milked the occasion. King Louis's cloak was sent to Damascus, where, on 20 April, the contemporary scholar and historian Abu Shama saw the governor put it on in public: 'It was of red woollen material lined with ermine, and it had a gold buckle.'[76] However, the negotiations between the captors and captured were not wholly one-sided, despite, as Joinville remembered, the crusaders living in constant fear of their lives from their guards' tactics of intimidation and threats of instant death. On hearing of the king's surrender, the Genoese, Pisans and others in Damietta were only dissuaded from leaving the city by the queen's promise to pay for their living expenses, including food, at a cost, allegedly, of 360,000 *l.t.*[77] This was to find an even more decisive role. With Damietta secure in Christian hands, Turan Shah was faced with the choice of his grandfather in 1221, a potentially costly siege or a profitable and peaceful agreement. Despite Egyptian attempts to include territorial concessions in the Holy Land, negotiations came down to an exchange of Damietta for the lives and freedom of the captives. This came at a high price. After lengthy bargaining, by the end of April it was agreed that the entire Christian army was to be ransomed for 800,000 bezants (400,000 *l.t.*), half payable before Louis left Egypt, as well as the surrender of Damietta. These stood as a form of war reparations. Christian supplies there were to be retained intact for collection later and prisoners on both sides, dating back to the Fifth Crusade, were to be returned. The territorial integrity of mainland Frankish Outremer was not questioned. Once agreement had been reached, Turan Shah moved his camp north near to Damietta to receive the city's surrender, taking his captives with him, still hostages for the first instalment of the ransom.[78]

The comparative civility with which the negotiations were conducted and the absence of punitive clauses in the treaty may have reflected, as western sources try to suggest, Egyptian respect for King Louis. More realistically, Turan Shah needed a quick, peaceful and neat resolution to the war. Further conflict would merely serve to emphasize his military dependence on the Bahriyya Mamluks, servants of his estranged father and no friends to his new regime, at the very time he was trying to insert his own mamluks and servants into positions of authority at court and in the army. Unfortunately for him, the peace itself removed the curb on these growing tensions. The Bahriyya Mamluks had largely been responsible for the defeat of the crusaders and for holding Egyptian morale together after the death of al-Salih Ayyub and the early setbacks at the battle of Mansourah. Now they faced exclusion rather than reward, as Turan Shah promoted his own mamluks and, perhaps shocking to the racism of white mamluk regiments, black eunuchs to head the royal household and royal guard. The Bahriyya forged an alliance with the former sultana, Shajar al-Durr, who saw her power disappear and status disparaged. On 2 May, the Bahriyya struck in a counter-coup against Turan Shah and his mamluks. After a botched initial assassination attempt, Turan Shah, in full view of terrified Christian prisoners, was hacked to pieces by the Bahriyya, among whom stood an ambitious young officer, Baibars al-Bunduqdari, the future nemesis of Frankish Palestine. The Bahriyya commander, Faris al-Din Aqtay al-Jamdar, cut out the young sultan's heart to show to King Louis while the rest of the body was dumped unceremoniously in the Nile. Authority was transferred to Shajar al-Durr, who for three months reigned as a sovereign queen, *malikat al-Muslimin* (queen of the Muslims), 'an event without precedent throughout the Muslim world'.[79] This proved controversial. In July 1250, she abdicated but retained influence by marrying her successor, a Turkish emir, Aybeg al-Turkumani. However, the military power of the regime and increasingly Egypt's political direction, despite the restoration of an Ayyubid sultan *fainéant* (1250–52), lay in the hands of competing mamluk regiments. Although it had failed to conquer Egypt, take Cairo or restore Jerusalem, Louis IX's crusade had played a significant part in ending the Ayyubid empire.

The new regime confirmed Turan Shah's treaty with the shocked and extremely nervous Frankish leaders. On 6 May Damietta was surrendered and King Louis released. Over the following two days, the ransom money was paid over, the only problem being not the king's credit but the availability of cash, solved by expedients such as raiding the coffers of the Templars (with their tacit complicity) for 30,000 *l.t.*[80] Both sides seemed eager to complete the business quickly and honestly, although Joinville complained that the Egyptians failed to honour their side of the bargain when they burnt the Franks' siege machines and stores of salt pork on pyres that lasted for three days.[81] With half the ransom paid and all the important prisoners released, Louis sailed directly to Acre, where he arrived on 12 or 13 May. Although most of his magnates, including his brothers, decided not to stay beyond the autumn passage, Louis, perhaps out of shame or embarrassment mingled with, or concealed by, piety and concern for the plight of the Holy Land, decided to remain in the east, intent on salvaging something from the Egyptian debacle.

Despite the enormous cost of the ransom, and the high price of maintaining his small army in Palestine (later estimated at over one million *l.t.*), Louis could clearly afford it. Helped by the subsequent agreement of the Egyptian government to cancel the second instalment of the ransom, Louis's line of credit with Italian bankers remained in excellent condition at least until 1252–3, possibly reflecting the sums still coming from France.[82] In the absence of the legitimate king of Jerusalem, Conrad II (i.e. Conrad IV of Germany), Louis could behave as *de facto* ruler. During his four-year stay, and supported by fewer than 1,500 troops of his own, he spent large sums on refortifications at Jaffa, Caesarea, Sidon and Acre. In 1252, he even agreed an alliance with Egypt that promised the return of Jerusalem and the lands west of the Jordan once, with French help, the sultan had subdued Damascus. This projected diplomatic revolution immediately foundered on a rare moment of pan-Islamic unity partly inspired by the advance of the Mongols further east. Louis's embassy under Andrew of Longjumeau had returned in 1251 carrying a demand from the Mongol regent, Oghul Qaimush, for annual tribute, not at all what the king had anticipated. On news of the conversion of a Mongol prince to Christianity, Louis despatched William of Rubruck on another embassy to the new Great Khan, Mongke.[83] Although primarily a missionary expedition, and despite Louis's care in not giving William accreditation to negotiate, the mission was regarded by some on all sides as another attempt to capture the chimera of a Franco-Mongol anti-Islamic alliance. This pursuit, as of the Christianization of the Mongols, proved an entirely false hope for Outremer as for the rest of Christendom. When Louis departed for home in 1254, he left a small garrison and committed himself to continued financial and military aid for the Holy Land. However, his vast expenditure of life and treasure had failed in almost every respect except, as contemporaries tried to see it, spiritual. Souls had been saved, but in death and defeat not triumph. Louis IX's crusade had proved the most spectacular of failures.

Both immediate and structural causes could be advanced to explain the disaster. Repeated tactical decisions reached during 1248–50 proved wrong. While there were good reasons for the delays in Cyprus in the winter of 1248–9 and again at Damietta between July and November 1249, they resulted in a lethal combination when tested by the campaign in the Nile Delta. While it is too simple to blame the unsatisfactory outcome of the battle of Mansourah on Robert of Artois, his actions point to a fatal mix of indiscipline and high morale. The subsequent stalemate from February to April 1250 exposed the weakness of Louis's strategic grasp as much as the torpor of his field tactics. He appeared to have no solution to the problem of his inability to dislodge the Muslims from Mansourah and lacked the flexibility to stage a tactical withdrawal. The shadow of 1221 lay heavy across his actions. Yet the failure to secure his rear defences and supply route to Damietta proved the most damaging omission of all, leading directly to the collapse of the expedition. Here, ignorance of local conditions and bad planning may have contributed to defeat. The Egyptians, in outmanoeuvring the crusader ships, relied on galleys, while the crusaders seemed to have depended more on larger transport vessels, including cumbersome cogs, excellent for transporting heavy cargoes at sea but vulnerable in the shallow narrows of the Delta. The Christians' lack of mastery in the waterways of the lower Nile sealed their fate. Despite the shipbuilding programme at Cyprus in 1249–50, the landings at Damietta indicated only a modest proportion of the fleet of the shallow-bottomed galley or landing craft variety. The numbers were inadequate for the task.[84]

However, plans and preparations should be seen not just in relation to execution but also purpose. Here the scale of Louis's defeat and responsibility for it was matched only by the size of his ambition. Louis saw Egypt as more than a gateway to Jerusalem. He intended it as a new

Christian Frankish colony in Outremer. His concept of the political and colonial needs of the crusade were consequently precise and radical. During the Fifth Crusade, there had been much debilitating debate as to whether to exchange conquests in Egypt for territory in Palestine. Something of this resurfaced in the discussions at Damietta in 1249 on whether to capture Alexandria or advance on Cairo. However, Louis was not interested in using Damietta as a bargaining pawn. Within days of the crusaders' occupation he had converted the mosques into churches. Before leaving in November 1249, he had established an archbishop and a permanent chapter of cathedral canons. Throughout, Louis treated Damietta as his and administered it as part of his domain. In the end he exchanged it for his own release from captivity. Louis saw himself as ruler of Damietta by right of conquest, the beginning of the far greater conquest of Egypt itself. Arabic sources refer to Louis's formal defiance to the Sultan in 1249: God will decide whether you or I ought to be master of Egypt.[85]

Understanding, if disapproval, of Louis's intentions may be reflected in Matthew Paris's implied criticism of the whole Egyptian strategy, which he characterized as a magnates' plot to subvert the proper concentration of the crusade on the recovery of Jerusalem and the Holy Land.[86] The English commentator was not unbiased, being hostile to the taxation necessary to fund such expeditions and suspicious of the motives of some *crucesignati*, not least Henry III, who took the cross in 1250 but tried his best to prevent many Englishmen from actually joining the expedition. However, Paris appears to have picked up Louis's desire to complement his conquest of Egypt with the conversion of the Egyptians.[87] In a good position to reflect attitudes as well as gossip at the French and English courts, Paris also repeated a claim of a monk of Pontigny, where the pope spent some time during these years, that Louis took with him to Egypt hoes, harrows, ploughs, ploughshares and other agricultural equipment, adding that Louis was distressed 'that he had not enough people to guard and inhabit the territory in Egypt which he had already occupied and was about to seize'.[88] Conquest, conversion and settlement appeared to be Louis's ultimate aims: the creation of a new Frankish state in Outremer, under Capetian rule, perhaps one of his brothers. Such a startling policy would fit the widely observed financial arrangements that supplied Louis with regular funds from the west. Such a scheme would explain the rejection of any compromise or the plan to take Alexandria rather than attack Cairo. The responsibility for the conduct and tactics of the Nile campaign were not the fault of Robert of Artois but the policy of Louis IX.

Here lay the fatal paradox. Louis's crusade was possibly the most clearly planned, best organized and most coherently mounted of all the larger expeditions to the east. This is not simply an impression created by the greater bulk of surviving archival evidence due to more efficient bureaucratic systems of written record keeping. Although their power should not be exaggerated, thirteenth-century governments possessed stronger tools of fiscal, political and administrative organization and control than their immediate predecessors. Louis himself possessed all the administrative vigour, personal bravery and studied piety associated with the ideal crusader. Yet he failed as dismally as the most unsuccessful of his predecessors. His crusade lacked adequate appropriate shipping or enough manpower to cope with Nile Delta warfare, still less lengthy sieges or lasting conquest and occupation. Less tangible but no less damaging, the ideology and conduct of the enterprise elevated precisely the barriers of culture and religion that directly militated against dissident political elements in Egypt (or elsewhere in the region) making any lasting common cause with the invaders. Joinville's later story of how some elements in the Egyptian elite after the murder of Tutan Shah wished to make Louis sultan represented the overheated imagination of an old warrior and storyteller. Yet it precisely touched a central weakness of the whole practice of thirteenth-century crusading in the Near East. Local Muslim rulers, dependent on their military, administrative, legal and religious elites, might, in certain circumstance, tolerate Franks as allies, even co-rulers, but never as masters.

Yet again, a crusade had shown itself ineffective against even the most limited of strategic targets. The impact of Louis's expedition on the wider conflicts of the Near East was marginal. The Ayyubid regime in Egypt had long relied on fractious mercenary groups. Louis's diplomacy, war or stay in Palestine exerted no influence on the Mongol advance or the prospects for Muslim resistance, still less Frankish survival. Yet, in contrast with the disillusion after the equally ignominious fate of the Second Crusade, Louis's expedition did not lead to an abandonment of enthusiasm for his cause. With crusading incorporated more into the devotional mentality of western Christendom than a century earlier, the reaction was shock at God's apparent disfavour and a desire to redeem sin, not apportion blame. As after 1221, instead of arguing that an Egyptian strategy was impossible, the legacy of Louis's campaign stirred planners, strategists and propagandists to examine how exactly Egypt could be conquered. The detailed advice composed over the following seventy-five years ostensibly tried to learn the lessons of 1248–50. This was most clearly seen in the work of Marino Sanudo Torsello, who based his plan (devised *c.*1306–21) on a long historical study of the eastern campaigns, including Louis IX's. His solution was a maritime trade blockade to weaken Egypt's economy; a small expeditionary force to secure Nile strongpoints followed by a professional army, fully equipped with appropriate shipping, to conquer the country. Only then would a large, mass army of *crucesignati* be launched to reshape the religious and political map of the Near East.[89] Sanudo, like Louis IX, identified the problems. But neither he nor the French king nor the long succession of other politicians and self-appointed experts could escape the reality that the freakish legend and myth of 1099 and its subsequent vigorous promotion had bequeathed an unwarranted optimism for an ideal that, pointless or not, was increasingly unattainable.

THE SHEPHERDS' CRUSADE 1251

Louis's crusade was the last great western campaign to reach the shores of the eastern Mediterranean until the arrival of Napoleon Bonaparte in Egypt in 1798. Its failure caused a sensation in the west, as it had in the Near East. Bad news travels fast. On 1 August 1250, Richard of Cornwall was sitting in the Exchequer at Westminster when he was brought the story of the death of William Longspee at Mansourah.[90] When the full extent of the disaster reached the west, unrest in Venice and other Italian cities was reported. France plunged into a sort of public mourning. For many, the grief was immediate and personal; for lost sons, brothers, husbands and fathers – and some mothers and daughters too. As he lay awaiting captivity in a hut near Sharamsah on 6 April 1250, Louis's head was cradled by a woman from Paris.[91] But in France reactions took a more aggressive turn, which revealed the extent of popular engagement in public affairs, the fragility of social and political control by the authorities and the existence of a wider civil society whose voice was usually drowned out by the deeds of their social, educational and economic superiors.

In the spring of 1251 a popular movement began to be organized in Brabant, Flanders, Hainault and Picardy, all areas of active, if in places confused, crusade preaching and fundraising. Rural bands of what clerical observers slightingly referred to as 'shepherds and simple people' gathered with the declared purpose of joining Louis in the Holy Land.[92] Critical of the failure of the nobility to achieve success in the crusade and hostile to those who had not even gone east, these 'pastoureaux' (literally shepherds) adopted the guise of religious processions, reminiscent of 1212. Marching on Paris, they carried holy banners, proclaimed their direct inspiration from the Virgin Mary and offered crosses and absolution of sins as they went. The influence of crusade preaching and Louis's religious propaganda that surrounded the raising of men, money and provisions were obvious from the symbols of the passion they carried on their flags, the cross and the lamb. The latter may even have helped provide them with their name.[93] The marchers were not inarticulate rabbles. Their mission spoke of ordered response to the crisis of Louis's defeat. Coming from liminal regions of France may have heightened their desire to occupy the centre of the political debate without the traditional networks of contact and exchange with that central authority. Their social critique matched the official line on collective sin, their increasing anti-clericalism a reflection on the prominent part in crusade preparations played by the clergy, especially the friars, for financial and administrative purposes.

Initially, the 'pastoureaux' appeared a credible force of active support for the beleaguered French king. The regency government under his mother, Blanche of Castile, welcomed them in Paris and provided them with supplies. Some, at least, apparently found the means to join the king in the Holy Land.[94] However, the implied social radicalism of their message soon drove elements of the movement beyond the pale of political respectability. Although characterized by observers as a single large army of protestors, it is likely that, as well as the main contingents from the north-east of the kingdom, there were separate and simultaneous outbreaks of popular enthusiasm across northern France, from Normandy to the Loire and into Berry. After the government decided to reject their call, some of these groups turned to violence and crime. There was trouble at Rouen in June. At Orléans, scholars were attacked. Everywhere, priests and friars were threatened. The 'pastoureaux' now appeared as armed criminal gangs, living off the land and terrorizing the population. At Bourges, a large body ran riot under a leader called 'the Master of Hungary', allegedly fluent in French, German and Latin, possibly a renegade monk, a characterization that served the purposes of disapproving observers by locating authority in traditional but perverted hands. This band assaulted Jews and looted the local synagogue before the city authorities and townspeople turned on them. 'The Master' himself was hacked to death and his followers dispersed, although some managed to continue their rampage as far south as Bordeaux.

Many aspects of these uprisings showed a clear and precise understanding and knowledge of the public policy of the French crown, witnessed by the symbols of the Passion, the request for validation and support from Blanche of Castile, the hostility to the venality of the clergy, the criticism of the nobility, and the appropriation of the mechanics of giving the cross and remitting sins. The attacks on Jews was entirely in keeping with Louis IX's own persecution, as was the general call to press political action into the service of God, who was presented as the chief instigator of policy. Although disapproving clerical commentators branded them as sexually hedonistic and criminal, out of social order and so out of moral control, the marchers seemed to possess discipline. The Master of Hungary claimed education. His targets could have been convincingly characterized to a far wider audience than the rioters as privileged spongers: Jews, scholars and clergy who appeared in cahoots with a political system whose venality ostentatiously conflicted with its stated goals. Yet this was no random proletarian revolt or social rebellion. The 'pastoureaux' declared their devotion to their king and his cause, claiming that they, instead of the traditional elites, were expressing and pursuing the best interests of royal policy. The uprisings' organization, cohesion and behaviour suggests the involvement of the politically rather than the economically marginalized, but not of the politically ignorant or innocent. The disturbances in 1251 revealed further evidence of the penetration of crusading practice into the mentalities of an increasingly diverse and sophisticated civil society, one educated by evangelism and taxation, energized by the circulation of detailed news of atrocities and disasters that, in the perspective of collective religious imagination, seemed not distant, but immediate and urgent. Just as such emotions underpinned and explained Louis IX's preparations from 1244 to 1248, so they produced the unrest and violence of 1251.

THE FAILED COUNTER-ATTACK OF LOUIS IX'S SECOND CRUSADE

Louis IX's unofficial protectorate over Frankish Palestine survived his departure in April 1254, embodied in the resident French garrison and the annual material and financial subsidies channelled east, some years thousands of livres, mainly derived from church funds and loans, although underwritten by the French government. Despite Joinville's prediction on the day they sailed away from Acre, that Louis 'had that day been reborn', entering a 'new life when he escaped from that perilous land', the king never forgot Jerusalem.[95] Instead, he cultivated the impression of a monarch whose gaze rested on the world of the spirit, a focus given physical expression in his and his court's continued declarations of devotion to the plight of the Holy Land. Added to his material power, this stance lent Louis enormous prestige and effectiveness as an international arbiter, especially as successive popes between 1254 and 1268 became locked into the destruction of the Hohenstaufen dynasty, a cause not seen by all Christians as of transcendent importance. Louis established a moral authority rare for a medieval layman. He became in some respects, *mutatis mutandis*, the Nelson Mandela of his day, a man of suffering, acquainted with grief, of seemingly unimpeachable integrity yet active in the temporal affairs of nations. Like many politicians, Louis fashioned his life to suit his public needs in a creation of art and piety.[96] This image acted as more than a pose; it framed practical politics, not least in a willingness to return to the east to reverse the decision of 1250.

Yet of far greater importance than Louis's personal enthusiasm for prospects for a new general crusade or the survival of Frankish Outremer were events in Italy and Syria. International attention and the resources of the western church were increasingly directed at exterminating the Hohenstaufen. The issues of control over the Sicilian church and the territorial integrity and security of the papal states in central Italy loomed larger in the policies of successive popes than did the Holy Land, for all the lip service paid to beleaguered Outremer. Alongside grants of crusading privileges to those who fought for the papacy against their Italian enemies, the priority was to find a papal champion. After a number of false starts, in 1265 agreement was reached with Louis IX's youngest brother, Charles of Anjou. He then proceeded to destroy first Manfred, Frederick's illegitimate son and ruler of Sicily, in 1266 and then, in 1268, Conradin, Frederick's grandson and titular king of Jerusalem. Until then, especially as England was only just emerging from a protracted and latterly vicious period of internecine conflict and civil war (1258–65), chances of a large eastern campaign were remote.

However, by the mid-1260s the outlook for mainland Outremer looked bleak. The structure of the kingdom of Jerusalem was slowly disintegrating. While John of Jaffa was composing his great lawbook commemorating a part historical, part imaginary world of legal niceties and juridical precedents, some institutions faced physical and legal annihilation. In 1255, Pope Alexander IV afforded diplomas of the abbey of Our Lady of Josaphat outside Jerusalem, renewing privileges with the same validity as the original grants because part of the abbey's archives had been destroyed by 'Saracens', thus endangering the very legal identity of the corporation.[97] Similar threats to the existence of the Latin settlement soon transferred to the level of high politics and diplomacy. The appearance of the Mongols in Syria radically altered the structure of power in the region, to the Franks' serious disadvantage. In February 1258, Hulegu (d. 1265), brother of the Great Khan Mongke (1251–9), captured Baghdad, killing the last Abbasid caliph, al-Musta 'sim. Moving on to Syria, the Mongols took Aleppo (January 1260) and Damascus (March 1260), ousting the Ayyubid ruler, al-Nasir Yusuf. Palestine was exposed. Mongols raids reached Ascalon, Jerusalem and the gates of Egypt. A Mongol garrison was placed at Gaza. Sidon was attacked and briefly occupied in August 1260. By then, most of the remaining Ayyubid and other princes left between the Euphrates and the Mediterranean had capitulated.[98] The Franks were divided how to respond. Bohemund VI of Antioch-Tripoli, briefly one of Outremer's most important power brokers, had already accepted Mongol overlordship, with a Mongol resident and battalion stationed in Antioch itself, where they stayed until the fall of the city to the Mamluks in 1268. The Frankish Antiochenes assisted in the Mongols' capture of Aleppo, thus in part achieving a very traditional Frankish target, and had received additional lands in reward. By contrast, the Franks of Acre saw no advantage in submission to the Mongols. Equally, they held aloof from outright military alliance with the new Mamluk sultan of Egypt, Qutuz, who was preparing an army to contest the Mongol conquest of Syria. Although many wanted to enlist in the Egyptian counter-attack, the Franks contented themselves with granting Qutuz safe conduct through their lands and supplying him with provisions.[99] Given the uncertainty of the outcome, the untrustworthiness of any alliance with Egypt and the universal contempt shown by the Mongols for any other group, such cautious neutrality was probably the least worst decision, far from the catastrophic strategic diplomatic blunder some have thought. This was no great missed opportunity. As Louis IX had discovered, and Bohemund VI was experiencing, there was nothing on their own terms for the Franks in a Mongol alliance. With Hulegu and the bulk of his forces having withdrawn eastwards, at Ain Jalut in southern Galilee on 3 September 1260, the Egyptians routed a smaller Mongol army under Kitbugha Nayan, who was killed. This victory, and Hulegu's preoccupation with consolidating his hold on Iraq and Iran, allowed the Mamluks to occupy Syria, ejecting the surviving Ayyubid princes. By the end of October, Qutuz had been assassinated by Baibars and the Bahriyya, who feared being passed over in the disposal of the Syrian spoils. Baibars was now installed as ruler of Egypt and Syria, more united than at any time since the death of Saladin in 1193.

Baibars saw in the eradication of the Frankish kingdom a means to consolidate his power as well as establish his credentials as a worthy Islamic ruler. A veteran of the drama of 1249–50, he rejected the accommodating policies of his Ayyubid and Mamluk predecessors. He rebuffed Frankish attempts at alliance in the early years of his sultanate (1260–77) and from 1265 began the systematic destruction of the kingdom, capturing in short order Caesarea, Arsuf, Toron and Haifa (1265); Saphet, Galilee, Ramla and Lydda (1266).[100] The complete loss of the kingdom looked an immediate possibility. Alarm revived half-dormant plans in the west for a new general crusade. The end of the English civil war in 1265 and Charles of Anjou's victory in Sicily in 1266 encouraged Pope Clement IV to revive plans for an eastern crusade begun under his predecessor Urban IV in 1263. Long-distance financial aid and sponsorship for garrisons, such as Henry III of England's promised 2,000 marks in 1264 to maintain a company of knights at Acre, were evidently insufficient to stem the Mamluk advance, which proceeded by sophisticated siege technology matched by military brutality. By September 1266, Louis IX had decided to take the cross once more, to lead what he and the pope, a former legal advisor to the French king, hoped would be an international league of recovery. On 25 March 1267, the Feast of the Annunciation, before the relics housed in the Sainte Chapelle, Louis, his three sons, his close family and most of the great nobles of France once more took the cross.[101]

Louis IX's second crusade was notable for its sophisticated methods of recruitment and its almost wholly nugatory results. Much of the process closely followed the precedents of the 1240s. Louis obtained a clerical tenth in France for three years. The collected deposits from legacies and redemptions were placed at the crusaders' disposal. Normal expenditure was trimmed. *Enquêteurs* investigated local grievances against royal agents. Towns were tallaged. In some regions, Jewish moneylenders were harried. As before, Genoa and Marseilles supplied ships, although at less exorbitant rates than in 1248.[102] However, the rising power of the Catalan ports was recognized in the arrangements of other crusade leaders. More significant, the king's fleet was commanded not, as in 1248, by Genoese admirals but by a Picard nobleman – with no previous maritime experience – Florent of Varennes. The king again acted as the expedition's central banker. He subsidized the veteran crusader Hugh IV of Burgundy, now contemplating his third eastern campaign. Clerical funds granted the king were diverted to Alphonse of Poitiers and the counts of Champagne, Brittany and Flanders. In 1269, Louis lent Edward of England 70,000 *l.t.* with a view to securing substantial English and Gascon involvement: 25,000 *l.t.* was earmarked for Gaston of Béarn.[103] On both sides of the English Channel, crusade leaders assembled their companies by means of formal contracts. In return for a fixed sum from his lord or commander, the contracting crusader was bound to provide a stated number of knights. Occasionally, the crusader would receive additional subsidies in the form of monetary gifts or free food. The contracts were backed by less formal ties of clientage, family and political ties and regional association. In such ways Louis engaged 325 knights and Edward of England 225, yet these only represented the core of, in the French case at least, a much more substantial army.[104] Alphonse of Poitiers alone raised perhaps as much as 100,000 *l.t.* towards his contingent of knights, crossbowmen, provisions and ships, raising the funds from the clerical taxes assigned him by the king, selling assets such as timber and levying a hearth tax on his subjects of the Midi. Judging from the level of noble commitment in France, Louis's second crusade army cannot, in expectation at least, have been much smaller than that of 1248, perhaps between 10,000 and 15,000 strong. Louis's second crusade witnessed another striking demonstration of the increasing power of the French state over nobles and regions. To drum up support, the king's itinerary in 1269 included areas of the kingdom previously free of royal visits.[105] In backhanded recognition of this royal authority, Joinville, who had this time refused to sign up, recorded that some French *crucesignati* felt they only took the cross to keep the king's favour rather than God's.[106] If so, the near unanimity of the higher nobility in following the king's lead speaks much for the strength of patronage over pious scruples or the purity of motives.

To the French levies were added contributions from Frisia, the Low Countries, Scotland, Aragon, England and Charles of Anjou, now installed as king of Sicily. The participation of James I of Aragon and Edward of England, especially the latter, owed much to the personal diplomacy and moral dynamism of Louis IX himself. Despite the opposition of his father, the ageing Henry III, and Pope Clement IV, Edward took the cross at Northampton in 1268.[107] He and his brother Edmund raised a significant force centred on the royal court with which well over half of those known to have been recruited in England possessed close formal links. However much the crusade may have helped unite the English baronage after the trauma of civil war, the enterprise was conceived and remained essentially as a royal and curial affair, as in France. Further sign of the commitment of the English government to the crusade lay in the strenuous and ultimately successful attempts by the court to obtain parliamentary approval for a tax on movables of a twentieth, only finally agreed in 1270. Whatever the tax supplied for the crusade – perhaps £30,000 – this represented a significant development in the newly restored consensual politics after the English civil war and confirmation of the fiscal role of the commons in Parliament, the first lay subsidy granted the English crown since 1237.[108]

If central funding and a network of contracts that embraced the English as well as French contingents gave Louis a uniquely influential position in ordering the expedition, this did not translate into control over the coordination of the campaign. In February 1268, Louis fixed his departure for May 1270. Yet, at one end of the scale, the king of Aragon embarked in June 1269, for his fleet to be wrecked by a storm, only a remnant of it actually reaching the Holy Land without the king.[109]

At the other, Charles of Anjou only took the cross in February 1270 and began to prepare his war fleet the following July. Even Edward of England missed the agreed muster by some months, only embarking in August 1270, while his brother, Edmund, set out in the winter of 1270–71. Numbers who actually participated, as opposed to the contractual estimates, appeared lower than the original rush of *crucesignati* in 1267–8 may have indicated. The driving force of the whole expedition remained the will and enthusiasm of King Louis. This was emphasized by the long papal interregnum after the death of Clement IV in November 1268. A successor was not elected until September 1271, so throughout its final preparations and the crusade itself, there was no pope. However guilty Louis may have felt over the disasters of 1250, his confessor claimed that the king's motives were more positive and altruistic, to achieve an act of such penitential severity that God would show mercy on the Holy Land.[110] In addition to the administrative and financial direction he gave, despite the extensive national and international response, Louis's personal decision on the strategy of the campaign, perhaps more than anything, lent the enterprise its particular character, some would say its especial futility.

While preaching began in 1267–8, led by cardinals who, appropriate to the character of the operation, had formerly been French royal councillors, the situation in the Holy Land deteriorated further, culminating in the fall of Jaffa, Beaufort, and, in a blood bath, Antioch to Baibars in May 1268. Initially Louis seems to have envisaged a repeat of the strategy of 1248–50, with a descent on Egypt as the likely destination of the new campaign. However, at some point in 1268 or 1269, Louis's attention turned in an entirely different direction, an attack on Tunis. This possessed a number of apparent advantages. All large crusade fleets, embarking from different places at different times, required a muster port. As all large fleets and armies had to await the harvest, embarkation for the east was usually deferred until the late summer or autumn sailing seasons. This in turn demanded a port to be found in which to collect the fleet and spend the winter: Lisbon 1147–8; Messina 1190–91; Zara 1202–3; Acre 1217–18; Limassol 1248–9. Tunis was within easier and safer sailing distance than Cyprus. Conquest of the city and region might assist the political ambitions of the new Sicilian king, Charles of Anjou, as the Hafsid emir Muhammed was harbouring renegade supporters of the ousted Sicilian Hohenstaufen. The emir was also an ally of the king of Aragon, a potential rival to Charles in the western Mediterranean. The possibility of an invasion of Tunisia may have persuaded James of Aragon to avoid integrating his army and fleet with Louis's. However, Charles's ambitions were focused eastwards, towards the Balkans and Byzantium. Despite later conjecture, the choice of Tunis as a target rested with Louis, not his brother. In Louis's eyes, the conquest of Tunis would deprive Egypt of an ally and act as a convenient base for an attack on the Nile in 1271, a geographic myopia of scale common enough in western European circles at the time. More specifically, Louis's close contacts with the friars may have led him to believe from the Dominicans that Tunis was ripe for conversion, a perception based on perennial missionary optimism and the largely friendly diplomatic contacts between Tunisia and western Christendom.[111] Such fantasies of conversion led to a series of ill-fated missions to north Africa in the late thirteenth and fourteenth centuries, the willingness to believe that Muslims could be brought to Christ acting as a form of cultural totem similar to modern enthusiasm for exporting western democracy. Friars seemed incapable of separating commercial from religious openness. Perhaps having got wind of Louis's thinking, the Tunisians sent an embassy to Louis in 1269, which may have furthered encouraged the king's thinking. While not of itself contradicting the nature of the crusade, the Tunis gambit was sufficiently sensitive to be concealed from followers until after his fleet had embarked. But with muster ports in Sardinia and western Sicily, a north African destination could hardly have come as a surprise. While hindsight condemned the whole idea, Louis's motives may have been quixotic but they were not without reason.

The rituals of departure in 1270 exactly copied those of 1248. On 14 March 1270, Louis received the oriflamme and the pilgrim's scrip and staff at St Denis. The following day, he entered Notre Dame in Paris as a barefoot penitent before walking to Vincennes, where he bade farewell to his wife. The first setback came at Aigues Mortes, where Louis found the promised ships were late, only arriving in late June, by which time sickness had already been incubated in the army. Leaving Aigues Mortes on 2 July, the French fleet reached Cagliari in Sardinia on 4 July, where they waited for other squadrons to assemble. There on 13 July Louis formally announced the destination of Tunis, where the fleet arrived on 17 July, effecting a landing the following day. On 24 July, the army moved its operations a few miles along the coast to Carthage in search of better terrain for the camp and adequate water. Further advance was delayed while Louis waited for the arrival of his brother Charles, who had only begun to equip his fleet in Sicily a few days earlier. High summer, poor diet and water contaminated by the immobile army soon stoked the outbreak of virulent disease, probably typhus or dysentery. The leadership was hit as well as the ordinary ranks. Louis's son John Tristan, born at Damietta in the dark spring days of 1250, died. The king and his eldest son, Philip, both fell ill. Lingering bedridden for a month, Louis died on 25 August 1270, just as the first detachments of Charles of Anjou's fleet were making land. Some said his last words were 'Jerusalem! Jerusalem!', although his confessor, who administered the dying king Extreme Unction, signally failed to mention such a neat end.[112]

With the new Philip III still convalescent, Charles of Anjou assumed command. Evacuation appeared the only option. By 1 November, after a debilitating period of negotiation and desultory skirmishing, Charles and Emir Muhammed agreed terms. In return for the handing over of prisoners, the emir's agreement to permit Christian worship and proselytizing, and a war indemnity of 210,000 gold ounces (*c.*500,000 *l.t.*), Charles agreed to withdraw, appropriating a third of the money. This angered some sections of the Christian army, not least Edward of England, who arrived off Tunis on 10 November, just as the crusaders were packing up to depart. The Christian fleet sailed for Sicily to decide on their next course of action, reaching Trapani on 14 November. Any decision on further campaigning was pre-empted by a storm on 15/16 November, which destroyed large numbers of ships and damaged many more. Perhaps as many as forty vessels were lost, including eighteen large transports, with over 1,000 lives. That effectively ended the crusade, only Edward of England insisting on proceeding to the Holy Land. By the time Philip III returned to his new kingdom, his train resembled a funeral cortège, bearing the bodies of his father, brother, brother-in-law, wife and stillborn son.[113]

The failure of the 1270 crusade, though dramatic and spectacular, did not mean the end of the crusade as a focus for monarchical aspirations. Some, like Alphonse of Poitiers before his death the following year, kept the flame burning. In 1271, the cardinals elected as pope Tedaldo Visconti, patriarch of Jerusalem, who was actually in Acre when he was elected as Pope Gregory X. Much of his reign, and those of his immediate successors, was occupied with prospects for a new general crusade to the east and galvanizing the kings of the west to join. Edward of England had done more. Reinforced by a few French nobles, Edward set off for Acre in the spring of 1271, despite attempts to persuade him to return to England, where his father Henry III was gravely ill. Characteristically, he refused, allegedly insisting that he would travel to Acre if necessary only with his groom Fowin for company.[114] As it was, his army was small, perhaps only 1,000 strong, carried in a small flotilla of just thirteen ships. Reaching Acre via Cyprus on 9 May 1271, Edward remained in the Holy Land for a year, joined by his brother Edmund in September 1271. He lacked the manpower to achieve any lasting or significant change in the Franks' position, arriving too late to prevent Baibars's capture of Crac des Chevaliers in April. Edward contented himself with pursuing the will of the wisps of a Mongol alliance with the il-khan of Persia and internal harmony within Frankish Outremer. He saw some action in defending Acre from Baibars's attack in December 1271 and launched a couple of military promenades into the surrounding countryside. The truce agreed by Hugh III and Baibars in May 1272 failed to persuade Edward of the futility of continued stay, an obstinacy that may have provoked the famous attempt on his life. Even before his departure in October 1272, some of his followers had begun to leave, including his brother, in May. While achieving almost nothing for Outremer, beyond the establishment of a small English garrison in Acre, Edward's crusade had proved massively expensive, perhaps over £100,000. During the crusade, he ran up debts of tens of thousands of livres.[115] However, in reputation and image, the crusade paid very handsome dividends which he and his eulogists were not slow in exploiting. Amid the increasingly fevered discussion around the courts of western Europe about how to save the Holy Land, Edward stood out as the only crowned head in the west to have actually gone there. In 1287, he even took the cross for a second time and began apparently serious preparations for a new expedition. Even so, as the only tangible assistance to reach Palestine from the great French crusade planned by Louis IX, Edward's crusade of 1271–2 represented very meagre pickings. In its way, far more potent, for the French monarchy although not for Palestine, was Louis IX's canonization in 1297. But even that was tinged with disappointment for one of those whose evidence had helped secure the king's elevation to sanctity. Joinville regretted Louis had only been gazetted as a confessor and not, as he thought only proper in the light of the king's acute sufferings on crusade, a martyr.[116]

THE LOSS OF THE HOLY LAND

For the rest of his life Edward I of England (d. 1307) protested his eagerness to return to the east, usually coupled with his insistence that he was too busy with vital affairs of state at home to leave just yet. While occasionally disingenuous, this excuse expressed the reality of late thirteenth- and fourteenth-century crusading. Louis IX had shown how the full resources of a kingdom allied to ecclesiastical funding could be directed very effectively towards the crusade. However, precisely these newly powerful central governments militated against the fulfilment of another such policy, as regimes became enmeshed in hardening intractable international conflicts and domestic administration. The experience of Louis's crusade alerted officials to the almost limitless expense of such enterprises, the accounts of Louis's campaigns being copied and studied by interested but anxious bureaucrats for more than half a century after his death.[117] The increasing bulk of works of theoretical planning or practical advice written from the 1270s began to expose very clearly the material difficulties facing any eastern expedition. This greater openness to the difficulties of crusading was summed up by a French diplomat, the crusade veteran Erard of Valéry, at the Second Council of Lyons in 1274, called by Gregory X to attempt to launch a new offensive. It would be like a small puppy yelping at a great mastiff.[118] The advice Gregory received before the council exposed how different theatres of the crusade, such as the Baltic, diverted interest and commitment. Even promoters of crusades in Europe against the Hohentaufen, such as the great Dominican preacher and canonist Humbert of Romans, noted how they engendered cynicism if not overt hostility among a wide if not necessarily deep coalition of observers from across western Europe. The Lyons Council authorized more church taxation and preaching of the cross, but the silence of the royal representatives and spokesmen for the military orders at the council when asked to advise on the best course of action spoke loudest.[119] Concern with the plight of the Holy Land had not declined, but action became harder to organize and, in consequence, undermined future commitment, a vicious cycle never thereafter escaped.

Attempts to organize a new crusade did not end in 1270. Preaching and clerical taxes were authorized in 1274 and 1291. Serious strategic thought was pursued, including suggestions (in 1274 and 1291) that the military orders should be amalgamated to exploit military and fiscal economies of scale and unity of purpose. In particular, the Second Council of Lyons appeared to promise a new beginning to efforts to restore Frankish rule in the Holy Land. Gregory X placed the eastern crusade at the heart of his diplomacy. Before leaving Acre after hearing of his election as pope in 1271, Gregory pointedly preached on the text 'If I forget thee, O Jerusalem, let my right hand forget her cunning' (Psalm 137 v.5). On reaching Europe, he summoned a general council to discuss church reform and plans for a new crusade, which he proposed to lead in person. Before the council convened in May 1274 at Lyons, Gregory sought advice from politicians and churchmen professionally involved. A number of treatises were submitted containing advice that varied from a catalogue of ecclesiastical, including crusading, shortcomings by a Franciscan, Gilbert of Tournai, a self-interested call by the bishop of Olmütz on behalf of the king of Bohemia to concentrate on the Baltic and eastern European crusading front to a plea by an Acre Dominican, William of Tripoli, for the conversion, not destruction, of the Muslims.[120] The council itself exposed the gap between intent and action. The decree *Constitutiones pro zeli fidei* (18 May 1274) expanded on its exemplar, Innocent III's *Ad Liberandam* of 1215, by instituting a clearer administrative structure for the collection of the proposed sexennial clerical tithe, establishing twenty-six specified collectories.[121] A voluntary lay poll tax was suggested. To provide the most favourable diplomatic context, union between the Roman and Greek Orthodox churches was negotiated, in part a response of the Byzantine emperor Michael VIII Palaeologus to his fears of isolation in the face of the aggressive ambitions of the previous papal favourite, Charles of Anjou, who was eyeing the Balkans with unconcealed purpose. Ambassadors from the Mongol khan were received by the council, its leader even undergoing a symbolic form of public Christian baptism.

However, only one western monarch bothered to attend, the ageing James I of Aragon. Despite his offer of a preliminary garrison force of 500 knights and 2,000 infantry to prepare for a subsequent large expedition, the political will was hardly overwhelming, despite strenuous efforts to excite general support.[122] Preaching was authorized by a papal bull of September 1274.[123] The clerical tax raised massive amounts in some areas such as Tuscany, testimony to new bureaucratic efficiency rather than overt enthusiasm.[124] As in 1215, money-boxes were set up in parish churches. Pope Gregory persuaded Philip III of France, Charles of Anjou and his preferred candidate for the imperial throne, Rudolf of Habsburg, to take the cross in 1275. A departure date was set for April 1277 when the pope and the new emperor would together embark for the east. Plans for a papal flotilla of about twenty ships were put in train. Yet the tepid reaction of delegates at Lyons proved a surer indication of the prospects for the crusade than the administrative, fiscal and diplomatic activity. Bureaucratic neatness was not enough. The lack of vocal support for the proposed expedition from the military orders and the French envoys at Lyons gave its own testimony. Gregory X's crusade simultaneously revealed how administratively effective papal leadership had become in the later thirteenth century and how politically and emotionally incapable it was to move the hearts of politicians and people. On Gregory's death in January 1276, the crusade plans were shelved and then abandoned. While the church taxes continued to be raised in places, the proceeds were diverted to papal wars, fought as crusades, in Italy. The Mongol alliance, despite six further embassies to the west between 1276 and 1291, led nowhere.[125] The prospect of an anti-Mamluk coalition faded as the westerners' inaction rendered them useless as allies for the Mongols, who, in turn, would only seriously be considered by western rulers as potential partners in the event of a new crusade which never happened. The union of the Roman and Greek churches was repudiated by the Orthodox faithful. It had in any case failed to curb Angevin aspirations for Balkan conquest at Greek expense. The activity of the 1270s set a pattern for the future, copied with an increasingly predictable monotony of frustration after the council of Vienne (1311–12), in the 1330s and the 1360s: papal or royal enthusiasm, commitment, taxation, distraction and abortion. The disintegration of Gregory's schemes confirmed the fears of even sympathetic onlookers, such as the well-informed networking Italian Franciscan Salimbene of Adam, that 'it does not seem to be the Divine Will that the Holy Sepulchre should be recovered'.[126]

Baibars's campaigns of 1265–71 had reduced the Frankish holdings in Palestine to a barely sustainable rump of a few castles and coastal cities clinging on to the shore of the Mediterranean with almost no hinterland. Not even Frankish superiority at sea could reverse the tide. By demolishing the places he captured, Baibars denied the prospect of reconquest. There would be no repeat of 1189–92, even though Christians retained bases in Cilicia and Cyprus. Of the campaigns of Baibars and his immediate heirs it has been said that they achieved what their predecessors, Persian, Arab, Turk or Frank, had not, 'the destruction of the ancient Syro-Palestinian city civilisation'.[127] The final act was postponed not by Frankish resolve or a new crusade, but by the tangled internal politics of the Mamluk empire and the Mongol threat to Syria, which continued into the early fourteenth century. A Mongol invasion was defeated at Homs in 1281, a new assault the next year only averted by the death of the aggressive il-Khan Abaqa from delirium tremens. His successor, Teguder, was a Muslim convert.[128] This freed Sultan Kalavun (1279–90) to resume his attack on the Franks. The great northern fortress of Margat fell in 1285; Lattakiah in 1287. Tripoli followed in 1289, after 180 years of uninterrupted Christian rule, the longest of any of the major Frankish conquests. It had been under Genoese control since the death of the last count, Bohemund VII, in 1287, and it was rumoured that the sultan's attack had been encouraged either by the Venetians or Pisans. Those who failed to escape – mainly non-nobles – were massacred; the city was demolished, a portent for the fate of Acre.[129]

Throughout the 1270s and 1280s, men and money were sent to the Holy Land by popes and western rulers. As the Frankish position in Palestine disintegrated, small companies led by well-connected crusaders appeared at Acre temporarily to stiffen local resistance and the permanent western garrisons funded by concerned, perhaps guilty kings in Europe: Countess Alice of Blois and Count Florent of Holland in 1287; John of Grailly in 1288; the Savoyard intimate of Edward I Othon of Grandson in 1290. None of these did anything to reverse the decline. The politics of western Europe militated against a new crusade just as firmly as the politics of the Near East. The intervention of Charles of Anjou's attempt to annexe the kingdom of Jerusalem in 1277 briefly seemed to offer a remedy.[130] Yet his ambition only served to challenge the unity of Outremer and provoke a damaging war in the west, known as the War of the Sicilian Vespers, after Sicily rebelled against Angevin rule in 1282. This pitted Aragon against Charles of Anjou and his French allies, smashing precisely the coalition assembled by Louis IX and sought by Gregory X. In 1285, Philip III of France died on crusade, like his father, but it had been against the Aragonese not the Mamluks. Edward I's priorities lay in the conquest of Wales (to 1284) shortly to be followed by his involvement in the Scottish succession, which increasingly dominated the last years of his reign (1290–1307). His alliance with France had become a distant memory as relations deteriorated into war over the status of Edward's French duchy of Gascony (1294). The legacy of the imperial interregnum (1250–73) prevented any unified German contribution. Although the last great Mongol attack on eastern Europe had ended in 1260, because of civil war breaking out in the Far East over the succession to the khanate, attempts to arrange an anti-Muslim alliance proved as elusive as before, while the rulers of eastern Europe occupied themselves with consolidating their own borders. Just as the power of kings promised more effective crusading, it largely precluded any alternative initiatives from their nobles. The gulf between capacity and policy came to match that between idealism and will.

The divisions of the west disrupted Outremer during Charles of Anjou's attempt to wrest the kingship of Jerusalem from the kings of Cyprus (1277–85). Yet even after Charles's death in 1285 and the restoration of a single nominal authority under Henry II of Cyprus and I of Jerusalem, no prospect of permanent defence on the mainland was possible without impractically massive outside assistance. As Sultan Kalawun tightened the noose, each Frankish lordship faced its own demise in autonomous desperation, some accepting Mamluk overlordship or condominium, others, like Tripoli, suffering conquest and butchery. The last act, begun by Kalavun in 1290 against Acre, continued after his death under his successor al-Ashraf Khalil. The siege of Acre lasted from 6 April 1291 until 18 May, when the city fell. The frenzied defence and countless acts of bravery – on both sides – ring in the memory.

Khalil's assault on Acre was designed to be final. The sultan, following preparations already put in train by his father, gathered troops, engineers and siege machines from across northern Syria, Damascus and Egypt. The well-maintained double walls of Acre presented a formidable obstacle, so the siege was to be a contest of throwing machines. One of

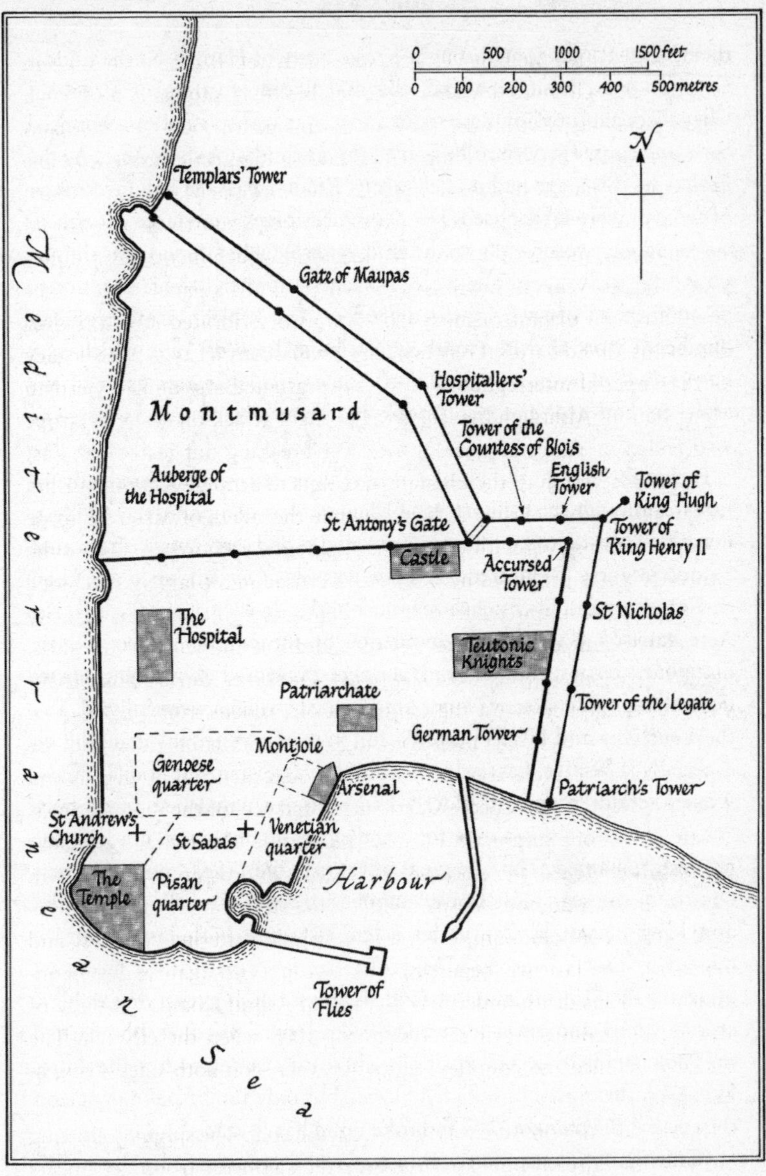
0
500
1000
1500 feet
0
100
200
300
400
500 metres
N
Templars' Tower
Gate of Maupas
Hospitallers' Tower
Montmusard
Tower of the Countess of Blois
English Tower
Tower of King Hugh
Tower of King Henry II
Auberge of the Hospital
St Antony's Gate
Castle
Accursed Tower
St Nicholas
The Hospital
Teutonic Knights
Patriarchate
Tower of the Legate
German Tower
Montjoie
Genoese quarter
Arsenal
Patriarch's Tower
St Andrew's Church
St Sabas
Venetian quarter
Harbour
The Temple
Pisan quarter
Tower of Flies
Mediterranean
Sea

23. Acre in 1291

them, a great mangonel brought by the army of Hamah on the middle Orontes from Hisn al-Akrad, the magnificent fortress of Crac des Chevaliers captured by Baibars in 1271, was transported in a hundred carts and took a month to be hauled the 125 miles or so to Acre. As the Franks by this stage had no field army, Khalil's passage and investment of the city were unopposed. His combined forces were large enough to surround Acre completely on the landward side. His strategy was simple: pound the walls to rubble, create breaches and then use his superiority of numbers to overwhelm the defenders. The Muslim army probably numbered more than the total civilian population of Acre, which may have stood at around 30–40,000. Some wild estimates claimed the attackers had over 200,000 troops. However large, numbers were the key.

Facing the sultan, the Franks in Acre were not without some advantages. Although the military establishment was comparatively modest, it was still substantial, perhaps 1,000 knights and sergeants with another 14,000 infantry. Reinforced by a few western crusaders, such as Othon of Grandson and his English regiment and a division from Cyprus, the Acre garrison was led and dominated by the military orders, whose discipline, resourcefulness and courage prevented the defence from descending into chaos or panic. Able-bodied civilians were enlisted, and the Venetians and Pisans played a full part, the Venetians manning an especially effective catapult. Accurately assessing the odds, many women, children and the elderly had been evacuated before the siege began, reducing the drain on food and emotion, but many, not least the poorest, remained. The one great advantage the Franks possessed was control of the sea. This allowed supplies to reach the beleaguered city, and King Henry of Cyprus-Jerusalem to arrive with last-minute, if limited, reinforcement on 4 May. The sea also provided a means of attacking the Muslim camps on land, as armoured ships carrying archers, crossbowmen and, in at least one case, a large mangonel, bombarded the flanks of the besiegers' positions where they came down to the shore. However, these attacks inflicted bloody but only superficial damage on the enemy; the mangonel soon broke up in heavy seas.

While the Franks could resist in reasonable security using the twelve towers that studded the outer walls of the city, without a massive infusion of new troops and in the absence of a land force they were doomed to wait for a seemingly inevitable end. Their only realistic chance of survival lay in disrupting the Muslims by inflicting unexpected or unacceptable casualties, thereby opening up the very real fissures in the political high command around the sultan (who was to be assassinated by members of his own government in Egypt only two years later). The spy network run by William of Beaujeu, Master of the Temple, was almost certainly well apprised of such tensions. The only military means to expose any Muslim rivalries was stubborn defence and repeated forays, sometimes at night, into the Muslim camps. These were vividly remembered by veterans such as Ismai 'il Abu'l-Fida, an Ayyubid princeling from Hamah, even if his sharpest memory concerned a botched night attack in which Frankish soldiers tripped over guy-ropes and one fell into an emir's latrine, where he was finished off.[131]

In reality, only a large western fleet (which did not exist) or a miracle could save Acre. As casualties grew, anxieties over the defenders' ability to man the whole length of the walls put a stop to the attacks on the Muslim camp. In desperation, soon after King Henry's arrival an attempt was made to negotiate with the sultan that only served to clarify that Khalil was determined on conquest not accommodation. As the weary days of May passed, Muslim sappers began to have increasing success in undermining the bastions and towers of the outer wall, all the time supported by a hail of missiles, including jars of explosive material, and arrows. By 16 May, the outer enceinte between the walls was abandoned.

The final Muslim assault on the now depleted, hungry and exhausted Frankish defenders came on 18 May, to the accompaniment of a blizzard of arrows and missiles and the encouragement of the usual military drums, cymbals and trumpets. The defences were soon penetrated and fierce street-by-street, hand-to-hand fighting ensued. Few escaped wounds; hundreds if not thousands were killed before the Christians broke for the port. There, ghastly scenes of mayhem, panic, confusion and despair marked the ragged evacuation of survivors. Too few boats caused overcrowding, capsizing and a nasty trade in selling places on the larger vessels. A Catalan Templar captain, Roger Flor, later famous as a freebooter across the Near East, allegedly made a fortune on money extorted from fleeing Frankish noblewomen. Western accounts are lit by stories of heroism and stoicism, none more moving than that displayed by the mortally wounded William of Beaujeu, and tales of rape and violent atrocities. Many of the leaders, including King Henry, managed to escape. Those that stayed were either slaughtered or captured to spend the rest of their lives as slaves or prisoners, the usual sequel to such military disasters. By the evening of 18 May, most of Acre was in Khalil's hands. The fortified Templar quarter, jutting out into the sea at the south-west angle of the city, managed to hold out for another ten days. An attempted parley ended in bloodshed, as Egyptian troops attempted to seize the women and boys sheltering in the Temple complex, and the Templars who had agreed terms with the sultan were summarily executed. Only the halt and the lame remained in the Templar buildings when the final moments came on 28 May. The only consolation afforded the last defenders of Frankish Acre – or perhaps the admiring but absent chronicler who described it – may have been that, as the sultan's troops advanced into the compound, its walls, which had been sapped for over a week, finally collapsed, burying victors and vanquished, perhaps appropriately, in a shared grave.

Once the final resistance had been cleared by the end of May, it became apparent that no immediate counter-attack or succour were possible. The sultan, according to one of his officers, after massacring all surviving defenders, commanded that the city of Acre be 'demolished and razed to the ground'.[132] There was to be no possibility of a repeat of the Third Crusade. By August all the remaining mainland bases had been surrendered or evacuated: Tyre, Sidon, Beirut, Tortosa and Athlit. One eyewitness of the final siege escaped the fall of Acre, an Arabic-speaking Frankish Cypriot who had served on the mainland for over twenty years, ending as the Master of the Temple's secretary and occasional secret agent. He recounted with hammer-blow clarity the heroic death of his employer and the last days of Frankish Acre. This man, whose only home was Outremer, put the events of 1291 in perspective: 'Thus was all of Syria lost . . . This time everything was lost so that altogether the Christians held not so much as a palm's breadth of land in Syria.'[133]

Lamenting western contemporaries did not know it. They and their successors for many generations refused to accept it. A century later, Cypriot noblewomen were still seen going about in public in deep mourning for the loss of Acre.[134] Yet, on its own terms, the attempt by western Europeans to establish and secure rule over the Holy Land and the Holy Places of their religion in the name of Christ had ended in failure.

The Later Crusades

25
The Eastern Crusades in the Later Middle Ages

The evacuation of Frankish holdings on the mainland of Palestine marked a period in the history of the crusades, but not their end. Over subsequent generations, the failure to mount a large, still less effective, western European military campaign against the Mamluks or, later, the Ottoman Turks, shifted the emphasis of wars of the cross while transforming their nature. They became diffused over widely separated front lines in Iberia, the Balkans, eastern, central and northern Europe, narrowly conceived and recruited political campaigns in Italy and small enterprises – often little more than piratical raids – in the Levant. The absence of international action altered the role of crusade ideology, rhetoric, liturgy, ceremony, politics and finance. Crusading did not decline after 1291. It changed, as it had over the previous two centuries since the First Crusade.

This explains the apparent contradiction of crusading throughout the later middle ages; its ineffectiveness failed to destroy sustained communal commitment to the idea or understanding of its ideology and ideals. This was not caused by some sort of collective escapism or mental atrophy. Rather, the crusade mentality, transmitted through long habit, current liturgy and constant renewal in fresh appeals for alms, tax, purchase of indulgences and, occasionally, armed service, framed a way of regarding the world. This mentality, widely dispersed through society, allowed the expression of faith and identity through social rituals and religious institutions without the necessity of individual political or military action. The relative scarcity of *crucesignati* was masked by cultural ubiquity. Independent of fighting and wars, crusading evolved as a state of mind; a means of Grace; a metaphor and mechanism for redemption; a test of human frailty, Divine Judgement and the corruption of society. Crusading became something to be believed in rather than something to do.

Holy war also remained a prominent feature of later medieval Europe for external reasons. The eastern Mediterranean outposts remained under threat. The Mamluk empire gradually consolidated its hold on its thirteenth-century conquests, resisting Mongol attacks on Syria around 1300 and widening its aggression to the seas and coasts of the northern Levant. The Christian enclave of Cilician Armenia, sporadically paraded as a possible base for reconquering the Holy Land, was finally annexed by the Mamluks in 1375. Cyprus remained a target for Egyptian attack far into the fifteenth century. Yet despite a flood of written advice, strenuous diplomacy and occasional assaults on the Levant coast, no major western campaign was assembled to reverse the verdict of 1291. Western European presence in Palestine was reduced to well-heeled pilgrim tourists, spies, merchants and visiting clergy. By the mid-1330s, the Franciscans were established as representatives of the Roman church in Jerusalem, under Mamluk licence.[1] Taking over the Latin sectors within the Holy Sepulchre, as well as the Coenaculum (Upper Room), the tomb of the Virgin Mary and the Grotto of the Nativity in Bethlehem, they devised a package of ritual site-seeing, rerouting the Via Dolorosa and inventing suitably moving ceremonies, including overnight vigils in the church of the Holy Sepulchre and, later, special knightly dubbings with a sword allegedly that of Godfrey of Bouillon. Christian military aggression against the Mamluks only interfered with this steady pilgrim trade. A treaty in 1370 between Egypt and Cyprus explicitly or implicitly secured lasting visiting rights for Latin Christian pilgrims, at a fixed price, providing the circumstances for the continued popularity of this form of religious adventure tourism, which, by 1400, had developed into a routine itinerary of chaperoned site-seeing. However, from the 1330s, a new power disrupted the thirteenth-century settlement. The land-based Ottoman sultanate of north-west Asia Minor gradually established itself as the greatest threat to the integrity of Christendom since the Mongols in the 1240s, and one that proved more durable and more immediate. By the time western Christendom began to succumb to ineradicable and violent religious schism in the sixteenth century, the Ottomans had conquered Greece, the Balkans, Asia Minor and the Mamluk empire, including Palestine, and were battering at the gates of Austria. There remained plenty of scope for anti-Muslim crusading.

IMAGINING THE CRUSADE

One of the most characteristic literary genres of the later middle ages could be described as 'recovery literature', books, pamphlets and memoranda concerned with the crusade, the restoration of Jerusalem and the advance of the Turks. The clerical and lay elites of western Europe found it almost impossible to let go of the Holy Land as a political ambition or vision of perfection. Throughout the fourteenth and fifteenth centuries, governments, moralists, preachers and lobbyists returned again and again to a subject in which practical and moral objectives were fused together. One early fourteenth-century master of the Hospitallers called the crusade 'the nearest route to Paradise'; another grizzled veteran insisted it could 'cure all ills and transform sadness into joy'.[2] The mountain of written advice thrown up in the two centuries after 1291 consistently associated the recovery of the Holy Land or the defence of the church with personal redemption, honour and the resolution of Europe's internal political, social and religious problems. Such ideas circulated as state papers as much as literary ephemera. All rulers contemplating a crusade demanded detailed advice and evidence from their own councillors or agents, from recognized interested parties, for instance the military orders or the Venetians, or from self-appointed experts and lobbyists who disseminated their ideas through networks of contacts, patronage and self-promotion. The former chancellor of Cyprus, Philip of Mézières (1327–1405), ran a corps of propagandists and supplied a stream of pamphlets and longer works. Marino Sanudo Torsello produced a large volume of history in support of his memoranda, engaged a lively scriptorium that produced maps and other crusade literature and exploited his own extensive links with courtiers in England, France, Avignon, Naples and Byzantium.[3] Such figures were taken seriously. Sanudo attended meetings of the French royal council in the 1320s that discussed his plans; seventy years later one of Mézières's agents received a grilling from the dukes of Burgundy and Gloucester over his crusade proposals.[4] These theorists, lobbyists and pamphleteers were not writing necessarily for their own amusement. The context was official interest and action. These writers inhabited the circles they wished to influence, lobbyists and their audience sharing an emotional susceptibility to crusade ideology. The practical intent of these schemes should not be minimized, even if their details fail to convince. Philip VI's doctor Guy of Vigevano's recipe for slug soup was a serious prescription for the avoidance of poisoning on crusade.[5]

The weight of crusade advice reflected a continuing confidence in prospect for the recovery of the Holy Land. Schemes were accompanied by elaborate explanations, with statistics, historical evidence and proofs that varied from the impressive to the banal and absurd. They contributed to setting the strategic orthodoxies that determined planning. The overwhelming fourteenth-century consensus advocated a series of seaborne expeditions to destroy the economic and political power of Egypt. A few voices, usually Iberian, advocated using the land route across North Africa to attack the Nile, but only the advent of the Ottoman threat to eastern Europe revived ideas of using the land route of the First and Second Crusades. Some doubts of the efficacy of mass crusades surfaced, suggested by experience and expense. Sanudo calculated the cost of the initial expeditionary force to Egypt at over 2 million florins, ten times the ordinary annual income of the papacy, an order of magnitude confirmed when governments themselves estimated costs of such campaigns.[6] This awareness of cost explains the often criticized concentration on methods of fundraising that accompanied any serious venture. However, financial problems failed to dissuade governments at least from investigating the possibilities of action, even if difficulties in raising the necessary sums acted as a material disincentive and political block.

However, theory rarely directed action. Neither Sanudo's ideas in the 1320s nor Mézières's in the 1390s were followed. When, half a century later, Bertrandon de la Broquière doubted the feasibility or wisdom of a crusade against the Turks, his employer, Duke Philip of Burgundy, ignored him in pursuit of his plans against the Ottomans.[7] Apart from identifying the difficulty of eastern crusading, the tendency of writers and lobbyists to couch their schemes in the widest context of international reconciliation indicated why their ideas remained unfulfilled. Discussing the obstacles to crusading hardly made them disappear. Equally limiting was the extraordinary conservatism of much crusade advice and theorizing. Rarely at any time in the later middle ages were schemes for eastern crusades uncoupled from the comfortingly familiar call for the recovery of the Holy Land, even when the clear danger came from the Ottoman Turks. Such traditional propaganda paralleled the flourishing Holy Land liturgies of masses, prayers and processions that persisted across western

Europe into the sixteenth century. Linking wars against the Turks with the historic struggle to recover the Holy Land increased the receptiveness of those, at least among courtly elites, whose pious and financial contributions were being sought.

Such traditionalism was never entirely shed by promoters of wars of the cross. However, the new threat of the Ottoman Turks coincided with and possibly provoked fresh interpretations of crusading among humanist historians and scholars, who sought to present the past as a model to inform present and future public behaviour. The drama and success of the First Crusade continued to inspire, but humanist crusade enthusiasts adopted a distinctive perspective. The Florentine chancellor Benedetto Accolti's long history of the First Crusade (1464–6) consistently referred to the Turks and other Muslims as 'barbari', barbarians, implying a classical comparison.[8] For humanist scholars, the crusades and their failure provided a commentary on the state of civil society in the west as well as the more familiar religious exegesis. On this reading, Latin Christendom had inherited the *imperium* of classical Rome, thus the conquest of Palestine was doubly a recovery, of religious space and imperial lands. For some apologists in this line of thought, not least Pope Pius II, who tried hard to organize a new general crusade, the two aspects of crusading united in the institution of the papacy, Christ's vicar and residual legatee of the Roman Empire. The rise of the Ottomans allowed the lack of successful crusading to stand as an illustration of the political as well as moral decadence of Latin Europe in contrast with the disciplined, united and successful Turks, forcing its retention as a central issue of public debate into the sixteenth century.

CRUSADES TO THE EAST

After 1291, and the failure of Nicholas IV's plans to launch an immediate new crusade to recover the Holy Land, international expeditions were seriously planned on three occasions.[9] The Council of Vienne (1311–12) authorized a sexennial clerical tax for the crusade. A year later Philip IV of France hosted an elaborate ceremony in Paris at which he, his sons and his son-in-law, Edward II of England, took the cross. Such gestures had become familiar in the courts of western Europe without necessarily indicating more than a desire for diplomatic respectability, like joining the League of Nations and about as effective. However, Philip invested propagandist effort and possible personal devotion to the cause of the Holy Land. The aura of St Louis was eagerly embraced. Active steps towards a crusade also secured legitimate access to church funds, otherwise highly contentious. While Philip's sincerity should not be dismissed too easily, his death and that of Pope Clement V in 1314, a papal interregnum (1314–16), the collapse of Edward II's political position after his defeat at Bannockburn (1314), and a European famine (1315–17) effectively ended the Vienne crusade. However, Philip V of France sought lay taxes for a new crusade and his successor, Charles IV, attempted to revive serious planning in 1323, sponsoring a flotilla for the east, although it never embarked.[10]

Between 1331 and 1336, Philip VI of France negotiated, planned and prepared for a new Holy Land expedition.[11] He took the cross in October 1333, having secured papal appointment as the church's 'Rector and Captain-general' and the desired massive financial subsidy from Pope John XXII the previous July. Philip jointly sponsored an anti-Turkish naval league with Venice, Byzantium and the Hospitallers (1332–4), and briefly toyed with a small preliminary expedition. However, French policy seemed more directed towards a new general *passagium* on the precedent of 1248 or 1270. While undoubtedly attracting the greatest chance of heavy papal subventions, such a strategy flew in the face of the realities of contemporary international politics. Only if Philip were able to engineer peace on his frontiers and across western Europe could his planned departure in 1336 be achieved. With the dispute between the papacy and the German king, Louis IV, unresolved, Italy at war and the Iberian monarchies disengaged, prospects seemed clouded. More damaging were relations between France, England and Scotland. Although Edward III of England had been involved in crusade diplomacy from at least 1332, the English attempts (1332–5) to subdue Scotland and oust Philip's ally David Bruce (1329–71) as king of Scots rendered serious cooperation impossible. A new pacific pope, Benedict XII, was reluctant to allow Philip any flexibility in how he spent (or, more properly, diverted or misspent) the crusade taxes. The French king, aware that the English might take advantage of his absence, made his departure for the east dependent on a settlement in Scotland. Raising men, money and materials also proved far more difficult than Philip had anticipated. The crusade project was cancelled in 1336. The fleet intended for the

Levant was subsequently directed to the Channel for the early preliminaries of the Hundred Years' War (1337–1453), a conflict that sounded the knell not just for Philip VI's crusade schemes but for any substantial international campaign in the eastern Mediterranean. Benedict XII's cancellation of the crusade removed a diplomatic restraint from both parties, which precipitated the outbreak of open hostilities a year later.

It has been argued that the somewhat sclerotic organization for the crusade before 1336 suggested a lukewarm attitude to the venture, especially among certain of the factions that dominated Philip VI's court, and that the crusade was abandoned because it looked increasingly risky. While the latter is self-evident, the accusation of a lack of commitment underestimates the chances Philip took, not least in expending political capital trying unsuccessfully to extract a lay subsidy in 1335–6. Equally, the crusade helped Philip establish the claim by his new royal dynasty, the Valois, to the authority inherent in the religion of monarchy created by his Capetian predecessors, especially St Louis. The administrative and diplomatic effort had been considerable, and reached beyond France in the embrace of clerical taxation and authorized preaching. What is more, as predicted by one French crusading hopeful, failure or deceit would attract 'la honte du monde', disgrace in the eyes of the world.[12] Reactions varying from resigned embarrassment to savage denunciation for hypocrisy echoed around the courts and commentators. Contemporaries accused Philip of using the crusade as a smokescreen behind which he prepared war against the English. Some ascribed his failures in that war to this supposed deceit. Decades later, Philip of Mézières, a boy in Picardy at the time, recalled clearly the unfortunate consequences of Philip VI's failure.[13] The memory was stitched into the narratives of recent events popular around 1400 on both sides of the Channel. The ambition of 1332 and, still more, the decision of 1336 remained to haunt the Valois kings of France.

The last concerted diplomatic effort to arrange a new general *passagium* directly against the Mamluks had to await the great truce in the Hundred Years War 1360–69. King Peter I of Cyprus (1359–69) was eager to enlist western aid for his ambitious policy to protect Cypriot trade in the Levant by destabilizing the Mamluk regime and its grip over the trade routes that passed through Alexandria.[14] Recent relaxation of papal embargoes on western commerce with Egypt stimulated Peter to bolder action. In 1361, he had taken the southern Turkish port of

Adalia. In 1362, tapping the traditional enthusiasms of western chivalry, Peter gave notice of a new campaign to recover the Holy Land, a declaration he followed with a personal visit to the major capitals of Europe, from England, Flanders and France to Poland and Bohemia. He had managed to gain Pope Urban V's support at a conference at Avignon in March and April 1363 attended by a large and distinguished gathering, including King John II of France, Amadeus count of Savoy, the Master of the Hospitallers and the English Thomas of Beauchamp earl of Warwick. The climax of the conference came with the reception of the cross by these luminaries and the new papal legate Elias of Périgord, Cardinal Talleyrand, a veteran diplomat. New crusade taxes were proposed, preaching authorized and indulgences offered. The protagonists at Avignon became immortalized in Andrea Bonaiuti's fresco of the Church Militant in St Maria Novella, Florence.[15]

The results of Peter I's grand tour of Europe in 1362–5 fell short of the extravagant hopes of the Avignon conference. John II and Cardinal Talleyrand both died in 1364. Crusade management devolved on to Peter I, and his advisors, the new crusade legate Pierre de Thomas (d. 1366), already legate in the east, and his chancellor, Philip of Mézières. Money from Pope Urban paid for a significant body of hired troops, including English mercenaries, possibly from the English Free Company based at Pisa. Leaving Venice in June 1365, Peter made his rendezvous with Cypriot and Hospitaller reinforcements in August, the combined fleet perhaps numbering 165 ships, capable of carrying a substantial body of men – as many as 10,000 has been suggested – and their horses. Recruits came from as far as Scotland, France, Geneva and England. The English mercenary contingent was commanded by an English noble, possibly the earl of Hereford.[16] However, the polyglot nature of the forces at King Peter's disposal did not tend to cohesion or unity of purpose, tactics or strategy. While the decision to attack Egypt's main port, Alexandria, was the king's, even on the first day of fighting one group of barons almost immediately suggested a withdrawal to avoid pointless casualties, implying that they thought the whole enterprise futile.

The campaign comprised a stunning victory, an embarrassing retreat and a huge, if tainted, profit. Against all expectations, Alexandria, one of the best-defended ports in the Mediterranean, fell by storm on the first day of fighting, 10 October 1365. Once inside the city, the Christians spent the following week massacring thousands of civilians in rapidly securing vast quantities of booty from one of the richest entrepôts in the world then known to Europeans. It was not a pretty sight; but it appeared, not least to Egyptian eyewitnesses, thoroughly effective, even if the parallels lay less with Constantinople in 1204 than with Damietta in 1249. Sudden success prompted an immediate row. Later apologists depicted King Peter, Pierre de Thomas and Mézières arguing for the retention of Alexandria as a lever to secure the return of Jerusalem. Others, equally well versed in crusade history, insisted the military position of the crusaders was untenable. Better to cut and run with the enormous booty than insist on a futile sacrificial gesture. Prudence prevailed, the Christians evacuating Alexandria on 16 October.

Peter possibly agreed with this analysis. He would have understood that without a promise of a massive relief force, the road from Alexandria led nowhere. Cypriot interests lay in disrupting Alexandrian trade to favour their own ports. By presenting the west with such a dramatic, startling and lucrative victory, the first on such a scale since 1249, Peter may also have hoped to provide impetus for fresh anti-Mamluk commitment at a time when popes and princes were increasingly distracted by the Turks further north. The novelty of Peter's crusade scheme of 1362–5 lay in the active leadership by an eastern Latin ruler of a western crusade, a coalition as obvious as it was rare. If Peter hoped to create a sensation, he succeeded. Encomiasts, such as Mézières, and the fashionable French poet and musician Guillaume de Machaut, in his verse epic *La Prise d'Alexandre* left vivid – if politically and morally pointed – accounts.[17] The English monastic chronicler Thomas Walsingham recorded that not only did the cost of spices rise as a consequence of the sack of Alexandria but many English and Gascons returned from Egypt with 'cloth of gold, silks and splendid exotic jewels in witness of such a victory achieved there'.[18] Despite criticism of the evacuation and the easily caricatured greed of the troops, the capture of Alexandria retained its lustre as a campaign honour whose renown Geoffrey Chaucer, who knew many of the real veterans, was careful to borrow for his Knight in the *Canterbury Tales*.[19]

Yet Peter I's strategy, whether of conquest or trade war, failed utterly. The 1365 crusade disintegrated with the evacuation; the next western crusading venture was conducted by the count of Savoy in 1366–7 in the Dardenelles and Black Sea. A few further Cypriot raids on the

Levantine coast over the next few years and another extensive western progress by King Peter in 1367–8 achieved nothing. Peter himself was assassinated in 1369, a victim of Cypriot feuding that rarely declined from the vicious. In fact, he had begun negotiations with the Mamluks in 1366. After his death, a Cypriot-Egyptian peace treaty was agreed. As it transpired, this ended the last crusade specifically directed at the Mamluks who controlled the Holy Land. Priorities changed, despite the cloak of traditional rhetoric. While both Cyprus and the Hospitallers of Rhodes regularly secured truces, treaties and accommodations with the Mamluks, the new power of the Ottoman Turks redirected the use of the crusade.

EXPANSION AND RETRACTION

Traditional eastern Mediterranean crusading operated in the context of a much wider application of wars of the cross. Crusade institutions – vow, cross, indulgence, privileges – continued to be associated with an expanding list of armed conflicts. The professionalism of recruitment and organization, by encouraging vow redemptions, alms and legacies, extended the social reach of involvement while risking the frustration of those forced to be non-combatant participants in an increasingly ritualized activity. By concentrating on the redemptive benefits of the cross to encourage donations, sermons *de cruce* lent themselves to wider penitential and eschatological themes than the crusade. By precept and analogy, crusading was stitched into the broad evangelism of the church and, hence, into religious experience, attitudes and expectations. The crusade also became a feature of state public finance. The availability of huge sums of money derived from church property through regular crusade clerical taxation and fundraising often proving irresistible to lay rulers.

The Registers of official correspondence of Innocent IV, a distinguished canon lawyer who himself wrote on the theory of just war, had shown just how extensively the crusade was applied to a variety of political conflicts.[20] Preaching of the cross was ordered against Frederick II; his son Conrad IV; the duke of Bavaria; Hohenstaufen supporters generally; Livs and Balts in Livonia and Prussia; Mongols; the irreligious in Sardinia; Muslims in Spain, Africa and Palestine; Greeks threatening the Latin Empire of Constantinople; alleged heretics in Italy, Lombardy and Bosnia; and Ezzelino of Romano. At other times, targets included the Drenther peasants in the diocese of Utrecht (1228–32); Stedinger peasants of the Lower Weser (1232–4); Russian Greek Orthodox (beginning in 1240); Finns (certainly in 1257 and from 1348); political opponents of the kings of England (1216–17 and 1265); Sicilians and Aragonese (1283–1302); Piedmontese cultic followers of the charismatic Fra Dolcino (1306–7); a gazetteer of Italian city states from 1255, including Venice (1310) and Milan (from 1360); the Canary Islands (planned in 1344); various Turkish emirs in the Aegean (from the 1330s); fourteenth-century mercenary companies, or *routiers* (from 1357), that fed on the opportunities and spoils of the Anglo-French and Italian wars; supporters of both sides during the Great Schism of the papacy (1378–1417), chiefly in the 1380s; Bohemian Hussites (from 1420); and, of course, the Ottomans. Of the scores of campaigns of the cross in the centuries after Louis IX's defeat in 1250 some answered urgent military necessity or traditional strategic ambition. Others were the result of allies' political pressure on the papacy to grant status and access to church funds to assist recruitment, diplomacy and war finance. The papacy was not necessarily a soft touch. Gregory IX instituted a careful investigation into the alleged heresy of the Stedinger peasants in the diocese of Bremen before authorizing a crusade to suppress then in 1232.[21] John XXII refused to accept the arguments of Philip V of France in 1318 that his enemies, the Flemish, were on a level with Saracens because, as excommunicates, their hostility to French policy impeded an eastern crusade.[22] John's successors remained reluctant to apply crusade formulae on behalf of the French during the Hundred Years War. Some popes were more enthusiastic for wars in the eastern Mediterranean; others for wars in Italy; others for a generally more pacific approach to Christendom's ills.

This expanded use of crusading followed changing patterns of international politics and diplomacy. Intractable disputes in the western Mediterranean between Naples, Sicily and Aragon in the late thirteenth century were superseded by bitter internecine Italian rivalries throughout the fourteenth century, driven by revived German imperial interest in the peninsula, papal absence in Avignon (1309–77) and the rise of the *signoria* in the endlessly competing city states of Tuscany and Lombardy. To all of these, crusading privileges were assigned at some stage. The

Hundred Years War may not have attracted crusading, except during the Great Schism, but much of the rhetoric advocating a negotiated peace was constructed in the context of first the recovery of the Holy Land and then defence against the advancing Turks. Far from an expression of cultural antiquarianism, the crusade retained practical resonance. It also continued to supply an ostensibly neutral and generally respected context and excuse for diplomatic settlement and compromise, from Scandinavia to the Mediterranean. Crusade talk was not necessarily cynical, hypocritical or sentimental double speak, although such elements existed. During the two long periods of truce between England and France in the 1360s and 1390s, crusade planning and action were conducted through the cooperation of former enemies. Failure to secure peace could elicit accusations of hindering the cause of the Holy Land or Christendom. Traditional formulae persisted into the sixteenth century.

Nonetheless, by the fifteenth century, the scope of crusading – action, institutions and rhetoric – had contracted, its nature changing as a consequence. Again, the dialectic of decline misses the point. Very crudely, in terms of material activity and international political attention, crusades to the Holy Land dominated the period 1188 to 1250; those in Italy from 1250 to the late fourteenth century; the wars with the Turks from the late fourteenth to the end of the sixteenth century.[23] The Italian and Turkish conflicts inevitably merged more seamlessly into their local, political, non-crusading settings than had the campaigns to Palestine or Egypt, even if the legal status was presented by the papacy as identical. Outside Iberia and, to a lesser extent after 1300, north-eastern Europe, the crusade was attached primarily to defensive operations: to resist Mamluks, Turkish pirates or the Ottomans; to extirpate the *routiers*; or to defeat those who, in papal eyes, were trampling on the church's rights and threatening its patrimony in Italy. Even where the military campaigns were offensive, such as in the Aegean in the 1330s and 1340s or during the Italian wars, the conventional justification remained that of defence, Christendom in danger. This persuasive device had formed part of the language of crusading since the 1090s. Yet before 1250 many of the wars supported by such justifications had actually been campaigns of aggression, notably the attacks of Egypt. After 1250, no similar offensives left the drawing board. Even the Nicopolis campaign of 1396, which saw a western European army fighting the Turks on the Lower Danube, was framed as part of the defence of Hungary, even if optimists hoped for a subsequent war of reconquest. By the fifteenth century the problem of crusading had become subsumed into the perceived problem of Europe, a question of cultural and political survival against what appeared, at least until the successful defences of Belgrade (1456) and Rhodes (1480), an inexorable force. As Pius II warned in 1463: 'Christendom is reduced to an angle of the world.'[24]

The strategic shift during the fourteenth century from plans to reinvade the Near East to desperate attempts to shore up the frontiers of Latin Christian Europe itself coincided with a contraction of crusading destinations. Louis IX's Egyptian campaign had no successors: it was the last occasion when a substantial land army from western Europe attempted to conquer or reconquer territory in the eastern Mediterranean. Nicopolis and Belgrade apart, all subsequent attacks on Mamluks and Turks represented either naval raids or rapid seaborne assaults, equivalent to the small, fast-moving scorched-earth sorties of the Hundred Years' War known as *chevauchées*. Of the attacks on Smyrna (1344), Adalia (1361), Alexandria (1365), Tripoli (1367, 1403) or Beirut (1403), only Smyrna was occupied (1344–1402). The exception was Rhodes, conquered and settled by the Hospitallers (1306–10). However, the success of the Hospitallers had not come as a result of a general crusade. Their presence in Rhodes until 1522 illustrated how Christian warfare in the eastern Mediterranean became a function of local interests – Venice, Genoa, Cyprus as well as the Hospitallers – rather than the imperatives of western Christendom. The elaborate fiscal administration established by the Second Lyons Council in 1274 was used as a universal system for less than half a century. The last general clerical crusade tithe, imposed and levied throughout Christendom, was granted by the Council of Vienne in 1312 and collected between 1313 and 1319. Thereafter the system was employed for regionally or nationally limited taxes. During the thirteenth century, central ecclesiastical administration of non-fiscal crusade matters, such as privileges, protection of property and legal immunities, was placed under the papal penitentiary, which acted as a sort of curial clearing-house. Yet this more coherent and more bureaucratic structure wholly failed to translate into crusade action.

Some of the main features of crusading enterprise of the thirteenth century and before fell away in the generations after 1250. The wars in the Baltic were almost exclusively subcontracted to the Teutonic Knights or to the kings of Denmark and Sweden. There was limited international participation in Iberian wars against the Moors, which, as well as being infrequent, had become the preserve of royal governments, until the later fifteenth century as much vehicles of finance and self-image as serious attempts to oust the Muslims from Granada. The mainly unsuccessful attempts by successive popes from the 1230s to launch crusades against the Greeks in defence of Latin Romania were compromised by parallel attempts at the union of the Roman and Greek Orthodox churches from the 1270s. After the death of Charles of Anjou in 1285, strenuous and persistent diplomatic efforts to involve the French royal family in Greece produced few tangible results. By 1320, despite the anti-Latin policies of the Byzantine emperor, Andronicus II, prospects for an anti-Greek crusade had effectively ended. Never popular in the west, such plans had consistently failed to be supported by extensive preaching or successful fundraising. After the 1320s, western policy turned to attempts to ally with the Greeks against Turkish pirates and acquisitive emirs in the Aegean. As with the Greeks, moves in the years before and after 1300 to accommodate another former enemy, the Mongols, removed another crusade target. The Mongol successor state of the Golden Horde in what is now southern Russia and the Ukraine began to operate within the orbit of the secular politics of eastern Europe, one competing power amidst the rivalries of Lithuania, Poland, Novgorod, Hungary and the Teutonic Knights. Only rarely could the interests of a Christian power extract a papal grant of crusade privileges against the Golden Horde, as in 1345, when the Genoese were defending their Crimean trading base at Caffa.[25] Only a very few new applications for crusading privileges appeared, such as the abortive plans and attempts to conquer the Canary Islands in 1344–5 and 1402, justified by the principle of the expansion (*dilatio*), not just defence, of the faith, later a potent argument employed in the European penetration of the Atlantic and the Americas.[26]

THE FALL OF THE TEMPLARS

As another symptom of contraction, one of the most prominent military, ideological and institutional features of active crusading was attacked and transformed. By 1291, the reputation of the military orders had long been equivocal. No observer could ignore their contribution to the cause of the cross on all fronts. Yet other clerical interest groups resented the orders for their papally protected privileges. Their demands for profit from their extensive estates in the west, although justified as a means of funding war in the east, aroused resentment from their tenants. Secular rulers, notably the kings of France, relied on their banking skills, especially those of the Templars, to help manage royal finance. Rulers regarded the orders' autonomy and supposed wealth with envy and suspicion even as they employed their leaders in secular government. The Masters and regional heads of the orders occupied important positions as representatives of large landed corporations in all the kingdoms of western Europe. In Spain, their autonomy was gradually eroded by the determined royal patronage and increasing control, until they became by the end of the middle ages almost an arm of the state. Hermann von Salza played a major political role in imperial politics under Frederick II and, as a prince of the empire, helped create a unique order-state in Prussia. In France, the Temple in Paris acted as a sort of national bank in the thirteenth century, closely integrated into servicing royal finances. In England the Priors of the Hospital sat in the House of Lords, some even acted as the king's treasurer, such as Joseph Chauncy (1273–80) or Robert Hales (1381), the veteran of the Christian attack on Alexandria in 1365 who paid for his involvement in government with his life at the hands of rebels in London during the Peasants' Revolt of 1381.[27]

However, the loss of the Holy Land in 1291 cast the very function of the orders into doubt. The Teutonic Knights, in the years around 1300, were vigorously attacked by the local Livonian church hierarchy, who accused them of cruelty, greed, friendship with pagans, larceny and violence against the church. The Knights were saved by their continuing role as defenders, with their blood and treasure, of the Christians of Livonia against the pagan Lithuanians. Even so, their escape from papal censure and suppression was a close-run thing.[28] The Order of St John could still claim their original hospitaller calling. Yet, almost from the earliest days of the militarized religious communities in the mid-twelfth century, writers had noted the rivalries and divisions between the orders, from the Egyptian wars of the 1160s to the civil wars of later thirteenth-century Outremer. Sermons and chronicles may have included elevating anecdotes of the special Christian heroism of members of the orders, yet the darker aspect of their reputation could not be dispelled, especially once mainland Outremer fell.

The loss of the orders' great fortresses in Syria and Palestine represented a potentially terminal threat to the orders' occupation. Reform was suggested at the Second Lyons Council of 1274. Scandal had never been far from some military orders, unregulated by local ecclesiastical authority and institutionally introspective as their calling made them. The suppression of the Swordbrothers in 1237 could be seen only as an extreme – or publicized – example of the pitfalls inherent in a corporate ideal that insisted on the awkward marriage of religious conventual exclusivity with close and necessary involvement in secular affairs – war, diplomacy, finance and property. Some of these temporal snares were common to all religious orders, many of which attracted similar complaints of corruption throughout the middle ages. However, the military orders were more vulnerable. Their vocation, perched at an extreme of cultural acceptability, had always been controversial in some quarters. Unlike other religious orders, the success of a military order could, in a sense, be tested by tangible, not just imagined spiritual, results. Defeat in the Holy Land indicated clear failure. The cause could only be God's displeasure, provoked by contumacious sin. The military orders thus stood as symbols – potential scapegoats – for the perceived moral failings of Christendom.[29]

Criticism, not all of it consistent, grew in scope after 1274. The orders were accused of being corrupt. Their ineffectual worldiness required the disendowment of their estates situated away from the frontlines. The orders should be amalgamated into one super-order to provide a well-funded, disciplined core for attempts to recover and defend the Holy Land. Some even argued that rule in a reconquered Holy Land should be vested in such a united order and its head, a *Bellator Rex*, recruited from one of the royal houses of the west. There was no consensus behind these ideas, the Master of the Temple, Jacques de Molay (1292–1314), for one arguing against union. Some critics appeared as enthusiastic for the idea of military orders as they were hostile to their practice. Others admired the model of an order-state pioneered by the Teutonic Knights. These ideas did not remain the preserve of theorists and lobbyists. In 1291, Nicholas IV instructed provincial church councils to consider the orders' future. At least four (Arles, Canterbury, Lyons and Norwich) supported a merger, as did Charles II of Naples, son of Charles of Anjou and a claimant to the throne of Jerusalem.[30] While between 1305 and 1307 the Masters of the Temple and Hospital added their own opinions, unsurprisingly supportive of their orders, the weight of advice 1290–1312 urged at least reform of the orders, if not union or a new order altogether.

The arrest, persecution, trials and final suppression of the Templars did not, therefore, come from nowhere.[31] Beginning with the arrest of all Templars in France on Friday 13 October 1307 (allegedly the origin for the ill-omen of Friday 13th), punctuated by torture, confessions, recantations and burnings, the sordid process was driven by officials of the king of France, appeased by the papal Curia and the other monarchs of western Europe. The attack culminated in the order's suppression by Clement V at the Council of Vienne in 1312 and the final, brusque execution by burning of the last Master in Paris in 1314. The assault on the Templars became notorious for the luridness of the accusations against them, the barbarism of the use of torture by French inquisitors, the inconsistent leadership of Clement V, the confused defence mounted by the order and the single-minded ruthlessness of Philip IV of France and his ministers, especially Guillaume de Plaisians and Guillaume de Nogaret. The ambitious but sporadically spendthrift Philip IV may have wanted control of Templar propertied wealth. He may also genuinely have believed them to have failed in their holy mission, to which he possibly held a sincere attachment.[32]

If so, he was by no means alone. Pious conviction, self-righteous brutality and myopic moral certainty are familiar partners. There existed sufficient belief in the justice of their cause among the French persecutors and the watching secular and ecclesiastical elites of western Christendom to sustain a campaign of oppression that reeked of hypocrisy, mendacity and avarice as well as cruelty. The charges of blasphemy, sodomy, irregular and obscene ceremonies, the common currency of formal ecclesiastical abuse, were lent added plausibility by the perception of dereliction of duty. The low grade of Templar membership, comprising a worryingly high number of dim, often elderly and politically inadequate minor nobility, did not enhance their defence or inspire confidence in the order's long-term value or viability. The garbled accounts of peculiar, half-remembered admission rituals may indicate some strange practices, not uncommon in closed, secretive elite male societies. Yet the confessions to the substantive charges appear mainly to have been extracted under torture, the trauma of public humiliation and sudden loss of liberty or the threat of violence. When led to the stake by his persecutors in 1314, the unfortunate Jacques de Molay insisted on his and his order's innocence of all charges, a protestation *in extremis* from an unsubtle man of apparent sincere faith that perhaps should command credence. Clement V refused to bow to French pressure to condemn the order, merely citing its irredeemable loss of reputation as the cause for its suppression in 1312 without a verdict of guilt or innocence. Clement even wrong-footed the French persecutors by granting the confiscated Templar property to the Hospitallers.

The Templar scandal exerted a significant influence on the future direction of the two largest surviving military orders. The Teutonic Knights narrowly avoided the similar, perhaps better-merited, fate of dissolution after another inquiry begun by Clement V in 1308. Fresh from having only just escaped condemnation by Boniface VIII, the order at Riga was briefly excommunicated in 1312–13. Hard lobbying and the order's role in Prussia and German imperial politics saved them, rather than any marked change in public or private behaviour, which continued to attract hostile comment, including a critical papal verdict in 1324 over the Livonian affair, before resurfacing prominently at the Council of Constance (1414–18).[33] The Hospitallers too were not immune to external scrutiny, some of it highly critical, at times menacing, as when Pope Innocent VI threatened to impose reform from without.[34]

Both orders learnt from the Templar debacle that protection lay in physical security. After 1291, the Hospitallers, like the Templars, had been based in Cyprus; the Teutonic Knights in Venice. Between 1306 and 1310, the Hospitallers conquered the island of Rhodes, transferring their headquarters there in 1309. The same year, the Master of the Teutonic Knights moved to the distant safety of Marienburg (Marlbork) in Prussia. Both orders were now settled in their own order-states. The timing was hardly accidental, precisely coinciding with the trials of the Templars. From these moves the orders gained protection and a restatement of their vocations as warriors of Christ on the frontiers of Christendom. Whatever the compromises with supposed enemies across the religious frontier – and there were many – the relocation of the military orders altered their role. The Teutonic Knights effectively abandoned the eastern Mediterranean while the Hospitallers created an independent eastern Mediterranean principality. Although still supported by estates across all of Europe – Rhodes receiving its western profits in the form of annual 'responsions' – both orders now operated behind their own palisades as sovereigns, at no one's beck and call except their own. By doing so, they helped shape the later medieval pattern of devolved and local campaigns in the east, which replaced the grand international expeditions of earlier generations in tackling the great new crusading venture of the later middle ages.

THE OTTOMAN TURKS

One of about ten emirates arising from the debris of the collapsed Seljuk sultanate of Rum in the later thirteenth century, the Ottomans fed on the carcass of the Byzantine empire.[35] While their rivals to the south engaged in piracy in the Aegean, attracting naval leagues under papal auspices in 1332–4 and 1343–5, leading to the capture and occupation of Smyrna (1344–1405) and a futile campaign by Humbert, dauphin of Vienne (1345–6), the Ottomans posed a different problem. Originating in the area around Bursa in north-west Asia Minor, the Ottomans, followers of Osman and his son Orkhan (1326–62), began to annexe lands along the Sea of Marmora, reaching the Bosporus and Dardenelles by the 1330s. While other Turkish mercenaries were defending Smyrna from the Christian Holy League, in 1345 Orkhan was hired by a claimant to the Byzantine throne, John VI Cantacuzene, to fight in Thrace during the imperial civil war, first against rival Greeks then against invading Serbs. The Ottomans soon secured their own bases in the Gallipoli peninsula, Gallipoli itself falling in 1354. An Ottoman empire was being created in Europe, not Asia, on land, not around easily accessible coasts.

Alarm at Ottoman advances in Thrace led to the first crusading coalitions to stop them. An offshoot of the crusade plans of Urban V and Peter I of Cyprus, a small expedition commanded by Count Amadeus VI of Savoy in 1366–7 succeeded in capturing Gallipoli and a number of Black Sea ports.[36] This hardly gave the Ottomans pause. Around 1369, they took Adrianople (Erdine), which became their capital. By the end of the century, after their defeat of Serbia at Kossovo in 1389, they dominated the Balkans between the Danube and Gulf of Corinth. While the spirited but ill-conducted crusade that was crushed at Nicopolis on the Danube in 1396 served only to consolidate Ottoman power, their defeat by Timur in 1402 spared central Europe immediate further assault. Under Murad II pressure was resumed. Gradually, assisted by confessional and political bickering among their Christian opponents, the Ottomans conquered the whole of the Balkans, as well as Asia Minor and Anatolia. The capture of the long-isolated Constantinople in 1453 by Mehmed II the Conqueror led to the absorption of the rest of Latin and Byzantine Greece by the mid-1460s and Venetian Negroponte in 1470. After a generation of relative peace after Mehmed's death, Selim I the Grim and Suleiman I the Magnificent conquered Mamluk Syria, Palestine and Egypt (1516–17), Belgrade (1521), Rhodes (1522–3) and most of Hungary after the crushing victory at Mohacs (1526). Vienna was besieged, but not taken, in 1529. This transformation of the political map of eastern Europe and the Mediterranean was conducted on the ideological terrain of the wars of the cross. Yet, the improbably successful defence of Belgrade in 1456 aside, no crusade had done much to prevent it.

Remarkably, compared with the number of sermons preached, taxes levied and indulgences sold, active crusading against the Turks remained a sideshow. Even at the height of the Ottoman threat to central Europe, when in 1463 Pius II was pointing to their presence 'from the Black Sea to Hungary, from the Aegean shore to the Danube', planners felt the need to associate their grander schemes of resistance with the pipe-dream of the recovery of the Holy Land.[37] Yet this was no distant war that relied on dedicated rhetorical fictions and religious empathy to render it immediate, as was the case with the Holy Land. The Greek émigré Cardinal John Bessarion argued, in 1463, that the Ottomans threatened 'our country, our homes, our children, our family, and our wives' as they wished 'to subjugate the entire world starting with Italy'.[38] Four years earlier, a papal legate told Henry VI of England that Ottoman dominance of the Danube threatened the Rhine and hence English interests directly. The later fifteenth-century English House of Commons feared lest the Ottoman conquests interrupt the supply of bowstaves from the Crimea.[39] Scare-mongering of Italy in danger did not appear fanciful when Otranto was briefly occupied in 1480. The chances of a Turkish conquest of Rome, of Italian Renaissance artists serving an Ottoman sultan were not entirely remote. As a barometer of their success, the demonized Turk replaced the Saracen as a western European catch-all bogeyman.

Yet this perception of the Ottomans as constituting a danger to the traditional integrity of Latin Christendom took generations to become established in the imagination and policies of the west, never fully eradicating the luminous image of the lost Holy Land as a metaphor of Christian failure. There were several reasons for this. The initial victims of Ottoman conquest were as liable to be schismatic Greeks as Catholics. The tangled politics of Byzantium, Latin Greece and the Christian Balkans lacked the resonance of the recovery of the Holy Land, which was sustained by a widespread liturgy of supplication, intercession and sacrament. Only in the fifteenth century did the Turk even compete for the prayers of the faithful.[40] Confusion and wishful thinking, often attendant on crusading, were rife. When Urban V authorized his new crusade in the east in 1363, he made no distinction between the Mamluks and the Turks.[41].

Conceptual obstacles paled beside practical difficulties. The early strategy (*c.*1332–67) of small naval leagues or modest amphibious attacks on the littoral of Greece and Asia Minor hardly matched the military resources of the Ottomans as they advanced into the Balkans. The Ottomans' was a land empire, not a thalassocracy. A further debilitating problem lay in the implacable enmity between potentially the most important providers of transport, the Genoese and the Venetians, the former as often as not actively allying with the Turks to steal material advantage over their ancient commercial rivals whose empire the Ottomans were eroding. The alternative, a mass land attack by western powers in conjunction with local rulers, never materialized, except in very attenuated forms in 1396, 1444 and 1456. Even the growing acceptance of a land route for a new crusade, while recognizing the plight of eastern Europe, was often justified in terms of Godfrey of Bouillon, not Mehmed the Conqueror.

THE TURKS AND BYZANTIUM

The nature of the Ottoman threat distinguished them from previous Asiatic opponents of Byzantium.[42] By 1300, the Ottomans had lost or adapted their steppe-based nomadic culture, which had first brought them to Asia Minor. Long before the establishment of their capital at Adrianople (Erdine), their political system revolved around a settled polity, no longer reliant on pasturage and a nomadic lifestyle. Being an

Ottoman depended on loyalty to the ruling dynasty not ethnic origin or identity: Ottoman, follower of Osman/Uthman, the eponymous, semi-legendary founder of the dynasty's greatness. As with Christian political communities, religious observance supplied the signifying social and propagandist glue. In this, the Ottomans copied the Byzantines. Just as Latins and Turks and other barbarians had perennially become Byzantine before 1204, so Greeks became Ottomans, including, after the fall of Constantinople in 1453, members of the imperial family itself and their courtiers. Although insistent on Islam, the Ottomans were not fighting religious wars, even if they relied on traditional *jihad* rhetoric. Their early proximity to the Byzantine frontier probably encouraged this, an inscription in their first capital Bursa describing Sultan Orkhan as a '*mujahid*, sultan of the *ghazis* (i.e. holy warriors), *ghazi* son of *ghazi*', a useful recruiting and disciplining ploy.[43] However, Ottoman policy was essentially secular: dynastic aggrandizement, wealth, power, domination, not conversion. They allied with peoples regardless of religion. They tolerated the faiths of their subjects provided they remained loyal. Ottoman success was a product of cultural similarity and contact with their neighbours and adversaries. The great fifteenth-century Albanian resistance leader and Christian hero Scanderbeg (d. 1468) had begun his career as an Ottoman hostage, becoming a Muslim in the service of Murad II, who gave him his name – Alexander Bey. He converted to Roman Catholicism to ease an alliance with the rulers of Naples across the Adriatic.[44] Western travellers who stayed at the Ottoman court, such as the Burgundian spy Bertrandon de la Broquière in the 1420s, did not depict them as barbarians. The French crusader Marshal Boucicaut, a veteran of Nicopolis, defender of Constantinople in 1399 and attacker of the Syrian coast in 1403, once offered to serve under Bayezid I (1389–1403).[45] While in the 1460s, Pius II and his agents were content to fall back on tired if lurid hyperbole of barbarism, the Turks as 'savage beasts in human form', Cardinal Bessarion recognized the rational secular imperative behind Ottoman policies: 'He invades foreign lands so as not to lose his own.'[46] The Ottoman conquest of Byzantium hardly fits a scheme of an immemorial clash of cultures or religion, Gibbon's 'World's Debate'.

The history of Asia Minor and the Balkans in the later middle ages cannot be explained in confessional terms. The rhetoric of religious confrontation imposed (and imposes) a pattern on events favoured by contemporary apologists, diplomats and polemicists that hardly corresponded to experience. Despite the individual and collective human tragedies inevitable in military conflict and conquest, the Ottoman advances did not constitute unalloyed disaster. Late medieval Byzantium had failed to bring order, peace and civility to the region once under its sway, a failure reaching back beyond 1204 into the twelfth century. The Ottomans restored the geographic, political and economic coherence of the old Greek empire. The Turks entered Europe as vassals and allies of the Byzantine emperor. The Ottoman empire as such, as opposed to the Ottoman dynasty, began in Europe, not Asia. Rival Greek imperial dynasties in the fourteenth century married into the Ottoman sultan's family. Serb Christian cavalry fought for the Turks at Nicopolis in 1396 (against crusaders) and at Ankara in 1402. Genoese helped Murad II defeat a dangerous western crusade in 1444. Christian allies fought with the Turks at the final storming of Constantinople in 1453, an event actually welcomed by some disaffected Greek Orthodox divines. Holy war remained largely a western luxury that Greeks and other inhabitants of the Balkans could ill afford. In the region of Thessalonica, the people's preferences expressed this complexity. Conquered by the Turks in the 1380s, the region was restored to Byzantine control in 1403. Under the Ottomans, direct taxation increased (via the *kharaj* or poll tax on non-Muslim 'People of the Book', Christians and Jews) but the rents paid by peasants to landlords decreased, lightening the net fiscal burden. After 1403, the Greeks maintained the Ottoman tax regime, two-thirds of proceeds going to the monks of Mt Athos, who, in 1384, had advocated support for the Muslim Turks against what they regarded as a heretical Greek emperor (John V Palaeologus).[47] Such cross-currents were typical.

The crusade against the Turks consequently failed to correspond with the political context or military requirements of the Ottoman advance. Western efforts fell into two general phases. The first, interrupted by the collapse of Ottoman power after their defeat by Timur the Lame in 1402, concerned the defence of Byzantium, a task that had failed utterly by the 1460s. The second, consequent on the first, lay in the defence of Latin Christian territories in eastern and central Europe. At the heart of the muddled western response to the Turk lay a reluctance to abandon the conceptual reassurance of Holy Land polemic even in the face of detailed advice and evidence of how Ottoman power worked from spies and veterans of Turkish wars. The traditional Manichaean designation of 'Christian' and 'infidel' wholly failed to encompass the reality of the politics of the Ottoman advance, let alone its military dimension. The old view of a Turkish conquest of the Byzantine Christian bastion weakened by Latin indifference or hatred of Greeks, of a Muslim enslavement of a resentful Christian peoples, does not match events. Unlike the wars to defend the Holy Land, here the compromises of political realities contradicted the imperatives of religious idealism.

The political fragmentation of the Balkans and Asia Minor in the thirteenth century provided the essential context for the creation of Ottoman power. The Byzantine empire of the twelfth century was replaced by rump successor Greek states at Nicaea (then, after its recapture in 1261, Constantinople), Epirus and Trebizond. These competed with established Latin territories in Greece, based in the statelets of Athens in Attica and Boeotia, Achaea in the Peleponnese and Venetian holdings in the Aegean archipelagos, at Euboea (or Negroponte) and ports scattered along the southern Peloponnese and Ionian coast. To the north the Bulgarians and Serbs maintained independent kingdoms, while successive kings of Hungary attempted to extend their authority south of the Danube into Bosnia and eastwards to Wallachia. In Asia Minor, a similar disintegration had occurred with the collapse of the Seljuk sultanate of Rum in the mid-thirteenth century. By the early fourteenth century, authority had devolved on to competing Turkish emirates, such as those of Aydin, Menteshe and Tekke along the west and south-west coast of Asia Minor, and the Ottomans in the north-west and Karaman in the south-east. To survive and thrive, each of these principalities from the Danube to the Taurus Mountains, including the enfeebled, renewed Byzantine empire, pursued a complicated round of shifting alliances and hostilities with and against their neighbours based on advantage, not cultural or religious affinity. The most fertile ground for Ottoman expansion proved to be in the Christian, especially Orthodox Christian Balkans, not in Muslim Anatolia. The fragmented political control concealed wide varieties in the nature of these competing powers. None of them, even *in extremis*, constituted fertile ground for new mass crusades. The Italian cities, although boasting long crusading traditions, appropriately operated their strictly commercial and imperial policies according to profit, not eternal salvation. The Latin states of Frankish Romania, ruled by a western military aristocracy scattered across central Greece and the Peleponnese, had never attracted western crusaders in any numbers. The Slav Balkan princes sought autonomy, not Latin or Roman Catholic domination. Help for Byzantium was complicated by religious suspicion on both sides and contingent on a unification of eastern and western churches that the Greeks, mindful of Latin behaviour since 1204, consistently repudiated.

Even when the menace of the Turks was recognized in the west, the obstacle of church union remained.[48] The price of a substantial western crusade, from the papacy's point of view, was Greek obedience to Rome, for Byzantine emperors a fatal dilemma. To secure western military aid on such terms risked alienating the people for whom they were seeking the aid in the first place. In principle, a form of ecclesiastical accommodation was feasible. Sections of the Armenian Orthodox church had entered into communion with Rome in the twelfth century. However, the legacy of 1204, the increasing equation of the Greek Orthodox church with the Byzantine state and its cultural identity, and the rise of a popular Greek mysticism known as the Hesychast movement in the early fourteenth century impeded reconciliation. Rome's inescapable insistence on papal supremacy institutionalized the division. The first attempt at reunion, at the Second Lyons Council of 1274, a diplomatic stunt by Michael VIII Palaeologus to secure a papal alliance against Charles of Anjou's designs on the Balkans, was repudiated by Michael's successor, Andronicus II, in 1282. However, after the civil wars of the 1340s and 1350s, the alternative to an alliance with the west was submission to the Ottomans. John V offered reunion in 1355 and visited Rome and the west in 1369, a journey repeated by Manuel II in 1400–1401 and John VIII in 1423. The renewed Ottoman pressure after 1420 persuaded elements of the Greek elite, led by the distinguished humanist scholar John Bessarion (1403–72), with the support of John VIII, to agree to church union at the Council of Florence in 1439.[49] Bessarion made his career in the west, for thirty years a loud advocate of a new crusade, later a cardinal of the Roman church and only narrowly defeated for the papacy itself in 1455. Bessarion embodied the possibilities of church reunification, but he operated on a rarefied plane of high politics, diplomacy and cosmopolitan scholarship. His accommodation held little appeal for the majority of his fellow Greek Orthodox countrymen. Moreover, the alternatives of the fourteenth century, church union or the Turk, were no longer realistic. The Ottoman Sultan Mehmed II the Conqueror wished to replace Byzantium, now little more than the city of Constantinople. Church union had no effect. The west provided inadequate aid. No pan-Christian alliance was possible in the shifting sands of Balkan politics: rational self-interest of local rulers and the power of the Ottomans made sure of that. Within Byzantium, the Union of Florence was generally repudiated, causing a damaging conflict between the Orthodox hierarchy and the last two emperors, John VIII and Constantine XI. The last Byzantine emperor never resiled from the Florence agreement, expelling anti-union clergy. In his city's final death agony in 1453 he was sustained by Italian troops, who proved more loyal than many of his Orthodox subjects. In a final irony of Byzantine history, the Orthodox patriarchate was restored to Constantinople by its Turkish conqueror.[50]

The drive towards church union failed to grasp the essentials of the Byzantine predicament. While continued economic and commercial prosperity sustained the noble and urban Byzantine elites, as well as the Italian commercial predators, for the Byzantine imperial government, irreversible loss of territory meant loss of revenues. Constant frontier warfare dislocated agriculture; necessarily higher taxes provoked peasant and aristocratic alienation from the imperial administrators in Constantinople. Lack of funds and manpower forced Byzantine rulers to abandon serious naval commitment, isolating them further. Compelled to hire land armies for protection and support in the regular civil wars, emperors and imperial claimants frequently found they could not pay their troops, who seized lands instead: the Catalan Company in central Greece in 1305–11; the Ottoman Turks in Thrace after 1345. This military dependency on private, non-imperial armies became entrenched by incessant political feuding. By the 1340s, the Byzantine emperor was so poor that he pawned the crown jewels in Venice, replacing the royal regalia with glass replicas. Donations for the upkeep of the great church of Saint Sophia went to pay Turkish mercenaries. Despite their cosmic pretentions, the Byzantine emperors became Ottoman dependants, then tributaries, by the 1380s vassals of the sultan. The still lucrative commercial system was run by others; at one point the Genoese controlled 87 per cent of Bosporus customs. The Orthodox church constituted the only robust, independent power in the Greek polity, which impeded western assistance. The contrast between ancient claims and contemporary debility was tellingly captured by a witness to Manuel II's visit to Henry IV of England at Christmas 1400:

> how grievous it was that this great Christian prince should be driven by the Saracens from the furthest East to the furthest Western Islands to seek aid against them ... What dost thou now, ancient glory of Rome?[51]

Yet, by the late fourteenth century, Greek emperors were more often than not allies and vassals of the Turks, not their implacable foes. Manuel himself, less than a decade earlier, had served for six months in the army of Sultan Bayezid I in Anatolia. Such were the contradictions of Byzantine survival.

By 1400, Byzantine emperors survived on sufferance. The Byzantine civil wars of 1346–54, between John V Palaeologus and John VI Cantacuzene made the Ottomans arbiters of the empire. Sultan Orkhan married a daughter of John VI in 1346, Muslim polygamy proving a diplomatic boon. John V's proposal for a new western crusade in 1355 coincided with some of the bitterest fighting of the Hundred Years War and renewed papal crusades in Italy. In 1358, John V recognized Ottoman power when one of his daughters married a son of Sultan Orkhan. Fresh attempts by John V to enlist western aid in the late 1360s only produced the limited intervention of Amadeus of Savoy's crusade in 1366–7. Once in control of most of the Balkans north of Attica and south of the Danube, Sultan Bayezid began an eight-year blockade of Constantinople in 1394. The western crusade of 1396 achieved nothing, although it temporarily drew some fire from the siege of Constantinople. The capital was reprieved for half a century by factors outside its control. These did not include the crusade. Until their wholesale adoption of gunpowder in the fifteenth century, the Turks lacked the ability to destroy the still-formidable walls of Constantinople. They also lacked control of the sea, depending on western allies such as the Genoese for shipping and technical expertise. Only in the decades surrounding the final attack on Constantinople did the Ottomans become a naval power, a fundamental prerequisite for achieving Mehmed II's goal of recreating a Mediterranean empire based on Constantinople. The loss of western naval hegemony ultimately sealed the fate of the maritime Latin east just as lack of military power doomed mainland Greece and the Balkans. In the fourteenth century, the Ottoman empire in Europe and Asia Minor had rested on a series of loose overlordships and alliances, with power delegated to vassals. By contrast, in the fifteenth century a highly centralized and disciplined Ottoman polity emerged after the restoration of the empire following Timur's withdrawal to central Asia and death in 1405, and the resolution by 1413 of the family power struggle in favour of Mehmed I. Acquiring a navy and cannon, the Ottomans restored their control over the sub-Danubean Balkans in a generation. Short of a miraculous revolution in western European priorities, the fall of Constantinople appeared inevitable.

THE CRUSADE OF NICOPOLIS

The western response to the Turkish conquests rarely reached the pitch of an armed crusade, despite sporadic papal appeals and offers of crusade privileges stretching back to the 1360s and 1370s. The expedition of Amadeus of Savoy in 1366–7, an adjunct of the papal-Cypriot schemes of 1362–5, exposed the limits of what could be achieved. Raiding, even occupying strategic maritime bases, such as Gallipoli or Smyrna, while helping the local interests of Latin rulers in the Aegean and in Rhodes, hardly impinged on the Turkish land advance. The prerequisite for any serious crusading venture lay in the establishment of peace in western Europe. The dissipation of efforts in the 1360s were overtaken by the resumption of the Hundred Years War in 1369 and the papal schism from 1378. Only after the Anglo-French truce of 1389, which ushered in a generation of wary peace, were new international schemes devised to fight the infidel. The first target, in keeping with aristocratic attitudes, was not the Turk at all, but a more traditional, if peripheral, foe.

In 1389–90, the Genoese took advantage of the truce to invite the French government of Charles VI to sponsor an expedition to capture the Tunisian port of al-Mahdiya. The Genoese probably hoped this enterprise would further their interests in the area after their own annexation of the island of Jerba, south of al-Mahdiya, in 1388. The French embraced this opportunity for unequivocally meritorious warfare. Lavish tournaments at Smithfield in London and especially at St Inglevert near Calais helped recruit English nobles in an appropriately chivalrous setting. The expedition was commanded by Charles VI's uncle, Louis II, duke of Bourbon.[52] In France recruitment was limited to 1,500, probably not including archers. The English contingent, made up mainly of well-placed but second-rank courtiers, was led by John Beaufort, an illegitimate son of Richard I's powerful uncle John of Gaunt, duke of Lancaster, who contributed twenty-five knights and 100 archers.[53] The Genoese supplied a fleet estimated as twenty-two galleys and eighteen transports. Although both Avignon and Roman popes offered indulgences, the al-Mahdiya expedition resembled a strenuous jaunt, on a par with the Baltic *reisen*, rather than a serious attempt to conquer territory in North Africa. Although there may have been processions and prayers for victory at home, no lay or ecclesiastical central funds were allocated or granted. Leaders were expected to be of gentle birth, capable of paying their own way. Despite the indulgences and the chroniclers' language of crusading, there is no clear evidence that a single participant actually took the cross.

Sailing from Genoa in July 1390, the Franco-English army besieged al-Mahdiya for nine weeks, fighting off relief attempts. Cooperation appeared good between the different elements in the army, Louis of Bourbon consulting the English, whose archers played a prominent role in the action. However, once peace terms were offered by the Hafsid ruler of Tunis, all contingents outside Duke Louis's household rejected his wishes and accepted them. The weeks before al-Mahdiya cost few lives; disease proving more lethal.[54] The campaign achieved nothing of concrete value, although it may have enhanced French links with Genoa. It is hard to locate the 1390 campaign within the tradition of the sporadic penetration of north Africa, conducted in this period largely by Castilians and Portuguese. Rather, it should be seen as part of Genoa's commercial strategy taking advantage of the Anglo-French truce of 1390. Both governments could appreciate the diplomatic benefits of this mechanism of reconciliation. Nobles and knights on both sides of the English Channel were eager to justify their status on exotic and laudable battlefields, not just in the service of crown and country. Many veterans of 1390 also found their way to Prussia and eastern Europe. The al-Mahdiya adventure provided a dress rehearsal for the Nicopolis crusade six years later.

The early 1390s saw a recrudescence of old-fashioned crusade dreaming. The victories of Bayezid I had brought him to the southern frontiers of Hungary, whose new king, Sigismund, sought military help from the west. This coincided with the emergence at the French and English courts of a new crusading policy. Promoted by the energetic veteran lobbyist Philip of Mézières, now settled in Paris, schemes were bandied about for a crusade that would seal the new peace between England and France, heal the papal schism and liberate the Holy Land. Individual commitment was secured through membership of Mézières's *New Order of the Passion* (*Nova religio passionis*), which between 1390 and 1395 attracted the patronage of Charles VI (although he lost his mind in 1392) and Richard II (1377–99), as well as scores of English and French knights. Through royal favour, personal diplomacy and targeted pamphleteering, Mézières and members of his order influenced the language of diplomacy, creating a discernible atmosphere of crusading enthusiasm and expectation.[55]

Coincidentally or not, concrete plans were put in train at least from 1392. The lead came from the Philip the Bold, duke of Burgundy, who used the crusade schemes to assert his power against his brothers for control of French affairs after the onset of Charles VI's madness. He was also probably a genuine enthusiast. By 1394 a plan had crystallized under which Duke Philip, his nephew and rival, Charles VI's younger brother, Louis, duke of Orléans and John of Gaunt would embark for Hungary the following year. Philip began collecting money from his lands in Burgundy and Flanders; Louis and Gaunt may well have received royal funds. By the end of the year, Gaunt had raised 1,500 men, although these may have been destined to police a Gascon revolt. Venice had been approached and Sigismund was expecting the army in 1395. As in 1390, crusade bulls were issued by Popes Boniface IX (Rome and Benedict XIII (Avignon), although the latter only in the spring of 1396, shortly before the expedition departed. Also in common with the al-Mahdiya expedition, there is no clear sign that any of those involved in this enterprise actually took the cross.[56]

However, delays in coordinating western aid with the plans of the Hungarians, diplomatic difficulties between England and France and domestic political problems, in Gascony and at the fractious French court, sabotaged this ambitious programme. The three putative leaders withdrew. Gaunt delegated his role to his bastard John Beaufort, the al-Mahdiya veteran. Philip the Bold appointed his son and heir John of Nevers to lead his troops. Louis of Orléans abandoned the project altogether. English involvement became peripheral. Beaufort may have joined the expedition when it embarked in the spring of 1396, but it is not certain. No unequivocal evidence of English participation exists. If individuals or private companies enlisted, it is unlikely they included a substantial or officially sponsored regiment.[57] The expedition devolved on to the household of John of Nevers, a circle of Burgundian knights and a smattering of French nobles sympathetic to the Burgundian faction at court, many of them with past or future experience of war in Prussia, Tunisia and Greece. The total of men at arms probably came to a few hundred, the whole Franco-Burgundian force to a few thousand, hardly Mézières's great redemptive crusade. Except as a make-weight for Sigismund's border defence, it is difficult to imagine what could be achieved by such a force. As well as its size, the decision to travel to Hungary by land severely limited its options, precluding action independent of Hungarian plans.

Although serious in intent, and courageous in battle, the leaders of this western army appear to have been seduced by wishful self-esteem, not sober strategy. Hopes of battering a path to Constantinople, of sweeping the Ottomans aside in one fell encounter or even, as some apparently envisaged, continuing to Jerusalem, were entirely illusory. Sigismund probably appreciated this, advocating a defensive strategy once the western army arrived in Hungary. Yet he played along with Burgundian fantasies to acquire powerful – and free – reinforcements. The policy was born of the crusade diplomacy after 1390 and the eagerness, demonstrated at al-Mahdiya, of French nobles to engage in what was still almost universally regarded as meritorious warfare far from home. The fourteenth century had witnessed the institutionalization of the cult of chivalry into a legion of secular orders, such as those of the Garter in England (1348) or the Star in France (1352). Many of these orders of chivalry, such as the Neapolitan Order of the Knot, dedicated to the Holy Spirit (1352), enjoined service in an eastern crusade on its members, an obligation that had more to do with personal self-image than the exigencies of Balkan politics or Levantine warfare. The 1396 campaign provided an occasion for the honouring of such commitments.[58]

Leaving Burgundy in April 1396, John of Nevers's army reached the Hungarian capital Buda late in July. Intent on forcing a hurried and incomplete response from Sultan Bayezid, the combined western and Hungarian army advanced down the Danube into occupied Bulgaria. After capturing the frontier fortresses of Vidin and Rahova, where the poorer, unransomable defenders were indiscrimately massacred, they laid siege to Nicopolis further downstream. Here Bayezid I's army caught up with them. On 25 September, the coalition Christian forces were destroyed by the Ottomans and their Serbian allies. The Christian allies took the initiative by seeking an assault against the advancing Turks. Refusing to remain as a powerful reserve and failing to coordinate their attack with the Hungarians, the French cavalry broke itself on the Turkish infantry and first rank of horse before reaching the main column of Turkish heavy cavalry, the *sipahis*, when they were cut to pieces. John of Vienne Admiral of France and William of La Trémoille Marshal of Burgundy were among the slain; John of Nevers, Philip of Artois constable of France, Marshal Boucicaut and Enguerrand of Coucy were among the captured. They later attracted huge ransoms, collectively perhaps as much as 500,000 francs. The Hungarians, deserted by their Wallachian and Transylvanian levies, fared little better at the hands of the Serbians under Despot Stephen Lazarevic. The Turkish victory was overwhelming and indisputable, as crushing a defeat of French arms as Agincourt nineteen years later, where exactly the same mistakes were made. There, as at Nicopolis, the French cavalry insisted on attacking a line of archers and infantry protected by rows of stakes. It says much for poor French generalship of the period: one of the chief tacticians at Agincourt was the Nicopolis veteran Marshal Boucicaut.[59]

The disastrous Nicopolis campaign has been described melodramatically as 'a final failure'. 'There would be no more crusades.'[60] Others have acknowledged the defeat as decisive as well as crushing. In confirming Ottoman military strength, and the adhesiveness of their Balkan clients, it exposed the ineffectiveness of western arms, traditional crusade strategies and the feeble hold Sigismund possessed over his allies. Only the irruption of Timur into western Asia in 1400 and his defeat of Bayezid in 1402 at Ankara saved Constantinople and central Europe. In Christian Europe, Nicopolis has been credited with Sigismund abandoning aggression against the Ottomans for his German and Bohemian interests and the disintegration of Anglo-French unity, with wide implications for the survival of Richard II's regime (it fell in 1399) and the renewal of the Hundred Years War (in 1415). However, both immediate and long-term effects can be exaggerated. Only a relatively small army had been engaged at Nicopolis. The popular court poet and chronicler Froissart was told only 700 French knights were involved.[61] The failure to coordinate the land attack with naval operations ran counter to contemporary experience and advice. The disaster of 1396 failed to disarm enthusiasm for fighting the infidel. Neither technically nor generically was Nicopolis the last crusade. Nicopolis did not lead to the conquest of Hungary, Bayezid's aggression turning eastwards in 1397–1400. The reaction to Nicopolis in France did not match that to other defeats during the Hundred Years' War. In England, chroniclers' almost universal silence indicates minimal impact. Nicopolis did not mark a watershed between crusading optimism and pessimism.

The response to the Nicopolis defeat did reveal how crusading was viewed. On their release from Ottoman captivity and return to France in 1398, John of Nevers and his companions were ecstatically received as heroes. The manner of their defeat had inspired a familiar round of hand-wringing introspection. On 9 January 1397 churches across France conducted grief-laden memorial services. Writers close to the French court and in contact with survivors were in no doubt that vanity and folly had led to the Frenchmen's destruction, although the bravery of individuals was accorded due praise. Nicopolis was transformed into a morality story of sin, redemption and heroism, a paradigm of the image of later medieval crusading itself. The well-informed official chronicler from the monastery of St Denis eschewed easy clichés in highlighting the contrast between the lavish feasts, ornate tents, gawdy clothes and loose women of the Christians with the God-fearing, prudent, discreet Bayezid, a suitable instrument of God's chastisement of sinners despite his 'Turkish superstition'.[62] Secular writers transmuted events into good stories with a didactic purpose. Froissart's almost wholly fantastical account of the 1396 campaign, written before 1402, emphasized the scale of the Ottoman threat, inventing threats by Bayezid to march on Rome and feed his horse on the altar in St Peter's.[63] This was no simple call to return to arms, but a polemic to end the papal schism and unite Christendom, precisely the Anglo-French policy that had preceded Nicopolis, a view that did nothing to disturb underlying assumptions about chivalric honour or the efficacy of holy war. Similar themes of folly, pride, Christendom's disorder, catastrophic defeat, the papal schism and a utopian desire to sweep the Islamic tide back as far as Jerusalem dominated the earliest literary response to the news of Nicopolis, Philip of Mézières's *Epistre Lamentable et Consolatoire* (*Letter of Lament and Consolation*), written by the veteran propagandist, now pushing seventy, in the first weeks of 1397.[64] Mézières's overlaying of pragmatic assessment of responsibility with revivalist cliché stood for a whole body of thoughtful contemporary opinion, mirrored in most other literary, historical, even diplomatic considerations of the eastern question. His ideas were not simply rhetorical flourishes or the eccentricities of a lonely, disappointed political has-been. Instead of flummery distractions, chivalry and holy war were inescapable weapons in the combat with Islam, a view the defeat at Nicopolis, in the hands of literary observers, at least, did much to reinforce. However, the response to Nicopolis confirmed a more damaging trait. Westerners' reactions were hobbled by a crippling solipsism that explored their own cultural disposition obsessively while failing in any sustained or serious fashion to comprehend or dissect the nature of their opponents. This, too, accorded with some of the longest traditions of crusading and did not end with the great defeat on the Danube.

BURGUNDY AND THE CRUSADE

The Nicopolis expedition had been a largely Burgundian affair, an element in the increasingly fevered power struggle around the throne of the insane Charles VI. The tradition of Burgundian leadership of western crusade planning continued until the end of the Valois line of dukes in 1477.[65] Burgundian writers, and others, repeatedly reminded fifteenth-century dukes of their gallant holy warrior ancestor John of Nevers, not least to deflect attention from his subsequent career as duke, a shifty, devious figure hardly inspiring pride, let alone honour or glamour.[66] As counts of Flanders as well as dukes and counts of Burgundy, the Valois dukes could lay claim to two of the grandest dynastic and regional crusading traditions. Their championing of the crusade and the need to tackle the eastern question served a similarly consistent political purpose. Once the prospect of dominating the French government evaporated after the English victories of 1415–20, Duke Philip the Good turned his attention to consolidating his autonomous authority in Burgundy, Flanders and the Low Countries. Although lacking the important asset of a crown, for over half a century Duke Philip and his son Charles the Rash sought to assert a role as independent rulers in the west, taking advantage of the Anglo-French war and a weak German empire. Leadership of the crusade enhanced self-image and status, allowing dukes a distinctive, independent diplomatic role. It also gave access to clerical taxes: Philip the Good received three grants of ecclesiastical tenths from his lands in the Low Countries between 1449 and 1455 alone. His crusade policy was further underpinned by huge ducal revenues in which even the massive Nicopolis ransoms made little dent.

However, to achieve these political, diplomatic and fiscal benefits, a crusade policy needed to be validated by action. Here the Burgundian dukes' record appears equivocal; energetic over many decades but always falling just short of substantial military commitment. In an apparent attempt to overcome the solipsist myopia of previous generations, spies were despatched on extensive journeys to the east to survey both the Turkish and Mamluk enemies in the 1420s and 1430s. Earlier crusade texts were collected and if necessary translated.[67] Philip employed Jean Germain bishop of Châlons (1436–61) as a pet court crusade expert for over twenty years, even supplying him with a translation of the Koran by the Venetian chaplain of Damascus, where Bertrandon de la Broquière had obtained a copy in 1433 during his reconnaissance tour of the Near East.[68] Germain peddled an erudite if muddled mixture of historical exegesis and vapid exhortation over two decades. Among other courtiers were eastern experts, such as Ghillebert of Lannoy (the spy sponsored by Philip the Good and Henry V of England in 1421) and Brocquière, and soldiers with experience of fighting the Turks, such as Geoffrey of Thoisy, with twenty years' active involvement in campaigns in north Africa, the eastern Mediterranean and the Black Sea from the 1440s to 1460s, or Waleran of Wavrin, a veteran of operations around the Black Sea in 1444–5. For decades, the Burgundian court attracted foreign crusade enthusiasts, lobbyists and diplomats, becoming a sort of clearing house for crusade schemes, however crackpot. When John Torcello, on behalf of John VIII Palaeologus, presented a plan for an anti-Turkish crusade to the Council of Florence in 1439 it was submitted for Burgundian scrutiny, only to be dissected and rejected by Duke Philip's expert, Brocquière, unsurprisingly given John's prediction that, following the defeat of the Turks, Jerusalem would fall within weeks.[69] Into the 1470s, any serious and many fanciful crusade schemes received an airing at the ducal court.[70]

Crusading found institutional expression through the ducal chivalric order, the Order of the Golden Fleece (1431). Key noble, court and military figures were knights or companions of the order, which acted as a permanent forum for testing and arousing enthusiasm. In the 1460s, its chancellor, William Filastre bishop of Tournai, led Burgundy's response to the crusade plans of Pius II; in 1473 the order's chapter supplied the setting for a new papal crusade appeal.[71] A generation earlier, Jean Germain acted as the order's chancellor and used its chapter meeting at Mons in 1451 to expand on his crusade ideas. One consequence of this meeting was the great Feast of the Pheasant, held at Lille on 17 February 1454 to promote Burgundian commitment to the eastern holy war. Constantinople had fallen the previous May; the duke was in the middle of active planning for an anti-Turkish expedition. The climax of the feast's entertainment consisted of a tableau including the Lamentation of the Holy Church, delivered to the duke and assembled knights, according to tradition, by one of the organizers of the revels, Oliver de la Marche, dressed as a woman, in a white satin frock and wimple, under a black cloak, perched in a castle carried on the back of a fake elephant that had been led into the hall by a grim-looking giant dressed as a 'Saracen of Granada'. (Oliver later explained the allegory; the elephant stood for exotic Constantinople; the castle, faith; the weeping lady, the church; and the giant, the Turk.) Once the affecting protest had finished, the Golden Fleece King of Arms (i.e. chief herald) entered with a live pheasant. On this remarkably or chemically quiescent bird more than 200 vows of varying implausibility were sworn to fight the infidel. One of the more sensible vows came from Ghillebert of Lannoy, the spy of thirty years before. The whole event was lavish beyond fancy; even Oliver de la Marche's professional eye noticed the excess of extravagance.[72]

The Vow of the Pheasant acted as the focus for a wider assault on the interests of the new crusade. The visual and ritual high-jinks of the Lille festivities were matched by widely circulated written memoranda, such as the Florentine James Tedaldo's eyewitness account of the fall of Constantinople; public assemblies of the Order of the Golden Fleece; religious ceremonies; verses, such as those of the Lamentation itself; and music, the great Burgundian composer Guillaume Dufay (*c.*1400–1474) writing a four-part motet on the same subject. Duke Philip was investing heavily in creating an atmosphere of engagement in which crusading, while not necessarily the most rational occupation, became respectable, accepted and unexceptional. However playful the crusade junketing, it was mirrored by a genuine, if sentimental, commitment to holy war, a prerequisite of princely stature.[73] In a forbidding international climate for organizing a crusading army, such ludic gestures kept the issue tangibly, excitingly alive.

Duke Philip's practical crusading achievements fell far short of the intoxicating and possibly intoxicated demonstrations at Lille. A striking feature of the Feast of the Pheasant was its secularity, despite the tableaux of the church and another of divine grace. Nobody took the cross; there were no clerics on view. Jean Germain had been banished to the margins. The morally dubious pagan progenitor of the Order of the Golden Fleece, Jason, featured in the Lille tableaux, not the biblical hero Gideon and his fleece moistened by heaven's dew promoted by Germain as the order's inspiration.[74] Yet without active promotion by the church, the court's obsession was likely to remain confined to itself. Popular engagement with the anti-Turkish posturing of the Burgundian court in the 1450s and 1460s only came with preaching, the sale of indulgences, local church processions and taking the cross. In practical terms, the Burgundian crusade activity fell into three categories; specific planning of grand crusades; general diplomatic encouragement; and regular, small-scale material and military assistance for Christian rulers in the east. Philip the Good's third marriage to the forceful Isabella of Portugal (1430) associated Burgundy with one of the continuing Iberian traditions of holy war, leading to plans for joint action, for example in Greece in 1436–7. John of Nevers had established good relations with the Hospitallers in Rhodes on his release from captivity in 1397–8. His son provided regular aid for Rhodes, as in 1441 and 1444, when Geoffrey of Thoisy assisted in the defence against the Mamluk attack on the island. Burgundian ships and men campaigned in the Black Sea in 1444 and 1445. In 1472–3 Charles the Rash promised to provide money and galleys to assist the Venetian plan for a two-pronged assault on the Ottomans. As so often, nothing came of this. A similar fate befell the two most intense efforts in crusade planning, 1451–4 and 1459–64.

THE CRUSADE OF VARNA

One of the most significant western interventions in eastern Europe attracted only modest Burgundian assistance. After church union was agreed at the Council of Florence (1439), Pope Eugenius IV attempted to coordinate relief for Constantinople. In 1442–3, the pope appointed a legate to eastern Europe, Cardinal Julian Ceasarini (previously a legate on the anti-Hussite crusade of 1431), and tried to orchestrate with Venice a western naval blockade of the Dardenelles while a Hungarian and Serbian army, under John Hunyadi of Transylvania (1440–56, regent of Hungary 1445–56), attacked Rumelia, as the European provinces of the Ottoman empire were known. With the Venetians holding aloof, no western flotilla had arrived to block Ottoman passage of the straits by the time the large Serbo-Hungarian force, strengthened by levies from Bohemia, Moldavia and some western volunteers, launched an attack through Bulgaria towards Thrace in the late autumn and winter of 1443–4.[75] It proved a great success. Nish and Sofia were taken and the Ottoman capital at Erdine (Adrianople) threatened, before the invaders retired to Belgrade. However, plans for 1444 were compromised by a contradiction in allied war aims. The Hungarians and Serbs sought their own advantage, security of frontiers for one, restoration of independence for the other. They had little interest and some suspicion of the legate's desire to relieve Constantinople. The locals were the more realistic. By the 1440s, much of Thrace had become thoroughly Turcified. There was no Byzantine empire to restore. Sultan Murad II exploited these divisions by offering peace terms to George Brancovic of Serbia (1427–56) and King Ladislas IV of Hungary. Brancovic accepted; Ladislas, after some equivocation, did not. The negotiations delayed assembling a new army, giving the Ottomans time to prepare their defences.

A western fleet of twenty-two or twenty-four galleys arrived in the Dardenelles in July 1444, mainly contributed by the papacy, Burgundy and Venice, manned by Venetians. Remaining immobile on station, the fleet totally failed to prevent Murad crossing the Bosporus north of Constantinople in October 1444 with a very large army. Neither did it make any attempt to harry the Black Sea coast or join up with the land army that advanced from the Danube to the Bulgarian port of Varna with just such an intention. The fleet's Venetian captain, Alvise Loredan, declined to risk his ships, provoke the Turks or assist the Hungarians, perhaps fearful of the competitive dangers of committing Venice too actively in the interests of other land powers. The Ottoman and Hungarian armies met on 10 November at Varna. Despite being heavily outnumbered, the Hungarians fought all day, the battle itself ending without either side gaining a clear advantage. However, losses were horrifying. King Ladislas and Cardinal Cesarini were both killed. Morale evaporated. The remnant of the Hungarian army under Hunyadi withdrew, leaving victory to the Ottomans. Varna confirmed Ottoman control of Rumelia while exposing the diplomatic fragility of their opponents. Peaceful accommodation, even under duress, seemed preferable to many Serbs, Hungarians and Poles, a point reinforced by Varna's catastrophic casualties and the passivity of the Venetian naval commanders. Aggression was not as obvious a reaction to Ottoman power along the Danube or in the Aegean as it appeared in the council chambers of Rome or the banqueting halls of the Low Countries. The reluctance of eastern rulers to agree among themselves, still less to fight at western behest, placed a bar to foreign aid. Hunyadi, now regent of Hungary (for Ladislas V), reflecting his own territorial vulnerability as lord of Transylvania, did pursue an aggressive policy. In 1448 he obtained crusade indulgences from Nicholas V for a foray into Serbia that ended in defeat by Murad II at Kossovo, the site of the great iconic Serbian defeat by Murad I in 1389. No western crusaders accompanied him. After Varna, eastern and central Europe was left largely to its own devices. Western rulers' political interests were concentrated in Greece, the Aegean and Cyprus; their emotional anxieties focused on Constantinople.

THE FALL OF CONSTANTINOPLE

In 1453, Mehmed II decided to risk a full assault on Constantinople, despite undefeated enemies on his eastern (Karaman) and western (Hungary) frontiers. The city would unite his empire, remove a potentially troublesome base for hostile troops and help define a universalist imperial ideology. Heavy artillery and temporary naval supremacy supplied the immediate means of conquest. The final siege by land and sea began in April 1453.[76] The last Greek emperor, Constantine XI, was politically and financially bankrupt, short of fighting men and bereft of allies willing to come to his aid, both Hungary and Venice holding back. His ramshackle, depopulated city was defended by a garrison of only a few thousand, afforced by Italian professionals. Constantine could only wait behind the great walls of the city and hope for relief that never came. After weeks of heavy pounding, the Turks moved in for the kill early on the morning of 29 May 1453, when the attackers swarmed into the breaches in the western land walls. The final scene saw the few defenders, the Italians prominent among then, in a desperate last stand within the walls. Constantine was killed in the press, his body possibly mutilated and his head taken as a trophy to the victorious sultan. The second sack of Constantinople may have been as damaging as the first in 1204. Perhaps as many as 4,000 Greek civilians died, about a tenth of the remaining population; many others were enslaved or ransomed. Within a decade, the last mainland Greek outposts had been engulfed; the surviving Latin holdings appeared even more precarious.

The Italian humanist Aeneas Sylvius Piccolomini, soon to be Pope Pius II, lamented at the news of Constantinople's conquest, 'a second death of Homer and Plato'.[77] A more traditional polemic of grief soon prevailed: the church in danger, the heritage of Christ defiled. To the same extent such reactions failed to stimulate a serious counter-attack, they missed the significance of the event. The mayhem, death and destruction, not least of artefacts and libraries, should not be ignored. Yet the human tragedy needs its own perspective. Greek cultural exchange with the west had flourished for generations. Greek learning was not something that reached western Europe in the luggage of Constantinopolitan refugees in 1453. The Byzantine state had comprehensively failed as a political institution. The fate of eastern Christendom lay not in the malignity of western holy warfare or diplomatic indifference, but in the operation of indigenous forces. The advent of the Ottomans was not the unalloyed disaster some have imagined, certainly not for the Ottomans, their allies, local Balkan groups they fostered and patronized, their Muslim subjects or even the Greek peasantry. Certain Greek elites suffered, but religious persecution played no part in fourteenth- or fifteenth-century Ottoman culture. Many Greeks who did not flee found Ottoman service, some even favour as converts to Islam. Ottoman culture, as eclectic and sophisticated as any in Europe and western Asia, introduced no new barbarism. The assumption of Christian superiority of culture or ethics is a damaging legacy of the age of colonialism and a feature of ill-informed modern demonization. The Ottoman triumph provided the lands of former Byzantium with security and a revived economy. By recreating the old territorial Byzantine empire, the Ottomans succeeded precisely where the crusaders of 1204 and generations of Greek rulers had failed. After 1453, Constantinople once again became the centre of the eastern Mediterranean world, resonant in its new name, Istanbul, 'in the city', 'downtown'.

The reaction in the west to the fall of Constantinople varied from genuine concern to ritual hysteria. In courts from Germany to the Iberian peninsula, elaborate plans were instigated for a new crusade. The papacy sought to galvanize Christendom in a new meritorious and redemptive cause through the assertion of papal leadership. Nicholas V issued a crusade bull, *Etsi ecclesia Christi* (30 September 1453). The German imperial *Reichstag* discussed the Turkish war on three occasions in 1454–5, Philip of Burgundy attending the diet at Regensburg in April 1454. The assembly at Frankfurt in November 1454 was addressed by Piccolomini, whose speech was widely circulated.[78] Large numbers of exhortatory pamphlets were produced, some using the new technology of printing. Nicholas V's successor, Calixtus III, maintained the momentum by authorizing preaching, clerical taxes and the sale of indulgences. The taxation aroused predictable clerical resentment. While the indulgence campaign proved financially effective, for example in England, the ubiquity of pardoners excited suspicion and encouraged widespread fraud.[79] Con men and crusading were not unfamiliar partners. Calixtus, despite age and debilitating gout, displayed obsessive energy in promoting the new venture, selling papal assets, including plate, dinner services and precious bindings from the volumes in the new Vatican Library created by his immediate predecessor. Galleys were constructed in the Tiber. Calixtus persuaded Alfonso V of Aragon (also king of Naples), whose secretary he had once been, to take the cross in November 1455. The German emperor Frederick III followed suit. Leadership of the crusade served the interests of his Habsburg family lands bordering Hungary while allowing Frederick to play a genuinely imperial role within Germany. In this company, Philip of Burgundy, even though he began to raise secular taxes for the crusade in his dominions, was conspicuous by his failure to take the cross, partly a reflection of his anomalous position as one of the richest and most powerful rulers in Europe who nonetheless remained subordinate to other monarchs. His French overlord, Charles VII, refused his cooperation or approval of the scheme.

In the autumn of 1454, Philip proposed an expedition for the following year. The lack of German response, Charles VII's opposition and the death of Nicholas V (April 1455) postponed action. Beyond raising money, hardly much of a burden for any prince, Philip did remarkably little in the way of military or naval preparations. The timetable slipped. Alfonso V suggested a massive amphibious attack for 1457 to no effect. Crucially, Venice, at peace with the Turks since 1454, refused to become involved. While the western powers dithered, Mehmed II extended Ottoman control over Serbia (1454–5) preparatory to an attack on Hungary and the middle Danube. The fantasies of the Burgundian nobles at Lille or German princes at Frankfurt or the courtiers of Alfonso V, saturated with images of the historic Holy Land wars of the cross, not only proved impossible to realize, they failed to address the actual threat to fellow Latin Christians on the Danube. The failure of western rulers to organize an international expedition of any significance after 1453 relegated traditional mass crusading to the lumber room of military strategy, as Jean Germain put it, 'the old expeditions and campaigns overseas that are called crusades (*croisiez*)'.[80] Western inaction confirmed that the only effective assistance crusading institutions could provide against the Ottomans lay in moral support, financial help, limited small-scale, mainly naval expeditions and the encouragement of locally based resistance.

BELGRADE 1456

The successful defence of Belgrade in July 1456 exemplified just such limited crusading.[81] Mehmed II advanced up the Danube in the summer of 1456, laying siege to Belgrade in the first week of July. He hoped, once the city had fallen, to press on to Buda before the campaign season ended. Facing him at Belgrade, the modest garrison was minded to come to terms. However, unexpected reinforcements arrived, led by John of Capistrano, a seventy-year-old Observant Franciscan with a long history of enthusiasm for crusading and moral rearmament. His interest in the recovery of the Holy Land and the Turkish question stretched back to the 1440s, part of his order's longstanding involvement in preaching against enemies of the church, including heretics and Jews. Well connected, John had visited the Burgundian court in March 1454 and attended the German imperial diet at Frankfurt in November. He began preaching the crusade. By the spring of 1455, John was in Hungary concocting with a probably sceptical Regent Hunyadi an absurd plan for a huge international crusade of 100,000 men. More constructively, John toured the region preaching and establishing his credentials as a religious reformer. Credibility among crusade preachers assumed great importance. A few years later Pius II acknowledged the damage from past deceit, corruption and idleness: 'People think our sole object is to amass gold. No one believes what we say. Like insolvent tradesmen we are without credit'.[82] Only ostentatious displays of simplicity and sincerity could anaesthetize such feelings. John exuded the right balance of personal holiness and practical direction.

John's preaching in Hungary, begun in May 1455 but reaching a crescendo of intensity between February and June 1456, was carefully orchestrated. Reflecting both his age and careful organization, progress was measured: 375 miles in fourteen months, less than a mile a day. In February 1456, in a well-publicized ceremony at Buda, John took the cross from the papal legate, John of Carvajal. According to John, at least, his evangelism was enormously successful, especially with 'the lesser folk'. Hunyadi's strategy appeared to have two elements. He concentrated on enlisting a reluctant nobility while John and his fellow preachers provided the focus for raising the general popular military levy, based on the so-called *militia portalis* system in use for a couple of generations.[83] This system of peasant military levy meant these non-noble recruits possessed at least rudimentary arms and probably some basic training. John's transparent sincerity mitigated any social or fiscal resentment a summons from the nobles may have aroused, his appeal deliberately transcending secular hierarchy. Little was left to chance. Local bishops lent their support. News of his preaching was carefully spread before his arrival. Sometimes, congregations were disappointed, one being kept waiting for over a week without John appearing. Recruits also came from outside Hungary, mainly Austria and Germany, including, apparently, hundreds of students from Vienna university, perhaps seeking a glamorously adventurous summer vacation away from the lecture halls. John's efforts formed only the centrepiece of a campaign that led to a summer of cross-taking in parts of Hungary, attracting very positive reports. Observers may have been pleasantly struck by the focus on raising men rather than the more usual touting for money. John's contribution may have been exaggerated in his own writing and the hagiographical accounts that soon clustered around the events of 1456. Nonetheless, he raised a significant army, perhaps some thousands strong, even if its cohesion suggests it was held together by more than the friar's personality alone.

Despite apologists' sentimental insistence on the wondrous and miraculous, John of Capistrano's crusader army, while not necessarily the collection of inspired and devoted civilian innocents of propaganda and legend, played an important role in the defence of Belgrade. They supplied numbers and vital morale. The Hungarian garrison was too small to combat the Turks outside the walls of Belgrade and, without relief, was unlikely to have withstood Turkish bombardment indefinitely. Mehmed may also have relied on the longstanding reluctance of elements in the Hungarian nobility to fight if an accommodation were available. The arrival of John's troops from 2 July onwards allowed for more aggressive tactics. They helped Hunyadi break the Turkish naval blockade around the city on 14 July. A week later, on the night of 21–2 July, they stood with the garrison in the breaches of the battered city walls to repulse the main Turkish assault. The following day, as Mehmed began to organize his retreat, they formed a major element in the counter-attack that swarmed over the Turkish forward positions, inflicting further heavy casualties and seizing large amounts of *matériel*. The success of John's recruiting effort seems to have wrong-footed Mehmed, whose plans depended on a relatively rapid seizure of Belgrade if his further targets were to be met. The crusaders' appearance in strength dashed hopes that his initial superiority of numbers and control of the rivers would force Belgrade's surrender. That Ottoman forces were stretched is confirmed by their precipitate withdrawal once the desperate ploy of a night-time frontal assault failed.

The well-attested tensions between John's crusaders and Hunyadi added lustre to the image of a providential force whose faith triumphed where military prowess and professionalism had failed. In fact, much of the antagonism between the two groups revolved around the disposition of booty and Hunyadi's lack of control over the crusaders, a consequence of the decision earlier in the year to give John a measure of autonomous authority over his recruits. However, John showed his understanding of the proper relationship of his army to Hunyadi when, the day after the Turks' departure, he summarily disbanded his troops when they tried to assert their independence by claiming sole credit for victory and, thus, ownership of its spoils.[84] John and his crusaders' reputation owed most to the search, then and since, for heroes who could be shown achieving temporal success through living up to the highest spiritual standards crusade rhetoric demanded. Undoubtedly, John's spiritual charisma helped bond his army together and to the cause. His banners spoke both of crusading and the morally strict programme of his order. Revivalism had perennially fuelled crusade enthusiasm, especially in default of the secular discipline or coercion of enforceable lay hierarchies and secular lordship. But such effervescent popular crusading tended to evaporate quickly, John of Capistrano's crusade proving no exception. His army disbanded and he himself died of the plague in October 1456. Thereafter garrisons and truces kept the Ottomans at bay and out of Hungary until the 1520s, not crusaders, indigenous or foreign.

The more conventional efforts of Calixtus III wholly failed to defend Hungary. His fleet only managed to set out in August 1456, meeting with modest success during a tour of duty that lasted until late 1457. Lemnos, Samothrace and Thasos were recovered in the Aegean; a Turkish fleet was defeated at Mytilene in the summer of 1457, and an uplifting but pointless raid was conducted down the Levantine coast to Egypt. Pope Calixtus milked these successes. The naval victories were commemorated by a medal, that at Belgrade by the institution in 1457 of general observance of the Feast of the Transfiguration on 6 August, the day news of the triumph had reached Rome a year before. It was also the date of the battle of Mytilene.[85] Yet such gestures did little to deflect the consolidation of Ottoman power south of the Danube and in Greece. The flow of the Ottoman advance may have been stemmed, but there was no counter-attack. The overwhelming presence of Turkish dominion from Serbia to Cilicia remained unaltered, a fact that preyed heavily on Calixtus III's successor, called by some 'the last crusader'.

THE CRUSADE OF PIUS II

By the time of his election as Pope Pius II in August 1458, Aeneas Sylvius Piccolomini (1405–64) had been promoting an anti-Turkish, anti-Muslim eastern crusade for over twenty years. A distinguished scholar, man of letters and experienced diplomat, Pius had been heavily engaged during negotiations in the earlier 1450s. On elevation to the throne of St Peter he immediately renewed calls for a crusade (October 1458), convening an international conference at Mantua (summer 1459–January 1460). Although the attendance at Mantua was meagre and the response decidedly tepid, Pius drove the meeting to agree on a new expedition, imagining at the end of it that he had a plan, with fixed promises of men and funding. Optimism soon ran into the sand. International prospects were poor. England had slipped into civil war. The new French king, Louis XI, continued his predecessor's hostility to Philip of Burgundy's participation. Louis had little time for his previous protector's posturing, regarding Philip as spoilt, arrogant and 'of no great intellect'.[86] In Italy, the succession to Naples dragged the pope into a conflict that pitted France against Aragon. Pius hardly helped. After 1453, he appeared to hanker after an old-fashioned general crusade to defeat the Turks and recover Jerusalem. This increasingly looked like code for enhancing papal supremacy rather than a serious military proposal. His and his advisors' language when discussing the Turks became crudely abusive. However, by placing the crusade at the centre of his pontificate, Pius was staking papal authority and even, as he admitted in 1462, respect for the church hierarchy itself.[87]

This explains the otherwise bizarre, pathetic or tragic coda to his reign. By early 1462, Pius had decided the only way to rescue his crusade and papal authority was to lead the expedition personally, to say to the faithful, 'Come with me,' not, 'Go on your own.' This represented the height of impracticality. Pius was prematurely old, a semi-invalid. A crusade, he very publicly acknowledged in 1463, would kill him. Perhaps he reckoned a heroic gesture of martyrdom would shake Christendom to reform where tens of thousands of his erudite words had not. Pius had come late to the priesthood, in his forties, after a successful public and private life as a layman; he had fathered a number of children. His mid-life conversion left him with an originality of perspective and freedom of thought denied his more institutionalized clerical colleagues. Freshness of vision, high intellect and impressive articulacy produced his remarkable elision of the crusade with papal supremacy and his own spiritual journey.

Prospects for action were better than in 1459. Philip the Good, although in his mid-sixties, recommitted himself to the venture. Venice was close to war with the Turks, reversing their neutrality of a decade earlier. Pius relaunched his crusade in October 1463, this time as a limited project directed at the Turks.[88] The full panoply of preaching, cross-giving, Holy Land indulgences, privileges and financial apparatus was rehearsed. The pope's leadership became central. To his cardinals Pius made no bones over his personal vocation: 'we shall in a sense be going to certain death', a noble end that may have appealed both to his religious faith and his classical imagination.[89]

The autumn of 1463 saw serious diplomatic efforts to gain material support. Pius negotiated with sceptical Italian states while securing a grand alliance between the papacy, Venice, Hungary and Burgundy. On 22 October Pius rather pompously declared war on Mehmed II. Ancona was fixed as the muster point for the international force. The Venetians would transport the army across the Adriatic to join either the Hungarians or Albanian freedom fighters under Scanderbeg. Typically, after another lavish crusade *fête* at Christmas 1463, Philip of Burgundy ratted, but did send a company of 3,000 men under his bastard Anthony, who set out for Ancona in May 1464. Other small contingents began to move south. The only cardinal to provide a galley was Rodrigo Borgia, nephew and protégé of the crusade fanatic Calixtus III, later Pope Alexander VI of ill-repute.[90] Given his notorious pluralism and greed, Rodrigo could certainly afford it. Pius himself assembled a fleet of galleys to meet him at Ancona before taking the cross at St Peter's on 18 June 1464, perhaps the only pope in office ever to do so to fight the infidel. Now seriously ill, he must have realized his mission to Ancona, whither he set out in late June, could only be *pour encourager les autres* and for the salvation of his own soul. The Venetian flotilla of twelve galleys commanded by the doge himself was late. Elements of the papal force, seeing how the land lay, began to desert. It was said that the curtains of Pius's litter had to be drawn to shield him from the sight of his disintegrating army.[91] On 14 August, soon after reaching Ancona, Pius, as he had expected, died. His crusade died with him.

The Ottoman problem did not. By 1481, when Mehmed the Conqueror died, Venice had lost its Aegean capital Negroponte (1470), the Hospitallers in Rhodes had narrowly survived a massive siege (1480), and Otranto, in southern Italy, had briefly been occupied. In Rumelia, there were no Turkish retreats, even if further conquest ceased under Bayezid II, only to be renewed with a vengeance by Selim the Grim and Suleiman the Magnificent. However, the crusade increasingly assumed a walk-on part in the drama. Bulls continued to be issued. Men still took the cross and rulers the money. The efficacy of the ideal continued to receive obeisance, sometimes genuine, sometimes not. In Hungary, recognized as 'the wall, bastion or shield' of Latin Christendom, defence was the priority.[92] Hunyadi's son, Matthias Corvinus, used crusading rhetoric to bolster his royal credentials as a monarch from a parvenu dynasty. However, income from papal crusade funds, while useful, made little impression on the cost of Hungary's military establishment. The recrudescence of crusade enthusiasm in the Iberian peninsula looked to other theatres of holy war, even when its promoters sought to associate them. When Charles VIII of France invaded Italy in 1494 to assert his claim to the kingdom of Naples, he placed the adventure in the context of a desire to fight the Turk and recover Jerusalem. The sincerity of the emotion need not be doubted, even if its implementation was outside practical politics. By initiating a sixty-year war in Italy, Charles VIII destroyed any serious chance to fulfil his ambition. His priorities were very clear. As for so many of his predecessors, the crusade became always the next thing to be done, always just one more military or diplomatic coup away.

Crusading refused to fade away. It still addressed central issues of politics, war, faith and community. International crusading remained a matter of courtly speculation, diplomatic trope and academic, and occasionally scholarly, debate. Popes continued to promote crusading with literary vigour, although the frequency and eloquence of their bulls were not matched by deeds. Increasingly the *cruciata*, through its taxes or sale of indulgences, became a matter of pious fiscality, in Spain a significant feature of public finance, jealously guarded by sixteenth-century monarchs. Indulgences remained popular. In England alone, between 1444 and 1502 there were twelve indulgence sales campaigns on behalf of crusades against the Turks. One of the earliest surviving pieces of English printing was an indulgence form issued to Henry and

Katherine Langley of London on 13 December 1476.[93] In 1464, a new curial finance department was established, the papal privy purse, specifically to receive crusade money. While the Ottomans presented a vital danger, talk of the recovery of Jerusalem remained the familiar small change of diplomatic parley and bombast, as in Francis I's attempt to impose an Italian peace in 1515. His later treaty with the Turks (1536) dealt a serious blow to the concept of a confessional foreign policy. Yet old habits died hard. In 1498, the Roman poet laureate promised the new French king Louis XII a Roman triumph and a greeting by Apollo if he liberated the Holy Land and Constantinople.[94]

The atmosphere more than the apparatus of crusading infected the language used to describe battles with the Turks. One account of the attack on Lesbos in 1501 is decorated by a lay crusade sermon supposedly delivered by the French king's lieutenant, compete with promises of papal indulgences, salvation, temporal and eternal honour and glory.[95] Ironically, on the eve of the Lutheran revolt against papal indulgences in 1517, the greatest challenge to the theology of crusading yet mounted, reassuring anachronism gave way to some appreciation of reality. None of the debates or decrees of the Fifth Lateran Council (1512–17), which discussed an *expeditio* against the Turks, mentioned Jerusalem.[96] The febrile and hostile politics of Italy, France and Spain prevented any but verbal activity. Religious disunion of a sort unknown in the west for centuries soon complicated responses to both crusading and the Turk. The greatest Muslim threat to Christendom, the advance of the Ottomans to the suburbs of Vienna in 1529, occurred in the same year German evangelical princes signed the 'Protest' from which the name Protestant derived. Thereafter, although many Protestants were far from squeamish about holy war or fighting the Turks, crusading assumed a partisan status, a weapon, if at all, of a splintered confessional affinity some, at least, of whose ideological assumptions and roots had been attacked if not hacked off. Crusade institutions remained in the papal armoury, especially in support of Habsburg campaigning around the Mediterranean. For the Roman Catholic faithful, the ideal still shone. Pope Paul III's summons to the great reforming council at Trent in 1544 announced its purpose: 'the removal of religious discord, the reform of Christian morals, and the launching of an expedition under the most sacred sign of the cross against the infidel.'[97]

But Paul hoped the council would abolish or restrict bulls for crusade indulgences, efforts thwarted by Spanish opposition for reasons of income not salvation. Yet that part of the game was up. Roman Catholic crusade apologists were increasingly reluctant to emphasize the offer of indulgences; their sale was abolished by Paul V in 1567. Crusading retained its place as an appropriate vehicle for Roman Catholics to use in fighting holy war. Yet religious division rendered its theology anathema to significant sections of Christian society who sought and found other ways and means to articulate and pursue violence in the name of their God.

26

The Crusade and Christian Society in the Later Middle Ages

Crusading mentalities did not wholly depend on active military engagement. The emotions sporadically summoned to support fundraising or recruitment were nourished by liturgy, literature, preaching, the sale of indulgences and taxation, from Cyprus to Greenland.[1] By the fourteenth century, planners and publicists assumed popular understanding and, for anti-Muslim crusades, sympathy. The familiarity of the crusading spawned recognizable social stereotypes: the 'ashy' *descroisié* or pontificating armchair crusader; the money-grubbing huckster and indulgence salesman; the power-seeking crusade preacher; the pious and chivalrous crusading knight; the faithful footslogger. The categories identified by Francis Bacon in his discussion of responses to holy war in the early seventeenth century boasted long histories: thoughtful theologians; fiery religious zealots; pragmatic soldiers; calculating courtiers; temporizing politicians.[2] In the later middle ages, crusading enjoyed greater prominence within western European society than on many frontiers with the infidel.

SOCIAL APPEAL

The wide social contact with crusading ideas and formulae transcended promotional special pleading and chroniclers' exaggeration. Philip of Mézières's final plan for his crusading Order of the Passion (1397) divided Christian warriors into three groups: kings and princes; common people; and, lastly, 'knights, squires, other barons, nobles, townsmen (*bourgeois*), merchants and men of honour of middling rank'.[3] On campaigns, humbler crusaders were naturally much in evidence. As in any army, officers needed men to command. The widely attested

Atlantic Ocean
ENGLAND
ENGLISH CRUSADES
For and against rebels
1215-1217
1263-1265
Evesham 1265
Lewes 1264
GERMANY
1239-1268
CHILDRENS CRUSADE 1212
SHEPHERDS' CRUSADE 1251+1320
Paris
CHILDRENS CRUSADE 1212
FRANCE
PIEDMONT CRUSADE 1306-1307
Milan
Venice
LOMBARDY
LANGUEDOC 1209-1229
ARAGON 1285
ITALY 1198-1418
Rome
SPANISH CRUSADES 1114-1492
Granada 1492
Mediter
1282-1302
SICILY
NORTH AFRICAN CRUSADES
1499-1578
Tunis
1270-1525
al-Mahdiya
1390

24. Crusades in Europe

0 100 200 300 400 500 miles
0 200 400 600 800 km
BALTIC CRUSADES
1147–1410
Tannenberg
1410
BOHEMIA
1420–1431
Hussites
ANTI-OTTOMAN
CRUSADES
1366–1699
Belgrade
1456
Nicopolis
1396
Varna
1444
Black Sea
Constantinople
ANTI-TURKISH
CRUSADES
1332–1571
Lepanto
1571
RHODES
CYPRUS
CRETE
nean Sea
Alexandria 1365

presence on crusades of squires, mercenaries and sailors causes no surprise. Perhaps more indicative were the urban citizens and working elites who displayed enthusiasm to join up. In the 1320s and 1330s citizens of northern French towns refused to pay crusade subsidies but protested their willingness to serve in person, encouraging fellow townsmen to follow suit.[4] Of course, these avowals may represent a traditional legal device to avoid novel fiscal demands, but they indicate how crusading remained a respectable public activity. More direct were the London apprentices who attempted to follow a crusade led by the bishop of Norwich against followers of the Avignon pope (i.e. the French) in 1382; or the eighty citizens of Ghent who took the cross, chose their own commander and set out for Venice in March 1464 (they were back by Christmas). Corporate pride sustained crusade traditions, in great commerical cities such as Venice, Genoa, Florence or London. Wine provided by the civic authorities of the small Flemish town of Axel in 1464 eased the tearful public farewells of the town's crusaders, who had just received the spiritual sustenance of the mass.[5]

Such occasional civic ceremonies were matched by more permanent demonstrations of crusade commitment: regular festivals, confraternities and gilds. Crusade interest in the 1330s at Tournai in north-eastern France may have been associated with the week-long festival of the Holy Cross that ended on 14 September, Holy Cross Day, a date closely linked with crusading.[6] While the lay orders of chivalry provided for the tastes and aspirations of the nobility, non-noble organizations emerged to cater for a wider public. Lay confraternities to channel devotion and material support can be found in France as early as the 1240s. In Italy, similar confraternities served the papalist cause. In Norfolk, England, in 1384 two gilds were founded, St Christopher's at Norwich and St Mary's at Wiggenhall, that began their meetings with prayers for the recovery of the Holy Land. If other English gilds' sponsorship of Jerusalem pilgrimages are a guide, these expressions of spiritual sociability could act as foci to arrange crusaders' practical needs as well as to give *crucesignati* members a good send off.[7]

The Parisian *confrarie* of the Holy Sepulchre demonstrated how interest could be fostered by overlapping local, political and social networks. Founded with a lavish ceremony on Holy Cross Day 1317 in the church of the Holy Cross in Paris, the confraternity's patron was Louis I count of Clermont and duke of Bourbon, grandfather of the 1390 al-Mahdiya commander and the French royal prince most frequently associated with French crusade plans for twenty years after 1316. Between 1325 and 1327, a church was built for the *confrarie*, dedicated to the Holy Sepulchre. This came to house a number of Holy Land relics, including three pieces of the True Cross, a key to one of the gates of Jerusalem, an arm of St George and a piece of stone from the Holy Sepulchre itself. Although attracting royalty and nobility, the core of the membership, apparently over 1,000 in the 1330s, were Parisian *bourgeois*, many of whom had taken the cross at Philip IV's great ceremony of 1313. The function of the confraternity was to provide these *crucesignati* with a way to structure and display their continued devotion and, no doubt, their special status and public association with the great. The patronage of courtiers lent snobbish value to membership as well as widening the circles of nobles' political clientage. The *confrarie* also acted as a charity, with the unachieved aim of founding a hospital for Holy Land pilgrims. Such institutions and buildings formed a tangible daily reminder of the *negotium crucis*, exploiting a variety of highly effective pressures: charity; the cult of relics; the elitism of a prominent civic social club; public display; the social allure of nobles and non-nobles mingling as *confrères*; the imprimatur of the church.[8] Such institutional context helped crusading continue as a social as well as religious phenomenon.

Before the gradual fading of realistic hopes of recovering the Holy Land, active planning could generate wider popular engagement, occasionally with disruptive consequences. Preaching, offers of indulgences and taxation could still ignite popular response from those on or beyond the margins of accepted political society. In 1309, in reaction to a small crusade expedition run by the Hospitallers, engaged in completing their conquest of Rhodes, apparently large numbers from England, the Low Countries and Germany took the cross and converged on Mediterranean ports. The papal-Hospitaller campaign, designed to relieve Armenia and Cyprus, only departed early in 1310. It had not been planned as a mass crusade, even if some hoped it would constitute an advance guard of much larger force, a dual strategy urged by contemporary theorists. In 1308, Pope Clement V had granted crusade privileges to those who helped the Hospitallers. A discrepancy arose between organizers and public. Official interest was in raising money to pay for a largely professional army; over two years in the archdiocese of York nearly £500 was collected, primarily from indulgences. However, the loss of the Holy Land in 1291, combined with more recent hopes of a Mongol liberation of Jerusalem, encouraged a wider participation. While hostile conservative chroniclers dismissed the recruits as unauthorized, underfunded and indisciplined, of lowly peasant or urban status, the social mix in this 'popular' crusade, as in 1212 and 1251, was broader than clerical snobbery and hierarchic defensiveness implied. From England, those licensed to depart for the Holy Land ranged from nobles to a surgeon. Some of the unofficial levies were sufficiently conversant with the political mechanics of crusading to petition the pope to summon a general crusade; he refused. Larceny and thuggery provided a familiar accompaniment to the progress of these bands southwards. As well as demonstrating the commonplace of violence and lawlessness on the fringes of mass demonstrations that disrupt the tenor of local communities, the alleged outrages reflected the crusaders' lack of funds and the impossibility of mounting a mass crusade without elite leadership and massive treasure. The existence of a pool of willing, if not particularly able, recruits cannot be doubted. The crusade industry had created its own market with customers unwilling to be fobbed off with spiritually passive or exclusively financial bargains.[9]

In 1320, the links between well-publicized official crusade policy and unauthorized crusade enthusiasm were just as clear. In the winter of 1319–20, Philip V of France held a series of conferences in Paris to discuss his crusade plans. A year earlier he had appointed Louis of Clermont as leader of the proposed French advance guard. In the spring, groups of so-called 'pastoureaux', indicating countrymen, if not literally shepherds, from northern France, converged on Paris around Easter. News of Philip's crusade plans may have penetrated these regions through the summonses to the winter assemblies, especially Normandy, Vermandois, Anjou, Picardy and the Ile de France. Economic conditions in some of these rural areas had been appalling. Peace with Flanders in 1319 and the hope generated by prospects of better times and a new crusade may have helped set these bands on the road to Paris. As in 1212 and 1251, many of those who set out were young men, with loose domestic ties, possibly without jobs or tenancies to sustain them through the severe agrarian depression. Yet their association with court policy was evident. A Parisian observer noted many of them came from Normandy, heavily represented at the crusade conferences.[10] Some marched behind the banner of Louis of Clermont, not improbably with his consent, hinting at the summons of the wider civil society in support of a troubled political elite. Pope John XXII expressed surprise that Philip V had acquiesced in the activities of the 'pastoureaux'.[11] Initially, churches gave them food and shelter. There was talk of using the marchers on a projected campaign to Italy by Philip V's cousin, Philip of Valois, the future Philip VI, hardly a task for a criminal mob. Parisians let them pass unmolested. The bands were well organized, some professing clear objectives, such as Aigues Mortes, whence they wished to sail to the Holy Land, indicating the power of nostalgia, precedent, history and legend, here the dominant memory of St Louis. As the bands headed towards the Midi, lack of assistance, realization of their isolation and resentment at the parasitic privileges of those deemed to have exploited or failed the crusade were channelled into violence. Wealthy laity and clergy were attacked; Jews were massacred. Such mayhem acted as a symptom as much as a cause of disintegration, a sign of the desperation to sustain themselves through acts of chastisement, in their eyes moral deeds that had to serve as substitutes for the greatest moral deed of all, the crusade.

The extent to which the French regime was complicit in encouraging the 'pastoureaux' in order to put pressure on the pope to grant crusade money to Philip V remains conjectural. Nevertheless, the French 'pastoureaux' did not operate entirely outside the perimeter of official crusade policy. They challenge any idea of popular enthusiasm for the Holy Land crusade declining or retreating into a day-dream for the chivalric classes. Neither were the 'pastoureaux' enacting a social revolt in disguise. The social critique was subtler, a shared acceptance with the elites of moral purposes coupled with harsh criticism of how those elites pursued them. Public failure, not social exploitation, lay at the heart of the grievances of 1320.[12]

The concept of the crusade could exceptionally be harnessed to radical social demands. In the spring of 1514, Archbishop Thomas Bakocz of Esztergom, with the vigorous assistance of the Observant Franciscans, hastily arranged a crusade in Hungary against the Turks, partly as a sop for his ego, battered by his narrow defeat at the papal conclave the previous year. Reminiscent of scenes in 1456, the preaching struck a chord with hard-pressed rural peasantry, townsmen and students. The economic situation was dire, hitting market towns and livestock herdsmen as much as peasants and tenant farmers. The crusade was sold as redemptive both spiritually and socially. The Hungarian nobility proved hostile, uninterested in supporting war with the Turks, eager to retain revenue designated for the defence of the Turkish frontier and angry at the potential loss of agricultural labour for hay making and harvest. Almost immediately, the crusaders turned on the nobles. Displaying a strong sense of community, the crusader army, led by the minor nobleman George Dozsa and allegedly numbering tens of thousands, began a reign of terror against nobles and their property across the Hungarian plain. Despite Archbishop Bakocz cancelling the crusade as soon as he saw how it was developing, the crusaders continued their rampage, while maintaining their devotion to the cross, crusading privileges, the king and the pope. As so often in sixteenth-century Europe, this was a very conservative social revolt. On 22 May 1514 an army of nobles was defeated, the crusaders finally being crushed only in mid-July at Timisoara (Temesvar). Atrocities had been committed on both sides, the final one the most horrific. Dozsa was placed on a burning stake, platform or throne, a red-hot iron 'crown' placed on his head and his followers compelled to bite chunks out of his burning flesh and drink his blood, all this accompanied by singing, dancing and a carnival atmosphere. Dozsa was being branded a traitor to nation, class and faith, precisely what he publicly denied. The 1514 crusade had been officially sanctioned. It attracted large numbers from a wide underclass of civil society with sensitive political antennae. They blamed the nobles – accurately – for failing to pursue the crusade, but took it further. The Hungarian nobles were branded as worse than Turks, a traditional charge levelled against those who impeded the *negotium Dei*. Only this time, those making these judgements were not popes, princes or prelates, but minor aristocrats and peasants who had taken too literally the message of the cross as a sign of emancipation.[13] It may be significant that one later Hungarian word for rebel, *kuruc*, is derived from *crux* and may enshrine a long cultural memory of the grim events of the spring and summer of 1514.[14]

The eccentric and gruesome Hungarian crusade revolt revealed the crusade as not necessarily the preserve of the social elites. However, it also illustrated how crusading motifs could be employed in contexts not essentially connected with holy war and, conversely, how initially tangential or non-crusading emotions and aspirations could find expression in crusade language and forms, however eccentrically or tendentiously construed, in this case by the radical Observant Franciscans. Equally, the behaviour of the Hungarian nobles in 1514 points to the absurdity of generalizing about crusade popularity or social embrace. The Hungarian elite became tepid at formal crusading at a time when the Habsburgs, heirs of the dukes of Burgundy but especially in their Iberian manifestation, eagerly employed the fully panoply of rhetoric, theology and privileges, tempered by their own brand of monarchical messianism. The Iberian revival found fewer echoes in fifteenth-century England when the collapse of the credibility of the Prussian crusade was not replaced by any new feasible object for action, except for those who became Hospitallers. In France, the crusade retained its lustre, but was inextricably caught up in the burgeoning religion of monarchy. As a bond of community and a justification for war, in many places and times crusading, having provided a model, became superseded. The very lack of such confidence in their share of national identity may have encouraged the less grand elements in Hungary to define their action against the Turks and then their nobles so tenaciously in terms of traditional crusading.

CONTINUING TRADITIONS

As in previous centuries, crusading continued to run in families and in regions. This could impose a sense of obligation, almost of responsibility, especially as stories of past crusading heroism circulated widely in literature, polemic and preaching. Parish churches and family homes were festooned with relics of past crusades and crusading ancestors. Tradition caused successive kings of France to be proclaimed as bearing an especial responsibility for crusading in the east, not least by themselves. The duty formed part of their kingship, a proprietorial association carefully nurtured by the first two rulers of the cadet Valois dynasty, Philip VI in the 1330s and John II in the 1360s. More junior branches of St Louis's descendants were no less infected, notably Louis I of Bourbon and his grandson Louis II, the al-Mahdiya commander. Across Europe similar family histories encouraged members from all stations of the nobility and aristocracy to maintain the tradition, some, such as the Beauchamps, Mowbrays and Percys in England, or the Briennes in Champagne, boasting holy war pedigrees that stretched in some cases from the early twelfth to the late fourteenth centuries. In the fourteenth century, families' engagement scarcely abated.[15] Although some used holy wars as a finishing ground for a knightly education, others found them sterner training. For casualties of Nicopolis or young Geoffrey Scrope of Masham in Yorkshire, killed in the forbidding wastes of Lithuania in 1362, as for those western recruits who fought with the Hospitallers in defence of Rhodes against the Mamluks in 1444, such as Daniel Habin of Majorca, who lost a hand, or Matthew of Transylvania, deprived of the use of his right arm, these wars were no games.[16] The decline in active crusading was the result of a reduction in opportunity not, as often asserted, the other way round. In relation to eastern crusades, at least, the continuing lure of the Holy Places alone testifies to lively interest. From the 1330s and entrenched by the 1370 Cypriot-Egyptian treaty, the Mamluk rulers of Palestine followed the precedent of Saladin in allowing western Christians access to the Holy Sites at a price. The fourteenth and fifteenth centuries witnessed a resurgence of large-scale western pilgrimages to Palestine and Egypt and a welter of published accounts of pilgrims' experiences as well as formal itineraries. Many of these pilgrims at other times also fought against the infidel, but not in the Holy Land.

Compensation for the absence of active crusading was found in the round of indulgences on offer and liturgies performed. Occasionally the crusading element in the prevailing cultural *milieu* found more targeted demonstration. In 1407–8, partly as a public relations exercise, the Hospitallers of Rhodes constructed the fortress of St Peter at Bodrum, classical Halicarnassus, on the mainland opposite Cos. To pay for the hugely expensive building work, which included reusing dressed stone from the nearby mausoleum, the Hospitallers launched an appeal, backed by papal indulgences. English contributions alone helped to pay for a tower on whose walls twenty-six coats-of-arms were set up in stone, including those of King Henry IV, his four sons and the families with recent or ancient crusade pedigrees, such as the Montagues, Courtenays, Nevilles, Percys, Beauchamps and Hollands. Possibly copied for an armorial roll, they may represent the chief contributors. One set of arms was those of the FitzHughs. Henry FitzHugh had sent equipment to Bodrum in 1409; Sir William, probably Henry's son, and his wife bought Bodrum indulgences in 1414. Bodrum retained strong links with the English section (or *langue*) of the Hospitallers throughout the fifteenth century, William Dawney and John Langstrother, later prior of the English Hospitallers, holding the command there in 1448 and 1456 respectively.[17]

Regional commitment varied but also demonstrated tenacious links with the past. The dukes of Burgundy played on their inheritance as counts of Flanders of the Flemish crusading legacy during attempts to arouse their subjects' support for a crusade in the 1450s. For a venture directed to the relief of Constantinople, it was convenient and appropriate to invoke the memory of Baldwin IX, the first Latin emperor. Each area seemed to require its crusade heroes – St Louis in France; Richard I in England; the Iberian champions of the *reconquista*, etc. – even ones with spurious credentials, such as St Ladislas in Hungary. The Low Countries, western Germany, Champagne and northern France, the heartlands of the First Crusade, remained fertile recruiting grounds. Grafting crusading enthusiasm on to social groups not attuned by long experience proved less easy, as the relative indifference of the Polish or Hungarian nobilities in the later fifteenth century testified. Long absence of concerted preaching or actual recruitment could relegate active crusading to an increasingly eccentric if no less sincere minority, as in England after the 1330s and even more after 1400. Conversely, as in Iberia in the later fifteenth century, crusade enthusiasm could be revived by government commitment and action. Either way, cultural recognition, once established, proved extremely tenacious, even when producing only fitful ignition of official or public activity.

One sign of this came in the way crusading acted as a mechanism of social advancement. Service in holy war acted as a means of entry to the ranks of the knightly and respectable for parvenus, a ticket of admission into the secular social elite. Such rites of social passage could include meritorious service in national or royal wars, but crusading, as indicated by the emphasis placed on it by numerous lay orders of chivalry, attracted especially rewarding recognition. Nicholas Sabraham, a veteran of Crécy in 1346, made his fortune at war for three decades, from the 1330s, on English campaigns in Scotland, France and Spain. He also fought in Prussia, joined Peter of Cyprus's crusade to Alexandria in 1365 and from there went to serve on Amadeus of Savoy's expedition of 1366–7 to the Dardenelles and Bulgaria. Most of the crusades offered few, if any, easy pickings. A professional soldier very different from the gilded crusading youths with whom he rubbed shoulders, Sabraham nonetheless was called to give evidence in a great armorial dispute held in the English Court of Chivalry in 1386, where he carefully described his crusading exploits.[18] They were a guarantee of his gentility of deed regardless of birth. Across the English Channel, Bertrand du Guesclin, the chief military commander and strategist under Charles V, by no means from the top drawer of the French nobility, attempted to enhance his status when fighting for French allies in Spain in 1366 by associating the Spanish war against the English with a crusade to Granada. Bertrand was even crowned 'king of Granada' by his employer, King Henry II of Castile.[19] The image of holy wars of the cross required little explanation or special pleading to attract admiration.

THE IMAGE OF CRUSADING

The commitment of individuals and communities to the ideals and occasional practice of crusading found expression in art and literature. At the end of Thomas Malory's *Morte d'Arthur* (finished 1469/70), Sir Bors, Sir Blamore, Sir Ector and Sir Bleoberis finish their careers fighting 'miscreants and Turks' in the Holy Land.[20] Judging by the contents of contemporary late fifteenth-century libraries, this was a historical but not cultural anachronism. Texts of crusade history and advice continued to be written, copied or, later, printed with undiminished energy into the sixteenth century, when new genres of vernacular literature emerged regarding the Turkish menace, particularly in Germany. Especially popular across Europe were histories and legends of the Holy Land crusades, not just with kings, princes and courtiers. Chronicles of Jerusalem, probably William of Tyre, found their way into the possession of local gentry in Norfolk and Bedfordshire in England. The Norfolk gentleman John Paston II owned a chronicle, in English, about Richard I. The printer William Caxton translated William of Tyre in 1481.[21] Historical knowledge was assumed. Entertaining Peter I of Cyprus to dinner in London in the winter of 1363–4, Edward III of England teased his guest that, if Peter succeeded in recovering Jerusalem, Cyprus, 'which my ancestor Richard entrusted to your predecessor to keep', should be restored to the English king.[22]

Contemporary news from the eastern front was equally avidly devoured, by word of mouth or in writing. Jean Waurin's account of the anti-Turkish wars of the 1440s reached the English court under Edward IV. Guillaume de Caoursin's eyewitness account of the siege of Rhodes (1480), with vivid woodcut illustrations, reached a wide international audience within a decade of its appearance, soon being translated, for example, into English in 1484.[23] Printers other than Caxton cashed in. The mid-fourteenth century pseudonymous compendium of crusade exhortation, pilgrim guide and stories of the mythic marvels of the east known as *The Travels of John Mandeville* remained an international best-seller for 200 years, transmuting into a series of at least fourteen separate versions in twelve different languages to suit contrasting tastes, purposes and regions. There was even a 'textless' pictorial 'Mandeville' derived from a Czech redaction. Some of its versions, at least, stressed the need for 'the right children of Christ . . . to challenge the heritage that Our Father left us and do it out of heathen men's hands'.[24]

Visual representations of crusading had long been popular. Many manuscript and printed books were embellished with especially luminous portrayals of famous crusading moments. Some of these suggest how, aesthetically, the past was hardly distinguished from the present, figures being shown in anachronistically contemporary dress. Late fifteenth-century illuminations depict Heraclius, the seventh-century Byzantine emperor whose return of the Holy Cross to Jerusalem opens William of Tyre's chronicle, sporting the heraldic device of fifteenth-century Habsburg German emperors. Stained glass, murals, sculpture and decorative tiles all provided media for commemorating a heroic past that allowed some to dream of a heroic future. In the 1390s, Thomas of Woodstock adorned his castle at Pleshey with fifteen tapestries on the romances of Godfrey of Bouillon.[25] Seventy years later, the demand for such artefacts led to the London merchant Sir Thomas Cooke being arraigned for treason because he refused to sell to Edward IV's mother-in-law an arras 'wrought in the most richest wise with gold of the story of the siege of Jerusalem'.[26]

Dramatic tableaux and ritualized plays supplied another medium to remind audiences of the significance of their crusading heritage. In 1378, Charles V of France entertained the emperor Charles IV of Germany in Paris with a lavish production of the siege of Jerusalem, possibly stage-managed by Philip of Mézières.[27] The impact of this presentation was later enshrined in manuscript illuminations of the event. On one level a wallow in shared chivalric nostalgia, the Paris production possessed a practical resonance. Both the French and German courts had been involved in actual crusade planning in the 1360s and were subject to more recent appeals for action against the Ottomans. Such play-acting could reduce the huge gap in time and circumstance, in a manner parallel to the static impression of time often given in church sermons; the past was somehow contemporary, whether biblical or crusading. These displays possessed purpose: to create a sympathetic atmosphere for the circulation of crusading ideas and to demonstrate continued official commitment, even of a generalized sort. Charles V was the first king of France not personally to be involved in crusading or crusade planning since Louis VI (d. 1137). The Paris *fête* asserted his credentials nonetheless. Elsewhere, such dramatic performances promoted more immediate causes, as at Mons in 1454, when the Burgundian court witnessed a pageant on the Fourth Crusade, Baldwin of Flanders and the 1204 capture of Constantinople.[28] These extravagant theatricals raise questions of seriousness and sincerity. They were showy entertainments, not recruiting platforms. Yet they revealed the cultural vivacity of crusading and a receptiveness to retaining at least a sentimentalized idealism within which wars of the cross could be thought of as possible as well as admirable. In the light of those who fought and died in such wars, this playfulness contained a serious message.

CRUSADES AND SALVATION

Evidence from popular devotional practices confirm that two central elements of the appeal of crusading retained potency throughout the later middle ages and beyond: the offer of remission of sins and fear of the infidel, usually couched in terms of the recovery of the Holy Land. Of all the continuities of crusading, its promotion by the church remained the clearest and most ubiquitous. The apparatus of privileges remained in place. Clerical taxation became habitual, if localized. The offer of indulgences remained part of a general penitential system, increasingly commercial as redemption of vows or even the performance of any particular meritorious act gave way to simple sale and payment. The doctrine of a Treasury of Merits, a sort of divine bank account laid up by God to be drawn on by the penitent faithful, was perfected by Clement VI. This further institutionalized crusading indulgences. Preaching, donations and legacies persisted. The chests set aside for contributions stayed in parish churches. The increasingly bureaucratic procedures of the papacy and local dioceses still administered the crusade, its promotion, privileges, organization and finance. At the most mundane, parochial level, the liturgy for the recovery of the Holy Land and appeals to God to turn back the infidel reached the daily lives of the faithful throughout Christendom until the Reformation tore it apart.

Recent research has identified large quantities of surviving manuscripts recording a range of associated liturgical rites centred on general or specific supplications for divine aid on behalf of the Holy Land or the Turks.[29] They reveal the extent of strenuous, regular religious activity, conducted in parish churches, monasteries and cathedrals across western Europe from the thirteenth to the sixteenth centuries, directed towards the object of crusading, the liberation of the Holy Land or defence against pagans, infidels or Turks. Although there are examples of papal orders to conduct Holy Land masses not being carried out, as in the diocese of Rouen in the 1330s, the nature and weight of the records suggest prayers and masses were not being copied out in some arcane collective antiquarian homage to past, dead usages but represent a set of living observances.[30] The Holy Land supplicatory devices appeared in a number of liturgical categories. The *clamor* to invoke God's help for the Holy Land was inserted in the mass between the consecration and the breaking of the Host before the Communion. It appeared in various standard forms in manuscript and printed missals from the thirteenth to the sixteenth centuries, those derived from the English dioceses of Salisbury, York and Hereford being particularly prominent. Associated with the rite of taking the cross, these prayers were inserted into the mass on special occasions. By contrast, normal celebrations of the Eucharist could be dedicated as a whole to the special votive aim of the recovery of the Holy Land. Provision for such special masses was included in the instructions for the preparations for a crusade by John XXII (1333), Urban V (1363) and Gregory XI (1373). Such special masses could be directed towards a particular crusade or, especially in the fifteenth century, to less precise assistance to the Holy Land. The later fifteenth century saw an increase in dedicated masses against the Turks, but they were also invoked against Hussites and, more vaguely, 'pagans' and 'infidels'.

A more remarkable use of masses for the Holy Land were the so-called Gregorian Trentals, originating in England in the later fourteenth century. These comprised clusters of thirty masses to be said for the soul of the dead after the death or burial of the testator who endowed the services. Within the mass, prayers were included for the liberation of the Holy Land alone or combined the liberation of the Holy Land with the liberation of the soul of the departed from 'the hands of demons', i.e. in purgatory. The destination of the soul and the Holy Land were equated, the pagans by analogy liturgically demonized. In England alone there survive eighty separate liturgical sources for this habit, as well as almost 150 wills, mainly from the fifteenth century. Calixtus III appears to have encouraged the practice during his crusade efforts in 1455. In England, at least, these daily masses could be sung 365 days a year.

Although such liturgies stretched the link between crusade ideology and crusade action to an extreme, they testify to the inescapable power and penetration of the image of the liberation of the Holy Land, which did not depend on sporadic official preaching or fundraising to hold the thoughts of the faithful. Further confirmation of this can be found in wills across western Europe, certainly in the fourteenth century, bequeathing money for the crusade as well as for Holy Land masses. However, the lack of association with active crusading suggests that the liberation of the Holy Land provided a spiritual metaphor, both for the liberation of the individual soul from the consequences of sin, as in the English Gregorian Trentals, and, more widely, for the struggle against the ungodly. This passive response was evinced most clearly by Holy Land bidding prayers. These were vernacular intercessory prayers said in parish churches across Europe on Sundays and feast days directly after the sermon. From the late thirteenth century they became a habitual part of the general supplicatory apparatus of church liturgy. They were far from calls to crusade, unlike elements elsewhere in the liturgy.[31] The only action prescribed for the recovery of the Holy Land was prayer, an ultimate distillation of the growing passivity that the extension of crusade institutions in the thirteenth century inadvertently encouraged. Once again, the recovery of the Holy Land appears as a symbol of God's favour and the acceptability of the prayers of the faithful. This tradition sustained the image of crusading as a central Christian devotional activity long after fighting for the cross had become a rarity. However, on all sides of the confessional divides that opened up in the sixteenth century, such externalized manifestations of corporate religion, using a physical act – the recovery of the Holy Land – as a means of securing grace and salvation, became increasingly unconvincing as more and more articulate believers turned towards systems of devotion that concentrated more directly on the interior personal experience of God and faith. Furthermore, different categories of 'ungodly' entered Christian demonology, replacing the old stereotypes and analogies, rendering crusade polemical imagery redundant.

Central ceremonies of crusading persisted. As in bidding prayers, the emphasis on the cross displayed in crusade sermons became integrated into more general evangelism and penitential exhortation centred on the cross's redemptive powers; parts of many crusade sermons were interchangeable with those concerned with moral reform. Sermons delivered or circulated in manuscript to provide models for local exhortation displayed a traditional formalism of structure and content, evident, for example, in England, in crusade sermons well into the fourteenth century. In fact, the heavily allusive metaphorical language of crusade was developed more by desk-bound or court-based propagandists, mostly laymen, than working preachers, who tended to operate within a tight academic tradition. Despite the crafted crusade preaching of, for instance, the fourteenth-century English Dominican John Bromyard, or the Frenchman Pierre Roger, the future Pope Clement VI, subsequently, the true heirs of the great crusade preachers of earlier generations were figures such as Mézières. Statistics of sermons in northern France between 1350 and 1520 indicate only a tiny proportion concerned the crusade, indulgences, Saracens or heretics.[32] The crusade preaching tour and sermon, like the sale of indulgences, became routine aspects of administration, no longer the necessary focal point of recruitment and propaganda, sometimes omitted altogether. The exception of John of Capistrano's popular evangelism in Hungary in 1456 exposed the contrast with other crusade initiatives where, if present at all, sermons were delivered to elite court audiences, with no thought to mass communication. Increasingly, the commonest public encounter came with the pardoner or indulgence salesman, not the preacher.

Other aspects of crusade organization, including privileges and taking the cross, similarly varied in intensity and application. Processions inspired by specific crusading campaigns were conducted at Douai regularly during the mid-fifteenth century. Such public demonstrations assumed greater significance in the absence of frequent recruiting drives. The near-permanent sale of indulgences, in many regions robustly popular in terms of profit, operated at a different, less intense level of public or personal involvement.[33] With fewer people actually taking the cross, the associated privileges tended to fall into disuse. One much exploited privilege of *crucesignati* allowed them to delay answering law suits, known as essoin of court. In his *Mirror of Justices*, Andrew Horn (d. 1328), fishmonger and Chamberlain of the City of London, described, as a matter of course, the essoin of crusaders engaged in 'a general passage to the land of Jerusalem'. By the end of the century, such assumptions may have became genuinely anachronistic. In France by the 1380s, for instance, the lawbook known as the *Grand Coutumier de France* omitted any mention of crusaders from its detailed list of essoins.[34] The habit of taking the cross had become too infrequent.

The ceremony of taking the cross, the defining ritual of crusading, remained available for the faithful, penitent or adventurous, but, as an active expression of interest in holy war, appears increasingly exceptional compared with earlier centuries. In December 1382, Bishop Henry Despenser of Norwich took the cross in St Paul's cathedral, London. He apparently had experienced some difficulty locating an order of service, given its recent rarity. In fact, copies of the ceremony existed in many English cathedrals and abbeys. Different English rites for taking the cross existed in York, Lincoln and Salisbury (Despenser found his version in the liturgy books of the monks of Westminster).[35] Although notable for their absence during the 1390 al-Mahdiya and 1396 Nicopolis expeditions, or as part of the Burgundian court's display of crusade enthusiasm in the 1450s, examples of individuals and groups taking the cross show how the practice continued, as among the Hungarian peasantry in 1456 or the citizens of Ghent in the 1460s. Individual vows to fight the infidel can be found from France and Bavaria in the fourteenth century to Englishman and Scotsmen in the 1450s and worsted weavers from Norfolk in 1499.[36] Rites for taking the cross continued to be copied into diocesan service books throughout the period, alongside the wider Holy Land liturgy. When Innocent VIII standardized the rite in the Roman Pontifical, he acknowledged the new circumstances of the Turkish advance when he changed the preamble to the ceremony from one restricted to those 'going to assist the Holy Land' to those wishing 'to assist and defend the Christian faith or the recovery of the Holy Land'.[37] The change indicated the pope believed or hoped the rite was in current use. Below the level of papal authorization, the cross could be given by local clergy to adventurers, such as Robert Almer at Canterbury in 1462, or to penitent robbers, a couple of whom received the cross at St Alban's in 1479.[38] The adaptability of the ceremony and institution was repeatedly confirmed, from new Iberian conquistadors to devout Roman Catholics fighting Protestant Huguenots in Toulouse during the French Wars of Religion in the 1560s. No less than Innocent III summoning the Fourth Lateran Council in 1213, Paul III was certain his congregation knew the significance of assuming the cross of Christ when he assembled the Council of Trent in 1544–5.[39]

By then, the whole idea of the redemptive merit of crusading had been challenged by critics of the Roman Church, mostly, but not exclusively, by Protestant confessional opponents. Ironically, central to the criticism lay the question of indulgences. Although those directed at serving the recovery of the Holy Land, the fight against the Turks or subsidizing the Hospitallers at Rhodes could still prove popular, the wide application and in places blatant racketeering involved threatened to discredit the whole system, as Pius II had warned.[40] Thus at the very core of the crusading practices, a *de facto* separation emerged between function – fighting the infidel – and method – the offer and sale of indulgences. This occurred at the same time as other dimensions of holy war asserted themselves across Christendom, some overtly associated with crusading, some less so, some not all. Hussites and Protestants could happily fight holy wars without the apparatus of Roman Catholic crusade theology. Prayers for aid against the Turks appeared in Edward VI of England's Protestant Prayer Book (1549, 1552). Just as not all prayers for the Holy Land indicated closet crusading, so not every expression of holy war, just war or hostility towards infidels came wrapped in formal crusading packaging. Even amongst Roman Catholics, the devolution of crusading to frontlines where combat was a matter of national survival, not religious duty, further diluted any ideological exclusivity the crusading may have possessed. The association of holy war with lay politics at once provided one of the commonest and most controversial battlefields for crusaders. As with indulgences, one of the most characteristic features of later medieval crusading proved one of the most self-defeating. To understand this, it is necessary to return to the thirteenth century.

CRUSADES AGAINST CHRISTIANS

Between the late thirteenth and early fifteenth centuries, crusades launched against Christians, in the heart of Christian society, formed the most consistent application of papal holy war. Inherent in the emergence of an ideology of holy war in the early middle ages, canonists and theologians in the thirteenth century, including Thomas Aquinas, further developed the doctrine of religious just war in Christendom. Henry of Segusio or Hostiensis argued that the *crux cismarina*, the crusade within Christendom, possessed more urgency and justice than the *crux transmarina*, or overseas crusade. In condoning papal policy, Hostiensis was reflecting traditional attitudes.[41] This did not absolve them from criticism and controversy. When preaching against the Hohenstaufen in Germany in 1251, Hostiensis himself discovered wide and deep opposition to preaching the cross against Christians.[42] Intellectually and legally valid, crusades against Christians never sat as comfortably in the mentalities of the faithful as wars against infidels. One of the key attractions of crusading lay in demonizing 'aliens' against whom the faithful could define their identity; crusades against Christians too often looked uncomfortably like crusades against themselves.

During the twelfth century, the papacy continued to sanction wars against its political opponents. Yet none, even the substantial expedition directed against the adventurer Markward of Anweiler in 1199, seems to have been accompanied by preaching, cross-taking or the full array of Holy Land privileges.[43] Only with the Albigensian crusade in 1209, directed to the Christian protectors of heretics as much as the heretics themselves, was the complete Holy Land apparatus employed, its equality with the eastern war confirmed in the bull *Excommunicamus* of the Fourth Lateran Council (1215). Innocent III's desire to offer the crusade indulgence as widely as possible and his encouragement of the idea of Christian society as a church militant constantly challenged by sin and temporal enemies made the incorporation of wars against Christians a logical step. Clerical crusade taxation for political conflicts appealed to secular rulers caught up in them, as well as providing the papacy with a mechanism of control and the capacity the vast sums of church money granted to initiate military action on its own behalf. This became useful with the acquisition under Innocent III and his successors of temporal Papal States in central Italy that required maintaining and defending.

The main wars of the cross against Christians in the thirteenth and fourteenth centuries revolved around the temporal position of the papacy in Italy, the defence of the Papal States, church rights, access to ecclesiastical wealth and fears of territorial encirclement. This last was no paranoid fiction. Thirteenth-century popes, such as Innocent IV, spent long periods in exile from Rome. A regularly peripatetic papacy presiding over an increasingly effective centralized bureaucracy and growing international recognition of papal ecclesiastical jurisdiction offered an irony not lost on papal adherents as much as opponents. Physical insecurity contradicted papal claims to temporal as well as spiritual plenitude of power. Directing crusades as a remedy implemented the ideological implications of papal ambition as well as confronting their material adversaries. Thus crusading became a major device in papal attempts to protect its vassals and allies. To achieve independence in Italy and primacy in Christendom, popes applied crusading to wars with the Hohenstaufen rulers of Germany and Sicily (1239–68), the Wars of the Sicilian Vespers to restore Angevin rule in Sicily (1282–1302), campaigns to secure papal interests in central and northern Italy during the evacuation of the papal Curia to Avignon (1309–77) and attempts to resolve by force the Great Schism (1378–1417), when two, then three popes claimed to be the legitimate successors of St Peter.

Papal ideology could easily become distracted to essentially secular conflicts, as in England in 1216–17 and 1263–5.[44] Between 1208 and 1214, England had lain under a papal interdict (which meant that the church ceased to function except for infant baptism and Extreme Unction) because of King John's refusal to accept Innocent III's nominee Stephen Langton as archbishop of Canterbury. John had been excommunicated (1209–13). In 1213, as part of the agreement that ended the interdict, John made England and Ireland fiefs of the papacy. After his attempt to win back lost lands in France in 1214, John took the cross in 1215, in part to gain protection against the growing threat of rebellion against his harsh financial exactions and roughshod management of his nobility. This failed to prevent England's slide into civil war, but the alliance with the Roman church persisted. After John's death, his nine-year-old heir, Henry III, reinforced his credentials as a deserving recipient of church assistance by taking the cross immediately after his coronation in 1216. The crusader's privilege paid dividends. In January 1216, Innocent III offered remission of sins to those who fought for King John; his opponents were branded as renegades hindering the crusade to the Holy Land. Indulgences were repeated by Honorius III in September 1216. Crusaders destined for the east were permitted to deflect their crusade vow to fight for the king. Contemporary chroniclers were unequivocal in describing royalists as *crucesignati*, the victors over the rebels at the crucial battle of Lincoln being depicted wearing the white crosses of the Angevins, albeit on their backs, not shoulders. Although the documentary evidence is more equivocal, it seems possible that a number of individuals took the cross to defend the English king in 1216–17. More certainly, eyewitnesses painted the conflict in explicitly crusading terms through language that sat comfortably with Innocent III's extended use of wars of the cross.

Half a century and a weight of crusades against Christians later, there was no doubt. In the autumn of 1263, in answer to an appeal from Henry III, Urban IV appointed Gui of Foulquois (subsequently Pope Clement IV) to negotiate peace between the king and his domestic opponents, if necessary by preaching the cross against them. The rebel victory at Lewes in May 1264 denied Gui access to England and, beyond excommunicating them, there is no sign Gui preached the cross. However, as Pope Clement IV, Gui renewed the royalist crusade. In the summer of 1265, Cardinal Ottobuono was instructed to preach the cross in north-west Europe and to raise a clerical tax in England, avoiding areas of southern Europe where Charles of Anjou's crusade to Sicily was being raised. In the event, the royalists crushed the rebels under Simon of Montfort at Evesham in August 1265 before any continental crusade force had been gathered. Nonetheless, the willingness of Urban IV and Clement IV to throw the full panoply of Holy Land crusading behind the political interests of their temporal allies reveals how far the war of the cross had become integrated into all aspects of papal secular policy, in the eyes of its promoters, synonymous, if only rhetorically, with the defence of the faith, i.e. the Roman church. This assumption, falling as a material burden on the whole church through taxation, grated on many, especially when it seemed to promise no end to conflict and bore few tangible benefits.

The war against the Hohenstaufen (1239–68) witnessed the most sustained pursuit of this policy.[45] It marked a final collapse of hopes for a papal–imperial alliance that had seemed attainable on a number of occasions between 1180 and 1230, not least during the youth of Frederick II, when he was a papal protégé and designated commander of the pope's crusade. The dispute derived from an intractable range of problems. The dynastic claims of Frederick to rule Sicily and the German empire, including rights over northern Italy, posed a potential challenge to papal independence. The creation of the Papal States inevitably led to tensions over frontier regions, especially the March of Ancona and the duchy of Spoleto. Local territorial rivalries were complicated by the special relationship of pope and emperor, symbolized by papal recognition and coronation of imperial candidates. Control of Sicily, as a papal fief, provided another focus of conflict, especially as Frederick and his successors governed the church in their lands with scant regard for papal supremacy and disdain for papal interference. The bitterness of papal hostility towards Frederick II in particular was a product of previously close attachment turning sour. A fundamental lack of trust in what Urban IV called a 'viper race' fuelled the tenacity with which the successive popes pursued Frederick and his heirs.

Earlier papally sponsored campaigns against Frederick II, such as that under John of Brienne in 1228–30, had been funded by clerical taxation. Frederick had twice been excommunicated, in 1227 and March 1239. However, only in the winter of 1239–40 did Gregory IX call for a formal crusade against the emperor. The pope's allies, the Lombard League of northern Italian cities, had been heavily defeated by Frederick in 1237. Imperial forces threatened Rome, where, as so often in the period, support for the pope remained fickle. By summoning a crusade, Gregory could expect to stiffen local resistance but also mobilize a larger coalition in northern Italy and Germany by making church funds available to those prepared to take the field against the emperor. The crusade, renewed in 1240 and 1243, was primarily preached in imperial lands north and south of the Alps. Anti-kings were established in Germany: Henry Raspe of Thuringia (1246–7), then William of Holland (1247–56). Ringingly endorsed by the First Council of Lyons (1245), these anti-Hohenstaufen crusades attracted many recruits, some defecting from Louis IX's crusade. The association of crusading to the political conflicts of Italy and Germany lent the anti-imperialist cause an element of institutional commitment and international appeal (or outrage, depending on the observer) they would otherwise not have enjoyed. However, the crusade's main contribution was financial: the church subsidized the war to destroy the Hohenstaufen, which would otherwise have been beyond the resources, let alone will, of the motley collection of secular lords ranged with the papacy.

On Frederick's death, attempts to reach an accommodation with his successors failed, and crusades were renewed against his heir, Conrad IV, and Frederick's illegitimate son, Manfred, regent (1250–58), then king, of Sicily. Increasingly, the focus of crusading fell on Italy and Sicily. In 1255 Alexander IV persuaded Henry III of England to accept the crown of Sicily on behalf of his second son, Edmund, hoping to add the resources of a secular kingdom to those of the church. English involvement proved abortive, as the financial obligations of the project and the extravagance of its ambition helped provoke opposition and civil war in England (1258–65). However, the scheme of hiring a secular prince to attack Manfred was revived by Urban IV and Clement IV, who secured the services of Louis IX's youngest brother, Charles of Anjou. After a lightning campaign in the winter of 1265–6, Charles defeated and killed Manfred at the battle of Benevento in February 1266. Two years later, Charles secured his position by victory at Tagliacozzo (August 1268) over Conrad IV's now teenage son and titular king of Jerusalem, Conradin. In October 1268, Charles had Conradin executed at Naples, the last of the male Hohenstaufen line.[46]

The baleful legacy of the crusades of conquest in southern Italy and Sicily infected the politics of the peninsula for generations. Opponents of papal interests became known as Ghibellines (*Ghibellini*), a nickname apparently derived from a twelfth-century Hohenstaufen war cry, 'Waiblingen', the name of a family estate in Swabia. Papal supporters and anti-imperialists, by deliberate contrast, were described as Guelphs, recognizing the long German opposition of the Welf family to the Hohenstaufen. Crusading became almost endemic in Italian politics, crusades being launched against Ezzelino and Alberic of Romano in 1255 and Sardinia in 1263. A new lease of papal energy followed the Sicilian uprising against Charles of Anjou in March 1282, known as the Sicilian Vespers, and the annexation of the island a few months later by Peter III of Aragon, whose wife was Frederick II's daughter.[47] In January 1283, a new crusade against Aragon was promulgated by Martin IV, to which Philip III of France was recruited. Philip's invasion of Aragon in

1285 ended in dismal failure. Having wasted the summer months in a fruitless siege of Gerona in north-east Catalonia and losing his fleet to the Aragonese navy, Philip was forced to retreat, during which he died. This debacle probably persuaded Philip III's son and heir, the inscrutable but single-minded Philip IV, to avoid such direct entanglements in the future. Further crusade bulls were issued when Frederick of Sicily, Peter III of Aragon's younger son, defied his elder brother James II of Aragon by retaining control of Sicily despite a papal-Aragonese agreement in 1295 restoring the island to the Angevins. This fresh round of crusades only ended with the Treaty of Caltabellotta in 1302 between Frederick of Sicily and the new papal claimant to the island, Charles of Valois, younger brother of Philip IV of France. Thereafter, there were no more crusades against Sicily. Although the crusade weapon may have helped destroy the Hohenstaufen, the final territorial settlement hardly matched papal aspirations; Sicily remained divided from the kingdom of Naples for another two centuries.

In the fourteenth century, Italian battlelines fragmented, especially with the papacy largely absent from the peninsula (from 1305, at Avignon from 1309 until 1377). Popes persisted in using the crusade to further their policies.[48] Twice aggressive attempts were launched to reassert imperial claims in Italy, by Henry VII (in 1310–13) and Louis IV (1328–30), German kings eager to acquire the traditional imperial title, the latter's move on Rome eliciting a crusade against him. Most Italian crusades in the period were applied to more local targets; Boniface VIII in dealing with his rivals the Colonna in 1297–8; the suppression of the Piedmontese heretical leader Dolcino in 1306–7; or preventing Venetian annexation of Ferrara (1309–10). John XXII showed himself particularly bellicose. The *signori* (military rulers of cities) of Lombardy, Tuscany and central Italy tended to be anti-papal Ghibellines, prominently the Visconti of Milan. Florence and the rump Angevin kingdom of Naples favoured the papal, Guelph, side. Regardless of the traditional crusade rhetoric, privileges, funding and accoutrements, such as red and white crosses adorning the banners of John XXII's Italian crusaders, self-interest, not principle or faith, determined action.[49] Thus in 1334 Guelph Florence combined with its rival, Ghibelline Milan, to thwart papal plans for a new Lombard puppet state. Only a very narrow, technical, partisan and increasingly unconvincing equation of the political interests of popes with the spiritual health of Christendom could endow these wars with religious significance. This did not prevent participants enjoying the crusader status and privileges on offer. The wars would have been fought in any case and men would have fought in them. The crusade merely added lustre; it hardly determined their practical nature. As in Spain, the crusade in Italy became increasingly a fiscal device, a means of raising money for war.

Major campaigns over the Papal States were organized by cardinal-legates Bertrand du Poujet after 1319 and Gil Albornoz after 1353. Crusades were instigated against Milan and Ferrara in 1321; Milan, Mantua and rebels in Ancona in 1324; Cesena and Faenza in 1354; and Milan again in 1360, 1363 and 1368. After 1357, a new element was introduced, with crusades directed to eradicating those mercenary companies not in papal pay, in 1357, 1361 and 1369/70. Huge sums were spent, especially by the spendthrift amateur war-monger John XXII. Yet outside Italy, the same popes were reluctant to apply crusading to other people's wars, such as those between France and England. Even in Italy, it is hard to see how the use of the crusade as a local coercive weapon, with strictly limited regional objectives, preaching, recruitment and impact, made much of a difference. They may not have been theoretical perversions of the institution of crusading. They were certainly enthusiastically embraced by those who were on the pope's side in the first place. They may have persuaded more to join the spiritual gravy train. They ensured the crusade remained embedded in western European experience, yet only on a limited scale. The Italian wars were not universal, even in propaganda. Although canonically legitimate – how could they not be, as popes determined what was canonical? – the papal crusades in Italy, and crusades against Christians generally, lacked the distinctive numinous historical resonance that gave holy wars elsewhere their particular spiritual charge.

As if to reinforce this, the early years of the Great Schism (1378–1417) saw crusades launched by both sides against each other. In 1378 the Roman pope Urban VI launched a crusade against his Avignon rival Clement VII. In 1383, a campaign against Flanders organized and led by Bishop Henry Despenser of Norwich gained funds and popular support by being granted crusade status by Urban VI as an attack on Clementists. Despite the panoply of cross taking, preaching, masses, processions, confessions and a massive campaign of selling indulgences, the 1383 expedition amounted to nothing more than an episode in the

Hundred Years War under another name. Its true nature was tellingly exposed as most of Despenser's Urbanist army spent its time ravaging Urbanist territory and besieging Urbanist towns.[50] A neat device to conduct a *chevauchée* on the cheap, the crusading elements of the 1383 Flanders crusade nonetheless disturbed some members of the English establishment wary of excessive ecclesiastical control over secular affairs and, as it transpired, rightly suspicious at the efficacy of the stratagem.[51] Official unease was cast in the shade by the English heresiarch John Wyclif's radical condemnation of Despenser's crusade and the sale of indulgences, *De Cruciata*, which portrayed the exercise as a corrupt and deceitful ploy, among other things to raise money.[52] Wyclif's opinion was not general. Schism crusading continued. In 1386, John of Gaunt received Urbanist crusade credentials to back his unsuccessful attempt to realize his wife's claim to the throne of Clementist Castile. The year before, at the battle of Aljubarrota, the victorious Urbanist Anglo-Portuguese troops had been fortified by receiving the cross from the bishop of Braga, while their defeated Castilian and Clementist foe had been offered indulgences from Clement VII by their spiritual advisors. However, at Aljubarrota, as with Despenser's crusade, the popularity of crusade images and privileges merged with a sense of national identity.[53] This lent such traditional gestures continuing potency but not in a traditional crusading context.

The death of the belligerent Urban VI (1389) and the withdrawal of active political support from the Avignon papacy by the French government in the 1390s effectively ended the use of the crusade as a weapon in the papal schism. The long-running succession dispute in the kingdom of Naples attracted crusade bulls in 1382 from Clement VII and in 1411 and 1414 from John XXIII, himself a former naval adventurer and military commander in the Neapolitan wars. However, the experience of the Italian wars of the previous century as well as the Schism wars dissuaded popes after the end of the Schism in 1417 from using the crusade to defend the Papal States. Only the aggressive Julius II revived the tradition of crusading in Italy (for which he was imperishably lampooned in Erasmus's *Julius Exclusus*) as well as granting Henry VIII of England's French war of 1512 crusading status.[54] The abandonment of crusades against political enemies perhaps signalled retrospective recognition of their futility and the damage they caused to the standing of both papacy and crusade. In the context of the growing dangers presented to Latin Christendom by the advances of the Ottomans, such applications of papal crusade theory appeared politically, militarily and financially self-defeating.

By contrast, where fighting for the cross appeared more appropriate, there was little hesitation. Five crusades were fought against the Hussite heretics of Bohemia (1420, 1421, 1422, 1431, 1465–71) and another planned (1428–9).[55] The Hussites, puritanical scriptural fundamentalists similar to Wyclif's followers in England, took their name from one of their early leaders, Jan Hus, a Prague academic who was burnt by the Council of Constance in 1415. The Hussites combined strong religious revivalism with a powerful sense of collective identity. The twin pillars of corporate unity rested on faith, expressed in rituals such as Communion in both kinds, which distinguished them from Roman Catholics, and nationality, demonstrated in the use of the written Czech vernacular. The mixture of political, social and religious rebellion forged a potent threat, which gave Bohemia a period of hard-fought independence for much of the fifteenth century. The serial failure of the crusades launched initially by Sigismund, the king of Bohemia and Hungary and the German emperor (d. 1437), and the indiscriminate brutality of the invading crusaders merely enhanced Czech appreciation of their own exceptionalist destiny, one holy war decisively repulsing another.

The sixteenth-century Reformation led to a fleeting revival of crusade schemes against the new heretics and schismatics, such as Henry VIII of England in the 1530s and his daughter Elizabeth I in the last years of the century, when Spain's attack in 1588 and Roman Catholic subversion in Ireland became associated with crusading.[56] Occasionally, popes, exasperated at compromises with confessional opponents, could threaten crusades against Catholic rulers such as Henry II of France, criticized by Julius III. The austere papalist militant Paul IV even waved the menace of a crusade against the Habsburgs Charles V and Philip II.[57] At the sharp local level of religious conflict, in the early years of the French Wars of Religion (1562–98), crusading motifs appeared among Catholic associations committed to combating the Huguenots. In Toulouse, Catholics defending the city from Huguenot attack in 1567 started wearing white crosses to symbolize their holy cause. The following year, 1568, Pius V granted these '*crucesignati*' plenary indulgences.[58] However, the general political approach to fighting Protestants, in Germany, France or England, avoided overt crusading, even if the circumstances of holy war were inescapable.

The absence of crusades against Protestants provided its own barometer of the decline of crusading as a living force within Christendom. To some extent this represented more a series of shifts in cultural emphasis than a wholesale abandonment of the crusading tradition. In 1536, elements of society in northern England rebelled against religious and political measures of the government of Henry VIII. At a crisis of the rebellion, the rebels were given badges of the Five Wounds of Christ that had been made for an English contingent sent to Cadiz to join a crusade to north Africa in 1511. Kept in storage ever since, they were now used to emphasize the religious legitimacy of rebellion, to the alarm of Henry's ministers, who suspected that the rebel leadership was trying to equate the uprising with a crusade. The 1511 crusade had ended in drunken brawls on the streets of Lisbon as the English, as many of their successors abroad, had found the local wine too intoxicating. The badges lent the rebels of 1536 no better fortune, but revealed how introspective religious priorities and ideas of holy violence could become. Thirty years later, crusade symbols were again on display, during the 1569 Northern Rebellion, like its predecessor in part a protest at religious change. However, by then few had any experience of crusading, unlike the leaders of the Pilgrimage of Grace. The resonances of the crusade had become fainter. Partly this charted the success of the Protestantizing policies of Elizabeth I; partly it revealed a significant change in perceptions of the Christian polity.[59]

With Christendom no longer confessionally united, nonetheless a sense of unity transcended the religious divide in the face of a common enemy, the Turk. This was one reason sixteenth-century anti-Protestant crusades failed to become more established. Both Lutheran and Roman Catholic addressed the Turkish threat to Germany in writing and action. Monks and Calvinists alike sought to extract from crusade histories lessons of faith and devotion.[60] Edward VI and his ministers called the Turks in 1552 'the old common enemy to the Name and Religion of all Christianity'.[61] In 1571, news of the great Habsburg Mediterranean naval victory over the Turks at Lepanto, seen by Roman Catholics as a crusading venture, was greeted with great enthusiasm in London, with sermons of Thanksgiving at St Paul's and bonfires and banquets in the streets 'for a victorie of so great importance unto the whole state of

Christian commonwealth'. One observer even hoped Protestant and Roman Catholic might reach a compromise so that they could pit their combined resources against the Turk.[62] This was remarkable given that England's monarch had only the year before been excommunicated and her subjects advised to overthrow her by the pope, who planned the coalition that achieved the Lepanto triumph. An increasingly secular concept of Europe, a continent shared by different confessional groups, supplanted the idea of a religiously uniform Christendom. In this new world, anti-Christian crusades held little meaning, let alone prospects for success outside a narrow closed circle of Spanish Habsburg strategists and their apologists at the papal Curia.

Even in their heyday, crusades against Christians had thrown up anomalies. The longevity of wars of the cross directed against Christians depended on cultural attitudes and an understanding of how the world operated that demanded formal religious sanction for what in other respects was secular behaviour. This mentality helps explain the eccentric phenomenon of what can only be called crusades against crusaders, on display among rebels in England in 1215–17,[63] anti-papalists in Germany in the 1240s,[64] during the Shepherds' Crusade of 1251 and with Simon of Montfort's radical anti-royalist idealists in 1263–5.[65] Such counter-crusades appear to be confined to the thirteenth century. Even though the English and the French smoothly incorporated holy war motifs into their propaganda and apologetics, and, later, both Hussites and Protestants were wholly familiar with justifications of religious warfare, the trappings of crusading had become at once undifferentiated and controversial through their use, some at the time argued overuse, in wars within Christendom. Victims and opponents naturally sought to distance themselves from what many asserted was an abuse. Crusades against Christians could seem tawdry rackets, distracting the faithful from the higher calling of the Holy Land or the defence of eastern and central Europe. In the thirteenth century many otherwise sympathetic to crusading opposed the papal wars in Italy: clergy resentful at taxation; English and French nobles reluctant to commute their vows; citizens of Lille in 1284; Florentines who refused to allow their crusade legacies to be diverted. Hostiensis, a passionate advocate of crusades against Christians, was forced to admit to widespread hostility to them in Germany.[66] Even Innocent IV recognized this when he insisted his order stop preaching the cross for the Holy Land to facilitate the war of the cross against Frederick II be kept secret.[67] The use of the Holy Land clerical taxes granted in 1274 and 1312 for the Italian wars looked like fraud. Those many, especially in the fourteenth century, who saw in crusading a means and expression of moral and spiritual regeneration, looked to wars with heretics and infidels, not fellow Christians. Numerous popes largely agreed, such as Gregory X, Nicholas IV, Benedict XII, Gregory XI and even Urban V, despite his use of crusades to tackle *routiers*. While certain popes and their apologists insisted that the Hohenstaufen and Italian crusades were necessary prerequisites for any successful eastern campaign, others, such as the Venetian lobbyist and habitué of the papal Curia Marino Sanudo or Philip of Mézières, argued instead that they constituted major impediments to the recovery of the Holy Land and defence against the Turks.[68] The coincidence of the gradual loss of the Holy Land after 1250 with the intensification of Italian crusading struck some as reprehensible. Anti-Christian crusading did not destroy the popularity of some holy wars of the cross, except in so far as it sharpened scepticism over papal motives and provided polemical ammunition for papal enemies, such as Wyclif or the influential political philosopher Marsilius of Padua in the 1320s. By the early fifteenth century, with papal plenitude of power compromised by schism, a sclerotic bureaucracy, political corruption and the growing assertion of national ecclesiastical autonomy, the Italian crusades appeared at worst objects of derision and at best irrelevant beyond the regional conflicts to which they were applied. When, in the last years of the fourteenth century, the English civil servant and poet Geoffrey Chaucer outlined the career of a perfect crusading knight, he pointedly omitted from his roll of honour the Italian crusades, with which he was personally most familiar. Whatever notional spiritual benefits the crusaders enjoyed, as a weapon of policy they failed to transcend normal secular constraints of politics and military action. A generation after Chaucer, the secular anti-Christian crusades were abandoned, not as ideologically corrupt so much as bad business. A century and a half later, they were joined by the crusades against schismatics and heretics.

CRUSADE AND NATION

In the early years of the fourteenth century, an obliging French cleric attempted to present a case for the king of France's war with the count of Flanders being regarded as holy, equivalent in merit to a traditional crusade. The French kings were holy because 'they esteem holiness, protect holiness and beget holiness'. Their victory over Flemish opponents characterized as rebels would be both just and pious because 'the king's peace is the realm's peace; the realm's peace is the peace of the church, knowledge, virtue and justice, and it is [a precondition for] the conquest of the Holy Land'. The French were following Maccabees (2:15, vv. 7–8) in seeking God's assistance, confident that those who died 'for the justice of king and realm will receive the crown of martyrdom from God'.[69] The argument embraced central elements of repeated attempts in the later middle ages to elevate national secular conflicts into holy wars, analogous or, occasionally, synonymous with crusading: monarchical holiness; the identification of king and nation; the providential destiny of a specially favoured *patria*; the consequent perfidy and evil of that nation's enemies; the translation of crusade and holy war privileges to lay warfare; the promise of salvation; and the testing of unrelated political contests against the requirements of the recovery of the Holy Land. The success of such efforts profoundly affected western political culture and marked one of the most significant of the crusade's legacies to succeeding generations.

The translation of crusading ideology and emotion to national conflicts in some senses saw a resurrection of the early medieval sanctified patriotism that had surrounded Christian rulers such as Charlemagne. However, the concept of holy war was now allied with stronger central control by governments of society and social ideas. The increasingly high costs of warfare and the techniques of centralized fiscal exploitation they provoked gave rulers added authority. Although the church had in many instances led the way in experimenting with techniques of public taxation and supplying justification for it, lay power benefited most, witnessed across Europe in England, France, Iberia, fifteenth-century Burgundy, the German regional principalities and the Italian city states. Political theory and propaganda followed suit. The fusion of the ruler and the ruled became crucial to developments in political identity, the lay power personifying or representing the people or nation. Two associated phenomena supported this creation of self-sufficient and self-regarding states: the perception of a people as Elect, whose public business was therefore meritorious on a transcendent not just temporal plane; and the assumption by rulers of what has been called a religion of monarchy, which both copied and usurped traditional ecclesiastical presentations of authority.

The scope for crusading to assume a national guise was thus greatly increased. The process could operate in three ways: through national pride in past involvement in crusades; formal crusades fought for national interests; and the elevation of the *patria* itself into a Holy Land, its defence being sanctioned by God and the Scriptures. Underpinning such a transformation lay the sacralization of war, its destinations and its participants inherent in crusading ideas and practices. Objects of crusading aggression were consistently couched in spiritual terms of the recovery of the lands of Christ (Palestine), His Mother (Livonia) or His disciples, such as James (Iberia) or Peter (any region extended papal protection or lordship, for example Prussia). By extension, the lands whence crusaders came assumed something of the numinous quality of the holy enterprise. As the universal homeland of these New Israelites or Maccabees, Christendom (*Christianitas*) became fragmented into distinct kingdoms, principalities or cities, *patriae*, these appropriated to themselves the concept of a Holy Land and the Old Testament images of the Chosen People. The consequent habit of equating national ambition with universal good formed a prominent part of the emergence of the nation state.[70]

In some instances, the link between traditional crusading and national crusades was immediate and direct. Although an idea that dated back at least to Urban II in the late eleventh century,[71] from the fourteenth, the idea of defensive bastions of Christianity (*antemurales*) standing on the frontier with the infidel was widely adopted along the borders with the Ottomans, from Poland and Hungary to the Adriatic. Apparently engaged in constant holy war, local rulers promoted national exceptionalism – and their own authority – though crusading imagery and the sacralization of their realms. Away from the frontline, myths and rituals of civic or national identity, as in Pisa, Genoa or Venice, proudly proclaiming their involvement in eastern crusades in public art, literature and municipal ceremonial. In Florence, crusading reinforced civic exceptionalism. The banner borne by Florentines at Damietta in 1219 became a revered relic in the church of San Giovanni. Florence repeatedly refurbished its crusade credentials, even responding positively, if cautiously, to Pius II's crusade appeal in 1463–4. This context of the crusade helping define distinctive civic identity and virtue probably helped the radical evangelist Girolamo Savonarola, who dominated Florence between 1494 and 1498, when he declared the city to be a New Jerusalem.[72] Although cities such as Florence or Venice may have been exceptional in the scale of crusade imagery on display, similar attention to their crusading past came from northern cities such as London or Cologne.

A parallel trend can be observed in the parade of canonized crusaders that adorned the royal genealogies of Europe: Charlemagne, universally regarded as a proto-crusader (canonized in 1166); Eric IX of Sweden (d. 1160; canonized 1167); Ladislas of Hungary (d. 1095; canonized 1192); Ferdinand III of Castile (d. 1252, whose cult was apparent soon after his death, even though he was officially canonized only in 1671); and, most famously, Louis IX of France (d. 1270; canonized 1297). Local secular 'saints' could be made out of crusader heroes, such as James of Avesnes, killed at Arsuf in 1191, or William Longspee, cut down at Mansourah in 1250.[73] In the absence of sanctified crusaders, local saints could be also pressed into service, such as Thomas Becket, whose shade was regularly invoked by Englishmen during the Third Crusade and who gave his name to a religious, briefly military, order at Acre. Such figures appeared as distinctively national or regional figures, the kings among them materially aiding the assertion of local royal dynasticism, all attaching an aura of sanctity to cities, regions or nations, helping mould a collective identity.

This incorporation of public religion, if not necessarily overt crusading, into assumptions of national self-image was reflected in the adoption across Europe of the cross as a national symbol, banner or uniform. It provided the sign of the Florentine *popolo*. Danish kings adopted the cross for their symbol around 1200. As already seen, at the battle of Evesham in Worcestershire in 1265, facing rebels wearing white crusader crosses, the royalists wore red ones. In the fourteenth century the red cross became the emblem of English troops in France and Spain and the national symbol, branded as the cross of St George. Apparently, some rebels during the so-called Peasants' Revolt of 1381 wore them. Yet iconographically red crosses remained associated with crusading, worn by crusaders in Prussia, on Despenser's crusade in 1383 and against the Hussites in the 1420s.[74] This elision of reference may not have been accidental. One description of Edward I of England's 1300 campaign against the Scots to Annandale and Carlaverock talked of him signing himself and his troops 'with the Lord's Cross', an unmistakable gesture in a war that observers on both sides equated with a holy war. In similar vein, Henry Knighton, a canon of Leicester, looking back from the 1390s on the French wars a generation earlier, depicted the English before the battle of Poitiers (1356) signing themselves 'with the Holy Cross'.[75] Overtones of holy war were convenient for Edward III, accused by many as responsible for scuppering the crusade plans of the 1330s and the first English king since Stephen not to take the cross for the Holy Land.

The most consistent hijack of the crusade for national objectives came from the French. By 1300, crusading had been claimed almost as a national prerogative, an enterprise in which the king of France held the major shareholding. A lavish illuminated manuscript produced at Acre *c.*1280 shows Louis IX attacking Damietta in 1249, the king and his followers emblazoned with the royal emblem of the fleur de lis. There is not a cross in sight.[76] Fashioned at the French royal court by a coalition of xenophobic clergy and smooth Roman lawyers, the ideologies of the crusade and the providential destiny of France and its monarch were woven into a legal imperialism backed by a form of apocalyptic royal, hence national, messianism. The argument deployed against the Flemish above was typical. The harnessing of the crusade semiotics of the Old Testament Israelites and Maccabees extended the transformation of a land of crusaders into a Holy Land in its own right. At least diplomatically, some were convinced. In 1311, Pope Clement V – a Frenchman from Gascony – declared: 'Just as the Israelites are known to have granted the Lord's inheritance by the election of Heaven, to perform the hidden wishes of God, so the kingdom of France has been chosen as the lord's special people.'[77] This tradition helped sustain French propaganda through the darkest days of defeat during the Hundred Years' War. In 1429, Christine de Pisan prophesied that Joan of Arc's recent victories over the English presaged her leading Charles VII to reconquer the Holy Land because God specially favoured the royal house of France. Joan, like Moses, would lead God's new people, the French, out of defeat and occupation.[78] In the manner of earlier crusaders, Charles was declared to be the fulfilment of the prophecy of the Last Emperor, whose career of world conquest would end with the laying down of his crown on the Mount of Olives in preparation for the Last Days. God directs the destiny of France; those who die in her cause will gain paradise. With or without the formal trappings, the ideology and mentality of crusading here permeated nationalist propaganda. This cocktail of prophecy, eschatology, holy war and the recovery of Jerusalem enlivened the rhetoric surrounding Charles VIII's invasion of Italy in 1494. Such justifications acted both as cover for political ambition and genuine inspiration. The potency of the identification of crusading with 'the Most Christian Kings' of France (a twelfth-century courtesy title bestowed by a grateful pope) was such that it survived the destructive Wars of Religion (1562–98) to find new literary expression from both Roman Catholic and Huguenot apologists of Henry IV (1589–1610).[79]

However, the appropriation of crusading mentalities did not lead to the application of formal crusade institutions to French wars. Popes consistently refused to elevate French conflicts with Flanders or England into crusades. Here the contrast with the otherwise closely parallel experience of late medieval Spain, in particular Castile, is most notable. An indigenous Iberian prophetic tradition nurtured by the *reconquista* encouraged a belief that the Iberian holy wars required ultimate fulfilment in the recovery of Jerusalem. Unlike the French, whose immediate enemies were fellow Christians, the Spanish faced Muslims, allowing papal grants of crusade privileges, especially taxation and indulgences, to flow more or less on demand. The expulsion of the Moors from Granada led to north African forays by Ferdinand of Aragon and his grandson Charles V (I of Spain). These not only attracted crusading privileges, but were cast by royal polemicists as preludes to the recovery of the Holy Sepulchre. Whatever the religious dimension, these were national campaigns in pursuit of local strategic conquest, political aggression and commercial advantage. However, for Charles's son, Philip II, the synergy of God's war and Spain's war occupied the centre of his world-view. The crusade, in the Mediterranean, north Africa, Europe or the Americas, imposed a specifically national responsibility in fulfilment of Spain's providential mission to lead the redemption of Christendom, whether the rest of Christendom approved or not.

While such conflation of the temporal and transcendent proved harder to pull off elsewhere, others played the same game. Reflecting on English success in the French wars, Chancellor Adam Haughton, bishop of St David's, insisted to Parliament in 1377 that 'God would never have honoured this land in the same way as he did Israel . . . if it were not that He had chosen it as His heritage'. A popular verse at the time reinforced the message; the pope had become French, but Jesus had become English. God's career as an Englishman lasted for centuries.[80] Such fancies and scriptural references connected with pre- and non-crusading traditions of the Old Testament and providential precedents for the defence of homelands. However, the congruence of language used to sacralize national warfare with concurrent crusade rhetoric made neat distinctions unconvincing. The intent of those English sources in describing crusaders against rebels in 1216–17 or the Montfortian *crucesignati* in 1263–5 as fighting 'pro patria' was clear. So, too, were the motives of writers such as Henry Knighton or the Scottish propaganda that equated their war of independence in the early fourteenth century with the Holy Land crusade. In England, liturgy, church processions and prayers similar to those devoted to the recovery of the Holy Land were directed in support of royal wars.[81] In the 1340s, those in royal service received the temporal privileges of essoin of court, exemption from taxation, moratorium on debt and pardon for crimes. It seems only the indulgences could not be transferred from crusading to national war. Even that may not have made too much difference, if Froissart, a close observer of the Anglo-French nobility, can be believed: 'Men at arms cannot live on pardons, nor do they pay much attention to them except at the point of death.'[82]

While numerous examples can be found of writers throwing a crusading mantle over secular warfare, the more powerful and lasting transference came where national wars were portrayed as of equal worth as crusading, as holy wars in their own right, independent of the Holy Land tradition. Just as the Hundred Years War fatally undermined practical efforts to raise a new eastern crusade, so it went far to replace crusading as the central public meritorious military act, even if many still hankered after the easy certainties of wars of the cross against infidels on far foreign fields. The construction of non-crusading holy war was a feature of fifteenth-century Europe where not all national wars were linked to the crusade tradition. While rejecting the theology and institutions of crusading, the Hussites in Bohemia self-consciously created their own holy land, renaming cult sites after places in Palestine, such as Mount Tabor or Mount Horeb. Within the pale of Catholic Christendom, similar reinventions were equally possible and plausible. In his description of the battle of Agincourt (25 October 1415), Henry V's chaplain had the king call the English 'God's people' as they donned 'the armour of penitence', exhorting them to follow the example of Judas Maccabeus.[83] Confession, absolution and taking Communion were familiar pre-battle morale-raising techniques, but the focus in this account is unambiguous. King Henry was God's soldier as well as the Lord's anointed. On his return to London after his victory, he was greeted by patriotic displays in praise of the blessed kingdom of England, its patron saints and holy kings.[84] While the crusade mentality and images infected the sacralization of political rule and patriotic identities in the later middle ages, national holy lands and holy wars acquired and projected an independent vitality. National crusades became the nations' wars.

THE WIDER WORLD

Medieval prophets and some post-medieval historians have not been shy to attribute sweeping consequences for the crusade, from a role in the Apocalypse to the opening of the west to new scholarly learning and fresh commercial markets. Such claims have prompted one modern historian to react by reducing crusading's contribution to western culture to the introduction of the apricot.[85] Yet it is undeniable that both practically and intellectually the traditional western European ambition of occupying Palestine encouraged sensitivity to Christendom's place in the wider world of the three classical continents of Europe, Asia and Africa. In turn this contributed to an inquisitive and acquisitive expansionism that characterized high and late medieval western European approaches to other peoples and regions near and distant. The extension of western European Christian culture and power to all other parts of the globe provided one of the major features of world history after 1500. In the origins of this process, which formed such as marked contrast to, say, the Chinese experience after 1400, the idealism and activity of crusaders in the four centuries after 1095 played a part.

The intellectual and physical, geographic aspects of the crusade's influence on European expansion cannot neatly be separated. Neither should it be exaggerated. The creation of Asiatic empires and the altering of trade routes; the development of the European economy, technology and commerce; or the transmission of classical and Arabic texts via Spain, Sicily, southern Italy and Byzantium ran distinct and parallel to the effect of the wars of the cross. However, crusading idealism led to significant political settlements of Latin Christians in the Near East and, in places, an obsessive European concern for western Asia and the eastern Mediterranean that would not have developed in the way it did without the distinctive dynamism of the crusade mentality and tradition. Politically, the nature of the Muslim powers of the Near East mattered to Frankish rulers and warriors. The acute interest in events further east during the Fifth Crusade stood as an extreme example of a more general concern, evinced, for example, in William of Tyre's lost history of the Muslim east. Although the irruption of the Mongols into western Asia and eastern Europe owed nothing to crusading, the European response did, in so far as successive missions were despatched to Mongol rulers in the thirteenth century at least in part to test prospects for an anti-Muslim alliance.

The Latin presence in the eastern Mediterranean and the need of prospective western crusaders for information stimulated a small industry of written information about Asia and north Africa from the thirteenth century. This sense of place and desire to acquire knowledge of it was encouraged and sustained by the increasing volume of Holy Land and Near East pilgrimage accounts after 1300, supplemented by memoirs of released captives or western spies, many of which were widely circulated and, in the fifteenth century, printed. While much of the writing about Asia and Africa was fanciful, non-empirical, inaccurate, hidebound by classical texts or vitiated by wishful thinking, it provided a way of looking at the non-Christian, non-European world that transcended mere tales of wonder (although these remained very popular throughout the later middle ages). Asiatic, Muslim and Mongol geography, politics, economy, sociology and demography came under increasingly familiar scrutiny, especially in the large numbers of 'recovery' treatises composed between the 1270s and 1330s.[86] These works, by such disparate figures as the Armenian Prince Hayton, who wrote about the Tartars (1307) or the French provincial lawyer Pierre Dubois, who worried about the demographic inequalities of Latins and Saracens

(1306–8), reflected both pragmatic and academic concerns about the nature of the outside world that went far beyond crusade planning.[87] The missions to the Mongols and the opening-up of China to western visitors after the Mongol conquest of 1276 added new geographic horizons, new intellectual challenges and, for some, a new crusading urgency. The introspective idealism of the need to recover Christ's heritage for Christendom was matched or replaced by a new understanding of the world context of the Holy Land, Christendom and Christianity itself. Such perceptions led directly to the development from the thirteenth century of the idea of crusading for the extension (*dilatio*) of the faith, not just its defence, a concept eagerly embraced and promoted by Iberian crusaders expanding their conquests along the shore of the Maghrib and into the north Atlantic in the fourteenth and fifteenth centuries. The effect of this aggressive concept of holy war, which even tolerated *de facto* wars of conversion previously outlawed, was powerfully displayed from the 1490s in the conquests in the Americas.[88]

Jerusalem and the Americas may appear opposite ends of the conceptual as well as geographic map. In fact the road to one led straight to the other. Christopher Columbus was an enthusiast for the recovery of Jerusalem. In later life, he construed his voyages to what he stubbornly viewed as part of the old world as fulfilling biblical prophecies of the reconquest of Jerusalem, notably Isaiah 60:9. In 1501, he wrote to his patrons, the Catholic monarchs of Spain, Ferdinand and Isabella, 'Our Lord wished to manifest a most evident miracle in this voyage to the Indies in order to console me and others in the matter of the Holy Sepulchre.'[89] Columbus, here and in his own work of prophecy, the *Libro de las profecias* (*Book of Prophecies*), a decade after his first voyage, was casting himself in an almost messianic role as the deliverer of Jerusalem. Such delusional hubris may have startled his royal sponsors, but it sprang from a lively current Spanish interest in outré prophecy, nationalism, the Holy Land and the crusade that the court and policies of Ferdinand and Isabella had done much to excite and foster. Columbus's interest was grounded on more than apocalyptic dreaming. His will of 1498 provided for a fund to be established in his home city of Genoa for the recovery of Jerusalem.[90]

Crusading, far from an anachronism, provided one impetus for the European age of discovery. One of the texts that Columbus may have consulted, and was certainly well known to members of his circle and people he met, was the pseudonymous John Mandeville's *Travels*. Its Prologue was unambiguous about the status of the Holy Land, Christ's heritage, as the centre of the world and about the Christian obligation to recover it by force. 'Mandeville's' account of his supposed travels to Jerusalem, the Near East, Asia and the fabulous Orient provided a rich mine of romance, history, theology, topography and geography. From the original as well as the many contrasting variants, different audiences could extract whatever they desired to inform their own interests, tolerant, bigoted, fanciful or topographical. For Columbus's circle, the focus on the crusade, which set the frame for 'Mandeville', would be of equal attraction as one of the book's most unequivocal claims: 'I say with certainty that one could travel around all the lands of the world, both below and above, and return to one's country'.[91] This assumption of the possibility of circumnavigation was supported by measurements. 'Mandeville' rejected the standard medieval calculation of the circumference of the earth, derived from Ptolemy of Alexandria, 20,245 miles, in favour of the more accurate 31,500 miles, Eratosthenes's figure included in the university textbook *De Sphaera* (1230×45) by John of Sacrobosco.[92] For Columbus, even if not directly influenced by 'Mandeville', which he may have been, science, cosmology and the crusade were complementary, not aspects of antagonistic cultures or hostile systems of thought. In contemplating ways of fulfilling the injunction to recover Christ's heritage, Columbus, like so many of his would-be crusader predecessors stretching back to Urban II's call to arms at Clermont, first sought to understand the world better, its natural phenomena, its diversity and its breadth as much as its eschatological destiny. Crusading remained embedded in western European culture for so long precisely for this reason. In presenting a spiritualized vision of reality, it recognized the temporal world and the actual experience of man while offering to transform both.

Conclusion

Popes today do not summon crusades. There are a number of reasons for this. One part of Christendom decisively rejected the theology behind the medieval wars of the cross in the sixteenth century. The Roman Catholic church itself refined its own teaching to modify its penitential practices in ways that undermined the fiscal and liturgical accoutrements of later medieval crusading. Crusade ideology had hardly developed since Innocent III. Based essentially on patristic and scholastic theology – and loosely at that – its justification looked increasingly awkward in the face of sixteenth-century scriptural theology and attacks founded on the New Testament. The increasing interiorization of faith, shared to some degree by all sides of the major confessional divides, militated against certain of the showier forms of medieval devotion that crusading exemplified, the increasingly controversial sale of indulgences merely being the most notorious. Men could and did still take the cross, perhaps even into the eighteenth century against Turks and Barbary pirates. The war of the Holy League against the Ottomans, 1684–99, was probably the last formal crusade. But these gestures were divorced from the communal round of devotional practices or cultural aesthetics. Although in times of crisis, such as the First World War, over-excited prelates can still urge their congregations to fight the good temporal as well as spiritual fight, and while the secular legalism of just war continues to attract advocates, most non-literalist Christian denominations now shun the tradition of holy war, some even pretending it was a kind of aberration. In the later twentieth century, the Roman Catholic church was careful not to embrace potentially violent (and certainly radical) theologies, such as Liberation Theology. John Paul II even apologized to victims of the crusades. The wars of the cross have become like a lingering bad smell in a lavishly refurbished stately home.

The protean development of the crusade as a weapon of policy and a mechanism of redemption – as was said of a departing crusader in 1197, 'to fight Saracens visible and invisible' – inevitably created diverse responses. The idea that the crusade 'declined' through growing unpopularity makes little conceptual or historical sense. Certain aspects of crusading – for example the sale of indulgences and the Italian wars – attracted criticism. But so did the inaction of western European rulers in the face of the loss of the Holy Land and the advance of the Turks. Neither led to the abandonment of the ideological foundations of wars of the cross. Indulgences continued to be bought. Crusading privileges usually managed to find some takers whatever the cause. Evidence of medieval public opinion is never neutral; to ignore the crusades' adherents is as absurd as to discount their critics. Crusading certainly did not decay through lack of interest. More damaging to its support as a way of conducting business were changing attitudes conditioned by external forces, such as the decline in the acceptance of the moral authority of the papacy, a phenomenon noticed by popes as much as by their critics in the fifteenth century. As crusading had always stood as part of the edifice of papal pretentions, their fates were intimately bound together. In a secular context, the gradual transformation from the late fifteenth century of military aristocrats from knights to officers, from warriors to gentlemen, a long process contingent on changing educational habits, social conditions, the requirements of the state and the conduct of war, left many of the traditional chivalric impulses redundant. Just as full plate armour became increasingly a matter of social prestige and show in the seventeenth century, so did the paraphernalia of crusading.

The crusade did not disappear from European culture because it was discredited but because the religious and social value systems that had sustained it were abandoned. Pragmatically, as a way of managing international relations it no longer suited the politics, diplomacy and war of the sixteenth and seventeenth centuries. This was not due to a moral failure, still less to any lack of 'modernity'; the most supposedly 'advanced' societies of the fifteenth century, the city states of Italy or the urban commercial communities of Low Countries, were enthusiasts, as were many humanist scholars. Yet, as the secular state captured many of the cultural functions previously centred on a religious vision of the world, in particular attitudes to civic, social and national identity, crusading, distinctive because of its essentially spiritual dimension, could seem misplaced. Even this was not inevitable; Habsburg Spain succeeded in integrating the crusade mentality into the burgeoning of new state power in the sixteenth century. However, by then crusading had increasingly become the preserve of antiquarians and confessional sectarians. Ways of looking at the world changed. Protestant though he was, Richard Hakluyt included a version of Mandeville's *Travels* in his first edition of *Navigations and Voyages* (1589), including the declaration 'the land of Jerusalem ... is ... worthier of being possessed than all lands of the world'. By the second edition, Mandeville had been dropped.

Fundamentally, the western Christian church lost its attempt to control civil society. In justice as well as government, secular authority emerged as the arbiter, guardian and enforcer of law. The tensions of church and state that had existed throughout the high and later middle ages were resolved by the triumph of the temporal state and the subservience of the Christian churches to lay power. Church jurisdiction remained, distinct yet absorbed into the public polity, in Protestant as well as Roman Catholic states of Europe, for example in the survival of church courts dealing with moral and testamentary issues. Religion hardly ceased to occupy a central, at times determinant, role in society. The Vatican City remains a church state – but it is the only one in Europe. Crusading had always been a public civic activity, a war, not just a prayer or a penance. With the failure of the papacy's long theocratic experiment, and as regional churches and churchmen lost their hold on the terms of political discourse, warfare became subject to secular rules and laws as well as leadership. By the early seventeenth century, theorists such as Gentili and Grotius elaborated international laws of war that explicitly discounted religion as sufficient just cause. This reflected the sanction of political events; the sixteenth-century French alliance with the Ottomans; the 1555 agreement at Augsburg accepting that the religion of each German principality be determined by that of its ruler; and the Treaty of Westphalia in 1648, which ended the great European Thirty Years' War by establishing an explicitly secular framework of international relations, a system of temporal nations in a secular Europe. Christianity thrived; Christendom was dead. With it died one of its most distinctive features, the crusade. Political and civil action now rested with secular states, civic justice a matter for laymen, not clergy, law and religion inhabiting different spheres of civil life, not even necessarily complementary or mutually dependent. Where civil justice was guaranteed by religious law and interpreted by religious scholars, the rational polity could remain the religious community not necessarily the secular state. Thus Islam's holy war, the lesser *jihad*, remains a modern phenomenon. The Christian crusade, except in the mouths of certain meretricious academics and unthinking politicians, does not.

The post-history of crusading is a subject of itself, as David Hume suggested in the eighteenth century, 'ever since engrossing the curiosity of mankind'. As opposed to polemicists for Reason, Colonialism, Imperialism, Medievalism, Nationalism, Capitalism, Freedom, Religion or Cultural Armageddon, who have severally and serially dominated popular interpretations of the crusades for much of the last four centuries, the historian is struck by the malleability of the crusade, its penetration into so many religious, political, social and personal interstices of medieval life. While the crusade did not define a society or a culture, it is impossible to grasp the nature or quality of the activity by looking at it in isolation, still less in relation to events centuries later. Few corners of Europe and the Mediterranean escaped entirely the touch of the wars of the cross. There are good grounds for associating crusading with some of the more intriguing developments of medieval western politics and society; the invention of Christendom, a European identity expressed in expansion and conquest; the acceptable rhetoric and performance of public violence with its consequent influence on the assertion of legitimate, sacralized, secular power; experiments in corporate government, of mechanisms in creating and ordering a wide political civil society; the growth of systems of public taxation. More obviously, crusading reflected aspects of attempts to establish a moral order in Europe run by a centralized church and the more successful efforts to expand the borders of the Latin Christian world. In providing an impetus to engage with far distant lands, the crusade both succeeded, as witnessed by the opening of the eastern Mediterranean to merchants and pilgrims, and spectacularly failed. Jerusalem was only briefly held, the politics of western Asia and the Near East only marginally inconvenienced.

As with any exercise in historical selectivity, which means all historical writing, extracting the thread of the crusade from the weave of the middle ages distorts both. Nonetheless, the experience of crusading is worth study if only because of the immediacy with which it addresses the observer. The world, assumptions and actions of crusaders and their contemporaries are irrecoverable but inescapable. Their deeds confront the historian directly, the sheer physical effort of so much of the endeavour; the inspirational idealism; utopianism armed with myopia; the elaborate, sincere intolerance; the diversity and complexity of motive and performance. Of equal if not greater power to move than the great set pieces of crusade history – Urban II at Clermont, the massacre at Jerusalem, Saladin at Hattin, Richard I at Acre, Louis IX at Mansourah – are the stories of the battered wives of absent crusaders, the evidence of ruined or enriched lives of veterans and survivors, the crosses etched into the stones of the church of the Holy Sepulchre or parish churches across Europe, intimate witnesses to the ambitions of those who sought to transform themselves and their world by taking the cross of their Saviour. As Josserand of Brancion prayed before he took the cross in 1248, 'Lord, take me from wars between Christians in which I have spent much of my life; let me die in your service so I may share your kingdom in Paradise'. Although the central cliché of aristocratic engagement with crusading, echoed in sources from the First Crusade onwards, the poignancy of these sentiments comes from the testimony of tens of thousands of corpses of men and women of all social stations. However wasteful of life and treasure, however narrow the original and sustaining aspiration to physical possession of the Holy Places, this was an ideal that inspired sacrifice at times on an almost unimaginable scale and intensity.

Yet sentimentality will not do. It hardly encompasses the subject. Too many died in the pursuit of sectarian ambition. Yet motives, like actions, can contradict without hypocrisy. While it is usually fruitless for historians to pursue the will of the wisp of private emotions, the question of what caused so many to change their lives so decisively persists. It is a fond myth of the religious that piety excludes greed, coercion, conformity and lack of reflection, that it is freestanding. The language of transcendence should not distract or dupe. Neither should it insist on judgement. Fighting for the cross was not necessarily more glamorous than paying taxes for it, only more strenuous. Both activities are open to reductive interpretations of unavoidable cultural or social compulsion. However, there can be no clear or sonorous summing-up. Wars destroy and create, even if in unequal measures for participants, victims and home communities. Explicable in collective terms as an expression or expressions of belief, anxiety, religious or social obedience, moral and material self-advancement, corporate solidarity and identity, solipsistic intolerance and expansive aggression, for each individual any choice involved in the crusade may or may not have caught 'the hidden wishes of God'. External manifestations can be observed. Yet the internal, personal decision to follow the cross, to inflict harm on others at great personal risk, at the cost of enormous privations, at the service of a consuming cause, cannot be explained, excused or dismissed either as virtue or sin. Rather, its very contradictions spelt its humanity.

Notes

The following abbreviations are used in the notes.

MGH	*Monumenta Germaniae Historica* (Hanover etc. 1826ff.)
MGHS	*Monumenta Germaniae Historica Scriptores*, ed. G. H. Pertz et al. (Hanover 1826ff.)
MGH SS	*MGH Scriptores in Folio et Quarto* (Hanover etc. 1826–1934)
PL	*Patrologia cursus completus. Series Latina*, ed. J. P. Migne (Paris 1844–64)
RHC	*Recueil des historiens des croisades* (Paris 1844–1906)
RHC Arm.	*RHC Documents arméniens* (Paris 1869–1906)
RHC Occ.	*RHC Documents occidentaux* (Paris 1844–95)
RHC Or.	*Documents orientaux* (Paris 1872–1906)
RHGF	*Recueil des historiens des Gaules et de la France* (Paris 1738–1876)

1: The Origins of Christian Holy War

1. *Recueil des chartes de l'abbaye de Cluny*, ed. A. Bruel, v (Paris 1894), 51–3, no. 3703; *Cartulaire de l'abbaye de Saint-Victor de Marseille*, ed. M. Guérard (Paris 1857), i, 167–8, no. 143.
2. H. Hagenmeyer, *Die Kreuzzugsbriefe aus den Jahren 1088–1100* (Innsbruck 1902), pp. 138–40, 141–2, 144, 146–9, 150, 151, 157, 160, 162; and pp. 136–7 for Urban's letter to the Flemish, J. and L. Riley-Smith, *The Crusades: Idea and Reality* (London 1981), p. 38.
3. *De expugnatione Lyxbonensi*, ed. C. W. David (New York 1936; reprint 1976), p. 81, as part of a comprehensive justification for holy war put in the mouth of the bishop of Oporto; for the identity of the author, H. Livermore, '"The Conquest of Lisbon" and its Author', *Portuguese Studies*, 6 (1990), 1–16.
4. From *De laude novae militiae*, *Sancti Bernardi Opera*, ed. J. Leclercq et al. (Rome 1963), pp. 214–15; J. and L. Riley-Smith, *Crusades*, p. 102.
5. S. Runciman, *A History of the Crusades* (Cambridge 1951–4), iii, 480.
6. Raymond of Aguilers, *Historia Francorum qui ceperunt Iherusalem*, RHC Occ., iii, 300, trans. J. H. and L. L. Hill (Philadelphia 1968), p. 128; for biblical citations P. Alphandéry, 'Les Citations biblique chez les historiens de la première croisade', *Revue de l'histoire des religions*, 99 (1929), 139–57, esp. p. 154, note 4; cf. Hagenmeyer, *Kreuzzugsbriefe*, pp. 153–5.
7. *Die Traditionsbücher des Benediktinerstiftes Göttweig*, ed. A. Fuchs (Vienna and Leipzig 1931), *Fontes rerum Austriacum*, lxix, no. 55.
8. For a summary, F. H. Russell, *The Just War in the Middle Ages* (Cambridge 1977), pp. 1–39.
9. St Augustine, *City of God*, bk XIX, c. 7; cf. bk I, c. 21, trans. H. Bettenson (London 1984), pp. 32, 862.

10. C. Erdmann, *The Origin of the Idea of the Crusade*, trans. M. W. Baldwin and W. Goffart (Princeton 1977), p. 19.
11. Bede, *Ecclesiastical History of the English People*, ed. B. Colgrave and R. A. B. Mynors (Oxford 1969), pp. 214–15, 231, 240–43, 251.
12. A. Bruckner and R. Marichal, *Chartae Latinae antiquores*, xii (Zurich 1987), 74, no. 543; P. D. King, *Charlemagne: Translated Sources* (Kendal 1987), pp. 223, 309–10; Einhard, *Vita Caroli magni imperatoris*, ed. L. Halphen (Paris 1981), pp. 22–8, trans. L. Thorpe as *Life of Charlemagne* (London 1969), pp. 61–4; M. McCormick, 'The Liturgy of War in the Early Middle Ages', *Viator*, 15 (1984), 1–23.
13. King, *Charlemagne*, pp. 78, 112; cf. Walafrid Strabo *c.*840/2 for St Martin's *cappa*, *De Exordiis et Incrementis*, MGH, Capitularia, ii (Hanover 1890), 515; and Notker the Stammerer, *Two Lives of Charlemagne*, trans. L. Thorpe (London 1969), p. 96.
14. P. Godman, *Poetry of the Carolingian Renaissance* (Oxford 1985), pp. 189, 255, 276–7; cf. K. Leyser, 'Early Medieval Canon Law and the Beginnings of Knighthood', *Communications and Power in Medieval Europe*, i, ed. T. Reuter (Woodbridge 1994); J. Nelson, 'Ninth Century Knighthood; the Evidence of Nithard', *Studies in Medieval History Presented to R. A. Brown*, ed. C. Harper-Bill et al. (Woodbridge 1989).
15. Godman, *Poetry*, pp. 128–9, 300–301, 302–3.
16. MGH, Epistolarum, v (Berlin 1898), p. 601 s.a. 853; vii (Berlin 1912), pp. 126–7, no. 150; Erdmann, *Origin*, p. 27.
17. *Annales Fuldenses*, ed. F. Kurze, MGH SS (Hanover 1891), p. 120, a. 891; C. J. Tyerman, *England and the Crusades 1095–1588* (Chicago 1988), p. 10 and note 4 for Alfred.
18. Abbo of St Germain, *De bello Parisiaco*, ed. G. H. Pertz, MGH SS (Hanover 1871), pp. 9–10, bk I, ll. 108–10; trans. Godman, *Poetry*, p. 313; for the Benedict story, Adelarius, *Miraculi S. Benedicti*, ed. O. Holder-Egger, MGH SS, xv–i (Hanover 1887), 499–500.
19. *The Dream of the Rood*, ed. B. Dickins and A. S. C. Ross (London 1954), pp. 20–35.
20. G. R. Murphy, *The Saxon Saviour* (New York/Oxford 1989), esp. pp. 6, 19–20, 58, 62, 65, 70, 71 et seq., 98, 99, 102–3, 105, 106, 109–10, 113.
21. *English Historical Documents*, i, ed. D. Whitelock (London 1955), 293–7.
22. *La Chanson d'Antioche*, ed. S. Duparc-Quioc (Paris 1977–8), i, 25–8 for passage; extracts J. and L. Riley-Smith, *Crusades*, pp. 72–3.
23. Aelfric, *Lives of the Saints*, ed. W. W. Skeat, Early English Text Society (London 1890), ii, ll. 688–704; cf. 966 foundation charter of King Edgar for New Minster, Winchester, quoted in R. W. Southern, *Western Church and Society in the Middle Ages* (London 1970), pp. 224–5 and similar views of the emperor, Louis the Pious, in 817, MGH, Capitularia, i, 349–51.
24. Aelfric, *Saints*, ii, 66–143, 324–5; Maccabees ll. 681–2 for quotation; Abbo of Fleury, *Passio Sancti Eadmundi*, in *Carolla Sancti Edmundi: the Garland of St Edmund King and Martyr*, ed. and trans. Lord F. Hervey (London 1907), esp. pp. 20, 26, 30, 32.
25. P. Rousset, 'L'idéal chevaleresque dans deux *Vitae* clunisienne', *Etudes de civilisation médiévale, Mélanges offerts à E. R. Labande* (Poitiers 1974), pp. 623–33; PL, 133, esp. cols. 647–8.
26. Ralph Glaber, *Historarium Libri Quinti*, ed. J. France (Oxford 1989), p. 61.
27. H. E. J. Cowdrey, 'The Peace and Truce of God in the Eleventh Century', *Past and Present*, xlvi (1970), 53 and, in general, 42–67; cf. a contrary perspective based on evidence from the Limousin, M. G. Bull, *Knightly Piety and the Lay Response to the First Crusade* (Oxford 1993).
28. The Penitentiary of Ermenfrid bishop of Sitten is translated by D. C. Douglas, *English Historical Documents*, ii (London 1963), 606–7; for Burchard of Worms, *Decretum Libri XX*, PL, cxl, esp. bk VI, *De Homicidiis*, e.g. chap. 23; cf. J. Gilchrist, 'The Erdmann Thesis and the Canon Law', *Crusade and Settlement*, ed. P. Edbury (Cardiff 1985), pp. 3–45.

29. Bonizo of Sutri, *Liber de Vita Christiana*, ed. E. Perels (Berlin 1930), esp. bk II, cc. 3, 43; bk III, c. 89; bk VII, c. 28; bk X, c. 79, pp. 35, 56, 101, 248–9, 336; cf. H. E. J. Cowdrey, 'Pope Gregory VII and the Bearing of Arms', *Montjoie: Studies in Crusade History in Honour of H. E. Mayer*, ed. B. Kedar, J. Riley-Smith, R. Hiestand (Aldershot 1997), pp. 21–35; I. S. Robinson, 'Gregory VII and the Soldiers of Christ', *History*, lviii (1973), 161–92.
30. Gregory VII to people of the archdiocese of Ravenna, 11 Dec. 1080, trans. E. Emerton, *The Correspondence of Pope Gregory VII* (New York 1969), p. 165.
31. Benzo of Alba, *Ad Heinricum IV. imperatorem*, ed. H. Seyffert (Hanover 1996), pp. 240, 242, 248 ('Cornefredus'), 300 ('Grugnefredus').
32. Orderic Vitalis, *The Ecclesiastical History*, ed. M. ChIbnall (Oxford 1969–80), iii, 216, 226, 260–62.
33. Emerton, *Correspondence of Gregory VII*, pp. 23, 25–6, 33, 39, 56–8, 60–61 for translations of some, but not all, the relevant letters of 1074 (cf. p. 165 for the 1080 reference to the 'enemies of the Cross of Christ'); Cowdrey, 'Gregory VII and Bearing of Arms', esp. p. 30 and note 35 for refs. to Gregory's Register, especially Gregory VII, *Regestrum*, ed. E. Caspar, MGH, Epistolae Selectae, 2, i–ii (Berlin 1920–23), bk I, nos. 46, 49; bk II, nos. 31, 37, pp. 69–71, 75–6, 165–8, 172–3; *The Epistolae vagantes of Pope Gregory VII*, ed. and trans. H. E. J. Cowdrey (Oxford 1972), no. 5, pp. 10–13; Cowdrey, 'Pope Gregory VII's "Crusading" Plans of 1074', *Outremer*, ed. B. Kedar, H. E. Mayer and R. C. Smail (Jerusalem 1982), pp. 27–40.
34. *Chanson de Roland*, v. 1015.
35. William of Tyre, *Chronicon*, ed. R. B. C. Huygens, Corpus Christianorum Continuatio Mediaevalis, lxiii (Turnhout 1986), bk I, cc. 1–2, pp. 105–7 (Rubric to first chapter: 'Quod tempore Eraclii . . . Homar . . . universam occupaverit Syriam'). Runciman, *History of the Crusades*, i, 3–5 has a famous purple passage on the fall of Jerusalem in 638; cf. a controversial alternative vision, P. Cronne and M. Cook, *Hagarism: the Making of the Islamic World* (Cambridge 1977), p. 51; for a conventional account, L. V. Vaglieri, 'The Patriarchal and Umayyad Caliphates', *Cambridge History of Islam*, ed. P. M. Holt et al. (Cambridge 1970), i, 62. Umar must have cut a striking figure; huge, with a long beard, he used to patrol the streets of Medina wielding a bullwhip.
36. R. Fletcher, *Moorish Spain* (London 1992), p. 75.
37. *Storia de' Normanni di Amato di Montecassino*, ed. V. de Bartholomaeis (Rome 1935), v. 12, p. 234; quoted in C. Morris, *The Papal Monarchy* (Oxford 1989), p. 142 and, for this period in general, pp. 79–153.
38. *Epistolae pontificum Romanorum ineditae*, ed. S. Löwenfeld (Leipzig 1885), no. 82, p. 43; Cowdrey, 'Gregory VII and Bearing of Arms', p. 28, note 31; Bull, *Knightly Piety*, pp. 72–8; A. Ferreiro, 'The Siege of Barbastro', *Journal of Medieval History*, ix (1983), 133–5.
39. Glaber, *Historiarum*, pp. 134–7; for Sergius's bull, Morris, *Papal Monarchy*, p. 146–7 and note 16; cf. A. Gieysztor, 'The Genesis of the Crusades: the Encyclical of Sergius IV', *Medievalia et Humanistica*, 5 (1949), 3–23, and 6 (1950), 3–34; for a Muslim view of western pilgrims *c.* 1047 Naser-e Khosraw, *Book of Travels (Saparnama)*, trans. W. M. Thackston Jnr (New York 1986), pp. 21, 35, 37–8.
40. Ademar of Chabannes, *Chronicon*, ed. P. Bourgain, *Opera Omnia*, i, Corpus Christianorum Continuatio Mediaevalis, cxxix (Turnhout 1999), bk III, cc. 38, 39, 45, 47, 52, 55, 65, 68, 69, pp. 159, 160, 165–7, 171, 174, 184, 188–9.
41. Glaber, *Historiarum*, pp. 37, 61, 83, 84–5, 118–21, 194–5, 196, 198–205, 206–7, 208–9, 212–15.
42. See discussion by J. Riley-Smith, *The First Crusade and the Idea of Crusading* (London 1986), pp. 18–19 and notes 27, 29; Gregory VII, *Regestrum*, bk II, no. 37, p. 173.

2: The Summons to Jerusalem

1. Sigebert of Gembloux, *Chronica*, MGHS, vi, p. 368.
2. Modern literature on the First Crusade is very extensive; for recent works in English in particular see Riley-Smith, *First Crusade*; idem, *The First Crusaders 1095–1131* (Cambridge 1997); J. France, *Victory in the East* (Cambridge 1994); Runciman, *History of the Crusades*, vol. i remains a compelling read.
3. Raymond of Aguilers, *Historia*, trans. J. H. and L. L. Hill, p. 15.
4. The phrase is that of the anonymous *Gesta Francorum*, ed. and trans. R. Hill (Oxford 1972), p. 1.
5. Bernold of St Blasien, *Chronicon*, MGHS, v. p. 462; for Alexius and the West, see esp. J. Shepard, 'Aspects of Byzantine Attitudes and Policy Towards the West', *Byzantium and the West c. 850–c. 1200*, ed. J. D. Howard-Johnston (Amsterdam 1988), pp. 102–18.
6. Bernold of St Blasien, *Chronicon*, p. 462.
7. R. Somerville, 'The Council of Clermont', in *Papacy, Councils and Canon Law* (London 1990), VII, p. 58 and passim; cf. ibid. V, 'French Councils of Pope Urban II' and VIII, 'The Council of Clermont and the First Crusade'; for Baldwin, Albert of Aachen, *Historia Hierosolymitana*, RHC Occ., iv, 626.
8. *Annales S. Benigni Divionensis*, MGHS, v, p. 43; *Annales Besuensis* (i.e. Blaise near Dijon), MGHS, ii, 250. For Urban's itinerary, A. Becker, *Papst Urban II* (Stuttgart 1064–88), ii, 435–57.
9. Hagenmeyer, *Kreuzzugsbriefe*, pp. 136–8; W. Wiederhold, 'Papsturkunden in Florenz', *Nachrichten von der Gesellschaft des Wissenschaften zu Göttingen* (Göttingen 1901), pp. 313–14; Fulk IV of Anjou, *Gesta Andegavensium peregrinorum*, RHC Occ., v, 345–6; Sigebert of Gembloux, *Chronica*, p. 367.
10. H. E. J. Cowdrey, 'Pope Urban II and the Idea of the Crusade', *Studi Medievali*, 3rd series, 36 (1995), 737–8; *Chroniques des comtes d'Anjou et des seigneurs d'Amboise*, ed. L. Halphen et al. (Paris 1913), pp. 100–101.
11. Geoffrey abbot of Vendôme, *Epistolae*, no. XXI, PL, clvii, col. 162; J. and L. Riley-Smith, *Crusades*, p. 38 for translation of Flemish letter; for the Clermont decrees, R. Somerville, *The Councils of Urban II, i: Decreta Claromontensia* (Amsterdam 1972) and above, note 7; J. D. Mansi, *Sacrorum Conciliorum nova et amplissima Collectio*, xx (Venice 1775), cols. 816–19.
12. William of Malmesbury, *Gesta Regum Anglorum*, ed. R. A. B. Mynors et al., i (Oxford 1998), pp. 593–4.
13. For a vivid reconstruction of Clermont, Runciman, *History of the Crusades*, pp. 107–8 and p. 108, note 1 for refs.
14. Gerald of Wales, *Journey Through Wales*, trans. L. Thorpe (London 1978), p. 75.
15. Hagenmeyer, *Kreuzzugsbriefe*, pp. 137–8; *Vita Altmanni episcopi Pataviensis*, MGHS, xii, 230; cf. Riley-Smith, *First Crusaders*, pp. 62–3, 81–3, 97. For penance and pilgrimage in crusade charters, ibid., esp. chaps. 3 and 4 and idem, *First Crusade*, esp. chap. 2.
16. Becker, *Papst Urban II*, ii, 352–62 (esp. pp. 352–3), 374–6, 398–9.
17. Urban to Bolognese, 19 Sept. 1096, Hagenmeyer, *Kreuzzugsbriefe*, pp. 137–8; J. and L. Riley-Smith, *Crusades*, p. 39.
18. Robert the Monk (of Rheims), *Historia*, RHC Occ., iii, 727–30.
19. Mansi, *Sacrorum Conciliorum*, xx, col. 816; Somerville, *Decreta Claromontensia*, p. 74; in general, H. E. J. Cowdrey, 'Pope Urban II's Preaching of the First Crusade', *History*, 55 (1970), 177–88; for the Bologna letter, J. and L. Riley-Smith, *Crusades*, p. 39.
20. Hagenmeyer, *Kreuzzugsbriefe*, pp. 136–7; J. and L. Riley-Smith, *Crusades*, p. 38.
21. Fulk of Anjou, *Gesta Andegavensium*, RHC Occ., v, 345; J. and L. Riley-Smith, *Crusades*, p. 39.
22. Tyerman, *England and the Crusades*, p. 13.
23. Henry of Huntingdon, *De captione Antiochae a Christianis*, RHC Occ., v, 374.
24. Glaber, *Historiarum*, pp. 200–201.

25. Adhemar of Chabannes, *Chronicon*, bk III, c. 47, pp. 166–7.
26. *Vita Altmanni*, p. 230.
27. Benzo of Alba, *Ad Heinricum IV. Imperatorem Libri VII*, MGHS, xi, 605, 606, 616–17, 652; MGHS, lxv, 144; J. Shepard, 'Cross-purposes: Alexius Comnenus and the First Crusade', *The First Crusade*, ed. J. Phillips (Manchester 1997), pp. 107–29 and note 5 above.
28. Cowdrey, 'Urban II and the Idea of Crusade', pp. 721–42; cf. G. J. C. Snoek, *Medieval Piety: From Relics to the Eucharist* (Leiden 1995), pp. 25–6, 35; Adhemar of Chabannes, *Opera*, PL, cxli, col. 110.
29. Snoek, *Medieval Piety*, p. 87.
30. *Winchester Annals*, *Annales Monastici*, ed. H. R. Luard, Rolls Series (London 1864–69), ii, 38.
31. Hagenmeyer, *Kreuzzugsbriefe*, pp. 142, 164; *Gesta Francorum*, p. 7 (for the date, often recorded as Sept. 1096, E. Jamison, 'Some Notes on the *Anonymi Gesta Francorum*', *Studies in French Medieval Literature Presented to M. K. Pope* (Manchester 1939), pp. 183–208.
32. R. Chazan, *European Jewry and the First Crusade* (Berkeley and Los Angeles 1987), p. 77; cf. S. Eidelberg, *The Jews and the Crusaders: The Hebrew Chronicles of the First and Second Crusades* (Madison 1977), pp. 21–115.
33. Baldric of Bourgeuil, *Historia Jerosolimitana*, RHC Occ., iv, 12.
34. Hagenmeyer, *Kreuzzugsbriefe*, p. 136.
35. Note 21 above; Hagenmeyer, *Kreuzzugsbriefe*, pp. 136–44, 176, 179; Urban's letters, J. and L. Riley-Smith, *Crusades*, pp. 38–40; for Limoges, RHC Occ., v, 350–53; for Amanieu, *Cartulaire du prieuré de Sainte-Pierre de la Réole*, ed. C. Grellet-Balguerie, *Archives historiques de la Gironde*, v (1863), 140.
36. Hill, *Gesta Francorum*, pp. 19–20.
37. Riley-Smith, *First Crusaders*, p. 62 and ref. note 41; PL, clvii, col. 162.
38. Hagenmeyer, *Kreuzzugsbriefe*, p. 138; cf. p. 154 for the leaders talking of pilgrimage in 1098; see note 15 above for pilgrimage motifs in charters.
39. *Notitiae duae Lemoviensis de praedicatione crucis in Aquitania*, RHC Occ., v, 350–53. For the importance of Christocentric festivals, see the deal between Cluny and Achard of Montmerle on 12 April, i.e. Easter Saturday, 1096, Bruel, *Chartes de Cluny*, v, 51–3.
40. Riley-Smith, *First Crusaders*, p. 75; France, *Victory*, p. 45.
41. For monkish touts, *Cartulaires de l'abbaye de Molesme 916–1250*, ed. J. Laurent (Paris 1907–11), ii, 83–4; *Cartulaire de l'abbaye de Noyers, Mémoires de la société archéologique de Touraine*, xxii (1872), ed. C. Chevalier, pp. 274–5; *Cartulaire du prieuré de Notre Dame de Longpont de l'ordre de Cluny*, ed. A. Marion (Lyons 1879), pp. 189–90; for the inculcation of a crusader's sense of sin, *Cartulaire Manceau de Marmoutier*, ed. E. Laurain (Laval 1911–45), ii, 86–9.
42. Hill, *Gesta Francorum*, p. 2.
43. Caffaro, *De liberatione civitatum Orientis*, RHC Occ., v, 49.
44. The chief primary sources for Peter are Albert of Aachen, *Historia*, RHC Occ., iv, 271–4; Guibert of Nogent, *Gesta Dei per Francos*, RHC Occ., iv, 142–3 (p. 140 for 'great rumour'); Anna Comnena, *The Alexiad*, trans. E. R. A. Sewter (London 1969), pp. 309–11; cf. Orderic Vitalis, *Ecclesiastical History*, ed. and trans. M. ChIbnall (Oxford 1969–79), v, 29. See E. O. Blake and C. Morris, 'A Hermit Goes to War: Peter and the Origins of the First Crusade', *Monks, Hermits and the Ascetic Tradition*, ed. W. J. Shields, Studies in Church History, xxii (1985), 79–109, which challenges the orthodoxy established by H. Hagenmeyer, *Peter der Eremite* (Leipzig 1879); the patriarch's letter is translated by E. Peters, *The First Crusade* (2nd edn Philadelphia 1998), pp. 283–4; I am grateful to Jonathan Shepard for discussion on some of these points.
45. Hill, *Gesta Francorum*, p. 2, 'The Gauls organised themselves into three parts. One group of Franks entered the region of Hungary, namely Peter the Hermit and Duke Godfrey . . .'

46. Riley-Smith, *First Crusaders*, p. 56.
47. Adhemar of Chabannes, *Chronicon*, bk III, *c.* 47, pp. 166–7; Gieysztor, 'Genesis of Crusades.
48. Albert of Aachen, *Historia*, p. 272; for Peter's retirement and foundation of the Augustinian abbey at Neumoustier near Huy, dedicated to the Holy Sepulchre and John the Baptist 'in remembrance and veneration of the church of Jerusalem', *Chronica Albrici monarchi Trium Fontium a monarcho novi monasterii Hoiensis interpolata*, MGHS, xxiii, 815; Giles of Orval, *Gesta episcoporum Leodiensium*, MGHS, xxv, 93.
49. Naser-e Khosraw, *Book of Travels*, p. 39; C. Cahen, 'La Chronique abrégé d'al-Azimi', *Journal Asiatique*, 230 (1938), 430; C. Hillenbrand, *The Crusades: Islamic Perspectives* (Edinburgh 1999), p. 50.
50. C. De Vic and J Vaissete, *Histoire générale de Languedoc*, v (Toulouse 1875), col. 737–8; Riley-Smith, *The First Crusade*, p. 21.
51. France, *Victory*, p. 194; Albert of Aachen, *Historia*, pp. 348–9; for Alexius and westerners see the articles by J. Shepard, 'Aspects of Byzantine Attitudes'; 'Alexius and the First Crusade'; 'When Greek Meets Greek: Alexius Comnenus and Bohemund in 1097–8', *Byzantine and Modern Greek Studies*, 12 (1988), 185–277; 'The English in Byzantium', *Traditio*, 29 (1973), 52–93. The Sicilian point I owe to Dr Jeremy Johns.
52. Orderic Vitalis, *Ecclesiastical History*, iii, 134–6; v, 156–9.
53. *Frutolfi et Ekkehardi Chronica*, ed. F.-J. Schmale and I. Schmale (Darmstadt 1972), p. 106. C. Haskins, 'A Canterbury Monk at Constantinople', *English Historical Review*, 25 (1910), 293–5; Shepard, 'Cross-purposes', pp. 116–22.
54. Duparc-Quioc, *La Chanson d'Antioche*, v, 3449.
55. J. and L. Riley-Smith, *Crusades*, pp. 44, 52.
56. Hill, *Gesta Francorum*, pp. 19–20.
57. *Jerusalem Mirabilis*, in R. L. Crocker, 'Early Crusade Songs', *The Holy War*, ed. T. P. Murphy (Columbus, Ohio 1976), pp. 78–98.
58. Guibert of Nogent, *Gesta Dei*, pp. 140–41.
59. By Riley-Smith, *First Crusaders*, esp. pp. 93–105.
60. RHC Occ., iii, 727–30.
61. Duparc-Quioc, *Chanson d'Antioche*, v, 7921.
62. Guibert of Nogent, *Gesta Dei*, p. 124.
63. Fulcher of Chartres, *A History of the Expedition to Jerusalem 1095–1127*, trans. F. R. Ryan, intro. H. S. Fink (Knoxville 1969), pp. 66–7.
64. These cited by Riley-Smith, *First Crusaders*, pp. 113–14.
65. Ralph of Caen, *Gesta Tancredi*, RHC Occ., iii, 605–6; for Thomas of Marle, Suger of St Denis, *Vita Ludovici Grossi regis*, ed. H. Waquet (Paris 1929), pp. 30–34, 174–8 and pp. 150–51 for Stephen of Blois; Guibert of Nogent, *Gesta Dei*, p. 79 for William; for Raimbold, PL, clxii, cols. 144–5 and C. J. Tyerman, *The Invention of the Crusades* (Basingstoke, 1998), pp. 11–12.
66. Quoted by Somerville, *Prolegomena* to the *Decreta Claromontensia*, in *Papacy, Councils and Canon Law*, VI, pp. 33–5.
67. Guibert of Nogent, *Gesta Dei*, p. 251; *Deeds of God through the Franks*, trans. R. Levine (Woodbridge 1997), p. 156.
68. *Vita Altmanni*, p. 230.
69. Sigebert of Gembloux, *Chronica*, p. 367; for his hostility to papal use of indulgences for war, MGH, *Libelli de Lite Imperatorem et Pontificum*, ii (Hanover 1892), 464.

3: The March to Constantinople

1. Sigebert of Gembloux, *Chronica*, p. 367; Albert of Aachen, *Historia*, pp. 274, 277, 289, 340; Raymond of Aguilers, *Historia* iii, 244; Hill, *Gesta Francorum*, pp. 2–3; Guibert of Nogent, *Gesta Dei*, p. 136 and passim; Riley-Smith, *First Crusade*, esp. pp. 111–12, 141–2, 147–8; Hagenmeyer, *Kreuzzugsbriefe*, pp. 141–2, 146; France, *Victory*, pp. 148, 210.

2. The best modern account of the campaign is France, *Victory*.
3. Raymond of Aguilers, *Historia*, trans. J. H. and L. L. Hill. p. 91.
4. The Lorraine and German expeditions are the prime concern of Albert of Aachen, *Historia*, p. 272 et seq. For chronology, see J. W. Nesbitt, 'The Rate of March of Crusading Armies', *Traditio*, 19 (1963), who amends H. Hagenmeyer, *Chronologie de la première croisade* (Paris 1902).
5. Guibert of Nogent, *Gesta Dei*, pp. 140–92 and 142–3 for his hostile account of Peter; cf. F. Duncalf, 'The Peasants' Crusade', *American Historical Review*, 26 (1920–21), 440–53, esp. p. 441.
6. Guibert of Nogent, *Gesta Dei*, pp. 183–4.
7. Anna Comnena, *Alexiad*, p. 286 and pp. 293–308; Shepard, 'Cross-purposes', esp. p. 115 for comments on this background.
8. Nesbitt, 'Rate of March', esp. p. 173; Albert of Aachen, *Historia*, pp. 278–82 for the size of the army and length of line in the Balkans.
9. Albert of Aachen, *Historia*, p. 280.
10. Albert of Aachen, *Historia*, p. 288.
11. Chazan, *European Jewry* p. 23 and, in general, pp. 1–37.
12. R. Chazan, '1007–1012: Initial Crisis for Northern European Jewry', *Proceedings of the American Academy for Jewish Research*, 38–9 (1970–71), 101–17.
13. Chazan, *European Jewry*, p. 36.
14. Runciman, *History of Crusades*, i, 137 and pp. 134–41 for the pogrom; cf. Chazan, *European Jewry*, pp. 50–136; the chief Jewish sources are translated by S. Eidelberg, *Jews and the Crusaders*, pp. 21–75, 79–93, 99–115. Emich of Flonheim used to be known to historians as Emich of Leinengen, A. V. Murray, 'The Army of Godfrey de Bouillon: Structure and Dynamics of a Contingent on the First Crusade', *Revue Belge de Philologie et d'Histoire*, 70 (1992), 315–22.
15. Eidelberg, *Jews and Crusaders*, p. 36.
16. Eidelberg, *Jews and Crusaders*, p. 50.
17. Albert of Aachen, *Historia*, p. 295.
18. Guibert of Nogent, *De vita sua*, ed. E.-R. Labande (Paris 1981), pp. 246–8; Albert of Aachen, *Historia*, p. 293; Ekkehard of Aura, *Hierosolymita*, RHC Occ., v, 20.
19. Eidelberg, *Jews and Crusaders*, p. 108 (the Mainz Anonymous); in general Chazan, *European Jewry*, pp. 72–84; cf. the awkward passages in Riley-Smith, *First Crusade*, pp. 53–7.
20. Eidelberg, *Jews and Crusaders*, pp. 21, 112.
21. Hagenmeyer, *Kreuzzugsbriefe*, pp. 138, 139.
22. Cf. Riley-Smith, *First Crusade*, p. 50.
23. Chazan, *European Jewry*, p. 145.
24. Tyerman, *England and the Crusades*, p. 19; Hagenmeyer, *Kreuzzugsbriefe*, pp. 137–8.
25. *Actes des comtes de Flandres 1071–1128*, ed. F. Vercauteren (Brussels 1938), pp. 65–6, no. 22; the count of Roucy is a witness.
26. Fulcher of Chartres, *History*, p. 74.
27. Preserved in mangled form by Anna Comnena, *Alexiad*, pp. 313–14.
28. 'Elias who had deserted from the emperor . . .', *Alexiad*, p. 314.
29. H. E. Mayer, *Mélanges sur l'histoire du royaume Latin de Jérusalem* (Paris 1984), pp. 17, 22–7, 43, 44, 49; Murray 'The Army of Godfrey de Bouillon', pp. 301–29, esp. pp. 314, 327.
30. Hill, *Gesta Francorum*, p. 2; G. Paris, 'La Chanson du pèlerinage de Charlemagne', *Romania*, 9 (1880), 1–50; J. Flori, '*Pur eschalier sainte crestienté.* Croisade, guerre sainte et guerre juste dans les anciennes chansons de geste françaises', *Le Moyen Age*, 97 (5th series vol. v, 1991), 171–87.
31. Albert of Aachen, *Historia*, p. 274.
32. Albert of Aachen, *Historia*, p. 311, and pp. 305–11 for the Constantinople stand-off.
33. This, at least, is the impression given by Albert of Aachen, who listened to them.
34. See now J. D. Howard-Johnston, 'Anna Komnene and the *Alexiad*', in *Alexios*

Komnenos, ed. M. E. Mullett and D. Smythe (Belfast 1996); J. France, 'Anna Comnena, the *Alexiad* and the First Crusade', *Reading Medieval Studies*, 10 (1983), 20–32.

35. Runciman, *History of Crusades*, i, 157–8.
36. On Bohemund's expedition, Hill, *Gesta Francorum*, pp. 7–9 et seq., whose author was with it; E. Jamison, 'Some Notes on the *Anonymi Gesta Francorum*'; on Bohemund's position on the crusade, J. Shepard, 'When Greek Meets Greek', *Byzantine and Modern Greek Studies*, 12 (1988), 185–276.
37. Marquis de la Force, 'Les Conseillers latins du basileus Alexis Comnene', *Byzantion*, xi (1936), 153–65; D. Nicol, 'Symbiosis and Integration; Some Greco-Latin Families in Byzantium', *Byzantinische Forschungen*, 7 (1979), 113–35; W. B. McQueen, 'Relations between the Normans and Byzantium 1071–1112', *Byzantion*, 56 (1986), 427–76.
38. Shepard, 'Greek Meets Greek' for these details.
39. Raymond of Aguilers, *Historia*, trans. J. H. and L. L. Hill, p. 22.
40. France, *Victory*, p. 98.
41. For Spain, Bull, *Knightly Piety*, p. 83.
42. Raymond of Aguilers, *Historia*, trans. J. H. and L. L. Hill, p. 18.
43. According to William of Poitiers, see Shepard, 'Aspects of Byzantine Attitudes towards the West'.
44. On Robert's crusade and career, C. W. David, *Robert Curthose, Duke of Normandy* (Cambridge, Mass. 1920); cf. William of Malmesbury, *Gesta Regum*, ed. W. Stubbs, Rolls Series (London 1887–9), ii, 433, 460, 461 for later myths and gossip.
45. France, *Victory*, p. 129.
46. Hagenmeyer, *Kreuzzugsbriefe*, p. 149.
47. Fulcher of Chartres, *History*, pp. 75–6.
48. J. H. Pryor, 'The Oath of the Leaders of the First Crusade to the Emperor Alexius Comnenus: Fealty, Homage', *Parergon*, 2 (1984), 111–41; France, *Victory*, pp. 107–21 for a trenchant account; cf. Shepard, 'Cross-purposes' and 'Greek Meets Greek'.
49. France, *Victory*, p. 154.
50. Anna Comnena, *Alexiad*, pp. 315, 325, 327, etc.
51. Raymond of Aguilers, *Historia*, trans. J. H. and L. L. Hill, p. 73.
52. Raymond of Aguilers, *Historia*, trans. J. H. and L. L. Hill, p. 24.
53. Anna Comnena, *Alexiad*, p. 329; cf. the embarrassed *Gesta Francorum*, p. 12.
54. Hagenmeyer, *Kreuzzugsbriefe*, p. 140.

4: The Road to the Holy Sepulchre

1. France, *Victory*, pp. 165–9 and, for Egyptian negotiations in general, pp. 211, 252–4 302, 304, 317, 325–6; cf. R. J. Lilie, *Byzantium and the Crusader States 1096–1204* (Eng. trans. Oxford 1993), chap. 1, pp. 1–60.
2. Ibn al-Qalanisi, *The Damascus Chronicle of the Crusades Extracted and Translated from the Chronicle of Ibn al-Qalanisi*, trans. H. A. R. Gibb (London 1932), p. 41; G. Dedeyan, 'Les Colophons de manuscrits arméniens comme sources pour l'histoire des croisades', *The Crusades and their Sources: Essays Presented to Bernard Hamilton*, ed. J. France and W. G. Zajac (Aldershot 1998), pp. 89–110; P. M. Holt, *The Age of the Crusades* (London 1986), p. 27 for the translation of al-Sulami.
3. Hill, *Gesta Francorum*, p. 21 and throughout the account of the siege of Antioch, pp. 28 et seq. For an account of the Christian communities in the Levant, see below pp. 226.
4. Emerton, *Correspondence of Gregory VII*, p. 94.
5. See the discussion and references in R. Ellenblum, *Frankish Rural Settlement in the Latin Kingdom of Jerusalem* (Cambridge 1998), pp. 20–22.
6. For brief general surveys, see Holt, *Age of Crusades* and R. Irwin, *The Middle East in the Middle Ages* (London 1986).
7. Hill, *Gesta Francorum*, p. 21.
8. Fulcher of Chartres, *History*, p. 85; for the best modern account of the battle and its

location, France, *Victory*, pp. 169–85, which also provides the most detailed narrative of the crusaders' campaigns in Asia Minor, Syria and Palestine.

9. Hill, *Gesta Francorum*, pp. 19–20.
10. Raymond of Aguilers, *Historia*, trans. J. H. and L. L. Hill, pp. 28–9; Hill, *Gesta Francorum*, p. 23; Fulcher of Chartres, *History*, pp. 87–8; Albert of Aachen, *Historia*, pp. 340–42.
11. Albert of Aachen, *Historia*, pp. 347–8.
12. Hill, *Gesta Francorum*, pp. 25–6.
13. On this Armenian strategy, France, *Victory*, pp. 190–96.
14. Fulcher of Chartres, *History*, pp. 88–92 (p. 90 for the number of knights).
15. For the *Chanson d'Antioche*, see the edition of S. Duparc-Quioc (Paris 1977–8); R. F. Cook, '*Chanson d'Antioche*', *chanson de geste: le cycle de la croisade est-il épique?* (Amsterdam 1980); for other stories, Tyerman, *England and the Crusades*, pp. 22–3; cf. the stained glass sequence on the crusade at St Denis, *c.*1146–7.
16. Anna Comnena, *Alexiad*, pp. 438–9.
17. For Bohemund's ambitions, J. Shepard, 'When Greek Meets Greek'; T. S. Asbridge, *The Creation of the Principality of Antioch 1098–1130* (Woodbridge 2000), pp. 15–42.
18. Raymond of Aguilers, *Historia*, trans. J. H. and L. L. Hill, p. 31.
19. Usamah Ibn-Munqidh, *An Arab-Syrian Gentleman and Warrior in the Period of the Crusades: Memoirs of Usamah Ibn-Munqidh*, trans. P. K. Hitti (reprint Princeton 1987), pp. 149–50.
20. Raymond of Aguilers, *Historia*, trans. J. H. and L. L. Hill, p. 35.
21. J. A. Brundage, 'Prostitution, Miscegenation and Sexual Purity in the First Crusade', *Crusade and Settlement*, ed. P. Edbury (Cardiff 1985), pp. 57–65.
22. Raymond of Aguilers, *Historia*, pp. 36–7; J. Richard, 'La Confrérie de la première croisade: à propos d'un episode de la première croisade', *Etudes de civilisation médiévale: mélanges offert à E. R. Labande*, ed. B. Jeannau (Poitiers 1974), pp. 617–22.
23. Hagenmeyer, *Kreuzzugsbriefe*, pp. 141–2, 144–6, 146–9.
24. Albert of Aachen, *Historia*, p. 435; France, *Victory*, pp. 209–20 and refs.
25. Hill, *Gesta Francorum*, pp. 34–5; Raymond of Aguilers, *Historia*, trans. J. H. and L. L. Hill, p. 37; cf. Shepard, 'Greek Meets Greek'.
26. Hagenmeyer, *Kreuzzugsbriefe*, p. 150.
27. Hagenmeyer, *Kreuzzugsbriefe*, p. 149; Raymond of Aguilers, *Historia*, trans. J. H. and L. L. Hill, p. 59; *Gesta Francorum*, p. 63.
28. Hill, *Gesta Francorum*, p. 46 and, for the author's apparently eyewitness and certainly dramatic account of the episode, pp. 44–8.
29. The butcher may have been a shepherd, according to the thirteenth-century Ibn al-Athir, *Arab Historians of the Crusades*, trans. F. Gabrieli (London 1984), pp. 6–7; for other references, France, *Victory*, p. 267.
30. Hagenmeyer, *Kreuzzugsbriefe*, p. 150.
31. Orderic Vitalis, *Ecclesiastical History*, v, 98; vi, 18.
32. A leading figure in these events left the most detailed record: Raymond of Aguilers, *Historia*, trans. J. H. and L. L. Hill, pp. 51–61, but cf. Hill, *Gesta Francorum*, pp. 57–60, 65–6 and the letters accepting the Lance's authenticity, of Anselm of Ribemont, July 1098, and the crusade leaders, Sept. 1098, Hagenmeyer, *Kreuzzugsbriefe*, pp. 159–60, 163; C. Morris, 'Policy and Visions: the Case of the Holy Lance at Antioch', *War and Government in the Middle Ages*, ed. J. Gillingham and J. C. Holt (Woodbridge 1984), pp. 33–45.
33. Dedeyan, 'Les Colophons', pp. 94–5.
34. Raymond of Aguilers, *Historia*, trans. J. H. and L. L. Hill, p. 52.
35. For Peter's later visions, Raymond of Aguilers, *Historia*, trans. J. H. and L. L. Hill, pp. 66–72, 76–8, 93–103; cf. France, *Victory*, p. 322; Morris, 'Policy and Visions', pp. 42–3; Runciman, *History of the Crusades*, i, 273–4.
36. Raymond of Aguilers, *Historia*, trans. J. H. and L. L., Hill, pp. 108, 110, 122–3, 128; on relics in general, cf. pp. 111–13.

37. Fulcher of Chartres, *History*, p. 106; Hill, *Gesta Francorum*, p. 67 and Orderic Vitalis, *Ecclesiastical History*, v, 108 for Herluin the interpreter; France, *Victory*, pp. 270–96.
38. Cf. Anna Comnena, *Alexiad*, pp. 348–50 with Hill, *Gesta Francorum*, pp. 63–5, Lilie, *Byzantium and the Crusader States*, esp. pp. 32–60.
39. Hagenmeyer, *Kreuzzugsbriefe*, pp. 161–5; cf. the earlier letter from the princes April/July 1098, which lacks anti-Greek vitriol, pp. 153–5.
40. Hagenmeyer, *Kreuzzugsbriefe*, pp. 155–6.
41. See note 1 above and refs. for Egyptian negotiations.
42. Raymond of Aguilers, *Historia*, trans. J. H. and L. L. Hill, pp. 74–5 ('peace of discord').
43. For cannibalism at Ma 'arrat *Gesta Francorum*, p. 80; Raymond of Aguilers, *Historia*, trans. J. H. and L. L. Hill, p. 81; in general, Guibert of Nogent, *Gesta Dei*, pp. 241–2; the main 'source' is the later *Chanson d'Antioche* which places the first outbreak at Antioch: L. A. M. Sumberg, 'The "Tafurs" and the First Crusade', *Medieval Studies*, 21 (1959), 224–46, esp. 235–46. Sumberg argues for a Flemish origin of the Tafurs and their 'king'. Albert of Aachen, usually a rich source for north-eastern Frenchmen, does not mention them.
44. Raymond of Aguilers, *Historia*, trans. J. H. and L. L. Hill, pp. 81–3; Hill, *Gesta Francorum*, p. 81.
45. For the events at Arqah, Raymond of Aguilers, *Historia*, pp. 87–113; Hill, *Gesta Francorum*, pp. 83–5; France, *Victory*, pp. 316–26 and pp. 326–31 for march to Jerusalem. For Urban II's alleged decree on the right of conquest, R. Somerville, 'The Council of Clermont and the First Crusade', *Studia Gratiana*, 20 (1976), 335–7, but cf. J. Richard, *The Crusades* (Cambridge 1999), p. 112.
46. Raymond of Aguilers, *Historia*, trans. J. H. and L. L. Hill, p. 113 comments on their rotting timbers.
47. Raymond of Aguilers, *Historia*, trans. J. H. and L. L. Hill, p. 116; Hill, *Gesta Francorum*, p. 87.
48. The best modern accounts are J. Prawer, 'The Jerusalem the Crusaders Captured', *Crusade and Settlement*, ed. Edbury, pp. 1–16; France, *Victory*, pp. 330–57.
49. Albert of Aachen, *Historia*, p. 470; Hill, *Gesta Francorum*, p. 90; Raymond of Aguilers, *Historia*, trans. J. H. and L. L. Hill, pp. 121–3.
50. Albert of Aachen, *Historia*, pp. 476–7.
51. *Gesta Francorum*, p. 91; Raymond of Aguilers, *Historia*, trans. J. H. and L. L. Hill, pp. 127–8.
52. S. Goitein, 'Contemporary Letters on the Capture of Jerusalem by the Crusaders', *Journal of Jewish Studies*, 3 (1952), pp. 165, 173 and, in general, pp. 162–77.
53. Raymond of Aguilers, *Historia*, trans. J. H. and L. L. Hill, p. 127; Hill, *Gesta Francorum*, p. 92; Goitein, 'Contemporary Letters', p. 172; idem, 'Geniza Sources for the Crusader Period', *Outremer*, ed. B. Kedar, H. Mayer, R. Smail (Jerusalem 1982), p. 312 and, generally, pp. 306–14.
54. See notes 52 and 53 above.
55. Hill, *Gesta Francorum*, p. 92; Raymond of Aguilers, *Historia*, trans. J. H. and L. L. Hill, p. 128.
56. The aftermath of the capture and the battle of Ascalon are dealt with contrastingly by Runciman, *History of the Crusades*, i, 289–302; France, *Victory*, pp. 356–66.
57. Fulcher of Chartres, *History*, p. 89; Murray, 'The Army of Godfrey de Bouillon', pp. 301–29.
58. A. E. Laiou, *Constantinople and the Latins: The Foreign Policy of Andronicus II 1282–1328* (Cambridge, Mass. 1972), pp. 130–99; K. Setton, *The Papacy and the Levant 1204–1571* (Philadelphia 1976–84), i, 163–4, 168–9, 441–56.
59. J. France, 'Crusading Warfare and Its Adaptation to Eastern Conditions in the Twelfth Century', *Mediterranean Historical Review*, 15 (2000), 49–66.
60. Hagenmeyer, *Kreuzzugsbriefe*, pp. 138–40, 144–6, 149–52, 156–60.

5: The Foundation of Christian Outremer

1. Translation in M. Biddle, *The Tomb of Christ* (Stroud 1999), pp. 92–4, generally pp. 91–5; for building dates, M. de Vogue, *Les Eglises de la Terre Sainte* (Paris 1860), esp. p. 218; for Fulk, William of Tyre, *Historia*, trans. E. A. Babcock and A. C. Krey, *A History of Deeds Done Beyond the Sea* (New York 1976, reprint of 1941 edn), ii, 62 (hereafter William of Tyre, *History*).
2. See the examples discussed by C. Morris, 'Picturing the Crusades', *The Crusades and their Sources*, ed. J. France and W. G. Zajac (Aldershot 1998), pp. 195–216; cf. Biddle, *The Tomb of Christ*.
3. H. W. C. Davis, 'Henry of Blois and Brian FitzCount', *English Historical Review*, 25 (1910), 301–3.
4. J. Delaville le Roulx (ed.), *Cartulaire général de l'ordre des Hospitaliers de S. Jean de Jerusalem 1100–1310* (Paris 1894–1906), no. 309, i, 222–3, no. 309; Robert of Rheims, *Historia Iherosolimitana*, RHC Occ., iii, 723.
5. B. Hamilton, *The Latin Church in the Crusader States* (London 1980), pp. 61–2; J. Richard, *The Crusades c. 1071–c.1291* (Cambridge 1999), pp. 100, 119; for the refashioning of the Holy Land in the twentieth century, see M. Benvenisti, *Sacred Landscape: The Buried History of the Holy Land since 1948* (London 2000).
6. In general for the 1100–1101 expeditions, Riley-Smith, *First Crusade*, pp. 120–34; Riley-Smith, *First Crusaders*, pp. 75–7 and passim; Runciman, *History of the Crusades*, ii, 18–31; J. L. Cate, 'The Crusade of 1101', *History of the Crusades*, ed. K. Setton (2nd edn Madison 1969–89), i, 343–67; cf. Hagenmeyer, *Kreuzzugsbriefe*, pp. 141–2, 144–55, 156–65, 174–9. For numbers, France, *Victory*, pp. 122–42; J. Riley-Smith, 'Casualties on the First Crusade', *Crusades*, 1 (2002), 13–28; Orderic Vitalis, *Ecclesiastical History*, iii, 182–3 (written before 1130) for his reference to the 1107–8 crusade as the third journey (*tercia profectio*) to Jerusalem, implying that the 1101–2 was regarded as the second.
7. *Cartulaire de St Cyr de Nevers*, ed. R. de Lespinasse (Nevers/Paris 1916), no. 96.
8. Orderic Vitalis, *Ecclesiastical History*, v, 324.
9. Hagenmeyer, *Kreuzzugsbriefe*, pp. 175–6, no. XX and pp. 144–6, 155–6 for the letters; Guibert of Nogent, *Gesta Dei*, p. 219 for their circulation.
10. Quoted by M. Angold, *The Byzantine Empire 1025–1204* (London 1984), p. 150; for Anna Comnena's gloss, *Alexiad*, pp. 355–7.
11. Albert of Aachen, *Historia*, p. 563.
12. Ekkehard of Aura, *Hierosolymita*, v, 30.
13. Hagenmeyer, *Kreuzzugsbriefe*, p. 150.
14. Fulcher of Chartres, *History*, pp. 284–8, 300–302; for general accounts of twelfth-century Outremer, J. Prawer, *The Latin Kingdom of Jerusalem* (London 1972); Richard, *The Crusades*, pp. 77–215; J. Riley-Smith, *The Crusades: A Short History* (London 1990), pp. 40–87; H. E. Mayer, *The Crusades* (2nd edn Oxford 1988), pp. 58–136, 152–95. The main western chronicle accounts are, up to the late 1120s, Fulcher of Chartres, Albert of Aachen and, thereafter, William of Tyre.
15. M. Benvenisti, *The Crusaders in the Holy Land* (Jerusalem 1970), pp. 14, 132; J. Riley-Smith, 'The Survival in Latin Palestine of Muslim Administration', *The Eastern Mediterranean Lands in the Period of the Crusades*, ed. P. M. Holt (Warminster 1977), pp. 9–22 and esp. p. 16.
16. Fulcher of Chartres, *History* pp. 132, 150; William of Tyre, *History*, i, 408; for the accounts of the Englishman Saewulf (1101x3) and the Russian abbot Daniel (1106x8), J. Wilkinson, *The Jerusalem Pilgrimage 1099–1185*, Hackluyt Society, NS, 167 (1988), 100, 108, 145, 148–50, 154, 162.
17. H. E. Mayer and M. L. Favreau, 'Das Diplom Balduins I für Genua und Genuas Goldene Inschrift in der Grabeskirche', *Quellen und Forschungen aus italianischen Archiven und Bibliotheken*, 55–6 (1976), 22 et seq.; other scholars still maintain the authenticity of both 1104 privilege and the inscription.

18. Caffaro of Genoa, *De Liberatione Civitatum Orientis Liber*, RHC Occ., v.
19. Richard, *The Crusades*, pp. 98–9.
20. Fulcher of Chartres, *History*, pp. 149–50.
21. Hillenbrand, *Crusades*, pp. 73–4 and, generally, pp. 69–76.

6: The Latin States

1. Fulcher of Chartres, *History*, pp. 271–2.
2. Apart from the general accounts by Riley-Smith, Mayer, Richard and Prawer (above chap. 5 note 14), see for the Muslim perspective Holt, *Age of Crusades*, pp. 23–59; C. Cahen, *La Syrie du Nord* (Paris 1940); and the chapters by H. S. Fink, R. L. Nicholson and H. A. R. Gibb in *History of the Crusades*, ed. Setton, vol. i. There is no surviving Edessan Latin chronicle, but cf. that of the Armenian Matthew of Edessa, trans. A. E. Dostourian, *Armenia and the Crusades* (New York and London 1993); William of Tyre et al. have much to say as well. On Edessa generally, J. B. Segal, *Edessa, 'The Blessed City'* (Oxford 1970).
3. On Antioch/Edessa relations, T. S. Asbridge, *Creation of the Principality of Antioch*, esp. pp. 50–91, 104–28.
4. William of Tyre, *History*, ii, 52.
5. H. Kennedy, *Crusader Castles* (Cambridge 1994), p. 18.
6. William of Tyre, *History*, ii, 201, cf. pp. 140–41.
7. In general and specifically, Asbridge, *Creation of the Principality*; Cahen, *Syrie du Nord*; Lilie, *Byzantium and Crusader States*; there survives an Antiochene chronicle by Walter the Chancellor, *The Antiochene Wars*, trans. T. S. Asbridge and S. B. Edgington (Aldershot 1999).
8. Although he was: Walter the Chancellor, *Antiochene Wars*, p. 163; Usamah, *An Arab-Syrian Gentleman*, p. 149; Ibn al-Qalanisi, *Damascus Chronicle*, p. 149.
9. Lilie, *Byzantium and Crusader States*, pp. 103–4; Mayer, *Crusades*, p. 115; Runciman, *History of the Crusades*, ii, 364–5 and note 1.
10. P. Deschamps, *Les Châteaux des Croisés en Terre Sainte* (Paris 1934–73), iii, 191–9; Asbridge, *Creation of Principality*, pp. 73, 175; Mayer, *Crusades*, p. 163.
11. Asbridge, *Creation of Principality*, pp. 176–7 and refs.
12. Cahen, *Syrie de Nord*, pp. 41–2, 343–4, 405, 540; B. Z. Kedar, 'The Subjected Muslims of the Frankish Levant', *Muslims under Latin Rule*, ed. J. M. Powell (Princeton 1990), pp. 137, 156–7; for Alan of al-Atharib, Asbridge, *Creation of Principality*, p. 169.
13. Cahen, *Syrie du Nord*, p. 278.
14. Walter the Chancellor, *Antiochene Wars*, pp. 87–9.
15. Mayer, *Crusades*, p. 192; Runciman, *History of the Crusades*, ii, 346–7; William of Tyre, *History*, ii, 235–6.
16. Richard, *The Crusades*, pp. 113–14.
17. Anna Comnena, *Alexiad*, p. 434 and 424–34 for text of treaty; Lilie, *Byzantium and Crusader States*, pp. 72–82; Asbridge, *Creation of the Principality*, pp. 94–103.
18. Lilie, *Byzantium and Crusader States*, passim.
19. William of Tyre, *History*, ii, 77–8.
20. Runciman, *History of the Crusades*, ii, 182–3 and refs.; William of Tyre, *History*, ii, 199.
21. J. H. and L. L. Hill, *Raymond IV Count of Toulouse* (New York 1962); Kennedy, *Crusader Castles*, p. 63.
22. Ibn al-Qalanisi, *Damascus Chronicle*, p.89.
23. For their fortifications, Kennedy, *Crusader Castles*, pp. 64–7; For the end of the Embriacos, below p. 732.
24. *Damascus Chronicle*, pp. 287–8; Runciman, *History of the Crusades*, ii, 287–8 for further refs.
25. William of Tyre, *History*, ii, 214; Holt, *Age of Crusades*, pp. 28, 39–40; B. Lewis, 'The Isma'ilites and the Assassins', *History of the Crusades*, ed. Setton, i, 99–132.

26. E.g. William of Tyre, *History*, ii, 192–3 (reactions after the debacle of the siege of Damascus 1148); ii, 418–20, 434–5 (for the tensions surrounding the visit of Count Philip of Flanders 1177, on which see B. Hamilton, *The Leper King and his Heirs* (Cambridge 2000), pp. 119–33).
27. Only one twelfth-century verse epic, the *Chanson des Chétifs*, originated in Outremer, at Antioch, probably at the court of Raymond of Poitiers (d. 1149), but other *chanson* cycles were known there as in the west; for a summary, Mayer, *Crusades*, pp. 192–3.
28. A. V. Murray, 'The Accession of Baldwin I of Jerusalem', *From Clermont to Jerusalem: The Crusade and Crusade Societies 1095–1500* (Turnhout 1998), pp. 81–102.
29. On titles, J. France, 'The Election and Title of Godfrey de Bouillon', *Canadian Journal of History*, 18 (1983), 321–30; cf. J. Riley-Smith, 'The Title of Godfrey de Bouillon', *Bulletin of the Institute of Historical Research*, 52 (1979), 83–6; A. V. Murray, 'The Title of Godfrey de Bouillon as Ruler of Jerusalem', *Collegium Medievale*, 3 (1990), 163–78; Richard, *The Crusades*, p. 78; H. E. Mayer, 'Latins, Muslims and Greeks in the Latin Kingdom of Jerusalem', *History*, 63 (1978), 175.
30. William of Tyre, *History*, i, 416; Mayer, *Mélanges*, esp. pp. 11, 17, 30–72.
31. William of Tyre, *History*, i, 487–8; for the Latin text, William of Tyre, *Chronicon*, bk 11, c. 14, p. 518.
32. Fulcher of Chartres, *History*, p. 222.
33. Fulcher of Chartres, *History*, p. 222; William of Tyre, who used Fulcher, removes all mention of non-Latins in his account.
34. S. Tibble, *Monarchy and Lordship in the Latin Kingdom of Jerusalem 1099–1291* (Oxford 1989); cf. the review by H. E. Mayer in *Göttingischen Gelehrten Anzeigen*, 245 (1993), 59–70.
35. H. E. Mayer, 'Angevin *versus* Normans: The New Men of King Fulk of Jerusalem', *Proceedings of the American Philosophical Society*, 133 (1989), 1–25.
36. E. de Rozière (ed.), *Cartulaire de l'église du Saint Sépulchre de Jérusalem*, v (Paris 1849), 17, no. 15; in general, H. E. Mayer, 'The Succession to Baldwin II of Jerusalem', *Dumbarton Oaks Papers*, 39 (1985), 139–47.
37. William of Tyre, *History*, ii, 47; as a boy in Jerusalem, William may have seen King Fulk in person.
38. William of Tyre, *History*, ii, 51.
39. Riley-Smith, *First Crusaders*, pp. 169–88.
40. C. J. Tyerman, *England and the Crusades 1095–1588* (Chicago 1988), pp. 50–51; cf. Hamilton, *The Leper King*, pp. 212–14.
41. P. Edbury and J. G. Rowe, *William of Tyre* (Cambridge 1988), pp. 61–84.
42. For a summary, J. Folda, 'Art in the Latin East', *The Oxford History of the Crusades*, ed. J. Riley-Smith (Oxford 1999), p. 141.
43. Alexander III, *Opera Omnia*, PL, 200, col. 1294; Hamilton, *The Leper King*, passim for a modern positive gloss on Baldwin.
44. William of Tyre, *History*, ii, 446, 460.
45. R. C. Smail, 'The Predicaments of Guy of Lusignan 1183–87', *Outremer*, ed. Kedar et al., pp. 159–76.
46. B. Z. Kedar, 'The General Tax of 1183 in the Crusading Kingdom of Jerusalem', *English Historical Review*, 89 (1974), 339–45; William of Tyre, *History*, ii, 486–7.

7: East is East and East is West: Outremer in the Twelfth Century

1. William of Tyre, *History*, ii, 397–8; E. Kohlberg and B. Z. Kedar, 'A Melkite Physician in Frankish Jerusalem and Ayyubid Damascus', in B. Z. Kedar, *The Franks in the Levant* (Aldershot 1993), chap. XII, pp. 113–15; C. Cahen, 'Indigènes et croisés', *Syria*, 15 (1934), 351–60; on William of Tyre, Edbury and Rowe, *William of Tyre*, esp. pp. 1–22 and passim for his historical interpretation.
2. *Livres des Assises de la Cour des Bourgeois*, c. 241, RHC Lois (Paris 1843), ii, 172.

3. Guibert of Nogent, *Gesta Dei*, p. 245; Orderic Vitalis, *Ecclesiastical History*, v, 136–7; Richard, *The Crusades*, pp. 144–5.
4. Ellenblum, *Settlement*, pp. 9, 14–19.
5. Fulcher of Chartres, *History*, pp. 149–50, 271–2; *The Travels of Ibn Jubayr*, trans. R. J. C. Broadhurst (London 1952), p. 325; Usamah, *An Arab-Syrian Gentleman*, p. 170.
6. A. de Barthélemy, 'Libre Exercise de commerce octroyé à un pèlerin champanois', *Archives de l'Orient Latin*, i (1881), 535–6; in general, Ellenblum, *Settlement*, passim; cf. Prawer, *The Latin Kingdom*; idem, 'Colonization Activities in the Latin Kingdom', *Crusader Institutions* (Oxford 1980), pp. 102–42.
7. *Le Cartulaire du chapitre du Saint-Sépulchre de Jérusalem*, ed. G. Bresc-Bautier (Paris 1984), no. 121, pp. 246–7; Hugh le Poitevin, *Chronique de l'abbaye de Vézelay*, *Monumenta Vizeliacensis*, ed. R. B. C. Huygens (Turnhout 1976), pp. 400, 402.
8. H. E. Mayer, 'Abu 'alis Spuren am Berliner Tiergarten', *Archiv für Diplomatik*, 38 (1992), 132–3; William of Tyre, *History*, ii, 292–4; note 1 above.
9. Ralph Niger, *De Re Militari et Triplici Via Peregrinationis Ierosolimitanae*, ed. L. Schmugge (Berlin 1977), pp. 186–7, 193–9; William of Tyre, *History*, ii, 192–3; for a rehabilitation of Heraclius, B. Z. Kedar, 'The Patriarch Eraclius', *Outremer*, ed. Kedar et al., pp. 177–204.
10. John of Würzburg, in *Jerusalem Pilgrimage*, ed. Wilkinson, Hakluyt Society NS 167 (1988), pp. 259, 266; John Phocas, *ibid.*, p. 324.
11. Theoderic, *Jerusalem Pilgrimage*, ed. Wilkinson, p. 310.
12. C. Kohler, 'Documents inédits concernant l'Orient Latin et les croisades', *Revue de l'Orient Latin* (Paris 1893–1911), vii, 1–9.
13. B. Z. Kedar's phrase, 'The Subjected Muslims of the Frankish Levant', *Muslims under Latin Rule*, ed. Powell, p. 174; idem, 'A Second Incarnation in Frankish Jerusalem', *The Experience of Crusading*, ii, ed. P. Edbury and J. Phillips (Cambridge 2003), p. 89.
14. Kemal al-Din, *Chronicle of Aleppo*, RHC Or., iii (Paris 1884), 597–8.
15. William of Tyre, *History*, ii, 374–5; the levels of military obligations were derived from lists collected by John of Ibelin in the mid-thirteenth century.
16. On lordships, Tibble, *Monarchy and Lordships*.
17. Prawer, 'Colonization', p. 140 and refs.
18. Wilkinson, *Jerusalem Pilgrimage*, pp. 120–71, 215–18, 220–22; for Jerusalem clergy and burgesses, see the witness lists in charters in R. Röhricht, *Regesta regni Hierosolymitani* (Innsbruck 1893, 1904), passim.
19. Wilkinson, *Jerusalem Pilgrimage*, pp. 264–5, 267, 273, 319, 330, 335–6.
20. Delaville le Roulx, *Cartulaire général de l'ordre des Hospitaliers*, no. 399, i, 272–3; Bresc-Bautier, *Cartulaire du Saint-Sépulchre*, no. 117, pp. 237–9; Ellenblum, *Settlement*, pp.74–82; Prawer, 'Colonization', pp. 119–21, 127–8.
21. Prawer, 'Colonization', pp. 140–41 and note 162; Ellenblum, *Settlement*, pp. 65–8.
22. Barthélémy, 'Libre Exercise', pp. 535–6; Ellenblum, *Settlement*, p. 84 and note 16; C. J. Tyerman, 'Who Went on Crusades to the Holy Land?', *Horns of Hattin*, ed. B. Z. Kedar (Jerusalem 1992), pp. 13–26; and, generally, pp. 82–5; Röhricht, *Regesta regni*, passim.
23. For a summary of legal processes with references to debated aspects, Mayer, *The Crusades*, chap. 8, pp. 152 et seq.
24. The phrase is Prawer's, 'Colonization', p. 105. For general discussions, Prawer, 'Colonization'; Ellenblum, *Settlement*, esp. Part II.
25. Discussed by Prawer, 'Colonization', p. 110.
26. *Cartulaire général de l'ordre des Hospitaliers*, no. 309, i, 222–3.
27. This is the central insight of Ellenblum, *Settlement*, pp. 111–44 and Part IV; cf. D. Pringle, 'Churches and Settlement in Crusader Palestine', *Experience of Crusading*, ed. Edbury and Phillips, ii, 161–78.
28. C. E. Bosworth, 'The "Protected Peoples" in Medieval Egypt and Syria', *Bulletin of the John Rylands Library*, 62 (1979–80), 11–36.

29. In general, the works of Prawer, Mayer and Riley-Smith; on Jews, J. Prawer, *The History of the Jews in the Latin Kingdom of Jerusalem* (Oxford 1988); for Muslim headman, Broadhurst, *Ibn Jubayr*, p. 317.
30. Broadhurst, *Ibn Jubayr*, p. 316; in general, Kedar, 'The Subjected Muslims of the Frankish Levant'.
31. Broadhursts, *Ibn Jubayr*, p. 322; William of Tyre, *History*, ii, 214; Fulcher of Chartres, *History*, p.146.
32. But see B. Z. Kedar, *Crusade and Mission* (Princeton 1984), pp. 75–6, note 95; in general pp. 74–83.
33. Broadhurst, *Ibn Jubayr*, pp. 321–2; Hillenbrand, *Crusades*, pp. 408–14.
34. Fulcher of Chartres, *History*, p. 232; Broadhurst, *Ibn Jubayr*, pp. 316–21, 323; Kedar, 'The Subjected Muslims of the Frankish Levant'; Mayer, 'Latins, Muslims and Greeks', pp. 175–92, esp. pp. 177–80.
35. Usamah, *An Arab-Syrian Gentleman*, pp. 164, 167–9; *Chronique d'Ernoul et de Bernard le Trésorier*, ed. L. de Mas Latrie (Paris 1871), pp. 82–4; B. Z. Kedar, 'The Samaritans in the Frankish Period', *Franks in the Levant*, ed. idem, chap. XIX, pp. 86–7; J. Drory, 'Hanbalis of the Nablus Region', *The Medieval Levant: Studies in Memory of Eliyahu Ashtor*, ed. B. Z. Kedar and U. L. Udovitch (Haifa 1988), pp. 95–112; E. Sivan, 'Refugiés Syro-palestiniens au temps des croisades', *Revue des Etudes Islamiques*, 35 (1967), 138–40.
36. William of Tyre, *History*, ii, 20–21, 76–7; Usamah, *An Arab-Syrian Gentleman*, pp. 93–6, 149–50, 159–60, 163–4, 169–70; Kedar, *Crusade and Mission*, pp. 74–83.
37. *Assises des Bourgeois*, c. 241, RHC Lois, i, 172; in general, Kedar, 'Subjected Muslims of the Frankish Levant'.
38. B. Z. Kedar, 'Gerald of Nazareth', *Franks in the Levant*, ed. idem, chap. IV, pp. 55 et seq.; Mayer, 'Latins, Muslims and Greeks', pp. 187–92; Runciman, *History of the Crusades*, ii, 232, 321–3; Röhricht, *Regesta regni*, no. 502; Ellenblum, *Settlement*, pp. 119–20, 125–8; Abbé Martin, 'Les Premiers Princes croisades et les Syriens jacobites', *Journal asiatique*, 12 (1888), 471–90; 13 (1889), 33–79; Dedeyan, 'Les Colophons', pp. 96–7 and note 38.
39. See the map, Ellenblum, *Settlement*, p. xviii and passim; D. Pringle, *Secular Buildings in the Crusader Kingdom of Jerusalem* (Cambridge 1997), esp. pp. 4–5; D. Pringle, *The Red Tower* (Edinburgh 1986).
40. Usamah, *An Arab-Syrian Gentleman*, pp. 95, 130.
41. Pringle, *Red Tower*, pp. 58–63; Tibble, *Monarchy and Lordships*, pp. 103–4, 108–10, 113, 141–3; Ellenblum, *Settlement*, pp. 198–204.
42. Ambroise, *Estoire de la Guerre Sainte*, trans. M. J. Hubert and J. L. Lamonte, *The Crusade of Richard the Lion-Heart* (New York 1976), ll. 7121–5, p. 281. (Hereafter Ambroise, *Crusade of Richard*.)
43. Hillenbrand, *Crusades*, pp. 342 and 343 for Abu Shama's account of Reynald of Sidon; Runciman, *History of the Crusades*, ii, 469; iii, 59, 489; for Ibn Shaddad's account of the bilingual diplomacy, Gabrieli, *Arab Historians*, pp. 228–9.
44. Röhricht, *Regesta regni*, no. 502; A. E. Dostourian, *Armenia and the Crusades: The Chronicle of Matthew of Edessa* (New York/London 1993), pp. 245–57.
45. For a useful summary, Mayer, *Crusades*, pp. 189–93 and refs.; and the articles by J. Folda and D. Pringle in J. Riley-Smith (ed.), *The Oxford Illustrated History of the Crusades* (Oxford 1995).
46. *De constructione castri Saphet*, trans. Kennedy, *Crusader Castles*, p. 194, but see n. 7 p. 211; Broadhurst, *Ibn Jubayr*, p. 322.
47. Usamah, *An Arab-Syrian Gentleman*, pp. 169–70.
48. Pringle, *Red Tower*, p. 178; *Cartulaire du Saint-Sépulchre de Jerusalem*, no. 117, pp. 237–9; G. A. Loud, 'Norman Italy and the Holy Land', *Horns of Hattin*, ed. Kazar, p. 52 and note 14.
49. Runciman, *History of the Crusades*, ii, 317 and note 2.
50. Cited by Mayer, *Crusades*, p. 183 and note 97.

51. See B. Z. Kedar's comments, *Horns of Hattin*, pp. 350–53, 359–60, 363 and J. Prawer's reaction, ibid., esp. pp. 365–6.
52. Cf. Prawer, *Latin Kingdom*, and Kedar, *Crusade and Mission*, p. 78.
53. Thietmar, *Peregrinatio*, *Peregrinationes Medii Aevi Quatuor*, ed. J. C. M. Laurent (Leipzig 1873), ii, 37.

8: A New Path to Salvation? Western Christendom and Holy War 1100–1145

1. Guibert of Nogent, *Gesta Dei* p. 124; Ekkehard of Aura, *Hierosolymita*, v, 39.
2. Riley-Smith, *First Crusaders*, p. 167 and, generally, pp. 144–68; Riley-Smith, *Oxford Illustrated History of the Crusades*, pp. 80–81.
3. H. W. C. Davis, 'Henry of Blois and Brian FitzCount', *English Historical Review*, 25 (1910), 301–3.
4. *Chronicon S. Andreae in Castro Cameracesii*, ed. L. C. Bethmann, MGH SS, vii (Hanover 1846), 544–5; in general, C. Morris, 'Propaganda for War', *Studies in Church History*, xx, ed. W. J. Shields (Woodbridge 1983), 79–101.
5. *Gesta Francorum*, pp. 50–56, 66–7; for the First Crusade histories, Riley-Smith, *First Crusade*, pp. 60–61, 135–52.
6. P. Rousset, *Les Origines et les caractères de la première croisade* (Geneva 1945); K. Skovgaard-Petersen, *A Journey to the Promised Land: Crusading Theology in the* Historia de profectione Danorum in Hierosolymam (Copenhagen 2001); R. Hiestand, 'Il cronista medievale e il suo pubblico', *Annali della facolta di lettere e filosofia dell'universita di Napoli*, 27 (1984–5), 207–27; Gunther of Pairis, *Historia Constantinopolitana*, ed. Comte Riant, *Exuviae Constantinopolitanae*, i (Geneva 1877), 60–66, now trans. A. J. Andrea, *The Capture of Constantinople* (Philadelphia 1997) (hereafter Gunther of Pairis, *Capture*); Gunther of Pairis, *Solymarius*, *Archives de l'Orient Latin*, i (1881), 555–61; for the abbot's presentation to Frederick I, Biblioteca Apostolica Vaticana, MS Vat. Lat. 2001, fol. 1 recto.
7. Orderic Vitalis, *Ecclesiastical History*, vi, 71, cf. pp. 68–9; Ekkehard of Aura, *Chronicon*, ed. G. Weitz, *PL*, 154, col. 987 for 1101 sermon; for 1108 appeal against the Wends, W. Wattenbach, 'Handschriftliches', *Neues Archiv* (1882), vii, 624–6, trans. J. and L. Riley-Smith, *Crusades*, pp. 75–7.
8. Gaimar, *Lestoire des Engleis*, ed. T. D. Hardy and C. T. Martin, Rolls Series (London 1888–9), i, 244–5; cf. William of Malmesbury, *Gesta Regum Anglorum*, ed. W. Stubbs, Rolls Series (London 1887–9), ii, 433, 460, 461.
9. Orderic Vitalis, *Ecclesiastical History*, vi, 352–5.
10. Quoted by Morris, 'Propaganda for War', p. 93.
11. D. Denny, 'A Romanesque Fresco in Auxerre Cathedral', *Gesta*, 25 (1986), 197–202.
12. See M. Biddle, *Tomb of Christ* (Stroud 1999), p. 31.
13. R. L. Crocker, 'Early Crusade Songs', *The Holy War*, ed. T. P. Murphy (Columbus 1976), pp. 78–98.
14. Sigebert of Gembloux, *Epistola Leodicensium adversus Paschalem Papam*, *Libelli de Lite Imperatorum et Pontificum*, ii, MGH (Hanover 1892), 451–2; D. Girgensohn, 'Das Pisaner Konzil von 1135 in der Überlieferung des Pisaner Konzils von 1409', *Festschrift für Hermann Heimpel* (Göttingen 1972), ii, 1,099–100.
15. Duparc-Quioc, *Chanson d'Antioche*, i, 171; Suger of St Denis, *The Deeds of Louis the Fat*, trans. R. C. Cusimo and J. Moorhead (Washington, DC 1992), pp. 37, 106–9.
16. Gouffier of Lastours, according to Geoffrey of Vigeois, *Chronicon*, *Receuil des historiens des Gaules et de la France*, ed. M. Bouquet et al. (Paris 1737–1904), xii, 428; the story describes a crusading Androcles and the Lion, the knight and the lion becoming inseparable after Gouffier had freed the beast from the clutches of a serpent. The tale is probably more exotic than true.
17. Orderic Vitalis, *Ecclesiastical History*, vi, 162.
18. Orderic Vitalis, *Ecclesiastical History*, vi, 287.

19. Suger, *Louis the Fat*, p. 84; *Gesta Ambaziensium Dominorum*, *Chroniques d'Anjou*, ed. P. Marchegay and A. Salmon (Paris 1856), pp. 181–205, esp. pp. 188–90, 193, 205; Orderic Vitalis, *Ecclesiastical History*, v, 168; vi, 158; Ivo of Chartres, *Epistolae*, PL, 162, cols. 144–5, no. 135.
20. Orderic Vitalis, *Ecclesiastical History*, vi, 240, 410.
21. Henry of Huntingdon, *Historia Anglorum*, ed. T. Arnold, Rolls Series (London 1879), pp. 262–3; Geoffrey of Monmouth, *Historia Regum Britanniae*, ed. A. Griscom and R. Ellis Jones (London 1929), pp. 437–8, trans. L. Thorpe, *The History of the Kings of Britain* (London 1966), p. 216.
22. PL, 163, col. 508, no. 25 for Gelasius's letter of 10 Dec. 1118; *Song of Roland*, trans. D. L. Sayers (London 1975), p. 135, l. 2197.
23. Snorri Sturluson, *Heimskringla*, trans. L. M. Hollander (Austin 1964), pp. 688–97; P. Riant, *Expéditions et pèlerinages des Scandinaves en Terre Sainte au temps des croisades* (Paris 1865), pp. 156, 161–3; William of Malmesbury, *Gesta Regum Anglorum*, ed. R. A. B. Mynors, R. M. Thomson, M. Winterbottom (Oxford 1998–9), i, 740–43.
24. *Annales Hildesheimensis*, ed. G. Waitz, MGH (Hanover 1878), pp. 50–51; Otto of Freising, *Chronica*, ed. A Hofmeister, MGH (Hanover and Leipzig 1912), p. 318; Ekkehard of Aura, *Chronicon*, col. 987; *Die Briefe Heinrichs IV*, ed. C. Erdmann, MGH (Leipzig 1937), pp. 39–40, no. 31.
25. Romuald of Salerno, *Chronicon*, in *The History of the Tyrants of Sicily*, ed. G. Loud and T. Weidemann, p. 231, cf. p. 242; *Materials for the History of Thomas Becket*, ed. J. C. Robertson and J. B. Sheppard, Rolls Series (London 1875–85), iv, 163, 174; Roger of Howden, *Chronica*, ed. W. Stubbs, Rolls Series (London 1868–71), ii, 17; F. Barlow, *Thomas Becket* (London 1986), pp. 258–9.
26. Robert of Ely, *De Vita et Miracula S. Canuti Ducis*, *Vitae Sanctorum Danorum*, ed. M. C. Gertz (Copenhagen 1908–12), esp. pp. 236–7.
27. Orderic Vitalis, *Ecclesiastical History*, vi, 379.
28. Walter of Thérouanne, *Vita Karoli*, ed. R. Koepke, MGH SS, xii (Hanover 1866), 540, and p. 568 for Galbert of Bruges's account; Ekkehard of Aura, *Chronicon Universale*, ed. D. G. Waitz, MGH SS, vi (Hanover 1844), 262.
29. John of Würzburg in *Jerusalem Pilgrimage*, ed. Wilkinson, p. 265; in general for references to early twelfth-century *crucesignati*, Riley-Smith, *First Crusaders*, pp. 148, 158–88.
30. For the military orders, A. J. Forey, *The Military Orders* (London 1992); J. Riley-Smith, *The Knights of St John in Jerusalem and Cyprus c.1050–1310* (London 1967); M. Barber, *The New Knighthood: A History of the Order of the Temple* (Cambridge 1994).
31. Orderic Vitalis, *Ecclesiastical History*, vi, 308–10; cf. Riley-Smith, *First Crusaders*, pp. 159–65.
32. *Anglo-Saxon Chronicle* sub anno 1128, trans. S. I. Tucker, *English Historical Documents 1042–1189*, ed. D. C. Douglas and G. W. Greenaway (London 1953), ii, p. 195.
33. Quoted Barber, *New Knighthood*, pp. 49–50; for Bernard's *De Laude*, *S. Bernardi Opera*, iii, ed. J. Leclercq and H. M. Rochais (Rome 1963), trans. C. Greenia, *Works of St Bernard*, vii (Kalamazoo 1977).
34. Thomas Aquinas, *Summa Theologiae* (Editiones Paulinae Rome 1962), Secunda Secundae, quaestio 188, articulus 3, p. 1,843, col. 2.
35. Barber, *New Knighthood*, pp. 26–7; E. Lourie, 'The Confraternity of Belchite, the Ribat and the Temple', *Viator*, 13 (1982), 159–76; for a translation of Saxo Grammaticus's account of the Roskilde confraternity in *Gesta Danorum*, bk 14.6, K. V. Jensen, 'Denmark and the Second Crusade', *The Second Crusade*, ed. J. Phillips and M. Hoch (Manchester 2001), p. 176.
36. Otto of Freising, *Gesta Frederici I Imperatoris*, trans. C. C. Mierow (New York 1966), p. 102: Otto, Conrad's half-brother, probably stayed there too.
37. J. Brundage, *Medieval Canon Law and the Crusader* (Madison 1969), pp. 157–8 and note 83.
38. In Eugenius III's bull of Dec. 1145, *Quantum praedecessores*, P. Rassow, 'Der Text der

Kreuzzugsbulle Eugens III', *Neues Archiv*, 45 (1924), 302–5; trans:. J. and L. Riley-Smith, *Crusades*, pp. 57–9.

39. Ivo of Chartres, *Epistolae*, PL, 162, cols. 170–74, 176–7, nos. 168–70, 173.
40. *Libellus de Vita et Miraculis S. Godrici Heremitae de Finchale*, ed. J. Stevenson, Surtees Society (1847), pp. 33–4, 52–7; William of Newburgh, *Historia rerum Anglicarum*, ed. R. Howlett, *Chronicles of the Reigns of Stephen, Henry II and Richard I*, Rolls Series (London 1884), i, p. 149; *Chartes de St Julien de Tours*, ed. L. J. Denis (Le Mans 1912–13), i, 87–8, no. 67; *Chronica de Gestis Consulum Andegavorum*, *Chroniques d'Anjou*, ed. Machegay and Salmon, p. 152.
41. *Decrees of the Ecumenical Councils*, ed. N. P. Tanner (London and Washington 1990), pp. 191–2 for Canon XX of 1123 Lateran Council, *Eis Qui Hierosolymam*; Ivo of Chartres, *Epistolae*, *PL*, 162, cols. 170–74, 176–7, nos. 168–70, 173.
42. *Epistolae pontificum Romanorum ineditae*, ed. Löwenfeld, no. 199, pp. 103–4; R. Hiestand, 'The Papacy and the Second Crusade', *The Second Crusade*, ed. Phillips and Hoch, p. 36; in general, Tyerman, *Invention of the Crusades*.
43. J. G. Rowe, 'Paschal II, Bohemund of Antioch and the Byzantine Empire', *Bulletin of the John Rylands Library*, 49 (1966), 165–202; for a full account possibly based on eyewitness evidence, Orderic Vitalis, *Ecclesiastical History*, vi, 68–73, 100–104.
44. Orderic Vitalis, *Ecclesiastical History*, vi, 70–71.
45. Anna Comnena, *Alexiad*, p. 422, 424–34.
46. Orderic Vitalis, *Ecclesiastical History*, iv, 264–5.
47. J. and L. Riley-Smith, *Crusades*, pp. 75–6.
48. For Urban's post-Clermont letter to the Catalan counts equating Spain and Jerusalem, J. and L. Riley-Smith, *Crusades*, p. 40. See below p. 662.
49. *Historia Compostellana*, *España sagrada*, ed. H. Florez, xx (Madrid 1791), 428, trans. Riley-Smith, *Short History*, p. 92; R. Fletcher, 'Reconquest and Crusade in Spain', *Transactions of the Royal Historical Society*, 5th series, 38 (1987), 31–47. See below, Chapter 20.
50. S. Barton and R. Fletcher, *World of El Cid: Chronicles of the Spanish Reconquest* (Manchester 2000), p. 250.
51. Robert of Ely, *De Vita S. Canuti Ducis*, pp. 234–41; Jensen, 'Denmark and the Second Crusade', pp. 165–72.
52. On this affinity, Riley-Smith, *First Crusaders*, pp. 169–88.
53. *Anglo-Saxon Chronicle*, sub anno 1128, *English Historical Documents*, ii, p. 195.
54. *Historia Ducum Veneticorum*, ed. H. Somerfeld, MGH SS, xiv (Hanover 1883), pp. 73–4; *Translatio mirifici Martyris Isidori a Chio insula in civitate Venetam*, RHC Occ., v, 322–3; William of Tyre, *History*, i, 548–56; ii, 7–21.

9: God's Bargain: Summoning the Second Crusade

1. Ibn al-Qalanisi, *Damascus Chronicle*, p. 271.
2. Gregory the Priest's Continuation of Matthew of Edessa's Chronicle, Dostourian, *Armenia and the Crusades*, pp. 243–57; in general, H. A. R. Gibb, 'Zengi and the Fall of Edessa', *History of the Crusades*, ed. Setton, pp. 449–62.
3. Holt, *Age of Crusades*, p. 42 and generally pp. 38–45.
4. E. Sivan, 'Réfugiés Syro-palestiniens', p. 142; Hillenbrand, *Crusades*, p. 115; C. Hillenbrand, '"Abominable Acts": The Career of Zengi', *The Second Crusade*, ed. J. Phillips and M. Hoch (Manchester 2002), pp. 111–32, esp. pp. 120–27.
5. D. S. Richards, 'Imad al-Din al-Isfahani', *Crusaders and Muslims in Twelfth-century Syria*, ed. M. Shatzmiller (Leiden 1993), pp. 133–46.
6. Hillenbrand, *Crusades*, pp. 150–61 and, in general, pp. 89–170; N. Elisséef, 'The Reaction of the Syrian Muslims after the Foundation of the First Latin Kingdom of Jerusalem', *Crusaders and Muslims*, ed. Shatzmiller, pp. 162–72.
7. Sivan, 'Réfugiés Syro-palestiniens', esp. p. 145; Hillenbrand, *Crusades*, pp. 69–71, 78–9; 114–15; Holt, *Age of Crusades*, pp. 24–5, 27–8.

8. Hillenbrand, *Crusades*, pp. 108–10.
9. Hillenbrand, *Crusades*, p. 110–11 and note 35; Hillenbrand, '"Abominable Acts"', p. 122.
10. Holt, *Age of Crusades*, p. 27; Elisséef, 'Reaction of Syrian Muslims', pp. 162–6; Hillenbrand, *Crusades*, pp. 69, 105–8; Richard, *The Crusades*, p. 124.
11. Otto of Freising, *The Two Cities: A Chronicle of Universal History to the Year 1146 AD*, ed. and trans. C. C. Mierow (Columbia 1928), pp. 440–3; R.-J. Lilie, *Byzantium and the Crusader States*, pp. 144–53; P. Magdalino, *The Empire of Manuel I Komnenos 1143–1180* (Cambridge 1993), esp. pp. 37–51.
12. E. Caspar, 'Die Kreuzzugsbullen Eugens III', *Neues Archive der Gesellschaft für ältere Deutsche Geschichtskunde*, 45 (1924), 285–305 (text 300–305); J. and L. Riley-Smith, *Crusades*, pp. 57–9.
13. R. W. Southern, 'England's First Entry into Europe', *Medieval Humanism and Other Studies* (Oxford 1970), p. 147; cf. M. Pacaut, *Louis VII et son royaume* (Paris 1964), esp. pp. 221–3.
14. Walter Map, *De Nugis Curialum*, ed. C. N. L. Brooke and R. A. B. Mynors (Oxford 1983), pp. 450–51.
15. Otto of Freising, *The Deeds of Frederick Barbarossa*, trans. C. C. Mierow (Columbia 1953), p. 70; Odo of Deuil, *De Profectione Ludovici VII in orientem*, ed. and trans. V. G. Berry (Columbia 1948), pp. 6–7.
16. *Abbreviationes Chronicorum* of Ralph of Diceto, *Opera historica*, ed. W. Stubbs, Rolls Series (London 1876), i, 256; A. Grabois, 'The Crusade of Louis VII', *Crusade and Settlement*, ed. Edbury, pp. 94–104.
17. *Cartulaire général de l'Yonne*, ed. M. Quantin (Auxerre 1854–60), i, 428–9, no. 277; cf. *Cartulaire du Chapitre de l'église métropolitaine Ste-Marie d'Auch*, ed. C. Lacave la Plagne Barris (Paris and Auch 1899), pp. 65–6, no. 64; *Archives administratives de la ville de Rheims*, ed. P. Varin, i (Paris 1839), 318–20, no. 95.
18. *Cartulaire de l'abbaye cardinale de la Trinité de Vendôme*, ed. C. Metais (Paris 1893–7), ii, 353–5, no. 520.
19. Ralph of Diceto, *Opera historia*, i, 256–7; *De Tributo Floriacensibus imposito*, RHGF, xii, 94–5; cf. letter of John abbot of 'Ferraricensis' to Suger, RHGF, xv, 497 and Peter the Venerable to Louis VII, RHGF, xv, 641–3.
20. Odo of Deuil, *De profectione*, pp. 20–21.
21. Odo of Deuil, *De profectione*, pp. 6–9; Otto of Freising, *Frederick*, p. 70; in general, W. Williams, *Saint Bernard of Clairvaux* (Manchester 1935), pp. 262–88; V. G. Berry, 'The Second Crusade', *History of the Crusades*, ed. Setton, pp. 463–512 and, especially, G. Constable, 'The Second Crusade as Seen by Contemporaries', *Traditio*, 9 (1953), 213–79.
22. Bernard of Clairvaux, *Letters*, trans. B. S. James, 2nd edn (Stroud 1998), nos. 32, 216, 217, 395, 396; Snoek, *Medieval Piety*, pp. 114–15.
23. Otto of Freising, *Frederick*, p. 70.
24. RHGF, xv, 439–40; Bernard of Clairvaux, *Letters*, no. 323, to Eugenius III, beginning 'God forgive you, what have you done?'
25. Odo of Deuil, *De profectione*, pp. 8–11; Bernard of Clairvaux, *Letters*, no. 391; cf. nos. 392–4.
26. Odo of Deuil, *De profectione*, pp. 8–9.
27. *Ex Chronico Mauriniacensis*, RHGF, xii, 88; letter from Bernard's secretary, Nicholas, to the count and barons of Brittany, RHGF, xv, 607.
28. RHGF, xv, 607.
29. Bernard of Clairvaux, *Letters*, no. 323; for his itinerary, Williams, *Bernard of Clairvaux*, esp. pp. 268–81, 397–8; J. Phillips, 'Bernard of Clairvaux, the Low Countries and the Lisbon Letter of the Second Crusade', *Journal of Ecclesiastical History*, 48 (1997), pp. 485–97.
30. *Papsturkunden für Kirchen im Heiligen Lande*, ed. R. Hiestand (Göttingen 1985), pp. 193–5.

31. PL 185, cols. 373–419; Otto of Freising, *Frederick*, pp. 75–6.
32. *Annales Rodenses*, ed. G. H. Pertz, MGH, xvi (Hanover 1869).
33. Otto of Freising, *Frederick*, p. 74; Williams, *Bernard of Clairvaux*, p. 266.
34. Bernard of Clairvaux, *Letters*, no. 393; Otto Freising, *Frederick*, p. 74.
35. Rabbi Ephraim of Bonn, *Sefer Zekhirah (The Book of Remembrance)*, *Jews and the Crusaders*, trans. Eidelberg, p. 122; in general on the attacks on Jews pp. 121–33; Otto of Freising, *Frederick*, p. 74.
36. RHGF, xv, 641–3; for William of Norwich, see R. Finucane, *Miracles and Pilgrims* (London 1977).
37. Bernard of Clairvaux, *Letters*, no. 393.
38. Ephraim of Bonn, *Sefer Zekhirah*, pp. 126–31.
39. Ephraim of Bonn, *Sefer Zekhirah*, p. 130; *Chevalier, Mult Estes Guariz*, *Les Chansons de Croisade*, ed. J. Bédier and P. Aubry (Paris 1909), p. 9.
40. Ephraim of Bonn, *Sefer Zekhirah*, pp. 123–4.
41. The phrase is Rabbi Ephraim's, *Sefer Zekhirah*, p. 127; Otto of Freising, *Frederick*, p. 75 for Radulf at Mainz.
42. Ephraim of Bonn, *Sefer Zekhirah*, p. 124; Bernard of Clairvaux, *Letters*, no. 393.
43. Otto of Freising, *Frederick*, p. 74.
44. Ephraim of Bonn, *Sefer Zekhirah*, pp. 122–3, and for the persecution in general, pp. 121–33.
45. A. Momigliano, 'A Medieval Jewish Autobiography', *History and Imagination*, ed. H. Lloyd-Jones et al. (London 1981).
46. *Annales Rodenses*, MGH, xvi, 718.
47. PL, 185, col. 383; *Annales Herbipolenses*, MGH, xvi, 3 (for the bishop of Würzburg's mission); F. Dolger, *Regesten der Kaiserurkunden des Ostromischen Reiches*, (Munich and Berlin 1924–65), ii, pp. 206–7, nos. 1348–50; for Franco-Byzantine diplomacy, RHGF, xv, 440–41; xvi, pp. 9–10.
48. Otto of Freising, *Frederick*, p. 78; in general, R. Hiestand, 'Kingship and Crusade in Twelfth Century Germany', *England and Germany in the High Middle Ages*, ed. A. Haverkamp and H. Vollrath (Oxford 1996), pp. 235–65; F. Lotter, 'The Crusading Idea and the Conquest of the Region East of the Elbe', *Medieval Frontier Societies*, ed. R. Bartlett and A. Mackay (Oxford 1989), pp. 267–306; J. Phillips, 'Papacy, Empire and the Second Crusade', *The Second Crusade*, ed. Phillips and Hoch, pp. 15–31.
49. Otto of Freising, *Frederick*, pp. 74–5; PL, 185, cols. 381–6.
50. Otto of Freising, *Frederick*, pp. 75–6.
51. PL, 185, col. 339.
52. Above notes 21 and 29; P. Jaffé, *Regesta Pontificum Romanorum*, ii (Leipzig 1888), 40–58 for Eugenius's itinerary; R. Hiestand, 'The Papacy and the Second Crusade', *Second Crusade*, ed. Phillips and Hoch, pp. 32–53; Phillips, 'Papacy, Empire and the Second Crusade', ibid., pp. 18–19, 25–6.
53. Odo of Deuil, *De profectione*, pp. 10–13; RHGF, xv, 440–41; xvi, 9–10.
54. Odo of Deuil, *De profectione*, pp. 13–16.
55. Odo of Deuil, *De profectione*, pp. 32–3.
56. *Chronicon Turonense*, RHGF xii, 473; C. Devic and J. Vaissete, *Histoire générale de Languedoc* (Toulouse 1872–1904), iii, 754; v, c.29; Odo of Deuil, *De profectione*, pp. 78–9.
57. Apart from *Quantum praedecessores*, cf. Odo of Deuil, *De profectione*, pp. 58–9, 130–31.
58. Odo of Deuil, an eyewitness, pp. 14–19.
59. Otto of Freising, *Frederick*, pp. 78–9; Berry, 'Second Crusade', pp. 478–9.
60. Otto of Freising, *Frederick*, p. 76; Bernard of Clairvaux, *Letters*, no. 394.
61. PL, 180, cols. 1203–4.
62. *Monumenta Corbeiensia*, ed. P. Jaffé, *Biblioteca rerum Germanicorum*, i (Berlin 1865), 245; E. Christiansen, *The Northern Crusades* (2nd edn London 1997), pp. 50–59.

63. Otto of Freising, *Frederick*, pp. 74–6, 79, 102; Odo of Deuil, *De profectione*, pp. 50–51, 92–3.
64. John of Salisbury, *Historia Pontificalis*, ed. M. ChIbnall (London 1956), p. 55; Hiestand, 'Papacy and Second Crusade', pp. 38, 41–2.
65. Otto of Freising, *Frederick*, p. 79.
66. Odo of Deuil, *De profectione*, pp. 114–15 and, generally, passim; William of Tyre, *History*, xvi, 24; for Itier of Magnac, ii, 176–7 supplementing Odo of Deuil, *De profectione*, pp. 122–3.
67. Runciman, *History of the Crusades*, ii, 262; David, *De Expugnatione Lyxbonensi*, pp. 56–7 (*mulieres*).
68. Odo of Deuil, *De profectione*, pp. 6–7, 22–3, 24–5, 28–9, 54–5, 70–71, 74–9.
69. Most of the gossip is from John of Salisbury, *Historia Pontificalis*, pp. 54–6.
70. John of Salisbury, *Historia Pontificalis*, p. 56 for the count's linguistic skills and friendship with Conrad III.
71. Odo of Deuil, *De profectione*, pp. 122–3; William of Tyre, *History*, ii, 176–7.
72. Bédier and Aubry, *Chansons*, p. 9.
73. Bernard of Clairvaux, *Letters*, no. 391.
74. David, *De Expugnatione Lyxbonensi*, pp. 52–7; for Templars, RHGF, xvi, 9–10; xv, 496; Odo of Deuil, *De profectione*, pp. 124–7; Tyerman, *England and the Crusades*, p. 31 and notes.
75. Löwenfeld, *Epistolae pontificum*, pp. 103–4, no. 199; Otto of Freising, *Frederick*, p. 76; local arrangements are dotted throughout surviving cartularies of religious houses.
76. *Chartes et documents pour servir à l'histoire de l'abbaye de Saint-Maixent*, ed. A. Richard, *Archives historiques de Poitou*, xvi (Poitiers 1886), 349–50, no. cccxxxi.
77. RHGF, xiv, 324.
78. RHGF, xii, 94–5.
79. *Register of St Benet of Holme*, ed. J. West, Norfolk Record Society, nos. 2 and 3 (1932), i, 54, 87, nos. 92, 155.
80. *Annales Rodenses*, MGH, xvi, 718–19.
81. Otto of Freising, *Frederick*, p. 102; RHGF xv, 496; Odo of Deuil, *De profectione*, pp. 122–5, 130–33, 136–7.
82. Phillips, 'Bernard of Clairvaux and the Low Countries'.
83. For translations of Winand's letter to the archbishop of Cologne and Duodechin's to the abbot of Disibodenberg, S. Edgington, 'Albert of Aachen, St Bernard and the Second Crusade', *The Second Crusade*, ed. Phillips and Hoch, pp. 61–7.
84. Odo of Deuil, *De profectione*, pp. 20–21.
85. David, *De Expugnatione Lyxbonensi*, pp. 56–7, 104–5, 176–7.
86. Odo of Deuil, *De profectione*, pp. 124–7.
87. David, *De Expugnatione Lyxbonensi*, pp. 56–7 and note 5, pp. 57–9.
88. *Chronicle of Pierre de Langtoft*, ed. T. Wright, Rolls Series (London 1866–8), i, 495.
89. David, *De Expugnatione Lyxbonensi*, pp. 176–7.
90. Quantin, *Cartulaire général de l'Yonne*, i, 437, no. 283.

10: 'The Spirit of the Pilgrim God': Fighting the Second Crusade

1. Otto of Freising, *Frederick*, pp. 25–7; Helmold of Bosau, *Cronica Slavorum*, ed. J. M. Lappenberg and B. Smeidler, MGH (Hanover 1937), p. 115; *The Chronicle of the Slavs*, trans. F. J. Tschan (New York 1966), p. 172.
2. Helmold, *Cronica*, p. 118; Otto of Freising, *Frederick*, p. 130; Henry of Huntingdon, *Historia Anglorum*, ed. and trans. D. Greenway (Oxford 1996), pp. 752–3; Eugenius III's bull *Divina dispensatione*, 11 April 1147, PL, 180, cols. 1,203–4; Bernard of Clairvaux, *Letters*, trans. James, no. 394.
3. Christiansen, *The Northern Crusades*, pp. 50–65; PL, 180, cols. 1,203–4; K. V. Jensen,

'Denmark and the Second Crusade', *The Second Crusade*, ed. Phillips and Hoch, pp. 164–5, 168 and refs.

4. Helmold of Bosau, *Chronicle*, pp. 187–8.
5. Helmold of Bosau, *Chronicle*, p. 180 and, for his account of the 1147 campaigns, pp. 170–82.
6. Vincent of Prague, *Annales*, ed. G. H. Pertz, MGH SS (Hanover 1861), pp. 662–3.
7. Vincent of Prague, *Annales*, p. 663.
8. What follows is based on the eyewitness accounts by Raol, *De Expugnatione Lyxbonensi*, ed. David; and by the writers of the so-called 'Lisbon Letter', ed. S. Edgington, 'Albert of Aachen, St Bernard and the Second Crusade', *The Second Crusade*, ed. Phillips and Hoch, pp. 62–7; cf. M. Bennett, 'Military Aspects of the Conquest of Lisbon', ibid., pp. 71–89.
9. David, *De Expugnatione*, pp. 160–61.
10. David *De Expugnatione*, pp. 100–104, 110–11 for Veils; for Flemish recruitment, J. Phillips, 'Bernard of Clairvaux and the Low Countries', pp. 485–97.
11. David, *De Expugnatione*, pp. 68–9, 98–9, 100–101; Edgington, 'Lisbon Letter', p. 63; Phillips 'Bernard of Clairvaux and the Low Countries', but the letter from Bernard to Afonso, Bernard of Clairvaux, *Letters*, no. 469, is probably a forgery.
12. David, *De Expugnatione*, pp. 78–9; and, for his sermon, pp. 68–85.
13. Possibly Raol himself, David, *De Expugnatione*, pp. 154–5.
14. Bédier and Aubry, *Chansons*, p. 8.
15. David, *De Expugnatione*, pp. 60–61, 68–85, 102–3.
16. David, *De Expugnatione*, pp. 100–11 for debate; for Raol's authorship and career, H. Livermore, 'The *Conquest of Lisbon* and its Author', *Portuguese Studies*, 6 (1990), 1–16.
17. David, *De Expugnatione*, pp. 110–15.
18. David, *De Expugnatione*, pp. 136–7.
19. *Loc. cit.*
20. Edgington, 'Lisbon Letter', p. 64.
21. For the Pisan, Edgington, 'Lisbon Letter', p. 64; David, *De Expugnatione*, pp. 162–3.
22. David, *De Expugnatione*, pp. 176–7 for pillage and murder.
23. David, *De Expugnatione*, pp. 178–81 and note 5 for Gilbert of Hastings.
24. Edgington, 'Lisbon Letter', p. 67, cf. Duodechin version, MGH SS, xvii, 28; *Annales Elmarenses, Les Annales de Saint-Pierre de Gand et de Saint-Amand*, ed. P. Grierson (Brussels 1937), pp. 111–12; G. Constable, 'A Note on the Route of the Anglo-Flemish Crusaders of 1147', *Speculum*, 28 (1953), 525–6.
25. N. Jaspert, 'Tortosa and the Crusades', *The Second Crusade*, ed. Phillips and Hoch, esp. pp. 90–91, 95, 97–100 and refs.
26. Odo of Deuil, *De Profectione*, esp. pp. 88–97; Helmold of Bosau, *Chronicle*, p. 174; John Kinnamos, *Deeds of John and Manuel Comnenus*, trans. C. M. Brand (New York 1976), p. 68; Conrad III to Wibald of Corvey, late Feb. 1148, *Die Urkunden der Deutschen Könige und Kaiser*, ix, *Die Urkunden Konrads III*, ed. F. Hausmann, MGH (Vienna, Cologne, Graz 1969), no. 195; in general, Berry, 'Second Crusade', *History of the Crusades*, ed. Setton, i, 483–512.
27. Kinnamos, *Deeds*, p. 60.
28. Odo of Deuil, *De Profectione*, pp. 94–5.
29. J. W. Nesbitt, 'The Rate of March of Crusading Armies in Europe', *Traditio*, 19 (1963), 177; for the German march, Otto of Freising, *Frederick*, pp. 79–81; Kinnamos, *Deeds*, pp. 58–68; Odo of Deuil, *De Profectione*, pp. 32–5, 40–51.
30. For Manuel's policy, Lilie, *Byzantium and the Crusader States*, pp. 145–63; Magdalino, *Empire of Manuel I Komnenos*, pp. 46–53.
31. Odo of Deuil, *De Profectione*, pp. 94–5.
32. Hausmann, *Urkunden Konrads III*, no. 195.
33. For a detailed if biased eyewitness account, Odo of Deuil, *De Profectione*, pp. 20–143.
34. Odo of Deuil, *De Profectione*, pp. 40–41.

35. Odo of Deuil, *De Profectione*, pp. 58–9, 54–5 for attacks on the bishop of Langres and William of Warenne.
36. Odo of Deuil, *De Profectione*, pp. 68–9.
37. Odo of Deuil, *De Profectione*, pp. 68–73.
38. Odo of Deuil, *De Profectione*, pp. 70–71.
39. Odo of Deuil, *De Profectione*, pp. 76–83.
40. Kinnamos, *Deeds*, p. 70.
41. The French march across Asia Minor is vividly and painfully described by Odo of Deuil, *De Profectione*, pp. 82–143; cf. Kinnamos, *Deeds*, pp. 70–71.
42. RHGF, xvi, 149; *O City of Byzantium, Annals of Nicetas Choniates*, trans. H. J. Margoulias (Detroit 1984), pp. 38–9.
43. Kinnamos, *Deeds*, pp. 70–71; Hausmann, *Urkunden Konrads III*, no. 195.
44. Odo of Deuil, *De Profectione*, pp. 122–3; cf. pp. 136–41.
45. Odo of Deuil, *De Profectione*, pp. 118–21; pp. 124–7 for Templar fraternity.
46. William of Tyre, *History*, ii, 179.
47. Ibn al-Qalanisi, *Damascus Chronicle*, pp. 281–2.
48. William of Tyre, *History*, ii, 179–80.
49. Otto of Freising, *Frederick*, pp. 101–2; William of Tyre, *History*, ii, 181–2; and note 24 above.
50. Hausmann, *Urkunden Konrads III*, no. 195; on the options in 1148, M. Hoch, 'The Choice of Damascus as the Objective of the Second Crusade', *Autour de la première Croisade*, ed. M. Balard (Paris 1996), pp. 359–69; idem, 'The Crusaders' Strategy against Fatimid Ascalon', *The Second Crusade and the Cistercians*, ed. M. Gervers (New York 1992), pp. 119–29; idem, 'The Price of Failure', *The Second Crusade*, ed. Phillips and Hoch, pp. 180–200; A. J. Forey, 'The Failure of the Siege of Damascus in 1148', *Journal of Medieval History*, 10 (1984), 13–23.
51. William of Tyre, *History*, ii, 181–3.
52. John of Salisbury, *Historia Pontificalis*, pp. 52–3; cf. the dark hints in William of Tyre, *History*, ii, 180–81.
53. Otto of Freising, *Frederick*, p. 102; Hausmann, *Urkunden Konrads III*, no. 195.
54. For the Acre council and the campaign of 1148, William of Tyre, *History*, ii, 184–95; cf. Otto of Freising, *Frederick* pp. 102–3; for the Jerusalem royal feud, H. E. Mayer, 'Studies in the History of Queen Melisende of Jerusalem', *Dumbarton Oaks Papers*, 26 (1972), 93–182.
55. Ibn al-Qalanisi, *Damascus Chronicle*, p. 283 and, for the siege, pp. 282–7.
56. Hausmann, *Urkunden Konrads III*, no. 197; William of Tyre, *History*, ii, 190–94; Otto of Freising, *Frederick*, p. 103; John of Salisbury, *Historia Pontificalis*, pp. 57–8; Berry, 'Second Crusade', p. 509.
57. Hausmann, *Urkunden Konrads III*, no. 197; William of Tyre, *History*, ii, 195.
58. Otto of Freising, *Frederick*, pp. 105–6.
59. RHGF, xv, 502, 508, 508–9, 509; John of Salisbury, *Historia Pontificalis*, p. 60; Kinnamos, *Deeds*, p. 72.
60. For the 1150 plan, Bernard of Clairvaux, *Letters*, nos. 399–400; T. Reuter, 'The "Non-crusade" of 1149–50', *The Second Crusade*, ed. Phillips and Hoch, pp. 150–63; Stephen of Paris, *Fragmentum Historicum de Ludovico VII*, RHGF, xii, 89–91.
61. Eugenius III's letter, PL, 180, col. 1414; Hadrian IV's letter, ibid., 188, cols. 1,615–17.
62. *Annales Herbipolenses*, MGH SS, xvi, 5. In general see E. Siberry, *Criticism of Crusading 1095–1274* (Oxford 1985).
63. Vincent of Prague, *Annales*, p. 663.
64. Otto of Freising, *Frederick*, pp. 103–6; for a translation of *De Consideratione*, II (PL, 182, cols. 741–5), J. Brundage, *The Crusades: A Documentary Survey* (Milwaukee 1962), pp. 122–4, p. 124 for quotation; Bernard of Clairvaux, *Letters*, no. 399.
65. *Vita Prima* of Bernard by his former notary Geoffrey, PL, 185, cols. 366–7.
66. William of Tyre, *History*, ii, 193.

67. Otto of Freising, *Frederick*, p.27; Helmold of Bosau, *Chronicle*, p. 174.
68. Brundage, *Crusades*, p. 123.

11: 'A Great Cause for Mourning': The Revival of Crusading and the Third Crusade

1. Gregory VIII, *Audita Tremendi*, October/November 1187, in response to news of the battle of Hattin, J. and L. Riley-Smith, *Crusades*, p. 65.
2. PL, 197, cols. 187–8; cf. William of Tyre, *History*, ii, 360, 417–23, 425, 434–5.
3. Gerald of Wales, *De Principis instructione*, *Opera*, ed. J. S. Brewer, Rolls Series (London 1861–91), viii, 207.
4. Ralph Niger, *De Re Militari*, pp. 193–4; cf. pp. 186–7 for other comments on the vices of the Jerusalemites.
5. William of Tyre, *History*, ii, 407–8.
6. For an equivocal eyewitness account, Ibn al-Qalanisi, *Damascus Chronicle*, pp. 317–21.
7. Ibn Munir of Tripoli, trans. Hillenbrand, *Crusades*, p. 150 and, in general, pp. 118–67; for the bathing incident, Holt, *Age of Crusades*, p. 44.
8. Translated in Gabrieli, *Arab Historians*, p. 71, and pp. 70–72 for a flattering appreciation.
9. Taken from the inscription on Nur al-Din's Aleppo/Jerusalem minbar, trans. Hillenbrand, *Crusades*, p. 152 and generally pp. 151–61.
10. William of Tyre, *History* ii, 235, and pp. 253–4 for the Cyprus raid.
11. On Manuel's Antioch policy, P. Magdalino, *The Empire of Manuel I Komnenos*, pp. 66–76; Lilie, *Byzantium and the Crusader States*, pp. 174–83.
12. Beha al-Din Ibn Shaddad, *The Rare and Excellent History of Saladin*, trans. D. S. Richards (Aldershot 2002), p. 45.
13. Accounts differ between Saladin's own, M. Lyons and D. Jackson, *Saladin: The Politics of Holy War* (Cambridge 1984), p. 47 and the version possibly given later by Saladin to his friend Ibn Shaddad, Ibn Shaddad, *Saladin*, p. 47.
14. According to Ibn al-Athir, Gabrieli, *Arab Historians*, p. 69; cf. Ibn Shaddad's more specious version, *Saladin*, p. 49.
15. The best modern biography is Lyons and Jackson, *Saladin*. His full name translates as 'the king, the governor, the goodness of the world and the Faith, father of Mustafa, Joseph, son of Ayyub, son of Shadhi the Kurd'.
16. *Itinerarium Peregrinorum et Gesta Regis Ricardi*, trans. H. Nicholson, *The Chronicle of the Third Crusade* (Aldershot 2001), p. 27 and note. (Hereafter *Itinerarium*).
17. Tyerman, *England and the Crusades*, p. 117 and note 26.
18. Ambroise, *Crusade of Richard*, ll. 5,499–5,500, p. 227; J. Gillingham, *Richard I* (New Haven and London 1999), pp. 188, 216, 262.
19. Gabrieli, *Arab Historians*, pp. 69, 119, 141; for Saladin's reputation in the Islamic world, Hillenbrand, *Crusades*, pp. 193–5, 592–600.
20. Lyons and Jackson, *Saladin*, pp. 87–90, 105–6; B. Lewis, *The Assassins* (London 1967), chap. 5.
21. Recorded by his secretary, Imad al-Din Isfahani, Gabrieli, *Arab Historians*, pp. 171–2.
22. M. Lyons, 'Saladin's Hattin Letter', *The Horns of Hattin*, ed. Kedar, pp. 208–12.
23. Ibn Shaddad, *Saladin*, pp. 28–9.
24. Tibble, *Monarchy and Lordships*, esp. pp. 134–5, 166.
25. William of Tyre, *History*, ii, 314.
26. William of Tyre, *History*, ii, 486–9; Kedar, 'The General Tax of 1183', pp. 339–45.
27. Most recently, B. Hamilton, *The Leper King*.
28. John of Ibelin, *Livre des Assises* c. xiii, ed. P. Edbury, *John of Ibelin and Kingdom of Jerusalem* (Woodbridge 1997), pp. 118–20.
29. The Old French Continuation of William of Tyre, trans. P. Edbury, *The Conquest of Jerusalem and the Third Crusade*, ed. idem (Aldershot 1998), p. 33; for the siege of Jerusalem, ibid., pp. 55–67; Mas Latrie, *Chronique d'Ernoul*, p. 175; *L'Estoire de Eracles*,

RHC Occ., ii (Paris 1859), p. 70; Nicholson, *Chronicle of the Third Crusade*, pp. 38–9 (fourteen is the number of knights given here); *Libellus de expugnatione Terrae Sanctae per Saladinum*, ed. J. Stevenson, Rolls Series (London 1875), pp. 241–51.

30. Roger of Howden, *Gesta Regis Henrici Secundi*, ed. W. Stubbs, Rolls Series (London 1867), i, 328.

31. As suggested by H. E. Mayer, 'The Beginnings of King Amalric of Jerusalem', *Horns of Hattin*, ed. Kedar, pp. 121–35.

32. William of Tyre, *History*, ii, 296–8 where the king is also accused of financial greed, a common charge against hard-pressed rulers.

33. Ibn Shaddad, *Saladin*, p. 90; Hamilton, *The Leper King*, p. 34, note 62.

34. On the state of Baldwin's health and the diagnosis of leprosy, see Piers Mitchell, 'An Evaluation of the leprosy of King Baldwin IV', in Hamilton, *The Leper King*, pp. 245–58.

35. P. Edbury, Propaganda and Faction in the Kingdom of Jerusalem', *Crusaders and Muslims*, ed. Shatzmiller, pp. 173–89; cf. Runciman, *History of the Crusades*, ii, 403–73.

36. On William of Tyre's prejudices, P. Edbury and J. Rowe, *William of Tyre: Historian of the Latin East* (Cambridge 1988).

37. The chronicle attributed to Ernoul; see now Edbury, *Conquest of Jerusalem*, pp. 1–8.

38. William of Tyre, *History*, ii, 417–34.

39. Hamilton, *The Leper King*, p. 139, note 50 for references.

40. Hamilton, *The Leper King*, p. 167, notes 40–41.

41. See the reconstruction in Hamilton, *The Leper King*, pp. 179–85.

42. William of Tyre, *History*, ii, 491–8 for the events of the 1183 campaign; Ibn Shaddad, *Saladin*, pp. 61–2.

43. William of Tyre, *History*, ii, 498–504, 507–9.

44. Edbury, *Conquest of Jerusalem*, pp. 11–16. For a convincing reconstruction of the events of 1184–5 based largely on the variant continuations of William of Tyre, Hamilton, *The Leper King*, pp. 198–210.

45. Ibn Shaddad, *Saladin*, pp. 68–9.

46. Edbury, *Conquest of Jerusalem*, pp. 24–30, 154–5; despite the continuations of William of Tyre's sympathetic glossing towards Raymond, the inference is unavoidable.

47. Ibn Jubayr, *Travels*, trans. R. J. C. Broadhurst (London 1952), p. 301 and generally on Outremer in the autumn of 1184, pp. 315–25.

48. For the events culminating in the battle at the springs of Cresson, Gabrieli, *Arab Historians*, pp. 114–18; Edbury, *Conquest of Jerusalem*, pp. 30–34, 156–7; Stevenson, *Libellus de expugatione Terrae Sanctae*, pp. 211–17. For the legends, Nicholson, *Chronicle of the Third Crusade*, pp. 25–6.

49. On the Hattin campaign, Gabrieli, *Arab Historians*, pp. 118–39; Edbury, *Conquest of Jerusalem*, pp. 34–49, 158–62; *Libellus de expugnatione Terrae Sanctae*, trans. Brundage, *Crusades*, pp. 153–63; Lyons and Jackson, *Saladin*, pp. 258–64; Lyons, 'Saladin's Hattin Letter'; R. C. Smail, 'The Predicaments of Guy of Lusignan 1183–7', *Outremer*, ed. Kedar et al., pp. 159–76; and, for the topography and details of the fighting itself, especially, B. Z. Kedar, 'The Battle of Hattin Revisited', *Horns of Hattin*, pp. 190–207.

50. Gabrieli, *Arab Historians*, p. 130.

51. Ibn al-Athir, Gabrieli, *Arab Historians*, p. 123.

52. Peter of Blois, *Passio Reginaldis Principis Antiocheni*, PL, 207, cols. 957–76.

53. Gabrieli, *Arab Historians*, p. 125.

54. For the siege and fall of Jerusalem, Ibn Shaddad, *Saladin*, pp. 77–8; Gabrieli, *Arab Historians*, pp. 139–75; Edbury, *Conquest of Jerusalem*, pp. 55–65, 162–3, 165–6.

55. Edbury, *Conquest of Jerusalem*, pp. 73–6.

56. For full references Gillingham, *Richard I*, p. 87, note 36.

57. Translated by J. and L. Riley-Smith, *Crusades*, pp. 64–7.

12: The Call of the Cross

1. *Pipe Roll 1 Richard I*, ed. J. Hunter (London 1844), p. 20; *Pipe Roll 3 Richard I*, *The Great Rolls of the Pipe* (Pipe Roll Society, London 1884–), pp. 28, 33, 58, 76.
2. For references, see Tyerman, *Invention of the Crusades*, esp. p.27.
3. Text in J. and L. Riley-Smith, *Crusades*, pp. 64–7; cf. Benedict of Peterborough, *recte* Roger of Howden, *Gesta Henrici Secundi*, ii, 15–19.
4. *Itinerarium*, pp. 43–4; Edbury *Conquest of Jerusalem*, pp. 73–5 for an account in a continuation of the chronicle of William of Tyre.
5. Gillingham, *Richard I*, p. 87, note 36 for a full list of references, esp. Ralph of Diceto.
6. *Historia de expeditione Friderici Imperatoris*, ed. A. Chroust, *Quellen zur Geschichte des Kreuzzuges Kaiser Friedrichs I*, MGHS (Berlin 1928), esp. pp. 5–15.
7. *De Profectione Danorum in Hierosolymam*, *Scriptores Minores Historiae Danicae*, ed. M. C. Gertz (Copenhagen 1970 reprint), ii, 464–8; in general pp. 457–92.
8. Gervase of Canterbury, *Historical Works*, ed. W. Stubbs, Rolls Series (London 1879–80), i, 389.
9. *Historia de expeditione*, Chroust, *Quellen*, p. 14, cf. p. 12 for Henry of Albano's summons 'ad curiam Iesu Christi'; Gilbert of Mons, *Chronicon Hanoniense*, ed. G. H. Pertz, MGHS (Hanover 1869), pp. 182–4.
10. *Epistolae Cantuariensis*, *Chronicles and Memorials of Richard I*, ed. W. Stubbs, Rolls Series (London 1865), ii, nos. 158, 167; cf. Gervase of Canterbury, *Historical Works*, i, 394 et seq. for the local context.
11. For the French nobles, Rigord, *Oeuvres*, ed. H. F. Delaborde, i, 83–4 and 84–5 for the March assembly in Paris; for Anglo-Norman sources for the Gisors meeting, Tyerman, *England and the Crusades*, p. 392 note 7 and, for English preparations in general, pp. 57–85.
12. Gerald of Wales, *Journey*, p. 201.
13. Roger of Howden, *Gesta Henrici Secundi*, ii, 44–5.
14. *Itinerarium*, p. 143.
15. E.g. the French landowner Heraclius of Montboissier, *Recueil des actes de Philippe Auguste*, i, ed. H. F. Delaborde et al. (Paris 1916), no. 286 (Dec. 1189).
16. Henry of Albano, *Tractatus de peregrinatione civitate Dei*, PL, 204, col. 353.
17. Peter of Blois, *De Hierosolymitana Peregrinatione Acceleranda*, PL, 207, col. 1063 and generally cols. 1,058–70, which is part of a longer piece, originally combined with *Dialogus inter regem Henricum secundum et abbatem Bonnevallensem*, PL, 207, cols. 975–88; cf. his other great crusade propaganda work, *De passione Reginaldi*, PL, 207, cols. 957–76.
18. Alan of Lille, *Sermo de cruce domini*, *Textes inédits*, ed. M. T. Alverny, *Etudes de philosophie médiévale*, 52 (Paris 1965), pp. 281–2.
19. J. and L. Riley Smith, *Crusades*, p. 66.
20. *Historia de expeditione*, Chroust, *Quellen*, p. 10.
21. Gerald of Wales, *Journey*, p. 114.
22. *De Profectione Danorum*, Gertz, *Scriptores*, p. 467.
23. Rigord, *Oeuvres*, p. 84.
24. *Cartulaire de l'abbaye Notre-Dame de Bonnevaux*, ed. U. Chevalier, *Bulletin de l'Académie Delphinale*, 4th series, ii (Grenoble 1889, dated 1887–8), no. 310, pp. 143–4.
25. For these tracts see above, notes 16 and 17.
26. Gerald of Wales, *Opera*, viii, 207.
27. Ralph Niger, *De Re Militari*, esp. pp. 194–9.
28. Reported to Henry II's court by Peter of Blois, Roger of Howden, *Gesta Henrici Secundi*, ii, 15.
29. *De profectione Danorum*, Gertz, *Scriptores*, p. 467; cf. K. Skovgaard-Petersen, *A Journey to the Promised Land* (Copenhagen 2001), esp. pp. 75–6.
30. A. Macquarrie, *Scotland and the Crusades 1095–1560* (Edinburgh 1985), pp. 27–32.

31. Gerald of Wales, *Journey*, p. 184.
32. *Ordinatio de predicatione S. Crucis in Angliae*, ed. R. Röhricht, *Quinti Belli Sacri Scriptores Minores, Société de l'Orient Latin*, ii (Geneva 1879), p. 24 and generally pp. 1–26.
33. Rigord, *Oeuvres*, p. 99.
34. Gerald of Wales, *De Rebus a se gestis*, trans. H. Butler, *The Autobiography of Giraldus Cambrensis* (London 1937), pp. 99–101. (Hereafter Gerald of Wales, *Autobiography*.)
35. Ibn al-Athir in Gabrieli, *Arab Historians*, pp. 182–3; Ibn Shaddad, *Saladin*, p. 125.
36. Gerald of Wales, *Journey*, pp. 1–209.
37. Gerald of Wales, *Journey*, p. 75; *Opera*, i, 74; *Autobiography*, p. 99.
38. Gerald of Wales, *Autobiography*, pp. 99–101, 104.
39. *Historia de expeditione*, Chrust, *Quellen*, pp. 11–13, 14; Rigord, *Oeuvres*, pp. 84–5.
40. Gerald of Wales, *Journey*, pp. 114, 185–6; *Opera*, vi, 55 'conversi sunt'.
41. Cf. Roger of Howden's account of a miraculous appearance of Christ on the cross in the sky near Dunstable, *Gesta Henrici Secundi*, ii, 47.
42. *Ordinatio*, passim, esp. pp. 18–26; for Gerald of Wales's anecdote, *Journey*, p. 172.
43. Roger of Howden, *Gesta Henrici Secundi*, ii, 26–8; for identity of Berthier, J. W. Baldwin, *The Government of Philip Augustus* (Berkeley and Los Angeles 1986), pp. 462, note 38 and 572 note 30.
44. Conon of Béthune, *Ahi! Amours, con dure departie*, Bédier and Aubry, *Chansons*, no. iii, pp. 32–5; cf. pp. 45–7, *Bien me Deusse Targier*.
45. *Actes des Comtes de Namur 946–1196*, ed. F. Rousseau (Brussels 1936), no. 28, pp. 61–4.
46. Ralph Niger, *Chronica*, ed. H. Krause (Frankfurt 1985), p. 288. For details of Frederick's crusade, *Historia de expeditione*, Chroust, *Quellen*, passim.
47. Roger of Howden, *Chronica*, iii, 8; for Philip II's deals, L. Delisle, *Catalogue des Actes de Philippe Auguste* (Paris 1856), no. 327A; Rigord, *Oeuvres*, p. 99; Delaborde et al., *Recueil des actes de Philippe Auguste*, i, no. 252; for Richard, Tyerman, *England and the Crusades*, pp. 75–85.
48. Ralph Niger, *Chronica*, p. 288; *Historia de expeditione*, Chroust, *Quellen*, p. 96.
49. Rigord, *Oeuvres*, p. 106, 116–17; Ambroise, *Crusade of Richard* ll. 4,575–99, 4,686–90; *Itinerarium*, p. 204; Roger of Howden, *Gesta Henri Secundi*, ii, 176; Richard of Devizes, *Chronicle*, ed. J. T. Appelby (London 1963), pp. 43–4; Gillingham, *Richard I*, p. 166.
50. Roger of Howden, *Gesta Henri Secundi*, ii, 32.
51. Jocelin of Brakelond, *Chronicle*, ed. H. E. Butler (London 1949), pp. 39–40, 51, 53–4, 123, 138–9; Tyerman, *England and the Crusades*, pp. 64–5, 78.
52. Roger of Howden, *Gesta Henri Secundi*, ii, 47–8 for a crooked collector in England, a Templar Gilbert of Hogestan; for a poetic accusation of official greed and fraud, perhaps by Conon of Béthune, *Bien me Deusse Targier*, Bédier and Aubry, *Chansons*, p. 45.
53. Delaborde et al., *Recueil des Actes de Philippe Auguste*, i, no. 252.
54. Delaborde et al., *Recueil des Actes de Philippe Auguste*, i, no. 237.
55. *Itinerarium*, p. 148.
56. Roger of Howden, *Gesta Henri Secundi*, ii, 32.
57. *Historical Manuscripts Commission, Report on Various Collections*, i (London 1901), pp. 235–6.
58. *Itinerarium*, pp. 48, 142.
59. Above, note 24.
60. *Itinerarium*, p. 48.
61. Arnold of Lübeck, *Chronica Slavorum*, ed. G. H. Pertz, MGHS (Hanover 1868), p. 127; cf. pp. 126–8.
62. Richard of Devizes, *Chronicle*, pp. 10–11, 15, 27–8 for backsliders.
63. E.g. Geoffrey FitzPeter, William Brewer and Hugh Bardolf, as well as Justiciar Hugh du Puiset, Tyerman, *England and the Crusades*, p. 65.

64. Tyerman, *England and the Crusades*, pp. 83–4.
65. Roger of Howden, *Gesta Henri Secundi*, ii, 132–3; cf. Richard of Devizes, *Chronicle*, p. 17.
66. Tyerman, *England and the Crusades*, pp. 64–75 for the details that follow.
67. *Itinerarium*, p. 48.
68. Gerald of Wales, *Journey*, p. 204.
69. Ambroise, *Crusade of Richard*, l. 5680; cf. Tyerman, *England and the Crusades*, pp. 61–3.
70. *Historical Manuscripts Commission, Fifth Report*, Appendix (London 1872), p. 462.
71. Roger of Howden, *Gesta Henri Secundi*, ii, 30. For Normans, *Itinerarium*, p. 99; Rigord, *Oeuvres* esp. pp. 83–4 for French.
72. Gilbert of Mons, *Chronicon Hanoniense*, ed. L. Vanderkindere (Brussels 1904), pp. 206–7.
73. Translation from *Historia de expeditione* by E. N. Johnson, 'The Crusades of Frederick Barbarossa and Henry VI', *History of the Crusades*, ed. Setton, ii (Madison 1969), p. 90, and for German recruitment that follows, pp. 50, 89–93.
74. *Historia de expeditione*, p. 22 and, for recruits, pp. 18–24; *Itinerarium*, p. 77.
75. B. Arnold, *German Knighthood 1050–1300* (Oxford 1985), pp. 24, 101.
76. *Narratio Itinere Navalis ad Terram Sanctam, Historia de expeditione*, pp. 179–96; *Chronica Regia Colonesis*, ed. G. Waitz, MGHS (Hanover 1880), p. 140 and pp. 142–4.
77. *Historia de expeditione*, pp. 96–8.

13: To the Siege of Acre

1. *Itinerarium*, p. 44; cf. p. 160 and note 62 refs.
2. The story is in the thirteenth-century Old French Continuation of William of Tyre, trans. Edbury, *Conquest of Jerusalem*, p. 66.
3. There is, at the time of writing, no modern scholarly account of the Third Crusade. See the general books by Mayer, Runciman, Riley-Smith, Setton (general editor), vol. 2.
4. Ibn Shaddad, *Saladin*, p. 81 and passim for Saladin and the Third Crusade; on Saladin, Lyons and Jackson, *Saladin*.
5. Thietmar, *Peregrinatio*, ii, 37. For Frankish rural settlement, Ellenblum, *Settlement*, and pp. 66–71 for Casal Imbert.
6. Ibn Shaddad, *Saladin*, pp. 90–91, 93, 95–7, 108; Edbury, *Conquest of Jerusalem*, pp. 71–3.
7. Gabrieli, *Arab Historians*, p. 182.
8. Ibn Shaddad, *Saladin*, passim, and p. 80 for his entry into Saladin's service.
9. Runciman, *History of the Crusades*, iii, 22.
10. Edbury, *Conquest of Jerusalem*, p. 169; Ibn Shaddad, *Saladin*, p. 91.
11. Ibn Shaddad, *Saladin*, p. 106.
12. The chronology of arrivals is largely derived from *Itinerarium*, pp. 71–83, possibly based on an eyewitness report.
13. Ibn Shaddad, *Saladin*, p. 104.
14. Waitz, *Chronica Regia Colonensis*, pp. 140–44; *Itinerarium*, pp. 73–4.
15. *Historia de expeditione*, Chroust, *Quellen*, pp. 23–4; *Itinerarium*, pp. 74–7, 81–3.
16. *Itinerarium*, p. 74; and pp. 25–6 and 34 for the uplifting stories of Templars Jakelin de Mailly and Nicholas at the battles of Cresson and Hattin in 1187 current at the siege of Acre.
17. *Itinerarium*, pp. 81, 83.
18. *Narratio Itineris Navalis ad Terram Sanctam, Historia de expeditione*, pp. 179–96; *Itinerarium*, p. 74.
19. Ibn Shaddad, *Saladin*, p. 106.
20. Ibn al-Athir in RHC Or., II-i, p. 15; Abu Shama, *The Book of the Two Gardens*, RHC Or., iv, 412.

21. Gabrieli, *Arab Historians*, pp. 204–6.
22. *Itinerarium*, p. 89; cf. Imad al-Din's shocked view of women warriors, Gabrieli, *Arab Historians*, pp. 206–7.
23. Ibn Shaddad, *Saladin*, pp. 118–20; *Itinerarium*, pp. 94–6; Edbury, *Conquest of Jerusalem*, p. 171.
24. Edbury, *Conquest of Jerusalem*, p. 94.
25. Ibn Shaddad, *Saladin*, pp. 106, 113–17, 121–2, 125 for the reception in Saladin's camp of news of German progress.
26. *Itinerarium*, p. 49; loc. cit. pp. 49–68 for a German source on Frederick's crusade and, for the most detailed contemporary account, *Historia de expeditione*, pp. 1–115.
27. From Henry, provost of Schäftlarn, Biblioteca Apostolica Vaticana, MS Vat. Lat. 2001 fol. 1 recto.
28. *Historia de expeditione*, p.39; Arnold of Lübeck, *Chronica Slavorum*, pp. 130–31; *Itinerarium*, p. 60; J. W. Nesbitt, 'The Rate of March', pp. 178–9.
29. Arnold of Lübeck, *Chronica Slavorum* pp. 10–21.
30. *Historia de expeditione*, pp. 15–16; Waitz, *Chronica Regia Colonesis*, p. 140; for spurious letters of defiance between Frederick and Saladin, *Itinerarium*, pp. 49–54.
31. Henry of Albano, *Tractatus de peregrinatione*, PL, 204, col. 360.
32. *Itnerarium*, p. 55.
33. *Historia de expeditione*, pp. 24–5; Ibn Shaddad, *Saladin*, pp. 114–16.
34. *Historia de expeditione*, pp. 85, 86; *Die Urkunden der Deutchen Könige und Kaiser*, x, pt IV, *Die Urkunden Friedrichs I*, ed. H. Appelt, MGH (Hanover 1990), pp. 301, 303.
35. In general, Angold, *Byzantine Empire*; iden, *The Fourth Crusade* (London 2003); Magdalino, *Empire of Manuel I Komnenos*; Lilie, *Byzantium and the Crusader States*.
36. Ibn Shaddad, *Saladin*, pp. 121–2.
37. A fifth was created at Philipoppolis, *Historia de expeditione*, pp. 34–5.
38. *O City of Byzantium, Annals of Nicetas Choniates*, trans. H. J. Margoulias (Detroit 1984), pp. 220–26. (Hereafter *Nicetas*.)
39. *Die Urkunden Friedrichs I*, pp. 302–6; cf. his letter of the same period to Leopold of Austria, pp. 306–7 and his earlier correspondence with Henry, pp. 301–2.
40. *Historia de expeditione*, p. 71.
41. *Nicetas*, pp. 233–4.
42. *Epistola de Morte Friderici Imperatoris*, *Historia de expeditione*, p. 175; *Iitnerarium*, pp. 60–61.
43. Edbury, *Conquest of Jerusalem*, p. 89, but cf. p. 76 for an opposite memory of Saladin fortifying these strongholds.
44. *Historia de expeditione*, pp. 91–2; *Epistola de Morte*, pp. 177–8; *Itinerarium*, pp. 65–6; Ibn al-Athir, in Gabrieli, *Arab Historians*, pp. 209–10; Ibn Shaddad, *Saladin*, pp. 113–17; Edbury, *Conquest of Jerusalem*, pp. 87–8.
45. *Itinerarium*, p. 67; Ibn Shaddad, *Saladin*, p. 125.
46. *Itinerarium*, p. 106; Ambroise, *Crusade of Richard*, ll. 3625–60, pp. 162–3.
47. For the marriage of Conrad and Isabella, Edbury, *Conquest of Jerusalem*, pp. 95–7, 171, 172–4; *Itinerarium*, pp. 100–102, 121–6; Ambroise, *Crusade of Richard*, pp. 177–80; Imad al-Din, *Conquête de la Syrie*, trans. H. Masse (Paris 1972), pp. 105–6.
48. Edbury, *Conquest of Jerusalem*, pp. 89–90; cf. H. E. Mayer, *Crusades*, p. 142 and note 71, p. 304.
49. Edbury, *Conquest of Jerusalem*, pp. 171–2.
50. *Itinerarium*, p. 143; this echoes the outrage of observers such as Henry of Albano and Peter of Blois.
51. In general on the Franco-English crusade, see Gillingham, *Richard I*, pp. 85–154; Tyerman, *England and the Crusades*, pp. 57–85; the main chroniclers include the *Itinerarium*; Ambroise; the Englishmen Roger of Howden, Ralph of Diceto and William of Newburgh; and the Frenchman Rigord.
52. *The Complete Peerage*, by G. E. C. (reprint Gloucester 1987), iv, 194 note a.

53. *Itinerarium*, p. 99, cf. pp. 74, 76, 82, 96–8; the Latin text is in *Itinerarium peregrinorum et gesta Regis Ricardi*, ed. W. Stubbs, Rolls Series (London 1864), p. 93; for Londoners, Tyerman, *England and the Crusades*, pp. 73–4, 183.
54. *Itinerarium*, p. 108.
55. Tyerman, *England and the Crusades*, pp. 68, 70–72, 179.
56. Delaborde et al., *Recueil des actes de Philippe Auguste*, i, 305–6, no. 252 (although some doubt on the authenticity of this act exists; see Baldwin, *The Government of Philip Augustus*, pp. 53–4 and note 86).
57. Gillingham, *Richard I*, p. 114.
58. Gerald of Wales, *Journey*, p. 184; Tyerman, *England and the Crusades*, p. 60.
59. Roger of Howden, *Gesta Henrici Secundi*, ii, 132–3; Richard of Devizes, *Chronicle*, p. 17.
60. For all the English financial and logistic preparations, Tyerman, *England and the Crusades*, pp. 75–83.
61. Roger of Howden, *Gesta Henrici Secundi*, ii, 90; William of Newburgh, *Historia rerum Anglicarum*, ed. H. C. H. Hamilton (London 1856), ii, 121; Richard of Devizes, *Chronicle*, p. 9.
62. Richard of Devizes, *Chronicle*, p. 15; a monk of St Swithun's, Winchester, he may have been close to royal servants in the city involved in the organization of the expedition; cf. Roger of Howden, *Gesta Henrici Secundi*, ii, 117.
63. Richard of Devizes, *Chronicle*, p. 28 for the size of the fleet.
64. Roger of Howden, *Gesta Henrici Secundi*, ii, 116–24 for a full account of Richard's fleet March–August 1190.
65. Roger of Howden, *Chronica*, iii, 8.
66. Hunter, *Pipe Roll 1 Richard I*, p. 5.
67. Rigord, *Oeuvres* i, 99; Delaborde, et al., *Recueil des actes de Philippe Auguste*, i, no. 292; *Codice diplomatico della repubblica de Genova*, ed. C. Imperiale de Sant'Angelo (Genoa 1936–42), ii, 366–8.
68. Roger of Howden, *Gesta Henrici Secundi*, ii, 113, 129; Rigord, *Oeuvres*, i, 106.
69. Roger of Howden, *Gesta Henrici Secundi*, ii, 83–4; William of Newburgh, *Historia Chronicles*, ed. Howlett, i, 294–9.
70. William of Newburgh, *Historia, Chronicles*, ed. Howlett, i, 308–24 has the fullest narrative; cf. R. B. Dobson, *The Jews of Medieval York and the Massacre of 1190*, Borthwick Papers, no. 45 (York 1974).
71. Chazan, *European Jewry*, pp. 139–42, 170–71.
72. Roger of Howden, *Gesta Henrici Secundi*, ii, 92–3.
73. Roger of Howden, *Gesta Henrici Secundi*, ii, 162–3.
74. Tyerman, *England and the Crusades*, p. 67 and p. 395 note 56 for refs.
75. *Itinerarium*, p. 151; Ambroise, *Crusade of Richard*, p. 44; Gillingham, *Richard I*, p. 128 and note 13.
76. *Itinerarium*, p. 151 for the collapsing bridge; for Philip see Roger of Howden, *Gesta Henrici Secundi*, ii, 157–9.
77. Roger of Howden, *Gesta Henrici Secundi*, ii, 112 and pp. 112–15 and 124–6 for Richard's cruise to Sicily; Howden was by this time in the king's company.
78. *Itinerarium*, p. 167; Ambroise, *Crusade of Richard*, p. 64. These two closely linked accounts of Richard's journey east seem to reflect versions of events derived from eyewitnesses. For an excellent modern narrative of events in Sicily, Gillingham, *Richard I*, pp. 131–44.
79. Ibn Shaddad, *Saladin*, pp. 145, 146; Ambroise, *Crusade of Richard*, pp. 191–2; *Itinerarium*, pp. 203–4.
80. Above, notes 62 and 63; the most vivid account of the Cyprus campaign is by Ambroise, *Crusade of Richard*, pp. 74–108; cf. P. Edbury, *The Kingdom of Cyprus and the Crusades 1191–1374* (Cambridge 1991), pp. 5–9.
81. 'Epistolae Cantuarienses', *Chronicles and Memorials of the Reign of Richard I*, Rolls Series (London 1864–5), ii, 347.

82. For the Cyprus deals, Edbury, *Cyprus*, pp. 7–9; Gillingham, *Richard I*, pp. 152–3, 196–7.
83. Ibn Shaddad, *Saladin*, pp. 150–51; cf. Ambroise, *Crusade of Richard*, pp. 108–18; *Itinerarium*, pp. 195–203; Roger of Howden, *Gesta Henrici Secundi*, ii, 167–9.

14: The Palestine War 1191–2

1. Edbury, *Conquest of Jerusalem*, p. 98 and, for the Palestine war generally, pp. 98–9, 104–21.
2. The main narratives for the events of 1191–2 by or derived closely from eyewitnesses include Ibn Shaddad, *Saladin*, pp. 145–234; *Itinerarium*, pp. 201–380; Ambroise, *Crusade of Richard*, pp. 114–18, 191–448; Roger of Howden, *Gesta Henrici Secundi*, ii, 169–92, 230–31. The best secondary accounts are Gillingham, *Richard I*, pp. 155–221, a vigorous, critical but admiring apologia for Richard I, and Lyons and Jackson, *Saladin*, pp. 295–361. On the siege, R. Rogers, *Latin Siege Warfare in the Twelfth Century* (Oxford 1992), pp. 212–35.
3. *Itinerarium*, pp. 208–10.
4. Roger of Howden, *Gesta Henri Secundi*, ii, 170; Ambroise, *Crusade of Richard*, p. 196; *Itinerarium*, p. 204; Ibn Shaddad, *Saladin*, p. 153.
5. Ambroise, *Crusade of Richard*, pp. 207–8; cf. pp. 203–4 for Philip doing the same thing; cf. *Itinerarium*, pp. 210, 213–14.
6. Edbury, *Conquest of Jerusalem*, pp. 108–9.
7. Roger of Howden, *Gesta, Henrici Secundi*, ii, 159; *Itinerarium*, p. 190.
8. *Itinerarium*, p. 202; Ambroise, *Crusade of Richard*, p. 115 for 'cœur de lion'.
9. Roger of Howden, *Gesta Henrici Secundi*, ii, 171–2.
10. Ibn Shaddad, *Saladin*, pp. 153, 155; *Itinerarium*, pp. 83, 92.
11. *Itinerarium*, p. 214, cf. p. 204; Ambroise, *Crusade of Richard*, p. 208.
12. Ibn Shaddad, *Saladin*, p. 162, cf. pp. 156–7.
13. Richard of Devizes, *Chronicle*, pp. 46–7.
14. Edbury, *Conquest of Jerusalem*, p. 179.
15. Edbury, *Conquest of Jerusalem*, p. 179; for Philip's reputation, see Gillingham, *Richard I*, pp. 164–6; for his return journey to Europe, see the account by Roger of Howden, who went with him as one of Richard's spies, *Gesta Henrici Secundi*, ii, 192–9, 203–6, 227–30.
16. Ibn Shaddad, *Saladin*, p. 163.
17. Edbury, *Conquest of Jerusalem*, pp. 179–80, to the abbot of Cîteaux on 1 October 1191.
18. Ibn Shaddad, *Saladin*, pp. 164–5.
19. Ibn Shaddad, *Saladin*, pp. 165.
20. *Itinerarium*, pp. 218–19.
21. Ibn Shaddad, *Saladin*, p. 173; for mutilation and execution, pp. 168–9.
22. Ibn Shaddad, *Saladin*, pp. 173–4.
23. For the battle, Ambroise, *Crusade of Richard*, pp. 249–73; *Itinerarium*, pp. 247–61; for the dragon banner, Ambroise, *Crusade of Richard*, p. 250 and, for the armed cart or tower on which it was carried, *Itinerarium*, p. 237 and Ibn Shaddad, *Saladin*, p. 170; armed war wagons became familiar in the early fifteenth century, for instance in the Hussite crusades.
24. Edbury, *Conquest of Jerusalem*, p. 180.
25. Tyerman, *England and the Crusades*, p. 165 and notes 53 and 54, p. 411.
26. Roger of Howden, *Gesta Henrici Secundi*, ii, 185–6; Ambroise, *Crusade of Richard*, p. 229; *Itinerarium*, p. 232; Ibn Shaddad, *Saladin*, p. 165.
27. See Gillingham, *Richard I*, pp. 179–80; cf. Ambroise, *Crusade of Richard*, p. 277, ll. 7,025–30.
28. The letter of 11 October 1191 is translated in Edbury, *Conquest of Jerusalem*, pp. 181–2.
29. For these diplomatic excursions, Ibn Shaddad, pp. 187–8, 191–2, 194–6, and Gillingham, *Richard I*, pp. 21, 184–9 and refs.

30. Ibn Shaddad, *Saladin*, p. 196.
31. Ambroise, *Crusade of Richard*, p. 291 and generally, pp. 289–91; Ibn Shaddad, *Saladin*, p. 193.
32. Ibn al-Athir, RHC Or., ii, pt i, 55–6.
33. Ambroise, *Crusade of Richard*, p. 303.
34. Ibn Shaddad, *Saladin*, p. 197; Ambroise, *Crusade of Richard*, p. 307; *Itinerarium*, p. 287.
35. Ambroise, *Crusade of Richard*, p. 303, ll. 7,783–4, cf. Ambroise, *L'Estoire de la Guerre Sainte*, ed. G. Paris (Paris 1897), col. 208.
36. Saladin's view was confided to Bishop Hubert Walter of Salisbury in September 1192, Ambroise, *Crusade of Richard*, p. 442.
37. Gillingham, *Richard I*, p. 192; cf. D. Pringle, 'King Richard I and the Walls of Ascalon', *Palestine Exploration Quarterly*, 116 (1984).
38. Ambroise, *Crusade of Richard*, p. 290; *Itinerarium*, p. 272. Richard's great-grandfather in the male line was Count Fulk V of Anjou, who became king of Jerusalem and the father of Baldwin III and Amalric.
39. For a full discussion, Gillingham, *Richard I*, pp. 197–202, 226–7.
40. Ibn Shaddad, *Saladin*, p. 198.
41. Ambroise, *Crusade of Richard*, pp. 355–64; *Itinerarium*, pp. 321–6.
42. Ambroise, *Crusade of Richard*, pp. 368–9; *Itinerarium*, p. 328.
43. Ambroise, *Crusade of Richard*, pp. 393–4; *Itinerarium*, p. 346.
44. Ibn Shaddad, *Saladin*, p. 211.
45. Ibn Shaddad, *Saladin*, pp. 211–12; the intelligence was excellent, cf. Ambroise, *Crusade of Richard*, pp. 377–9.
46. Ambroise, *Crusade of Richard*, p. 393; *Itinerarium*, p. 346.
47. Ibn Shaddad, *Saladin*, p. 212.
48. Ibn Shaddad, *Saladin*, p. 223 and pp. 219–26; Ambroise, *Crusade of Richard*, pp. 399–426; *Itinerarium*, pp. 349–69.
49. *Sine feminalibus* in Latin, Stubbs, *Itinerarium*, p. 415.
50. Ibn Shaddad, *Saladin*, pp. 228–33.
51. Ambroise, *Crusade of Richard*, pp. 363–4; *Itinerarium*, p. 325.
52. Ambroise, *Crusade of Richard*, p. 444.
53. Ibn Shaddad, *Saladin*, p. 26; William of Newburgh, *Historia*, *Chronicles*, ed. Howlett, p. 374; cf. pp. 372–81, 379–81 for general reflections.
54. Ambroise, *Estoire de la Guerre Sainte*, ed. G. Paris (Paris 1927), l. 12,255, col. 329.
55. Albert von Johansdorf, a German minnesinger, quoted by Siberry, *Criticism of Crusading*, p. 193.
56. Gislebertus of Mons, *Chronicon Hanoniense*, ed. L. Vanderkindere (Brussels 1904), p. 272.

15: 'Ehud's Sharpened Sword'

1. Judges 3:16; Ehud was an Israelite hero who killed Eglon, king of the Moabites.
2. Sermon 1213×1218 for the Fifth Crusade, trans. by J. and L. Riley-Smith, *Crusades*, p. 134.
3. J. and L. Riley-Smith, *Crusades*, pp. 77–8 (letter to Waldemar II of Denmark for 'the Lord's war'), 79 (letter to Philip II 1207), 119–24 (*Quia Maior*), p. 119 for the Matthew text: the italics are mine; *Selected Letters of Pope Innocent III concerning England 1198–1216*, ed. C. R. Cheney and W. H. Semple (London 1953), p. 4 ('ab obsequio Iesu Christi', describing Richard I's crusade); cf. p. 91, to Leopold VI of Austria, who has taken the cross 'to follow Christ'.
4. J. and L. Riley-Smith, *Crusades*, p. 123.
5. Translation by C. Morris, *The Holy Land, Holy Lands and Christian History*, ed. R. N. Swanson, Studies in Church History, 36 (Woodbridge 2000), p. xvi.

6. Gerald of Wales, *Journey*, p. 114; James of Vitry, *Letters*, ed. R. B. C. Huygens (Leiden 1960), p. 77; Gunther of Pairis, *Historia*, p. 66, cf. *Capture*, p. 73; Caesarius of Heisterbach, *Dialogus Miraculorum*, ed. J. Strange (Cologne, Bonn and Brussels 1851), i, 12–13; James of Vitry, *Historia Occidentalis*, ed. J. F. Hinnebusch (Friburg 1972), pp. 20–21.
7. Cheney and Semple, *Selected Letters of Innocent III*, pp. 207, 208, 216, 218, 219.
8. Quoted in J. Gilchrist, 'The Lord's War as the Proving Ground of Faith; Pope Innocent III and the Propagation of Violence', *Crusaders and Muslims*, ed. Shatzmiller, p. 69 and generally pp. 65–83.
9. On this see Tyerman, *Invention of the Crusades*, pp. 27, 50, 76–83, 86; M. Markowski, 'Crucesignatus: Its Origins and Early Usage', *Journal of Medieval History*, 10 (1984).
10. J. and L. Riley-Smith, *Crusades*, p. 139.
11. J. and L. Riley-Smith, *Crusades*, pp. 119–29.
12. Tyerman, *Invention of the Crusades*, pp. 14–15 and note 35; the 1198 bull sent to England is included in Roger of Howden, *Chronica*, iv, 70–75.
13. J. and L. Riley-Smith, *Crusades*, pp. 145–8.
14. J. and L. Riley-Smith, *Crusades*, p. 123, and pp. 119–24 in general for what follows.
15. J.-M. Canivez (ed.), *Statuta Capitulorum Generalium Ordinis Cisterciensis ab anno 1116 ad annum 1786* (Louvain 1933–41), i, 122, 172, 181–2, 208, 210, 268, 270, etc.; Snoek, *Medieval Piety*, pp. 168–9 and refs.
16. J. and L. Riley-Smith, *Crusades*, p. 124; *Councils and Synods with Other Documents Relating to the English Church*, gen. ed. F. M. Powicke (Oxford 1964–81), ii, 175.
17. The letter from the patriarch of Jerusalem on behalf of the First Crusaders at Antioch, January 1098, is translated in Peters, *The First Crusade* pp. 283–4; Roger of Howden, *Chronica*, iii, 317–19; iv, 165–7; cf. C. Cheney, *Hubert Walter* (London 1967), pp. 124–32.
18. Royal Commission on Historical Manuscripts, *Fifth Report*, Appendix (London 1872), p. 462; idem, *Report on Various Collections*, i (London 1901), 235–6; Roger of Howden, *Chronica*, iv, 108–12; Tyerman, *England and the Crusades*, pp. 168–72.
19. *Coutumiers de Normandie*, ed. E. J. Tardif (Rouen 1881–1903), iii,, 91; cf. for general discussions of privileges, J. Brundage, *Canon Law and the Crusader*; Tyerman, *Invention of the Crusades*, pp. 55–62; idem, *England and the Crusades*, pp. 187–228; S. Lloyd, *English Society and the Crusade 1216–1307* (Oxford 1988).
20. Delaborde, et al., *Receuil des actes de Philippe Auguste*, nos. 228, 1360; Rigord, *Oeuvres*, i, 84–8.
21. *Curia Regis Rolls* (London and Woodbridge 1922–), iii, 193.
22. Tyerman, *England and the Crusades*, pp. 71, 135, 204, 219, 221.
23. F. M. Stenton, 'Early Manumissions at Staunton', *English Historical Review*, 26 (1911), 95–6; P. R. Hyams, *Kings, Lords and Peasants* (Oxford 1980), p. 32 and note 37.
24. *Curis Regis Rolls*, x, 293; *Bracton's Note Book*, ed. F. W. Maitland (London 1887), ii, 159–60, 196; J. Brundage, 'The Crusader's Wife: A Canonistic Quandary', *Studia Gratiana*, 12 (1967), 427–41.
25. Cheney and Semple, *Selected Letters of Innocent III*, pp. 144–7.
26. Christiansen, *The Northern Crusades*, p. 98.
27. J. D. Mansi, *Sacrorum Conciliorum nova et amplissima collectio*, xxii (Venice 1778), cols. 231–3.
28. For a full contemporary account, Arnold of Lübeck, *Chronica Slavorum*, pp. 195–212; cf. Waitz, *Chronica Regia Colonensis*, pp. 157–61.
29. *Nicetas*, pp. 261–3.
30. Jaffé, *Regesta Pontificum Romanorum*, ii, nos. 17,226, 17,270, 17,274; Ralph of Diceto, *Ymagines Historiarum*, *Opera Historica*, ed. Stubbs, ii, 132–5; Waitz, *Chronica Regia Colonensis*, p. 157.
31. Edbury, *Conquest of Jerusalem*, p. 139 and, generally, pp. 136–45.
32. Arnold of Lübeck, *Chronica Slavorum*, p. 195.
33. On these negotiations, Edbury, *Cyprus*, p. 33 and refs.

34. *Die Register Innocenz' III*, ed. O. Hageneder et al. (Graz-Cologne, Rome and Vienna 1964–), i, no. 336; cf. Roger of Howden, *Chronica*, iv, 70–75.
35. Geoffrey of Villehardouin, *The Conquest of Constantinople*, trans. M. R. B. Shaw (London 1963), p. 29.
36. Runciman, *History of the Crusades*, iii, 130.
37. J. Crosland, *William Marshal: Knighthood, War and Chivalry* (London 2002), pp. 78–81; *Histoire de Guillaume le Maréchal*, ed. P. Meyer (Paris 1891–1901), ll. 11,373–688.
38. See Innocent III's letter, 5 November 1198, C. Tyerman (ed.), *An Eyewitness History of the Crusades*, Folio Society (London 2004), iv, *The Fourth Crusade*, 4.
39. Roger of Howden, *Chronica*, iv, 76–7.
40. James of Vitry, *Historia Occidentalis*, pp. 89–90; cf. pp. 96–101; for Fulk, see Roger of Howden, *Chronica*, iv, 76–7; Ralph of Coggeshall, *Chronicon Anglicanum*, ed. J. Stevenson, Rolls Series (London 1875), pp. 80–83, 130, 131 for a very flattering account; Winchester Annals, *Annales Monastici*, ed. Luard, ii, 67–8 for a hostile view; Villehardouin, *Conquest*, pp. 29, 38; Robert of Clari, *The Conquest of Constantinople*, trans. E. H. McNeal (New York 1966), pp. 31, 34, 38.
41. According to Gunther of Pairis, *Capture*, p. 67.
42. Robert of Clari, *Conquest*, p. 31 and p. 38 for the alleged use of Fulk's money; James of Vitry, *Historia Occidentalis*, p. 101. For other accounts of Fulk, his controversial personality and the disposal of his money, see the *Devastatio Constantinopolitana*, the account of the crusade by the so-called Anonymous of Soissons, and the colourful chronicle by the Cistercian Alberic of Trois Fontaines, trans. A. J. Andrea, *Contemporary Sources for the Fourth Crusade* (Leiden 2000), pp. 213, 233, 293; and Mas-Latrie, *Chronique d'Ernoul*, p. 233.
43. Tyerman, *England and the Crusades*, pp. 160–70 and refs.
44. Roger of Howden, *Chronica*, iv, 111; J. and L. Riley-Smith, *Crusades*, pp. 145–8.
45. Innocent III, Hageneder et al., *Register*, i, no. 555; ii, no. 212; E. Kennan, 'Innocent III and the First Political Crusade', *Traditio*, 27 (1971), 231–49; N. Housley, 'Crusades against Christians', *Crusade and Settlement*, ed. Edbury, pp. 27–8.

16: The Fourth Crusade: Preparations

1. Villehardouin, *Conquest*, p. 93. In general, D. E. Queller and T. F. Madden, *The Fourth Crusade: The Conquest of Constantinople* (Philadelphia 1997); M. Angold, *The Fourth Crusade* (London 2003).
2. At least once he rather belatedly found out about the violence and pillage, see his letter of 12 July 1205, translated in Andrea, *Sources*, pp. 163–8.
3. Andrea, *Sources*, p. 294.
4. Villehardouin, *Conquest*, pp. 29–31.
5. J. and L. Riley-Smith, *Crusades*, pp. 145–8.
6. For Germany, Gunther of Pairis, *Capture*, pp. 67–72 and p. 149 note 28 and ref. For the British Isles, Tyerman, *England and the Crusades*, pp. 96, 160, 162, 163, 167, 168, 170; A. Macquarrie, *Scotland and the Crusades*, pp. 32–3.
7. Andrea, *Sources*, pp. 19–21.
8. Ralph of Coggeshall, trans. Andrea, *Sources*, p. 280; Mas-Latrie, *Chronique d'Ernoul*, p. 338; cf. *Devastatio Constantinopolitana*, trans. Andrea, *Sources*, p. 213.
9. Gunther of Pairis, *Capture*, pp. 67–77, 149 note 28; placing the sermon less plausibly given the subsequent chronology of Martin's crusade in 1200, C. Maier, 'Kirche, Kreuz und Ritual', *Deutches Archiv für Erforschung des Mittelalters*, 55 (1999); Villehardouin, *Conquest*, pp. 38–9, 51.
10. Gunther of Pairis, *Capture*, p. 68.
11. Villehardouin, *Conquest*, p. 29.
12. For biographical information, J. Longnon, *Les Compagnons de Villehardouin* (Geneva 1978).

13. Robert of Clari, *Conquest*, pp. 33–4, 102, 117–18.
14. *Deeds of the Bishops of Halberstadt*, trans. Andrea, *Sources*, p. 246 and, generally, pp. 246–64.
15. Andrea, *Sources*, p. 250.
16. Hugues de Berzé, *S'Onques nus hom pour dure departie*, written in Lombardy in June 1202, Bédier and Aubry, *Chansons*, pp. 126–9.
17. Andrea, *Sources*, p. 186.
18. Villehardouin, *Conquest*, pp. 36–7; Robert of Clari, *Conquest*, p. 34; J. and L. Riley-Smith, *Crusades*, p. 147 ('in stipendia bellatorum' in Latin, Roger of Howden, *Chronica*, iv, 111); Andrea, *Sources*, p. 188.
19. Villehardouin, *Conquest*, pp. 40–41, 52–3.
20. A. Wauters (ed.), *Table chronologique des chartes et diplômes imprimés concernant l'histoire de la Belgique* (Brussels 1866–1965), iii, 174.
21. Andrea, *Sources*, p. 247.
22. Tyerman, *England and the Crusades*, p. 96 and p. 400, note 35 and refs.; Baldwin, *The Government of Philip Augustus*, pp. 96 and 480 note 62.
23. Tyerman, *England and the Crusades*, p. 191.
24. According to the contemporary *Devastatio Constantinopolitana*, Andrea, *Sources*, p. 213.
25. *Collection des principaux cartulaires du diocese de Troyes*, vi, *Cartulaire de Montier-le-Celle*, ed. C. Lalone (Paris-Troyes 1882), pp. 10–11, no. 9; *Pèlerins Champenois en Palestine*, ed. A. de Barthelemy, *Revue de l'Orient Latin*, 1 (1898), p. 366.
26. *Chartes de Chapitre de Sainte-Waudru de Mons*, ed. L. Devillers (Brussels 1899–1913), i, no. XLV, pp. 84–6.
27. Röhricht, *Regesta*, pp. 202–3; for the possible reply suggesting negotiation not war, J. Bongars (ed.), *Gesta Dei Per Francos* (Hanover 1611), pp. 1,125–9.
28. For the text of the treaty, G. L. Tafel and G. M. Thomas, *Urkunden zur alteren Handels- und Staatsgeschichte der Republik Venedig* (Vienna 1856–7), i, 362–73; cf. Villehardouin, *Conquest*, p. 33.
29. Villehardouin, *Conquest*, pp. 40, 52–3.
30. Andrea, *Sources*, pp. 33–9; cf. J. M. Powell, 'Innocent III and Alexius III: a Crusade Plan that Failed', *The Experience of Crusading*, i, ed. M. Bull and N. Housley (Cambridge 2003), pp. 96–102.
31. Andrea, *Sources*, pp. 46–54, 61–4.
32. Villehardouin, *La Conquête de Constantinople*, ed. E. Faral, i (Paris 1961), p. 14.
33. Robert of Clari, *Conquest*, p. 37; Roger of Howden, *Chronica*, iv, 73.
34. The Anonymous Monk of St Nicholas of the Lido, *Historia de Translatione*, RHC Occ., v, 253–78 and above pp. 255–6.
35. Tafel and Thomas, *Urkunden*, i, 362–73; Villehardouin, *Conquest*, pp. 33–5. Cf. the insightful discussion by J. Pryor, 'The Venetian Fleet for the Fourth Crusade and the Diversion to Constantinople', *Experience of Crusading*, ed. Bull and Housley, i, 103–23.
36. E.g. the Anonymous of Soissons reflecting, perhaps, the views of Bishop Nivelo concerning the Venetians' 'excessive' demands, Andrea, *Sources*, p. 233; cf. Robert of Clari, *Conquest*, pp. 37–41.
37. Robert of Clari, *Conquest*, p. 40.
38. Pryor, 'Venetian Fleet', esp. pp. 114–17 and note 6; *Nicetas*, pp. 295–6; the *Devastatio Constantinopolinana* and Hugh of St Pol, Andrea, *Sources*, pp. 186–201, 212–21.
39. Angold, *Fourth Crusade*, pp. 52–8 is a sensitive reading.
40. *Nicetas*, p. 295.
41. Andrea, *Sources*, p. 23.
42. William of Tyre, *History*, i, 552–6.
43. Villehardouin, *Conquest*, pp. 35–41 for this and what follows.
44. Gunther of Pairis, *Capture*, pp. 76–7; Villehardouin, *Conquest*, p. 45.
45. Villehardouin, *Conquête*, p. 42.

46. Villehardouin, *Conquête*, p. 42 cf. Queller and Madden, *Fourth Crusade*, pp. 25–7 and refs. for a different view of Boniface as a 'brilliant choice'; I am grateful to Dr Jean Dunbabin for her thoughts on the French royal dimension.
47. *Gesta Innocenti*, chap. 83, PL, ccxiv, col. 132; Villehardouin, *Conquest*, p. 38; Baldwin, *The Government of Philip Augustus*, p. 481 note 1. King Philip could have argued he was formally involved, his putative approval having been anticipated in the Treaty of Venice, Tafel and Thomas, *Urkunden*, i, 367.
48. Gunther of Pairis, *Capture*, pp. 107–8. Boniface's fame was also gilded by a personal publicist, his friend the troubadour Raimbaut of Vaqueiras.
49. Villehardouin, *Conquest*, pp. 37–8; Tafel and Thomas, *Urkunden*, i, 369.
50. Villehardouin, *Conquest*, p. 45.
51. Gunther of Pairis, *Capture*, pp. 76–7; Villehardouin, *Conquest*, p. 45; *Devastatio*, probably reflecting a Rhinelander experience, Andrea, *Sources*, p. 213.
52. Villehardouin, *Conquest*, p. 41.

17: The Fourth Crusade: Diversion

1. Andrea, *Sources*, p. 166 and for the whole letter, pp. 163–8.
2. The main narratives are Villehardouin, Robert of Clari and Gunther of Pairis; important shorter accounts by Hugh of St Pol, the Anonymous of Soissons, the author of *The Deeds of the Bishops of Halberstadt* and the *Devastatio Constantinopolitana*, are translated in Andrea, *Sources*, pp. 186–264; the useful *Chronicle of Novgorod* is translated by J. Gordon, *Byzantion*, 43 (1973), 297–311; cf. Innocent's letters and his *Gesta* in PL, 214.
3. Villehardouin, *Conquest*, p. 42; Robert of Clari, *Conquest*, p. 40.
4. Andrea, *Sources*, p. 213.
5. Robert of Clari, *Conquest*, p. 40; Villehardouin, *Conquest*, p. 42.
6. Villehardouin, *Conquest*, p. 43; Robert of Clari, *Conquest*, p. 41; Andrea, *Sources*, pp. 213, 233; Gunther of Pairis, *Capture*, pp. 77–8.
7. Robert of Clari recorded 36,000 marks, *Conquest*, p. 41.
8. Villehardouin, *Conquest*, pp. 43–4.
9. Robert of Clari, *Conquest*, p. 42.
10. Villehardouin, *Conquest*, p. 43; Andrea, *Sources*, p. 250 and pp. 35–48; for Innocent's correspondence cf. Gunther of Pairis, *Capture*, p. 78.
11. Villehardouin, *Conquest*, pp. 47–8.
12. Robert of Clari, *Conquest*, p. 44.
13. Peter of Les Vaux-de-Cernay, *The History of the Albigensian Crusade*, trans. W. A. and M. D. Sibly (Woodbridge 1998), p. 58, and pp. 57–9 for the events at Zara in general; Peter was Abbot Guy's nephew.
14. Villehardouin, *Conquest*, p. 54.
15. For the term, Villehardouin, *Conquête*, ed. Faral, p. 200; Robert of Clari, *La Conquête de Constantinople*, ed. P. Lauer (Paris 1924), p. 81; Andrea, *Sources*, pp. 188, 213. For clarifying thoughts and discussion of this and related points on the structure of the army, I am indebted to a paper by Jonathan Riley-Smith given in Oxford in January 2004.
16. Villehardouin, *Conquête*, ed. Faral, p. 100.
17. Villehardouin, *Conquête*, ed. Faral, pp. 148–52.
18. Gunther of Pairis, *Capture*, p. 78.
19. Robert of Clari, *Conquête*, p. 16.
20. PL, 214, cols. 1,123–5; Andrea, *Sources*, pp. 35–9.
21. Villehardouin, *Conquest*, p. 50.
22. For useful surveys, Angold, *Byzantine Empire* and *Fourth Crusade*; Magdalino, *Empire of Manuel I Comnenus*; J. Harris, *Byzantium and the Crusades* (London 2003).
23. Villehardouin, *Conquest*, p. 99.
24. *Nicetas*, p. 296.

25. As in C. Brand, *Byzantium Confronts the West* (Cambridge, Mass. 1968); but cf. more nuanced views, e.g. A. M. Bryer's in D. Baker (ed.), *Relations between East and West in the Middle Ages* (Edinburgh 1973).
26. Quoted in Angold, *Byzantine Empire*, p. 150.
27. Matthew Paris, *Chronica Majora*, ed. H. R. Luard, Rolls Series (London 1872–84), v, 284–7.
28. *Nicetas*, pp. 323–4.
29. Andrea, *Sources*, pp. 163–8.
30. PL, 214, cols. 130 et seq., chap. 82; cols. 1,123–5; Villehardouin, *Conquest*, pp. 44–5.
31. See note 30.
32. See his correspondence, Andrea, *Sources*, pp. 35–98.
33. Andrea, *Sources*, p. 188.
34. Gunther of Pairis, *Capture*, pp. 90–91.
35. Villehardouin, *Conquest*, p. 52; Robert of Clari, *Conquête*, p. 40.
36. *Devastatio Constantinopolitana*, Andrea, *Sources*, p. 216.
37. Andrea, *Sources*, pp. 46–59.
38. Andrea, *Sources*, p. 48.
39. Andrea, *Sources*, pp. 62–3.
40. For the disputes at Corfu, Villehardouin, *Conquest*, pp. 54–6; Robert of Clari, *Conquest*, pp. 58–9, 66; Andrea, *Sources*, pp. 188 et seq., 216 et seq., 250.
41. *Nicetas*, p. 297; Andrea, *Sources*, p. 254.
42. Andrea, *Sources*, p. 255.
43. The phrase in Innocent III's in his letter of November 1202, above, notes 20 and 30.
44. Andrea, *Sources*, p. 199.
45. Robert of Clari, *Conquest*, p. 67.
46. *Nicetas*, p. 301.
47. Villehardouin, *Conquest*, pp. 74–5.
48. Robert of Clari, *Conquest* p. 81, who has 36,000 marks as the debt against Villehardouin's possibly more informed 34,000, p. 43.
49. Villehardouin, *Conquest*, pp. 76–7.
50. Villehardouin, *Conquête*, ed. Faral, p. 200.
51. Villehardouin, *Conquest*, p. 77.
52. Villehardouin, *Conquest*, p. 78; Hugh of St Pol, Andrea, *Sources*, pp. 199–201.
53. Villehardouin, *Conquest*, p. 78–9; Robert of Clari, *Conquest* pp. 81–2; *Devastatio Constantinopolitana*, Andrea, *Sources*, p. 218; *Nicetas*, p. 304.
54. *Nicetas*, pp. 302–4.
55. *Nicetas*, p. 305.
56. *Nicetas*, pp. 304–6; Villehardouin, *Conquest* pp. 81–3; Robert of Clari, *Conquest* p. 82.
57. *Nicetas*, pp. 306–12, p. 309 for the murder; Villehardouin, *Conquest*, pp. 83–6; Andrea, *Sources*, p. 105, for the lurid details in Baldwin of Flanders's circular after his election as emperor.
58. Anonymous of Soissons, writing before 1207 with material from Bishop Nivelo, Andrea, *Sources*, p. 234.
59. Tafel and Thomas, *Urkunden*, i, 445; Andrea, *Sources*, pp. 140–44; Villehardouin, *Conquest*, p. 88; Robert of Clari, *Conquest*, pp. 91–2.
60. Villehardouin, *Conquest*, pp. 84–5; Mansi, *Sacrorum Conciliorum*, xxii, cols. 231–3.
61. Robert of Clari, *Conquest*, p. 94.
62. Villehardouin, *Conquest*, pp. 91–5; Robert of Clari, *Conquest*, pp. 99–102; *Nicetas*, pp. 314–25; Nicholas Mesarites in Brand, *Byzantium*, p. 269; Gunther of Pairis, *Capture*, pp. 106–13; Andrea, *Sources*, pp. 100–112, 221, 235–7, 255, 261–3; *Chronicle of Novgorod*, pp. 309–10.
63. Gunther of Pairis, *Capture*, p. 107, perhaps special pleading to exonerate his abbot of guilt by association; a usefully calm discussion is by Angold, *Fourth Crusade*, pp. 111–13 and refs.

64. The phrase is Gunther of Pairis's, describing his abbot, *Capture*, p. 111; the figures are discussed in Queller and Madden, *Fourth Crusade*, pp. 294–5; cf. Villehardouin, *Conquest* pp. 94–5.
65. Angold, *Fourth Crusade*, pp. 111–12; cf. *Nicetas*, pp. 323–5.
66. Robert of Clari, *Conquête*, p. 81 for the phrase 'quemun de l'ost'; Robert of Clari, *Conquest*, pp. 100–102.
67. Villehardouin, *Conquest*, pp. 94–5; *Devastatio Constantinopolitana*, Andrea, *Sources*, p. 221; Robert of Clari, *Conquest*, pp. 101–2.
68. Villehardouin, *Conquest* p. 93.
69. Andrea, *Sources*, pp. 100–112. For the Latin Empire, Angold, *Fourth Crusade*, part 2, esp. pp. 113–50; P. Lock, *The Franks in the Aegean 1204–1500* (Harlow 1995); D. Jacoby, 'The Encounter of Two Societies', *American Historical Review*, 78 (1973), 873–906.
70. PL, 215, cols. 1,372–5, of March 1208; the initiative may have come from Theodore Lascaris; see Angold, *Fourth Crusade*, pp. 195–8.
71. Robert of Clari, *Conquest*, pp. 86–8.
72. Alberic of Trois Fontaines, Andrea, *Sources*, p. 306 and note.
73. Angold, *Fourth Crusade*, pp. 148, 237–40.
74. Gunther of Pairis, *Capture*, pp. 109–12, 119–27; Angold, *Fourth Crusade*, pp. 228–47.
75. Andrea, *Sources*, pp. 235–7, 261–3; Robert of Clari, *Conquest* p. 5.
76. Ralph of Coggeshall, *Chronicon Anglicanum*, pp. 201–3, trans. Andrea, *Sources*, pp. 288–90. In general, M. Barber, 'Western Attitudes to Frankish Greece in the Thirteenth Century', *Latins and Greeks in the Eastern Mediterranean after 1204*, ed. B. Arbel et al. (London 1989), pp. 111–28.
77. Andrea, *Sources*, p. 108.
78. Runciman, *History of the Crusades*, iii, 477.

18: The Albigensian Crusades 1209–29

1. Peter of Les Vaux-de-Cernay, *Historia Albigensis*, translated as *The History of the Albigensian Crusade* by W. A. and M. D. Sibly (Woodbridge 1998), p. 197. (Hereafter PVC.)
2. In general, in English, A. P. Evans, 'The Albigensian Crusades', *History of the Crusades*, ed. Setton, ii, 277–324; W. L. Wakefield, *Heresy, Crusade and Inquisition in Southern France, 1100–1250* (London 1974); J. Sumption, *The Albigensian Crusade* (London 1978); M. Barber, *The Cathars* (London 2000).
3. Mainly on the evidence of mishaps and losses, including the death of Louis VIII, Roger of Wendover, *Flores Historiarum*, ed. H. G. Hewlett, Rolls Series (London 1886–9), ii, 315.
4. Wakefield, *Heresy*, p. 245.
5. Barber, *Cathars*, passim; for general surveys, M. D. Lambert, *Medieval Heresy* (2nd edn Oxford 1992); idem, *The Cathars* (Oxford 1998); R. I. Moore, *The Origins of European Dissent* (Oxford 1985).
6. William of Newburgh, *Historia*, ed. Howlett, pp. 131–4; J. Sayers, *Innocent III* (London 1994), p. 157 and note 55.
7. P. Biller, 'The Cathars of Languedoc and Written Materials', *Heresy and Literacy 1000–1350*, ed. P. Biller and A. Hudson (Cambridge 1994), p. 63 and, generally, pp. 61–82.
8. For a summary, see L. M. Paterson, *The World of the Troubadours* (Cambridge 1993), pp. 249–52 and refs.
9. William Pelhisson, *Chronicle*, trans. Wakefield, *Heresy*, p. 210.
10. William of Puylaurens, *Chronicle*, trans. W. A. and M. D. Sibly (Woodbridge 2003), p. 12 (hereafter WP); Barber, *Cathars*, pp. 21–2 and note 43, and passim for Sacconi; Wakefield, *Heresy*, pp. 139, 143 and 192 note 4 for Robert; PVC, p. 18 for Theodoric.
11. See the important article by B. Hamilton, 'Wisdom from the East', *Heresy and Literacy*, pp. 38–60.
12. For the St Félix Council, Barber, *Cathars*, esp. pp. 21–2 and 71–3.

13. Wakefield, *Heresy*, pp. 68–81.
14. WP, p. 25.
15. WP, pp. xxix–xxx and notes for a discussion of the term.
16. WP, p. 22.
17. Paterson, *World of Troubadours*, pp. 70–71; Barber, *Cathars*, pp. 55–8.
18. Wakefield, *Heresy*, p. 52.
19. *La Chanson de la croisade contre les Albigeois*, trans. J. Shirley, *The Song of the Cathar Wars* (Aldershot 1996), pp. 84–5. (Hereafter *Song*.)
20. Decree 27.
21. Gervase of Canterbury, *Historical Works*, i, 270–71.
22. Barber, *Cathars*, p. 52 and note 62.
23. PVC, p. 117; WP, p. 40; *Song*, p. 41.
24. A point made in order to damn Raymond VI by WP, pp. 16–18.
25. Mansi, *Sacrorum Conciliorum*, xxii, cols. 231–3.
26. WP, p. 12 and note 36 to refs. to the narratives of the 1181 expedition.
27. *Ketzer und Ketzerbekampfung im Hochmittelalter*, ed. J. Fearns (Göttingen 1968), pp. 61–3.
28. PVC, p. 8.
29. On Innocent III, Barber, *Cathars*, esp. pp. 115–20; Wakefield, *Heresy*, pp. 86–91.
30. PL, 215 cols. 358–60 for Arnold Aimery's appointment; col. 362 for talk of the spiritual virtue of the 'material sword'.
31. See, for example, PVC, pp. 16–22; WP, pp. 23–9.
32. PVC, p. 19.
33. Innocent's letter is translated in J. and L. Riley-Smith, *Crusades*, pp. 78–80.
34. PVC, pp. 31–8 for Innocent III's account; cf. *Song*, p. 13 for the culprit.
35. PVC, p. 33.
36. PVC, pp. 31–8.
37. See papal letters in PL, 215, nos. clvi–clviii; Siberry, *Criticism of Crusading*, p. 107 and note 215.
38. *Recueil des Chartes de l'abbaye de Cluny*, ed. Bruel, v, nos. 4,452–3, pp. 826–8.
39. PVC, p. 116.
40. Tyerman, *England and the Crusades*, p. 164 and ref.
41. Quoted Riley-Smith, *Oxford History of the Crusades*, pp. 10–11.
42. *Sigeberti Gemblacensis chronica auctarium Mortui Maris*, ed. G. H. Pertz, MGH SS, vi (Hanover 1844), p. 467.
43. N. P. Tanner, *Decrees of the Ecumenical Councils* (London and Washington 1990), p. 234.
44. WP, pp. 35–6, 39; *Song*, p. 32.
45. PVC, p. 97.
46. Loc. cit.
47. Roger of Wendover, *Flores*, ii, 312–13.
48. *Anecdotes historiques, légendes et apologues d'Etienne de Bourbon*, ed. A. Lecoy de la Marche (Paris 1877), pp. 36–7.
49. PVC, p. 209.
50. Translated in PVC, Appendix F, p. 308.
51. PVC, pp. 250–51 and note 29; Wakefield, *Heresy*, p. 73.
52. For a clear narrative, Sumption, pp. 77–87.
53. PL, 216, cols. 97–9.
54. PVC, p. 56.
55. PVC, p. 60.
56. PVC, pp. 44–5 and note 75 and refs.; *Song*, pp. 13–18; WP, p. 32 (misdates Raymond's overtures to Philip II and Otto IV).
57. Translated WP, Appendix A, pp. 127–9; for a full discussion in English of the massacre and the sources, PVC, Appendix B, pp. 289–93.

58. WP, p. 128.
59. Caesarius of Heisterbach, *Dialogus Miraculorum*, ed. J. Strange (Cologne etc. 1851), i, 302.
60. WP, p. 128.
61. *Song*, pp. 19–22; PVC, p. 291.
62. For a discussion of this, see Barber, *Cathars*, pp. 133–5.
63. PVC, p. 189, quoting a papal letter of 21 May 1213.
64. PVC, pp. 299–301, Appendix D, for mercenaries; 144; *Song*, pp. 181–9; WP, pp. 64–5.
65. PVC, pp. 62–3.
66. PVC, pp. 84–5, 117, 120; WP, pp. 40–41; *Song*, pp. 41, 48; H. C. Lea, *A History of the Inquisition* (New York and London 1888), i, 162.
67. PVC, p. 70, 71–2, 163, 237–8 and note 98.
68. WP, pp. 65–6; *Song*, pp. 181–3.
69. Quoted by M. Routledge in Riley-Smith, *Oxford History of the Crusades*, p. 109.
70. *Song*, pp. 26–8; PVC, pp. 55–9 and Appendix C, pp. 294–8; J. R. Maddicott, *Simon de Montfort* (Cambridge 1994), pp. 1–5.
71. See Innocent III's letters of January and May, PVC, pp. 186–9, 308.
72. PVC, pp. 154, 228 and note 50, 232, 234 and note 90.
73. PVC, p. 95.
74. WP, p. 58.
75. PVC, pp. 98–9 and 90–100; *Song*, pp. 34–6.
76. PVC, pp. 63–4 and note 105.
77. WP, p. 42, precipitated by the treachery at Castelnaudary in 1211 of William Cat, a former intimate; cf. PVC, pp. 134–5.
78. Translated PVC, pp. 320–29.
79. PVC, p. 310; for the correspondence, pp. 308–11.
80. PVC, pp. 186–9; J. and L. Riley-Smith, *Crusades*, p. 122.
81. PVC, pp. 203–17; *Song*, pp. 68–71 and WP, pp. 45–9 are later but informed.
82. PVC, pp. 242–5.
83. *Song*, pp. 74–5.
84. Translated PVC, pp. 311–12.
85. WP, p. 56.
86. *Song*, p. 172 (and cf. p. 176 for a wonderfully hostile obituary notice); PVC, pp. 276–7; WP, pp. 61–2.
87. WP, p. 65.
88. R. Kay, 'The Albigensian Twentieth of 1221–3', *Journal of Medieval History*, vi (1980), 307–16.
89. *Chronicon Turonense*, RHGF, ed. Bouquet et al., xviii, 314; cf. Siberry, *Criticism of Crusading*, p. 131 and refs. to Honorius III's letters and bulls.
90. Its terms are translated in WP, Appendix C, pp. 138–44.
91. For a useful recent summary, Barber, *Cathars*, pp. 141–75, which has full references.
92. Wakefield, *Heresy*, pp. 179–89, 193.
93. WP, pp. 107–8; Barber, *Cathars*, pp. 154–8 and refs.
94. An incident made famous by E. Le Roi Ladurie, *Montaillou* (Eng. trans. London 1978), a rather misleading work (cf. comments by L. E. Boyle, 'Montaillou Revisited', *Pathways to Medieval Peasants*, ed. J. Raftis (Toronto 1981), pp. 119–40); for a scholarly recent discussion of the revival, Barber, *Cathars*, pp. 176–202.
95. See J. H. Mundy, *Society and Government at Toulouse in the Age of the Cathars* (Toronto 1997).
96. G. Langlois, *Olivier de Termes: Le Cathare et le croisé* (Toulouse 2001) for a recent study (note 509, p. 269 corrects the date of his death usually cited) and for other 'Cathar crusaders', ibid., pp. 121ff; WP, p. 111; Barber, *Cathars*, p. 164; Wakefield, *Heresy*, p. 187 and p. 213 (William Pelhisson's chronicle: 'there were at that time [1229] many who had taken the cross to go overseas because of their acts against the faith').

97. WP, p. 67 and note 93.
98. WP, p. 111–12, note 26 and refs.

19: The Fifth Crusade 1213–21

1. J. and L. Riley-Smith, *Crusades*, pp. 91–2.
2. The best modern account is J. M. Powell, *Anatomy of a Crusade 1213–21* (Philadelphia 1986).
3. On the general phenomenon, M. Clanchy, *From Memory to Written Record* (London 1979).
4. PVC, p. 50; Legates' report, WP, p. 127.
5. Above pp. 525, 530, 540–41, 542, 547, 551–2, 554.
6. In general, P. Raedts, 'The Children's Crusade of 1212', *Journal of Medieval History*, 3 (1977), 279–323 and, especially, G. Dickson, 'La Genèse de la croisade des enfants (1212)', *Bibliothèque de l'Ecole des Chartes*, 153 (1995), 53–102 and idem, 'Stephen of Cloyes, Philip Augustus and the Children's Crusade of 1212', *Journeys towards God: Pilgrimage and Crusade*, ed. B. N. Sarget-Baur (Kalamazoo 1992), pp. 83–105.
7. PVC, pp. 142, 150–51.
8. Waitz, *Chronica Regia Colonesis*, p. 234; cf. translation in E. Peters (ed.), *Christian Society and the Crusades 1198–1229* (Philadelphia 1971), p. 36.
9. *Sigeberti Gemblacenses chronica auctarium Mortui Maris*, ed. W. Pertz, MGH SS, vi, 467; *Annales Admuntenses*, ed. W. Wattenbach, MGH SS, ix, 579–93.
10. PVC, p. 151; for the Cologne version see note 8 above.
11. See note 6 above.
12. For the sources, with stories of heavenly letters and visions of Christ, see Dickson, 'Stephen of Cloyes', pp. 84–6 and notes 7, 27, pp. 98, 101.
13. Wattenbach, *Annales Admuntenses*, p. 592.
14. See translation in PVC, p. 308.
15. Quotation from *Quia Maior*, trans. J. and L. Riley-Smith, *Crusades*, pp. 120–21. The full text is at pp. 119–24.
16. Robert of Courçon, *Summa*, x, 15, cited by J. W. Baldwin, *Masters, Princes and Merchants: The Social Views of Peter the Chanter and His Circle* (Princeton 1970), ii, 148–9 note 37, and see i, 211; cf. Russell, *Just War*, pp. 225–6 and note 37.
17. See Innocent's letter to members of the German clergy, *c.*May 1213, trans. J. and L. Riley-Smith, *Crusades*, pp. 130–31; for a list of crusaders being kept by one Master Hubert in England, Roger of Wendover, *Flores historiarum*, ii, 323.
18. J. and L. Riley-Smith, *Crusades*, pp. 131–2 for Innocent's correspondence and pp. 134–5 for an example of James of Vitry's preaching; for the abbot's letter book, F. Kempf, 'Das Rommersdorfer Briefbuch des 13 Jahrhunderts', *Mitteilungen des Österreichischen Instituts für Geschichtsforschung, Erganzungsband*, 12 (1933), 502–71.
19. *Magna Carta*, Clauses 52, 53 and 57.
20. On England, Tyerman, *England and the Crusades*, pp. 135, 136, 139; for Frederick, Powell, *Anatomy*, pp. 3, 23, 74, 75.
21. PL, 216, col. 830, no. xxxv.
22. For some of the letters of summons, see PL, 216, cols. 823–31.
23. Tanner, *Decrees*, p. 234.
24. Tanner, *Decrees*, pp. 267–71; J. and L. Riley-Smith, *Crusades*, pp. 125–9.
25. Delaborde et al., *Recueil des Actes de Philippe Auguste*, no. 1,360.
26. Official hostility was reflected in Guillaume le Breton's comments, R. Röhricht, ed., *Testimonia Minora de quinto bello sacro*, *Société de l'Orient Latin*, iii (Geneva 1882), 78–9 (trans. Powell, *Anatomy*, p. 35).
27. Cf. Powell, *Anatomy*, pp. 44–5 and note 50.
28. The forum for implementing Clause 12, 'no scutage or aid shall be imposed . . . unless by the common counsel of our kingdom', was explained in Clause 14, which details the

composition and summoning of a representative assembly of clerical and lay magnates and all tenants-in-chief.

29. Oliver of Paderborn, *Die Schriften des Kölner Domscholasters*, ed. H. Hoogeweg (Tübingen 1984), pp. 285–6, the account in a letter to the count of Namur; for other copies circulated, D. U. Baratier, 'A Propos de Jacques de Vitry', *Revue Bénédictine*, 27 (1910), 521–4, and for a translation, J. and L. Riley-Smith, *Crusades*, pp. 135–6; for the story in Oliver's account of the Damietta campaign, Peters, *Christian Society*, pp. 60–61.
30. Waitz, *Chronica Regia Colonensis*, pp. 192–3.
31. Burchardus Urspergensis, MGH SS, xxiii, 378–9.
32. E. Baratier, 'Une Prédication de la croisade à Marseille en 1224', *Economies et sociétés au moyen age: Mélanges offerts à Edouard Perroy* (Paris 1973), pp. 690–69.
33. James of Vitry, *Lettres*, p. 77; cf. his own misogynist *exemplum*, from his *Sermones Vulgares*, ed. T. F. Crane (London 1890), p. 56.
34. *Registro del Cardinale Ugolino d'Ostia*, ed. G. Levi (Rome 1890), esp. pp. 128–33; cf. pp. 7–9, 11–13, 19–24, 101, 109–10, 113–14, 138–40, 152–3; Powell, *Anatomy*, esp. pp. 33–50 (for Courçon's mission to France), 67–87.
35. *Ordinatio de predicatione S. Crucis in Angliae*, *Quinti Belli Sacri Scriptores Minores*, ed. R. Röhricht, *Société de l'Orient Latin*, ii (Geneva 1879), vii–x and 1–26; p. 24 for the definition of *exempla*.
36. Röhricht, *Ordinatio*, p. 22.
37. C. T. Maier, *Preaching the Crusades* (Cambridge 1994), pp. 118, 173. For Frisian pole-vaulters, J. A. Mol, 'Frisian Fighters and the Crusade', *Crusades*, 1 (2002), pp. 107–8.
38. Powell, *Anatomy*, esp. p. 35 and above, note 26.
39. Powell, *Anatomy*, pp. 38–9 for a discussion, and refs. at note 22, p. 48; Abbot Gervase of Premontré's account of popular unease, RHGF, xix, 604–5; Delaborde et al., *Recueil des Actes de Philippe Auguste*, no. 1360. For the agreement with Genoa for transport by the counts of Nevers and La Marche, *Annales Genuenses*, Rohricht, *Testimonia minora*, p. 238.
40. E.g. Tyerman, *England and the Crusades*, pp. 217–24.
41. James of Vitry, *Lettres*, p. 116.
42. Tyerman, *England and the Crusades*, pp. 95–101, 133–44, 180, 201, 205, 211, 227, 329.
43. For Savaric in Languedoc, and a note of his other crusading exploits, PVC, p. 130 and note 12.
44. E.g. by Oliver of Paderborn, *Capture of Damietta*, trans. Peters, *Christian Society*, pp. 49–139. (Hereafter Oliver of Paderborn.) (The Latin text is in Hoogeweg's 1894 Tübingen edition.)
45. Tyerman, *England and the Crusades*, pp. 98–9 and p. 401 notes 49 and 50 for refs.
46. Frederick's role is exhaustively discussed in Powell, *Anatomy*, passim.
47. Powell, *Anatomy*, p. 116.
48. James of Vitry, *Lettres*, pp. 73–4.
49. Thomas of Split, *Historia pontificum Spalatensis*, ed. L. von Heineman, MGH SS, xxix, 577–9, for Andrew's crusade; for the Venice treaty, *Monumenta spectantia historiam Slavorum meridionalium*, i (1868), 29–31; T. Van Cleve, 'The Fifth Crusade', *History of the Crusades*, ed. Setton, pp. 387–9; J. R. Sweeny, 'Hungary and the Crusades', *International History Review*, 3 (1981), 467–81.
50. The two main sources are the *Gesta Crucigerorum Rhenanorum* and *De Itinere Frisonum* in Röhricht, *Scriptores Minores*, pp. 29–56 and 59–70.
51. Oliver of Paderborn, p. 61 and pp. 53–9 for the Palestine campaigns of 1217–18. In general, also, see Röhricht, *Scriptores Minores* and *Testimonia Minora*; for Ibn al-Athir, see the extracts in Gabrieli, *Arab Historians*, pp. 255–66, and, for French translation, RHC Or., ii–i, and Abu Shamah's compilation, RHC Or., v. Powell, *Anatomy*, pp. 128–93 provides a thorough analytical account of the war in Palestine and Egypt with full references to eastern as well as western accounts and some discussion of sources.

52. Thomas of Split, *Historia*, pp. 578–9.
53. Mas Latrie *Chronique d'Ernoul*, pp. 414, 436; James of Vitry, *Lettres*, pp. 100, 102; Patriarch Aymar of Jerusalem's 1199 advice to Innocent III on Damietta, Bongars, *Gesta Dei Per Francos*, p. 1,128.
54. For this curious incident, J. M. Powell, 'Francesco d'Assisi e la Quinta Crociata', *Schede Medievali*, 4 (1983), 68–77; Kedar, *Crusade and Mission*, pp. 126–31.
55. Oliver of Paderborn, p. 62.
56. The *Eracles* Continuation of William of Tyre, RHC Occ., ii, 329.
57. Oliver of Paderborn, pp. 80, 104; cf. p. 115 for his *largesse* on the advance in July 1221.
58. *Epistolae selectae saeculi XIII*, ed. C. Rodenberg, MGH SS, i, no. 124, pp. 89–91 dated 24 July 1220. For a tabulation of the sums received and sent, Powell, *Anatomy*, p. 100.
59. RHC Occ., ii, 349.
60. Oliver of Paderborn, p. 102.
61. Oliver of Paderborn, pp. 122–3; E. Blochet, 'Extraits de l'histoire des patriarches d'Alexandrie relatifs au siège de Damiette', *Revue de l'Orient Latin*, II (1908), 260.
62. Letter trans. Peters, *Christian Society*, p. 141. Cf. James of Vitry, *Lettres*, pp. 150, 152; Oliver of Paderborn, p. 89.
63. As emphasized by Oliver of Paderborn, p. 124.
64. See the convenient table, Powell, *Anatomy*, p. 117 and the discussion pp. 166–72 and 187.
65. Oliver of Paderborn, pp. 107–8, perhaps somewhat *ben trovato*.
66. As revealed by James of Vitry, *Lettres*, p. 106; Oliver of Paderborn, p. 65 is modestly reticent.
67. Ibn al-Athir, Gabrieli, *Arab Historians*, p. 257.
68. Powell's guess, *Anatomy*, p. 148.
69. Ibn al-Athir, Gabrieli, *Arab Historians*, pp. 257–8.
70. RHC Occ., ii, 336.
71. Oliver of Paderborn, pp. 122, 125; Ibn al-Athir, Gabrieli, *Arab Historians*, p. 261.
72. Ibn al-Athir, Gabrieli, *Arab Historians*, pp. 257–8 and 260.
73. Ibn al-Athir, Gabrieli, *Arab Historians*, p. 260; Oliver of Paderborn, p. 108.
74. The gloom on the Ayyubid side is well captured by Ibn al-Athir, no friend to the dynasty, Gabrieli, *Arab Historians*, pp. 257–61.
75. Oliver of Paderborn, p. 114, figures based on those from the 'estimators of the army'.
76. Oliver of Paderborn, p. 105.
77. Above note 54 and Kedar, *Crusade and Mission*, passim.
78. Oliver of Paderborn, pp. 85–6; Blochet, 'Histoire des patriarches', p. 253; *Eracles*, RHC Occ., ii, 341–2; James of Vitry, *Lettres*, pp. 124–5; Ibn al-Athir, Gabrieli, *Arab Historians*, p. 260. Cf. Ernoul, p. 435.
79. Ibn al-Athir, Gabrieli, *Arab Historians*, p. 262; Oliver of Paderborn, p. 124.
80. See the end of the first section, addressed to Cologne, finished soon after the fall of Damietta in November 1219, Oliver of Paderborn, p. 89.
81. James of Vitry, *Lettres*, p. 141.
82. James of Vitry, *Lettres*, pp. 135, 139; cf. William of Tyre, *History*, bk V, chap. 10.
83. For these prophetic works and the rumours of 'David' and 'Prester John', Oliver of Paderborn, pp. 89–91, 112–14; James of Vitry, *Lettres*, pp. 141–53; Ibn al-Athir, Gabrieli, *Arab Historians*, p. 260; P. Pelliot, 'Deux passages de la *La Prophétie de Hanna, fils d'Isaac*', *Académie des Inscriptions et Belles Lettres, Mémoires*, 44 (1951), 73–96; cf. J. Richard, 'L'Extrême-Orient légendaire au moyen âge', *Orient et Occident* (Paris 1976), no. XXVI; Mayer, *Crusades*, p. 226; Powell, *Anatomy*, pp. 178–9.
84. Ibn al-Athir, Gabrieli, *Arab Historians*, p. 264.
85. Richard of San Germano, *Chronica*, quoted by Powell, *Anatomy*, p. 196. For a survey of other reactions, see Siberry, *Criticism of Crusading*, pp. 34–5, 85–6, 102–3, 107–8, 152–3, 165, 193.
86. John of Tubia, *De Johanne Rege Ierusalem*, *Scriptores Minores*, ed. Röhricht, pp. 138–9;

Eracles, RHC Occ., ii, 346, 348–9. Oliver of Paderborn provides a highly sanitized account, pp. 95–7.

87. Oliver of Paderborn, p. 104.
88. Oliver of Paderborn, pp. 101–2, 103–4; *Eracles*, RHC Occ., ii, 347, 349; Ernoul, in Röhricht *Testimonia Minora*, 300–301.
89. Van Cleve, 'Fifth Crusade', pp. 422–8; Powell, *Anatomy*, pp. 180–91. Cf. Oliver of Paderborn, pp. 114–34, and the letters recorded by Roger of Wendover, trans. pp. 142–5; *Eracles*, RHC Occ. ii, 350–52; Gabrieli, *Arab Historians*, pp. 261–6.
90. Peters, *Christian Society*, p. 144; cf. a similar image Oliver of Paderborn, p. 123.
91. Oliver of Paderborn, p. 132.
92. See below pp. 745–7.
93. Tyerman, *England and the Crusades*, pp. 99–101.
94. Although some resistance to further preaching was recorded in Germany, H. Hoogeweg, 'Die Kreuzzpredigt des Jahres 1224', *Deutsche Zeitschrift für Geschichtswissenschaft*, 4 (1890), 72–3.

20: Frontier Crusades 1: Conquest in Spain

1. Trans. Holt, *Age of Crusades*, p. 27.
2. Trans. J. and L. Riley-Smith, *Crusades*, p. 40.
3. In general, see now J. F. O'Callaghan, *Reconquest and Crusade in Medieval Spain* (Philadelphia 2003); for the myth, P. Linehan, *History and the Historians in Medieval Spain* (Oxford 1993).
4. R. Fletcher, *Moorish Spain* (London 1992), a very accessible introduction, esp. pp. 35–8, based on R. W. Bulliet, *Conversion to Islam in the Medieval Period* (Cambridge, Mass. 1979).
5. The central study of the crusade bulls from the eleventh to the twentieth century is J. Goni Gaztambide, *Historia de la bula de la cruzada* (Vitoria 1958).
6. As in R. I. Burns, *The Crusader Kingdom of Valencia*, 2 vols. (Cambridge, Mass. 1967) and his other pioneering works on the region.
7. See texts quoted by O'Callaghan, *Reconquest*, p. 5.
8. O'Callaghan, *Reconquest*, pp. 185–7.
9. Quoted, Fletcher, *Moorish Spain*, p. 75.
10. Glaber, *Historiarum*, pp. 82–5.
11. D. Wasserstein, *The Rise and Fall of the Party Kings* (Princeton 1985); for a corrective view of Spain and holy war, Bull, *Knightly Piety*.
12. Trans. Fletcher, *Moorish Spain*, p. 99.
13. Fletcher, *Moorish Spain*, pp. 100–110; idem, *The Quest for El Cid* (London 1989).
14. Trans. O'Callaghan, *Reconquest*, pp. 8, 30.
15. A. Ubieto Arteta, *Coleccion diplomatica de Pedro I de Aragon y Navarra* (Zaragoza 1951), p. 115 note 9.
16. O'Callaghan, *Reconquest*, p. 24 and note 6, p. 228; in general, R. Fletcher, 'Reconquest and Crusade in Spain c. 1050–1150', *Transactions of the Royal Historical Society*, 37 (1987), 31–47.
17. The phrase is R. Menendez Pidal's, *La España del Cid* (Madrid 1947), i, 147.
18. E. Emerton, *The Correspondence of Gregory VII* (New York 1969), p. 6; O'Callaghan, *Reconquest*, p. 29.
19. Contacts that impressed Bishop Pelayo of Orviedo (1101–30, 1142–3) in his *Chronicon regum Legionensium*, trans. S. Barton and R. Fletcher, *The World of El Cid* (Manchester 2000), pp. 87–8.
20. See, for example, the texts in Barton and Fletcher, *World of El Cid*, passim.
21. O'Callaghan, *Reconquest*, pp. 31–2 for translation; cf. Riley-Smith, *First Crusade*, pp. 18–20.
22. Ubieto Atreta, *Diplomatica Pedro I*, pp. 113 note 6 and 115 note 9.

23. *Historia Silense*, in Barton and Fletcher, *World of El Cid*, pp. 50–52.
24. *The Poem of the Cid*, ed. and trans. R. Hamilton, J. Perry and I. Michael (London 1984); Barton and Fletcher, *World of El Cid*, pp. 90–147 for the *Historia Roderici*.
25. See the discussion of this by R. Bartlett, *The Making of Europe* (London 1994), pp. 240–42.
26. See the discussion by N. Housley, *Religious Warfare in Europe 1400–1536* (Oxford 2002), esp. pp. 75–82, 201–4.
27. Mansi, *Sacrorum Conciliorum*, xxi (Venice 1776), col. 284; for a narrative, O'Callaghan, *Reconquest*, pp. 32–41.
28. J. and L. Riley-Smith, *Crusades*, p. 74.
29. R. Fletcher, *St James's Catapult* (Oxford 1984), pp. 298–9.
30. E. Lourie, 'The Will of Alfonso I', *Speculum*, 50 (1975), 635–51; A. Forey, 'The Will of Alfonso I', *Durham University Journal*, 73 (1980), 59–65; O'Callaghan, *Reconquest*, p. 40.
31. Caffaro, *Annales Ianuenses* and the *Ystoria captionis Almarie et Turtuose*, ed. L. T. Belgrano, *Fonti per la Storia d'Italia*, ii (Rome 1890), 33–5, 79–89; G. Constable, 'The Second Crusade as Seen by Contemporaries', *Traditio*, 9 (1953), 226–35; Eugenius III, 'Epistola et privilegia', PL clxxx, cols. 1,203–4.
32. *Coleccion de documentos ineditos de la Corona de Aragon*, ed. P. Bofarull et al. (Barcelona 1847–1910), iv, 314–15, no. 128; cf. N. Jaspert, 'Tortosa and the Crusades', *The Second Crusade*, ed. Phillips and Hoch, pp. 90–110.
33. Fletcher, *Moorish Spain*, p. 123.
34. O'Callaghan, *Reconquest*, pp. 62–4, and cf. pp. 59–61.
35. Above, notes 33 and 34.
36. In general see Forey, *The Military Orders*, pp. 23–32.
37. O'Callaghan, *Reconquest*, pp. 148–9.
38. For a recent discussion, O'Callaghan, *Reconquest*, pp. 70–76; for the financial precedents, ibid., pp. 152–76.
39. O'Callaghan, *Reconquest*, pp. 102, 119; in general see Bartlett, *Making of Europe*, esp. pp. 197–242.
40. See P. E. Russell, *Prince Henry the Navigator* (New Haven and London 2000); idem, 'Some Fifteenth Century Eyewitness Accounts of Travel in the Atlantic Ocean before 1492', *Historical Research*, 66 (1993), 115–28.
41. In general, see J. Muldoon, *Popes, Lawyers and Infidels* (Liverpool 1979).
42. Housley, *Religious Warfare*, esp. pp. 75–82, 201–4.
43. Toribio Motolinia, *History of the Indians of New Spain*, trans. E. A. Foster (Berkeley 1950), pp. 110–17. I am grateful to J.- J. Lopez Portillo for bringing this incident to my attention.
44. Quoted Housley, *Religious Warfare*, p. 202.

21: Frontier Crusades 2: the Baltic and the North

1. Bernard of Clairvaux, *Letters*, no. 394, p. 467; see above pp. 292–3, 304–5.
2. J. and L. Riley-Smith, *Crusades*, pp. 75–77.
3. Above pp. 221, 243–7.
4. Above pp. 251–3; in general, Lotter, 'The Crusading Idea'.
5. H. Richter, '*Militia Dei*', *Journeys Towards God*, ed. B. N. Sargent-Baur (Michigan 1992), pp. 107–26.
6. The best general account is by Christiansen, *Northern Crusades*; see also W. Urban, *The Baltic Crusade* (2nd edn Chicago 1994) and Bartlett, *Making of Europe*; A. V. Murray (ed.), *Crusade and Conversion on the Baltic Frontier 1150–1500* (Aldershot 2001), esp. the bibliography pp. 278–85, with important refs.
7. See note 1 above; Lotter, 'The Crusading Idea', p. 292; see rebuttals of Lotter in reviews by H. E. J. Cowdrey, *English Historical Review*, 94 (1979), 166–7; and J. Brundage, *Speculum*, 54 (1979), 172–3.

8. Jensen, 'Denmark and the Second Crusade', p. 169. This is the tone of much of Helmold of Bosau's account, below, note 9.
9. Helmold of Bosau, *Chronicle*, pp. 169, 176–7.
10. Otto of Freising, *Deeds of Frederick Barbarossa*, p. 76, cf. p. 79 for the rejection of Henry the Lion's suit at Frankfurt; above, pp. 292–3.
11. Helmold of Bosau, *Chronicle*, p. 180.
12. Jaffé, *Monumenta Corbeiensia*, p. 245; above pp. 305–8.
13. Jensen, 'Denmark and the Second Crusade', esp. pp. 165–72; see, in general, T. Riis, *Les Institutions politiques centrales du Danemark 1100–1332* (Odense 1977).
14. *De Profectione Danorum*, Gertz, *Scriptores*, ii, 465–7.
15. Trans. Christiansen, *Northern Crusades*, p. 69, and ref. note 37.
16. PL, 200, cols. 860–61.
17. Helmold of Bosau, *Chronicle*, p. 188.
18. Henry of Antwerp, *Tractatus de captione urbis Brandenburg*, ed. O. Holder-Egger, MGH (Hanover 1880), p. 484; trans. Bartlett, *Making of Europe*, p. 35.
19. Helmold of Bosau, *Chronicle*, p. 221.
20. Cf. trans. J. and L. Riley-Smith, *Crusades*, p. 77.
21. On the 1172 pilgrimage, Arnold of Lübeck, *Chronica Slavorum*, p. 10; generally, Helmold of Bosau, *Chronicle*, pp. 233, 242–5, 254–64, 266–7, 274–5, 281–2; Christiansen, *Northern Crusades*, pp. 61–2, 69–70, 72; Bartlett, *Making of Europe*, pp. 268, 274–8.
22. Arnold of Lübeck, *Chronica Slavorum*, p. 215.
23. Henry of Livonia, *Chronicon Livoniae*, ed. L. Arbusow and A. Bauer (Hanover 1955) (cf. trans. J. Brundage, *The Chronicle of Henry of Livonia* (Madison 1961)), XIV, 11; Christiansen, *Northern Crusades*, p. 95.
24. Henry of Livonia, *Chronicon*, p.9.
25. Innocent III to Valdemar II, J. and L. Riley-Smith, *Crusades*, p. 78.
26. For summaries, Forey, *The Military Orders*, esp. pp. 32–9; Christiansen, *Northern Crusades*, pp. 79–83, 99–103, 128.
27. Gregory IX, *Registres*, ed. L. Auvray et al. (Paris 1890–1955), no. 2,097 (cf. nos. 2,098–2,102); Henry of Livonia, *Chronicon*, pp. 23, 29, 31, 34, 92, 132; Christiansen, *Northern Crusades*, esp. pp. 127–8; Bartlett, *Making of Europe*, p. 195.
28. Christiansen, *Northern Crusades*, pp. 95–7, 221–2, 224–5.
29. Trans. Christiansen, *Northern Crusades*, p. 128.
30. See, e.g., refs. and trans. of Bacon's *Opus Maius* and Humbert's *Opusculum tripartitum*, Christiansen, *Northern Crusades*, p. 152.
31. Arnold of Lübeck, 'De conversione Livonie', *Chronica Slavorum*, pp. 212–31; Henry of Livonia, *Chronicon*, pp. 6–12 et seq.
32. PL, 215, cols. 428–30.
33. Christiansen, *Northern Crusades*, p. 98; Bartlett, *Making of Europe*, p. 268 for Riga's Fifth Crusade contribution.
34. For Livonia, W. Urban, *Baltic Crusade*; Christiansen, *Northern Crusade*, esp. pp. 93–104.
35. For Livonia after 1300, W. Urban, *The Livonian Crusade* (Washington, DC 1981). In general, N. Housley, *The Later Crusades* (Oxford 1992).
36. Apart from the general surveys, see T. Lindkvist, 'Crusades and Crusading Ideology in the Political History of Sweden', *Crusade and Conversion*, ed. Murray, pp. 119–30; Jensen, 'Denmark and the Second Crusade'.
37. PL, 200, cols. 860–61.
38. Henry of Livonia, *Chronicon*, p. 43.
39. Christiansen, *Northern Crusades*, esp. pp. 109–13, 132–7.
40. See note 39 and ibid., pp. 177–98.
41. For refs. to the *Revelationes S. Brigittae*, Christiansen, *Northern Crusades*, p. 276 note 135 and pp. 190–92.

42. W. Urban, *The Prussian Crusade* (Lanham 1980); Christiansen, *Northern Crusades*, pp. 104–9 and pp. 199–226.
43. Gregory IX, *Registres*, no. 2,097.
44. *Codex Diplomaticus Prussicus*, ed. J. Voigt (Königsberg 1836–61), i, 59–60.
45. See, apart from the general works cited, M. Burleigh, 'The Military Orders in the Baltic', *New Cambridge Medieval History*, v, ed. D. Abulafia (Cambridge 1999), pp. 743–53.
46. E. N. Johnson, 'The German Crusade in the Baltic', *History of the Crusades*, ed. Setton, iii, esp. pp. 572–3.
47. *Epistolae saeculi XIII e regestis pontificum romanorum*, ed. G. H. Pertz and C. Rodenberg, MGH, ii (Berlin 1887), no. 5.
48. Voigt, *Codex Diplomaticus Prussicus*, i, 59–60.
49. Alexander IV, *Registres*, ed. C. Bourel de la Roncière et al. (Paris 1895–1953), no. 3,068.
50. In general, Urban, *Livonian Crusade*; Christiansen, *Northern Crusades*, pp. 138–98; A. Ehlers, 'The Crusade of the Teutonic Knights Reconsidered', *Crusade and Conversion*, ed. Murray, pp. 21–44.
51. Bruno of Olmütz's *Relatio*, ed. C. Hofler, 'Analecta zur Geschichte Deutschlands und Italiens', *Abhandlungen der historischen Classe der Königlich Bayerischen Akademie der Wissenschaften*, 3rd series, 4 (1846), 1–28.
52. *Liv-, Esth-, und Curländisches Urkundenbuch*, ed. F. G. Bunge (Revel and Riga 1853–1910), ii, no. 630.
53. In general, W. Paravicini, *Die Preussenreisen des europäischen Adels* (Sigmaringen 1989–).
54. G. Chaucer, *General Prologue* to *The Canterbury Tales*, ll. 52–4.
55. For what follows, Tyerman, *England and the Crusades*, pp. 266–76; M. Keen, 'Chaucer's Knight, the English Aristocracy, and the Crusade', *English Court Culture in the Later Middle Ages*, ed. V. J. Scattergood and J. W. Sherborne (London 1983).
56. *Calendar of Patent Rolls* (Public Record Office, London 1901–), *1367–70*, pp. 24, 56, 57, 58, 64, 72, 127, 128.
57. *Calendar of Papal Registers*, ed. W. T. Bliss et al. (London 1893–1960), iv, 19.
58. J. Capgrave, *De Illustribus Henricis*, ed. F. C. Hingeston, Rolls Series (London 1858), p. 99; cf. Ehlers, 'Crusade of the Teutonic Knights'.
59. Tyerman, *England and the Crusades*, p. 272 and note 55 for ref. to Henry's accounts.
60. *Calendar of Close Rolls* (Public Record Office, London 1902–), *1374–77*, p. 11.
61. For these commercial aspects, Tyerman, *England and the Crusades*, pp. 272–4.
62. In general, Christiansen, *Northern Crusades*, pp. 227–58; M. Burleigh, *Prussian Society and the German Order 1410–66* (Cambridge 1984).
63. See the discussion, Christiansen, *Northern Crusades*, pp. 231–41.

22: Survival and Decline: the Frankish Holy Land in the Thirteenth Century

1. In general, Holt, *Age of the Crusades*, esp. pp. 53–106, 138–53; Irwin, *Middle East*, esp. pp. 21–84.
2. E.g. Runciman, *History of the Crusades*, iii, passim. Cf. Mayer, *Crusades*, esp. pp. 247–59, 272–88.
3. Edbury, *Cyprus*.
4. *Eracles*, RHC Occ., ii, 313–15, 318, 347–8, 349.
5. E.g. John of Jaffa's *Livre des Assises* (1264×66).
6. See the work on Acre by D. Jacoby, *Studies on the Crusader States and on Venetian Expansion* (Northampton 1989).
7. J. Riley-Smith, *The Feudal Nobility and the Kingdom of Jerusalem 1174–1277* (London 1973), p. 48 and refs.; Mayer, *Crusades*, pp. 278–9.
8. D. Jacoby, 'Montmusard, Suburb of Crusader Acre', *Outremer*, ed. Kedar et al., pp. 205–17.

9. Matthew Paris, 'Itinéraire de Londres à Jerusalem', ed. H. Michelant and G. Raynaud, *Itinéraires à Jerusalem* (Geneva 1882), p. 137.
10. *Eracles*, p. 428 mentions the Frankish army at the battle of Gaza included 600 knights, more or less exactly the figure estimated as the kingdom's levy in the 1180s. For trade, E. Ashtor, *Levant Trade in the Later Middle Ages* (Princeton 1983).
11. Riley-Smith, *Feudal Nobility*, pp. 175–84, 208–9; Edbury, *John of Ibelin* pp. 67–8.
12. Willibrand of Olbenburg's description of the Ibelin palace in Beirut, which he visited in 1212, *Peregrinatores medii aevi quatuor*, ed. J. C. M. Laurent (Leipzig 1864), pp. 166 et seq.
13. Marino Sanudo Torsello, *Secreta Fidelium Crucis*, ed. J. Bongars (Hanau 1611), ii, 1–33 (Book I).
14. Mayer, *Crusades*, pp. 278–9.
15. D. Jacoby, 'L'Expansion occidentale dans le Levant: les Vénitiens à Acre dans la seconde moitié du treizième siècle', *Journal of Medieval History*, 3 (1977), 225–64.
16. Trans. Kennedy, *Crusader Castles*, pp. 190–98, at p. 194.
17. *Les Gestes des Chiprois*, RHC Arm. ii (Paris 1906), bk III, trans. P. Crawford, *The Templar of Tyre: Part III of the 'Deeds of the Cypriots'* (Aldershot 2003), chap. 382.
18. John of Joinville, *The Life of St Louis*, trans. M. R. B. Shaw, *Chronicles of the Crusades* (London 1963), p. 252.
19. See Crawford, *Templar of Tyre*, pp. 4–5.
20. Holt, *Age of Crusades*, p. 93.
21. Above p. 509.
22. E.g. above, note 9.
23. Matthew Paris, *Chronica Majora*, iv, 488–9.
24. Gregory X, *Registres*, ed. J. Guiraud and E. Cadier (Paris 1892–1906), nos. 160–61; cf. no. 220; this advice is discussed by P. Throop, *Criticism of the Crusade* (Amsterdam 1940).
25. M. Barber, 'The Crusade of the Shepherds in 1251', *Proceedings of the 10th Annual Meeting of the Western Society for French History*, ed. J. F. Sweet (Lawrence 1984); G. Dickson, 'The Advent of the *Pastores* (1251), *Revue Belge de Philologie et d'Histoire*, 66 (1988), 249–67.
26. For the treaties, see T. Van Cleve, 'The Crusade of Frederick II', *History of the Crusades*, ed. Setton, ii, 455–6; P. Jackson, 'The Crusades of 1239–41 and Their Aftermath', *Bulletin of the School of Oriental and African Studies*, 50 (1987), 32–60.
27. *Eracles*, pp. 427–31; cf. pp. 562–6 for the Rothelin Continuation version.
28. Holt, *Age of Crusades*, esp. pp. 86–8, 91–2, 102; Irwin, *Middle East*, pp. 37–102; C. Cahen, 'The Mongols and the Near East', *History of the Crusades*, ii, 715–32.
29. For references to the arrivals of foreign troops, *Eracles*, pp. 441–78; C. J. Marshall, 'The French Regiment in the Latin East 1254–91', *Journal of Medieval History*, 15 (1989); on Geoffrey of Sergines, J. Riley-Smith, *What Were the Crusades?*, (3rd edn London 2003), pp. 77–80; for Olivier of Termes, Langlois, *Olivier de Termes*, pp. 128–34, 137–42, 211–32.
30. J. R. Strayer, 'The Crusade of Louis IX', *History of the Crusades*, ed. Setton, ii, 508.
31. Gregory X, *Registres*, nos. 802–3; *Eracles*, p. 462.
32. Tyerman, *England and the Crusades*, p. 125 and note 59, p. 405.
33. In general, Runciman, *History of the Crusades*, iii, 76–104, 171–233, 293–348, 387–423; Mayer, *Crusades*, esp. pp. 239–59, 272–88; Riley-Smith, *Feudal Nobility*, passim; Edbury, *John of Ibelin*, pp. 1–103; idem, *Cyprus*, pp. 23–100; Holt, *Age of the Crusades*, pp. 60–66, 82–104.
34. *Eracles*, p. 305.
35. Charles of Anjou, who in 1277 bought Maria of Antioch's claim to the throne of Jerusalem, below pp. 731–2, 817–18.
36. *Eracles*, p. 220; Runciman, *History of the Crusades*, iii, 93 and note 2.
37. Edbury, *Cyprus*, p. 32.

38. Edbury, *Cyprus*, pp. 39–73.
39. *Eracles*, pp. 306–10.
40. See above chapter 19.
41. The main source, if heavily biased against the Hohenstaufen and in favour of the Ibelins, is Philip of Novara, *The Wars of Frederick II Against the Ibelins*, trans. J. La Monte and M. J. Hubert (New York 1936).
42. Riley-Smith, *Feudal Nobility*, pp. 177–84.
43. P. Jackson, 'The End of Hohenstaufen Rule in Syria', *Bulletin of the Institute of Historical Research*, 59 (1986), 20–36; D. Jacoby, 'The Kingdom of Jerusalem and the Collapse of Hohenstaufen Power in the Levant', *Dumbarton Oaks Papers*, 40 (1986), 83–101.
44. Above note 11. Simon played the leading role in establishing the Commune of England in 1258.
45. Cf. Riley-Smith, *What Were the Crusades?*, pp. 77–80.
46. Jacoby, 'L'Expansion occidentale'.
47. Edbury, *John of Ibelin*, esp. pp. 96–7; Riley-Smith, *Feudal Nobility*, pp. 215–7.
48. Edbury, *John of Ibelin*, esp. p. 96; for examples, see Gabrieli, *Arab Historians*, pp. 312–16, 323–33.
49. Ibn Furat's chronicle trans. M. C. Lyons and J. Riley-Smith, *Ayyubids, Mamlukes and Crusaders*, ii, 104–5, 113, 135, 164; *Eracles*, pp. 462, 479; Runciman, *History of the Crusades*, pp. 342–3; idem, 'The Crusader States 1243–91', *History of the Crusades*, ed. Setton, ii, 580, 584, 586; Riley-Smith, *Feudal Nobility*, pp. 28, 224; Edbury, *Cyprus*, pp. 91, 96 and note 84.
50. On John and his lawbook, Edbury, *John of Ibelin*, passim, esp. pp. 58–106. The text of John's book is in RHC Lois, i.
51. John of Joinville, *Life of Louis*, pp. 203–4, 269–70, 295, 297.
52. Edbury, *John of Ibelin*, p. 106. For the redating of 'Bracton', *De Legibus et consuetudinibus Angliae*, ed. and trans. S. E. Thorne (Cambridge, Mass. 1968–77).
53. H. Buchtal, *Miniature Painting in the Latin Kingdom of Jerusalem* (Oxford 1957); J. Folda, *Crusader Manuscript Illumination at Saint-Jean d'Acre 1275–91* (Princeton 1976); idem, 'Art in the Latin East', *Oxford Illustrated History of the Crusades*, ed. Riley-Smith, pp. 66–90.
54. E.g. Kennedy, *Crusader Castles*; D. Pringle, 'Architecture in the Latin East', *Oxford Illustrated History of the Crusades*, ed. Riley-Smith, pp. 160–83.
55. A. Jotischky, *The Perfection Solicitude: Hermits and Monks in the Crusader States* (Philadelphia 1995).
56. John of Joinville, *Life of Louis*, p. 297.
57. For a commentary, Edbury, *Cyprus*, esp. pp. 39–73 and idem, *John of Ibelin*, pp. 1–103.
58. Riley-Smith, *Feudal Nobility*, pp. 220–28; Edbury, *Cyprus*, pp. 90–100; Mayer, *Crusades*, pp. 282–7.
59. *Gestes des Chyprois*, Arm. ii, Bk iii, and Crawford, *Templar of Tyre*, chap. 410; Gabrieli, *Arab Historians*, p. 343.
60. Gabrieli, *Arab Historians*, pp. 326–33.
61. See below, pp. 818–22.
62. Ludolph of Suchem, *Liber de Itinere Terrae Sanctae*, ed. F. Deycks (Stuttgart 1851), p. 89.

23: The Defence of the Holy Land 1221–44

1. Waverley Annals, *Annales Monastici*, ed. Luard, ii, 295.
2. *Regesto del cardinale Ugolino d'Ostia*, ed. G. Levi (Rome 1890).
3. Baratier, 'Une prédication de la croisade à Marseille', pp. 690–99.
4. *Archives de l'Hôtel Dieu de Paris*, ed. L. Briele (Paris 1894), no. 203, pp. 87–8.
5. E.g. the 1237 case of Peter of Erdington's land in Shropshire, *Curia Regis Rolls* (London 1922–), xvi, 31 no. 115.

6. Roger of Wendover, *Flores*, ii, 323.
7. N. Vincent, *Peter des Roches* (Cambridge 1996), p. 234.
8. Tyerman, *Invention of the Crusades*, p. 86 and notes 249–51 for refs.
9. S. Lloyd, 'Political Crusades in England c.1215–17 and c.1263–5', *Crusade and Settlement*, ed. Edbury, pp. 113–20; Tyerman, *England and the Crusades*, pp. 144–51.
10. F. M. Powicke, *The Thirteenth Century* (Oxford 1962), p. 80.
11. Theobald of Champagne, *Seigneurs, sachiez: oui or ne s'en ira* l. 18 'the ashy people will remain behind', trans. M. Routledge, *An Eyewitness History of the Crusades*, ed. C. J. Tyerman, Folio Society (London 2004), iv, 269; Rutebeuf, *La desputizions dou croisié et dou descroisié* in *Onze poèmes concernant la croisade*, ed. J. Bastin and E. Faral (Paris 1946), pp. 84–94.
12. Vincent, *Peter des Roches*, p. 252 and refs. at note 118.
13. In general, T. C. Van Cleve, *The Emperor Frederick II of Hohenstaufen* (Oxford 1972), pp. 158–233; idem, 'The Crusade of Frederick II', 429–62; D. Abulafia, *Frederick II* (London 1988), pp. 148–201; Mayer, *Crusades*, pp. 228–38.
14. Van Cleve, *Frederick II*, p. 229.
15. Above p. 491.
16. The contemporary Ibn Wasil's account in Gabrieli, *Arab Historians*, pp. 267–8, 269–70; Maqrizi, *Histoire d'Egypte*, trans. E. Blocquet, *Revue de l'Orient Latin*, 9 (1901), 509–10 seems based on this.
17. MGH *Constitutiones et Acta publica Imperatorum et Regum*, iv (Hanover 1896), ed. L. Weiland, IV-ii, 129–31, no. 102.
18. Richard of San Germano, *Chronica*, ed. G. H. Pertz, MGH SS, xix (Hanover 1866), 347–9, cf. pp. 343–4; Vincent, *Peter des Roches*, pp. 238–9 and refs. notes 52 and 53.
19. Vincent, *Peter des Roches*, pp. 233–4.
20. Above, note 13.
21. Vincent, *Peter des Roches*, pp. 229–58; K. R. Giles, 'Two English Bishops in the Holy Land', *Nottingham Medieval Studies*, 31 (1987), 46–57; Lloyd, *English Society*, in index under 'Peter des Roches', 'William Brewer', etc.; Tyerman, *England and the Crusades*, pp. 99–101.
22. *Calendar of Patent Rolls 1225–32*, pp. 90–91; Vincent, *Peter des Roches*, pp. 235–9 for Bishop Peter's finances.
23. Roger of Wendover, *Flores*, ii, 323; *Calendar of Liberate Rolls* (Public Record Office, London 1916–64), *1226–40*, p. 93 for Aubigny.
24. A. Forey, 'The Military Order of St Thomas of Acre', *English Historical Review*, 92 (1977), 481–503.
25. Holt, *Age of Crusades*, pp. 63–5; cf. R. S. Humphreys, *From Saladin to the Mongols: The Ayyubids of Damascus* (Albany 1977).
26. John of Joinville, *Histoire de St Louis*, ed. N. M. Wailly (Paris 1868), pp. 69–70.
27. Gabrieli, *Arab Historians*, p. 268.
28. Sibt Ibn al-Jauzi, Gabrieli, *Arab Historians*, pp. 273–4; cf. pp. 272–3 for Ibn Wasil's account.
29. Giovanni Codagnelli (a Piacenza notary fl. 1200–30), *Annales Placentini*, ed. O. Holder-Egger, *Scriptores Rerum Germanicarum* (Hanover 1901), pp. 85–6.
30. J. L. Huillard-Bréholles, *Historia Diplomagtica Friderici Secundi* (Paris 1852–61), iii, 23–30; Gregory IX, *Registres*, nos. 178–9.
31. According to the hostile Philip of Novara, *Wars of Frederick II*, p. 73; for preparations, Richard of San Germano, *Chronica*, pp. 348–9.
32. Roger of Wendover, *Flores*, ii, 351–2 and generally, pp. 364–73. For the events of 1227–9, *Eracles*, pp. 363–75; Philip of Novara, *Wars of Frederick II*, pp. 73–92 (who emphasizes Frederick's confrontation with the Ibelins in Cyprus).
33. For these and other exchanges, *Eracles*, pp. 369–72; Gabrieli, *Arab Historians*, pp. 267–75.
34. Translations, Van Cleve, *Frederick II*, p. 217 and see notes 3 and 4.

35. Van Cleve, *Frederick II*, p. 217 note 5.
36. Gabrieli, *Arab Historians*, p. 270.
37. Van Cleve, *Frederick II*, pp. 219–20, reconstructs the treaty that has not survived.
38. Gabrieli, *Arab Historians*, p. 271; in general pp. 270–71, 273–4.
39. Gerold's encyclical letter condemning Frederick is translated in Peters, *Christian Society*, pp. 165–70, taken from Matthew Paris's version.
40. Riley-Smith, *Feudal Nobility*, pp. 171–2.
41. Trans. Peters, *Christian Society*, pp. 164–5.
42. Richard of San Germano, *Chronica*, p. 355.
43. Gabrieli, *Arab Historians*, p. 270.
44. Roger of Wendover, *Flores*, ii, 372; trans. Peters, *Christian Society*, p. 156.
45. Above pp. 725–7.
46. Gabrieli, *Arab Historians*, p. 275.
47. Philip of Novara, *Wars of Frederick II*, p. 91; cf. pp. 87–92 for opposition to Frederick.
48. Van Cleve, *Frederick II*, p. 528 and note 1.
49. The Rothelin Continuation of William of Tyre, *Eracles*, pp. 526–7, and, for what follows, pp. 526–56 and, for Eracles Continuation itself, pp. 413–22, trans. J. Shirley, *Crusader Syria in the Thirteenth Century* (Aldershot 1999), p. 38 and, generally, pp. 38–58, 123–9.
50. For 1239–41, apart from the general surveys for background, S. Painter, 'The Crusade of Theobald of Champagne and Richard of Cornwall', *History of the Crusades*, ed. Setton, ii, 463–85; Lloyd, *English Society*, esp. pp. 22, 58, 83, 86, 90, 92–3, 136, 149, 151, 178, 182; Tyerman, *England and the Crusades*, pp. 101–8; P. Jackson, 'The Crusades of 1239–41 and Their Aftermath', *Bulletin of the School of Oriental and African Studies*, 50 (1987), 32–60.
51. Theobald of Champagne, '*Seigneurs Sachiez: oui or ne s'en ira*', trans. Routledge, *Eyewitness History of the Crusades*, ed. Tyerman, iv, 268.
52. Roger of Wendover, *Flores*, iii, 104–7; Gregory IX, *Registres*, nos. 2,180–9.
53. Gregory IX, *Registres*, no. 2,664.
54. Gregory IX, *Registres*, nos. 3,923, 3,926.
55. Tyerman, *England and the Crusades*, pp. 104–6 for Richard's financial arrangements.
56. Gregory IX, *Registres*, no. 4,107; Painter, 'Crusade', p. 466.
57. Matthew Paris, *Chronica Majora*, iii, 368–9.
58. Matthew Paris, *Chronica Majora*, iv, 7; Dunstable Annals, *Annales Monastici*, ed. Luard, iii, 152.
59. Tyerman, *England and the Crusades*, pp. 104–5; Painter, 'Crusade', p. 466.
60. *Eracles*, pp. 527–8; Thomas Wykes, *Chronicon*, *Annales Monastici*, ed. Luard, iv, 86–7.
61. Matthew Paris, *Chronica Majora*, iii, 620; in general, Tyerman, *England and the Crusades*, pp. 102–4, 107.
62. Lloyd, *English Society*, pp. 83–4, 136; Tyerman, *England and the Crusades*, pp. 103–4.
63. Painter, 'Crusade', p. 469.
64. The most detailed account is in the Rothelin continuation of William of Tyre, *Eracles*, pp. 531–46; trans. Shirley, *Crusader Syria*, pp. 41–50, p. 46 for quotation.
65. Eracles, p. 554; Shirley, *Crusader Syria*, p. 57.
66. Painter, 'Crusade', p. 482.
67. Gregory IX, *Registres*, nos. 3,363, 3,633, 4,027, cf. 4,315.
68. Burton Annals, *Annales Monastici*, ed. Luard, i, 265–7; Matthew Paris, *Chronica Majora*, iv, 38–43.
69. Mathew Paris, *Chronica Majora*, iii, 620.
70. Trans. Routledge, *Eyewitness History of the Crusades*, ed. Tyerman, iv, 290; cf. Shirley, *Crusader Syria*, p. 55.
71. Matthew Paris, *Chronica Majora*, iv, 71.
72. Lloyd, *English Society*, Appendix 5 for the contract and pp. 135–7 for a discussion of it.

73. *Eracles*, p. 532; Shirley, *Crusader Syria*, p. 42.
74. *Eracles*, pp. 531–2; Shirley, *Crusader Syria*, p. 41.
75. *Eracles*, pp. 533–6, 538–9; Shirley, *Crusader Syria*, pp. 42–4, 45–6.
76. The best analysis of these manoeuvres is Jackson, 'Crusades of 1239–41'.
77. *Eracles*, p. 554; Shirley, *Crusader Syria*, p. 57.
78. Matthew Paris, *Chronica Majora*, iv, 138–44.
79. Above p. 726.
80. D. Pringle, 'King Richard I and the Walls of Ascalon', pp. 143–6.
81. *Eracles*, p. 421; Shirley, *Crusader Syria*, p. 129.
82. Matthew Paris, *Chronica Majora*, iv, 107, 143–5, 211–12, 218.
83. *Eracles*, p. 556; Shirley, *Crusader Syria*, p. 58.

24: Louis IX and the Fall of Mainland Outremer 1244–91

1. See above Chapter 22.
2. *Eracles*, p. 564 and generally pp. 561–6; Shirley, *Crusader Syria*, p. 65 and pp. 62–6.
3. Holt, *Age of the Crusades*, p. 66; Irwin, *Middle East*, pp. 18–19.
4. A. Potthast, *Regesta Pontificum Romanorum* (Berlin 1874–5), no. 11,491, 31 Dec. 1244.
5. The classic, if not necessarily accurate, account, written over sixty years later, is John of Joinville, *Life of Louis*, p. 191; cf. Matthew Paris, *Chronica Majora*, iv, 397–8 for mystical implications of the cross; cf. Tyerman, *Invention of the Crusades*, pp. 82–3. For modern general discussions in English, see especially W. C. Jordan, *Louis IX and the Challenge of the Crusade* (Princeton 1979), esp. pp. 3–13; J. Richard, *St Louis: Crusader King of France*, ed. S. Lloyd, trans. J. Birrell (Cambridge 1993), pp. 99–112; Strayer, 'Crusades', pp. 487–508.
6. Matthew Paris, *Chronica Majora*, iv, 397–8; v, 3–4; for William, see P. Biller, *The Measure of Multitude* (Oxford 2000), chap. 3, and esp. p. 85.
7. Potthast, *Regesta*, no. 11,492; Matthew Paris, *Chronica Majora*, iv, 410–12; cf. p. 391 for a meeting between Louis, Innocent IV and another future crusader, the duke of Burgundy, at Cîteaux on Holy Cross Day, 14 September 1244.
8. Potthast, *Regesta*, no. 11,491; T. Rymer, *Foedera*, (3rd edn London 1745), 1-i, 148–9 (crusade bull to Henry III, 23 Jan. 1245); F. M. Delorme, 'Bulle d'Innocent IV pour la croisade', *Archivum Franciscanum Historicum*, 6 (1913), 386–9; cf. Maier, *Preaching*, p. 62 et seq.
9. *Analecta Novissima Spicilegii Solesmensis*, ed. J. P. Pitra (Paris 1885–8), ii, 331–2 (Odo of Châteauroux's Sermon XII); in general for his crusade sermons, nos. XI, XII, XIV, XV, pp. 328–33.
10. Tyerman, *England and the Crusades*, esp. pp. 111–13 and refs.
11. Maier, *Preaching*, p. 70 and, generally, pp. 62–70.
12. Innocent IV, *Registres*, ed. E. Berger (Paris 1884–1921), no. 2,935.
13. Maier, *Preaching*, pp. 67, 140–42; Eudes Rigaud, *Regestum visitati*, ed. E. Bonnin (Rouen 1853), p. 733; Tyerman, *Invention of the Crusades*, pp. 44–5.
14. Maier, *Preaching*, pp. 101–2.
15. For recruitment, Jordan, *Louis IX*, pp. 14–34, 65–104; Richard, *St Louis*, pp. 99–112; Strayer, 'Crusades', pp. 487–93.
16. Jordan, *Louis IX*, p. 66.
17. Innocent IV, *Registres*, no. 2,644.
18. *Etablissements et coutumes, assises et arrest de l'échiquier de Normandie au treizième siècle*, ed. M. A. J. Marnier (Paris 1839), p. 201; *Layettes du Trésor des Chartes*, ed. A. Teulet et al. (Paris 1863–1909), ii, no. 3,560.
19. John of Joinville, *Life of Louis*, p. 192.
20. See especially Jordan, *Louis IX*, pp. 35–64; R. Bartlett, 'Louis IX, Towns and Enquêteurs Réformateurs', *Journal of Medieval History*, 5 (1979).

21. Jordan, *Louis IX*, p. 49.
22. RHGF, xxi, 404. For finances, Jordan, *Louis IX*, pp. 65–104.
23. For figures and calculations, Jordan, *Louis IX*, pp. 94–9.
24. RHGF, xxi, 540; Innocent IV, *Registres*, no. 3,708.
25. Eudes de Rigaud, *Regestum visitati*, p. 733.
26. Innocent IV, *Registres*, no. 3,708.
27. Maier, *Preaching*, p. 67.
28. See the case of Hugh of Rodez, Maier, *Preaching*, pp. 143–5.
29. RHGF, xxi, 532–40; Jordan, *Louis IX*, pp. 79–82; Strayer, 'Crusades', pp. 490–91.
30. John of Joinville, *Life of Louis*, p. 198.
31. Jordan, *Louis IX*, pp. 100–102, and table p. 102.
32. RHGF, xxi, 513–15, trans. J. and L. Riley-Smith, *Crusades*, pp. 149–52 for the 1250–53 expenses; cf. Jordan, *Louis IX*, pp. 78–104; Strayer, '*Crusades*', pp. 492, 504.
33. A. Jal, *Pacta Naulorum, Documents historiques inédits*, ed. M. Champollion-Figéac (Paris 1841–3), i, 605–9; ii, 51–7; L. T. Belgrano, 'Une charte de nolis de S. Louis', *Archives de l'Orient Latin*, 2 (1884), 231–6.
34. Jal, *Pacta Naulorum*, ii, 66–7; RHGF, xxi, 283, cf. pp. 223–4, 260–84.
35. John of Joinville, *Life of Louis*, pp. 320–1; Jal, *Pacta Naulorum*, p. 63; Strayer, 'Crusades', p. 492; Jordan, *Louis IX*, p. 103.
36. Matthew Paris, *Chronica Majora*, v, 93; WP, pp. 112–3.
37. John of Joinville, *Life of Louis*, p. 197; Jordan, *Louis IX*, p. 76 note 82 for discussion and refs. re. salt pork.
38. John of Joinville, *Life of Louis*, p. 191–2, 194–7.
39. John of Joinville, *Life of Louis*, p. 195.
40. Richard, *St Louis*, pp. 99–112 summarizes Louis's plans, preparations and departure; for the relics of the Passion, see Angold, *Fourth Crusade*, pp. 237–40.
41. John of Joinville, *Life of Louis*, p. 197. For modern narratives and discussion in English of the Egyptian campaign, Strayer, 'Crusades', pp. 493–504; Richard, *St Louis*, pp. 113–52; Holt, *Age of Crusades*, pp. 82–4; Irwin, *Middle East*, pp. 19–27. The most vivid chronicle account is John of Joinville, *Life of Louis*, pp. 195–264; the Rothelin continuation of William of Tyre included an important letter from Jean Sarasin and other details, *Eracles*, pp. 566–71, 589–623; Shirley, *Crusader Syria*, pp. 66–9, 85–108.
42. John of Colonna, RHGF, xxiii, 19 for the vessels.
43. For a recent discussion, P. Jackson, *The Mongols and the West* (London 2005), esp. chaps. 3–7.
44. Jackson, *Mongols*, pp. 87–93 and refs.
45. Described by the well-informed Jean Sarasin, *Eracles*, pp. 569–71; Shirley, *Crusader Syria*, pp. 68–9; John of Joinville, *Life of Louis*, pp. 197–8, 282–3; cf. Jackson, *Mongols*, pp. 98–100.
46. John of Joinville, *Life of Louis*, p. 288, and generally pp. 282–8.
47. See the lurid but serious fascination shown by Matthew Paris throughout his *Chronica Majora*, e.g. iv, 76–8, 270–77, 386–9; for his drawing of alleged Mongol cannibalism, M. R. James (ed.), 'The Drawings of Matthew Paris', *Walpole Society*, 14 (1925–6), no. 86. For the cultural and intellectual significance of such opening of the east to direct western scrutiny, Biller, *Measure of Multitude*, chap. 9, esp. pp. 227–35.
48. For numbers, Strayer, 'Crusades,' pp. 493–4.
49. On this contingent, Tyerman, *England and the Crusades*, pp. 108–10; Lloyd, *English Society*, p. 137, and notes 105–6 for refs.
50. *Eracles*, p. 571; Shirley, *Crusader Syria*, p. 69.
51. John of Joinville, *Life of Louis*, pp. 203–4.
52. John of Joinville, *Life of Louis*, p. 214.
53. *Eracles*, p. 592; Shirley, *Crusader Syria*, p. 87.
54. Ibn Wasil, Gabrieli, *Arab Historians*, pp. 286, 288 and, generally for the Nile campaign, pp. 284–302.

55. John of Joinville, *Histoire* (French text), p. 140; John of Joinville, *Life of Louis*, p. 262 omits the detail that the Frenchman had come to Egypt with the Fifth Crusade.
56. John of Joinville, *Life of Louis*, p. 210.
57. After her own interlude in power in the summer of 1250, she promptly married her successor, the Turkish emir Aybak.
58. *Eracles*, pp. 594–5; Shirley, *Crusader Syria*, p. 89.
59. For the timber for war machines, John of Joinville, *Life of Louis*, pp. 213–17; *Eracles*, p. 600; Shirley, *Crusader Syria*, pp. 92–3.
60. For the victory and defeat at Mansourah, John of Joinville, *Life of Louis*, pp. 218–42; cf. the Rothelin version, *Eracles*, pp. 599–616; Shirley, *Crusader Syria*, pp. 92–103; Gabrieli, *Arab Historians*, pp. 288–95.
61. Gabrieli, *Arab Historians*, p. 90.
62. John of Joinville, *Life of Louis*, p. 225.
63. John of Joinville, *Life of Louis*, p. 222.
64. John of Joinville, *Life of Louis*, p. 224.
65. John of Joinville, *Life of Louis*, p. 222.
66. P. Cole, D. L. d'Avray, J. Riley-Smith, 'Application of Theology to Current Affairs: Memorial Sermons on the Dead of Mansourah and on Innocent IV', *Historical Research*, 62 (1990), 227–47, esp. Odo of Châteauroux's sermon on 2 King's 1:18, David's lament over Jonathan.
67. For the Longspee heroics and early legend, Matthew Paris, *Chronica Majora*, v, 76–7, 105–9, 116–17, 130–34, 138–44, 147–75, 201–4 (p. 154 for 'manifest martyr'), 254, 280–81. S. Lloyd, 'William Longspee II: The Making of an English Hero', *Nottingham Medieval Studies*, 35 (1991), 41–69 and, with T. Hunt, 36 (1992), 79–125.
68. Gabrieli, *Arab Historians*, p. 291.
69. John of Joinville, *Life of Louis*, p. 239.
70. Gabrieli, *Arab Historians*, p. 292; John of Joinville, *Life of Louis*, p. 237; *Eracles*, p. 610; Shirley, *Crusader Syria*, p.99.
71. *Eracles*, p. 611; Shirley, *Crusader Syria*, p. 100.
72. Quoted Richard, *St Louis*, p. 125.
73. John of Joinville, *Life of Louis*, p. 243.
74. Ibn Wasil, Gabrieli, *Arab Historians*, p. 294.
75. Richard, *St Louis*, p. 125; John of Joinville, *Life of Louis*, captures the chaos, dejection and fear, pp. 240–44.
76. Abu Shamah, *Livre des Deux Jardins*, RHC Or., v (Paris 1906), 196; cf. Gabrieli, *Arab Historians*, p. 302, from Maqrizi's fifteenth-century compilation.
77. John of Joinville, *Life of Louis*, p. 263; an exaggerated sum.
78. John of Joinville, *Life of Louis*, pp. 246–50.
79. Ibn Wasil's comment, Gabrieli, *Arab Historians*, p. 298; for the coup, pp. 295–8; John of Joinville, *Life of Louis*, pp. 251–6.
80. John of Joinville, *Life of Louis*, pp. 258–60.
81. John of Joinville, *Life of Louis*, p. 256.
82. Above pp. 777–9. And chap. 22, p. 727.
83. *The Mission of Friar William of Rubruck*, ed. P. Jackson with D. Morgan, Hakluyt Society, 2nd series, no. 173 (London 1990), pp. 1–55 (Introduction); pp. 59–278 for the friar's report to Louis IX; Jackson, *Mongols*, pp. 99–100.
84. A possible reading of Joinville's account: why was the king wading up to his chest? Why did the southerly wind matter so much on the march south in November 1249? Cf. similar doubts Matthew Paris, *Chronica Majora*, vi, *Additamenta*, p. 154; Guillaume de Nangis, RHGF, xx, 370.
85. The sense of Maqrizi's account of the defiance and refusal to contemplate a negotiated accommodation, Gabrieli, *Arab Historians*, p. 301.
86. Matthew Paris, *Chronica Majora*, v, 105–6.
87. Matthew Paris, *Chronica Majora*, v, 160–61; cf. Richard, *St Louis*, pp. 119, 127.

88. Matthew Paris, *Chronica Majora*, v, 107; vi, 163; cf., v, 116–7 for money sent to Louis from the west. For Arabic hints of the same policy, Gabrieli, *Arab Historians*, pp. 294, 299, 300–301.
89. *Liber Secretorum fidelium Crucis*, *Gesta Dei Per Francos*, ed. Bongars, vol. 2.
90. Matthew Paris, *Chronica Majora*, v, 147; for other reactions v, 170–73, 254, 280–81. Cf. trans., R. Vaughan, *Chronicles of Matthew Paris* (London 1984), p. 239, and p. 256 for Italian disturbances.
91. John of Joinville, *Life of Louis*, p. 241.
92. The *Chronicon* of St Laud of Rouen, RHGF, xxiii, 395. In general, M. Barber, 'The Crusade of the Shepherds in 1251', *Proceedings of the 10th Annual Meeting of the Western Society for French History*, ed. J. Sweet (Lawrence 1984), pp. 1–23; G. Dickson, 'The Advent of the *Pastores* (1251)', *Revue Belge de Philologie et d'Histoire*, 66 (1988), 249–67.
93. For some primary sources, the chronicles of Primat, John of Colonna and St Laud, RHGF, xxiii, 8–9, 123–4, 395–6; Matthew Paris, *Chronica Majora*, v, 246–54, p. 248 for emphasis on the Lamb as a symbol; Salimbene of Adam, *Chronicle*, ed. and trans. J. L. Baird (Binghampton 1986), p. 453.
94. Matthew Paris, *Chronica Majora*, v, 253.
95. John of Joinville, *Life of Louis*, p. 318.
96. See, apart from Jordan and Richard, J. Le Goff, *St Louis* (Paris 1996).
97. *Chartes de Terre Sainte provenant de l'Abbaye de Notre Dame de Josaphat*, ed. H.-F. Delaborde (Paris 1880), pp. 105–6, no. L.
98. Jackson, *Mongols*, esp. pp. 113–28 for a recent survey; cf. Holt, *Age of Crusades*, p. 86–92; Irwin, *Middle East*, pp. 30–36.
99. *Eracles*, pp. 635–8; Shirley, *Crusader Syria*, pp. 117–19.
100. For Baibars, Irwin, *Middle East*, pp. 37–61; Holt, *Age of Crusades*, pp. 90–98. The best account of his campaigns is by Ibn Furat, *Ayyubids, Mamluks and Crusaders*, ed. and trans. U. and M. C. Lyons and J. S. C. Riley-Smith (Cambridge 1971).
101. The best detailed modern narrative is Richard, *St Louis*, pp. 293–332; cf. Strayer, 'Crusades', pp. 508–18; Jordan, *Louis IX*, pp. 214–18.
102. Jal, *Pacta Naulorum*, i, 516 et seq. The main French chronicle accounts are by the St Denis monks Primat, RHGF, xxiii, 39–61 and the associated account by Guillaume de Nangis in his biography of Louis IX, RHGF, xx, 438–62.
103. *Diplomatic Documents (Chancery and Exchequer)*, i, ed. P. Chaplais (London 1964), no. 419.
104. Lloyd, *English Society*, chap. 4, 'The Crusade of 1270–1272: A Case Study' and Appendix 4 contain the best account of the organization of the expedition; cf. Strayer, 'Crusades', pp. 509–13, 515; Richard, *St Louis*, pp. 306–15; Tyerman, *England and the Crusades*, pp. 124–32.
105. On these preparations, Richard *St Louis*, pp. 315–29.
106. John of Joinville, *Life of Louis*, p. 345.
107. Thomas Wykes, *Chronicon*, *Annales Monastici*, ed. Luard, iv, 217–18.
108. J. R. Maddicott, 'The Crusade Taxation of 1268–70 and the Development of Parliament', *Thirteenth Century England*, ed. P. Coss and S. Lloyd, ii (Woodbridge 1990).
109. *Eracles*, pp. 457–8.
110. The Dominican Geoffrey of Beaulieu, RHGF, xx, 20, and generally pp. 20–24.
111. An aspiration confirmed by Louis's Dominican confessor Geoffrey of Beaulieu, RHGF, xx, 21, 25.
112. The pleasing legend is in William of Saint-Pathus, *Vie de St Louis*, ed. H.-F. Delaborde (Paris 1899), pp. 153–5; but cf. Geoffrey of Beaulieu, RHGF, xx, p. 23 and Guillaume de Nangis, RHGF, xx, 460–61, confirmed by the testimony of another eyewitness, one of Louis's sons, Peter of Alençon, John of Joinville, *Life of Louis*, p. 349; for Geoffrey administering the last rites, Primat, RHGF, xxiii, 57.
113. Richard, *St Louis*, pp. 329–32; Strayer, 'Crusades', pp. 516–17.

114. Tyerman, *England and the Crusades*, pp. 131 and 407; for Edward's crusade, above note 104 and pp. 720, 722.
115. Lloyd, *English Society*, pp. 144–8; Tyerman, *England and the Crusades*, pp. 126–30.
116. John of Joinville, *Life of Louis*, p. 163, cf. p. 351.
117. E.g. by the officials of Philip VI in the 1330s.
118. Mayer, *Crusades*, p. 283; Throop, *Criticism*, p. 232 and passim.
119. Throop, *Criticism*, pp. 229–30 for the account by James I of Aragon, who was there.
120. For a discussion of these, Throop, *Criticism*, pp. 69–213; but cf. Siberry, *Criticism of Crusading*, for a different view, on which see Mayer, *Crusades*, pp. 320–21.
121. Ed. H. Finke, *Konzilienstudien zur Geschichte des 13 Jahrhunderts* (Munster 1891), Anhang, pp. 113–17; trans. N. Housley, *Documents on the Later Crusades 1274–1580* (Basingstoke 1996), pp. 16–21. See the comments of Riley-Smith, *Short History*, pp. 176–8.
122. Throop, *Criticism*, p. 228.
123. Gregory X, *Registres*, no. 569.
124. P. Guido, *Rationes decimarum Italiae nei secoli XIIIe Xiv. Tuscia: la decima degli anni 1274–1290*, *Studi e Testi*, LVIII (Vatican City 1932), esp. pp. xli–xliii.
125. Jackson, *Mongols*, pp. 165–95.
126. Salimbene of Adam, *Chronicle*, pp. 504, 505.
127. Mayer, *Crusades*, p. 286.
128. Holt, *Age of Crusades*, p. 102.
129. *Gestes des Chiprois*, iii, and Crawford, *Templar of Tyre*, chaps, 473 and 474; Runciman, *History of the Crusades*, iii, 405–6.
130. Above, chapter 22, p. 732; the best Frankish local account is that of the Templar of Tyre, trans. Crawford, chap. *Templar of Tyre*, 396–516.; cf. Ibn Furat, *Ayyubids*.
131. Ismai il Abu'l-Fida, trans. Holt, *Age of Crusades*, p. 104; for an inside view on the siege of Acre, Crawford, *Templar of Tyre*, chaps. 482–508; cf. Runciman, *History of the Crusades*, iii, 414, note 2 for western sources; Gabrieli, *Arab Historians*, pp. 344–50.
132. Holt, *Age of Crusades*, p. 104.
133. *Gestes des Chyprois*, iii and Crawford, *Templar of Tyre*, chap. 513.
134. Runciman, *History of the Crusades*, iii, 423; Mayer, *Crusades*, p. 287.

25: The Eastern Crusades in the Later Middle Ages

1. J. Moorman, *A History of the Franciscan Order* (Oxford 1968), p. 436.
2. B. Kedar and S. Schein, 'Un projet de "passage particulier" ', *Bibliothèque de l'Ecole des Chartes*, 137 (1979), 221; Philippe de Mézières, *Epistre Lamentable*, ed. K. de Lettenhove in Froissart, *Chroniques*, xvi (Brussels 1872), 491.
3. Philippe de Mézières, *Le Songe du Vieil Pèlerin*, ed. G. W. Coopland (Cambridge 1969); N. Iorga, *Philippe de Mézières (1327–1405) et la croisade au XIVe siècle* (Paris 1896); C. J. Tyerman, 'Marino Sanudo Torsello and the Lost Crusade: Lobbying in the Fourteenth Century', *Transactions of the Royal Historical Society*, 5th series, vol. 32 (1982), 57–73.
4. John Froissart, *Chronicles of England, France, Spain etc.*, trans. T. Johnes (London 1839), ii, 584–8; Tyerman, 'Sanudo'.
5. Bibliothèque Nationale (Paris), MS Latin 11015 fols. 32 recto–54 verso for Guy's treatise, fols. 39 recto–41 recto for the section on poisons.
6. Bongars, *Gesta Dei Per Francos*, ii, 30–31, 36–7, 75–7; F. Cardini, 'I costi della crociata', *Studi in memoria di Frederigo Melis* (Naples 1978), pp. 179–210; N. Housley, 'Costing the Crusade', *The Experience of Crusading*, i, ed. M. Bull and N. Housley (Cambridge 2003), 48.
7. *Le Voyage d'Outremer de Bertrandon de la Brocquière*, ed. C. Schéfer, *Recueil de voyages et de documents pour server à l'histoire de la géographie depuis le xiiie jusqu'à la fin du xvie siècle*, xii (Paris 1892), 267–74, esp. p. 274.
8. Benedetto Accolti, *De bello a Christiani contra Barbaros Gesta*, RHC Occ., v, 532–3 et

seq.; cf. a useful summary, M. Meserve, 'Italian Humanists and the Problem of the Crusade', *Crusading in the Fifteenth Century*, ed. N. Housley (Basingstoke 2004), pp. 13–38.

9. For a useful general survey, N. Housley, *The Later Crusades* (Oxford 1992).
10. C. J. Tyerman, 'Philip V of France, the Assemblies of 1319–20 and the Crusade', *Bulletin of the Institute of Historical Research*, 57 (1984), 15–34; idem, 'Sed Nihil Fecit? The Last Capetians and the Recovery of the Holy Land', *War and Government in the Middle Ages*, ed. Gillingham and Holt, pp. 170–81.
11. C. J. Tyerman, 'Philip VI and the Recovery of the Holy Land', *English Historical Review*, 100 (1985), 25–52.
12. Philip V to Louis count of Clermont, July 1319, Archives Nationales (Paris) MS JJ 60, no. 100.
13. Philippe de Mézières, *Songe du Vieil Pèlerin*, i, 399.
14. P. Edbury, 'The Crusading Policy of Peter I of Cyprus', *Eastern Mediterranean Lands*, ed. P. M. Holt (Warminster 1977), pp. 90–105; idem, *Cyprus*, pp. 161–79; Setton, *Papacy and the Levant*, i, 225–84.
15. Reproduced in Riley-Smith, *Oxford Illustrated History of the Crusades*, opposite p. 276.
16. Tyerman, *England and the Crusades*, pp. 289–93; A. Luttrell, 'English Levantine Crusaders 1363–1367', *Renaissance Studies*, 2 (1988), 143–53.
17. Philippe de Mézières, *The Life of St Peter Thomas*, ed. J. Smet (Rome 1954); Guilluame de Machaut, *La Prise d'Alexandre*, ed. L. de Mas Latrie (Geneva 1877), now trans. J. Shirley and P. Edbury, *The Capture of Alexandria* (Aldershot 2004).
18. T. Walsingham, *Historia Anglicana*, ed. H. T. Riley, Rolls Series (London 1863–4), i, 301–2.
19. *Canterbury Tales*, General Prologue, l. 51.
20. Tyerman, *Invention of the Crusades*, p. 139 note 41.
21. Maier, *Preaching*, pp. 52–6; cf. pp. 167–9 for the Drenther crusade.
22. E. Baluze, *Miscellaneorum*, i (Paris 1678), 165–95.
23. See below pp. 343–74, 894–905.
24. D. Wilkins, *Concilia Magnae Britanniae et Hiberniae* (London 1733–7), iii, 588 (Oct. 1464); cf. the future pope using the same phrase in 1454, L. d'Achéry, *Spicilegium* (Paris 1723), iii, 795–6.
25. Tyerman, *Invention of the Crusades*, p. 37 and note 20; Setton, *Papacy and the Levant*, i, 202.
26. Muldoon, *Popes, Lawyers and Infidels*, passim and esp. pp. 88–91, 119–31; Housley, *Later Crusades*, pp. 288, 308–10.
27. Tyerman, *England and the Crusades*, pp. 289, 293, 355.
28. Christiansen, *Northern Crusades*, pp. 147–51.
29. In general, Forey, *The Military Orders*, pp. 204–41.
30. For opinions and refs., A. Leopold, *How to Recover the Holy Land* (Aldershot 2000), esp. pp. 19, 34, 78, 178–9.
31. The best account is M. Barber, *The Trial of the Templars* (Cambridge 1978); cf. Barber, *New Knighthood*, pp. 280–313.
32. S. Schein, 'Philip IV and the Crusade: A Reconsideration', *Crusade and Settlement*, ed. Edbury, pp. 121–6.
33. Christiansen, *Northern Crusades*, pp. 151, 231–41.
34. Forey, *The Military Orders*, p. 240.
35. On the Ottomans, C. Imber, *The Ottoman Empire 1300–1481* (Istanbul 1990); H. Inalcik, *The Ottoman Empire: The Classical Age 1300–1600* (London 1973); on Byzantium, D. Nicol, *The Last Centuries of Byzantium 1261–1453* (London 1972).
36. Setton, *Papacy and the Levant*, pp. 195–223; E. L. Cox, *The Green Count of Savoy* (Princeton 1967).
37. Wilkins, *Concilia*, iii, 587. For a recent discussion, N. Bisaha, 'Pope Pius II and the Crusade', *Crusading in the Fifteenth Century*, pp. 39–52.

38. *Documents on the Later Crusades 1274–1580*, ed. N. Housley (Basingstoke 1996), p. 149.
39. Tyerman, *England and the Crusades*, p. 320.
40. A. Linder, *Raising Arms: Liturgy in the Struggle to Liberate Jerusalem in the Late Middle Ages* (Turnhout 2003), pp. 179, 189–90.
41. Setton, *Papacy and the Levant*, p. 245; Housley, *Later Crusades*, p. 40.
42. Above, note 35.
43. Quoted Housley, *Later Crusades*, p. 64.
44. Housley, *Later Crusades*, pp. 90–91 provides a convenient potted account.
45. Schéfer, *Voyage d'Outremer*, esp. pp. 181–99, when he met Murad II; for Boucicaut, *Le livre des Faicts de bon Messire Jean le Maingre dit Boucicaut*, ed. M. Petitot, *Collection des mémoires relatives à l'histoire de France*, vi and vii (Paris 1819).
46. Meserve, 'Italian Humanists', pp. 26–7, 35.
47. N. Oikonomides, 'Byzantium between East and West', *Byzantium and the West*, ed. J. Howard-Johnston, Byzantinische Forschung, xiii (Amsterdam 1988), 326–7 and note 17. The situation in Greek cities was far more resistant.
48. In general, D. Geanakoplos, 'Byzantium and the Crusades', *History of the Crusades*, ed. Setton, iii, 27–103; J. Gill, *Byzantium and the Papacy 1198–1400* (New Brunswick 1979); Nicol, *Last Centuries of Byzantium*.
49. R. Manselli, 'Il cardinale Bessarione contro il pericolo turco e l'Italia', *Miscellanea franciscana*, 73 (1973), 314–26.
50. S. Runciman, *The Fall of Constantinople* (Cambridge 1965).
51. Adam of Usk, *Chronicon*, ed. and trans. E. M. Thompson (London 1904), pp. 57, 220.
52. J. Cabaret d'Oronville, *La Chronique de bon duc Loys de Bourbon*, ed. A. M. Chazaud (Paris 1876), pp. 218–57; Froissart, *Chronicles*, ii, 434–49, 465–77, 481–4; generally Setton, *Papacy and the Levant*, i, 329–41.
53. Tyerman, *England and the Crusades*, pp. 278–80.
54. Cabaret d'Oronville, *Chronique*, p. 257; some French nobles also died on the way home.
55. J. J. N. Palmer, *England, France and Christendom* (London 1972), esp. pp. 180–210; Tyerman, *England and the Crusades*, pp. 294–301; cf. Philippe de Mézières, *Letter to Richard II: A Plea Made in 1395 for Peace between England and France*, trans. G. W. Coopland (Liverpool 1975).
56. E.g. in the main official French chronicle source, *Chronique du religieux de Saint-Denys, contenant le règne de Charles VI*, ed. L. Bellaguet (Paris 1839), ii, esp. 428–9; in general A. S. Atyia, *The Crusade of Nicopolis* (London 1934); Setton, *Papacy and the Levant*, i, 341–69; Housley, *Later Crusades*, pp. 73–81.
57. Tyerman, *England and the Crusades*, pp. 300–301 and refs.
58. M. Keen, *Chivalry* (New Haven 1984), esp. pp. 179–99, esp. p. 195 (Order of the Ship); for Order of the Knot and the crusade, Bibliothèque Nationale (Paris), MS Fr. 4274, fol. 6, reproduced E. Hallam (ed.), *Chronicles of the Crusades* (London 1989), p. 2.
59. A point made by J. Paviot, 'Burgundy and the Crusade', *Crusading in the Fifteenth Century*, ed. Housley, pp. 71 and 204 note 11.
60. Runciman, *History of the Crusades*, iii, 462.
61. Setton, *Papacy and the Levant*, i, 352.
62. *Religieux de Saint-Denys*, ii, 498.
63. Froissart, *Chronicles*, ii, chap. xci and p. 654.
64. Mézières, *Epistre*, pp. 444–523.
65. J. Paviot, *Les Ducs de Bourgogne, la croisade et l'Orient* (Paris 2003); cf. R. Vaughan, *Philip the Good* (London 1970), pp. 268–74, 334–72.
66. E.g. Olivier de la Marche, *Mémoires*, ed. H. Beaune and J. d'Arbaumont (Paris 1883–8), i, 83–4.
67. Paviot, *Ducs de Bourgogne*, pp. 201–38, esp. p. 238 for Duke Philip's lack of books on the Turks.

68. For a summary, J. Paviot, 'Burgundy and the Crusade', pp. 71–3, 75–7, 79–80; *Discours de voyage d'Oultremer*, ed. C. Schefer, *Revue de l'Orient Latin*, 3 (1895), 303–42.
69. Torcello's *Avis* and Brocquière's assessment Schefer, *Voyage d'Oultremer*, pp. 263–74; cf. *Oeuvres de Ghillebert de Lannoy*, ed. C. Potvin (Louvain 1878).
70. R. J. Walsh, 'Charles the Bold and the Crusade', *Journal of Medieval History*, 3 (1977), 53–87.
71. Housley, *Later Crusades*, p. 108; Walsh, 'Charles the Bold', p. 56.
72. M.-T. Caron, *Les Vœux du faison, noblesse en fête, esprit de croisade* (Turnhout 2003), esp. pp. 120–25; pp. 133–67 for vows (p. 153 for Lannoy's); Paviot, *Ducs de Bourgogne*, pp. 129–35; pp. 308–13 for Oliver de la Marche's account; cf. la Marche, *Mémoires*, ed. J. A. C. Buchon (Paris 1836), p. 494–6.
73. Paviot, *Ducs de Bourgogne*, p. 238: 'la croisade chez Philippe le Bon etait un rève chevaleresque'.
74. Paviot, *Ducs de Bourgogne*, p. 132.
75. O. Halecki, *The Crusade of Varna* (New York 1943); Housley, *Later Crusades*, pp. 85–9.
76. Runciman, *Fall of Constantinople*, for an elegant and elegiac account.
77. Quoted, Bisaha, 'Pius II and Crusade', p. 40.
78. Bisaha, 'Pius II and Crusade'; J. Helmrath, 'The German *Reichstage* and the Crusade', *Crusading in the Fifteenth Century*, ed. Housley, pp. 53–69.
79. W. R. Lunt, *Financial Relations of the Papacy with England*, (Cambridge, Mass. 1939–62), ii, passim for indulgence and taxation returns; Housley, *Later Crusades*, pp. 99–103.
80. *Voyage d'Oultremer*, p. 339.
81. J. Hofer, *Giovanni da Capestrano* (L'Aquila 1955); N. Housley, 'Giovanni da Capistrano and the Crusade of 1456', *Crusading in the Fifteenth Century*, ed. idem, pp. 94–115; Housley, *Later Crusades*, pp. 103–4, 408–10. For the impact, note the Middle English romance *Capystranus*.
82. Setton, *Papacy and the Levant*, ii, 235.
83. J. M. Bak, 'Hungary and Crusading in the Fifteenth Century', *Crusading in the Fifteenth Century*, ed. Housley, p. 117.
84. Housley, 'Capistrano', p. 108, for a somewhat different slant.
85. Housley, *Later Crusades*, pp. 104–5 for a summary; cf. 'Capistrano', p. 111
86. Quoted Housley, *Later Crusades*, p. 108; in general, now, Bisaha, 'Pius II and Crusade'.
87. Above, note 86.
88. Wilkins, *Concilia*, iii, 587–94; see French version at the Burgundian court, Caron, *Vœux du faison*, 167–85.
89. Bisaha, 'Pius II and Crusade', pp. 50–51.
90. M. Mallett, *The Borgias* (London 1969), p. 92.
91. Runciman, *History of the Crusades*, p. 467.
92. Piccolomini to Calixtus III in 1458, quoted Bak, 'Hungary and Crusading', p. 119; cf. N. Housley on the *antemurale* image, *Religious Warfare in Europe 1400–1536* (Oxford 2002).
93. Tyerman, *England and the Crusade*, pp. 315–16.
94. Jean d'Auton, *Chronique de Louis XII*, ed. R. de Maulde la Clavière (Paris 1889–95), i, 396–7; Tyerman, *Invention of the Crusades*, pp. 95, 152 note 292.
95. D'Auton, *Chronique*, ii, 166–7.
96. N. Tanner, *The Decrees of the Ecumenical Councils* (London and Washington, DC 1990), pp. 595, 607, 609–14, 651, 653–4, 796–7.
97. Setton, *Papacy and the Levant*, iii, 486.

26: The Crusade and Christian Society in the Later Middle Ages

1. E. Riant, *Pèlerinages des Scandinaves en Terre Sainte* (Paris 1865), p. 398; apparently the Greenlanders paid the crusade tax in walrus tusks.
2. *The Works of Francis Bacon*, ed. J. Spedding et al., vii (London 1859), pp. 1–36.
3. Mézières, *Epistre*, pp. 467, 473.
4. *Archives administratives de la ville de Rheims*, ed. P. Varin ii (Paris 1843), 273–4, 665.
5. Thomas Walsingham, *Historia Anglicana*, ed. H. T. Riley, Rolls Series (London 1863–4), ii, 95; Paviot, *Ducs de Bourgogne*, pp. 171–2.
6. Giles de Muisis, *Chronicon majus*, ed. J. J. Smet, *Recueil des Chroniques de Flandres*, ii (Brussels 1841), 216.
7. Innocent IV, *Registres*, no. 2,644; N. Housley, 'Politics and Heretics in Italy: Anti-Heretical Crusades, Orders and Confraternities 1200–1500', *Journal of Ecclesiastical History*, 33 (1982), 193–208; Tyerman, *England and the Crusades*, pp. 261, 285.
8. *Chronique parisienne anonyme de 1316 à 1339*, ed. A. Hellot, *Mémoires de la société de l'histoire de Paris*, xi (1885), 29–30; 102–3; X. du Boisrouvray, 'L'Eglise collégiale et la confrérie du St Sepulchre à Paris 1325–1791', *Positions des thèses de l'école nationale des chartes* (Paris 1953), pp. 33–5; for full refs., C. J. Tyerman, *The French and the Crusades 1313–1336* (unpublished Oxford DPhil thesis 1981), pp. 138–41.
9. S. Schein, *Fideles Crucis; The Papacy, the West and the Recovery of the Holy Land 1274–1314* (Oxford 1991), chap. 7, pp. 219–38; Tyerman, *England and the Crusades*, pp. 240–42; Housley, *Later Crusades*, pp. 27–8.
10. Hellot, *Chronique parisienne anonyme*, p. 46 and generally pp. 46–8.
11. John XXII, *Lettres secrètes et curiales relatives à la France*, ed. A. Coulon et al. (Paris 1900–), no. 1,116.
12. In general, M. Barber, 'The Pastoureaux of 1320', *Journal of Ecclesiastical History*, 32 (1981), 143–66; Tyerman, 'Philip V of France', 15–34; Tyerman *French and Crusades*, pp. 99–101.
13. N. Housley, 'Crusading as Social Revolt: The Hungarian Peasant Uprising of 1514', *Journal of Ecclesiastical History*, 49 (1998), 1–28; J. M. Bak, 'Hungary and Crusading in the Fifteenth Century', *Crusading in the Fifteenth Century*, ed. Housley, esp. pp. 117, 126–7.
14. The suggestion is that of Dr L. S. Ettre, to whom I am grateful for sharing it.
15. A. S. Atiya, *The Crusade in the Later Middle Ages* (London 1938), pp. 420, 441, 443, 445, 450, 458, 465–6, 522, 527; *History of the Crusades*, ed. Setton, iii, 85–7, 306–9, 652–3.
16. Tyerman, *England and the Crusades*, pp. 268, 271, 274, 292; St John's Gate MSS, L. H. Butler Papers, Notes, Calendars and Transcriptions from the Archives of Malta, A. O. M. 356, fols. 232 verso, 237 and 242.
17. Tyerman, *England and the Crusades*, pp. 314–15, 355 and refs.
18. *Scrope and Grosvenor Controversy*, ed. N. H. Nicolas (London 1832), collated by C. G. Young (Chester 1879), i, 124–5; in general, Tyerman, *England and the Crusades*, pp. 274, 281, 289, 292, 429 note 91, 431 note 132; cf. M. H. Keen, 'Chaucer's Knight, the English Aristocracy and the Crusade', *English Court Culture in the Later Middle Ages*, ed. V. J. Scattergood and J. W. Sherborne (London 1983), 45–61.
19. Housley, *Later Crusades*, p. 282.
20. Sir Thomas Malory, *La Morte D'Arthur*, ed. S. H. A. Shepherd (New York 2004), p. 697; cf. pp. 149 and 689 for Arthur's own crusading ambitions.
21. Tyerman, *England and the Crusades*, esp. pp. 304–6.
22. *Chronique de quartre premiers Valois*, ed. S. Luce (Paris 1852), p. 128.
23. Tyerman, *England and Crusades*, p. 305; cf. for Burgundian book collection, Paviot, *Ducs de Bourgogne*, pp. 201–38.
24. See now R. Tzanaki, *Mandeville's Medieval Audiences* (Aldershot 2003); for crusading Prologue, e.g., M. C. Seymour (ed.), *Mandeville's Travels* (Oxford 1967), pp. 1–4.
25. A. Goodman, *The Loyal Conspiracy* (London 1971), pp. 81–2, cf. p. 78 for more

crusade memorabilia. For the Heraclius heraldry, see MS n. 98 in the Royal Academy exhibition 2003–4, 'Illuminating the Renaissance: The Triumph of Flemish Manuscript Painting in Europe', by the 'Master of Edward IV' (RA Catalogue by S. McKendrick et al., London 2003); for Heraclius as a king of France in the fourteenth century, Bibliothèque nationale de France, ms Fr. 2813, *Grandes Chroniques de France*, fol. 70 verso.

26. A. Gransden, *Historical Writing in England c. 550 to the Early Sixteenth Century* (London 1974–82), ii, 231–2.
27. Housley, *Later Crusades*, p. 393; Keen, *Chivalry*, p. 216.
28. Paviot, 'Burgundy and Crusade', p. 73; the 1378 scene was illustrated in the contemporary *Grandes chroniques de France*, Bibliothèque nationale de France, ms Fr. 2813, fol. 473 verso.
29. Linder, *Raising Arms*.
30. Linder, *Raising Arms*, p. 102; cf. pp. 363–4.
31. Linder, *Raising Arms*, p. 359.
32. Discussed Tyerman, *Invention of the Crusades*, pp. 72–4.
33. E. g. Lunt, *Financial Relations*.
34. Tyerman, *Invention of the Crusades*, p. 62.
35. *The Westminster Chronicle*, ed. and trans. L. C. Hector and B. F. Harvey (Oxford 1982), 32–3 (cf. pp. 34–7 on the sale of indulgences); J. A. Brundage, '*Crucesignati*: The Rite for Taking the Cross in England', *Traditio*, 22 (1966), 289 ff.
36. Tyerman, *Invention of the Crusades*, pp. 76–83; idem, *England and the Crusades*, pp. 307–9.
37. M. Andrieu, *Le Pontifical Roman au moyen âge* (Vatican 1940), iii, 30, 228, 243, 330; M. Purcell, *Papal Crusading Policy* (Leiden 1975), p. 200.
38. *Literae Cantuariensis*, ed. J. Brigstocke Sheppard, Rolls Series (London 1887–9), iii, 239, no. 1,051; *Registrum Abbatiae Johannis Whethamstede*, ed. H. T. Riley, Rolls Series (London 1872–3), ii, 191–2.
39. Above p. 873.
40. Trans. Setton, *Papacy and the Levant*, ii, 235.
41. Above, Chapter 1 and refs.; for Hostiensis, *Suma Aurea* (Venice 1574), pp. 1,141–2; Russell, *Just War*, p. 205.
42. See Mayer's acute commentary, *Crusades*, pp. 320–21.
43. Housley, 'Crusades against Christians'.
44. For what follows, S. Lloyd '"Political Crusades" in England', Tyerman, *England and the Crusades*, chap. 6, pp. 133–51.
45. In general, J. R. Strayer, 'The Political Crusades of the Thirteenth Century', *History of Crusades*, ed. Setton, pp. 343–75; N. Housley, *The Italian Crusades* (Oxford 1982), who rather avoids some central issues by beginning the study in 1254; the biographies of Frederick II by Van Cleve and Abulafia.
46. See J. Dunbabin, *Charles I of Anjou* (London 1998).
47. S. Runciman, *The Sicilian Vespers* (Cambridge 1958).
48. In general, Housley, *Later Crusades*, chap. 8, pp. 235–66; N. Housley, *The Avignon Papacy and the Crusades 1305–78* (Oxford 1986).
49. Housley, *Italian Crusades*, p. 137 and note 116 for contemporary contrast with Holy Land crosses.
50. Tyerman, *England and the Crusades*, pp. 333–40 and refs.
51. Hector and Harvey, *Westminster Chronicle*, pp. 33, 36–7, 39.
52. John Wyclif, *Polemical Works in Latin*, ed. R. Buddensieg (London 1883), ii, 582.
53. P. E. Russell, *English Intervention in Spain and Portugal in the Time of Edward III and Richard II* (Oxford 1955), esp. pp. 173–525; J. Edwards, 'Reconquista and Crusade in Fifteenth-century Spain', *Crusading in Fifteenth Century*, ed. Housley, p. 167.
54. Tyerman, *Invention of the Crusades*, p. 103; idem, *England and the Crusades*, p. 359 and note 74; Setton, *Papacy and the Levant*, iii, 1–141 for an exhausting discussion of Julius II.

55. For a summary, Housley, *Later Crusades*, pp. 249–60 and 482; idem, *Religious Warfare*, pp. 33–61.
56. Tyerman, *England and the Crusades*, pp. 359–67.
57. Tyerman, *Invention of the Crusades*, p. 103.
58. Housley, *Religious Warfare*, pp. 195–7.
59. Tyerman, *England and the Crusades*, pp. 343–5, 351–2, 362–7.
60. R. C. Schwoebel, *The Shadow of the Crescent: The Renaissance Image of the Turk* (Nieuwkoop 1967); J. W. Bohnstedt, *The Infidel Scourge of God: The Turkish Menace as Seen by German Pamphleteers of the Reformation Era*, Transactions of the American Philosophical Society (Philadelphia 1968), 1–58; M. J. Heath, *Crusading Commonplaces* (Geneva 1986); Tyerman, *Invention of the Crusades*, pp. 100–109.
61. G. Burnet, *History of the Reformation*, ed. E. Nares (London 1830), iv, 32.
62. R. Holinshed, *Chronicles of England and Ireland* (1587, reprint London 1808–9), iii, 262–4.
63. Tyerman, *England and the Crusades*, p. 137 and refs. note 18.
64. *Albert von Beham und Regesten Papst Innocenz IV*, ed. C. Hofler (Stuttgart 1847), pp. 16–17.
65. Above, note 44.
66. Above, notes 41–2, for Hostiensis; for Lille, *Lois et coutumes de la ville de Lille*, ed. E. B. J. Brun-Lavainne and J. Roisin (Lille 1842), pp. 308–9; for Florence, F. Cardini, 'Crusade and "Presence of Jerusalem" in Medieval Florence', *Outremer*, ed. Kedar et al., p. 341.
67. *Epistolae Saeculi XIII*, ed. Pertz and Roderberg pp. 161–2. no. 214.
68. Tyerman, *Invention of the Crusades*, p. 33 and note 9; cf. Mézières's *Songe du Vieil Pèlerin*.
69. Trans. Housley, *Documents*, pp. 31–5.
70. C. J. Tyerman, *Fighting for Christendom* (Oxford 2004), esp. pp. 183–9; idem, *England and the Crusades*, chap. 12; Housley, *Religious Warfare*, passim (see index under '*antemurale Christianitatis*' and 'national feeling').
71. In 1089 regarding Tarragona south of Barcelona; see trans. and ref. O'Callaghan, *Reconquest*, p. 31.
72. Cardini, ' "Presence of Jerusalem" ', passim; Housley, *Later Crusades*, pp. 107–8; idem, *Religious Warfare*, pp. 30–31, 80–83.
73. James is lauded in contemporary sources such as Ambroise and the *Itinerarium* and appears in thirteenth-century *exempla*; for Longspee above, pp. 793–4.
74. Tyerman, *England and the Crusades*, p. 327 and refs. notes 7 and 8.
75. *Annales Regis Edwardi Primi*, a St Alban's fragment printed in William Rishanger, *Chronica*, ed. H. T. Riley, Rolls Series (London 1865), p. 439; Tyerman, *England and the Crusades*, pp. 332–3 and refs. note 30.
76. Bibliothèque nationale de France, ms Fr. 2628, fol. 328.
77. Trans. Housley, *Religious Warfare*, p. 27.
78. Trans. Housley, *Documents*, pp. 132–3.
79. C. J. Tyerman, 'Holy War, Roman Popes, and Christian Soldiers: Some Early Modern Views on Medieval Christendom', *The Medieval Church: Universities, Heresy and the Religious Life*, ed. P. Biller and R. B. Dobson (Woodbridge 1999), esp. pp. 301–5.
80. *Rotuli Parliamentorum* (London 1767–77), ii, 362; Tyerman, *England and the Crusades*, esp. 326–33 for what follows.
81. Cf. A. K. McHardy, 'Liturgy and Propaganda during the Hundred Years War', *Studies in Church History*, 18, ed. S. Mews (Oxford 1982), 215–27; W. R. Jones, 'The English Church and Propaganda during the Hundred Years War', *Journal of British Studies*, 19 (1979), 18–30.
82. Froissart, *Chronicles*, i, 756.
83. *Gesta Henrici Quinti*, ed. F. Taylor and J. S. Roskell (Oxford 1975), p. 79.
84. Taylor and Roskell, *Gesta Henrici Quinti*, pp. 101–13.

85. J. Le Goff, *La Civilisation de l'Occident médiéval* (Paris 1964), p. 98; but cf. M. Balard's very brief summary, 'Notes on the Economic Consequences of the Crusades', *Experience of Crusading*, ii, ed. Edbury and Phillips, pp. 233–9.
86. In general, Leopold, *How to Recover the Holy Land*, Housley, *Later Crusades*, chap. 13; more interesting, the brilliantly original P. Biller, *The Measure of Multitude* (Oxford 2000), Part 2, 'The Map of the World'; cf. Tzanaki, *Mandeville's Audiences*.
87. Hayton, *Flos historiarum terre orientis*, RHC Arm., ii, 113–363; Pierre Dubois, *De Recuperatione Terrae Sanctae*, ed. C. V. Langlois (Paris 1891), trans. W. Brandt, *The Recovery of the Holy Land* (New York 1956).
88. In general, Muldoon, *Popes, Lawyers and Infidels*.
89. Trans. Housley, *Documents*, pp. 169–73; for Columbus's increasingly messianic mentality and some of its cultural context, A. Milhou, *Colon y su mentalidad mesianica* (Valladolid 1983).
90. C. Colon, *Los cuatro viages del admirante y su testamento* (Madrid 1964), pp. 213–14.
91. M. H. Letts, *Mandeville's Travels: Text and Translations*, Hakluyt Society, vols. 101–2 (London 1953), ii, 332.
92. Letts, *Mandeville's Travels*, ii, 334; cf Tzanaki, *Mandeville's Audiences*, p. 90, and for circumnavigation, pp. 88–91.

Select Further Reading

This is far from an exhaustive bibliography, merely an indicative one, primarily of obvious sources and secondary works in English. For more detailed pursuit of the subject, the notes should be consulted.

General

Sources

J. Bédier, *Les Chansons de croisade* (Paris 1909)
J. Brundage, *The Crusades: A Documentary Survey* (Milwaukee 1962)
F. Gabrieli, *Arab Historians of the Crusades* (London 1984)
J and L. Riley-Smith, *The Crusades: Idea and Reality* (London 1981)

Secondary

M. Barber, *The New Knighthood: A History of the Order of the Temple* (Cambridge 1994)
J. Brundage, *Medieval Canon Law and the Crusader* (Madison 1969)
K. Erdmann, *The Origin of the Idea of the Crusade*, trans. M. W. Baldwin and W. Goffart (Princeton 1977)
J. Flori, *La Guerre sainte* (Paris 2001)
A. J. Forey, *The Military Orders* (London 1992)
J. Goni Gaztambide, *Historia de la bula de la cruzada* (Vitoria 1958)
C. Hillenbrand, *The Crusades: Islamic Perspectives* (Edinburgh 1999)
P. M. Holt, *The Age of the Crusades: The Near East from the Eleventh Century to 1517* (London 1986)
B. Z. Kedar, *Crusade and Mission* (Princeton 1984)
M. Keen, *Chivalry* (New Haven 1984)
H. E. Mayer, *The Crusades* (2nd edn Oxford 1988)
J. Muldoon, *Popes, Lawyers and Infidels* (Liverpool 1979)
J. Richard, *The Crusades* (Cambridge 1999)
J. Riley-Smith, *What Were the Crusades?* (3rd edn London 2003)
J. Riley-Smith (ed.), *The Oxford Illustrated History of the Crusades* (Oxford 1995)
S. Runciman, *A History of the Crusades* (Cambridge 1951–4)
F. H. Russell, *The Just War in the Middle Ages* (Cambridge 1977)
K. Setton (ed.), *A History of the Crusades* (2nd edn Madison 1969–89)
E. Siberry, *Criticism of Crusading 1095–1274* (Oxford 1985)
C. J. Tyerman, *England and the Crusades 1095–1588* (Chicago 1988)
C. J. Tyerman, *The Invention of the Crusades* (Basingstoke 1998)
C. J. Tyerman, *Fighting for Christendom: Holy War and the Crusades* (Oxford 2004)

First Crusade

Sources

Albert of Aachen, *Historia Hierosolymitana*, RHC Occ., iv

Anna Comnena, *The Alexiad*, trans. E. R. A. Sewter (London 1969)

S. Eidelberg, *The Jews and the Crusaders: The Hebrew Chronicles of the First and Second Crusades* (Madison 1977)

The First Crusade ed. E. Peters (Philadelphia 1998)

Fulcher of Chartres, *A History of the Expedition to Jerusalem 1095–1127*, trans. F. R. Ryan (Knoxville 1969)

Gesta Francorum, trans. R. Hill (Oxford 1972)

H. Hagenmeyer, *Die Kreuzzugsbriefe aus den Jahren 1088–1100* (Innsbruck 1902)

Raymond of Aguilers, *Historia Francorum qui ceperunt Iherusalem*, trans. J. H. and L. L. Hill (Philadelphia 1968)

Secondary

A. Becker, *Papst Urban II* (Stuttgart 1964–88)

M. Bull, *Knightly Piety and the Lay Response to the First Crusade* (Oxford 1993)

R. Chazan, *European Jewry and the First Crusade* (Berkeley and Los Angeles 1987)

J. France, *Victory in the East* (Cambridge 1994)

J. Riley-Smith, *The First Crusade and the Idea of Crusading* (London 1986)

J. Riley-Smith, *The First Crusaders 1095–1131* (Cambridge 1997)

Twelfth-century Outremer

Sources

Beha al-Din Ibn Shaddad, *The Rare and Excellent History of Saladin*, trans. D. S. Richards (Aldershot 2002)

P. Edbury, *The Conquest of Jerusalem and the Third Crusade* (Aldershot 1998)

Ibn al-Qalanisi, *The Damascus Chronicle of the Crusades Extracted and Translated from the Chronicle of Ibn al-Qalanasi*, trans. H. A. R. Gibb (London 1932)

The Travels of Ibn Jubayr, trans. R. Broadhurst (London 1999)

Usamah Ibn-Munqidh, *An Arab-Syrian Gentleman and Warrior in the Period of the Crusades: Memoirs of Usamah Ibn-Munqidh*, trans. P. K. Hitti (reprint Princeton 1987)

William of Tyre, *A History of Deeds Done Beyond the Sea*, trans. E. A. Babcock and A. C. Krey (New York 1976, reprint of 1941 edn)

Secondary

M. Benvenisti, *The Crusaders in the Holy Land* (Jerusalem 1970)

C. Cahen, *La Syrie du Nord* (Paris 1940)

R. Ellenblum, *Frankish Rural Settlement in the Latin Kingdom of Jerusalem* (Cambridge 1998)

B. Hamilton, *The Leper King and His Heirs* (Cambridge 2000)

H. Kennedy, *Crusader Castles* (Cambridge 1994)

R.-J. Lilie, *Byzantium and the Crusader States 1096–1204* (trans. Oxford 1993)

M. Lyons and D. Jackson, *Saladin: The Politics of Holy War* (Cambridge 1984)

J. Phillips, *Defenders of the Holy Land. Relations between the Latin East and the West 1119–87* (Oxford 1996)

J. Prawer, *The Latin Kingdom of Jerusalem* (London 1972)

J. Prawer, *Crusader Institutions* (Oxford 1980)

R. Rogers, *Latin Siege Warfare in the Twelfth Century* (Oxford 1992)

R. C. Smail, *Crusading Warfare* (Cambridge 1956)

H. S. Tibble, *Monarchy and Lordship in the Latin Kingdom of Jerusalem 1099–1291* (Oxford 1989)

Second Crusade

Sources

De expugnatione Lyxbonensi, ed. and trans. C. W. David (New York 1936, reprint 1976)
Odo of Deuil, *De profectione Ludovici VII in orientem*, ed. and trans. V. G. Berry (Columbia 1948)
Otto of Freising, *The Deeds of Frederick Barbarossa*, trans. C. C. Mierow (Columbia 1953)

Secondary

G. Constable, 'The Second Crusade as Seen by Contemporaries', *Traditio*, 9 (1953), 213–79
M. Gervers, *The Cistercians and the Second Crusade* (New York 1992)
J. Phillips and M. Hoch (eds.), *The Second Crusade* (Manchester 2001)

Third Crusade

Sources

Ambroise, *Estoire de la Guerre Sainte*, trans. M. J. Hubert and J. L. Lamonte, *The Crusade of Richard the Lion-Heart* (New York 1976)
Gerald of Wales, *Journey through Wales*, trans. L. Thorpe (London 1978)
Itinerarium Peregrinorum et Gesta Regis Ricardi, trans. H. Nicholson, *The Chronicle of the Third Crusade* (Aldershot 2001)

Secondary

J. Gillingham, *Richard I* (New Haven and London 1999)

Fourth Crusade

Sources

A. J. Andrea, *Contemporary Sources for the Fourth Crusade* (Leiden 2000)
Geoffrey of Villehardouin, *The Conquest of Constantinople*, trans. M. R. B. Shaw (London 1963)
Gunther of Pairis, *Historia Constantinopolitana*, trans. A. J. Andrea, *The Capture of Constantinople* (Philadelphia 1997)
Nicetas Choniates, *Annals*, trans. H. J. Margoulias, *O City of Byzantium* (Detroit 1984)
Robert of Clari, *The Conquest of Constantinople*, trans. E. H. McNeal (New York 1966)

Secondary

M. Angold, *The Byzantine Empire 1025–1204* (London 1984)
M. Angold, *The Fourth Crusade* (London 2003)
J. Harris, *Byzantium and the Crusades* (London 2003)
P. Lock, *The Franks in the Aegean 1204–1500* (Harlow 1995)
D. E. Queller and T. F. Madden, *The Fourth Crusade: The Conquest of Constantinople* (Philadelphia 1997)

Innocent III and the Fifth Crusade

Sources

Oliver of Paderborn, *Capture of Damietta*, trans. E. Peters, *Christian Society and the Crusades 1198–1229* (Philadelphia 1971)

Secondary

J. Powell, *Anatomy of a Crusade 1213–21* (Philadelphia 1986)

Thirteenth-century Outremer and the Crusades

Sources:

Continuation of William of Tyre, trans. J. Shirley, *Crusader Syria in the Thirteenth Century* (Aldershot 1999)

Ibn Furat, trans. M. Lyons and J. Riley-Smith, *Ayyubids, Mamlukes and Crusaders* (Cambridge 1971)

John of Joinville, *The Life of St Louis*, trans. M. R. B. Shaw, *Chronicles of the Crusades* (London 1963)

Philip of Novara, *The Wars of Frederick II against the Ibelins*, trans. J. La Monte and M. J. Hubert (New York 1936)

The Templar of Tyre: Part III of the 'Deeds of the Cypriots', trans. P. Crawford (Aldershot 2003)

Secondary

P. Cole, *Preaching of the Cross to the Holy Land* (Cambridge, Mass. 1991)

P. Edbury, *The Kingdom of Cyprus and the Crusades 1191–1374* (Cambridge 1991)

P. Edbury, *John of Ibelin and the Kingdom of Jerusalem* (Woodbridge 1997)

R. Irwin, *The Middle East in the Middle Ages* (London 1986)

W. C. Jordan, *Louis IX and the Challenge of the Crusade* (Princeton 1979)

S. Lloyd, *English Society and the Crusade 1216–1307* (Oxford 1988)

C. T. Maier, *Preaching the Crusades* (Cambridge 1994)

J. Richard, *St Louis: Crusader King of France*, ed. S. Lloyd, trans. J. Birrell (Cambridge 1993)

P. Throop, *Criticism of the Crusade* (Amsterdam 1940)

Crusades in Europe

Sources

Helmold of Bosau, *Chronica Slavorum*, trans. F. J. Tschan, *The Chronicle of the Slavs* (New York 1966)

Henry of Livonia, *Chronicle of Livonia*, trans. J. Brundage (Madison 1961)

Peter of Les Vaux-de-Cernay, *The History of the Albigensian Crusade*, trans. W. A. and M. D. Sibly (Woodbridge 1998)

The Song of the Cathar Wars, trans. J. Shirley (Aldershot 1996)

William of Puylaurens, *Chronicle*, trans. W. A. and M. D. Sibly (Woodbridge 2003)

Secondary

M. Barber, *The Cathars* (London 2000)

R. Bartlett, *The Making of Europe* (London 1993)

E. Christiansen, *The Northern Crusades* (2nd edn London 1997)

J. F. O'Callaghan, *Reconquest and Crusade in Medieval Spain* (Philadelphia 2003)

J. Sumption, *The Albigensian Crusade* (London 1978)

W. Urban, *The Livonian Crusade* (Washington, DC 1981)
W. Urban, *The Prussian Crusade* (Lanham 1980)
W. Urban, *The Baltic Crusade* (2nd edn Chicago 1994)
W. L. Wakefield, *Heresy, Crusade and Inquisition in Southern France 1100–1250* (London 1974)

Later Middle Ages

Sources

N. Housley (ed.), *Documents on the Later Crusades 1274–1580* (Basingstoke 1996)
William of Machaut, *The Capture of Alexandria*, trans. J. Shirley and P. Edbury (Aldershot 2004)

Secondary

A. S. Atiya, *The Crusade in the Later Middle Ages* (London 1938)
M. Barber, *The Trial of the Templars* (Cambridge 1978)
N. Housley, *The Italian Crusades* (Oxford 1982)
N. Housley, *The Avignon Papacy and the Crusades 1305–78* (Oxford 1986)
N. Housley, *The Later Crusades* (Oxford 1992)
N. Housley, *Religious Warfare in Europe 1400–1536* (Oxford 2002)
N. Housley (ed.), *Crusading in the Fifteenth Century* (Basingstoke 2004)
C. Imber, *The Ottoman Empire 1300–1481* (Istanbul 1990)
A. Leopold, *How to Recover the Holy Land* (Aldershot 2000)
A. Linder, *Raising Arms: Liturgy in the Struggle to Liberate Jerusalem in the Late Middle Ages* (Turnhout 2003)
D. Nicol, *The Last Centuries of Byzantium 1261–1453* (London 1972)
J. Paviot, *Les Ducs de Bourgogne, la croisade et l'Orient* (Paris 2003)
S. Runciman, *The Fall of Constantinople* (Cambridge 1965)
K. Setton, *The Papacy and the Levant 1204–1571* (Philadelphia 1971–84)

Select List of Rulers

Papacy

Gregory VII 1073–85
(Anti-pope Clement 1080–1100)
Victor III 1086–7
Urban II 1088–99
Paschal II 1099–1118
Gelasius II 1118–19
Calixtus II 1119–24
Honorius II 1124–30
Innocent II 1130–43
(*Anti-pope Anacletus 1130–38*)
Celestine II 1143–4
Lucius II 1144–5
Eugenius III 1145–53
Anastasius IV 1153–4
Hadrian IV 1154–9
Alexander III 1159–81
Lucius III 1181–5
Urban III 1185–7
Gregory VIII 1187
Clement III 1187–91
Celestine III 1191–8
Innocent III 1198–1216
Honorius III 1216–27
Gregory IX 1227–41
Celestine IV 1241
Innocent IV 1243–54
Alexander IV 1254–61
Urban IV 1261–4
Clement IV 1265–8
Gregory X 1271–6
Innocent V 1276
Hadrian V 1276
John XXI 1276–7
Nicholas III 1277–80
Martin IV 1281–5
Honorius IV 1285–7
Nicholas IV 1288–92
Celestine V 1294
Boniface VIII 1294–1303
Benedict XI 1303–4
Clement V 1305–14
John XXII 1316–34
Benedict XII 1334–42
Clement VI 1342–52
Innocent VI 1352–62
Urban V 1362–70
Gregory XI 1370–78
Urban VI 1378–89
(*Avignon Clement VII 1378–94*)
Boniface IX 1389–1404
(*Avignon Benedict XIII 1394–1423*)
Innocent VII 1404–6
Gregory XII 1406–15
Alexander V 1409–10
John XXIII 1410–15
Martin V 1417–31
Eugenius IV 1431–47
(*Anti-pope Felix V 1439–49*)
Nicholas V 1447–55
Calixtus III 1455–8
Pius II 1458–64
Paul II 1464–71
Sixtus IV 1471–84
Innocent VIII 1484–92
Alexander VI 1492–1503
Pius III 1503
Julius II 1503–13
Leo X 1513–21
Hadrian VI 1522–3
Clement VII 1523–34
Paul III 1534–49
Julius III 1550–55
Marcellus II 1555
Paul IV 1555–9

Germany

(**denotes also Holy Roman Emperor*)

Henry IV* 1056–1106
Henry V* 1106–25
Lothar III* 1125–37
Conrad III 1138–52
Frederick I* 1152–90
Henry VI* 1190–97
Philip of Swabia 1198–1208
Otto IV* 1198–1214
Frederick II* 1212–50
Conrad IV 1250–54
(Competed rule 1247–73)
Rudolf I 1273–91
Adolf of Nassau 1292–98
Albert I 1298–1308
Henry VII* 1308–13
Louis IV* 1314–47
Charles IV* 1346–78
Wenzel 1378–1400
Rupert 1400–1410
Sigismund* 1410–37
Albert II (I of Hungary) 1438–9
Frederick III* 1440–93
Maximilian* 1493–1519
Charles V* 1519–55

Byzantine Empire

Alexius I 1081–1118
John II 1118–43
Manuel I 1143–80
Alexius II 1180–83
Andronicus I 1183–85
Isaac II 1185–95; 1203–4
Alexius III 1195–1203
Alexius IV 1203–4
Nicholas 1204
Alexius V 1204
Latin Empire of Constantinople:
- Baldwin I 1204–5
- Henry 1205–16
- Peter of Courtenay 1217–18
- Robert of Courtenay 1221–8
- Baldwin II 1228–61
- John of Brienne (co-emperor) 1231–7

Michael VIII 1261–82
Andronicus II 1282–1328
Andronicus III 1328–41
John V 1341–7, 1354–77, 1379–90, 1390–91
John VI 1347–54
Andronicus IV 1376–79
John VII 1390
Manuel II 1391–1425
John VIII 1425–48
Constantine XI 1448–53

France

Philip I 1060–1108
Louis VI 1108–37
Louis VII 1137–80
Philip II 1180–1223
Louis VIII 1223–6
Louis IX 1226–70
Philip III 1270–85
Philip IV 1285–1314
Louis X 1314–16
John I 1316
Philip V 1316–22
Charles IV 1322–8
Philip VI 1328–50
John II 1350–64
Charles V 1364–80
Charles VI 1380–1422
Charles VII 1422–61
Louis XI 1461–83
Charles VIII 1483–98
Louis XII 1498–1515
Francis I 1515–47

England

William I 1066–87
William II 1087–1100
Henry I 1100–1135
Stephen 1135–54
Henry II 1154–89
Richard I 1189–99
John 1199–1216
Henry III 1216–72
Edward I 1272–1307
Edward II 1307–27
Edward III 1327–77
Richard II 1377–99
Henry IV 1399–1413
Henry V 1413–22
Henry VI 1422–61
Edward IV 1461–70
Henry VI 1470–71
Edward IV 1471–83
Edward V 1483
Richard III 1483–85
Henry VII 1485–1509
Henry VIII 1509–47
Edward VI 1547–53
Mary I 1553–58
Elizabeth I 1558–1603

Sicily

Roger I 1062–1101
Simon 1101–5
Roger II 1105–54
William I 1154–66
William II 1166–89
Tancred 1189–94
William III 1194
Henry I (VI of Germany) 1194–7
Frederick I (II of Germany) 1197–1250
Conrad I (IV of Germany) 1250–54
Conrad II (Conradin) 1254–8
Manfred 1258–66
Charles I 1266–85 (Naples only 1282–5)
Naples:
Charles II 1285–1309
Robert I 1309–43
Sicily:
Peter I (III of Aragon) 1282–5
James I (II of Aragon) 1285–96
Frederick II 1296–1337
(these kingdoms continued independent until the sixteenth century)

Castile

Ferdinand I 1036–65
Sancho II 1065–72
Alfonso VI 1072–1109
Urraca 1109–26
Alfonso VII 1126–57
Sancho III 1157–8
Alfonso VIII 1158–1214
Henry I 1214–17
Ferdinand III 1217–52
Alfonso X 1252–84
Sancho IV 1284–95
Ferdinand IV 1295–1312
Alfonso XI 1312–50
Peter I 1350–69
Henry II 1369–79
John I 1379–90
Henry III 1390–1406
John II 1406–54
Henry IV 1454–74
Isabella 1474–1504
Ferdinand V (II of Aragon) 1475–1516
as Spain:
Charles I (V of Germany) 1516–56
Philip II 1556–98

León

Ferdinand I 1037–65
Alfonso VI 1065–1109
(1109–57 as Castile)
Ferdinand II 1157–88
Alfonso IX 1188–1230
Ferdinand III 1230–52
(from 1252 as Castile)

Aragon

Sancho I 1063–94
Peter I 1094–1104
Alfonso I 1104–34
Ramiro II 1134–7
Petronilla and Ramon Berenguer 1137–62
Alfonso II 1162–96
Peter II 1196–1213
James I 1213–76
Peter III 1276–85
Alfonso III 1285–91
James II 1291–1327
Alfonso IV 1327–36
Peter III 1336–87
John I 1387–96
Martin I 1396–1410
Ferdinand I 1412–16
Alfonso V 1416–58
John II 1458–79
Ferdinand II 1479–1516
(from 1516 as Castile/Spain)

Hungary

Ladislas I 1077–95
Coloman 1095–1116
Stephen II 1116–31
Bela I 1131–41
Geza II 1141–62
Stephen III 1162, 1163–72
Stephen IV 1162–3
Bela III 1172–96
Emeric 1196–1204
Ladislas II 1204–5
Andrew II 1205–35
Bela IV 1235–70
Stephen V 1270–72
Ladislas III 1272–90
Charles 1290–95
Andrew III 1290–1301
Wenceslas III 1301–4
Otto of Bavaria 1304–8
Charles Robert 1308–42
Louis I 1342–82
Sigismund 1387–1437
Albert I 1438–9
Ladislas IV 1439–44
Ladislas V 1444–57
Matthias Corvinus 1458–90
Ladislas VI 1490–1516
Louis II 1516–26

Ottoman Empire

Osman d. 1326
Orkhan 1326–62
Murad I 1362–89
Bayezid I 1389–1403
Mehmed I 1413–21
Murad II 1421–51
Mehmed II 1451–81
Bayezid II 1481–1512
Selim I 1512–20
Suleiman I 1520–66
Selim II 1566–74

Jerusalem

Godfrey of Bouillon 1099–1100
Baldwin I 1100–1118
Baldwin II 1118–31
Fulk 1131–43 and Melisende 1131–52
Baldwin III 1143–63
Amalric 1163–74
Baldwin IV 1174–85
Baldwin V 1185–6
Guy of Lusignan 1186–92; with his wife Sybil 1186–90, daughter of Amalric
Isabella I 1192–1205; with Conrad I 1192; Henry 1192–7; Aimery 1197–1205
Maria 1205–12
John of Brienne 1210–25
Isabella II 1212–28; with Frederick (II of Germany) 1225–8
Conrad II (IV of Germany) 1228–54
Conrad III (Conradin) 1254–68
Hugh I (III of Cyprus) 1268–84
John 1284–5
Henry I (II of Cyprus) 1285–1324

Antioch

Bohemund 1098–1105
Tancred regent 1101–3 and 1105–8; prince 1108–12
Roger of Salerno 1113–19
Baldwin II of Jerusalem 1119–26; 1130–31
Bohemund II 1126–30
Fulk of Jerusalem 1130–36
Raymond of Poitiers 1136–49
Constance 1149–53; 1161–63
Reynald of Châtillon 1153–61
Bohemund III 1163–1201
Bohemund IV 1201–16; 1219–33
Raymond Roupen 1216–19
Bohemund V 1233–52
Bohemund VI 1252–68

Tripoli

Raymond IV of Toulouse, I of Tripoli 1102–5
William-Jordan 1105–9
Bertrand 1109–12
Pons 1112–37
Raymond II 1137–52
Raymond III 1152–87
Bohemund IV of Antioch 1187–1233
Bohemund V 1233–52
Bohemund VI 1252–75
Bohemund VII 1275–87

Edessa

Baldwin I of Boulogne 1098–1100
Baldwin II of Le Bourcq 1100–1118
Joscelin I of Courtenay 1119–31
Joscelin II 1131–50
(Joscelin III titular count 1150–88)

Valois Dukes of Burgundy

Philip the Bold 1363–1404
John the Fearless 1404–19
Philip the Good 1419–67
Charles the Rash 1467–77

Index